Religion in America

ADVISORY EDITOR

Edwin S. Gaustad

Life and Correspondence

OF THE

Rev. William Smith, D.D.

VOL. I.

Engraved by John Sartain, Phila.

WILLIAM SMITH, D.D.

FIRST PROVOST OF THE COLLEGE OF PHILADELPHIA

ÆT. 30.

From the original painting by Benjn. West, in the collection of the
Historical Society of Pennsa.

S.A. GEORGE & CO. PHILA

Life and Correspondence

OF THE

Rev. William Smith, D.D.,

First Provost of the College and Academy of Philadelphia.
First President of Washington College, Maryland. President of the St. Andrew's Society of Phila-
delphia. President of the Corporation for the Relief of the Widows and Children of
Clergymen in the Communion of the Church of England in America.
Secretary of the American Philosophical Society, etc., etc.

WITH COPIOUS EXTRACTS FROM HIS WRITINGS.

BY HIS GREAT GRANDSON,

HORACE WEMYSS SMITH.

Member of the Historical Society of Pennsylvania.
Editor of the "Miscellaneous Works of Richard Penn Smith," of "The York-Town Orderly Book,"
"Andreana," etc., etc.

VOL. I.

PHILADELPHIA:
PUBLISHED BY S. A. GEORGE & CO.,
15 NORTH SEVENTH STREET.
1879.

Entered according to Act of Congress, in the year 1878, by

S. A. GEORGE & CO.,

In the Office of the Librarian of Congress, at Washington, D. C.

163018

Belmont University Library

AAX-6818

LD
4525
1755
.862
1972

YOUTHFUL VENERATION

FOR

MY GREAT-GRANDFATHER

MADE HIM THE

ALPHA OF MY LIFE.

AGE AND FILIAL AFFECTION HAVE MADE MY GRANDCHILDREN THE OMEGA.

I Therefore Dedicate these Volumes to

RICHARD PENN AND RUSSELL MOORE SMITH,

WHOM I LOVE,

HOPING THAT THE BRIGHT FAME OF OUR ANCESTOR

MAY BE TO THEM

THE GUIDING INSPIRATION

OF

THEIR LIVES.

PREFACE.

REMEMBRANCE of a majority of mankind perishes at their death. The tomb in closing over their mortal remains separates them forever from the busy world. Another body has been consigned to the dust out of which it was framed; another

> "Soul, exiled and journeying back to-day,"

has completed its pilgrimage in the flesh. Another life, like a falling star, has glittered and suddenly gone out. Death is indeed oblivion. In some deep-loving heart, a silent and a sweet forget-me-not may linger; but time soon effaces this last memorial, and no relic then remains on earth of the life that once has been. Yet it is not so with the great actors on this world's stage. They cannot be accounted dead as common men die, whose remembrance is buried with them. In their deeds and works they beget a second and a mightier existence, which fills like air the universe of mind. Their good or bad qualities excite the admiration or disgust of future generations; their achievements form the most attractive materials of history, and furnish the poet with the noblest themes of song. Yet all fame cannot be considered precious. There is the glittering and delusive brilliancy as well as the pure and steadfast flame; and when we sit in judgment on the

dead, reviewing their actions, but often knowing nothing
of the motives that produced them, or the chances that
gave a development different from that at first intended,
how difficult does it become to award a fair and righteous
verdict! Frequently biography displays but the skeleton
of the subject, in which we look in vain for the full exposition of the man. More frequently it is an unqualified
panegyric, overloaded with details which interest no one
beyond the writer of the book.

Upon the death of my father, the late Richard Penn
Smith, A. D. 1854, I found among his papers this note
from the late WILLIAM RAWLE, Esquire,* the oldest of that
name, and the first President of the Historical Society of
Pennsylvania. It had been written by that excellent man
and accomplished lawyer in execution of a scheme of large
usefulness, which, in the year 1826, he planned and
marked out, and which assigned to particular standing
committees that he was authorized by the Society to
appoint, certain duties designed to preserve and to present
the history of men and of events that had done honor to
Pennsylvania, whether in its Aboriginal, its Swedish, its
English, or its Independent condition:

HISTORICAL SOCIETY OF PENNSYLVANIA, January 2d, 1826.
DEAR SIR:—As President of the Historical Society, I hereby appoint
you one of the committee to collect biographical notices of persons distinguished among us, and I request you to take, as one of your subjects,
your grandfather, Dr. William Smith. Besides the mention of personal
anecdotes relating to him, it will give you an opportunity to notice the
provincial politics in which he took so active a part, and also much of
the literary history of the colonies.
Your sincere friend,
WILLIAM RAWLE.
RICHARD PENN SMITH, Esq.

---

* Mr. Rawle died A. D. 1836.

I wish, indeed, that my honored father, whose vocation was letters, and who was qualified beyond the common for the office of Dr. Smith's biographer, had been able to find time for this pious labor. But literary engagements of a constantly pressing kind prevented his doing that which he felt was a duty, sooner or later, by some of Dr. Smith's descendants, to be performed.

In the course of survivorship, the task has fallen upon me. I have devoted myself through many years to the work, and have discharged it thus far, and in this first volume, as well as my moderate abilities would allow. The second volume will follow, without much delay, if my life and health are spared.

The book to which I have been most indebted in preparing this work is the second volume of the "Historical Collections relating to the American Colonial Church," in which are found many letters of Dr. Smith; transcripts made in England under the direction of the late Rev. F. L. Hawks, D. D., and recently, with many other documents of value, given to the Church in those beautiful volumes of the Rev. William Stevens Perry, D. D., now the honored Bishop of Iowa. The high office which Dr. Perry at present fills is of course one where his usefulness will be of a kind quite different from that which marked him in the office where he so long, previously to coming to it, labored. But the preservation of the Church's history, and the history of those holy and humble men of heart that through the ages all along have been her servants, is a high and holy office too; and it would be difficult to overestimate the value of Dr. Perry's services in this department of ecclesiastical labor.

To a manuscript "History of Parishes on the Eastern Shore of Maryland," by the Rev. Ethan Allen, I have to acknowledge great obligation.

I must acknowledge my obligation also, in many cases where, from abridging, enlarging or modifying it, I have not indicated a quotation, to the very useful "History of Philadelphia," by Thompson Westcott, Esquire, still in a course of publication through a weekly paper.

Of parts of the writings of my father, as of Dr. Smith himself, I have made frequent use, without other acknowledgment than this; as I have generally so altered them as to make them accommodate themselves to the history I am writing.

I am under obligations to the Right Reverend the Diocesan of Pennsylvania, Dr. Stevens, who has assisted me, not only by permission to consult his valuable library, but by information or right judgments imparted to me by conversation on certain matters connected with portions of my book, where my own knowledge was defective or my impressions uncertain.

To the Hon. Horatio Gates Jones, of the Senate of our State, I have been much indebted. The monograph entitled "*Ebenezer Kinnersley, and his Connexion with Early Discoveries in Electricity*"—delivered some time since in Boston, afterwards in Providence, R. I., as also in this city, and fully reported in the Boston and Providence papers—I regard as a most careful, accurate and valuable paper on an ancient and recondite topic closely connected with the fame of the old College of Philadelphia.

I must also express my thanks for his counsel and encouragement to the steady friend of nearly my whole life, the Hon. Benjamin Harris Brewster, lately the Attorney-General of Pennsylvania ; the learned lawyer, the eloquent advocate, the true, generous and faithful MAN. Had his acute and accomplished mind and his elegant pen found leisure in the midst of his ceaseless professional labor to devote themselves for a short time—as without venturing to propose the office, I have sometimes wished they could —to writing the life of Dr. Smith, different indeed and far better would have been the character of these volumes. But I have done what I could.

I have also to acknowledge much courtesy in the preparation of my book from Mr. Lloyd Smith, the learned Librarian of the Philadelphia Library; from Ferdinand J. Dreer, Esq., from William Kent Gilbert, M. D., from Robert Coulton Davis, whose immense collections of autographs have been most kindly opened to me, and have liberally contributed to the profit of my readers.

I ought perhaps to tender my thanks to other persons ; but it is possible that in the long term which has passed since I began my work, the names of some of my many benefactors have escaped me.

I do not suppose that in a work so large as mine I have escaped falling into occasional errors. To any one who will communicate errors to me in a kind spirit, I shall be obliged. And any errors, in whatever spirit communicated, I shall endeavor to correct.

The portrait of Dr. Smith, which is prefixed to this volume, is from an original by Benjamin West, which I had the pleasure to present to the Historical Society of our State, on its coming, some years ago, into the hall which, by the wise liberality of the Managers of the Pennsylvania Hospital, that Society now occupies. That hall was originally built to receive a large historical picture called *Christ Healing the Sick*, presented by West to the Hospital; in his day, as now, admirably managed by representatives of that venerable and honored "Religious Society of Friends," of which West himself was a member. It seemed to me that an original portrait of Dr. Smith, by the great artist himself, would be a suitable memento for such a place. The history of the picture is not without interest. I give some notice of it in an appendix. (See Appendix VI.)

H. W. S.

FALLS OF SCHUYLKILL,
    December 10th, 1878.

CONTENTS.

CHAPTER I.

CHAPTER II.

CHAPTER III.

CHAPTER IV.

CHAPTER V.

CHAPTER VI.

CHAPTER VII.

CHAPTER VIII.

CHAPTER IX.

CHAPTER X.

CHAPTER XI.

CHAPTER XII.

CHAPTER XX.

CHAPTER XXI.

CHAPTER XXII.

CHAPTER XXIII.

CHAPTER XXIV.

CHAPTER XXV.

CHAPTER XXVI.

CHAPTER XXVII.

CHAPTER XXVIII.

CHAPTER XXIX.

CHAPTER XXX.

CHAPTER XXXI.

CHAPTER XXXII.

CHAPTER XXXIII.

CHAPTER XXXIV.

CHAPTER XXXV.

LIFE AND CORRESPONDENCE

OF THE

REV. WILLIAM SMITH, D. D.

CHAPTER I.

Origin, Youth, and Early Education—Duncans of Camperdown—Emigrates to America—College of Mirania—Early Publications—Prologue—Dr. Franklin to Dr. Smith—Acquaintance with Dr. Samuel Johnson—Dr. Franklin to Dr. Smith—Call to the Academy of Philadelphia—Dr. Smith to the Trustees—Accepts the Provostship—Governor de Lancey—Dr. Smith to Governor de Lancey—Dr. Franklin to Dr. Smith—Sails for England.

William Smith, D.D., first Provost of the College and Academy of Philadelphia, was by birth a Scotchman, born upon the banks of the river Don, within a few miles of Aberdeen, in Aberdeen shire. His father was a gentleman of some means, living upon a country estate which he had inherited from his father, James Smith, who was the first of the family born in Scotland. The following genealogical account of his ancestors (which is a matter of record in the University of Aberdeen) has been kindly furnished by a gentleman* connected with that institution, and I have every reason to believe it correct, as I have the same in the manuscript of Dr. Smith from 1630 down :

John Smyth, afterwards *Smith*, a descendant of *Sir Rodger Clarendon*, son of Edward the Black Prince ; born in the year 1500 ; sheriff of the counties of Essex and Herts, in the thirtieth year of the reign of Henry VIII. He married Agnes Charnock, of an ancient Lancaster family, succeeded by their son,

---

* James Webster, Esq.

2

Sir William Smith, who died in 1631, leaving an only son,

William Smith, who was born in 1620, and the father of

James Smith, who was born in Scotland in 1651, a noted astronomer, and father of

Thomas Smith, born in Aberdeen in 1692, and married Elizabeth Duncan, of the Camperdown family, by whom he had issue,

William Smith (the subject of this memoir), who was born September 7th, 1727, baptized in the old Aberdeenshire Kirk, October 19th of the same year, and

Isabella Smith, born 1728; who died single, at the family seat, Falls of Schuylkill, Pa., 1802.

Thomas Smith, by a second marriage, with a Miss Margaret Campbell; had issue

Charles Smith, who came to America, but returned to London, where he died;

Thomas Smith, who likewise came to America, where he filled a prominent place in the history of Pennsylvania, became Judge of the Supreme Court, and died in 1811; and

James Smith, who sailed for America, but was lost overboard.

The family of Duncan of Lundie, from whom the wife of Thomas Smith was descended, is known as that of Camperdown, and is of remote antiquity; it was originally designated of Seaside, and there is an authenticated heraldic tradition which accounts for the crest, a dismantled ship, now borne over the arms of Camperdown. A member of the family, who lived some two hundred years ago, having been supercargo on board a vessel bound from Norway to his native place, Dundee, was overtaken by a tremendous storm, in which the ship became almost a complete wreck, and the crew were reduced to the utmost distress. Contrary, however, to all expectations, they were enabled to navigate their crazy, crippled bark into port, and the parents of the thus fortunately rescued son immediately adopted the crest alluded to, in commemoration of the dangers their heir had so providentially escaped from.

The first of the name of whom I can get any account is Alexander Duncan, Esq., of Lundie county, who married a daughter of Sir Peter Murray, Bart., of Auchtentyre; he had issue,

1st. Elizabeth (who married Thomas Smith in 1724);

2d. Adam, born 1725, who early in life adopted the naval profession and afterwards was celebrated as the hero of Camperdown.

I find the following notice of him in " Burke's Peerage:"

Adam Duncan, having adopted the naval profession, entered into that service about the year 1746, under Robert Haldane, then captain of the Shoreham frigate. In three years afterwards we find young Duncan a midshipman, on board the "Centurion," of fifty guns, a ship ordered to be equipped to receive the broad pendant of Commodore Keppel, who was appointed commander-in-chief on the Mediterranean station. In 1755 Mr. Duncan obtained his lieutenancy, and was appointed to the "Norwich," a fourth-rate, commanded by Captain Barrington. On the 21st September, 1759, he was advanced to the rank of commander, and in the year 1761 made post-captain, and appointed to the "Valiant," of seventy-four guns, in which ship, under the broad pendant of Admiral Keppel, he acquired considerable reputation at the capture of the "Havannah." In 1789 Captain Duncan was promoted to be Rear Admiral of the Blue, and, passing through the intermediate grades, was appointed, 14th February, 1799, Admiral of the White. During the greater part of this interval, however (up to the year 1795), singular as it may appear to posterity, the great merits of Admiral Duncan continued either unknown, or at least unregarded. Frequently did he solicit a command, and as frequently did he experience disappointment. It has even been reported that this brave man had it once in contemplation to retire altogether from the service, on a very honorable civil employment connected with the navy ; at length, however, the cloud burst, and Admiral Duncan was constituted, in 1795, Commander-in-chief in the North seas. He accordingly hoisted his flag on board the "Prince George," of ninety-eight guns, but afterwards removed to the "Venerable," of seventy-four. In this command he had the honor of achieving a splendid victory off Camperdown, 11th October, 1797, over the Dutch fleet under Admiral De Winter, and was elevated to the peerage, 30th October, 1797, in the dignities of Baron Duncan of Lundie, and Viscount Duncan of Camperdown. His lordship had a grant at the same time of a pension of £3,000 per annum for the life of himself and his next two successors in the peerage. He married Henrietta, second daughter of the Rt. Hon. Robert Dundas, of Arniston, lord-president of the Court of Session, and niece of Henry, first Viscount Melville, by whom he had issue.

Creations.—Viscount and Baron, 30th October, 1797. Earl, 12th September, 1831.

Arms.—Gu., a representation of the gold medal conferred upon the first viscount by George III., for the victory off Camperdown, ensigned with a naval crown, and subscribed "CAMPERDOWN," between two roses in chief, and a buglehorn in base, ar., strung and garnished, az.

Crest.—A dismasted ship, ppr.

Supporters.—Dexter, a female figure, crowned with a celestial crown, a scarf across her garments, resting her exterior hand upon an anchor, the other holding a palm branch ; sinister, a sailor, holding in his exterior hand the union flag, with the tricolored flag wrapped round the staff.

Mottoes.—Above the crest, "Disce pati;" under the shield, "Secundis dubiisque rectus."

Seats.—Camperdown, Forfarshire, and Gleneagles, Perthshire."

Adam Duncan came to America, and I have been informed spent some time with Dr. Smith, while he resided at the corner of Fourth and Arch streets. This must have been about the year 1763 or 1764.

In a short account of his life, Dr. Smith mentions having entered the parish school at the age of seven and remaining until March, 1735, when he was taken charge of by the Society for the Education of Parochial Schoolmasters. Where this school was situated I am not able to ascertain, but he was instructed under their care until the beginning of the year 1741, when he entered the University of Aberdeen, and resided there for the full term of years required for his first degree, which he received in March, 1747, and left the institution.

I find him in London under date "January 31st, 1750," when he published *A Memorial for the Established or Parochial Schoolmasters in Scotland, addressed to the great men in Parliament, etc. By William Smith, as Commissioner of said Schoolmasters.* In July of the same year he wrote and published *An Essay on the Liberty of the Press.*

The following is the first note in his handwriting I have found:

October 30th, 1750. Published in the *Scot's Magazine* for this month a scheme for augmenting the salaries of Established or Parochial Schoolmasters in Scotland, dated at Abernethy, November 5th, 1749.

The whole of the year 1750 he passed in London, and I have every reason to believe that during that time he acted as clerk for the Honorable Society for the Propagation of the Gospel.

Mr. Smith's efforts in regard to the schools in Scotland do not appear to have been successful, and the project itself was soon after abandoned. On the 3d day of March, 1751, he embarked for New York, accompanying as tutor two young gentlemen who were returning to their native country. He bore with him strong letters of recommendation to Governor de Lancey from the Archbishop of Canterbury, who had been the governor's preceptor at the University of Cambridge. On the 1st of May he landed in New York city, and took up his residence in the house of Colonel Martin, on Long Island, as tutor to his two children, whom he had accompanied from England. Here he remained until August, 1753. While he resided here I find nothing that he published except an Essay upon "Education," which appeared in a New York newspaper on November 7th, 1752; a "New Year's Ode" on January 1st, 1753; and a pamphlet entitled *A General Idea of the College of Mirania*. This was intended as a sketch for a proposed college in New York. The principles laid down in this pamphlet were eventually used by Dr. Smith himself in the subsequent establishment of the College and Academy of Philadelphia. He says he received his publication from the hands of the printer on April 1st, 1753, and sent a copy to the Rev. Richard Peters, at Philadelphia, and to Dr. Benjamin Franklin, who was at that time President of the Board of Trustees of the Academy and Charitable School of that city, a charitable school which had greatly prospered since its foundation four years before, and which had received a charter from the Provincial Government on the 13th day of July, 1753. At this date he does not appear to have met with either Dr. Franklin or Mr. Peters.

The *Idea of the College of Mirania** was printed by J. Parker and W. Weyman, in New York, at the desire and expense of some gentlemen in that city, for private distribution. This motto and preface were appended to it in the London edition of 1759:

"*Quid Leges sine Moribus vane proficient.*"—HORACE.

The "Preface" begins thus:

The following idea of a seminary of learning, adapted to the circumstances of a young colony, was drawn up and published at the desire of some gentlemen of New York, who were appointed to receive proposals relative to the establishment of a college in that province; and as it contains a pretty exact representation of what the author is now endeavoring to realize in the seminary over which he has the honor to preside in another colony, he thought that it might be no improper introduction to the subsequent account of that seminary.

In a performance written in so early a period of life, and designedly offered as a plan for improvement, the reader will not look for perfection.

---

* The *Idea of the College of Mirania* was republished in both editions of Dr. Smith's Sermons in London, and in the Philadelphia edition.

In this edition, however, some redundancies are retrenched, and some faults corrected, into which want of experience, hasty publication, and too easy assent, had drawn the author.

The annexed prologue was published with the pamphlet:

PROLOGUE

SUPPOSED TO HAVE BEEN SPOKEN AT THE OPENING OF THE COLLEGE
OF MIRANIA.

It comes! it comes! the *promis'd* æra comes!
Now Gospel Truth shall dissipate the glooms
Of Pagan Error—and with cheerful ray
O'er long-benighted realms shed heavenly day.
Hark! the glad Muses strike the warbling string,
And in melodious accents thus they sing:
"Woods, Brooks, Gales, Fountains, long unknown to Fame,
At length, as conscious of your future claim,
Prepare to nurse the *philosophic thought*,
To prompt the *serious* or the *sportive* note!
Prepare, ye *Woods*, to yield the Sage your shade,
And wave ambrosial verdures o'er his head!
Ye *Brooks*, prepare to swell the Poet's strain,
Or gently murmur back his am'rous pain!
Haste, O ye *Gales*, your spicy sweets impart,
In music breathe them to the exulting heart!
Ye *Fountains*, haste the inspiring wave to roll,
And bid *Castalian* draughts refresh the soul!"

'Tis done—woods, brooks, gales, fountains, all obey;
And say, with general voice, or seem to say,—
"Hail, Heaven-descended, holy Science hail!
Thrice welcome to these shores; here ever dwell
With shade and silence, far from dire alarms,
The trumpet's horrid clang and din of arms;
To thee we offer every softer seat,
Each sunny lawn and sylvan sweet retreat,
Each flower-verg'd stream, each amber-dropping grove,
Each vale of pleasure and each bower of love,
Where youthful nature with stupendous scenes,
Lifts all the powers, and all the frame serenes—
Oh! then, here fix—earth, water, air, invite,
And bid a new Britannia spring to light."

Smit deep, I antedate the golden days,
And strive to paint them in sublimer lays.

Behold! on periods, periods brightening rise,
On worthies, worthies crowd before mine eyes!
See other Bacons, Newtons, Lockes appear
And to the skies their laureat honors rear!
Amidst undying greens they lie inspir'd,
On mossy beds, by heavenly visions fir'd;
Aloft they soar on Contemplation's wing
O'er worlds and worlds, and reach th' Eternal King!
Awak'd by other suns, and kindling strong
With purest ardor for celestial song,
Hark! other Homers, Virgils touch the string,
And other Popes and Miltons, joyous, sing;
Find other Twit'nams in each bowery wood,
And other Tibers in each sylvan flood!

Lo! the wild Indian, soften'd by their song,
Emerging from his arbors, bounds along
The green Savannah, patient of the lore
Of dove-ey'd Wisdom, and is rude no more.
Hark! even his babes Messiah's praise proclaim,
And fondly learn to lisp Jehovah's name!

Oh! Science! onward thus thy reign extend
O'er realms yet unexplor'd till time shall end;
Till deathlike ignorance forsake the ball,
And life-endearing knowledge cover all;
Till wounded slavery seek her native hell,
With kindred fiends eternally to dwell!
Not trackless deserts shall thy progress stay,
Rocks, mountains, floods, before thee shall give way;
Sequester'd vales at thy approach shall sing,
And with the sound of happy labor ring;
Where wolves now howl shall polish'd villas rise,
And towery cities grow into the skies!
"Earth's farthest ends our glory shall behold,
And the new world launch forth to meet the old."

Upon receiving this publication, Dr. Franklin writes the following letter to Dr. Smith:

PHILADELPHIA, April 19th, 1753.

I received your new piece on Education, which I shall carefully peruse, and give you my sentiments of it, as you desire, by next post.* If it

---

* The above is copied from the original among the "Smith Papers." But Dr. Franklin, in his autobiography, at this point inserts the following:

"I believe the young gentlemen, your pupils, may be entertained and instructed

suits you to visit Philadelphia, before your return to Europe, I shall be extremely glad to see and converse with you here, as well as to correspond with you after your settlement in England; for an acquaintance and communication with men of Learning, Virtue and Public-Spirit, is one of my greatest enjoyments. I do not know whether you ever happened to see the first Proposals I made for erecting this Academy. I send them enclosed. They had (however imperfect) the desired success; being followed with a subscription of Four Thousand Pounds, towards carrying them into execution. And as we are fond of receiving advice, and are daily improving by experience, I am in hopes we shall, in a few years, see a perfect institution!

I am very respectfully, etc.,
B. FRANKLIN.

MR. WILLIAM SMITH,
    Long Island [near New York].

Provost Stillé, in a memoir of Dr. Smith, speaks of the effect that this pamphlet had upon Dr. Franklin and upon Mr. Peters, and I am satisfied from the correspondence that the trustees of the Academy were determined to secure the Doctor's services from the time they had seen this publication.

While living in New York Dr. Smith had formed the acquaintance and was on the most intimate terms with the celebrated Connecticut divine, the Rev. Dr. Samuel Johnson, the father and first President of the College of New York. It appears that two years before, Dr. Franklin had consulted Dr. Johnson about a plan of education for the college, and urged him to undertake the presidency of it, which proposal, although it was in many respects agreeable to the Doctor, he finally declined.

About this time Dr. Johnson had written a work on Ethics,

---

here, in mathematics and philosophy, to satisfaction. Mr. Alison (who was educated at Glasgow) has been long accustomed to teach the latter, and Mr. Grew the former; and I think their pupils make great progress. Mr. Alison has the care of the Latin and Greek school, but as he has now three good assistants, he can very well afford some hours every day for the instruction of those who are engaged in higher studies. The mathematical school is pretty well furnished with instruments. The English library is a good one; and we have belonging to it a middling apparatus for experimental philosophy, and propose speedily to complete it. The Loganian Library, one of the best collections in America, will shortly be opened; so that neither books nor instruments will be wanting; and as we are determined always to give good salaries, we have reason to believe we may have always an opportunity of choosing good masters; upon which, indeed, the success of the whole depends. We are obliged to you for your kind offers in this respect, and when you are settled in England, we may occasionally make use of your friendship and judgment."

which was published in London.   To this Dr. Smith appended a
" Philosophical Meditation and Religious Address to the Supreme
Being, for the Use of Young Students in Philosophy."

The life of the Rev. Dr. Johnson has been twice written and
published: first by the Rev. T. B. Chandler, and latterly by the
Rev. Dr. Beardsley, in which will be found the correspondence
and full account of these transactions.

On May 3d the following letter was written by Dr. Franklin to
Dr. Smith :

SIR: Mr. Peters has just now been with me, and we have compared
notes on your new piece.   We find nothing in the scheme of education,
however excellent, but what is in our opinion very practicable.   The
great difficulty will be to find the Arastus,* and other suitable persons
in New York, to carry it into execution ; but such may be had if proper
encouragement be given.   We have both received great pleasure in the
perusal of it.   For my part, I know not when I have read a piece that
has so affected me—so noble and just are the sentiments, so warm and
animated the language—yet, as censure from your friends may be of
more use than praise, I ought to mention that I wish you had omitted
not only the quotation from the *Review*,† which you are now justly dissatisfied with, but all those expressions of resentment against your
adversaries, in pages 65 and 79.   In such cases the noblest victory is
obtained by neglect, and by shining on.

Mr. Allen has been out of town these ten days, but before he went he
directed me to procure him six of your pieces, though he had not and
has not yet seen it.   Mr. Peters has taken ten.   He proposed to have
written to you, but omits it as he expects so soon to have the pleasure
of seeing you here.   He desires me to present his affectionate regards
to you, and to assure you that you will be very welcome to him.   I shall
only say to you that you may depend upon my doing all in my power
to make your visit to Philadelphia agreeable to you.   Yet, methinks I
would not have you omit bringing a line or two from Mr. Allen.   If
you are more noticed here on account of his recommendation, yet as
that recommendation will be founded upon your merit, known best
where you have so long resided, their notice may be esteemed to be as

---

* The name given to the principal or head of the ideal college, the system of
education in which hath nevertheless been nearly realized, or followed as a model, in
the College and Academy of Philadelphia, and some other American seminaries, for
many years past.

† The quotation alluded to (from the *London Monthly Review* for 1749) was
judged to reflect too severely on the discipline and government of the English Universities of Oxford and Cambridge, and was expunged from the following editions of this
work.

much "*on the score of something you can call your own,*" as if it were merely on account of the pieces you have written.   I shall take care to forward your letter to Mr. Miller by a vessel that sails next week.   I proposed to have sent one of the books to Mr. Cave, but as it may possibly be a disappointment to Mr. Miller if Cave should print it, I shall forbear, and only send two or three to some particular friends.   I thank you for your information concerning the author of the dialogues.   I had been misinformed ; but saw with concern, in the public papers last year, an article of news relating that one Mr. Fordyce, the ingenious author of *Dialogues on Education,* perished by shipwreck on the coast of Holland, in returning home from his tour to Italy.   The sermon on the "Eloquence of the Pulpit " is ascribed, in the *Review* of August, 1752, to Mr. James Fordyce, minister at Brechin.

I am, with great esteem, sir,

Your most humble servant,

B. FRANKLIN.

Addressed to MR. WILLIAM SMITH,
Long Island.
Free : B. FRANKLIN.

At a meeting of the Trustees of the College, held on the 25th of May, "*It being proposed that Mr. William Smith, a gentleman lately arrived from London, should be entertained for some time upon Trial to teach Natural Philosophy, Logic, etc., in case he will undertake the same, it was agreed to, and Mr. Franklin and Mr. Peters are desired to speak with him about it.*"*

Dr. Smith must have visited Philadelphia shortly after the date of the above, as we will see by the following :

Dr. Smith to the Trustees of the Philadelphia Academy.

PHILADELPHIA, June 5th, 1753.

GENTLEMEN : Having received the utmost satisfaction in visiting your academy, and examining some of its higher classes, I could not be easy till I had testified that satisfaction in the most public manner.   The undeserved notice many of you were pleased to take of me during my short stay in your city, and the honor the academy (when I first went into it) did me, in making one of the youth speak a copy of verses, which I lately wrote to promote the Interest of Science in a neighboring Province, might claim my most grateful acknowledgments.   But what I now offer is a Tribute paid to merit of a more public nature.   A few private Gentlemen of this city have in the space of two or three years projected, begun, and carried to surprising Perfection, a very noble

---

* Minutes of the Trustees, page 40.

Institution; and an Institution of that kind, too, which in other countries has scarce made such a figure in the space of some centuries, though
founded by Kings and supported at public Expense. Prosecute, Gentlemen, yet a little longer, prosecute your generous Plan, with the same
spirit; and your own Reputation, with that of your academy, shall be
established, in spite of every obstacle, on a Bottom immortal, and never
be shaken. A succession of good men and good citizens shall never be
wanting in Pennsylvania to do Honor to your memories, and diffuse
spirit and happiness through the country. The virtues to be chiefly
inculcated on your youth, in order to obtain this end, you know better
than I. They are, however, modestly hinted in the following Poem,*
from a mouth that cannot fail to give them new Importance.

The Performance is far inferior to the subject; but an Apology will
not mend it, as I can have *no time to improve it during my stay in
America.* I beg your acceptance of it as it is at present, together with
my promise of rendering it more worthy the subject when more leisure
shall enable me so to do. That success of your undertaking may exceed
your most sanguine Hopes, is my earnest Prayer, as it is my firm persuasion that such a fair Beginning cannot fail of the most lasting good
consequences.

I am, gentlemen, with great sincerity and esteem,
Your most obliged humble servant,
WILLIAM SMITH.

By this it will be seen that Mr. Smith anticipated an early return
to England. He must have received and accepted an offer from
Messrs. Franklin and Peters, provided some arrangement could be
made for his support. This and to obtain holy orders were the sole
objects of his visit.

The next date at which I locate him is on October 1st, under
which date he writes the following letter to Governor de Lancey:†

---

* The poem here spoken of was published with this letter by Dunlap in quarto; a
copy is in the Philadelphia Library, No. 3032.

† This James de Lancey was the son of Stephen de Lancey, a French Huguenot
gentleman from Caen, in Normandy, who fled from persecution in France. Settling in
New York in 1686, he married a daughter of M. Van Cortlandt, and was thus connected with one of the most opulent families in the province. He was also an active
member of the House of Assembly during the administration of Governor Hunter. His
son James was sent to Cambridge University, England, for his education, and bred to
the profession of the law. On being elevated to the bench, such were his talents and
application, he became a profound lawyer. While at Cambridge he attracted the
attention of his tutor (afterwards the Archbishop of Canterbury), and upon Mr. Smith
leaving London for America, the then archbishop gave him letters of introduction to
de Lancey, who was then the Lieutenant-Governor of the Province of New York.
From this introduction a friendship and intimacy arose, which continued until the death
of de Lancey, in the year 1760, July 30th. He died suddenly from an attack of asthma,

NEW YORK, October 1st, 1753.

HONORED SIR : When your grandson engaged me to dine with your honor to-day, I had forgot that I had several days ago engaged myself to Mr. Walton, who has asked some of my friends on my account. I hope, therefore, this will excuse me to your honor for to-day, as I shall take the first opportunity of waiting on your honor for your commands before I embark for England.

Your honor's most obedient,
And most humble servant,
WILLIAM SMITH.

To the Honorable Lieutenant-Governor,
Present.

On October 13th he sailed for England.

Dr. Franklin to Dr. Smith.

PHILADELPHIA, November 27th, 1753.

DEAR SIR : Having written you fully, *via* Bristol, I have now little to add. Matters relating to the academy remain in *statu quo.* The trustees would be glad to see a rector established there, but they dread entering into new engagements till they are got out of debt ; and I have not yet got them wholly over to my opinion, that a good professor, or teacher of the higher branches of learning, would draw so many scholars as to pay great part, if not the whole of his salary. Thus, unless the proprietors (of the province) shall think fit to put the finishing hand to our institution, it must, I fear, wait some few years longer before it can arrive at that state of perfection, which to me it seems now capable of ; and all the pleasure I promised myself in seeing you settled among us, vanishes into smoke.

But good Mr. Collinson writes me word that no endeavors of his shall be wanting ; and he hopes, with the archbishop's assistance, to be able to prevail with our proprietors.* I pray God grant them success.

My son presents his affectionate regards, with,

Dear sir, yours, etc.,
B. FRANKLIN.

P. S.—I have not been favored with a line from you since your arrival in England.

---

being found by one of his little children sitting in his library in the last agonies of death. He was buried in Trinity Church-yard.

* Upon the application of Archbishop Herring and P. Collinson, Esq., at Dr. Franklin's request (aided by the letters of Mr. Allen and Mr. Peters), the Hon. Thomas Penn, Esq., subscribed an annual sum, and afterwards gave at least £5,000 to the founding or engrafting the college upon the academy.—Note by Franklin.

CHAPTER II.

Arrives in London—Archbishop Herring to Dr. Smith—Address to the
Society for the Propagation of the Gospel in regard to the German
Protestants—Archbishop Herring concerning the German Emigrants
in Pennsylvania—Dr. Smith ordained Deacon and Priest in the Episcopal Church.

On the 1st of December Dr. Smith landed in London, and
mentions writing a letter to Archbishop Herring, giving a circumstantial account of the death of Sir Danvers Osborne, Governor of New York. To which he received the following answer;
the original is in the Maryland Church Papers, from which
copies of everything connected with Dr. Smith have been kindly
furnished by the Rev. E. A. Dalrymple, S.T.D., of Baltimore:

Archbishop Herring to Dr. Smith.

CROYDEN HOUSE, December 10th, 1753.

SIR: I thank you for your particular account of the sad accident in
New York. It was very happy for the city that its government devolved
on the Chief Justice, who, I promise myself, will recommend himself by
the care in his Lieutenancy to further favor from the King.

I have read over your Mirania, and am pleased with the Design. It
is a very comprehensive one, and if you cannot execute the whole you
must go as far as you can. When you form it into a plan for public use,
you will cut off some of those Luxuriances which perhaps are more of
amusement than instruction. You see I am somewhat free with you.
I shall be glad to find that the schemes for yourself are like to succeed,
being confident you will do your duty conscientiously.

Your friend,

THOS. CANTAUR.

To DR. WILLIAM SMITH,
London.

On December 13th Dr. Smith addressed the following letter to
the Society for the Propagation of the Gospel:

LONDON, December 13th, 1753.

MY LORDS AND GENTLEMEN: For many years past incredible numbers
of poor protestants have flock'd from divers parts of Germany & Swit-

zerland to our Colonies, particularly to Pennsylvania. Their melancholy situation, thro' want of instructors & their utter inability to maintain them, with the distressing prospect of approaching darkness & idolatry among them, have been represented to their fellow-protestants in Europe in the most moving terms.

Indeed it is deeply affecting to hear that this vast branch of the protestant Church is in danger either of sinking into barbarian ignorance, or of being seduced at last from that religion for which they and their fathers have suffered so much. And should ever this be their misfortune, their Liberty itself, with all their expected use to these nations, will be entirely lost. Besides this, their having no opportunity of acquiring our language, & their living in a separate body, without any probability of their incorporating with us, are most alarming considerations.

In these circumstances, the Scheme you have engaged in, to send instructors among these people, is of the greatest importance. The influence of a faithful clergy to form the social temper, to keep up a sense of religion, & guide such a people in their duty, is obvious. Nor is the institution of Schools for the education of their children a point of less, but perhaps still greater, importance.

Without Education it is impossible to preserve a free government in any Country, or to preserve the Spirit of Commerce. Should these Emigrants degenerate into a state little better than that of wood-born savages, what use could they make of English privileges? Liberty is the most dangerous of all weapons, in the hands of those who know not the use & value of it. Those who are in most cases *free* to speak & act as they please, had need be well instructed how to speak and act ; and it is well said by *Montesquieu*, that wherever there is most Freedom there the whole power of Education is requisite to good Government. In a word, Commerce & Riches are the offspring of Industry & an unprecarious property ; but these depend on Virtue & Liberty, which again depend on Knowledge & Religion.

But further, Education, besides being necessary to support the Spirit of liberty & commerce, is the only means for incorporating these foreigners with ourselves, in the rising generation. The old can only be exhorted and warn'd. The young may be instructed and form'd. The old can neither acquire our Language, nor quit their national manners. The young may do both. The old, whatever degree of worth they acquire, descend apace to the grave, & their influence is soon lost. The young, when well instructed, have their whole prime of life before them, & their influence is strong & lasting.

By a common Education of English & German Youth at the same Schools, acquaintances & connexions will be form'd, & deeply impress'd upon them in their cheerful & open moments. The English language & a conformity of manners will be acquired, & they may be taught to feel the meaning & exult in the enjoyment of liberty, a home & social endearments. And when once these sacred names are understood & felt at the heart;—when once a few intermarriages are made between the chief families of the different nations in each county, which will naturally follow from School-acquaintances, & the acquisition of a common language, no arts of our enemies will be able to divide them in their affection; and all the narrow distinctions of extraction, &c., will be forgot—forever forgot—in higher interests.

In the day of danger should any attempt be made to seduce our Germans, all the endearments of acquaintances formed in the open moments of youth & joy, rushing upon the heart & resuming their early place in it, will teach every one to reason thus—

"What! shall I draw my sword, & perhaps sheath it next in the "bosom of my dear friend & school-fellow? shall I commence the "deadly foe of him who once bore my fault & the punishment due to "it? of him who once was the dear partner of my soul & all my "youthful sports? of him whose more practised arm once snatched me "from death, when, sporting in the limpid wave & launching beyond "my depth, I was borne by the headlong current to instant fate? can I "forget him with whom I received the first impressions of virtue, & "reasoned so oft upon the difference of governments, & the excellency "of our own, inculcated upon us in so many lessons?"—Or, perhaps, a dearer tye, with eloquence irresistible, claims to be heard in words like these—"What! shall I divide myself forever from him, whom, tho' "born of English parents, I introduced as my dear school-fellow to my "father's house, which gave rise to an acquaintance that issued in his "marriage of my sister? he, in return, brought me acquainted in his "family. The eyes of his cousin thrill my heart with emotions not to "be described. Her every look is animated kindness towards me—I am "full of dear hopes—And shall I desert them and be miserable? no; I "will not.—Hence traitor! quickly from my sight, thou that persuadest "me to it, or the sword thou wouldst have me draw against my best "friends shall this instant open a passage to thy insidious heart. I "know no enemy but thee who striv'st to seduce me from my happi-"ness, which is wrap't in those my relations & acquaintances.—What "tho' they are English, & I of a different extraction from them? so am "I from thee & thy busy countrymen. The generous people among "whom I live have admitted me to an equal share of their high privi-"leges, & I can have no interest which they have not:—I *feel* I am "happy in what I enjoy at present; what can I more? but, by the "change thou striv'st in vain to make me risk, I can only hope to "be so."

It was intermarrying in this manner that saved the infant Roman State from a dreadful war, & occasioned the incorporation of two different nations. And the neglecting to concert proper measures for more frequent intermarriages between the *Scots & Picts* hindered them from ever incorporating; so that it was a fatal resolution which Buchanan tells us the latter entered into—*Providendum ne peregrini secum post miscerentur.* The nations pursued one another with inextinguishable hatred till the *Picts* were totally extirpated.

But besides these advantages already mentioned, by means of a right education of the vulgar, such a spirit may be promoted thro' all ranks, as is best suited to the particular genius of every government in our colonies. Every government has its fundamental active principle, as every man is thought to have his ruling passion, as the spring of his actions; & therefor, as Mons. de *Montesquieu* well observes—"The "laws of education being the first impressions we receive, & those that "prepare us for civil life, each (school or) particular family should be "governed according to the plan of the great family that comprehends "the whole."—Nor is this all. Education, when thus uniformly conducted thro' a whole country, in subordination to the public sense, may not only be made to preserve the grand principle of government, whatever it is, but also to mend or change a wrong principle.

Thus, if the spirit of a people is too pacific, as in some of our colonies, it may be gradually changed by a right institution of the laws of education. Means may be contrived to fire the boy-senator by displaying the illustrious actions of the greatest heroes in the sacred struggle for freedom. He may be rationally convinced that without self-defence society cannot long subsist in the centre of aspiring foes.

On the other hand, if the spirit of a people is too martial or barbarous, as was the case of Numa's Romans, such a spirit, by means of education, as well as by his religious Polity, may be softened & tempered. Youth may be taught to relish the softer arts, & take enjoyments in peace & virtuous industry, far superior to those that are falsely look'd for in the unbounded licentiousness of war. They may be early taught to abhor offensive war, & to esteem a brave & steady self-defence (& that too after all possible forbearance) all that is consistent with the general ties of humanity. Indeed there is little danger any of our colonies should be soon seized with the madness of heroism, which has deluged the earth with so much human blood. The heart must have been long petrifi'd & train'd up in deeds of violence, before one can think of attacking peaceful, unsuspecting neighbors, thro' mere lust of rule, without being eternally pierced with all the unsufferable pangs of wounded humanity!

It was by a scheme of polity similar to this sort of education, that the wise *Numa* blended a vast mixed multitude into one social body. When he was called to the administration his country was in a condition as unformed & feverish as the most uncemented of our colonies. Like them, infant Rome had opened her sheltering arms, inviting alike the poor & rich, the industrious & idle, the good & the profligate, of all

countries to her embrace.   Thus her small territory was soon deluged
with a promiscuous multitude, differing in all things, language, manners,
& extraction.

The great lawgiver saw this, & knew how great address as well as
labor would be required to form his infant country.   This made him
shrink from the toils of government (now-a-days so passionately courted)
& earnestly desire to close his days in his philosophic retirement.   At
length, however, he was prevailed upon to sacrifice *private ease* to *public
good*.   Quitting his little farm, he came to his high station, breathing
justice, breathing *peace*, breathing *piety;* merciful of disposition,
serene of temper, beneficent of heart, plain & sanctified of manners, the
favorite of heaven.   He well knew that a small territory of people
vigorously & uniformly pursuing a common interest, is a body far
stronger & more powerful, than the greatest numbers, dissipated, uncemented & differing in all pursuits.   Hence he made it the invariable
object of his administration rather to incorporate the mixt multitude, &
form their temper to a correspondence with that sort of government he
proposed among them, than to acquire any accession of territory or
people.   With this view he dexterously employed the mild & social
aspects of religion to tame & humanize the savage nature, to open the
reserved heart, & wake public affections.   And indeed the religion he
instituted was marvellously adapted to these beneficent purposes.   Consisting of many public festivals, it frequently congregated the people &
brought them acquainted.   In these festal moments of mirth & sacrifice,
they felt their hearts open towards one another ; distrust & reserve
were laid aside ; strict friendships were formed, & the social flame
catch'd from breast to breast.—Then would they talk, exultant, of
freedom, prosperity, a common-weal, & *a common*-country !   And while
these sacred names rushed upon their thoughts, every narrow distinction
gave room & was at last totally expelled by them.   Difference of manners,
language, & extraction, was now no more.   Every one saw himself
leagued with his neighbor, wherever born, in the common interest of
Rome, & looked down with contempt on every mean distinction that
would drive this interest from the heart.   The rising generation acquired
a conformity in all things.   No distinction remained but between a
virtuous and vicious citizen.   No contest but between *Romans & Romans*
concerning their pre-eminence in public worth.—*Cives cum civibus de
virtute certabunt.*

From what has been said, it appears that, in the present circumstances
of the people under consideration, nothing but a common education of
youth, can obviate the inconveniences justly dreaded.   It is only this
that can incorporate them, by teaching them a common language, giving
rise to acquaintances & intermarriages, influencing their genius ; & pre-

3

serving, forming, or altering the principle of Government among them as public weal requires.

The next things are the method of education, the government of the Schools, & the means of supplying & maintaining them in proper masters.

The method of education is a point too important to be handled in the bounds of this letter, & shall be the subject of a separate essay.   It is obvious that it must be calculated rather to make good subjects than what is called good scholars.   The English language, together with writing, something of figures, & a short system of religious & civil truths & duties, in the *Socratic* or *catechetic* way, is all the education necessary to the people.   These things therefore must be left open to everybody without price; but all other less necessary branches of literature may have quarterly fees laid upon them, to prevent the vulgar from spending more time at school than is necessary.   It is generally thought that the knowledge of *ethics*, civil & religious, is not to be acquired without languages, & laborious discussions, for which the bulk of mankind has neither leisure nor capacity.   But nothing can be a greater mistake than this; & it is to be feared nothing has contributed more to the present general corruption of morals.   Can it be possible that those great Truths & Duties, the knowledge & practice of which God intended as the means of making man happy & keeping Society together, are any other way above the vulgar reach, than as they have been made so by the imaginary distinctions & perplexing reasonings of men themselves? No.   These truths & duties are founded on the most simple principles, the most obvious relations, & from thence may be deduced at no great expense of Time or Genius, without the aid of learned languages and laborious researches.   The general principles of our common Christianity may, in a very short Compass be laid before youth, & the truths & duties thence resulting press'd home upon them as truly amiable for their own intrinsic beauty & happy tendency.   The use & end of Society, the different forms of Government, the excellency of our own, with all the horrors of civil & religious tyranny, may be displayed to them; and from thence all social duties might be deduced, by a chain of the most clear & natural consequences.   All this might be taught at leisure hours by a good master, during the 3 or 4 years the people otherwise spend in learning to read, write, &c. ; & it is hardly to be conceived how much such early impressions would contribute to make good men as well as good subjects.   It is of little importance to Society how many *recluses* should know the theory of *ethics*, when they seldom launch into busy scenes of real life; but the virtue & practice of the vulgar is the strength of the State, so that without making these topics, above mentioned, a part of education, such schools will be wanting in the main point, the forming good Subjects.

 2. With regard to the Government of the Schools, it is of the greatest

use, in smaller Societies, where it is practicable, to have all places of Education uniformly govern'd by one sett of men, that so youth may be everywhere trained up in subordination to the public Sense. This trust can only be executed by men residing on the spot, & therefore 6 or 7 principal Gentlemen in Pennsylvania may be appointed Trustees-general for providing foreign protestants in that & other Colonies, with Ministers and Schoolmasters.

One or more of these Trustees, is once every year to visit all the Schools & examine the Scholars, giving a small premium to one or more boys, born of German Parents, who shall best deliver an oration in English, or read an English Author, nearest to the right pronunciation. Let another premium be given to that boy, whether English or German, who shall best answer to some questions concerning religious & civil duties, on the plan already sketched out.—And now, what a glorious Sight will it be to behold the Proprietor, governor, or other great men, in their summer Excursions into the country, entering the schools & performing their part of the visitation. This will be teaching indeed like those ancient Fathers of their Country, who deign'd to superintend the execution of the laws they made for the education of youth, as the rising hope of the State.

But further, as the success of all Schools depends on good discipline, & keeping up emulation, these Trustees-general should substitute six deputy-trustees for every School, 3 of them being English, & 3 Germans, for the sake of forming more connexions. These deputies should visit the Schools & bestow premia as above, one every month, transmitting an account of such visitations to the Trustees-general, & these last sending once or twice a-year an account of the whole state of the Schools to the Society in London. This scheme cannot fail of helping up discipline & emulation.

3. The Masters for such Schools can only be found & educated in America. They must understand the English & high Dutch, with Mathematics, Geography, Drawing, History, Ethics, with the Constitutions & interests of the Colonies. Now, strangers cannot be thus qualified. For tho' they understood both languages, we could not be sure of their principles ; nor would they for several years know the Genius of the people, or correspond with the general Scheme of Polity in the education of youth ; nay, they might be sent from the *palatinate* or *Switzerland* to counterwork it, & defeat the desired Coalition. Clergymen, Schoolmasters, Physicians, &c., have a natural influence over the people in the Country, & the constant importation of strangers of these professions is impolitic. Such Men should be educated under the Eye of the public in the colonies where they are wanted ; & thus we will not only be certain of their principles, but also have them complete masters both of the English & German languages.

It is a happy circumstance, in Pennsylvania in particular, that there is a flourishing Seminary, where such men may be educated ; & happier still that the hon^{ble} proprietary is to make a foundation for maintaining & educating constantly some promising Children of poor Germans as a Supply of well-principled Schoolmasters, that must be acceptable among their friends.

4. With regard to the maintenance of these instructors, that must come in a great measure from you. 'Tis true monies already collected in Holland, England, & Scotland will be no more than sufficient for a fair beginning ; but you cannot fail of success in your application to the public Charity, to enable you to prosecute your Undertaking—an under-taking of far greater importance to the British—the Protestant Interest —than can be well imagined at this distance.

Figure to yourselves upwards of 100,000 Strangers settled in our terri-tory, chiefly by themselves, & multiplying fast ;—Strangers indeed to everything of ours ; strangers to our Laws and manners ; strangers to the sacred sound of liberty in the land where they were born, & unin-structed in the right use & value of it in the country where they now enjoy it ; utterly ignorant & apt to be misled by our unceasing enemies & surrounded with such enemies to mislead them ; &, what is worst of all, in danger of sinking deeper & deeper every day into these deplorable circumstances, as being almost entirely destitute of instructors, & unac-quainted with our language, so that it is scarce possible to remove any prejudices they once entertain. Nay, such prejudices may be daily increased among them, unknown to us. They import many foreign books ; and, in Pennsylvania, have their Printing houses, their news-papers, and of late their Bonds & other legal writings, in their own language. In courts of Judicature, Interpreters are constantly wanted, thro' the vast increase of German business, & may soon be wanted in the Assembly itself, to tell one-half the Legislature what the other half says.

If these things alarm our ears, it will also awaken our pity to think we hear the following daily lamentations of these poor people—

"Alas ! how long shall we be the most miserable of mortals ? Driven " from our friends & natal soil by the fiery scourge of persecution, we " committed ourselves to the mercy of the Seas, & sought a better home " in an unknown corner of the World. We penetrated the howling "wilderness, & sat down in places before untrod by Christian foot, "where only savage beasts prowled round us, content to suffer the " worst of difficulties, for the sake of religious liberty & a good con-" science. But, O deplorable situation ! we are again threatened with " all those dangers from which we fled. On the one side Popery, & on " the other heathen-ignorance, make dreadful approaches towards us. " The French-Germans, well supply'd with missionaries, are our near " neighbors ; and if we should escape their snares, who shall save our " Children—Our Children ! O piercing thought ! did we mention our

" Children ? These helpless innocents are the rising hopes of a large
"branch of the Protestant interest, coming forward into the world like
" grasshoppers in multitude. Upon their instruction it greatly depends
" whether our heathen neighbors, in whose original soil we dwell, shall
" at last embrace the truth, & flourish long in all that exalts, all that
" embellishes Society ; or whether, on the other hand, a great part of
" the new world shall fall either back to its original barbarism or under
" the dreary reign of popery. But alas ! we see our dear little ones,
" whose fate is to decide this, rising round us like wild branches, with-
" out one hand to form or guide them. Their tender Souls ripen only
" in ignorance & are exposed an early prey. We ourselves are unable
" to instruct them, and are moreover obliged to face the piercing North,
" or sultry South, toil all the day long, & to provide for their infant
" calls of hunger, without having one moment to spare for the nurture
" of their tender Minds."

This is the alarming situation, & these the moving lamentations of
those unhappy Emigrants. To you, ye noble Patriots ! they address
themselves. To you their helpless Children lisp their tender plaint
thro' my Pen. And surely we ought to regard them from Motives of
honor, humanity & good policy. These people are now become British
subjects, & have many shining virtues. Their industry & frugality are
exemplary. They are excellent husbandmen & contribute greatly to the
improvement of a new Country. They possess a vast tract of our territory, & by proper instruction, might be made a great support of trade
& agriculture in our Colonies, & thus encrease the riches & strength of
Britain.

What a patriot work must it then be, to contrive means for making
them flourish long with ourselves in well-ordered society ; to incorporate
& mingle them in equal privileges with the sons of freedom ; to teach
them to value & exult in the conscious enjoyment of these privileges, &
make a provision for improving their natures and training them up for
eternal scenes !

This is not the work of any particular party. It is a British work.
It does not regard a handful of Men of this or that denomination,
happily escaped the jaws of persecution ; but its success is to determine
whether an incredible number of fellow-protestants, of many different
denominations, shall fall into the grossest ignorance ; shall be seduced
by our indefatigable rivals ; shall live in a separate body ; shall turn our
trade out of its proper channel by their foreign connexions, & perhaps
at last give some of our Colonies laws and language ;—Or, whether, on
the other hand, they shall adopt our language, our manners, our interests,
& incorporate with us in one enlightened happy Society.

Upon the whole, those who delight in Offices of Charity, could never
have found a more useful or meritorious way of bestowing it than upon
the instruction of such a vast encreasing multitude of young & old

Subjects, in order to make them good men & useful members of the community. The effects of such a Charity will be felt thro' many a brightening Æra, & roll'd down in a tide of happiness, gently diffusing itself to glad the hearts of unborn millions, in the untutor'd parts of the earth.

Thus, instead of hearing the sound of lamentation & sorrow among a vast people, wandering without Shepherds in a dry & barren land, we shall hear the voice of Joy among them. They & their posterity, thro' long-succeeding generations, shall be happy & enlightened ; so that, in the sublime strains of the Prophet, The wilderness and solitary place shall be glad for them ; and the desert shall rejoice & blossom as the rose.

I hope to be a pleased spectator of part of this happiness ; and if I have been too much warm'd with the prospect of it, take it as a sure pledge that I will decline no labor, as oft as you honor me with an opportunity of helping to bring it about.   I am,

My Lords & Gentlemen,

Your most faithful, humble Servt,

WILL. SMITH.

Upon this paper, a copy of which seems to have been sent to Archbishop Herring, his Grace made an endorsement thus :*

The Design of helping the German Emigrants in his Majesty's Colonies seems as great and as necessary to be put in Execution as any that was ever laid before the British Nation, and the neglect of it may occasion such mischief to us as is inconceivable and may probably be Irreparable.

To recomm'd it therefore to the Publick, is on All accounts not only expedient but necessary ; And the method of doing it will be in as short and comprehensive a way as possible.

1.—To State the Fact and make it Clear by Authentic Truths, that such Numbers of Germans have emigrated as are reported ; if not so many, what the Numbers are.

2.—To Inform the world where in particular they came from ; what was the cause of their Removal ; of what sort the People are as to Religion, Tempers, Circumstances, Occupations, &c., and for what Reasons they quitted their native Country.

3.—To point out their present place and Situation ; the Country and People which they border upon ; in what Manner they Subsist at present ; what provision is made for their due Government, and what for the exercise of their Religion.   These things and others of equal consequence being *clearly and precisely* known, they will all of them probably

---

* From the Smith MSS., endorsed "Archb'p Herring's Remarks on the Scheme for Instructing the German Emigrants."

furnish convincing Arguments that they are Objects highly worthy our Attention. It will then be necessary to be as exact in Pointing out the Methods which become us as *Christians*, as *Men*, as *Britons*, to pursue, in order to lay the foundation of their becoming a good People and usefull Subjects of our Colonies and Government.

How it may be requisite to show :

1.—What has been done for them? How incomprehensive the Means of private Collections are to Attain fully so Great and desirable an End, which seems worthy the Immediate care of some Parliamentary Provision.

2.—To suggest a Method of ranging & sorting the great number of People, so as to render them Governable and tractable in a right way by dividing them into districts under the inspection of proper Magistrates, the easy controul of Laws, and the Institution of Christian Pastors and Schoolmasters.

3.—To show the necessity of a regular Education form'd upon a Large and Generous plan of religious Liberty, consistent with the national Establishment of the Mother Country, to instill and propagate the notion that these Germans are to become one with us, and that it were best for both to have, in time, one common Language. This will be the natural effect of a common Education, which of course leads men on to Friendships, Intermarriages, and a general blending of Interests. Care should be taken that there be no affectation, in their Education, of aiming at high degrees of science, but that their Religion be plain and Practicable, and such as all Christians agree in ; and that their knowledge be suited to their occupation. There will be room enough left under these general regulations to attend to any distinguish'd genius.

The Arguments to enforce this good Plan will be drawn, not from general considerations, but the particular interests of our Colonists, which would bleed under the Mischief, if such a Number of Sober and useful protestant People be Abandoned to be made the Prey of French Papists and Jesuits, or become Mixed with the Tribes of Indians who are under the pay and influence of the French.

From Dr. Smith's diary I make the following extracts :

December 21st, 1753. I was ordained deacon, in the palace at Fulham, by Dr. John Thomas, Bishop of Lincoln, at the request and in the presence of Dr. Thomas Sherlock, then Bishop of London, but in a very declining state of health.

23d. I was ordained priest, at the same place and at the same request, by Dr. Richard Osbaldeston, Bishop of Carlisle.

26th. Started to the North, to see my honored father.

31st. Preached in the kirk in which I was baptized.

CHAPTER III.

Origin of the Society for the Education of the Germans in America—Dr. Chandler's Letter to the Trustees—Bishop of Oxford to Dr. Samuel Johnson—Spandenberg—Dr. Franklin to Dr. Smith—Dr. Smith's Return Home—Dr. Smith to Dr. Chandler—Treaty with the Indians— Saurs' Attacks upon the Trustees of the German Schools—Dr. Smith to Dr. Peters.

March 15th, 1754. Under this date Dr. Smith mentions being at a meeting of the Society for the Propagation of the Gospel. The purport of this meeting will be explained in the correspondence which follows. A number of worthy noblemen and gentlemen in England being now apprehensive that the ignorance of the German emigrants, settled in Pennsylvania, etc., might render them liable to be led away from the British interests by French emissaries, and being also greatly desirous to give them means of continuing the free exercise of that religion among them, for the free exercise of which they migrated from the land of their nativity to these parts, the said noblemen and gentlemen for these reasons formed themselves into a society, and requested Dr. Samuel Chandler, an English Dissenter of prominence and whom they made their Secretary, to address a letter to certain gentlemen in Pennsylvania, appointing them their trustees, etc. Dr. Chandler accordingly wrote a letter as follows (a manuscript copy of which, made by Dr. Smith, is in the possession of Dr. J. H. Brinton, his great-grandson, to whom I am indebted for much of the information in this work):

London, 15th March, 1754.

To the Honorable James Hamilton, Esq., Lieutenant-Governor of Pennsylvania; William Allen, Esq., Chief Justice; Richard Peters, Esq., Secretary of Pennsylvania; Benjamin Franklin, Esq., Postmaster-General; Conrad Weiser, Esq., Interpreter, and the Rev. William Smith.

Gentlemen: The number and destitute circumstances of the German Protestants settled in Pennsylvania and Maryland, have engaged some very worthy gentlemen to form themselves into a Society for their relief, and particularly to provide them with a few German ministers and some English schoolmasters, that the elder among them may not be destitute of needful instruction, and the younger may be brought to the knowledge of the English language ; that they may become better subjects to the British Government and more useful to the Colonies, where Providence has now fixed their habitation.

The Society consists of the Right Hon. Earl of Shaftesbury ; Right Hon. Lord Willoughby, of Parham ; Right Hon. Sir Luke Schaub, Bart. ; Right Hon. Sir Josiah Van Neck, Bart. ; Thomas Chitty, Esq., Thomas Fluddyer, Esq., Aldermen of the City of London ; Benjamin Amory, LL.D., James Vernon, Esq., John Bance, Esq., Robert Fergusson, Esq., Nathaniel Paice, Rev. Dr. Birch, Rev. Mr. Caspar Weitstein, Rev. Mr. David Thomas, minister at Amsterdam, and myself, whom they honored to appoint as their secretary. His Majesty and her Highness the Princess of Wales have with truly royal and princely generosity contributed to the encouragement of this design, and the Church of Scotland has made a very liberal collection toward promoting the same excellent work ; and we are endeavoring to obtain a further supply by means of a subscription from some benevolent noblemen and gentlemen of the city of London. Thus, from our first beginnings, we are encouraged to hope that we shall gather a sum sufficient for assisting these poor Protestants for some few years in the above-mentioned instances, till they are brought into a more regular state, and better able to take care of themselves and their families. The honorable Society, earnestly desirous to apply the moneys they collect in the most effectual manner for his majesty's service, the benefit of the Colonies, and the welfare of these poor people, could think of no method so likely to carry on these salutary views as the opening a correspondence with some worthy gentlemen of knowledge, interest, and experience in Pennsylvania ; and as they know of none in whose honor, integrity, and prudence they can better confide, gentlemen, than in yours, they have unanimously, with the advice of the honorable proprietor, resolved that you be desired to accept of the inspection and management of the whole charity as their trustees in Pennsylvania, and particularly to assist with your encouragement and counsel the Rev. Mr. Michael Schlatter, whom the Society has ordered, with a yearly salary of £100 sterling, under your direction, to be their supervisor and visitor of the schools they have agreed to erect in the following places, viz., Reading, York, Easton, Lancaster, Skippack, and Hanover, where, as they are informed by a letter from the worthy secretary to the honorable proprietor, now before me, the Germans are being settled. The intention of the schools is to instruct their youth in the English language and the common principles of the Christian religion and morality. The schoolmasters for these schools should understand both the German and the English languages, and we are encouraged to hope by Mr. Schlatter that proper persons for this purpose may be found in the province, the choice of which we must beg leave to devolve upon you, as we have an entire confidence in your disposition to promote so good a work, and judgment in the conduct of it. The yearly salary of each of these masters we are willing to allow for some years in any sum not exceeding £20, and the proportion to each we beg you would determine for us; and, indeed, that you would transact the whole of this important affair, as you shall judge it most expedient to accomplish the good intentions that are before us. As to German ministers, we have as yet appointed none, because, as you are well acquainted with the circumstances of the Germans settled among you, we are willing to act with your advice, which will in great measure determine us as to the numbers that shall be sent over, the places they shall settle at, and the stipend that shall be yearly allowed them. This advice, therefore, we earnestly request, and indeed that you will be so good as to send us such information, from time to time, of what may be proper for us to do the most effectually to secure the good ends we aim at, and of the success that shall attend the measures we take in concert with you if it shall please God happily to prosper them. The account transmitted to me as their secretary shall be regularly laid before them, the honorable Society.

We are sensible, gentlemen, that such a correspondence will occasion you some trouble; but when we consider the importance of the service, the benevolence of your dispositions, and the worth of your characters, we promise ourselves your kind assistance in a work which we know must have your entire approbation and best wishes. As for myself, 'tis my great pleasure I have so honorable an introduction to the acquaintance of gentlemen, whose characters I so honorable esteem, and on whose friendship I should place the greatest value.

I have the honor, in the name of the Society, to be

Your most humble servant,

S. CHANDLER.

Favored by the hand of the
REV. WILLIAM SMITH.

A letter which follows shows the impression made by young Mr. Smith on Dr. Secker, then Bishop of Oxford, afterwards Archbishop of Canterbury.*

DEANERY OF ST. PAUL'S, March 19th, 1754.

GOOD DR. JOHNSON: I should have returned you my hearty thanks before now, if extraordinary business had not put it partly out of my power and partly out of my thoughts, for your favors by Mr. Smith. He is, indeed, a very ingenious and able, and seems a very well-disposed young man, and if he had pursued his intention of residing awhile at Oxford, I should have hoped for more of his company and acquaintance.

---

* Life of Dr. Samuel Johnson, by Rev. Thomas Bradbury Chandler, D.D., of New Jersey, page 176.

Nor would he, I think, have failed to see more fully what I flatter myself
he is convinced of without it, that our universities do not deserve the
sentence which is passed on them by the author whom he cites, and
whose words he adopts on page 84 of his *General Idea of the College of
Mirania*. He assures me they are effaced in almost all the copies. I
wish they had not been printed, or that the leaf had been cancelled.
But the many valuable things which there are in that performance, and
in the papers which he published in New York, will atone for this blemish
with all candid persons. . . .

I am, with great regard and esteem, Sir,

Your loving brother and humble servant,

THOMAS OXFORD.

The Society referred to in Dr. Chandler's letter was not the first
Society in London which was intended for the benefit of the Germans in America; for upon the arrival of Spangenberg * in London,
whither he went in the spring of 1741, to superintend the Moravian
Brethren's religious movement in England, he proposed the formation of a society in aid of their foreign missions. To this he was
encouraged by friends of the Brethren, who were deeply interested
in the success of their great work among the heathen, and who
desired an opportunity of contributing of their means statedly, and
of co-operating otherwise towards its support. On the 5th of May,
1741, accordingly, a board of directors was appointed, and on the
8th of the same month the Society was organized by electing
Adolph von Marshall Secretary, and William Holland Servitor. A
collection which was taken up on this occasion amounted to six
guineas. The board, or committee, consisting of James Hutton,
Rev. George Stonehouse, John Ockershausen, John Bray, and
Spangenberg, met on every Monday. The first Monday in each
month was fixed for the so-called "general meeting" of the So-

---

* Spangenberg, Augustus G., *alias* Joseph, and Eve Mary, late Immig, m. n. Ziegel-
bauer, his wife. Augustus Gottlieb Spangenberg, who for almost twenty years was at
the head of the American branch of the Moravian Church, was born July 15th, 1704,
in Klettenberg, Hohenstein, Saxony, and was the son of the Lutheran clergyman of
that place. He studied theology at Jena, and in 1732 was appointed a professor at
Halle. Thence he went to Herrnhut, in 1733, and became Zinzendorf's trusty assistant
in the religious movement to which he devoted his life. Spangenberg was four times
in America: from 1735 to 1739 in Georgia and Pennsylvania; from 1744 to 1749 in
Bethlehem and Philadelphia; from 1751 to 1752 in Pennsylvania and North Carolina,
and for the last time from 1754 to 1762. He returned to Europe in July of the last-
named year, and until his death held a seat in the Unity's Elders' board. He died at
Berthelsdorf, September 18th, 1792.

ciety, at which funds were collected, and reports and letters from the Mission were communicated. Although the number of actual members of the Society was only twenty, two hundred persons were present at the first of these meetings, which was held on the 15th of May. Dr. Doddridge was an early associate and also a corresponding member, and Whitfield occasionally addressed the general meeting. For upwards of ten years this association rendered the Brethren's Mission important service; providing to a large extent for the support of the Moravian missionaries in the British West India Islands. It was dissolved in 1751. For the "Regulations," according to which its operations were conducted, the reader is referred to Benham's *Memoirs of James Hutton*, p. 70.

In 1766 a second organization for the furtherance of the Gospel, and in aid of Moravian missions, was effected, through the instrumentality of Hutton and others, among friends of the Brethren resident in the British metropolis. It is still active, and for many years has met the entire expense incurred in conducting the Esquimaux Mission in Labrador.

Spangenberg had visited America in 1735, and well understood the condition of the Germans in that country. He came to Philadelphia a second time, in 1744, to labor for their good. A full account of his and the Society's acts will be found in the publications of the Moravian Historical Society, published at Nazareth, Pennsylvania, 1877.

But to return to the subject of our memoir. On the 5th of April, 1754, Dr. Smith sailed from London in the ship "Falcon," bound to Philadelphia. During the voyage he wrote several essays on education, which were afterwards published in the *Antigua Gazette*.

Dr. Franklin (in his Life) mentions having written the following to him, which, I suppose, he never received:

PHILADELPHIA, April 18th, 1754.

DEAR SIR: I have had but one letter from you since your arrival in England, which was but a short one, *via* Boston, dated Oct. 18th, acquainting me that you had written largely by Captain Davis.—Davis was lost, and with him your letters, to my great disappointment.—Mesnard and Gibbon have since arrived here, and I hear nothing from you. My comfort is, an imagination that you only omit writing because you are coming, and propose to tell me everything *viva voce*. So not knowing whether this letter will reach you, and hoping either to see or hear from you by the "Myrtilla," Captain Budden's ship, which is daily expected, I only add, that I am, with great esteem and affection,

Yours, etc.,
B. FRANKLIN.

MR. SMITH.

Dr. Smith, in his diary, says:

May 22d, 1754. Landed in Philadelphia. Put up at the Ton Tavern,* on Chestnut Street, kept by Joseph Osborn.

24th. I was this day inducted Provost of the College and Academy of Philadelphia, and Professor of Natural Philosophy.

25th. Commenced teaching in the philosophy class, also ethics and rhetoric to the advanced pupils. I have two classes, a senior and a junior one.

May 30th. On having delivered Mr. Chandler's letter to his Honor, the Lieutenant-Governor, to whom it was directed, his Honor communicated it to the other gentlemen appointed as trustees; but as several of them were then setting out as commissioners from this province to the Indian treaty at Albany, they could not have a meeting upon the business recommended to them by the honorable Society till the return of the said commissioners; therefore, the trustees requested me in their name to write to the Rev. Mr. Chandler, secretary of the said Society, and acknowledged the receipt of his letter.

Dr. Smith did this, as follows:

PHILADELPHIA, May 30th, 1754.

REV. SIR: As soon as I arrived at Philadelphia (which was on the 22d instant) I delivered your letter to Governor Hamilton, and his Honor communicated it to the other gentlemen to whom you were pleased in the name of the honorable Society to address it. Messrs. Peters and Franklin are to be sent out on Monday next as commissioners from this province to the general treaty, to be held with the Five Nations at Albany, in New York, on the 14th of next month; we cannot, therefore, do anything in the business you so generously recommend to us until their return, especially as Mr. Weiser attends them. In the meantime, however, the gentlemen have desired me to assure you in their name that they are sensible of the honor done them by the illustrious Society,

---

* The One-Ton Tavern stood upon the northeast corner of Third and Chestnut Streets. The old building had a porch at its front door on Chestnut Street, and it stood as high in its reputation as a hostelrie as any one in the city. It was kept by Joseph Osborn until about 1770, when the sign was changed to the Cross Keys, a name it continued to bear for a long period after the Revolution.

and that they will decline no labor in the execution of their important trust. Their general interest as Britons, their particular interest as Americans, and their sincere desire of promoting every charitable design, all concur to engage them to do everything experience and advantage of their situation shall enable them to do. The affairs of the Germans become every day more interesting. You have doubtless heard of the encroachments of the French upon the Ohio, and can guess at their designs. The severity of their government has hitherto retarded the migration of Europeans to settle their colonies, while ours have been the constant asylum of distressed foreigners of all countries. Thus they have despaired of ever drawing numbers from Europe to render their colonies equal in strength to ours. Hence, they have turned their eyes upon the vast body of Germans settled in the back part of this province, etc., hoping that many of these Germans who have been born in this country, may be drawn over to them, as they are entirely ignorant, and have not the same notions of French government that their European parents had.

These schemes seem to have been long laid and uniformly pursued, and if they keep possession of the Ohio it will probably be too successful. For as the generality of these Germans place all happiness in a large farm, they will greedily accept the easy settlements which the French will be enabled to offer them. Thus, vast numbers will be induced to go over to the enemy, and others who have come from many parts of Europe and settled lands without any title or patent, will accept such from and promise allegiance to the French. Should this scheme succeed (as from the backwardness of some of our colonies, and the slowness of all of them to concert proper measures of defence, it perhaps may) it will be of far greater advantage to the French than the same acquisition of hands fresh from Europe, because all that is taken *from* us is thrown into the scale *against* us, which is a double advantage to them and a double loss to us. Now, nothing can prevent this dreadful evil and secure the British trade and interest in these colonies but a union of our strength and counsels, together with a proper instruction of these poor emigrants. Whenever we can teach them to distinguish between French and English governments, especially if they are also united to us by a common language, it is to be hoped that no efforts of our enemies will ever be able to draw them from us. Considered in this light, we think the scheme you have engaged in for the instruction of these poor foreigners, and blend them with ourselves in the most inestimable privileges and interests, is one of the most generous and most useful that ever engaged the attention even of Britons. You may depend, then, on our hearty endeavor in the execution of it, as we are fully convinced that so many illustrious names as are with you engaged in it, can never be either without interest or inclination to support it.

In the name and at the desire of your trustees, I have the honor to sub-scribe myself,   Reverend Sir, your affectionate brother,
And most obliged servant,
WILLIAM SMITH.

P. S.—As soon as the return of the commissioners from Albany shall enable us to do anything of consequence, you may expect to hear from us in full, in answer to yours. I offer my most grateful respects to all the worthy members of your Society for their kind notice of me while in London.   W. S.
To REV. MR. SECRETARY CHANDLER.

The treaty mentioned in this letter was held June 19th, 1754.

The object of this treaty or meeting at Albany appears to have been to prevent the Six Nations from going over to the interests of the French. The day appointed had been the 14th, but the commissioners did not all arrive until the 19th. The commissioners from the several colonies were:

James de Lancey, Joseph Murray, William Johnson, John Chambers, William Smith, for the Province of New York.

John Chandler, Samuel Wells, Thomas Hutchinson, Oliver Partridge, John Worthington, for Massachusetts.

Theodore Atkinson, Richard Wibird, Meshech Weare, Henry Sherburne, for New Hampshire.

William Pitkin, Roger Wolcott, Elisha Williams, for Connecticut.

Stephen Hopkins, Martin Howard, for Rhode Island.

John Penn, Richard Peters, Benjamin Franklin, Isaac Norris, for Pennsylvania.

Benjamin Tasker, Benjamin Barnes, for Maryland.

There seems to have been much dissatisfaction on the part of the Indians at this treaty, as but about one hundred and fifty were present; but the commissioners succeeded in making the famous purchase from them of the Wyoming lands.*

June 24th. Dr. Smith makes mention of being at the theatre, at which time Hallam closed his house with a performance for the benefit of the charity schools, performing two pieces, viz., " The Provoked Husband," and " Miss in Her Teens."

On the 9th of this month (July) nine chiefs of the Six Nations

* The most perfect account of this treaty which I have been able to find, is in the " Life and Times of Sir William Johnson, Bart.," by William L. Stone, vol. 1, chap. 14.

signed a deed never to sell any lands in Pennsylvania, as the same
is bounded by New York, except to the Penns as proprietors of
Pennsylvania. This deed and treaty he looked upon as very important.

About this time the following articles which we have translated
appeared in Mr. Sauer's* newspaper. They were the signal of a
determined and long-continued opposition of that gentleman to all
Dr. Smith's schemes for educating the poor Germans.

June 26th. We hear that ambition, etc., has made a provision in the
Academy of Philadelphia for Germans who have no mind to get their
living by honest labor, probably under the pretext of raising lawyers,
preachers, and doctors, since so little honesty comes in from abroad.
But as human weakness values things that come from far much more
than what is daily in view; and, whereas, one has liberty in Pennsylvania to call a shilling a shilling, those that have got their learning from
empirics shall expect but little encouragement in this country, since
"a prophet himself has no honor in his own country."

July 1st. If a countryman or farmer in Pennsylvania should have no
paper money to pay his debts with, and the sheriff should proceed to
sell the plantation for ready money to the rich man, and if this rich
man should let it again to the poor man at a high rent, so that the poor
man should become a servant and scarce have sufficient bread for all his
toil, this would be unjustly making one live in want and another to fare
in abundance and lasciviousness.

Now, there walks a rumor in darkness (which I can neither believe

---

* Christoph Sauer, Sr., died in the year 1758. He was a native of Germany, where
he was born in the year 1693. He came to Philadelphia in 1724, went to Germantown, and afterwards removed to Lancaster county. In 1731 he went back to Germantown and established himself as a farmer and medical practitioner, he having acquired
a knowledge of medicine by his previous studies. An anxiety to supply his countrymen in Pennsylvania with Bibles printed in the German language made him, in consequence of his appeals to his countrymen in Germany, the trustee and agent for the
distribution of such Bibles and religious books as they might send over. This turned
his attention to the necessity of finding facilities for the printing of books and papers
in the German language, and made him a printer. He procured a press and type, and
published his first book, an almanac, in August, 1738. In August, 1739, he published
the first number of a religious and secular paper, which was continued during his lifetime, and was afterwards called the *Germantown Gazette.* He published a religious
quarterly in February, 1746, which afterwards became a monthly magazine, but was in
time discontinued. In 1743 he published the first edition of the Bible in the German
language ever printed in this country. He made his own type, did his own binding,
manufactured his own paper and his own ink. Whilst engaged in these avocations he
found time to sell books and medicines, and was one of the first agents for the sale of
the Franklin stove.

nor prove), that the honorable proprietaries and the representatives should have in view to make the Germans their servants, and in this respect would allow no paper money to be made till they had obtained their end, and outwitted or forced the Germans to sell their plantations.

We now give a letter showing some of a Provost's trials:

Dr. Smith to Dr. Peters.

PHILADELPHIA, 18th July, 1754.

DEAR SIR: As we have not heard from you this Post, I am at some loss how to direct to you, but presume this will find you at New York. I wish your congress with the Indians may turn out to the advantage of the British cause, which has received a fatal Blow by the entire defeat of Washington, whom I cannot but accuse of Foolhardiness to have ventured so near a vigilant enemy without being certain of their numbers, or waiting for Junction of some hundreds of our best Forces, who were within a few Days' March of him. But perhaps what *is* (in this case) *is right;* as it may open the eyes of our Assembly.

As I hope soon to see you I shall say nothing about the Academy. A Resolution which my worthy Friend, Col. Martin, is like to take, affects me much, as it must be attended with an irreparable Loss to his children, for which Reason and none other, you may endeavour, as I have already done, to divert him from it; and I doubt not his good sense will take it in this Light both from you and me. I know his children. They know and I hope love me. Now in about a twelvemonth their Education will be finished on the plan I have proposed. What is most useful in Logic they have already acquired. Moral Philosophy we have begun, and against the vacation in October shall have completed what we intend. Greek and Latin they continue to read at proper Hours, together with two Hours every Day at Mathematics. From October till February or March we shall be employ'd in reading some ancient Compositions critically, in applying the Rules of Rhetoric and in attempting some Imitations of these most finished Models in our own Language. This I take to be the true way of Learning Rhetoric; which I should choose to put off until after the study of natural Philosophy had we any apparatus ready, because in order to write well we should have at least a general notion of all the sciences and their relations one to another. This not only furnishes us with sentiments but perspicuity in writing, as one science frequently has Light thrown upon it by another. In the Spring we shall spend 5 or 6 weeks in such experiments in nat. Philosophy as we shall be able to exhibit. The rest of the summer may be usefull spent in the Elements of civil Law, the reading of History and the study of the Ends and Uses of Society, the different Forms of Government, &c., &c. All this I hope we shall be able to give our higher Class

4

a sketch of, several of whom, particularly Mr. Martin's sons, have capacity enough for such a course of Reading. ╳Now, sir, I appeal to you whether, for the sake of one year, it would be prudent in Mr. Martin to change his sons' Masters and Method? Would he consult their Interest if, for that short time, he should interrupt the many acquaintances they are forming at our academy, which may be of use to them while they live, and which they cannot expect at New York, where there will not be for some time above 8 or 10 Boys (unless they depart from the odd plan they have proposed), and not one Boy can be classed with Mr. Martin's sons.

All this I say upon the supposition their Education could be completed as well in New York as here. But this is impossible at first. For Dr. Johnson only pretends to teach Logic and Moral Philosophy, both which the Martins will have gone thro' before Dr. Johnson begins, and should he begin them again, his Logic and his Morality are very different from ours. There is no Matter by his scheme. No Ground of Moral Obligation. Life is a Dream. All is from the immediate Impressions of the Deity—Metaphysical Distinctions which no Men and surely no Boy can understand. I fear much will come in the place of fixing virtue on her true Bottom and forming the Taste of elegant writing. But further, whom have they at New York for Mathematics or nat. Philosophy, which are not the Dr's. province? Whom for teaching the Belles Lettres? Where is their apparatus? Where a sufficient number of Students for public school acts & Disputation? Thus, then, you see if Mr. Martin takes his sons from this place he must fix them at New York so far advanced that they cannot carry them one step farther, and therefore I wonder what could induce Dr. Johnson, whose worth and Integrity I know, to strive to persuade Mr. Martin to remove his sons from a Seminary where they have reaped great Benefit, & where their Education must soon be finished To me, who know what they have done, what they can do and what they want to do, it clearly appears such a step would absolutely mar their Education and I doubt not it would appear so to you. I have stated the case to Col. Martin, but could say a Thousand things more if I saw him. I beg you to speak to him, if you should go to Long Island on purpose. You love doing good, and you never can have such an opportunity of serving that Gentleman, who, not having a liberal education, may be easily misled in a point the most important of all others. Did I not see it in this light I would scorn to say one word on the subject. 'Tis true, I had reason to think what I have already done for his sons would make him glad of finishing their studies under one who knows and loves them; but if their Interest were not at stake, his Design of removing them would only so far affect my pride as to make me resent the usage with Silent Contempt. I would never wish that the Character of our Academy or mine in particular should want any other Basis but what is intrinsic and may be seen by all.—My Compliments to our dear Franklin. We are in hopes he will return with you. I beg also to be remembered to Mr. Penn, Mr. Norris and all your company, as also to the Gov'r'mt and as many of my New York Friends as are pleased to think of me. The clergy there I do not forget. Excuse my haste & the length of this, which flows from honest zeal for the wellfare of my dear pupils.*

Yours affectionately,
WILLIAM SMITH.

CHAPTER IV.

ACCOUNT OF THE COLLEGE, ACADEMY, AND CHARITABLE SCHOOL OF PHILADELPHIA IN PENNSYLVANIA.

THE institution over which Mr. Smith had been called upon to preside, the Academy of Philadelphia, had been founded in the year 1749 by a number of citizens of that city, prominent among whom was Benjamin Franklin. In 1750 he as president of the trustees drew up and presented the following paper to the Common Council of Philadelphia:

The trustees of the Academy have already laid out near £800 in the purchase of the building, and will probably spend near as much more in fitting up rooms for the schools and furnishing them with proper books and instruments for the instruction of youth. The greatest part of the money paid and to be paid is subscribed by the trustees themselves, and advanced by them, many of whom have no children of their own to educate, but act with a view to the public good, without regard to sect or party. And they have engaged to open a charity school within two years for the instruction of poor children, gratis, in reading, writing, and arithmetic, and the first principles of virtue and piety.

The benefits expected from this institution are:

1. That the youth of Pennsylvania may have an opportunity of receiving a good education at home, and be under no necessity of going abroad for it, whereby not only considerable expense may be saved to the country, but a stricter eye may be had over their morals by their friends and relations.

2. That a number of our natives will hereby be qualified to bear magistracies, and execute other public offices of trust, with reputation to themselves and country, there being at present great want of persons so qualified in the several counties of this province; and this is the more

---

* From the original in the archives of the Historical Society of Pennsylvania.

necessary now to be provided for by the English here, as vast numbers of foreigners are yearly imported among us, totally ignorant of our laws, customs, and language.

3. That a number of the poorer sort will hereby be qualified to act as schoolmasters in the country, to teach children Reading, Writing, Arithmetic, and the Grammar of their mother tongue, and being of good morals and known character, may be recommended from the Academy to country schools for that purpose—the country suffering very much at present for want of good schoolmasters, and obliged frequently to employ in their schools vicious imported servants or concealed Papists, who by their bad examples and instructions often deprave the morals or corrupt the principles of the children under their care.

4. It is thought that a good Academy erected in Philadelphia, a healthy place, where provisions are plenty, situated in the centre of the Colonies, may draw numbers of students from the neighboring provinces, who must spend considerable sums among us yearly in payment for their lodging, diet, apparel, etc., which will be an advantage to our traders, artisans, and owners of houses and lands. This advantage is so considerable that it has been frequently observed in Europe that the fixing a good school or college in a little inland village has been the means of making it a great town in a few years; and, therefore, the magistrates of many places have offered and given great yearly salaries to draw learned instructors from other countries to their respective towns, merely with a view to the interest of the inhabitants.

Numbers of people have already generously subscribed considerable sums to carry on this undertaking; but others, well disposed, are somewhat discouraged from contributing by an apprehension lest when the first subscriptions are expended the design should drop.

The great expense of such a work is in the beginning. If the Academy be once well opened, good masters provided, and good orders established, there is reason to believe (from many former examples in other countries) that it will be able after a few years to support itself.

Some assistance from the corporation is immediately wanted and hoped for; and it is thought that if this board, which is a perpetual body, take the Academy under their patronage and afford it some encouragement, it will greatly strengthen the hands of all concerned, and be a means of establishing this good work and continuing the good effects of it down to our latest posterity.

Upon consideration of this petition the council agreed to give £200 in cash towards erecting and supporting the said Academy and school, and also £50 per annum for five years; with an additional £50 yearly during the same time for the right of nominating and sending one scholar, each year, from the charity school to the Academy, to be instructed in any or all of the branches of learning taught therein. The merchants of London contributed £100 to the same object.

It now became necessary to find a building in which to hold the school. Among the unoccupied buildings in the city at this time was one on the west side of Fourth Street, below Mulberry, called the "New Building," which had been put up largely upon credit by an association, as a place in which Whitfield could preach, and also for the purpose of a charity school. The visits of Whitfield not being regular, the enterprise did not succeed. In 1749 Edmund Woolley and John Coats petitioned the Assembly for the passage of a law giving them a right to sell the building, alleging that the debts were not only unpaid, but that the original trust, that a charity school should be held there, had not been complied with.

This building was thus secured by the school and alterations were forthwith commenced, and partitions dividing it into classrooms were put up. In December the following announcement was made:

Notice is hereby given that the Trustees of the Academy of Philadelphia intend (God willing) to open the same on the first *Monday of January* next; wherein youth will be taught *Latin, Greek,* English, French and German languages, together with History, Geography, Chronology, Logic, and Rhetoric, also Writing, Arithmetic, Merchants' Accounts, Geometry, Algebra, Surveying, Gauging, Navigation, Astronomy, Drawing in Perspective, and other mathematical sciences; with Natural and Mechanic Philosophy, etc., agreeable to the *Constitution* heretofore published, at the rate of £4 per annum and twenty shillings entrance.

Of this Academy, at the opening David Martin was rector; Theophilus Grew, mathematical master; Paul Jackson, professor of languages; and David James Dove, teacher of the English school.

On the 8th of January, 1750, the exercises of the opening took place. The trustees met and waited on the governor, who accompanied them to the hall in the new building, where the Rev. Mr. Peters preached an excellent sermon to a crowded audience. The rooms not being complete, the schools were opened the next day at Mr. Allen's house in Second Street. The free school was opened in September. In August, Mr. Dove, one of the masters of the Academy, proposed to open a school for young ladies at five o'clock in the evening, to continue three hours, "in which," said the proposals, "will be carefully taught the English grammar, the true way of spelling and pronouncing properly, distinctly, and emphatically, together with fair writing, arithmetic, and accounts. Price, ten shillings entrance and twenty shillings per quarter."

In Maxwell's edition of the works of Dr. Smith (Philadelphia, 1803) I find the following account of the Academy:

In the year 1749, a few private gentlemen of Pennsylvania, observing the vast accession of people to that place from different parts of the world, became seriously impressed with a view of the inconveniences likely to arise from their being destitute of the necessary means of instruction. As sundry circumstances rendered it improbable that any-thing could be speedily done among them, in a public way, for the advancement of knowledge, and at the same time but very few of so great a multitude could afford the expense of educating their children in distant places, they saw with concern that their country was not only in danger of wanting a succession of fit persons for the public stations of life, but even of degenerating into the greatest ignorance.

To prevent these dreadful evils, they published proposals for erecting the English, Latin, and Mathematical schools of this institution, under the name of an Academy,* which was considered as a very proper foundation on which to raise something farther, at a future period, if they should be successful so far. And in order to carry this design into execution, twenty-four persons joined themselves together as trustees, agreeing never to exceed that number.

The scheme being made public, with the names of the gentlemen con-cerned in it, all was so well approved of that in a very short time the subscription for carrying it on amounted to £800 per annum, for five years; a very strong proof of the public spirit and generosity of the inhabitants of that place.

In the beginning of January, 1750, the three schools above mentioned were opened, namely, the Latin, the Mathematical, and English school. For it had always been considered as a very leading part of the design to have a good school in the mother-tongue, and to have a person of abilities intrusted with the care of it.

Oratory and the correct speaking and writing of English are branches of education too much neglected, as is often visible in the public per-formances of some very learned men. But, in the circumstances of this province, such a neglect would have been still more inexcusable than in any other part of the British dominions. For being made up of so great a mixture of people, from almost all corners of the world, necessarily

---

* Many gentlemen of the first rank in the province gave their countenance to this design, as soon as it was mentioned to them, and afterwards became trustees for it; but those on whom the chief care of digesting and preparing matters rested were Thomas Hopkinson, Tench Francis, Richard Peters, and Benjamin Franklin, Esqrs.; by the latter of whom the original proposals were drawn up and published.

speaking a variety of languages and dialects, the true pronunciation and writing of our own language might soon be lost without such a previous care to preserve them in the rising generation.

At the opening of the above schools, which were intended to be preparatory to the higher parts of learning, a suitable sermon was preached by Mr. Peters, provincial secretary, from St. John viii. 32, "And ye shall know the truth, and the truth shall make you free."

This reverend and worthy gentleman (who, amid all the labors of his public station, as well as the many private labors in which his benevolence continually engages him, has still made it his care to devote some part of his time to classical learning and the study of divinity, to which he was originally bred) took occasion, from these words of our blessed Saviour, to show the intimate connection between truth and freedom, between knowledge of every kind and the preservation of civil and religious liberty.

The institution thus begun continued daily to flourish, and at length the trustees applied for a charter of incorporation, which they obtained in July, 1753, from the honorable proprietors; who, at different times, have contributed in lands and money to the amount of £3,000 sterling, for carrying on the design; a very noble and even princely benefaction, truly worthy of persons so closely concerned in the essential interests of the country.

Things having proceeded thus far, it was soon found that many of the youth, having gone through their course of grammar learning, would be desirous of proceeding to philosophy and the sciences; and this being represented to the trustees, they began to think of enlarging their plan as they had promised at the beginning. They were very sensible that the knowledge of words, without making them subservient to the knowledge of things, could never be considered as the business of education. To lay a foundation in the languages was very necessary as a first step, but without the superstructure of the sciences would be but of little use for the conduct of life.

In consideration of this they determined to complete the remainder of their plan, and applied for an addition to their charter, by which a power of conferring degrees and appointing professors in the various branches of the arts and sciences was granted to them. By this means a college was added to and ingrafted upon their former academy; a joint government agreed upon for both; the style of the trustees changed to that of "Trustees of the College, Academy, and Charitable School of Philadelphia, in Pennsylvania," and the professors constituted under them into one body or faculty, by the name of "the Provost,* Vice-Provost, and Professors, of the College and Academy of Philadelphia." This charter bears date May 14th, 1755.

---

* It was about a year before the obtaining this additional charter, viz., May 25th, 1754, that the author was settled as head of this seminary.

Having given a short account of the rise of this institution, I proceed now to give a view of the different branches thereof, as they are at present, and shall begin at the lowest, which consists of two charity schools.   In one of them forty girls are taught reading, writing, sewing, etc.   In the other eighty boys are taught reading, writing, and arithmetic, in order to fit them for the various sorts of business and mechanic arts.

The second branch is properly an English academy, and consists of two parts : an English and writing school, and a school for the practical branches of the mathematics, drawing, etc.   In the former, besides writing, the pupils are taught the mother-tongue grammatically, together with a correct and just pronunciation.   For attaining this a small rostrum is erected in one end of the school, and the youth are frequently exercised in reading aloud from it, or in delivering short orations, while the professor of English and oratory stands by to correct whatever may be amiss, either in their speech or gesture.

Besides this rostrum, which is in their private school, there is also a large stage or oratory erected in the college hall, where the speakers appear on all public occasions, before as many of the inhabitants as please to attend.

This part of the institution is of singular benefit.   It corrects unbecoming bashfulness, etc., gives the youth presence of mind, habituates them to speak in public, and has been the means of producing many excellent young orators, that have occasionally entertained large audiences ;* and it is hoped will soon become an honor and an ornament to

---

* A number of the students and scholars, with very just applause, performed the "Masque of Alfred" by way of oratorial exercise, before the Earl of Loudon and the governors of the several Colonies, who met at Philadelphia in the beginning of the year 1757.

The choice of this performance was owing to the great similarity of circumstances in the distress of England under the Danish invasion and that of the Colonies at this time under the ravages and incursions of the Indians.   The whole was applied in an occasional prologue and epilogue ; and at any time a sufficient number of speakers may be found to perform any piece of this kind, in a manner that would not be disagreeable to persons of the best taste and judgment.   Mr. Sheridan, it is to be presumed, never heard of the constitution of this seminary, when he asked the following question in his introductory discourse to *Lectures on Elocution*, etc. :

"To instruct our youth," says he, "in the arts of reading and writing, there are many seminaries everywhere established throughout this realm, but who in these countries ever heard of a master for the improvement of articulation, for teaching the due proportion of sounds and quantity of syllables in the English language, and for pointing out to his pupils by precept and example the right use of accents, emphases, and tones, when they read aloud or speak in public ? "

Now, the professor of English and oratory, mentioned above, is exactly such a master of articulation as this, and has been employed in the College and Academy of Philadelphia from its first foundation.   And if the many advantages that have arisen from this part of the plan were sufficiently known, they would furnish one very convincing argument in favor of the point, which Mr. Sheridan is so worthily striving to accomplish in behalf of the language and elocution of his country.

their country in the various stations to which they may be called. This attention to public speaking, which is begun here with the very rudiments of the mother-tongue, is continued down to the end; and especially in the philosophy schools, where the youth frequently deliver exercises of their own composition, at commencements, examinations, and other public occasions.

The third and highest branch of the institution is the college, in which the learned languages and the sciences are taught, as in other colleges and universities, though on a plan somewhat different. It consists of the Latin and Greek schools and three philosophy schools. An account of the whole follows.

LATIN AND GREEK SCHOOLS.

FIRST FORM or STAGE. Grammar. Vocabulary. Sententiæ Pueriles. Cordery. Æsop. Erasmus.

N. B. The youth to be exact in declining and conjugating; and to begin to write exercises, for the better understanding of Syntax. Writing, reading, and speaking of English to be continued likewise, if necessary.

SECOND STAGE. Selectæ é Veteri Testamento. Selectæ é Profanis Auctoribus. Eutropius. Nepos. Metamorphosis. Latin exercises and writing continued.

THIRD STAGE. Metamorphosis continued. Virgil with Prosody. Cæsar's Comment. Sallust. Greek Grammar. Greek Testament. Elements of Geography and Chronology. Exercises and writing continued.

FOURTH STAGE. Horace. Terence. Virgil reviewed. Livy. Lucian. Xenophon or Homer begun.

N. B. This year the youth are to make themes, write letters, give descriptions and characters, and to turn Latin into English, with great regard to punctuation and choice of words. Some English and Latin orations are to be delivered, with proper grace both of elocution and gesture. Arithmetic begun.

Some of the youth, it is found, go through these stages in three years, but most require four, and many five years; especially if they begin under nine or ten years of age. The masters must exercise their best discretion in this respect.

Those who can acquit themselves to satisfaction in the books laid down for the fourth stage, after public examination, proceed to the study of the sciences and are admitted into the philosophy schools, by the name of Freshmen or novitiates, with the privilege of being distinguished with an undergraduate's gown. The method of study prosecuted in these schools for the term of three years follows, and the portion of reading allotted for each month is particularly distinguished.

VIEW OF THE PHILOSOPHY SCHOOLS.

Forenoon.

| | INSTRUMENTAL PHILOSOPHY. | |
FIRST YEAR.	*Lecture I.*	*Lecture II.*
Freshmen. May 15. First term. Three months.	Lat. and Engl. exercises cont.	Common arithm. reviewed. Decimal arithmetic. Algebra.
Second term. Three months.	The same.	Fractions and extract. roots. Equations, simple and quadrat. Euclid, first six books.
January. Third term. Four months.	Logic with Metaphysics.	Euclid a second time. Logarithmical arithmetic.
Remarks.	N. B. At leisure hours disputation begun.	
SECOND YEAR. Juniors. May 15. First term. Three months.	Logic, etc., reviewed. Surveying and dialling. Navigation.	Plain and spherical Trigonom.
Second term. Three months.	Conic sections. Fluxions.	Euclid, 11th book. ———— 12th " Architecture, with Fortificat.
	MORAL PHILOS. begun.	NAT. PHILOS. begun.
January. Third term. Four months.	Viz., Compend. of Ethics.	Viz., gener. propert. of body. ———— Mechanic powers. ———— Hydrostatics. ———— Pneumatics.
Remarks.	N. B. Disputation continued.	N.B. Declamation and public speaking continued.
THIRD YEAR. Seniors. May 15. First term. Three months.	Ethics continued. Natural and civil Law.	Light and colors. ——Optics, etc. Perspective.
Second term. Three months.	Introduction to civil History. —to Laws and Government. —to Trade and Commerce.	Astronomy. Nat. Hist. of Vegetables. ———— of Animals.
January. Third term. Four months.	Review of the whole. Exam. for Degree of B. A.	Chemistry. Of Fossils. Of Agriculture. N. B. Through all the years, the French language may be studied at leisure hours.

VIEW OF THE PHILOSOPHY SCHOOLS.—*Continued.*

	AFTERNOON. Classical and rhetoric studies.	PRIVATE HOURS. Books recommended for improving the youth in the various branches.
FIRST YEAR.	*Lecture III.*	
Freshmen. May 15. First term. Three months.	Homer's Iliad. ———— —— — Juvenal.	Spectator, Rambler, etc., for the improvement of style, and knowledge of life.
Second term. Three months.	Pindar. Cicero, select parts. Livy resumed.	Barrow's Lectures. Pardie's Geometry. Maclaurin's Algebra. Ward's Mathematics. Keil's Trigonometry.
January. Third term. Four months.	Thucydides, or Euripides. Well's Dionysius.	Watt's Logic and Supplement. Locke on Human Understanding. Hutcheson's Metaphysics. Varenius's Geography.
Remarks.	N. B. Some afternoons to be spared for declamation this year.	Watts's Ontology and Essays. King de Orig. Mali, with Law's Notes. Johnson's Elem. Philosophy.
SECOND YEAR. Juniors. May 15. First term. Three months.	Introduction to rhetoric. Longinus critically. ———— —— ——	Vossius. Bossu. Pere Bohours. Dryden's Essays and Prefaces. Spence on Pope's Odyssey. Trapp's Prælect. Poet. Dionysius Halicarn. Demetrius
Second term. Three months.	Horace's Art Poet. critically. Aristot. Poet., etc., critically. Quintilian, select parts. COMPOSITION begun.	Phalereus. Stradæ Prolusiones. Patoun's Navigation. Gregory's Geometry, on Fortification. Simson's Conic Sections. Maclaurin's and Emerson's Fluxions.
January. Third term. Four months.	Cicero pro Milone. Demosthenes pro Ctesiphon.	Palladio by Ware. Helsham's Lectures. Gravesande. Cote's Hydrostatics.
Remarks.	N. B. During the application of the rules of these famous orations, imitations of them are to be attempted on the model of perfect eloquence.	Desaguliers. Muschenbroek. Keil's Introduction. Martin's Philosophy. Sir Isaac Newton's Philosophy. Maclaurin's View of do. Rohault per Clarke.
THIRD YEAR. Seniors. May 15. First term. Three months.	Epicteti Enchiridion. Cicero de officiis. Tusculan Quæst. Memorabilia Xenoph. Greek.	Puffendorf by Barbeyrac. Cumberland de Leg. Sidney. Harrington. Seneca. Hutcheson's Works. Locke on Government. Hooker's Polity.
Second term. Three months.	Patavii Rationar. Temporum. Plato de Legibus. Grotius de Jure, B. and P.	Scaliger de Emendatione Temporum. Preceptor. Le Clerc's Compend of History.
January. Third term. Four months.	Afternoons of this third term, for composition and declamation on moral and physical subjects.—Philosophy acts held.	Gregory's Astronomy. Fortescue on Laws. N. Bacon's Discourses. My Lord Bacon's Works. Locke on Coin. Davenant. Gee's Compend. Ray Derham. Spectacle de la Nature. Religious Philosopher. Holy Bible, to be read daily from the beginning, and now to supply the deficiencies of the whole.

Concerning the foregoing plan, it is to be remarked that life itself being too short to attain a perfect acquaintance with the whole circle of the sciences, nothing can be proposed by any scheme of collegiate education, but to lay such a general foundation in all the branches of literature as may enable the youth to perfect themselves in those particular parts to which their business or genius may afterwards lead them; and scarce anything has more obstructed the advancement of sound learning than a vain imagination, that a few years spent at college can render youth such absolute masters of science as to absolve them from all future study.

Those concerned in the management of this seminary, as far as their influence extends, would wish to propagate a contrary doctrine; and though they flatter themselves that by a due execution of the foregoing plan they shall enrich their country with many minds that are liberally accomplished, and send out none that may justly be denominated barren or unimproved, yet they hope that the youth committed to their care will, neither at college nor afterwards, rest satisfied with such a general knowledge as is to be acquired from the public lectures and exercises. They rather trust that those whose taste is once formed for the acquisition of solid wisdom, will think it their duty, and most rational satisfaction, to accomplish themselves still farther by manly perseverance in private study and meditation.

To direct them in this respect, the last column contains a choice of approved writers in the various branches of literature, which will be easily understood when once a foundation is laid in the books to be used as classics, under the several lectures. For these books will not be found in this last column, which is only meant as a private library to be consulted occasionally in the lectures, for the illustration of any particular part, and to be read afterwards for completing the whole.

In the disposition of the parts of this scheme a principal regard has been paid to the connection and subserviency of the sciences, as well as to the gradual opening of young minds. Those parts are placed first which are suited to strengthen the inventive faculties, and are instrumental to what follows. Those are placed last which require riper judgment, and are more immediately connected with the main business of life.

In the meantime it is proposed that they shall never drop their acquaintance with the classic sages. They are every day called to converse with some one of the ancients, who, at the same time that he charms with all the beauties of language, is generally illustrating that particular branch of philosophy or science to which the other hours of the day are devoted. Thus, by continually drawing something from the most admired masters of sentiment and expression, the taste of youth will be gradually formed to just criticism and masterly composition.

For this reason composition, in the strict meaning of the term, cannot well be begun at an earlier period than is proposed in the plan. The knowledge of mathematics is not more necessary, as an introduction to natural philosophy, than an acquaintance with the best ancient and modern writers, especially the critics, is to just composition; and, besides this, the topics or materials are to be supplied, in a good measure, from moral and natural philosophy.

Thus it is hoped that the student may be led through a scale of easy ascent, till finally rendered capable of thinking, writing, and acting well, which are the grand objects of a liberal education. At the end of every term some time is allowed for recreation, or bringing up slower geniuses.

No doubt those who compare this plan with what is laid down in the preceding essay will think the term of three years too scanty a period for the execution of everything here proposed. And it must be acknowledged that a longer period would be necessary. But circumstances must always be regarded in the execution of every plan, and the reason of confining the execution of this to the term of three years hath been mentioned in the postscript to the former number.

THE WHOLE IN ONE VIEW.

SCHOOLS.	MASTERS.
College. ⎰ Three Philosophy Schools. ⎱ Latin and Greek Schools.	The Provost and Vice Provost. ⎰ The Professor of Languages, three Tu- ⎱ tors, a Writing-master, etc.
Students and scholars in this part about 100.	
Academy. English School.	⎰ The Professor of English and Oratory, ⎱ with one Assistant and a Writing-master.
School for practical branches of Mathematics.	The Professor of Mathematics.
Scholars in this part about 90.	
Charity Schools. ⎰ School for Charity Boys. ⎱ School for Charity Girls.	One Master and one Assistant. One Mistress.
Scholars in this part 120.	
In all, 310.	

THE CHIEF MASTERS ARE—

William Smith, D. D., Provost of the Seminary and Professor of Natural Philosophy; Francis Alison, D. D., Vice-Provost and Professor of Moral Philosophy; Ebenezer Kinnersley, M.A., Professor of Oratory; John Beveridge, M.A., Professor of Languages; Hugh Williamson, M.A., Professor of Mathematics.

THE PRESENT TRUSTEES ARE—

Richard Peters, Esq., President of the Board, by annual election; the Honorable James Hamilton, Esq., Lieutenant-Governor of the Province; the Honorable William Allen, Esq., Chief Justice; William

Coleman, Esq., Third Judge of the Supreme Court; Alexander Sted-
man, Esq., First Judge of the Common Pleas; Edward Shippen, Esq.,
Judge of the Admiralty; Benjamin Chew, Esq., Attorney-General; Ben-
jamin Franklin, Esq., LL.D.; Joseph Turner, William Plumsted, Abram
Taylor, William Coxe, Thomas Willing, Esqrs., Aldermen of the city of
Philadelphia; Drs. Thomas Cadwalader, Thomas Bond, Phineas Bond,
William Shippen, Physicians; Messrs. John Inglis, Thomas Leech,
Thomas White, Samuel McCall, Philip Syng, Gentlemen; The Reverend
Jacob Duché, one of the ministers of Christ Church.   One seat vacant.

Thus we see that this institution is placed on a most enlarged bottom,
being one great collection of schools, under a general government; in
which all the branches and species of education are carried on that can
be conceived necessary for any community, whether in the learned professions, in merchandise, in the mechanic arts, or inferior callings.   It
may, therefore, be proper now to give a short sketch of the methods by
which discipline and good order are preserved, among such a variety of
schools, students, and scholars.

The chief power is, by charter, lodged in twenty-four trustees, who
must all be resident not only within the province, but within five miles
of the city.   All matters of higher import are to be decided by their
counsel and direction; and all laws are either to be made by them, or
receive a final sanction from them.   No student can receive the honors
and ordinary degrees of the College without a previous examination in
their presence, and a mandate under their privy seal and the hands of a
majority of them.   Nor can even an honorary degree be conferred without a like mandate, under the said privy seal and the hands of at least
two-thirds of the whole body; which regulations must always be a
means of preventing a prostitution of those degrees and honors to the
illiterate and undeserving, which should be the reward of real learning
and worth.

In order to do their duty as trustees more effectually, they set apart
the second Tuesday of every month for visiting and examining the
schools, conversing and advising with the masters, encouraging the
students according to their several degrees of merit, and making such
regulations as may be thought necessary.   All the schools have their
turns of these visitations, which are truly calculated to keep up the spirit
of the institution, and promote diligence, emulation, and good behavior
among the scholars.

Besides these stated meetings, their president, who is chosen annually,
has a power of calling other meetings on any particular occasion.

Under these trustees the principal masters are constituted into a
faculty or common body, with all the powers necessary for the ordinary
government of the schools and good education of the youth.   They are
to meet, in faculty, at least once in every two weeks, and at such other
times as the provost or senior member present shall think fit to call

them, or any two members desire him so to do. At these meetings they
are to inquire into the state of the schools, and see that the several
parts of education be regularly carried on, and the laws of the institution duly executed and observed. They have also power to enact
temporary rules and ordinances, to be in force as laws, till the first
ensuing meeting of the trustees; before whom they are then to be laid,
in order to be altered, amended, or confirmed, or left probationary for
a longer period, or wholly laid aside, as they shall think fit.

By this method all laws either do or may take their rise from masters,
who being daily present in the institution know best what regulations
and orders may be wanted. At the same time, as these regulations are
to receive their last sanction from the trustees and visitors, who are men
of experience, influence, and probity, and have children of their own
to educate, we may be certain that nothing can obtain the force of a
standing law but what is found salutary and good upon trial.

By the present rules the faculty of masters meets every Thursday noon,
and all the schools are assembled before them, that they may examine
the weekly roll, and call delinquents to account. As many of the youth
are too big for corporeal punishment, there are small fines by the laws
agreeable to the nature of the offence and the custom of other colleges.
Whatever money is thus raised from the slothful and refractory in fines,
is appropriated in rewards to the diligent and obedient; so that any
youth, who has once been a delinquent, may have an opportunity of
getting back, by future care, what he forfeited by former neglect.

These rewards and punishment are both administered in the most
public manner; and, in short, the whole discipline is so reasonable and
just, that any youth who might desire to break through the rules of this
institution in his younger years can hardly be expected to submit to the
rules of civil society itself when grown up.

As to the plan of education, great care has been taken to comprehend
every useful branch in it, without being burdensome or launching into
those that are unnecessary.

The principal masters are men who have severally given specimens of
their skill in those particular parts of literature which they profess. Nor
is it any objection, but rather an advantage, particularly to the youth
intended for business and public life, that the building is within the
city. By good rules and good example, the morals of youth may
be as easily preserved in a great and well-policed city as in a small
village, if we can suppose any place to continue small where such a
seminary is once founded. When I speak so I would be understood to
mean when the youth all lodge in the houses of their parents, or in
lodgings within the walls of the College; a proper number of which
are now erecting at a very considerable expense.

In this institution there is a good apparatus for experiments in natural
philosophy, done in England by the best hands, and brought over from

thence in different parcels. There is also in the experiment-room an electrical apparatus, chiefly the invention of one of the professors,* and perhaps the completest of the kind now in the world.

This is a faithful though brief account of the whole Seminary, and what a blessing must it prove to the continent of America in general, as well as to the province in which it is founded? What advantages may not the youth reap amid so many opportunities of improvement and so many incitements to industry, where the masters transact everything by joint advice, where all possible regard to religion and morality is kept up, and the whole open to the visitation and frequent inspection of a number of gentlemen of rank and character?

May there never be wanting a succession of such gentlemen to take the trust and care of it; and may it continue, to the latest times, a shining light to the world around it and an honor to the province, as long as any memorial of virtue and letters shall remain among mankind!

CHAPTER V.

MEETING OF THE TRUSTEES OF THE SOCIETY FOR THE EDUCATION OF THE GER-
MANS—DR. MUHLENBERG TO DR. FRANKLIN—VARIOUS SCHOOLS ESTABLISHED
—DIFFICULTIES WITH SAUER, ETC.

ON the 10th of August, 1754, the Governor, having called a meeting of the trustees of the Society for Propagating Christian Knowledge among the Germans settled in Pennsylvania, the trustees met at the house of William Allen, Esq., in Mount Airy, to take into their consideration the business so warmly recommended in the letter from the secretary, dated London, March 15th. There were present James Hamilton, Richard Peters, Benjamin Franklin, and William Smith.

The following resolutions were passed:

That an English school be erected and opened with all possible expedition at each of the following places, viz.: at Reading, York, Easton, Lancaster, Hanover, and Skippack.

That, for the better government of these schools, a certain number of the most reputable persons residing near every particular school be ap-

---

* Mr. Kinnersley.

pointed deputy trustees, to visit that school, superintend the execution of the scheme of education in it, and use their interests in the support of it.

That six, eight, or ten be appointed for every school, and that, to render the scheme more catholic and unexceptional, part of these trustees for each school shall be colonists, part Lutheran Germans, and part Englishmen of any Protestant profession whatever.

That against next meeting the present members endeavor to inform themselves what persons may be fittest to be employed under them as trustees, and that proper steps be taken to engage such persons in the interest of the scheme, hoping that by means of such persons a schoolhouse and dwelling-house for the master may be immediately erected by the inhabitants of the particular divisions for which each school is to be established, without putting the honorable Society or their trustees to any expense or trouble on this head.

The difficulty of finding proper schoolmasters skilled in both languages coming next under consideration, Dr. Smith informed the trustees that there were several poor children in the Academy that spoke English and German, who might in a few years be qualified to serve as schoolmasters, and that if a few could be found to begin the work immediately, there would be no difficulty of finding a constant supply by encouraging such children to continue at the Academy by the benefaction of the proprietaries,* whenever their parents, who live chiefly in the city of Philadelphia, shall become tired of their maintenance.   He also further informed the trustees that he had conversed with a young man named Magaw, born in this colony, who came well recommended, and who could be well qualified in six or eight months at the Academy to take charge of a school,† and that he had prevailed upon the Rev. Mr. Brunnholtz,‡

---

* The Hon. Thomas Penn, Esq., empowered his secretary (Mr. Peters) to lay out £50 sterling per annum upon the education of some young men in the Academy, in order to fit them for schoolmasters, and left the choice of them and the disposition of his bounty entirely to the trustees.   Thirty pounds of this fifty were his own proper gift; ten pounds were bestowed by Lady Juliana Penn, his wife, and ten pounds by Richard Penn, Esq., per annum.

† This was afterwards the Rev. Samuel Magaw, D. D., Rector of St. Paul's Church, and Vice-Provost of the University.

‡ Rev. Peter Brunnholtz was a native of Germany.   He came to Germantown some time before the year 1750, at which time he had charge of the German Lutheran Church at that place, and also took charge of St. Michael's Church in Philadelphia, officiating on alternate Sabbaths at each church.   John Helfrich Schaum, who taught school in Philadelphia, filled the pulpits at Philadelphia and Germantown during the intervening Sabbaths.   Brunnholtz died July 5th, 1757.

5

member of the Lutheran congregation in this city, to board Mr.
Magaw in his house, to watch over his morals, and assist him in
making further progress in the German language, provided the
trustees would admit him to the proprietaries' bounty.

It was agreed that Mr. Magaw be admitted, and Mr. Brunnholtz
made acquainted that the trustees would stand engaged for his
lodging and board; also, that further inquiry should be made in
order to find three or four more young men who, together with
Mr. Magaw, might be qualified to open a few schools next spring.

A letter from the Rev. Mr. Henry Muhlenberg, of Providence,
in the district which at present is Montgomery county, to Benjamin
Franklin was read, the purport of which was as follows:

That he rejoiced much in hearing an illustrious society at home
had undertaken to carry on a scheme for promoting the knowledge
of God among the Germans in Pennsylvania, and for making them
loyal subjects to the sacred Protestant throne of Great Britain, and
that he was pleased the management of the said charity was intrusted to such impartial persons; but, as by long experience he
was acquainted with almost all the corners of Pennsylvania, and
with the temper and circumstances of his countrymen, he much
feared some ill-minded persons would strive to defeat so just and
noble a view, as they had of late done many others, to the offence
of many thousand ignorant but well-meaning souls, unless proper
means were taken to prevent it. Mr. Sauer, he observed, who
printed a German newspaper, which was universally read by the
Germans all over Pennsylvania and the neighboring colonies, made
haste to prejudice them against the scheme, as might be seen by
the extracts from his paper.

Mr. Muhlenberg further observed that Mr. Franklin had at
great expense set up another German press, in order to rescue the
Germans out of Mr. Sauer's hands and the hands of those whose
interest it was to keep them in ignorance, but that for want of a
German printer with sufficient skill and correspondence to a
proper interest made to support Mr. Franklin's undertaking, Mr.
Sauer kept the advantage, continuing to turn them against their
clergy and everybody that endeavored to reduce them to order in
Church and State affairs. That he, Mr. Muhlenberg, himself once
attempted to buy a press, on purpose to serve his countrymen and
instil sound notions in them concerning the inestimable privileges,

spiritual and temporal, which they enjoyed under the Protestant throne of Great Britain, but by reason of his large increasing family and narrow circumstances he had been obliged to drop his design, and now beheld his poor countrymen as much poisoned as ever with notions that might produce unhappy consequences in very remote periods.   That he saw no way to cure this growing evil unless the Society, or their trustees in Pennsylvania, should be at the expense of buying a press and making a proper interest to support a newspaper, almanacs, etc.   That he would undertake the direction of such a press under the trustees; that he would use his whole influence among his people and brethren to support it, and that a person might be got who could manage the press and serve as schoolmaster at the same time.   He did not doubt of the success of the scheme, since he had a large correspondence with pious German ministers and congregations in Pennsylvania, New York, New England, New Jersey, Maryland, Virginia, Carolina, and Georgia, who could be engaged to support it without putting the Society to any expense, especially if the printing-house was in a country where there was no house-rent to pay, and where the same persons might serve as schoolmasters and chief printer. He further lamented the riots, disloyalty, and irreligion which were nursed among his countrymen by their being stirred up against pious and regularly ordained clergy, while vicious vagabonds coming on without orders and credentials were indulged; many of them being justly suspected to be more in French than in British interests.   That many people without discretion traded with the English government.   One who named himself Charles Rudolph, Prince of Wurtemberg and minister of the Gospel, was a stroller of this kind.   Yet it could be proved that he made a conspiracy with the Indians against the English, and escaped the gallows in Georgia by stealing a boat and running over to the Spaniards, and was infamous all over America for riots and breaking jails; nevertheless, he was followed as a Lutheran, and sometimes as a Calvinist minister.   Another, named Engelland, in Germany, turned Roman Catholic.   While under the hands of the hangman, he was reprieved at the intercession of the Jesuits after receiving eighty lashes at the gallows; was banished to the Spanish Netherlands for stealing and carrying off children; and now about Lancaster and York he breeds dissensions, etc., by passing as a Lutheran minister. " There were many more of the same sort which," said Mr. Muhlenberg, " we shall never get rid of, nor reduce the people to proper order, until our gracious superiors are pleased to demand proper credentials of all who exercise the ministry, and not suffer vagabonds to laugh at *us*, who are regular clergymen, by saying it is a free country, and by turning liberty into licentiousness." Mr. Sauer (Mr. Muhlenberg said), in his newspaper, was a professed adversary to all regularly ordained clergy, and drew people to Quakerism; for he often told the people that clergy of all kinds were tools of tyrannical governors, to awe the mob.*

Mr. Muhlenberg's letter was accompanied by these translations from Mr. Sauer's paper of September 1st, 1754:

TRANSLATION.

In our number 159 we mentioned that a high school or college was to be erected at Philadelphia for the benefit of the Germans in the city of Philadelphia, Lancaster, York, Reading, Easton, etc., and that the Germans by degrees may become one nation with the English, and so make all of English ministers only. These accounts further tell us this was done out of fear; the multitude of Germans might make up or form themselves into one separate people or body, and in time of war go over to the French, and join with them to the hurt and prejudice of the English nation.

Then follow Mr. Sauer's remarks:

The new Society in England deserves praise for being so liberal and so kind as to teach the Germans the English tongue gratis. But if Slatter has accused the Germans to such a degree, and represented them as if they were a nation of so roguish and mischievous a disposition, that in time of war they would probably join the French and villanously espouse their cause, he has most certainly acted with great imprudency, to the disadvantage of the King, as well as of himself. None, indeed, will permit himself to think that many Germans could be so treacherous as he perhaps may think. The Irish, the Swedes, and the Welsh keep their languages, yet for all that are not looked upon as a disloyal people. Oh, that truly pious schoolmasters in the English tongue might be given them, who could be to them a pattern of a true Christian life ! Then

* It is proper to add that though Mr. Sauer was a good deal embittered in this matter of educating the poor Germans, and dangerous, in the respects spoken of by Mr. Muhlenberg, to the government, he was in private life a respectable man, and doubtless, in his views about clerical ordination, conscientious.—ED.

still some hopes would be left, some good might proceed therefrom ; for it is true piety only that makes men to be faithful towards God and their neighbor.   The preacher Solomon says, chap. ix., v. 18, " Wisdom is better than weapons of war ; but one single artful and wicked man destroyeth much good."   The wicked man may either preach English or German, yet it is to no purpose or benefit, for no soul shall be mended thereby, nay, not himself.

Then he goes on as follows :

Since it has been now for many years past a matter of praise in Europe, and the English newspapers now boast of the exceedingly mild government under which we live in Pennsylvania (for which reason so many Germans are induced to come over here from Europe, and for the future more may come), necessity itself requires that all countries, and more especially Philadelphia county, should take it into their considera-tion how to choose such mild assemblymen on 1st October next ensuing, as in a dangerous and critical conjuncture of things will preserve the liberty of the land, and that this land may not fall short of that glory and praise in Europe, and that the inhabitants may not be burdened for the future with paying heavy taxes in an unnecessary manner.

The representations of the Rev. Mr. Muhlenberg coinciding with the views of the trustees, it was unanimously resolved that a short account of the real design of the Society should be written and couched in the most unexceptionable language.   Dr. Smith was accordingly desired to prepare a draft of the same and lay it before the trustees when finished, in order that when it had their approbation it might be printed in English and Dutch, and a proper number of copies sent to the deputy or assistant trustees, to be dispersed in the country among the people.

It was also resolved to purchase a German printing-house, and make proper interest to begin and support a newspaper, yearly almanacs, and other small pieces.   Mr. Franklin then told the Board that a few days before a printer, of good character, well skilled in English and German, had applied to him to purchase his German printing-house, in order to attempt something for his own livelihood and the service of his countrymen, but that if the trus-tees thought it best to have the press under their own direction, he would endeavor to engage the printer in their service, both as a schoolmaster and printer, and that, in order to encourage so useful a work, he would dispose of his press to the trustees at £25 *less* than any two impartial judges would value it at.

This proposal of Mr. Franklin was agreed to, and it was recommended to him to engage the printer, by offering him a house, and a few acres of land, and £20 sterling, as a schoolmaster, per annum, and wages for everything he might be further employed in as a printer.

It was further agreed that Dr. Smith should act as secretary, take charge of all papers concerning this undertaking, and keep a record of the proceedings of the trustees, so that copies of them might from time to time be transmitted to the Society in London, and to the proprietaries.

On the 23d of August, 1754, the trustees of the Society met at the Governor's house, at Bush Hill, when there were present the Governor, Richard Peters, Benjamin Franklin, Conrad Weiser, and William Smith.

Dr. Smith laid before the trustees two petitions, which he had received by the hands of Mr. Muhlenberg; the first, entitled the " Petition of the Vestrymen and Wardens in the name of the German Lutheran Congregation, at New Providence, about Perkiomen and Skippack, in the county of Philadelphia." The petitioners offered the trustees their new-built school-house, which was well situated for the convenience of the children of the several Protestant denominations. This petition was subscribed by John Schrack, Anthony Heilman, Jacob Schrack, Valentine Sharrar (now Sherer), John Heebner, John Heilman, Nicholas Custer, Hieronymus Haas, Michael Bastian, Conrad Yost, Nicholas Seidel.

The second petition—entitled the " Petition of the Vestrymen and Wardens in the name of the Lutheran (German) Congregations, at New Hanover, in the county of Philadelphia "—by permission of their former benefactors, His Majesty's German chaplain, the Rev. Fred. Ziegenhagen, and August Frank, D. D., offered the new-built large school-house, very conveniently situated in the middle of the township. This petition was signed by George Geiger, Andrew Kepner, Valentine Geiger, George Beck, Michael Schweinhard, Adam Wardman, Casper Singer, Henry Krebs, Michael Schlonecker, George Burchard, Matthias Hollebach, John Rinker, Nicholas Miller, Matthias Richard, John Wingel, John Seidel.

The trustees passed this resolution :

That the thanks of the trustees in the name of the honorable Society be returned to the Rev. Mr. Muhlenberg, and the several vestrymen and wardens for their kind endeavors to promote this useful undertaking by the offer of a school-house, and which offer would be accepted of by the trustees, provided the German Calvinist congregations in the same township signify their approbation, and concur in the choice of and situation of these school-houses; it being the resolution of the trustees, according to their instructions from the honorable Society, to manage the whole undertaking in such an equal and impartial manner as that no parents, of what denomination soever, shall have any reasonable objections against sending their children to any school that may be established upon this charity.

The trustees therefore recommended it to Mr. Muhlenberg to have a meeting with the chief men and ministers of the Calvinist congregation in the township, that he with them might fix on the Lutheran or any other school-houses for the common benefit of their helpless children, the trustees stating that they would not hesitate in accepting any offer or the coming into any measure that might be agreed upon in common by the said Calvinist and Lutheran congregations, between which they always hoped to see a perfect Christian harmony.

Mr. Muhlenberg, being acquainted with this resolution, replied that in his part of the province such a harmony had always subsisted, and that he would endeavor and did not doubt to obtain the concurrence of the Calvinist congregation in the choice of the two school-houses offered, as they are both situated in places fixed upon by the Society to erect schools in, and there being no other school-houses in these parts fit for the purpose.

The trustees then proceeded to consider who would be the most fit persons to act as assistant or d puty trustees for the several schools. It was desirable that the persons selected should reside near these schools. Among many that were recommended for this purpose the following persons were preferred, many of them being personally known to the Governor and the Secretary, Mr. Peters, and almost all of them by Mr. Conrad Weiser. They were accordingly written to.

For Lancaster.—Edward Shippen, Esq. (English), President; Mr. Adam Simon Kuhn, Mr. Otterbein, Mr. Sebastian Graff (Calvinist), Mr. Gera (Lutheran), Mr. James Wright, Mr. John Bär.

For New Providence and Skippack.—Mr. Abram Sahler, Dr. John Diemer (Calvinist), John Schrack, Nicolaus Küster (Lutheran), Henry Pawling, Esq., Mr. Robert White, John Coplin (English).

For Reading.—Mr. James Read, Prothonotary, Francis Parvin, Esq. (English Quaker), James Seely (English Presbyterian), Mr. Isaac Levau, Mr. Samuel High (Calvinist), Mr. Hans Martin Gerick, Mr. Jacob Levan (Lutheran), Mr. Sebastian Zimmerman.

For Easton.—Mr. Parsons, Mr. Lewis Gordon, Mr. John Chapman, Mr. John Le Fevre, Mr. Peter Trexler.

For New Hanover, Frederick Township.—Andrew Kepner, Henry Krebs (Lutheran), Henry Antes, Esq., Mr. John Reifsnyder (Calvinist), John Potts, Esq., William Maugridge, Esq. (English.)

For York.—Nobody was as yet recommended, but Mr. Weiser engaged in his journey to the frontiers in the service of the government, to converse with the proper persons in regard to the school to be fixed at York.

A question arose among the trustees whether one Calvinist and one Lutheran minister should not be joined with each of the above sets of assistant trustees for every school, upon which it was observed by Mr. Weiser that so great was the jealousy of the people at present against the clergy in general, that such a measure at first might be a hindrance to the scheme, especially as these jealousies are daily fomented, as was further confirmed by different articles which he called attention to in Mr. Sauer's paper. On the other side it was observed that the clergy, in all countries, were reckoned fit persons to superintend the education of youth, and that if the Germans had prejudice at present against clergy of all kinds, it was one great design of the undertaking of the Society to remove such prejudice, and promote a sense of religion and a greater regard to their clergy among the Germans, without which there was little probability of rendering them peaceable, industrious, and governable subjects. However, it was—

Resolved, That at present the opinion of other gentlemen proposed as deputy trustees, etc., be taken on this subject, and that Mr. Smith be appointed to write a joint letter to each of the above sets of deputy or assistant trustees, in order to know their sentiments on this and every other part of the scheme as far as it is yet advanced.

Mr. Franklin informed the trustees that he had, according to his engagement, spoken to the German printer mentioned at the last meeting, but that the said printer seemed rather inclined to take the press on his own risk, and print such for the trustees at a rea-

sonable rate as they should think proper. But it was decided that
this proposal was contrary to the intention of the trustees, and
that it was absolutely necessary, in order to their design, that they
should have the sole direction of the press and newspaper on their
own hands, or the hands of such persons as they should appoint
for that purpose, and that Mr. Franklin should acquaint the printer
with this resolution.

CHAPTER VI.

First Sermon in Christ Church, Philadelphia, on the Death of a Pupil—
Verses of Compliment by the Students and Friends—Hopkinson, Magaw,
Duché, Barton, and Jackson—Hymn by Dr. Smith—Society for the Education of Poor German Protestants—Particulars about it—Dr. Smith
to Rev. Henry Muhlenberg—Muhlenberg to Dr. Smith—Petitions from
New Hanover—Henry Antes—Dr. Smith's Letter to Rev. Messrs. Reiger
and Stoy—Answer—Letter from W. Parsons to Dr. Peters—Letter
from Christopher Sauer—Dr. Smith a Statesman and True Son of
the Church.

The affectionate interest taken by Dr. Smith in his pupils was
manifested in many ways. We have an evidence of one of the
ways in a sermon preached in Christ Church, Philadelphia, September, 1754, on the death of one of them, William Thomas
Martin, a truly promising youth, who died at Philadelphia, August
28th, 1754, while a student in the Senior Philosophy Class of the
College. He was the second son of the Hon. Josiah Martin, Esq.,
of Antigua, and cousin to Samuel Martin, Esq., member of Parliament for Camelford, Treasurer to the Princess Dowager of Wales,
and Secretary of the Treasury. The sermon, which is preserved
in Dr. Smith's printed sermons,* gives evidence of those same
oratorical powers seen in his later discourses. It produced a
great impression, due, doubtless, in part, to a highly effective manner of delivery. It brought forth the following stanzas from the
fellow-students and friends of Mr. Martin, which were sent to Dr.
Smith in the graceful fashion of the day. As a record of this and
of our early college literature, as much as for any poetical merit
which the pieces have, we insert them:

* Vol. I., p. 5.

TO THE REV. MR. WILLIAM SMITH,

ON HEARING HIS SERMON UPON THE DEATH OF HIS HOPEFUL PUPIL,
OUR DEAR FELLOW-STUDENT, MR. WILLIAM THOMAS MARTIN.

BY A FELLOW-STUDENT.

I call no aid, no muses to inspire,
Or teach my breast to feel a poet's fire;
Your soft expression of a grief sincere,
Brings from my soul a sympathetic tear.
Taught by your voice, my artless sorrows flow;
I sigh in verse, am eloquent in woe,
And loftier thoughts within my bosom glow.
For when, in all the charms of language drest,
A manly grief flows, genuine, from the breast,
What gen'rous nature can escape the wounds,
Or steel itself against the force of melting sounds?
O could I boast to move with equal art
The human soul, or melt the stony heart;
My long-lov'd friend should through my numbers shine,
Some virtue lost be wept in every line;
For virtues he had many—'Twas confest
That native sense and sweetness fill'd his breast.
But cooler reason checks the bold intent,
And, to the task refusing her consent,
This only truth permits me to disclose,
That, in your own, you represent my woes;
And sweeter than my song is your harmonious prose!

FRANCIS HOPKINSON.

COLLEGE OF PHILADELPHIA, September 5th, 1754.

BY A FELLOW-STUDENT.

And is your Martin gone? Is he no more,
That living truth, that virtue seen before?
Has endless night already hid the ray,
The early promise of his glorious day?
That grief, great *Mourner*, in such strains exprest,
Shews he was deep implanted in your breast.
Yet hark! soft-whispering reason seems to say,
Cease from your sorrows, wipe these tears away.
He's gone, he's past the gloomy shades of night,
Safe landed in th' eternal realms of light.
Happy exchange! to part with all below,
For worlds of bliss where joys unfading flow,
And sainted souls with love and rapture glow.

SAMUEL MAGAW.

COLLEGE OF PHILADELPHIA, September 6th, 1754.

BY A FELLOW-STUDENT.

While for a pupil lost your sorrow flows,
In all the harmony of finish'd prose;
While melting crowds the pious accents hear,
Sigh to your sighs, and give you tear for tear;
We, too, in humble verse, would treat the theme,
And join our griefs to swell the general stream.
For we remember well his matchless power,
To steal upon the heart and cheer the social hour.
　　Ah, much lov'd friend, too soon thy beauties fade!
Too soon we count thee with the silent dead!
Thou, late the fairest plant in virtue's plain,
The brightest youth in wisdom's rising train;
By genius great, by liberal arts adorn'd,
By strangers seen and lov'd, by strangers mourned;
Blest in a tender brother's friendly breast;
And in paternal fondness doubly blest!
Art thou now sunk in death's tremendous gloom,
Wrapt in the awful horrors of a tomb?
Ah me! how vain all sublunary joy!
Woes following woes, our warmest hopes destroy!
But hark!—some voice celestial strikes mine ear,
And bids the muse her plaintive strains forbear.
"Weep not, fond youths,"—it cries, or seems to cry,—
"He lives, your Martin lives, and treads the sky;
From care, from toil, from sickness snatch'd away,
He shines amid the blaze of heaven's eternal day."

JACOB DUCHE.

COLLEGE OF PHILADELPHIA, September 7th, 1754.

BY A FRIEND.

　　Check, mournful preacher! check thy streaming woe,
Pierce not our souls with grief too great to know;
He joys above whom we lament below.
Snatch'd from our follies here, he wing'd his way,
To sing hosannas in the realms of day.
With him the fight of life and death is o'er,
And agonizing throes shall pain no more;
No more shall fell disease, with wasteful rage,
Blast the fair blossoms of his tender age;
Transplanted now, he blooms a heav'nly flow'r,
Where spring eternal decks yon amaranthine bower.
　　Thy pious sorrows, Smith, to future days,
Shall bear his image, and transmit his praise.

Still, still I feel what thy Discourse imprest,
When pity throb'd, congenial, in each breast;
When deep distress came thrilling from thy tongue,
And sympathizing crowds attentive hung.
To mourn for thy lov'd pupil all approv'd;
On such a theme 'twas virtue to be mov'd.
Whoe'er these tender pages shall explore,
Must learn those griefs the pulpit taught before.

THOMAS BARTON.

COLLEGE OF PHILADELPHIA, September 7th, 1754.

BY ONE OF THE TUTORS.

O Death! could manly courage quell thy power,
Or rosy health protect the fatal hour;
Could tears prevail, or healing arts withstand
Th' unsparing ravage of thy wasteful hand;
Then Martin still had liv'd a father's boast,
Nor had a mother's fondest hopes been lost;
Then, Smith, thy darling youth, thy justest pride,
With virtue's first examples long had vi'd.
But he is blest where joys immortal flow;
Cease, tears, to stream! be dumb the voice of woe!
Releas'd from vice, in early bloom set free
From the dire rocks of this tempestuous sea,
The youthful saint, in heaven's ambrosial vales,
With glory crown'd, etherial life inhales.
No more let grief repine, or wish his stay,
In this dark gloom, this twilight of our day.
Rather we'll hail him fled from night's domain,
Array'd in light to tread the azure plain.
There science dwells:—before the mental eye
Nature's stupendous works unfolded lie;
There wisdom, goodness, power diffusive shine,
And fire the glowing breast with love divine.

PAUL JACKSON.

COLLEGE OF PHILADELPHIA, September 7th, 1754.

Dr. Smith had some poetical talent. One evidence of it was a hymn composed by him, and sung at the church after his discourse. It is thus:

Father of all! still wise and good
    Whether thou giv'st or tak'st away;
Before thy throne devoutly bow'd
    We hail thy providential sway!

Save us from Fortune's hollow smile,
　　That lures the guardless soul to rest ;
A round of pleasure is but toil,
　　And who could bear a constant feast ?

Sometimes thy chast'ning hand employ
　　Gently to rouse us, not to pain !
Sometimes let sorrow prove our joy,
　　And scatter folly's noisy train !

Oft let us drop a pensive tear,
　　O'er this much suffering scene of man ;
Acute to feel what others bear,
　　And wise our own defects to scan.

Teach us, while woes and deaths are nigh,
　　To think on thee, and weigh our dust.
Well may we mark the hours that fly
　　And still find leisure to be just.

We have already spoken of the interest taken by Dr. Smith in giving an education both in the English language and in good religious morals to the poorer class of Germans in Pennsylvania. The following correspondence is in reference to the subject. We give, first, a letter by him to the Rev. Mr. Henry Muhlenberg, pastor of the Lutheran congregation at New Providence, Pennsylvania, on a point connected with this subject, where difficulty was feared and where delicate management was required. We cannot but be struck by the entire directness and candor of Dr. Smith in his mode of dealing with it.

This correspondence, along with Minutes of the Proceedings of the Trustees, were sent by the Rev. Thomas Barton (who, on the 9th of October, 1754, sailed for England) to the Rev. Mr. Chandler, already mentioned; a copy of them being enclosed for prior perusal by the Proprietaries.*

PHILADELPHIA, October 23d, 1754.

REVEREND SIR : In answer to the petition you and your vestry were pleased to lay before us, dated 1st and 4th of August last, I inclose you the resolution of the trustees taken from the minutes of our last meeting. You will see by them that we have a just sense of the pains you have taken in this affair, and we should be extremely glad to find it consistent

---

* For some account of the Rev. Thomas Barton, a poetical piece from whose pen we have given *supra*, p. 75, and whose name and letters frequently occur in this volume, see Appendix No. I.

with the design of the honorable Society to accept your school-houses; but we apprehend that it may be easy for you to bring the Calvinist congregation to concur in the same choice, when they are made acquainted with the catholic and generous plan on which it is proposed to establish the schools. In order, therefore, that you may have a just view of the design, I inclose you a sketch of it which I have drawn out for some Calvinist ministers who wanted to be informed of the design, and which I propose to give to their classis, who are to meet next week in this city. In the meantime I shall beg you to proceed as follows: The extract from the minutes, together with the above sketch of our design, be so kind as to translate into your own language, and get a number of copies made. Give some to Mr. Leidig, the Calvinist minister, and next Sunday let him, as well as you, give notice to the chief persons of your respective congregations to meet in the school-house or church the day following, and it would be well if each of you would prepare your people by opening up a little of the design, and explain the importance of a religious education in your sermons. At the time of the meeting put the translated papers into the hands of some of your most moderate and sensible laymen to explain to the people; and if the matter is managed skilfully, I hope by God's blessing the eyes of the people will be open to their interest, and you will agree to have your children educated in the same school, on the same common uncultivated principles of religion and virtue. Such a Christian harmony well becomes those who are heirs of the same common salvation. Our design is truly catholic, no compensation is intended, and I hope you will urge all the people to remember what is insisted upon in the inclosed papers, namely, that if by any ill-timed discord they shall defeat the benevolent design of the Society, they will be accountable to God not only for their own ignorance but for all that ignorance and misery which they will thereby entail upon their unhappy children. It is not our intention to strive against the stream; and in case you shall not agree to accept the schools on that generous and free bottom on which we are resolved to fix them, we must establish them among those who will; but from your zeal and interest we hope better things, and that you will set a noble example of moderation and unanimity to others. I pray God give you success in return for all your labors. You may depend on the good-will of the trustees, and with regard to myself I shall be glad of any opportunity of verifying, by more than words, how sincerely I am

Yours, etc.,

WILLIAM SMITH.

Mr. Muhlenberg's Answer to the Preceding Letter.

PROVIDENCE, October 29th, 1754.

REVEREND SIR: I had the pleasure of your kind letter of October 23d and 24th, with your obliging answer from the minutes, together

with the other papers. In obedience to your orders I had a meeting in
mine own house with Mr. Leidig, and the chief men of the Reformed
Calvinists at New Providence, and several honest men of other denominations. I explained the undeserved munificence of the illustrious
Society and the fatherly cares of the honorable trustees, which made a
deep impression on the minds of all present, so that they unanimously
agreed to concur in the choice of our Lutheran school-houses as the best
situated for our children of all denominations; and they also promised
to prepare an humble petition to signify their entire approbation of the
truly catholic and charitable design. Thus much for New Providence.
Yesterday we had a meeting in the offered school-houses at New Hanover, at which the Rev. Mr. Leidig, Henry Antes, Esq., and the chief
men of both Calvinists and Lutheran congregations and of some other
persuasions were present. I began with prayer, and then gave them a
brief historical account of the excellent and ever-to-be-praised charity.
I concluded with recommending Christian unanimity, and then delivered a translation of your answer and order out of the minutes, and all
your other papers into the hands of Henry Antes, Esq., who, being a
man of great reputation and influence, was attentively heard while he
explained the same to the people. After conferring a little together
they all melted at once into tears of joy, uttered many thankful expressions, and agreed in Christian harmony in the choice of our Lutheran
school-house, and offered also their own school-house, which is only
about sixty poles distant, to be added when our children of all denominations should grow too numerous to be contained in one house. The
Calvinists and other denominations then asked us Lutherans to sell two
or more acres of our church and school land, where, if need be, we
might erect one large building for such a charitable design in time to
come. We answered that we would readily bequeath the left and most
convenient corner of our church land for so Christianlike an institution,
which aimed at the common benefit of the State and Christ's Church.

Mr. Leidig, who goes down to Philadelphia this day to meet the
trustees, will present you with both the petitions. The whole meeting
agreed to recommend the present Lutheran and Calvinist schoolmasters
to the honorable trustees as worthy to be taken into their service; as
the said schoolmasters bear good characters, and have instructed the
children of several Englishmen in the English tongue. If you should
not think them quite perfect in English, they are willing to come this
winter to Philadelphia to be perfected. One of those schoolmasters,
who resides in our township, called Cornelius Rabatan, is a true-born
Englishman, a Presbyterian bred, and wants no instruction, for besides
his native English he speaks indifferent good French and Dutch. He is
much beloved by people of all persuasions, for his decent and Christian
behavior. He was sent to town, but missed your reverence; when you
were lately on a journey to New York; but he waited on Mr. Secretary

Peters and was well received. Him in particular, if it would please the trustees to appoint during his good behavior, I can assure you a vast number of German and English children of all persuasions would flock to him; and I know divers parents who have been already inquiring where to lodge their children and board them, for the school at New Providence, when it shall be opened.

May God prosper your kind endeavors, and those of the other worthy trustees, for the benefit of a vast multitude of helpless souls, which is the prayer of   Yours, etc.,

                                                            HENRY MUHLENBERG.

To REV. MR. SMITH.

The petitions referred to in Mr. Muhlenberg's letter were as follows:

PETITION FROM NEW HANOVER.

The petition of the ministers, elders, and chief men of the German Calvinist Congregation, and of some other Protestant denominations in the township of New Hanover and county of Philadelphia, humbly showeth: That whereas, by our gracious superiors, preparation is being made to establish a number of charity schools for the children of every German denomination, in order to instruct them in the German and English languages and to render them fit for becoming true worshippers of God in Christ, most loyal and dutiful subjects to the sacred Protestant throne of Great Britain, and thankful to the illustrious benefactors here and at home; and that, whereas the minister, vestry, and chief men of the Protestant Lutheran Congregation, our beloved neighbors and fellow-citizens of the township and county aforesaid, have humbly implored the honorable trustees to make their and our children jointly an object of their intended charity, and have offered a most suitable house in the midst of the township, between two large evangelical meetings, very suitable for so noble an institution, we, the humble petitioners join, therefore, with our beloved neighbors, the said Lutheran and other denominations, in humbly beseeching that it may please the illustrious benefactors to make our very numerous youth the object of their clemency, and to fix their intended charity on the helpless children of all denominations in the said offered school-house or place, and in case the said house should become too small for our said children we readily offer our school-house also, and being altogether of one mind and in Christianlike harmony, think to provide the most suitable place for so noble an institution. Moreover, your humble petitioners recommend, under the illustrious benefactors and two well-behaving and beloved schoolmasters, or either of them who has made the best progress in the English language, and may be rendered more perfect for the purpose, if they have been already among us in our mean circumstances, they are willing to improve themselves with their utmost endeavors in the English language and to assist in so good a work. May the Lord inspire the catholic spirit of our gracious superiors and illustrious benefactors always to keep in mind our numerous and helpless children and school-masters, since a fine harvest is to be hoped. We shall endeavor to join in a Christian harmony, to pray for our most gracious sovereign, King George II., and all that are in authority under him, especially for our illustrious benefactors.

Conrad Dodderer, John Philip Leidig, V.D.M., John Muller, Dieter Bucher, George Palzgreff, Valentine Kyle, Jacob Barnard, Andrew Smith, Frederick Rymer, Henry Smith, Bernard Dodderer.

Testes: Henry Muhlenberg, V.D.M., Henry Antes.*

NEW HANOVER, October 28th, 1754.

PETITION FROM PROVIDENCE.

The petition of the minister, elders, and principal members of the German Reformed Congregation, and of some other Protestant persuasions in the township of Providence, in and about Perkiomen and Skippack, humbly showeth (as in the foregoing petition), and prays that the trustees will accept of the offered Lutheran school-house, in the midst of said township, as most convenient, and therein to make the children of all denominations in and about the places above mentioned the object of the honorable Society's bounty, and that at the common request of all denominations Cornelius Rabatan be chosen as schoolmaster, to whom vast numbers would flock. The humble petitioners pray, etc.

John Umstead, John Hendricks, Gilwig Ewalt, Matthias Koplin, Samuel Lane, David Robeson, John Philip Leidig, V. D. M., Edward De Haven, Nicholas Bonn, William Howe, John Penebacker, Joseph Kendall, Valentine Haus.

Testes: Henry Muhlenberg, V.D.M., John Schrack, John Koplin, Abram De Haven.

We return now to the correspondence.

Dr. Smith to the Rev. Messrs. Reiger and Stoy.

PHILADELPHIA, September 30th, 1754.

REVEREND SIRS: An account being desired of me concerning the design now carrying on, for the benefit of the Germans in Pennsylvania, I shall beg leave to lay before you the following hasty sketch of it, which may suffice to give you some idea of it till my leisure, and the return of the other trustees, who are now absent, shall permit us to

---

* For some account of Mr. Antes, see Appendix No. II.

6

give an ample account of all the parts of it in print; and this you may expect soon, both English and Dutch.* A considerable sum of money has been raised in Scotland for the instruction of the destitute German Protestants in this and the neighboring provinces, and the said money is committed to the management of an illustrious society of noblemen and gentlemen in London.

The said Society in London, as they would neither bestow their bounty on any who do not deserve it, and as they cannot at such a distance judge who are most deserving, that they may not be imposed upon in this important matter, they have therefore intrusted the management of the whole scheme to us, whose names follow, as trustees general in Pennsylvania: James Hamilton, William Allen, Richard Peters, Benjamin Franklin, Conrad Weiser, Esq., and the Rev. William Smith. They have also appointed the Rev. Mr. Schlatter, under the direction and with the advice of the said trustees, to act as superior of the schools that are to be erected, and assist in the execution of the whole scheme.

This Society is endeavoring to raise a much greater sum of money in England, and have resolved to apply the same towards the encouragement of pious and peaceable ministers and schoolmasters, beginning first in Pennsylvania.

We, the said trustees, therefore, are empowered to increase the yearly salaries of pious and well-behaved ministers among you, and will accordingly do the same, especially if all things are amicably settled between you and Mr. Schlatter, for as few of you are personally known to us we must depend in some measure upon his resolution.

We are likewise to establish some schools for the education of youth, both in the English and German languages and in the principles of our common Christianity. Such schools will be on the most catholic bottom, and are intended equally for the benefit of all denominations. Calvinist children may use their own catechism; for with regard to religious tenets no compulsion or constraint will be offered to the consciences of any persons however scrupulous.

The schoolmasters are to be men of good character, and such as may be approved by all denominations and parties. Their salaries will be paid regularly by us, and for the more immediate government of the schools, men of good character residing among yourselves will be nominated. As this is a truly charitable and pious undertaking, without which the labors of you who are preachers will have but little success, we hope all good men, and particularly you who are ministers of the blessed Gospel, will join to support it; and all ministers who do zeal-

---

* When, in this correspondence, the word *Dutch* is used, the reader will understand that the emigrants from Germany, or their descendants, are spoken of, and not Hollanders, of whom, in the interior of Pennsylvania, there were not many.

ously promote this pious design, and assist us in the execution of it, may expect particular regard and encouragement. The place fixed upon for the school-houses are Lancaster, York, Reading, Easton, Skippack, and Hanover; unless, by any difficulties or discords raised among the different persuasions in those places, we should be obliged to fix them elsewhere, among those who may be more deserving. But this we only hint, by the by, and we have no reason to think any persons will be so infatuated as not cheerfully to concur in a design so disinterested as that of the honorable Society in London.

The cries of a vast multitude of despairing souls reach the ears of the good and pious in Britain and Holland. A proper sum is raised for their relief. The management of it is in the hands of persons of worth and credit. Any change proposed by yourselves to the more effectual application of this charity will be readily listened to.

The cause of the true undefiled religion and of the Protestant interest is concerned. Ignorance, which is the sure forerunner of superstition and of civil and religious tyranny, is the enemy to be rooted out; and can we then expect any persons will be so wicked and inhuman to throw any obstacle in the way of a design so friendly to all the better interests of mankind as this? If there are any such persons, certainly they must reflect that their memory would be held in abhorrence by posterity, and that they would be accountable in the sight of God for all that misery and ignorance, which such a conduct would be the means of entailing upon their helpless children perhaps to latest generations, as you gentlemen cannot but think it your duty to inculcate a contrary conduct. We shall be glad to have your advice from time to time in the management of the whole design now opened, and your answer as a classis to the following queries (to be transmitted to the Society) will much oblige us:

1. Query. What are the particular salaries of every Calvinist minister in this province, and how much do they fall short of a competent, decent, and independent living?

2. How many more Calvinist ministers may be immediately wanted in Pennsylvania, and in what places, that we may be able to compute the expense of the whole undertaking?

3. How many more schools than those above mentioned may be wanted, and what are the proper places to fix them in?

I shall conclude all with recommending to the reverend classis to point out some worthy young men to be trained for schoolmasters immediately. The education of such young men in theology shall be under any clergyman the classis may appoint. In other branches of science they shall be instructed gratis, or at an easy rate, either in this city or perhaps at some country school. It is further recommended to the reverend classis to fall upon some method of educating a supply of good men in this country for the ministry, because it is inconvenient and expensive to send to Germany for them, and there is great danger in being deceived by bad men of irregular lives, since those will be most inclined to come here who could not live or have been involved in quarrels in their own country. But on the other hand, if men are born and educated in this country we shall be sure of their merit. They will be inured to the climate, and not only the manners of the people, but how to suit their temper; and it is to be hoped may be the means of preventing differences on both sides. Any countenance or encouragement we can grant to a scheme of this nature you may very readily command. Your answer to the above will oblige the trustees and reverend gentlemen in their name.

Your brother and faithful servant,

WILLIAM SMITH,

Secretary.

Answer to the Preceding Letter.

PHILADELPHIA, October 1st, 1754.

REVEREND SIR: We have received your respected letter, and have considered all the contents, particularly the queries therein proposed to us; but as such like weighty matters require a fuller consideration than the present time would allow of, we have desired our reverend brother, Mr. Schlatter, to give your reverence such an account as the want of some more particular acquaintance (and Mr. Schlatter's late absence), for this present time will possibly afford to be given. But we will more particularly consider the whole at our next classis, which will be held, D. V., next spring in Lancaster, and Mr. Schlatter, who still communicates with us, and is acquainted with the most notable circumstances of the most places of this and other adjacent provinces, will be desired to communicate to your reverence then, as we hope, a fuller account of the whole. We conclude this, our short answer, with all the thanksgiving we are able to express, and recommend us for the future to the benevolent care of the honorable Christian Society in London, and their general trustees in these parts, in the name of our classis.

JOHN BARTHOLOMAUS REIGER.*

WILLIAM STOY.†

TO REV. WILLIAM SMITH,
Secretary.

---

* The Rev. John Bartholomaus Reiger, born in Ober-Engelheim on the Rhine, January 10th, 1707; graduated at Heidelberg, and came to America September, 1731; settled in Lancaster, Pa., and had charge of the German Reformed congregation at that place. He died March 11th, 1769, aged 62 years.

† William Stoy (pronounced Sto-e) was born at Herborn, Germany, on March 14th, 1726. He was a German Reformed preacher, having been ordained by the Classis at Amsterdam, and came to America with Michael Schlatter in 1752. He took charge of the congregation at Tulpehocken; afterwards came to Philadelphia, and then removed to Lancaster. Later in life he resided at Lebanon, where he died September 14th, 1801, aged 75 years.

The Minutes of the Trustees sent with this correspondence state that, notwithstanding that circumstances were on the whole encouraging, the accounts from some places were not so promising. This the trustees say proceeded from the want of some persons of interest to explain the design; for as the people were extremely ignorant, they were in every district led by a few on whom they have placed implicit confidence. From Easton, William Parsons, Esq. (one of the persons nominated assistant trustees for the school proposed there), had sent the following letter to Mr. Peters, which the trustees placed in their minutes and sent to Mr. Chandler and the Penns, "for its good sense," as they say, "and particularly to show to the Society one necessary part of the undertaking, which had not yet come under consideration, and concerning which it was desirable to have speedy directions; namely, some English schools for girls."

William Parsons to the Rev. Richard Peters.*

EASTON, October 18th, 1754.

To RICHARD PETERS, ESQ.

SIR: I am under some difficulty about the plan of a school-house, but am clearly of the opinion that we neither ought to ask nor suffer the people to contribute either money or labor to it; they are so perverse and quarrelsome in all their affairs that I am sometimes ready to query with myself whether it be men or brutes that these most generous benefactors are about to civilize.

Nevertheless, seeing so many great and worthy personages, out of their abundant humanity and goodness, have been pleased to set on foot so

---

* William Parsons was brought up a shoemaker. He came to Philadelphia some time prior to 1735, at which time he was Librarian of the City Library. In 1743 he was appointed Surveyor-General, and resigned in June, 1748, on account of ill health. In 1749 he was a Justice of the Peace in Lancaster county. He went to Easton to reside in 1752; and was appointed Major of all troops to be raised in Northampton county, with Easton as his head-quarters. He held the office of Prothonotary, Clerk of the Courts, Recorder, Clerk of the Commissioners, and Justice of the Peace. He died at Easton in December, 1757.

The Rev. Richard Peters, sometimes called Richard Peters, *Esquire*, came to this country in Holy Orders, A. D. 1735, and in 1736 was made the assistant to the then Rector of Christ Church (Mr. Cummings). Some misunderstanding arising between the Rector and himself, he resigned the place and was made Secretary of the Provincial Land Office of the Province. His brother, William Peters, and other members of his family were long influential persons in the Proprietary Government. In December, 1762, on the death of the then Rector of the United Churches, the Rev. Dr. Jenney, he was elected Rector, and so remained until September 23d, 1775. He died July 10th, 1776.

benevolent an undertaking, I will not be negligent in doing whatever they shall be pleased to recommend to me, though I am well assured that whoever is any way concerned in building or directing the schools will be exposed to perpetual insults and the most ignominious treatment even from those very persons for whose benefit they are laboring. This, I say, is the real sentiment of my mind, and not to discourage or show any unwillingness to do to the utmost of my power whatever the gentlemen trustees shall desire of me in the management of the affair. One thing I think has not been sufficiently attended to—the principal directions in forming the plan. As mothers have the principal direction in bringing up their young children, it will be of little use that the father can talk English if the mother can speak nothing but Dutch to them; in their case the children will speak their mother-tongue. It therefore seems to me quite necessary that there should be English schoolmistresses as well as schoolmasters, and the girls should be taught something of the use of the needle, as well as to read and write (if writing should be thought necessary for girls). By the use of their needles the mistresses will have an opportunity of teaching them and making them fond of the English dress, which will have great influence on their minds all their lives after, and if the young women affect the English manner in their dress and speaking, I need not mention how industrious young men will be generally to appear in their habit, and to speak the language which they think the most agreeable to the female world. It is the same in this respect in regard to low as well as to high life. Nature is the same in every station, and we differ only as we are educated.

WILLIAM PARSONS.

Dr. Smith to Archbishop Herring.

PHILADELPHIA, October 19th, 1754.

MY LORD: I now make use of the liberty your grace permitted me. At present, however, I cannot enter, as I intend afterwards to do, upon the state of our colonies and the proposed schools among the Germans, both which are become very interesting. As the French are daily encroaching behind us, and taking possession of the vast fruitful country upon the Ohio, they will be able to offer our Germans easy settlements, which these last will accept of, as they are an ignorant people that know no difference between French and English government, being wanton with liberty, uninstructed in the use of it, and placing all happiness in possessing a large piece of land. Now, this will be a far greater advantage to the French than peopling their colonies from Europe (which the severity of their government would never suffer them to accomplish). For however many by these means they take from us, so many they add to themselves, which is a double advantage to them, especially as such hands are old inhabitants and accustomed to the climate. This is a scheme which the French for a number of years have been pursuing to establish their empire in America. The Indians are going over to the French in these parts, because the latter, having possession by means of their forts, can protect them ; and whenever they come a little nearer, the Germans will submit and go over also for protection, caring for nothing but to keep possession of the estates they have settled.

Now, I can see nothing that can prevent these dreadful calamities, or subject these back-settlers to any form of government (as they are like to degenerate into savages) but to fix schools and a regular clergy among them, in order to open their eyes to the blessings they enjoy and the dangers they incur by a change. I wish, then, the honorable Society for Propagating the Gospel, instead of sending more missionaries to New England, where they are not wanted so much, would erect some missions among those back-settlers I speak of, who are quite destitute and in great danger, as bordering upon the French and the Indians. The bearer, Mr. Barton, comes with a petition from a vast number of these back-settlers, but I am in doubt whether the Society will make a new mission for him. If he has any difficulty, I have desired him to apply to your grace ; otherwise not to be troublesome, as your time and health are of the greatest public importance.

For the same reasons the proposed schools among these back-settlers is a very important undertaking, as your grace was thoroughly convinced when you generously contributed to the support of them. They are, indeed, so important that we are entirely of your grace's opinion, "*that they should be made the object of some parliamentary provision,*" and we humbly hope your grace may be a great means of making them so, for though private contributions may begin, they cannot long enough be supported on such a precarious footing. We have a good prospect of their success ; and as I have been appointed a trustee, and chosen secretary by the other trustees, for the management of the scheme, I have transmitted Mr. Chandler a full account of our progress.

As your grace has condescended to peruse some other compositions of mine, I have enclosed one of my first sermons, which I could not avoid printing, though made at a few hours warning. It had a very great effect from the pulpit, and has been well received from the press. In compositions of this kind I carefully avoid those *luxuriances* which your grace kindly blamed under the name of *agreeable.*

I hope and pray that this may find your grace's health perfectly restored. Last post, Mr. de Lancey was well and easy in his government. I wish it may be long his. Should your grace ever think it worth while to honor me with any commands, Mr. Miller will find a conveyance ; or Mr. Penn, whom I have frequent letters from, as he never misses an opportunity of writing to somebody or other here.

I beg pardon for the length of this letter. I did not intend to give your grace the trouble of turning over the leaf when I begun ; but as it comes from a great distance I hope I shall be excused.

With the sincerest gratitude and respect, I remain, my lord,

Your grace's most dutiful son, and

Obedient, humble servant,

WILLIAM SMITH.*

To His Grace, the Lord Archbishop of Canterbury.

P. S.—The Rev. Mr. Schlatter, who is safely returned, just now called upon me, and in the tenderest manner begs me to present his most grateful and most dutiful respects to your grace.

An extract from the Minutes of the Trustees will continue our record on this subject of schools for the Germans.

December 10th, 1754. A meeting of the trustees was called. Present: Messrs. Allen, Peters, Weiser, and William Smith. Mr. Smith read the memorial he had prepared, entitled "A Brief History† of the Rise and Progress of the Scheme carrying on for the Instruction of Poor Germans and their Descendants," etc., and Mr. Schlatter being present, the same was approved of, and fifteen hundred copies ordered to be printed in English and Dutch, to be distributed for the information of the public. A petition was brought down from Reading, in the terms of the former petition, signed by the minister and chief men, both of the Calvinist and Lutheran persuasions and some English in that township. Agreed that a school be opened in Reading, as soon as possible, in consequence of said petition.

Ordered, that copies of as many of these minutes as have not been sent before be now sent to the honorable Society and the Proprietaries, and that Mr. Smith write to them with said copies.

Of the memorial to the Germans there were published :

English copies, ...	800
Dutch "	1,000
Dutch and English copies, ...	500

2,300 in all.

150 English copies were sent to Mr. Chandler, in London, by Captain Budden, 20 to the Proprietaries, and 30 to other persons of distinction, making, with 150 distributed to persons in this and the neighboring provinces, 350 in all.

---

* From the original draft in his own handwriting. See Perry's Historical Collections, Diocese of Pennsylvania.

† Penn Papers in the Historical Society of Pennsylvania.

Of the Dutch copies, Mr. Schlatter received   .   325
Mr. Weiser and the Lutheran clergy, .   .   .   275
All of which have been properly distributed
   among the Dutch, with about 70 Dutch and
   English, ...   70
And upwards of 300 copies have been given away
   to sundries, ...   300

Making in all, ... 1,320
Remaining on hand, about   1,000
                                          2,320

At a meeting of the trustees, held December 26th, 1754, a petition was received from the Reformed and Lutheran congregations
of Vincent township, Chester county, praying for a school in that
place, where it was represented that there were a great number of
poor children. It was therefore agreed that a school should be
erected, and that Louis Ache, who came well recommended,
should be schoolmaster. It was further agreed that he should be
taken into the academy, at the expense of the Proprietaries, to be
better qualified in the English tongue. The following persons
were recommended as deputy trustees for the township:

Calvinists { Sebastian Wagner.   Lutherans { Michael Heilman.
           { Peter Stager.   { Conrad Shriner.

           English { Samuel Hover.
                   { Richard Richardson.

At the same meeting a petition was received from the Lutheran
and Reformed congregations in the township of Upper Salford,
now Montgomery county, praying for a school, and recommending
the Rev. Frederick Schultz, the Lutheran minister, as a schoolmaster, a gentleman, it was observed, who was capable of teaching
the English language. It was agreed that a school be immediately
begun, and that Mr. Schultz be appointed master. This having
been signified to the people and Mr. Schultz, they began to be impatient of waiting until the other schools were opened, and sent
Mr. Schultz and the Rev. Mr. Weiss* in the end of February, to

---

* Rev. George Michael Weiss, or Weitzius, was a native of the Palatinate on the
Rhine, came to America in the year 1727, and settled at Schippach, in Montgomery
county. He had charge of various Reformed congregations in the States of Pennsylvania and New York. He died about 1763, and was buried in the church at New
Goshenhoppen. Upon his tomb is the simple inscription :

                     Hier ruhet der Ehr :

                     Herr Weiss.

obtain leave to open the school immediately. Finding it inconvenient to get a meeting of the trustees, and being afraid of raising
jealousies by opening the school before the others who had petitioned sooner, Mr. Smith wrote to the congregations that it was
proposed at all times to open the Society schools with a sermon
by Mr. Schlatter, or some other fit person, as becoming at the
undertaking of such pious designs; and that in the first week of
April—as the season would not permit it sooner—that and some
other schools would be opened in the Society's name, with due
form and solemnity. By a letter from the Rev. Mr. Weiss, of
March 4th, 1755, it appears that the people were satisfied to wait
till the time named by the trustees.

A petition was also received, January 15th, 1755, from the township of Tulpehocken and Heidelberg, in the counties of Lancaster
and Berks, asking for a school; but as the congregation seemed
to differ about the situation of the school-house, it was agreed to
delay the answer to this petition until the site should be fixed.

At the same time a petition was received from the borough of
Lancaster, as follows:

To the Trustees-General of the Charitable Scheme for the instruction of Poor Germans in the Province of Pennsylvania:

The Petition of divers of the inhabitants of the Borough of Lancaster
in behalf of themselves, and others of the German nation residing in the
said Borough, and parts adjacent, humbly sheweth that the number of
poor Germans in these parts is very considerable, as well as those who
are of ability to pay for the education of their children, if proper schools
for that purpose were opened, and your Petitioners, having a just and
lively sense, not only of the many Benefits attending a competent Knowledge of the English language, in their commerce and intercourse with
divers persons unacquainted with the German tongue, but also of the
pleasures resulting from an unity of Languages, greatly conducive to an
unity of sentiments, do Humbly pray that they may partake of the
bounties of the charitable Society in London; that a school may be
opened in this Borough by the Trustees-general for teaching the English
language in Pursuance of the said Charitable Scheme, and that the said
Trustees would be pleased to appoint and send a sober, discreet and
religious Gentleman, capable of fulfilling this trust and answering the
benevolent intentions of said Society. As divers of the inhabitants of
this Borough are desirous of having their Children instructed in the
Latin and Greek Languages, but from the smallness of their numbers are
unable to support a master for that purpose, your petitioners request
that a gentleman acquainted with these learned languages may be ap-

pointed, that the desires of these inhabitants may be gratified, but in a way not prejudicial to the principal design.

As there are two German schools—one of the Lutheran, and the other of the Calvinist Congregations—already in this town ; and the Germans are unable to educate their own poor children in the German languages together, as it would occasion confusion ; your petitioners pray that the charity designed for this purpose may be given to the masters of the respective Congregations.

Posterity, whose welfare and happiness will be chiefly increased by this charitable Institution, will doubtless be filled with the warmest sense of gratitude to the authors of this Benefaction, and as your petitioners are unanimous in their wishes for the success of it, their utmost efforts will not be wanting in the promoting of it.*

LANCASTER, December 28th, 1754.

And to induce the trustees to send a Latin schoolmaster, who might have the assistance of an usher, to instruct such poor Germans as should be sent to the school, some of the most substantial inhabitants, English and German, made a subscription of money. The list of subscribers (A. D. 1755) is as follows :

A LIST OF THE SUBSCRIBERS FOR THE LATIN MASTER FOR THREE YEARS.

Edward Shippen, for two scholars, though he has none to send, . . . per annum, £ 6 o o	
Simon Kuhn, ... 6 o o	
George Gibson, ... 6 o o	
Michael Utt, for one scholar, ... 3 o o	
Emanuel Carpenter, for one scholar, . . . 3 o o	
George Ross, " " " . . . 3 o o	
George Craig and James Wright, . . . 3 o o	
£30 o o	

A LIST OF THOSE THAT SUBSCRIBE FOR ONE YEAR.

Michael Gross, for one scholar, . . £ 3 o o	
Jacob Good, " " " . . . . 3 o o	
William Ilvon, no scholar, ... 1 10 o	
Jacob Eicholtz, for one scholar, . . . 3 o o	
John Jacob Loeser, no scholar, . . . 1 10 o	
Bernard Hubley, for one scholar, . . . 3 o o	
£15 oo o	

Jacob Huber, ⎫
Sebastian Graff, ⎬ promise to pay £3 each for one year.
George Graff, ⎭

* This petition was signed by the Calvinist and Lutheran ministers, and by fourteen of the chief men of the place in the name of the rest.

In the beginning of the year 1755 it was determined by the trustees of the Society for the Education of Germans that the Rev. Dr. Smith should prepare a Letter of Instruction for the Rev. Mr. Schlatter, with which Mr. Schlatter should take a journey through the several parts of the Province. The Letter of Instruction, thus prepared, was as follows:

Dr. Smith and others to Mr. Schlatter.

PHILADELPHIA, February 12th, 1755.

REV. SIR: As you are appointed visitor of the intended schools to be opened by us for the benefit of the poor Protestant Germans, you will please observe the following general directions in the journey you are now about to begin through the several counties of this Province:

1st. According to the terms of the printed case, you will please converse with the People on the spot, and assist them with your advice in any designs they may project in order to obtain the Society's Bounty for encouraging schoolmasters among them.

2d. You may receive the proposals and petitions of persons deserving the Benefit of a school in the terms of the printed case; assist and direct the people in choosing the fittest places to fix the school in; and with your advice and that of their several ministers, let them recommend Catechists and Deputy Trustees in their Petition. The Calvinists two or three for each school, and the Lutherans an equal number, unless perhaps there be any places where the latter are not so numerous.

3d. If any of your own Clergy are straitened by the smallness of their livings, and have anything to propose concerning the augmentation of them, you are desired to bring their proposals to us; and if you can recommend them as pious, industrious men, and friends to the benevolent designs of the generous society, they will be immediately relieved and assisted according to the tenors of the printed case. We rely on your own Judgment as to every other thing not mentioned, and hope you will keep a correct diary of every material transaction, that when you return you may lay the proper information before us, to enable us to answer the expectation of those who repose so important a trust in us (any proposals made for a school to instruct your ministers will be encouraged). You are desired to acquaint Mr. Richard Jacob and the eight other gentlemen who favored us with a letter concerning the schools at New Providence, That as we have not yet opened that school in the society's name, we leave it to Mr. Muhlenberg, Mr. Leidig, and them, with your advice, to fix the numbers to be admitted into the schools. We cannot open it till the month of April, but we shall give the master a sufficient Gratuity for any poor children he teaches, and the subscribers to the school shall not be desired to pay anything more than

they shall think reasonable. The Master at present should not take
more than he can manage, and afterwards we shall settle all these matters by Rules, either when the schools grow numerous to get assistant
masters in them, or open new schools as far as the society's fund will
extend. We pray God to direct and strengthen you in your fatiguing
journey, and are, Rev. Sir,   Yours, etc.,

JAMES HAMILTON,
WILLIAM ALLEN,
RICHARD PETERS,
WILLIAM SMITH.

TO REV. MR. SCHLATTER.

On the 16th of February, 1755, Mr. Schlatter opened a school
at New Providence, Philadelphia county; Charles Cornelius Rabatan being master at a salary of £25 (and £10 to his wife), to teach
18 poor children reading and sewing.

On the 1st of March following, he opened one at Upper Salford,
Philadelphia, the Rev. Frederick Schultz being appointed master at a
salary of £30 per annum. On the 5th of March he opened one at
Reading. On the 1st of April Mr. Conrad Weiser, for the Society,
opened a school at Tulpehocken * and Heidelberg, in the counties of
Lancaster and Berks; Mr. John Davis, from Ireland, being master at
a salary of £30 per annum. On the 8th of May a school was opened
at Vincent Township, Chester county, Mr. John Lewis Ache being
master. Mr. Schlatter allowed him a salary of but £20 per annum,
as he had been instructed for some time at the Public Academy in
Philadelphia, at the expense of the Society.

On the 16th of May a school was opened in Easton, Northampton county. Mr. William Parsons was appointed trustee, and Mr.
John Middleton master, at a salary of £30 per annum. On the 1st
of July one was opened in the borough of Lancaster, the Rev. Mr.
Samuel Magaw being appointed master, and it was agreed that he
should be permitted to teach the learned languages to the children
of those persons who had subscribed for that purpose; and to
enable him to employ an usher, he was allowed £25, to be paid by
the trustees.

What we have already put before our readers shows that the
idea—the intellectual conception—of educating the poor Germans,

---

* Tulpehocken (a branch of the Schuylkill in Berks county) corrupted from *Tul-
pewi-hacki*, signifying, *the land of turtles.*

so far as England was concerned, was Dr. Smith's. The following receipts, found among Dr. Smith's papers for the year 1755, show that on him, too, fell the labor of detail:

Received, June 23d, 1755, of the Rev. William Smith four pounds, being in part of what the Trustees of the Free School shall allow me as Catechist to the schools near me.

£4 0 0.   GEORGE MICHAEL WEISS.

Received, June 25th, of the Rev. William Smith four pounds, being in part of what the Trustees of the Free School shall allow me as Catechist to the children in the free schools near me.

JOHN CONRAD HEINER, *V.D.M.*

July 2d, 1755, Received from Mr. William Smith five pounds eight shillings, as part of what the Society shall allow me as Catechist to the Lutheran children in the free schools near me.

JOHN FREDERICK HANDSCHUH,
Minister of the Lutheran Congregation at Germantown.

July 24th, 1755, Received from the Rev. Mr. Smith fifteen pounds, as Catechist to the Society's free schools at New Providence, New Hanover, Vincent, and Reading, commencing from May 1st, 1755.

HENRY MUHLENBERG.

Sept. 9th, Received Five Pounds Eight Shillings.

FREDERICK HANDSCHUH.

Received, for the use of the Calvinist Congregation in the City of Philadelphia, the sum of fifteen pounds.   MICHAEL SCHLATTER.

We have already spoken of the bitter aversion entertained by some of the Germans in Pennsylvania to the establishment of the schools promoted by Dr. Smith, and especially of the opposition by Christopher Sauer, the well-known German printer of Germantown. The following letter, written by him (in German), is in the collection of his respected descendant, Mr. A. H. Cassel, of Montgomery county, Pennsylvania. I give a translation—the direction being lost, I cannot now tell to whom it was written:

GERMANTOWN, September 6th, 1755.

DEAR FRIEND: I received your letter, and answer it by the bearer. I have been thinking since you wrote to me whether it is really true that Gilbert Tennent, Schlatter, Peters, Hamilton, Allen, Turner, Schippin, Schmitt, Franklin, Muhlenberg, Brumholz, Handschuh, &c.,

have the slightest care for a real conversion of the ignorant portion of the Germans in Pennsylvania, or whether the institution of free schools is not rather the foundation to bring the country into servitude, so that each of them may look for and have his own private interest and advantage.

Concerning Hamilton, Peters, Allen, Turner, Schippin and Franklin, I know that they care very little about religion, nor do they care for the cultivation of mind of the Germans, except that they should form the militia and defend their properties. Such people do not know what it is to have faith and confidence in God; but they are mortified that they cannot compel others to protect their goods.

Tennent may believe, if he pleases, that his religion is the best; and if it is possible that, with the assistance of Schlatter, English preachers may receive a salary in being called for the Germans; that such preachers should be educated in Philadelphia, or even if such ministers should be formed and polished in New Jersey, then has Tennent the honor, and Schlatter is provided for. But the Germans will no doubt elect for the Assembly, on account of their benefactors, Hamilton, Peters, Schippin, Allen, Turner, &c., &c.

These make a law, together with Robert Hunter Morris, for the building of a fortress for the militia, with a garrison; stipulate a salary for the ministers and schools, so that it will not be necessary to write a begging letter to Halle (in Germany) of which they are ashamed afterward, and are considered as liars, when the reports are printed. Thus *the poor Germans* are the pretext, that every one may succeed in his purposes.

I am here, as it were, hidden in a corner, where I hear the words and thoughts of many.

The one says: "I feel uneasy about having my children educated out of the funds of the poor, as I do not need it, being able to pay for it."

Another says: "Where so many children come together, there they learn more evil from others than what is good; I will therefore teach myself my children writing and reading, and I am sorry that so many children come to see my own ones."

Others again say: "If the German children learn to speak English and come in society with the English, then do they wish to be clothed after the English fashion, and there is much difficulty and trouble to remove from their minds these foolish notions."

I hear others say: "We, poor people, have no advantage from the benevolence of the king and of the Society, if they do not build a school-house or keep a teacher at the distance of every ten miles. For, if a child is obliged to go to school and come from further than five miles, it is too far to do so every morning and evening; the children cannot be boarded, nor can we give them clothes to go to school with others of higher rank, and therefore this advantage is only for the rich and the English. Should people make petitions for their temporal and eternal ruin?"

I have a small English book on the principles of the Freemasons; my copy, printed in England, is the 3d edition. I find its teachings very far from the kingdom of Jesus Christ. Indeed, they are the very hindrance of it. The people, who are the promoters of the free school, are Grandmasters, Wardens among the Freemasons, and their pillars. I think they intend something else, from what they think to be their best.

If they give Zübly a call, I will say that I was mistaken; for, if they desire to oppose the influence of sectarian imagination, and only wish to promote the truth as it is in Christ, then Zübly is one among the thousand. However, I apprehend they fear him, for in the pamphlet there is a passage, as follows: "There is nothing the Quakers more fear than "to see the Germans pay any regard to regular ministers. Whenever "they know any such minister in good terms with his people, they "immediately blame him by means of this printer, and distress him by "dividing his congregation and encouraging vagabonds and pretended "preachers, whom they every now and then raise up; this serves a "double end." When I consider the principles of the Freemasons from this pamphlet, which a goldsmith, one of their members, lent to Heron, and who lent it to me, I do not know what judgment to make of the eulogy of Prof. Schmitt * concerning the author of the book, "The Life of God in the Soul of Man."† I consider it only as having a political purpose and tendency.

May God turn it to good and to His glory. For your part, do as much as you can for its promotion; and if it should be printed, unexpectedly, in German and English, to which they would, perhaps, willingly consent, then I keep my promise, and still remain a debtor to God and to my neighbor, the whole human race.

Your friend,

Chr. Sauer.

It will be remembered that the trustees in Philadelphia for educating the poor Germans resolved to buy a printing press. We have in a letter, which is below, some account of the cost.

Dr. Smith to Mr. Secretary Chandler.

Philadelphia, October 3d, 1755.

Sir: This day I have drawn upon you by order of the Trustees for £109.8.4, payable to Benjamin Franklin, Esq., or order, being in part the value of the Dutch press, the account of which is as follows, having been valued by an impartial hand:

---

* Meaning Dr. Wm. Smith.
† Dr. Smith caused this excellent work of Scougal to be translated into German.

1761½ lbs. of Types of various sizes and sorts, at 2s. per lb., one with
  another, 76 patterns, chases, cases, frames, letter-boards, etc., etc.,
  complete in all...£236 3
By deduction of Mr. Franklin's subscription.........£25
  "   Mr. Allen's   "   ....£25..................   50
                                                              ⎯⎯⎯⎯⎯
                                                              £186 3*

Mr. Hamilton will probably subscribe something; but he was not at
our last meeting. What he does subscribe shall be brought into our
general account. The German newspaper succeeded well; there being
upwards of 400 subscribers, and more daily coming in. But it is so
very low that it will do no more than clear itself, and that not until
the year's end; so that there must be a considerable advance for paper
and for the director of the Press. But after the first year all this may
be saved, and we must ease you in the other articles; for the paper
may do more good to the design than several schools, because the Director has express orders not to meddle with any of the disputes in this
province, but to strive in every paper to say something to improve and
better his countrymen and to confirm them in the Love and Knowledge
of the Protestant Religion and civil Liberty. There are also 3,000 Dutch
almanacs for 1756 printed, by which article we shall be gainers.

I have the honor to subscribe myself, reverend sir,

Your affectionate brother, etc.,

WILLIAM SMITH.

To Mr. Chandler.

We have given at a length and with a detail which, we fear, may
prove tedious to some of our readers, an account of this work of
rendering our German emigrants and their children fit to be citizens of a British colony. It was a great work. The statesmen
of the day looked upon it as such: for so vast was the German
population in parts of the province, that it seemed to some uncertain whether the colony founded by William Penn, under the
charter of a Stuart King, would not finally become a province of
Germans. Their religion—many of them being Mennonists,
Dunkers, Omish, etc.—was as far removed from that of the
Church of England as was their language from that of English
people. The matter of this foreign ethnology and mixed faith is
very particularly spoken of by Mr. Wallace, President of the
Historical Society of Pennsylvania, in his discourse of March
11th, 1872, at the inauguration of the new hall of that Society.†

---

* Equivalent to £109 8s. 4d. sterling.
† Page 12.

7

He refers to this passage in Edmund Burke's Account of the European Settlements in America.*

Pennsylvania is inhabited by upwards of 250,000 people; half of whom are Germans, Swedes, or Dutch. Here you see Mennonists . . . and the Dumplers, a sort of German sect that live in something like a religious society, wear long beards and a habit resembling that of friars. . . . It was certainly a very right policy to encourage the importation of foreigners into Pennsylvania, as well as into our other colonies. But it has been frequently observed, and, as should seem, very justly complained of, that they are left still foreigners, and likely to continue so for many generations. And they have schools taught, books printed, and even the common newspaper in their own language : by which means, as they possess large tracts of the country without any intermixture of English, there is no appearance of their blending and becoming one people with us. This is certainly a great irregularity, and the greater, as these foreigners, by their industry, frugality, and a hard way of living, in which they greatly exceed our people, have in a manner thrust them out in several places; so as to threaten the colony with the danger of being wholly foreign in language, manners, and, perhaps, even inclinations. In the year 1750 were imported into Pennsylvania and its dependencies 4,317 Germans, whereas of British and Irish but 1,000 arrived ; a considerable number, if it was not so vastly overbalanced by that of the foreigners.

I do by no means think that this sort of transplantations ought to be discouraged ; I only observe, along with others, that the manner of their settlement ought to be regulated, and means sought to have them naturalized in reality.

Dr. Smith's work was, therefore, the work of a statesman attached to his sovereign, and of a pious man attached to the religion of his church. For though, on this last matter, no provision was made for the inculcation of specific tenets of the Church of England, and indeed all such inculcation was carefully avoided, people educated in such schools as we have spoken of, and in which a man like Dr. Smith was a founder and leader, would necessarily be brought, in some degree, under his influence, and, without specific action on his part, gravitate more or less towards his own political principles and forms of faith. The Rev. Mr. Muhlenberg, of the Lutheran Church, who was a co-worker with him, sincerely respected the Church of England, and afterwards was even a trustee of the venerable corporation, established A. D.

---

* Burke's Works, Vol. IX., p. 345—Boston edition of 1839.

1769, for the relief of the widows and children of its clergymen. Moreover, a portion of that church has always been disposed, I think, to recognize the validity of the Lutheran orders; as the church generally, I believe, does the validity of the Swedish and Moravian. Thus, even if the whole body of poor Germans passed into the Lutheran Church, a great gain—one almost quite satisfactory—was made to the Church of England, on their previous forms of faith; or, rather, on their previous want of all faith.

When we consider that at this time Dr. Smith was but twenty-eight years old, we cannot but see in his efforts a vigorous, comprehensive, and forecasting mind as well as fine executive power. That he had already made a great impression upon the best minds of Philadelphia, is shown by the fact that he had preached four times in this year in the conservative pulpit of Christ Church.

CHAPTER VII.

CHARTER OF THE ACADEMY ENLARGED AND POWER TO CONFER DEGREES GIVEN—DR. SMITH'S SALARY FIXED AT £200—VARIOUS CORRESPONDENCE: ARCHBISHOP HERRING; DR. BEARCROFT; SECRETARY CHANDLER.

UP to this time nothing of a positive kind had been agreed on by the Academy for the support of Dr. Smith; and unless it could be elevated in character, Dr. Smith was not satisfied to remain in it. He therefore represented to the trustees that it would increase the reputation of the institution if it had the power of conferring degrees on such students and other persons as by their learning should merit them; observing that several ingenuous young men, not finding that they could get here that testimony to their acquirements, had left the Academy to go to other schools. He proposed, in short, to convert the Academy into a College. The trustees accordingly desired Dr. Smith and Mr. Allison to draw up such clauses as should properly amend the charter. They did this. The amendments were approved by the trustees. On the 14th of May a new charter was granted to the Academy, confirming the charter of July 13th, 1753, and giving the institution power to confer degrees. In this charter the institution is called a College,

Belmont University Library

and the names of Dr. Smith and Dr. Allison appear as Provost and Vice-Provost, as if appointed by the Governor himself.

On the 11th of July the salary of the Provost was fixed by the trustees at £200, and it was ordered that it should begin from the time of his first being employed in the Academy.

We have now a variety of interesting letters, which we give in sequence. They need no explanatory statements to introduce them. They explain themselves.

Archbishop Herring to Dr. Smith.

CROYDON HOUSE,
SURRY, January 19th, 1755.

REV'D SIR: As I was much out of order, & at some distance from London, Mr. Palmer did not call upon me, but sent your Letter. I find the Society have shewn a proper regard, & I am confident any man who comes to that Board wth your recommendation will be treated with all proper distinction. I am glad of this opportunity of professing to you, that I have the most honourable opinion of your character, & the utmost confidence, that you do all you can by a faithful & conscientious discharge of your Duty.

It gave me a particular pleasure to be assured, That the Gentlemen of New York have pitch'd upon you for President of their New College, to which I wish all possible success for the Advancement of our Common Religion & the good of the Publick Weal. The Trustees will do me honour in naming me in their charter, & they may be satisfied, that I neither have nor can have anything more in my view and at my Heart, than to support the Establishment of the ch. of England, in conjunction with the Act of Toleration. I hope all Dissenters of your & our side of the great water are convinced, that as they never did, so it is hardly to be imagin'd, they ever can, live under a milder Government both in Church & State, than they do at present, & if ever it should seem good to our Government to send Bp^s into America, for Ecclesiastical purposes only, it will not be looked upon, as I could hope, as an unreasonable Step; as the Case now stands with us, & you feel it. The church of England is the only set of Xtians in America, that do not enjoy their full Rights and Privileges in the Exercise & Polity of their Religion. Many of the Dissenters of Rank in England have a just sense of this matter and have declar'd it to me; so that if there are with you any active men of a different spirit, they will do well to consider, that as Peace is next to Truth, the best thing in Society, so Dissention & animosity are the worst. I hope your charter will be settl'd upon a Just Plan, & I am convinced that your Lieutenant Governor in

---

* Maryland Papers.

Belmont University Library

this as all other affairs, wh. come before him, will act w'th honesty & courage & prudence. I beg the favour of you to pay him my most affectionate respects. I am very sorry to hear that Mr. Whitefield's Preaching at Boston has been the occasion of such contention as appear'd there in last October.

I am, Rev'd Sir, yr. assur'd Friend,
THOS. CANTAUR.

The Rev. Dr. Bearcroft to Dr. Smith.

LONDON, February 17th, 1755.

REVEREND SIR: Mr. Barton,* God willing, will be the bearer of this, having happily succeeded in his petition thro' your Recommendation, and that of those other worthy Persons who bore witness to his merit, wch from the proofs of his Learning & good Conduct he hath by no means lessen'd here, & I make no doubt but he will prove a good & usefull Missionary in your Province, wch I am very sensible the back parts of it stand very much in need of; may God of His mercy in due time supply them! & as I make no doubt but that nursery of Learning, over wch you preside, will, by God's Blessing on your worthy Endeavours join'd to those of your good Brethren, hereafter send forth Labourers into it. I thank you for the truely pathetick sermon preached by you at the death of one of your best Pupils;† it is a debt we must sooner or later all pay, & may we all duely think of it! In ye mean time let us be all duely carefull in our several Stations to promote true Religion here, & we shall reap a glorious Recompence hereafter.

I remain, S^r,
Your affectionate Servant, &
Brother in Christ,
PHILIP BEARCROFT.

P. S.—It will always give me pleasure to hear of your Success & of the state of Learning & Religion in your Province.

To THE REV^D. M^R. SMITH IN PHILADELPHIA.

Dr. Smith to Mr. Secretary Chandler, D. D.

PHILADELPHIA, Aprile, 1755.

REV. DEAR SIR: I had your several Favors by M^r. Barton, & shall lay them before the Trustees general, on the Return of such of them as are now gone to Alexandria in Maryland, to assist at the Congress between General Braddock, & the several Colony-Governors.

All Parties continue disposed to the Schools in the same Manner as

---

* The Rev. Thos. Barton, who was now returning to America. See supra, p. 77, and Appendix No. I.

† See supra, p. 73.

when I wrote you last. The Calvinist Cœtus has addressed us in the most respectful Manner, & seem entirely satisfyed.

At the Time I received your Orders, we had about eighteen Petitions for Schools before us, & had agreed to grant a greater Number of them than that limited in your Letter. We must, therefore, to save our Honor, take the Liberty to depart a little from that mode of appropriating this year's Funds, which is prescribed in your Letter. There will not be such pressing Occasion for such a large Number of Girl-Schools at first, nor perhaps for such a large Sum to the Ministry, many of whom are tolerably provided for. We hope, therefore, still to be able to maintain twelve Schools for Boys this Year, without passing the Bounds you have fixed in the Expence. As the Schools are the main Part of the Design, it would be imprudent to throw a Damp upon them at first setting out.

I sincerely thank you for your Professions of Friendship for me. I have had many instances of the Goodness of your Heart, & shall strive for a Continuance of your Favor, by those upright Methods which first recommended me to it. You may be sure I will very readily benefit myself by the Proffer you make of your good Offices for me in England.— Whenever you can serve me, I know no person to whom I would sooner lay myself under Obligations. Favors from you will be doubly such. The Delicacy of your Sentiments will never permit you to confer them, with the too common Insolence of flattered pride ; and the Warmth of your Affections will bid you Share the Joy you Give !

You do me great Honor in mentioning my Name in the same Line, & in the same advantageous Light, with the name of my much admired Friend, M^r. Franklin—your approbation of my Sermon likewise gives me a sensible Pleasure ; but as to your Apprehensions that we are seducing the Masses from their beloved English Haunts to our American Wilds, and your Threats of letting in the French upon us, to drive them back (seeing their coy *Ladyships* will never deign to dwell with Slaves), I can only look upon it as a Compliment ; & that such a refined one as mocks a Reply. I am now more than ever convinced that you are in no Danger from us being rivaled in the Affections of those fair Ladies you mention with so much Tenderness. In vain have I had Recourse to all the Misses of my Acquaintance. I can find none among them that has Warmth of Fancy enough to return your Compliment without disgracing us.

But I have rambled from the main Purport of this Letter, which was not to enter into any private Affairs of our own, but to make known to you the State of the Old Presbyterian Congregation in this City ; the members of which have lately addressed you, to provide them with a Minister. This Letter was to have attended their Address ; but I could not, at that Time, find leisure.

It would be needless to give you a minute Account of the Occasion of the late Separation among the Presbyterians in these Colonies. When M^r. Whitfield first came to these Parts, among several of his Doctrines, many run away with that of an instantaneous sort of Conversion or *new Light,* the Signs of which were Falling into Fits, Faintings, &c., &c.— To such an enthusiastic Pitch many well-meaning Persons of a warmer Temper could no Doubt work themselves up, & might, perhaps, mistake their own Enthusiasm for the inward Operations of the holy Spirit. But Persons of a cooler & more sedate Turn could not believe in the Possibility of such a sudden Change from the most vicious to the most virtuous Course of Life, unless by a Miracle, which was not to be expected in common Cases. Those last rather believed that the Spirit of God co-operating with, and strengthening, our honest Endeavours, the Heart and Affections must be purified and rendered fit for Heaven, not instantaneously, but by a course of Holiness stedfastly persisted in, & gradually approaching nearer to that Degree of Perfection required in the Gospel. This, in the ordinary Course of Things, they considered as the subordinate Means, & the Redemption by Christ as the meritorious Cause of eternal Salvation.

Hence, I presume, arose the original Distinction between New Light, & Old Light Presbyterians, by which the two Parties are now vulgarly denominated. The former followed Whitfield ; and he & they did not fail to "deal Damnation round" on the other side, as well as on all Persuasions different from theirs. But tho' this began the Difference, it was widened & continued by Matters relating to Church Government, as will appear in the Sequel.

With the same Degree of Extravagance with which Whitfield condemned his Adversaries, he extolled his Adherents, tho' they had nothing to recommend them but their blind Attachment to his Doctrines. Among others, he proposed the two Tennents & some others to his Followers in this City as the only Gospel Ministers. One of them is a Man completely accomplished in all the Degrees of Ignorance & Weakness. The other I need not tell you of. He is the same you saw in the Character of a *Sturdy Beggar,* & who came recommended to you (as you told me) under the uncommon Name of *Hell-fire T——nt.*

Upon the Strength of Whitfield's Recommendation this Man left his little Congregation in New Jersey & came to this Town an itinerant, as it was thought, on his Master's Plan. He was sure to have the greater Part of Whitfield's Mob after him ; and of Course more than one-half of the Presbyterian Congregation follow'd, & stuck by him, as he professed himself a Presbyterian. Several others of the lower Sort did the same from other Congregations.

Tennent, finding he was like to have a greater Harvest in Philadelphia than elsewhere, projected & accomplished a Settlement for Himself in this City, to the great Disappointment (as I have been told) of M^r. Whitfield, who expected in Tennent an Itinerant only, & a Man after his own Heart.

As this Settlement was a Manifest Intrusion into M^r. Cross's Congregation, in Contempt of all Order & Right, M^r. Tennent had no way to justify it but to pretend that himself & several others of his Kidney who made the like Intrusions & Settlements in other Places, being a Majority, were the Synod, & those who adhered to the old Doctrines were Separatists. In Consequence of this the New Lights associated themselves into a kind of independent Synod, protests were entered, pamphlets published, & the Difference widened without any probability of a Reunion, but by the entire Submission of the Tennents, &c., who are certainly the Separating or Seceding party, which is not very like to happen, as they think themselves by far the strongest, & hope soon to swallow up the other Side by their Numbers.

To accomplish this, their first Method was to take Men from the Plough to the Pulpit in a few Months, by which Means they deluged the Country with their Teachers, having no higher Idea of the sacred Function than to think any person qualified for it who could *cant* out a few unintelligible sounds concerning Conversion, Saving Grace, Reprobation, Election, &c. ; without ever striving to adorn the Heart with the Christian Virtues of Meekness, Peace, Charity, Long-suffering, Kindness, and Forgiveness. On the contrary these Virtues, altho' some of the brightest Ornaments of the Christian Character, seemed to be industriously banished, & the Souls of the People soured, by the Orthodox Cursing, Railing, & Anathematizing, they daily heard from the Pulpit.

Tho' the Party were thus continually encreasing in Numbers & Biggotry, yet they soon began to think that they never could establish themselves in the Opinion of the world without consulting at least the Appearance of human Learning, which at first they thought unnecessary to the Character of a Gospel-Preacher. To complete their Scheme, therefore, they founded a Seminary, called the Jersey College, & have even got the Dissenters in England & Scotland, as you know, to contribute to the support of it, though a Nursery of Separation from themselves. You knew the design, but did not oppose it, being pleased, as I myself was, to see Learning encouraged in America, in any Stands whatever ; for true Learning, if they have Recourse to it, will in process of Time bring them to see that the Essentials of Religion do not consist in any of those little party-Tenets about which they contend so warmly.

But in the mean Time the old Presbyterians are in a difficult Situation. It would be giving up the Justice of their Cause should they accept of Ministers from a Seminary set up against them, & they would in a few years be entirely lost among the New Party, & so fall into the Trap laid for them. On the other Hand, they have no Seminary of their own nearer than New-haven, in Connecticut, & with the small Livings (made yet smaller by their Divisions) they find it impossible to answer the growing Calls of Congregations, by sending to G. Britain or Ireland for Ministers.

To redress these inconveniences, some of them have spoke to me about
a project for ingrafting a Seminary upon our Philadelphia-College,
which is erected upon the most extensive & catholic Bottom. The
Scheme is this. They propose to collect about 12, or £1400, not to be
laid out in raising superb Edifices like their Jersey-Brethren, but to the
more humane & useful Purposes of maintaining yearly 6 or 7 poor
Students of Genius & Piety to learn the Sciences & receive their
Degrees under the Professors of our College, and to read Divinity at
the same time under the eldest Minister of the Oldest Presbyterian
Congregation, who is to have a small Salary for his pains out of the
Fund. The Candidates for these Burseries are to come recommended
from the old Synod, & where more than the stated Number offer, the
most Deserving to be preferred after due Examination in the public
Hall of the College.

I thought proper to give you a Sketch of this Design beforehand, to
know your Opinion of it. I shall afterwards do myself the Honor to
join in the Application for your Encouragement of it, upon wch they
must chiefly depend. Whatever you do for this, will be done for those
who are really, not nominally, Presbyterians. It will also be the best
Means of Union, & reducing the separating Party to Reason. For when
they see the old Party in a Capacity of maintaining their Ground, a
Treaty may then be entered into on a more equal Footing than at
present, when the New-Lights soon expect to have all, by means of their
prolific Seminary. Besides this, it will always, or at least for a long
Time, be impossible to raise Clergy in America without Burses to
encourage poor Students. Those who can be at the Expence of a liberal
Education will hardly breed their Sons to the *Starvings*, not Livings, of
the Generality of Ministers, in a Country where their money may be
laid out to so much more advantage, any other way whatsoever.

In the mean Time the Congregation in this City can see no Way so
good as applying to you for a Minister. M^r. Cross, the present worthy
Minister, is very infirm, & his valuable Assistant, M^r. Alison, is not
only engaged in one of the most important Offices in our College, but
also so subject to pleuritic Disorders that it is feared his Life will be but
of a short Date. At the Time I am writing this he is so ill, that his
physicians think him in imminent Danger, & if he recovers I think they
will advise him against frequent Preaching for the future. Both he &
M^r. Cross are willing to see the Congregation supplied in their Life-
Time with an able Laborer, who may animate & support their just
Cause, when they are laid in Dust. This they think the more necessary, as the new Party have even had the Assurance to think of putting
one of their Number into that Congregation.

To defeat this Design at present was not difficult, as they are capable
to encourage an able Man to come over to be at the Head of the affairs
of the Old Party, & to superintend the Students in Divinity, should the

foregoing plan take Effect. Since M^r. Tennent purged M^r. Cross's Congregation, the Remainder are some of the most substantial & sensible People of this place, & still a large Body. A Minister among them will be admitted into the genteelest Company in Town ; & what they have promised they will overpay.

Among others of this Congregation, you are not a Stranger to the Name of M^r. Allen, the chief Justice of this Province. Your own Ralph Allen, tho' a more public, is not a more valuable Character than his. Has your Allen an affluent Fortune and a correspondent Generosity? So has ours! Has your Allen inflexible Honesty, great public Spirit, & private Worth? Ours is admired for the same!

Permit me, then, if it may have any weight, to join him & the rest of the Congregation in Soliciting your Dispatch of the Affair. You may know, partly from this Letter, how pressing the Occasion is. They have put great Confidence in you; but they know the Character in which they have confided.

What they expect from you, if Possible to find such a one, is a Copy, or at least an honest tho' distant Imitation of yourself—A Gentleman & a Scholar; of good Sense & masculine Piety ;—not a rigid Predestinarian, nor yet presumptuously excluding God from the Government of his own world ;—fixed in his own Principles, yet not breaking the sacred Ties of Benevolence with those that differ from him;—& to crown all, a good & zealous Defender, as well as Ornament, of our common Christianity.

Should you succeed in this, you will have one good work more to reflect upon. The Congregation will have the Blessing of a faithful Pastor & of an agreeable Friend.

I am yours, &c.

W. SMITH.

CHAPTER VIII.

MASONIC CELEBRATION AND SERMON ON ST. JOHN'S DAY, 1755—DR. SMITH TO
REV. THOMAS BARTON—TO THE ARCHBISHOP OF CANTERBURY—MR. BARTON
TO DR. SMITH—GEORGE STEVENSON TO DR. SMITH—POLITICAL EXCITE-
MENTS—VARIOUS PAMPHLETS PUBLISHED.

IN the year 1755, of which we now write, General Braddock
was carrying on his expedition to the Ohio, and the spirit which
afterwards caused the Declaration of Independence had just begun
to show itself. The Masonic Order, which had existed in America
in an organized form since about 1730, had now become an important body. In 1754 it began the erection of its fine Lodge,
which long gave to one of the thoroughfares of Philadelphia its
title of Lodge Alley, and some of the most important citizens of
Philadelphia were active members of the body. They were, indeed, a body of the highest character. John Penn, Benjamin
Franklin, William Allen, James Hamilton, Thomas Cadwalader,
Thomas Bond, John Swift, William Plumsted, William Franklin,
John Wallace, Alexander Hamilton, Thomas Lawrence, Edward
Shippen, Joseph Shippen, Henry Bell, Charles Stedman, John Kidd,
Thomas Boude, Samuel Mifflin, Richard Hill, Jr., and others not less
respected, were the active persons of the Lodge in this day. Old
Philadelphia had few better names. Dr. Smith took part in all
their transactions. He had been made a Mason prior to his coming
to Philadelphia, though where or at what time I do not know.

The Grand Lodge of 1755 determined to celebrate St. John's
Day, being the 24th of June, with a ceremony worthy of their now
established importance; and that the occasion might be the more
impressive, requested Dr. Smith to deliver a sermon. Dr. Smith
agreed to do so, meaning to make it "an earnest exhortation to
religion, brotherly love, and public spirit in the present dangerous
state of affairs."

On St. John's Day the brethren met at the Lodge room—Governor Tinker, of Providence, in the Bahama Isles, being apparently
with them—and proceeded in state to Christ Church, preceded by

the band of music attached to one of the regiments stationed at Camp Town.   They went in the following order: *

1. The Sword-bearer.

2. Two Deacons, bearing wands tipped with gold.

3. Grand Secretary and Grand Treasurer, bearing the Bible and Constitution.

4. The Preacher.

5. The Grand Master, supported by two brethren of rank and distinction.

6. The Deputy Grand Master, supported in like manner.

7. The two Grand Wardens.

8. The members of the Grand Lodge.

9. The three orders, Doric, Ionic, and Corinthian, carried by three Tylers.

10. The three Masters of the three regular Lodges of the city.

11. The two Wardens of the First Lodge.

12. The two Wardens of the Second Lodge.

13. The two Wardens of the Third Lodge.

14. The three Secretaries of the three Lodges.

15. The three Treasurers of the three Lodges.

16. The visiting brethren, walking two and two.

17. The members of the First, Second, and Third Lodges, walking two and two.

18. The six Stewards, with their rods, walking two and two.

19. The Grand Master's, Governor Morris's, Governor Tinker's, and others of the brethren's coaches and chariots, empty.

When the procession came opposite Market street the echoes of the town were waked by the thunder of cannon, fired as a salute from the vessel of a brother, which lay opposite Market street, handsomely decorated with colors.

When the brethren entered the church, they were seated in pews which had been reserved for them in the middle aisle.   Prayers were said by Rev. Dr. Jenney, the rector of the church, after which Dr. Smith delivered his discourse.   The text was from the 1st Epistle of Peter xi. 17 : *Love the brotherhood.   Fear God.   Honor the king.*   The object of the discourse was to show that the observance of these three grand duties was not only the duty of

* See Westcott's " History of Philadelphia," a work published as yet in a weekly newspaper, but deserving a better form.

the ancient Society of Free Masons, but of societies of every kind.
After the services the members of the Order withdrew; the cannon
again fired a salute from the Delaware; the people again gazed at
the drawn swords of the Tylers, and at the badges and jewels of
the brethren; and with the band gayly playing the tune of the
"Entered Apprentice's Song," the Lodges returned to their hall.

A meeting was there held in form. Through the kindness of
Charles E. Meyer, Esq., I am furnished with a copy of the official
minute:

At the Grand Anniversary and General Communication of Free and
Accepted Masons, held in the Lodge Room, in Philadelphia, on Tuesday, the 24th of June, A. M. 5755 & C. Æ. 1755.

PRESENT—The Right Worshipful W. Allen, Esq., G. M.; B. Franklin,
Esq., D. G. M.; Dr. T. Bond, G. S. W.; J. Shippen, G. J. W.; W.
Plumsted, Esq., G. Treas.; W. Franklin, G. Sec.

Members of Grand Lodge—Hon. R. H. Morris, Esq.; Dr. T. Cadwalader, Esq.; J. Hamilton, Esq.; T. Boude.

Visiting Brethren—His Excellency J. Tinker, Governor of Providence;
John Penn, Esq., etc., and also the Masters, Wardens, and Members of
the Three Regular Lodges.

Upon motion made, it was unanimously agreed:

That the thanks of this General Communication be given to our Reverend Brother, MR. WILLIAM SMITH, for his sermon, preached this day,
before the Fraternity of Free and Accepted Masons in this city, and that
he be requested to give a copy of the same for the press.

WILLIAM FRANKLIN, Grand Secretary.

In the whole, 130 brethren.

Later in the day the brethren dined together, and indulged in
large expressions of loyal and fraternal sentiment.

We were now in the horrors of a French and Indian war. The
religious Society of Friends were still the governing power of the
province. They would do nothing to defend the people by arms.
Braddock had been defeated with terrible slaughter. The matter
became a religious controversy as much as a political and social
one. The missionary clergy of the Church of England—devoted,
as they mostly were, to the crown—publicly censured the conduct
of the Quaker rulers, and called upon the people "to arm," and
defend their homes. Among these clergy was the Rev. Thomas
Barton, of whom we give some account in our Appendix No. I—a
missionary at Carlisle of the Society for the Propagation of the

Gospel, for our then frontier counties of York and Cumberland. This gentleman preached at Carlisle, and at other places in the counties just named, just after Braddock's defeat, a sermon full of loyal feeling. He entitled it UNANIMITY AND PUBLIC SPIRIT, and naturally it had a complexion somewhat political. He was on intimate relations with Dr. Smith, and being urged by the people of his parishes to print the sermon, he sent it in MS. to Dr. Smith, to ask his judgment upon it, and to ask from him his views "on the office and duty of Protestant ministers, and the right of exercising their pulpit liberty in the handling and treating of civil as well as religious affairs, and more especially in times of public danger and calamity."

Dr. Smith wrote to him a letter as follows. Mr. Barton printed his sermon soon afterwards, with this letter as a preface :*

PHILADELPHIA, 21st August, 1755.

MY DEAR SIR : I have carefully read the sermon that came enclosed to me in yours of the 15th instant ; and cannot but think the subject well chosen, and highly seasonable. The thoughts you have chiefly dwelt on, are truly interesting ; and their frequent intrusion shews a mind more deeply impressed with its subject, than attentive to external niceties and method. But, for this very reason, perhaps, the sermon may be more generally useful to such readers as want to have the same truths set in various points of view ; so that I have been very sparing in my proposed alterations of method. Some transpositions and abridgments I have, however, offered to your consideration, agreeably to the confidence you are pleased to repose in me.

There is, if we could hit upon it in composition, a certain incommunicable art of making one part rise gracefully out of another ; which, although it is to be seen by a critic only, will yet be felt and tasted by all. To please in this respect is well worth our warmest endeavours. We are debtors alike to the wise, and the unwise ; the learned Greek, and the foolish Barbarian. None but a few choicer spirits, have sense and goodness enough, to be captivated by the naked charm of Religion. Vulgar souls need to be roused from the lethargy of low desire, and to have their love of God and goodness, excited and enflamed. Hence, Religion must be taught, as it were, to breathe and to move before them, in all the grace and majesty of her most winning and attractive form.

We shall, therefore, err greatly, if we flatter ourselves that it will cost us less labour to preach or write to the ignorant, than to the intelligent.

---

* The sermon is in 8vo., and the title-page states that it is sold by B. Franklin and D. Hall at the new printing office in Philadelphia ; by W. Dunlap in Lancaster, and in York county by the author.

To please and profit the latter, requires sense only. To please and profit the former, requires sense and art both.

I am obliged to you for your kind expressions towards me. An intercourse of compliment would ill suit the seriousness of our characters; and, in regard to any small services I have been able to render you, I am more than repaid in observing that I have, in some measure, been instrumental in supplying our poor back-settlers, with a minister of the blessed gospel; who, in this day of our visitation, will, to the best of his abilities, stem the tide of popular vice and folly, and disdain to appear cold to the cause of his God, his king, or his protestant country.

I know, however, that your appearing warm in these grand concerns, will even procure opposition to your ministry, as well as objections to all sermons of this kind. You will hear it said—"That a minister profess-"ing to be a disciple of the meek and blessed Jesus, should confine "himself to subjects purely spiritual and eternal. What have the clergy "to do with civil and temporal concerns? And as to blowing the "trumpet of war, and declaiming against popery, a subject so long ago "exhausted, what purpose can it serve, but to kindle the flame of perse-"cution, and banish Christian charity from the habitations of men?"

These objections will seem plausible to many, though they will not so much be levelled against any particular performance, as against every protestant minister in general, who shall have the noble resolution to discharge the important duties of his office, in the present emergency. I shall, therefore, endeavour to strip such objections of their false varnish, and shew that to admit them in their full force, tends clearly to involve the world in error and slavery.

It is indeed a melancholy consideration that such a task should be necessary at this day, even under the happy auspices of liberty and a reformed religion. But I know that, in the course of your duty here, you will find arguments still wanting to combat prejudices of this kind, and even to plead before very partial judges the cause of a protestant ministry. And it is our good fortune that such arguments may readily be produced, even upon principles of reason and good policy, if those of a higher nature should be refused.

We may grant that, in the infancy of time, when men lived in a dispersed state, it was possible that every one might be priest as well as king in his own family. Not being as yet collected into larger societies, men were not then engaged in that constant round of action, which hath since been the lot of their short-lived posterity. Their manners were more simple; the distinctions between right and wrong were less perplexed; and they had leisure to attend not only to the dictates of a heart less corrupt, but also to those positive injunctions, received occasionally from God himself, conversing face to face, or handed down from their first parents, in pure and faithful tradition.

But although in these times of simplicity, as they are described to us, we may suppose every man capable of discovering his own duty, and offering up the pure and spiritual worship of his own heart, yet such a worship was too refined, abstracted and solitary, to last always. Human affairs soon became more complicated. Societies were necessarily formed; and this sacred intercourse of individuals, with the Father of Love, soon began to decay. The avocations of life made many forget it; and many more were too much sunk in ignorance and indolence, to mark those displays of wisdom, power and goodness, which ought to raise it in the breast. Such persons could see the sun set and rise, and could turn their sight upon the spacious sky, without adoring the Maker's greatness, or extolling his wisdom. They could wander, with unconscious gaze, in the midst of nature, neither listening to her voice, nor joining in her grand chorus to creative goodness.

Now it was easy to foresee, that this defection of individuals from their Almighty Parent, might not only spread itself into general corruption, but involve particular societies in temporal misery. It, therefore, became necessary to institute a social worship, by which all the members of a community might be assembled, in one solemn act, to give some public mark of that homage of heart, which was universally agreed to be due to the supreme head of the social system.

From this time, then, a chief ruler, to administer law and superintend the public weal, was not a more salutary institution, than the separate institution of an order of men to preside in these solemn acts of devotion, and to form the minds of the people to the knowledge both of law and duty. For action follows opinion; and, in order to act right, we must first learn to think right.

Thus, the priesthood seems to rest on the same foundation with society itself, and takes its rise from the necessity of human affairs, which requires some institution for assisting the busy, rouzing the indolent, and informing all. Without this, every other institution for the good of mankind would be found imperfect; and there never was a society of any kind that did not find it necessary, under some name or another, to appoint certain persons, whose particular business it might be, to study and explain what was conceived to be the great interests of that society, especially to such of its members as had less opportunity or ability of informing themselves.

We see, then, that the office of such an order of men (call them priests, or by any other name) is important in its original, and noble in its design; being nothing less than the great design of making men wise and happy—wise in knowing and happy in doing what God requires of them.

But what is it that God requires us to know and to do as the means of happiness? Is it not to know and do homage to him as our supreme good, and to know and do our duty in the several relations he hath appointed us to sustain?

Shall those, then, who are called to instruct mankind be told after this, that things belonging to civil happiness fall not within their sphere? Hath not God himself joined the table of social duties to that of religious ones? Hath he not, in his benevolent constitution of things, made temporal wisdom and happiness introductory to that which is eternal? And shall we perversely put asunder what God hath so kindly joined? Or is it not evidently our duty, as teachers, to explain to others their great interests, not only as they are creatures of God, but also as they are members of a particular community?

The contrary doctrine would soon pave the way to entire wretchedness. For what nation hath ever preserved a true sense of virtue, when the sense of liberty was extinct? Or, in particular, could the protestant religion be maintained, if the spirit of protestant liberty were suffered to decay? Are they not so intimately connected, that to divide them would be to destroy both?

Indeed, languid and remiss as many of our profession are said to be, yet to them is greatly owing what sense of virtue and liberty is still left in this remote part of the globe. Had not they, or some of them at least, from time to time, boldly raised their voice, and warned and exhorted their fellow-citizens, mixing temporal with eternal concerns, most certainly popish error and popish slavery (perhaps heathen error and heathen slavery) had long ere now overwhelmed us! Where, then, would have been the blessings purchased by our reformation and glorious revolution? Or, where would have been that inestimable liberty of conscience, which, as the best things may be most readily abused,—

> " Now views with scornful, yet with jealous eyes,
> " Those very arts that caused itself to rise? "
>   POPE.

But further, in favour of the point in question, I might here also bring the sanction of God himself, and plead the example of our blessed Lord and master, that great high-priest and best preacher of righteousness, who had a tear—yes, a heart-shed tear—for the civil distress incumbent over the very country that crucified him, and would have led its inhabitants to shun their temporal as well as their eternal misery.

But this I pass over, as I know you will have to deal with those who will be for trying everything at the bar of what they call impartial Reason. I have, therefore, hinted such reasons as I think will hold immutably true, in societies of every kind, even in the most enlightened, and far more so in those that are circumstanced as we are at present.

We are a people, thrown together from various quarters of the world, differing in all things—language, manners, and sentiments. We are blessed with privileges, which to the wise will prove a sanctuary, but to the foolish a rock of offence. Liberty never deigns to dwell but with a prudent, a sensible and manly people. Our general conduct, I fear, will scarce entitle us to this character in its proper degree. We are apt either to grovel beneath the true spirit of freedom; or, when we aim at spirit, to be borne, by an unbridled fierceness, to the other extreme; not keeping to that rational medium, which is founded on a more enlarged and refined turn of sentiment. Add to all this, that an enterprising enemy behind us is ready to seize every advantage against us. We are continually advancing nearer to one another in our frontier settlements, and have here no surrounding ocean, or impassable barrier between us.

Now, in such a situation, what can ever unite us among ourselves, or keep us a separate people from our crafty foes, but the consciousness of having separate interests, both civil and religious? It should, therefore, be the constant endeavour of the clergy, in all their public addresses, to inspire every bosom with a rational zeal for our holy protestant faith, and an utter aversion to all sorts of slavery, especially in the present emergency.

How far a just sense of our inestimable privileges, will contribute to exalt the genius of one people above another, is evident from the conduct of our brave countrymen, in the colonies to the northward. Their preachers have been long accustomed to dwell much upon the rights of Britons and of protestants. In consequence of this, to their immortal honour, they are now acting, as one man, like Britons and protestants, in defence of those rights.

Among us, on the contrary, where the few, who ought to explain those noble subjects, labour under many disadvantages, which I need not mention to you, a quite different temper and spirit are to be seen. We either think it unlawful to act at all in the assertion of these sacred rights; or if we act, it is only with half a heart, as if but half informed with that sublime spirit, which is kindled by the love of truth and freedom, and burns in the bosom, like some pure ethereal flame, lighting the soul to deeds of virtue and renown.

Every endeavour, therefore, to kindle up this all-enlivening flame, and exalt our country's genius, is truly worthy a preacher's character, notwithstanding ten thousand such frivolous cavils as those above mentioned; every one of which falls of course, on the removal of the fundamental one. For, having already shewn, that it becomes those who are placed as watchmen on the walls of our holy Zion, to "cry aloud and spare not," on the approach of everything that can "hurt or make us afraid," either in our civil or religious capacity; surely no warmth can be unseasonable at a time when all that we account dear or sacred is threatened with one indiscriminate ruin.

Those who are in good earnest, in the great work of instructing others, will suit themselves to seasons and occasions; and for a preacher to neglect the present opportunity of making impressions of holiness, and diffusing a just sense of those excellent privileges, which are but too little understood, though fully enjoyed among us, would be the most unpardonable breach of duty.

It were, no doubt, sincerely to be wished, that the harsh voice of discord, and the clangor of the trumpet, could be forever hushed in the world. And we, in particular, who preach the kingdom of the Messiah, cannot but prize and even adore peace, as it is the chief of blessings, and auspicious to religion and all the best interests of mankind. But the greater this blessing is, the more necessary it often becomes to assert it against those who delight in violence and blood. There is no unmixed felicity in this imperfect state. It was only in Eden and the state of innocence, where the rose bloomed without its thorn; and till we are admitted into a kingdom of universal righteousness, we must not look for the blessings of peace, entirely free from the miseries of war. While we have public sins, we must expect public chastisements.

With regard to the last objection, which I said might probably be levelled against such sermons as yours, I would observe, that I think the subject of popery can never be exhausted, while the danger of it remains; and though it may be a subject well understood by those who have been long blessed with faithful Protestant pastors; yet this cannot be the case with those who have had so few advantages of this kind as your infant congregations.

Indeed, that you should be more than ordinarily alarmed at this most singular crisis, is not to be wondered at. For, while we sit as yet safe in our metropolis, your situation on the frontiers is most dreadful; and our last accounts from you are truly distressing to humanity—The army sent to your protection, defeated, retreating and leaving you defenceless behind them! murderers stealing through midnight darkness, and polluting the bed of rest* with savage death! Our poor back-settlers, who, after much hardship and toil, had just begun to taste ease and comfort, daily forced from their habitations, leaving their unreaped harvests to the spoiler; and—what is far more severe—leaving, some a beloved wife, some an affectionate husband, some a tender parent, a brother or a son—leaving them bleeding beneath the unrelenting hand of merciless barbarians!

In such a case, shall we be silent to avoid the imputation of too much warmth? Shall we expose ourselves to worse than persecution, for fear of stirring up a persecution of others? The rest of the foregoing objections would only lead us to give up all concern for the civil rights of our fellow-citizens; but this goes farther, and, under an extraordinary shew of benevolence, would induce us tamely to yield up our sacred truth and religious rights also, for fear of being thought rude and uncharitable to such as seek to rob us of them. Surely we may guard

---

* The inhuman butcheries and outrages of the Indians.

against *slavish* and *erroneous* doctrines, without any breach of our Christian charity towards those who have unhappily embraced such doctrines. And surely we may strive to awaken in every protestant bosom a due sense of our exalted privileges, and a noble resolution to defend them against every foreign invader, without kindling the flame of persecution against any of those who have peaceably sheltered themselves amongst us, upon the faith of a rational toleration.

Most certainly, my friend, all this may be done ; and I think it has been clearly shewn that all this ought to be done by every minister, and more especially those of our national church, which is the great bulwark of the protestant interest. And, indeed, we who belong to that church, can want no farther arguments on this head when we have the example of that great and good prelate* who now presides over it. In his *civil* capacity, I need not mention the noble stand which he made in his diocese of York, during the late rebellion. It will never be forgotten by Englishmen. And, in his *episcopal* capacity, when that danger was over, if you read his sermon preached at Kensington, on the Fast-day, January 7th, 1747, you will there find him as strenuously engaged for the preservation of the public virtue of his country, as he had been before for the preservation of its public liberty ; considering the one as inseparable from the other, and breathing forth that candid benevolence to his species, together with that tempered zeal for the protestant religion, and the rights of the British nation, which distinguish his character.

And here I cannot forbear the transcribing a paragraph of a late most excellent letter, which I had the honour to receive from him by your hands. It is not foreign to the subject we are now upon ; and I persuade myself that you will make the same good use of it, which, by the help of God, I shall strive to do. He says :

> You will not only maintain, but certainly increase your credit, by promoting the interest of your country and the honour of religion ; in which I will venture to call it the *golden rule* of conduct, to keep strictly to the spirit of protestantism, and to preserve the dignity of our establishment, in the temper of every reasonable degree of liberty.——

This is a *golden rule* indeed ; and while we frame our conduct by it, we need not be awed by the faces of men, but boldly proceed to warn and exhort them in every species of duty. It is true, we have but few temporal advantages, in these parts, to support us in such a noble cause, but yet we are not left destitute of the most animating motives. Whilst others are proposing, and justly proposing, to themselves the palm of high renown, for bravely subduing and maintaining a rich and spacious country for the name of Britain and liberty, we may consider ourselves even in a still higher light, as subduing it to the name of Christ, and

---

* Archbishop Herring.

adding it to his everlasting kingdom ! Compared to this, the glory of temporal conquests and foundations is but unsubstantial air, and short-lived renown !

Hence, then, my friend, were it my lot to be in your situation, at this perilous season, methinks I should consider myself as one who had advanced to the very frontiers of those places to which the gospel hath yet reached, and among the first who had unfolded its everlasting banners in the remotest parts of the West. Recede I would not, nor give back a single inch to the gloomy reign of Heathenism and Error ; but would strive to subject still more and more to the kingdom of God and his Christ. To see the fire and vigour of youth spent in such a work, is indeed a most lovely spectacle, because they are spent in his service who gave us both youth and fire ! And if we exert ourselves manfully in such a cause, who knows, but at length, through Almighty assistance, a flame may be kindled which shall not only exalt every bosom among us to an equality with the foremost of our neighbours, but shall also burn, and catch, and spread, like a wide conflagration, till it has illuminated the remotest parts of this immense continent !

I would not, however, be understood from anything here said, to think it expedient for ministers of the gospel to interfere any farther in civil concerns than is just necessary to support that spirit of liberty, with which our holy religion is so inseparably connected ; for such a conduct might engage us in broils, ruffle our tempers, and unfit us for the more solemn part of our duty. Nor do I think we ought to dwell any farther on the errors of others, than just to enable those, with whom we are connected, to shun them ; lest, instead of the spirit of true holiness, a spirit of vain-glory, self-righteousness, and hypocritical-pride, should be promoted.

'Tis true, as hath been already said, that we can never be too much upon our guard against the growth of a corrupt and slavish religion among us, but we may be in as much danger, on the other hand, from infidelity, a morose and censorious spirit, and a neglect of the practice of all religion. Hence, then, though on proper occasions, we are to rise with a noble contention of soul, against vice and error ; yet still our favourite subjects ought to be on the brighter side of things—to recommend the love of God and our neighbours, together with the practice of every social and divine virtue.

I would just observe farther, though, in such circumstances as the present, sermons from the press may be sometimes both necessary and seasonable, yet I am far from thinking that this will be our most effectual method of serving religion, in general. We shall be vastly more useful in this cause by being much among the people committed to our care, and knowing how to accommodate our private as well as public instructions to their various dispositions and necessities.

That the author of every good gift may enable you to be more and more useful in this and everything else that can adorn the character of a preacher of righteousness, is my sincere wish, as I cannot think myself indifferent to anything that affects the credit of your ministry.

I am, etc.,
WILLIAM SMITH.

In the same spirit which prompted the preceding letter, Dr. Smith now writes* to the Archbishop of Canterbury; and gives some account of the conduct of the Society of Friends which had provoked the publication of Mr. Barton's sermon.

PHILADELPHIA, October 22d, 1755.

MY LORD: I take the Liberty of enclosing a Copy of a petition to his Majesty, subscribed by the principal Gentlemen of this City, & sent by this Conveyance to be presented. Copies of the same are now subscribing in the several Counties throughout the Province, & will be sent also to England as soon as possible.

The purpose of the Petition will be found truly interesting. Our Situation at present is such as never any Country was in. The Province is powerful in Men, in Money, and in all Sorts of Provisions. From twelve to twenty Thousand Men might be raised on an Emergency: & we could find Provisions for six Times that Number. And yet we have not a single Man in Arms, but our Lives & our all left at the Mercy of a Savage Crew, who are continually Scalping around us & among us. While I am writing this I hear of a large Number cut off on our own Frontiers. The Winter approaches & the King's Troops have left this Province, so that we have a most melancholy Prospect. —'Tis extremely distressing to think that we have Strength sufficient; & yet, by the very Government that owes us Protection, to be restrained from making Use of those Powers, which God & Nature gave us, to repel Violence, and prevent the Inroads of Injustice & Iniquity into the World.

'Tis far from being my desire to see any Sett of Men hampered by real religious Scruples; but surely if these Scruples unfit such Men for that which is the chief End of all Government (the Protection of the Governed), they ought in Conscience to resign to those who are better qualified. The Lives and properties of the People are things too sacred to be trifled with. And yet while our Government rests in the hands of *Quakers*, they must trifle on the Subject of Defence. They will suffer no Body to share power with them, & as they themselves can take no Part of a Military Power, so they are determined never to suffer it in the Province; & some of them say they would sooner see the Enemy in the Heart of the Country. For this Reason, when they are called upon to put the Frontiers in a posture of Defence, they con-

---

* From the original draft among the Smith MSS.

tinually introduce some Dispute about Money & privilege to evade the Question & amuse the People; Altho' no Money is required by a Militia-Law, but only the Authority & Sanction of the Government.

'Tis upon the same plan that they abuse every Clergyman who strives to rouse the attention of the people to their present Danger. If we endeavour to distinguish between the Popish & Protestant Religions in Order to keep the People firm to the British Interest at this Perilous Season, we are said to be of a biggoted and persecuting Spirit. If we exhort to a manly Defence of our inestimable Liberty, we are said to be Dabblers in Politics, & not Ministers of the meek and blessed Jesus. They are afraid of seeing a Spirit of Virtue and Freedom raised among the People, which would spurn those Quietist & non-resisting Principles which at present sway the Government of this Province.

For my Part I shall with my whole Influence oppose such Principles, which tend to subvert all Society. My Conscience, & Charity to our poor suffering back-Inhabitants, would not permit me to act otherwise. For this Reason, upon the general consternation that followed General Braddock's Defeat, I wrote to the Missionaries on the Frontiers as far as I knew them, exhorting them to make a noble Stand for Liberty, and vindicating the Office & Duties of a Protestant Ministry against all the Objections of the Quakers & other Spiritualists who are against all Clergy.

This Letter was soon after published & dispersed by the Rev^d M^r. Barton, together with a Sermon of his suited to the Times. The Letter I enclose, as it is short. It had a good Effect, especially as it described what I conceived to be the Duties of the Ministry in Times of public Calamity and Danger. I humbly beg your Grace to peruse it, because I found it necessary to make use of your Grace's Name & illustrious Example, in Order to give a Sanction to the Conduct recommended. Your Grace will perceive, in the last seven Pages, how good an Use I have made of those noble Principles of Liberty & Moderation, which your Grace was pleased to recommend to me as a Golden Rule of Conduct. I hope I shall be forgiven the Freedom I have taken in quoting that Rule, since it was intended for the Interest of our holy Religion & excellent Establishment. If this Letter shall but receive your Grace's Approbation, I shall prefer it to every other production that I have been capable of, because it was so seasonable & has been so useful in furnishing my Brethren with arguments.

As the Letter mentions your Grace's Sermon on the fast Day at Kensington, a very ingenious Lutheran Minister is now translating it into Dutch, to be printed for the Use of our Germans, among whom are Shoals of Roman Catholics. The Translator is extremely capable of the work, & it will be highly seasonable.

I would just observe farther that the following petition was written by me. I endeavored to keep clear of all Party Reflexions & to make it general. As I love my Country I cannot help giving what Assistance I can to bring it into Order, & I hope his Majesty & his most hon^{ble} Council will think our Case worthy of their serious Consideration. I doubt not it will be thought worthy of your Grace's particular Countenance, who cannot but think yourself affected with whatever affects so many of his Majesty's Subjects, however distant. Your Humanity is as conspicuous as all your other public Virtues. It will do me singular Honor to be favoured now & then with a few Lines under your Grace's Hand, in whose Life & Well-being I think myself so nearly interested. M^r. Penn will find a Conveyance. I am,

Your Grace's Most obedient Servant & dutiful Son
WILL. SMITH.

P. S. Please to excuse the little Ceremony with which I am obliged to write, while Truth, Sincerity, & the profoundest Respect appear at Bottom.

The following letters—one from Mr. Barton, the other from George Stevenson—though from different places, are on the same general subject :

The Rev. Thomas Barton to Rev. Dr. Smith.

CARLISLE, November 2d, 1755.

REV'D SIR : Since I last wrote you I have been engaged in one trouble after another. We have had nothing here but alarms upon alarms. The back-settlers are daily passing through this Town, and leaving their long-toiled-for possessions to the rude spoiler ; Women and Children hanging about their Husbands, imploring them to escape. In short, sir, every circumstance is heightened with the most shocking Accounts. A Letter from Harris's Ferry last night acquainted us that Andrew Monteur and Monachatouth were sent for to the big Island, who found there six Delawares and four Shawanese Indians, who informed them that they had received the Hatchet from the French to destroy the English, which they resolved to make use of while there remained one alive. Monachatouth is now upon his way to Philadelphia with some important Reports to the Governor. We are building a small stockade here, in which most of the country people are engaged. This town is particularly threatened, and we expect to be attack'd every Hour. I saw Yesterday a copy of a Petition to the citizens and Merchants of Phil^a for a Subscription. This Petition was directed to William Allen, Wm Plumsted, and Richard Peters, Esqrs., Messrs. Israel Pemberton, W^m. West, Samuel Hazard, and yourself. I mean the Petition intended to request these Gentlemen to hand it about. Whether it will be sent or no, I cannot tell. If volunteers will go out against the Enemy, I am ready to be one. I know not where I shall be this day week.   But wherever I am, I shall always be,   Revd Sir,

Your affectionate, hum^ble Servt,

THOMAS BARTON.

P. S. By advices just received from two Gentlemen in this County, we are assured that the great Cove is quite destroy'd, the Houses burnt, and the Inhabitants murder'd.   We are in the most unhappy situation —nothing but crys and confusion.   I wish the gentlemen of Philadelphia would enter into a Subscription for us.   We shall otherwise be inevitably ruined.

*George Stevenson to Rev. Dr. Smith.**

YORK, Wednesday, 5th November, 1755, 3 o'clock, P. M.

REV^D D^R S^R : The grand *Quære* here now is, whether we shall stand or run ? most are willing to stand, but have not Arms nor Ammunition ; this is the Cry of the People.

I have sent repeated Petitions to the House, Letters to the Governor, to M^r. Peters, & one to M^r. Allen, but no Answer ; for my own Part, I am in the greatest Distress.   The whole Country run to me, and I have neither Arms nor Ammunition to give them, nor can Credit nor Money buy these things.   With the Assistance of the Justices, M^r. Lishy, & some principal Men on the Spot, I spirit up the People all I can.   We have sent fifty-three Men to Harris's last Monday from this Town.   Such as have Arms stand ready, and we watch Night & Day.   People from Cumberland are going thro' this Town hourly in Droves, and the Neighbouring Inhab^ts are flocking into this Town, defenceless as it is. For the Distress of the People Westward, refer you to M^r. Dougherty, the Bearer.   Schools, I can neither think nor say ought about.

I beg a few Lines to tell me what you see & hear, & whether any Relief is to be speedily expected from our Rulers.

Perhaps I may not be here to receive your Letter, but be sure write, for if I fly, it will not be to Quakers ; I will go to Maryland.   Excuse this Trouble.   I must add that M^r. Barton heads a Comp^y, M^r. Bay another, &c., &c.   I am, D^r S^r, with great Esteem,

Y^r most obed^t H^ble Servt,

GEORGE STEVENSON.

The REV'D MR. SMITH.

The state of things mentioned in the several letters preceding produced, of course, a great deal of feeling, both in England and here. Many pamphlets were written. Mr. Westcott, in his "History of Philadelphia," describes them. So far as he speaks of those relating to Dr. Smith, we profit by his labors:

---

* Penna. Archives.

William Smith, Provost of the College, published, in pamphlet form, a representation of the condition of the Province according to the views of the Governor's party.   The following was the title :

A Brief State of the Province of Pennsylvania, in which the conduct of their Assemblies is impartially examined, and the true cause of the continual encroachments of the French displayed; more especially the secret design of their late and unwarrantable invasion and settlement on the river Ohio.   To which is annexed an easy plan of restoring quiet in the public measures of the province and defeating the ambitious views of the French in time to come.   In a letter from a gentleman who has resided many years in Pennsylvania, to his friend in London.   Third edition, London.   Printed for R. Griffith, in Paternoster Row, 1756.

This paper began by describing the condition of the colony.   It was said that, in staples and provisions, it produced enough to maintain itself and one hundred thousand men besides ; that four hundred vessels sailed from Philadelphia annually ; that the inhabitants were computed to be two hundred and twenty thousand—one-third Germans, two-fifths Quakers, more than one-fifth Presbyterians, and some few Baptists. Complaints were made of the conduct of the Quakers.   It was said that the Government was in fact more a pure republic than when there were not more than ten thousand souls in the colony ; that the inconveniences under such a state of affairs must continually increase with the numbers of the people, till the Government at last became so unwieldy as to fall a prey to any invader, or sunk beneath its own weight unless a speedy remedy was applied.   It was declared that the Assembly had made itself independent of the Proprietaries.   By voting or withholding the salaries of the Governors from them, it was alleged that they had wrested from the Governors the right of appointment to many offices.   It was suggested that Christopher Sauer was a popish emissary, in the pay of the Quakers.   He had told the Germans in his paper that there was a design to enslave them, and to force their young men to be soldiers; that a military law would be made, heavy taxes enforced, and all the miseries they suffered in Germany would be renewed.   The consequence was that the Germans voted with the Quakers, were under the control of that party, and always voted to keep them in power.   Sauer was accused of attacking other preachers.   One-fourth of the Germans were supposed to be Roman Catholics.   The author of the pamphlet advocated, as measures of reform, the passage of an Act of Parliament

To oblige all those who sit in the Assembly to take the oath of allegiance to His Majesty, and perhaps a test or declaration that they will not refuse to protect their country against all His Majesty's enemies ;

To suspend the right of voting for members of the Assembly from the Germans until they have sufficient knowledge of our language and Constitution ;

      *   *   *   *   *   *   *   *   *   *

To encourage Protestant schoolmasters among the Germans, in order to reduce them into regular congregations; to instruct them in the nature of free government, the purity and value of the Protestant faith, and to bind them to use a common language and the consciousness of a common interest;

To make all bonds, wills, and other legal contracts, void, unless in the English tongue; that no newspapers, almanacs, or periodical paper, by whatever name it may be called, be printed or circulated in a foreign language; or, at least, if allowed, with a just and fair English version of such foreign language printed in one column of the same page or pages, along with the said foreign language.

The publication of this pamphlet was speedily followed by others on both sides of the controversy. Among them are to be specified several of interest and ability. One was:

An Answer to an invidious pamphlet entitled "A Brief State of the Province of Pennsylvania," wherein are exposed the many causes of assertions of the author or authors of the said pamphlet, with a view to render the Quakers of Pennsylvania and their Government obnoxious to the British Parliament and Ministry, and the several transactions most grossly misrepresented therein set in their true light. London. S. Bladen. 1755.

In this publication the action of the Governors was attacked. It was alleged that they had endeavored to get the disposal of the public money into their own hands. The opinion of George Croghan, an "Irish papist," was quoted to the effect that the importation of Germans was a great benefit in settling the colonies. The passages in the "Brief State" which attributed immense power to Christopher Sauer, were ridiculed. It was said that Sauer had been useful in teaching the people their rights The objections against the Germans were asserted to be false and malicious.

This was followed by another pamphlet by Dr. Smith, after Braddock's defeat, entitled:

A Brief View of the Conduct of Pennsylvania for the year 1755, so far as it affected the general service of the British colonies, particularly the expedition under the late General Braddock, with an account of the shocking inhumanities committed by incursions of the Indians upon the Province in October and November, which occasioned a body of the inhabitants to come down while the Assembly were sitting, and to insist upon an immediate suspension of all disputes and the passing of a law for the defence of the country; Interspersed with several interesting anecdotes and original papers relating to the politics and principles of the people called Quakers; being a sequel to a late well-known pamphlet, entitled "A Brief State of Pennsylvania." In a second letter to a friend in London. London. R. Griffith. 1756.

It had this motto:

To see the sufferings of my fellow-creatures,
And own myself a man—to see our Senators
Cheat the deluded people with a sham
Of Liberty, which yet they never taste of.
All that hear this are villains, and I one,
Not to rouse us at the great call of Nature,
To check the growth of these domestic spoilers,
Who make us slaves, and tell us 'tis our charter.—SHAKESPEARE.

In this pamphlet the dangers of the inhabitants were set forth. It was said that a militia law was wanted ; that the answer to the " Brief State " was written by one—formerly an attorney's clerk—who was convicted of forgery, sentenced to be hanged, transported to Pennsylvania, was not allowed to plead as an attorney here, and at the end of the time of his banishment went home ; that the day before the military bill was passed, four hundred inhabitants, chiefly Dutch of the best sort, came down from the back parts of Philadelphia county in a peaceable and orderly manner, not knowing what was done, and created an alarm ; the governor sent for the sheriff, &c. ; that the military tax would not have cost " the people two pence each, one with the other."

There were other pamphlets on the subject, but none that I know of by Dr. Smith.

On Christmas day of 1755 I find Dr. Smith in New York, and preaching in Trinity Church, in that city. After such conflicts as he had gone through with "the Friends" at home, we are not surprised at his seeking a little enjoyment on a great festival elsewhere.

CHAPTER IX.

The Curriculum given on Pages 56–63 Adopted in 1756—Characterized by the Provost Stillé—Charges made against Dr. Smith—All Examined and all Refuted—Action of the Trustees—Letter of David Hall..

The curriculum which we have given *supra*, pages 56–63, under the date 1754, was conceived and written out by Dr. Smith nearly at that time. Being now, A. D. 1756, requested by the trustees of the College and Academy to prepare a Plan of Education for these institutions, he reproduced it, as already given by us at the pages named. It was adopted, and continued in use during the time he was its Provost. In 1776 it was adopted by the Rev. James Madison, in the College of William and Mary, in Virginia; and A. D. 1782 by Washington College, Maryland.

In regard to this Plan of Education the Provost Stillé, than whom there can be no more competent judge in America, says:

It is impossible to read this " Plan," remembering that a century ago all plans of education on this continent were experiments to be tried

under circumstances wholly novel and peculiar, without being struck
with the sagacity, judgment, and far-reaching views of its author.   Its
best eulogy is, that it has formed the basis of our present American
College system.   He set out with the sound principle so frequently forgotten in our day, but quite as true now as it was then, " that nothing
can be proposed by any scheme of collegiate education, but to lay such
a general foundation in all branches of literature as may enable the youth
to perfect themselves in those particular parts to which their business or
genius may afterwards lead them ; and scarce anything has more obstructed the advancement of sound learning than a vain imagination that
a few years spent at college can render youth such absolute masters of
science as to absolve them from all future study."   The *curriculum* of
study, both in the choice of subjects and in the order in which they
were taken up, was not unlike that which until recently formed the general system of instruction in all our American Colleges.   The period of
study extended over three years, and during that time Juvenal, Livy,
Cicero, Horace's *Ars Poetica*, Quintillian, and the Tusculan Questions
were read in the order given.   In Greek, the Iliad, Pindar, Thucydides,
Epictetus, and Plato de Legibus formed the text-books.   In Mathematics, the course was quite as extended as that now pursued in any
College in the country, while in the department of Natural Philosophy,
Chemistry, Hydrostatics, Pneumatics, Optics, and Astronomy occupied
the attention of the students during a large portion of the Junior and
Senior years.   A good deal of time was given also (much more than in
the present College course) to instruction in Ethics, and in Natural and
Civil Law, as illustrated by History.

It may be safely affirmed that in 1756 no such comprehensive scheme
of education existed in any College in the American colonies.   We have
Dr. Smith's own authority for saying, that this scheme did not exist
merely on paper, but that it was faithfully carried out in its details, and
with the most brilliant results, during the whole period of his connection
with the College.   This statement is confirmed so far as the instruction
in Natural and Moral Philosophy is concerned, by an examination of
the note-books of the lectures (which are still preserved) which he
delivered on those subjects.

We now pass to a new matter.   The political opposition arising
out of the French and Indian war had brought with them personal
animosities towards him.   His pen, when animated by a sense of
wrong, could be sharp and incisive ; and he had not failed to exhibit in their true light and genuine colors the disastrous effects
which the conduct of the Assembly of Friends had produced upon
the Province.   In addition to this he was now the recognized
champion of the Proprietaries' interests—interests to which there

had arisen a strong opposition, Dr. Franklin being the real, though not much avowed leader of it. The result was numerous attacks, mostly anonymous, through the newspapers, on Dr. Smith's official and even his personal conduct. He was charged, among other things, with using his official place to teach to his classes doctrines inconsistent with those recognized by the Charter and Constitution of the Province, and, as some persons considered, with religion itself. Dr. Smith was desirous that all the charges should be investigated, as he felt sure that they would be all refuted. Accordingly a meeting of the trustees was called for the 5th of July, 1756. It was moved by one of the trustees that examination be made into their foundation, as the reputation of the Academy might be affected by them; and it appearing to the trustees that in justice to their own character, as well as that of their Provost, such an examination was very proper, it was referred to Mr. Peters, Mr. Taylor, and Mr. Stedman, to make full inquiry into this matter, and report the same at the next meeting of the trustees, that it might then be considered what ought further to be done.

Upon hearing of the proposed investigation, the students of the Senior Philosophy Class presented to the trustees the following paper, which the trustees ordered to be entered on their minutes:

To the Trustees of the College of Philadelphia :

GENTLEMEN : Whereas, several unjust and malicious Insinuations have lately appeared in the public Papers and been spread through the City by the Heat of Party against the Rev^d Mr. William Smith, Provost of this College, some of them designed to misrepresent his Conduct and injure his Credit with Respect to the Pupils under his Care ; we whose names are hereunto subscribed being such of the Students of the Senior Philosophy Class as are now in Town, think it our Duty, in Justice to the Character of our respected Tutor, to certify to you that for near the space of two years last in which we have been under his immediate Care, he never did, in any of his Lectures, take Occasion to introduce any Thing relating to the Parties now subsisting in this Province, or tending to persuade us to adopt the Principles of one side more than another. We further beg Leave to certify to you that, in the whole Course of his Lectures on Ethics, Government and Commerce, he never advanced any other Principles than what were warranted by our standard Authors, Grotius, Puffendorf, Locke, and Hutcheson ; writers whose sentiments are equally opposite to those wild notions of Liberty that are inconsistent with all government, and to those pernicious Schemes of Govern-

ment which are destructive of true Liberty.   That he readily embraced
every opportunity of applying Morality to the sublime Truths of Religion and Christianity—on which subjects he always dwelt with a peculiar
and affecting warmth, cautiously avoiding all Party Distinctions and
controverted Subjects; as a sufficient Proof of which, we now lay our
notes of the Lectures, which he delivered upon the several Branches of
Morality, before the Trustees; and any other persons willing to inspect
the same may also be favoured with them, upon application to any of us:

JACOB DUCHE, JR. (in his 19th year),
JAMES LATTA (in his 21st year),
FRANCIS HOPKINSON (in his 19th year),
HUGH WILLIAMSON (in his 21st year).

PHILA., June 21st, 1756.

The committee appointed to examine into the charges made a
report in writing.   It was thus:

REPORT.

Agreeable to an Order of the Trustees of this College and Academy,
at their last meeting, Setting fourth that several Insinuations had lately
been inserted in the public Papers, injurious to the Character of the
Revd Mr Smith, and that the same, if just, might be of Disadvantage to
this Institution, we, to whom it was referred as a Committee to inquire
into the grounds of these Insinuations, do report, that we have perused
the Publications made in the late News papers and are of Opinion that
nothing therein insinuated ought to prejudice the College and Academy;
because, on examination, it must appear to every one, as it really does
to us, that no single Master can, by the Constitution of the College
and Academy, carry on any separate or party-Scheme, or teach any
principles injurious to Piety, Virtue, and good Government, without an
evident failure of Duty in the whole Body of Trustees and Masters;
the general Scheme of Education being fixed, a part of it assigned to
every Master, The Visitations of the Schools by the Trustees monthly,
and in the Interim between their Meetings, the Government, the
Morals, and the Education of the whole Youth committed to the
Faculty, which consists of the Provost, Vice-Provost, and Professors,
who have it in charge to examine into and report to the Trustees at
their Stated Meetings whatever shall appear wrong in any of the Professors, Masters or Scholars.

We have likewise, at the Request of the Trustees, examined and
inquired into the Conduct of the Rev^d Mr. Smith, and do report that,
during his Employment in his present Station as Provost of the said
College and Academy, it has been becoming and satisfactory to us.
His Application, his Abilities and Labours in the Instruction of his
Pupils, have been attended with good success, and approved by the

Trustees and Audience, at the late public Examination of the Senior
Philosophy Class, who are now recommended for Admission to their
first Degree ; moreover, such of this Class as are now in Town, consisting of Young Men from nineteen to twenty-one years of age—from a
motive of Gratitude and Justice to Mr Smith's Character, which they
think had been aspersed and injuriously treated—have laid before us
their Note-Books, which contain the Substance of his Lectures to them
on the Subject of Religion, Morality, and Government, which were
taken at the Time they were delivered, and were always open to the
view of the Trustees at their monthly or occasional visitations ; and
have voluntarily presented to the Trustees an Ample Testimonial of his
Conduct towards them whilst they were his Pupils. From these facts,
and our own personal Knowledge of Mr. Smith, we are of Opinion that
he has discharged his Trust as a capable Professor and an honest man,
and that he has given sufficient Evidence of the goodness of his
Principles.

This report, having been fully considered, was unanimously
approved by the trustees, who ordered the same, with the minutes
relating thereto, to be published in the *Pennsylvania Gazette*, a
paper owned and edited by Dr. Franklin and Mr. David Hall ; but
of course controlled by the former.

The report, with its accompanying minute, was left by some of
the trustees with Mr. Hall, to be inserted in the *Gazette*. He
returned them, with the following letter. The letter reveals the
beginning of an estrangement, which afterwards grew wider,
between Dr. Smith and Dr. Franklin. Dr. Smith's friends subsequently adverted to Dr. Franklin's action in this matter as one
evidence among others—exhibited more strongly from 1761 to
1763—that he or his known friends were willing to break down
the College which he had himself founded, in order to break
down a man who in it was now rising into political importance,
and threatened in that department to become more potential than
himself.

David Hall to the Trustees.

July 15th, 1756.

GENTLEMEN : Upon considering the Paper you left with me this
morning, and finding in it notice taken of some Insinuations published
to the Disadvantage of Mr Smith ; but as those Insinuations were not
published in our Paper, and as it has some Relation to the Party Disputes that have for some time subsisted, which we have carefully
avoided having any concern with, I cannot but think it more proper
to publish this by the same Channel through which the Disputes have

hitherto been carried on on both sides ; especially as, in all Probability, there will be some answer or Remark offered upon it, which we should be under a necessity of publishing if we printed this, and be thereby engaged in an affair which we all along have been endeavouring to avoid. I therefore *return* it to you in Time, that it may be published in the other paper, if thought proper, and am

Your very humble Servt,

DAVID HALL.

CHAPTER X.

QUARREL WITH ROBERDEAU, ETC.—FAST SERMON IN CHRIST CHURCH—MR. BAR-
TON TO DR. SMITH—DR. SMITH VISITS HUNTINGDON—LETTER OF MR.
BARTON TO DR. BEARCROFT—TRUSTEES TO THE SOCIETY—DR. SMITH TO
DR. BEARCROFT—DR. SMITH TO BISHOP SECKER—ACRELIUS LEAVES AMERICA
—DR. SMITH TO DR. BEARCROFT.

DURING the year 1756 the feeling between the Assembly and the adherents to the Proprietaries continued to run high, and among the latter Dr. Smith was prominent. Being on one occasion at the Coffee House (the Merchants' Exchange of that day, then recently established by Col. Bradford, and still standing at the southwest corner of Front and Market, a place which was for a long time the head-quarters of all genteel strangers and of our Provincial officers, as well as of our active citizens in private life), Dr. Smith was charged by some one of a circle with which he was conversing with an excessive devotion to the Proprietary party. He denied any excess of devotion.

One of the company, Mr. Daniel Roberdeau, made a public statement of what Dr. Smith had said, and Dr. Smith denying very positively that Mr. Roberdeau had rightly reported him, Roberdeau made an affidavit that what he (Roberdeau) had said was true. Singular enough to add, he went to Dr. Jenney, the rector of Christ Church, an aged man, never entering much into Dr. Smith's plans, and to the vestrymen and wardens of the church, and to the Rev. William Tennent and the elders of the New Presbyterian Church, and to seventy merchants, etc., of Phila-delphia, and procured from them a certificate that, in their opinion, he (Roberdeau) was " an honest man "—the most ridiculous part

9

of the whole matter being that the allegation against Dr. Smith was
that he had used these words:

I am not of one party more than another.   I only dress the sentiments of the Proprietary side in proper language, and if it were not that
there are men of sense among the friends of the people, I would do the
same by them.

The matter became a town-talk.   Gilbert Tennent was a Presbyterian, and personally no friend of Dr. Smith.   His elders
followed their master, and the " seventy merchants," being all personal friends of Roberdeau, and probably selected on that account,
were not good witnesses against Dr. Smith; independent of which
there was no question about whether Mr. Roberdeau was "an
honest man."   Dr. Smith would, doubtless, have been willing himself to certify that he was so.   The only question was whether he
had rightly understood what Dr. Smith—in an animated conversation, in which several persons participated, and had got disputatious
and " altogethery "—had really said.

The testimony of the whole body of signers to the certificate was
of no relevancy to the issue, seeing that none of them were at the
Coffee House at the time when the conversation occurred.   And,
as respected the Rev. Mr. Gilbert Tennent and his elders and the
"seventy merchants," Dr. Smith paid no great regard to it.   As
respected, however, the rector, minister, vestry, and wardens of
Christ Church, he felt somewhat aggrieved.   They had been
guilty of great forgetfulness of what was due to a minister of the
church whose faith they themselves professed.   He blamed them
to their face, as did most judicious men.   It is agreeable to add
that they made the best *amende* that they could.   It was in a
document, in the Historical Society of Pennsylvania, thus:

Whereas, the vestry of Christ Church, in this city, have been blamed
as if their late Certificate to the character of Mr. Daniel Roberdeau, now
a Member of Assembly of this Province, had been granted to give him
an Advantage over the Rev. Mr. Smith in the Dispute between them,
we, the subscribers, members of said vestry, think ourselves bound to
declare for ourselves severally, that when we signed the said Certificate
we had no such Intention, and imagined that it was to be made use of
in the Common Method of such Certificate, and not to be inserted among
any public or Party Papers, with the View to prejudice a Gentleman for
whose Character as a minister of the Church of England we have the

greatest tenderness, and who, during his Residence among us, has discharged the office of Provost of the College and Academy of this city
with Reputation, and has occasionally officiated in the Congregation to
which we belong, much to the satisfaction of the audience; nothing that
we know of having ever been said to his Prejudice till the appearance
of some Party Papers, during our late unhappy Debates, to which we
paid the less Regard, as the true Character of men are to be taken from
their Life and Conversation, and seldom to be learned from Papers of
that nature.   Signed by the Vestry of Christ Church, Phila.

The truth was that good Dr. Jenney, who was now seventy years
old, and had been struck with paralysis, had lost, in some degree,
his mental power; and that his worthy assistant, Mr. Sturgeon,
without age or paralytic stroke, had no such superabundance of
his own as to be able to supply his rector's calamity.   Rector,
assistant, and corporation generally, had about this time, from the
infirmity of the head of the corporation, fallen into the hands of a
political party opposed to Dr. Smith.   The whole history is given
at pages 215–261, further on in this book, in a letter of Dr. Smith to
the Archbishop of Canterbury.   The *amende* was soon made more
publicly honorable; for the government of Pennsylvania, having appointed the 21st of May, 1756, as a day for a public fast, Dr. Smith
was invited by Dr. Jenney to preach in Christ Church.   His sermon, which is printed in his collected works,* was on "hardness of
heart, and contempt of God's merciful visitations," which he declared to be "the certain forerunners of more public miseries."
He applied the subject to the colonies in a parallel between their
state and that of the Jews in many remarkable instances, alluding
pathetically to the misery under which the Province was groaning
in consequence of Braddock's defeat, and the inroads of the French
and savages on the distressed and hapless frontier; a subject which
seems to have taken possession—as it might well take possession—of the mind and heart of Dr. Smith as a Christian and a
patriot.

Dr. Smith sought to promote the cause of the crown not only
from the pulpit, but apparently in some political organizations in
the interior.   We thus interpret the first part of the following letter.
The questions before the country were questions of life and death;
of the supremacy of infuriated savages, with the tomahawk in

---

* Vol. II., p. 91.

their hands, or of a civilized government protecting its citizens from them.   In such a moment he felt that his rights and duties as a man and as a citizen were not destroyed by his profession as a minister.   His views of the duties of the clergy in such a case are already given in his letter to Mr. Barton.*

It appears from this letter, we may add, that Dr. Smith was himself contemplating a journey towards the frontier.   He afterwards made it, as appears by his own letter (*infra*) of November 1st, 1756, to the Bishop of Oxford, and by a letter which we now give, from Mr. Barton to Dr. Bearcroft, the Secretary of the Propagation Society.   Though the letter of Mr. Barton does not all relate to Dr. Smith, it all relates to a subject in which he interested himself, and it all has connexion with our proper subject.   In this visit Dr. Smith went as far west as Huntingdon, on the Juniata.   He was accompanied by Mr. Secretary Peters, George Croghan, and Conrad Weiser.   The object of the visit appears from the letter of Mr. Barton to have been in the interest of the Free Schools, but I find no account of his having established a school at Huntingdon. In a memoranda made by him at this time he mentions having baptized upwards of an hundred persons, many being children brought by their parents more than fifty miles, in order to receive the sacrament.   In a list of their names I find that of Brotherline, Parkerson, Edmerson, Sell, Swank, Dean, Weston, Spanogle, Nearhoof, Drake, Prigmore, Ingard, Shirly, Hoffman, Westbrook, etc., etc.

It were but fair to suppose that the Rev. Mr. Barton was the first Episcopal clergyman stationed at Huntingdon.   At that time there could have been none farther west.

The Rev. Mr. Barton to Rev. Dr. Smith.

CARLISLE, September 23d, 1756.

REV⁰ DEAR SIR: I wish I had received yours sooner, I would have recommended to you to procure a letter from Mᵣ Alison to Mᵣ Thompson, and one from Mᵣ Tennant to Mᵣ Bay.   I am afraid the Scheme is come too late; The Country has already settled a Ticket so that it will be no easy Matter to prevail upon them to change it.   However, rest assured, I shall use my utmost Endeavour; as will also Mr. Lishy; who has been with me about it.

I am not surprised that all is Confusion with you, for the British In-

* Supra, p. 110.

terest seems to totter !   Braddock defeated !—Minorca taken !—Oswego
destroyed,—I had like to have said sold !—Our Fellow Subjects daily
murder'd, & carried into Savage Captivity ;—and a great Part of Pennsylvania already depopulated & laid waste !

The present War seems big with Ruin !   God knows what may be the
Issue, but the English Colonies on this Continent have Reason to dread
the sad Effects of it.   We are Ten Times the Number of the Enemy,
but our Misfortune is, that we do not cherish that Harmony & Unanimity that was formerly wont to make Englishmen terrible.

Some of our petty Colonies are, at this Time, aiming at separate
Interests & independent Glory ;—Some think the Danger at a Distance,
and therefore will not be concern'd ;—Others either swarm with Papists,
or are govern'd by a Set of Men whose religious Principles are contrary
to the very Nature & Design of Government, & will not part with their
peaceable Testimony to rescue the Country from Destruction.

As you will no Doubt have a full Account of Mr Armstrong's Expedition to the Kittannon in the Papers, I shall only observe to you, that
the famous Captain Jacobs fought, & died, like a Soldier.   He refus'd
to surrender when the House was even on Fire over his Head ; And
when the Flame grew too violent for him, he rush'd out into the Body
of our Men flourishing his Tomahawk, & told them he was born a Soldier, & would not die a Slave.

If you should come as far as York, I should be glad to see you, having
some affairs to communicate to you.   I faithfully assure you that I am,
Your affectionate Friend & Servt,

THO. BARTON.

TO THE REVD MR WILLIAM SMITH.

Mr. Barton to the Rev. Dr. Bearcroft.

HUNTINGDON IN PENNSYLVᴬ, Novr 8th, 1756.

REVEREND SIR : It gives me a real concern that I have never been
able to send you any accounts since I entered upon my mission till now.
Our distresses here have been such that in short I knew not what to
write or what to do.   These considerations will I hope still support me
in your esteem and incline The Hon'ble Society to pardon me, as I
intend to be the more particular now to atone for my past silence ; I
foresee a long letter and must therefore bespeak an indulgence.

After a short and very agreeable passage I arriv'd at Philadelphia
about the 16th of April, 1755, and immediately wrote to the people of
Huntingdon who came generously with their waggons and brought away
my effects.   As soon as I settled my affairs and visited my friends I set
out for this place about the latter end of May, when I was received with
a hearty welcome, and was much pleased to find the poor people fill'd
with gratitude under a due sense of the weighty obligations they were
under to the Hon'ble Society for the favors confer'd upon them, and

what pleased me still more was, to hear that they had struggled hard to keep alive some sense of religion among their children by meeting every Sunday and getting one of the Members to read prayers to them.

My first business was to visit and make myself acquainted with the State and members of the Congregation at York, Huntingdon and Carlisle, and having settled Wardens & Vestrymen in each, they all met and according to their numbers agreed mutually that I should officiate three Sundays in six at Huntingdon, two at Carlisle and one at York. Upon hearing that within the limits of my mission there were large numbers of the Communion of the Church of England in the Settlements of Canogochieg, Shippensburg, Sharmans Valley, West Penns-Borough and Marsh Creek, I determined to visit each of those places four times a year to prepare them for the Sacrament of the Lord's Supper and to baptize their Children.

I had the pleasure to see my hearers encrease daily; which amounted to such a number in a few weeks at Huntingdon that I have been sometimes obliged to preach to them under the Covert of the Trees, and when it was my turn at Carlisle, I am told that people came 10, 50 and some 60 miles. The Dissenters also (who are very numerous in these parts) attended constantly & seemed well disposed, always behaving themselves decently and devoutly. The more rational part of them appear well reconciled with our Church and some of the principal of them offer'd generously to subscribe to me.

I now began to consider myself (as the Rev^d M^r. Provost Smith expresses it in a letter to me), "as one who had advanced to the very frontiers of the Messiah's Kingdom and among the first who had unfolded his everlasting Banners in the remotest part of the West."

From the advantage of my situation bordering upon nations of Savages I entertained strong hopes that it might please the Lord to make me a happy Instrument to subject some of these poor ignorant Creatures to the Kingdom of God and of Jesus Christ, and hearing that a number of them were come down from the Ohio to Carlisle to dispose of their furr and Deer Skins, I made it my business to go among them and endeavour as much as possible to ingratiate myself into their good opinion. Next morning I invited them to Church, and such of them as understood any English came and seemed very attentive the whole time. When I came to visit them in the afternoon those that had been at Church brought all their Brethren to shake hands with me; and pointing often upwards discoursed with one another some time in their own language, I imagine they were telling them what they had heard, and indeed I observed them to be pleased with the relation.

This gave me reason to think that the Indians were willing to be instructed and were susceptible of good impressions; and if they found Missionaries divested of sinister and selfish motives they could easily be prevailed upon to exchange their savage barbarity for the pure and peaceable religion of Jesus.

Just when I was big with the hopes of being able to do service among these tawny people we received the melancholy News that our forces under the Command of General Braddock were defeated on the 9th of July as they were marching to take Duquesne, a French Fort upon the Ohio. This was soon succeeded by an alienation of the Indians in our Interest, and from that day to this poor Pennsylvania has felt incessantly the sad effects of Popish Tyranny and Savage Cruelty! A great part of five of her Counties have been depopulated and laid waste and some hundreds of her sturdiest Sons either murdered or carried into barbarous Captivity.

At a time of such publick calamity and distress, you may easily conceive, Revd Sir, what must be my situation whose fortune it was to have my residence in a place where these grievances were felt most. I repine not, however, at my Lot in being placed here; but rather esteem it a happiness, since I hope I may say God has enabled me to do some service to our pure Protestant Religion, in spite of its most inveterate Enemies.

Tho' my Churches are Churches militant indeed, subject to dangers and trials of the most alarming kind, yet I have the pleasure every Sunday (even at the worst of Times) to see my people crowding with their Muskets on their Shoulders; declaring that they will dye Protestants and Freedmen, sooner than live Idolaters and Slaves. The French King has rather served than injured the Protestant Cause in these parts, For the people have seen so much of the cruel Barbarities of those who call themselves the subjects and allies of His Most Christian Majesty, that they detest the very name of Popery.

Among a people thus disposed I should think myself extremely happy, were they barely able to keep me above want, which at present, indeed, they are not. It is but a little time since these Counties were erected. They were chiefly settled by poor people, who, not being able to purchase lands in the interior parts of the Country, came back where they were cheap. Many of them were so low at first, that two families were generally obliged to join in fitting out one Plough; and before they could raise a subsistence were necessitated to run in debt for a Stock and for what maintained them in the Interior. As soon as they became industrious, the fertile soil gave them a hundred fold, and in a little time rais'd them to affluence and plenty. When they were just beginning to feel the comforts and taste the fruits of their industry, a barbarous and cruel enemy came and ruined them! The County of Cumberland has suffered particularly, and the condition of its remaining shatter'd Inhabitants is truly deplorable! Many of them are reduced to real poverty and distress; groaning under a burden of calamities; some having lost their Husbands, some their Wives, some their Children; and all, the labour of many years! In this Condition (my Heart bleeds in relating what I am an Eye-witness to), they now wander about, without Bread of their own to eat, or a house to Shelter themselves in from the Inclemency of the approaching winter! They have left many thousand Bushels of Wheat and other Grain behind them in their Barns and Store-houses, which must become a Spoil to the Enemy, while the just owners of it must either beg or Starve! Since I sat down to write this Letter, I have received accounts that a poor family had fled for refuge into this Country above six months ago, where they have remained ever since ; but finding they could not subsist, chose, a few days ago, to run the risk of returning home to enjoy the fruits of their labour, where they had not time to unlode their Cart before they were seized by Indians, and murdered.

Carlisle is the only remains of that once populous County. They have a Garrison of about 100 Men, but how long they will be able to defend themselves is very uncertain, as the Enemy have threatened that place in particular. They still have their share of my ministrations, and seem extremely thankful to the Honble Society, upon whose bounty I am chiefly supported.

By the reduction of Cumberland the County of York is become the frontier, and should the Enemy carry their ravages this far, I shall be a considerable sufferer, for upon my arrival at Huntingdon, I found the Glebe still under its native woods, and the people not able to make any improvement upon it. This put me under the necessity of purchasing a small plantation and building on it at my own expense, by which means I embarrass'd myself in debt, in hopes the people would assist me in paying for it, which, indeed, they promised to do. But this dismal turn in our affairs renders it impracticable. From York I have still less to expect, as the Town is chiefly inhabited by Dutch, and not many of our Communion among them. Upon the whole, I believe the people will be able to do very little for me, till we have some favourable change. I do not design, Revd Sir, by anything I have said, to derogate from the merit of my good parishioners; that would be ungrateful, as I have reason to think that they are a worthy, well-disposed and kind sort of people, who possess the greatest friendship and esteem for me, and am persuaded would willingly do anything in their power to afford me an easy support and maintenance.

This mission in a few years would have vyed with the ablest in this province, as it was in a flourishing state and could not contain less than 2,000 persons, Members of the Church of England ; but so melancholy is the transition, that it cannot afford to build one Church ; so that I officiate sometimes in a barn, sometimes in a waste house, or wherever else convenience offers.

I have baptized since my arrival 160 Infants, 10 Adults, and an Indian Girl, who has been brought up in a Christian family since her Infancy ;

after due examination and instruction. The Number of my Communicants is 58, which I have but little expectation of encreasing, till this Storm is blown over! But I assure you, Rev⁴ Sir, no endeavours of mine shall be wanting to bring many to Righteousness. Whatever hardships or discouragements may attend my Ministry, I hope I shall ever keep in view the importance of my undertaking, and always strive to answer the pious and laudable designs of the Honble Society in appointing me their missionary ; by doing all in my power to promote the Glory of Almighty God and the Salvation of Mankind. I received lately from the hands of D^r. Jenney the Society's Instructions to their Missionaries in North America, which are very seasonable and justly adopted to our present circumstances ; and if duly observed and properly inforced, may do infinite service to our bleeding Country.

I have often observed and indeed regretted it as a misfortune that our Missionaries in this part of the World are so little acquainted with one another, And though in the 12th instruction of the Society's collection of papers, it is recommended to them to " keep up a Brotherly correspondence by meeting together at certain times as shall be most convenient for mutual advice and assistance," yet no such thing is observ'd and I dare affirm that many of them have never had an opportunity of conversing with four of their Brethren since they left England. How many advantages we shall lose by such a neglect at this time of publick and emminent danger, I shall submit to the judgment of the Honble Society.

M^r. Provost Smith has been lately up here to settle Free Schools, who is the only Episcopal Clergyman, beside M^r. Secretary Peters, that I have had the happiness of seeing in these Counties since I came into them. M^r. Smith has been pleased to communicate to me the Honble Society's design to extend their care to the instruction of Indian Children at the Academy in Philad^a. Which good scheme I believe M^r. Smith will heartily endeavour to put into execution & do everything in his power to make it answer the glorious ends proposed by it. If I can assist him in any part of it, he shall always find me ready and willing to do it. Happy had it been for us had this scheme been resolved upon many years ago. For it is probably from the neglect of this necessary duty of instructing the Indians, that these Colonies derive the greater part of the Miseries they now sadly groan under.

While the French were industrious in sending Priests and Jesuits among them, to convert them to Popery, we did nothing but send a set of abandon'd profligate men to trade with them who defrauded and cheated them, and practic'd every vice among them that can be named, which set the English and the Protestant Religion in such a disadvantageous light, that we have reason to fear they detest the name of both.

It is said by some of our Brethren who have lately escaped from captivity that they heard the Indians say they thought it no Sin to Murder the English, but rather a meritorious Act, and if it was a Sin the French had old Men among them who could forgive all Sins.   Others observe that they crossed themselves every Night and Morning and went to prayers regularly.   That they often murmur'd and said the English it was true had often made them trifling presents, but that they took care they should never carry them many Miles before the Traders came after them, to cheat them, giving them only a little Rum in return.   Whereas the French always paid them well for their Skins, &c. ; built houses for them ; instructed their children and took care of their wives when they went to war.

By such neglect and such treatment have we forfeited an alliance that would in all probability have secured to us a quiet enjoyment of our possessions and prevented the dreadful consequences of a Savage War.

Several Sachims or Indian Kings in their Treaties formerly with this Government earnestly solicited that no European should be permitted to carry Rum to their Towns; Upon which an Act was pass'd by the Governor and Assembly of this Province, prohibiting any person under a penalty of Ten pounds, to sell, barter, or give in exchange, any Rum or other Spirits to or with any Indian within the province.   But the difficulty of producing proof against offenders, as they were chiefly far back in the Woods, where they would deal clandestinely out of the view of any but themselves, made this Act not answer the good intentions of the Legislature.   So that the Traders still continued to sell strong Liquors to the Indians, whereby they were often cheated and debauch'd to the great dishonor of Almighty God, Scandal of the Christian Faith, and hindrance of propagating true religion among them.   Yet I don't despair but some methods may be fallen upon to reclaim them, and make them sensible that their attachment to the English will be their truest interest, and greatest happiness.

And indeed (in my humble opinion) nothing can promise fairer to produce these happy effects than this scheme proposed by the Hon[ble] Society.   In the conversion of Indians many difficulties and impediments will occur, which European Missionaries will never be able to remove.   Their Customs and manner of living are so opposite to the Genius and constitution of our people that they could never become familiar to them.   Few of the Indians have any settled plan of habitation but wander about, where they can meet with most success in hunting, and whatever Beasts or Reptiles they chance to take are food to them.   Bears, Foxes, Wolves, Raccoons, Pole Cats and even Snakes, they can eat with as much cheerfulness as Englishmen do their best Beef and Mutton.   But such hardships are easily surmounted and such an austere life made agreeable, by such as from their infancy have been accustomed to them.   So that Indian boys educated at the Academy under the care of able Masters, where they can be visited by their relations and taught every thing necessary for them to learn, at an easier expence than in any of the Universities in Europe, will be first to be employed in this Grand and Glorious work and the most likely to succeed in it.

However defective these thoughts may be, I have ventured, Revd Sir, to communicate them freely ; and if I have luckily dropt any hint that can be improv'd to the advantage of this important scheme, I shall esteem it a happiness; As I shall always think it my duty to pay the highest regards to the Honble Society's directions.

I might justly incur the censure of ingratitude, did I conclude this Letter without presenting my most hearty thanks, which I sincerely do, to that Hon'ble Body for appointing me their Missionary. And I shall ever retain a grateful sense of the many friendships and favours wherewith I was honour'd when in London by particular Members of it.

I am, Revd Sir, &^{c}.

THOMAS BARTON.

We now come back to the agreeable topics of the schools for poor Germans and of educating Indian children ; the progress of the former and the practicalness of the latter is interestingly told in the following letters, the first one doubtless from the pen of Dr. Smith as much as the last.

The Pennsylvania Trustees to the Society in London.

PHILADELPHIA, September 24th, 1756.

To the Right Honourable and worthy Members of the Society for promoting religious Knowledge and the English Language among the German Emigrants in Pennsylvania, &c.

MOST WORTHY LORDS AND GENTLEMEN : We have been duly honoured with your several Letters thro' the Hands of your worthy Secretary and Fellow Member, the Reverend D^r. Chandler, part of which have been directed to Us jointly, and part to the Reverend M^r. Smith. We have, from Time to Time, faithfully endeavoured to follow your Orders and Instructions, and beg Leave to assure You of the sensible Pleasure it gives Us to find our Conduct approved by such an honourable Body of Men, in the Management of so useful and excellent a Charity. But nothing, in this whole Business, gives Us more real Satisfaction than to be so strongly assured, in your Letter of January 28th, 1755,—" That " the whole of what you aim at is, not to proselyte the Germans to any " particular Denomination, but (leaving all of them to the entire Liberty " of their own Judgments in speculative and disputed Points) to spread " the knowledge of the avowed uncontroverted Principles of Religion " and Morality among them, to render them acquainted with the " English Language and Constitution, to form them into good Subjects " to His Majesty King George, whose protection they enjoy, and make

" them Friends to the Interests of that Nation which hath received them
" into her Bosom, blessed them with Liberty, and given them a Share
" in her invaluable Privileges."

Such a noble and generous Declaration is truly worthy of the noble
and generous Spirits from whence it comes. It is worthy of Men who
have embarked on a Principle of Doing Good for its own Sake, and
who, by their Birth, Education, and liberal Turn of Mind, are elevated
far above the narrow Distinctions that blind the Vulgar. We have likewise the Honour to assure You, that such a Declaration is also perfectly
agreeable to our Sentiments, who, by Reason of our Publick Situation
in this Country, could never have engaged in the Management of any
partial Scheme. Nor indeed would such Scheme have answered, in any
Shape, your pious and noble Design. For whatever is proposed for the
Benefit of the German Emigrants must, in its Nature and Plan, be as
Catholic and General as their Denominations are various; especially as
far as regards the Education of their Children ; in which Point they are
exceeding jealous and tenacious of their respective *Dogmas* and *Notions.*

We ought long ago to have addressed You in this public Manner, but
have been hitherto prevented ; partly by the great Distress of our
Country and the frequent Absence of many of Us from Town ; and
partly by the necessary Time it took to give You a Notion of the Expence,
and settle Accounts of various Articles and different Commencements,
in such a manner as to commence from stated Periods in Time coming.
Nevertheless, although these Things have delayed this public Letter, and
may perhaps sometimes have interrupted the Course of our more private
Intelligence, yet We have not been wanting in our Attention to the
Progress of the Schools. It will appear by the Minutes sent You to June
16th last, and by those which accompany this Letter, that Messieurs
Smith and Schlatter have done their Part ; and some of Us in our
Journey to the Frontiers have also occasionally visited several of the
Schools.

Upon the whole, they are in as promising a State as can reasonably be
expected in a Country so much harrassed by a Savage Enemy, and subject to so many Alarms to disturb that Peace and Tranquillity which are
so essentially necessary to the Cultivation of Knowledge. You are
already informed that three of the Schools We had planted have for some
Time past been entirely broken up, being near the Frontiers, where the
People for near a year have been flying from Place to Place, and but
little fixt in their Habitations. The other Schools remain much in the
same State as when You received our last Minutes; and We are now
not without Hopes of enjoying more internal Quiet for the future and
keeping our Enemy at a greater Distance.

Along with this, You will receive the Remainder of the Minutes and
a State of the Accounts to July 1st, by which You will find, that, including the Purchase of the Press, £600, the Sum already drawn for is

expended for one Year and a half, excepting a very small Balance, and the Outstanding Debts, which We shall give Credit for as fast as they can be collected in. We must now continue to draw £100 Quarterly, till We receive your further Orders. This will do our Business, and We hope so good a Work will not be suffered to drop for want of that Sum. The carrying on the printing Work has been expensive at first setting out ; but great part of that will in Time be defrayed by the debts due in the Country. And 'tis also to be considered that the distributing religious Books was part of our Design ; for which Reason We were at a considerable Expence with the Dutch Copy of the " Life of God in the Soul of Man," 500 Copies of which are yet remaining, and the other 500 are gone out among the People, and have proved most acceptable at this Time.

Permit Us to assure You that We shall at all Times think Ourselves happy in contributing every Thing in our power, under so illustrious a Society of Men, to the forwarding such an excellent Design, for the Honour of Great Britain, and the Benefit of those poor People who have taken Refuge under her Wings, and with due Care may be preserved as his Majesty's most faithful Subjects, and zealous Defenders of the Protestant Cause.

We have the Honour to be

Your most obedient and most humble Servants,

BENJAMIN FRANKLIN,	JAMES HAMILTON,
CONRAD WEISER,	WILLIAM ALLEN,
WILLIAM SMITH,	RICHARD PETERS.

Dr. Smith to the Rev. Dr. Bearcroft.

PHILADELPHIA, November 1st, 1756.

REVᴰ AND WORTHY Sᴿ : Your Favour of March 25ᵗʰ, in the name of the Society for Propagating the Gospel in Foreign Parts, I received about the first of Septʳ, and have spoken to several proper Persons relating to the Scheme you propose "of instructing & maintaining a Number of " Indian Children at the Academy at Philadelphia under my Care at " the Expence of the Society, with a View to initiate the said Children " in the Principles of Christianity." I have observed in a letter to my Lord Bishop of Oxford, of this Date, how much pleasure it would give me to contribute towards so good a Design, and a Design so perfectly agreeable to the original Plan of the worthy Society ;—" The " glorifying the Name of Jesus, by the further Enlargement of his " Church, and particularly by spreading his everlasting Gospel among " the Heathen Natives of America ; as well by Instructing and civilizing " those of them that are grown up, as by laying a Foundation for edu- " cating, cloathing, and training up their Children in the knowledge " of morality, true Religion, the English Tongue, & in some Trade,

" Mystery, or Calling, should they be disposed to follow it." I have further hinted in that Letter that, altho' Almighty God has not thought fit hitherto to give any remarkable Success to the pious labours of the Society in the great Work of Converting the Indians, yet as such a Conversion, if ever it is accomplished, must probably begin in the rising Generation, it would be well if, in every Frontier Colony, there were a Provision made in the most public Place of it for maintaining and educating a Number of Indian Children ; and who knows the Time when, or the Means by which, God may be pleased to bless the great Work at last ? I have also in the said Letter hinted several other Things on this Head, which I need not repeat here, as his Lordship is a constant and worthy Member of the Meetings of the Society, at which this important Scheme will be further deliberated.

I proceed then to your Query as to the Expence of such an Under-taking. This, indeed, it is not possible exactly to answer. However, they may be cloathed, fed and educated for about £20 Sterl. one with another. But then there is a considerable Expence which, perhaps, you have not thought of. Wherever we have Indian Children, their Parents will be coming down twice or thrice a Year to see them ; and must be maintained, not only during their Stay, but on their Journey, Going and Coming, besides receiving a considerable Present every Time, which is an Article not to be dispensed with. This Expence, however, I believe the Province would defray very willingly ; and on that Head Mr. Penn is to be consulted. I should be glad to be informed what Number the Society would propose to maintain of these Children, and under what Regulations, that I might be able to settle all the Parts of the Plan with the Trustees of our College and Academy, and to fall upon Means of defraying any Expences that may arise over and above the Society's Allowance. If it was thought advisable, some of them might be placed in the Country at the Charity-Schools lately created among the Germans, in the Management of which I am concerned. But tho' this method would be something less expensive, yet I should not think it so advisable, because the farther distant from their Parents, and the more public the place is at which these Children are placed, so much better would it be in the political Consideration of attaching them more strongly to our Interest, by giving them Opportunities of seeing and knowing the principal Persons in our Government.

Another Expence will be in getting them to consent to such an Edu-cation. And this is only to be done by getting our Government here to engage its Credit for their good Usage, and making it worth the Pains of the Provincial Interpreter to go among them & use his Influ-ence for that purpose ; that so the Parents may be gradually reconciled to part with them.

Now there is a greater chance of getting all this done by making such a Provision in our public Academy than any where else that I know.

This Province has always preserved its Faith remarkably with the Indians. The chief Men in the Province are engaged in the Trustee-ship of our Academy, and its Foundation is on the most catholic and liberal Plan.

I find D^r. Jenney is not very fond of the Design, and says that our Trustees have little Regard for Religion. But the Truth is that from the first he has opposed the Institution, because it was not made a Church Establishment & all the Masters to be of that Persuasion. His Zeal for the best Church on Earth is certainly commendable; but it may be carried too far. Had our College been opened on that Plan in such a Place as Philadelphia, the Students would indeed have been a very scanty Number. The People would not have borne even the Men-tion of such a Design at first. However the Church, by soft and easy Means, daily gains Ground in it. Of Twenty-four Trustees fifteen or sixteen are regular Churchmen; and when our late additional Charter was passed, I, who am a Minister of the Church of England, had the Preference to two other Ministers of other Persuasions of longer Stand-ing than me in the Institution, and was made Provost of the same by the unanimous Voice of the Trustees. We have Prayers twice a day, the Children learn the Church-Catechism, & upon the whole I never knew a greater Regard to Religion in any Seminary, nor Masters more thoroughly possessed of the truth of our common Christianity. And glad should I have been could I have dispelled Doctor Jenney's Preju-dices, and persuaded him to be convinced with his own Eyes. But he never would set a Foot within our Gates.

You will not think that I mean by this to throw any Reflection on a Gentleman so much my superior in years. I would only endeavour to prevent your being prejudiced against our Institution by any Thing he may say from a well-meant Zeal to have the Church established faster in this Province than the Temper of the People will allow. If any Thing farther than my Word be necessary concerning our Academy, I can get all the Clergy in the Country to Certify to its Credit, and to the Expediency of your Proposal for educating Indian Children at it. And, indeed, if the weight of the Trustees, their Authority in the Govern-ment, and the Reputation of our College and Academy cannot engage the Indians to consent to the Design, certainly the Credit of a Church Vestry or any private School will be ineffectual. I hope soon to be favoured with the Society's further Commands on this Head that I may know how to frame my Conduct accordingly.

This will be delivered to you by the Rev^d M^r. Acrelius, a learned Swede, and late Commissary to the Swedish Churches on Delaware, who now returns to considerable Preferment in his native Country, as the Reward of his past faithful Labours. He is a sincere Friend to the Church of England, and has been useful to many of our destitute English Congregations, particularly Newcastle, by preaching and using our Service in English.   He is well acquainted with the State of all our Missions in this Province; and it may be worth the while to inform yourself concerning some of them, particularly Chester and Newcastle. He is a worthy and discerning Man, and as he is never to return among us, must be impartial.*   Along with him there goes a young Gentleman of the name of McKean, of whom I have a good Character from people of Reputation.†   I wish you could serve him in any Degree.

I was at Newcastle lately, and find all the People mightily set upon having M^r. Cleaveland for their Missionary; and at their pressing Instances he now supplies them, as he is kept out of his Mission at Lewes by a most worthless Fellow of the Name of Harris.   I wish M^r. Cleaveland may be ordained at Newcastle, which he will soon render a flourishing Congregation, as he is a worthy Man & a popular Preacher. As for the People of Lewes they deserve no Notice till they return to their Senses and discharge their present irregular Minister, which they will soon do if left to themselves.   I hear that a whole Revolution is proposed among the Missions, M^r. Craig for Oxford, M^r. Ross for Newcastle, & M^r. Cleaveland for Lancaster.   Such a Step I fear will not be agreeable to all the parties concerned, and particularly to Newcastle, which in that case you will find will be reduced to great Distraction. D^r. Jenney would be willing to have M^r. Craig near him; but Lancaster perhaps would not like the change.   But these Things are not my Business any farther than as an impartial Spectator that regards the Interest of the Church.

M^r. Barton is indeed a most worthy & useful Missionary.   He is the Darling of his People, & has been obliged for a twelvemonth past sometimes to act as their Captain & sometimes as their Minister.   He has been the means of keeping them together at the Risk of his Life, when they would otherwise probably have been dispersed all over the Continent.   They are under continual Alarms from the Savages, and I believe able to pay him but little.   I have just been up among them.   They do all they can for M^r. Barton; but if the Society do not grant him some Gratuity over his Salary, in these distrest Times, I fear he must leave them & seek a Living elsewhere.   For on any Alarm his House is their Rendezvous, and the Number of poor becoming every Day a greater Burden, who being driven from their Houses and Homes would melt the hardest Heart into the kind Offices of Charity.   I shall always rejoice if in my present Station I can be any way instrumental in executing any of your Commands, or promoting the great Work in which you are so assiduously engaged.   May God prosper and direct all

---

* For a further account of Acrelius, see *infra*, pp. 148–9.

† This was a brother of Thomas McKean, afterwards Chief-Justice and Governor of Pennsylvania. He became a useful missionary of the Church of England in New Jersey.

the Designs of the worthy Society to his own Glory, which is the unfeigned Prayer of

Worthy Sir, Your most Affectionate Brother

and Obedient humble Servant,

WILLIAM SMITH.

P. S.—Direct to Wm Smith, Provost of the College and Academy of Philadelphia.

We have now two noble letters; on subjects partly political and partly religious, the one topic at this time interfusing itself inseparably with the other.

Dr. Smith to the Bishop of Oxford (Dr. Secker).*

PHILADELPHIA, November 1st, 1756.

MY LORD : The Misery and distress of this unhappy province, bleeding under the Murderous knives of a savage enemy, instigated and led on by popish cruelty, have been so unspeakably great, and the confusions arising from a Quaker Government, obstinately persevering in their absurd pacific Polity, while the sword of the enemy was at our throats, have so thoroughly engrossed my attention, and engaged my weak endeavours to defeat such wicked principles, and procure relief to a miserable people; that I hope to be excused for not having sooner returned my humble acknowledgments for the honour of Your Lordship's letter of February the first, 1755, by the Reverend M^r. Barton.

I am extremely rejoiced that the worthy Society are so well convinced of the importance of sending Missionaries to the Frontier of our Colonies ; and that they took in good part my endeavours to set that matter in a true and striking point of view.   The more I consider it, the more I see its importance to the Protestant interest.   If the people of the Frontiers were duly sensible of our inestimable privileges, and animated with the true Spirit of Protestantism, they would be as a wall of brass round these Colonies ; and would rise with a noble ardour to oppose every attempt of a heathen or popish enemy against us.   For none were ever brave without some principle or another to animate their conduct ; and of all principles, surely a rational sense of British freedom and the purity of our holy religion, is the noblest.   Indeed nothing but such a sense, propagated and spread to the utmost verge of our Colonies, can keep our people from being drawn off and mixing with our popish enemies the French, who are still coming nearer and nearer to us, and have lately planted a fine Colony of German and other Catholics on the Ohio, near where it falls into the Mississippi ; from whence they now supply all their Garrisons on that river, and which will undoubtedly

---

* "American Colonies MS."   Lambeth Palace, No. 1123, II., No. 105.

10

prove a drain or colluvies to receive many of our disaffected Germans and others.

It was from apprehensions of this kind, that I took the liberty to write so fully to the Society when M^r^. Barton went for holy orders; and since that we have still farther accounts of the growing state of the said French-German Colony. It was from the same apprehensions I so warmly pressed, and so earnestly engaged in, the scheme for planting English schools among our Germans, which now flourish as well as the distracted state of the Country permits; and Your Lordship may depend, that they shall always be conducted with "a due regard to the interests of the Church of England." For, in truth, it is but one part of the same noble scheme in which the venerable Society are engaged; and wherever there are Missionaries near any of the schools, they are either employed as Masters, or named among the deputy trustees and Managers of the school. In short, till we can succeed in making our Germans speak English & become good Protestants, I doubt we shall never have a firm hold of them. For this reason, the extending the means of their instruction, as far as they extend their settlement, is a matter that deserves our most attentive consideration. I am pleased therefore that your Lordship, and the Society, have given me leave to mention such other places on the frontiers as may be fit to place Missionaries in, so that the Kingdom of Christ may keep pace in its growth, with the growth of the English Colonies. This liberty I shall not fail to make due use of, and likewise to offer a scheme for uniting with the church, all the German Lutherans of this Country; which I am sure would easily take effect. But this is not the time for anything of that nature. Our frontiers at present are so far from extending themselves, or wanting the erection of New Missions, that I fear some of those already erected must fall. Poor M^r^. Barton has stood it upwards of a year, at the risk of his life, like a good Soldier of Jesus Christ, sometimes heading his people in the character of a clergyman, and sometimes in that of a Captain, being often obliged, when they should go to church, to gird on their swords and go against the enemy. If he and two worthy presbyterian Ministers, had not stood it out, I believe all the parts beyond Susquehanah, where his Mission lies, would have been long ago deserted. I ventured out three weeks ago to visit him and some of our German schools in his neighbourhood, and found him universally beloved by his people. But their love is the most they can give him in their present distrest state; and therefore I wish your Lordship would move the honourable Society, to make him some gratuity above his Salary in these troublesome times. I am sure he both wants and deserves it.

I enclose a letter which I sent him after Braddock's defeat, and which he printed with a Sermon. I hope Your Lordship will think it worth perusal, as it agrees so nearly with the sentiments contained in the excellent instructions lately sent over from the Society—But, alas! we are here in a sad situation. To meddle with the duty of defence, or paying taxes, or supporting our invaluable rights, will in this province infallibly expose us to party rage. The Quakers, although their own preachers dare publickly propagate notions of non-resistance, non-payment of taxes, and other rebellious doctrines, yet they are sure to wreak their utmost vengeance against us, if we venture, in consequence of our duty, to oppose such poisonous tenets. I have ever been exposed to the Martyrdom of my character on this account; but I remain yet unhurt; and were it otherwise, I should glory in suffering in so good a cause. It is true, I shall never meddle otherwise in such matters, than becomes a good subject, who is a friend to Government, yet at the same time I scorn to burn incense on the altar of popular folly, or to be a silent spectator of my country's ruin. To conceive Your Lordship, however, with what temper I have managed my part of the opposition to such destructive tenets, I enclose a paper called Plain Truth, which I hope your Lordship will also peruse, as it will give a most striking representation of the present state of the province, and the moderation as well as warmth of those arguments by which we are obliged to combat the doctrines that have so long most unnaturally tied up our hands, and exposed us to be passively Slaughtered by a cruel foe.—

I had the honor to receive a letter lately from the Revd Dr Bearcroft in name of the Society, relating to a plan for educating some Indian Children at the College and Academy of Philadelphia. This I think a most excellent proposal and perfectly agreeable to the great original design of the Society; namely—"The glorifying the name of *Jesus,* by the further enlargement of his church, and particularly the spreading his everlasting gospel among the heathen natives of America, as well by instructing and civilizing those of them that are grown up, as by laying a foundation for educating, clothing and training up their children in the knowledge of morality, true religion, the English tongue, and in some trade, mystery or lawful calling, should they be disposed to follow it." This the Society have been frequently attempting in various places, and though God has not yet been pleased to grant any remarkable degree of success, yet still the design is worthy of being persisted in. For if ever the savages are converted to Christianity, their conversion must begin among the rising generation by a more general education of their children, since the few that have been hitherto educated by us, are but as a drop of tincture thrown into a large collection of waters, and lost therein; being too inconsiderable to have any effect. It would be well, therefore, if in every Colony, bordering on any Indian Nations, there were a provision for educating such of their Children as can be persuaded to accept of it, and the more publicly this is done, so much the better; who knows the time when, or the means by which, the Lord may be pleased to bless the great work. If but one savage should be truly illu-

minated with the true spirit of Christianity, it is worth all the expense—
Perhaps even that *one* might convert thousands—and after all, if they
should return, like the sow to her wallowing in the mire, yet still their
being publicly educated among us, will give them connections with us,
and at least leave some impressions of humanity among them, especially
to such of us as they may have known at school.

The great difficulty is to persuade them to accept of such an offer.
The Government must be security for their good treatment; and none
but the provincial interpreters with the credit of our Governors and
great men, can prevail on them to trust us with their children.   In this
view, the College and Academy of Philadelphia has a fair chance.   The
province have never broke faith with the Indians, and the chief men in the
province are engaged in the trust and direction of our Academy.   We
have now two Indian Children of a considerable family who have been
at it these two years, and can now read and write English, &c., and if
any body can engage more to come, it is Mr Weiser,* our interpreter
and the credit of the Trustees of the Academy.   As I have the honor
to be Provost of it, nothing shall be wanting on my part in so good a
work.   I have mentioned the terms to Dr Bearcroft more fully, to which
I beg leave to refer Your Lordship for such points as are not here mentioned, and perhaps this letter may be of use with regard to some things
I have not had time to mention in his.   I enclose a view of the College-
part of our institution by which your Lordship will see that our plan is
an extensive and liberal one.   The Academy is the lower part of it,
confined to the English language, writing and the mechanic arts.

The bearer of this is the Revd Mr Israel Acrelius, a learned Swede,
who has been several years Commissary to the Swedish Congregations
on Delaware, and now returns to considerable preferment in his own
Country, as a reward of his faithful labours.   He is well entitled to the
honour of Your Lordship's Notice, and knows the state of all the Missions in this province perfectly well.   There is a good deal of confusion
in some of them, and as he is an impartial person, his account will no
doubt be of weight should he be called upon.   He has often preached
in English, and made use of our service.   His chief abode was near
Newcastle, which now apply to have Mr Cleveland for a Missionary, as
he could not find admittance at Lewes, whither he was sent by the Society, which deserves no further notice till they discharge the disorderly
and worthless man who has excluded Mr Cleveland.   The people of
Newcastle are very fond of Mr Cleveland† and he is a worthy man, and
will prevent the church from going to pieces, as I fear it otherwise will,
if three or four removes are made in our Missions, which I hear pro-

---

* See Appendix No. III.

† Rev. Mr. CLEVELAND died at Newcastle, Del., of dropsy, in 1757. *Society's
Abstract for* 1758, p. 45.

posed, without any good reason that I can learn.   There are many other circumstances that deserve consideration before such removes are made, which I have no call to mention, as I am but little connected with what relates to Missionaries—I leave all to Mr Acrelius,* who will be on the spot, and can have no interest in being partial, as he is never to return to this place.

I hope Your Lordship will excuse the length of this letter, and take in good part the freedom wherewith I speak my honest sentiments, relating to the weighty subject it treats of.   When Your Lordship can spare a few Moments from the important duties of your station, to favor me with any future commands in return to this (which I shall earnestly expect) the Honourable Mr. Penn, at his house in spring Garden will find means to convey it.   I have the honour to be

My Lord
Your Lordship's most
dutiful Son & Servant

My Lord of Oxford —   WILLIAM SMITH.

Dr. Smith to Rev. Dr. Bearcroft.

PHILADELPHIA, Novr 5th, 1756.

Since I wrote you the 2^d Instant, the enclosed were sent me from M^r. Barton's three Congregations to be forwarded to you.   As I took the Liberty warmly to recommend these Congregations to the ven^ble Society, from a Conviction that nothing can preserve our Frontiers *separate* from a popish encroaching Enemy, except a sublime Sense of British Religion and Liberty, spreading itself along as far as our Colonies spread ; so it

---

* Rev. ISRAEL ACRELIUS, whose name and labors have recently been made familiar to us by the admirable translation, published by the Historical Society of Pennsylvania, of his history of the Swedish settlements on the Delaware, came to America in Nov., 1749, and resided in this country more than six years.   On his return to Sweden, he resumed the pastoral duties at Fellingsbro, and died in 1800, at the advanced age of 86 years.   In the year 1759 he published, in Sweedes, the work just spoken of, relating to the early history of the settlements on the Delaware river, entitled " Beskrifning om de Svenska Församlingars Forna och Närwarande Tilständ, utdet sa kallade Nya Sverige, sedan Nya Nederland, men nu fortyden Pennsylvanien, saunt nastliggande orter wid Alfwen Delaware, West Jersey och New Castle County uti Norra America.   Utigfwen of Israel Acrelius, fordetta Probst ofwer Svenska Forsamlingar i America och Kyrkoherde uti, Fellingsbro, Stockholm : 1759." [Description of the present and former state of the Swedish Congregations in New Sweden so called, since New Netherland and now Pennsylvania, and in the neighbouring parts on Delaware Bay, West Jersey and New Castle county, in North America.   Published by Israel Acrelius, late Provost of the Swedish churches in America, and Pastor at Fellingsbro, Stockholm : 1759.]   Sm. 4to, pp. 534.   This work is divided into eight books ; the first three contain the civil and political history of the country under the Swedish, Dutch and English governments, to the time when the author wrote ; the five last are devoted to the ecclesiastical affairs of the Swedish congregations.

gives me Pleasure, and I am sure it will give the worthy Society Pleasure, to see so much Fruit, by the blessing of God, already sprung up in the new Mission of York & Cumberland, even amid all the Horrors of a most desperate War, with the bloodiest of all Enemies, a Race of merciless Savages. Our People now, inspirited by their zealous Missionary, & kept constantly in mind of their holy Protestant Religion & inestimable Privileges, exert themselves manfully for the Cities of their God against a Popish & Savage Enemy; and I am sure were not the Sense of these Blessings to be extended backwards, as far as our Settlements extend, nothing could prevent our People from being seduced by busy Jesuits, & mixing gradually with our French Foes. The whole Country is, therefore, under the highest Obligation to the Society for this New Mission, both in a civil & religious Light; and will be under still higher for every new one that is opened on the Frontiers. They will be as so many Watch-Towers, from which our faithful Missionaries "would cry aloud & spare not, on the Approach of every Thing that could hurt our holy Zion." I have promised my Lord B^p of Oxford, in Answer to a Letter of his Lordship's on that Subject, that whenever I know of any other Places on the Frontiers, deserving the Society's regard, I shall humbly propose the same; but that at present we cannot tell where our Frontiers will be;—so unsettled is our State.

I observe M^r. Barton's several Congregations have modestly hinted at their Inability to perform their Engagements. Yet I am sure they will do their best, & M^r. Barton does not complain; tho' when I was lately back in Company with our Governor to the Frontiers, I could learn that he was much pinch'd; & therefore I doubt not you'll kindly consider what I hinted in mine of the 2^d Instant, for the Presbyterians and other Dissenters are chiefly the Men that must defend this Country, & it is reasonable they should have their Share in the Government of it.

I did my Part to unite all the Protestants in one Interest, by publishing and distributing the enclosed Paper, called Plain Truth. It contains a most striking State of the Province, and is allowed on all Sides to be one of the best Papers that have appeared here. It has done much Good; but there is still much to do. Read it attentively and let me know your Sentiments concerning it; particularly the Note at the Bottom of last Page. This Assembly will not give us any Militia Law, better than the last which was justly repealed.

I wish this may find you well. You have been extremely sparing of your letters of late. I long daily to hear from you. Along with this you will receive Duplicates of the Minutes and Accounts to July 1st. I have also drawn upon you for the Quarter from July 1st to Octr 1st, 1756, £100 Ster., in two Bills; the one payable to B. Chew, Esqr, Attorney-general of this Province, or his Order, for £93.7.10 Ster. The Balance of £6.12.2 I have drawn as a Present to a Brother of mine, whose Apprenticeship being expired, I think deserves that

token of my Esteem.   I have advanced the Value & shall give Credit
accordingly.   I have desired my Brother to present it to you in Person,
& hope you'll give him your best advice with Regard to his Conduct.
I hope you will find him as I left him ; Modest and virtuously disposed.
I have no time to keep a copy of this, and hope you'll preserve it, as it
contains my free and catholic Sentiments on subjects of Importance.   I
say keep a Copy ; for it is probable I may see you sooner than you expect.   I offer you the continuance of my sincerest good wishes, and
am,   Revᵈ Sir,

Your affectionate Brother & Serv't,

WILLIAM SMITH.

CHAPTER XI.

AFFAIRS OF THE COLLEGE—FIRST EXAMINATION—LIST OF THE STUDENTS—FIRST
   COMMENCEMENTS—CHARGE BY DR. SMITH—DR. SMITH PREACHES TO THE
   FORCES UNDER GENERAL STANWIX PREVIOUS TO THEIR MARCH AGAINST THE
   FRENCH AND INDIANS AFTER BRADDOCK'S DEFEAT—DR. SMITH TO GOV.
   SHARP—DR. SMITH TO DR. MORGAN—DR. PHILIP BEARCROFT TO DR.
   SMITH—THE AMERICAN MAGAZINE.

THE beginning of the year 1757 found the College of Philadelphia established as one of the principal institutions of learning in
the colonies ; in some respects, perhaps, as the first.   In January
of this year a public examination was held, at which the " Masque
of Alfred," with a Prologue and Epilogue, as altered and prepared
by Dr. Smith for the occasion, was represented by the students.
The performance was honored by the presence of Lord Loudon
and the governors of several of the colonies, who met at Philadelphia in the beginning of that year.

The " Masque of Alfred " was selected for the representation on
account of the great similarity between the distress of England
under the Danish invasion, and that of the Colonies in 1757 under
the ravages and incursions of the Indians, a matter which, as we
have already seen, took deep possession of Dr. Smith's faculties,
mental and of the heart, and which he kept before the public in
every way.

The following is a list of the youth belonging to the institution
at that time :

PHILOSOPHY SCHOOL.

SENIOR CLASS.

John Allen.	Samuel Morris.	Thomas Mifflin.
Andrew Allen.	William Greenway.	Lindsay Coates.
James Allen.	Joel Evans.	Robeson Yorke.
Joseph Reade.	John Cadwalader.	James Murray.
John Morris.	Lambert Cadwalader.	Tench Tilghman.

JUNIOR CLASS.

Samuel Keene.	Abraham Walton.	James Cruikshanks.
John Chew.	John Luke.	William ———.
Philemon Dickinson.	John Stevens.	Hugh Hughes.
Alexander Lawson.	Alexander Wilcox.	Mark Grime.
William Paca.	William Gibbes.	John Searle McCall.
Samuel Powel.	Richard Peters.	Andrew Hamilton.

LATIN SCHOOL.

Benjamin Baynton.	John Murgatroyd.	John Diemer.
Thomas Bond.	Samuel Inglis.	Henry Elves.
William Hamilton.	Thomas Lawrence.	Thomas Coombe.
Jasper Yeates.	Samuel Nicholas.	Francis Moore.
Henry Dalter.	Perry Frazier Child.	Benj. Alison.
John Neilson.	Robert Strettell Jones.	Anthony Morris.
George Thomson.	John O'Kill.	John Johnson.

MATHEMATICAL SCHOOL.

Nathan Armitage.	John Sharpe.	William Hockley.
Henry Benbrige.	John Wilcox.	John Reade.
James Coots.	John Yeates.	Samuel Correy.
John Dunbavin.	Andrew Yorke.	George Ogle.
George Emlin.	William Karst.	Philip Francis.
Nathaniel Evans.	Thomas Hopkinson.	Abraham Denormandie.
James Gorrel.	James Haston.	Gillis Sharp.
John Jepson.	George Rundle.	Joseph Syng.
John Inglis.	George Davis.	John White Swift.
Charles Knight.	William White.	Thomas Tresse.
Thomas Maybury.	Thomas Murgatroyd.	John Wooden.
Cornelius ———.	James Sayer.	Thomas Moore.
Charles Pratt.	John Benezet.	Thomas Woodcock.
Thomas Plumsted.	Edward Welsh.	John Fullerton.
Thomas Philipe.	John Ord.	
Samuel Penrose.	William Davis.	

ENGLISH SCHOOL.

Andrew Bell.	Henry Keppele.	William Rush.
James Bingham.	Mathew Jackson.	Samuel Smith.
John Bingham.	Joseph McIlwaine.	Alexander Fullerton.
Phineas Bond.	William McIlvaine.	William Falkner.
Joseph Conyers.	William Merrifield.	John Montour.
John Deering.	George Morgan.	Richard Stanley.
Richard Duncan.	Robert Montgomery.	
George Gostelowe.	Lindley Murray.	

This list makes a fine show certainly in the case of an institution so recently established and so little endowed.

On the 17th of May, 1757, the commencement of the College took place. Six students received the degree of Bachelor of Arts. They were Paul Jackson, Jacob Duche, Hugh Williamson, Francis Hopkinson, James Latta, and John Morgan; nearly every one of whom subsequently became eminent either in scholarship, in the church, in statesmanship, or in medical science.* I believe that a part of them had been acting as ushers or teachers in the institution. Dr. Smith always regarded the maxim, *Doce ut discas*, as one founded in truth.

He delivered the following charge:

GENTLEMEN: You now appear as candidates for the first honours of this institution. The free spirit that it breathes permits us not to bind you to us by the ordinary ties of oaths and promises. Instead thereof, we would rely on those principles of virtue and goodness which we have endeavoured to cultivate. Suffer me, therefore, ere you go, to sum up all our former labours for you, in this place, by one last and parting charge.

Surely—to live is a serious thing! And you are now about to step into life, and embark in all its busy scenes. It is fit, then, that you should make a pause—a solemn pause—at its portal, and consider well what is expected from you, and how you are prepared to perform it.

On the one hand, you will have all the dangers and indiscretions of youth to grapple with, at your first setting out in the world. Raw and un-experienced in its ways, you will be apt to consider yourselves as set loose from the reins of discipline, and to look abroad in it with conscious rapture, and the most buoyant hopes. The fulness of blood, the strength of passion, the constant call of pleasure, and the harlot-form of vice, will be apt to bear down that sober wisdom and cool reflection, which are your best guard. At every glance, elysian scenes and fairy

---

* The present Society of the Alumni, under the encouragement of the Faculty, and especially of Professor McElroy, an active member of it, have done great good service to the College by their recently published List of the Graduates; a work which, considering that it was what in fact might be called a first effort to make a complete work of the sort, was surprisingly full and accurate; though not content even with so good a degree of progress, I am told, that a new printed list is in preparation. May I take leave to suggest to the excellent Society of the Alumni, that after this their work shall be accomplished, there yet remains another, a volume like Professor Samuel Davies Alexander's " Princeton College in the 18th Century; " a work which shall give short biographical sketches of such of our early graduates as have left a name behind them. Princeton herself, rich as she is in honored names in early times, has no more in number, nor any higher in fame, than our own old College of Philadelphia.

prospects will open before you ; seemingly so variegated with beauty and stored with pleasure, that the choice will perplex you.   But, alas ! these lead not all to the bowers of joy ! many will only seduce you from the path of virtue, by false appearances of happiness, and draw you on, through meades of unreal bliss, to the fool's paradise ; a deceitful region, which proves at last to be but the valley of the shadow of death, where snakes lurk under the grass—

> And, mid the roses, fierce repentance rears
> Her horrid crest *—

On the other hand, you will find the world inclined to make but small allowances for the slips of youth.   Much—very much—will be expected from you.   Your superior opportunities of knowledge, the many specimens of genius you have already exhibited, will give your friends and country a right to expect everything from you that is excellent or praiseworthy.

Oh ! then, let no part of your future conduct disgrace the lessons you have received, or disappoint hopes you have so justly raised !   Consider yourselves, from this day, as distinguished above the vulgar, and called upon to act a more important part in life !   Strive to shine forth in every species of moral excellence, and to support the character and dignity of beings formed for endless duration !   The Christian world stands much in need of inflexible patterns of integrity and public virtue ; and no part of it more so than the land you inhabit.

Remember that superior talents demand a superior exercise of every good quality ; and that, where they produce not this salutary effect, it were far better for the world to be forever without them.   Unless your education is seen conspicuous in your lives, alas ! what will be its significancy to you, or to us ?   Will it not be deemed rather to have been a vain art of furnishing the head, than a true discipline of the heart and manners ?

If, then, you regard the credit of this institution, which will travail in concern for you, till you are formed into useful men ; if you regard your own credit, and the credit of the many succeeding sets of youth, who may be fired to glory by your example ; let your conduct in the world be such, at least, as to deserve the applause of the wiser and better part of it.   Remember you are the first who have received the honours of this seminary.   You have been judged doubly deserving of them.   O ! think, then, what pain it would give us, should we be disappointed in you, our first and most hopeful sons !   What a reproach would it be to have it said that, under us, you had obtained all sorts of learning, and yet had not obtained wisdom—especially that wisdom, which has for its beginning the fear of God, and for its end everlasting felicity.

---

* Thomson.

But we have every reason to expect far better things of you. And, in that expectation I shall beg leave to propose a few rules, which, being well observed, will contribute greatly to your success in life. They shall be confined to two heads.

1st, How to live with yourselves, and your God.

2dly, How to live with the world.

Perhaps this may be deemed a very needless work at this time. But my heart yearns towards you. I cannot easily part with you. And though I should only repeat what you have often heard in the course of our lectures in this place; yet, being laid together in one short view, and delivered before such a number of witnesses, 'tis probable the impression may be so much the deeper. And, that it may be so, I shall not amuse you with high drawn characters and visionary precepts; the creatures of fancy's brain, worked up beyond the life. Such may allure the eye, but they will not sway the practice. They may induce despair, but they will not quicken industry. I shall, therefore, confine myself to the living virtues, as they are within the ordinary reach of humanity, when assisted by divine grace and goodness. For it is they alone that can influence the conduct, and excite to imitation.

First, then, in living with yourselves and your God, let it be your primary and immediate care, to get the dominion of your own passions, and to bring every movement of the soul under subjection to conscience, reason, and religion; those three lovely guides set over the human conduct. Let your wishes be moderate, solicitous about nothing so much as the friendship of your God, and the preservation of your virtue and good name!

Accustom yourselves to an early industry in business, and a wise reflection upon human life. Beware of idleness, and the pernicious influence of bad habits. Possess yourselves of just and elevated notions of the divine character and administration, and of the end and dignity of your own immortal nature. Oh! consecrate to your God the first and best of your days! When you enjoy health of body, strength of mind, and vigour of spirits, then is the heart a noble sacrifice, and best worthy of being presented to the great Creator of heaven and earth.

But, alas! when the prime of our years have been devoted to the ways of pleasure and folly, with what confidence can we offer to our God the dregs of vice and iniquity; an old age broken with infirmity, and groaning under the load of misery? Though heaven be all merciful, and even this last offering not to be neglected; yet, to a generous mind, there is something peculiarly painful in the thought. And certainly, when the soul is fittest for pleasure, then also it is fittest to be lifted up, in manly devotion, to its adorable maker!

That your souls may be the more disposed to this exalted intercourse, continue to adorn them with every divine grace and excellence. As far as your circumstances will permit, continue through life the votaries of

Wisdom; and never drop your acquaintance with those sciences into which you have been initiated here. But, in the prosecution of them, weigh well the strength of the human understanding. Keep to subjects within its reach, and rather to those which are useful than curious. In your inquiries, never suffer yourselves to be drawn from the main point, or lost in a multitude of particulars. Always keep first principles in view; life is short; we can go but little farther, and that little will then only be of use, when clearly deduced from them.

For this reason, beware, above all things, of valuing yourselves much on any temporary acquisitions, or falling into the error of those who think they shew the depth of their wisdom, by disregarding that sublime system, brought down from heaven by the Son of God. Poor is the extent of human science at best; and those who know the most, know but just enough to convince them of their own ignorance. Vain, then, must they be who would be thought wise for despising the dictates of eternal wisdom, and would build up the pride of knowledge upon their ignorance of things of the most lasting consequence.

Such empty smatterers can have but small pretensions to common wisdom, much less to the exalted name of philosophy. The true votaries of this divine science will ever disclaim them.

Though we honour human reason, and think human virtue the glory of our nature, yet your education here will teach you to fix your hopes on a far more solid foundation. It will convince you that reason, when unenlightened, may be fallacious; and consequently that virtue, by it alone directed, will be devious. There are mists, diffused before the temple of happiness, which are only to be penetrated by the purer eye of religion.

Hence, then, you will be disposed to seek a sublimer wisdom than any that is to be attained by mere human efforts, confined to the works of nature alone, those fainter exhibitions of the Deity! You will see the necessity of studying his character, as exhibited in his holy oracles. There you will receive such august impressions of him, as will correct your philosophy, humble the pride of reason, and lay you prostrate at his feet. You will be taught to renounce your own wisdom, however excellent; and your own righteousness, however distinguished. You will' be made to rejoice in the name of Christian, and triumph in the glorious relation you bear to Jesus, as shedding the brightest lustre round the human character. And consequently you will love to inculcate his holy religion, as a scheme of wisdom salutary to mankind, unfolding their best interests, training them up for eternity, and conducting them to the supreme felicity and perfection of their nature!

Thrice happy you, when by divine grace you shall have obtained this dominion over yourselves, and through the Redeemer's merits are thus united to the supreme good; every wish resigned, and every passion raised to the throne of your father and your God! then, and not

till then, you will have truly learned to live with yourselves, and with
him that made you; till, after the close of your pilgrimage here, you
are finally admitted to live and rejoice with him for ever!

I am now, in the second place, to offer you a few plain directions,
how to live with the world. And on this subject I shall be but brief.
For, being once initiated into the true enjoyment of your own nature,
and actuated by a deep sense of God's universal presence, all your
other actions will be duly influenced thereby.

With regard to benevolence, that great law of Christ, and fruitful
source of all social virtue, why should I recommend it to you? If you
truly love God, you must necessarily love all his creatures for his sake,
and disdain a narrow unfeeling heart, coiled up within its own scanty
orb. Your charity will be of the most exalted and fervent kind; extending itself beyond the vulgar attachments of family and friends,
embracing the whole human species and ready to sacrifice every temporal consideration to their good.

Actuated by such liberal sentiments as these, you will always be
ready to do good and communicate freely your superior knowledge.
Your counsel and your assistance, your hand and your heart—will never
be refused, when demanded for the benefit of others, and in a virtuous
cause. Or rather, you will never let them be demanded, but freely
prevent the readiest wish. Modest merit will be the object of your
peculiar regard; and you will always rejoice when you can produce it
to public view, in an amiable and advantageous point of light.

Believe me, my dear youths, you can acquire no authority so lasting,
no influence so beneficial, as by convincing the world that you have
superior talents, joined to inflexible virtue, and unconfined benevolence.
Compared to such a foundation as this, the proud structures of vulgar
ambition are but rottenness, "and their base built on stubble." A
confidence placed as above, will give you a kind of dominion in the
hearts of others, which you will, no doubt, exert for the noblest purposes; such as reconciling differences, enforcing religion, supporting
justice, inspiring public virtue, and the like.

To this benevolence of temper, you are to add prudence, and a strict
regard to the grace of character and proprieties of life. If you would
be very useful in the world, beware of mixing too indiscriminately in
it, or becoming too cheap in the vulgar eye. But, when you are in it,
be affable to all, familiar with few, cautious in contracting friendships,
stedfast in preserving them, and entering into none without the clearest
virtue for their foundation and end.

Maintain such dignity of conduct, as may check the petulance of
vice, and suffer none to contemn you; yet shew such modesty of temper, as may encourage virtue, and induce all to love you. Preserve a
cheerfulness of countenance, never affecting to appear better than you
are; and then every good action will have its full weight. It is dis-

honouring God, and discouraging goodness, to place virtue in a down-cast look, or in things external. The Christian life, far from being gloomy and severe, was meant to exalt the nature of man, and shew him in his best perfection—happy and joyful !

When you mix in company, you will often have occasion to be dis-gusted with the levity, 'tis well if not the vice, of the general run of conversation. Strive, therefore, as often as you can, to give it a chaste and instructive turn ; regarding always the propriety of time and place. And if, on any occasion, an ingenuous honesty of nature, and an abhor-rence of vice and dissimulation, should oblige you to bear your testimony against what you hear, let it be evident to all that you are offended, not at the persons but at the things. Great delicacy is requisite in such cases ; and you must blame without anger, in order to remove the offence, and not to wound the offender.

'Tis true, sometimes an animating conviction of a just cause, an un-disguised love of divine truth, and a consciousness of superior knowl-edge, will, in the best of men, on such occasions, produce a seeming warmth of expression, and keenness of expostulation ; especially when heated by opposition. But if, from the general tenor of your conduct, you have convinced the world of the goodness of your heart, such starts of passion will be forgiven by your friends, or considered only as the fire from the flint ; "which, being smitten, emits its hasty spark, and is straightway cool again."

It will be your wisdom, however, to preserve the serenity of your temper ; to avoid little disputes ; and to raise yourselves above the world, as much as possible. There are really but few things in it, for which a wise man would chuse to exchange his peace of mind ; and those petty distinctions, that so much agitate the general run of man-kind, are far from being among the number.

But some things there are, nevertheless, which will demand your most vigilant attention ; and some occasions, when to be silent or consenting would be a criminal resignation of every pretension to virtue or man-hood.

Should your country call, or should you perceive the restless tools of faction at work in their dark cabals, and plotting against the sacred interests of liberty ; should you see the corrupters or corrupted imposing upon the public with specious names, undermining the civil and reli-gious principles of their country, and gradually paving the way to certain slavery, by spreading destructive notions of government—then, oh ! then, be nobly rouzed ! Be all eye, and ear, and heart, and voice, and hand, in a cause so glorious ! "Cry aloud, and spare not," fear-less of danger, undaunted by opposition, and little regardful of the frowns of power, or the machinations of villainy. Let the world know that liberty is your unconquerable delight, and that you are sworn foes to every species of bondage, either of body or of mind !

These are subjects for which you need not be ashamed to sacrifice
your ease and every other private advantage——For certainly, if there
be aught upon earth suited to the native greatness of the human mind,
and worthy of contention ; it must be——To assert the cause of religion
and truth ; to support the fundamental rights and liberties of mankind ;
and to strive for the Constitution of our country, and a Government by
known laws, not by the arbitrary decisions of frail impassioned men.

If, in adhering to these points, it should be your lot, as, alas ! it has
been the lot of others, to be borne down by ignorance, to be reproached
by calumny, and aspersed by falsehood, let not these things discourage
you—

> All human virtue, to its latest breath,
> Finds envy never conquer'd but by death.
> The great Alcides, every labour past,
> Had still this monster to subdue at last.—POPE.

While you are conscious of no self-reproach, and are supported by
your own integrity, let no earthly power awe you from following the
unbiassed dictates of your own heart. Magnanimously assert your
private judgment where you know it to be right, and scorn a servile
truckling to the names or opinions of others, however dignified. With
a manly and intrepid spirit, with a fervent and enlightened zeal, persevere to the last in the cause of your God, your King and your Country. And, though the present age should be blind to your virtue, or
refuse you justice, let it not surprize you——

> The suns of glory please not till they set ;   POPE.

and the succeeding age will make ample amends to your character, at a
time when the names of those who have opposed you will be forgotten,
or remembered only to their lasting dishonour.

Nevertheless, though you must not expect to escape envy, or to receive
the full applause of your virtue in your own day; yet there will always
be some among the better few ready to do you justice, and to judge
more candidly. Perhaps, it may be your lot to be singularly favoured
by your friends, in this respect. But be not too much elevated thereby.
The real good man, as he will never be more undaunted than when
most reviled and opposed in his great career of justice, so he will never
be more humble than when most courted and applauded.

The two great rocks of life, especially to youth, are prosperity and
adversity. If such meet with any degree either of success or difficulty
in the world, before they have learned great self-denial, they are apt, in
the one case, to be blown up by an overweening conceit of their own
importance ; and, in the other, to be borne down by a timid distrust
of their own abilities. Both dispositions are equally prejudicial to
virtue—the former so far as it tends not to excite emulation, and inspire

to worthy actions; and the latter so far as it checks the native ardor of the soul, and ties it down to inglorious pursuits. But the same means will correct both. A larger commerce with the world, and a frequent viewing ourselves through a more impartial medium, compared to others of equal or greater merit, will bring down the one, and raise the other, to its just and proper standard. What was pride before, will then be converted into a sense of honour, and proper dignity of spirit; and what was timidity or self-distrust, will be turned into manly caution, and prudent fore-sight.

Time will not permit me to add more. Happy shall you be, if, by attending to such maxims as these, you can pass your days, though not with the highest approbation of others, at least with full satisfaction to yourselves! Happy, if in the eve of life, when health and years and other joys decline, you can look back with conscious joy upon the unremitting tenor of an upright conduct; framed and uniformly supported to the last on these noble principles——Religion without hypocrisy, generosity without ostentation, justice tempered with goodness, and patriotism with every domestic virtue!

Ardently praying that this may be your lot, I shall take leave of you in the words of old Pollonius to his son—

> The friends you have, and their adoption try'd,
> Grapple them to your soul with hooks of steel.
> But do not dull your palm with entertainment
> Of each new-hatch'd unfledg'd comrade.   Beware
> Of enterance to a quarrel————
> Give every man your ear, but few your voice.
> Take each man's censure, but reserve your judgment.
> This above all—to your own-selves be true,
> And it must follow, as the night the day,
> You cannot then be false to any man.—SHAKSPEARE.

These things I have sketched for you as the outlines of your duty. I pretend not to go farther. It is not my present business to offer a perfect plan for the conduct of life. Indeed my experience in it has been too small for such an arduous work. And I hope to be judged rather by what I have said, than by what could not properly be said, on such an occasion.

As for the rest, I shall commit you to the best of masters. Be sure, in all things, to learn of Christ. In following him you cannot err. And to do so will be your interest, and your greatest glory, at a time when human wisdom shall fail, and of the things that now are, virtue—immortal virtue—shall be the great and chief survivor!

Farewell! my blessing season these things in you.—SHAKSPEARE.

This charge was published in a pamphlet at the time. Appended to it was an oration in Latin, by Paul Jackson, a tutor in the College. The pamphlet had the following preface : *

Whether the Partiality of Private Friendship has made the Author of the following Charge too Sanguine in favour of the young gentlemen to whom it was delivered, Time will best shew. He has annexed a Latin oration by one of them, which will be a sufficient Specimen of the Gentleman's abilities who composed it. Other specimens might also be produced, which would redound greatly to the credit of the other young gentlemen, were any thing farther necessary than the ample Testimony they have already received from an institution which 'tis hoped will never prostitute its Honours to the Undeserving.

The eyes of the country were at this date—April 5th, 1757— turned to the forces under General Stanwix, who, after the dreadful defeat of General Braddock, were assembled to go to the defence of our frontier towns and settlements, then bleeding under the devastations of the French and their savages. It was expected that they would go directly against Fort Duquesne on the Ohio, but they were obliged to act only on the defensive for this year. A great part of them, however, were present at the reduction of the place in the year following, under Brigadier-General Forbes. They were a noble body of men, equally brave and humane, and with a noble commander. Having happily got possession of Fort Duquesne in November, 1758, General Forbes sent a part of his army to Braddock's field, some twenty miles away, on the banks of the Monongahela, to bury the sad remains of the dead that had lain there upwards of three years. This solemn scene was made yet more solemn by the tears of the soldiers, many of whom had lost their fathers, brothers, and dearest relatives in that fatal spot.

Just before their march, Dr. Smith, at the request of General Stanwix, preached to them, in Christ Church, a sermon, from Luke iii. 14, on " The Christian soldier's duty, the lawfulness and dignity of his office, as a servant of the public, for the defence of his country, and for the maintaining and asserting true religion and liberty." It was a fine, showy discourse, with something of the

---

* The title reads thus : "A Charge Delivered May 17th, 1757, at the First Anniversary Commencement in the College and Academy of Philadelphia, to the Young Gentlemen who took their Decrees on that Occasion, by W. Smith. To which is added an Oration in Latin, by Paul Jackson. 12mo. B. Franklin and D. Hall, Phila. 1757."

trumpet's sound; such as might be expected on an occasion so much calculated to rouse indignation, pity, and patriotism. It was immediately printed and widely circulated.

The following letter, from the admirable collection of autographs owned by Mr. F. J. Dreer, shows that the ardor of Dr. Smith in the cause of his country did not cease with the delivery of his discourse.

Dr. Smith to Governor Sharp, of Maryland.

PHILADELPHIA, April 27th, 1757.

SIR: I have taken the Liberty to enclose a Composition of mine for your Excellency's Perusal, and shall think myself happy if I shall appear to have been sufficiently animated with the sublime and interesting Subjects it treats of. My ambition is to acquit myself zealously for promoting the King's Cause, in the Estimation of the Discerning Few, among which Number M^r. Sharp will always be one.

If, after Perusal, your Excellency shall think that 10 or 12 copies might be of use among your Provincial Officers *for kindling that noble Enthusiasm, that unconquerable Passion for Liberty and the Protestant Faith*, mentioned in the sermon as the true Principle of a British Soldiery, I shall, on having the Honour of a Line from your Excellency, send that, or any other number, either to your Excellency, or to M^r. Green. I have some Hopes of seeing Annapolis this summer, & have the honour to be   Your Excellency's most obed^t humble S^t,

WILLIAM SMITH.

HIS EXCELLENCY, GOVERNOR SHARP.

Among the graduates of this year we have mentioned John Morgan. He went, it would seem, almost at once into service in the army; at this time, of course, in some other capacity than the medical; one in which he afterwards became eminent, and indeed one in which he served, for a short time, even in the then existing war, but towards its close.

Dr. Smith to Mr. Morgan.*

PHILADELPHIA, May 1st, 1757.

MY DEAR SIR: We long impatiently to see you down here. It was thought best by M^r. Peters, M^r. Young, & your Friends here, that you should obtain your Leave from Major Burd than apply to the Governor, as all the other officers have been down occasionally on the same Footing. M^r. Peters writes to the Major, & you may come down

* For this letter, as for the last, I am indebted to my kind friend, Mr. Ferdinand J. Dreer.

either by Leave, or as a recruiting officer, which last M^r. Peters thinks
best, as you will be less hampered in Point of Time on that Plan.   In
whatever shape you come, pray come soon if the Service should not
suffer, which I think it cannot.   I am

Yours,

W. SMITH.

In the midst, however, of all the stirring scenes of this epoch,
we find Dr. Smith intent upon the great work of education.   The
following letter—an answer to one given *supra*, pp. 141–5—shows
this fact.   It appears from it too, that Dr. Smith had sent copies
of his different discourses to Dr. Bearcroft.

*Dr. Bearcroft to Dr. Smith.**

CHARTER-HOUSE, July 1st, 1757.

REV'^D SR: Your letter by Mr. Acrelius, a very worthy Divine, hath
been maturely considered by the Society;† and after consulting Mr.
Penn, who professes to approve of the Education of Indian Children
in your College, & promises, what in him is, to countenance and help
forward that design as much as the present turbulent times in Pennsylvania will admit, the Society are come to the Resolution of advancing as far as £100 sterling per annum, by way of trial for the
Education of as many Indian Children as that sum will maintain in the
College, if their parents will consent to put them under *your* care and
Direction; and the particular Regulations concerning them are left to
you; taking along with you the approbation of the Trustees of the
College.

I much approve of your courage in bearing a Publick Testimony
against those Quaker Doctraines that are subversive of all order and
Society, in spite of all the obloquy malice hath and will throw out
against you for it; and you may depend upon my best endeavours to do
you Justice; if I meet with any thing of that nature here.   I am glad
Mr. Barton has proved himself so worthy a Missionary, and so very
proper a one for the dangerous time and place in which his Mission is.
The Society are most sensible of his good conduct, and to give him a
substantial proof of it, they have given him a Gratuity of £20, as they
have likewise to Mr. Acrelius, £30, for the many good services done
by him during his residence in Pennsylvania, to the members of our
Church.   Mr. Robert McKean, who came over with him, is appointed
Missionary to the Church of New Brunswick, in New Jersey, and will
be the bearer of this.

---

* From the original MSS.
† The Society for the Propagation of the Gospel.

I cannot conclude without particular thanks for the Entertainment I received from your Epilogue, and the account of the College Exercise; and that you may go on, and prosper, and bring much fruit to Perfection, is the hearty wish of, Mr. Provost,

Your very faithful, humble servant,

PHILIP BEARCROFT.

To the Rev'd Mr. SMITH, Provost of the College for the Education of Youth, in Philadelphia.

Soon after his arrival in Philadelphia Dr. Smith became acquainted with Mr. William Bradford, distinguished from his grandfather of the same name, by whom the art of printing was introduced, A. D. 1684, into our middle colonies, and from his accomplished son William, Attorney-General of the United States under Washington, as "Colonel Bradford." Colonel Bradford was, at this time, the largest bookseller, printer, and publisher in Philadelphia; and probably the largest in the middle colonies. He was also owner, editor, and publisher of the *Pennsylvania Journal.* He was an enthusiastic, active and efficient man in whatever he undertook; and his enterprises were numerous. Sincerely devoted through a long life to the honor of his country in every department, and fertile in such resources as would advance it, he had been for some time contemplating the establishment of a monthly periodical. His uncle, Andrew Bradford, had begun one, A. D. 1741, but the time was not then ready for it, and like a rival enterprise undertaken by Dr. Franklin in the same year, it was discontinued after a short experience. The difficulty for any new work had been to find a suitable editor. That, indeed, was the difficulty with the old one. Although Bradford had long known Dr. Smith, their relations, till of late, had not been intimate. Franklin as well as Bradford was a bookseller, printer and publisher; and the Provost's earlier relations of business had been with him. However, in the matter of the defence of the country and of the doings of the Assembly of Friends, Bradford was the strong supporter of Dr. Smith. In truth Dr. Smith was now fighting, A. D. 1757, in the New French war, a battle which Bradford had begun, A. D. 1744, in the Old one; for Bradford was one of the earliest and most active of the " Philadelphia Associators " of that day; a Lieutenant in a company which assisted to build and man its battery. Indeed, from youth to old age, he had but

one idea about the Society of Friends, so far as their capacity to
govern the Province was concerned; and though he was much
less animated in expression than Dr. Smith, he was not a bit less
decided in view, or energetic in action.   One purpose of the new
periodical would be to support the cause of the Crown against
France, and the interest of the Penns against the Society of
Friends and Dr. Franklin.   Both editor and publisher were,
therefore, "hearted" in the new work.   The parties saw in each
other their required complements; and with such a literary support as Dr. Smith,—both ready and able with his pen, methodical
in business, and with talents formed equally to gratify the learned
and to attract those aspiring to learn,—Bradford felt that he could
safely begin his work.   Its first number came forth in October,
1757.

The title-page announces that the Magazine is " By a Society
of Gentlemen."   No doubt we may believe what the Magazine
itself declares; that it received great assistance from the neighboring Governments, and particularly from two or three ingenious
gentlemen in Maryland.   It is undeniable, nevertheless, that its
conduct clustered largely around the College and Academy of
Philadelphia; and that the accomplished Provost of that College
and Academy both largely animated and largely supported it.
The design embraced Literature, Science, History, Politics, Moral
Essays, and Current News, both Foreign and Domestic.

Ebenezer Kinnersly, distinguished as an Electrician, and whose
discoveries in Electrical Science "the very ingenious Mr. Franklin "[*] is said to have appropriated in a way not quite honorable,[†]
writes upon this subject of his studies, then a small one, but now
astonishing the earth.[‡]   Thomas Godfrey, "a phenomenon for
natural or intuitive knowledge in the abstruse parts of Mathematics and Astronomy," speaks upon the Quadrant,[§] of which
useful instrument, *he* and not Hadley, as our British friends would
pretend, was the inventor.   Professor Winthrop, of Cambridge,
in New England, treats of the Causes of Earthquakes.[‖]   Other
persons give us essays on other parts of Science.   One on the

---

[*] Page 112.

[†] Page 639.   For some account of Kinnersly, see Appendix No. IV., where I insert
a sketch from the pen of the Hon. Horatio Gates Jones, LL.D.

[‡] Page 627.   [§] Pages 475, 527.   [‖] Pages 23, 111.

Noctiluca Marina, or the luminous appearance of the ocean in the night-time.* A second on the Causes of the *Aurora Borealis*.†
A third on uncommon Sea-Animals,‡ including the *Sea-Snake*, "a great and amazing monster;" and, huger still, the KRAAKEN, an animal so vastly large that they who accept implicitly the sea-serpent are compelled to pause, the writer tells us, when they come to this great superior. Poetical pieces; Observations upon the Fine Arts; upon new publications at home and abroad, all appeared with regularity; and Dr. Smith, himself, contributed a series of beautiful moral essays, under the title of " Theodore, the Hermit." The tone of the work was thoroughly loyal to the Crown; and not in the least favorable to the Government of the Province by the Religious Society of Friends, or the irreligious society of the French and Indians. The literary part, the typography, paper and press-work, were all in advance of the day. The subscription list too was very large; the periodical having the double advantage of Dr. Smith's extensive knowledge of literary persons, and of Bradford's possession of all the posts; a matter long in his hands and obtained through the distribution of his newspaper.

The magazine makes a fair octavo volume of twelve numbers and a supplement. Dr. Smith's political troubles, and a purposed voyage to England made necessary, as we hereafter state, by them, arrested the continuance of it, although both pecuniarily and in reputation to editor and publisher, it was more profitable than such things commonly are.

The ability to edit as Dr. Smith did edit this work, in the midst of such anxieties and occupations as engaged his time and thoughts, indicates an order of talent not usual.

---

* Page 24.   † Page 25.   ‡ Page 32.

CHAPTER XII.

Illegal Arrest, Trial, Conviction and Imprisonment of Dr. Smith by
    the Assembly of Friends—His Spirited Conduct—Appeals to the
    King in Council—Accounts of the Matter in Letters from the Rev.
    Mr. McKean to Dr. Bearcroft, and from Dr. Smith to the Bishop of
    London—A Letter from Dr. Jenney, Rector of Christ Church, Phila-
    delphia—Dr. Smith Teaches his College Classes in the Walnut St.
    Gaol—Mr. Moore Remains in Office, Being Absolved by the Governor
    from Charges of Mal-practice.

WE come now to one of the most memorable years among the
many memorable ones, which marked the long and much varied life
of William Smith, Provost of the College and Academy of Philadelphia. The record which we have now to make presents a melancholy proof of the weakness of human professions ; and shows that
the Religious Society of Friends, which, when out of civil power,
could complain pathetically of the abuses of civil rulers, when in
power could carry those abuses to a point which hardly any spiritual
governors in Protestant lands at any time equalled. The history
of the particular proceeding which prompts our remark has
enough both of political instruction and of dramatic interest to
justify an account of it somewhat in detail.

William Moore, Esquire, of Moore Hall, in Chester county in
Pennsylvania, the first Judge of the Common Pleas, and one of the
Justices of the Peace for Chester, had long distinguished himself
as an active magistrate and an advocate for the defence of his
country. In opposing the principles of the Religious Society of
Friends on the subject of defensive war, Mr. Moore became very
obnoxious to them. In consequence of this, the House of Assembly, in August, 1757, called him to answer before them to
sundry petitions previously procured by some of their own members (as was said) from divers persons—convicts in his own court,
Roman Catholics and others—charging him, in sharp terms, with
injustice in the execution of his office.

Mr. Moore delivered a respectful memorial to the House, setting
forth his innocence as to the matters charged ; but denying their

authority to try him for his conduct as a magistrate, since they could neither examine upon oath, nor give any legal judgment *per pares*, and because all the matters charged against him were cognizable by common law. If the Assembly could try him, he might be tried and punished twice for the same offences—if guilty of any.

On receiving this memorial the House, in Mr. Moore's absence, proceeded to take the oaths or affirmations of all the petitioners *ex parte* in support of their several petitions; and, without other proof than these, they laid an address before the Governor charging Mr. Moore with oppression, injustice and corruption in office, and praying his immediate removal therefrom. This address of theirs the House caused to be published in their official organ, the *Pennsylvania Gazette.*

To this address the Governor answered that he would speedily appoint a day to hear Mr. Moore and his accusers face to face, and if found guilty of any mal-conduct, they might depend on his immediate removal; but that no man should be condemned unheard.

The annual dissolution and the election of a new Assembly—which was to take place on the 1st of October of this same year 1757—followed on the back of this; and Mr. Moore, fearing the address of so weighty a body as the Assembly, if passed unanswered, might prejudice him with the Governor, who was now to be his judge, determined to present a counter-address in his own vindication; and as the Assembly that had so maliciously and so unjustly accused him, as he conceived, had no longer an existence, he thought that he might exercise great freedom in saying everything relative to their conduct which could tend to justify his own. He accordingly presented the following address to Governor Denny. The date of this was October 29th, 1757; nearly a month after the adjournment.

May it Please Your Honour: Whereas the late Assembly of this Province, upon a Number of groundless and scandalous Petitions, most shamefully procured against me by one or more of their Members, from sundry Persons of mean and infamous Characters, did, on the 28th of September last, present to your Honour, and order to be published in the common Gazette, a most virulent and slanderous Address, charging me, in the bitterest Terms, with divers Misdemeanours and corrupt

Practices in my Office, without exhibiting any other Proof thereof than
their own unjust Allegations, founded on the Evidence of the said Petitioners procured as above, and taken *ex parte* before themselves, who
were invested with no legal Authority for so doing.   And whereas, at
the same Time that the aforesaid late Assembly presented and published
such heavy Charges against me, they did most unjustly suppress and keep
back from your Honour and the World, my Memorial delivered to them
in my own Defence, six Days before their presenting or publishing their
aforesaid Address, endeavouring as far as in their Power, to prepossess
your Honour against me, by a partial Representation of my Case, and
to make the World condemn me unheard, as they themselves have in
effect done, thereby acting a Part unworthy of any public Body, except
the most oppressive.   Wherefore, for your Honour's Satisfaction, and
in Justice to my own Reputation, least the aforesaid Address should fall
into the Hands of any Persons who may not know the Character of the
late Assembly, nor the particular Motives of their Rancour against me,
I beg Leave to make some further Remarks, and hope to be indulged
therein with all that Justice, Patience and Candor, which are due to
one who is pleading his Cause against the severest and most grievous
Accusations, and in Points the most nearly affecting his Character and
Interest.

I. It appears from the Minutes of Assembly, November 1757, page
54, that the Country being then in the utmost confusion and distress,
the Savage Knife of the Enemy hourly plunged into the Breasts of the
miserable Frontier Inhabitants, I join'd with many others (who were
too deeply affected with the Sufferings of their bleeding Fellow-Subjects, to be silent), in Representing to the Assembly, " the ill effects of
" the Disputes in which they were then engaged, the alarming Situation
" of the Country thro' the Want of a Militia Law, and the terrible De-
" struction made on our Frontiers on that Account ; beseeching the
" Assembly at the same Time, that if their Consciences tied them up
" from doing their Duty in Points of such high Consequence to the
" Preservation of the Lives and Properties of the People committed to
" their Protection, to resign their Seats to others."   That I not only
signed such a Petition as this, in Conjunction with Thirty-five of my
Neighbours, dated November 5th, 1757 (as is set forth in the aforesaid
Minutes), but also drew up the same with my own Hand, I readily own ;
and think I should not have been acquitted in my own Conscience if I
had neglected such an Act of Duty to my distress'd and suffering Country
at that Time.   From the Day of delivering the aforesaid Petition, I
may justly date the Commencement of the Virulence of the Party against
me.   To the same Cause is to be attributed all the Petitions procured
against me by one of the Members, or rather Tools, of the late Assembly,
thro' the most unjustifiable Practices, many of them, at a Tavern, and
at a Time when the Petitioners were render'd incapable of reading or

knowing what they signed ; and by the same Methods might have been made to sign Petitions against their nearest and most innocent Relations.

II. As to the Address itself, it appears to agree well enough with the Motives of its Authors and Abettors. It is from Beginning to End, one continued string of the severest Calumny and most rancorous Epithets, conceived in all the Terms of Malice and Party Rage, exaggerated and heaped upon one another in the most lavish Manner.

III. It asserts evident Falsehood, in saying that I refused to obey a Summons from the House to answer to the Charges against me. For, in the first place I never had any Summons, but only a private Notification from the Clerk, acquainting me of the Day fixed for hearing the Evidence against me. In the second place, I did appear before the House, and delivered to them my Reasons for declining to be tried before them, where my Cause could not be cognizable, as they had it not in their Power finally to acquit or condemn me. Tryals by our Peers (and not by the Parties against us) I take to be one of the highest Privileges of an Englishman ; which if I had submitted to give up, in my Case, by agreeing to be tried by a House of Assembly, and even by my Accusers themselves, I ought not only to have been deemed void of all Reason, and unworthy of the Commission I have the Honour to bear, but my Name would have deserved to be had in Reproach among all Freemen ; and a House of Representatives, who should be the Guardians of Liberty, ought to have been the last Persons to propose such an Infringement of the Rights of a British Subject. By these Considerations, founded on the Principles of Freedom, and a Love of our excellent Constitution, my Conduct was actuated, tho' it would otherwise have been much more agreeable to me, to have confronted those Slanderers of my Character, and vindicated myself, as I am desirous of doing before your Honour, or any impartial and legal judicature.

IV. The last Thing I would observe with Regard to the conduct of the late Assembly in my Case, is, that it must be an Inlet and Encouragement to much false swearing, if the Evidence of such partial and corrupt Witnesses is taken in their own Cause, *coram non judice*, where they are not punishable by Law for perjury. For in such Cases, where such Persons have been procured to assert Facts by way of Petition, and are afterwards, contrary to their Expectations, call'd before a publick Body to support them, the Necessity they are under to justify their own conduct must convince every discerning Man, that, in such a Situation, the Transition from asserting to swearing falsely, will be no difficult Matter amongst them.

Upon the whole, it may be submitted, whether the Character drawn of me by the late Assembly, does not perfectly agree with their own Conduct, viz.: "That, regardless of the impartial and just Discharge "of their Duty, and wickedly and corruptly through an avaritious Dis-

" position (to usurp Powers that do not belong to them) and designedly
" oppress and injure me, they have misbehaved themselves greatly, by
" taking Wages of the publick under colour of their Office, where no
" Services were done their Country, and by encouraging the bringing
" in a Number of petty suits before them by corrupt and wicked Prac-
" tices (in order to gratify their Party Rancour), to the great Scandal
" of Justice, Derogation of the Laws, and grievous distress of his Ma-
" jesty's Subjects." It may also be submitted whether it would not
have redounded more to their Credit, if, instead of making use of their
Power to sit as the Persecutors of those who have opposed their unjustifiable Measures, they had employed their Time, and the publick Money
to better Purposes, by taking pity on the Sufferings of their distress'd
Constituents, and putting their Country into a Posture of Defence.
Had they done so, it might have saved the sheding much innocent
Blood, and prevented strife and contention among Neighbours.

The Treatment I have received, in having my Name branded in the
publick Gazette, before I had Time to be heard by your Honour, or
tried by my Peers, I hope, will justify the Freedom I have used with my
Opponents on this Occasion. Sorry I am to think, that their Conduct
has been so diametrically opposite to that Justice and Humanity which
heretofore distinguish'd their Predecessors in Assembly, and which yet
distinguishes the sober and better parts of the Inhabitants of this Province. Will not the perusal of such virulent and malignant Papers induce
the World to think that Pennsylvania is no longer the Land of brotherly Love, Forbearance and Meekness, but of the most bitter Persecution and severe Calumny? For my part, I doubt not of being able to
justify my Conduct to your Honour and the World; and while that is
the Case, I am little solicitous about the censure of an Assembly, whose
particular Talent and Character are known to have been Slander and
Obloquy. And it is a favourable Circumstance for me, that in the
same Gazette, that has conveyed to the public their unjust attack upon
my Character, they have exhibited a Message to your Honour, which
will be a standing Monument of Scurrility and Abuse, seldom equall'd
in a civilized Country. And I had no Reason to expect that any greater
Regard would be shewn to me on falling under their Displeasure, than
they have already shewn to your Honour, your worthy Predecessors,
and to all the Members of your Council without Exception, who have
been loaded from Time to Time with the severest Reproaches that
Malice could invent or bestow, not even refraining to brand them with
the Names of Tyrants, Oppressors, &c., as is well known both here and
abroad. After such Considerations as these, I am so far from thinking it
my Misfortune to have been marked out as an Object of their Resentment, that were I so vain as to desire my Name should be transmitted
to Posterity, I think it could not be done in a Manner more advantageous to my Character, than in the Proceedings of the late Assembly;

provided it appeared that I had borne any constant Testimony against them, and that they had spoke ill, not well of me.

I shall not trouble your Honour any further on this Subject at present, hoping that what I have said will be sufficient to shew the Spirit by which my Accusers have been actuated, and to prevent the Consequences which they must have intended by their Misrepresentations of me.   I am

Your Honour's most obedient and Most humble Servant,

WILLIAM MOORE.

PHILADELPHIA, October 29th, 1757.

As the Assembly had published their address in the *Pennsylvania Gazette*—which was carried on by their own printer, Mr. Hall—Mr. Moore thought it proper to convey his answer through the same channel.   He therefore carried his address to the printer of the *Gazette*, who refused to insert it until after he had consulted and obtained the leave of the Speaker and several members of the old House, who were chosen again into the new one, which had not yet met.   Permission having been granted, the address was afterwards published in that paper.   It was soon afterwards published also in the *Pennsylvania Journal*, the well-known paper of Colonel William Bradford.   After it had been thus published, both by Mr. Hall and by Colonel Bradford in their respective papers, Mr. Moore applied to Dr. Smith to have it inserted in the German newspaper which Dr. Smith had been instrumental in establishing for propagating religious knowledge and the English tongue among the German emigrants in Pennsylvania.

In consequence of this application, Dr. Smith, happening to meet the German translator of that newspaper, spoke with him about inserting the address, saying that there could be no harm in printing what the Assembly's printer had done so long before, and what Colonel Bradford had also done, and that the Germans ought to see everything that was in the English papers.   The translator was of the same opinion, took the copy from the English papers, and translated it into the German without Dr. Smith having anything more to do in the matter.

Soon after this—viz., in the beginning of January, 1758—the new Assembly met for business, and the first thing they did was to issue warrants for taking Messrs. Moore and Smith into close custody.   Both Mr. Moore and Dr. Smith were accordingly—in the face of some of the most distinguished people of the city—

arrested by the Sergeant-at-arms of the House on the 6th of January, 1758, at the Coffee-House, where they happened to be. Dr. Smith was lodged in the old jail at the southeast corner of Sixth and Walnut streets. Mr. Moore was carried before the Assembly and ordered to prepare for his trial at their bar*—first, with respect to his conduct in the magistracy, in answer to the petitions that had been presented against him; and, secondly, for writing and publishing a virulent paper, entitled "An Address," etc., reflecting on the conduct of a former House, and which the present House had resolved to be a libel against their Constitution and the very being of Assemblies in general.

As to the first, Mr. Moore still denied the authority of the House to try him as a magistrate, for the same reasons that he had before denied it on in his address to the Governor; and, with respect to the second, he owned that, when he found his character so injuriously treated by the former Assembly, he thought it his duty, as far as he could, to remove the aspersions which they had thrown upon him; that he did write and publish the address which the present House termed a libel; that it was settled law, as appeared by "Coke's Second Institute," page 228, that nothing published in a course of justice to procure a man's own right could be taken for scandal, or be punishable as a libel; and that this was his case, who had not published his address maliciously and to traduce the Assembly, but to defend himself against a printed address of theirs praying the Governor to remove him from the magistracy as guilty of maladministration therein; that the address was written before the present House had a being, and therefore could be no contempt or libel against them; and that, if it was a libel against the Constitution or government in general, there were known laws and forms of proceedings in such cases, which he considered could neither be abrogated nor suspended, nor in any way prevented in their effects, by any single part or branch of the Legislature.

Immediately upon this the Assembly, with the forms and solemnity of a court of judicature, sentenced Mr. Moore to the common jail on account of his refusal to be tried before them, for his con-

---

* The House took Mr. Moore into custody the day before his hearing was to have come on before the Governor in consequence of the address of the former House. This was apparently done to prevent his having an opportunity of clearing himself, unless he would agree that the Assembly had jurisdiction to try him.

duct in the magistracy, and on account of his writing and publishing his said address, and reflecting on a former House in a document which they termed a libel against all Houses, etc. They commanded, at the same time, the sheriff of the county and city "not to pay regard to any of His Majesty's writs of *Habeas Corpus* that should be to him directed in the case of William Moore, as he should answer at his peril."

This done Dr. Smith was next brought to the bar of the House, and charged with " *abetting and promoting the writing and publishing of a libel entitled the Address of William Moore,*" which he answered immediately by pleading his entire innocence of the matters charged.

The House replied that they had sufficient proof of the charge, and that he must prepare to take his trial before them upon the same.

To this Dr. Smith answered that, as the gentleman who had signed the address had already acknowledged himself the sole writer and publisher thereof, and was punished for the same by the House, it seemed strange that they should look for any other publishers or writers; that he could easily prove his own innocence, but that he had hoped, when they considered the matter in all its consequences, they would not insist thereon; that the address had been written against a House not in being; that it had been the policy of all wise nations to leave it in the power of every subject to arraign the conduct of their highest officers when they swerved from their duty; that the meanest plebeian in Rome might have impeached a Consul at the expiration of his term; that the best check which the British nation enjoys against those clothed in superior power is the right of animadverting freely on their conduct, within the bounds and spirit of law, whereof a jury of themselves are the judges; that if the Assembly should proceed so far as to call men to account for what had been said concerning a preceding dissolved House, they might by the same rule call them to account for censuring any House that had subsisted a century ago, and by this means tie up the tongues and pens of men forever, sanctify the most iniquitous measures, and render it impossible even to write a history of former times without being subject to the prosecution of every future enraged House of Assembly; that the liberty of the press was concerned in Dr.

Smith's case; that if he had done anything, it was as a director of a newspaper, in which he had been exercising his best judgment, as was his duty; that two other persons had printed it, particularly the Assembly's own printer, and by the advice of several of their members; that they all stood on the same footing, and if they had offended against the laws, they should be tried by the laws and the verdict of their peers; that if the Assembly should try the matter, they had no law to proceed by, and were moreover the parties pretending to be injured, which rendered them very unfit to be judges; and that they might certainly trust their cause to the ordinary courts of justice and an impartial jury of their constituents.

Having said this, Dr. Smith was ordered to withdraw a little; and, being soon called in again, he was acquainted that the House had resolved that they would hear no arguments tending to call in question their jurisdiction and right to try the publication of a libel; that they had appointed the Tuesday following to begin his trial, and that he might have the assistance of counsel, if he desired it, and would name those he intended to employ.

Dr. Smith, considering that if, after hearing this resolve, he should still decline their right of trying him on the matters charged, it would be called a contempt of a House then in being—for which they would have voted a commitment, which, as he conceived, was all they had in view—told them that he must be guided by the determination of the House, and that he would choose the Attorney-General for his counsel, who was his particular friend, as well as a gentleman of whose abilities he had a high opinion. He also named two other lawyers—John Ross and William Peters—to be employed with the Attorney-General.

The House replied that he was welcome to the two other lawyers, but that the Attorney-General could not be permitted to plead at their bar in behalf of any prisoner, as they judged it inconsistent with the nature of his office and qualification.

Dr. Smith now prepared for his defence, which he had resolved to confine to two points:

First. To show that the paper was not a *libel*, even against the Assembly whose conduct it reflected on; and

Second. That if it was a libel, it was contrary to all precedents, and unwarranted by any law for a succeeding House to take cognizance thereof.

But, to his surprise, the first thing he heard at the bar of the House on the day of trial was the following resolve, viz.:

The counsel for Dr. Smith shall not be permitted to adduce any arguments to show that the address of William Moore is not a libel, OR to call in question the right of this House to take cognizance thereof.

This was, in fact, condemning him unheard, and depriving him of both points of his defence. The nature of the crime was predetermined against him; the jurisdiction of the House was not to be impeached; no matters of law were to be pleaded in his behalf. So that nothing was left but the examination of the evidences, and he was to be a sort of silent spectator of a mock trial before this new-erected judicature.

The examination of the evidences took up many days; Colonel Bradford and Mr. Hall both testifying that they had printed the address in their respective papers before it was in the other.

On summing up the whole, it appeared that of near twenty persons who had been consulted and applied to by Mr. Moore— some in writing and some in publishing his address—Dr. Smith was the most innocent, having had no hand in the writing and but very little in the publishing, namely, some occasional conversation with the German translator, who was the third publisher, and who had not published it until many weeks after both Mr. Hall and Colonel Bradford had done so.

The House now adjudged Dr. Smith "guilty of promoting and publishing a false, scandalous, virulent and seditious libel against the late House of Assembly of the Province, highly derogatory of and destructive to the *privileges of the Assembly*."

Dr. Smith was now thus addressed by the Speaker:

Mr. Smith: The House, having inquired into the charge against you, have found you guilty of promoting and publishing a libel, entitled " The Address of William Moore, Esquire," and do order you to be committed to the gaol of this county till you make satisfaction to *this* House.

Immediately after the sentence, Dr. Smith rose and tendered to the House an appeal to the King. The House rejected the appeal and returned it to him. On his desiring that the tender and refusal might be entered on their minutes, they asked him, with anger, if they were to be directed by him how to keep their minutes. The Speaker then read a form of an acknowledgment made by the Bishop of Bristol in King James the First's time, and insinuated that the same would be sufficient from Dr. Smith. Dr. Smith now rose, and, with great dignity, said :

Mr. Speaker : I cannot make acknowledgments or profess contrition. No punishment which this Assembly can inflict on me would be half so terrible to me as suffering my tongue to give to my heart the lie.

This last sentence was uttered with much emotion ; — the speaker striking his breast with his hand as he spoke. The lobbies were crowded with people, all of more or less importance in our then little town : Thomas Willing, Lynford Lardner, Richard Hockley, William Peters, John Wallace, John Bell, James Young, Captain Vanderspeigle, Charles Osborne, and others, some of them officers of the crown, and all friends both of Dr. Smith and the Proprietaries ; several of them, too, being Masons, as Dr. Smith himself was.* Dr. Smith's bold defiance of the Assembly, uttered with an effect highly dramatic, and set off by the Provost's noble face and person, brought out a storm of applause from the auditors. When this had subsided, and the House had vindicated its dignity by an arrest and fine of several of the parties, Dr. Smith was taken to jail. The warrant of commitment was thus :

PENNSYLVANIA, *ss.*

To James Coultas, Esq., Sheriff of the City and County of Philadelphia.

The House of Assembly of the Province of Pennsylvania hath this day adjudged William Smith for promoting and publishing a false, scandalous, virulent and seditious libel *against the late House of Assembly of this Province, and highly derogatory of and destructive to the rights of this House and the privileges of Assembly.* These are, therefore, in behalf and by order of the said last-mentioned House of Assembly, to require and charge you to receive the said William Smith into your custody within the common jail of your county, under your charge, and him therein safely to keep and detain until you shall receive further orders from this House.

Hereof fail not, as you shall answer the contrary at your peril. Given under my hand this 25th day of January, in the year of our Lord 1758.

THOMAS LEECH, Speaker.

---

* Thomas Lawrence, Charles Osborne, John Bell and John Wallace were all Masons. John Wallace was apparently at one time Treasurer of the Lodge. (See *The Grand Lodge of the Most Ancient and Honorable Fraternity of Free and Accepted Masons of Pennsylvania.* Philadelphia, 1877. p. xxxii.

The *charge* against Dr. Smith, it will be remembered, was for publishing a *libel*, entitled, etc. The publishing of a libel is a common law offence. It involves no matter of privilege, and is punishable by the courts of common law. But condemnation by the Assembly for an offence punishable at common law would have been void. This was soon seen by the Assembly, and the defect was sought to be remedied by an allegation of a breach of privilege. The warrant of commitment alleged a new offence—a breach of privilege ; one of which the House was the judge.

Dr. Smith now gave notice to the Speaker of the Assembly of Friends that he would not leave things where the Friends had placed them :

SIR : As I do not think that the refusal of your House to receive *or admit the appeal* which I tendered to them on Wednesday, the 25th instant, can either deprive His Majesty of his royal prerogative to hear appeals from any judgment in this Province, nor any of his subjects of their right *to make such appeal*, I think it proper to acquaint you and this House of Assembly that I am still determined *to lay my appeal*, case and complaint, before his Majesty in Council, and to prosecute the same, in such manner as I shall be advised in order to obtain that redress which I have reason to hope from the royal clemency and justice.

I am, sir, your most humble servant,
WILLIAM SMITH.

To Thomas Leech, Esq., Speaker of the House of Representatives of the Freemen of Pennsylvania.

The judgment and commitment for an offence not charged ; the erection of itself, by the Assembly, into an extraordinary judicature whose authority was not to be questioned, and the denial by it of Dr. Smith's appeal, were obviously unconstitutional acts. An act equally unconstitutional is exhibited in an order which we copy from the Journal of the Assembly.

Such orders were hardly made even in the days of bad kings.

January 25th, 1758.

ORDERED, That M^r. Speaker do give in charge to the Sheriff to keep his prisoner, William Smith, Provost of the Academy of Philadelphia, agreeable to the directions of the commitment to him delivered ; and *that he do not obey any writ of Habeas Corpus, or other writ whatsoever,* that may come to his hands, for Bailing and discharging him from his custody on any pretence whatsoever, *and that this House will support him in obedience to this order.*

The Friends, in directing the Sheriff to pay no attention to the King's Writ of Habeas Corpus, quite forgot themselves. They ought to have remembered that the Sheriff, by whomsoever appointed or elected, was the King's officer, bound of necessity to obey the King's writs directed to him; that this very office was instituted for executing them; so that their commanding him not to obey such writs was commanding him not to be a Sheriff, which at the same time they allowed him to be; and consequently was the absurdest of absurdities. The adjectitious clause about the *Habeas Corpus* was obviously made under fear that Dr. Smith might seek relief through the Courts; and the Assembly mean thus to obviate his act.

If the strange behavior of the Friends through all this matter did not proceed from ignorance, it proceeded from the intolerance which would confound law and justice to gratify revenge, and a lust of power. Unfortunately there were too many reasons to fear that it proceeded from the last.

Dr. Smith being resolved to attempt every legal method to attain his liberty before he should trouble the Crown officers in England with the exhibition of a case so little creditable to the Legislature of the Province, now, February 4th, 1758, sought relief, though he was aware of the technical difficulties which the Assembly had here put in his way, from the Judicial and the Executive powers at home.

He first addressed the Judicial Power:

TO THE HON. WM. ALLEN, CHIEF-JUSTICE OF THE PROVINCE OF PENNA.

The Humble Petition of William Smith, of the City of Phila.
     Sheweth:

That your Petitioner is a Prisoner confined in the county gaol of Philadelphia, and, as he avers, unduly deprived of his liberty; your petitioner therefore prays your Honour to grant him his Majesty's Writ of Habeas Corpus, returnable immediately, or as your Honour shall think proper, so that your petitioner shall either be discharged or bailed, as the nature of his case upon the return of said writ shall require.
     And your petitioner will pray, &c.,
                 WILLIAM SMITH.

To this petition, the Chief-Justice made the following answer:

On view of a copy of the Petitioner's Warrant of Commitment, it appearing to me that, among other things, the Petitioner is committed by the House of Assembly of this Province for *a breach of Privilege*, I do not think myself authorized in granting a Habeas Corpus, and in bailing the Petitioner during the sitting of the House, and therefore am obliged to reject the prayer of the Petitioner.   WILLIAM ALLEN.

He now appealed to the Executive:

To WILLIAM DENNY, Esq., Lieutenant-Governor, and Commander-in-Chief of the Province of Penna., and Counties of Newcastle, Kent, and Sussex, on Delaware.

The humble Petition of William Smith, of the City of Philadelphia, Clerk,

        Sheweth:

That your Petitioner is a Prisoner confined in the county Gaol of Philadelphia by order of the House of Assembly of this Province, and, as he conceived, unduly restrained of his liberty, and by the Chief-Justice refused his Majesty's Writ of Habeas Corpus.

Your Petitioner therefor prays your Honor to grant him such Redress and Relief as your Honor, on Consideration of his case, which will be laid before your Honor, shall think suitable and just.

            And your Petitioner shall Pray, &c.,

                                        WILLIAM SMITH.
    PHILA., Feb. 4th, 1758.

Governor Denny's action appears by his endorsement on this petition:

The unhappy Situation of the Petitioner moves me with great Compassion, but if I have a Power* in any Shape to interpose in this matter, I do not incline to exercise it, as it might, at this critical Juncture, endanger the safety of the whole Province.

                                        WILLIAM DENNY.
    Feb. 6th, 1758.

There, therefore, remained nothing for Dr. Smith to do but to appeal to the King in council; and although that would involve a voyage to England, waiting the law's delay, with perhaps the insolence of office, etc., this step he resolved to take. The oppressor's wrong had already come—wrong not to him alone, but to his college, his country and his King—and he was determined to have it redressed.

In the meantime he went to prison.

Such proceedings as these which we have described—a clergyman of the Church of England, the Provost of the College and

---

* The power here spoken of as perhaps existing was that of a dissolution of the Assembly.

Academy, a Trustee and Chief Director of all the German schools,
put into the Walnut Street gaol—made something of a stir among
the gentlemen of Philadelphia.   It made a stir, in fact, over the
land.   We give a letter from a minister in New Jersey (a brother
of Thomas McKean, afterwards Chief-Justice and Governor of
Pennsylvania), and one from Dr. Smith himself about it:

The Rev. Mr. McKean to Dr. Bearcroft.*

NEW BRUNSWICK IN NEW JERSEY, Feb⁥ 5, 1758.

REV⁰ SIR: Since my arrival here I have wrote you by two different
Conveyances, one by the Pacquet, and the other by means of a friend
via Ireland.   In them I have troubled you with a particular account of
my Voyage and other proper occurrences, as also the kind reception I
have met with and the happy prospect I have as yet in my mission.

What I have further to communicate by this opportunity is, that the
Rev⁰ M⁰. Thompson at Chester in Pennsylvania had left that Mission
before my arrival in America, and 'tis said is gone to some of the West
India Islands.   The cause of his going away I am uncertain of, tho',
some have said, it was in consequence of a report spread by some means
or other that he was removed from the Society's service.   The Hon'ble
Society's Letter for that Gentleman I have now in my possession and
will return it or otherwise dispose of it, as soon as you will honor me
with your pleasure on that head.

An extraordinary Affair has lately happened in Philadelphia, of which,
Sir, I must also beg the indulgence to inform you; the cause of Reli-
gion, the Church of England and the Liberty of that Province (Penn-
sylvania) seeming to be highly concerned in it.   The Case is thus.
A certain William Moore, a Justice of the Peace and President of the
Court in one of the Counties of that Province, having distinguished
himself about two years ago in opposing the measures of the Quaker
Assembly, by joining with many others in strongly soliciting a Militia
Law, which was refused, became an object of the Quakers' resentment.
Some time before the last General Election of Representatives for that
Province, M⁰. Moore was summoned before the then House of Assembly
in consequence of some Petitions presented against him for maladministration in his Office.   He appeared and delivered in a Memorial in his
own defence.   The Dissolution of the then Assembly approaching,
they thought proper to publish to the World in the *Gazette*, the charges
and accusations against Moore, omitting his Memorial of Defence.
After that Assembly was dissolved, Moore thinking himself aggrieved
by that publication presents an Address to the Governor, setting forth
the injuries he had received and praying that the Governor would make

* Lambeth MSS.

enquiry into his conduct and if guilty to punish him accordingly. This Address was sent to M^r. Hall, Printer to the Assembly, who after consulting three of the principal Members whether he might publish it, and obtaining their consent, printed the same in his *Gazette.* After this another Printer, W^m. Bradford, published it in a weekly paper of his. Some weeks after the Rev^d M^r. Smith, one of the Trustees of the Schools erected in that Province for the propagating Religion and the English Language among the German Emigrants and Director of a German Press set up for conveying proper intelligence to these people and promoting the noble design of making them good Subjects, was applied to by several Germans and others who had heard of the aforementioned Address to reprint the same. Accordingly it was translated into the German Language and printed. The present Assembly, consisting mostly of the same Members with the former, looking upon this Address as containing things very severe on their conduct, Voted the same " a seditious and scandalous Libel," in consequence of which they arrested M^r. Moore by their Serjeant at Arms ; had him before their House where he confessed his being the Author of the Address, and was thereupon by them sentenced to prison 'till the 1st of October next and was accordingly committed to the Common Gaol.

But this proceeding, which is here looked upon as a most .extraordinary stretch of power and contrary to the constitution and fundamentals of an English Government, did not satisfy the incensed Assembly.

The Rev^d M^r. Smith has long been an object of the Quakers' hatred upon several accounts. They have suspected him for exposing to the World their pernicious conduct in refusing to defend the Country against the dreadful devastations and cruel barbarities of the Savages. He is, you know, Sir, at the head of the College and Academy, which has all along met with the greatest opposition from that party as they justly fear it will be a means of promoting true Religion and Loyalty and thereby exterminate their power. And what is still as vexatious and grating to them, and has met with the same opposition, is the scheme of the German Schools. These people (the Germans), who compose a large body in the Province, the Quakers had formerly under their direction and therefore were willing to keep them in ignorance. M^r. Smith has been extremely assiduous in promoting this great design and for this reason also has been marked out as an Enemy to their interests and projects.

The reprinting this paper (the Address) was conceived by the Assembly as a proper handle by which they might lay hold on M^r. Smith and thereby wreak their vengeance on him. He was in pursuance of a Resolve to this purpose Arrested, brought to the Bar of their House and after a sham Tryal of several days, was committed to close confinement in the Common Gaol " for " (as they expressed it) " promoting and publishing a Libel," while the two Printers who had published the

same a Month before were past unnoticed.   The clamor of the People
was however so great that they would have willingly dismissed M^r. Smith
upon making a submission, but this he nobly refused, and when he
received his Sentence declared as he was not conscious of any crime
" his Lips should not give his Heart the Lie ; " when M^r. Smith delivered this Speech the Audience gave a general clap in applause of his
conduct.

This the Assembly construed into a contempt and had several persons
arrested and brought before them, who after some slight submissions
were discharged.   M^r. Smith now appealed from this extraordinary and
new erected Court of Judicature (who assume to themselves greater
powers than the House of Commons in England) to his Sacred Majesty
and offered to give any Bail to prosecute the same, but this Appeal was
refused, and he is still confined, the Sheriff being ordered by them not
to execute a Writ of Habeas Corpus, if such an one should be issued
for this persecuted Gentleman's relief.   The Case however will be laid
before His Majesty; but in the meantime M^r. Smith bears the loss
and injury, yet still is in good spirits considering the cause for which
he suffers.

I hope Revd Sir, you will pardon my troubling you with such a long
detail of this affair as I thought it a duty I owed to the cause of the
Church, Religion, and the Province that gave me Birth to represent it
to you, and believe me, Sir, I am so little a politician and meddle so
seldom with such affairs, that I would not have presumed to say a word
on this head to you if it had not appeared a case of the most engaging
and important nature, and a severe stroke levelled at the interests of the
Church of England thro' the person of M^r. Smith.   This is a true state
of the Case and unless protection from your quarter of the World can
be had, which it is not doubted will be given, it cannot be conceived
where these daring attempts may end.

Revd Sir, Your most Obedient and most Humble Servant,

ROBERT McKEAN.

*Dr. Smith to the Bishop of London.**

(EXTRACT.)

PHILAD^A COUNTY GAOL, Feb^{ry} 7th, 1758.

MY LORD :   This will be delivered to your Lordship by M^r. Jacob
Duché, a Young Gentleman of good Fortune, bred up in our College
under me.   He has distinguished himself as a Scholar and Orator on
many Public occasions, and from the most disinterested motives has
devoted himself to the Church.   He proposes to spend some time at the
University in England and goes from this place in company with M^r.
Hamilton, our late Governor.   He is in every respect a Youth of the

* Lambeth MSS., No. 1123.

most hopeful parts and not unworthy the Honor of your Lordship's protection and notice.

I have heretofore hinted the persecuting spirit of the Quakers against all those who had the courage to avow themselves strenuous Advocates for the Defence of this His Majesty's Colony in opposition to those pernicious principles that would tamely resign all our sacred rights, civil and religious, into the hands of a savage and popish enemy.

Against me in particular they have had a long grudge, supposing me the Author of some Pamphlets published in London to alarm the Nation of the dreadful consequences of suffering such men to continue in power at this time. But finding no pretext to distress me, though lying on the watch for three years, the Assembly at last called me before them and committed me to gaol for having reprinted a Paper (in the German Newspaper under my direction as a Trustee for a Society in London) which had been printed four weeks before in both the English Newspapers, and in one of them by the Assembly's own Printer after consulting the Speaker and two other leading Members.

This appeared so partial that on my rather chusing to go to Gaol than make any acknowledgments to the House when I saw the other Printers passed over, together with the Members and ten other gentlemen who had advised the Author therein and some of them eminent Lawyers as may appear in the Depositions—I say, my Lord, this appeared so partial that on the refusal aforesaid the Audience set up a loud clap of applause. Every person of impartiality exclaimed against the Sentence of the House ; a Majority of the Church Vestry and other leading Gentlemen petitioned them not to send a Clergyman of the Church to Gaol, offering any Sum Bail for me. But all this was refused unless I would meanly belie my conscience and acknowledge wrong where I had done none. I accordingly appealed from this strange sentence to His Majesty in Council, at the earnest desire of every person here who wishes to see the Privileges of Assemblies explained and the Liberty of the Subject ascertained.

Indeed, my Lord, there seems an end of all liberty both of Writing and Preaching here, if our Assemblies will be both Judges and Juries in their own case, taking upon them to Try Common Law Offences, Examine upon Oath and refuse a Trial by Peers. They likewise fixed the nature of the Crime as well as their own right to try it, refusing to hear any arguments on that head. The Trial lasted 13 days, and my Gaol is as comfortable as a Gaol can be, being crowded with Visitors from Morning to Night.

We are determined to push the Appeal with vigor, a large Sum being raised for that effect. D^r. Chandler will wait on your Lordship to propose a meeting between your Lordship, D^r. Nichols, D^r. Bearcroft, M^r. Penn and M^r. Hamilton, to concert the proper measures for defeating this Quaker persecution, in which all Churches and all Friends of Liberty are concerned.

I presume therefore to beg your Lordship's countenance therein. The Case and Depositions will be laid before your Lordship, and if you do not find it the cause of Religion, Liberty and persecuted Innocence, I request no favor.

I am,

Your Lordship's

Most Dutiful Son and Servant,

W. Smith.

P. S.—I have sent your Lordship a small Charge delivered to my Pupils, together with an American Magazine which contains some account of my affair, and shall continue to send that Magazine for your Lordship's amusement during the war.

That we may not be suspected of a wish to paint out any shades, specks, or spots upon the character of Dr. Smith, we give the following letter from the Rector of Christ Church, preserved among the manuscripts at Lambeth. The reader will have an account of Dr. Jenney and of this letter further on in this volume. See pages 215–262; 286.

Dr. Jenney to the Archbishop of Canterbury.

(EXTRACT.)

PHILADELPHIA, November 27th, 1758.

MAY IT PLEASE YOUR GRACE: The general joy of every friend of our Church at the exaltation of your Grace to the See of Canterbury could not but reach these parts and affect us here, as we are told it did those at home, particularly it gave me the greatest pleasure who have long ago been informed of your excellent Administration in the See of Oxford, from whence we cannot help expecting the like or greater advantages from one in a more exalted station from whence more good may redound to the Church.

As your Grace hath always been a most zealous Member of the Hon'ble Society for propagating the Gospel, &c., so your present situation puts it in your power to exert your pious disposition in this way more than formerly, and we of this Province have more than ordinary reason to mention this, because we cannot help observing mistakes in the Abstracts of that Ven'ble Body which we apprehend arise from misrepresentations from hence.

But what I am most concerned for & apprehensive of evil consequences from, is the practice of some Clergymen here to intermix what is their true and real business with Politics in civil affairs and being so zealous therein as to blame and even revile those of their Brethren who cannot approve of their conduct in this particular. I am very sorry to be forced to name one William Smith, who 'tis said is gone to England with this view, and without doubt will wait upon your Grace. He hath always been exceedingly busy in Church in New York and this Province ever since A. D. 1744, since when he was admitted into the Hon'ble Societie's service, and I have not heard that I have ever in all that time been charged with a fault or any indiscretion ; and I am very unwilling to have my reputation called in question now the first time when my great age and infirmities make it impossible that I can hold out long. I would not care to go out of the world in the ill opinion of any, especially so great a Man in station and character as your Grace.   He pretends to be a great intimate of the Hon'ble M^r. Thomas Penn, our Proprietor, and several other great Men whose favours he boasts of, but I am in hopes that no great Man will support him in his misrepresentation of me without giving me an opportunity to clear myself.   And I humbly pray that his forwardness will not prevail upon your Grace in particular to entertain anything amiss of me who am not conscious to myself of having done anything to deserve it.

I humbly thank God to prosper your Grace's Labours in his service. I earnestly pray your favorable Opinion of me and am,

> May it please your Grace,
> Your Grace's most dutiful Son and
> most Obedient Humble Servant,
> ROBERT JENNEY.

We come back, however, to the beginning of 1758. The Provost was still in gaol.   With the head of the College in a place so unlike the grove of Academus, and so little convenient for instruction, an alumnus of this day would, perhaps, wonder how the classes could get along, or how, indeed, the College could exist. There was no difficulty in the year 1758 about such a matter: never, at least, where Dr. Smith was the Provost, and the classes such as attended upon him.   "The mind is its own place."   The minutes of the College, under date of February 4th, 1758, have this entry :

The Assembly of the Province, having taken Mr. Smith into Custody, the Trustees considered how the inconvenience from thence arising to the College might be best remedied ; and Mr. Smith having expressed a Desire to continue his Lectures to the Classes which had formerly attended them, the students also inclining rather to proceed in their Studies under his care, they ordered that Said classes should attend him for that Purpose at the usual Hours in the Place of his present confinement.

On his arrest by the Sergeant-at-arms at the Coffee House, January 6th, 1758, Dr. Smith was kept in confinement until the

25th of the month, when he was sentenced to jail. He here remained eleven weeks; being liberated about the 11th of April, by
order of the Supreme Court on the adjournment of the Assembly.
The Assembly meeting again, however, new warrants of arrest and
commitment were issued. These, however, were not executed.
But the Assembly meeting again in September, 1758, Dr. Smith
was again arrested, and kept in confinement until the end of the
session, when the House was dissolved. He then, in some way,
got free. However, on the meeting of a new Assembly, this new
body issued a warrant to take him into custody for not having
made satisfaction to the former House. Whether he was actually
found on this new warrant, I do not discover.

CHAPTER XIII.

Dr. Smith obtains a Commission for Godfrey, the Poet—Makes an Address
to the Colonies—Marriage with Miss Moore—Thanksgiving Sermon
—Sails for England.

THE spirit of active usefulness which marked Dr. Smith's character did not forsake him even under great anxieties and troubles.
We almost recall in him the exiled Duke of Ardens.

> ————" Happy is your Grace,
> That can translate the stubbornness of Fortune
> Into so quiet and so sweet a style."

He had discovered, while editing the *American Magazine,* a young
man named Thomas Godfrey, a son of the inventor of the quadrant,
who possessed high poetical genius. He greatly interested the
Provost, who published in the *Magazine* Godfrey's earliest poem,
and after his death—too soon for his friends and the literature of
the country—collected and published his writings. Godfrey,
the father, who was a glazier, was very poor, and could do
nothing for his son. The son—who was a man of genius for
poetry and the fine arts—could do little for himself. Such a
case was sure to interest Dr. Smith ; and we find among his papers
the evidences that he was now trying to obtain from the Governor
a Lieutenant's commission for the unfriended youth. He obtained

it, and Godfrey joined the Pennsylvania forces now being raised for an expedition against Fort Duquesne.

Dr. Smith's literary and intellectual powers, in spite of his troubles at this time, were equally active with the affections of his heart. He now—in June, 1758, on the opening of the campaign of that year—wrote and published a paper, entitled: "An Earnest Address to the Colonies." It was addressed particularly to those of the southern district, and was written and published at the desire of Brigadier-General Forbes, when levying forces for the expedition against Fort Duquesne, which was afterwards taken by him.

This document, which produced a good effect, may, perhaps, reward the reader's perusal:

BRETHREN AND COUNTRYMEN : I am now to address you, in the most solemn manner, on the present posture of affairs, and the duty we owe to his sacred majesty, to our holy religion, and to our latest posterity, on this important occasion. As I would be understood by all, I shall not affect a vain parade of words, or pomp of style. Brevity and perspicuity shall be my principal aim.

The almighty Author of our nature has thought fit to create man a needy and dependent being, incapable of subsisting in a solitary state with any degree of happiness. In order to his well-being, a mutual interchange of good offices with his fellow-creatures is absolutely necessary.

Hence the origin and foundation of civil societies, which are nothing else but certain bodies of men linked together by common compact or agreement, for the better securing themselves against want, and defending themselves against danger. In consequence of this compact, every individual is under the most solemn obligations to contribute what he can, for the general welfare, and preservation of the community, whereof he is a part ; and when this is done with zeal, fidelity, and an elevated sense of duty, it is denominated public virtue and love of our country ; than which, human nature boasts of no qualities that are more amiable or more divine. Both reason and religion inculcate this in the strongest terms. A narrow, selfish spirit is odious to God and man ; and no community ever subsisted long where such a spirit disgraced its members. It is scarce to be conceived how great a difference public virtue makes in the state of nations. Animated by it, the smallest remain powerful and safe ; while, without it, the most populous are despicable and weak.

The little state of Sparta was an illustrious proof of this. To acknowledge no lord or master ; to live independent and free ; to be governed by their own laws and customs ; to preserve themselves from corruption, selfishness and effeminacy; and to be the avengers of justice and the scourges of tyranny—were the highest wishes which Spartans knew; and, whenever they were called to exert themselves on this score, they declined neither toils nor dangers nor sufferings. The blaze of public spirit then shone illustrious from bosom to bosom, till it had effectually subdued and consumed the enemies of their country. Their very women shared the holy flame; and whenever the trumpet sounded the alarm of war, one fitted out a husband, and another a son; charging them, by all the ties of love and honour and duty, not to disgrace the dignity of the Spartan name, and either to chastize the insolence of their enemies, or perish in the glorious attempt.

Seeing, then, my countrymen, such was the virtue of a Spartan, and even of a Spartan woman, what may not be expected from Britons; who, added to all the advantages which the former enjoyed, have that of the Christian religion and its everlasting prospects to animate and inflame their conduct? We are, or might be, the happiest and most enlightened people in the world; and, by consequence, we ought to be the bravest.

Were we to cast our eyes over this globe, and to take a view of the condition of our fellow-creatures in other countries; how should we bless our lot, and how dear would the name of Britons become to us!

Not to mention many parts, even of Europe itself, where the common people are in a manner the property of their lords, and on little better footing than their cattle themselves; I might carry you through Asia and Africa, to shew you the deplorable state of human nature in those countries, groaning under a race of monsters that disgrace their very shape; and in a condition so completely miserable, that you have neither seen nor can imagine any thing of the kind. The wild savage, that roams the American wilderness, is infinitely happier than they.

But I shall not take up your time with these eastern scenes of servitude and woe. Thanks be to God! we are as far removed from the danger of them, as we are from the place of their existence. Our apprehensions are from another quarter. Our ambitious French neighbours on this American continent, are the only people on earth, from whom we have any thing to fear. It may, therefore, be proper to give you a sketch of the situation we should be in, under their government and power.

And, on this head, I would observe, first, that among them you would in vain look for that happy equality and security which you now enjoy. All the property of the subject lies, among them, at the absolute disposal of the sovereign; and the poor labourer has no encouragement to be industrious or get before hand in the world, since he can neither be certain to comfort himself thereby, nor those with whom he is most nearly connected.

You have frequent opportunities of being informed of the manner in which the French are forced to live near ourselves in Canada. You know on what poor fare all who can bear arms among them, are obliged to follow their arbitrary leaders through these inhospitable American woods ; seldom enjoying a comfortable meal, unless by chance they can seize it from us, which makes them the more eager to dispossess us of these happy settlements, and to reap the fruit of our labours.

But, added to all their other miseries, the greatest is, that they are not only deprived of freedom of body, but even of mind. Instead of being permitted to pour forth the genuine worship of the heart, according to the dictates of their own conscience, before the great Creator of heaven and earth, they are obliged to pay a mock adoration to those "who are no gods!" Instead of putting their trust in his mercies through the only Mediator Jesus Christ, they are taught to put a vain confidence in relicks, and departed spirits, and those who can afford no help. Instead of following the plain dictates of common sense and the light of their own understandings, they must submit to be hood-winked, and to have their consciences ridden, by a set of priests and jesuits and monks and inquisitors, swarming in every corner !

But how different is the case among us ! We enjoy an unprecarious property; and every man may freely taste the fruits of his own labours, "under his vine and under his fig-tree, none making him afraid." If God has blessed us with the good things of this life, we need not fear to make an appearance answerable to our condition; and what we do not spend ourselves, the laws will secure to our children after us. The king, upon his throne, cannot exact a single farthing of our estates, but what we have first freely consented to pay by laws of our own making. We cannot be dragged out, in violation of justice and right, to wade in seas of blood, for satiating the avarice or ambition of a haughty monarch. We need not fear racks, nor stripes, nor bonds, nor arbitrary imprisonments, from any authority whatsoever; or could such prevail for a time *above law*, yet, while the constitution remains sound, we may be sure the very act would soon destroy itself, and terminate at length in the utter ruin of the projectors.

It is our happiness too that our minds are as free as our bodies. No man can impose his own dogmas or notions upon our consciences. We may worship the God of our fathers, the only living and true God, in that manner which appears most agreeable to our own understandings, and his revealed will. The Bible is in our hands; we are assisted by an orthodox gospel-ministry; we may search and know the words of eternal life; and, what is equally valuable, we may convey what we know to our children after us, no man having it in his power to wrest their education from us.

This, my dear countrymen, is happiness indeed ! and what still enhances it, is the consideration that we are not only called to enjoy it ourselves, but perhaps to be the blessed instruments of diffusing it over this vast continent, to the nations that sit " in darkness and the shadow " of death."

Surely the thought of this ought to rouse every spark of virtue in our bosoms. Could an ancient Spartan rush into the field of death, upon the motives mentioned above? and is there any danger which a Briton ought to decline for the sake of these inestimable privileges? or shall a French slave and popish bigot, at this day, do more for the glory of his arbitrary lord, than a freeman and Protestant, for the best of kings, and the father of his people?

This land was given to us for propagating freedom, establishing useful arts, and extending the kingdom of Jesus. Shall we, then, be false to such a trust, or pusillanimous in such a divine cause? We have hewn out habitations for ourselves in an uncultivated wilderness; and shall we suffer them to fall a prey to the most faithless of enemies? We have unfurled the Messiah's banner in the remotest parts of the earth; and shall we suffer the bloody flag of persecution to usurp its place? We have planted the blessed Gospel here; and shall we suffer heathen error to return where the glad tidings of salvation have once been preached?

No, countrymen! I know your souls disdain the very thought of such a conduct; and you would rather suffer ten thousand deaths (were so many possible) than be guilty of that which would entail infamy on yourselves, and ruin on your latest posterity.

Your readiness to join in the measures concerted for your safety, and to strike a decisive blow against the enemy, may much determine your future happiness and safety as a people; and I may well trust, when so much is at stake, you will not be backward in offering your service for a few months, under a General of humanity, experience, and every amiable accomplishment. I hope even to hear that our women will become advocates in such a cause, and entitle themselves to all the applauses so long ago paid to their Spartan predecessors!

I would not now wound you, with a disagreeable recapitulation of our past misconduct and fatal indolence, especially in these southern colonies. Many a time has it been in our power to crush out this dangerous war with a single tread of our foot, before it blazed up to its present height—But this we sadly neglected; and, perhaps, the all-wise disposer of events meant to shew us that, when our affairs were at the worst, he was mighty to save.

Never was the Protestant cause in a more desperate situation, than towards the close of last campaign. The great and heroic king of Prussia stood ready to be swallowed up of the multitude of his enemies. The British nation was torn to pieces by intestine divisions; its helm continually shifting hands; too many bent on sordid views of self-interest; too few regarding the public good; Minorca lost; Hanover overrun; our secret expeditions ending in disgrace; our forts in

America destroyed; our people captivated or inhumanly murdered, and our fleets dispersed and shattered before the winds.

Yet even then, when no human eye could look for safety, the Lord interposed for the Protestant Religion. In the short space of two months, the king of Prussia extricated himself from his difficulties, in a manner that astonished all Europe, and will continue to be the admiration of ages to come! And had we only done our part in America at that time, the pride of France would have been effectually humbled, and we should probably now have been rejoicing in an honourable peace.

But as that was not the case, the nation, in concert with the king of Prussia and other Protestant powers, has been obliged to make one grand push more for the general cause in the present campaign; and if that is unsuccessful, God knows what will become of our liberties and properties. This we may lay down as a certain truth, that the expense of the present war is far too great to be borne long by the powers concerned in it. The British nation is labouring under a heavy load of taxes. These colonies are likewise drained to the utmost, and sinking under the burden, as we all feel. Peace, then, of some kind or other, must be a desirable event; and upon our success this campaign it may depend, whether we shall dictate a peace to the French, or they to us. Should the latter be the case, (which God forbid!) it would be a fatal peace to us.

Rise then, my countrymen! as you value the blessings you enjoy, and dread the evils that hang over you, rise and shew yourselves worthy of the name of Britons! rise to secure to your posterity, peace, freedom, and a pure religion! rise to chastize a perfidious nation for their breach of treaties, their detestable cruelties, and their horrid murders! remember the cries of your captivated brethren, your orphan children, your helpless widows, and thousands of beggared families! Think of Monongahela, Fort William Henry, and those scenes of savage death, where the mangled limbs of your fellow-citizens lie strewed upon the plain; calling upon you to retrieve the honour of the British name!

Thus animated and roused, and thus putting your confidence, where alone it can be put, let us go forth in humble boldness; and the Lord do what seemeth him good!

Dr. Smith's whole life would seem to have been one of incident and romance. We have mentioned the extraordinary manner in which he was arrested, tried and imprisoned for what might be called an accidental connexion with William Moore, Esq., though he had long known and respected him. Both were co-laborers in the cause of the country. Both were prisoners—fellow-prisoners —in its behalf. The matter ended, in this part of it, according to

rules of the drama.   The daughter of Mr. Moore, Miss Rebecca
Moore, was a frequent visitor to her father's cell.   Dr. Smith,
who had before this time known her many excellent qualities of
understanding and had been already interested in her beauty, was
deeply touched by her sweet devotion to her much wronged parent.
An engagement of marriage was completed; and after the libera-
tion of the prisoners, the ceremony of marriage itself was performed, June 3d, 1758, at Moore Hall, the house of the lady's
father, by the Rev. William Currie, the Rector of St. David's
Church, Radnor, Delaware county.   To this alliance Dr. Smith
was indebted for a well-assorted and happy connexion.   It was
every way judicious : family, fortune, and external circumstances,
combined with considerations of feeling to make it wise.   A year
or two before this time he had made a purchase of property at the
Falls of Schuylkill; a spot at which he continued to make purchases till 1767, when he owned about sixty acres.   He built the
mansion-house, still standing, in the year of his marriage or soon
afterwards.*

Happy public events seemed soon to crown private felicity.
The British arms now began to retrieve the disasters of Braddock's Field, and we find, too, among Dr. Smith's works printed
at this time, *A Thanksgiving Sermon*, preached, September 17th,
1758, at *Bristol*, in *Pennsylvania*, on the signal Success of his
Majesty's Arms in *America*, during the Campaign, 1758.   The
text, from Exodus xv. 1, is appropriate: "I will sing unto the
LORD, for he hath triumphed gloriously."

During these months of trouble, anxiety, joy and thanksgiving,
Dr. Smith was busy in getting ready his appeal to the Crown,
for supporting it by evidence and for pressing it forward.   It was
a great work.   He had demanded from the Assembly copies of
its records.   They were not given.   He supplied the want by the
affidavits of witnesses, who were cognizant of facts of his arrest,
trial and imprisonment.   The appeal had gone on before him to
England; and on the 1st of April, 1758, had been referred to the
Attorney-General at this time, Charles Pratt, afterwards well
known both in England and America; and the Solicitor-General,

---

* It is agreeable to add that a portion of this estate still remains the property of the
present writer; his son and his grandchildren making six generations (male) who have
resided on it.

13

the gifted and ill-fated Charles Yorke.   He was now ready to sail, and before the King himself defy the Religious Society of Friends in assembly assembled, in committee represented, or in individuality individualized.

In the meantime the case of Mr. Moore—the original cause of the whole trouble—had been disposed to the satisfaction of himself and Dr. Smith.   The Governor, with advice of Council, appointed Thursday, the 24th of August, 1758, for the hearing of the charge of malpractice made by the Assembly against him, and ordered the fact to be notified to the parties concerned, and to the witnesses on both sides.

The parties having appeared at the time appointed, in the Council-chamber the Governor opened the hearing in the following words:

" Several Complaints were made against Mr. Moore, for Mal-practices as a Magistrate ; I sit here, as my predecessors have done, not to determine as a Court of Judicature, but to satisfy my own Conscience of the Truth or Falsehood of the Charges.   I am now ready to hear every Thing the Complainants have to offer, or that Mr. Moore can say in his Defence ; that I may thereby be enabled to judge how far he is fit to be a Minister of Justice, under a Commission from this Government."

All the 24th and the day following were spent in hearing the parties on both sides, and examining their evidences; and on Saturday, the 26th, the Governor, with the unanimous concurrence of his Council, acquitted Justice Moore, addressing himself as follows :

MR. MOORE : It is now near twelve Months since I received an Address from the Assembly of this Province, charging you with oppressive, extortionate, and illegal Practices, in the Office of a Justice of Peace for the County of Chester, which you have long had the Honour of holding, and requesting that I would remove you from that and all other Offices you enjoyed under this Government.   From the Moment I received this Address, I determined to make the strictest Enquiry into the Truth of the several Charges that were made against you, and to put an End to any Tyranny and Oppression which, in the Course of that Enquiry, it might appear the People had suffered from you ; and of this I gave the Assembly the strongest Assurances.   I therefore soon afterwards appointed a Day to hear you and your Accusers Face to Face, of which I gave them and you Notice.   The Reasons, why I did not make this Enquiry on that Day, and which have occasioned it to be so long

delayed, are so generally known, that I need not now make Mention of
them.   The Assembly, at my Request, furnished me with Thirty-two
Petitions preferred against you, several of which containing Complaints
of a mere private Nature, I do not think they properly lie before me,
and have therefore referred the Parties, who conceive themselves injured,
to seek Redress in the Courts of Law, in the ordinary Course of Justice.
. . . As to those which regard your Conduct as a Magistrate, I have
spent two Days with Patience and Attention in hearing every Thing that
could be alledged against you in support of them.   I am very sensible
of the Difficulties and Hardships you must necessarily have been under,
in producing Witnesses to defend yourself against Charges of this
Nature, especially when I consider that several of the Transactions complained of are of many Years standing.   It is, however, a great Pleasure
to me, to find that you have been able to surmount all these Difficulties,
and to acquit yourself of every Matter charged against you in the Execution of your Office, which you have fully done to my Satisfaction ;
and I think myself obliged, in Justice to your injured Character, in this
public Manner to declare, That the Petitions appear to me to be entirely
groundless ;   That you have acted in your Office with great Care,
Uprightness, and Fidelity ; and are so far from deserving Censure and
Disgrace, that, in many Instances, you merit the Thanks of every good
Man, and Lover of Justice.

So far things were going well.   But the work of the Assembly
was not yet undone.   Nothing but the King in Council could undo
that.   Dr. Smith was now going to England.

CHAPTER XIV.

DR. SMITH sailed for England about the beginning of December,
1758. He arrived in London on the 1st day of January in the
new year. The Provost Stillé gives the following account of his
arrival :

He brought with him something of the prestige of a political martyr,
and he had also gained a reputation as a writer which had extended
beyond the limits of the Province. It was just at this period that the
elder Pitt was planning a campaign to drive the French from North
America, and thus complete in this country that destruction of French
power, which his ally, Frederick the Great, had begun in Germany. It
was the era of preparation for the conquest of Quebec, the cession of
Canada, and the final overthrow of the French on this Continent. The
Minister had infused into all classes his own bitter hostility to France,
and something of his inflexible purpose to humble her by sea and on
land. In such a state of public feeling it may well be supposed that a
man who was looked upon as having undergone persecution and imprisonment (whatever might be the pretext alleged for it), because in the
hour of danger he had urged, with unflinching boldness, the duty of
defending a distant portion of the empire against a French invasion,
would be received, wherever he went in England, with sympathy, if not
with enthusiasm.

Thomas Penn, one of the Proprietaries, had been his warm personal
friend ever since he had come into the Province, and he was by far the
largest contributor to the funds of the College. He was at that time
engaged before the Privy Council in one of his many quarrels with the
Assembly of the Province, and he zealously aided Dr. Smith in bringing
his business (which was, in truth, only one of the branches of the same
controversy) to a speedy and favorable conclusion. But the principal
service which he rendered him was placing him in communication with
men of rank and fortune, who were at that time interested in the affairs

of the colonies, eager for information, and well-disposed to aid in developing their resources.

Another means of bringing him into relation at that time with persons of position and influence in England, was his connection with a Society for promoting the establishment of schools among the German settlers on the frontiers of this Province. This Society, formed several years before, was composed of prominent noblemen and gentlemen both in England and in Scotland, who were impressed with a fear lest the Germans should be led astray from the British interest by French and Popish emissaries, and had collected a considerable fund, both for the establishment of schools where their children might be taught the English language, and for the supply of true Protestant ministers among them.

But the favorable reception of Dr. Smith in England at that time was due not merely to the interest he excited as a political martyr, and to his efforts to make our German settlers good subjects and sound Protestants, but also in no small measure to his literary reputation. Provincial literature, at that time, it may be unnecessary to say, had not attracted much attention at home. It appears, however, that certain of Dr. Smith's writings had passed the ordeal of the dispensers of literary fame in those days,* and that their judgment was not unfavorable. An edition of his sermons had been published in London, in 1759, and a second edition was called for in 1763—a fact significant in itself of their literary value, for a volume of Sermons is not at any time very attractive reading, and in the middle of the last century, in England, sermons by a provincial author must have forced their way into notice by the weight of their own merit alone. The "Critical Review" speaks of one of these sermons (a funeral sermon) as "containing strokes equal to any in the *Oraisons Funèbres* of Bossuet!" It goes on to say:

Our judgment of this author, on the whole, is that what he says seems to come from the heart, and consequently cannot fail of affecting all who are not as void of pity as of public spirit.

The judgment of the "Monthly Review" was not less favorable, even if more discriminating:

The principal design of these discourses is to show the value of the blessings arising from the enjoyment of the Protestant religion and civil liberty. They are written in an excellent spirit, and in a sprightly and animated manner; the language is clear and forcible, the sentiments generally just and often striking.

The Doctor found numerous of the dignified English clergy ready to pay him honor. One of the most gratifying evidences of their disposition was given him in a recommendation dated the 12th of March, 1759, to the University of Oxford, from the Arch-

---

* The Monthly and The Critical Reviews.

bishop of Canterbury, and the Bishops of Durham, Salisbury, St. Asaph, Gloucester and Oxford, to confer upon him the Doctorship of Divinity. The recommendation shows what evidences of merit and service were required in 1759 at Oxford, for an honor which now, in *this* our country, is disgracefully scattered round the land.

TO THE UNIVERSITY OF OXFORD.*

The underwritten Representation in behalf of William Smith, Cl., M.A., of the University of Aberdeen, and now Provost of the College of Philadelphia, in America,
Humbly sheweth,

That the said William Smith was regularly bred at the University aforesaid, and left the same in March, 1747, having resided the full Term of Years there required.

That in the year 1750 he was sent to London (on a Scheme soon afterwards laid aside), to solicit the Parliament for a better Establishment of the Parochial Schools in Scotland, and was particularly recommended to the then Archbishop of Canterbury.

That after this he accompanied some young Gentlemen to America, and resided upwards of two years at New York, having carried with him Letters of Recommendation from the said Arch-Bishop to Lieutenant-Governor Delancey of that place, who had been his Grace's pupil at Cambridge.

That in 1753, he visited the City of Philadelphia, in Pennsylvania, and was invited to take Care of a laudable Seminary of Learning, just founded there; to which he consented, on Condition of being allowed time to enter into holy Orders.

That towards the End of the year he did accordingly return to England, and was regularly admitted into the holy Orders of Deacon and Priest, by the Lord Bishop of London; having brought back ample Certificates of his good Behaviour in America, as well to the aforesaid Arch-Bishop, as to several other Bishops and Dignitaries of our Church; and particularly to his Grace the present Arch-Bishop, then in the See of Oxford.

That in May, 1754, he returned to Philadelphia, and with the Assistance of the Other Persons concern'd, immediately applied himself to regulate the Seminary under his Care, agreeably to the Circumstances of the Province; and having modelled it into the form of a College, with an Academy subordinate thereto, and obtain'd a Charter of Incorporation, he was appointed Provost of the same, which Office he has discharg'd ever since (being near the space of five Years), and given several Public Specimens of his Abilities and diligence therein.

---

* Printed from original pamphlet in possession of Dr. J. H. Brinton.

That he has had the Pleasure to see the Seminary rising and flourishing under him, even beyond Expectation; so that it now contains near 300 Students and Scholars, from different parts of America (whose circumstances would not permit of an Education in their mother-Country). And besides himself as Provost, there is also a Vice-Provost (who is a Doctor of Divinity from Glasgow), with three Professors in the Sciences, and five Tutors or Assistants; with a Power of conferring the usual Degrees in Arts, &c., as appears more fully from the printed account of the Institution.

That the said William Smith is also a Trustee for the Free Schools, lately erected, among the vast Body of his Majesty's German Subjects on the Frontiers of Pennsylvania, and Colonies adjacent, by an honourable Society in London; in order to instruct the Children of the said Germans, in the English Tongue and Principles of Protestantism, and defeat the wicked Designs of the French and Papish Emissaries that swarm among them; to which pious Work his sacred Majesty has been a generous and constant Benefactor.

That in Consequence of this Trust, the said William Smith has, besides the Youth of the College, upwards of 700 Children continually under his care, in different parts of the Country; that he visits them frequently in their several schools, pays the Master's salaries, and superintends the Execution of the whole Design.

That he has, to his best Abilities, employed the Influence which he derives from these important Trusts, in order to promote Religion, Learning and good Government in those valuable parts of his Majesty's Dominions, and particularly to advance the pious Designs of the venerable Society for propagating the Gospel; having kept a constant Correspondence with many of the Members, bred up several young Men, who now make a Figure in their Service, and several more are coming forward under him, who (being of less confined circumstances) propose to finish their Education in the most liberal manner at the English Universities.

That during all the late Disturbances in America, he has shown himself a most faithful subject to his Majesty's just Government, taking every Opportunity to excite the People to the Defence of their inestimable Possessions, and to discourage that pernicious Doctrine too prevalent there, viz. : "That it is unlawful for Christian men to wear Weapons and serve in the Wars," A Doctrine which has occasion'd the spilling much innocent Blood in Pennsylvania, enabled the French to establish themselves on the Ohio, within its Borders, and was the main source of that War whose Flames involve all Europe.

That, in particular, when the unhappy General Braddock was defeated and slain; when the French and their savages broke in upon our Frontiers, carrying Death and Desolation along with them, and the whole Province was in Danger of being lost to the Crown of Great Britain,

the hands of near 300,000 Inhabitants being tied up by the absurd
Principles of their Rulers, who under pretence of Religion refused all
warlike measures for Defence ; the said William Smith was among the
Number of those who exerted themselves signally, on that Occasion, to
rouse the People to a sense of their Duty; and join'd in laying an
humble Representation of their distress'd State before his sacred
Majesty in Council, by which means a temporary Relief was obtain'd
and several of those who were scrupulous of bearing arms or voting
money for the Public Defence were obliged to resign their Seats in
Assembly.

That their Successors harboring Resentment against those who had
been concern'd in these necessary Transactions, and particularly
desirous to prejudice the Free Schools and Seminary of Learning under
the said William Smith (the Propagation of Knowledge and Freedom
of Inquiry being unfriendly to their dark System and Views) did about
a Twelvemonth ago, in the most unprecedented manner, set themselves
up above the Laws ; by their own sole authority, without any due Form
or Process, and without the Benefit of a Jury, trying, condemning, and
imprisoning several of his Majesty's liege subjects, for alleged offences
against former dissolved Assemblies ; and even presumed to suspend
Acts of Parliament by commanding his Majesty's High Sheriff not to
obey any Writs of Habeas Corpus, that might be issued in behalf of the
Persons so imprisoned.

That a Number of the principal Inhabitants of Pennsylvania, considering these outrageous Proceedings as subversive of the very Fundamentals of Liberty, did determine to support an appeal from the same
to his sacred Majesty in Council, which appeal was accordingly made,
and full accounts of the whole transmitted under the Great Seal of the
Province ; and the said William Smith (who had been a principal
Sufferer in this affair) is now in England to sollicit its speedy Determination which is soon expected ; his Majesty having been graciously
pleas'd to refer it to his Attorney and Solicitor-General, who have
engaged to make their immediate Report thereon.

Now, whereas these things (many of which are of public Notoriety)
have been represented to us by Persons in whom we can well confide,
and whereas the said William Smith is personally known to most of us,
and is placed in a station in America that gives him an Opportunity of
being extensively useful to the Interests of Religion, Learning, and
good Government in those valuable Parts of his Majesty's Dominions,
to which he is about to return, We, whose Names are underwritten,
think that it may contribute to the advancement of those Interests to
confer on him, by your Diploma, the Degree of Doctor in Divinity :
and we beg Leave to recommend him to your Grace and Favour for the
same, not doubting but he will make it the Care of his Life to behave

worthy of so honourable a mark of your Distinction, and the hope we entertain concerning him.

Thos. Cant,
R. Duresme,
John Sarum,
R. Asaph,
J. Glocester,
Z. Oxford.

London, 12th March, 1759.

On the 27th of March, 1759, Dr. Smith, in consequence of the foregoing recommendation, received his diploma.

We have occasionally seen diplomas from our American colleges —those particularly in small towns—where the Latin was a product of the college which conferred them. We doubt whether it would have stood the test of Lilly or old Ruddiman. We give the copy of the diploma from Oxford, and we add to it the copy of one which the Provost had previously received from his *Alma Mater*, the University of Aberdeen. If our own colleges will all confer their degrees in Latin as good as that of either of these degrees, and on persons no less distinguished by ability and learned than William Smith, they will make fewer mistakes than some of them do make.

VICE CANCELLARIUS (vacante Cancellarii munere) Magistri et Scholares Universitatis Oxon : omnibus ad quos hoc præsens scriptum pervenerit ; salutem in Domino sempiternam.

{ Seal of the University. }

Cum eum in finem gradus Academici, a majoribus nostris prudenter instituti fuerint, ut viris qui de Religione, Republica et Literis opitime sint meriti, publici honores decernerentur— Cumque præclarè nobis compertum sit, non modo ex amplissimorum Præsulum testimoniis, perquam honorificis ; verum etiam ex ipsâ rerum gestarum famâ, reverendum et egregium virum *Gulielmum Smith*, ex Academiâ Aberdonensi in Artibus magistrum, et Collegii apud Philadelphiam in Pennsylvaniâ Præpositum ; per complures annos, in provinciis Americanis, ita fuisse versatum, ut omnes sacri concionatoris partes cumulatè adimpleverit, juveniles animos optimarum Artium studiis et disciplinis excoluerit, propriæ etiam eruditionis atque ingenii, plurima exhibuerit specimina : necnon, in gravissimo rerum discrimine, popularibus suis auctor, atque hortator acerrimus, extiterit, ut, contra Gallorum impetus iniquissimos, arma pro Rege, pro Libertate, et communi omnium salute, capesserent ; atque, adeo, cum suo ipsius damno, virum sese bonum, patriæque amantem, ostenderit :—

Nos igitur, hisce rationibus, virique Ornatissimi nominis et virtutis famâ commoti; in frequenti Convocatione doctorum, magistrorum, regentium et non regentium (conspirantibus omnium suffragiis) die vicesimo secundo mensis Martii, Anno Domini millesimo septingentesimo quinquagesimo nono habitâ; eundem egregium virum, *Doctorem in sacra Theologia*, renunciavimus et constituimus; eumque, virtute præsentis Diplomatis, singulis juribus, privilegiis et honoribus, ad istum Gradum quaqua pertinentibus, frui et gaudere, jussimus.

In cujus rei testimonium, Sigillum Universitatis Oxon commune, Præsentibus opponi fecimus.

DATUM in domo nostræ Convocationis, die vicesimo septimo mensis Martii Annoq Domini, prædicto.

DIPLOMA FOR THE DOCTORSHIP OF DIVINITY FROM THE UNIVERSITY OF ABERDEEN.

UNIVERSIS et SINGULIS, in quacunque Dignitate constitutis, quorum hæc nossê interest, Senatus Inclytæ Universitatis et Collegii Regii Aberdonensis, S. I. D. S.

Noveritis nos, ea Auctoritate, quam summi ac potentissimi Principes almæ huic Universitati amplissimam indulsere, Tabellarum præsentium Latorem, Reverendum ac Eruditum Virum, Magistrum GULIELMUM SMITH, Verbi Divini Ministrum, et Academiæ Philadelphiensis Præpositum; SACROSANCTÆ THEOLOGIÆ DOCTOREM et MAGISTRUM constituisse, creâsse, proclamâsse, renunciâsse, ex Senatus Academici Decreto, promovente Reverendo Viro Doctore JOANNE CHALMERS, dicti Collegii Principalis, et S. S. Theologiæ, Professore primario, (Omnibus quæ Dignitatis Ratio, aut Academiæ Consuetudo postulat, rite peractis); Nec non eidem Potestatem fecisse, docendi, legendi, scribendi, commentandi, omniaque id genus alia præstandi, quæ hic aut alibi uspiam S. Th. Doctoribus et Magistris, concedi solent: Omnibusque Honoribus, Dignitatibus, et Privilegiis ipsum afficisse et ornâsse, quibus affici et ornari solent, qui ad illum Dignitatis Gradum, ullibi terrarum legitima Ratione evehuntur. Quod ut felix faustumque sit, Deum ter Opt. Max. comprecamur. In cujus rei fidem, Tabellas hasce, communi Universitatis Sigillo, et Chirographis nostris muniendas curavimus. Aberdoniæ, e dicto Collegio Regio, Anno A. C. M,DCC,LIX, Die vero Mensis Martii decimo.

JO. CHALMERS, Promotor.

> JO. LUMSDEN, S. T. P.
> JO. GREGORY, M. P.
> AL. BURNET, Sub. Principalis.
> THO. GORDON, Hum. Lit. P.
> RODERICUS M'LEOD, P. P.
> THO. REID, P. P.
> GEO. GORDON, L. L. : O O. P. R.
> JO. LESLIE, Gr. L. P.

These were agreeable incidents of his presence in England. But the great matter for which he went abroad was not a University degree. His conviction as a libeller of the Assembly of his Province, and a person who had committed a breach of its privileges, remained of record, unreversed and not annulled, made void and of none effect; which in taking his appeal he was resolved that they should be.

But alas! "the law's delay!" He had foreseen it and here it was. His appeal had been sent to his Majesty in April of 1758, or thereabouts, and graciously referred to his Attorney-General and his Solicitor-General. But there it stayed; neither officer had taken it up. The Attorney-General was infirm, and Dr. Smith was informed by some of those attending the Privy Council, that when applied to despatch this business, he declared that he could not "lose the benefit of the country air during the holidays on any consideration whatever." This was a little like "the insolence of office."

Dr. Smith now prepared a petition to the Attorney-General. He set forth the facts of his case, as we have less perfectly related them on pages 167–180; showed the illegality and public perils of such proceedings as those of the Assembly of Pennsylvania. "The House," he said, "in this mock trial, resolved that what I did was *libel*, and that THEY had power to punish for it. Had they resolved it *High Treason*, they could have punished me as well." He now, in language full of independence, dignity and pathos, proceeds to urge the Crown officers to attend immediately to the subject. After speaking of the delays encountered by him, he says:

I make no doubt, Sir, but a matter of this kind has its Difficulties; and am sensible of the Multiplicity of Business in which your important Station engages you at this time: But what I suffer, and what every zealous friend of the Government may expect to suffer from these People, is no way alleviated thereby. Hard, indeed, would it be if there could be *Right without Remedy*, and if a body of men in any part of his Majesty's Dominions could range at Pleasure thro' the wide Fields of Oppression in any part of Majesty's Dominions, in that old abolished Star Chamber manner, banishing, persecuting and imprisoning his best subjects from year to year, without Jury or any known Process of Law, and no Relief within our Constitution.

Twice have Mr. Moore and I suffered imprisonment on the same score. For no sooner were we released by the Judges of the King's Bench,* in April last, on the adjournment of the house, than they met again, and issued fresh warrants to take us into custody. These, 'tis true, were not then executed, not knowing what might be the Issue of the Affair in England. But having met a 3d time in September last, and hearing that nothing was then done, we were forthwith taken into Custody, and kept till the end of the sessions and annual Dissolution ; where it was thought the affair would rest, and the sentence expire with the house that made it. But herein we were deceived. For no sooner did the new house meet, in November last, than without any new Sentence or Offence, and without requiring any Satisfaction to be made to themselves, *they* also issued warrants to take us into Custody for *not having made Satisfaction to the former House,* altho' we had suffered the alternative of their Sentence, viz. : Imprisonment till the end of their sessions, and entire Dissolution.

Finding no End to these Proceedings, and that I must either be banished from my country or be a Prisoner for Life in it, or—which is still worse—submit to acknowledge in an American Assembly a Power above Law, and contrary to our great Charter of Privileges, I found myself obliged to embark for this Place, where I arrived the first Day of January last, having left Mr. Moore a Prisoner in his own House, and every Lover of Liberty in the Province anxious what might be the Issue of these strange Proceedings. Since I have been here, my Solicitor has been assiduous in representing my case, and I have waited with all becoming Patience, abstaining from every appearance of public appeals or Complaints ; nor do I now come to make any, but to beg & beseech you by the Ties of Humanity, by your Hatred to Oppression, and Love of Justice and Liberty so often signalized, that you will bring this matter to some speedy Issue. I am sure you will think the delay of Justice in any case hard, but in mine it is particularly so. I am driven from my Family and Bread by a Jurisdiction new to us, and am forced to leave a Seminary of Learning with near 300 Scholars that were under my care, as well as a number of Public free schools, with about 700 scholars more, all which must suffer greatly in my Absence ; and, indeed, it is but too obvious that this Persecution of me is intended, if possible, to destroy these useful Institutions and drive me from that country, as the spreading of Knowledge there does not suit the views and Policy of the *Ruling Party.*

In a Word, Sir, such is my present Situation that to stay much longer here would be certain Ruin to all my affairs there ; and to return without some decision in my case would only be continued Imprisonment to me and the ground of more oppression to the rest of the country. In such Circumstances I hope you will not think a few moments of your time ill

---

* He thus designates the Supreme Court of the Province.

bestowed in doing what is in your Power to prevent so much Evil. What it is you can do, it would ill become me so much as to hint. This only I know that at present our assembly are so doubtful of their Conduct that any certain assurance of its being deemed illegal and highly disagreeable to his Majesty, who disdains oppression, would check their Progress effectually. But while they pass uncensured; 'tis hard to say to what Lengths their Boldness may proceed; certain I am that they have no Precedent for their conduct in the Transactions of the British Parliament; or if there be any Similitude to it, it was in warm Times not to be drawn into imitation; and it is also conceived that there is great difference between the august Representative Body of this Nation, acting by virtue of *undenied* Powers co-eval with our Constitution; and these subordinate assemblies, whose Powers were expressly delegated to them by particular Grants for particular Ends; and tho' a Power seemingly above Law might in some Instances be safely vested in so wise and numerous a Body as the British Parliament, who could not be supposed to follow the Dictates or gratify the Revenge of one or two Individuals, yet in these lesser assemblies, which are generally influenced by a very few leading men, every power of this kind (except what is essentially necessary to their Being) will be found dangerous in the highest Degree; all which (earnestly begging your speedy Determination) is humbly submitted by

Sirs, your most obedient humble Servant,

WILLIAM SMITH.

LONDON, April 30th, 1759.

A document like this was likely to have an effect, if any document whatever would have it. The law officers of the Crown took up the case, brought it before the Lords of the Committee of Council for Plantation Affairs, before whom both Dr. Smith and the Assembly of Pennsylvania were heard by Council. The counsel for Dr. Smith presented the arguments which he had presented to the Assembly. We need not repeat them.

In answer to them it was insisted for the Assembly—

"'That all Courts of Justice, and all branches of a Legislative Body, had a right to punish Contempts against themselves, and that the House of Commons in England had always asserted and exercised such right.

"'That the libel in question was a manifest contempt of the authority of the Assembly, arraigning their publick acts, and charging. the whole Body with injustice, oppression, and calumny, and as such, was the highest breach of Privilege, tho' not so called in the charge.

" 'That if it be once admitted that this libel was an Offence of this kind, and properly cognizable by the Assembly, it was highly improper to suffer the point of jurisdiction to be argued, on the nature of the paper to be debated at the Bar, wherein the Assembly had followed the example of the House of Commons in Great Britain.

" 'That according to the reasoning of the Council for the petitioner, as the Assembly, by the laws of Pennsylvania, meet and are dissolved annually, every House of Assembly would be subject to the scandal & abuse of every libeller, who would be content to wait till the dissolution; or if he presumed to insult them even during their sitting, might be sure to escape with impunity, by keeping out of the way till they were dissolved.

" 'That, though the Order to the Sheriff might be irregular, yet that it was made upon a presumption, that if the Writ of Habeas Corpus had issued, the prisoner must have been remanded, because it is a Commitment in Execution, and not bailable.' "

The Attorney & Solicitor-General gave it as their Opinion to the Lords of the Committee, that the paper in question was a libel, and that if it had been published whilst the Assembly was sitting, which it had aspersed, they would have had a right to have punished the authors & publishers thereof. But after that Assembly was dissolved, that kind of Jurisdiction ceased, and that the subsequent Assembly had no right to take up the consideration of this offence as a Contempt to themselves, who were not then in being, and consequently, could not be aimed at, described, or calumniated, by a Libel published before their election.

That this objection appeared upon the face of the warrant of commitment, and that the Distinction had been frequently taken with respect to proceedings for contempt, even by the House of Commons in Great Britain. But that even supposing the jurisdiction of that House in similar cases might be extended further, according to the Law and usage of Parliament, that this extraordinary power ought never to be suffered in inferior Assemblies in America, who were not to be compared, either in power or privileges, to the Commons of Great Britain, and that it was observable that the Assembly themselves had studiously avoided to declare the libel to be a contempt, or breach of Privilege, either in the charge or sentence pronounced, notwithstanding that the contempt to themselves, the then existing Assembly was the only legal, or colourable ground upon which they could take cognizance of the matter, in order to punish the Offender.

And lastly, that they were of Opinion that it was a high and unwarrantable invasion, both of His Majesty's Royal Prerogative, and of the Liberties of the Subject, to order the Sheriff not to Obey His Majesty's Writ of Habeas Corpus, and that, as Mr. Smith was guilty of no offence against any Assembly then in being, and no Assembly had a right to proceed against him for a contempt to any former Assembly; and as the Law had provided sufficient remedy in all cases of illegal and Arbitrary commitments, it was their opinion that the petitioner should be directed to seek redress (as he should be advised), in the proper Courts of Justice, in His Majesty's Province of Pennsylvania; and that His Majesty, if it was His Royal pleasure, might graciously issue His Orders to the Governor of Pennsylvania, to take care that in all Cases, His Majesty's Writ should issue free according to Law, and that all Officers of Justice and others, should be protected in the due Execution of them, and that no person or persons whatsoever, should presume to disobey the same.

The Lords of the Committee, taking the Petition & Report, and the whole matter into their consideration, agreed in opinion with His Majesty's Attorney and Solicitor-General, upon all the points above stated.

On the same day, at White Hall, the Privy Council were assembled. The record of its proceedings yet exists. There were present at the Council the Archbishop of Canterbury, the Lord President, the Earl of Cholmondely, the Earl of Kinnoul, the Viscount Falmouth, and Lord Berkley of Stratton.

A Report from the Lords of the Committee of Council for Plantation Affairs was now read. It gave an account of the whole affair of Mr. Moore and Dr. Smith in substance as we have presented it, and in a great part in the same language; stated the opinion as above given of the Law Officers of the Crown; and their own agreement in opinion with those officers. It ended with a recommendation for a report accordingly, and for proper warning to the Assembly and Governor of Pennsylvania for the future.

The Privy Council, after listening to the whole, give their Judgment and Declaration as follows:

The Lords of his Majesty's most honourable privy Council, this day took the said Report into consideration, and were pleased to approve thereof, and do hereby, in his majesty's name, declare His high displeasure at the unwarrantable behaviour of the House of Representatives of Pennsylvania, in assuming to themselves powers which do not belong to them, and invading both his majesty's Royal Prerogative, and the Liberties of the Subject; and their Lordships do, therefore, hereby order that the Governor, or Commander-in-Chief, for the time being, of the said Province of Pennsylvania, do forthwith signify the same to the said Assembly accordingly, and take the utmost care, and use all the means in his power to support the Laws and His Majesty's Prerogative against all usurpations and encroachments whatsoever, by the Assembly of that Province, at all times and upon all occasions; and that the Governor or Commander-in-Chief, for the time being, do likewise take care that, in all cases, His Majesty's Writs do issue freely according to Law, and do protect all Officers of Justice, and others, in the due execution of them, and that no person or persons, whatsoever, do presume to disobey the same; and that, with regard to the petitioner, their Lordships are hereby further pleased to direct that he do seek redress (as he shall be advised) in the proper Courts of Justice, in the Province of Pennsylvania, whereof the Governor, or Commander-in-Chief, of the said Province of Pennsylvania, for the time being, and all others whom it may concern, are to take notice, and govern themselves accordingly.

Dr. Smith went to his bed that night a happy man. The climate of England agreed with him. Officially, he had been honored. Politically, he had been maintained. In the matter of fact and of law he had been justified. He now got ready to go home: having been in England something over eight months. Soon after his arrival in Philadelphia the Governor of Pennsylvania summoned the Assembly, and sent to them the following polite communication; one which it is probable Dr. Smith and his friends enjoyed quite as much as the Assembly.

MESSAGE FROM THE GOVERNOR.

GENTLEMEN: Having been served by the Reverend Mr. William Smith, Doctor of Divinity, with an order made by his Majesty's most Honourable Privy Council, on the 26th of June last, upon the petition and Appeal of the said William Smith to his Majesty, complaining of Certain Hardships, and Oppressions, alleged to have been suffered by him from the Assembly of this province, for the Year 1758; I herewith lay before you both the said Original Order and the petition of the said Doctor Smith to me thereupon.

And as I am therein commanded, in the King's name, forthwith to signify to you his Majesty's High Displeasure at the unwarrantable behaviour of the said Assembly, in assuming to themselves powers which did not belong to them, and invading both his Majesty's Royal Prerogative, and the Liberties of the people, I do in obedience to the order, hereby signify the same to you accordingly.

JAMES HAMILTON.

February 13th, 1760.

While it may be inferred, from what has been said, that Dr. Smith during his stay in England was much occupied with the matter of his appeal to the Crown, and somewhat also with the collegiate ceremonies incident to his double doctorships—it would be an error to suppose that he was not equally occupied with the interests of his College in Philadelphia. He had been brought into new, strong and valuable relations with men of power, both in Church and State; and he was "sowing," says Dr. Stillé, "the seed which produced a plentiful harvest when he came three years afterwards to England to gather it."

CHAPTER XV.

COMMENCEMENT-DAY, A. D. 1759—VISIT OF THE GOVERNOR TO THE COLLEGE—
NAMES OF SOME OF THE GRADUATES.

THE Commencement-Day of 1759 was the only important event connected with the College which we have to note for that year. The newspapers of the time gave us a pretty full account of it; and at the same time bring before us a vision of antique gentility in style and manners as completely passed away in this our day and land, as has passed away the day in which the scene itself was exhibited.*   The account is thus:

On Tuesday the 11th instant, the honourable James Hamilton, Esq., our Governor, was pleased to visit the College and Academy of this City, whereof his honour is a Trustee, and being received at the Gate, was conducted up to the Experiment Room, to take his Place among

---

* The Commencement-Day of this year was in December, and therefore later than usual. It was deferred until Dr. Smith should have returned. However, not to interrupt a narrative in our next chapter which runs through near two years, we give the account of the Commencement, disregarding order of time.

the other Trustees, who attended him from thence to the public Hall, followed by the Masters, Tutors, Graduates and Students, in orderly Procession; where, being seated, the following Address and congratulatory Verses were delivered, in the Presence of a large Number of the Citizens, viz.:

    1. The *Address*, by the Provost, attended by the rest of the Faculty.

    2. The *Latin Verses*, by the Rev. Jacob Duché, A. B., (public Orator of the College, Assistant Minister of Christ Church, and Chaplain to the Right Hon. the Earl of Stirling) attended by a Deputation from the Graduates and Philosophy Schools.

    3. The *English Verses*, by Mr. William Hamilton, attended by a Deputation from the lower Schools.

THE ADDRESS BY THE PROVOST.

To the Honourable JAMES HAMILTON, Esq., Lieutenant-Governor of the Province of Pennsylvania, and Counties of New Castle, Kent and Sussex, on Delaware. The humble ADDRESS of the FACULTY of the College and Academy of Philadelphia.

MAY IT PLEASE YOUR HONOUR,

We the Provost, Vice-Provost and Professors of the College and Academy of Philadelphia, being met in Faculty, together with the Tutors, Graduates and Scholars of the same, humbly beg Leave to congratulate your Honour, on your second Appointment to the Government of this Province; and to offer our sincerest Wishes that it may be attended with all that Satisfaction to yourself, and Advantage to the Public, which your former *candid* and *uncorrupt* Administration gives us Ground to expect.

No Persons in the Community have greater Reason to rejoice in this Event, than we who are concerned in this Seminary. The Advancement of true Religion and sound Wisdom hath always been considered by every liberal Spirit, as one of the firmest Foundations of good Government and civil Order. The Sciences never had any Enemies but such as have at the same time been Enemies to the human Race; and, in a Country professing Humanity and Gentleness of Manners, the Interests of Learning and Knowledge will be among the last Sacrifices attempted in any Administration.

Our Hearts would suggest much on this Occasion—but we forbear every Retrospect which might damp our present Joy, as we can truly say that the Streams of Knowledge with us have never been polluted, or suffered to deviate from their right Course; so we trust their Sources will never be diminished or dried up, notwithstanding any Attempts for that End, so long as the Love of Virtue and useful Arts is capable of opening or influencing the hearts of Men.

To you, Sir, who are a Trustee of this Seminary, it would be needless to enter into Particulars. Had you not known it to be generous in its

Plan, free in its Constitution, and well-calculated to promote the great Ends of liberal Education, we are very certain that your Name would never have appeared in the List of its Patrons; nor should we now have had the very great Honour of saluting you at once, cloathed with the Authority of Government, and seated in your Place among your Fellow-Trustees here.

It is our Happiness, who now address ourselves more immediately to you, that we have heretofore received Marks of your Approbation; and that the Seminary under our Care hath been continually growing in its Reputation by Means of the many promising Youths, which it hath had the good Fortune to raise. In our several Spheres, we have ever made it our Endeavour, as it is our great Duty, to break through the Fetters of Prejudice; to promote sound Literature in all its Branches; to advance the Interests of true Protestantism and undisguised Christianity; and to propagate an enlightened Zeal for the Public, a steady Loyalty to our gracious King, a thorough Veneration for our excellent Constitution, and a sovereign Regard for Liberty, Laws and civil Order.

In the Continuance of such Pursuits and Endeavours as these, we cannot but expect your Countenance, Sir, who have already given us more—your Example both in public and private Life!

We shall only add, that the Time is approaching (and may it fast approach!) which will put an End to this tedious War; and with it, perhaps, under your prudent Administration, to those domestic Troubles that have been equally prejudicial to the Muses here. Then may we hope that general Benevolence and Harmony will be restored; the interests of Learning flourish, and the Lamp of Knowledge burn brighter and brighter, till its benign Rays have reached and illuminated the remotest Parts of this Continent!

Signed in Name and by Order of the Faculty,

WILLIAM SMITH, *Provost.*

COLLEGE OF PHILADELPHIA, December 11, 1759.

THE LATIN VERSES BY THE REV. JACOB DUCHÉ.

AD VIRUM DIGNISSIMUM JACOBUM HAMILTON, PENSYLVANIÆ PRÆFECTUM, JUVENTUTIS ACADEMICÆ LAUREA DONATÆ & DONANDÆ CARMEN SALUTATORIUM, A REV. JAC. DUCHÉ, A. B. PUB. ORATORE HABITUM. AUTHORE JOAN. BEVERIDGE, A. M. LING. PROFESS.

Nos tibi devoti juvenes, dynasta verende,
Totaque Pieriæ nutrix Academia turbæ,
Jam reduci studiis plausuque assurgimus omnes;
Quæcunque optaris cedant et fausta precamur.
    Multa quidem læti tibi nos debere fatemur
Hactenus, atque agimus memori tibi pectore grates;
Pluraque sed vestri monumenta & pignora amoris
Fas & jura sinunt; quum Rex moderamina rerum

Commisit fascesque sacros, curamque salutis
Communis, statuitque Patres qui fœdere justo
"Aut premere, aut laxas scires dare jussus habenas."
Et merito ; quoniam virtutum lucidus ordo
Circumstat ; decorant stabili constantia vulta,
Intemerata fides, quondam fugitivaque virgo,
Nunc Astræa redux, pretioque potentior omni.
   Ad te confugiunt castæ, tua cura, Camœnæ,
Quas furor insanus, quas implacabilis error,
Invidia, aut asius ficto suo crimina vultu
Dissimulans, metuensque diem, motimine **magno**
Obruere ardebant.   Sed tu tutare jacentes,
Erige languentes, & rebus consule lapsis.
Exitio fœtum, quoties inimica Camœnis
Ora ferox tollat, Lernæum comprime monstrum.
   Sic te Numen amet, sic & Parnassia pubes
Nomen HAMILTONI longum diffundat in ævum ;
Post monumenta dabit multo potiora metallis ;
Quæ neque civilis rabies, neque sera senectus,
Flamma vorax, imbres, neque fracto fulgura cœlo,
Nec furor armorum poterunt abolere nefandus.
   Nunc fore speramus, (quid non sperare licebit
Sub tali auspicio) Pallas quas condidit arces
Ut colat ipsa suas ; studiisque dicata juventus
Floreat æternum ; resonet clamoribus æther,
Plausibus & lætus, tibi quos Helicona colentes
Ingeminent—Audin' ?—Nonne hinc Schulkillius **amnis**,
Hinc Delavarus item, sedesque paterna salutant ?
   Quo feror ?—aut ubi sum ?—Redeo. Te, Satrapa, **grati**
Te curatorem, patremque fatemur amicum.
Ergo tuæ vigili curæ nos, nostraque cuncta
Credimus experti ; neque res erit illa pudori.
   Vive, vale, musis sed vivito semper amicus,
Vive decus patriæ, nostrum decus.—Ite Camœnæ,
Protinus hæc nunquam perituris addite chartis.

THE ENGLISH VERSES BY MR. WILLIAM HAMILTON.*

SPOKEN BY MR. W. HAMILTON, ATTENDED BY A DEPUTATION OF
SCHOLARS FROM THE LOWER SCHOOLS.

Once more we strike the long neglected Lyre—
New Prospects rise, and sudden Transports fire.
Once more we bid bright *Wisdom's* joyous Train,
Fearless advance along the peaceful Plain ;

---

* He was at this time about fourteen years old.

With Wreathes of Roses strew the chearful Way,
And pour from Hearts sincere the rapt'rous Lay,
Bid *Discord* fly, the Rage of *Party* cease,
And hail the glad Return of HAMILTON and Peace.
 O ! Friend to Science, Liberty and Truth,
Patron of Virtue, Arts and rising Youth ;
Indulge our weak Attempts ! with Smiles approve
This humble Boon of Gratitude and Love.
 And you, ye tuneful Sisters, sacred Nine !
'Tis yours with Skill the Laureat Wreath to twine ;
To bid unfading Garlands richly bloom,
And give to honest Praise its best Perfume.
 Haste, gentle Maids, your honour'd Patron greet,
And lay your fragrant Chaplets at his Feet !
Your sprightliest Mien, and brightest Aspect wear—
No *venal* Foe to *polish'd Arts* is here !
Far other Scenes now wake your warmest Joy ;
Far other Thoughts your favourite Chief employ.
Beneath his softer Sway shall Virtue shine,
And Crouds of Vot'ries bend at Wisdom's Shrine !
 Hail, happy Patriot, gen'rous, good and great !
On Thee the Sons of Science humbly wait.
O ! midst the Toils of Rule, and public Care,
Still may we hope thy wonted Smiles to share ;
Still deign to visit this our lov'd Retreat,
Where every Muse has fix'd her every Seat.
So may some Bard sublime, in future Days,
Rise from these Walls, exulting in thy Praise ;
With Hand advent'rous snatch the Trump of Fame,
And give to latest Times thine honour'd Name.

The above Address and congratulatory Verses being delivered, his HONOR was pleased to make the following ANSWER:

GENTLEMEN OF THE FACULTY : I Thank you for this kind Address of your Body, and for the Marks of Regard shewn to me by the Youth educated under your Care.

I should think myself greatly wanting in the Duties of my Station, if I did not countenance every Institution for the Advancement of useful Knowledge : And I am so sensible of the particular good Tendency of this Seminary, whereof I became an early Promoter, that I shall always be happy in affording it every reasonable Degree of Encouragment in my Power.

I am glad to find it growing in Reputation, by Means of the Youths raised in it, and doubt not but it will continue to do so, under the Direction of Gentlemen, who have given unquestionable Proofs of their Capacity, and, on that Account, have received the highest honours from some of the most learned Societies in Great Britain.

Among the graduates for this year were several who became distinguished ; among them Andrew Allen, a member of the Provincial Council, 1769–1775; Attorney-General, 1769; delegate to Congress, 1776: James Allen, described by Graydon, as "a man of wit and pleasantry, and who, for the gratification of his ambition, determined to be a man of business—the only road, in Pennsylvania, to honors and distinction;" Samuel Keene, born A. D. 1724, a clergyman of prominence in the Episcopal Church in Maryland, concerning whom see *infra*, p. 246: William Paca, of Maryland, delegate to Congress, 1774–1779, and *signer of the Declaration of Independence;* State Senator of Maryland, 1777–1779; Chief-Justice of Maryland, 1778–1780; Chief Judge Court of Appeals Maryland, 1780–1782; Governor of Maryland, 1782–1786; Judge of the District Court of the United States, 1789–1799: Samuel Powell, Trustee of the College; Speaker of the Senate of Pennsylvania; Mayor of Philadelphia; who, the Provost Stillé tells us, attended, with Dr. Smith, a levee of George III.

CHAPTER XVI.

Dr. Smith's Return—Birth and Baptism of his First Child, William Moore Smith—The Rev. William Macclanechan—His History, and a Correspondence by and about him, in which Dr. Smith, Macclanechan himself, Eighteen Presbyterian Ministers, and Dr. Secker, Archbishop of Canterbury, participate—St. Paul's Church, in Third street, Philadelphia, founded.

Dr. Smith landed in Philadelphia on the 3d of October, 1759. On the 13th his son, who had been born on the 1st of June previous during his absence, was christened in Christ Church, by the reverend rector, Dr. Jenney; the god-fathers being the Rev. Richard Peters, D. D., and the Rev. Mr. Duché. The child received the name of his mother's father, William Moore.

In a preceding chapter—the one before the last—we had to do with political excitements. We now come to one of an ecclesias-

tical sort; and one which, in its day, made much of a disturbance.
Its effects, too, remained, and perhaps do remain; some of them
good, we may hope; some the reverse of it.   It will be seen with
what vigor Dr. Smith came to the rescue of a venerable, reverend
brother, enfeebled by age and infirmities, and of an honored parish
brought almost to the throes of dissolution from the ambitious
schemes of an ecclesiastical demagogue, who was leading a numerous, though not highly enlightened class in it to insubordination
to the spiritual pastors and masters to whom it was their duty to
submit themselves; not drawing up their minds—as they, with
self-complacence, thought—to heavenly things, at all, but alluring
them, by flowery paths, to a most dangerous downfall.

The Reverend WILLIAM MACCLANECHAN was apparently a native
of Ireland.   He emigrated from that country in 1736, with a
number of Presbyterian families, to Portland, Maine, where he
was installed as their pastor, but his congregation being unable
to support him, he moved to Georgetown, east of Portland, where
he officiated until 1744, when he went to Massachusetts.   He is
found in 1747–8, at Chelsea, until 1754, when he conformed to
the Church of England in Boston.   In the following year he went
to London, and on the recommendation of Governor Shirley, was
there ordained deacon and priest.   He was then appointed Missionary, by the Society for the Propagation of the Gospel, to
Georgetown, in Maine, at which place he remained from May,
1756, to December, 1758, and then went to Virginia, leaving his
family in New England.   After entering into some engagements
with a Parish in Virginia, as he was returning to remove his family from New England there, he was invited to preach in *Christ
Church, Philadelphia;* where he was much admired by a great
number of the Congregation, who seemed desirous of obtaining
for him a settlement in their Church.   The Rev. Dr. ROBERT
JENNEY, the Rector of it, had then, through age and indisposition,
become incapable of much duty.   But he had one Assistant, the
Rev. Mr. Sturgeon; and an application of the Vestry had
been made to the Bishop of London, Dr. Sherlock, in favor
of a young gentleman born and educated in *Philadelphia*—Mr.
JACOB DUCHÉ, requesting his Lordship to ordain him for another
Assistant.

The advocates for Mr. Macclanechan, notwithstanding, insisted on *his* being appointed a Lecturer, or Assistant Extraordinary, offering to support him by private subscription. Accordingly in May, 1759, about seventy-four members of the Congregation applied to Dr. Jenney and the Vestry for that purpose. The Doctor answered, " That he was willing, with the consent of the " Church-Wardens and Vestry, that Mr. Macclanechan should " have the use and liberty of his Pulpit to preach in, *during the* "*pleasure*, of himself, the said Dr. Jenney, the Church-Wardens "and Vestry:" And the Vestry added, that " he shall have this " use, *during pleasure*, as a *Lecturer only.*"

But, on June 19th following, a Majority of the Vestry met, and, the Rector not being present, proceeded " to *fix and establish* the " said Mr. Macclanechan as an *Assistant;*" and they agreed to address the Bishop of London, requesting his Licence for that Purpose, "according," as they said, " to the practice and custom " of this Church in such cases used and approved."

An address was accordingly sent some time after, to the Bishop of London, dated Oct. 3d, 1759, and on the 11th of the same month, Dr. Jenney, joined by most of the Episcopal Clergy in the Province, sent a Counter-Address to the Bishop, setting forth, that his Lordship had already, " on the Application of the Church-Wardens and Vestry, been pleased to ordain and licence the Rev. Mr. Duché (since arrived and settled) as an Assistant with Mr. Sturgeon in Christ Church—that more than two Assistants were unnecessary—that Dr. Jenney's former Consent to Mr. Macclanechan's having the Use of his Pulpit was only *during Pleasure*—that Mr. Macclanechan had since given him and many others Offence, by his railing in the Pulpit against his Brethren, as not preaching the Articles of the Church—and that this and other sufficient causes (which were assigned), had moved him, in conjunction with his Brethren of Pennsylvania, to request his Lordship not to permit Mr. Macclanechan to settle among them."

The Bishop of London, having received both the Address and Counter-Address, refused his Licence to Mr. Macclanechan. But, before this letter had come to hand, Dr. Jenney had sent one to Mr. Macclanechan, forbidding him his Pulpit ; upon this Mr. Macclanechan obtained the use of part of the *State-House* in Philadelphia, and set up a separate Congregation. Dr. Smith in about eight weeks after his arrival in Philadelphia, wrote a long letter to the Archbishop of Canterbury, Dr. Secker, giving him a full account of what had taken place.

Mr. Macclanechan's friends, finding that they could obtain no Countenance from the Bishop of London, but that the Bishop desired Mr. Macclanechan to withdraw from *Philadelphia* to *Virginia*, where his more proper duty lay, also addressed Dr. Secker, professing a regard for the doctrines and Articles of the Church, and setting forth " that they were about to erect a new " Place of Worship, to be called *St. Paul's Church*, and praying " his Grace to take them under his Protection and Patronage, as " the Bishop of *London's* Indisposition rendered him incapable " of Business." EIGHTEEN PRESBYTERIAN MINISTERS, " unsolicited by the gentleman concerned," also addressed the Archbishop praying that Macclanechan might be " inducted " and settled in *Philadelphia.* This address Mr. Macclanechan accompanied by a long letter of his own, complaining of the treatment which he had received from the authorities of Christ Church.

The Church Clergy of Philadelphia, being informed of the Address of the Presbyterian Ministers, applied to their *Synod*, then sitting at Philadelphia, for a Copy of it; and to know who among them subscribed it, or whether it was the Act of their whole Body. The Moderator of the Synod sent a copy of the Address, but declined giving the names of the subscribers, saying it was not a synodical Act, and that the Synod could not answer for the private correspondence of their Members.* The Archbishop, however, in the month of October following, sent over the original Address, in which the names of the subscribers appeared in their own Hand-Writing; and the names became known.

The matter, so painful in its general character, was not without its ridiculous incidents. On the 30th of April, 1760, under the impression that " it might contribute to the general service of religion," Dr. Smith caused " a free and voluntary meeting or Convention " of the clergy " of Pennsylvania and the Provinces

---

* In a Synod of 1761, where Macclanechan's matter came up again, it was observed that Presbyterians did not approve of ministers being " inducted " into churches; " for induction, in a legal sense, is what we disapprove of." " Induction " being a pro- ceeding and term of the Church of England alone, the idea naturally arose that Mr. Macclanechan, or some Church-of-England man, himself drafted the paper which the eighteen Presbyterian ministers, " unsolicited by the gentleman concerned," signed.

annexed," to assemble in Philadelphia. We speak of the Convention further on. He presided. Several clergymen were present; among them the Rev. Mr. Macclanechan, sitting as one of the assistant ministers of Christ Church. A committee was appointed to prepare an "Address" to the Bishop of London; an address, of course, chiefly of form and compliment. The Address was prepared, and Macclanechan, with the other clergy, signed it. Just after this a letter, from an authentic source, and that day received, was laid before the Convention, by which it appeared that the Bishop of London had refused to give a license to Mr. Macclanechan to act as an assistant minister in Christ Church. Upon this it was moved and carried, as the sense of the Convention, that, while Mr. Macclanechan might still sit in the Convention as a clergyman of the Church of England, he could not sit as a representative of the church just named. Macclanechan now asked that his name might be erased from the Address to the Bishop, which he had signed. The Convention refused to let it be erased. Thereupon, Macclanechan bounced up and jerked the Address out of the hands of the Secretary, meaning to tear or cut his own name out. Dr. Smith, who was then thirty-three years old, and at that time of his life distinguished by physical strength, stepped from his Chair, and very quickly, though without exhibiting the strain of a single muscle, pinioned, by pressure, one of Macclanechan's arms to his body, while, with his own two hands, he wrenched open the hand of Macclanechan which was holding the Address, and kept it; the whole operation being performed with as much neatness as if, at Mr. Macclanechan's request, Dr. Smith had been adjusting a sleeve-button. Having thus possessed himself of the manuscript, injured only by a small corner, with a few unimportant words on it, torn off, Dr. Smith resumed his seat, and went on with the duties of the Chair, as if nothing had taken place; Macclanechan, in the meantime, with a very literal observance of Dogberry's rules to his Watch, going out of the room protesting that the Convention was a parcel of crafty and designing men, and that he would have nothing to do with them. " He would take no note of them, but let them go, thanking God that he had got rid of knaves."

It was the wisest thing that he could do.

It may be added that, seeing how violent a man Mr. Macclan-

echan was, and how much in the nature of a mob his followers
were, the Convention appointed a Standing Committee, composed
of Dr. Smith, and the Rev. Messrs. Sturgeon and Duché, to look
after the interests of the Church in Philadelphia; *ne quid detri-
menti capiat.*

We give a few letters on the subject above generally spoken of.
They are not all letters either from or to Dr. Smith; but they are
all letters immediately connected with Dr. Smith's letters, in that
they are all upon subjects on which his letters are written, and in
which he was a principal, and. as we say, the most efficient actor.

Dr. Smith to Archbishop Secker.

PHILADELPHIA, Nov. 27th, 1759.

MY LORD: I did myself the Honour to write to Your Grace by last
New York Packet, and mentioned the surrender of St John's, which I
must now contradict, as a piece of false intelligence ; for the early setting in of the cold weather obliged Genl Amherst to return without
accomplishing his design.   The French still hold that Fort as well as
Montreal, and perhaps may stand it out till next Spring ; but all these
lesser places must soon follow their Capital, *Quebec*.

Having Your Grace's permission and Commands to write at all times
freely about the state of Religion and our Church in these Colonies, I
am sorry that I have so soon occasion to write a very long and, I fear,
disagreeable letter on this head.   But Duty calls, & I hope Your
Grace will ever believe me incapable of any sinister Motive on such an
occasion.

I value Your Grace's favor and protection above every other earthly
Consideration.   It saved me in the worst of times, & from the worst
sort of oppression.   My Antagonists are brought to sufficient confusion,
and he who was like to be borne down, unheard, as a foe to his Country,
is received back again into it, in the more agreeable light of an acknowledged Advocate for Civil Order and public liberty.

Such a happy turn as this accomplished chiefly, My Lord, by Your
Grace's goodness, is not to be repaid by words or single acts, but by
the gratitude of a whole life ; and whenever I am found capable of
making the least unworthy return, or of abusing Your Confidence in a
single instance, I may justly be accounted among the worst of mankind.

Indeed, in the present fatal division in which I found our Church at
my arrival (which I hinted at in my last, and now to give a circumstantial account of,) it is impossible that I should have any particular
interest.   The Church here can do nothing to place me in a more
honorable or advantageous station than I hold at present.   All sides,
since my arrival, have desired my interest, but I have held it most

prudent to take no other public part, except to support the Rev^d D^r. Jenney in his just Orders, and to prevent matters (as far as I can) from running to extremity, till we receive a proper interposition of Your Grace's and our Diocesan's authority, by which alone the matter can be accommodated. As a foundation for such an interposition, I now proceed to my account; which I must begin a considerable way backwards, to give the more perfect idea of the whole.

The Chief Powers of this Government were originally in the Quakers, who were a Majority of the first settlers. But, in process of time, by the accession of men of other persuasions, they not only became a minority; but do not now even exceed one-fifth part of the whole. The number of souls, in this Province & Territories, is thought to be at least 250,000; and the state of Religious Persuasions, agreeable to the best Calculation I can make, from ample materials in my hands, is as follows, viz:

1. Of the Church of England about.................................... 25,000
2. Quakers.. 50,000
3. English, Scotch and Irish Presbyterians, Covenanters, &c.............. 55,000
4. English Anabaptists... 5,000
5. German Anabaptists, or Menonists, and other Quietist Sects........... 30,000
6. German Lutherans, who are well inclined to be incorporated into the Church of England... 35,000
7. Swedish Lutherans, who use the Liturgy & discipline of the Church in most Articles... 5,000
8. German Presbyterians or Calvinists, who style themselves the *Reformed*.. 30,000
9. Roman Catholics, English, Irish and German....................... 10,000
10. Moravians, and a small German Society called Donkers, about......... 5,000

In all... 250,000

Notwithstanding this great disparity, the Quakers still hold the Chief places in the Government, which, from the above state, it is obvious they could not do by their own single interest. They have, therefore, made it their invariable rule (agreeable to the Maxim, *Divide* et *impera*) to divide and distract all other Societies, and to take off some men among them, who have been found mean enough to be so dealt with; and in proportion to the reluctance with which other Societies bear their being excluded from their just share of public Trust, does this subtle political body exert their dividing arts; from which cause proceed most of the confusions and distresses felt by the Ministers & Missionaries of the Church here, and the Continual Clamor kept up against them as *Hirelings*, &c., by this crafty levelling sect, and their Mercenary Adherents.

Now, My Lord, no religious Society here so well deserves the exertion of this Quaker policy, as the Congregation of Christ-Church in this City, which is already numerous enough to fill three large Churches, & consists of many of the most opulent and respectable families in the place. The Quakers, therefore, have always endeavored to get the

Ministers of that Church in the Interest of their unconstitutional policy (knowing the influence it would have on the other Ministers in the Province); and, when that could not be done, to give them as much uneasiness as possible, by stirring up part of their Congregations against them, and rewarding such disturbers with places & other Emoluments; particularly, procuring them to be elected Members of their Provincial Assembly.

The use of these observations will appear immediately, My Lord, for, this being a just view of the Quaker Policy, Your Grace will not wonder that when there is a prospect of a vacancy in so considerable an Office as the *Rectorship* of Christ Church here, that Party should stir themselves to fill it up with a person devoted to their interest, and to exclude every one whom they judge Capable of uniting and Confirming the Congregation in those laudable principles of Religion and Government, which are the Glory of our English Church.

In that light, My Lord, I flatter myself they did me the Honor to consider me, when they first endeavored to foment differences between the Rev. Dr Jenney's Assistant and me, by telling him that it was intended, on the D^{rs} decease, to put me over him in the Church, & offering to support him against me with their whole interest. The poor Credulous Man gave too much Ear to this; notwithstanding that he had little reason to expect to succeed Dr Jenney himself, having neither abilities nor consequence enough for the task, and knew moreover that my station as Head of the College put me above any anxiety about other Preferment here. The story, however, served the ends of the party, to weaken us by jealousies, and was the true cause of the part * Mr. Sturgeon acted during the grand struggle with the Quakers and their adherents about the King's Service and the defence of the Country, throwing himself wholly into the hands of that party, and doing sundry unfriendly things against me at their instigation, such as writing to Your Grace, &c., which I never knew of till my return, and do most heartily forgive him, notwithstanding the unkindness of his conduct in endeavoring to hurt me with Your Grace, at a time when I was so unjustly oppressed in the Cause of public *liberty*, and had no other support but the goodness of that Cause, and the favor of good and discerning men. Nevertheless, I should not so much as mention these things now, were they not connected with my subject, or could they do him any injury. But he has smarted sufficiently for his error, and is fully sensible of it, as the sequel will shew. For no sooner did the party find a man, whom they thought fitter for their purpose than Mr Sturgeon, than they threw him entirely off, and became his bitterest enemies.

---

* I mention Mr. Sturgeon only; for Dr. Jenney, for three years, has been incapable of going abroad, or doing anything but what he was advised to by those about him, who too often imposed upon his weakness.

This happened about last April, while I was in England. One Mr Macclanechan, who had been many years a dissenting Preacher in New England, having on some misunderstanding with his brethren, lately become a Convert to the Church of England, was employed by the Ven^{ble} Society in an itinerant Mission on the Frontiers of that Colony. This Station, however, was not very agreeable to his vagrant temper; for, by the best accounts I can obtain (of which the Society may more certainly inform themselves) he was not very constant in his attendance on his Mission, but was much on the ramble for better preferment. He spent much of his time in and about Boston, affecting the Methodist manner and doctrines to captivate the Multitude, and had his Eye chiefly on Dr Cutler's Congregation, where by reason of the D^{rs} age and infirmities, he had most frequent opportunities of preaching. But his manner becoming at length extremely exceptionable, and his designs being discovered by an application of many of the people to have him settled even during the D^{rs} life, as his Coadjutor and successor, which was like to be attended with much Confusion to that as well as the other Episcopal Congregations there, the Doctor, with much spirit, upon the advice of his brethren, not only rejected the proposal, but refused him any further use of his pulpit, which example was followed by all the other Clergy, which left him no opportunity of doing further hurt there.

The consequence of this was a determination to move Southward, and accordingly he went to Virginia, notwithstanding he was all this while in the pay of the Society. At Virginia he made some agreement to settle in a parish, and the people, in consideration of his pretended poverty and inability to move his family from New England, advanced him Money in bills of Exchange to the value of about £75. With this Money, he was on his way Northward about April last, and called at this City to turn his bills into Cash, where he was asked to preach. The novelty of his manner, his great noise and *extempore* effusions, both in praying and preaching, struck sundry of the lower sort of people, and made the party I have been describing, catch at him eagerly as one providentially sent among them, and much fitter for their purpose than poor Mr Sturgeon; whom they no doubt found too Conscientious to go the lengths they wished, and if they should have succeeded in getting him at the head of the Church, could never have been of much service to them; being but an unengaging preacher, averse to public bustle, and of but indifferent abilities, though otherwise a man of much apparent piety, that has taken much pains in his Office, & where he has erred, I believe was rather led away by bad advice, than any unworthy design in himself.

But, to return, it was accordingly proposed to Mr Macclanechan to lay aside all thoughts of returning to Virginia, and to settle at Philadelphia. To a man who was on the hunt for preferment, this Overture was acceptable enough, and he consented to embrace it, notwithstanding his Contract with the Virginians, his acceptance of their Money, and perhaps his being at the same time in the Society's pay, during all these peregrinations, whereof their own accounts will best inform them. The matter was accordingly proposed to the Vestry here ; but Dr Jenney and they objected that there was no vacancy; that there was one assistant in the Church already, and they had some months before addressed the Lord Bishop of London for another, namely the Rev. Mr Jacob Duche, that amiable Youth whom I had the honor of introducing to your Grace, whose Character stands so high in Clarehall where he finished his studies; a Youth that had been bred up in our College here, born in the bosom of our Church and of the highest expectations that ever any Youth brought into the Ministry; having the most Captivating Eloquence and every engaging accomplishment. They further added, that his arrival, to enter upon his Office, was then every day expected ; that the Church would then be fully supplied during Dr Jenney's life ; that a third assistant was an unusual as well as an unnecessary thing in a single Church; that the funds were already insufficient to maintain the rector and his two Assistants which they had already employed ; that the new Church which they were building would not be ready for some years, and that it was uncertain who the Contributors might be inclined to employ in it ; that Mr Macclanechan was a stranger to every body in this City, and that his manner and doctrines were moreover very exceptionable to the Rector and the principal people in the Congregation.

This did not satisfy the party. They then mustered their whole Force amounting to about 70 persons, signed a paper and came to the Vestry while sitting, insisting that Mr Macclanechan should be employed, and offering to maintain him by private subscription. This number, tho' but a handful compared to the body of the Congregation, took the Vestry off their guard when some of its principal members were absent, and extorted a kind of Conditional promise of granting Mr Macclanechan the occasional use of the Church along with Dr Jenney's two Assistants, till the matter could be otherwise accommodated ; provided he should procure sufficient testimonials of his Character, which was now much questioned on account of two letters received from the Revd Messrs. Brown and Chandler, two worthy Missionaries in New Jersey.

Dr Jenney, however, still refused his assent, declaring that he wanted no other Assistant, and had a particular dislike to Mr Macclanechan ; nor would he leave his Chamber to be present at some of the meetings on this Occasion. This incensed Mr Macclanechan's party; some of the leaders of which found means to force themselves to a Conference with the poor dying gentleman, threatening to keep back all their Pew-Money, out of which his Salary was paid, and to starve him alive if he did not comply ; with other language too insolent & barbarous to be

used by any but such a party, to a poor old servant of the Church, who
had already one foot in the grave. And all this was done with Mr Macclanechan's assent and approbation; the Consequence of which was, as
they pretend, that Dr Jenney gave his Consent to what had been agreed
upon, tho' he himself says he does not know what he did on the occasion, having been so ill-used; nor does it signify, since it was done so
irregularly, and not in a meeting of the Vestry.

Matters being brought so far, Mr Macclanechan proceeded soon after
to New England to bring his family and Certificates; but he brought
none of any moment, but a letter from Messrs Caner and Troutbec; the
purport of which was merely negative, viz., "that they did not know
enough of Mr Macclanechan to give any character of him, but hoped
the people of Philadelphia who had employed him would find no exception to his moral behaviour." This is the substance of all they said,
which he procured from them, under pretence that his settlement at
Philadelphia was already fixed, and that it would be hard and unkind to
disappoint him, by refusing him a few lines from at least some of his
brethren. Such a letter, however, seemed strange from men living in
Boston, who, whatever they might pretend, could not be strangers to
the man who had made so much disturbance in several of their Congregations; and indeed it did Mr Macclanechan no service here, more
especially when it was found that Governor Pownall was so far from
consenting to join in a character of him, that with his own hand he tore
off the Province-Seal from one formerly drawn up. Nor can Mr Caner
be excused for not writing all he knew about him, except by considering
that he was told everything at Philadelphia was concluded upon, & that
it would be only making more disturbance to write the whole matter.
Added to this, perhaps, they were not ill-pleased to get fairly rid of him
at Boston, for it is now known that neither they nor any of the other
Clergy there, had for some time past allowed him any use of their
pulpits.

Lame as this letter was, yet as it contained nothing directly for or
against him, the violence of the party procured his admission into the
Church on his return, which was about the beginning of September, a
week after Mr Duche's arrival, and a month before mine. In drawing up
the Minute of Vestry for his admission, he was artfully called an
Assistant to Dr Jenney, and it was so entered, but without the D^rs joining in it, or any other regular form; every thing being in the utmost
Confusion, and some of the Chief Vestry men absenting themselves.

Soon after this an address was framed to the Bishop of London, for
his Lordship's approbation of Mr Macclanechan's settlement here, and
the extension of his license to this Province. It was intended also that
this address should be an act of the Vestry, but Dr Jenney's absolute refusal to sign it disappointed them. Never at loss, they then called
themselves the Vestry without their Rector, and set forth in the body of

the address that he was consenting to what they did, out by reason of indisposition could not sign his name, which was so far from being true that by the same ship, and on the same day, both the D^r and his Assistants wrote to the Bishop against granting the license to Mr Macclanechan. Several of the leading men of the Vestry were privy to all this, when they suffered the address of Mr Macclanechan to pass them; and their reason for doing it was that they knew it would be ineffectual without the D^rs hand to it, and they thought it best to procure a little temporary quiet, by seeming to Comply; knowing that the Bishop's rejection of the address would enable them to act the proper part when necessary.

So far had matters gone before my arrival, when at New York I received the first notice of them from the Revd Dr Johnson, and the Revd Mr Barclay; who lamented much the distractions of our Church, and gave me some sketch of Mr Macclanechan's Character and behaviour to the Northward; adding that neither they nor any of the Clergy there would allow him their Pulpits, he being an avowed Methodist and follower of Whitfield's plan; occasioning much confusion wherever he came. And, indeed, the first time I heard him open his mouth in the Pulpit, it sufficiently confirmed what they had said. With a huge stature, and voice more than *Stentorian,* up he started before his Sermon; and, instead of modestly using any of the excellent forms provided in our Liturgy, or a form in the nature and substance of that enjoined by the 55th Canon, he addressed the Majesty of heaven with a long Catalogue of epithets, such as "Sin-pardoning, all-seeing, heart-searching, reintrying God"—"*We thank thee that we are all here to-day and not in hell*"—Such an unusual manner in our Church sufficiently fixed my attention, which was exercised by a strange extempore rhapsody of more than 20 minutes, and afterwards a Sermon of about 68 Minutes more; which I think could hardly be religion; for I am sure it was not Common Sense. I have heard him again and again, and still we have the same wild incoherent rhapsodies, of which I can give no account, other than that they consist of a continual ringing the Changes upon the words Regeneration, instantaneous Conversion, imputed Righteousness, the new Birth, &c.—But I find no practical use made of these terms, nor does he offer anything to explain them, or to tell us what he would be at. In short, My Lord, it would make the Ears of a sober Christian tingle to sit and hear such Preachments.

Thus did I find matters at my arrival, the next day after which I waited on Dr Jenney and delivered Your Grace's letter, which I found threw him into tears, & made him cry out he had been much abused by designing men. He did not offer to shew me the Contents, but thanked me for all my past Candor to him; said he would always do me justice while he lived, & hoped I would not join Mr Macclanechan and his party who wanted to take the bread out of his mouth. I told him

15

that he might depend I should do every thing in my power to make him easy while he lived, and to keep the Peace of the Church, which I could appeal to himself I had never offered to disturb, even when used ill by it.   He said that was very true, and he hoped God would bless me for it ; then he proceeded with many tears to report the substance of· what I have set forth above concerning Mr Macclanechan, which seemed to affect him so much that I thought it best to beg his wife to try to compose his Spirits, and found means myself to slip away from him abruptly—His Case is indeed worthy of Compassion, and I am sure I shall slip no opportunity of administering him all the Comfort in my power.

The day following Mr Sturgeon Came to see me, and made very sincere acknowledgments for the part he had been unguardedly led to act against me—A few hours afterwards Mr Macclanechan came also.   He spoke much of his popularity, the *Call* he had from the people to be their Minister, which he pretends gives the only right title.   The Bishop's authority he spoke of very disregardfully, and said it could never bind the people.   I replied that however that matter might be, it was certainly binding on him and me, who were of the *Clergy ;* that the Bishop pretended no authority over the people, but that if he did not think fit to grant his license to any Clergyman, or withdrew it when granted, I presumed that such Clergyman would not be warranted to officiate or enjoy any of the benefits belonging to a Clergyman of the Church of England ; and that, in this light, the Bishop's approbation was necessary to the removal as well as settlement of the Clergy here ; else they were quite independent, and our Church wholly void of discipline.   He hardly seemed to allow this reasoning, and as it was in my own house, I chose to drop the dispute.

When I see him he behaves civilly, but has too little regard to truth in his Conversation, and Continually calumniating his brethren. Several of his party had made repeated attempts to draw me to their side, telling me how easy it might now be to crush Mr Sturgeon, who had formerly been my enemy.   But, as I thank God who has not made me revengeful in my nature, so I tremble at the thoughts of supporting a man who is aiming to intrude himself into the Congregation of another, in a manner that would put an end to all order, and destroy us as a Church here.

This, my Lord, is a faithful account of every thing that I can recollect in this affair worthy Your Grace's notice, in order to give a perfect idea of it.   Nothing now remains but to subjoin Copies of some necessary papers.

In my last I sent Your Grace a copy of the Remonstrance of the Clergy of this Province, drawn up against Mr Macclanechan before my arrival, and a Copy has also been sent to my Lord Bishop of London ; both which I presume having got safe to hand, I shall not now insert it. It was signed by Dr Jenney, his two Assistants Mr Sturgeon and M^r

Duche; by Mr Reading Missionary at Apoquiminink, Mr Neil Missionary at Oxford, Mr Inglis Missionary at Dover, and Mr Carter Missionary at the Bahama Islands, who was here for his health and a witness to all the transactions. It sets forth the manner of Mr Macclanechan's introduction as above, his want of Conformity to the rules and liturgy of the Church, the Confusions he is like to make, the little security any of them will have for the enjoyment of their living if such a precedent is suffered, his violence of temper, the bad light in which he stands with all the Clergy, wherever he has come &c.—

Soon after this remonstrance, Dr Jenney thought it necessary to give the following written Order. The occasion of it was, as set forth in it, owing to the exceeding ill temper of Mr Macclanechan, his disputing duty and precedency with the settled Assistants, & particularly obliging Mr Duche to put off his Surplice when about to assist in administering the holy Sacrament, and that in so indecent a manner that if Mr Duche had not been possessed of the meekest temper, it would have given much scandal on that solemn occasion—

COPY OF DR. JENNEY'S ORDER FOR REGULATING THE DUTY OF HIS CONGREGATION.

November 1st, 1759.

" To the Revd Mr William Sturgeon to be Communicated.

" Forasmuch as it hath pleased Almighty God, by a long Indisposition,
" to render me incapable of officiating to my Congregation in person,
" and I am now supplied with two Assistants, both regularly appointed,
" *licensed* and received, with my approbation and consent, namely the
" Revd Mr Wm Sturgeon, and the Revd Mr Jacob Duché; and whereas
" sometime after the appointment of the latter of my said Assistants and
" his being licensed and approved by the Bishop, agreeable to the joint
" request of me and my Vestry, the Revd Mr Macclanechan was pro-
" posed and with much importunity pressed upon me, as a third Assis-
" tant notwithstanding my *known dislike to the man*, which I sufficiently
" testified by *declining to sign any address to the Bishop* for licensing
" him to this place, seeing neither the necessity for another assistant nor
" the funds for his support, but have nevertheless for peace-sake (on
" hearing that he was to be supported by a private subscription) agreed
" to allow him the *occasional Liberty* of my Pulpit along with my said
" two Assistants, till the Bishop's pleasure is known in this matter;
" which liberty he has abused by disputing precedency with my two
" Assistants aforesaid—

" Now, therefore, as far as in me lies, to prevent any further con-
" fusion and strife, I have thought fit, agreeable to the authority which
" I enjoy as Rector and Incumbent of Christ-Church in this City, and
" vested with the power of an Ordinary in matters merely Ecclesiastical
" therein, to appoint, direct and ordain as follows; viz.

"That the duties of Preaching and reading Prayers in the forenoon
"& afternoon of every Sunday shall be performed alternately by the
"three persons aforesaid; the Revd Mr Sturgeon my first Assistant
"taking the first turn, the Revd Mr Duché my other Assistant taking the
"second, and the Revd Mr Macclanechan aforesaid the third, till the Bish-
"op's Pleasure is known in this matter, or till my further orders therein :
"Provided always, and it is the express condition of this order, that
"every person officiating in my Church Conform himself to the Order
"of Prayer & Rites ecclesiastical as established in our Church, and
"hitherto used in my said Congregation, without either diminishing,
"mixing or adding any thing in the matter or form thereof, or using
"any other prayer before or after Sermon than is well warranted by the
"Canons and Rubrick of the Church : And with respect to the rest of
"the Parochial duty, such as the Administration of the Sacraments and
"so forth, I do ordain that in all cases where Precedency is necessary,
"it shall be in favor of my two settled and licensed Assistants afore-
"said.

"And lastly, whereas the Ven^{ble} Society for propagating the Gospel,
"out of their pious Concern for the Salvation of Souls, and with the
"express approbation of me and my Vestry, do pay an yearly Salary to
"my first Assistant aforesaid, as a *Sunday-Night's* Catechist to the Ne-
"groes, which duty he has been necessarily obliged for some time past
"to discontinue, but is now at leisure to resume the same ; I do therefore
"think it expedient that he do resume the same accordingly, and for
"that end I do appoint him the entire use of my Pulpit on Sunday
"evenings as usual.*   Given under my hand at Philadelphia this day
"& year above said.

"Rob^T Jenney."

The same day that this order was given, and a few hours only afterwards, the following letter was sent to Dr Jenney by Mr Macclanechan's
party, which they hoped would have reached him time enough to
prevent the order, by throwing the blame of all the differences on him
and his Assistants.   The manner in which it is written will convince
your Grace how different the spirit of that party is from that of the D^r
and his friends—

"To the Revd Dr Robert Jenney, Rector of Christ Church &c.

"Rev^D Sir : Since your disability to serve this Congregation in public
"it hath pleased Almighty God to send among us his worthy and pious
"Servant the Revd Mr Macclanechan, whom the members of the Church,
"in Conjunction with the Vestry and your assent heartily received
"and established him to be Your Assistant, and from whose labors we

---

* This part of the Order was necessary, because Mr. Macclanechan & his people
wanted to have the Pulpit on Sunday Evenings for a lecture.

" have the utmost reason to hope for a general reformation of manners ;
" and in consequence of his settlement he continued to officiate to the
" great satisfaction of the Congregation, and a Manifest appearance of
" adding to our numbers—Permit us, Revd Sir, now to acquaint you that
" from the late behaviour of his brethren towards him, and from divers
" reports (which we are averse to believe) you and they treat him in such
" a manner as if you proposed to seclude him from further service among
" us.   The sudden change of the Evening lecture and Service to make
" way for M^r. Sturgeon's Catechetical Lectures to the Negroes, when no
" Negroes were called for, expected or attended is a plain evidence of
" what we fear and apprehend.   Nor can we conceive the necessity of
" taking up the Church on Sunday evening for M^r. Sturgeon to Catechize
" a few Negroes, when wanted for the service of the Congregation,
" which may be equally well done at the School-house, or any other
" private place.

   " Wherefore, Revd Sir, as you cannot serve us yourself, we must pray
" your best Offices to promote harmony and peace among us ; and in
" order thereto we have a right to expect the public as well as private
" good offices of this gentleman, M^r. Macclanechan among us ; and
" rest assured as we pay our Clergy, we have right, and shall insist on
" the service of such who we conceive can serve us.

   " We have been further informed that M^r. Duché the younger yester-
" day forbad * M^r. Macclanechan more to officiate in any parochial
" duties, he not having the Lord Bishop of London's License for so
" doing.   The Report amazes us, and we would hope it is without
" foundation.   But allow us to say, in M^r. Macclanechan's present state
" and settlement among us, we shall ever consider him invested with
" all the powers necessary for the discharge of any duties pertaining to
" his Office, *as fully as if he had his Lordship's License;* and we shall
" consider, support and maintain him accordingly, notwithstanding
" what M^r. Duché or any other can say to the contrary ; his Lordship's
" *License means nothing here, as we humbly apprehend, without a*
" *previous presentation from the people.*   This we insist on, and is what
" the late Lord Bishop of London acknowledged ; and M^r. Duché would
" do well to consider, before he meddles with other men's matters,
" whether he ever had such a presentation from the Congregation"—
        Signed by the same people mostly, that first addressed the
     Vestry in favor of M^r. Macclanechan.†

---

   * This was an invention of Mr. Macclanechan's own ; for Mr. Duché never said
any thing of the kind, but in conversation insisted that no person could be Dr. Jenney's Assistant without his own consent & the Bishop's License or Approbation.

   † A sentence written along the margin in the volume of London Documents, from
which this letter is copied, says : " On receiving this strange paper Dr. Jenney sent for
Mr. Macclanechan to ask if it was delivered with his privity ; and he owned that
it was."

The usual way of settling all Congregations here, where the right of nomination is not in the Governors of the Province, or in the Society, is for the Vestry to recommend and the Bishop to approve: But an independent Right of the people to *call, settle* and *induct*, without any control, was never heard before M^r. Macclanechan brought it with him from the Dissenters and Congregationalists of New England. And indeed, if such a call of the people be necessary, he is on a bad footing; for he has nothing of that kind to shew in his own favor, or to transmit to the Bishop.

Moreover, what these people may pretend about the authority of the Bishop here, the royal Charter of the Province, by which we hold our liberties has put the matter out of doubt. For there, in the very grant of the Province, King Charles the 2nd of blessed memory, makes the Bishop of London's authority, for the time being, absolutely necessary, to the establishment of every Episcopal Congregation; nor would our laws, made in consequence of that Charter, know any Minister to be of the Church, that had not his Lordship's License and approbation.

" Our further pleasure is—that if any of the inhabitants of the said
" Province, to the number of twenty, by writing, or by any person de-
" puted by them, shall signify their desire to the Bishop of London
" for the time being, that any Preacher or Preachers *to be approved* by
" the said Bishop, may be sent unto them for their instruction, that
" then such Preacher or Preachers may reside within the said Province
" &c."

But I shall weary Your Grace with this very tedious account. I shall therefore conclude it with begging Your Grace's directions as soon as may be convenient. Any letter to me will be carefully forwarded, if sent to the Honble Thomas Penn, Esqr, at his house in Spring Garden. I would further beg Your Grace to be pleased to speak with D^r. Nichols, or whoever may have the care of the Affairs of the Bishop of London for the time being; because this account to Your Grace is more circumstantial than any other sent on this occasion.

I hope Your Grace will find cause to advise that M^r. Macclanechan do forbear any further duty in D^r. Jenney's Congregation or during his life, seeing he has intruded himself into it against the Doctor's will, and without a vacancy, as is fully proved by the Doctor's own letters, and the papers he has signed; that the said M^r. Macclanechan do either return to his Mission if the Society think fit to receive him, or go to Virginia, or wherever else he can be provided for in a regular way. This matter, it is hoped, will require no great time for consideration, as every day increases our confusion; nor does any thing farther seem necessary to prove M^r. Macclanechan's intrusion, than the letters and papers signed by the incumbent himself and his brethren, which will admit neither of answer nor palliation. We pray for speedy directions, and that they may be forwarded to such persons as may be thought fit to communicate them faithfully and see them executed. The bearer of this, who comes well recommended for an itinerant Mission in New Jersey, and with sufficient bonds & testimonials from the people, will take great care of any letters he may be trusted with for the Decision of this Affair. But in the meantime I must again request Your Grace's private directions as soon as Convenient. Your Grace may depend on the utmost temper and prudence on our part.

I had some other things to mention to Your Grace; but this has carried me to such a length that I must postpone them to another occasion. I am, with all duty and humility,

Your Grace's ever grateful & obliged
Son & Servant,
WM. SMITH.

His Grace of Canterbury.

P. S. Since concluding the above, D^r. Jenney and M^r. Sturgeon have been so good as to send the annexed paper, to be forwarded to Your Grace; by which it will appear that their too easy attention to some of my enemies, and not any imprudence or warmth of mine, occasioned any misunderstanding that might ever have been between us; which I do not know that it ever proceeded farther than a little jealousy on their part. But with every thing on this head, I have now for ever done, and shall never trouble Your Grace more on that score; hoping that I have done nothing more than a good man, anxious for every thing that affects his Character, ought to have done.*

Indeed it is quite obvious that all the affair in Christ Church was a matter of weakness, jealousy and ambition. Good old Dr. Jenney, who in his years of health and vigor had done true and laudable service in Christ Church, had now become old and was paralyzed. Dr. Smith was a showy orator, a man of charming manners, and Dr. Jenney thought that before death should deliver, Dr. Smith might oust him. Pious Mr. Sturgeon, though probably he did not think more highly of himself than he ought to think, still naturally hoped, in so conservative a cote as Christ Church, that preferment would not by letter and affection go, but

"——By the old gradation, where each second
Stood heir to the first."

He hoped that when, in the order of God's wise Providence, his venerable superior might be gone to his eternal reward, he, Mr.

---

* This postscript doubtless refers to the certificate in Roberdeau's matter and to Dr. Jenney's letter to the Archbishop of Canterbury (See *supra*, pp. 131–185). The annexed paper referred to in the postscript is not found.—EDITOR.

Sturgeon, might himself become the Reverend Rector. He too was jealous, therefore, of Dr. Smith. But behold! As soon as Dr. Smith went to England, where he now was, the Rev. Mr. Macclanechan spies out the prospects of advancement for *somebody* in Christ Church, and gravitates towards Philadelphia, where he alarms and terrifies both Dr. Jenney and Mr. Sturgeon. As we shall see by the sequel, they were both finally indebted to Dr. Smith, whom they had both disliked, been jealous of and sought to injure, for deliverance at last from the jaws of the lion.

Dr. Jenney to the Rev. Mr. Macclanechan.

JUNE 17, 1760.

REV^D SIR: About a twelvemonth ago, having been much solicited by sundry persons in my congregation, I granted you the occasional use of my Pulpit. You must certainly know that the only conditions upon which it was in my power to grant this were your conforming yourself to the Canons and Discipline of our Church, procuring sufficient Testimonials of your former conduct, & obtaining the Lord Bishop of London's License and Approbation for your removal to this place, but tho' you have had sufficient time you have not only produced no such License or Approbation, but on the contrary I am sufficiently assured that your whole conduct is so much disapproved of that you will never obtain any License, so that I might have been well warranted in denying you my Pulpit some time ago. But I must now tell you that your late conduct has been such that even if you were Licensed to preach here, I could not allow you any more use of my Pulpit till I had laid the matter before your Superiors; and therefore you are to take notice that you are henceforth to desist from Preaching in my Church or Congregation. My reasons for this I shall transmit to those who have the proper authority to take cognizance of them.

May God forgive you the disturbances you have made in my Congregation and the uneasinesses you have added to those which the Hand of Heaven and Infirmities of Age had already laid upon me.

Sir, Your Humble Servant,

ROBERT JENNEY.

Dr. Jenney to the Wardens and Vestrymen of Christ Church.

[Enclosing the letter which precedes.]

JUNE 17, 1760.

GENTLEMEN: I take this opportunity of laying before you a Letter which I have this day sent to the Revd Mr Macclanechan notifying my determination of refusing him the further use of my Pulpit and of transmitting the reasons of my conduct to those who have the proper cognizance of them.

To you Gentlemen who have been witnesses to the manner of this man's introduction among us, and the confusions which he has ever since occasioned, it would be needless to say much at present. At the desire of many of you, tho' with much reluctance of mind, I allowed him the occasional use of my Pulpit upon the only conditions on which it was in my power to receive him, namely, his conformity to the canons and discipline of our Church, and his obtaining the approbation and License of the Lord Bishop of London for his settlement here. But with respect to the latter you will see by authentic proofs which I lay before you, in how bad a light he stands with his late employers, the Society at home, & how unlikely it is, that he should ever receive any License or Countenance to settle here. And in regard to his conformity to our Church, it is submitted to you, how agreeable to the canons are his Extemporary Praying & Preaching, his railings and revilings in the Pulpit, his leaving our Church and his duty during the time of divine service, & carrying many of the Congregation with him to other Societies. These things added to his known connexions with those who do not belong to our Church, and have an evident interest in dividing and distracting it, might have long ago justified my withholding my Pulpit from him. But of late his aspersions of the whole Body of our Church and Clergy, their Doctrines and Principles, their Lives & Writings, have been so bold and indiscriminate that I should have thought myself wanting in every duty had I suffered my Pulpit to be any longer employed for such purposes.

I trust therefore that I shall meet with your approbation & support in what I have thought necessary to do for the interest & Preservation of that Church wherein by the Grace of God I have been for fifty years a conscientious & I hope a faithful Minister.

I am, with much regard and esteem

Gentlemen, Your Afflicted

Minister & Faithful Servant,

ROBERT JENNEY.

Minute of the Vestry of Christ Church.

The Vestry taking the foregoing Letter into consideration and knowing the facts therein contained to be true, *Resolved*, that this Vestry do approve of D^r. Jenney's having refused M^r. Macclanechan the use of his Pulpit until the Lord Bishop of London's pleasure be known upon the matter.

A committee which had been appointed by the Convention which we have already mentioned to assist Dr. Jenney in his troubles—Dr. Smith being undoubtedly the author of it, as he was also its effective member—supported him by a certificate as follows :

The Committee upon reading the aforesaid letters took that opportunity of testifying their hearty approbation of the measures which D^r. Jenney had taken in respect to M^r. Macclanechan. They think the Doctor would have been highly to blame had he permitted his pulpit any longer to be made use of for the purposes of railing against our clergy, & thereby weakening and overturning our happy establishments. Were it necessary the Committee could heartily join with D^r. Jenney in vouching for the Facts charged against M^r. Macclanechan, and could of their own knowledge add many others which would sufficiently shew him to be no Friend to our Church & unfit to receive any countenance in it.

WILLIAM SMITH,
WILLIAM STURGEON,
JACOB DUCHÉ.

PHILADELPHIA, June 27th, 1760.

"The Lord Bishop of London's pleasure" and his displeasure both, were soon made known by a letter, which though anterior in date to the two preceding letters, did not arrive in Philadelphia till three days after they had both been written. The Bishop's letter came, of course, as a powerful support to the act of Dr. Jenney, who was now guided largely by Dr. Smith.

The Bishop of London to Dr. Jenney and others.

LONDON, March 25th, 1760.

GENTLEMEN : I am expressly commanded by the lord bishop of London with his hearty commendation to you, to let you know that he has received your several letters and addresses to him relating to the Settlement of ministers in the church of Phil^a, and after having well considered the circumstances of your case, his lordship is firmly of opinion that two assistant ministers are sufficient for your church. Mr. Sturgeon has been many years among you, and has well supplied the duties of the church during the indisposition of your worthy minister, Mr. Jenney ; and now of late, since the duty is increased, his lordship has at your request, ordained a very promising young gentleman, Mr. Duché ; and at your request likewise has licensed him to be another assistant in the same church. In justice, therefore, to those two gentlemen, who have devoted themselves to your service, and in regard to your own recommendations of them, which have been strong in their favor, his lordship thinks proper that they shall be the officiating ministers in Philadelphia, and no other.

In respect to Mr. Macclanechan, his lordship has many reasons why he cannot license him in the parts of Pennsylvania. He was ordained and licensed to a mission in the Society's service, from which he has withdrawn himself in a manner that does him no credit ; since that, he has engaged himself to a parish in Virginia, and has received such marks of their favour that he ought to think himself under obligations to serve them. It is incumbent on him, therefore, to return thither, in order to obtain a proper Settlement from the governor and commissary of that province, in the parish where he may be appointed to serve ; and not to give any disturbance in the congregation where ministers are already settled and established.

Therefore, gentlemen, the bishop desires, and expects it from you that you give Mr. Macclanechan no encouragement to remain in Pennsylvania; but on the contrary that you assist him in removing back again to the place where his duty calls him, and where he ought to be. His lordship orders me to assure you of his hearty good will and affection for you. With his sincere prayers for the welfare and prosperity of your church and country, I am, gentlemen, with the greatest respect and esteem, your most obedient and faithful humble servant,

SAMUEL NICOLS,
Secretary to the Bishop of London.

The vestry directed that Mr. Macclanechan should be furnished with a copy of this letter, and that it should be read in church on the next Sunday morning, the 22d of June.

We come now, in order of date, to the

Letter of Eighteen Presbyterian Ministers to the Archbishop of Canterbury.

PHILADELPHIA, May 24th, 1760.
MAY IT PLEASE YOUR GRACE :

Encouraged by the amiable and excellent character we have had of your Grace as a sincere & catholick Friend to truth & practical Religion, we, ministers of the Presbyterian Denomination in the Province of Pennsylvania, New Jersey & New York, providentially convened in Philadelphia, *Unsolicited by the Gentleman concerned,* beg leave in the most respectful manner to address your Grace in the only way which our distance will admit as Witnesses & Petitioners for what we cannot but account the common cause of Truth & Religion and one of its successful & popular Advocates in these parts, namely, the Revd Wm Macclanechan. This Gentleman has for some time past officiated in Philadelphia as Assistant to the Rev^d D^r. Jenney, and has given such publick specimens of his zeal for the Doctrines of Christianity as contained in the articles of the Church of England, and so remarkable a blessing has attended his ministry in some striking instances of unquestionable Reformation from Vice and Infidelity, that, from what we personally know or have heard of him, we cannot but look upon him as worthy of our warm and hearty recommendation; and we beg leave to assure your Grace that, tho' we will not be accountable for any man's prudentials in every step of his conduct, even in carrying on the best design, nor presume to determine future contingencies, yet it is our humble opinion that his continuing to officiate in Philadelphia will greatly tend to advance our common Christianity; and therefore we most earnestly pray your Grace would use your utmost influence to have him *inducted* and settled in said city.

We are encouraged & even constrained thus far to intermeddle in this affair by our disinterested regard to those fundamental Doctrines of the Christian Religion & Protestant Reformation, in which we are so happy as to agree with that Church over which your Grace presides, & to the cause of Virtue & practical Piety; a Regard so warm & extensive that no differences in lesser matters, nor any selfish attachments to a party can extinguish; and by the candid invitation of the Society for Propagating Christian Knowledge in Foreign Parts, that the Inhabitants of these Plantations would transmit to them such accounts of their Missionaries as might enable them to form a just estimate of their character & conduct. And did your Grace but fully know the circumstances of this affair, you would be sensible that perhaps no application was ever made to your Grace with more unquestionable and self-evident disinterestedness & impartiality. Praying for your Grace's happiness and extensive usefulness, we are, may it please your Grace,

Your Grace's most respectful
and most Humble Servants,

JOHN ROGERS,	JAMES FINLEY,
ABRAHAM KETELAS,	JOHN ROAN,
ABNER BRUSH,	JOHN MOFFAT,
ALEXANDER McWHORTER,	ROBERT SMITH,
ROBERT KENNEDY,	GILBERT TENNENT,
WILLIAM TENNENT,	CHARLES TENNENT,
SAMUEL DAVIES,	JOHN BLAIR,
MOSES TUTTLE,	CHARLES McKNIGHT,
BENJAMIN CHESTNUT,	WILLIAM RAMSEY.

The Synod, as we have stated, disowned the act of these eighteen brethren pressing for the "induction" and settlement of Mr. Macclanechan. Presbyterians did not know what "induction" meant.

With this letter, another, now following—from the Rev. Mr. Macclanechan himself—was sent to the Archbishop.

MAY IT PLEASE YOUR GRACE:

I here present you with a brief Narrative of my Conduct and Circumstances, since I entered into the Gospel Ministry in the Church of England; with a brief and honest Account of the State of Religion in the Plantations, so far as I have been acquainted with it.

In the Year 1755, I went to London for holy Orders, well recommended by [to] many Persons of Distinction, among whom your Lordship was one. I had the Pleasure of being kindly received, by many dignified Clergy of our Church. I was ordained Deacon and Priest, in about a Month after my Arrival, and was appointed an itinerant Missionary on the Eastern Frontiers of the Massachusetts Bay in New-England. The Spring Ships bound for [New] England sailed, before I was ready to take a Passage in one of them; by which Means I was detained above four Months in London. Unwilling to spend my Time idly, and St. Ann's Church, in Lyme house, wanting a Minister, I cheerfully undertook the Duty; and (blessed be God) I laboured not unsuccessfully. And I was warmly invited to continue there. But the poor Inhabitants of the Eastern Frontiers in New-England wanted me more, and I thought had a better Title to me; for which Reason I declined settling in that amiable Church, where Ease, Pleasure, and Profit would have been my Portion; and chose rather, for a Time, to preach the Gospel to the Poor in the Wilderness, where I knew Dangers and Difficulties would await and surround me. During my Stay in London, I preached in sixteen Churches; and the Rev'd Dr. Bearcroft, without my Request, certified that my Behaviour in London was worthy the good Character transmitted from New-England.

I embarked at Gravesend the 8th of August, and arrived at Boston the 10th of October following.

I did not think it safe to move my wife and Eight Children, on the Eve of the Winter, to the Wilderness, especially as there was no Place prepared by the People for my Reception. I therefore brought my Family to Boston, and wintered there. During this Time, I was not forgetful, nor negligent, of my Duty as a Clergyman of the Church of England: I preached at Stoughton, Needham, Watertown and Woburn. These Places enjoyed not the public Worship of God according to our Liturgy: I hope my Labours were not entirely lost in those Places. I was the first Church of England Clergyman that had ever preached in Watertown; and without Vanity, I may say, that I was the Instrument of opening up to the People there the Excellency of our Church Service, and bringing them to be Members of the Church of England. I laid the Foundation; may God enable the Gentleman that is now settled there faithfully and successfully to do his Duty.

As early as I could with Safety, I embarked for Kennebec; where I was kindly received by the poor Inhabitants; and to their Service I entirely devoted myself. I preached twice every Sunday, and frequently on Week Days. I travelled among the People, visiting them, and baptizing their Children, and doing them every good Office in my Power. The War with the French and Indians becoming very hot, I lived in an old dismantled Fort, without Arms, Ammunition or Soldiers ; and there was not an English Inhabitant on the Western Side of Kennebec River, between me and Quebec.

In this Dangerous Situation I continued, travelling not less than 1000 or 1200 Miles every Year, in the Discharge of the several Duties of my sacred Function. I was allowed £50 sterling annually from the Society : A great Part of this Sum I was obliged to spend in maintaining the Men who rowed me from Place to Place ; the Remainder was no Ways sufficient [to] support my Family. I frequently wrote to the Rev'd Dr. Bearcroft, and begged that my difficult and dangerous Circumstances might be laid before the Society. I received several Letters from the Doctor, but no encouragement of being appointed to any other Place. At length, almost worn out with Fatigue, and myself and Family being daily in Jeopardy of being killed or captivated by the cruel Enemy, I resolved to take a Tour to the Southward, and see what Providence would do for me. I took a Passage to Virginia, and there being many vacant Parishes, I was soon appointed to one, where I performed I believe to the Satisfaction of the People. I found I might be provided for in that Colony, and had a Prospect of doing Service ; and therefore thought it my Duty to hasten to the northward, to deliver my Family from the Danger of the common Enemy. I must here beg Leave to inform your Grace that I received no Sum of Money from the Church where I preached, to enable me to bring my Family to that Part, nor even Pay for the Time I served them in my sacred Office. This I am obliged to acquaint You with, because it has been represented to the Lord Bishop of London, that I was under strong Obligations to return to Virginia, because of many generous Donations to support me and my Family. This Report is malicious and false, which will soon appear in a very public Manner. This Digression I thought necessary, because 'tis possible that the same Story has been or may be conveyed to your Grace.

On my Journey to New-England, I arrived at the oppulent City of Philadelphia, where I paid my Compliments to the Rev'd Dr. Jenney, Minister of Christ's Church in that City, and to the Rev'd Mr. Sturgeon, Catechist to the Negroes. The Doctor for a long Time has been incapable of doing Duty in the Church ; and at that Time Mr. Sturgeon happened to be indisposed and incapable of doing Duty. I was invited by the Doctor and Mr. Sturgeon to preach, and I accordingly preached fore and Afternoon, for which I received the Thanks of these Gentlemen. I intended the Tuesday following to have pushed on my Journey, but was persuaded to spend another Sunday with them. Accordingly

I preached fore and Afternoon again, and Mr. Sturgeon read Prayers. On Monday several of the Congregation paid me a Visit, and expressed their very warm Desires, that I should continue for some Time to preach and perform the other Duties of my Function, on Probation, with a View to settle with them ; to which I consented, and proceeded according to an Act of Vestry in my Favour.   The 19th of June the Vestry again met, and with the Advice of the Congregation elected, settled, established and confirmed me an assistant Minister to the Rev'd Dr. Jenney, and voted to address his Lordship the Bishop of London for his Licence to me to this Church, so being I produced good Testimonials of my moral and religious Life in the Places where I had lived.   I procured ample Testimonials of my christian Behaviour, from the People among whom I had laboured in the Society's Service, and from many Gentlemen of Distinction, both of the Church and Presbyterians, who had been acquainted with me for many Years.   These Credentials I laid before the Vestry, who unanimously approved of them, and accordingly wrote a Letter to the Bishop of London for his Licence for me.   I likewise wrote a Letter to his Lordship, and to Dr. Bearcroft, and I doubted not of being favoured with a Licence.   But alas ! While I thought all was well, and had no Mistrust of any Plot or Design against me ; then were the crafty employed, in contriving Means to dissuade his Lordship from sending me his Licence.   God knows what Art and low Cunning they have used, and how they have abused the good old Bishop, and (I doubt not) many other Clergy.   Several Letters and Addresses have been sent to the Bishop of London, as if from the Vestry and Parishioners, recommending strongly the Rev'd Messrs. Sturgeon and Duché as Assistant Ministers to Dr. Jenney, and desiring that I might be dismissed.   This Fallacy, this unparalleled Piece of Perfidy, will in a fair and reputable Manner be laid before your Grace, by a Multitude of the honest and worthy Members of the Church of England in this City. To their clandestine Addresses his Lordship, the Bishop of London, has given great Credit.   For their Request is granted, and Messrs. Sturgeon and Duché are appointed Assistant Ministers to Dr. Jenney, and I am dismissed.   The good Bishop has not thought proper to answer the honest Letter sent to him by the honest Vestry regularly assembled, nor to my Letter.   This is a little surprising, if his Lordship received our Letters ; and as Dr. Bearcroft, to whom they were inclosed, informed me that he forwarded them, I cannot think how they could have miscarried.   However, the one Party is favoured, and their Request granted ; and the other despised and condemned without a hearing. His Lordship's Letter discharges all People from giving any Encouragement to me to live in any Part of this Province, and charges them to assist in moving me to Virginia.   But before this extraordinary Letter arrived, Dr. Jenney, and a Majority of his Vestry, assembled, in three Hours from the Time the Warning was given, and dismissed me ;

declaring that they were well assured that his Lordship's Letter would
be to the same Purpose.

Is this the Reward of my arduous Labours? No. Heaven has, and
will reward me. Have I been often in Danger, by Sea,and Land, and
among the merciless Savages; and am I now in Perils among false
Brethren, of whom I might have expected better? They have done me
much Wrong: the Lord forgive them. I am unwarrantably and cruelly
thrust out of the Church; but, Glory be to God, not out of the Church
of Christ. I am dismissed from this Church, without being allowed to
speak for myself; and the Doors are shut against me for preaching the
Doctrines of the Gospel, the Faith of our holy Church. Blessed be the
Lord, who has thought me worthy to suffer for his Name's Sake.

Ought I then tamely and cowardly to submit to the despotic Act of
this superannuated Ruler with a Majority of the Vestry, many of them
being as much prejudiced against the Articles of our Church, as they are
against me the Preacher of them? Shall I now cease to preach a crucified Christ, according to the Power that was given me, by the Bishop
and Presbyters of the Church of England; when, in my Ordination they
so solemnly laid their Hands on my Head, and I as solemnly promised
(by divine Aid) to preach them, and to banish all strange Doctrines?
No, no; God being my Helper, I will not, I cannot, I dare not. Woe
be to me, if I preach not the Gospel; not with enticing Words of Man's
Wisdom, but in Demonstration of the Spirit and of Power.

One Door has been shut against me; God has opened another. I was
dismissed by the Doctor and Vestry, in Manner aforesaid, on Wednesday; the Bishop's Letter arrived the Saturday following; and I read
Prayers and preached at the State-House on Sunday, to above, perhaps,
Five Thousand Hearers. The Benefit of assembling, in this spacious
Building, for the public Worship of God, we shall enjoy, till the Church
be built, which will be with all possible Expedition.

For this Blow at Christian Liberty makes all good Men pity and help
us. This alas! will render Prelacy contemptible in this Part of the
World: For a free People will ever esteem it their Privilege, to choose
their own Minister; a Right, which they in the Plantations will not
care to give up. Let not my Lord imagine, that I write thus through
Disregard to our Church. God forbid. I am grieved at my very Soul,
that our holy Church, by such an unwarrantable Procedure, is thus
wounded. Let none imagine, that we are about to erect a Church
separate from the Church of England. No; we shall strictly adhere to
her Liturgy, Doctrines and Discipline.

Thus I have informed your Grace of my Conduct and Circumstances,
from my entering into the sacerdotal Office to this Day.

By your Grace's Letter to Dr. Johnson, of which I have had the
Favour of a Copy, I am emboldened to give You an imperfect, but
honest, and melancholly Account of the State of Religion in our
Churches in the Plantations, so far as I am acquainted.

We have in our Churches a Form, but little of the Power, of Godliness; nay, in many Places the Power thereof is derided. Arminianism is become the most fashionable Doctrine, and is highly applauded among us. In short, the Church of England is far from flourishing in the Plantations; and the Cause is very obvious.

Missionaries are sent here to propagate the Gospel, who have never studied Divinity. These are to instruct and guide Souls in the Way to Heaven; these indeed are blind Guides. What will the Consequence be? The Ditch must be their Portion. Is it not a Pity, that such Novices should be sent to instruct poor Sinners, who, instead of endeavouring to convince them of their ruined State by Nature and Practice, preach up the Dignity and Purity of Nature; instead of shewing poor Sinners the Need of a Saviour, they make thems*elves* their own Saviours! How many Clergymen have we in the Plantations, who never had a Thought of entering into the Ministry, till they failed in the Business they were brought up to: Some to the Law, some to Physick, and others to Merchandize or Shop-Keeping! when they could not live by their Employments, being ignorant or imprudent, then their Friends consulted; saying, what shall we do to provide for our poor unhappy Relations? When all Methods failed, then it is proposed; let us procure them Recommendations, and send them home for holy Orders. This melancholly Truth is too plain to be doubted; and Dissenters have Reason to say, that, instead of propagating the Gospel, the Church Clergymen are propagating the Errors of Arminius, and are artfully and industriously introducing Deism.

The Donations of Christian People to the Society are improperly appropriated, not only in being bestowed on Men unfit for the Gospel Ministry, but in appointing Missions, where they have no Claim to the Society's Charity, and in neglecting the Frontiers, East and West; which ought principally to be taken notice of, and provided for.

While I am speaking of the Frontiers, permit me to beg your Grace's Favour in Behalf of the poor Inhabitants on the Eastern Frontiers of the Massachusetts Bay in New-England: Three at least ought to be sent to those Frontiers.

One to George Town and Harpswell, one to Frankfort and Withcossit and Newcastle, and another to Walpole, Harrington, Townsend and Pemmaquid; and indeed a fourth would be necessary at Miesscingquois, Broad Bay and George's. But above all, Care should be taken to send worthy Ministers, of sound Principles and good Morals.

Thus have I plainly and faithfully informed your Grace of the melancholly Condition of Religion in the Churches in these Parts. Were I to give you a particular Account of the erroneous Doctrines which are propagated in the Plantations, it would fill many Sheets.

Your Grace fills the highest Office in the Christian Church, and you are able and likely to do the most good. I have no View but the

16

Enlargement of my Lord and Master's Kingdom; this, by his Grace, I shall labour.

My highest Ambition is, and ever shall be, to win Souls to Christ. I therefore seek Refuge and Protection in your Grace, from that Contempt and Rage to which I am exposed, and which I have undergone, for preaching faithfully the Doctrines of our holy Church.

I humbly beg, that if I am charged with any Crime or Misdemeanor, I may know the Faults of which I am accused, and my Accusers; and have the Liberty of speaking for myself. If I am guilty, let me suffer; but if I am the honest Man and faithful Minister of the Gospel of Jesus Christ, I shall enjoy the Felicity of your Grace's Smiles. This will silence the screaming Owls; this will still the swelling Waves, the rushing Billows and mighty Tempest, that is [*are*] raised against me.

That your Grace may long continue, a great Ornament to Christianity, and an Instrument, in the Hand of our great Lord and Master, of doing much good in his Church, is, may it please your Grace, the hearty Prayer of   Your Grace's dutiful Son

and most obedient Servant,

WM. MACCLANECHAN.

Dr. Smith to Archbishop Secker.

PHILADELPHIA, July 1, 1760.

MY LORD: Before my return from England, the Clergy of this Province had agreed that it might be of Service to Religion & promote Harmony & better acquaintance with one another to hold a free & voluntary Convention at Philadelphia. They accordingly met here May 1, being the time of our public Commencement, and did me the honor of chusing me their President, as D^r. Jenney was unable to discharge that office. And herewith I transmit a copy of their Minutes, together with a humble tender of our Duty in a joint Address, which is enclosed to your Grace.*

On perusal of the minutes your Grace will be pleased to observe that a like friendly meeting is purposed next May; before which I hope to have the Honor of hearing from your Grace, in answer to our said humble Address, that such Meetings, when held only for the purposes of Religion, & conducted with mutual temper and love, without any vain parade, or assuming powers & authorities which we have not, will meet with your Grace's countenance & approbation, as they have also been countenanced by our present worthy Governor and the Government here.

Our last Meeting was productive of the best consequences, in attaching us closely to each other, at the present crisis; and I hope, on the

---

* An account of the Convention, with a Copy of the Addresses, including that of the Archbishop, is given further on. See pages 262–273.

face of our proceedings which lie full and genuine before your Grace, there will appear all the marks of temper and decorum of conduct.   To preserve this at every future Meeting shall be my earnest endeavour, so far as any influence of mine extends.

Along with the minutes of the Meeting or Convention your Grace will receive the Minutes of such transactions as have come before five of us, who were men appointed to be a standing committee to assist and advise D^r. Jenney in his present troubles, and to do such other things as might be for the general good of the Church.   There is also an ample state of the Missions, &^{c}., transmitted by us; all which Papers are sent under cover to D^r. Bearcroft, to be by him presented to your Grace.

I have already troubled your Grace sufficiently on the affair of M^r. Macclanechan, & as I hope this shall be the last time I shall have occasion to mention his Name, I shall briefly lay everything concerning him in one view, from the time of his coming into our Church to the 17th June last, when he left it to set up a private Meeting or Conventicle of his own; that so your Grace may be taken in nothing unprovided or uninformed.   These particulars I am enabled to give by Letters from M^r. Caner and M^r. Apthorp; the former of whom has promised to write to your Grace in confirmation of what he has wrote to me.

M^r. Macclanechan, he tells us, had various Removes among the Presbyterians, owing to his own imprudent and restless Temper, till about four years ago he offered himself to the Church, recommended by M^r. Shirley to the Kennebecque Mission, on account of his robust constitution; to which he was appointed in the beginning of the year 1755, from which time his salary commenced.   While in London he made an acquaintance with D^r. Ward, & got a quantity of his Quack Medicines, with which he embarked, purporting to settle wherever he could in the double capacity of Quack Doctor and Quack Preacher. In his way he stop'd at Halifax and endeavoured to settle himself as a Physician there, as I am informed.   But matters not answering, he left that & got to Boston the September following, near 7 months after his appointment to his Mission.   When he came to Boston, instead of proceeding to Kennebeque, M^r. Caner writes that he took a House on Lease for three years & began to practise as a Physician, pretending to perform extraordinary Cures, by means of certain Nostra.   At the same time D^r. Cutler being indisposed, he made a party to force himself in the D$^{r's}$ congregation.   M^r. Caner seeing this remonstrated to M^r. Macclanechan that he would write to the Society if he did not proceed to his Mission (for which he was receiving his Salary), and forbear disturbing other Congregations.   At length, vizt: the May following, 18 months after his appointment, he went to Kennebeque for the first time. As soon as he was gone, M^r. Caner learned that he was deeply in Debt, which soon brought him back to Boston with a view to take the Benefit of the Act of Insolvency. M^r. Caner, thinking that this would bring a reflexion on the Church, writes me that he once more sought M^r. Macclanechan out (who appeared now only on Sundays), and assured him that if he proceeded in that manner he would be obliged to write to the Society & procure his dismission. He asked what he could do, seeing his creditors prevented his going abroad to discharge the duties of his mission, and his Family were in a suffering condition. M^r. Caner advised him to endeavour to get a Living in the back parts of Maryland or Virginia, where, by good Economy, he might maintain his Family & save something to pay his Debts justly. He took the hint, went to Virginia, made an Agreement for a Cure as he says of £150 ster: p^r ann^m, obtained half a Year's Salary in advance, and was in the way to bring his Family, when unluckily he hit upon this Town, forgot all his engagements to the People of Virginia, as he had before done to the Society, & looking on Philadelphia as a better place to exercise his double profession, determined to settle here. M^r. Caner, by Letter, once more remonstrated to him his want of Talents for such a place as Philadelphia and his unfaithfulness to his former engagement, all to no purpose.

All this happened during my absence in England. As for the rest your Grace has been already informed of it. During the Winter his chief aim was in all his preaching to run down the Clergy and persuade the People that he himself was the only sound Divine. He scarce ever staid to hear any of the other Preachers in our Church, but when it was not his own turn to officiate, went to another Society of Swedes in Town, preached in their meeting & carried his Followers with him, whom he had also brought to hear nobody but himself. When the Presbyterian Synod met he associated much with the New Light part of them, as they are called, & procured an Address from them to your Grace in his favour, a Copy of which with our Letter on the subject is in our Minutes. Whether they have sent the original I know not, but happening to have a larger interest with the members of that Synod than M^r. Macclanechan, having been long connected with the principal men among them (one of whom, D^r. Allison, is Vice-Provost of our College), I obtained a Declaration from their Body disowning their public knowledge of the matter, so that it passed over as a private affair. How many signed it perhaps your Grace will better know; but I think they must have been a small number in comparison of the whole, there being about 50 members at their Synod. By an Address, sent at the desire of a large part of them to D^r. Chandler, he is requested to assure your Grace that they are in good harmony with the regular Ministers of our Church, that they disapprove all meddling in our affairs on the part of their Brethren, and that Gilbert Tennent and others who address in favour of Macclanechan have been long disturbers of their own Societies. The truth of this D^r. Chandler well knows.

Soon after this M^r. Macclanechan preached two such extraordinary
Sermons charging the whole body of our Church & Clergy with Heterodoxy, excepting a few worthy Divines on the other side of the Atlantic
(who, we were made to understand, were persecuted for their *Faith*),
that he lost all the Vestry that had before applied to have him licensed;
and they joined D^r. Jenney in resolving to allow M^r. Macclanechan no
more of the Pulpit to be employed for such purposes, as railing
against our Clergy & Establishment, and so enraged were they, that
tho' the matter had been put on the issue of the Bishop's Letter they
would not wait that issue; being determined that even if he was
licensed they would not sit under such Ministry. The Bishop's Letter,
which was a very full one, came a few days afterwards & was intimated
to him, desiring his removal to perform his engagements in Virginia;
but he refused: and the Quakers, who love to divide in order to rule
our Church & have been at the bottom of all the troubles in it, & particularly the opposition to me, immediately opened their State House or
Public Room where the Assembly meets, in order to give it M^r. Macclanechan; who, in return, does their Business for them in trumpeting
forth the errors of our Church, the Corruption of our Priests, &^c.

The number that followed M^r. Macclanechan from our Church to his
Conventicle are but inconsiderable: & as they were the tools of the
Quaker Party to distract and divide, we think such a purgation a happy
incident. The Church is as crouded as ever on Sundays & great numbers are not able to get Pews. And as for my particular opponents
they are now fairly gone. They are about Building a Place of Worship
for M^r. Macclanechan, and still will be hardly enough to sollicit a
Licence for him, by every misrepresentation of all the regular Clergy
both here & in Boston. But I hope your Grace will think it proper
that such proceedings that tend to destroy all order shall never have
any countenance. The Quakers and their open adherents are the chief
people who contribute to encourage this schism. One of the oldest
Quakers in the Province has procured the Ground on which the House
is to be built, so that by the turn this affair has taken, your Grace has a
fresh proof, were any necessary, that the state I gave of these matters
in all my former representations was just. God, who knows the heart,
sees that I have no self view in these matters. Some of my own
Brethren, by the arts and Jealousy of party, had heretofore been misled
& drawn in to insinuate such things. But they have been convinced by
experience & suffered for their mistake; and if they had now 20 hands
each would subscribe to the truth of what I have said. Indeed I had
much more opportunity of seeing further into these matters than they.
The opposition that was early made to me & to our College, led me to
trace the sources from whence it sprung; & I soon saw that the same
hands were at work to weaken & divide our church by some of her own
unworthy members, who drew many weak people in with them. But it
is time to quit this subject.

The Bearer of this, M^r. Samuel Keene, is of a good family in Maryland, where he is to be provided for in the Church. He is a Youth of as great decorum of character as I have ever met with; prudent, sensible and well accomplish'd in all useful Literature, according to his years. He has had a regular and full Education in our College, of which he is a Bachelor of Arts; and he will give your Grace the utmost satisfaction in every enquiry that your Grace may be pleased to make in respect to the State of Religion and Learning here.*

The Hon'ble James Hamilton, the worthy Governor of this Province, has given me his leave to request that he may be proposed & accepted as a member of the Society, and I hope he may be honour'd with your Grace's approbation. He will give proper directions to his Correspondent in regard to the Present he intends, and his annual Subscription, on which head I have wrote to D^r. Nichols.

Should your Grace find leisure to honour me with any commands, M^r. Penn will take care of the Conveyance, unless there should be some particular person bound thither. I have not yet had the Honour of anything immediately from your Grace since I left England.

I am, may it please your Grace,

Your Grace's most dutiful Son & Servant,

WILLIAM SMITH.

From Archbishop Secker to the Rev. Mr. Macclanechan.

LAMBETH, October 9th, 1760.

SIR: I received, on the 23d of August, a Letter from you; and another from several Persons at Philadelphia, who profess themselves to be Members of the Church of England, and desirous of having you for their Minister. When they were written is not expressed. I received also, at the same Time, a Letter in your Favour, dated May 24th, 1760, from Eighteen Presbyterian Ministers, convened at Philadelphia. Why any of these have been sent to me, I know not. The Superintendency of the Church at Philadelphia belongs neither to me, as Archbishop of Canterbury, nor to the Society for Propagating the Gospel, of which I am President: But hath always been exercised by the Bishop of London. And he is well known to be very capable of Business, though the Writers

---

* *Samuel Keene*, D.D., to whom, on page 214, we have before referred, was a native of St. Paul's, Baltimore county, Md., brought up in the church, ordained in 1760, and became the incumbent of St. Ann's, Annapolis; in 1767, of St. Luke's, Queen Ann's Co.; in 1779, Rector of Chester Parish, Kent Co.; in 1781, of St. John's, Queen Ann's Co.; in 1783, of Dorchester Parish, Dorchester Co.; in 1791, of St. Luke's, Queen Ann's, and in 1805, of St. Michael's, Talbot Co.; a member of the Examining, Superintending and Standing Committees; delegate to the General Convention, and visitor of Washington College; died in 1810, *Anno Æt.* 76, Whig.— *Allen's Maryland Clergy.*

of the second Letter above deny it.   But even were he incapable, the Application made to me would be irregular.   However, I would willingly hope that it doth not proceed from Disregard to that venerable Person, or from Inclination to throw Things into Disorder ; or from any worse Cause than Inconsiderateness, or Want of right Information.   If good Opinion of me in any Respect hath contributed to produce it, I wish I deserved it better ; and shall be heartily glad, if it produces also a serious Attention to what I shall now, for the Sake of Religion, and of all Parties concerned, say on the Subject.   Though I have neither Leisure nor Desire to intermeddle in other Men's Matters, They, who have called me to it, I trust will excuse me for it.

Previously to the Business now in Question, you speak of your Behaviour as a Missionary ; and I follow you in that the more readily, as it relates to the Society.   You were appointed March 21st, 1755 : And your Salary commenced from Christmas preceding : But you did not embark for America till August.   You say it was for want of a Ship : And I make no objection, though the Time seems long.   You landed at Boston October 10th, and there you stayed till May following, because you did not think it safe to carry your Family on the Eve of Winter to the Place of your Mission, where no House was provided for you.   But might not you have gone without your Family, as you did at last, no House being still provided for you ?   However, I pass over this also. Nor will I enter into what hath been reported of your hiring a House at Boston for a year, some say for Three Years, as if you proposed to fix there ; or of your attempting to procure a Settlement in Dr. Cutler's Church, till you were forbidden his Pulpit.   The Society, on Complaint of your Delays, had stopt your Salary : but on your Writing from your Mission, promising Diligence, and expressing your Hope to be continued, they restored it, December, 1756.   And on your requesting, not, as you say, frequently, but twice—June and October, 1758—to be removed, they ordered you £10 each Time, as an Encouragement to stay ; fearing from your Representation, that a Successor of sufficient Resolution and Activity could not easily be got.   The People of Frankfort say, that you stayed with them but till December, 1758 ; and it was not till the Middle of that Month that your first Request to be removed came before the Society.   So that you did not wait to see whether they would remove you or not, though your Followers, in their Letter to me, say, that you patiently waited for an answer, without Effect, for a long Time. You first went to Virginia, of which I shall take Notice afterwards ; then to Philadelphia ; From which City you sent, June 22d, 1759, your first Notification to the Society of your resigning your Mission, and desired to have your Salary paid till Midsummer, alledging that it wanted but Two Days of the Time.   This the Society granted of Course ; not suspecting that you had left the place of your Mission Six Months before, which you ought fairly to have told them.   And thus you received your

Salary for Four years and a half, besides Gratuities of £20, and were but Two years and a half upon your Mission.

At Philadelphia the Vestry chose you, about Seven Weeks after your Arrival, Assistant to Dr. Jenney. And by accepting their Choice, you appear to have understood that the Right of Chusing was in them. Then You and They applied to the Bishop of London for a Licence to authorize you to officiate as such. And by so doing you acknowledged that their Choice was ineffectual without his Confirmation of it, which accordingly you call a Favour. Now it being a Favour, he might refuse it. And therefore, since he hath refused it, you ought to acquiesce in his Refusal.

But you say it was procured by God knows what Art and low Cunning; that several Letters were sent to him, as if from the Vestry and Parishioners, recommending strongly M^r. Sturgeon and M^r. Duché as Assistant Ministers, and desiring that you might be dismissed; that this Fallacy, this unparalleled Piece of Perfidy will be laid before me in a fair and reputable Manner, by a Multitude of Members of the Church; that the Request of these clandestine Addresses hath been granted, M^r. Sturgeon and M^r. Duché appointed, and you dismissed. Now I cannot learn, upon Inquiry, that any one such Letter was written to the Bishop, as from the Vestry and Parishioners. And if any was written by others, they might at least have as good a Right to remonstrate against You to Him, as You have to remonstrate against the American Clergy in general to me: Nor was their Letter any more clandestine, than yours. Nor hath he grounded his Refusal on their Remonstrance. Nor could the Two Gentlemen before mentioned be recommended to him now as Assistants, and appointed by him on that Recommendation; because M^r. Sturgeon was appointed long ago,* and M^r. Duché was recommended before you came to Philadelphia, which You could scarcely fail to know, though You write as if both these Things were quite otherwise. What You mean, therefore, by charging any Persons with unparalleled Perfidy, or even with Fallacy, on this Occasion, I cannot guess. For surely You have not poor D^r. Jenney in View, who can only be charged with Weakness, and that in your Favour. He granted you, as he saith himself, the occasional Use of his Pulpit with great Reluctance of Mind, being much solicited; but others say, terrified by the Violence of your Party. However, seeing more of You afterward, and recovering Courage, he refused to sign the Application for a Licence, and signified to the Bishop that he disapproved you. I see no crime in this. And I am sure that your Followers, to whom you refer me, have not laid before me any Perfidy or Fallacy of any one: But have only asserted, without attempting to prove, or intimating their Reasons for believing it, that many have endeavoured to poison the Mind

---

* Mr. Sturgeon had been Assistant Minister to Dr. Jenney ever since 1747.

of the Bishop by a Misrepresentation of Facts.   Now considering how excessively angry You are apt to be, when any Thing is charged upon You; surely you ought to be very careful, and exhort those whom you have taken under your Direction, to be very careful never to charge others at Random.

His refusing to licence you was the legal Exercise of a discretionary Power, vested in him.   And he is not bound to set forth the Reasons why he exercised it in this Manner.   He hath, however, set forth in D^r. Nicholl's Letter one Reason, which supersedes the Need of any others.*   That the Church was already provided with two Assistants, approved by it and licenced by him, and wanted no more.   To this he hath added, that you had engaged yourself to a Parish in Virginia, which your Adherents, in their Letter to me, deny; upon whose Information they deny it, unless your own, I know not.   Yet you say, that you were appointed to a Parish there, which was scarce done without some Engagement on your Part.   He further adds, that you had received such Marks of Favour—meaning probably in Money, though that is not expressed—that you ought to think yourself obliged to serve them. But you affirm that you received no Money from the Church where you preached; either to enable You to bring your Family thither, or to pay for your Services there.   Whether you received any from any particular Members of the Church, or other Persons in those Parts, on either of these, or any like Accounts, You do not say.   Nor do I say more than this: That I wonder how the Report should prevail, if nothing passed to give Rise to it; that the Bishop's preceding Objection against licencing You was sufficient, whatever becomes of the Present; and that supposing You had not engaged yourself in Virginia, still it was much fitter You should go thither, where You say there were many vacant Parishes, than stay at Philadelphia, where every Place was filled.

Besides these Reasons, the Bishop signifies that he had others: but specifies no others, excepting that you had withdrawn yourself from the Society's Service, in a Manner that did You no Credit; of which I have spoken before.   Probably he thought it a further Reason, and surely with good Cause, that D^r. Jenney had not put his Name to the Recommendation from the Vestry.   But if he credited any Thing written to him against You, besides what I have just now mentioned, he hath had so much Tenderness for you, as to decline expressing it.   For which you make him an ill Return, in saying that he hath condemned You and your Party without a Hearing.   Whereas in Truth he hath heard You; that is, he hath taken Notice of all that you laid before him, and hath not condemned You, only he hath thought your Request unreasonable. He hath also at the same time very kindly proposed, not only that You should be settled in Virginia, which I presume would be a very comfort-

---

* See this letter *supra*, p. 234.

able Settlement, but likewise that the Church of Philadelphia should assist you in moving thither.   This last, indeed, you seem to represent, as if he had required that they should assist in moving You thither against your Will.   But I hope you could not mean to pervert his Intention so unthankfully and unfairly.

You say that what he hath done will, alas, render Prelacy very contemptible in your Part of the World.   Now I can neither see, that he hath done any Thing amiss, nor apprehend, that the refusal of one Licence by one Prelate, were it ever so unjustifiable, would render Prelacy itself contemptible in any Part of the World.   He who thinks it will, must entertain a very mean Opinion of it, how much soever he may profess to be concerned for it.   But on the other Hand, denying a Bishop's Right to refuse a Licence, or maintaining that his Presbyters may officiate where they please, and even from new Churches without it, is rendering episcopal Government contemptible indeed.

You say, that You are cruelly and unwarrantably thrust out of the Church, meaning Dr. Jenney's.   Now from what he and others have said, I rather conceive, that cruel and unwarrantable Steps have been taken to thrust You into it.   But certainly you were not thrust out. For You were never legally admitted.   And now the Vestry, which had once approved you, on further Trial disapproves You.   I think only Two, out of the Fifteen who recommended you, have subscribed the Letter, written to me, as still adhering to you.   You alledged indeed, that the Vestry, which disapproved you, had only three Hours Notice of the Meeting.   But however that be, the Majority of the whole must have been satisfied with what was done, else unquestionably the Vote, then passed, would before now have been repealed.   You alledge also, that the Vestry agreed to your Dismission before the Bishop's Letter came. But you own that they declared they did it, on being well assured, as the Event shewed they were, that the Bishop would not Licence you. There are likewise other Reasons for your Dismission, given by Dr. Jenney, and allowed by the vestry; Which you have doubtless seen in his Letter to them, though you have not chosen to mention them in your Letter to me: And which ought to have restrained you effectually from calling it, as you do, very unbecomingly, the despotic Act of a superannuated Ruler.

He saith, that your extemporary Prayers and Preaching are not agreeable to the Canons.   Now the 55th Canon requires, that before Sermon the Minister shall move the People to join with him in Prayer, in the Form or to the Effect there expressed, as briefly as conveniently may be. And if, instead of that, he makes a long Prayer, or one in a different Form and to a different Effect, he disobeys the Canon.   And from such Disobedience very great Mischiefs have arisen in the Church, and may again.   Next to such Liberties taken in Prayer, those of extempore Sermons are dangerous, unless the Preacher be very prudent, and mild in his Temper. For the Passions of other Preachers hurry them to say Things, which it may be hoped they would not, were they to consider them previously. Or at least their Discourse being written by them, would testify concerning itself. And the 53^d Canon directs, that "if any Preacher shall particularly and of Purpose oppose or argue against any Doctrine, delivered by another Preacher, in the same or a neighbouring Church, without the Bishop's Order, the Church Wardens or Party grieved shall, because upon this there may grow much Offence and Disquietness, signify it to the Bishop, and not suffer him to preach any more, unless he promise to forbear such Matter of Contention, till the Bishop's further Order." Now Dr. Jenney affirms, and the Vestry admits, that You have done worse, than what is here restrained ; that you have used "Railings and Revilings in the Pulpit;" and boldly and indiscriminately aspersed "the whole Body of our Church and Clergy, their Doctrines and Principles, their Lives and Writings;" and made Disturbances ever since You were admitted. These things undoubtedly you will deny; nor do I assert them. But many Persons of very good Credit, both Clergymen and Laymen, who had sufficient Opportunities of knowing, assert them. And as the Governors of the Parish saw your Behavior in this Light, what could they do less, than forbid your Preaching again till the Bishop's Pleasure should be known? Would you in their Case have done less? And more they did not.

You maintain, that dismissing you is a Blow at Christian Liberty And your Followers profess to be alarmed on this Occasion for their religious Rights and Privileges, in which their Peace on Earth, and their everlasting Welfare are most intimately concerned. Yet neither You nor they directly specify what Branch of this Liberty or of these Rights, You apprehend to be endangered. I presume, however, that the Meaning of both is intimated in those words of yours, that a free people will ever esteem it their Privilege to chuse their own Minister ; a Right, which they in the Plantations will not care to give up. But where in Scripture do you find this declared, either to be a Part of Christian Liberty, or a Right of the Christian Laity? Or where do our Laws make it the Privilege of a free People? If it were, they would soon find Cause to grow weary of it. But scarce any Parishes in England or Ireland chuse their Parish Minister. I believe, few episcopal Congregations in America do; and I am told, that of Philadelphia doth not. Lecturers indeed, who are Assistant Ministers, the People often chuse; Only their Choice is of no Avail, unless the Incumbent and Bishop approve it. But in Dr. Jenney's Church, I conceive, the Vestry are authorized to act for the People in the Choice of an Assistant. Else why were You chosen by the Vestry? And have they not the same power to vote against You, as to vote in your Favour? You were never chosen by the People. And therefore, if they have the sole Right of chusing, You were never duly chosen at all. You will say perhaps, what your Adherents say, that the Majority of the Congregation is for you.   But the other side say the contrary: And there is no regular Method of putting this Question to the Trial.   But if there were: Suppose you were settled, as Incumbent of a Parish, with two Assistants, and thought you wanted no more; but some of your People had a Mind to a third; Would you think it right, that they should put it to the Vote, whether you should have a third, and whether it should not be such a particular Person; and that they should fix that particular Person upon you, against your Liking, and against the Liking of the Bishop, agreeing with you?   I presume not.

But suppose further, that a Number of your Parishioners, not being able to carry their favourite Point, should break off from your Church, and set up another; would You think this right also?   Let your Conscience speak.   Your Adherents desire me, that they may not be stigmatized with the opprobrious Names of Schismatics, Separatists, &c. &c. I am not disposed to give harsh Names: But indeed I can give no good one to such Practices, as theirs.   If Persons may withdraw from a Congregation, of which they are Members, merely because they cannot get some Person, whom they have in Admiration, to be appointed an Assistant in it; how many other Pretences for withdrawing may they and others make with equal Reason; and what End can there be to Divisions and Confusions?

Yet your Followers profess great Zeal for the Peace of the Church. And you profess great grief, that it is wounded; and declare in your own Name, and theirs, that You will strictly adhere, not only to the Liturgy and Doctrines, but to the Discipline of the Church of England. Pray, Sir, consider.   Can you adhere to the Discipline of the Church of England whilst you act in Defiance of the Bishop, the Minister of the Parish, and the Vestry, on Principles that tend to the Dissolution of all Churches, and the Subversion of all ecclesiastical Order?   How could such an Imagination come into your Mind?   And how can You request me to countenance such Proceedings?

But, it seems, You have a further, and much mightier Plea to make. You affirm that the Doors are shut against you for teaching the Doctrines of the Gospel: And intimate, that you are required to cease from preaching a crucified Christ though the Bishop had given you Power to do it; and though you had solemnly promised at your Ordination, that you would do it, and would banish all strange Doctrines.   But consider: The Power given You was "to preach the Word of God . . . . in the Congregation, where you should be lawfully appointed thereunto." Now you have not been lawfully appointed to preach statedly at Philadelphia.   And why could not your Promise have been as well and better performed in Virginia, where you might have been lawfully appointed? Consider further: On what Grounds do you affirm, that the Doors are shut against you for teaching the Doctrines of the Gospel?   I hope you do not account your Bishop an Enemy to them: And besides, his Reasons for declining to licence You are not in the least founded on the Doctrines, which you teach. Nor, I believe, have you been charged in any Letter to him, nor certainly are you charged in Dr. Jenney's Letter to the Vestry on your Dismission, with false Tenets, but with railing Accusations. And of this Charge You have in your Letter to me, gone a great way towards proving yourself guilty.

You say, many of the Vestry are as much prejudiced against the Articles of our Church, as they are against You the Preacher of them. Now I suppose You preached them from the first. Yet they do not appear to have disliked you till a considerable Time after. And therefore it must be presumed, that not your preaching the Doctrine of the Articles, but other Things produced their Dislike. By calling yourself the Preacher of the Articles, You seem to think yourself the only Preacher of them in that Church. And accordingly your Followers say, that excluding You, forces them to hear Men whose Doctrines, not being agreeable to the Articles of the Church, cannot please, nor their Lessons convey Instruction. Now they made no such Complaint of their Ministers before: So that you must probably have been, as Dr. Jenney's Letter represents you to be, the Accuser of your Brethren. And were this Accusation proved, your request might have been carried further: That they should be expelled or silenced, as well as You admitted. But no proof is produced: Nor do any other Persons join with your new Congregation in the Charge. Even the Presbyterian Ministers, whom I mentioned at first, have abstained from doing that. They recommend you indeed (and I hope interfered so far with a good Design) as a peculiarly useful Preacher. But whether from their own Knowledge, or from whose Information, they have omitted to express. And I understand, that they were by far the smaller part of the Assembly.

You say, one Door has been shut against you, but God hath opened another. And he hath, indeed, permitted another to be opened; But he permits many unjustifiable things to be done. You observe to me, seemingly with great Pleasure, that in four Days after your Dismission by the Vestry, and the very next Day after the Bishop's Letter of Refusal came, You preached to a large Audience. Surely you should rather have feared to take so very hasty a step, which looked so undutiful, and threatened such Disorders. You say, that all good Men pity and help you and your Party. If so, there are no good Men amongst your Opposers: But they deserve a still worse name than that of Screaming Owls, which you have given them. Do you really think that? Your Adherents boast of the Promise of the most generous and charitable Aid of the People of every Denomination, towards building you a church: Which, they assure me, arises from their being Witnesses to the whole Transaction, and to the unkind Treatment which you have received, and from a real Concern for Religion in general. They likewise mention it as an irrefragable Proof, not only of your Popularity, but of your Importance to the Cause of Religion in Philadelphia, that the Representatives of the People have favored you with the occasional Use of the State-House, and that you are still followed by a Multitude of People of all Denominations. Now certainly few or none of these have been Witnesses to the whole, or any great Part, of what hath been transacted chiefly in Vestries and Letters: But must have taken up with Reports; in spreading of which, the Ignorant and the Partial are usually the busiest and the loudest. I am very sensible that a Minister of the Gospel should have a good Report of them which are without But mere good Opinion I apprehend, would not excite in the Breasts of Dissenters of all Sorts at once so very warm a Zeal in favour of a Minister of the Church of England, as they are said to shew at present, without his taking some undue Methods of courting them, or their hoping to gain some Advantage to their common Interest, by such Behavior. These several Sects, differing so widely from us and from one another, cannot all of them approve your Doctrines ; and therefore it is not for your Doctrines, that they applaud you. I would not think uncharitably of any of them: But I cannot help remarking, how much more Charity your Followers have for them, than for the Ministers and Members of the Church, which they have left. The latter, they suspect, do every thing from a wrong Principle: The former, they are clear, do every thing from a right one. But is it not very natural to imagine, that a large Proportion of these Multitudes may flock after you solely from an idle Curiosity, and Fondness of Novelty? And that more than a few may encourage you, because they promise themselves, that dividing our Church at Philadelphia will weaken, if not overturn it; and perhaps promote their political Views at the same time? Ought you not to suspect the Promises, and even the Gifts of such: Nay, to suspect your own Cause for being supported by them, instead of glorying in that support? And ought it not to give you a further Distrust of your Proceedings, that no one Clergyman of the Church of England in America hath declared himself to approve them: And that the Convention of Clergymen, which met at Philadelphia last May, have strongly expressed their Disapprobation of your Behavior both in that Convention and out of it ; and have signified, that they would not suffer You to preach in any of their Pulpits? Which is the more probable Presumption of the Two? That You are in the wrong, or that all the rest of the Clergy are?

Indeed if your own Account of yourself and them is to be taken, the whole Body of them is not to be put in Competition with you. For you tell me, in general and definite Terms, that Missionaries are sent over to propagate the Gospel, who have never studied Divinity, but are Novices; who instead of convincing Men of their ruined State by Nature and Practice, preach up the Dignity and Purity of Nature ; and instead of shewing poor Sinners their Need of a Saviour make themselves their own Saviours.   You speak of many Clergymen in the Plantations, who never had a Thought of entering into the Ministry, till they failed through Ignorance or Imprudence, in the Business to which they were brought up, and then were sent home for Holy Orders.   And you add, that Dissenters have good Reason to say, that instead of propagating the Gospel, the Church Clergymen are propagating the Errors of Arminius, and are artfully and industriously introducing Deism.   You do not indeed directly assert, that all besides yourself, are such: But You make no Exception; nor even hint that there is a single one.   Pray, Sir, reflect a little: Can these be the Words cf Truth and Soberness?   I hope and believe, that even the Dissenters, whom You quote on this Occasion, I mean the more considerable Part of them, would not express themselves so harshly and crudely about the Clergy, as you do. Some are sent Missionaries when they are young, and possibly you might be as young when you had your first Ordination.*   Some are less qualified than we could wish: But however, they appear upon Examination not unqualified.

We send the best we can: We promise ourselves, that they will improve: And we question, whether you can direct us, at least no Body hath yet directed us, where to get better.   We have sent out many excellent ones: And there are many such now.   That any Americans have failed in secular Employments, and then come hither for Orders I never heard before: And that any of our Missionaries have I do not think.   They come usually from the Colleges in those Parts: They come always well recommended.   We must act upon Recommendations: And it would be much righter to caution us against unfit Persons, when they offer themselves, than to reproach us with them afterwards.   I trust, that none of our Clergy in America are such in Point of Doctrine, as you make the Generality of them to be.   But of this I am sure, that the contrary ought to be presumed concerning them all: that it appears concerning several of them from what they have written: And that since we are directed by the Apostle, "against an Elder receive not an Accusation, but before two or three Witnesses:" we ought not to receive an Accusation, much less so improbable an Accusation, against the Elders of a whole Country, on the Credit of one Witness; especially of one, who hath so much Need to be reminded of the same Apostle's other Direction, "Let all Bitterness, and Wrath, and Anger, and Clamour, and Evil-speaking be put away from you."

I suppose you will plead, that the Society have in Print and I have in a private Letter which you have seen, desired faithful Accounts of our Missionaries.   But we mean particular Information, where Cause is given for any, of which we shall always take due Notice; not indiscrim-

---

· * Mr. Macclanechan was bred among the Dissenters, and was a preacher among them many years before he conformed to the church.

inate Invectives, which never do Service. And besides, we cannot think one of your immoderate Vehemence a very fit Person to furnish us with Information about them; above all, at a Time, when so many of them have manifested their Disapprobation of your Conduct; but that indeed a due Sense of Propriety must have shewn you the Unseasonableness of attempting it.

However, not satisfied with condemning our American Brethren, You censure likewise the Society. For you tell me that the Donations of Christian People to it are improperly appropriated; not only by our employing unskilful and heterodox Missionaries, to which I have answered already; but by appointing Missions in Places, which have no Claim to our Charity. I conceive You do not mean, that the whole or nearly the whole of their Donations is thus misemployed; though You boldly speak at large, as if You did; but some part only. And what Part You have in View, is not clear. If You apprehend that we give Salaries to Missionaries, where the Congregations could and would maintain them without our Help; and if this be any where true, as it possibly may, we have not been apprised of it, though we have both formerly and lately desired that we might. And asserting it in general, is of small Use, without notifying the Congregations particularly. But were even that done also we must hear what they have to urge in their own Defence, before we judge; and Persons, who have not been made acquainted with their Defence cannot be sure that we judge amiss. If You mean, that we maintain Missionaries for those, who have no Claim to them, because there are Ministers of other Persuasions in their Neighborhood, Our Answer is, that where professed Members of the Church of England assure us, that they cannot in Conscience communicate or join in Worship with these other Ministers, either the Service of the Church of England must be provided for them, or they must have no public Service at all, which last our Society was established to prevent.

You charge us likewise with neglecting the Frontiers. Now I believe, that whenever any competent Number of the Inhabitants of the Frontiers hath applied to us, or the Case of any hath been represented by others (and we cannot know these Matters of ourselves), we have endeavoured to assist them, as far as we were able. But our Stock of Money hath often been very low; and procuring Missionaries for such Places is very difficult; especially in Time of War. You are a Man of singular Courage and Hardiness; * Yet you would not stay upon one of those Missions. And you know that we readily voted you extraordinary Encouragment. I flatter myself therefore, that we have not been much to blame on this Head; and surely of all Men you have no Right to be our Accuser.

---

* Mr. Macclanechan went home recommended in these words to the Society by Governor Shirley.

You add a Request for four new Missions, which You specify. Few persons, I believe, will think You peculiarly intitled either to make Request, or give Advice to us. But we are willing to hear: I wish you were equally so. An Inquiry into what you propose will, in all Likelihood, be ordered. The Result of it cannot be foreseen at present.

I think I have now gone through every Thing, that is material, in your Letter; And my deliberate Judgment upon the whole is, that You ought not to have made the Separation, which You have done; but to have quitted Philadelphia, when the Bishop's Refusal of a Licence came, first begging Pardon for the Uneasiness, which you have stirred up there. This, I am fully satisfied was your Christian Duty. Whether it would have been worldly Wisdom also, Time will shew: I do not take upon me to prognosticate. But possibly some, who have been hurried into subscribing, may change their Minds before they have paid much of their Money. Or supposing the Church built, or the Liberty of using the State-House continued, what is no longer new may fail after a while to draw the expected Numbers together: Your Singularities and your intemperate Heat, may gradually disgust such as once were pleased with them; and they who delight in you now, as an Instrument of making Breaches in our Church, may come to Slight you when the Work is done, or when you have miscarried in it, whichsoever may happen. So after doing much Harm, You may be laid aside, or little regarded; and wish, even for the Sake of your temporal Interest, that you had gone and settled in a regular Manner, where you were invited.

But, for the Sake of an infinitely more important Interest, I beg you would consider the solemn Promise, which you have made, "reverently to obey your Ordinary, and other chief Ministers to whom the Charge and Government over you is committed;" and "to maintain and set forward, as much as in you lieth, Quietness, Peace and Love amongst all Christian People." But if you turn a deaf Ear to this Intreaty, I must then beg your Followers, for whose Perusal, as well as yours, this Letter is intended, to remember and observe St. Paul's Rule, "Mark them which cause Divisions and Offences, and avoid them." As I have written these Things, if I know my own Heart, in the Spirit of Meekness, I hope you will read them with the same: And not be kindled by them into that "Wrath of Man," which "worketh not the Righteousness of God." Part of them, I am sensible, must give you Pain. But "faithful are the Wounds of a Friend," and I am very sorry, that you have allowed me no other Way of approving myself

Your Sincere Friend,

THO. CANT.

To the REV. MR. MACCLANECHAN, at Philadelphia.

17

Archbishop Secker to Dr. Smith.*

LAMBETH, October 12th, 1760.

GOOD DR SMITH : Having received a long Letter from Mr. Macclanechan, & another from his Followers, I have written to him a very long
answer, which I have told him is intended for their perusal also.   And
I have order'd copies of them all to be made for you.   God grant, that
the pains, which I have taken, may be some service.   I am very much
obliged to you for your Account of him.   You will see, that there are two
or three small chronological mistakes in it.   And all mistakes should be
avoided, but especially all Exaggerations, in speaking of an Opposer.
Such things give him great Advantages.   And they, who in any part of
a Controversy either carry their Assertions too far, or use too harsh or
vehement Expressions, cannot with so good Grace or near so good Effect,
remark & expose the Faults, of which the other side is guilty.   I hope,
therefore, that Mr. Macclanechan's Heat will induce those, who speak
or write or act against him to be very cool, & upon their Guard to take
the Benefit of his not being so.   I hope, likewise, that his Accusations
of the Clergy as not preaching the Doctrines of the Gospel, will induce
them, not only to give cautions against any erroneous Opinions into
which he may have fallen, which should be done with the utmost circumspection ; but much more, diligently to indicate whatever Truths
border upon his Errors, and whatever Articles he charges them with
denying or slighting.   For they will greatly discredit him by thus con-
victing him of false Accusations, provided they do it with mildness.
And indeed I think it hath been a pretty general Defect amongst us,
that we have not insisted sufficiently in our Discourses on the peculiar
Doctrines of Christianity, nor enforced sufficiently our practical Exhortations with peculiarly Christian motives.   This hath furnished the
Methodists & others with a Handle for representing us, as mere moral-
izers, and as hoping to obey God's Commands by our own Strength
and be saved by our own good Works.   Doubtless they wrong
us : but they will seem to be in the right, and to be the more scriptural
& orthodox preachers, unless we dwell oftener upon the fallen Condition of Man, on the Efficacy of Faith, & the necessity of sanctifying
Grace.   Doing this, we shall discredit their Imputations upon us ; &
remonstrate with Weight against the Extremes, into which they run.
Many of the Tutors in our Universities have sadly neglected instructing
their pupils in Theological knowledge : of which all should have a good
Tincture : but all, who are intended for Orders, a very strong one.   It
is indeed the chief thing, that they should learn : the only one, absolutely necessary.   I hope due Care is taken about it in your College.
Had I been consulted beforehand about your Convention, I should

---

* From the Original in the Maryland Papers.

have been much afraid of its giving Offence: though I am very sensible, that you may as allowably meet to hold friendly Conferences, as any other Set of Men.   God be thanked, that you have a Governor, who hath viewed the matter in so just a Light.   You will certainly be careful, in your future meetings, neither to give Him, nor the people of any Denomination, nor the Bishop, any Umbrage.   Indeed I think you would have done better, if you had asked his Opinion previously, whether you should take this Step.   And I wish, that you had addressed yourselves to Him only, and not to me also.   Yet I know you meant no Disrespect to Him, and great Civility to me : for which I desire you, good D^r. Smith, to return my very hearty Thanks to the whole Assembly, at their next meeting, and assure them of my earnest Desire to do good offices to every one of them in particular, as well as to join with them in serving our Common Cause.   No one hath more at Heart the Establishment of Bishops in America.   Few persons, if any, have taken more pains to convince those, on whom it depends, of the need & usefulness of it.   But the Time for it is not yet come.   God grant it may soon.   Disposing the Laity of our Church to desire it, and the Dissenters of all Sorts to acquiesce in it, is the best thing that can be done on your Side of the water to hasten it.   Without this, pressing for it will only retard it.

I am very much obliged to the Members of the Convention for their Account of the several Missions : and should be extremely glad to have the like Accounts concerning every one, that is under the care of the Society.   They would assist me very much in making for my own use an orderly Notitia of the whole, to which I could readily on all occasions have Recourse.   I must endeavour to make such a one as soon as I have Leisure : for till then I shall not have so distinct a Notion, as I ought, of many particulars.   Amongst other things I have seen Hints from several Quarters, that we maintain Missionaries in some places, where the Congregations might well maintain Ministers for themselves. If you can give or procure me any certain Informations relating to this matter, or any other which is of Consequence to the Society, they will be received very thankfully by

Your loving Brother

THO. CANT.

Who, after reading a letter so truly Christian in its tone, so thoroughly that of a gentleman, but must feel that had all parties been animated and actuated by the spirit which is breathed in *it*, a painful history would have been avoided!

Out of all this disturbance arose, as the reader will have already discovered, the church in Philadelphia called St. Paul's.   The fundamental articles of the new organization were drawn by John

Ross, Esq., and kept the dissentients more strictly within the Church of England than perhaps all of them knew. It was agreed that the house, "when built, shall be used and employed as a house of public worship forever, wherein shall be read, performed, and taught the liturgy, rights, ceremonies, doctrines and true principles of the established Church of England, according to the plain, literal and grammatical sense of the thirty-nine articles of the said church, and none other whatsoever; and the same house is hereby agreed forever hereafter to be styled and called by the name of St. Paul's Church." Its origin, parochially considered, however, was schismatical. Mr. Macclanechan was its first rector, but was not licensed by the Bishop of London. He continued in the parish only about two years—two years of agitation and discomfort. He afterwards settled himself in Maryland, where he lived, it is said, to confess some of his errors. His followers at St. Paul's, it would seem, became convinced, too, of the rashness of their proceedings.

On Mr. Macclanechan's going away, the Rev. Hugh Neil officiated there with good spiritual effects. He went to Maryland in 1767. He had previously been at Trinity Church, Oxford; and, as we infer from a passing remark in Dr. Buchanan's valuable historical sketch of that parish—where he has himself so long ministered with usefulness and honor—was distinguished more by active qualities than by any great refinement or education. In that respect he was perhaps suited to Mr. Macclanechan's new parish. However, his services here were apparently disinterested, and he appears, from the records of the Convention, already mentioned, to have had no sympathy whatever with the late rector's turbulent disposition and his apparent purposes. On the contrary he was a confidential agent of Dr. Smith.

In this state of things the church went through a good many troubles, spiritual and fiscal. Its doors were often closed. One or more lotteries were made to assist it in the way of finance. At last, in 1772, the vestry being very desirous to be reconciled to the Bishop of London, a respectable gentleman named William Stringer, for whom they procured strong testimonials to the Bishop from the regular clergy of Philadelphia and New York, went to London in December of the year just named. The vestry gave assurance to the Bishop that they were not schismatics, but firmly attached to the Church of England. They say :

We do with the utmost sincerity declare that we hold and strictly adhere to the true faith, principles and practice of that excellent church. We have not the least intention of introducing any novelty, unless the doctrine of grace and justification by the righteousness of Christ be esteemed such, which your Lordship's gracious character forbids us to think you will admit. We have never admitted the least innovation in the excellent service of the Church of England, nor permitted any to officiate in our church, nor applied to any for that purpose, but the regular clergy here. We have chosen rather to keep the doors shut than to admit any other ; and, being thus destitute and distressed, we should have been greatly dispersed but for the singular, disinterested service of the Rev. Mr. Neill, now removed to Maryland.

On the faith of the letters and assurances, Mr. Stringer was ordained by the Bishop of London. He returned in the spring of 1773 to Philadelphia; and on the 4th of May was unanimously elected Rector of St. Paul's Church. After Mr. Stringer's departure for orders, the United Churches—Christ Church and St. Peter's—interested themselves in the congregation, and Messrs. Peters, White, Coombe, and Duché officiated alternately, during his absence, in his church. He accordingly found things, when he returned, on a good basis, and he entered upon his sacred duties with earnestness and regularity. At the commencement of the Revolutionary war he was still in charge of St. Paul's, performing his duties with sincerity and good results. During parts of its existence the church has exhibited some " taste and tincture " of its irregular origin ; but, under a succession of pious men, including the Rev. Joseph Pilmore, D. D., and the truly respectable Rev. Dr. Samuel Magaw, and with the wise episcopal control exercised over it in critical times by Bishop White, it has been retained in the communion of the Church, with a considerable measure of usefulness.

The devotion which Dr. Smith ever gave to his College and Academy was not abated during this year by the business or the troubles of the Church, which we have just mentioned. The Annual Commencement took place in May, and its interest was heightened by religious accessories. Anthems and psalms were sung by the charity scholars, the sweet voices of the children being accompanied by an organ, provided for them by the liberality of certain citizens.

Among the graduates of the College were: Patrick Alison, of Lancaster county (born 1740; died 1802), afterwards a tutor in the College, who, in 1762, studied divinity, and received the degree of Doctor of Divinity in 1782; Thomas Bond, M.D.; Robert Goldsborough, of Maryland, afterwards, A. D. 1768, Attorney-General of the State; he died in 1788; John Johnson, one of the tutors in 1763; and Thomas Mifflin, whose history is sufficiently well known.

On the 18th of November of this year (1760) the second child of Dr. Smith was born. He was baptized on the 6th of the following March, by Dr. Jenney, in Christ Church; Rev. Dr. Peters and Mr. Thomas William Moore being sponsors. He was named Thomas Duncan—Duncan being, as we have already stated, in the beginning of this volume, the maiden name of Dr. Smith's mother.

CHAPTER XVII.

The First Convention of the Church in Pennsylvania — Dr. Smith Preaches the Opening Sermon—Parts of it in MS. Approved by Bishop Newton, the Author of the Work on the Prophecies—Addresses to the Governor, the Penns, the Archbishop of Canterbury, and the Bishop of London—Dr. Smith to Dr. Bearcroft, Secretary of the Propagation Society.

On Wednesday, the 30th of April, 1760, in pursuance of an opinion which had been expressed in the autumn of the previous year by sundry of the Episcopal clergy of Pennsylvania and the counties then annexed to it, and which now constitute the State of Delaware, that it might contribute to the general service of religion to have a free and voluntary meeting or Convention, to confer together on such subjects as the particular situation of their congregations might require, the following gentlemen came together, viz.: Doctor Jenney, Rector of Christ Church, Philadelphia; Doctor Smith, Provost of the College in Philadelphia; Mr. George Craig, Missionary at Chester; Mr. Philip Reading,

Missionary at Apoquiniminck; Mr. Thomas Barton, Missionary at Lancaster; Mr. William Sturgeon, Assistant Minister and Catechist to the Negroes in Philadelphia; Mr. William Macclanechan, another of the Assistant Ministers in Christ Church, Philadelphia; Mr. Charles Inglis, Missionary at Dover; Mr. Hugh Neill, Missionary at Oxford, and Mr. Jacob Duché, likewise an Assistant Minister in Christ Church, Philadelphia. There were present also Mr. Samuel Cook and Mr. Robert McKean, two Missionaries in New Jersey, of the Society for the Propagation of the Gospel, with the kind intention of giving their advice and assistance in promoting the designs of the Convention.

It was agreed that Dr. Jenney, Rector of Christ Church, ought naturally to preside at the .Convention, and the same was notified to him; but he, excusing himself from acting on account of his great bodily indisposition, recommended Dr. Smith for that purpose. Dr. Smith was accordingly unanimously chosen. James Humphreys, Esq., one of the Vestrymen of Christ Church, was appointed Secretary or Clerk.

It was agreed that a copy of an address should be prepared to present to the Governor; Messrs. Thos. Barton and Jacob Duché were appointed to prepare it. It was also agreed that a copy of an address should be prepared to the Archbishop of Canterbury (Secker), to congratulate his Grace on his elevation to that high office, and to make an humble tender of the Clergy's duty to him. Messrs. Reading, Barton and Macclanechan were appointed to draw the same.* It was also agreed that a state of the missions within this Province should be transmitted with the same; also that an address should be sent to the Bishop of London, with a like state of the missions.

Dr. Smith was requested to preach a sermon before the Convention in Christ Church on Friday, May 2d, 1760. The Rev. Mr. Macclanechan declined to join in the request, and offered to produce reasons for the said dissent against next meeting. Notwithstanding Mr. Macclanechan's refusal to join in the civility to Dr.

---

* Mr. Macclanechan did not meet the Committee to assist in drawing the said address, and wanted his name to be erased from it the day after it was signed. As my reader has had enough of this gentleman—reverend or irreverend—I do not present the discussions had about him in this Convention. It was here that Dr. Smith took the Address to the Bishop of London out of his hand. See *supra*, p. 218.

Smith, Dr. Smith preached his sermon at the time and place appointed. His text was the 8th verse of the 2d Psalm, "Ask of me and I shall give thee the heathen for thine inheritance; the utmost parts of the earth for thy possession." This sermon was made applicable more particularly to the conversion of the heathen *American*, and to the Final Propagation of Christianity and the *Sciences* to the ends of the earth. It was published at the request of the Convention, with a dedication as follows: "To the Most Reverend, his Grace, Thomas, Lord Archbishop of Canterbury, President; and to all the honourable and venerable members of the Society, for propagating the Gospel in foreign parts."

Dr. Smith says in this dedication that it may be thought a very needless labor to attempt a proof—that the interests of Christianity will be advanced, by promoting the interests of Science; which was one design of the Sermon. But he asserts that it had been his misfortune, in his endeavors for the latter, to meet with men, who, seeming to consider the advancement of knowledge and free inquiry as unfriendly to their dark system, had set themselves up, with rage truly illiberal, to stifle the infant Sciences in America. For this reason, Dr. Smith thought "he could not do a better service than by endeavouring to shew them, at large, that they were, in effect, waging war, not only with everything elegant and useful in life, but even with the extension of our common Christianity, the prosperity of our country, and the best interests of our species." He adds that "if, in the prosecution of this design, he hath been led into a more particular analysis of the Sciences than some may judge needful in a discourse of this kind, he hopes the circumstances of the case will be his plea." "It may also be some apology," he continued, "that it was delivered before a learned body of Clergy."

An agreeable circumstance connected with the discourse (which is preserved in Dr. Smith's collected works)* is one which he mentions in this dedication: to wit, that Bishop Newton, "that truly learned Prelate, who had himself written so excellently on the accomplishment of the Prophecies, condescended to peruse and make some corrections in the discourse, respecting the explanation of some passages of Prophecy, before the present edition was committed to the press."

---

* Vol. II., p. 311.

The thanks of the Convention were voted to Dr. Smith "for his excellent sermon preached before them," and he was requested to print it.

On Saturday evening, May 3d, Dr. Smith reported to the Convention that his Honor the Governor had sent down a box containing 200 of the second volume of the Bishop of London's Sermons, being his Lordship's generous gift, for the use of the Churches in Pennsylvania; and that his Honor desired a proper distribution might be made of them to the several members present; to be given away by them on their return home in such manner as they thought might best answer his Lordship's pious designs; and accordingly it was agreed to distribute them as follows, viz.:

To his Honor the Governor,	8
To the Rev^d D^r. Jenney, for the use of Christ Church,	60
To M^r. Craig, for the Mission of Chester,	10
To M^r. Reading, for the Mission of Apoquimininck,	12
To M^r. Ross, for the Mission of New Castle,	6
To M^r. Inglis, for the Mission of Dover and Lewis,	18
To M^r. Barton, for the Mission of Lancaster and over Susquehanna,	30
To M^r. Curry, for the Mission of Radnor,	12
To M^r. Neill, for the Mission of Oxford,	12
To M^r. Campbell, for the Mission of Bristol,	6
To Doctor Smith,	6
To M^r. Richard Peters,	6
To the Ministers of other Denominations,	14
	200

The Convention, after requesting Dr. Smith to transmit the addresses to the Archbishop, the Bishop of London, and to the Proprietaries, adjourned on Monday, May 5th, agreeing that the next Convention should be held in Philadelphia, on the last Wednesday in April, 1761, requesting Mr. Curry to prepare a sermon for the occasion, and in case of his refusal that Mr. Craig would do so.

It took care, also, as a final act, to leave its powers in " Commission," Dr. Smith, Mr. Sturgeon, Mr. Craig, Mr. Neill, Mr. Duché (together with the Rev. Dr. Jenney when able), having been appointed "a Committee for the transacting of such matters as may be of general concern to the Church in Pennsylvania *at the present crisis.*" The power had obvious reference to the case of Mr. Macclanechan, and the weak condition of Dr. Jenney.

The different addresses directed by the Convention to be made were all made. I give them below. They all have an interest. Old John Adams's sour, cynical, envious nature, which made him badly emulous of every great man, and whose jealousy of Washington and Hamilton destroyed the purest political party which our country ever had, and in the end brought political ruin on himself, could see in Dr. Smith only "a man distracted by a strong passion for lawn sleeves, and a stronger passion for popularity." Others, whether possessed of the gift of charity or only of the spirit of truth, will readily admit that whatever of humanity may have belonged to Dr. Smith's motives, his *acts* in these matters were those of propriety and usefulness. His addresses to the civil authorities were due to them; for both James Hamilton and the Penns ever exhibited kind dispositions towards the Church of England. To the Archbishop of Canterbury and Bishop of London, they were equally due. For the Church in America never had a prelate more devoted to its interests than was Archbishop Secker, whose efforts to give to us an Episcopate before the Revolution were constant, and brought upon him much obloquy from Presbyterians and other dissenters; and it had few more devoted than Sherlock, whose sermons were among those that all true churchmen could read with profit.

THE ADDRESS TO THE GOVERNOR.

To the Honorable James Hamilton, Esqr., Lieutenant-Governor of the Province of Pennsylvania & Counties of New Castle, Kent & Sussex upon Delaware.

The Humble Address of the Clergy of the Church of England in the said Province and Counties now convened in the City of Philadelphia.

MAY IT PLEASE YOUR HONOR:

We, the Episcopal Clergy of the Province of Pennsylvania and Counties annexed, being now met in voluntary Convention, beg leave to embrace this favorable opportunity to congratulate your Honor upon your second appointment to this Government, and to testify the Joy we feel upon so favorable and happy an event.

The Reputation with which you formerly discharged this important Trust is still fresh in our Memories, and while we reflect on the blessings we once enjoyed from your happy administration, we cannot but esteem it our particular felicity that we can again call you our Governor.

Permit us, sir, to assure you of our firm Attachment to his Majesty's sacred person, Family & Government, and that we are heartily disposed and shall at all times esteem it a most essential part of our Duty whilst we are propagating the interest of Religion & Virtue, to inculcate obedience to our most Gracious Sovereign and to all who are put in authority under him.

Actuated by such principles as these we cannot entertain any doubts of receiving your Honor's patronage and protection both in our collective and single capacities. The close connexion between Religion and Civil Government, between the Increase of Virtue and the Prosperity of a Nation might be alone sufficient to afford us these sanguine expectations. But when we consider your Honor is a professed Member of the Church of England, and well affected to her Doctrines and Discipline, we have still greater reason to entertain these hopes.

To consider the State of Religion in General and the Situation and the Circumstances of our own Church in particular, and to confer together upon the most proper means of promoting the one and advancing the other, is the sole design of our present Meeting. And in this we do but comply with the particular instructions of that Venerable Society in whose service, under that of our Lord & Master Jesus Christ, most of us here present are engaged. Remote as we are from the immediate influence and jurisdiction of our Ecclesiastical Superiors (which we have too frequently the greatest reason to lament), it was matter of the highest joy and gratitude to us to hear your Honor publickly declaring upon a former occasion that you would afford all the countenance & protection in your power to the Church of England.

May we, sir, be so happy as to recommend ourselves to your just regard by our prudent conduct & steady endeavours to promote a sense of Piety & true Religion among the People committed to our care and may you long live a blessing to us all! May your Administration be made easy & happy to yourself & continue to be distinguished by a firm adherence to Justice, Right and Law and an unshaken Zeal for our Constitution, both in Church and State.

> ROB'T JENNEY, Rector of Christ Church,
> WILLIAM SMITH, President of the Convention,
> GEORGE CRAIG,
> PHILIP READING,
> WILLIAM STURGEON,
> HUGH NEILL,
> THO. BARTON,
> CHAS. INGLIS,
> WM. THOMPSON,
> JACOB DUCHÉ.

All the members of the Convention (Mr. Macclanechan excepted) waited on the Governor and presented the Address. To which the Governor was pleased to return an answer in the following words:

Reverend Gentlemen, I am extremely obliged to you for this very kind address. You may be assured of my constant protection and readiness to do everything in my power which may tend to the advantage of the Protestant Religion and of the Church of England. And I shall at all times be pleased with the opportunity of seeing and conferring with you on any matters which you shall judge serviceable to the Church in general or to any of yourselves in particular.

After which the same members of the Convention went in a body to Christ Church, when evening prayer was said, and where Dr. Smith preached a sermon.

THE ADDRESS TO THE HONORABLE PROPRIETARIES.

To the Honorable Thomas Penn & Richard Penn, Esq^{rs}., true and absolute Proprietaries of the Province of Pennsylvania and Counties of New Castle, Kent and Sussex on Delaware.

MAY IT PLEASE YOUR HONORS:

We, the Clergy of the Church of England, in the Province of Pennsylvania and Counties annexed, having met together in free and voluntary convention to confer on such matters as we thought might be conducive to the general service of Religion, beg leave to embrace so favorable an opportunity to assure you of our sincere regards to the honorable Proprietary family.

At the same time that we do this we beg leave also to express our grateful sense of the many invaluable privileges which, as members of community, we enjoy under the Charter granted to this Province by your Honorable and Worthy Father, whose memory we regard, and our sincere Resolution to take every opportunity in our power to promote its best interests.

We are persuaded this will ever be the most effectual means of recommending ourselves to your Favour and countenance, which we hope to be so happy as to enjoy, while our best endeavours will be directed at deserving them.

Wishing you every Felicity, temporal and eternal, We are may it please your Honors,

Your most obed^t & affectionate humble serv^{ts}.,

(Signed as is the address to the Governor).

PHILADELPHIA, May 5th, 1760.

The Rev. Messrs. Cooke and McKean desired leave to add the following words:

We, the Subscribers, Missionaries in New Jersey, assisting in this Convention, beg leave to join with our Reverend Brethren in the sincere testimony they have given of their Regards to the Honble Proprietary Family.

SAMUEL COOKE, ⎫
ROBERT MCKEAN, ⎰ Missionaries in New Jersey.

The original MS. of the document above given is among the Penn papers in the Historical Society of the State.

THE ADDRESS TO THE ARCHBISHOP OF CANTERBURY.

To the most Reverend His Grace Thomas, by Divine Providence, Lord Archbishop of Canterbury, Metropolitan, & Primate of all England.

The Humble Address of the Missionaries and other Clergy of the Church of England residing in & near the Province of Pennsylvania.

We, the Missionaries and other Clergy of the Church of England, residing in and near the Province of Pennsylvania, having conven'd in the City of Philadelphia, beg leave to present our most humble Duty to your Grace and to assure you of our zealous Attachment to the interest of that Church in whose service we have the honor to be engaged.

Your Grace's Elevation to the Primacy of all England cannot give greater pleasure to any than to your obedient Sons now joining in this Address.

In the accomplishment of this event we see the good Providence of God in behalf of the Protestant cause clearly manifested ; the character of Defender of the Faith in our Sovereign amply exerting itself; the wisdom of the present glorious Administration every way justified ; and the purity of our Religion amiably recommended in the truly primative & Apostolical Example of your Grace under God and the King the present Head of our Church.

To assure the Government under whose protection we reside of our inviolable attachment to his present most glorious Majesty and his illustrious House, To confer mutually on such subjects as are best adapted to our duty as Ministers ; To assist each other with such comfort & counsel as the exigencies of our respective Congregations may require, are the sole points we have in view in our present voluntary Convention. And we herewith transmit to your Grace a Copy of our Proceedings as also a brief State of the several Missions. We have nothing more at heart than the Glory of that God whom we serve, and the Salvation of those whose Souls are committed to our charge.

The state of Religion in North American Colonies becomes more & more the subject of high importance.   And it must not be dissembled to your Grace that the Church of England here is far from bearing the most favorable aspect.   This we humbly conceive is owing to those hardships under which our Church peculiarly labours.   Indeed nothing but the good Providence of God together with the Excellency of its Constitution ; the most assiduous & extensive labours of the Missionaries, and the Aids of the Venerable Society for Propagating the Gospel whom we pray God to bless & preserve, hitherto secure the visibility of our Church.   For while every other Denomination is guarded by some plan of Discipline, we alone are left without that necessary assistance, without a Head to guide us with counsel, an authority to correct abuses, or a Jurisdiction to appeal to for ascertaining the just privileges of our Ministry and Congregations.

It is with concern, my Lord, we are compelled to observe, that the more flourishing and populous our Colonies become, the more alarming is our situation.   Seminaries of Learning are now erected in many of the most noted Provinces, particularly in the City of Philadelphia under the conduct of Professors of approved worth, whose Abilities are every way equal to such a Task.

The Inhabitants of this Country of European Extraction are quite deprived of the benefits arising from the Episcopal Office & particularly of the Apostolical Rite of Confirmation.   Very few have either inclination or capacity to attend to those essential differences by which the Constitution of our Church is distinguish'd.

The inconvenience of Passing & repassing the dangerous Atlantic, being added to these difficulties, will we apprehend induce many to Educate their Children to the Dissenting Ministry rather than ours, so that our Church will not have such full advantages from these Seminaries of Learning as she otherwise might have.

These, my Lord, are the chief of those points which have fallen under our present consideration, and which principally retard the growth of our Church.   It is needless for us to point out the remedy of these evils to a Prelate of your Grace's penetration and judgment or to say that the appointing a Bishop or Bishops in America would with the divine assistance be the most effectual method to remove these difficulties.

We shall therefore detain your Grace no longer than just to crave your Blessing and Direction on these and all other deliberations for the advancement of Christ's Kingdom in general and the good of this particular Branch of his Church.

And that the Era of your Grace's Primacy in the Church Militant may be rendered eminently glorious by introducing the Episcopal Character into America & that your Grace, after a good old age, may be

numbered in the choir of Apostles & Confessors in the church triumphant is the unfeigned prayer of

> My Lord,
>
> > Your Grace's most dutiful Sons &
> >
> > > Most obedient humble servants,

ROBERT JENNEY, Rector of Christ Church, Phila.
WILLIAM SMITH, President of the Convention.
GEORGE CRAIG,
PHILIP READING,
WILLIAM STURGEON,
HUGH NEILL,
THOMAS BARTON,
WILLIAM MACCLANECHAN,
CHAS. INGLIS,
JACOB DUCHÉ,
WILLIAM THOMPSON,
SAMUEL COOKE, } Missionaries in New Jersey.
ROBERT MCKEAN, }

THE ADDRESS TO THE LORD BISHOP OF LONDON.

To the Right Reverend Father in God, Thomas, by Divine Permission, Lord Bishop
of London.

The Humble Address of the Missionaries and other Clergy of the
Church of England residing in & near the Province of Pennsylvania.

May it please your Lordship,—

We, the Missionaries and other Clergy of the Church of England in
& near the Province of Pennsylvania, having convened in the City of
Philadelphia, beg leave to present our most humble Duty to your Lordship, our lawful & just Diocesan, offering at the same time our most
devout thanks to Almighty God who has so long preserved your Lordship's Life and Faculties through a truly venerable old age, as an Ornament to our Church & Nation.

The State of Religion in the Northern Colonies in America becomes
more and more a subject of importance. It must not be dissembled to
your Lordship that the Church of England here is far from bearing the
most favorable aspect. This we conceive is owing to those hardships
under which our Church particularly labours. Indeed nothing but the
good Providence of God together with the excellency of its constitution,
the most assiduous and extensive Labours of the Missionaries & the aids
of the Venerable Society for propagating the Gospel whom we pray God
to bless and preserve, hitherto secures the visibility of our Church ; for
while every other denomination is guarded by some plan of discipline,
we alone are left without that necessary assistance, without a Head to
guide us with Counsel, Authority to correct abuses or a jurisdiction to
ascertain the just privileges of our Ministry and Congregations.

To do the best in our power under such circumstances as these, we thought it might conduce to the advancement of Religion in general, and the situation of our Church in particular, to confer together in a voluntary & free Convention upon the most proper means of promoting the one & advancing the other; and herewith we transmit to your Lordship a Copy of our Proceedings and a general account of the State of the Missions in this Province.

Among many other inconveniences which we think greatly disturb the peace of our Church, that of the want of order in moving from one Mission or Congregation to another is like to become a very great one. As we think it indecent as well as hurtful to Religion for Ministers to leave their Congregations abruptly without others to supply their places, so we humbly apprehend that it would greatly tend to promote peace & good order if it was a standing Rule that there should be no removal from one Mission to another without the Society's express Leave nor from one Congregation or Province to another without your Lordship's particular Licence for that purpose, after your Lordship has been furnished with authentick Documents for judging of the necessity of such a removal and the fitness of such a person to supply the vacant cure; a method similar to this has ever been observed in our Mother Country, as we apprehend to the great advantage of the Church.

With the utmost gratitude we acknowledge the receipt of 200 Volumes of your Lordship's most excellent & valuable Sermons, sent down to us this day by his Honor the Governor of this Province; and we have unanimously made such a division of them among the several Missions & Episcopal Congregations in this Province as we judged would most effectually answer your Lordship's benevolent designs.

Praying for your Lordship's Blessing, Advice & Directions in these and all matters relating to the discharge of our Sacred Functions & that your Lordship having finished your mortal Course on Earth may be translated to the Kingdom of our Great Lord and Master,

> We are, my Lord,
> Your Lordship's most dutiful Sons
> & obedient servants,
>
> ROBERT JENNEY, Rector of Christ Church, Phila.
> WILLIAM SMITH, President of the Convention.
> GEORGE CRAIG,
> PHILIP READING,
> WILLIAM STURGEON,
> HUGH NEILL,
> THOMAS BARTON,
> WILLIAM MACCLANECHAN,
> CHAS. INGLIS,
> JACOB DUCHÉ,
> WILLIAM THOMPSON,
> SAMUEL COOKE, ⎫
> ROBERT McKEAN, ⎬ Missionaries in New Jersey.

We now give two letters : one recording a missionary's troubles; the other asking for a mission at Reading:

Dr. Smith to Rev. Dr. Bearcroft.

REV^D AND DEAR SIR : I had intended you the trouble of a long Letter by this Conveyance ; but a severe and indeed dangerous disorder in my blood, Lungs, &^c., catch'd by the extreme heat and fatigue of a Journey to supply some vacant congregations the first Sunday of this month, hath saved you that trouble. I am to-day, for the first time, able to sit it, and hope to get those few lines sent down after the Ship, as also a few more to the good Archbishop ; but if I should miss that, I beg you would present my duty and excuse to his Grace. I shall send a large packet to his Grace by Captain Hammit, a Ship of Force, that sails in about a fortnight, and I am the more desirous that this should be made known, as my last Letters to his Grace, I find have been carried with the Ship into France, and his Grace may think it strange that I have never acknowledged the receipt of his most excellent Letters and papers of Novr last.

I have ordered a Brother of mine, to whom I have remitted a Bill of M^r. Barton's on M^r. Pearson for £25, to pay you three Guineas, which is my subscription as a Member of the Society for a year and a half preceding Ladyday last, or if it must be paid to the Treasurer, you will give my Brother directions in that case, that a proper Entry may be made. Govr Hamilton has not heard that any Notification of his Election has been made to M^r. David Barclay. When he does he will order what is genteel and proper to the occasion.

Poor M^r. Barton, your worthy Missionary at Lancaster, is in a deal of trouble on account of M^r. Pearson's protesting his Bill of £50 due at Christmas, 1760, and I cannot but think he has been unkindly used. The case is exactly this :

M^r. Barton being in Philadelphia about 1st of December, and being obliged to be home to his congregation before Christmas, drew for his whole Salary Decr 5th, but dated his Bill the 25th, the day it was due, knowing that in that Season he could have no other opportunity. This the Missionarys who come to Town but once or twice a year often do, namely, draw a few weeks before or after their Bills are due, but date them at the time of their being due. It happened now that Barton's Bill, being thus transacted and in the Merchant's hand and the Ship hurrying away for fear of the Ice, and having a short winter passage of about twenty days, the Bill arrived and was presented in about 10 or 12 days after its date, viz. : about January 8th, as the protest shows. M^r. Pearson refused the Bill, it was noted for non-acceptance, and 30 days afterwards being presented a second time was still refused, and finally

18

protested ; on which a damage of upwards of Eleven Guineas, by the Laws of this province, has fallen on M^r. Barton, which is a heavy deduction out of £50. I have just settled the matter for M^r. Barton with the Merchant without suffering it to make noise, and have paid him the damages which I hope the Society will generously make good to him again. The original Bill he has drawn over again.

I am, dear Sir,

Your affec^e humble serv^t, &^{c}.,

W^M SMITH.

Dr. Smith to Rev. Dr. Bearcroft.

PHILADELPHIA, 26th August, 1760.

REV^D SIR : I wrote to you a long letter by M^r. Keene about 7 weeks ago, with a full account of every thing concerning Macclanechan, and a copy of the Minutes of the late Meeting of our Clergy, together with an address to His Grace of Canterbury ; all which I hope have been duly received. Macclanechan gains no ground in the Church, and we have lost but two or three Men of any note (one of which is John Ross, who has not acted like a member of your Body & son of a regular Clergyman as he is, being the chief founder of all this trouble in order to be at the head of a party). The Quakers and their adherents are the chief support of this Schism, agreeable to their maxim, *Divide et impera ;* but we think it will not hold long, especially as that shining youth, M^r. Duché, is so much more popular than Macclanechan, who only draws the lower sort, and of these more from the Presbyterians & Baptists than from us.

Enclosed I send you a petition from one of our back Counties, which I hope will merit the Society's attention. The Subscribers of it are personally known to me. I was present and preached to them by their own invitation, the day of its date when they made the subscription ; and I knew them both able and willing to make good their engagements. The first Gentleman who signs, M^r. Bird, is worth 1,000 guineas per annum in Iron works. The place is 60 Miles from Philadelphia. It is the Chief Town of Berks County, settl'd chiefly with Germans lying on the frontier, & no English Minister has ever yet resided in it. The Romish Priests are busy among the people on the one hand, and the Sectaries dependent on the Quaker on the other. You will observe that in the transactions of our late Convention the whole Body of the Clergy of this province recommend Reading as a place fit to open a Mission in. There is an Old Swedish Settlement about 15 Miles lower towards Philadelphia, that petitions along with the Town of Reading, and hath a Church ready built, and I do give it as my honest and most candid Judgment that I know of no place where a Mission is more wanted. I enclose you M^r. Barton's account of the place, who has preached there since I was up, and beg you will lay the whole, together with the enclosed Letter, before the Archbishop, previous to your doing anything in the Society.

I enclose you my sermon before the Clergy at their Convention, which, being on a subject which is a favourite one with you, and placing some points perhaps in a light somewhat new, I hope you will bestow a candid Reading upon it. I shall beg to hear from you as soon as may be convenient, in regard to the people of Reading who have put their affair into my hands and will in due time expect their answer from me. The Hon'ble M^r. Penn's agents here have promised a fine lot, whereon to erect their Church; and from M^r. Penn himself you will receive this.   I am, Revd Sir,

Y^r affec^t humble serv^t, &^c.,

WILLIAM SMITH.

CHAPTER XVIII.

ACTION OF THE TRUSTEES IN REGARD TO THE PENN DONATION—COMMENCEMENT
AT THE COLLEGE—CONVENTION OF THE CHURCH CLERGY HELD IN PHILADEL-
PHIA—ERECTION AND DEDICATION OF ST. PETER'S CHURCH, AT THE SOUTH-
WEST CORNER OF PINE AND THIRD STREETS.

ON the 10th of February, 1761, Dr. Smith brought before the Trustees of the College a matter of importance to him in the way of his annual support. It was in the form of a communication to the Board, and thus:

To THE TRUSTEES OF THE COLLEGE, &C., OF PHILADELPHIA:

About seven years ago when the state of the Academy made it neces-sary to open schools in the higher branches of learning, the President and some of the Trustees applyed to the Honble Thomas Penn, Esqr., setting forth the narrowness of their Funds, and begging his assistance to enable them to employ a fit person to instruct the youth in the Art of Science. Mr. Penn accordingly ordered £50 pr. annum for that end, and the Trustees settling £200 pr. annum more, made £250 for the Provost's salary.

In the year 1756 Mr. Penn was so well pleased with the success of the Institution that in a letter to the Provost he mentioned his design of changing the temporary sum he paid into a permanent Grant of his fourth of Perkajie Manor, containing about 3,000 acres.

In the year 1759, the Provost being in London, put Mr. Penn in mind of his former promise, and our present worthy Governor adding his Sollicitations to the same effect, the grant was readily and chearfully made. The Provost saw from the Tenor and Preamble of the grant that £50 Subscription was to cease from that date (viz. : the beginning of July, 1759), and consequently that his salary would in the meantime be so much diminished, and mentioned that matter to the Governor. But it was thought best to leave this wholly to the future care and justice of the Trustees, and say nothing then that might stand in the way of so kind a Donation. The Provost, therefore, assures himself the Trustees will be very sensible that both his circumstances as well as the circumstances of the Times are so much altered since the first settlement of this salary that must find the whole of the sum which he then enjoyed a very scanty Allowance to subsist him now, any way conformable to his station in the College and his Character which he thinks it necessary to sustain for its good.

The Trustees, with a just liberality, ordered that the £50 per annum should now be paid out of the Academy Funds, to commence from the date of Mr. Penn's deed.

The Commencement at the College took place on the 18th of May. The clergy, who were attending the Convention, went to it in a body. Dr. Smith preached in the College Hall before them, the Trustees, and the pupils. There were thirteen graduates, among them Jasper Yeates, born in 1745, a member of Convention of Pennsylvania which ratified the Federal Constitution; Judge of the Supreme Court of Pennsylvania from 1791 to 1817, in which year he died; Alexander Wilcocks, afterwards Recorder of Philadelphia; Abraham Ogden; Joseph Shippen, and Henry Waddell, a well-known clergyman of the Episcopal Church in New Jersey, afterwards honored with the degree of D. D.; Tench Tilghman,* and Richard Peters.†

---

* Colonel Tench Tilghman went out from Philadelphia a captain of a light infantry company during the Revolution. He served in the "flying camp," in 1776, and in August of that year he joined the military family of Washington, having been appointed an aid-de-camp by the commander-in-chief. Colonel Tilghman conveyed to Congress the intelligence of the surrender of Cornwallis. He died at Baltimore, in April, 1786, in the forty-third year of his age. Colonel Tilghman married a daughter of Matthew Tilghman, of Maryland. Margaret, the offspring of this marriage, married Tench Tilghman, of Talbot county, Md., who had one son, who was also called by the favorite family name of Tench. Wllliam Tilghman, Chief-Justice of Pennsylvania, was connected with the family.

† Richard Peters, known afterwards as "Judge Peters," was born at Blockley, in

From some loose papers of Bishop White, it appears that a second Convention was held in this year. The Bishop gives us their names: The Rev. Dr. Smith, and the Rev. Messrs. Campbell, Craig, Reading, Sturgeon, Neill, Barton, Inglis, Thomson, Duché, Chandler (of New Jersey), and Keene (of Maryland). This, says Dr. Dorr, from whose History of Christ Church* we get our information about this Convention, " was a large number of clergy-men to assemble at that early day, when there was but one Epis-copal congregation in Philadelphia." The Rev. Dr. Smith was again elected President. Mr. Macclanechan does not appear in the record. Archbishop Secker, it will be remembered, in his letter to Dr. Smith, † after being informed about the Convention of 1760, had expressed some fear that the Conventions of the clergy might offend the Government in Pennsylvania, and requested him to be careful in any future meeting not to give umbrage to him or to any-body. Dr. Smith, with Mr. Reading, were accordingly now appointed to wait on the Governor to request his approbation of the meeting, and his " protection " during its sittings. The two gentlemen, after waiting on the Governor, reported " that he was " pleased to say that he could have no possible objection to the " clergy meeting together, and that we might depend on his coun-"tenance and protection at all times." Mr. Craig preached a sermon suitable to the Convention on Friday, the 22d.

We come now to a historical event in the history of the Philadelphia churches—the dedication of St. Peter's Church.

On the 1st of August, 1754, as appears by the original petition preserved among the Penn Papers in the Historical Society of Pennsylvania, William Plumsted, John Wilcocks, Charles Sted-man, John Inglis, John Baynton, Phineas Bond, Thomas Bond, Redmond Conyngham, Philip Benezet, John Swift, Thomas Law-rence, Thomas Coombe, John Nixon, Enoch Hobart, William

---

June, 1744, and was the nephew of the Reverend Richard Peters, Secretary of the Proprietary Government for many years, and afterwards Rector of Christ Church. He received his education at Philadelphia, at the Academy, and studied law. He probably commenced practice about the year 1765. He was captain in the Revolutionary army; Secretary of the Board of War, 1776–1781; delegate to Congress in 1782; Speaker of the Legislature of Pennsylvania. He was a man of great wit and good humor, lively and sportive. He was a good Latin and Greek scholar, and had a fair knowledge of the French and German languages. After the Revolution he was appointed by Washington a Judge of the United States District Court. He died in 1828.

* Page 123.   † *Supra,* pp. 258–9.

Peters, Samuel McCall, Archibald McCall, George McCall, William Bingham, and several other persons in this day less well known, though persons of great respectability, presented a petition to the Proprietaries, stating that the members of the Church of England in this city had grown so numerous that the present church (meaning Christ Church) was little more than sufficient to accommodate one-half the families of that persuasion with seats; that it was judged most proper that another church should be built towards the south end of the city; that no vacant ground was to be had so commodiously situated for the purpose as a part of a certain lot, 104 feet, extending from Second street to Fourth, on the west side of Pine, which belonged to the Proprietaries; and praying the Proprietaries to grant them that lot on the west side of Third street for a church and yard for the use of the members of the Church of England in and about the city.

In due time the grant was made, and the present Church of St. Peter's was built; a venerable monument indeed! the only church in Philadelphia, said Bishop De Lancey, which the spirit of change, ambitious of improvement and covetous of ease, has left undesecrated by any remodelling hand;—its interior arrangements almost the only remnant of the early taste and judgment of our fathers as to interior church architecture, convenience and arrangements.

The history of this church, including the history of its erection, is full of interest. I have reason to believe that ere long—if the Parish of St. Peter's shall sufficiently encourage the undertaking— we shall have it presented by a faithful antiquary of our city; to whom, with the Rev. William White Bronson, we are already indebted for the publication of the Epitaphs in the Church-yard; a descendant from one of the honored men whose names I give, at the bottom of the preceding page and at the top of this.* I do not trespass, therefore, on ground so rightfully occupied.

By the middle of August, 1761, the building was completed and handed over to the congregation. Dr. Dorr in his history of Christ Church† continues our narrative:

---

* I refer to Mr. Charles Riché Hildeburn, a great-grandson of John Swift, Esq., the last Collector of the Port of Philadelphia under the Crown.

† Sermon, Philadelphia, September 4th, 1861, at the Centennial Celebration of the Opening of St. Peter's Church, page 13.

On August 19th, at a meeting of the Committee appointed to prepare a plan for the opening of St. Peter's Church, Dr. Jenney acquainted the vestry that he had applied to the Rev^d M^r. Richard Peters
to preach at the opening of the church, and that he and his assistants
thought the compliment due first to D^r. Peters, not only in regard
to his abilities but also for his many services that he had done the
church, and in particular for having procured many generous subscriptions for St. Peter's Church.   But he declining the offer on account of
his present engagements in public business, it was judged that no
other person was so well qualified for that duty as the Rev. Dr. Smith,
not only on account of his abilities but likewise for the service that
he has been to our church in this part of the world, at home, &c.; all
of which the vestry approved of; therefore it was resolved that *Dr.
Smith* be requested to preach the opening or dedication sermon, and
that the said opening and dedication take place on the 4th day of September, 1761.

Accordingly on Friday, September 4th, 1761, that being the
day appointed for the opening of the church, the officiating
clergy, and several of their brethren, together with the church-
wardens and vestrymen, met at Christ Church, from whence they
walked in regular procession in the following order: Clerk and
Sexton; Questmen; Vestrymen, two by two; the Church-Wardens; Clergy who are to officiate; other Clergy—to the Governor's house.   At the Governor's house they were joined by his
Honor and some members of his Council.   These taking their
places with the Wardens and just before the officiating clergy, all
went on to St. Peter's Church.

The service, as we learn by a record of Dr. Smith, began with
the following sentences, followed as we show:

Thus saith the Lord: The Heaven is my Throne and the earth my
Footstool.   Where is the House that ye build unto me? and where is
the place of my rest?—*Isaiah.*

From the rising of the sun even unto the going down of the same,
my name shall be great among the Gentiles; and in every place incense
shall be offered unto my name, and a pure offering: for my name shall
be great among the Heathen, saith the Lord of hosts.—*Malachi.*

The wilderness and the solitary place shall be glad, and the Desert
shall rejoice and blossom as the rose.—*Isaiah.*

Where two or three are gathered together in my Name, there am I in
the midst of them.—*St. Matthew.*

2. An occasional Prayer from the Reading-Desk.

3. Morning Prayer of the Church, as usual.

4. Proper Psalms, 84th, 122d, 132d.

5. The Lessons, viz. } 1 Kings, ch. viii.
                     } St. Matthew, ch. xxi. to verse 14th.

[N. B.—Thus far (except reading the Absolution) was by the youngest officiating Minister.*]

6. An occasional Prayer, with a Baptism, at the Fount, by Dr. Smith.

7. The remainder of the Morning Service (using only, instead of the Collect for the Day, that for St. Peter's Day, and the last for Good Friday) by the eldest Missionary† present.

8. Occasional Prayer, with the Communion Service.

9. The Epistle. Haggai, ch. ii. to verse 10th.

10. The Gospel for St. Peter's Day.

[N. B.—This part of the Service was performed at the Altar, by the eldest officiating Minister.‡]

To this succeeded the Sermon. The text was:

I have surely built thee an house to dwell in, a settled place for thee to abide in forever. . . . But God, indeed, dwells on earth. Behold, the Heaven and Heaven of Heavens cannot contain thee: how much less this house that I have builded? The Lord our God be with us as he was with our fathers: let Him not leave us or forsake us. . . . That all the people of the earth may know that the Lord is God, and that there is none else.—[1 Kings, ch. viii., 13, 27, 57, 60 verses.]

" Everything," says a contemporary narrative,§ " was conducted with the utmost decency, order and solemnity, and after the sermon the words of the text, which had been previously composed into an anthem, were elegantly sung by a number of ladies and gentlemen, to the vast satisfaction of everybody present."

The reader knows, of course, that at this date we had no prescribed form for the Consecration of Churches.

At a meeting of vestry held in St. Peter's Church, September 7th, 1761, three days after the celebration, it was

Resolved, That the thanks of this Board be given to the Rev. Dr. Smith for his excellent Sermon preached at the opening of St. Peter's Church, the 4th instant; and the Church-wardens are ordered to return him the thanks of this Board accordingly, and to request the favour of him to furnish a copy of the said Sermon to be printed.

---

* The Rev. Mr. Duché.   † The Rev. Mr. Neill.   ‡ The Rev. Mr. Sturgeon.
§ Pennsylvania Gazette of September 10th, 1761.

The sermon was printed by Franklin. The preface deserves insertion here :

It was an ancient custom, not only among the Jews, but even among the Gentiles, long before the coming of Christ and the establishment of Christianity, to separate from common use, by certain formal Rites of Dedication, their Temples, Altars, and Places of religious Worship. And we find God himself expressly approving this custom in respect to the Jews (who were his peculiar people, and blessed with a more adequate knowledge of His Name) inasmuch as he vouchsafed his special Presence, in the places so separated and dedicated by them. Of this, the chapter, from which the text of the following discourse is taken, furnishes sufficient evidence ; and, in the third verse of the succeeding chapter, God expressly tells Solomon :

I have heard thy prayer and thy supplication—I have hallowed this house which thou hast built, to put my Name there forever; and mine Eyes and mine Heart shall be there continually.

Agreeably to this, the Primitive Christians, even in the most difficult times (as we have the utmost reason to believe), did not resort to any place for stated worship, till they had first separated or set it apart, if not by public rites, yet at least by peculiar Thanksgivings, and Prayers for a sanctified use thereof. And, in the more prosperous days of Christianity, when kings and potentates became converts to its Truths, these Separations were performed with far greater ceremony, and distinguished by the more pompous names of Dedications, Consecrations, and the like ; in all which acts, " the common prayers of the Church were not looked upon as sufficient, without special Panegyrical Orations, and forms of Adoration and Praise, more peculiar to the Occasion."*

This custom was very early introduced into our mother country ; for we find Austin himself, who has been styled the Apostle of our Ancestors, agreeably to his instructions, converting such idol-temples, as were fit for use, into Christian Churches, by the Rites of Consecration. And, in after-times, it was expressly provided, that all Churches, &c., should be Consecrated within two years after they were finished ;† nor do our laws take any notice of Churches or Chapels, as such, till they are formally Consecrated.‡

Now, it is to be presumed that, in these laws and regulations, our forefathers were actuated by the same pious motives that influenced

---

* See Bingham's Eccles. Antiquities; who gathers this from Eusebius, who has preserved an Oration delivered on one of these occasions.

† ——ut omnes Cathedrales Ecclesiæ, et Conventuales, ac Parochiales, a tempore Perfectionis ipsarum, infra Biennium, per Diœcesanos ad quos pertinent, vel eorum Auctoritate per alios, Consecrationes acciperent.

‡ V. Coke Inst., 4.

the primitive Christians; namely the hopes (grounded on the Old Testament, and more particularly on the New) that God would be specially present with them, to hear their prayers and pardon their offences, in those places thus separated to His Service, and dedicated to His name. And thus run the preambles of these very laws themselves :

Domus Dei, materiali Subjecto non differens a privatis, per Mysterium Dedicationis invisibile, fit Templum Domini, ad expiationem Delictorum & divinam Misericordiam implorandam.*

And therefore it was but fit that the performance of a service so solemn and ancient, agreeably to the same laws, should be reserved to the highest dignitaries of the Church ; namely the Bishops, or those having their immediate authority.

In this Country, then, where our Church is far removed from the Government of her Bishops, and where it hath not yet been the Method (nor indeed would Circumstances always admit) before a stated use of our newly-erected places of Worship, to solicit a special Authority for separating them to God's Service, in the express manner of any approved Ritual ; all we can do is to preserve so much of the original design of the thing as Presbyters may warrantably perform ; and which, in such circumstances, may be thought more immediately necessary for Edification. We may meet on a fixt day ; and in conjunction with the common Service of the Church, may use such particular Forms of Prayer and Sermons, as may be suitable to the Occasion ; professing, before God and the World, our humble Desire of setting apart such Places to his Service, and keeping them continually sacred to that pious End.

Thus much is in the Power of every religious Society ; and thus much, at least, as Members of the Church of England, it is our particular Duty to do, with all possible Solemnity, Gravity, and Love to God, whensoever we devote any particular Place to his Service ; in Order that, forever afterwards, when we enter therein, we may consider ourselves as entering into the Place where He hath promised to manifest His more immediate Presence ; and behave ourselves when there (as the primitive Christians are† said to have done in their Places of Worship) with the utmost Reverence and Devotion, as in the Palace of the Great King.

These were the Principles kept in View at the Opening of St. PETER's CHURCH in this City ; and the best testimony for the conduct of that Solemnity, is the Approbation it met with, even from some who came prejudiced against every thing of that Kind.

---

* Vid.. De Consecr. and Reform. Eccles. 52 Hen. 3.   Gibson's Cod.
† Chrysostom.

CHAPTER XIX.

DETERMINATION OF THE TRUSTEES OF THE COLLEGE TO SOLICIT FUNDS IN ENGLAND
FOR ITS SUPPORT—APPOINTMENT OF DR. SMITH AS THEIR AGENT—LETTER OF
INSTRUCTIONS—LETTER OF CREDIT TO DAVID BARCLAY & CO.

THE scale upon which it was indispensable to keep the College, if it was to be such an institution as both faculty and trustees desired to have it, made more money necessary than could be raised on this side of the Atlantic. It was therefore resolved, in the autumn of 1761, that Dr. Smith should go to Great Britain, to endeavor to procure it there. He had now two children, and little or no inherited property. His voyage would be in winter. Nevertheless he was willing to serve the institution by going abroad for this object, or in any other manner, and stated that "he would make all the despatch he could in preparing himself for it, and had good hopes, from what had passed between him and some persons of distinction in England, of answering the expectation of the trustees in this matter."

The trustees accordingly, at a special meeting on the 17th of December, 1761, unanimously agreed that his present salary should be paid to his order in his absence; that £150 currency should be advanced to him towards the expense of his voyage, of which he was to give an account, and that he should be furnished with a credit on Messrs. Barclay & Sons to the extent of £100 sterling. If he should prove successful in obtaining money, he was to pay it, from time to time, into the hands of Messrs. Barclay, for the use of the Academy, and give them a list of the contributors from whom he had received it ; all to be transmitted to the trustees as opportunity should offer. The trustees were further of opinion that, if in six months after Dr. Smith's arrival in England, he should meet with no suitable success, nor see any probability of his succeeding, he should not stay, but return to Philadelphia in the first good vessel that should offer.

The Rev. Mr. Ewing having agreed to supply Dr. Smith's place in his absence upon a proper compensation, Mr. Peters and Mr.

Stedman were desired to confer with him, and to settle the sum that should be allowed him.

The president then delivered to Dr. Smith the following Instructions and letter to Messrs. Barclay:

Instructions to Dr. Smith.

PHILADELPHIA, December 17th, 1761.

REV'D SIR: You will herewith receive an Instrument, under the seal of the Academy, authorizing you to sollicit Contributions in Great Britain and Ireland for its support, together with the Trustees' address to the Proprietaries of this Province, requesting their Countenance and advice to you in the Prosecution of this Charitable Application, and a Letter to the Eldest of them for Liberty to sell the Perkasie Lands.

You are sensible we have proceeded in this affair very much by your advice, and in expectation of the hearty concurrence of our Honourable Proprietors, and therefore we trust and desire you will lose no time, either in embarking for England, or, when there, in setting about and carrying on this good work with your utmost zeal, prudence and assiduity, first waiting on the Proprietors, that by their Council and Recommendation you may be enabled to make a good beginning. Do not neglect to let Mr. Thomas Penn know that as Lands are now at a high price, owing to our present happy flow of wealth, if he be inclined to favour our application for the sale of the Perkasie Estate, the sooner he sends his Orders the greater benefits will be likely to accrue to the Academy.

If Mr. Franklin should be in England on your arrival, we desire you will wait upon him, lay before him your several Papers, acquaint him with our necessities, consult with him, and desire he will give you all the assistance in his power, and we doubt not but he will readily advise and assist you, and by his means you may be recommended to many persons of wealth and Distinction.

If any other of the Trustees should happen to be in England whilst you are engaged in this business, you are to consult with them from time to time, as occasion may require.

The Treasurer is ordered to pay you the sum of £150 currency, which is advanced towards the charge that may attend the service, and we trust you will lay it out with the utmost frugality, and be careful to keep an exact account of every expense that you shall be put to in the prosecution of this business.

Mr. Peters on our behalf has given you a Credit on Messrs. Barclay & Co. as far as £100 sterling. If you arrive safe there may be no use for it, but in case you shall fall into the hands of the Enemys, it may be of use to obtain a decent support and a quick Exchange and Conveyance to England.

If in six months after your arrival in England you shall not meet with Encouragement nor see any prospect of it, we would have you lose no time but take the first opportunity that shall offer of returning home.

But if you shall meet with good success, we think it too great a risque for you to carry large sums of money about you, and therefore order you whenever the sum collected becomes considerable to pay or order it to be paid into the hands of Messrs. Barclay & Co., whom we have appointed our Agents for the receipt of all sums that shall be collected on this occasion, sending them always along with the money or order an exact List of the names of such as you shall have received it from, which List we would have transmitted to us from time to time that we may know how you go on. You will not fail to write full accounts of your proceedings to us by every opportunity.

What further occurs necessary to give you in Instruction we shall send by Letter, having only to add that we most heartily pray for your safe arrival and good success.

Signed by order and on behalf of the Trustees.

RICHARD PETERS, President.

To the Rev^{d}. WILLIAM SMITH,
Provost of the College of Philadelphia.

The Trustees to David Barclay & Co.

PHILADELPHIA, December 17th, 1761.

GENTLEMEN : The Trustees of the Academy finding their Funds likely to fail, and not being able to put their Institution on any durable footing by private subscriptions, have determined to send D^{r}. Smith over to England to sollicit the public spirited people of Great Britain for Contributions, and we hope, Providence favouring our pious and charitable design, he will be able to collect as much as being paid on ground rents or put out to Interest will furnish us with an annual Revenue that will support it forever.

They have desired me to give D^{r}. Smith a Credit with your House for any sum not exceeding £100 sterling. It is imagined he will not want any money if he arrives safe, but if he should be taken by the enemy, and should find it necessary to draw on you in order to obtain a decent support or to procure his discharge and a conveyance to England, I desire you will furnish him to the amount of that sum out of any money in your hands.

The Trustees have appointed you their Agents for such sums as shall be collected for the use of the Academy, and have ordered Dr. Smith not to keep any large sums of money in his hands, but when his Collections amount to anything considerable to pay or cause the money to be paid to you, with an exact List of the Names of such as he has received it from, which Lists and an exact account of the sums put into your hands from time to time we desire you would transmit to us as opportunity serves.

We hope you will not have much trouble in this Agency, and that your former goodness and friendship for all concerned in the management of this Institution, and your regard for the Improvement of the people of this and the neighbouring Provinces in all useful Literature, will engage you to accept of this business and to give Dr. Smith all the assistance in your power. I write this at the instance of the Trustees, and am with a very sincere esteem,

Gentlemen,

Your most humble servant,

RICHARD PETERS,

President of the Trustees and by their order.

To Messrs. DAVID BARCLAY & SONS.

CHAPTER XX.

DR. SMITH PREACHES SERMON IN CHRIST CHURCH ON THE DEATH OF DR. JENNEY —NOTICE OF—LETTER OF DR. SMITH, ETC., TO DR. BEARCROFT—SAILS FOR ENGLAND—BIRTH OF A DAUGHTER (MRS. GOLDSBOROUGH)—MISS GRÆME, AFTERWARDS MRS. FURGUSON—COMMENCEMENT OF 1762—ACCOUNT OF IT FROM COL. BRADFORD'S PENNSYLVANIA JOURNAL.—NOTICE OF WILLIAM HAMILTON, OF THE WOODLANDS, AND NOTICE OF SAMUEL JONES.

JUST fifteen days before leaving Philadelphia to go to New York, whence he was to sail for England, a pathetic duty was to be discharged by Dr. Smith.

We have spoken much of Dr. Jenney, Rector of Christ Church. Of English origin, though born, I think, A. D. 1687, in Ireland, where his father was Archdeacon of Wannytown, and educated at Trinity College, Dublin, he came in 1715 to America as a Missionary from the Society for Propagating the Gospel. In 1717 he became Chaplain to the Fort at New York, either in form, or in fact as an assistant to Dr. Vesey, the Rector of Trinity Church. In 1722 he was Minister of the church at Rye, Westchester county, New York, and from 1728 to 1742 in charge of the church at Hempstead, Long Island. In November of the year last named he became Rector of Christ Church; and with a license from Edmund Gibson, then Bishop of London—the well-known author of the *Codex*—entered on his duties. For the last few years of his

life paralytic disorder and asthmatic affection precluded any efficient
influence on his flock. He died January 5th, 1762, aged 75 years;
his closing years having been clouded with sorrows, some of which
we have mentioned.

Although Dr. Smith, from causes which the reader will remember,* might naturally have felt less than others all that so touching an
old age and death would inspire, he came forward at once to testify
his reverent sympathy for the aged Rector. On the 10th he preached
a funeral sermon on him. It is from that awful text, "Give an
account of thy stewardship; for thou mayest be no longer steward."† The sermon has a grand solemnity suited to the occasion.
Towards its conclusion the preacher says:

> We are met here to perform the last obsequies to the body of our de-
> ceased pastor; a man venerable in years and who was a striking pattern
> of Christian resignation under a long and severe illness. Those who
> knew him best in that situation know that his chief concern was not for
> himself but for the distressed and perplexed state of his Congregation.
> I can with truth say that he was a man of strict honesty, one that hated
> dissimulation and a lie; exemplary in his life and morals, and a most
> zealous member of our Episcopal church.

He is buried in the middle aisle of the church where he so long
ministered.

In or about the year 1732 the sum of £300 sterling was bequeathed by one Mr. Jauncey to the Society for the Propagation
of the Gospel, to be by them disposed in the best manner for the
conversion of infidels. This money, with its interest, was afterwards appropriated by the Society for the use of "the minister of
the Church of England at Philadelphia, Pennsylvania, for the time
being; and the same was laid out in South Sea Annuities, till
lands can be purchased in Pennsylvania." The ministers of
Christ Church probably received the interest up to 1759, but the
pious gift was never fixed in lands. In the year last named the
Rector and Wardens wrote to Dr. Bearcroft, Secretary of the
Society, praying that the Society would authorize them to draw

---

* See supra, p. 129–185.

† The sermon was published soon after it was delivered. The title is, "The Last
Summons, a Sermon Preached in Christ Church, Philadelphia, on January 10th, 1762,
at the Funeral of Robert Jenney, Rector of the said Church. *A. Stewart, Philadelphia*, 1762."

on the Society's Treasurer for the above-mentioned sum, with its advance, if there was any, in order to purchase a piece of land, which they proposed to lease on ground-rent. This request the Society granted, and authorized Dr. Smith, Jacob Duché, John Ross and Evan Morgan, for, and in the name of, the said Society, to purchase lands in the Province of Pennsylvania to the amount of such sum as should be raised by the sale of £300 new South Sea Annuity Stock; the annual rent of such land to be and remain to the sole use and behoof of the minister of Christ Church for the time being, and his successors forever." The letter which now follows, gives a sequel to the history. St. Peter's Church had now become united in one corporation with Christ Church.

Dr. Smith and others to Dr. Bearcroft.

PHIL^A, Jany 12th, 1762.

REV^D SIR : We have received the Honorable Society's Letter of attorney authorizing us or the major part of us to contract for lands in this province to the value of £300 Sterling, to be vested in the Society for the use of the parson of Christ's Church forever. In pursuance whereof we have agreed with our Honorable proprietor, Thomas Penn, Esqre, his agents here, for a Lot of Land in this city which we conceive will well answer the uses intended, a plott whereof you will herewith receive. The Rev^d M^r. Richard Peters, late Secretary to our proprietor and Governor, has most generously offered the sum of £100 Sterling, and proposes to obtain from others the like sum in voluntary contributions to inlarge the lot purchased by us in the name of the Society. Two fifth parts of which large Lott he proposes to be settled and vested for the use of the parson of St. Peter's Church, lately erected in this city, of which we heartily approve and gratefully acknowledge his benevolence. We, in behalf and in the name of, and as Attornies to the Society, have entered into Articles of agreement with the agents of our proprietors for the purchase of this great lott, and obtaining a title in the name of the Society for the uses aforesaid, but the title deed in full form we have at present declined receiving (tho' offer'd to us), until we have further advice from and approbation of the Society. To render these donations useful when the title is vested, some persons thereto authorized must sell and lett this Grand Lott into smaller Lotts under certain yearly Ground Rents forever, and perhaps the tenants at times may prove troublesome and refuse payment, the Society will be often put to trouble to renew their power; their attorney may dye; and the dues to the parson be long withheld, suits at Law may happen for the Recovery of those rents, and no attorney from the Society here to prosecute such suits, &^c. In consideration therefore of the many difficultys which may arise in carrying on these Charities, to have their full and intended effect, we pray the advice and consent of the Honorable Society hereupon, and that we may be permitted to receive our title in the name of any of the Corporations of this City for the uses aforesaid, an exemplified Copy of which deed we shall carefully transmit to your Board, and this mode of title, we humbly conceive, will obviate every objection against our ready and speedy recovery of the rents issuing out of the several Lots to be granted. Whatever the Society shall determine hereupon and advise us thereof, we shall cheerfully acquiesce under.

And now, Reverend Sir, as we have so far ratified our agreement for this purchase by sealing articles for the same, we pray the Honorable Society will be pleased to order a transfer to be made to our Honorable proprietor, Thomas Penn, Esqre, for the £300, New South Sea annuities Stock, his agents here having agreed that he will accept the same in payment for this Lot,

We are, with due regard, &^{c}.,

Wm. Smith,
John Ross,
Evan Morgan,
Jacob Duché.

It is agreeable to add that, from this pious bequest of Mr. Jauncey, made A. D. 1732, the Churches of Christ Church and St. Peter's are to this day, A. D. 1879, in part supported.*

On the 25th of January, Dr. Smith left Philadelphia for New York, where he remained until the 13th of February, on which day he sailed for England. On the 4th of July, while he was in England, his wife was delivered of a daughter, who was baptized Williamina Elizabeth, in Christ Church, on the 4th of August, by the Rev. Dr. Peters, who, on the 8th of January previous, had been elected its Rector. Mr. Sturgeon, with Mrs. Williamina Moore, grandmother of the child, and Miss Elizabeth Græme, of Græme Park, were sponsors. This daughter in after life was one of the Ladies of the *Mischianza*, and became the wife of the Hon. Chas. Goldsborough, of Maryland, and the ancestress of an honored race. Miss Elizabeth Græme afterwards became Mrs. Elizabeth Furguson, and is well known in American history by her connection with the asserted effort of the British Government to purchase the allegiance of General Reed with ten thousand guineas and a good office. Mrs. Furguson's husband joined the

---

* See Dr. Dorr's History of Christ Church, page 372.

royal side. She was a lady of intelligence and wit. A translation of Fenelon's "Telemaque" into English blank verse by her hand is in MS. in the Philadelphia Library. Later in life she went to England for benefit to her health, and kept a journal of her travels, which was much sought for by her friends. In Nathaniel Evans' Poems are some specimens of the versification of Miss Græme, under the signature of "Laura." Mrs. Furguson died in 1801, and is buried by the south side of Christ Church.

Dr. Smith sailed for England from New York on the 13th of February, 1762. The Commencement of the year took place in his absence; but his mind was everywhere. He took care, even when occupied before the King in Council with matters of the gravest interest to himself, to attend even to the details of what was to be done in his darling College.

The *programme* of exercises for the day is in Latin. A copy, with great numbers of valuable papers—including "Compositions" by the boys of the Academy—sent by Dr. Smith to the Penns in England, to keep them apprised of and interested in the College and Academy—is preserved in the Penn Papers in the Historical Society of Pennsylvania—as, indeed, what documents of value in our early history are not? It is a huge broadside, nearly two feet long by more than a foot wide, and all printed in what printers call display, and of impressive style. I can give only the heading:

VIRIS PRÆCELLENTISSIMIS,

THOMÆ PENN ac RICHARDO PENN, Armigeris,

Provinciæ *Pennsylvaniæ*, nec non Comitatuum *Novi Castelli, Cantii* et *Sussexiæ*, ad fluvium *Delaware* veris atque solis Proprietatiis;

VIRO DIGNISSIMO, Literis humanioribus ornatissimo

JACOBO HAMILTON, Armigero,

Prædictæ Provinciæ et Comitatuum, VICE-GUBERNATORI Præclarissimo, nec non hujus Collegii and Academiæ *Philadelphiensis*, Curatori;

Cæterisque VIRIS ORNATISSIMIS

Richardo Peters, *Præsidi;* Gulielmo Allen, Johanni Inglis, Samueli McCall, Josepho Turner, Benjamino Franklin, Gulielmo

Shippen, Phillipo Syng, Phineæ Bond, Abrahamo Taylor, Thomæ Bond, Gulielmo Plumsted, Thomæ White, Gulielmo Coleman, Thomæ Cadwalader, Alexandro Stedman, Benjamino Chew, Edvardo Shippen, jun., Gulielmo Cox, Thomæ Willing, et Jacob Duché, ejuidem Collegii et Academiæ CURATORIBUS amplissimis, Artiumque ingenuarum PATRONIS humanissimis;

Toti denique *Senatui Academico* dignissimo, nempe Reverendo GULIELMO SMITH, S. T. P., Collegii and Academiæ PRÆFECTO; Reverendo FRANCESCO ALISON, S. T. P., Collegii Vice-Præfecto et Academiæ RECTORI; Reverendo JOHANNI EWING, A. M., Philosophiæ Naturalis Professori; Reverendo EBENEZERO KINNERSLEY, A. M., Linguæ Anglicanæ et Oratoriæ Professori; JOHANNI BEVERIDGE, A. M., Linguarum Professori· et HUGONI WILLIAMSON, A. M., Matheseos Professori:

Hæc Philosophemata sub VICE-PRÆFECT Moderamine (DEO opt. max. favente) discutienda.

Juvenes in Artibus initiati.

SAMUEL CAMPBELL,	GULIELMUS HAMILTON,	JOANNES PORTER,
JOHANNES COOKE,	SAMUEL JONES,	STEPHANUS WATTS.

Summâ cum observentiâ M. D. D. D. C. Q.

Then follow the Theses, to wit: Theses Gramaticæ; Theses Rhetoricæ; Theses Logicæ; Theses Metaphysicæ; Theses Physicæ; Theses Morales, and Theses Politicæ. The Theses Metaphysicæ being De Ente, De Mente Humana, and De Deo ; and the Theses Morales, De Ethica and De Jurisprudentia Naturali.

One of the Theses Metaphysicæ, that De Ente, runs thus:

Quicquid non habet existentiam, nec essentiam habet. *Ergo*, Omnes essentiæ rerum in mente Dei ab eterno existere non potuerunt.

Another is:

Origo mali solvi potest, salvis DEI attributis.

We are not quite sure, though we understand Latin, that we understand these Theses.

However, another is more intelligible. It is among the Theses Politicæ:

Militibus dubitantibus an bellum sit justum, nec ne, Militandum est.

A sentiment which shows plainly enough that, however catholic may have been the basis of the College, the Religious Society of Friends had very little to do with prescribing its Theses Politicæ.

We are thus informed after the list of Theses:

Ante Theses indice notatas, ventilandas Oratio habita est salutatoria; cæteris autem Exercitiis pro tempore ad finem perductis, Oratio succcesserit valedictoria. Commitiis Academiæ *Philadelphiensis* habita ad xv Junii Cal. Salutis Anno MD.CCLXII.

There was a power of Latin here, to be sure! and rugged names—harder than Gordon, Colkitto, Macdonnel or Galasp—"that would have made Quintillian stare and gasp." We feel, indeed, as we read the huge *programme*, in the original, with the " Catologus eorum qui ad aliquem Gradum in Collegio Philadelphiensi admissi fuerunt," and the "Stelligeri qui e vitâ decesserunt," some anxiety to know how all turned out, with the Provost absent, on this eventful day. Happily Colonel Bradford, who, from his now intimate relations with Dr. Smith, probably witnessed the whole scene, gives us this very satisfactory account of all in his paper of May 27th. It appears from this account that in these early times a commencement was the affair of a *whole day*. Dining at 6 and 7 o'clock had not then come into fashion:

On Tuesday, the 10th instant, a public Commencement was held at the College in this city in the Presence of a learned, polite and very brilliant Assembly: every Part of the public Hall was crowded with spectators. His Honour, the Governor, who is one of the Trustees of this Institution, was pleased to attend the whole Day. A great Number of the Clergy, of different Denominations, together with many other Gentlemen of Learning, and the first Distinction, from the neighbouring Parts were likewise present.

The Exercises were opened in the morning with a Salutatory Oration in Latin by one of the Candidates: This was succeeded by a forensic Disputation, which gave very high Satisfaction to the Audience, as it was on a subject that greatly interested many of them, and as the Disputants discovered a great deal of Sprightliness, wit and good sense, in the course of the Debate. A Latin Syllogistic Disputation concluded the morning Exercise.

In the afternoon two English Orations were pronounced. A Syllogistic Disputation in Latin succeeded. The Degrees were then conferred by the Vice-Provost, and a *Solemn Charge* delivered from the pulpit to the Candidates. The Valedictory Oration was then spoken with much

Elegance and Tenderness, and the young orator met with deserved applause. A *Dialogue* and *Ode* on the accession and nuptials of his Majesty closed the whole performance.* The ode was written and set to music by one of the sons of this institution,† and excellently performed by a set of gentlemen who kindly and generously employed their agreeable Talents to do Honour to the occasion.‡

The following Gentlemen were Admitted to Degrees at this commencement : Samuel Campbell, John Cooke, William Hamilton, Samuel Jones, John Porter, and Stephen Watts, to the Degree of Bachelor of Arts.

John Beard, Nathaniel Chapman, William Edmiston, and William Hamilton, to the Degree of Master of Arts.

Henry Merchant, formerly a student in this institution, having pronounced an elegant spirited English oration upon the study of the law, was admitted to a Master's Degree; also the Rev. Mr. Morgan Edwards, the Rev. Mr. Joseph Mather, the Rev. Mr. John Simonton, and Mr. Isaac Smith, of *Nassau College*, now Student of Physic, to the Honorary Degree of Master of Arts. And Mr. Thomas Pollock, Tutor in the Academy, to the Honorary Degree of Bachelor of Arts.

Every thing was conducted with the utmost Decency and order. The candidates acquitted themselves in every part of their exercises to the satisfaction of all present, and have derived considerable Honour to themselves, and to the institution.

Among the graduates, as the reader will have observed, was " Gulielmus Hamilton," and Samuel Jones. The former was afterwards known as of "the Woodlands," and long its hospitable, refined, and well-educated proprietor. He had been in the academy from childhood, and spoke in public there when under nine years old. Dr. Griswold, in his "Republican Court, or American Society in the Days of Washington," says of him :

From his youth he seems to have possessed a high degree of taste. On graduating, A. D. 1762, at the Academy of Philadelphia, he gave a fête at the Woodlands to his college friends, among whom were young

---

* The Dialogue and Ode were published in a 4to form, with the following title : "An Exercise, Containing a Dialogue and Ode, On the Accession of His Present Gracious Majesty George III., Performed at the Public Commencement in the College of Philadelphia, May 18th, 1762. Phila.: Printed by William Dunlap, in Market Street. MDCCLXII.

† Francis Hopkinson, distinguished alike by his genius in music and by his literary accomplishments.—Ed.

‡ It thus appears that the Orpheus Club of the College, now led with so much science and taste by one of the brothers Neilson, had an early and honorable origin. It is more ancient than the nation, and may now celebrate its 116th anniversary.—Ed.

men afterwards known as Judge Yeates, Judge Peters, Mr. Dickenson Sergeant, the Reverend Dr. Andrews, Bishop White and others. The beautiful edifice, for which his place has since been celebrated, was not then erected, and his entertainment was necessarily spread in a temporary building.

It is an interesting fact that this lovely place and "beautiful edifice," to which Dr. Griswold refers, then almost miles away from the College and Academy—which were in Fourth Street below Arch —are now, though clothed with the pathetic interest of a resting-place of the dead, in immediate view of the University of Pennsylvania; and that upon ground owned by this very graduate of 1762 now stands, in 1879, the institution from which he received his literary honors.

Samuel Jones chose another lot in life. His was perhaps the wise part. He devoted himself to the ministry, and obtained in it a good degree.*

---

* He was born at Cefen y Gelli, Bettus parish, Glamorganshire, Wales, January 14th, 1735, and was brought to America by his parents in 1737. His father was the Rev. Thomas Jones, who was ordained pastor of Tulpehocken Church, Pennsylvania, in 1740. Samuel Jones was ordained to the work of the ministry on January 8th, 1763, he being at that time a member of the First Baptist Church. He became pastor of the united churches of Pennepack and Southampton in 1763. In 1770 he resigned the care of Southampton Church and devoted himself entirely to the Pennepack Church until his death, which occurred February 7th, 1814. He was buried in the rear of the church. He received the degree of Master of Arts from the Rhode Island College in the year 1769, and he obtained the degree of Doctor of Divinity from the University of Pennsylvania in the year 1788. During his ministry he established a school and academy for the young for tuition in theology on his farm near Pennepack Church, and was successful as a teacher. His printed works were "The Doctrine of the Covenant," a sermon preached in 1783; "Century Sermon," preached in October, 1807, before the Baptist Association; and a small broadside on "Laying on of Hands," which was replied to by the Rev. David Jones, of the Great Valley Church.

CHAPTER XXI.

Dr. Smith arrives in London—Dr. Smith to the Secretary—Reference to the Provost Stillé's Life of Dr. Smith—Extracts from it—Address by the Trustees to the People of Great Britain—Sir James Jay, an unwelcome Fellow-Laborer—Kindness of the Archbishops, Bishops, Mr. Penn, and Others—A Royal Brief—History of Dr. Smith's and Sir James Jay's—His Majesty's Fiat for it—Letters of Dr. Smith and Dr. Jay to the Clergy—Dr. Smith to the Archbishop of York—Begins his Work of Travel and Collections—Sermons published in London.

We have already mentioned that Dr. Smith sailed for England, February, 1762. He arrived in London early in March. He was in England two years and some months. This part of his history has been so admirably told by his successor of our own day, the Provost Stillé, in that short life of the Provost Smith—by which, as in so many other ways, he has done such good service to the University of Pennsylvania—that I am almost afraid to go over the same ground with him. In doing so I shall do best by using much of his language. I shall use also Dr. Smith's private memoranda. Without other acknowledgment, therefore, than this, I avail myself both of Dr. Stillé's facts and his words, interposing, in places, documents which were not open to him, and come to me only by hereditary title.

The Provost Stillé tells us that Dr. Smith was furnished with an address from the trustees, prepared by the Rev. Mr. Peters, President of the Board.

The document—endorsed, "An Humble Representation, by William Smith, D. D., Provost of the College, Academy, and Charitable School, of Philadelphia, in behalf of said seminary and by appointment of the Trustees thereof"—we give here:

To all Charitable Persons and Patrons of Useful Knowledge.

While this happy Nation is exulting in a Series of the most important Successes, and hath given Protection and even Increase to her Dominions in the remotest Parts of the World; while all are ready to consider our distant Colonies and Acquisitions as an inexhaustible source of future Wealth and Grandeur to the Public; and in that favourite View, think no Toil or Treasure too much for their Preservation; there is one view, more important still, in which every serious Mind will delight to consider them, namely, as promising to become an immense addition to the Kingdom of Christ, and to the Protestant Church and Interest upon Earth, and, indeed, unless they are cultivated in this latter view, it is to be feared they will scarce answer our expectations in the former.

A numerous and increasing People, left to Ignorance, unenlightened by the blessed Gospel, Strangers to the humane Arts, and to the just use of rational Liberty, would not only be a very unprofitable, but even a dishonourable Appendage to the British Government, and the greatest of all Glories that can accrue to this Kingdom, from a Dominion so widely extended, will be to make use of the Opportunities thereby given her for the Advancement of Divine Knowledge, and to be found a chosen Instrument in the Hands of Providence, for calling New and heretofore unexplored Countries to the Enjoyment of every Thing that can exalt Humanity, at a Time when so many of the Old have fallen again into their original Barbarity.

Those that love to do Good, and to lay Foundations for Posterity, may, in this great work, find ample scope for their generosity; and what should animate us the more is the amazing Pains which we find the Emissaries of a false Religion have taken, and the many Establishments which they have made under a public Sanction, in all the Parts of America that have been subjected to them; while we can boast of little this way beyond the pious Labours of particular Societies, and a few Seminaries of Learning, chiefly of a private Establishment. Yet, these Societies and Seminaries, it is hoped, are, thro' divine Assistance, kindling up and spreading a light, which shall in the End shine to the remotest parts of the New World.

Among the several Seminaries which have been erected with this noble view, that extensive one, comprehending the College, Academy and Charitable School of Philadelphia, in Pennsylvania, hath in a short time made a most rapid Progress. It was begun about twelve Years ago by a few private Gentlemen, who, observing the vast Accession of People to that Place from different Parts of the World, became seriously impressed with a View of the Inconveniences likely to arise from their being destitute of the necessary means of Instruction. As sundry Circumstances rendered it improbable that any Thing could be speedily done among them, in a public Way, for the Advancement of Knowledge, and at the same Time but very few of so great a Multitude could afford the Expense of educating their Children in distant Places, they saw with Concern that their Country was not only in Danger of wanting a Succession of fit Persons for the public Stations of Life, but even of degenerating into the greatest Ignorance.

In this Situation, therefore, they had recourse to private Subscriptions, and through the Blessing of Almighty God, and the Liberality of Individuals, though unassisted by any public Encouragement, the Design has been attended with remarkable Success. Many excellent Youths, that would otherwise have been without the Opportunities of a liberal Instruction, have already been raised in this Institution as well for the sacred Office of the Ministry, as for the civic Professions of Life; and many others, of more enlarged Circumstances, after acquiring the first Rudiments of Literature there, are now finishing their Education in this Kingdom, at the Universities and Inns of Court.

The Seminary consists at present of near Two Hundred Students and Scholars, besides Eighty Boys and Forty Girls educated on Charity. It is governed under a Corporation of Twenty-four Trustees, by a Provost, Vice-Provost, and three Professors, assisted by six Tutors or Ushers, besides two Masters and a Mistress for the Charity Schools. Very great Sums have, from Time to Time, been contributed for its Support by private Persons within the Province; besides to the Amount of near £3,000 Sterling, in Lands and Money, by the honourable proprietary Family. But although the greatest Economy hath been used in every Part of the Design, and nothing attempted but what the Circumstances of so growing a Place seemed absolutely to require, yet the necessary Expence attending so large an Undertaking hath greatly exceeded all the Resources in the Power of the Trustees; and as the Charge of the Institution is now more than £400 sterling nearly above its Income, they have just Apprehensions of seeing its Funds in a few Years wholly exhausted, and a Period put to its Usefulness, after all their Labours for its Support, unless they can speedily procure the Assistance of generous and well-disposed Persons in distant Parts.

Under these Difficulties they cannot but in the first Place turn their eyes to the known Benevolence and Charity of the Mother Country. And when they consider how far most of the Seminaries, that have been erected in the Colonies, were in their Infancy indebted to the Liberality of pious Persons in Great Britain and Ireland, they cannot doubt but a Seminary placed in one of the most important Cities and central Provinces in America, and which promises to be of so much service to the general Cause of Literature and true Christianity, will in this particular Crisis meet with all due Encouragement.

With these just Hopes, the Trustees of the said Seminary have nominated the Writer of this to solicit and receive the Benefactions of Charitable and benevolent Persons for its Use; and they do hereby promise that whatever may be bestowed for that pious End, shall be most faithfully applied, and due Care taken to preserve Lists of the

Contributors, and to perpetuate their Names in the Institution with Gratitude, to the latest Generation.   WILLIAM SMITH.

LONDON, 1762.

P. S. As many pious Persons and Friends of Literature, whom the Writer of this cannot possibly know of, nor wait upon at their respective Places of Abode, may be desirous of contributing to this useful Seminary, they will be pleased to observe that Benefactions will be received for it by the following Gentlemen, Bankers, viz. : Sir Charles Asgill and Company, Lombard Street, and Messrs. Drummond and Company, at Charing-Cross.

The Form of a Legacy for this Seminary is :

To the Trustees of the College, Academy and Charitable School of Philadelphia, in the Province of Pennsylvania; to be applied towards the support of the said Seminary.

And such Legacy, we ought to add, should be bequeathed and paid out of personal Estates only.

Dr. Smith was also furnished with a special recommendation and appeal to the Penns to aid the enterprise in England. Thomas Penn was called the principal Patron of the College (and well he might have been, for he contributed to its support during his lifetime nearly £4,500), and it is evident that great reliance was placed upon his influence with his friends in England.

On reaching London he at once waited upon those to whom he looked for aid in his design. " Mr. Thomas Penn," he says, "received me with his usual kindness, and said that he was glad to see me on the scheme of a collection, and would forward it all in his power. It is impossible, indeed, for me to express how hearty and zealous Mr. Penn is in this business. He has put himself down for £500 sterling."

Dr. Smith was aware, before proceeding to collect funds, that there were two ways before him in England for raising money: one—that practised then and since in our own country—of going to all persons of every class indiscriminately who might be supposed to be liberally inclined towards an American college, and by direct application to them to get what money they chose to give ; the other—a way more official and dignified—to proceed by " Brief," as it is called in England. " The Brief," Dr. Stillé tells us, "was the technical term given to letters patent written in the royal name to the incumbent of every parish in England (at that time about *eleven thousand five hundred* in number), directing him

to recommend to his congregation some charitable object which
the King was particularly desirous of promoting, and authorizing
collections to be made by specially appointed Commissioners
'from house to house'—these are the words of these Briefs—
throughout the kingdom in aid of the undertaking." It had been
the practice to issue such Briefs only in cases of great general
interest; such, for instance, as when deep sympathy was excited
for the Protestant refugees who flocked to England after the
revocation of the Edict of Nantes, or when succor was asked for
the inhabitants of portions of the country which had suffered from
the overwhelming disasters of famine or pestilence. In later years
it had been the custom to appeal to the public in this way for the
support of such societies as that for Propagating the Gospel in
Foreign Parts, as well as for various undertakings of a charitable
sort in the Colonies. Dr. Smith, under the impression that a
collection by means of a Brief would injuriously restrain his own
personal application, was at first not disposed to proceed in that
way. However, finding that the proceeding by a "Brief" had
many advantages, and advantages so great as to outweigh all
disadvantages, and that he would still be at liberty to appeal to
individuals when he thought he could best aid his design by so
doing, he rather resolved to apply for the Royal Document.

On the 19th of March, 1762, he waited upon the Archbishop of
Canterbury, Dr. Secker, now so well known to him by correspondence, who most cordially assured him that he would do
everything in his power to forward his design by mentioning it to
his friends, and contributing to it in person, asking if there was
anything else that he expected from him; but telling him, if he
intended to apply for a Brief, that there had been so many applications of that sort of late, that he feared it would produce but
little.

He made his business known soon afterwards to the Archbishop of York, and to several of the most eminent of the other
Bishops. "They all declared," he says, "their readiness to concur
with the Archbishop of Canterbury in any scheme his Grace
might propose for countenancing and forwarding the design."
Nor did he forget to invoke the powerful aid of Rev. Dr. Chandler, at that time the most eminent dissenting minister in England, and at all times most kindly attached to him.

" That gentleman," writes Dr. Smith, " sent for me this week,
" and told me that though he had been afraid that all his Court
" interest was gone with the Duke of Newcastle, yet he had been
" with the present Minister Lord Bute, who had most graciously
" received him, and told him that none of the charities which the
" Doctor was concerned in should suffer from the late change, and
" that if there was any good design that the Doctor could recom-
" mend it should be mentioned to the King, who was graciously
" disposed to favor all pious and laudable undertakings. Upon the
" Doctor's return he told me all this, and frankly offered to recom-
" mend our College, and make the first trial of his interest in its
" behalf as a most catholic and laudable foundation, it being in
" this view that the Doctor loves to speak of it in all places."

Dr. Chandler accordingly wrote a warm letter of recommendation to Lord Bute.

But the pleasing prospect which his kind reception had opened
before Dr. Smith was soon clouded by an unforeseen occurrence.
He writes under date of July 10, 1762:

Just now I am so disconcerted that I know not what to do. I had
proposed setting out in a day or two with Mr. Powel to proceed
leisurely through the several trading towns and places to the northward
as far as Edinburgh; but Dr. Jay, from New York, which he left June
1st, has just called on me, and told me that, some business of his own
calling him to England, the people of the College at New York had
applied to and empowered him to solicit money for them.

Dr. Smith was indignant at what he considered an unfair interference with his plans.* A month later, when his anger was a
little cooled, he writes:

Here was a strange clashing of interests and applications, and the
common friends of both Colleges were afraid that both schemes might
be defeated by this method of doing business, and that the public
would be disgusted with such frequent applications, and so close upon

---

* Dr. Jay, of whom frequent mention is made in later parts of our narrative, was
the gentleman better known afterwards as Sir James Jay, Knight. He was the fourth
son of Peter Jay and Mary Van Cortland, and brother of the Hon. John Jay. He was
born in 1732, and bred a physician. On his visit to England as agent of King's College, New York, now Columbia College in that city, he received from King George III.
the honor of Knighthood. He remained several years in England, where he became
involved in a suit in chancery, arising out of the collection for the College, but returned to America previous to the Revolution. He died October 20th, 1815.—ED.

the heels of each other. A proposal was made to unite both designs, but I thought my own interest best, provided the good Archbishop shared his countenance equally, and we could agree to keep at a good distance from each other; nor could I well stomach the thought of being concerned with people who had followed so close upon us as if on purpose to interfere with and prevent our success.

After a good deal of negotiation, during which Dr. Smith's friends, Mr. Penn, Dr. Chandler, and the Archbishop of Canterbury, convinced him that as the New York College had applied for a Royal Brief, it must be a joint one for the benefit of both, or else the whole scheme would be ruined, and that nothing would be gained by their entering upon the same field as rivals, it was agreed that *a joint application on behalf of both Colleges* should be made to the King. " His Majesty," says Dr. Smith, " expressed " his approval of the plan, and said he would do something to " begin the design, that to King's College in New York he would " order £400 sterling, and that in respect to the College in Phila- " delphia, he observed that it had a liberal benefactor in our Pro- " prietors, who stood as it were in his room, but that he must not " suffer so good a design to pass without some mark of his regard, " and therefore would order £200 sterling for us."

The first formal step towards procuring a Royal Brief was to present a petition to the King in Council. Dr. Smith knew something about proceedings before the King in Council already. He had learnt it from his Friends, the Quaker Assembly. His intercourse with the King in Council on that occasion had left most agreeable impressions of both. He gives the following lively account of the circumstances, under which his prayer on this his second application to His Majesty was granted:

The glorious 12th of August (the 1st of August O. S.), remarkable heretofore for so many good things, viz. : the battles of the Boyne * and Minden, and the accession of the present Royal family, became again remarkable for the birth of a young Prince,† the reception of the riches of the Hermione, a larger prize than Anson's, and· if small things may be mentioned with these, the ordering and passing of our Brief, which three things happened before nine o'clock on Thursday morning. The Prince was born at half-past seven, the treasure passed by the palace a little after eight, and the Council that met before nine to register the

* The battle of the Boyne was fought July 1st (not August 1st).
† Afterwards George IV.

birth did our business. We had fixed beforehand with the Archbishop
that the Council of State officers, that should immediately meet on the
joyous occasion of the Queen's delivery, would not only be the most
favorable moment for us, but also the most honorable, if any such
business could be introduced. The good Archbishop engaged to try
what could be done, and I got the clerks of the Council to promise me
early notice to attend with the petition. The event, however, happened
sudden and easy to the Queen, as every Briton had prayed it might,
and before I could hear of it, and had huddled on my gown to run to
St. James' with my petition, the Council was convened in the King's
closet. I meditated whether it was proper to send in anything under
cover to the Archbishop while in the royal presence, and as I was perplexing myself about this, the Council rose. I immediately saw his
Grace, who wished me double joy on the birth of the Prince, and the
completion of our business, of which he had not been unmindful. For
before he went into the Council he desired Lord Egremont, who presides in Lord Granville's absence, to propose it. His Lordship doubted
whether anything of business had ever been introduced on such an
occasion. Lord Bute, who was very willing to have our business
through, observed that there was on the present occasion one other
piece of business to be done, viz.: qualifying Lord Berkeley as Constable of the Tower, and that ours might also be done. The King
having signified his royal pleasure that the petition should be granted,
it was unanimously and without more difficulty agreed to.

An American reader in the year of grace 1879 may perhaps
like to see a little of the Royal Machinery as it was put in motion
at the interview in the closet just described. We present to him
therefore one of the preliminary instruments. What a farce it all
seems to be! A half a word from the Archbishop of Canterbury
before breakfast—as in the chatter of the closet courtiers were
making felicitations and gossip was getting ready to be set a going,
men bowing round and women pushing in—good old George III.
kissing his new-born baby—destined to be such a plague to him
—though in the end a much better king than many others who have
been more praised—and everything is done! "Fiat!" And a
document comes forth as if his Majesty had most laboriously,
most conscientiously, consulting much, pondering much, resolving
slowly, resolving wisely, had arrived at the great conclusion.
But there was no "farce" in the matter. So things are done
in England. Ministers are Majesty. Majesty is Myth. Yet
all works well, and if the Fictions of Government were made

realities, the Government would fall to pieces in a week.   Here is
the Fiat for the Brief:

AT THE COURT OF ST. JAMES'S.

The King's most excellent Majesty in Council :

Whereas there was this day read to His Majesty at this Board the joint
Petition of William Smith, Doctor in Divinity, Agent for the Trustees
of the College, Academy and Charitable School of Philadelphia, in the
Province of Pennsylvania, and Provost of that Seminary; and of James
Jay, Doctor in Physic, Agent for the Governor of the College of the
Province of New York, in the City of New York, in America,—Setting
forth, That the great growth of these Provinces and the continued accession of People to them from the different parts of the World, being
some years ago observed by sundry of his Majesty's good subjects there,
they became seriously impressed with a view of the inconvenience like
to arise among so mixt a multitude, if left destitute of the necessary
means of instruction, differing in Language and Manners, unenlightened
by Religion, uncemented by a common Education, Strangers to the
human Arts, and to the just use of Rational Liberty.

That these considerations were rendered the more alarming by sundry
other circumstances, and particularly the amazing pains which Popish
Emissaries were every day perceived to take for the propagation of their
peculiar Tenets, and the many Establishments which they were making
for this Purpose in all the parts of America belonging to them; while
his Majesty's numerous subjects there, and particularly in the two important and central Provinces aforesaid, remained liable to their corruptions by being spread abroad on a wide Frontier, with scarce a possibility of finding a sufficient supply of Protestant Ministers and Teachers
for them, so long as opportunities were wanting to educate them there,
and but few men of proper qualifications here could be induced to
exchange their hopes in these Kingdoms for a laborious Employment in
a remote Wilderness, where they were to expect but small secular advantage to reward their toil.   That these inconveniences began to be greatly
felt, not only by the Society for propagating the Gospel in Foreign
parts, but also by the various Denominations of other Protestants, in
his Majesty's Colonies, so that the good purposes which they severally
had in view for the Support and Extension of the Reformed Religion in
these remote Countries were like to be grievously affected by the want
of fit persons to send forth as Instructors and Teachers.   That from a
deep sense of these growing Evils the two Seminaries aforesaid, distant
about 100 Miles from each other, were begun in two of the most important and populous trading Cities in his Majesty's American Dominions,
nearly at the same time and with the same view—not so much to aim at
any high Improvements in Knowledge, as to guard against total Ignorance, to instill into the Minds of Youth just principles of Religion,

Loyalty and Love of our excellent Constitution; to instruct them in
such branches of Knowledge and useful Arts as are necessary to Trade,
Agriculture, and a due improvement of his Majesty's valuable colonies;
and to assist in raising up a succession of faithful Instructors and Teachers to be sent forth not only among his Majesty's Subjects there but also
among his Indian Allies, in order to instruct both in the way of truth,
to save them from the Corruptions of the Enemy, and help to remove
the Reproach of suffering the Emissaries of a false Religion to be
more zealous in propagating their Slavish and Destructive Tenets in that
part of the world than Britons and Protestants are in promoting the
pure form of Godliness, and the glorious plan of public Liberty and
Happiness committed to them.

That for the better answering these great and important purposes the
aforesaid Seminaries are under the direction of the chief Officers of
Government: sundry of the Clergy of different Denominations and
other persons of Distinction in the respective cities where they are
placed; and their usefulness has been so generally felt and acknowledged
that amidst all the calamities of an expensive war, near ten thousand
pounds sterling have been contributed in each of the said Provinces to
their support and some hundreds of Youth continually educated on
charity and otherwise.   But as Designs of so extensive a nature have
seldom been completed (even in the most wealthy Kingdoms) unless by
the united generosity of many private Benefactors and often by the particular Bounty of Sovereign Princes, the Petitioners are persuaded it
will not be thought strange that all the power of individuals in young
Colonies should be found inadequate to such a work, and that the Governor and Trustees of the said Seminaries should have the just apprehension of seeing all that they have raised for their support speedily
exhausted and an end put to their usefulness, unless they can procure
assistance from distant places, as the expense of each of them is four
hundred pounds sterling yearly above their Income; the defraying of
which would require an additional Capital of above Six Thousand
Pounds Sterling a piece.   That, under such circumstances, at a time
when the signal success of his Majesty's Arms in America opens a new
field for the advancement of Divine Knowledge there and renders the
Design of such Seminaries more peculiarly important, it was hoped that
Benefactors would not be wanting to give that kind assistance to pious
Foundations in his Majesty's Colonies, which has always been so readily
done upon every Design of the like kind in these Kingdoms, and seldom
denied to Protestant Brethren even in foreign Nations.   That the Petitioners being accordingly appointed to sollicit and receive such assistance,
and being sensible that the highest satisfaction which his Majesty's
known piety and humanity can derive from the Prosperity and Extension
of his Dominions will be to see these advantages improved for enlarging
the sphere of Protestantism, increasing the number of good Men, and

bringing barbarous Nations within the Pale of Religion and Civil life, they are, therefore, encouraged humbly to pray, That his Majesty will be pleased to direct that a ROYAL BRIEF may be passed under the Great Seal of Great Britain, authorizing them to make a Collection throughout the Kingdom from house to house, for the joint and equal benefit of the two Seminaries, and Bodies Corporate aforesaid. His Majesty taking the same into his Royal Consideration, and being willing to give encouragement to every Design that may tend to the good of his Colonies and the advancement of Religion and Virtue, is graciously pleased with the advice of his Privy Council, to order as it is hereby ordered.

That the R't Honorable the Lord High Chancellor of Great Britain do cause Letters Patent to be prepared and passed under the great seal for the Collections of the Charity of all well-disposed persons for the Assistance and Benefit of the said two Seminaries, according to the prayer of the said Petition.

W. SHARPE.

Dr. Smith now, on the 18th of August, enclosing a copy of the order above given, writes, near midnight, with delight to his Trustees in Philadelphia:

This is a very ample and honourable Order, and as the Chancellor was present at its being granted, there is no doubt but he will comply with it; and it shall be presented to him on Monday for that end. After that Dr. Jay will take one end of the Kingdom and I the other, and as each shall apply in the name of both Colleges, and people be under no fear of second applications, they will undoubtedly give more than could be got for any one of them, and thus both be gainers in the end; for neither of us could on our own separate plan have had time to go through half the Kingdom. Jay is an active and sensible young fellow. It is now late at night and I must break off abruptly to reach the mail.

August 15th, he writes further:

The Archbishop's goodness to our College has been so great that I beg he may have a handsome address of Thanks under all your hands and the public Seal. My Letters will furnish you with instances enough of his condescension and kindness, which are to be acknowledged. Dr. Chandler deserves the same mark of your regard, and particularly for his letter to Lord Bute, so very kind in behalf of our College, as well as particularly kind in respect of his recommendation of me; both of which have produced the best effects.

All things now seem to go smooth; only do not let your expectations be too high. It is agreed that the names of every Contributor be published here before we leave England.

20

The Brief was issued on the 19th of August. With many of
those fine words of preamble which Edmund Burke describes as
familiar to the College of Heralds, and come from " a pen dipped
in the milk of human kindness," it authorized certain great persons
(if I remember), the Archbishops of Canterbury and York; the
Lord Bishops of Winchester, of London, and of St. David's ; the
Hon. Thomas Penn, Esquire; the Reverend Samuel Chandler,
Doctor of Divinity; Barlow Trecothick, Esquire; Sir James Jay,
Knight; and William Smith, Doctor of Divinity, etc., or *any* five
of these persons, to appoint agents "to collect funds from door to
door," for the joint benefit of the Colleges of New York and
Philadelphia.

We can well conceive with what emotions the breast of good
Dr. Smith was inspired as, at a later day, he left the precincts of
royalty carrying in his hand that fair, white parchment, with its
gold and rubricated letters, the rich scarlet ribbon hanging
smoothly from its folds, with the royal seal dangling from the
ribbon ends.

But possession of the precious document was not all that the
case needed.   In itself it was what the lawyers call *damnosa
hereditas.*   " The expense of the Brief," writes the Doctor, " will be
£100, the Chancery Fees being high ; which, with former expenses,
I fear will leave little above £300 of the cash I sent Mr. Coleman
an account of by Mr. Franklin. . . . Mr. Penn's £500 sterling is
to be paid in Philadelphia." The object, therefore, now was to
make the Brief operative. The original, of course, could not be
sent to each one of the eleven thousand five hundred clergymen of
every grade in England. The plan of the thing had no such purpose. Briefs have a purpose of their own, as well as a purpose for
charities. The plan is to send a stamped copy to each of the eleven
thousand five hundred of the clergy who are to make the appeal
under it. The stamps bring as much to the Crown as the Brief
sometimes does to the charity. Besides this, " Brief Layers " follow
all Briefs. The American reader will, perhaps, hardly know
what a " Brief Layer " is. He does not know that it would be
thought beneath the dignity of a person holding a Royal Brief,
especially of a Doctor of Divinity and a Knight, to perform any
details incident to it himself. All that must be done by " Brief
Layers." They were now, August 24th, 1762, appointed by Dr.

Smith and Sir James Jay, two of the commissioners to whom the Brief was directed. We give the Power of Attorney: *

WHEREAS, upon the joint Petition of us, William Smith and James Jay, the former of us Agent for the Trustees of the College, Academy and Charitable School of Philadelphia, in the Province of Pennsylvania, and the latter Agent for the Governors of the College of the Province of New York, in the city of New York in America; his Majesty with the advice of his most hon^ble privy council has been graciously pleased to grant his Royal Brief or Letters Patents under the great Seal for Collecting the Charity of well-disposed Persons from House to House throughout this Kingdom for the joint and equal Benefit of the said two Seminaries of Learning and Bodies Corporate: Now, Know all men by these Presents that we do hereby authorise and appoint JOHN BYRD, JOHN HALL and JOHN STEVENSON, in the Borough of Stafford, in the County of Stafford, Gentlemen, to cause a sufficient number of the said Briefs or Copies thereof to be printed, and to give a Receipt for the same as the Law directs; and when the said Copies shall be Signed by us or some one of us, we do further appoint the said Persons to see them stamped as the Law directs; and to pay all the Fees for such stamping, and also the expence of the Letters Patents and of the printed Copies thereof, & to bring us an account of the same as soon as possible, in order to have it settled and allowed by us; and we further appoint the said John Byrd, John Hall, & John Stevenson to lay down and dispose the said Briefs in all Parishes & Places where the same by the said Letters Patents shall be required to be laid, and to take up and receive back the same together with the money thereupon collected, and to pay the same to the Trustees therein named for the uses aforesaid; deducting out of the same the sum of Six Pence a Parish chapel or meeting for every Brief duly certified and endorsed, which shall by them be collected and received back from all Places (except within the city of London & weekly Bills of mortality and therein the sum of twelve Pence) as the full salary and Charge for Laying down, collecting and receiving back the said Briefs, with the money thereupon collected and the Payment of the same to the Trustees and all other Trouble of management whatsoever. In witness whereof we have hereunto set and subscribed our Hands this twenty-fourth of August, one thousand seven hundred and sixty-two.

WILLIAM SMITH,
JAMES JAY.

Dr. Smith now lost no time in beginning his work. While the Brief Layers were performing the mechanical parts of the work, he was at the more difficult work of exercising influence. The

---

* From the original, in the possession of William Kent Gilbert, M. D.

following letter shows with what vigor and effectiveness and at the same time with what tact, good breeding and delicacy he was trying to carry forward his schemes :

Dr. Smith to the Archbishop of York.

LONDON, 26th August, 1762.

MY LORD : Having by the kind interposition of the Arch[b] of Canterbury obtained a joint Brief for our College & that of New York, attended with Signal Marks of the Royal Favor and Bounty, it is our duty to consider by what means the said brief may be made the most effectual for our Purpose ; especially as two objects are united in one, and the Sum which we want very considerable. If the Clergy should interest themselves no more than in the common run of Briefs, and raise us only the common sum of £800 or perhaps £1000, this, when divided, would go but a short way. But on the contrary, if they could be induced to take the matter to heart, & improve the arguments suggested by the Brief, it is hoped the Business might be made very popular, and the Collection Considerable. Now, my Lord, if it could any way be notified to the Clergy that the Design of this Collection is particularly approved by our good Archbishops & that your Grace considers the Encouragement of these American Seminaries, as particularly connected with your pious and noble Designs for the Propagation of the Gospel there, I am well persuaded it would be the means of doubling our Collection. Thus much, if only annexed by way of Testimonial or Certificate to a short printed account of the two Colleges, and dispersed along with the Brief, which the undertakers promised to do, would answer our end. The enclosed Clause from our Brief shews that there is no Impropriety in this ; though we do not desire any Thing for particular Dioceses, nor by way of Injunction or Command to the Clergy ; but only something to notify an Approbation of the Design by your Grace as above. For we have not time to apply to each particular Bishop upon the plan pointed out in the clause, before the season of laying down the Brief, which will commence in a few weeks.

Permit me, my Lord, just to hint one Thing more which the Secretary of Briefs told me ; viz.—That the enclosed Clause has only been inserted in such Briefs as are given by orders of Council, for promoting & preserving the Protestant Religion in Foreign Parts & where the Collection is all over the Kingdom ; so that there is no Danger that any Thing done in this affair can be drawn into Precedent to give Trouble in future Briefs granted on the common Plan for Losses within the Kingdom, rebuilding Churches, &c. In short, all that we humbly request is only such a Certificate in favour of our Colleges as we should have ventured to ask, even if we had proceeded without a Brief, on a common printed case of our wants. These things are most humbly and dutifully submitted to your Grace, which I have taken the Liberty to do, after having just come from the Archbishop of Canterbury, who was pleased to say he would write to your Grace on this subject, and that there might be no Impropriety in my sending a few Lines at the same time. With the utmost Gratitude to your Grace for your past Kindness, and a sincere Desire in all Things to prove myself not unworthy of its Continuance,

I am, &c.,

WILLIAM SMITH.*

To His Grace, the Lord Archbishop of York.

By the time that the Brief Layers had stamped and addressed their copies of the Brief, Dr. Smith had prepared for himself and Sir James Jay a letter to be sent with each copy; a letter explaining more particularly than did the Brief itself the object of the collection, and urging upon the clergyman to whom the copy of the Brief was sent, the importance of his aiding it by his personal influence and, where practicable, by preaching a sermon having special reference to it. I give this fine document, even though it iterate somewhat—as was unavoidable—thoughts already expressed in other like documents by the pen of the great Provost.

To all the worthy and Reverend the Clergy and Ministers of the Gospel into whose hands his Majesty's Royal Brief, for the Colleges of Philadelphia and New York, shall come:

LONDON, 9th Sept., 1762.

REVEREND AND WORTHY GENTLEMEN: As you will herewith receive his Majesty's Royal Brief or Letter Patent, for making a collection from House to House among the People under your Ministry, for the two Colleges lately established in the Cities of New York and Philadelphia, we thought it our Duty to submit to your perusal such further account of the Design and Usefulness of these Seminaries, as might enable you, upon due information, to give them that Encouragement, which we are persuaded your Christian zeal will induce you to bestow upon every Scheme for the advancement of Religion and useful Knowledge.

At a time when this happy Nation is exulting in a Series of the most Important Successes, and hath given Protection and even Increase to her Dominions in the remotest Parts of the Earth ; while all are ready to consider our distant Colonies and Acquisitions as an inexhaustible Source of future Wealth and Grandeur to the Public, and think no toil or Treasure too much for their Preservation, there is one View more important still, in which we know you will delight to consider them, namely, as promising

---

* From the original draft among Dr. Smith's MSS.

to become an immense Addition to the Kingdom of Christ, and to the Protestant Church and Interest upon Earth. And, indeed, unless they are cultivated in this latter View, it is to be feared, they will scarce answer our Expectations in the former. It would be needless to enumerate to you the lamentable Consequences of leaving a vast and increasing Multitude of our fellow-Subjects, in a remote corner of the Earth, a prey to Ignorance, open to the Corruptions of a vigilant Enemy, and continually exposed to false Notions of Religion and Government for want of due Opportunities of Instruction in those that are true. Liberty does not deign to dwell but where her fair companion Knowledge is ; nor can government be administered but where the principles of Justice, Virtue, Sobriety, and Obedience for the Lord's Sake are upheld.

It is of the utmost consequence, therefore, to this Nation that our Colonies should be made an Object of Civil and Religious Culture ; and that all necessary Knowledge should not only be propagated among our own people there, but also among the Heathen around them, in order to root out their Notions of Barbarity, Murder, Rapine, Cruelty and Revenge, which are so fatal to us on every difference with them. Without due care in this respect, these immense Countries can never be rendered of full use to these Kingdoms. Their advantages of Soil, Climate and Situation, would not be improved for the Extension of our Commerce. They would be in danger of becoming not only a very unprofitable, but even an unwieldy and dishonorable an Appendage to this Monarchy, and, in the End, be so far from enlarging the Church of Christ and giving fresh strength to the Protestant Interest, as to fall perhaps into the opposite Scale of Superstition and Idolatry.

But it is for the honour of this Nation that, even in an Age wherein Christianity hath lost much of its Influence on the Lives of Men, several publick Societies have been formed, and noble contributions made, in order to prevent these fatal Evils, to support Religion in our Colonies, and extend its sacred Influence to the very ends of the Earth. Much has been done by these truly pious Bodies, and particularly by that venerable Society incorporated for this Purpose. But neither of them had proceeded far in their work, before they found the harvest to be indeed great, but the Labourers few ; that it would be impossible, with the small encouragement in their power, ever to induce a sufficient number of able Instructors to go from these Kingdoms to supply the growing Calls of our Colonies ; and that if there were better opportunities of instruction there, more of the natives would be fitted for this Work ; which they would undertake with many advantages above such as go from hence. And therefore these Societies have always been desirous to promote useful Seminaries of Learning in the Colonies as one of the surest Foundations for the Support and Advancement of true Christianity in them.

Now no Institutions can be better calculated to answer these good purposes, or better deserve publick Regard, than the Colleges above-mentioned. They are placed in two of the most important Cities of America, in Central and populous Provinces; and being intended for the benefit of a very mixt body of Men, they are founded on an enlarged bottom, and put under the most unexceptionable Direction. The Chief Officers of Government; the Magistrates, the Clergy, and other principal gentlemen, are concerned in the management of them. And it is truly edifying to behold, in this Instance, to what an amiable Height the divine Virtues of Love and good Understanding may be carried by Men, tho' otherwise differing in pursuits and opinions, when engaged in any great and publick work, actuated by the Christian Principles, and blest with an enlarged and liberal Turn of Mind.

Near four hundred Youths are continually educated in them; of whom about Sixty are intended for the learned Professions, and particularly to furnish a Supply of Ministers and Teachers for the different Societies of Christians in these parts. The Remainder are chiefly designed for Merchandize, Trade, Navigation, and the Mechanic Professions; and the Academy and lower Schools in the Philadelphia Seminary are wholly intended for raising up Youth in this way. Belonging to this Seminary there is also a Charity School for eighty Boys and forty girls; as there is likewise at New York a Charity School for near the same number, supported at the Expense of those who are the chief Contributors to the College there. Thus many excellent youths, who would otherwise have been destitute of all opportunities of a sufficient Instruction, are continually rendered useful in both Provinces; and, among those of more enlarged Circumstances, a far greater Number than ever was known at any former Period, for acquiring the first Rudiments of learning there, have been induced and enabled to finish their Education in this Kingdom at the Universities and Inns of Court.

But a great Check has been given to these Undertakings by the Ravages of a destructive War, which laid waste a considerable part of both Provinces, increased the Expense of these Institutions, dispirited many of their friends, and forbid them to expect any speedy assistance from their own Legislatures, on account of the vast load of Public Debt accumulated for the Defence of the Country. They have, therefore, been severally obliged to have recourse to the known Benevolence and Charity of the Friends of Religion and Learning in these Kingdoms; and have joined both applications in one, in order that from the importance of the objects, pious and well-disposed persons may be induced to contribute more liberally without fear of future sollicitations for any thing of the like Kind from that part of the World.

These things, therefore, having in the first place been represented to our most pious and excellent Sovereign, he was graciously pleased out of his princely Zeal for the advancement of Religion and useful

Knowledge in every part of his extensive Dominions, to order his Letters Patent for making a Public Collection for the joint Benefit of these Seminaries, accompanied with a Royal Bounty of £600 as an example to his good Subjects. And accordingly the two worthy Archbishops, such of the Bishops as we have found in town, with sundry persons of Eminence, Clergy, and others, of Different Denominations, have made a beginning by most liberal Contributions, and have afforded us well grounded Hopes of a due Measure of further success.

As to you, Gentlemen, who are the Ministers of God's Word, and always foremost in every Design for the Instruction of Mankind, we can well depend that this so laudable an undertaking will meet with your particular Countenance and assistance. The kind Providence of God seems to have great things in view, by calling the British Nation to the Possession of the most important part of America; and the greatest of all the Glories that can accrue to this Kingdom from a Dominion so widely extended, will be to make use of the opportunities thereby given her for the advancement of divine Knowledge, and to be found a chosen Instrument in these latter days for calling New and heretofore unexplored Countries, to the enjoyment of everything that can exalt Humanity, at a time when so many of the old have fallen again into their original Barbarity. Should we once become indifferent in this respect, and begin to consider our vast American Settlements as given to us merely for advancing our Secular Interests, and not for enlarging the Sphere of Protestantism and increasing the number of good men, we may have reason to fear that Divine Providence would leave us to ourselves, and raise up worthier Instruments for accomplishing his own eternal purposes of Love towards those so long benighted and forlorn regions.

But, blessed be God! it is yet no part of the Character of this Nation to be indifferent to works of Charity and public Spirit; and in this light, we trust, the present important undertaking for the Benefit of these infant Seminaries, will have a just claim to be considered. Here, indeed, those who love to do good and to lay Foundations for Posterity, will find ample Scope for their Generosity; and we know that in you, Gentlemen, they will have kind and ready prompters.

What we would in a more especial manner pray of you is, that, together with your good offices to make our Brief as effectual as possible, in regard to the pious purposes for which it is granted, you would likewise give it all the dispatch your convenience will admit of. And we hope our particular circumstances will be our plea for this humble request, being at three thousand miles distance from the places of our abode, and obliged at great expense to our Constituents, to wait the issue of this business.

We should likewise be glad, if it were convenient, to have the names of our Benefactors returned with the Briefs, that they may be perpetuated with gratitude, in these Seminaries, to the latest generations.

Praying that every Happiness may attend you, as the Reward of all your pious Labours, we are, with the utmost Respect,
        Reverend and worthy Gentlemen,
            Your most obedient, and most humble Servants,
                                WILLIAM SMITH,
                                JAMES JAY.

With the stamped copy of the Brief and a copy of this letter sent as *avant coureurs,* Dr. Smith and Sir James Jay set off from London on the 29th of September, 1763, to perform their work; Dr. Smith preparing to make a journey to the north of England and to Scotland, his native land, while Sir James went to scour the south and western plains.*

We now let the Provost and the University tell their own story. They both tell it charmingly in a sequence of letters unfortunately broken in parts, but still held sufficiently together to present to the intelligent reader a narrative of fulness and order.

CHAPTER XXII.

TRUSTEES TO DR. SMITH—DR. SMITH TO TRUSTEES—DR. SMITH TO DR. PETERS—
DAVID GARRICK TO DR. SMITH AND MR. JAY—PERMISSION TO RETURN
HOME—DR. PETERS TO DR. SMITH—DR. SMITH VISITS THE KING IN PERSON
AT ST. JAMES—THE UNITED CHURCHES—BISHOP OF LONDON TO VESTRY—
DR. SMITH TO VESTRY OF CHRIST CHURCH—DR. PETERS TO DR. SMITH.

The Trustees of the College to Dr. Smith.

PHILADELPHIA, January 11th, 1763.

SIR: The President has communicated to us such parts of your Letters as give an Account of your proceedings in the Business committed to your charge, and by these it appears to us that you have acted with great care and judgment in the several Difficulties that have occurred. Since Dr. Jay was sent over to sollicit contributions in favour of the New York College, and an opposition between the two Seminaries might

---

* The 2d edition of his sermons were published in London soon after he left that city, but not for sale, as I think; since all the copies which I have ever met with—and they are several—contain a Presentation; and as I find no mention in his cash account (which is particular) of having paid either for any printing of the edition, or for particular copies, I am led to believe that they were printed by the liberality of Mr. Penn.

have hurt both, we very much approve of your agreeing with him to join the two Charities together, and to make a joint application to his Majesty for a special Brief for the benefit of both.

The Birth of the Prince gave a favourable opportunity for doing it, and we are obliged to you for pushing the Brief in the Council that was called on that joyful occasion. As we have been so fortunate as to obtain such a Brief, we do not in the least doubt but by the Continuance of your unwearied diligence and personal attendance at the principal places where the Collections will be made, all sorts of people will be duly informed of the usefulness of the Charity, and be Spirited up to give generously.

We would not therefore have you to think of coming home one moment sooner than the expiration of the Time limited in the Brief for the collections. We are sorry you will be so long absent from your Family, but we hope the same zeal which moved you to undertake this Business, will animate you to continue in it as long as you can be of any service, and never to remit your personal sollicitations wherever they can turn to account.

You must be sensible that if the Collections be left to the Management of the Parish Officers in the ordinary Course of business, little can be expected from the sort of people who think these matters burdensome, and hurry them over anyhow so as they can rid their hands of them. This makes it necessary for you to attend yourself wherever you can, and where you cannot we must recommend it to you to engage some good person of interest who lives upon the spot where the Collection is to be made to attend for you, and to take care that the Charities be carefully collected and no persons left unsollicited.

As Mess.rs Barclay did not choose their names should be made publick you did well to take their advice as to the Gentlemen you have employed in their places, they being Bankers of established character.

We desire you will continue to give us full accounts of your proceedings by every opportunity that offers, and please to let us know particularly what success you had in your private applications before you joined with Dr. Jay, and as there is very little Money in the Treasurer's hands, the sums paid on account of Lotteries being mostly disposed of either in the payment of Salaries or in the new buildings, which are near finished, we desire to know when we may draw and for what sum.

Whenever we receive your Accounts of what is done, we shall write to you on all points that we shall find to be material, and we desire you may not return till you have our express orders for so doing. We thank you for the unwearied pains you have taken in this business and we hope you will persevere to the end. Wishing you the enjoyment of your health and success, we are

Your sincere friends, &c.

[Signed by a Committee of the Trustees.]

It will be remembered that Dr. Smith, immediately on getting the Fiat for the Royal Brief, had written to the Trustees, saying that both the Archbishop of Canterbury's and the Rev. Dr. Chandler's goodness to the College had been so great, that a handsome vote of thanks ought to be sent to both of them under the hands of the Trustees and the public seal of the College.*   This was now done : and no doubt in a genteel and elegant way; as Dr. Peters, the President of the Board of Trustees, was capable of doing it.   We find in the minutes of the 11th of January, 1763, an entry as follows :

At a meeting of the Trustees, the President was ordered to affix the lesser Seal of the Academy to the Addresses to the Archbishop and Dr. Chandler and to sign them in behalf of all the Trustees, and to enclose them, with their letter to the Proprietor likewise signed by the President in their behalf, in Dr. Smith's Letter, with Directions to him to present them to each person in the very best and most respectful manner.

We resume our correspondence :

Dr. Smith to Trustees.
April 12th, 1763.

Since my letters by Mr. Duché I have only wrote once, having been but five days in London since the end of September, as you will see by the following short account of what I have been doing.   But as I believe the ship by which I did write, although she left this place six weeks ago, has not yet left the Channel, I shall begin as far back as September 29th.†   On that day, which was as soon as we could get all the eleven thousand five hundred Briefs signed and stamped, I set out for Edinborough, and from thence went 100 miles farther north to see my aged and good Father.   As my business urged I was obliged to do so much violence to myself as to stay only a few days with him.   This act of duty I hope the Trustees will not think was throwing away their time.   If they should, it is the only fortnight, or indeed the only moment I have lost to them.   But it cannot well be called loss.   One gentleman of that neighbourhood, Sir Arch⁴ Grant, gave ten pounds sterling to the Design, and will collect somewhat more for us.   The University of Aberdeen also propose doing something.   When at Edinborough I waited on Dᵣ. Robertson, Dᵣ. Wishiart, Dᵣ. Cumming, Dᵣ. Jordain and others.   They were well disposed to serve us, but think their joint Interest, tho' at the Head of the Church of Scotland, will not be able next assembly, at least, to procure us a National Collection.   For they have had three public collections for America within

---

* See *supra*, p. 305.   † A. D. 1762.

these few years and one of these is now on foot for the conversion of
the Indians, on the Petition of a Society lately erected by Law at
Boston. Another, viz., M^r. Beaty's, is but just finished. However,
the Gentlemen above mentioned are to write to me on this head, and
readily agreed to countenance a private collection, which may produce
almost as much as the public one, if that could not be obtained. Provost
Drummond, who is the most popular Magistrate they have ever had,
will give his countenance to the same. D^r. Morgan is now collecting
somewhat occasionally for us, and M^r. Inglis will join him; D^r. Alison
will not lose a moment in procuring Letters for the Scots Clergy,
whether we apply publickly or privately; and let them be here in April
with your Instruction on this Head. I fear the College of New York
may be some Impediment in getting the public collection in Scotland;
for they have instructed Dr. Jay to apply also, and as the King has
joined us here, I cannot separate them in Scotland, if the application
be made now. In my mind it might be delayed for a year or two, and
made afterwards by a petition sent from the Trustees at Philadelphia
without sending anybody over to sollicit for it. Let these things be
immediately considered, and an answer sent me to the whole.

At Glasgow I found the same encouragement as at Edinborough
among the Clergy, who professed themselves pleased with the Catholic
Plan of having Professors, &c., of different Persuasions, and told me
that the Party in the Church of Scotland to whom that would be an
objection were not many. But I would not stay to make any particular
collection either here or at Edinborough, only prepared matters. My
being detained so long at London before I could set out for the North,
and being obliged to be at Oxford in November, hampered me much in
time. However, it was necessary on account of the success of the
Brief to make the Tour. On my return, I visited all the principal
Clergy in the Towns on or near the great Road, and wrote Letters to
others. In places where it was thought my presence would assist the
Collection, we agreed to delay it till March, when I promised to go
down again, especially to Yorkshire. In places of less note I left it to
the Clergyman himself to read the Brief, and make the most of it,
after having waited on some leading persons and engaged their assistance to make the Collection. Thus, in about six weeks from my setting
out I got back to London to meet Dr. Jay, who had taken a like tour
southward on the same plan. Neither of us could stay to do much
more than put the Brief in a fair way; and that end has been answered
very effectually. After two or three days' stay in London we set out
again for Oxford, thinking it a compliment due to them to be both
there. From Oxford we went to Gloucester, and to the manufacturing
Towns in that County: Dr. Jay taking part of them and myself the
other part, so as to meet at Bath, which we did a day or two before
Christmas, and then proceeded to London, where the Briefs are now to

be read in those full months—January and February. Bristol we have delayed to the end of February, and Bath afterwards. Dr. Jay will go thither while I go to the North in March. This is a general sketch of what we have done and are to do. To copy the particulars of our Journal would be taking time from business of more importance: for we now find before us near forty Letters unanswered, and a continual attendance on the Clergy of London necessary; every one of whom (being near 200) we must see within this fortnight, and before they can read the Brief, which we are to give them with our own hand. Many principal people are also to be waited on before the Brief is read in their particular Parish, because we hope they will give more to one of ourselves than to a Brief which some persons have resolved never to contribute to on account of the abuses which they conceive are committed by the Brief-Layers. But we have taken care that nothing of this can happen in our case.

From the above account you will see that neither our Plan nor our time would permit us to collect much money, yet we have not been unsuccessful even in this respect. I shall subjoin an account of what we have got since our schemes were united even amidst all the hurry in travelling, chiefly for the sake of the Brief.

Collected by Dr. Jay, from our parting, Sept. 29th, to our meeting again, Nov. 20th, per list entered in his book and in mine and reciprocally signed. £121 12 6

Collected by Dr. Smith, during the aforesaid period................. 187 6 0

From Nov. 25th to Dec. 25th collected as follows, viz.,

Collected jointly from the University of Oxford...................... 161 18 0

Collected jointly in the City of Gloucester........................ 35 16 0

Collected by Dr. Smith among the Clothiers at Stoude, where he preached and had the Brief read.. 49 11 6

N. B.—This was given independent of what the Vicar collected by the Brief, which made about £15 more, to be returned in the usual way to the Brief Collection, at the Spring Visitation.

Collected by Dr. Smith at Uley, Dwelsey and Weston Underedge, other Cloathing Towns independent of the Brief....................... 65 6 6

Collected by Dr. Jay at Hamton, Tadbury and Painswick............. 33 4 6

Her Royal Highness the Princess Dowager of Wales through Lord Boston and Sir Charles Hardy..................................... 100 0 0

In the whole....................................... £754 15 0

Dr. Smith to Dr. Peters.

LONDON, 24th April, 1763.

DEAR SIR: I received the kind Letter which the Trustees did me the honour to send me, and shall be attentive to its contents. At present, however, for the same reason mentioned to you in the beginning of the Letter relative to your own business, I must defer giving any very particular answer to it.

The Addresses of the Trustees to the Arch Bishop, M^r. Penn, and D^r. Chandler, were delivered, and kindly received. I shall leave this place by the 12th of May at farthest, having kept back the Collection at York, Liverpool, and some other considerable Towns. From thence I shall cross over to Ireland, and try to get away for America by Sepr 1st, for I will by no means take a Winter passage. The Trustees may depend that I shall leave nothing undone that requires my presence, and shall rather stay another Winter, how irksome and inconvenient soever, than desert the good Cause which I have carried on so far with success.

I shall, before I leave London, give you particulars of everything. At present our Collection goes on well in the several parishes of this City, and I take the usual pains to get proper Preachers. In a most divided Kingdom, by a happy Fate, the leaders of all sides have been induced to contribute. We have in our List the names of the Duke of Newcastle, Lord Bute and M^r. Pitt; and both Universities have been liberal. From Lady Curzon, who happened to be one of my audience when I preached at Curzon Street Chapel (commonly called Mayfair Chapel), I received one hundred pounds. My friend, Mr. Dawkins, readily gave fifty pounds, and Col. Barre has been kind in introducing me to sundry persons.

But you must not think that all this produces very great sums. We are, by the Brief, entirely prevented from applying to the Middling rank of people, for if we were to go to them (which indeed is hardly possible in any large degree) none of the Parish Ministers would be at the pains to carry round the Brief; and then, as to people of Fortune who can afford something extraordinary, it is almost impossible to get at them, or to get anything from them, but by particular Interest—they are so harassed with an Infinity of Charities; and then when they are disposed to give, you must call twenty times perhaps before the matter is finished, so you see the Brief must greatly interfere with all our private attempts to collect, not only as barring our Applications to all that set of people who could be most readily got at, but likewise furnishing others with an excuse to put us off by saying they have given or will give to the Brief.

On Summing up my book I find that, including M^r. Penn's benefaction, I have seventeen hundred pounds to the Credit of our College without the Brief Money, our share of which will certainly amount to as much more, so that if our Share of what may be got in Ireland should be six hundred pounds, we shall thus get £4,000, which is the most that ever I flattered myself could be done, even when I thought to have the whole Kingdom to myself alone, and therefore I cannot but be thankful to Providence. Of the £1,700 already coming to our share, £500 is ordered by M^r. Penn to be paid to the Trustees, £650 are in M^r. Barclay's hands, having paid him £100 yesterday, since he wrote to advise you of what he had received; £25 I paid at D^r. Alison's desire, for which I enclose the Draught drawn on him, and about the same sum I paid for M^r. Duché. The remainder, £500, is partly at Cambridge, partly in Benefactions sent to our different Bankers, not taken out of their hands, and partly going to my expenses, and the expense of our Brief and printed papers. This Sketch, I hope, will suffice till I have more leisure.

I wonder you should desire to know what I collected before D^r. Jay came over. I sent an exact list of it to M^r. Coleman by M^r. Franklin, and he received it.

On Wednesday next we are to have a Benefit Oratorio at Drury Lane, and M^r. Beard leaves his own house to perform for us at the other; and will give a Benefit himself next Winter, but could not do it now on account of a week lost to him, at His House, viz.: Covent Garden.

M^r. Garrick has been exceedingly kind in the matter, and gave his house at first asking, and was sorry that the season was so far advanced, and that he had no night disengaged sooner.* The principal performers, Vocal and Instrumental, serve gratis, and we are favoured with the Boys from the Chapel Royal, and every other mark of distinction. M^r. Tyers even put off the opening of Vaux Hall, which was fixed on Wednesday next, in order to favour us.

We now find an entry in the Minutes of the Trustees as follows, indicative of their continued and increasing confidence in Dr. Smith's good judgment, as well as in his disinterested zeal for the interests of the College.

May 23d, 1763.

At a meeting of the President and Trustees of the College a letter from D^r. Smith was read, desiring that he might be left at liberty to return home when he should think proper. It was agreed to withdraw that part of our last letter which directed him to stay in England till he should have our further orders, and to leave him at his liberty as desired, after consulting with M^r. Penn and such Trustees as shall happen to be in England.

---

* It is probable that Dr. Smith may have taken letters of introduction to Mr. Garrick, and sent them to him, with a note indicating a purpose to call on him. I find among Dr. Smith's papers a note (undated) thus:

"Mr. Garrick presents his Respects to Dr. Smith and Dr. Jay, and will not give "them ye trouble of calling in Southampton street, as his being at home is quite un- "certain on account of his business at the Theatre, but Mr. Garrick will take ye first "opportunity of paying his respects to Them at the News Gate."

Addressed:

To the Rev. Dr. Smith and Dr. Jay, at the News Gate, corner of Duke's Court, London.

In May, 1763, Dr. Smith writes to the Trustees, desiring them to send him an Address to the King and to Lord Bute. In writing he tells them that the New York people had shown themselves wiser than ours of Philadelphia. *Their* agent had brought such Addresses as Dr. Smith now asked for. He adds "what," says the Provost Stillé, " is just as true and apposite now as it was a hundred years ago :"

I know not how it is that *our* College, as a body, is so diffident and apt on the first motion to beat down any proposal that has anything great in it. It was thought once that we were too little an object for national notice here. Time and a fair trial have taught us better on that head. Had I at first desired an Address from the Trustees to the King, I think it would not have been granted. Yet a College of less note set out with such an Address. Public bodies should have no shame of this sort ; I speak not this to blame what is past, but rather to persuade you to lift up your heads, and rather fail in great attempts than be found too diffident.

Dr. Peters now writes in form again:

Dr. Peters to Dr. Smith.

PHILADELPHIA, 27th May, 1763.

SIR : I have laid before the Trustees the Letters and Papers received from you since my public Letter of the 11th January last*, which was wrote by their order and in their Behalf. These Letters, which bear date the 8th of January, 12th of February, and first of March, have been considered,† and I am directed by the Trustees to return you their Thanks and to acquaint you that they much approve the several measures you have taken in the business committed to your care, and rejoice in the success that is likely to attend them. They are sensible of the indefatigable pains you have taken in that infinite variety of private sollicitations that you have found necessary to make, and cannot but be pleased to observe the easy access you have to persons of the first Rank and Influence in the kingdom, and how well you have availed yourself of this Indulgence. It is with particular pleasure they take notice of the zeal wherewith so many eminent members of the Church, excited by your judicious and warm address sent along with the Royal Brief, have served this Institution. They desire that as occasion serves you will not fail to return the hearty Thanks of the Trustees to every worthy person, who has been in any wise serviceable to you in this Charity. Was it possible for them to distinguish them according to their respective Merits they would spare no pains to do it. They think themselves

---

* *Supra*, p. 313.   † None of these letters have come to my hands.—ED.

particularly obliged to Dr. Brown for his most excellent Sermon, and thank you for the extract from it.

Agreeable to your request the Trustees have herewith sent Addresses to his Majesty and Lord Bute under the Seal of the Corporation, which they desire may be presented by you with a due observance of all the Forms used on these Occasions, and they hope and desire such of the Trustees as can conveniently be got together will accompany you. They thought it would be expected from them to express their own Sentiments of the Royal Goodness, otherwise they would have instructed and authorized you to have done it for them.

If there be anything else that occurs to you as necessary or becoming the Trustees to do in order to testify their Respect and Gratitude to their Benefactors, you may be assured, on the least information of it from you, every thing of this sort will be done on their part and transmitted as soon as opportunity serves.

The Trustees observe what you say of the good disposition you found in several of the Clergy and Gentlemen in Scotland in your letter of the 8th January, which did not arrive till the 18th March. Mr. Inglis & Dr. Morgan will be able to advise you whether it is best to proceed now to ask private Charities, or to stay as you think it would be better, till some time hence. Whatever you do, Mr. Elliott can be of great assistance, and will we doubt not cheerfully give it, and furnish all necessary Letters and Recommendations from his Relations, who are numerous and have great Interest. Dr. Alison has been consulted, and as the time of the Session of the General Assembly is over for this year, and indeed he thinks with you that little would be got at this time on a General Brief, he advises private Sollicitations, and has sent you some Letters to his Friends among the Clergy, which you may use or not as you shall think best.

You have mentioned in your last Letter that the Bishops and other persons of distinction in Ireland would assist a Collection in that Kingdom. If after you have done all you can in England you chuse to try your Address with the People of that Kingdom who are noted for their generosity and public Spirit, it will be a further Service done to the Academy and very agreeable to the Trustees.

They are not insensible of the inconveniences that must arise to their own affairs as well as to yours in desiring as they do in mine of the 11th January that you would not come away till you have their express orders for so doing; and therefore do cheerfully consent according to your desire to withdraw this instruction, being well assured from what you have done, and the abundant Testimonies you have given of your great zeal to serve this Institution, that you will not leave England whilst there remains any thing material to do which will require your personal Attendance: so that you are now left to your own discretion and the advice of Mr. Penn and those who have shewn themselves such hearty

Friends to you and the Institution, to return home at what time and in what manner you please.

The Trustees have empowered me to draw for £500 Sterling on Messrs. Barclay for the use of the Academy, and the Bills go by this Conveyance, you will therefore take care that they be duly honoured.

I am, Rev. Sir, &c.,

RICHARD PETERS.

Fortified with his Address to the King, Dr. Smith was taken on the 5th of August by Mr. Penn to St. James'. Mr. Inglis, on the part of the Trustees, and Mr. Powel, on the part of the Graduates, also went. The King asked in a kind manner several questions about the College, and the success of the collection. He also received Mr. Inglis and Mr. Powel very graciously. Dr. Smith, in one of his letters, says that he had almost got Mr. Powel Knighted, but thought it would be idle, and be considered as a design to separate him from his old friends, the Quakers at home; a thought which the Doctor says he would scorn in regard to any of his pupils. Moreover, he did not know whether it would be agreeable to Mr. Powel; and, therefore, gave it to be understood that he desired no honors, but only to testify gratitude.

Notwithstanding the incessant demand made while in England upon his time and attention by the affairs of the College, Dr. Smith was ever ready to assist the church and his friends connected with it in America in every way that he could. On the 6th of December, 1762, Mr. Peters was elected Rector of the *United Churches*—as Christ Church and St. Peter's, now made one corporation, were called—in the place of Dr. Jenney, deceased. Mr. Sturgeon was also elected an assistant minister. A notification was immediately made of the fact to the Bishop of London, and certificates sent by the vestry from both the assistant ministers, Mr. Sturgeon and Mr. Duché, to show to his Lordship the propriety of the choice, and their satisfaction with it. In their letter to the Bishop of London, the vestry say·

We are very sensible that it is Mr. Peters' duty to wait upon your Lordship, and he is very desirous of doing it; but as we are circumstanced his absence would be very detrimental to our churches. Therefore, we most humbly request, since your Lordship's licence in the ordinary form cannot be obtained, that you would be graciously pleased to signify your approbation of our choice in any manner your Lordship shall think proper by a letter under your own hand and seal to Mr.

Peters himself. This practice, we can assure your Lordship, has heretofore been observed by your pious predecessors.

The vestry also asked the confirmation of Mr. Sturgeon's election to be assistant of the *United* Churches. After testimony to his devotion to his ministerial duties for fifteen years, " with sobriety and unwearied diligence, and to the utmost of his ability," they add that " he long since married a gentlewoman of this city, by whom he hath a large family of children, and his connexions are chiefly here ; and here in our service he has spent the prime of his life." The letter of the vestry was sent by Mr. Peters to Dr. Smith, to be presented to the Bishop of London. There was sent with it a draft of a charter for the recently erected St. Peter's Church, hoping that it would be passed by Mr. Penn, then in London.

The Bishop of London, writing at Fulham, May 24th, 1763, in answer to the letters from the vestry, says :

From the credentials that have been transmitted to me . . . concerning Mr. Peters' moral Character, I can entertain no doubt but it is altogether unexceptionable, and therefore I do approve him to be your rector in the churches aforesaid. *I depend upon it Mr. Peters will embrace the first convenient opportunity of coming to England, and he will find me disposed to grant him a license in due form.*

Dr. Smith also writes, and, among other things, explains the Bishop of London's letter :

Dr. Smith to the Vestry of Christ Church.

LONDON, June 4th, 1763.

GENTLEMEN : The Rev. M^r. Peters, your rector, having done me the honor to transmit, through my hands, your address to the lord bishop of London, I lost no time in delivering the same, and have at length received his lordship's answer, most cordially approving your choice of M^r. Peters, and also giving his approbation of M^r. Sturgeon, in regard to his general good character, though he has not quite escaped his lordship's censure in the affair of the irregular marriage complained of. You will perceive that his lordship insists on it, as necessary both for M^r. Peters and M^r. Sturgeon to come to England, to be regularly licensed ; and this the strict rules of the Church would require. But as one sea voyage of six thousand miles, backwards and forwards, for ordination, is already a burden under which our American Church groans grievously, his lordship is far from expecting that the clergy will increase this burden by coming a second, third, or fourth time, as often as there may be any new bishop, or any new appointment for a clergyman himself. His lordship only thinks that, as this is regular, his insisting on it may help to place in a stronger light the inconveniency of our not enjoying on the spot the full rights of a Christian Church ; as to the good discipline of the clergy, and keeping up a succession in the holy office of the ministry ; and trusts that these and the like things may lead the administration here to consider seriously at last of this matter. But the time seems yet at a distance ; and indeed while things are so unsettled at home, we cannot be much thought of abroad.

I thought it necessary to be thus particular in regard to the paragraph in the bishop's letter ; and if you make any record of it in your books, as I doubt not you must, it will be extremely proper to enter likewise this explanation, or the substance of it, lest it should have a construction put upon it which it was not meant to bear, namely, as subjecting the American Clergy to new inconveniences, which might deter many from taking holy orders in our Church.

I have seen the draft of your charter, which is a good one ; only *I think power should have been reserved to the Vestry, if they should ever find it convenient, to constitute a separate head for each church, under such regulations as they might think proper. A time may come when they would find this a very necessary power.* A few words would have conveyed it to them, and if they should never have occasion to use it, it would have stood very innocently on the face of the charter. Mr. Penn seems well disposed to pass the charter and oblige the people of the Church, as soon as he has received his solicitor's advice as to the law parts of it. If any solicitation of mine be necessary, it shall not be wanting in this or any other business where I can serve the general cause of religion, or the particular one of your Church.

I rejoice to hear of the Christian harmony that subsists among you ; and am sure that under so good a man as M^r. Peters, and his assistants, it must continue to flourish ; which is the sincere prayer of,

Gentlemen, your affectionate humble servant,

WILLIAM SMITH.

The part of this letter in italics is interesting as showing by how much forecast the mind of Dr. Smith was distinguished. For the want of such a power as he mentions, Christ Church and St. Peter's were long incommoded; so much so that, at last, an appeal had to be made to the Legislature for relief. On the 5th of February, 1829—sixty-two years after the date of Dr. Smith's letter— the churches were erected into corporations with a separate head for each.

Dr. Peters to Dr. Smith.

PHILADELPHIA, June 1st, 1763.

DEAR SIR : Your public Letters are acknowledged in my public Letter and I have likewise wrote a very long private one. This is to return to you my Thanks for your kind services on receiving my Letter, acquainting you with my appointment to the Rectory of the Church. You will see by my other Letters on this Subject that I have placed an entire confidence in you, and did not chuse any other person should have any thing to do in my affairs. I know your trouble (which is already too great for any one man) will be much increased by this unforeseen choice of me. But I know, too, that affection makes all this easy ; and I can pronounce boldly that you have as much for me as one friend can have for another. I measure your Breast by my own towards you. Glad shall I be should we jointly be able to promote the real advancement of Religion and serve our Church, which wants people that will take pains as well as talk for her Interest. I do not chuse to say any more now, as you will give me a better opportunity on receiving your answer to my letters wrote along with the addresses and the Vestry's Letters to the Bishop of London. May the Almighty preserve your Health, Spirits and Zeal for the public good. I am, Dear Sir,

Your most Affectionate Humble Servant,

RICHARD PETERS.

To REVD. DR. SMITH.

We are now in the month of September, 1763. Dr. Smith was getting ready to sail for Ireland, where he hoped to make some collections. We shall follow him thither ; but must first break the unity so far as to go for a single day—Commencement Day—to Philadelphia.

CHAPTER XXIII.

COMMENCEMENT OF THIS YEAR—WATCHED AFTER BY DR. SMITH IN ENGLAND, AS MUCH AS IF HE HAD BEEN AT HOME—ACCOUNT OF IT IN THE LIVERPOOL PAPERS.

THE reader will remember that in the address on Commencement Day of 1759, by the Provost* to the Governor (the Hon. James Hamilton), the Provost says :

---

* *Supra,* 211.

The time is approaching (and may it fast approach!) which will put an end to this tedious war; and with it, perhaps, under your prudent administration, to those domestic troubles which have been prejudicial to the Muses here.

The time did not *fast* approach. The war was the Seven Years' War. It began in 1756, and ended only in 1763. But it came at last; a joyful peace it was. Dr. Smith, with his capacity to turn incidents to advantage, availed himself of it for his Commencement of 1763. And to make the thing operate with its fullest value, he inserted in the *Liverpool Advertiser*, of July 21st of that year, a dialogue and ode on the peace, which had been transmitted to him from across the ocean. We give it from an original paper in the Historical Society of the State. The verses were from the pen of the Rev. Nathaniel Evans.

AN EXERCISE

CONTAINING A DIALOGUE AND ODE ON PEACE, PERFORMED AT THE PUBLIC COMMENCEMENT IN THE COLLEGE OF PHILADELPHIA, MAY 17, 1763.

Oh Stretch thy Reign, fair PEACE! from Shore to Shore,
Till.Conquest cease, and Slavery be no more;
Till the freed INDIANS in their native Groves,
Reap their own Fruits, and woo their fable Loves!—POPE.

Pacatumque reget; patriis virtutibus orbem.—VIRGIL.

A DIALOGUE, &c.
HORATIO, PALEMON, PHILANDER.

Horatio. WHEN flourish'd *Athens* with the *Grecian* reign
And liv'd her Heroes, an illustrious Train;
When by her Arms each neighb'ring State was sway'd,
And Kings an Homage to her Warriors pay'd,
E'en then those Chiefs who all the World subdu'd
Low'r'd their proud Fasces to the *Learn'd* and *Good:*
And with less Glory in the Rolls of Fame
Shines ev'ry Hero's than each Sage's Name.
Hail, blest *Ilissus!* in whose sacred Shade
The Muses warbl'd, and the Graces stray'd;
There the deep *Stagyrite* his Pupils taught,
And Godlike *Plato* lay intranc'd in Thought.
This joyful Day in Miniature we've shew'd
Scenes that enraptur'd *Athens* would have view'd;
Science triumphant! and a Land refin'd,
Where once rude Ignorance sway'd th' untutor'd Mind;

Of uncouth Forms no more the dark Retreat,
Transform'd to Virtue's and the Muse's Seat.
Welcome ! thrice welcome, ye who grace our *Dome*,
To *Wisdom's Schools* so throng'd the Sons of *Rome*,
So oft with *Greeks* the fair *Lyceum* shone,
Whose Taste applauding they approv'd their own.

Come, then, my Friends, your Notes mellifluous pour,
And the soft soul of Harmony explore.
With melting Strains the happy day prolong,
What more enchanting than the Charms of Song?

Palemon. JOYOUS we join thee in the choral Lay,
To add new Transports to this blissful Day;
To trace the Muses to their hallow'd spring,
Catch the sweet Sounds, and as they fire us, sing.
The pleasing Theme, PHILANDER, shall be thine,
To wake the Raptures of th' immortal Nine,
Say, in thy Breast what sprightly Thoughts arise,
Illume thy Face, and kindle in thy Eyes?

Philander. NOT with more Pleasure o'er the fragrant Lawn,
Sports the fleet Hare, or bounds th' exulting Fawn,
When to black Storms succeeds the solar Ray,
And gilds each Beauty of the smiling Day,
Than my Heart gladdens at the Dawn of PEACE;
As Wrath subsides, and War's loud Tumult cease.
GEORGE gave the Word—and bade Mankind repose !
Contending Monarchs blush'd that they were Foes :
Old Warriors now with Rage shall glow no more,
But reap the Fields their Valour won before.
Such is the Subject which my Soul enjoy'd,
In my Eyes sparkled, and my Thoughts employ'd;
And sure no Theme more fitting could we chuse
Our Friends to glad, and fire each youthful Muse.

Horatio. AUSPICIOUS Theme ! for which shall be display'd
The richest Chaplets of th' *Aonian* Shade.
How bright the Scene ! unsullied Days arise,
And golden Prospects rush before my Eyes !
Hail smiling Goddess ! in whose placid Mien
Celestial Bliss with ev'ry Grace is seen ;
O'er thy smooth Brow no rugged Helmet frowns,
An Olive-Wreath thy shining Temple crowns.
Far shalt thou banish barb'rous Strife and Woe,
With purple Vengeance to the Realms below.   [wield,

Palemon. STERN Chiefs no more their crimson'd Blades shall
Nor deadly Thunders bellow o'er the Field ;
Satiate of War, the battle-breathing Steed
Peaceful shall range the Grove and verdant Mead :

No Drum shall animate the Soldier's Breast,
Nor piercing Fife arouse him from his Rest,
The Trump shrill-sounding and the clang of Arms
Shall shake the Plain no more with dire Alarms.

Philander. THE useless Rampart shall its Strength resign,
And o'er the Bastion spread the curling Vine;
Th' aspiring Ivy round old Towers shall stray,
And in the Trenches harmless Flocks shall play;
The crystal Streams shall flow without a Stain,
The Groves bloom Spotless and each flow'ry Plain.
Countries oppress'd by War's destructive Rage
Again revive to bless a milder Age;
In the same Fields where Groves of Lances rose
The furrow'd Grain shall golden Ranks compose.

Horatio. OH haste, fair PEACE! begin thy pleasing Reign,
Come, with each lovely Virtue in thy Train!
Then pure Religion's Precepts shall prevail,
Impartial Justice poise her balanc'd Scale;
Bright Liberty shall wanton in the Breeze,
Innoxious Pleasure, philosophic Ease,
Heart-chearing Mirth, and Plenty ever gay,
With rosy Joy shall tend thy gentle Sway!

Palemon. HASTE then, O haste, thy soft'ning Pow'r renew,
Bless ev'ry Clime, the *Old-world* and the *New!*
In friendly League unite each distant shore,
And bid Mankind with Anger burn no more:
COMMERCE shall then expand without control,
Where Coasts extend, or farthest Oceans roll;
These spacious Realms their Treasures shall unfold,
And *Albion's* Shore shall blaze with *Indian* Gold.

Philander. HAIL! happy *Britain*, in a Sovereign blest
Who deems in Kings a virtuous Name the best;
Guardian of Right and sacred Liberty,
Rome's glorious* NUMA shall be seen in Thee;
Beneath thy smile fair SCIENCE shall increase,
And form one Reign of LEARNING and of PEACE.
E'en we who now attempt the Muse's Shell
Great GEORGE'S kind Munificence can tell,
Tho' far, far distant from his glorious throne,
Yet has our Seat his regal Bounty known.
So universal shines the God of Day,
Each Land enlight'ning with his genial Ray.

---

* Vid. Plut. vit in Num.

Horatio. Enough, my Friends! Ye sweeter Numbers flow,
And let the deep-ton'd swelling Organ blow,
Ye tuneful Quire your dulcet Warblings join,
And soothe the attentive Soul with Harmony divine.

ODE.

I.   Smiling Pleasure's festive Band
      Swift descends to bless our Land,
      Sweet Content and Joy and Love
      Happy Off-springs from above!
No more fell *Discord* calls aloud to War,
Her crimson Banners flaming from afar.

Chorus.   Blest *Æra* hail! with Thee shall cease
             Of War the wasting Train;
             On thee attendant white-rob'd *Peace*
             In Triumph comes again.

II.   Where the grim Savage Devastation spread,
           And drench'd in Gore his execrable Hand;
       Where prowling Wolves late wander'd o'er the Dead,
           And repossess'd the desolated Land:
       There beauteous Villages and wealthy Farms
           Now variegate the far-extended Plain;
       And there the Swain, secure from future Harms,
           Delighted views his Fields of waving Grain.

Chorus.   Blest *Æra* hail! with Thee shall cease
             Of War the wasting Train;
             On Thee attendant white-rob'd *Peace*
             In Triumph comes again.

III.   Haste! ye Muses and explore
        The tawny Chief on *Erie's* Shore;
        Or among the Forests wide
        That imbrown *Ontario's* Side.
        Bid him quick his Bow unbend,
        Hateful War is at an End.
And bid the *Sire of Rivers*,* as he runs,
The Joy proclaim to all his swarthy Sons.

Chorus.   Blest *Æra* hail! with Thee shall cease
             Of War the wasting Train;
             On Thee attendant white-rob'd *Peace*
             In Triumph comes again.

---

* *Sire of Rivers* is a translation of the word Mississippi.

IV.   MAY *Britain's* Glory still increase,
    Her Fame immortal be,
  Whose Sons make War to purchase *Peace*,
    And conquer to set free.
  Such Pow'r, like the bright Star of Day,
    Invades the Realms of Night,
  Before whose Beam, each Beast of prey
    To Darkness speeds his flight.
  Still may it grow, till round the earthly Ball
  Science and *Liberty* illumine all!

Chorus.   BLEST *Æra* come! when War shall cease
    With all her wasting Train;
  And *Justice*, *Innocence* and *Peace*
    Shall ever more remain.

There were nine graduates at this Commencement; among them Jonathan Dickinson Sergeant, born in Princeton, N. J., 1746; delegate to Congress from New Jersey, 1776; Attorney-General of Pennsylvania, 1777–80; died in the yellow fever of 1793; a man deserving honor for his own merits, and worthy of remembrance as the father of that upright and eminent lawyer of Philadelphia, long beloved by the community, and, with Mr. Binney and Mr. Chauncey, the pride of its Bar—JOHN SERGEANT.

We now shift the scene, and find ourselves in Dublin, to which city Dr. Smith sailed from England in September, 1763.

CHAPTER XXIV.

DR. SMITH ARRIVES IN DUBLIN—SICKNESS—RECEIVES HIS DEGREE OF D.D. FROM THE UNIVERSITY OF DUBLIN—DR. MARTIN TO DR. SMITH—LEAVES DUBLIN —POWER OF ATTORNEY FROM THE ARCHBISHOP OF CANTERBURY AND OTHERS TO CLOSE ACCOUNTS WITH THE BRIEF LAYERS—DR. FRANKLIN AND DR. SMITH.

UPON the arrival of Dr. Smith in the city of Dublin, in September, 1763, he was taken seriously ill; so much so that his friends gave up hopes of his recovery. When the Hon. Thomas Penn was informed of the Provost's illness, he and Lady Juliana Penn were immediately by his side, and remained with him until he was in a condition to be removed.

He made a strong impression in Trinity College, Dublin, which hastened to add its Doctorship to those which he had received in 1759 from Aberdeen and Oxford.

The diploma is a short one; an *ad eundem*. Its words are these: The critical scholar may compare its Latinity with that of the diplomas of England and Scotland given on previous pages:

OMNIBUS AD QUOS PRÆSENTES LITERÆ PERVENERINT.

SALUTEM,

Nos Præpositus et Socii Seniores Collegii Sacrosanctæ et individuæ *Trinitatis Reginæ Elizabethæ*, juxta Dublin, Testamur; Reverendo viro GULIELMO SMITH gratiam concessam fuisse pro gradu Doctoratus in Sacra Theologia, apud nos Dublinienses, quem apud Oxonienses habet: In cujus rei Testimonium, singulorum manus, et Sigillum, quo in hisce utimur, apposuimus.

Nono Die Januarii, A. D. 1764.

GUL. CLEMENT,
Vice Præpositus.

J. STOKES,
W. MARTIN,
[SEAL.]   THOAKER WILDER,
THOS. LELAND,
GUL. ANDREWS,
A. MURRAY.

Dr. Martin, who I suppose was a Fellow, had informed Dr. Smith of the Degree conferred. Upon which it would seem that Dr. Smith sent him a letter of thanks, inquiring also what fees were to be paid; sending also one of the Liverpool papers containing the Dialogue and Ode which made part of the Exercises at the College of Philadelphia in this year.

Dr. Martin replies:

D^r. Martin is obliged to D^r. Smith for the two pieces which he has sent him; he will read them with much pleasure.

The University of Dublin takes *no fees* for degrees *ad eundem*. He heartily wishes the Doctor a happy voyage, whenever he sails.

TRINITY COLLEGE,
Thursday Morning.

Dr. Smith was prevented by his illness from leaving Dublin till the 7th of March, 1764. He then went to Stoke, the seat of his kind friend, Mr. Penn, where he remained until he had fully recovered.

It was now time for Dr. Smith to turn his face to the westward. He had been in England two years and some months.

The Commissioners named in the Royal Brief had executed a Power of Attorney in form, to enable him to close all accounts with the Brief Layers. As it is not every day that our readers— even those who belong to the law—see a Power executed by Archbishops, Bishops, Proprietaries and Aldermen, I give the document entire. I have no belief that Graydon's Book of Forms, or any more fashionable like volume, contains a safer one to follow.

POWER OF ATTORNEY.*

Whereas His present most Gracious Majesty King George the Third, by certain Letters patent under the Great Seal of Great Britain, bearing date at Westminster, the 19th day of August in the second year of his Reign, Did, upon the joint petition of William Smith, Doctor in Divinity, Agent for the Trustees of the College Academy and Charitable School of Philadelphia, in the Province of Pennsylvania, and Provost of that Seminary, and of James Jay, now Sir James Jay, Knight, Doctor of Physick, Agent for the Governors of the College of the Province of New York in America, Grant to the Governors and Trustees aforesaid a public Collection from House to House throughout the Kingdom of Great Britain, called England and Dominion of Wales, for the joint and equal benefit of the said Two Seminaries and Bodies Corporate for the preservation of the Protestant Religion in those countries, and Did therein Authorize, Nominate and appoint us whose Names and Seals are hereunto set, Together with divers other persons in the said letters patent particularly named, Trustees and Receivers of the charity to be collected by virtue thereof, with power to any five or more of us to give Deputations to collectors to be chosen by the Petitioners as therein mentioned, And to make and sign all necessary orders for the due and regular collection of the said Brief, and to dispose and distribute the money to be collected by virtue thereof in such manner as might best answer the ends for which the said Letters patent were intended, as by the said Letters patent may now at large appear. *And Whereas* five of the said Trustees in the said Letters patent named Did, by a certain instrument in writing under their Hands and Seals bearing date the 13th day of April last, at the nomination of said Petitioners, Testifyed by a writing under their Hands and Seals, appoint John Byrd, John Hall and John Stevenson of Stafford, in the County of Stafford, Gentlemen, Collectors of the said Letters Patent or Brief for the purposes aforesaid, and in pursuance thereof They, the said John Byrd, John Hall and

---

* From the original, in the possession of William Kent Gilbert, M. D.

John Stevenson, have Collected and received divers sums of money which now remains in their Hands to be accounted for.

Now Know all Men by these Presents, That in order finally to settle the accounts of the moneys collected by virtue of the said Letters Patent or Brief, and to appropriate the same to the uses in the said Letters Patent mentioned, We, whose names are hereunder written, being five of the Trustees appointed by the said Letters Patent, Have in pursuance of the Power thereby given to us, Nominated, Constituted, Authorized and Appointed, and by these presents *Do* Nominate, Constitute, Authorize and Appoint, and in our place and stead put William Smith, Doctor in Divinity, of the city of Philadelphia, Pennsylvania, and Barlow Trecothick, Esquire, Alderman of the city of London, our True and Lawful Attorneys, jointly and severally for us and in our Names, but to and for the use and purposes in the said Letters patent mentioned, To ask, demand and receive of and from the said John Byrd, John Hall and John Stevenson, the collectors appointed as aforesaid, their Heirs, Executors and Administrators, and of and from all other person and persons whom it doth or may concern, All sum and sums of money which have already been collected or shall hereafter be collected by them or any of them, or by their or any of their agents by virtue of said Letters patent, and to examine all and every the Brief Returns and Indorsements thereof, and to state, settle, adjust and allow the Charges and Disbursements of the said Collectors, or any of them, in the management of the Briefs according to an Agreement in that behalf made between the said William Smith and Sir James Jay, and Thomas Stevenson and John Stevenson, Jr., Agents or Attorneys for the management of the said Briefs, under the said John Byrd, John Hall and John Stevenson, and upon receipt of any sum or sums of money, or the Balance of the said accounts from the said collectors for us and in our names, or in the names of all or a sufficient number of the said Trustees, acquittances or other sufficient discharges for the same, to make, sign, seal, and deliver, and further to act, do, and perform all and every matter and Thing whatsoever necessary and requisite to be done in and about the premises, and we do also authorize and impower the same Thomas Penn and Barlow Trecothick, or either of them, for the purposes aforesaid, to make and depute one or more Attorney or Attorneys under them, and such Deputies from Time to Time at pleasure to displace and others to substitute, and we do hereby promise and agree to allow, ratify and confirm all and whatsoever our said Attorneys, their Deputies or substitutes shall jointly or severally lawfully do or cause to be done in the premises by virtue of these presents, so long as they shall continue in Great Britain or Ireland, for it being our meaning and intention, That when they or either of them shall embark for America, then our Power of Attorney shall cease and determine.

In Witness thereof we have hereunto set our Hands and Seals this

13ᵗʰ day of May, in the year of our Lord one Thousand seven Hundred and Sixty Three.

Sealed and delivered by the Arch-
bishop of Canterbury in the pres-   THO. CANT.   [SEAL.]
ence of
    CHRIS. HARGRAVE,
    THOS. PARRY.

Sealed and delivered by the Lord
Bishop of London in the presence of   RIC. LONDON.   [SEAL.]
    WILLIAM DICKES,
    RICHARD NELSON.

Sealed and delivered by the Lord
Bishop of St. David's in the pres-   S. ST. DAVIDS. [SEAL.]
ence of
    RICHARD BRADON,
    THO. ALLEN.

Sealed and delivered by Thoˢ.
Penn, Esq., in the presence of us.   THO. PENN.   [SEAL.]
    DAVID CHEVAUX,
    WILLIAM SALMON.

Sealed and delivered by Barlow
Trecothick in the presence of us.   BARLOW TRECOTHICK. [SEAL.]
    JOHN THOMLINSON, JR.,
    T. APTHORP.

That the Brief Layers had not used the whole fund in stamps, commissions and like expenses appears by a receipt, which follows:

Received, London, April 4th, 1764, of Messʳˢ. Byrd, Hall and Stevenson, by the hands of Messʳˢ. Thomas & John Stevenson, the sum of Six Hundred Pounds on further account of the Brief for the Colleges of Philadelphia and New York, making with former Payments above mentioned, the sum of *Nine Thousand Six Hundred Pounds* in the whole now paid on account of this Brief. We say received by virtue of the within Power of Attorney.

£9,600 in all.   WILLIAM SMITH, for himself,
                    and SIR JAMES JAY.
    Witness:
BARLOW TRECOTHICK,
WM. NEATE.

We must regard the work done by Dr. Smith as a great achievement. John Adams describes him, in 1774, as "soft, polite, insinuating, adulating, sensible, learned, industrious, indefatigable." And hardly anything short of all these qualities would have done what he did, when he did it.

" The list of persons who preferred to give directly to the Agents rather than to the Brief Commissioners," says the Provost Stillé, in speaking of Dr. Smith's work, " now lies before me, and it is a most curious and interesting document. It embraces more than eight hundred names of people of every rank and condition in life, residing in widely distant portions of the kingdom, from the ' King's most sacred Majesty,' who contributed £200, and the Princess Dowager of Wales, who gave £100, to ' Master Tommy Ellis,' who offered his mite of two shillings and sixpence! In the list are to be found, as has been said, the names of both Archbishops and of all the Bishops, and of very many of the clergy, one of whom, Rev. Dr. Tew, Rector of Bolden, near Newcastle, gave £100. There is also a long array of noblemen, including the Dukes of Devonshire and Newcastle, the Duchess of Argyle, the Earls of Shelburne, Dartmouth, Temple, Chesterfield, and Shaftesbury, Lords Bute, Clive, Grosvenor, Spencer, Gage, etc. Each of these historical personages made a liberal donation. Among the contributors was the Right Hon. William Pitt, who gave £50."

The various Colleges of the University of Oxford gave £163, although Dr. Smith complains in his diary " that at St. John's and Baliol, Dr. Franklin's friends were very averse." At the University of Cambridge he collected £166. Liverpool gave £211, Halifax, £52, Birmingham, £127, Bristol, £112, Gloucester and the neighboring towns, £85. These amounts are made up of small sums, far the larger portion of them not exceeding a guinea each, contributed by several hundred different persons; and the labor attending such a collection can only be estimated by those who have had experience in such undertakings. In this way were gathered for the two Colleges about £2,400.

It is " not pleasant," to use the expression of the Provost Stillé— it is not pleasant to record that the only man in England and America by whom the great effort of the College and its then Provost was opposed, thwarted and injured, was Dr. Benjamin Franklin; himself at the time a Trustee of the College, and also the Provincial Agent, that is to say the accredited agent of his Province to the British Government; a capacity in which he had gone to England in 1757, and was there in 1762, after Dr. Smith arrived, though then about to come home. The Provost Stillé says:

Dr. Franklin was still one of the Trustees of the College, and Dr. Smith's instructions directed him to be guided in a great measure by his advice on his arrival in England. He found, however, that the Doctor was about embarking for home, and either could not or would not do anything more than give him a general introduction to his friends. Dr. Smith soon discovered that Franklin's dislike for *him* was a far stronger feeling than sympathy with the *business which had brought him to England.*

Dr. Smith, as we have already seen, in two colleges of that University which had recently given to him its high honors, now "found *Dr. Franklin's* friends very averse" to giving anything. These men must have been Churchmen. By what statements he operated on *them* we do not know. How he operated on Dissenters Dr. Smith himself tells us. In giving an account of his general success, and his occasional want of it, he thus writes:

An eminent Dissenter called on me, and let me know that Dr. Franklin took uncommon pains to misrepresent our Academy, before he went away, *to sundry of their people,* saying, that it was a narrow, bigoted institution, put into the hands of the Proprietary party as an engine of government; that the Dissenters had no influence in it (though, God knows, all the Professors but myself are of that persuasion), with many things grievously reflecting upon the principal persons concerned in it; that the country and Province would readily support it if it were not for these things; that we have no occasion to beg, and that my zeal proceeds from a fear of its sinking, and my losing my livelihood. . . . The virulence of Dr. F. on this subject betrayed itself, and disgusted the gentleman, who had procured me forty guineas to the design.

As the whole claim for support in England was based on the catholicity and wide character of the scheme of the College, Dr. Franklin struck his blows just where he thought that they would inflict a mortal wound.

These statements—assuming the "eminent dissenter" to have spoken the truth, and Dr. Smith to have correctly reported him— were untrue in fact, were made in violation of Dr. Franklin's duty as a trustee, and were alike dishonorable to him, malicious and vindictive.

1. *They were untrue in fact.* No one can have read this book, even so far as the page where I now write, and not see that the College was not "a narrow, bigoted institution," in which "Dissenters had no influence." The Vice-Provost, and Professor of

Moral Philosophy, Dr. Alison, was a Presbyterian Clergyman, a leader in his sect; Dr. Ewing, Professor of Natural Philosophy, and the now acting President, a Presbyterian Clergyman also; Mr. Kinnersley, Professor of Oratory, was a Baptist Clergyman, as his father had been before him. John Beveridge, Professor of Languages, and Hugh Williamson, Professor of Mathematics, were Dissenters as much as they were anything. The only Churchman in the Faculty, Dr. Smith, was so liberal in his ideas that, as will be seen hereafter, he was inclined to admit as ministers of the Church of England the whole body of the Lutheran clergy in Pennsylvania, without further ordination than what they had.* It is plain he never sought to use the College as an instrument of advancing the Church. In fact, so far as education was concerned, he obliterated the Church as a distinctive element of it. This was one of the difficulties between him and Dr. Jenney. In speaking of Dr. Jenney's dislike of the College, he says:†

I find D‍ʳ. Jenney is not very fond of the Design, and says that our Trustees have little regard for religion. But the truth is, that from the first he has opposed the Institution, *because it was not made a Church Establishment & all the Masters to be of that persuasion.* His zeal for the best Church on earth is certainly commendable; but it may be carried too far. Had our College been opened on that plan in such a place as Philadelphia, the Students would indeed have been a very scanty Number. The People would not have borne even the Mention of such a Design at first.

As respected the trustees, many were known Dissenters. William Allen, afterwards Chief-Justice of Pennsylvania, and a leading man in the Board, was a Presbyterian. Franklin was anything and all things. William Coleman, another trustee, was his most valued friend, but not a Churchman. The President of the Board indeed was Richard Peters, a Clergyman of the Church of England, but a man as void of anything narrow or bigoted in his heart or mind as any man that ever lived. He was a man of large fortune, untrammelled by domestic ties in America, and his whole life seems to have been a series of kind, hospitable and beneficent acts to people around and about him. No biography of him has yet been published, but I speak with knowledge of what I assert. As for his churchmanship it was so broad—its exterior tints were

---

* See *infra*, p. 402-3.   † *Supra*, p. 143.
22

so mild and so affected from colors outside of them—that no man could see its edges or tell where the church ended and the sects began. In 1769—a few years later than the time we are speaking of, but still showing what his *spirit* always must have been, being then the Rector of the United Churches—he was invited to take a leading part in the dedication of the great Lutheran Church, then recently built on Fourth Street above Arch. He did so. Now listen to him as, from the pulpit of that majestic edifice, he speaks to the thousands of every name and of many tongues that were seated before him.*

Your Invitation to the Ministers and Members of the Episcopal Church, to mix their Devotions with yours, and to partake of the Joy you must needs feel on bringing this large Building to such an admired and astonishing Perfection, fills us with an high Sense of your Brotherly Love to us in Christ Jesus. It reminds us of the Love and tender Affection which subsisted between the first Christian Churches, and which makes so large and delightful a Part of the Apostolic Epistles recorded in Scripture. All those numerous Congregations, which in divers and distant Parts, and under various Forms of Divine Worship, were brought together by the Apostles and first Preachers of the Gospel, had nothing afflictive or joyous in their Affairs, but what they were all alike Sharers in. As often as Occasion called them to distant Places, they went with the utmost Cheerfulness into one another's Churches, and joined together in Communion of Prayer and Exhortation. And is it not much to be lamented, that the same affectionate Intercourse does not prevail now? Do we not all worship the one God and Father of All—the one Son and Redeemer of All—the one Holy Ghost and Sanctifier of All? What though Churches are built in different Forms, what though Ministers wear different Habits, what though every national Church has a different Mode of Expression in the Compilement of their Articles and Prayers—has not Christ Jesus provided one and the same strong Cement of Love and Charity to tie and keep all these his different Members together? Should the Differences be Reasons for Enmity, Distance, or separate Interests? What does the Spirit of Christ say to us all on this Occasion? "As the Body is one, and hath many Members, and all the Members of the one Body, being many, are one Body, so also is Christ, for by one Spirit are we all bap-

---

* A sermon Preached in the New Lutheran Church of Zion, in the City of Philadelphia, at the instance of the Ministers, Wardens, and Vestrymen of the incorporated Congregation of St. Michael's. On the 26th day of June, 1769. By the Rev. Richard Peters, Rector of Christ Church and St. Peter's in the said City. Philadelphia. Printed by John Dunlap at the *Newest Printing Office*, in Market Street, the Third Door below Second Street. MDCCLXIX.

tized into one Body, whether we be Jews or Gentiles, whether we be bond or free ; and have been all made to drink into one Spirit.''

We heartily wish this Union of Hearts, this Communion of affectionate Intercourse, was general among Protestant Churches.   And we have a very sensible Pleasure in being able publicly to declare, that between your Church, the Swedish Church, and our own Episcopal Church, there has always been, from the very first, a kind and loving Participation of Divine Service and Brotherly Offices.   May the good God bless this disinterested friendly Union! and may we all use our own earnest Endeavours to inspire the same Zeal into our Children, that we may forever continue in the sincere Love of one another, and in an open undisguised Participation of Worship and Instruction.

If this was churchmanship, it was churchmanship "with a difference."   Except as the Book of Common Prayer—the index and conservatory of her true principles—kept him in right line, such a man could hardly have kept himself with the Church at all. Certainly he was not "narrow" nor "bigoted."

I say, therefore, that Dr. Franklin's statements, if made, were untrue in point of fact.

2. *They were in violation of his duty to the College, and dishonorable.   I should say also in violation of his duty as agent of the Province.*

Franklin was at the time when he was thwarting the effort of the Trustees, a member of their Board, and the Agent of the Province.   His position as a Trustee of the College made it obligatory, while he held that position of honor, to advance the purposes of the Trustees, and not privately to thwart them.   In addition, as the Provost Stillé tells us, " Dr. Smith's instructions directed him to be guided in a great measure by Franklin's advice on his arrival in England."   The Trustees said in those instructions :

If Mr. Franklin should be in England on your arrival, we desire you will wait upon him, lay before him your several Papers, acquaint him with our necessities, consult with him, and desire he will give you all the assistance in his power ; and we doubt not but he will readily advise and assist you, and by his means *you may be recommended to many persons of wealth and Distinction.*

It is plain, from this, that the Trustees looked upon Dr. Franklin as a friend.   He was bound, therefore, "in double trust," both as a Trustee of the institution, and as one specially looked to in a foreign land and in an official post. And, withal, he was the Agent of the Province, bound to do everything to promote learn- ing, science, and the arts, in all parts of it, everywhere.

3. *Franklin's action was malicious and vindictive.*

From about the year 1754 Dr. Franklin had been an active partisan in the political disputes that then arose between one class of persons in Pennsylvania and the Proprietaries. He managed his weapons like a practised combatant, and was opposed by Dr. Smith with more than equal strength and skill. His object was to break down the Proprietary title of the Province, as derived from William Penn, and to vest it in the British Crown—to take it from a family ever beneficent to this Province, and vest it in the Government which so soon afterwards began to oppress us. He did not succeed in that object, and he seems to have cherished on that account an animosity towards Dr. Smith.

The Provost Stillé tells us, too, that Dr. Smith opposed the granting of a Doctor's degree by the University of Oxford to Franklin. We are not enabled by an exhibition of Dr. Smith's objections, as assigned, to judge whether his action was blame- worthy, excusable, or to be justified and commended.

But there was a deeper cause, I think, than any of these things. In the year 1757–8—the era of our early electrical discoveries— there was a person in the Faculty of the College—somewhat Franklin's junior—named Ebenezer Kinnersley. "He was," says Dr. Stillé, "a man of remarkable attainments," and is reported to have been "the first person who delivered a course of lectures on scientific subjects in this city." Dr. Stillé adds:

He had assisted Dr. Franklin in his first experiments in electricity, and is thought to have deserved more credit for their results than he received.

There is no doubt whatever, I believe, that Franklin, a Trustee of the College, a member of the power which appointed its Fac- ulty, and the senior of Kinnersley, was on terms of intimacy with him ; that he and Kinnersley made joint experiments and joint discoveries ; but that Kinnersley, experimenting also by himself at home, *made other discoveries which were his own exclusively, but which he communicated to Franklin.* All the discoveries which were made anywhere, or by any one, were communicated to the public by the pen of Dr. Franklin alone, and chiefly by letters to his friend, Peter Collinson, in London. Europe soon resounded with the name of FRANKLIN. The name of Kinnersley was honored only within the College walls : *

In this state of things, Dr. Smith, in the year 1758, in giving out a Prospectus of his College, and exalting the advantages which it offered from the merits of its Professors, when he came to the department of Kinnersley, in speaking of the Professor there, said :

He is well qualified for his Profession, and has moreover great merit with the learned world in being the chief Inventor of the Electrical Apparatus, as well as *author of a considerable part of those discoveries in Electricity, published by Mr. Franklin, to whom he communicated them.* Indeed Mr. Franklin himself mentions his name with honor, though he has not been careful enough to distinguish between their particular discoveries. This perhaps he may have thought needless, as they were known to act in concert. But though that circumstance was known here, it was not so in the remote parts of the world to which the fame of these discoveries has extended.

I do not think that Dr. Smith in this statement, which, if too broad, was not without foundation, meant to do injury to Franklin. His purpose, rather, was to do justice to a man of real merit whose modesty was too great to allow him to do justice to himself, and to place the merits of the College upon their proper basis. But Franklin was deeply offended.

He soon exhibited his feelings to the Provost in these lines, which he wrote on the title page of a benevolent pamphlet by Dr. Smith, printed in 1759, and under the author's name. *Tantænè animis cælestibus iræ !*

> Full many a *peevish, envious, slanderous* elf
> Is in his works, Benevolence itself.
> For all mankind, unknown, his bosom heaves,
> He only injures those with whom he lives.
> Read then *the man.* Does truth his actions guide?
> Exempt from *petulance,* exempt from *pride ?*
> To social duties does his heart attend—
> As son, as father, husband, brother, *friend ?*
> Do those who know him love him? If they do
> You have *my* permission—you may love him too.†

---

* There its honors increase. Through the generous efforts of a Senator of Pennsylvania—the Hon. H. G. Jones—a memorial window has been recently erected in the new University to the memory of this early and gifted Electrician.

† "Loyalist Poetry of the Revolution," edited by the late Winthrop Sargent. I

Such an effusion was malignant and vindictive; denigratory simply. In law it was libellous, and if Franklin had himself printed it in his lifetime instead of leaving it in his library for others to print—after he was dead—he might have been convicted of an offence, for which in his day, I think, an institution not far from his own house, called the Pillory, was the punishment, and for which Dr. Smith, if he had been inclined, could have retaliated in a way about as refined as the Doctor's own in the original offence.

We *now* have the secret of Dr. Franklin's active, though apparently clandestine opposition to the work of the Trustees and Dr. Smith. Rather than have *Dr. Smith* succeed, he was willing to break down an institution which he had himself brought into being, and which his friends were now seeking to rear; one, too, which his official place in it and special confidence put in him by the Trustees, made it obligatory on him, in honor and duty, to specially protect and assist. To gratify this personal spite he was willing, in this unavowed way, to deprive the city of Philadelphia of an institution which would make her queen among cities, a centre of learning, science and the arts; an institution by which the Province that he was representing would be elevated and dignified among the Provinces of America, and by which the people of the whole country, if it were successfully established, would forever receive, as they are now receiving, benefits of incalculable value.

I have seen a statement made by William Allen, afterwards Chief-Justice of Pennsylvania, not a Churchman, but as I have said a "Dissenter," in a letter of the 4th of February, 1758, to Mr. Paris, an agent of the Penns, which last-named persons were apparently indisposed to think that Dr. Franklin could be ever other than all that he professed to be. The letter says:

I have the pleasure of your agreeable favors of the 14th of October and the 3d of May, in which I duly observe your thoughts of our great Squire Franklin; that he is not likely to distress our Proprietors, and they will be neither cajoled nor bullied by that spark.

---

have seen with my own eyes the pamphlet to which Mr. Sargent refers. I know Dr. Franklin's handwriting as much as any one now living can know it; and the verses are undoubtedly in his chirography.—H. W. S.

Whatever his fair pretences are, I have been *so often in the Assembly witness to his envenomed malice* that I am quite sure he will do them and their friends all the mischief a very wicked heart is capable of.

I have seen a letter by the elder Adams, written late in life, in which he characterized Franklin as "the base flatterer of the King of France." Mr. Allen, in referring to Franklin's "fair pretences" to the Proprietaries and to "his envenomed malice," believed, it is plain, that Franklin was capable of flattering chiefly when he meant to destroy.

The popular estimate of Franklin—the estimate merely popular I mean—is that he was a man free from all unworthy passions, of a calm, elevated, serene nature, to whose heights no malignant or unworthy passions ever rose. This estimate places him beside Washington—in purity, in honor, in personal dignity, and in political integrity—and makes him worthy to stand there. "Franklin and Washington. Washington and Franklin. United in worth. Let them never be separated in fame."

With this estimate any one whom Dr. Franklin has deliberately characterized as peevish, envious and a slanderer; injuring those with whom he lived, while professing benevolence to all the world beside; his actions not guided by truth; himself petulant and proud; a bad son, a bad father, a bad husband, a bad brother, and a bad friend, hated by all who know him—any one thus characterized by HIM can surely deserve, but little, the respect of posterity.

But I have a word to say about the epigrammatist himself. It was a little bit unwise for the runaway apprentice from his father and brother to speak of a bad son and a bad brother; not very safe for him who had acted as Franklin did to the family of Mr. and Mrs. * * * *, to speak of "injuring those with whom he lived;" considerably dangerous for a man who "took to wife"* a woman that he had once abandoned—and who, on his own showing, might perhaps be claimed at any time, by another man as *his*,— so much as to whisper "husband."

Dr. Franklin was not always engaged in bringing thunder from heaven, nor in wresting the sceptre from tyrants. He kept much

---

* It is in this way that Dr. Franklin mentions his marriage. No particulars of the thing are given.

other company than that which he met in the Congress of 1776 and the Convention of 1787. He did not grow up amidst the elegancies of Versailles, and in the nation of gallant men, the nation of men of honor and cavaliers. His education was among associations coarse, and if he tells the truth about the causes of his running off, worse; associations calculated to vulgarize his nature even if heaven had given to him one, in itself, elevated and refined. He came, a runaway, at the age of seventeen, to Philadelphia, and during much of a long life lived there. His steps were in many ways and many walks in that place. He was in trade of many kinds: dealing in lamp-black and chimney jambs, as well as in books, in stationery, in newspapers and stationers' blanks. He was long in local politics, and in several stations there, humble as well as more high. He was in boards of business, of science, and of humanity. He was in active every-day life in that city for over thirty years. The people of Philadelphia were as familiar with his face, his frame, his ways, his deeds—private as well as public—as they were with the streets of their little town; and it is a fact, undeniable of any, that in that city of his longest residence and most active and busy career, there were ever many men—men who could weigh the motives and actions of their fellow-citizens with impartiality and truth—who largely disesteemed him. In a popular election of 1764 he was set aside in favor of an honorable citizen, of whom it was never said that he courted popularity, and who on a memorable occasion openly defied it. So, too, some of the best citizens of Philadelphia protested publicly against his appointment as Colonial Agent, charging him with being the author of many of the calamities which had then befallen the Province.*   There was, in short, nothing in the character of Dr. Franklin in the days in which they both lived, that for active usefulness, disinterested effort, elevated sentiment, or generous qualities—and most of all as respects his conduct as a son, brother, father, husband, neighbor and friend—could in the least outweigh the character of Dr. Smith.

Mr. Sparks, to whom literature and history are so much indebted for his edition of Franklin's works, has considered himself at liberty in discharging an editorial office entrusted to him by the

---

* See Appendix No. V.

people of America, and designed to present to the world in their
most dignified form the writings of one of its great representatives,
to omit the malignant libels which Franklin wrote and preserved,
but never dared to print in their lifetimes, upon his friends or his
rivals, and to suppress without a notice, at the places of his having
done so, passages of obscenity and irreligion which dishonor
Franklin's earlier character and writings. In reference to his duty,
Mr. Sparks was quite right in his omission of such passages;
though perhaps not so absolutely right in failing to indicate at the
proper places a suppression of some sort. His task was in a great
degree national, and neither the reputation of our country nor the
proper pride of its people could gain anything by exhibiting
Franklin as a man who at any time of his life was deficient in
moral sense, or who could so far forget himself as to write with
malignity, coarseness and obscenity.

But while Mr. Sparks, in discharging a special duty, did right to
do what he did, others do equally right—in discharging a duty
still more special—to speak of Franklin's writings as he made and
as he left them. The statements of Dr. Franklin as to the narrow
and bigoted character of the old college impugn directly the
candor and even the veracity of Dr. Smith; for he was collecting
money only upon representations that it was catholic and liberal.
Dr. Franklin's characterization of him in verse goes to every
part of his character. And both the representations and the
characterizations I find put by others and without my agency
into print.

In such a case any descendant of Dr. William Smith is quite
free, indeed is bound to speak of Franklin as our Philadelphia
fathers—his best judges—knew him and as in truth he was. If
the men of this generation had nothing but the beautiful edition
of his works that comes from the city to which by birth he belonged, and to which the Legislature of Pennsylvania, in not adopting him for one of the Statues with which Congress has recently
allowed her to do honor to her statesmen—seems disposed to have
him relegated—they might still think, as they read in a charming
autobiography an account of the way in which *Franklin* reached
the summit of worldly honor, and as they consider how purely
"wisdom for a man's self"—a depraved thing, *right earth*, as Bacon
calls it—is the animating spirit of all that Poor Richard ever taught

LIFE AND CORRESPONDENCE OF THE

his countrymen—that by the history, counsels and example of no
one man has American character been so much educated to those
*un*enviable features which signalize it to the eyes of Europe.

But they would still, perhaps, have some difficulty to comprehend what JOSEPH DENNIE—"whose genius was *catholick* as it was
confessedly splendid"*—and others, the best educated and loftiest
men of Franklin's later days, have meant by charging him with
having "clubbed with Deists," with "foisting dull jokes into
manuals of catholic piety," with sneering at the most moral and
religious tracts extant in any language from a mere spirit of levity
or the natural and spontaneous modesty of *im*moral philosophy.†
They would be at a loss to know, if they ever hear it, how in the
city of his early life and longest residence the man who received
the homage of two continents, and stood before kings, has left
behind him, as a fitting distinction, the traditionary title of "The
old Rogue;" to understand how in the summer breezes of Twy-
ford and the cooling shades of Passy he was still carrying out,
through twenty years, the same purpose; and, habitually "regardless of literary reputation" in general, was covering up with apparent calmness and candor, in the most careful of his writings,‡
—the manuscript "erased, corrected on every page, filled with inter-

---

* So characterized by N. Chapman, M. D. John Quincy Adams, in inscribing his
tombstone, says that "as the first editor of the Port-Folio he contributed to chasten
the morals and to refine the taste of the nation," that "to an imagination lively not
licentious, a wit sportive not wanton, and a heart without guile, he united a deep sensibility, which endeared him to his friends, and an ardent piety which, as they humbly
trust, recommended him to his God."

† See "The Port Folio," Vol. I., p. 165, No. 21, Paper of May 23d, 1801, and "The
European Magazine" of July, 1804, p. 115, for a letter, as written by Dr. Franklin,
the original of which was long preserved in Philadelphia by the late Mr. E. D. Ingra-
ham, to whom it came from the late Rev. James Abercrombie, D.D. (who received it,
it is said, from the late Mr. Collinson Read), and see "Franklin's Works," Boston,
1840, Vol. VII., p. 17, for the same letter as published by Mr. Sparks.

‡ Franklin's Autobiography was begun when he was visiting Dr. Shipley, at Twy-
ford, in 1771, and resumed at Passy in 1784, and again in 1788 (*Works, Boston*, 1840,
Vol. I, pp. 148, *nn.*) "Few writers," says Mr. Sparks, "have been so regardless of
literary reputation as Franklin . . . The fame of authorship appears rarely to have
been among the motives by which he was induced to employ his pen." (*Preface to
Franklin's Works, Vol. I.*) His "Autobiography" seems to have been an exception.
Mr. P. Jul. Fontaine, in whose possession the original manuscript of it was in 1836,
thus describes it: "*Il est entièrement* ecrit de la mais dè l'auteur, *raturé, corrigé à
chaque page, rempli d'intercalations, d'additions et les marges couvertes de notes.*"
(*Manuel de lamateur d'Autographes, Paris*, 1836, *p.* 337.)

lineations and additions; its margins covered with notes"—the offences of his early life, the intrigues of his trade, the aims and arts of his local politics in an autobiography which, by concealing, coloring, substating and overstating should make—upon the basis of generally admitted fact—whatever impression,—whether a true one, or one false—it was its author's design to leave; and though dishonesty demonstrable, should largely pervade it, would still present a relation of such extraordinary interest—a narrative written with such inimitable art—as that no one, in any time to come, would ever attempt to write a biography of the man who is its subject, with truth.

With what magnanimity—with what freedom from all resentments—in fact, with what perfect, absolute sweetness of nature Dr. Smith acted towards the character and memory of Franklin, after all that we have described, this will be seen hereafter.* Dr. Smith's conduct in 1790, on the death of this great citizen, places him high in the rank of Philosophers; much more, it establishes his title to that "excellent gift," the brightest possession of the Christian.

In the next chapter we shall revert to our main subject. When we departed from it for the purpose of paying our tribute of justice to Dr. Franklin, we left Dr. Smith getting ready, after great success with his collection, to return to Philadelphia.

---

* See Vol. II., in my account of his oration on the death of Dr. Franklin.

CHAPTER XXV.

BEFORE setting sail for America, Dr. Smith, pressed as he was
for time, found enough of it to address a letter to the Bishop of
London, upon a matter having direct practical importance in
America. The parochial clergy, in 1764, to the northward and
eastward of Maryland—in number perhaps seventy—were all,
except those in Boston, Newport, New York, and Philadelphia,
missionaries of the Society for the Propagation of the Gospel.
Through that society it was that the Church of England gave to
us "a long continuance of nursing care and protection."

Dr. Smith to the Bishop (Obaldiston) of London.

LONDON, April 17, 1764.

MY LORD: The Society for Propagating the Gospel have long found
themselves under Difficulties in carrying on their Good Designs, for
want of some Societies of Correspondence in America to give them due
Intelligence of Things necessary, and two or three Agents under them
to take Bonds from the People for the effectual Payment of the Sums
subscribed, to take Care of the Libraries sent by the Society into these
Parts, and do such other Things as they may be instructed from Time to
Time.

The Society have now before them Proposals for remedying these Inconveniences upon a Plan almost wholly the same with that which I had
the Honor to lay before your Lordship near two years ago. This Plan
has been well considered by the two Archbishops, the Bishops of Durham and Winchester, who with your Lordship, the Secretary, and
myself were appointed a Committee for that Purpose; & the Bishop of
Winchester has wrote to your Lordship on the Subject. The Society are

to meet on Friday next to take this matter before them & come to proper Resolutions upon it.

At present it is proposed to have but three Agents, viz., one for Massachusetts, Rhode Island, & New Hampshire, one for New York and Connecticut, & one for Pennsylvania & New Jersey; these being the Countries where the chief of the Societies lie. In each of these Districts it is proposed to have some of the Principal Gentlemen as a Society to advise & assist these Agents & to transmit faithful Accounts to your Lord^p & the Society. The Business of the Agents will be a Business of Labor, and not of Profit or Power. They are to sollicit larger Subscriptions from the People, to take Bonds for the Payment in the Society's Name, & see that these Contracts are duly fulfilled; & they can do nothing without advice. Much Good may also be expected from the corresponding Societies, not only in the Article of giving faithful Intelligence, but likewise in Countenancing those who are to execute whatever Orders your Lordship or the Society may give; and when that happy Time arrives when it shall please God to bless us with the Government of Bishops on the spot, these Societies will no doubt be the first to take them by the hand, & to support them in the Discharge of their Office. Another material Benefit expected from this Design is the establishing more Missions & Schools among the Indians, which it is feared can never be done effectually till some leading Men in America are thus associated to assist the Society in it.

If it be agreeable to your Lordship, I believe it will fall to my Share to set this Design on foot for Pennsylvania & New Jersey. I am to set out on Friday evening next for Falmouth, to embark for America in the Packet, & would take Bath in my Way to pay my Duty to your Lordship if you think it convenient. It is at the earnest Desire of the Missionaries of our Parts that I would take any share of this Business, & they have fully signified their good-will to me in an Address to your Lordship. Many of them have been my Pupils, & I have the Happiness to be well in their Esteem.

I hope your Lordship's Health is so well restored as that I may be honored with two or three Lines from your Lordship or D^r. Parker before Friday; as the Society would be willing perhaps to do something farther in this Matter before I go.

I am, &c.,

WILLIAM SMITH.

We have seen in a former chapter that, unless grossly misrepresented, Dr. Franklin had sought to impress the minds of people in England that the College "was a narrow, bigoted institution of government, put into the hands of the Proprietary party as engine of government, and that Dissenters had no influence in it." Nothing, as we have said, could be more untrue. But Dr. Smith

well knew that these misrepresentations were not the less dangerous because they were false. He was a man distinguished by
foresight. He saw into the future, as he was informed of the
present. I do not doubt that he had in his mind as a possible,
and perhaps as a probable result of Dr. Franklin's misrepresentations, such consequences as followed in November, 1779, when,
under the same allegations that Franklin made in 1762, the " Dissenters " abrogated the charter of the College and entered into its
estates; allegations as much unfounded at the one time as they
were at the other, and not more so. Just before Dr. Smith embarked for America, therefore, he sought, so far as he could, to
ensure the perpetuation of that "free and catholic plan" in the
management of the College, which he had urged upon those to
whom he applied for money as one of the very strongest reasons
for its support. Just before he embarked, he went to his friend,
Dr. Chandler, stated to him, no doubt, the fears which he had of
what might be the effect of Dr. Franklin's representations that the
College was a narrow and bigoted institution, and suggested that
something should be done which might counteract them.

It was resolved that the two persons, Dr. Chandler and himself,
should go to Lambeth Palace and see Archbishop Secker, and
take his judgment on the matter. This they did, and at Dr. Smith's
suggestion a letter to the Trustees was prepared and signed by the
archbishop, praying that the ancient liberal base might be preserved; and Dr. Chandler and the Penns subsequently put their
names to it. It was thus:

Archbishop Secker and others to the Trustees.

April 9th, 1764.
To THE TRUSTEES OF THE COLLEGE OF PHILAD^A.

GENTLEMEN: We cannot omit the opportunity which Doct^r Smith's
Return to Philadelphia gives us of congratulating you on the great Success of the Collection which he came to pursue, and of acknowledging
your obliging Addresses of Thanks to us for the Share we had in recommending and encouraging this Design. Such a Mark of your attention
to us will, we doubt not, excuse our hinting to you what we think may
be further necessary to a due Improvement of this Collection and the
future Prosperity of the Institution under your Care.

This Institution you have professed to have been originally founded
and hitherto carried on for the general Benefit of a mixed Body of
People. In his Majesty's Royal Brief, it is represented as a Seminary

that would be of great use " for raising public Instructors and Teachers, as well for the Service of the Society for Propagating the Gospel in Foreign Parts, as for other Protestant Denominations in the Colonies." At the time of granting this Colleçtion, which was sollicited by the Provost, who is a Clergyman of the Church of England, it was known that there was united with him a Viceprovost who is a Presbyterian, and a principal Professor of the Baptist Persuasion, with sundry inferior professors and Tutors, all carrying on the Education of Youth with great Harmony; and People of various Denominations have hereupon contributed liberally and freely.

But Jealousies now arising lest this Foundation should afterwards be narrowed, and some Party endeavour to exçlude the Rest, or put them on a worse Footing than they have been from the Beginning, or were at the Time of this Collection, which might not only be deemed unjust in itself, but might likewise be productive of Contentions unfriendly to Learning and hurtful to Religion, We would therefore recommend it to you to make some Fundamental Rule or Declaration to prevent Inconveniences of this kind; in doing of which, the more closely you keep in view the Plan on which the Seminary was at the time of obtaining the Royal Brief, and on which it has been carried on from the Beginning, so much the less Cause we think you will give for any Party to be dissatisfied.

Wishing continual Prosperity and Peace to the Institution, We are with great Regard,

Gentlemen,

Your faithful Friends and Servants,

THO. CANT,

THO. & RICH^D PENN,

SAM^L CHANDLER.

The following little correspondence, on the eve of Dr. Smith's leaving London, does so much credit, both to Mr. Thomas Penn and to Dr. Smith, that I cannot forbear inserting it :

Mr. Thomas Penn to Dr. Smith.

SPRING GARDEN, Ap^r 9th, 1764.

SIR : The great Zeal with which you have sollicited the Contributions for the Benefit of the College of Philadelphia must entitle you to the Regard and Esteem of every Person that wishes well to the Province of Pennsylvania : And, as I am perfectly sensible of it, I was willing to make my Acknowledgements to you for it, & to assure you of my Friendship on all Occasions; as a Token of which I desire your Acceptance of the enclosed Draft on my Banker for fifty Pounds, & am,

Your affec^t Friend,

To REV^D DR SMITH.   THO. PENN.

Answer to the Foregoing Letter.

LONDON, Ap^r 9th, 1764.

HON^D AND WORTHY SIR: The kind Sense which you have express'd of my sincere & well-meant Endeavours to serve the College of Philadelphia, makes an Impression on my Heart, which no Length of Time can erase. The Hopes of obtaining your Approbation in the End, animated me thro' a Series of Labors and Difficulties, which would have cool'd an ordinary Zeal; and the best Reward I can enjoy is the Prospect you give me of your future Protection & Countenance, while you think I continue to merit it.

I was far from wishing, or having any immediate Need of, the generous Mark of your favour which accompanied your most obliging Note; but the Manner of bestowing it was so truly honorable to me, that I do with the utmost Gratitude receive it.

I have never gone in the least Instance out of my Way to make Use of the Opportunities I might have had here for benefiting myself; chusing to rely solely on your Goodness, as Head of the Country where I live, to make my Settlement easy & useful in it.

Nothing but that Regard which every Man must feel for a growing Family, and the Fears of Leaving them, after a Life of the greatest Labor, in a worse Situation than the Children of the meanest Tradesman, would have induced me to open my Heart to you in the free Manner I did this Morning; & your truly kind Intentions of future Kindness to me will send me home happy in the View of my own Situation, & happy in the Issue of my Endeavours for the Service of the College.

Please to accept my Assurances, that so far as my Judgment or Abilities can carry me, you shall ever find me, in all Prudence, earnest to promote the best Interests of the Country with which you are so closely connected, & which I know you & your Family will always consider as inseparable from your own Interests.

There were several Gentlemen with me when your Servant delivered your kind Note, or I would have answered it immediately. I am, with great Gratitude & Regard,   Hon^d Sir,

Your most obliged & obd^t
Humble Servt,

TO THE HON^BLE THO^S. PENN, ESQ^R.   WILL. SMITH.

Dr. Smith embarked at Falmouth early in May, 1764, freighted with letters of honor from his friends, for America. We give a few:

Mr. Thomas Penn to the Trustees of the College.

LONDON, April 12th, 1764.

GENTLEMEN: As D^r. Smith, your worthy Provost, is now on his departure for Pennsilvania, I take this opportunity by him to acknowledge the receipt of your Letter of the 11th of January, 1763, and to do justice to his conduct in the execution of the Commission you gave him the charge of.   With regard to the first, I should not have thought myself worthy the regard of such People, whose good opinion every honest Man would covet, had I omitted any opportunity of serving such a Cause as the advancement of your College, from whence so great advantages will, in all probability, be derived to the Inhabitants of Pennsilvania ; the Subscription was the Act of the Proprietors, which you will take notice of in your Books, as by your Letter to me I apprehend you conceived it to be my private benefaction.

With regard to D^r. Smith's conduct in his sollicitations for subscriptions, I think he merits the highest commendations and that he has laid great obligations on every Man who has the welfare of this Institution at heart ; he has been so constantly attentive to this object, and so zealously concerned to establish it effectually, that no other seemed to have any place in his thoughts, or any labour to be regarded that was necessary to serve the Cause.

His Success has been great, and I make no doubt of your care so to place the Money out that the principal Sum may be secured so as always to remain a fund, the Interest of which only, or the Produce of Land purchased with that Money, may be applyed to the Support of the College, this being what the Contributors fully depend.

I make not the least doubt but that the College will now, under your direction, be carried on so as effectually to answer every reasonable expectation, which I most heartily wish, and assuring you of my good offices wherever they will contribute to so good a purpose,

I remain, Gentlemen,

Your very affectionate Friend,

Tho. Penn.

The Messrs. Penn to the Trustees.

London, Ap^r 12th, 1764.

Gentⁿ : In Compliance with your Request in your Address to us, we have given our Assistance to D^r. Smith for putting forward your Intention of Collecting money for the Use of the College of Philadelphia ; and have had the Pleasure to find that, by the benevolent dispositions of ye People of this Country, and the constant Attention & Labor of D^r. Smith, a very large Sum of Money has been collected, to which we have added £500 Sterling ; which together will be at least as large a Sum of Money as the most Sanguine did expect.

We heartily wish you Success in your Endeavours for the Improvement of Mankind, for wch Purpose you may be always assured of our Encouragement.   We are, with great Regard, Gentlemen,

Your very affectionate Friends,

Tho. Penn,

Richd Penn.

To the Trustees of the College of Philadelphia.

23

Archbishop Secker to the Rev. Mr. Peters.

LAMBETH, April 13th, 1764.

GOOD M^R. PETERS : I rec^d and read your Letter of ye 22^d October w^t great Pleasure. But I have had the Gout almost, if not quite, ever since ; wch hath attack'd not only my Feet, but my Hands, in such a Manner, that for a long Time I was not able to write so much as my Name, and now I can write but very little, without doing myself Harm.

However, I cannot let D^r. Smith go without sending you a Line by Him. Providence hath bless'd our Endeavours here, for the Benefit of his College, much beyond my Expectation. And indeed his Abilities and Diligence have been the chief Instruments of the Success.

Dissenters have contributed laudably ; but the Members of the Church of England, and particularly the Clergy, have been proportionably more liberal. Doubtless they were induced to it by the Allegation in the *Brief*, that this Seminary, and that of New York, would be extremely useful in educating Missionaries to serve the Society for propagating the Gospel. And therefore I hope the Trustees of the College of Philadelphia will be careful to make Provision, that all such as are designed for Clergymen of our Church shall be instructed by a Professor of Divinity who is a Member of our Church ; which may surely be done without giving any Offence to Persons of other Denominations : a Fault that by all Means should be studiously avoided ; as I doubt not, thro' your Prudence, it may and will. And with due Precaution, the Thing is necessary to be done.

My Hand admonishes Me that I have gone my Length. I have many Things to say to you ; but must postpone them till we meet, if it please God to give us Life and Health for it. I have heard within these few Days that you have been very ill. May the Father of Mercies preserve you for the Good of his Church.

> I am,
> With very great esteem,
> Your loving Brother,
> THO. CANT.

Mr. Chandler to the Rev. Richard Peters.

REV^D & DEAR SIR : I hope our good Friend, D^r. Smith, will deliver this safe & in good Health into your Hand, and that he will find you entirely recovered from every Indisposition & thoroughly established in your Health, which I know will be very pleasing to Him, & will give the highest Satisfaction to me. The D^r. has been indefatigable in his Endeavours to serve the Philad^a College, & greatly successful. He well deserves the sincerest Thanks of all the Trustees, of the several Professors & Masters, & all who wish well to the College, and indeed, in general, of all ye Friends of Knowledge & Learning.

I cannot help further recommending him to the Esteem of all our common Friends in Philadᵃ in that he hath not only exerted himself with an unremitting Zeal in Reference to the Collection, but hath shown an honest & public Concern for the future Peace & Prosperity of the College.

As there have been some Suspicions entertained on both Sides that the present Constitution of it may be altered, and the Professors & Masters, now of different Denominations, in Time may all be of one prevailing Denomination to the Exclusion of those of the other, by the Art & Power of the Prevailing Party ; and as the Doctor justly apprehended this would be contrary to the Intention of those who have contributed towards the Support of the College (who have been of all parties amongst us) and inconsistent with the Prosperity of yᵉ Institution itself, by his Desire, I waited, Monday last, on the good Archbᵖ of Cantʸ, where, with the Dʳ., we freely debated this Affair for an Hour together. His Grace, a Friend to Liberty, and highly approving the present Plan on which the College is established, gave his Opinion that this Plan should be preserved without Alteration. I had the Honor entirely to agree with the Archbᵖ, and, on Dʳ. Smith's proposing to him that a Letter to the Trustees representing our Judgment in this Affair, & signed by both of us, might be of some Weight to keep Things on their present Footing and prevent all future Jealousies on either Side, he readily assented to it.

A Letter to this Purpose was read & signed by us Both, wᶜʰ the Dʳ. will have the Pleasure of shewing You. I do not expect that I can be considerable enough in myself to have any great Influence in an Affair of this Nature. But as my Judgment is supported by that of so worthy a Prelate, and as I apprehend, by the Reason of the Thing itself, I hope it will, as his Judgment, have the good Effect of preventing all future Jealousies, and of establishing Peace & Harmony amongst all the worthy Professors, & of promoting Religion, Learning, and Liberty, which I pray God may long continue to flourish in that Seminary.

As the [free] Schools, &c., in Pennsylvania are now at an End, tho' I could have obtained his Majesty's Bounty for the Continuance of them, had it been of any Consequence to have upheld them longer, you, Sir, and the rest of our worthy Trustees, have my most sincere and warm Thanks for the Care and Integrity you have shewn in this Affair ; and I will take Care you shall have all due Acknowledgments of the Society upon their first Meeting.

Your last Account I have recᵈ, agᵗ which there can be no possible Exception. We have got some Moneys left, which I shall use my Endeavors shall for the most Part be applied to the Use of the College. You will do well to appropriate whatever outstanding Debts may come in, to the Use of the Charity School ; for which Purpose I intend to keep in my Hands a small Sum that yet remains with me ; for which I shall

desire at a proper Time to be drawn on.   I have honored your Draught
to Messrs. Barclay for £100.   I am, with the sincerest Affection and
esteem,   Rev^d & Dear Sir,

Your, &c.,

SAM. CHANDLER.

TO REV^D. M^R. PETERS.

From Dr. Llewelin to Rev. Dr. Edwards, Philadelphia.

(EXTRACT.)

SOUTHAMPTON STREET, BLOOMSBURY, April 12th, 1764.

 * * * I congratulate you also on the extraordinary Success of our
common Friend, Dr. Smith.   You ought to welcome him Home with
Ringing of Bell, Illuminations, and Bonfires.   The Professors of the
College in Particular (for which he has collected upwards of £6,000
Sterling) ought to meet him at least Half Way from New York, &
from thence usher him into Philadelphia with all the Magnificence and
Pomp in their Power.   The Scholars, Students, and Fellows should all
attend the Cavalcade, in their proper Order and Habits ; and the Procession should march thro' the principal Parts of the City, and termi-
nate at the Lecture Room, or rather Hall, where Verses and Orations
in various Languages should be delivered in Praise of Knowledge and
Learning,—in Praise of the Liberality and Generosity of the Mother
Country, of the Unanimity & Harmony of her Colony of Pennsylvania,
& especially of the Catholic College of Philad^a, with Vows for its
Continual Prosperity and Success.

As a Baptist, as a Friend of Learning, as a hearty Approver of a Plan
so free and open, I would add my Wish *quod felix faustumque sit.*   As
a Graduate of the College, as a dutiful Son of this *Alma Mater*—you
will readily join in every Act of Rejoicing on this Account.

If it was in my Power to make any Laws for this Seminary, or any
Alteration in its settled or intended Plan, it should only be that the
Professors should rank, or become Provost, &c., according to their
Seniority or Standing in the College, in future Elections.   I should
wish this, not only as it may open a Way for you *ad Cathedram*, but as
it seems to me to be more fair & equal, & more consistent with the Rest
of the Plan.   But as it is, it is a very good Thing, & I wish all concerned may duly improve it, & be ever careful to preserve it from any
Alteration for the worse.

From Rev. Dr. Stennet to the Rev. Mr. Morgan Edwards, Philada.

(EXTRACT.)

LONDON, Ap^r 12, 1764.

 * * * D^r. Smith, you see, has met with extraordinary Success.
I wrote particularly on those Matters in one of my last.   The Plan is,

I think, exceeding good. What some have feared is, lest it should, in Time, be perverted. But Dr. Smith assures us every possible Method will be taken to prevent an Abuse of the Institution.

What he proposes relative to our Interest in your Parts is the raising a Sum to furnish Exhibitions for the Encouragement of such a Number of young Persons as shall be thought needful to send to the College. You are to have your own Divinity Tutor. If you can agree upon any Scheme of this Sort, & can raise any Thing among you towards it, it may be very well. But you are best Judges yourselves. If any Assistance could be given you by your Friends here, I sh⁴ rejoice in promoting it. But I am not authorized from any to give you Assurances of this Sort. You know pretty well how it is with our Interest here.

Upon the return of Dr. Smith the Trustees met and unanimously voted to him their thanks for the zeal which he had shown in the collection of funds for the College, and publicly acknowledged that they, as well as all friends of learning, were under the greatest obligations to him. They voted him also for his services an annuity of £100 currency *for life*, which, I believe, he received until his death.

Almost in this same moment, in which the Trustees were thinking and acting with this generous justice towards him, he was thinking of the permanent welfare of the College. Dr. Franklin's misrepresentations preceded that gentleman—went with him— stayed behind him. So untruth always courses. The first thing to be done by Dr. Smith was to show explicitly that the statements of the Colonial Agent had no foundation.

The letter of Archbishop Secker, the Messrs. Penn, and Dr. Chandler, was put before the Trustees at the earliest date. They now make the following record:

The Trustees being ever desirous to promote the peace and prosperity of this Seminary, and to give satisfaction to all its worthy benefactors, have taken the above letter into their serious consideration, and perfectly approving the sentiments therein contained, do order the same to be inserted in their books, that it may remain PERPETUALLY DECLARATORY of the present wide and excellent plan of this institution, which hath not only met with the approbation of the great and worthy personages above mentioned, but even the royal sanction of His Majesty himself.

They further declare that they will keep this plan closely in their view, and use their utmost endeavors that the same be not narrowed, nor the members of the Church of England, or those dissenting from them (in any future election to the principal officers mentioned in the aforesaid letter), be put on any worse footing in this Seminary than they were at the time of obtaining the Royal Brief. They subscribe this with their names, and ordain that the same be read and subscribed by every new trustee that shall hereafter be elected, before he takes his seat at the board.

RICHARD PETERS, President, etc.

This Declaration was signed by all the Trustees then in office, and by all who were subsequently elected under the College Charter.

For the present Dr. Franklin's efforts to break down the College had failed. From a *causa proxima*, at least, he was relegated into a *causa remota*, a *causa causans;* and President Reed, in due time, became his successor.

There was a convention of the Clergy of the Province of New Jersey and of their Brethren from New York and Pennsylvania held at Perth Amboy, in September of this year (1764).

It was the third convention of the Clergy in this region, and was a sort of general convention, or one at least of the Clergy of the Middle States—New York, New Jersey, Pennsylvania, and the "Lower Counties" (what is now known as "Delaware")—all sending ministers. Dr. Smith presided at it. We have no record of its proceedings that I know of beyond incidental allusions— one of a painful kind—further on in Dr. Smith's letters. From them we learn that it was harmonious, and approved of the plan of Corresponding Societies, Agencies, etc., as recommended by Dr. Smith in the letter already given on page 349. It seems to have ordered an Address to Dr. Terrick (as I suppose it was) on his then late translation to the See of London. Bishop Terrick wrote no great deal, and his name has passed into tradition. But he was a most amiable and benevolent man. Many of our clergy—including the excellent Robert Blackwell—were ordained by him; and Dr. Smith felt peculiar regard for him as a warm friend and liberal benefactor of the church in America.

The year 1764 was signalized by great heats of party between the supporters of the Proprietary government and those who opposed and wished to change it. John Dickinson, with Dr. Smith, belonged to the former party; Joseph Galloway, with Dr. Franklin—whose confidential friend he was—to the latter. Dickinson and Galloway were members of the Assembly; both were able men, and both made able speeches. These were afterwards printed—the speech of Dickinson, with a preface by Dr. Smith, and the reply of Galloway, with one by Dr. Franklin. It is stated by the late William Rawle* as remarkable that, able as were the speeches, the prefaces were more admired than they were.

Mr. William Thomson Read,† after speaking of the great ability of all the papers, says:

It seems to me, however, that Smith and Dickinson have the advantage in the main argument, showing, as they do, very clearly the inexpediency and folly of relinquishing the existing Charter, inasmuch as, from the temper of the British Parliament to the Colonies, so far from its being likely that new privileges would be conferred, it was unlikely that those enjoyed would be retained.‡

We have seen by the exordium of a discourse already given§ of the Rev. Dr. Peters, Rector of the United Churches, how fraternal was the feeling in early days between the United Churches—Christ Church and St. Peter's—and the Lutheran Church in Philadelphia. We have evidence of the good ground which existed for this friendly feeling by the Church of England to them in the following document, which was transmitted to the English Archbishops and to the Bishop of London, with a certificate which will be found appended to it. Dr. Smith's early efforts to educate the Germans in English—not at all by forcing the church upon them, but by leaving them free to adopt it only when and as they liked—was now beginning to bear good fruits.

---

* " Recollections of the Pennsylvania Bar," p. 167.

† Life of George Read, p. 19.

‡ John Dickinson was the eldest son of Samuel Dickinson and Mary Cadwalader, born in Maryland, in 1732. It is not known where he received his education, except that William Killen (afterwards Chief-Justice and Chancellor of Delaware) was for some time his tutor. In addition to the "Farmers' Letters," by which he is most extensively known, he wrote nine letters signed "Fabius," advocating the ratification of the Constitution of the United States, and fourteen, under this same signature, to inform his fellow-citizens in regard to the French Revolution still in progress, and foster and increase friendly feeling for the French people. He was a consistent Quaker, to which Society he belonged, living in a liberal style as suited his ample fortune. When he retired from public life he went to reside in Wilmington, Delaware, where he died, on the fourteenth day of February, 1808. He was interred in the Friends' burying ground. *No stone marks his grave.*

§ *Supra*, p. 338.

To the most Reverend and Right Reverend Fathers in God, Thomas, Lord Archbishop of Canterbury, Robert, Lord Archbishop of York, and Richard, Lord Bishop of London.

The Petition of the Representatives of the High German Church called S^t. George's Church in the city of Philadelphia,

In all Humble Manner Sheweth,

That your Petitioners and other members of this Congregation have at very great expence erected an handsome brick church in the said City for the service of Almighty God, being eighty feet in length and fifty-two feet in breadth.

That your Petitioners have felt the inconveniences which have too often arisen in our Churches by being under the jurisdiction of a Cœtus here or a foreign Synod in Holland or Germany, are desirous of being under the protection of the Lord Bishop of London or whatever other Bishop our most gracious Sovereign may be pleased to appoint over this part of America.

That your petitioners have therefore got a Declaration of Trust for the uses of the said Church duly executed by Nine of the twelve trustees of the Ground (which they are advised is sufficient in Law), empowering fourteen members of the Congregation in conjunction with the said Trustees or a majority of them and the said Fourteen (whose names are subscribed) to frame, settle and finally conclude upon fundamental Articles and Rules for the good order and future government of the said Church forever.

That in pursuance of the trust so reposed in us, we, your petitioners by and with the consent of the Congregation have agreed upon the following fundamental articles, viz. :

First, " That from and after Easter, which shall be in the year of our Lord one thousand seven hundred and sixty-six, no Minister shall be capable of officiating in the said Church or of being chosen to the office of Minister thereof without first receiving Episcopal Ordination nor without being specially licenced or approved for the same by the Lord Bishop of London for the time being or whatever other Bishop His Majesty may be pleased to invest with Episcopal Jurisdiction over this part of America."

Secondly, "And we do hereby further provide that such Licence or approbation on the part of the Bishops as aforesaid shall only be given to such Minister or Ministers as the Representatives of the said Congregation or a majority of them known by the name of Consistory shall nominate and recommend to the Bishop for that purpose."

Thirdly, "And we do further ordain and settle it as a Fundamental constitution of the said Church and Congregation that the Liturgy and Service of the Church of England or a translation thereof in the German as used in the King's German Chapel and none else, be used in the said Congregation of the said Church."

Fourthly, "And we do hereby with the approbation, consent and advice of the Congregation nominate, appoint and recommend the Reverend M^r. Frederick Rothenbuhler to be the fixed and settled Minister of the said Church, provided he shall receive Episcopal Ordination and be licenced, qualified and approved agreeable to the Tenor hereof."

That your petitioners in pursuance of the said Articles had proposed to send our present Minister, M^r. Rothenbuhler (who was educated and had Calvinistic Ordination at Berne, in Switzerland), to receive Episcopal Ordination from the Lord Bishop of London, if thought worthy of the same, and to solicit the benefactions of pious and well-disposed persons in England to enable us to pay off a debt of above a Thousand pounds sterling, contracted in building the said Church (which is not yet near finished in the Inside), for which Debt the Estates and Houses of many of your poor Petitioners are mortgaged and no means left in their power to clear the same, having raised everything they could by contributions among their Friends in this city and Province.

That our said Minister would have embarked for England immediately, but was advised by the Episcopal Clergy of this city first to transmit the state of our case and obtain the approbation of your Graces and of your Lordship for the same.

Your petitioners therefore humbly pray (as they are the first German congregation in this country who have solicited to be taken under the Protection of the Church of England and united with her), that their case may be favourably received and that they may be informed whether their Minister may be permitted to proceed to England in the Spring agreeable to the Articles aforesaid, and whether your poor petitioners may not have hopes by Royal Brief or otherwise of obtaining assistance from pious and well disposed persons in England in their present distressed state of circumstances; and your petitioners as in duty bound shall ever pray, &c.

CONRAD ALSTER,	FREDERICK SCHREYER,
JOHN HANG,	CONRAD SCHNEIDER,
VALENTINE KERN,	JOHN GAUL,
JOSEPH JOB,	JACOB ROTH,
CHRISTIAN ROTH,	ABRAHAM FRIOTH,
SIGMUND HAGLEGAUSS,	SAMUEL MAUS,
PETER FIESS,	GEORGE FODEL,
JOHN FRICK,	JACOB BECKER,
JOHN WOLF,	JACOB KLEISLY,
CHRISTIAN ALBERGER,	JACOB BARR.

———— ————,*

ST. GEORGE'S CHURCH, Philadelphia, October 21st, 1764.

* Illegible.

DR. SMITH'S CERTIFICATE APPENDED.

PHILADELPHIA, October 22d, 1764.

MY LORDS: Give me leave to certify that the above is a true state of the aforesaid Congregation and Church and that the subscribers, whose names I have annexed in English, are the regular Representatives of the Congregation. It would not become me, who have been so lately a Beggar in England myself, and so highly favored by the countenances of your Graces and your Lordship, to become a speedy or warm solicitor for others. But if by any means something could be done for these poor people, they are really objects of Charity and their case worthy of Notice. The Congregation is very considerable in number, the greatest part of them are but of low circumstances and any countenance given to a German Congregation on this plan may be of happy consequence among their numerous countrymen in this Province. The answer to their Petition may be transmitted under cover to,

My Lords, Your most dutiful son and obliged humble Servant,

WILLIAM SMITH.

We now have the Bishop of London's reply (through Dr. Smith) to the Address of the Convention upon his recent translation:

FULHAM, November 10th, 1764.

REV'D SIR: I take the first opportunity of expressing to you and the rest of the Clergy, who have been pleas'd to favour me with their Congratulations upon my Translation to the See of London, my sincere Acknowledgments of so early a Testimony of their Regard and Attention. You, sir, will be so good as to assure them in return, that as I come to that station (in which His Majesty's Goodness has thought fit to place me, however undeserving of it); with a due sense of the Importance of that part of my Duty, which by Custom & long Usage is more particularly connected with the See of London—the Care of spiritual Concerns in the Plantations, so it shall be my constant Endeavour to make use of any Influence, which my Situation may give me, in forwarding every Measure that may be thought the most conducive to the more general Advancement of Religion and Virtue in the World.

No one can be more sensible than I am of the peculiar disadvantages attending the Church of England in America, for want of a more perfect & Compleat Establishment. And I should have great Satisfaction if I could in any Degree be instrumental in promoting a measure, which, upon true Principles of Liberty, seems to me to be founded in Reason and Equity. But we can only declare and humbly represent our own Sentiments; we must leave it to the superiour Wisdom of Government to judge how far and when such a Measure may be seasonable;

and we must acquiesce with all Duty in the Determination, however it may interfere with our own private opinions and wishes.

All that I can promise with any assurance, is my own Care & Attention to the Concerns of the American Churches, so far as they are thought to belong to my Station; and a cheerful readiness to assist with my best Advice, any of the Clergy who may think proper to apply to me, as the State of Religion in their several Parishes may require.

I shall hope, likewise, that they will, as opportunities offer, give me any information which may better enable me to discharge my Duty, however imperfectly at this distance. For I most earnestly desire (and in Duty I owe it to the best of kings, who plac'd me in the Relation I now bear to you,) to answer, in every possible way, that great and good Purpose (which He has most sincerely at Heart); the Success and influence of true Religion in the remotest parts of His Dominions. As you are at the Head of that Convention of the Clergy, who have given me so acceptable a Proof of their regard, I must desire you to convey my grateful sense of it in what manner you may think proper, and assure them of the Affection which I bear to them.

I am, Revd Sir, Your loving Brother,

LONDON.

To REV. DR. SMITH, Provost of the College at Philadelphia.

CHAPTER XXVI.

COMMENCEMENT AT THE COLLEGE—REV. GEORGE WHITFIELD THERE—WILLIAM (AFTERWARDS BISHOP) WHITE A GRADUATE—RETURN OF DR. MORGAN TO AMERICA—HIS INAUGURAL ADDRESS—ADDRESS IN VERSE BY MR. NATHANIEL EVANS, ON TAKING HIS DEGREE—COL. HENRY BOUQUET—DR. SMITH WRITES THE HISTORY OF HIS EXPEDITION IN 1764 TO OHIO—THE WORK MUCH ADMIRED—DIFFERENT EDITIONS—DR. SMITH'S LETTERS ABOUT THE CONVENTION OF 1764—THE STAMP ACT—"AN INDEPENDENT EPISCOPAL CHURCH" —DR. SMITH COLLECTS AND PUBLISHES THE POEMS, ETC., OF THOMAS GODFREY, THE YOUNGER.

THE Annual Commencement this year (1765) took place at the College on Fourth street below Arch, on the 30th and 31st of May. Although the Church Clergy of Philadelphia would not now invite Whitfield to preach in their *Churches*, Dr. Smith invited him to deliver a Sermon in the College Hall at the Commencement. Indeed, as the edifice in which the College was held was originally built as a church for Whitfield, there seemed some special propriety in asking him to address the Classes. Whitfield thus speaks of the College:

It is one of the best regulated institutions in the world. Dr. Smith read the prayers for me; both the present and the late Governor with the head gentlemen were present, and cordial thanks were sent to me from all the Trustees for speaking to the children and countenancing the institution.

This Commencement marks an important event in the history of the College. Dr. John Morgan, of whom we have made some mention among the graduates of 1751, now proposed to establish a medical school in the College. He was born in Philadelphia in the year 1736. After graduating he studied medicine under Dr. Redman, and subsequently entered the Provincial Army during the French war as a surgeon. After four years' service in the army he went to Europe, where he studied in London, under Hunter and Hewson, and graduated as M. D. at Edinburgh in 1763. Dr. Morgan and William Shippen had been companions in London, and it is believed that they agreed together upon the plan of establishing a medical school in Philadelphia. Dr. Morgan was desirous to have the influence of the College in favor of medical instruction, and he brought with him a letter to the Trustees of the College from Thomas Penn, recommending Dr. Morgan's plan for introducing "new professorships into the academy for the instruction of all such as shall incline to go into the study and practice of physic and surgery, as well as the several occupations depending upon these useful and necessary arts." He also had letters from Mr. Hamilton and Dr. Peters, former members of the Board of Trustees of the College, who were then in England, as also Dr. Fothergill, Dr. Hunter, Dr. Watson and Dr. Cullen, distinguished British physicians.

The Trustees, says Mr. Westcott, to whose valuable " History of Philadelphia" I am indebted for this whole account, received the application of Dr. Morgan with favor, and, after due consideration, on the 3d of May, 1765, unanimously elected him Professor of the Theory and Practice of Physic. At this commencement of the College in this year, he delivered an inaugural address entitled "A discourse upon the institution of medical schools in America." In that address he prophetically said:

Perhaps this medical institution, the first of its kind in America, though small in its beginning, may receive a constant increase of strength and annually exert new vigor.   It may collect a number of young persons of more than ordinary abilities, and so improve their knowledge as to spread its reputation to distant parts.   By sending these abroad fully qualified, or by exciting an emulation among men of parts and literature, it may give birth to other useful institutions of a similar nature; or, by its example, it may occasion to arise numerous societies of different kinds, calculated to spread the light of knowledge through the whole American continent wherever inhabited.

Thus was the Medical Department of the College, since so renowned, begun.

Among the graduates of this year was one whose name deserves from all a special honor.   I refer to him who afterwards was the *Rev. John Andrews, D. D.*   This excellent man was born in Maryland, April 4th, 1746.   In his boyhood he was educated under the care of the Newcastle Presbytery, at Newark, Delaware. After graduating he taught school in Lancaster county, Pennsylvania, and studied divinity under the Rev. Thomas Barton, missionary at that place.   He was ordained in England, in February, 1767, and sent by the Society for Propagating the Gospel to Lewes, in Delaware.   In 1784 he was made Principal of the Episcopal Academy, at Philadelphia, and afterwards Provost of the University of Pennsylvania.   He died A. D. 1813, aged 68 years. There was also another, named James Sayre, a Scotchman by birth, who, also, if I remember rightly, became a clergyman.   He refused to approve the doings of the General Convention in regard to the Book of Common Prayer; entering his protest upon the record.   He became dissatisfied with the Episcopal Church, and afterwards apostatized, joining the Methodists.   He died somewhere about 1798, *ætat* 60, in Fairfield, Connecticut, leaving a wife and seven children, who continued to be zealous and useful Episcopalians.

The most noteworthy, however, of all the graduates was *William White*, son of *Col. Thomas White*, of England, and Esther Hewlings, of Burlington, New Jersey.   His history, as well as his praises, are in all the churches, and, indeed, over all the land.   We need repeat neither.

At this commencement the Master's degree was conferred on several graduates of a former year; among them on Mr. Nathaniel

Evans, a young gentleman of great piety and attainments. He
took orders in the church, and for some years was at the Gloucester
mission, New Jersey, in the service of the Society for the Propagation of the Gospel; the predecessor in that place—with the
exception of a very short time when the Rev. Mr. Griffith was
there—of the Rev. Robert Blackwell. He died at the age of 26,
"a dutiful and only son of aged and affectionate parents." On
receiving his Master's degree he spoke an address to the Trustees
of the College and Academy. We give it here:

'Twas nobly done! The Muse's seat to raise
In this fair land, and earn immortal praise!
To civilize our first fam'd fires began,
'Twas yours to prosecute the glorious plan;
They peopled deserts with unwearied toil,
Establish'd laws and till'd the fruitful soil;
'Twas yours to call in each refining art,
T' improve the manners, and exalt the heart;
To train the rising race in wisdom's lore,
And teach them virtue's summit to explore.

What land than this can choicer blessings claim,
Where sacred liberty has fixt her name;
Where o'er each field gay Plenty spreads her store,
Free as yon * river laves the winding shore;
Where active Trade pours forth her jovial train
O'er the green bosom of the boundless main;
Where honest Industry's bright tools resound,
And Peace her olive scepter waves around?
To such a state fair Science to convey,
And beam afar the philosophic day;
To make our native treasures doubly blest,
Was sure a scheme to fire each worthy breast;
Was fit for gen'rous patriots to pursue,
Was fit for learning's patrons—and for you!
As from the east yon orb first darts his ray
O'er heaven's blue vault, and westward bends his way,
So Science in the orient climes began,
And, like bright Sol, a western circuit run;
From eastern realms to Greece was learning brought,
Whate'er Pythagoras or Cadmus taught;
Her form illustrious Athens did illume,
And rais'd the genius of imperial Rome;

* The Delaware.

From Latium's plains she sought Britannia's shore,
And bid her barb'rous sons be rude no more ;
Fierce nations roam'd around the rugged isle,
Till Science on its fields began to smile ;
Fair Cam and Isis heard no muse's strains,
Their shades were trod by wolves and fiercer Danes,
Till with the Arts Augusta's grandeur rose,
And her loud thunder shook the deep's repose.
Just so, in time (if right the Muse descries)
Shall this wide realm with tow'ry cities rise ;
The spacious Delaware, thro' future song,
Shall roll in deathless majesty along ;
Each grove and mountain shall be sacred made,
As now is Cooper's hill and Windsor's shade.

Flushed with the thought I'm borne to ages hence,
The muse-wrought vision rushes on my sense.
Methinks Messiah's ensign I behold
In the deep gloom of yonder shades unroll'd,
And hear the Gospel's silver clarion sound,
Rousing with heav'nly strains the heathen round ;
Methinks I hear the nations shout aloud,
And to the glory-beaming standard crowd ;
New inspirations shake each trembling frame,
The Paraclete pours forth the lambent flame—
In renovating streams on ev'ry soul,
While through their breasts celestial transports roll.
Stupendous change ! methinks th' effects appear ;
In the dark region sacred temples rear
Their lofty heads ; fair cities strike my sight,
And heaven-taught Science spreads a dazzling light
O'er the rough scene where error's court was found,
And red-eyed slaughter crimsoned all the ground.
Oh haste, blest days ! till ignorance flee the ball,
And the bright rays of knowledge lighten all ;
Till in yon wild new seats of Science rise,
And such as you the arts shall patronize !
For this your names shall swell the trump of fame,
And ages yet unborn your worth proclaim.

Nothing, I think, in the character of Dr. Smith, is more striking
than the variety and versatility of his powers ; and the slight degree
in which anything external operated in the way of a perturbation
of them. Whether engaged in severe work, or surrounded by

political excitements, or made anxious by economical solicitudes, or suffering—as he must have suffered—by misrepresentations of his purposes and acts, he was ever able to work, and to work steadily, and to work well; to give out what he knew upon an old subject, or to acquire matter for exhibition in a new.

In the year 1765 he formed, at Philadelphia, the acquaintance of Colonel Henry Bouquet, and at his request, and from facts narrated orally by him, or derived from papers which he furnished, prepared the volume known as " Bouquet's Expedition against the Indians ;" a work which had, when it appeared, an immense popularity in America, Great Britain, and over the Continent. It places Dr. Smith higher as a " narrator" or historian, I think, than his discourses place him as a pulpit orator.

But " Who was Colonel Henry Bouquet, and what Indians did he go against in 1764 ? " This is a question which, when speaking of this remarkable book, I have been constantly asked. It would be a question disgraceful to the inquirer, were it not a sad fact that there never has been a History of Pennsylvania yet written. I mean a history which should inspire general interest among the people of our State, and invite and reward a study of our colonial annals. The fault has not been wholly with our writers. Since the death of the venerable Samuel Hazard, some years ago—to whose labors we owe the publication of our earlier colonial records and State archives—our State, until lately, has been somewhat perhaps to blame. Until lately, I say; for now, indeed, under the animating zeal of such men as Dr. Eagle, Mr. Linn, Mr. Quay, and a few gentlemen at Harrisburg, the Legislature is putting into print all our historical manuscripts, and putting before the writers of Pennsylvania the means of knowing what her history—a great history—is. Nor ought I to pass, without words of high praise, that recently established journal, *The Pennsylvania Magazine of History and Biography*, published by the Historical Society of the State from the resources of that " well-managed fund," which has deservedly attracted the praise of the chief magistrate of our Commonwealth.*

---

* " The Centennial celebration has attracted particular attention to State history, with the gratifying result that this Commonwealth has not been behind others in providing liberally for the preservation of its true source. The labors of the Historical Society of Pennsylvania in this direction are worthy of especial notice. Its well-managed

Let us say then, first, a few words of Colonel Henry Bouquet.

HENRY BOUQUET was born at Rolle, a small town in the Canton of Vaud, on the northern borders of the Lake of Geneva, Switzerland, in or about the year 1719. In 1736, being then seventeen years old, he was received a cadet in the Regiment of Constant, in the service of the States-General of Holland, and in 1738 obtained an ensign's commission in the same regiment. He soon went into the service of the King of Sardinia, and distinguished himself as First Lieutenant, and afterwards as Adjutant, in the memorable and ably conducted campaign which that great prince sustained at this time against the combined forces of France and Spain. The written reports which he made—equally scientific, truthful and interesting—attracted the attention of the Prince of Orange, and that prince induced him to enter the service of the Republic. Bouquet accordingly, about 1748, went to the Hague, where he was made Captain Commandant, with the rank of Lieutenant-Colonel in the regiment of Swiss guards just then formed in that place; and, along with Generals Burmania and Cornabe, was appointed to receive from the French all the places in the Low Countries that, in pursuance of the treaty of Aix-la-Chapelle, were to be given up; as also to make arrangements for the return to the Republic of prisoners then in the hands of the French. This work being all happily accomplished, he travelled for some time in France and Italy along with Lord Middleton. On his return to the Hague, he pursued, every moment which his regimental duties allowed, his military studies, paying especial attention to Mathematical studies, which so much form military science. When the Seven Years' war broke out, in 1756—that war which in Pennsylvania we call the French and Indian war—England wishing to send troops to America, a corps called the "Royal American" was raised, composed of four battalions of 1,000 men each; the ranks to be formed, in a great measure, of the Germans and other continental settlers of Pennsylvania and Maryland, under the orders of one chief. Fifty of the officers might be foreign Protestants, but, in any case, men of capacity and experience. Bouquet

Publication Fund has contributed to historical resources the correspondence of Penn and Logan; the History, by Acrelius, of our Swedish Settlers upon the Delaware before the time of Penn; and Heckewelder's Indian Nations; and the Historical Map of Pennsylvania."--*Extract from the Message of Governor Hartranft, January,* 1877.

was one of the first persons to whom attention was directed, and he agreed to serve in a brigade as Lieutenant-Colonel. In 1763, after the conclusion of the Seven Years' war, the *Indian* war broke out. Bouquet, having distinguished himself in it, in the campaign of 1763, was appointed Colonel of Infantry and Brigadier-General in the expedition made in the same war against the Indians in Ohio. It is this campaign which constitutes the chief subject of the work of Dr. Smith.

But let us give a little of the history which preceded.*

The general peace, concluded between Great Britain, France and Spain, in 1762, at the end of the Seven Years' war, was universally considered as a most happy event in America. To behold the French, who had so long instigated and supported the Indians, in the most destructive wars and cruel depredations on our frontier settlements, at last compelled to cede all Canada, and restricted to the western side of Mississippi, was what Pennsylvania had long wished for, but what her people had scarcely hoped to see accomplished. The precision with which our boundaries were expressed, admitted of no ground for future disputes, and was matter of exultation to every one who understood and regarded the interest of these Colonies. The Province had now the pleasing prospect of entire security from all molestation of the Indians, since French intrigues could no longer be employed to seduce, or French force to support, them. Unhappily, however, it was disappointed in this expectation. Our danger arose from that very quarter, in which we imagined ourselves most secure; and just at the time when we concluded that the Indians were entirely awed, and almost subjected by our power, they suddenly fell upon the frontiers of our most valuable settlements, and upon all our outlying forts, with such unanimity in the design, and with such savage fury in the attack, as the Provinces had not experienced, even in the hottest times of any former war.

The reason of this uprising of the Indian tribes seems to have been a jealousy of our growing power, heightened by their seeing the French almost wholly driven out of America, and a number of forts now possessed by us, which commanded the great lakes

* A large part of what follows for some pages is taken, with little or no change of language, from the Introduction to Dr. Smith's "Expedition."

and rivers communicating with them, and awed the whole Indian country. They beheld in every little garrison the germ of a future colony, and thought it incumbent on them to make one general and timely effort to crush our power in the birth.

The different Indian nations surrounding our settlements were in that day powerful, and their situation with respect to each other not unfavorable to a strong combination. The Shawanese, Delawares and other Ohio tribes, took the lead in this war; their scheme appears to have been projected with much deliberate mischief in the intention, and more than usual skill in the system of execution. They were to make one general and sudden attack upon our frontier settlements in the time of harvest, to destroy our men, corn, cattle, etc., as far as they could penetrate, and to starve our outposts, by cutting off their supplies, and all communication with the inhabitants of the Provinces. In pursuance of this bold and bloody project, they fell suddenly upon our traders whom they had invited into their country, murdered many of them, and made one general plunder of their effects, to an immense value. The frontiers of Pennsylvania, Maryland and Virginia, were immediately overrun with scalping parties, marking their way with blood and devastation wherever they came, and all those examples of savage cruelty, which never fail to accompany an Indian war. All our out-forts, even at the remotest distances, were attacked about the same time; and the following ones soon fell into the enemies' hands, viz.: Le Boeuf, Venango, Presqu' Isle, on and near Lake Erie; La Bay, upon Lake Michigan; St. Joseph's, upon the river of that name; Miamis, upon the Miamis river; Ouachtanon, upon the Ouabache; Sandusky, upon Lake Junundat, and Michilimackinac. Being but weakly garrisoned, trusting to the security of a general peace so lately established, unable to obtain the least intelligence from the Colonies, or from each other, and being separately persuaded by their treacherous and savage assailants that they had carried every other place before them, it could not be expected that these small posts could hold out long; and the fate of their garrisons is terrible to relate. The news of their surrender, and the continued ravages of the enemy, struck all America with consternation, and depopulated a great part of our frontiers. The Provinces now saw most of those posts, suddenly wrested from us, which had been the great object of the late war, and one of the principal advantages acquired by the peace. Only the forts of Niagara, the Detroit and Fort Pitt, remained in our hands, of all that had been purchased with so much blood and treasure.

The Indians had early surrounded Fort Pitt, and cut off all communication from it, even by message. Though they had no cannon, nor understood the methods of a regular siege, yet, with incredible boldness, they posted themselves under the banks of the Ohio and Monongahela, at the junction of which stood the fort, and continued, as it were, buried there, from day to day, with astonishing patience; pouring in an incessant storm of musketry and fire-arrows; hoping at length, by famine, by fire, or by harassing out the garrison, to carry their point. Captain Ecuyer, who commanded there, though he wanted several necessaries for sustaining a siege, and the fortifications had been greatly damaged by the floods, took all the precautions which art and judgment could suggest for the repair of the place, and repulsing the enemy. His garrison, joined by the inhabitants and surviving traders who had taken refuge there, seconded his efforts with resolution. Their situation was alarming, being remote from all immediate assistance, and having to deal with an enemy from whom they had no mercy to expect. The fort remained all this while in a most critical situation. No account could be obtained from the garrison, nor any relief sent to it, but by a long and tedious land-march of near 200 miles beyond the settlements, and through those dangerous passes where the fate of Braddock and others still rises on the imagination.

Colonel Henry Bouquet was appointed by General Amherst, the Commander-in-Chief, to march to the relief of the fort, with a large quantity of military stores and provisions, escorted by the shattered remainder of the Forty-second and Seventy-seventh regiments, lately returned in a dismal condition from the West Indies, and far from being recovered of their fatigues at the recent siege of Havannah. General Amherst, having at that time no other troops to spare, was obliged to employ them in a service which would have required men of the strongest constitution and vigor. Early orders had been given to prepare a convoy of provisions on the frontiers of Pennsylvania, but such were the universal terror and consternation of the inhabitants, that when

Colonel Bouquet arrived at Carlisle, nothing had yet been done. A great number of the plantations had been plundered and burnt by the savages; many of the mills destroyed, and the full-ripe crops stood waving in the field, ready for the sickle, but the reapers were not to be found! The greatest part of the county of Cumberland, through which the army had to pass, was deserted, and the roads were covered with distressed families, flying from their settlements, and destitute of all the necessaries of life. In the midst of that general confusion the supplies necessary for the expedition became very precarious, nor was it less difficult to procure horses and carriages for the use of the troops. The commander found that, instead of expecting such supplies from a miserable people, he himself was called by the voice of humanity to bestow on them some share of his own provisions to relieve their present exigency. However, in eighteen days after his arrival at Carlisle, by the prudent and active measures which he pursued, joined to his knowledge of the country, and the diligence of the persons he employed, the convoy and carriages were procured with the assistance of the interior parts of the country, and the army proceeded. Their march did not abate the fears of the dejected inhabitants. They knew the strength and ferocity of the enemy. They remembered the former defeats even of our best troops, and were full of diffidence and apprehensions on beholding the small number and sickly state of the regulars employed in this expedition. Without the least hopes, therefore, of success, they seemed only to wait for the fatal event, which they dreaded, to abandon all the country beyond the Susquehanna.

In such despondency of mind, it is not surprising, that though their whole was at stake, and depended entirely upon the fate of this little army, none of them offered to assist in the defence of the country, by joining the expedition; in which they would have been of infinite service, being in general well acquainted with the woods, and excellent marksmen.

It is obvious that the defeat of the regular troops on this occasion would have left the Province of Pennsylvania, in particular, exposed to the most imminent danger, from a victorious, daring, and barbarous enemy; for (excepting the frontier people of Cumberland county) the bulk of its industrious inhabitants was composed of merchants, tradesmen and farmers, unaccustomed to arms, and owing to the influence of the Society of Friends in our Legislature, the Province was without a militia law. The Legislature had ordered seven hundred men to be raised for the protection of the frontiers during the harvest; but what dependence could be placed in raw troops, newly raised and undisciplined? Under so many discouraging circumstances, Colonel Bouquet (deprived of all assistance from the Provinces, and having none to expect from General Amherst, who had sent him the last man that could be removed from the hospitals) had nothing else to trust to but about five hundred soldiers of approved courage and resolution indeed, but infirm in health, and entire strangers to the woods, and to this new kind of war. A number of them were even so weak as not to be able to march, and sixty were carried in wagons to reinforce the garrisons of the small posts on the communication.

Meanwhile Fort Ligonier, situated beyond the Allegheny Mountains, was in the greatest danger of falling into the hands of the enemy before the army could reach it. The stockade being bad, and the garrison weak, they had attacked it vigorously, but had been repulsed by the bravery and good conduct of Lieutenant Blane, who commanded there. The preservation of that post was of the utmost consequence, on account of its situation and the quantity of military stores it contained, which, if the enemy could have got possession of, would have enabled them to continue their attack upon Fort Pitt, and reduced the army to the greatest straits. For an object of that importance, every risk was to be run; and Colonel Bouquet determined to send through the woods, with proper guides, a party of thirty men to join that garrison. They succeeded by forced marches in that hazardous attempt, not having been discovered by the enemy till they came within sight of the fort, into which they threw themselves, after receiving some running shot. This post being secured, Colonel Bouquet advanced to the remotest verge of our settlements, where he could receive no sort of intelligence of the number, position, or motions of the enemy. This indeed was often a very embarrassing circumstance in the conduct of a campaign in this country. The Indians had better intelligence, and no sooner were they informed of the march of our army than they broke up the siege of Fort Pitt, and took the route by which they knew we were to proceed, resolved to take the first advantageous opportunity of an attack on the march.

In this uncertainty of intelligence under which Colonel Bouquet labored, as soon as he reached Fort Ligonier, he determined to leave his wagons at that post, and to proceed only with the pack-horses. Thus disburdened, the army continued their route. Before them lay a dangerous defile at Turtle Creek, several miles in length, commanded the whole way by high and craggy hills. This defile he intended to have passed the ensuing night, by a double or forced march, thereby, if possible, to elude the vigilance of so alert an enemy, proposing only to make a short halt in his way to refresh the troops, at Bushy Run. When they came within half a mile of that place, about one o'clock in the afternoon (August 5th, 1763), after a harassing march of seventeen miles, and just as they were expecting to relax from their fatigue, they were suddenly attacked by the Indians, on their advanced guard: which being speedily and firmly supported, the enemy was beat off, and even pursued to a considerable distance. But the flight of Indians, in war, is often a part of the engagement, rather than a dereliction of the field. The moment the pursuit ends, they return with renewed vigor to the attack. Several other parties, who had been in ambush in some high grounds which lay along the flanks of the army, now started up at once, and falling with a resolution equal to that of their companions, galled our troops with a most obstinate fire. It was necessary to make a general charge with the whole line to dislodge them from these heights. This charge succeeded; but still the success produced no decisive advantage, for as soon as the Indians were driven from one post, they still appeared on another, till by constant reinforcements they were at length able to surround the whole detachment, and attack the convoy which had been left in the rear. This manœuvre obliged the main body to fall back in order to protect it. The action, which grew every moment hotter and hotter, now became general. Our troops were attacked on every side; the Indians supported their spirit throughout; but the steady behavior of the English troops, who were not thrown into the least confusion by the very discouraging nature of this service, in the end prevailed; they repulsed the enemy, and drove them from all their posts with fixed bayonets. The engagement ended only with the day, having continued from one o'clock without any intermission.

At the first dawn of light on the next morning the Indians began to declare themselves all about the camp, and, by shouting and yelling in the most horrid manner, endeavored to strike terror by an ostentation of their numbers and their ferocity. They then went to attack them after this, and, under the favor of an incessant fire, made several bold efforts to penetrate into the camp. They were repulsed in every attempt, but by no means discouraged from new ones. Our troops, continually victorious, were continually in danger. They were besides extremely fatigued with a long march, and with the equally long action of the preceding day; and they were distressed to the last degree by a total want of water, much more intolerable than the enemy's fire. Tied to their convoy, they could not lose sight of it for a moment, without exposing, not only that interesting object, but their wounded men, to fall a prey to the savages, who pressed them on every side. To move was impracticable. Many of the horses were lost, and many of the drivers, stupefied by their fears, hid themselves in the bushes, and were incapable of hearing or obeying orders. Their situation became extremely critical and perplexing, having experienced that the most lively efforts made no impression upon an enemy, who always gave way when pressed, but who, the moment the pursuit was over, returned with as much alacrity as ever to the attack. Besieged rather than engaged, attacked without interruption and without decision, able neither to advance nor to retreat, they saw before them the most melancholy prospect of crumbling away by degrees, and entirely perishing without revenge or honor, in the midst of those dreadful deserts. The fate of Braddock was every moment before their eyes, but they were more ably conducted. The commander was sensible that everything depended upon bringing the Indians to a close engagement, and to stand their ground when attacked. Their audaciousness, which had increased with their success, seemed favorable to this design. He endeavored, therefore, to increase their confidence as much as possible. For that purpose he contrived the following stratagem. Our troops were posted on an eminence, and formed a circle round their convoy from the preceding night, which order they still retained. Colonel Bouquet gave directions that two companies of his troops, who had been posted in the most advanced situations, should fall within the circle; the troops on

the right and left immediately opened their files, and filled up the
vacant space, that they might seem to cover their retreat. Another
company of light infantry, with one of grenadiers, were ordered
"to lie in ambuscade," to support the two first companies of
grenadiers, who moved on the feigned retreat, and were intended
to begin the real attack. The dispositions were well made, and
the plan executed without the least confusion.

The Indians fell into the snare. The thin line of troops, which
took possession of the ground which the two companies of light
foot had left, being brought in nearer to the centre of the circle,
the barbarians mistook those motions for a retreat, abandoned the
woods which covered them, hurried headlong on, and advancing
with the most daring intrepidity, galled the English troops with
their heavy fire. But at the very moment, when, certain of success, they thought themselves masters of the camp, the two first
companies made a sudden turn, and sallying out from a part of
the hill, which could not be observed, fell furiously upon their
right flank.

The Indians, though they found themselves disappointed and
exposed, preserved their recollection, and resolutely returned the
fire which they had received. Then it was the superiority of combined strength and discipline appeared. On the second charge
they could no longer sustain the irresistible shock of the regular
troops, who, rushing upon them, killed many and put the rest to
flight.

At the instant when the Indians betook themselves to flight, the
other two companies, which had been ordered to support the first,
rose "from the ambuscade," marched to the enemy, and gave
them their full fire. This accomplished their defeat. The four
companies, now united, did not give them time to look behind
them, but pursued the enemy till they were totally dispersed.

The other bodies of Indians attempted nothing. They were
kept in awe during the engagement by the rest of the British
troops, who were so posted as to be ready to fall on them upon
the least motion. Having been witnesses to the defeat of their
companions, without any effort to support or assist them, they at
length followed their example and fled.

This manœuvre rescued the party from the most imminent
danger. The victory secured the field, and cleared all the adja-

cent woods. But still the march was so difficult, and the army had suffered so much, and so many horses were lost, that before they were able to proceed, they were reluctantly obliged to destroy such part of their convoy of provisions as they could not carry with them for want of horses. Being lightened by this sacrifice, they proceeded to Bushy Run, where, finding water, they encamped.

The Indians, thus signally defeated in all their attempts to cut off this reinforcement upon its march, began to retreat with the utmost precipitation to their remote settlements, wholly giving up their designs against Fort Pitt; at which place Colonel Bouquet arrived safe with his convoy, four days after the action, receiving no further molestation on the road, except a few scattered shot from a disheartened and flying enemy.

Here Colonel Bouquet was obliged to put an end to the operations of this campaign, not having a sufficient force to pursue the enemy beyond the Ohio, and take advantage of the victory obtained over them, nor having any reason to expect a timely reinforcement from the Provinces in their distressed situation. He was therefore forced to content himself with supplying Fort Pitt and other places on the communication with provisions, ammunition, and stores, stationing his small army to the best advantage he could against the approach of winter. The Indians in the meantime retreating into what is now Ohio, reformed, and reinforced and fortified themselves with rapidity and skill. To dislodge and destroy or conquer them was the work of the campaign of 1764, described in the " Expedition " of Dr. Smith.

The military knowledge, the literary skill and the patriotic zeal of Dr. Smith were never better illustrated than in this work. The narrative is comprehensive in thought, rich in fact and brilliant in style ; and so little did he value literary fame that the book, published anonymously, was for nearly a century attributed to Mr. Hutchins.

The work of Dr. Smith was first printed at Philadelphia in quarto—some copies on fine demi-paper at 10s. the copy, and some on common paper at 8s. The title is upon the page which faces this.

A N
HISTORICAL ACCOUNT
OF THE
EXPEDITION
AGAINST THE

OHIO INDIANS, in the YEAR 1764.

UNDER THE COMMAND OF

HENRY BOUQUET, Esq;

COLONEL of Foot, and now BRIGADIER GENERAL in AMERICA.

INCLUDING

His Transactions with the Indians, relative to the delivery of their prisoners, and the preliminaries of PEACE.

WITH AN

INTRODUCTORY ACCOUNT

Of the Preceeding Campaign, and Battle at BUSHY-RUN.

TO WHICH ARE ANNEXED

MILITARY PAPERS,

CONTAINING

Reflections on the war with the Savages; a method of forming frontier settlements; some account of the Indian country, with a list of nations, fighting men, towns, distances and different routs.

The whole illustrated with a Map and Copper-plates.

Published from authentic Documents, by a Lover of his Country.

PHILADELPHIA:

PRINTED and sold by WILLIAM BRADFORD, at the LONDON COFFEE-HOUSE, the corner of Market and Front-streets.   M.DCC.LXV.

The work was illustrated with three copper plates in the best style of old English engraving. 1. A general plan of the country on the Ohio and Muskingum River, with the road through which Col. Bouquet passed (Engraved Designs.) 2. A plan of the Battle at Bushy Run. 3. Plans of the line of march, encampment, disposition to receive the enemy and general attack, to explain the military papers. There is in addition a plan in letter-press meant to explain the way in which frontier townships might defend themselves.

The work had an immense popularity. Soon after its appearance it was published in a handsome quarto in London in 1776, with maps and two charming engravings, one by Grignion, after Benjamin West, a particular friend and early protegé of Dr. Smith, who exerted his pencil to effect for this work. The maps, however, are not near as fine as in the Philadelphia edition. It was also translated into French, and published in Paris; also, A. D. 1769, in 12mo. in Amsterdam. The Amsterdam edition has the maps and engravings after the same two pictures of West. In 1867— just one hundred and two years after it appeared from the old London Coffee-House—coming back to the country from which it originated, it was handsomely printed in Cincinnati, Ohio, by Robert Clarke & Co., from the London edition; with photo-lithographic copies of the maps and engravings in it. The work for some years was supposed to be written by Thomas Hutchins, but there is no doubt now, that Dr. Smith was its author.*

The French translator pays to Dr. Smith and his work this high compliment:

" Si j'ai su atteindre à la moitié seulement de l'elegance et du pathétique de l'original Anglois, ma copie doit plaire et toucher. C'est deja beaucoup. Si jai renou fidelement ce qu'il y a d'instructif, elle sera utile ; et peu de feuilles ferent se que des volumes ne font pas toujours, de renfermer l'agréable avec le solide.

N'oublions pas de faire remarquer une autre grace particuliere à ce livret, celle de la nouveauté. Un ouvrage rempli de goût, de sentiment et de vues, écrit et imprimé originairement en Pensylvanie (naguere un désert) a réellment de quoi piquer la curiosité, exciter même la surprise de ceux qui, n'ayant qu'une connaissance imparfaite dés Colonies Septentrionales de l'Amerique Anglaise, ignorent que quelques-unes de celles-ci ne sout plus qu'improperement appellées du nom modeste de Colonies ;

---

* See *infra*, p. 392.

que ce sout deja des peuples nombreux, des Etats croisants, que ont leur villes du premier et du second ordre, leurs bourg et villages ; des formes de Gouvernment calculées pour le plus grand bonheur des cito-yens, des ecoles publiques, des bibliotheques, des gazettes et des jour neaux.''

This volume in this its first American form has become a jewel in the case of Bibliophiles.   Robert Clarke & Co. apparently never saw it.   A copy of it was sold October 29th, 1878, by Messrs. M. Thomas & Sons, at auction, in my presence, for $52.

We have mentioned in our last chapter that a convention of the church was held in the autumn of 1764 at Perth Amboy.   We now have some mention of it.   Who Mr. Morton was, with whose case the convention was so much occupied—further than that he seems to have been a missionary who had got into some trouble with a young lady—I must leave it to some person more of an ecclesiastical antiquary and lover of *la chronique scandaleuse* than I am, to inform my readers ; if, indeed, they wish to know.

Dr. Smith and Others to the Secretary of the Society for the Propagation of the Gospel.*

ELIZABETH TOWN, Jan'y 11th, 1765.

REVᴰ SIR : At a convention of the clergy of this Province and some of their Brethren from New York and Pennsylvania, held at Perth Amboy in Septʳ last, among other things the case of Mʳ. Morton (agree-able to the Society's pleasure formerly signified) came under their con-sideration, and they would at that time have presented the Venerable Society with the unexpected termination of that affair as it had been laid before them—but in the course of the enquiry certain evidence of a very material nature, being then inattainable, a full account was deferred till that could be procured.   Of this the Honorable Society was informed by our general Letter, and that a Committee was appointed to finish this business, and report the Issue of the whole matter.

From the evidence and vouchers produced at the late Convention it appeared that the prosecution against Mʳ. Morton had been withdrawn by his adversary, who had also given him a full and final Release, and that the only motive influencing the plaintiff to this conduct, mentioned in the papers respecting this settlement, was a scruple of conscience restraining him from an injurious act.   But it being moved that a report had prevailed of Mʳ. Garrison's declaring that he had received from one Charles Steuart, Esqʳᵉ, a sum of money for compromising this dispute, the Convention upon the whole came to the following Resolution : That

---

* This letter was drawn up by the Rev. Mr. McKean.   See following letter.—Ed.

if M^r. Morton could make it appear to their satisfaction that the said Charles Steuart, Esqre, did not give any money with the consent or privity directly or indirectly of the said M^r. Morton, it is the unanimous opinion of this Convention M^r. Morton stands fairly acquitted of the charges brought against him in all its parts.

That this matter might be determined as early as possible—we, the subscribers, were appointed a Committee by our Brethren as signified in the above-mentioned general letter. For this purpose, Sir, we had a meeting at Trenton, where we were attended by M^r. Steuart and have now the Honor, through you, of acquainting the Venerable Society with the result of our enquiries.

M^r. Steuart, being solemnly interrogated, returned us the following answers, viz. :

1. "That the desire of an accommodation arose from M^r. Garrison, who solicited him to effect a meeting between him and M^r. Morton ;— that he at first declined intermeddling, but on M^r. Garrison's repeated solicitations and declarations of his uneasiness, and desire of having the affair settled, he undertook to speak to M^r. Morton, and accordingly proposed a meeting, which M^r. Morton, suspecting (as he said) some evil design, refused, but on his urging his opinion of M^r. Garrison's sincerity in the overture, M^r. Morton agreed to meet, but not without the presence of witnesses.

2. "That he did not give M^r. Garrison any money to procure the said accommodation with the consent and privity of M^r. Morton, directly or indirectly, but so far from it that M^r. Morton declared to him both before and on the day they met, that if M^r. Garrison would not voluntarily, honorably and without the least overture from him release all matters of accusation whatever, he would not agree to any accommodation, nor enter on that subject with him.

3. "That at the meeting, M^r. Garrison readily and freely offered and gave M^r. Morton a full release of all actions and causes of action either in respect of himself or daughter ; but that after the matter was thus concluded and not before, upon M^r. Garrison's privately urging and bewailing his distressed circumstances, the necessity he was under of immediately paying costs, and his inability thereunto, and otherwise bespeaking his pity, he did from a disinterested, generous and charitable view, and from a regard to Religion and the peace of his neighbourhood promise and afterwards pay him a sum of money to assist him in his difficulties, and prevent any subsequent complaints, and that this was all done without the consent or privity of M^r. Morton either directly or indirectly.

4. "That he had never received any reimbursement of the said money from M^r. Morton or from any person on his account, nor did expect or claim any such reimbursement.

5. "And lastly, that he believes M^r. Morton knew nothing of this transaction of his with Garrison, till about ten or twelve days after the

Meeting; that M^r. Morton and M^r. Grandin came to him in apparent uneasiness and disturbance and informed him of a Report prevailing of his having given M^r. Garrison a sum of Money to effect the accommodation and desired to know whether he had given any money, at which time he related the circumstances of that matter, as he before declared, at which M^r. Morton expressed great uneasiness and disapproved of what he had done, as it might be construed to his disadvantage. M^r. Steuart concluded by adding that he should never have mentioned this transaction had not M^r. Garrison been influenced by some evil-minded people to report the affair in an injurious and unjust light."

These declarations of M^r. Steuart were taken from his own mouth, and were in due form of question and answer by us reduced to writing in proper minutes, and were afterwards repeatedly read and assented to before us by M^r. Steuart, in testimony of which we subscribed our names to the said minutes, and from those minutes the foregoing account is almost literally extracted, as conveying the fullest and most perfect view of this particular.

A copy of the release and a Letter to the Attorney General, both which we know to be genuine, we herewith enclose, as likewise a determination of M^r. Morton's Churchwardens and Vestry, after a particular scrutiny into the many scandalous reports propagated by Bad people concerning the accommodation.

Thus, Sir, have we faithfully laid before you the evidence offered to us on this very disagreeable subject. The Honorable Society will determine as it appears to them with their usual candour and uprightness. We cannot conclude, however, without observing, that as we have it in our power with full confidence to say, that from all accounts M^r. Morton's behaviour in every other respect and circumstance still continues unblemished, and that he is yet diligently and usefully employed in the duties of his mission, we cannot therefore but be greatly pleased at this termination of his late misfortunes.

But we would with submission add, that we are of opinion that though he may be in some measure usefully employed where he is, yet we apprehend not so extensively as he might otherwise have been, or as he may be in some other place, besides that we apprehend he cannot be so happy among his enemies as if removed somewhere out of their reach.

This, with everything herein offered, we humbly submit to the paternal regard of the Honorable, able and Venerable Society, and are with a due sense of their goodness to us, and of the trust reposed in us,

> Revd Sir,
>
> Their & your most obed^t Serv^{ts},
>
> WILLIAM SMITH,
> COLIN CAMPBELL,
> SAM^L COOKE,
> ROB^T M^{c}KEAN,
> LEO^D CUTTING.

The Same to the Same.

(EXTRACT.)

PHILADELPHIA, May 8th, 1765.

DEAR & WORTHY SIR:

     *   *   *   I am not clear in one expression in our joint letter, which says that the convention at Amboy judged that if this enquiry to be made of M^r. Steuart should terminate in M^r. Morton's favor, "he stood fairly acquitted of the charge brought against him in all its parts." Tho' I presided at the Convention, and attended close to everything before us, I do not remember any conditional or other decision to have been made. Tho' we thought M^r. Morton legally acquitted, yet it was too general an opinion among us founded on good grounds, that he had by imprudences in his behaviour to the Girl (tho' I really believe not of a criminal nature), given advantages against himself, and therefore we all wished that he might be removed to a distant place where he might not lie under these or any other imputations to hurt his usefulness. But as M^r. McKean drew the committee's Letter with all the minutes before him, he knew best what was in them, and I may have forgot particular words ; and therefore made no scruple to sign my name.

M^r. Whitfield is here, but will receive no invitation from us to preach in our Churches, being determined to observe the same conduct as when he was here in October last, which our superiors in England have approved.

He has turned his Georgia Hospital into a College, and is to solicit a Royal Charter and Grant of Lands for it, If a proper security is made for a Church of England Head of his College. However Catholic and wide his scheme may be otherwise, it may be of service to grant his request, But if he intends it otherwise as a nursery of his own particular Tenets, which tend to hurt order and a regular ministration of the Gospel, I should be sorry ever to see it established. He declares this is far from his intention. I shall have some conversation with him on this Head and shall write to the Archbishop.

I am, Worthy Sir, &^{c}.,

W. SMITH.

We observe in the year to which we have now arrived something of a cessation of correspondence between Dr. Smith and the higher clergy of England. We were now in the memorable year of the Stamp Act, and political feeling between the colonies and the mother country was operating to refrigerate the sentiments which lead to pleasant letter-writing. Dr. Smith, in common with nearly all America, opposed the Act as highly impolitic and unjust. Writing to Dr. Tucker, the celebrated Dean of Gloucester—

the same who shortly after declared that the severest punishment which could be inflicted upon the rebellious Colonies would be to " let them depart in peace "—under date of December 18th, 1765, he says:

With regard to the Stamp Act, or any act of Parliament to take money out of our pockets, otherwise than by our own representatives in our Colony legislatures, it will ever be looked upon so contrary to the faith of charters and the inherent rights of Englishmen, that amongst a people planted, and nursed, and educated in the high principles of liberty, it must be considered as a badge of disgrace, impeaching their loyalty, nay, their very brotherhood and affinity to Englishmen, and although a superior force may, and perhaps can, execute this among us, yet it will be with such an alienation of the affections of a loyal people, and such a stagnation of English consumption among them, that the experiment can never be worth the risque.

The spirit of political opposition which the Stamp Act called forth infused itself both soon and strongly into the church.

We have mentioned three Conventions of the Church as having been held—two at Philadelphia, in Pennsylvania, in 1760 and 1761, and one in New Jersey, in 1764, at Perth Amboy. Dr. Smith presided at all. These were all harmonious and useful, further than that Mr. Macclanechan was a disturber of the first one. A fourth one was held in 1765, which made some excitement. Dr. Smith was not at it. We must enlarge a little at this point.

The reader will have already seen that the want of Bishops resident in America was a want which was felt by all our early clergy. Many of the English Bishops also acknowledged that it was very desirable that the Church should be completed in the Colonies by the presence of its highest order as well as by the presence of the two lower orders. The Bishop of Landaff, in a sermon before the Propagation Society, in 1767, and Archbishop Secker oftentimes, and once specially in a letter to Walpole, urged the matter in England with earnestness. But up to this date the matter took no form offensive to any one.

Among the American clergy earliest and most active in urging an American Episcopate was Dr. Samuel Johnson, of Stratford, Connecticut. He had been urging it from as far back as the year 1727 or thereabouts. In the year 1766 he addressed himself to the Rev. Thomas Bradbury Chandler, D. D., a man of energy and

25

parts, to bring the matter before the public by some printed work. Dr. Johnson was at this time afflicted by a tremor in the hand— some sort of paralysis, I suppose—which made it difficult for him to use his pen.   Dr. Chandler accordingly undertook to make a printed appeal to the public in behalf of the Church of England in America.   While he was engaged on his tract, the clergy of New York and New Jersey met in voluntary convention at Shrewsbury, and assisted by some of their brethren from the neighboring prov- inces, took into consideration the propriety of what Dr. Chandler was engaged in.   "After a thorough discussion of the point"— according to Dr. Chandler's own account—they were unanimously of opinion that fairly to explain the plan on which American Bishops had been requested; to lay before the public the reasons of this request; to answer the objections that had been made, and to obviate those which might otherwise be conceived against it, was not only proper and expedient, but a matter of necessity and duty.

The Convention accordingly voted that something to this pur- pose should be published; and Dr. Chandler was appointed to do it, with liberty, however, to make the time of doing it convenient to himself.

I suppose it, too, to have been the fact, that Dr. Chandler had his appeal nearly ready for the press, and desired the support of the Convention in bringing it out.

The English Bishops having apparently done all that they could do, and the ministry having refused to comply with their wishes, this action of the clergy in New Jersey had a little the aspect of insubordination.   And when Dr. Chandler's printed book, called "An Appeal to the Public, in Behalf of the Church in America," came forth—as it did from the press of James Parker, of New York, in 1767—with rather a fierce motto from Justin Martyr, " *We desire a fair trial.   If we are guilty, punish us: If we are inno- cent, protect us* "—a considerable disturbance was raised.   A regular battle of pamphlets, periodicals and newspapers began.   The book from beginning to end was most respectful, and asked nothing not proper to be asked.   The Presbyterians, however, saw nothing in it but the "likeness of a kingly crown;" and were thrown at once into convulsions.   Indeed, had the Tiara itself been seen sailing into Boston Bay or along Long Island Sound, and the

Beatissimo Padre under it, those in Massachusetts and Connecticut would have hardly been more excited. But the thing somewhat alarmed our own Church. An "appeal!" From whom? From what? Plainly from the English Bishops, the English Crown, and the English Ministers. An appeal to what? To whom? Plainly to laity and clergy everywhere; in short, to general justice. Suppose, then, that the English Bishops, Crown and Ministry, who had always professed a readiness to listen to appeals *to* them, would not be constrained to act on appeals *from* them? What then? The answer was obvious. You acknowledge some foreign Episcopates.—The Swedish, the Moravian. We will apply to them. We will apply to the Non-Juring Bishops; most of them now Scotch. We will set up an independent American Episcopal Church. The Church was thus in a sort of rebellion before the State was. As we have said, there was not a word in the Appeal which could properly be found fault with by any one, ecclesiastical or lay, in either England or here. Some resolutions of the Convention were possibly more open to remark.

The matter, by good fanning, soon came to a great flame. Dr. Chandler's appeal to the public was answered by the Rev. Charles Chauncy, D. D., pastor of the First Church of Christ, in Boston, a Presbyterian clergyman. Dr. Chandler then published his "Appeal Defended," in answer to Dr. Chauncy's " Misrepresentations." Dr. Chauncy replied to this. And Dr. Chandler published his "Appeal further Defended." Six pamphlets by the two gentlemen. Dr. Chauncy, moreover, in "A Letter to a Friend," published in 1767, made his remarks on the Bishop of Landaff's sermon, and William Livingston, in 1778, came to his aid with "A Letter to the Right Reverend Father in God, John, Lord Bishop of Landaff, Occasioned by his Lordship's Sermon on the 20th of February, 1776, in which the American Colonies are loaded with great and undeserved reproach." "A Lover of Truth and Decency" got at both gentlemen, and defended his lordship's sermon from " the gross Misrepresentations and Abusive Reflections contained in Mr. William Livingston's Letter to his Lordship," and made " Observations" besides on Dr. Chauncy's remarks. "An Anti-Episcopalian" printed "A Letter concerning an American Bishop." Two periodical papers—*The American Whig* and *The Centinel*—were set up to oppose the matter. *The American Whig* was answered by "A Whip for the American Whig;" *The Centinel* by "The Anatomist." Bishop Porteus wrote a "Life of Archbishop Secker," and "A Defence of his Letter to Mr. Walpole on American Bishops." This was followed by "A Critical Commentary on Archbishop Secker's Letter to Mr. Walpole concerning Bishops in America." And this again by "A Free Examination of the Critical Commentary." In Virginia some of the Episcopal clergy —the Rev. Mr. Henley, the Rev. Mr. Watkin, the Rev. Mr. Hewitt and the Rev. Mr. Bland—publicly and formally protested against an application for an American Episcopate; calling the plan of introducing them as "a pernicious project." And the House of Burgesses —most of whose members were professed Episcopalians—on the 12th of July, 1771, resolved that the thanks of the House be given to the said gentlemen for the wise and well-timed opposition they had made to the pernicious project of a few mistaken clergymen for introducing an American bishop; "a measure by which much disturbance, great anxiety and apprehension, would certainly take place among his Majesty's faithful American subjects." And Mr. Richard Henry Lee and Mr. Bland were directed to acquaint them therewith.

The "protesters" in Virginia were all regularly ordained ministers of the Church of England. That church was the established one of the State. Most of tne Legislature professed to be Episcopalians. One of the writers in Virginia speaks of the Church in Virginia as an independent society, making no part of the Church of England. One of them, the Rev. Mr. Henley, thus speaks of Archbishop Secker,* who had always desired that we should have an episcopate :

As to Secker, he is laid in his grave. Disturb not his slumber. His character, no more than his body, can endure the keen question of the searching air. Unless you would give another proof of your friendship, cause him not to stink to futurity.

"Mr. Camm" answered the Protesters; and to counteract such doctrines as were coming from Virginia, a regular "Address" was made by a committee of the clergy of New York and New Jersey, who had been at the convention in the latter State, "to Episcopalians in Virginia, occasioned by some late Transactions in that Colony Relative to an American Episcopate."

---

* Purdie & Dixon's Virginia Gazette, of July 18th, 1771.

I speak only of such pamphlets as I have seen. There were doubtless others; while periodical journals and the newspapers were filled with the discussion.

From this little history of a most unreasonable and unaccountable excitement, both in the Church and out of it, from 1767 till the Revolution, the reader will better understand some allusions in subsequent letters of Dr. Smith. It seems that he went into the fight himself.*

I have alluded, on a former page,† to that gifted child of genius, Thomas Godfrey, the younger—poet, musician and dramatist— and to Dr. Smith's procuring for him a lieutenancy in the army, then stationed at Fort Duquesne. His name forms part of the literary honor of Pennsylvania; but the spirit of our antiquaries has of late given so many early productions to the country, that I am not sure all my readers are as well acquainted with the name of Godfrey the younger, as they probably are with that of the father, whose name is immortalized as the inventor of the quadrant, though the honor of the discovery was taken by another. I more willingly give some account of him, as I find one written by my own father, Richard Penn Smith. He says:

Of the exact time of his birth, there is no record: but his intimate friend, the Rev. Nathaniel Evans, states that he was born in the year 1736, in the city of Philadelphia, and that at an early age he was made an orphan by the death of his ingenious, though neglected parent. On this melancholy event, he was placed among his relations, and received from them the rudiments of an English education. He was afterwards apprenticed to a watch-maker; but it appears that he never was pleased with the pursuit selected for him by those who had the control of his early life.

His taste for poetry displayed itself in youth; and the productions of his muse were communicated to the world through the pages of the *American Magazine,* edited by the Rev. Dr. Smith. The benevolent feelings of Dr. Smith prompted him to extend his favourable regards to one, who had thus exhibited no inconsiderable talent in an

---

* When Bishop White went, after the Revolution, to be consecrated in England, some of his friends, fearing that it might expose him to indignity, begged him not to take, on his return, the title of Bishop. Hence he was long called by many Doctor White. He used to tell this anecdote himself. " But now," said he, speaking in the year 1834, " we have a score of bishops, in every part of the country; including, among the Methodists, a *black* bishop."

† Page 187.

art which himself admired and could properly appreciate. He encouraged Godfrey to cultivate his abilities, and not only supplied him with much valuable information, but also introduced him to the society of a number of his students, already endeared to him by their excellent dispositions and accomplishments.

Among these were Francis Hopkinson, Benjamin West, afterwards President of the Royal Society of Painters, and Jacob Duché, who subsequently became a clergyman and officiated as Rector of St. Peter's Church, in Philadelphia. With West our poet formed a close intimacy, which ripened into a strong and mutual friendship. Like this illustrious artist, Godfrey had early shown a taste for painting ; but was dissuaded from pursuing it as a profession by his relatives. Whether it was from congeniality of feeling towards the art which West had determined to pursue throughout his life, or a similarity of temper and disposition, the young painter appears to have been the favourite with our subject. It is related by Galt, in his life of the above distinguished artist, that Godfrey would frequently compose his verses under a clump of pines, which grew near the upper ferry of the Schuylkill, to which spot he sometimes accompanied West, and their mutual friends, to angle. In the heat of the day he used to stretch himself beneath the shade of the trees, and repeat to them the verses as he composed them.*

Through the exertions of Dr. Smith, our poet received a lieutenancy in the Pennsylvania line, destined for an expedition against Fort Duquesne, now Pittsburgh. He continued with the army to the end of the campaign ; and, amid the toils and privations of a border contest, he found seasons for engaging in his favourite pursuit. It was when garrisoned in Fort Henry that he wrote a poetic epistle, in which he describes the horrors of savage warfare ; the miseries of the frontier inhabitants, and the dreadful carnage of Indian massacres. The description, although agonizing, is given with poetic force ; and is valuable for being the first production of the kind published in America, on a subject so painfully interesting.

A short time subsequent to the termination of his military engagements, he was induced to accept a commission as a mercantile agent, and went to North Carolina. During his residence there he composed a tragedy, entitled "The Prince of Parthia." This drama, which, in many portions, is indicative of no little genius in that department of literature, is not calculated for representation on the stage, being deficient in scenic effect. It, however, contains much merit, and has the honour of being the first tragedy written and published in our country.†

Godfrey, on the death of his employer, returned to Philadelphia, and,

---

* There was long in my father's possession a portrait by West of his young friend.

† It was the *first* play by an American author performed by any regular theatre in America ; it was acted on the 24th of April, 1767, at the Philadelphia Theatre.

having continued there for some time, was induced to sail as supercargo to the island of New Providence. Having completed his commissions, he revisited North Carolina, where, soon after his arrival, he was seized by a violent malignant fever, and in a few days was summoned to pay the debt of nature. He died on the 3d of August, 1763, and in the twenty-seventh year of his age.

"Thus hastily was snatched off," observes Mr. Evans, " in the prime of manhood, this very promising genius, beloved and lamented by all who knew him! The effusions of his muse flowed with a noble wildness from his elevated soul. Free and unpremeditated he sung; unskilled in any precepts but what were infused into him by nature, his divine tutoress. But whatever desert he may be allowed as a poet, it will be rendered still more conspicuous by his character as a man. His sweet and amiable disposition, his integrity of heart, his engaging modesty and diffidence of manners, his fervent and disinterested love for his friends, endeared him to all those who shared his acquaintance; and have stamped the image of him, in indelible characters, on the hearts of his more intimate friends."

Dr. Smith collected the various poems of Godfrey, and published them, together with "The Prince of Parthia," in a volume of 223 quarto pages.

CHAPTER XXVII.

Dr. Smith to Sir William Johnson—Dr. Smith to Dr. Chandler—A Visit from Colonel Barré—The Commencement of this Year—The Graduates—Mr. John Sargent's Prize Medal awarded to Dr. Morgan—Dr. Smith's Early Connection with the Town of Huntingdon, in Pennsylvania—Dr. Smith to the Bishop of London—Dr. Smith takes Charge of Oxford Church, Pa.—Dr. Smith to the Bishop of London.

We now introduce a new correspondent—the well-known Sir William Johnson, the Superintendent of Indian Affairs in New York. We see, in a letter from Dr. Smith to him, the first evidence of that desire for the acquisition of *lands*, which, by degrees, made a feature in Dr. Smith's character and history. It was a prevailing disposition of the day.

PHILADELPHIA, January 13th, 1766.

HONOURED SIR: The several voyages I have made to England, and various other interruptions, have for a long time past deprived me of the Pleasure of writing to you; but no one had all the while been more sensible of the important services you have done your country, nor more sincerely rejoiced in the reward conferred on them by a most gracious Sovereign. I have in my way likewise been endeavoring to be of some use, and have been enabled to raise, from first to last, in Lands and money, a capital of about £9,000 sterling for our College. It gives me much satisfaction to hear from my good Friend, M^r. Barton (who most greatfully acknowledges your civilities to him), that you made kind enquiries after me, and were pleased to remember me.

M^r. Barton, who is a very valuable man, informed me that you had recommended him for a grant of some Lands from your Government, and he generously offered me to share with him. If, by your goodness, any thing would be done this way, or any Tract worth recommending, I believe I have interest enough in England, and perhaps also in New York, to make it Effectual. I am sorry your modesty suffers so few of your numerous Services to transpire especially in your conduct of Indian affairs. I much want to have materials for a Complete account of all the Indians and their countries that are connected with us since the conquest of Canada and the general Peace. M^r. Croghan has favoured me with his last Journal, and some other things which would be of great use. If you should favour me with any thing in this way, it shall not be misapplied nor used in a manner that would be any discredit to you. Mr. Croghan set out the day before I expected he would, else I proposed sending you a copy of Bouquet's Expedition to Muskinggum, which I drew up from some papers he favoured me with, and which is reprinted in England, and has had a very favourable reception. But I presume you may have received it before. I send this letter after M^r. Croghan to New York, and on his return should take it as an Honor to hear from you, being with the utmost Deference and Esteem, Hon. Sir,

Your most obedient

Humble Servant,

WILLIAM SMITH.

Sir William answered this letter, and apparently in an interesting way. I do not find his letter, but we can gather parts of it in a letter from Dr. Smith to Dr. Chandler in England, which follows:

Dr. Smith to Dr. Chandler.

PHILADELPHIA, March 3d, 1766.

MY DEAR SIR: I have mentioned everything which I think of immediate consequence in the enclosed letter to his Grace, which you will no doubt have the perusal of; only I must trouble you with one thing which I did not recollect till after the enclosed was sealed up, viz., to propose the worthy S^r W^m. Johnson, Bar^t, his Majesty's Superintendant for Indian Affairs, as a member of the Society.

In this letter to me he writes "with satisfaction on the success of our College, which he says he observes with greater pleasure as the Church of England is weak in these parts and held in to much contempt by the blind zealots of other communions who may one day repay with a heavy hand, whatever severity they at any time suffered or rather brought on themselves in England. As a specimen of their good inclinations and charity (continues he in his letter to me), I send you a copy of a petition, some new Settlers here (near Mount Johnson), yesterday put into my hand requesting that I would patronize and assist them; but they met with the first refusal I ever gave such applications from any reformed denomination; the misrepresentations and Falsehoods in their petition were so gross I thought it would be worthy of your perusal."

This petition at which Sr William is so angry was from a sort of Scots Covenanters addressed to the Dutch Kirk at Schenectady in Sr William's Neighborhood, in which they say—

That altho' our Fathers be originally from Scotland, yet after residing some years in Ireland, being there *oppressed in our consciences by the vigorous impositions of superstitious Episcopacy & Archbishops* we set sail from Ireland in *May*, 1764 (to be sure you would have thought they came more than a century ago), & God hath provided us a settlement in *Batten Kiln*, but we have been 3 half years destitute of a Kirk, &^{c}.,—and as God did in the bloody days of Charles the 2nd put it into the hearts of your fathers in Holland to shelter our ancestors who fled from the long 25 years persecution in Scotland so we hope, &^{c}.

The design of all this was to work on the Dutch at Schenectady and make them believe these people fled from persecution in Ireland even as late as 1764—no wonder a man of S^r W$^{m's}$ goodness rejected their Petition. The intention of the above extracts of his Letters is to show that he would be a worthy Member of the Society for which I beg he may be proposed. I am,

Dear & Worthy Sir, &^{c}.,

WILL. SMITH.

The Annual Commencement at the College took place on the 20th of May. Dr. Smith, as usual, prepared a Dialogue and two Odes, which were published with the following title: "*An Exercise* containing *A Dialogue and two Odes*, performed at the Public Commencement in the College of Philadelphia, May 20th, 1766. It was printed by William Dunlap, in Market Street, MDCCLXVI;" a person who soon afterwards became a clergyman of the Church of England; though, as will appear in the sequel, he was more relished by Dr. Smith in the Printing-Office than in the Pulpit.*

---

* See *infra*, p. 403.

While Dr. Smith was preparing this Exercise Col. Barré was his visitor and guest, and the joyful news of the Repeal of the American Stamp Act was received in Philadelphia.

This Commencement was attended by the Board of Trustees, comprising the Governor, Chief-Justice and most distinguished men of the Province. After the business of the Commencement was finished, it was resolved, "that as Francis Hopkinson (*who was the first scholar* entered in this seminary at its opening, and likewise, one of the first who received a degree in it) was about to embark for England, and has always done honor to the place of his education by his abilities and good morals, as well as rendered it many substantial services on all public occasions, the thanks of this institution ought to be delivered to him in the most affectionate and respectful manner; and Mr. Stedman and the Provost were desired to communicate the same to Mr. Hopkinson accordingly, and wish him a safe and prosperous voyage."

The graduates were numerous; among them were—

Robert Andrews, Samuel Boyd, M. D., died 1783; *Hans Hamilton.*

Phineas Bond, Jr., born July 15th, 1749, and died in England in 1815.

Thomas Hopkinson, a young man of abilities, who afterwards studied divinity and was licensed to preach in Pennsylvania in 1773. He afterwards went to Virginia.

John Montgomery was another graduate. He took orders in the Church of England and was licensed to Maryland, where he established himself.

James Tilghman, a native of Maryland, educated to the law, and practised in that Province. By marriage to the daughter of Tench Francis, he assumed an interest in Pennsylvania which drew him to this Province. He came to Philadelphia in 1762, where he soon received the favor of the Proprietary family, and was made Secretary of the Land Office. In January, 1767, he became a member of the Proprietary and Governor's Council.

Thomas Coombe, born in Philadelphia in 1747. He became one of the Assistant Ministers at the United Churches. He translated some of Beveridge's Latin poems. In 1775 he published in London a poem entitled "The Peasant of Auburn; or, The Emigrant," which was afterward republished in Philadelphia by Enoch Story. It is dedicated to Goldsmith, and was apparently designed as a continuation of the poem of "The Deserted Village." Coombe takes his emigrant to the banks of the Ohio, "where," says Mr. Westcott, "Indian atrocities seem to show that it would have been much better if the emigrant had not deserted Auburn, or had at least chosen some more favorable place of exile." But on the breaking out of the war, he rather for a time espoused the popular side, but afterwards became a royalist, and finally retired to England. He never returned. Bishop White mentions that when he was consecrated Bishop at Lambeth, Mr. Coombe, his old associate in the United Churches, was present.

This Commencement is memorable in the annals of the College, from the award of Mr. Sargent's gold medal to Dr. Morgan, for a prize essay. The following advertisement explains the nature of this honor:

COLLEGE OF PHILADELPHIA, March 6th, 1766.

WHEREAS, John Sargent, Esq., Merchant of London and Member of Parliament, hath presented to this College a Gold Medal for the best English Essay on the reciprocal advantages of a perpetual union between Great Britain and her American Colonies, notice is hereby given by order of the Trustees, that the said Medal will be disposed of at the ensuing Commencement in May, for the best Essay that shall be produced on the subject proposed, by any one of those who have received any degree or part of their education in this College; and, as the said subject is one of the most important which can at this time employ the pen of the patriot or scholar, and is thus left open to all those who have had any connection with this College, either as students or graduates, it is hoped for the honor of the Seminary, as well as their own, they will nobly exert themselves on a subject so truly animating, which may be treated in a manner alike interesting to good men, both here and in the Mother country.

From nine performances which were presented, the Committee of Trustees selected that of Dr. Morgan, and, immediately after the valedictory oration, "the Hon. John Penn, Esq., Governor of the Province, as President of the Trustees of the College, delivered the medal to the Provost, ordering him to confer it in public agreeably to their previous determination. The Provost accordingly acquainted the audience that the same had been decreed to John Morgan, M. D., F. R. S., &c., Professor of the Theory and Practice of Physic in the College of Philadelphia, and then requested Dr. Morgan to deliver his dissertation in public, which being finished, the eulogy accompanied the conferring of the medal." *

The sweet name of Thomas Secker now returns. His letters show how sincere was the love of this pious prelate for the Church in America, and how sincerely it was his wish to give to us an Episcopate of our own. Political causes prevented our having it.

The Archbishop of Canterbury to Dr. Smith.

LAMBETH, August 2nd, 1766.

GOOD DR. SMITH: It is long since I wrote to you : Sickness and business have had their shares in preventing me, but the chief hindrance hath been that I could say nothing determinate concerning [MS. lost]. Our principal American ecclesiastical settlement of Quebec was almost made [a basis?] on which a Bishop might easily be grafted. But that was opposed by one great man as not favourable enough to the Papists. Then the Ministry changed. We were to begin again; and could get nothing but fair words though the King interposed for us. Now it is changed once more, and whether we shall fare better or worse for it I cannot guess. I have begged the Bishop of London to take out a commission. He is backward; but I hope at length to prevail, and then we may set up our corresponding Societies.† There were no improper expressions in the Address of the Connecticut or of the New York and New Jersey clergy; but they came when both you and we were on fire about the Stamp Act; and so were not presented. But the King was apprised of the contents of them, and desired they might be postponed.

The Bishops have expressed their good wishes to Mr. Wheelock's School,‡ but declined contributing to it, as the Society designs to set up one in imitation of it, which Sir William Johnson, who desires to be a member of the Society, presses as peculiarly seasonable. We have sent to ask his advice, and Mr. Barton's, and shall be glad of yours and every Friend's, in what place or places, under what masters or Regulations, we may best begin the work. I was at first for sending Indians to Mr. Wheelock, to be afterwards Episcopally ordained; but Mr. Apthorp was

---

* The essay was published, with others, under the title, " Four Dissertations on the reciprocal advantages of a perpetual union between Great Britain and her American Colonies, written for Mr. Sargent's Prize Medal, to which by desire is prefixed an Eulogium, spoken on the delivery of the medal at the public Commencement of the College of Philadelphia, May 20th, 1766. Philadelphia: Printed by William and Thomas Bradford, at the London Coffee-House, 1766."

† These were probably the Societies recommended by Dr. Smith, just previous to his leaving England for America, in a letter to the Bishop of London, of April 17th, 1764. See the letter, *supra*, on p. 348.

‡ This, I suppose, was what became Dartmouth College.

clear that they would all turn out Presbyterians. Mr. Whitfield hath got such hold of Lord Dartmouth, who was first Lord of Trade till a few Days ago, that I laboured in vain to oppose his scheme for the Orphan House. But if it be not completed, I hope it may now be altered. I wrote a long Letter to Mr. Duché in December, in answer to one from him about his religious notions. I hope he hath communicated it to you, and hath at least received no harm from it. I considered Mr. Peters as some way superior to the compliment of a Doctor's Degree; but if you find he would like it, and think it would be useful, I can easily obtain it on your sending me word, where he was educated, what Degree he hath, what age he is, &c. I condole with you on the sad loss of Messrs. Wilson and Giles and your Brother, which I mentioned to the King as one argument for American Bishops.* You will have had an account from Dr. Barton of what the Society have on the occasion, and I hope you will find that sooner or later, such care, as we can, hath been taken, or will be taken, of every thing which you have recommended to us; particularly we shall be mindful of what Mr. Peters and you desire concerning Sussex and Kent Counties. Mr. Neill hath been directed not to give his assistance any longer to Mr. Macclanechan's congregation, as they have made no application to the Bishop of London. The clergy at New York have been alarmed with a Report that the American Dissenters are uniting themselves with the Kirk of Scotland, in hopes of obtaining by their means some new privileges from our Parliament. I do not apprehend any danger of that sort. Pray write frequently and fully about everything, though I should write seldom and briefly. Yet I will endeavour to mend in that respect, if I am able. But at least be assured that I shall take much notice of your Information and advice, and that I am,

With great Regard,

Your loving brother,

Tho. Cant.

On September 6th, Dr. Smith having purchased a tract of land on the Juniata, at the mouth of Standing Stone † Creek, went there

---

* These were two young men who died on their voyage to England to get orders. It appears that up to the year 1767 fifty-two young gentlemen had sailed for Holy Orders. Forty-two returned safely. Ten, Messrs. Bradstreet, Browne, Miner, Dean, Checkley, Colton, Johnson, Usher, *Giles* and *Wilson*, lost their lives in the attempt. *Address from the Clergy of New York and New Jersey to the Episcopalians in Virginia. New York:* 1771. P. 48—Note.

† The *Standing Stone,* a landmark for trader and Indian travelling through the wilds of Western Pennsylvania in the middle of the last century, is first mentioned in records by Weiser in his Journal to Logstown. "Aug. 18, 1748," he writes, "had a great rain in the afternoon, and came within two miles of the Standing Stone." When the town of Huntingdon was laid out a few years prior to the Revolution, this historic column

with his brother, Thomas Smith, afterwards a Judge of the Supreme Court of Pennsylvania, to survey it. The place is where the town of Huntingdon now stands. A small settlement or trading-post, called Huntingdon, was upon the tract. Mr. Day, in his " Historical Collections of Pennsylvania," states that the name Huntingdon was given to it by Dr. Smith, who having received when in England a large contribution to his College from the Countess of Huntingdon, named the town with her title, as a token of his grateful estimation of her liberality. There is no foundation for this story. Dr. Smith did, however, lay out the town now called Huntingdon, in regular lots, and sold them on ground-rent. The spot had been a trading-post, commonly called Huntingdon, after the township in which it was. The absence of foundation for the story of Mr. Day appears in the following petition from this region, where the name of Huntingdon appears as early as 1748, before Dr. Smith came to America, and where it appears that numbers of English people were settled at that early day :

To the Honorable Society for Propagating the Gospel in Foreign Parts, &c.

The humble Petition of the Inhabitants of the Townships of Huntingdon and Tyrone, commonly called Conninaga, on the West side of the River Susquehana, in the Province of Penselvania.

May it please your Honours Graciously to look upon our Humble Petition for a minister of yᵉ Church of England & send us one to reside amongst us, & whereas we are sensible that itt is our duty to do yᵉ best we can toward his maintenance we transmit, enclosed with this, our Subscription for that purpose which we promise to renew & pay every year as long as he shall reside & officiate amongst us, & we make no doubt of yᵉ Subscription encreasing when we have a minister upon yᵉ spot who by his prudent conduct may recommend himself to those who at present are not so warm in yᵉ cause as we, but yet well minded to itt. Besides this Subscription we have purchased a Tract of Land of an hundred and eighty acres to remaine a Glebe for yᵉ use of yᵉ minister excepting as much thereof as shall be thought proper for a church yard or Burying Ground & we have built a small church already, which we have called Christ Church, of thirty feet long & twenty wide upon the same Tract. Besides there is another Tract of Land upon the Banks of Susquehana about Twenty miles distant given to yᵉ use of minister for the time being of yᵉ said church & to remain for ever a Glebe, containing One Hundred

---

was still, though mutilated, at its place. There is a " Standing Stone " in the Susquehanna, opposite the village of that name, in Bradford county, and there were Standing Stones at other places.

Acres, by the late M^r. John Huggins in his will he having dyed less than
two years past.   We have further to add that there are a good number
of People members of our church at a place called Connidaiguinam
about Twenty miles from us who offer to join with us, & are willing to
pay ye missionary your Honours shall please to send in proportion to
ye share of the service that he will allow them.   We humbly pray that
your Honours will take this our humble Petition into consideration and
according to your wonted piety & charity send us a missionary to whom
we promise to pay great regard which we think is due to his sacred character.   We are in a starving condition for ye spiritual nourishment of
our Souls nor can we ever hear Divine Service without travelling many
miles.   M^r. Locke is the nearest by much & he above Forty miles from
us.   We dread to think of our children being brought up in ignorance
as to all Divine Knowledge & it cuts us to the very harte to see our poor
Infants dye without being made members of Christ by Baptism.   We
are not willing to take up much of your Honours' time and therefore
state our case as briefly as we can.   We pray God to put itt in your
Hearts to consider us & that he will reward your pious & charitable
care for ye churches in America is the hearty prayers of

May it please your Honours,

Your most obedient & humble Servants.

October ye 3 day, 1748.

What became of the ancient Christ Church, mentioned in this
early petition, I am not able to say.   The place, however, is rendered interesting to churchmen by its later history as by its earlier.
On this spot it was that on the 14th of August, 1836, the saintly
JOHN WALLER JAMES, Rector of Christ Church, Philadelphia,
having attained but the age of 31 years, rendered up his spirit.
He had been the assistant of Bishop White ; and on his death,
July 17th, 1836, was elected Rector of the church.   Availing himself of a short season of leisure afforded to him by the alterations
which, at that time, were making in the church edifice, he left Philadelphia to visit his aged parents in Pittsburgh.   Before arriving at
Huntingdon he was taken ill, and stopped in that place.   After a
short term of severe suffering he died.   His last words were :

"I wish to say to the dear people of my charge, 'Remember the
words I spake unto you, while I was yet alive.   The same truths make
me happy in the prospect of death and heaven.'"

The people of Christ Church, Philadelphia, to whom Mr. James
had deeply endeared himself by his lovely character and devotion
to their welfare, erected a memorial chapel, meant to commemo-

rate the place of his death and their own affection for his memory.*

Dr. Smith to the Bishop of London.

PHILADELPHIA, 13ᵗʰ Novʳ, 1766.

MY LORD: The last time I did myself the Honor to write to your Lordship was by Mʳ. Evans.† I cannot now let the Bearers, Mʳ. Samuel Magaw and Mʳ. John Andrews, go without a few lines. They were educated and graduated under me, and I hope on Examination will do credit to our College. Their Letters to Doctor Burton ‡ mention their Destination, viz. : Dover and Lewes, on Delaware, and their Testimonials to your Lordship will certify their moral character.

Mʳ. Macclanechan's or Sᵗ. Paul's Congregation in this City I believe will now at last write to your Lordship. When we know that what they write has your Lordship's approbation, then will be time enough for us to take notice of them. I know they will make strong professions of their attachment to the Church as they do to us here. They will complain that the Missionaries (who indeed are but thin here and have Business enough of their own) do not supply them. But while their conduct contradicts their professions, while they look only to Mʳ. Whitefield to send them a Minister and want our Clergy to be convenient Instruments to keep them together till they can have a Minister of this stamp to divide and tear us to pieces, I cannot think we owe them any Service. They will even profess to your Lordship that they will have no Minister without your Licence ; but they will try their Minister first, and if they like him, then they will ask a Licence. If your Lordship gives it, all will be well ; if you refuse it for reasons *they* do not think sufficient, what will they do then ? I have asked them the question and they say they would not give their man up ; which was the case with Mʳ. Macclanechan, whom they kept, tho' refused a Licence, till at last they quarrelled with him. This was their conduct before. I hope they are now coming to a better sense, which we sincerely wish for and strive to promote. Your Lordship will be able to judge from their address and we shall be guided, as in Duty bound, by your advice, wᶜʰ we hope to have as soon as possible.

I think after all they will not ask your Lordship to provide a minister for them, but will still look to the old Quarter, tho' I hope I may be

---

* Some thirty years ago the writer resided for some time in the town of Huntingdon. It was here he was married—it was before the Pennsylvania Railroad or telegraph was made—when it took eight or ten days to write to Philadelphia and get an answer. The recollection of the days spent in the *"Ancient Borough"* are replete with pleasant memories, as they were among the happiest of his varied life.

† Nathaniel Evans, the young man whose address at the College we have quoted on page 365–6 ; and of whom we give a particular account further on.

‡ Secretary, I believe, of the Society for the Propagation of the Gospel, in place of Dr. Bearcroft, who, I presume, was no longer living.

deceived and shall be glad to find myself so.   They are now neither numerous nor of much Note, but are still worthy to be brought into the Bosom of our Church, if it can be done.   Those among them who are true Churchmen, have generally fallen off.   The rest are a mixt sort, chiefly for an Independent Church of England—a strange sort of Church, indeed ! But the Notion gains too much Ground here even among some of the Clergy.   I believe your Lordship will perceive something of this kind not altogether pleasing, if the resolves of a majority of last Jersey Convention should come before you against Commissaries, &c., prefer- ring thereto a kind of Presbyterian or Synodical self-delegated Gov- ernment by Conventions, which I fear will end in Quarrels by every one's striving to be uppermost in their turn and never could have been thought of, but as an expedient for friendly converse and advice, till something better could be done.   I could not attend that convention, being the day our College met after vacation, and the place at 80 miles distance.   I attended and presided in the year 1764, when all was har- mony and the Design of Commissaries, corresponding Societies, &c., approved of.   M^r. Peters attended now and bore his testimony against these Resolves as not becoming Missionaries especially, and Servants of the Society, and perhaps he may give some account of the matter to your Lordship.   He was milder, I believe, than I should have been, for I think I should never have sat among them if they had put one of their own number in the Chair, while a member of the Society, a Clergyman of respect^ity, was present.

I am, Your Lordship's dutiful son and Servant,

WILLIAM SMITH.

About this time—some time, I mean, in 1766—Dr. Smith, not- withstanding his other labors, found time to preach frequently in Trinity Church, Oxford ; a church at some distance from Philadel- phia ; and he continued to preach there for many years.   For the sake, too, of procuring for it certain advantages in law, he suffered himself to be elected rector; though parochial duty was not greatly to his taste, and the less so because it necessarily interfered with his duties as Provost.   Dr. Buchanan, its present respected incumbent, to whose excellent historical sketch of the Parish I have already referred,* gives all that I believe any one can now tell us on the subject.   He says :†

A few months after the removal of Mr. Neill, in 1776, the vestry invited the Rev. Dr. William Smith, of the "College of Philadelphia," and a gentleman eminent for his learning and abilities, to accept the

---

* See *supra*, p. 260.   † Page 31.

charge of the congregation ; and he, " in consideration of the difficulties they were labouring under," consented to do so for a time, or until they could obtain another minister. He continued to officiate here certainly till 1770, and most probably for several years longer.

In 1770 the church wardens and vestrymen, in a communication addressed to the Society in England, write concerning him :

We are likewise to acknowledge that, since Mr. Neill's removal, the mission hath been supplied, with the approbation of the Society, by the Revᵈ. Dʳ. Smith, who, notwithstanding his many engagements, hath been constant in his attendance upon us & zealous for the good of the congregation.

In the remainder of the letter, as they speak of a fact much to his credit, and of a change and improvement in the church building, which was probably soon after made, I shall make a further quotation from it :

We are now about putting a new roof on the church, and propose erecting a gallery ; for defraying the expence of which, as it would be too great for us at present, Dr. Smith hath generously agreed to appropriate (with the Society's leave) one half of the two years' rent of the Glebe due to him, and also one half of the present year's rent.

Dr. Smith probably continued to officiate for them—at least occasionally—until his removal from Philadelphia to Maryland, about the year 1779. Nothing, however, is known in reference to the point ; for the book containing the parochial Records for several years from 1770 was lost about the year 1782.

We have now an interesting letter, one which shows how far from " narrowness " and " bigotry " were the views of the first Provost, although he does no more " than just to mention the *facts* and the accession it might bring to our Church." I do not find, however, that his suggestion received any countenance from the Bishop of London. Nor would it be covered by Dr. White's tract of " The Case of the Episcopal Churches in the United States Considered ; " a tract which expresses views applicable to a very special case indeed ; one incident to a long war of English colonies, like that which was our Revolution ; the case of a church wholly unable to procure Episcopal ordination—on the point of being extinguished, the extinguishment followed by a cessation in its communion of all religious ordinances and services whatsoever ; a declaration of the necessity of Episcopal ordination whenever it can be had, and a determination to procure it at the earliest date practicable, preceding the whole arrangements contemplated.*

---

* When Dr. White issued this tract there was no prospect of a peace with England ; and even if a cessation from war was secured, no prospect of any such relations with Great Britain as would give to us an Episcopate. On the first prospect of a peace with

The presence, however, in any great numbers, of regularly ordained ministers like the Rev. William Dunlap, I do admit,
might tend to justify a little a laxity of notions such, perhaps, as,
with such able clergy as were in the Lutheran Church in Pennsylvania, invaded, for a short time, the mind of Dr. Smith.

Dr. Smith to the Bishop of London.

PHILIDELPHIA, Decr 18, 1766.

MY LORD : This will be delivered to your Lordship by M^r. Bryzelius,
who has had ordination among the German Lutherans here and has
maintained a good character as a preacher among them. He comes to
London for Episcopal Ordination, in pursuance of the desire of the
Society to M^r. Peters and myself to send some person capable of officiating in English and German in Nova Scotia, and his Credentials are
signed by the Reverend M^r. Muhlenberg, the head of the numerous Body
of the Lutherans in this Province, and the Reverend D^r. Wrangel, Commissary to the Swedish Congregations, both men worthy of all Credit
from your Lordship. M^r. Bryzelius is a sedate and sensible man of
good education and strong Constitution, and has already acquitted himself with such prudence among the Germans that we have no doubt of
his future good conduct. He has often preached among our English
Congregations to their satisfaction.

There is an extreme good disposition among the Lutheran Clergy
here to be united to our Church, and tho' M^r. Bryzelius has agreed to
go to England and request what they consider as the Re-ordination, yet
this matter staggers many of them even as a point of conscience ; seting
aside the risque and distance of the Seas.

Your Lordship knows this is no new scruple among reformed persuasions that are desirous of Union with our Church. I think the majority
of the great Divines concerned in the comprehension Scheme in King
William's time seemed to be inclined to a concession that " those who
had not had an opportunity of Episcopal Ordination, but had been
ordained beyond Seas in any of the reformed Churches, be not required
to re-ordination to render them capable of preferment in our Church."
It is said also that there was an act of Q. Elizabeth of the same Import,
but whether intended as temporary in favor of those of our Nation ordained abroad in the former times of trouble, or for what other reason
I am not sufficiently versed in these matters to say. D^r. De Laune and
M^r. Whittington, we are told, were both admitted to Livings, the latter
to the Deanery of Durham, tho' ordained at Geneva, and had Judgment

---

Great Britain he called in all the copies which he could find of the tract. I think that
when he issued it, he and Dr. Blackwell, assistant minister with him in the united
churches of Christ Church and St. Peter's, were the only two Episcopal Clergymen in
Pennsylvania. At one time they were certainly so.

in Law that his Title to his Living was not thereby invalidated for want of Episcopal Ordination.

The Lutheran Ministry in America, willing to conform to our Church, have more to urge in their own favor, for those I have spoken of above being then in England, had an opportunity of Ordination from Bishops, but the latter have not without an expence and risque in crossing the Seas, which few will be able to undergo.

Whether, then, anything could be done to receive them without this is a matter which must be with your Lordship and our Superiors, and which it becomes not us any further to meddle with than just to mention the facts and the accession it might bring to our Church.

My last to your Lordship was by M^r. Andrews and M^r. Magaw, both educated in our College, since which another, M^r. Edmiston, educated with them, has sailed for Maryland on the same Errand. I hope it will appear to your Lordship that they are all well grounded in their education.

Your Lordship will give me the Leave in all humble Duty to mention an affair by which our Church, I fear, will suffer a little in the sight of her adversaries here. One William Dunlap, a Printer in this place, having also a printing press in Barbadoes, having gone to that Island after his Business, applied here for recommendations for orders which we could not give, as he had no education but reading and writing, as well as for other reasons. He did, however, it seems, procure Letters from some Clergy in Barbadoes, tho' they could not have known him above a year. No doubt they thought and your Lordship thought that, in the remote and new settled Islands, a pious man, without the learned languages, &c., might be useful, and with that view we hear your Lordship received him. Had he staid there in the West Indies, it might have been all well. But he is now in Philadelphia preaching in S^t. Paul's Church, and in a place where Presbyterian preachers have all some Learning, where the Laity, too, have learning, and where some things are remembered to his disadvantage, particularly the affair of a Lottery which a few years ago he had and was like to have been brought into Law trouble about it. His Printing Press, too, he still carries on, and it is seldom a " prophet has honor in his own country."

The man always appeared to me a simple, inoffensive man, whom I never could have thought of recommending for Orders, tho' I know no harm of him; only I wish he had not come here.

I mentioned St. Paul's Congregation in my last. No doubt your Lordship has received their Letters. A few days ago M^r. Whitefield sent them a letter telling them that he had prevailed on a Clergyman (they say M^r. Chapman, of Bath and Bradford) to come to them. Surely he will wait on your Lordship, tho' some here say not. I have some acquaintance with him. M^r. Evans, after preaching twice to them, declined any further Service and is properly applied to the Business of his own Mission. I have yet little expectation of the Regularity from that Congregation, but I hope I may be deceived.

Your Lordship's goodness will excuse the Freedom I have mentioned M^r. Dunlap's affair as it is only to yourself, thinking it my Duty to do it, because if any other persons should come without Testimonials from the place where they properly reside and are known, Care may be taken to inquire concerning them. I need not mention that I would not have any public notice taken of the hints I have given, for M^r. Dunlap was bred under M^r. Franklin, now in England, in his Printing Office, and married some Relation of his, and his knowledge of our writing any thing now might only make differences. I hope prejudice will wear off and M^r. Dunlap be useful in some place, tho' not in this Town.

I am, Your Lordship's most dutiful son and Servant,

W^M. SMITH.

CHAPTER XXVIII.

CORRESPONDENCE—DR. SMITH TO THE SECRETARY OF THE PROPAGATION SOCIETY —WILLIAM DUNLAP IS ORDAINED A CLERGYMAN BY THE BISHOP OF LONDON —DR. SMITH'S REMARKS ON HIM—COMMENCEMENT DAY, 1767—DEGREES OF MASTER CONFERRED ON DAVID RITTENHOUSE AND JAMES WILSON—DR. SMITH DELIVERS A COURSE OF LECTURES IN THE WINTER OF 1767-8 ON NATURAL AND EXPERIMENTAL PHILOSOPHY FOR THE BENEFIT OF MEDICAL STUDENTS— ASSUMES TEMPORARY CHARGE OF CHRIST CHURCH—IS ELECTED TEMPORARY CHAPLAIN OF THE 18TH OR ROYAL IRISH REGIMENT—CORRESPONDENCE—DR. SMITH AND OTHERS TO THE BISHOP OF LONDON—DR. SMITH TO THE SECRE- TARY OF THE PROPAGATION SOCIETY—TO THE BISHOP OF LONDON—TO THE SECRETARY OF THE PROPAGATION SOCIETY—TO SIR WILLIAM JOHNSON—COM- MENCEMENT IN THE DEPARTMENT OF ARTS OF 1768—COMMENCEMENT IN THE MEDICAL DEPARTMENT—WAS THE FIRST IN THE UNITED STATES.

WE continue our extracts from Dr. Smith's correspondence. They disclose some curious particulars about the Church clergy; particularly about William Dunlap, whose imprints are known to the Bibliophiles of Philadelphia. It is probably to some such cases as that of Spencer that Bishop White refers in his "Case of the Episcopal Churches in the United States Considered," and where he speaks of the "scandal sometimes brought on the Church by the ordination of low and vicious persons," "generally," he adds in a note, "by deceptions on the Bishop of London;" one of the proofs, as he considers, of the attachment of our church people to episcopacy, as it subjected them to such, among "many inconveniences," inci- dent to having to send "three thousand miles for ordination."

Dr. Smith to the Secretary of the Propagation Society.

(EXTRACT.)

PHILADELPHIA, May 1st, 1767.

REV^D AND WORTHY SIR: I have by Col. Croghan & with him & M^r. Peters's advice laid before Sr Wm Johnson a scheme something different, much more extensive & what he is pleased to think better, than any other for propagating the Gospel and the arts of Civil life among the Indians. Col. Croghan is just returned from him & he has sent me by him a few lines to let me know he will write fully to me as soon as the Indians then at his house were departed.

I shall in my next send you copies of the papers; & no doubt S^r W^m himself will write anew on the subject.

You did well to give M^r. Sturgeon the answer you did, for I assure you, on my own knowledge there are not more than two heads of families, & those of but poor characters, that are inclined to hear him in Oxford Mission. Time may make it otherwise. M^r. Barton is the person they desire, but they cannot yet encourage him. I have as often as I could be spared from Philadelphia & generally once a fortnight supplied Oxford since M^r. Neill's departure, & in order to recover their Glebe lands, rent their pews & do other things necessary, have suffered them to vote & enter me on their Books as their Minister till September next, or longer, if it suits me & the Society approves. But I would not have you make any entry of anything of this on your public minutes till you hear from them or me.

I am exceeding sorry & our Church suffers much by the too easy admittance of some men of indifferent character & no abilities into holy orders. One Dunlap, a Printer of this Town, who had no education & could scarce read English, has been ordained. One Spence or Spencer, who was publickly carted thro' New York & was otherwise of very bad character, to our prodigious astonishment we hear is also ordained. No Church on this Continent will receive him.

One Shippen & one of the name of Sayre, both born in this Town of reputable Parents, but who have been spendthrifts & behaved very wildly, we hear are gone home for the Gown.

I know the B^p of London is a most worthy and venerable Prelate, but I fear has been deceived in some recommendations. When young men or other candidates for orders come from America & bring nothing from any of the Clergy of the Province where they lived or were born, they ought always to be suspected. I do not say my recommendation or any other particular man's is necessary; but surely that of two or three reputable Clergymen, who have known the person recommended for at least two or three years, is requisite by your own Rules.

I am, worthy Sir,

WM. SMITH.

The Same to the Same.

(EXTRACT.)

PHILADELPHIA, Septr 1, 1767.

Rev^D & Worthy Sir: I have in several late Letters informed you that since M^r. Neill's departure in October last, I have twice in three weeks supplied the Mission at Oxford in order to prevent that old and respectable Mission from dwindling away, and as the act of our Assembly, which was made for selling the old and purchasing the New Glebe, required that there should be a Minister to constitute a Vestry & do any legal act, I was obliged last February to let the people nominate me their Minister, in order that we might proceed to get possession of the Glebe for the use of the Church, and I accordingly consented to supply them for one year or till you appointed another, unless so far as M^r. Peters's indisposition might require my assistance in Town, which has been but seldom till within these few weeks past.

I have got possession of the Glebe & have leased it for one year, to commence from the first of June last, but this year's rent will not be sufficient to make the necessary repairs to the house and fences, which are suffered to go to great ruin. I have also let out the Pews and done everything to make the Mission worth M^r. Barton's acceptance, who has an unanimous invitation from the people. He was down here last week, but has not given his answer whether he will accept, as he fears he will change for the worse.

In the meantime I shall give them what help I can, but as nothing can be got this first year from the Pews nor from the Glebe, M^r. Neill's Tenant being insolvent, I shall receive nothing and shall be considerably out of Pocket in my frequent visits, besides Sundays, unless the Society should be pleased to give me some consideration, as they did D^r. Cooper, for supplying West Chester.*

I find by a Letter from the Lord Bishop of London that D^r. Franklin recommended M^r. Spencer for Orders, which is astonishing, as he well knew the shameful Character he bore at New York. The same D^r. Franklin recommended, as I am told, one M^r. Dunlap, a Printer, who is constantly thrown in our dish by the Presbyterians, & you say he has recommended M^r. Sturgeon to Oxford, where I assure you nobody would go to hear him, nor would they receive him; so that you see I had some reasons to give you hints concerning that Gentleman's recommendations, who may have political, but is not like to have religious motives for them.

I am, Rev^d and Worthy Sir, &^{c}.,

WM. SMITH.

---

* This is West Chester, in New York.

The Commencement Day of 1767 took place on the 17th of November. Dr. Smith prepared for the occasion "An Exercise, containing a Dialogue and two Odes." The exercises in a former year were printed by William Dunlap, in Philadelphia. But, as we shall see directly, he had now turned clergyman. Those for this year were printed by William Goddard, who for a short time was established as a printer and publisher in Market Street, Philadelphia; a man of far superior education and capacity in every way to Dunlap.

Among the graduates were *Jacob Bankson*, *James Cannon*, afterwards Professor of Mathematics, from 1779 to 1796, in the College; *Francis Johnston*, a Colonel, A. D. 1778, in the Revolutionary army, and who died A. D. 1815; *Joshua Maddox Wallace*, son of Mr. John Wallace, originally of Drumellier in Scotland, afterwards of Philadelphia. He was born in the city just named October 4, 1752, and received his primary education in Newark, Delaware. Immediately on his graduation in the College at Philadelphia, he acted for a short time as tutor there. On the occupation of the city he went to New Jersey, and resided in Burlington till his death, in 1819. He was a Judge of the Common Pleas for Burlington county, N. J., 1784; member (1787) of the Convention of New Jersey which ratified the Constitution of the United States; a member of the Assembly of New Jersey; Trustee from 1799–1819 of Princeton College; Representative of New Jersey in the General Conventions of the Episcopal Church for the years 1786, 1795, 1808, 1811, 1814, and 1817; President of the Trustees of the Burlington Academy; President of the Society of New Jersey for the Suppression of Vice and Immorality; President of the Convention held in New York, May, 1816, by which the American Bible Society was formed. This graduate was a grandson on the maternal side of Joshua Maddox, Esquire, one of the founders and first trustees of the College.

A name, very eminent in the science of jurisprudence, comes too within the class of this year. I refer to that of Edward Tilghman. This great man was a native of Maryland, born at Wye, on the Eastern Shore, December 11th, 1750. He received his education, literary and classic, at Philadelphia. He went to England about the year 1770–71, and was entered as a student at the Middle Temple in the latter year. He remained in England probably during the entire war, and was admitted to the Bar of Philadelphia on the 22d of June, 1785. After his admission, he gradually rose into practice, and continued in the exercise of his profession until his death, November 1st, 1815. During this time he held no office, and was content to be a lawyer. Governor McKean offered him the Chief-Justiceship, upon the death of Chief-Justice Shippen; but he declined it, and threw his influence in favor of his cousin, William Tilghman, who is recognized as an ornament of the Bench. Edward Tilghman was a deep-read lawyer, particularly well versed in the abstruse doctrines of devises and contingent remainders.

The honorary degree of *Master of Arts* was bestowed upon two men—both eminent, but eminent in different branches of science— David Rittenhouse and James Wilson. William Barton, nephew of the former,* tells us that the Provost, in conferring these degrees, addressed the two candidates in form. To Rittenhouse he said:

SIR: The trustees of this College (the Faculty of Professors cheerfully concurring) being ever desirous to distinguish real merit, especially in the natives of this province—and well assured of the extraordinary progress and improvement which you have made, by a felicity of natural genius, in mechanics, mathematics, astronomy, and other liberal arts and sciences, all which you have adorned by singular modesty and irreproachable morals—have authorized and required me to admit you to the honorary degree of Master of Arts in this Seminary. I do, therefore, by virtue of this authority, most cheerfully admit, &c.

Some address, suited to his proficiency in other branches, was made to Wilson. Wilson, however, had no biographer, and we have no special record of the address which was made to him. *Sacrâ vate caret.*†

The Medical Department of the College from its origin always much interested Dr. Smith. He could look into the seeds of

---

* Life of Rittenhouse, page 157.

† *James Wilson* was a Scotchman, born in 1742, and educated at Edinburgh. He came to America in 1766, studied law, and was admitted to the Bar about the year 1770. His talents were early conspicuous, and he was entrusted with important public interests. He was a Signer of the Declaration of Independence, and of the Constitution of the United States. He was appointed by Washington a Judge of the Supreme Court of the United States. His eminence at the Bar, and his public services of many kinds, especially in the Federal Convention, were high. No record of them can be made in a note like this.

time, and say which grain will grow and which will not. Early
in the year he united with the physicians in the Board of Trustees,
and with Drs. Morgan and Shippen in framing a " Code of
Rules" for it. They were submitted to the Board of Trustees in
May, 1768, and at once adopted by it.

Later in the year he devoted himself to giving lectures on Natural and Experimental Philosophy. We give his printed announcement. It is a proof of the extraordinary variety of his attainments
and the versatility of his talents.

COLLEGE OF PHILADELPHIA, December 17th, 1767.

At the request of the Medical Trustees and Professors, the subscriber
having last winter opened a course of Lectures on Natural and Experimental Philosophy, for the benefit of the Medical Students, which he
hath engaged to continue this winter on an extensive plan, notice is
hereby given that on Monday, the 28th inst., at 12 o'clock, it is proposed to deliver the Introductory Lecture at the College. As these
lectures are instituted and given gratis, with the view to encourage the
medical schools lately opened, and to extend the usefulness and reputation of the College, any gentlemen who have formerly been educated in
this Seminary, and are desirous of renewing their acquaintance with the
above mentioned branches of knowledge, will be welcome to attend
the course.

To the standing use of the large apparatus belonging to the College,
Mr. Kinnersley has engaged to add the use of his electrical apparatus
which is fixed there, and to deliver the lectures on electricity himself,
as well as to give his occasional assistance in other branches; so that
with these advantages, and the many years' experience of the subscriber in conducting lectures of this kind, it is hoped the present
course will answer the design of its institution and do credit to the
Seminary.   W. SMITH.

N. B.—An evening lecture in some branches of Mathematics, preparatory to the philosophical course, is opened at the College.

We arrive at the year 1768.

He now, for a short time, in the beginning of this year, took
charge of Christ Church. The cause of his doing this is interestingly stated in the following extract from Dr. Dorr's history
of that parish. Dr. Peters, before becoming the Rector of this
church, had long been Secretary of the Provincial Land Office of
Pennsylvania, and had there been brought into intimate relation
with Indian affairs.

FEBRUARY 16th, 1768.

The Rector (Dr. Peters) informed the vestry that there was to be an Indian Treaty held at Fort Stanwix for the settlement of a boundary line between the Indians and his Majesty, and other matters of importance; and that the Governor and Council had desired that he would attend, from the belief that his long experience in Indian affairs would enable him to be of great service there; but as he thought with them that he might be of some service, being personally acquainted with Sir William Johnson, and having received letters from M[r]. Croghan, Sir William's deputy, expressing their opinion that his attendance would be serviceable, he had consented to go; and that his friend, Dr. Smith, had been kind enough to promise to do his (Dr. Peters') duty during his absence.   The vestry expressed satisfaction, &[c].

In the spring of 1768 the 18th Regiment, commonly called the " Royal Regiment of Ireland," was at Philadelphia.   It was composed of the survivors of the 60th and 42d regiments and of those of Montgomery's Highlanders.   Their loss, while under Col. Bouquet here and in the West Indies, had been thirteen officers, twelve sergeants, and three hundred and eighty-two rank and file.   James Wemyss—an uncle of Dr. Smith's wife—was the second officer in command.   Dr. Peters having now returned from Fort Stanwix, Dr. Smith was elected the temporary chaplain.   He preached a series of sermons; most or all of them being delivered in the "Great Hall of the College" before the regiment.   The first was delivered on the 7th of April—the last in the summer; being a " Farewell to the Regiment," then under marching orders.   It was at this time commanded by Col. Wilkins, who had been a school-mate of Dr. Smith at Aberdeen.   Five of the sermons are in Dr. Smith's Works.*   The subject of them is the Christian Soldier's Duty— his whole duty in a free State, under a Government and Laws, human and divine, in times of Peace as well as of War; as a servant of his God, as a servant of his King, and as a member of society; interested alike with his fellow-citizens in all that concerns the peace, order and prosperity of his country.   They embrace, of course, a wide range of topics, and the topics are grandly handled.   We should be delighted to make extracts from these sermons; but our space forbids.

---

* Vol. II., pp. 155–251.

We will now resume our correspondence.

Dr. Peters, Dr. Smith and Mr. Duche to the Bishop of London.

PHILADELPHIA, April 22nd, 1768.

MY LORD: We have presumed to address your Lordship concerning two hopeful young Gentlemen who are desirous of presenting themselves to your Lordship for Holy Orders, viz. : M^r. John Montgomery and M^r. Thomas Coombe. They have both had a regular education in our College, the former having been about five years in it, and the latter more than ten years. Both have taken their Bachelor's Degree, and this Summer will be of standing for and admitted to their Master's Degree.

We have great want of Clergymen in these parts, and both the young Gentlemen could be immediately provided for. M^r. Montgomery, if the Society approve of it, has an opportunity of being settled in the Mission of Oxford, which with the approbation of the Society D^r. Smith hath supplied once every Fortnight since M^r. Neill left it in October, 1766, and which he would be glad to be released from the fatigue of as soon as convenient. M^r. Coombe can be provided for several ways, and both would have been recommended Home this Summer, if they were of the age required. But in this matter neither they nor we would dissemble with your Lordship. M^r. Montgomery is twenty-two years next August, and M^r. Coombe twenty-one about the same time, tho' each of them will be a year older before they can return to America, should they be allowed to embark from hence next September.

Our humble request to your Lordship therefore is to know by a few lines as soon as possible "Whether this want of the full age might not be dispensed with in regard to America, without being made a hurtful Precedent to others who have not so well improved their time." We know it will subject us to disagreeable solicitations, but we have the resolution, 'tis hoped, to withstand them where there may not be equal merit.

If the rule can in any case be dispensed with on account of the necessities of the Church here, we would recommend it in this case, for both the Gentlemen and three others nearly of their age have for two winters past attended Divinity Lectures under D^r. Smith, and have acquitted themselves so well in delivering their Sunday Evening Exercises, that seldom fewer than a thousand persons have attended to hear them. They are well versed in Composition, and are excellent Speakers, M^r. Coombe in particular being admired for his Talent in this way, nor have we the least Doubt of their prudence, and shall be ready to give, as we think they will be ready to receive, our best advice at their first setting out in Life.

We say nothing of their accomplishments in the Languages and liberal Sciences, as we are persuaded they will give your Lordship satisfaction in that, and no way sink in your opinion the favorable Idea you have been pleased to form concerning the education of such Youth as have come already under your Lordship's notice from the College of this City.

We submit the whole to your Lordship's Wisdom and are,
   Your Lordship's most dutiful sons & Servants,
           RICHARD PETERS,
           WILLIAM SMITH,
           JACOB DUCHÉ.

P. S.—What is particularly desired is whether they may be permitted to come home next Fall, viz.: about September, or whether they must be obliged to wait longer and how long, so as to have Priest's Orders, for they cannot well afford the expence or time for two Voyages to London.

              APRIL 24th, 1768.

TO THE LORD BISHOP OF LONDON :

Since writing the above it hath been rumoured that one M^r. Chambers, born in this Town, educated a Presbyterian in New Jersey College, hath gone into Maryland, got a title to a Curacy from one Adams, I think, and some of the Maryland Clergy to sign his Credentials, deceaved, I suppose, by his College Certificate, which is full ; but it is three years since he left College and they know nothing of Him during that time, he having been in this province, nor yet the Cause of his leaving the Presbyterians, nor a very high charge against him at Lancaster about a month ago, in this Province, which made him quit that and go to Maryland, as the Rev^d M^r. Barton, the Society's Missionary there, informed me. This, if true, must render him wholly unworthy of Holy Orders. I have wrote to him not to venture to embark till this is cleared up, but if he is gone I pray your Lordship may suspend doing anything concerning Him, and you shall have an Authentic Account, which is a charge of having a Bastard, the Truth or untruth of which your Lordship shall receive by a letter in less than two weeks after this date. In any case his Testimonials should have been from this Province, for he is an entire stranger in the place where he now is.   W. SMITH.

We have already—at page 386—spoken of the disturbance raised by Dr. Chandler's appeal, and the petition of the Clergy at the New Jersey Convention for an American Episcopate. The following extract of a letter from Dr. Smith to the Bishop of London, and written, I suppose, about this time, refers to this matter. I am not able to state where or how Dr. Smith contributed "his mite" to the contest—I presume through the newspapers. I have no knowledge of any pamphlet by him on the subject, though I know of many by others.

(EXTRACT.)

I wrote your Lordship that I had much reason to fear the extraordinary warmth of the Jersey Conventions might do hurt. Their addresses and Dʳ. Chandler's appeal about Bishops for America, tho' in the main well done, have raised a great Flame. There is nothing but writing in every Newspaper. I could not approve of any Appeals to the Public here about Bishops, as thinking such Appeals *Coram non Judice* and only provoking Strife. However, the Church here is now very rudely treated by a malevolent set of Writers, and tho' I could have wished our side had not given any cause, yet they must not be left unsupported, and I am determined now to contribute my mite, for great openings are given to detect their shameful misrepresentations. The time does not allow me to add more, but only to beg leave to subscribe myself,

Your Lordship's most dutiful son and Servant,

WM. SMITH.

Dr. Smith to the Secretary of the Propagation Society.

(EXTRACT.)

PHILADELPHIA, May 6ᵗʰ, 1768.

DEAR AND WORTHY SIR,

* * * The Presbyterians from one end of the Continent to the other are attacking the Church about American Bishops. I never liked appealing to the publick here about it, as it was an appeal *Coram non Judice*, nor did I like the too great zeal of our late Jersey conventions, for which they thought me too cold. However, Dʳ. Chandler's Pamphlet, tho' too long and sometimes foreign to the purpose in it, is on the whole such as he can support, and tho' I wish he had not published it, yet it is well defensible and he shall not be left to stand alone, for the virulence of his antagonists is now not to be borne.

I am, Worthy Sir, &ᶜ.,

WM. SMITH.

Dr. Smith to the Bishop of London.

PHILADELPHIA, May 6ᵗʰ, 1768.

MY LORD: In a postscript to a Letter which I wrote to your Lordship about ten days ago, I mentioned with sorrow the information I had that one Chambers, born in this City and educated a Presbyterian in New Jersey College, who had left Lancaster, in this Province, on a charge of having a Bastard, had gone into Maryland and got a title to a curacy from one Adams, with a certificate to your Lordship from some Maryland Clergy, none of whom could have known him above a fortnight.

In that letter I promised your Lordship that I would get the truth of the story from the Reverend Mʳ. Barton, the Society's worthy Missionary at Lancaster, and write as soon as I received it, adding a humble request that your Lordship would suspend doing anything in Chambers's affair till you should hear further.

I have since received a letter from M^r. Barton with a Deposition in the affair from one of the Magistrates of Lancaster Borough, and find the story too true. The deposition is that of Mary Kalleren before James Bickham, Esquire, dated 16th Feby., 1768, who does depose and say, &^{c}., "That the Bastard child, wherewith she is pregnant, was begotten upon her by Joseph Chambers, late of Lancaster, Schoolmaster, who is the Father thereof and none else." On this Deposition Chambers ran off from Lancaster.

M^r. Barton in his letter of May 3^d writes thus: "I am really sorry to hear Chambers has got off; the Church will be ruined by such things. I enclose you the Deposition taken before M^r. Bickham. The Girl is since delivered and declared that Chambers and none else was the Father of her child. This she did in the *Pains and Perils of Child Birth*, which the Law deems the highest Testimony to convict a man of the crime of *Bastardy*. Chambers, after he went off, likewise wrote to M^{rs}. Stout, whose Servant the Girl is, to 'provide her with Lodging, necessaries, &c.,' for all which he would pay. But had M^{rs}. Stout taken his word, she would have been left in the Lurch for this as well as he has done for his Board, &c.

"Capt. Singleton, from Newark (where Chambers lived before), is here at present and says this is not the first crime of the sort in him. In short, he is a person of no valuable qualifications, has read nothing and can scarce write three lines correctly. His passions are violent and his conceit insufferable He seems to prefer a life of Dissipation to anything serious, and discovers a fondness for Drink, Gaming and Low Company. If these charges require proof, they may be soon had. I beseech you send off *Duplicates* and even *Triplicates* of Letters to the Bishop, else he will carry his point, as he is a bold, importunate man."

I think, my Lord, a worse Character can hardly be given. I pray God this may come time enough to your Lordship's hand, and I cannot but repeat what I once before took the liberty humbly to suggest, that whenever a Man comes recommended from any other Province or place but where he last resided, or where the Clergy who recommended do not certify three years' personal knowledge, there ought always to be suspicion. I wish I knew what method your Lordship would take to prevent Impositions of this sort. I know of none, but requiring the hands of some two or more Clergymen in each province whom your Lordship can confide in, as indispensably necessary in each Certificate from that Province. Perhaps Chambers may go to some other Bishop, but I hope your Lordship will take care they be apprized of him.

Your Lordship's most dutiful Son and Servant,

W. SMITH.

Dr. Smith to the Secretary of the Propagation Society.

(EXTRACT.)

PHILADELPHIA, August 20th, 1768.

DEAR & WORTHY SIR,

* * * I have an opportunity of *preaching* a great many times & baptizing numbers of children at a place fifty miles from any settled Minister, and hardly ever visited but when I see them.* Great numbers of them are Church people that have come from the back of Maryland, & the settlement of Religion in that part of the Country will soon be an object worthy of the Society's Notice.

I am in haste, Dear & worthy Sir, &c.,

WM. SMITH.

Dr. Smith to the Secretary of the Propagation Society.

(EXTRACT.)

PHILADELPHIA, Octr 22, 1768.

REV^D & WORTHY SIR : I enclose you a letter I have received from the Churchwardens of Bristol & of another Congregation now building a Church in Bucks County in this Province, about 25 miles from Philadelphia, who are greatly encouraged by many *Quakers*, who at this day declare themselves highly desirous of seeing the Church flourish from a fear of being overrun by Presbyterians.

The present favorable disposition to the Church in this vastly populous Province should be considered, and when you reflect that we have but 6 or 7 Missionaries in the whole of it, we hope it will be thought that some additions here are as necessary as in any place where they have been lately made, and you will consider that from my knowledge of the state of the Society's Funds I have always been backward in recommending anything new, tho' I see this Province has suffered by it, while others have been pushing forward.

We are to have 3 different Charters, one from New York, one from New Jersey, & one from our Pennsylvania Governor, so that in which Province soever we meet, as convenience requires, we are still a Corporation in that Province, & can let out our money accordingly where interest and security may be best.† These Charters will be passed in a few weeks; & all we want is the Society's sanction & consent to the two following clauses which I send you beforehand, not having time to copy the whole, & believing that D^r. Auchmuty's full copy will soon reach you along with our public Letter. The design is so truly good

---

* Huntingdon, Pennsylvania.

† Dr. Smith here refers to the Corporation for the Relief of the Widows and Children of Clergymen in the Communion of the Church of England; an institution in which he greatly interested himself, and of which we give an account further on.

that I am not under the least doubt of its meeting with the sanction of the benevolent & worthy Society.   The clauses are the 2^d & 3^d, viz. :

2^d. That there be deducted as the yearly rate of each Missionary three pounds sterling out of the Salary such Missionary receives from England, and that the Treasurer of this Corporation have power to draw on the Treasurer of the Society for the Propagation of the Gospel for the yearly contributors of the several Missionaries who shall subscribe to this scheme.

3^d. And whereas the Fund would suffer & uncertainties arise by vacancies in Mission—that humble application be made to the Ven^{ble} Society to allow the £3 Rules to continue during the vacancies, & if the Society could be further prevailed on to suffer the rents of Glebes or other rents & Interest money (not particularly appropriated) to come to the stock during such vacancy, the capital might be considerably assisted thereby.

By allowing this the Glebes, &c., which are generally neglected and seldom come to any good during vacancies, would be properly look'd after by this Corporation & be found in better order for the next Incumbent.

The rest of the scheme relates to the proportioning the Annuities between the Widows & children; to the payment of the annual rates of Ministers who are not Missionaries, & who are to pay one penny in the pound for every day's default, in consideration that the rates of the Missionaries being to be drawn for in one Bill on the Society are always sure pay at the day, which is the first Wednesday after the Feast of S^t. Michael in every year.

That worthless man Joseph Chambers is, I hear, gone to Ireland to try for orders.   Can nothing be done to prevent it?   Pray write to some of the Bishops to put them on their guard, if it is not too late.

Dear & worthy Sir, &c.,

WILLIAM SMITH.

Dr. Smith to Sir William Johnson.

PHILA, December 17th, 1768.

HON^D SIR: I take this opportunity of M^r. Maclay to trouble you with a few lines, hoping that, after the hurry of the important services in which you have been engaged for so many months past, you may now find leasure to favor me with a few lines upon subjects that I have formerly written to you upon.   Mr. Peters tells me you were kind to say you would write to me soon, & says he had a good deal of conversation with you about Church affairs, and that you are truly attentive to them; and indeed the Church stands in need of such friends as you.

I should be glad to know whether any lands be reserved for the Church and Indian Missions upon the plan formerly mentioned.   I think I have heard that you have appropriated some land for that purpose in your own part of the country.   Pray how much, and where situated?   Is there any thing secured on the Ohio or its waters for

27

making an attempt there, which could be conducted under your direction by proper persons from this place? Mr. Murray would be glad to know what the encouragement is at Schenectady, because that will determine him whether to move or not. He has lately married a woman with some little fortune and good family in this city. Mr. Peters and I have talked seriously about supplying you with proper persons for the Indian Mission, and on the whole submit to you whether it were not best to have one or two pious young men of sound principles and good education, not exceeding 22 years of age, to be sent immediately to spend two years under your direction as Catechists and schoolmasters, till they acquire the language; others, if found fit, to be sent for orders. We have two such now, who can speak both German and English, educated in our College, of exemplary good behavior; one of them, on account of his grandfather, Conrad Weiser, perhaps, might be particularly acceptable to the Indians. He is also the son of a most worthy man, the Rev^{d} Mr. Muhlenberg, who married Weiser's daughter, and is at the head of the Lutheran Churches in this Province, and is willing his son should go on this business and take orders in the Church. The other is Equally well qualified. I believe Mr. Peters will write on this subject. I wish, by your interest, a small grant of 12 or 15,000 acres of land could have been or could yet be got for Mr. Barton and me. I know you wish us both well; I have seen your kind professions of friendship to Mr. Barton, and have also had the like from you to myself, altho' I never had any opportunity of making you any return except in what care I took of your son *Sir* John, which was done with affection and esteem. Many persons have been favored in large grants of this kind. We want only a small one; and if you could yet help us to it in a good place or near any thing of your own, we would cheerfully pay the cost and zealously forward the settlement. I beg, by Mr. Maclay, you'll favor me with a few lines on the several particulars above, which will be gratefully acknowledged by

Hon^{d} & worthy Sir,

Your most Obliged Servant,

William Smith.

P. S.—We have Erected a philosophical society here, whereof you are chosen a member. I hope you will permit me the honor of saying you accept of it. Our year's transactions will soon be published, and I shall send you a copy.

To the Honble Sir William Johnson, Bart.

The Commencement of 1768 in the Departments of Arts took place in the College Hall early in June. It was attended by the various public bodies. Among the graduates were William Bingham, born A. D. 1751; a Trustee, 1791; Delegate to the Continental

Congress, 1787–1788; Senator of the United States from Pennsylvania, 1795; President of the Senate, *pro tem.;* Commercial Agent of the United States, during the Revolution, to St. Martinique; Benjamin Duffield; Edward Duffield; Adam Kuhn. This last gentleman was born at Germantown in 1741, and was the son of a physician who had emigrated from Germany. He became a physician. He went to Europe at the age of twenty, and studied botany and *materia medica* in Sweden under Linnæus. Afterward he studied medicine at Edinburgh, and received the degree of Doctor of Medicine in 1767. He was appointed a Professor in the Medical Department of this College.

The Medical Commencement of this year, being the first public commencement of any medical school in America, was held in the College Hall, on Saturday, June 21st. The ceremonies attending it are thus minutely detailed upon the Minutes of the Board of Trustees:

This day may be considered as the *Birth-day of Medical Honors in America.* The Trustees being met at half an hour past nine in the forenoon, and the several Professors and Medical Candidates, in their proper Habits, proceeded from the Apparatus Room to the Public Hall, where a polite assembly of their fellow-citizens were convened to honor the Solemnity.

The Provost having there received the Mandate for the Commencement from his Honor the Governor, as President of the Trustees, introduced the business of the day with Prayers and a short Latin Oration, suited to the occasion. The part alluding to the School of Medicine is in the following language:

Oh! Factum bene! Vos quoque Professores Medici, qui magno nummi, temporis et laboris sumptu, longâ quoque peregrinatione per varias regiones, et populos, domum reduxistis et peritiam, et nobile consilium servandi, et rationali praxi, docendi alios servare valetudinem vestrûm civium. Gratum fecistis omnibus, sed pergratum certé peritis illis medicis, qui artis suæ dignitatis conscii, praxin rationalem, et juventutis institutionem in re medicâ liberalem, hisce regionibus, ante vos longé desideraverunt.

To this succeeded—

1. A Latin oration, delivered by Mr. John Lawrence, *"De Honoribus qui in omni ævo in veros Medicinæ cultores collati fuerint."*

2. A dispute, whether the Retina or Tunica Choroides be the immediate seat of vision? The argument for the retina was ingeniously maintained by Mr. Cowell; the opposite side of the question was supported with great acuteness by Mr. Fullerton, who contended that the Retina is incapable of the office ascribed to it, on account of its being easily permeable to the rays of light, and that the choroid coat, by its being

opaque, is the proper part for stopping the rays, and receiving the picture of the object.

3. *Questio, num detur Fluidum Nervosum ?* Mr. Duffield held the affirmative, and Mr. Way the negative, both with great learning.

4. Mr. Tilton delivered an essay "On Respiration," and the manner in which it was performed did credit to his abilities.

5. The Rev. Provost, Dr. Smith, then conferred the degree of Medicine on the following gentlemen, viz. :

John Archer, of New Castle; David Jackson, of Chester; Benj. Cowell, of Bucks County; John Lawrence, of East Jersey; Saml. Duffield, of Phila. ; Jonathan Potts, of Phila. ; Jonathan Elmer, of West Jersey ; James Tilton, of Kent Co., Del. ; Humphrey Fullerton, of Lancaster ; Nicholas Way, of Wilmington.

6. An elegant valedictory oration was spoken by Mr. Potts " On the Advantages derived in the Study of Physic from a previous liberal education in the other sciences."

Dr. Smith then addressed the graduates in a Brief Account of the present state of the College, and of the quick progress in the various extensive establishments it hath already made. He pointed out the general causes of the advancement as well as the decline of literature in different Nations of the world, and observed to the Graduates, that as they were the first who had received medical honors in America on a regular Collegiate plan, it depended much on them, by their future conduct and eminence, to place such honors in estimation among their countrymen ; concluding with an earnest appeal that they would never neglect the opportunities which their profession would give them, when their art could be of no further service to the body, of making serious impressions on their patients, and showing themselves men of consolation and piety, especially at the awful approach of death, which could not fail to have singular weight from a lay character.

Dr. Shippen, Professor of Anatomy and Surgery, then gave the remainder of the charge, further inviting the Graduates to support the dignity of their Profession by a laudable perseverance in their studies, and by a Practice becoming the character of gentlemen ; adding many useful precepts respecting their conduct towards their patients, charity towards the poor, humanity towards all ; and with reference to the opportunities they might have of gaining the confidence of the sick, and esteem of every one who by their vigilance and skill might be relieved from suffering, and restored to health.

The Vice-Provost concluded the whole with Prayer and Thanksgiving.

CHAPTER XXIX.

Birth of a Fourth Son—Sir William Johnson to Dr. Smith—The Corporation for the Relief of the Widows and Children of Clergymen in the Communion of the Protestant Episcopal Church in Pennsylvania—A Clerical Life Insurance Company and Savings Bank—Its Solid Character and Great Usefulness—Dr. Smith the Founder of it, a. d. 1769, and Largely the Author of its Early Successful Establishment—Is Elected President of it, a. d. 1783, and continues to be so until 1789— The Gloucester Mission—Dr. Smith assists at an Indian Treaty and Preaches to the Indians.

On the 25th of January, 1769, Richard, the fourth son of Dr. Smith, was born.   He was baptized in Christ Church on the 19th of March by the Rev. Dr. Peters; Dr. Smith and Richard Hockley, Esq., Receiver-General of the Province, being sponsors.

We have now a reply from Sir William Johnson to Dr. Smith's letter of December 17th, 1768, already given by us on page 417 :

Sir William Johnson to Dr. Smith.

JOHNSON HALL, Jany 3^d, 1769.

SIR : The return of M^r. McClay affords me a good opportunity of answering your favor of last month on the subjects you mention on some of which M^r. Peters & I have conversed, and to whom I have wrote fully the other day as well concerning M^r. Murray, as of the Two Young men you mention for Orders your Sentiments on which I greatly approve.

I long since informed the Society that if his Majesty's permission was obt^d I would use my Interest to get a valuable Tract of Land for the Church but have never since received any thing concerned it, I however lately secured a purchase made by myself for these purposes, & if the Society will use their Interest to obtain the Royal Grant, I will still endeavor to get a large purchase to the Northward where the Line is not yet Closed.

M^r. Barton and yourself may be well assured of my friendly regards, and of my inclination to do you any good office in my power, I am likewise Sensible of your care of my Son, and your good inclinations towards him, and wish I could obtain the Tract you require in a Convenient place.   The Line as I before observed is not closed to the Northward so that Lands there must lye till his Majesty's pleasure is known, and for the rest it is Ceded to the King by the late Treaty, so that it is hard to know what will be the Channell for Patents in future, and the fees here are Extremely high—at the late Treaty nothing was done with regard to Lands but what related to the boundary, or had been before determined on, should any Tract answer that may be had on a reasonable lay worthy your attention, I shall be very Glad to serve you in it.   I am much obliged by the honor done me in Choosing me a Member of the Philosophical Society, and altho' my Necessary Avocations must deprive me of much of the pleasure I might otherwise receive as one of that Body.   I cannot but accept it with many thanks, heartily wishing that their Institution may be attended with that Utility to the public & Reputation to the founders which may be reasonably expected from the Transact^{ns} of Gentlemen who apply to studies of such importance.

Be assured, Sir, of the perfect esteem with which I am always yours, &c.,   WILLIAM JOHNSON.

We still have letters indicative of still continuing trouble at St. Paul's.   The evil that Macclanechan did, lived after him, or at least lived after his leaving Philadelphia.   We have already given an account of the matters spoken of in the letter above.*

PHILADA, 22 Feby, 1769.

DEAR AND WORTHY SIR : *   * As for Trenton, they have applied for Mr. Thomson, as I wrote you before, & as for Glocester, Mr. Fayerweather would not be able to live on the income ; and nothing will do there but turning it into an itinerant Mission for the whole County with some active young man.

I have no other particular to add ; only to beg, as I cannot by this ship write to the Bishop of London, that you would wait on his Lordship & inform him that the congregation of St. Paul's, on receiving a Letter from Mr. Chapman that he was coming out with his Lordship's Licence and telling them that when he shall come out, Mr. Stringer, whom they now have at St. Paul's, cannot continue under him, & blaming them for employing a man ordained irregularly in London by some Greek or foreign Bishop—I say, on receiving this letter of Chapman's—which I think was not blameworthy—a majority of the congregation got offended at Chapman & passed a sort of confused vote to keep *Stringer* even if Chapman should come.   But the Trustees of the Church & all men of sense declare that *Chapman*, having now the Bishop's Licence & everything they require, must be received as their Minister ; & this the other party of them are so sensible of, that they trust only on being able in a letter they have written to Mr. Chapman, to discourage his coming out ; for they could not barefacedly contradict their

---

* *Supra*, pp. 214–261.

own pressing former invitations to him.   I was desired by some leading
men to write M^r. Chapman & assure him that he would be received;
but I did not chuse to put any letter of mine in his power.   I beg then
you may let the Bishop know this state of the case ; & if Mr Chapman
comes I think he should be encouraged, as it seems now the only thing
that can make that a regular Church & keep it from continuing in a
state of separation.   I think the Bishop should see M^r. Chapman before
he sends any answer.   Only as little use as possible should be made of
my name.   This matter deserves serious consideration.

M^r. Stringer seems a peaceable good man, tho' I am told all his
sermons are in one strain & only in the way of Romaine, &c.   But
were his orders regular, I believe he might be made a useful Missionary ;
and he says he is willing to be employed wherever he can serve the
cause of religion.   I am, dear & worthy Sir, &c.,

                                                  W^M. SMITH.

" Mr. Stringer " was undoubtedly " a peaceable good man ; " his
sermons a little too much " in the way of Romaine " to be agreeable to Dr. Smith's logical head and highly educated taste ; but
probably very much to the taste of some of his parishioners.   He
became satisfied that the " Greek or foreign Bishop," who ordained
him, had no good authority, and he submitted to the Bishop of
London and was properly ordained.

There exists in Philadelphia a society known as " The Corporation for the Relief of the Widows and Children of Clergymen in
the Communion of the Protestant Episcopal Church in the Commonwealth of Pennsylvania."   The institution is a clerical life
insurance company, and a clergyman's saving bank for the benefit
of his widow and children.   But it differs from most life insurance
companies and from most savings banks in this : that the clergyman insuring his life or depositing his money in this corporation,
purchases a right in favor of his widow and children to have such
a portion of any profits above what is necessary to keep the company solid, as the directors in their discretion may see fit to give
to them.   The legal power of the directors in distributing the
surplus is an absolute one, but is controlled against all abuse by
their characters, their moral duty, and their responsibility to public
opinion.   The corporation is so opulent, that what it gives away
year by year in bounty far exceeds what it gives away year by
year in contract ; and this has been the case for many, many years.

Its somewhat privately published fiscal statements, which a director kindly lends me, disclose the relations of the two heads, since 1865, as follows :

	Legal Claims.	Gratuities Voted.
1865 and 1866	$1,463.38	$6,660.00
1867	200.00	2,205.00
1868	1,566.96	4,100.00
1869	1,223.72	4,400.00
1870	360.00	8,625.00
1871	2,198.88	6,150.00
1872	1,542.50	6,425.00
1873	360.00	7,625.00
1874	360.00	8,075.00
1875	662.57	9,225.00
1876	5,522.52	8,925.00
1877	2,635.24	8,975.00
	$18,095.77	$81,390.00

I have not yet seen any report of payments for the year 1878.
The assets of this company by the Report of May, 1878, were thus :

	Par.	Market Value.
Ground Rents	$69,480.49	$82,124.28
State of Penna. 6% Loan	57,000.00	64,020.00
do. 5% Loan	35,600.00	39,338.00
City of Philada. Loans	46,000.00	51,980.00
United States 6% Loans	38,600.00	41,919.00
do. new 5% Loan	10,000.00	10,400.00
Bonds and Mortgages	117,366.67	117,366.67
City of Philada. Warrants	9,670.79	9,670.79
Cash	1,295.56	1,295.56
	$385,013.51	$418,114.30

Nominal Amount of all Outstanding Engagements—

Policies of Annuitants in expectancy	$2,666.67	
Policies of Endowments	179,618.91	
Deposits on Interest	2,351.64	
Value of Annuities now payable	1,154.91	
		$185,792.13
		$232,322.17

Here is a company of unparalleled beneficence, of extraordinary strength ! It was *bound* to pay $18,095.77. It *has* paid $99,485.77. It has all its investments in a form convertible in a day—almost in an hour—into cash ; and if all its outstanding engagements—in expectancy and others—came upon it at once, it could pay them all and have a balance of nearly twice as much as they all amounted to.

To the founders of no institution have the clergy of Pennsylvania greater cause to be thankful. Of no institution may our city and State be more justly proud.

The late Hon. Horace Binney was long a principal manager of the company, and for many years its president. Resigning the office in his ninety-third or ninety-fourth year—though still remaining a member—he was succeeded by the Hon. Peter McCall, its present worthy head.

The directors of this company are citizens of Philadelphia. The well-known names of most of them testify to its vital energy and action to-day : The Rev. H. J. Morton, D. D., Peter Williamson, James M. Aertsen, Richard R. Montgomery, Thomas Robins, Charles Willing, M. D., John Wm. Wallace, LL. D., John Welsh, Ellis Yarnall, the Rev. D. R. Godwin, D. D., George W. Hunter, George H. Kirkham, the Rev. Thomas F. Davies, D. D., Edwin M. Lewis, the Rev. Eugene A. Hoffman, D. D., P. Pemberton Morris, Robert M. Lewis, Henry S. Lowber, W. Heyward Drayton.

One century in the history of this company—which was founded A. D. 1769—has been written by one of its members, Mr. John William Wallace, A. D. 1869. He entitled the narrative "A Century of Beneficence." After giving, with particularity, the annals of the corporation from its foundation up to the date when he was writing, with a list of all the directors, the dead and the living, he says :

I forbear to set out ostentatiously the many names eminent in the social history of the Colonies and the Republic. The list of our earlier members discloses them all; and shows that there were few persons eminent in such history, in either of the three Provinces or States, who were not members of this Society, if members of the Church at all. Some of them were "leaders of the people by their counsels;" and some of them "rich men, furnished with ability, living peaceably in their habitations." Some have left a name behind them, "that their praises might be reported;" and some have now "no memorial," and are "perished, as though they had never been"—but all alike were "honored in their generation, and the glory of their times."

In the hundred years which have passed since the original Society was incorporated, the roll presents the names of near 250 members. Many of them have performed, for years, great, laborious, and responsible service. *But not one, that I have heard of, has ever asked or has ever been willing to receive one cent of compensation ; and, by a rule of the Society, reciting this honorable fact, it is now ordained that no member, for any service rendered, ever shall.*

The Society has proved of signal benefit in the cases of numerous families of the clergy departed this life. They have invariably received all that their fathers or husbands contracted for. In the earlier history of the body its contracts were based upon a scheme so much more for the interests of the clergy who should first come upon the fund than of the fund itself, that nothing but accidental facts and the fact that the Society was continually asking and continually receiving donations, saved it from disaster. But even then the families of the clergy subscribing received great additions from the surplus; as *ex. gr.*, in one case where the Society paid to one family, for thirteen years, $400 a year, where the sum contracted for was but $80. Since 1835, when the Society was placed on a safer basis, the same liberal administration has prevailed, and the family of one clergyman, who recently insured his life for $100, by making a single payment of $49.52, which compounded at the rate of five per cent. to the date of his death, amounted to but $68.14, has received an annual payment of $500. In the same way the child of a deceased clergyman, who had paid for two years $8 a year, receives lately over and above all that she was lawfully entitled to claim, an annual sum of $200 by way of bounty. These are but three instances of many. In no instance through the whole century, as we learn from a recorded statement given us by the oldest member of the body, has the corporation enforced a forfeiture against any person whatever. It has allowed the contributors to change from one form of contract to another, where the by-laws permitted, and it has cancelled contracts where the pecuniary interests of the corporation opposed it. The whole administration of the concerns of the corporation has been, for the entire century, as much distinguished by liberality as by prudence and by justice. What higher praise can be given to the administration of any corporation intrusted with interests like those of this!

And now we ask—since the foundations of the Society were laid one hundred years ago, and since it has been thus honorable and thus useful—who was its founder? by whom was it brought into being? who watched over all its earlier years, and assisted in primitive days to give to it the basis of that wonderful strength which it now confessedly enjoys and has long enjoyed? "The members of the corporation," said Mr. Binney in 1851, "do not administer their own bounty, but the very moderate bounty of a former age, successfully accumulated through a course of years

by the fidelity and gratuitous care of the successive managers of
the trust."

Who were the actors in this "former age?" What hand had
any of *them* in "successfully accumulating through a course of
years, by fidelity and gratuitous care," the capital of the solidly
opulent society of this day?

The historian of the corporation, whom I have already quoted,
and whose language I use where I am able to do so, tells us:

Although efforts at the elucidation of what mortal men call "chances,"
engaged, towards the end of the 17th century, the attention of Huygens,
Pascal, Bernouillé, and others, the actual subject of insuring lives, and
granting annuities upon them, is a thing of modern institution. In
France, until the time of De Moivre, several of whose brilliant results
were left to us without a knowledge of the steps by which he attained
them,[*] the thing was forbidden by law as against the principles of
morality and nature. The oldest English company goes back, I believe, no further than to 1706: in which year the Amicable Society was
established at Sergeants' Inn, London, and notwithstanding the "Table
of Mortality," as it was then called, prepared thirteen years before by
the great astronomer and mathematician, Dr. Halley, it was not until
the time of Dr. Richard Price, a non-conforming minister of eminence,
in the middle of the last century, that even in England the subject was
much considered on true principles, if even then it was fully so. Dr.
Price's essays on the subjects of "Reversionary Payments," of "Schemes
for Providing Annuities for Widows and Persons in Old Age," and on
"The Method of Calculating the Values of Assurances on Lives,"
mark, I think, the date when the thing began to be understood in
England. In our own country, no general essay towards it was made,
even theoretically, till 1772, when William Gordon, of Roxbury, Massachusetts, printed a pamphlet of 35 pages, entitled, "*The Plan of a
Society for making Provision for Widows by Annuities for the Remainder
of Life; with the Proper Tables for calculating what must be paid by
the several Members in order to secure the said Advantages.*" In the
preface to this tract, Gordon states that one of the motives to his publication was the fact "that there were no general societies of this nature
in America." I am not aware that his tract caused the establishment
of any one anywhere, or even that it attracted any public notice.
Indeed, the statement made by Dr. Price—esteemed perhaps as a writer
on the subject of life insurance, and who, more than any man of his day,
was familiar with the history and management of these institutions—
that of all those established in England, but one, the Amicable, already

---

[*] See "The Quarterly Review," vol. 64, p. 285.

mentioned, had, up to his day, "stood any considerable trial from time and experience," and who records it as the result of his observations, derived from the showings of "melancholy experience," "that *none but mathematicians* were qualified for forming and conducting schemes of this sort"—would have been quite enough to have deterred most prudent men in Philadelphia, in 1769, for wishing to participate in such schemes, either as managers or as parties contracting.

That such an institution as the one which we are describing—a Clerical Life Annuity Company—did not in 1769 originate from suggestion or providence of the clergy in the Middle Provinces generally, is, I apprehend, quite certain.

Who then was the individual, equally humane and intelligent, so far in advance of the country, and we may even say of the day also, in which he lived, that first conceived as practicable in this new region, and for the benefit of a small and special class, this sort of beneficent scheme; a scheme originating in an idea, which it is only in our days and under the vicissitudes of commercial life in times when these vicissitudes have been greatly multiplied, that even the secular classes have carried into effect among themselves; a scheme "which although founded on self-interest, is yet the most enlightened and benevolent form which the projects of self-interest ever took," and which among the clergy, as among all others who have resorted to its more solid administrations, has proved of vast advantage to families thus solaced in their afflictions, and but for such solace dependent and destitute alike? Was the idea in the case of our own corporation original in the Colonial Church itself, or did we derive it from some other religious body among us, or did it come from the mother Church in England? . . .

Nothing which I have had leisure to look into just now enables me to say with confidence where the idea of our own Society originated, or by whom it was originally inspired. Indications, I think, rather point to Dr. WILLIAM SMITH, already named, as the first mover among the Episcopal clergy in this scheme of beneficence for the families of his reverend brethren; a man of a bold and original cast of thought, of active usefulness, and of great powers of giving effect to all that he undertook; highly admired both at home and abroad for his eloquence, and whom, as I suppose, nothing but some of those infirmities which often attend superior genius, though happily, as splendid proofs in the Church attest, not inseparable from it, prevented from arriving at the honors of the Episcopate itself.*

---

* The Right Rev. William Stevens Perry, now Bishop of Iowa, in his invaluable "Historical Collections of the American Colonial Church," referring to Mr. Wallace's monograph, says that the letter of Dr. Smith, *supra*, on page 416, and which I take from his Collections, "fully confirms the inference made by that gentleman, unaided by direct proof, that this celebrated clergyman was the moving spirit in this work of

The Society, in its origin, was an institution of the three Provinces of Pennsylvania, New York and New Jersey, and had charters from all three. The first meeting which began to give it form
was at Elizabethtown, in the last-named State. The first meeting
under the charter was by adjournment from Burlington, N. J., to
Philadelphia. Arriving in the last-named city, the first action
of the Society seems to have been attendance on divine worship
in Christ Church, in which venerable temple, historic in the annals
of the Church and State alike, Dr. Smith, whose name stood first
in order among those of the clergy in the charter, and who had
been appointed preacher for the occasion, proceeded to deliver his
discourse. It was taken from three texts,* all relating to the
fatherless and the widows; selected in such number, the preacher
says, to show how rich are the sacred oracles of God, as in exalted
lessons of benevolence in general, so particularly in that amiable
branch thereof which he is to recommend to the regard of those
present. " Through the whole inspired books of the Old Testament, as of the New, we shall scarcely find," he declares, "a writer
who hath not made the cause of the fatherless and widows peculiarly his own."

His discourse has been more than once printed, and was widely
circulated at the time. It is an eloquent tribute to the "charity"
of the gospel; and were any preacher of this day seeking to
recommend to hearers before him a society like the corporation
whose objects we have described, perhaps the eloquence of no day
would furnish better language than that which the first Provost
and first preacher used, one hundred and ten years ago. Thus he
speaks :

You well know the situation and circumstances of the clergy in these
Northern Colonies. Except in a few places, their chief support depends
on the bounty of our fellow-members of the church in Great Britain.
The additional support which our clergy receive from their congregations is small and exceedingly precarious; decreasing sometimes, in

---

beneficence." Indeed, Dr. Smith himself, in a Sermon found in his works (vol. ii., p.
417), says, by way of quieting some fears of persons "long accustomed to view every
transaction of our Church with a jealous eye," and who might therefore " conceive
more to be intended by the undertaking than was expressed," " if it may have any
weight with them—that everything relative to the design, from the beginning, has passed
through his *own hands*," " assisted by a few others appointed for that purpose."

  * Job xxix. 11-13; Jeremiah xix. 2; and St. James i. 27.

nominal, often in real value; while the expense of every necessary in life is proportionately increasing. Decency, a regard to character, to their own usefulness, to the credit of religion, and even to *your* credit among whom they minister, require them to maintain some sort of figure in their families above those in common professions and business; while certain it is, on the other hand, that any sober, reputable tradesman can turn his industry to more account than they. I am far from mentioning these things as complaints. I know they are of necessity in many places, and I trust none of my brethren among the clergy will ever make their calculation in this way, but keep their eye on their Master's service, looking forward to "the recompense of reward." Yet what I mention is so far necessary, as it shows, incontestably, the great propriety of the design before us.

It certainly requires little attention to what passes around us, to see that the families of our deceased clergy are often left among the most distressed in their vicinity. The father, by strict economy and good example, may be able to support them in some degree of reputation during his own life, although not to flatter them with the hopes of any patrimony at his death. By his own care, and some conveniency of schools, he may give the sons the rudiments of an education for his own profession, or some other useful one in the world. The mother, with the like anxious care, and fond hopes of rendering the daughters respectable among their sex, may employ her late and early toil to train their minds to those virtues, and their hands to that diligence and industry, which might one day make them the sweet accomplished companions of worthy men in domestic life.

But alas! amidst all these flattering dreams and fond presages of the heart, the father, perhaps, in his prime of years and usefulness, is called from this world. The prop and stay of all this promising family is now no more! His life was their whole dependence, under God, even for daily bread! His death leaves them destitute—destitute, alas! not of bread only, but even of counsel and protection upon earth!

Fatal reverse—Ah! little do the world in general, and especially they who bask in the easy sunshine of affluence and prosperity—little do they know the various complicated scenes of private anguish and distress. Here they are various and complicated indeed!

The bereaved and disconsolate mother, as soon as Christian reflection begins to dry up her tears a little, finds them wrung from her afresh by the melancholy task that remains to her. She is now, alas, to reduce the once flattering hopes of her tender family, to the standard of their present sad and humbled condition! Hard task, indeed! The son is to be told that he must no more aspire to reach the station which his father filled; and the daughter is to learn that, in this hard and selfish world, she must no longer expect to become the wife of him, to whom she once might have looked on terms of equality. The son, perhaps, must descend to some manual employ, while even the poor pittance necessary to settle him in that, is not to be found; and the daughter must serve strangers, or be yoked, perhaps, in marriage for mere bread; while the mournful mother without the slow-procured help of friends, can scarce furnish out the decent wedding-garment!

What did I say? the decent wedding-garment and a marriage for mere bread? This were an issue of troubles devoutly to be wished for! But, ah me! The snares of poverty in a mind once bred up above it— shall every unguarded, unprotected female be able to escape them? Alas! no. . . . The picture here drawn is no exaggerated one; and when the children of clergy, in low circumstances, are in an early age deprived of both parents—then are they orphans indeed! and every distress, every temptation falls upon them with aggravated weight!

To be fathers then, to such fatherless children; to take them by the hand and lead them out, through the snares of the world into some public usefulness in life, that the name and memorial of our dear brethren and faithful pastors, deceased, may not be wholly lost upon earth— I say, to do this, and give some gleam of comfort to the afflicted widows and mothers that survive—must surely be one of the most delightful actions of a benevolent mind; and this, my brethren, is the glorious object of the charity for which we are incorporated, and which we have undertaken to solicit and conduct.

At the conclusion of the sermon, a collection, called in the printed account of the day, "a very generous one," and amounting to £40 10s. Pennsylvania money,—equivalent, I believe, to about $140,—was made, we are told, "at the church doors for the benefit of the charity." And the members of the corporation having continued in church till the congregation was dispersed, went then in a body to wait on the Hon. Governor Penn, with an address of thanks for his having granted them a charter of incorporation; an address similar to that, which, when in New Jersey, they had presented to Governor Franklin, when he had done the same thing.

In view alike of his superior years, his high social position in the Province, his distinguished official place as Rector of Christ Church, his most amiable character and his liberality to the fund, to which in its origin and in a single sum he gave £200 of our Pennsylvania currency, Dr. Peters was properly elected the first President. But Dr. Smith seems to have been the animating spirit of the Society everywhere; and though the Society owed much in New York to the excellent Samuel Auchmutty, Rector of Trinity Church, New York, and in New Jersey to the Rev. Samuel Bradbury

Chandler, D.D.—and in all three Provinces to many besides these three—Dr. Smith appears to have been the man who was most looked to for *work ;* the man who, having planned the general scheme of things, carried them, through all their details, into effect; the man who, most of all, all looked to for the collection of funds. The Historical Tract to which I have referred gives a list of the early contributors to the corporation; and shows that, through Dr. Smith's agency more than through that of any other person, its treasury was kept full, and the foundation laid of that noble wealth which still continues to diffuse its blessings to the widows and children of our clergy; and which, though he be dead, makes him yet to speak.

He interested his powerful friends in it, and also his youthful ones; several of these, graduates of the College. Among the first Directors I find the names of John Penn, James Hamilton, Benjamin Chew, James Tilghman, Alexander Stedman, Samuel Powel, Francis Hopkinson, Thomas Barton, Thomas Duché, Samuel Magaw and John Andrews. He made all his friends everywhere and of all kinds useful; and the Rev. Henry Muhlenberg, not a minister of the Church of England at all, was brought in by him as a Director. Thomas Hopkinson, one of the early graduates, was Treasurer of the Corporation. In the same way as to contributions: The Society for the Propagation of the Gospel contributes £30. The Lord Bishop of London contributes £20. John Dickinson, Esquire, £13 10s. Sir William Johnson, Bart., £9 7s. 6d. These were all in particular Dr. Smith's friends; and we find the corporation's printed accounts for 1772, in which year Dr. Smith collected and caused to be printed the literary remains of the Rev. Nathaniel Evans, of whom we have already spoken, the following entry, showing how much he preferred the Society's interest to his own.

To Rev⁴ Dr. Smith, for the consideration paid to him by Mr. John Dunlap, for the privilege of printing the Poems of the Rev⁴ Nathaniel Evans, late Missionary for Gloucester county, New Jersey £20

Dr. Peters died on the 10th of July, 1776, and during the revolution the Society was prostrated. On the re-establishment of peace, "Dr. Smith," says Mr. Wallace, "now venerable for his years and deserving such honor from his long and great service to the Society, was appointed President."* The first thing to be done was to raise up the Society from the prostration in which the war of the Revolution had left it. The names of two-thirds of the ancient members had disappeared from the records during the revolutionary term. And though younger men—William White and Robert Blackwell and others—in after times most efficient actors in the body—had now come above the horizon, and were truly interested in the reorganization of the corporation, Dr. Smith entered into the subject with the ardor and energy of youth; ready to spend and to be spent in what promoted the welfare of the church and the welfare of the widows and children of its faithful ministers. The Society still was one throughout the three States. The first formal meeting after the peace was on the 10th of October, 1784, in New York. Dr. Smith, after the adjournment of the meeting, remained behind in that city to preach there on the following Sunday, both forenoon and afternoon—at St. Paul's in the morning, and in the afternoon at St. George's—"which," says Mr. Wallace, "he did with so good effect as to have added £112 19s. 10d.† to the corporate moneys. From 1783 to 1789 Dr. Smith was indefatigable in his efforts to place the Society upon a wide, strong and enduring basis. He had excellent coadjutors, in such men as the two I have named, Dr. White and Dr. Blackwell—one of whom had been chaplain to the American Congress and the other a chaplain and surgeon at the Valley Forge—and among the laity in men like Jasper Yates, Richard Willing, John Wilcocks, Samuel Powel, Edward Tilghman and Alexander Wilcocks. The Society was at last firmly re-established. Alexander Hamilton, Gouverneur Morris and Robert Morris—then residents of Philadelphia—were all among its Directors, giving to this ancient institution of the clergy—most of them, at the outbreak of the Revolution, loyalists —the countenance of names which secured it and its possessions from political disturbance. He had founded the Society. He had given twenty years of his life to its service. He saw it vigorous and flourishing. The narrative of Mr. Wallace continues:

The year 1789 is to be signalized by the retirement of Dr. Smith from the presidency of the corporation. He had been, as I suppose, more

* Century of Beneficence, page 41.
† The money was currency of New York, I suppose.

than any one else, its author; he had certainly been for twenty years one of its most active and efficient friends; alike in labors of the pen, of the pulpit, of his providence, and his personal agency. The minutes now record that he informed the corporation that he wished, on account of his advanced age, to decline the honor of being continued their president. The thanks of the corporation were given to him for his long and faithful services as president; and the Rev. Dr. White, who had been a member of the Society since 1772, and had now recently been consecrated to the episcopate, was elected to the place.

Although Dr. Smith was at this time sixty-two years old, and his years—in the case of a man of less vigorous general health—would have been a sufficient reason for his asking a dismission, I rather think that in putting his resignation on the ground of "advanced age," the *full* reason, as was decorous, was hardly assigned. He had an exquisite sense of "place, priority, degree," and I suppose that he thought that it did not well become a Presbyter to preside, in a body so largely composed of the clergy, where a Bishop was constantly present. It is certain that, in the place of a director merely, his efforts to assist the Society were hardly less vigorous than ever. Bishop White now became President.

The corporation of which we speak grows year by year in importance. If its usefulness increases, as it has been increasing for the last twenty years, its beneficence will be great indeed! Let all honor be paid to the many men who have assisted to build, to protect and to serve it! But let the name of its chief founder, William Smith, never be forgotten.

The death of Mr. Nathaniel Evans left vacant the " Gloucester Mission "—one which embraced Coles's Church, at Waterford—an ancient and important church, in Waterford Township, near Morestown, New Jersey. Dr. Smith always interested himself much in it.

Dr. Smith to the Secretary of the Propagation Society.

(EXTRACT.)

PHILADᴬ, Augˢᵗ 10ᵗʰ, 1769

REVᴰ AND WORTHY SIR: Mʳ. Lyon has come to see Glocester Mission. Mʳ. Peters & I—as it lies directly over against this city on the Jersey side of Delaware—went over to introduce him, but he does not seem wholly satisfied to settle there as that part of the Mission which makes the Glocester Congregation having been hastily gathered by Dʳ. *Wrangel,* of many *Presbyterians* & Quakers, has fallen considerably off by the

Settlement of a Presbyterian Preacher among them & we did not find that they could engage to raise more than £15 in lieu of £45 they at first engaged to me in behalf of M^r. *Evans.* The *Waterford* Congregation, which is the other part, is more zealous and steady & have increased their subscription £8 or £10 more than at first, being now about £56. M^r. *Andrews* being at Philad^a last week at the same time with M^r. *Lyon* gave so favorable account of the good disposition, liberal contributions, large numbers of people & great importance of the Lewes Mission, with his reluctance to leave it unprovided, that he persuaded M^r. Lyon to go down with him to visit it ; not doubting if he should find it more to his advantage, have a prospect of doing more good & prove acceptable to the people but the Society would indulge him with that place instead of Glocester where the people cannot suffer so much by a delay as being within reach of the Philadelphia Churches. M^r. Lyon seems hardly fit to bear the climate & fatigues of the Lewes Mission. What his determination will be I cannot tell, till he returns up ; and then I do not expect to be in Town as our College vacation begins next Monday and I cannot deny myself my annual ramble towards the frontiers of this Province.

Believe me to be, dear & worthy Sir,

W^M. SMITH.

On the 14th of August, 1769, Dr. Smith went, at the request of Mr. Penn, to assist at an Indian Conference, which was to be held at Fort Augusta. On the 20th he preached to the Indians, Isaac Hill acting as his interpreter.

Coming back to the College, the chief feature of Commencement Days—June 28th and 29th—this year is the Medical Department.

The Degree of Bachelor of Medicine was conferred on James Armstrong, Josias Carroll Hall, John Hodge, John Houston, Thomas Pratt, Alexander Skinner, Myndert Veeder, and John Winder.

The Medical Exercises were the following:

An oration in honor of Medicine, by Mr. Hall.

A Forensic Dispute, whether Medicine had done most good or harm in the world, by Messrs. Alexander Skinner and John Hodge.

An oration on the most probable method of obtaining a good old age, by Mr. John Winder.

The *Pennsylvania Gazette*, of July 6th, 1769, speaking of these discussions, says :

In the composition of these exercises the young gentlemen gave full proofs of learning, as well as a thorough acquaintance with their subjects and the History of Physic, and they were honored with the close attention and warm approbation of the audience. Mr. Skinner's part of the Forensic Dispute, in particular, seemed to afford singular entertainment, from the candid freedom which he took with his own Profession, and the very humorous manner in which he attempted to prove that Medicine had done more harm than good in the world; which Position of his was, however, very seriously and fully replied to by Mr. Hodge. To this succeeded a very solemn and interesting charge, in which the Provost addressed himself chiefly to the graduates in the arts, adding, with respect to the graduates in Physic, that he had prevailed on a gentleman of their own Profession, whose precepts would receive Dignity from his years and experience, to lay before them what he thought requisite as well for the honour of the College, as for promoting their own future honour and usefulness in life. This part was accordingly performed by Dr. Thomas Bond, in a manner so truly feeling and affectionate that it could not fail to make a serious impression on those for whom it was designed.

In the Department of Arts we find, among the graduates, John D. Coxe, born in Philadelphia, in 1752; died in 1824; President Judge of the Court of Common Pleas at Philadelphia; an upright and learned magistrate, whose name is still remembered with honor by the bar; Joseph Swift, born A. D. 1752, in Philadelphia; died in 1826; a Lieutenant in the British Army.

CHAPTER XXX.

Transit of Venus—Formation of the American Philosophical Society—Its Charter and Fundamental Rules Drawn by Dr. Smith—He an Active Member of it—His Observations at Norriton with David Rittenhouse of the Transit—His Accounts of it—Correspondence with Rittenhouse; with Nevil Maskelyne, the Astronomer Royal; with Lord Stirling, on the Transit—Correspondence with Rittenhouse about a Comet—The Silk Society—Dr. Smith a Manager and Subscriber to it.

The year 1769 was one memorable in the history of the celestial bodies. The attention of astronomers and learned men had been for some time directed to an expected Transit of Venus over the sun's disc, which, it was predicted, would occur in this year. It was an event which no human being then living on our earth could ever live long enough to behold a second time. It could not occur again for one hundred and five years; that is to say, not till the year 1874. An intense anxiety prevailed throughout Europe for the results of observations throughout the world—so beneficial to science—if the weather and the sky should prove favorable. And the preparations were not bad. The Assembly voted £100 sterling; Thomas Penn sent one telescope;* another was procured by Franklin, who was now in England.

In America the body most looked to for obtaining true results of the great phenomenon was the American Philosophical Society. This Society, which soon became eminent over our own country and Europe, was formed in 1769. There had been two societies called scientific before this in Philadelphia—the American Society and the Philosophical Society. Both were in a state of decline. The expected Transit animated every man of science; and it was resolved to consolidate the two associations, and to give new activity to the united body. Dr. Franklin, to whom, had he been in Philadelphia, all would naturally have looked for guidance, was, as we have said, now in England—our Provincial Agent. He had left us in 1764, and did not return till 1775. But Dr. Smith never failed to see and to profit of opportunities—" opportunities which are the help of wise men's fortunes and the tests of the incapacity of fools." Transits of Venus were not affairs of every day. If *rightly improved*, it would make Philadelphia, in the eyes of Europe and America, a centre of sciences; her College the cynosure of eyes. He did improve it. And the American Philosophical Society rose into fame. Philadelphia was looked upon with reverence by men of learning, and the College of Philadelphia was ranked with universities which numbered the students by thousands. "Of this great Society," Dr. Smith, as their Provost, Stillé tells us, "was a founder. *He* drew its charter and fundamental laws, carried on its chief correspondence with various parts of the world, and superintended the publication of the first volume of its transactions."

As early as the 7th of January, 1769, the Society met at the College and appointed a Committee to observe the great phenomenon which calculations led to believe would be seen on the 3d of June following. The Committee was composed of the following

---

* Mr. Penn directed that, after its use for the purpose of observing the Transit, it should be given to the College. It was so given, and is still preserved among the astronomical apparatus of the Institution.

persons: the *Rev. John Ewing, Joseph Shippen, Jr., Esq., Rev. Dr. William Smith, Mr. John Lukens, Esq., Owen Biddle,* John Sellers, William Poole, Mr. Thomas Prior, Hugh Williamson, M.D., Mr. David Rittenhouse, James Alexander, James Pearson, and Charles Thomson.*

"The gentlemen thus nominated," says Mr. William Barton,† the nephew and biographer of Mr. Rittenhouse, "were distributed into three committees, for the purpose of making separate observations at three places. These were the city of Philadelphia, Mr. Rittenhouse's residence in Norriton, and the Light-House at Cape Henlopen, on Delaware Bay. Dr. Ewing, an able mathematician and very respectable astronomer, had the principal direction of the observatory in the city, which was erected on this occasion in the State-house garden; and Mr. Owen Biddle, a person of much ingenuity, had charge of superintending the observations at Cape Henlopen. Associated with Mr. Rittenhouse, on the Norriton Committee, were the Rev. Dr. Smith, well known as an astronomer and eminently skilled in mathematics; Mr. Lukens, then Surveyor-General of Pennsylvania, who possessed considerable abilities in the same department of science; and Mr. Sellers, a respectable member of the Provincial Legislature for the county of Chester. The Rev. Mr. Thomas Barton voluntarily attended at Norriton on this occasion, and rendered such assistance as they could to the Committee."

It will, perhaps, surprise the reader to find Dr. Smith, whom he has considered chiefly as a pulpit orator, a scholar, a college professor, a military historian and military critic, a statesman, or possibly a courtier, named by one of the first scientific societies of Europe or America as one among a number of men of pure

---

* Owen Biddle died March 10th, 1799, aged sixty-one years. He was born in Philadelphia, and engaged in commercial business, in partnership with his brother, Clement Biddle. He signed the non-importation resolutions of October 25th, 1765. He was a member of the Committee of the City, Northern Liberties, and Southwark, in 1774, and of the Committee of Safety of 1775, the Council of Safety of 1776, and of the Constitutional Convention of 1776. During the Revolution he was one of the eighty Philadelphia merchants who became bound for certain provisions of the army, amounting to more than two hundred and sixty thousand pounds sterling. He was an active member and officer of the American Philosophical Society, and one of the members of the Committee of that Society which observed the Transit of Venus, June 3d, 1769. Mr. Biddle's station, at that time, was at Cape Henlopen. He was a member of the Board of War in 1777.

† Life of Rittenhouse, page 102.

science, to give to the world the results of a great celestial phenomenon. Yet he was properly so named; and he will appear as
able and ready in Astronomical Science as he was in any other
situation or business whatsoever.

On the 1st of June, 1769, Dr. Smith and Mr. Lukens were at
Mr. Rittenhouse's dwelling in Norriton, about twenty miles from
Philadelphia; not reached then as easily as now. In a letter to
the Society, dated July 20th, he says:

As Mr. Rittenhouse's dwelling is so far off, our other engagements did
not permit Mr. Lukens or myself to pay much attention to the necessary
preparations; but we knew that we had entrusted them to a gentleman
on the spot, who had joined to a compleat skill in Mechanics, so extensive an astronomical and mathematical knowledge, that the use, management, and even the construction of the necessary apparatus, were perfectly familiar to him. Mr. Lukens and myself could not set out for
his house till Thursday, June 1st; but, on our arrival there, we found
every preparation so forward, that we had little to do but to examine
and adjust our respective telescopes to distinct vision. Mr. Rittenhouse
had fitted up the different instruments, and made a great number of
observations, to ascertain the going of his Time-Piece, and to determine
the latitude and longitude of his observatory. The laudable pains he
hath taken in these material articles, will best appear from the work
itself, which he hath committed into my hands, with a modest introduction; giving me a liberty, which his own accuracy, care and abilities,
leave no room to exercise.

Dr. Smith describes the telescope used by himself on this occasion as "a Gregorian Reflector, about 2 f. focal length, with a
Dollond's Micrometer, made by Nairne, having four different magnifying powers, viz., 55, 95, 130, and 200 times; by means of two
Tubes containing eye-glasses that magnify differently, and two
small Speculums of different focal distances."

He continues:

"It hath been mentioned before, that it was on Thursday afternoon,
"June 1st, that Mr. Lukens and myself arrived at Norriton, with a
"design to continue with Mr. Rittenhouse 'till the transit should be
"over. The prospect before us was very discouraging. That day,
"and several preceding, had been generally overcast with clouds, and
"frequent heavy rains; a thing not very common for so long a period
"at that season of the year, in this part of America. But, by one of
"those sudden transitions, which we often experience here, on Thurs-
"day evening the weather became perfectly clear, and continued the

"day following, as well as the day of the Transit, in such a state of
"serenity, splendor of sunshine, and purity of atmosphere, that not the
"least appearance of a cloud was to be seen.

"June 2d, and the forenoon of June 3d, were spent in making the
"necessary preparations, such as examining and marking the foci of our
"several telescopes, particularly the reflector, with and without the
"micrometer. The reflector was also placed on a polar axis, and such
"supports contrived for resting the ends of the refractors, as might give
"them a motion as nearly parallel to the equator as such hasty prepa-
"rations would admit. Several diameters of the Sun were taken, and
"the micrometer examined by such other methods as the shortness of
"the time would allow."

The sun was so intensely bright on the Day of the Transit, that,
instead of using the coloured glasses sent from England with the Reflector, I put on a deeply-smoked glass prepared by Mr. Lukens, which
gave a much more beautiful, natural, and well-defined appearance of the
Sun's Disk. The smoked glass was fastened on the Eye Tube with
a little bees-wax, and there was no occasion to change it during the
whole day, as there was not the least cloud, or intermission of the Sun's
splendour.

That each of us might the better exercise our own judgment, without
being influenced, or thrown into any agitation by the others, it was
agreed to transact everything by signals, and that one should not know
what another was doing. The Situation of the Telescopes, the two
Refractors being at some distance without the Observatory, and the
Reflector within, favoured this design.

Two persons—Mr. Sellers, one of our Committee, and Mr. Archibald
McClean, both well accustomed to matters of this kind—were placed at
one window of the Observatory, to count the clock and take the signal
from Mr. Lukens. Two of Mr. Rittenhouse's family, whom he hath
often employed to count the clock for him in his observations, were
placed at another window to take his signal.* My Telescope was placed
close by the clock, and I was to count its beats, and set down my own
time.

Preliminaries being settled, we prepared at two o'clock to sit down to
our respective Telescopes ; or (I should rather say) lie down to the
Refractors, on account of the Sun's great height.

As there was a large concourse of the inhabitants of the county, and
many from the city, we were apprehensive that our scheme for silence
might be defeated by some of them speaking, when they should see any
of the signals for the Contacts ; and therefore we found it necessary to

---

* I believe that this clock is the same one that now stands in the hall of the Historical Society of Pennsylvania, and known as "Mr. Rittenhouse's Clock;" obviously
an astronomical one.

tell them that the success of our observation would depend on their keeping a profound silence 'till the Contacts were over. And to do them justice, during the 12' that ensued, there could not have been a more solemn pause of silence and expectation, if each individual had been waiting for the sentence that was to take his life.

The contact was now coming on.   Dr. Smith thus proceeds:

The power kept on the Gregorian Reflector, for observing the contacts, was the same which we had been using, and were again to use, with the Micrometer, magnifying 95 times. I had therefore a large field, taking in about half the Sun's Disk; and the instrument was so firmly supported, with its axis in a polar direction, that it could not be shaken by any motion on the earthen floor of the observatory, and required only an easy movement of one part of the rack-work to manage it. With these advantages, any part of the Sun's limb could be readily kept in the middle of the field, without neglecting, every 4" or 5", to cast my eye on all other parts of the limb on both sides, where there was any possibility of the contact to happen.

Within half a minute of the time calculated for the 1st contact by Mr. Rittenhouse, I spoke to the counters at the windows to be very attentive to those who were to give them the signals from the Telescopes out of doors; and turning my eye closely to the part of the Sun's limb where Venus was expected, I had viewed it stedfastly for several seconds, without having occasion to change my field, when I was suddenly surprized with something striking into it, like a watery pointed shadow, appearing to give a tremulous motion to all that part of the limb, although the Telescope stood quite firm, and not the least disturbance or undulation were perceptible about any other part.

The idea I had formed of the contact was, That Venus would instantaneously make a well-defined black and small impression or dent on the Sun. But this appearance was so different, the disturbance on the limb so ill-defined, undulatory, pointed, waterish, and occupying a larger space than I expected, that I was held in a suspense of 5" or 6" to examine whether it might not be some skirt of a watery flying cloud.

Perceiving this shadow (atmosphere, or whatever else it was) to press still forward on the limb, with the same tremulous pointed appearance, the longest points towards the middle, I began to count the beats of the clock for either 15" or 16", when a well-defined black dent, apparently occupying a less space on the Sun's limb, became distinctly visible. I then quitted the Telescope and turning to the clock, noted the time it then showed, which was 2ʰ. 12' 5".

About 22" sooner than this (viz. the 16" I counted, and the 5" or 6" in which I remained in doubt at the beginning) was the first visible impression on the limb which my Telescope would shew; and I also marked that time down; viz., 2ʰ. 11' 40" to 43". If this first impression is to be taken for the external contact, I think it may be judged of almost to a single second by persons having equally good eyes and Telescopes; which cannot be done, as I apprehend, to several seconds, either with respect to the internal contact, or even with respect to the moment of the first distinct black dent, commonly marked for the external contact. In both these, some differences may well happen among the best observers, from their different manner of judging, in respect to a circumstance of such exquisite nicety.

Whether a Telescope of larger powers than what I made use of, might not have sooner shewn this first shadowy impression (that preceded the distinct black contact) I will not take upon me to determine; though, from the time given by Mr. Rittenhouse, I think it would. But this I can be sure of, that I saw the first stroke of it perceptible through my Telescope, having that part of the Sun's limb in full and steady view; and I might have noted the time to a single second, if I had expected it in that way.

As to the internal contact, the thread or crescent of light, coming round from both sides of the Sun's limb, did not close instantaneously about the dark body of the planet, but with an uncertainty of several seconds; the points of the threads darting backwards and forwards into each other, in a quivering manner, for some space of time, before they finally adhered. The instant of this adhesion I determined to wait for, with all the attention in my power, and to note it down for the internal contact; which I did, at 2^h. $29'$ $5''$ by the clock; a few seconds later than Mr. Lukens, who judged in the same way. And even then, though the points of the thread of light seemed to close, yet the light itself did not appear perfect on that part of the limb till about $12''$ afterwards; and I apprehend that a person who had waited for the perfection of this small thread of light, would have given the contact that number of seconds later than I did, although I was later than the others.

After the first contact, having quitted the Telescope to note down my time, the gentlemen who counted for us, and several others now in the observatory, were impatient to see Venus before she had wholly entered on the Sun; an indulgence not to be denied them, as the Reflector was most convenient for them. For this reason I did not sit down to it again till within $5'$ or $6'$ of the internal contact, and consequently saw none of those curious appearances on that part of the planet off the Sun, mentioned by my associates. But their account may be fully depended on, as both of them are well accustomed to celestial observations, and are accurate in judgment as well as sight. The small differences in the times of our contacts, it is presumed, may be easily reconciled, from the different powers of our Telescopes, and other circumstances mentioned in the manner of judging. At any rate, we have set them down faithfully.

As to the first disturbance in the Sun's limb, it may be worthy of consideration, whether it was really from the interposition of the limb of Venus, or of her atmosphere. One cannot easily imagine it to be the former without supposing her limb and body much more ragged and uneven than they appear when seen on the Sun. An atmosphere is a much more probable supposition, not only from the faint and waterish color at first, but the undulatory motion above mentioned, which might arise from the growing density of the atmosphere, pushing forward on the Sun, and varying the refraction of his rays, as they pass in succession through it.

If such an atmosphere be granted, it will probably account for the tremulous motion in the thread of light creeping round Venus at the internal contact; which may be thus prevented from closing and adhering quietly till this atmosphere (or at least its densest part) has entered wholly on the Sun, and consequently the coincidence of the limbs be past. For, though the atmosphere of Venus (as far as we could possibly judge) be not visible on the Sun; yet that part of it which is surrounding, or just entering, his limb, may be visible; having, if I may so express it, a darker ground behind it.

But these are only hasty conjectures, submitted to others; although, if they have any foundation, it would make some difference in the time estimated between the contacts. And, therefore, those astronomers who may happen to be in the world at another transit, will perhaps think it best to fix on some general mode of pronouncing with respect to the contacts; either by neglecting this atmosphere altogether, or taking their time from the appearance and disappearance of its effects on the Sun's limb. In either case, it is presumed the times of different observers having nearly the same altitude of the Sun, and equal advantages of weather and instruments, would not differ so much as has been the case hitherto, even among eminent astronomers at the same place.

When Venus was fully entered on the Sun's limb, and we had compared the different papers on which our contacts were written down, and entered them in our book, we prepared for the Micrometer and other observations.

Of the Micrometer measures, the 2d, 5th, and 18th distance of the nearest limbs of the Sun and Venus; the 1st in a chord parallel to the equator, the 1st and 6th of the diameters of Venus; and the 1st and 4th of the diameters of the Sun, were taken by Mr. Rittenhouse. The 3d and 16th distance of the nearest limbs, the 3d diameter of Venus, and the 2d of the Sun, were taken by Mr. Lukens. All the other Micrometer measures were taken by myself, while Mr. Rittenhouse applied himself to take the appulses of the limbs of the Sun and center of Venus to the cross hairs of his equal altitude instrument, Mr. Lukens writing down the observations and their exact time.

The Micrometer measures were all separately reduced to their value in minutes and seconds by Mr. Rittenhouse, and by myself, making the proper allowance for the error of adjustment of the instrument. Many more Micrometer measures might have been taken ; but had we made the intervals between them much shorter than 8 or 10 minutes, they would have been of little use in the projection, and would have crowded it too much. Nor could we have bestowed the same care in setting the instrument, reading off the vernier, etc., if a much larger number had been taken.

In order to judge of the error of the Micrometer (if any) Jupiter's diameter was not only taken with it both ways, viz. : to the right and to the left, but Mr. Rittenhouse likewise took a *mean* to the right of 10 diameters of a white painted circle about 330 yards distant, and also a *mean* of as many to the left. This work was performed early in the morning before sunrise; when the air was free from all tremulous motion ; and the result gave an error of adjustment of 1″, 12 to be subtracted from all the Micrometer measures.

It was once intended still further to confirm the work of the following delineation, by applying the observations of the appulses of the limbs of the Sun and center of Venus, mentioned to have been taken above. But the lines necessary for this would have confused the figure ; and the Micrometer observations being found so exact, any further use of the others than to try how well they would agree, was thought to be needless, especially as the fractions of seconds in them could not be estimated, so as to come up to the accuracy of the Micrometer. For this reason, they are not set down.

We proceed to give some interesting correspondence on the subject of the Transit and of the observations on it, and on another astronomical phenomenon.

Dr. Smith to Mr. William Barton.

PHILADELPHIA, July 8th, 1769.

DEAR SIR: M^r. Jesse Lukens left my house on Tuesday evening at half an hour past 6, where he waited till I scrawled out a pretty long letter to M^r. Rittenhouse, for whom my esteem increases the more I see him ; and I long for an opportunity of doing him justice for his elegant preparations to observe the Transit, which left M^r. Lukens and me nothing to do but to sit down to our telescopes. This justice I have already in part done him, in a long letter to the proprietor (Thomas Penn, Esq.,) yesterday, and I hope M^r. Rittenhouse will not deprive us of the opportunity of doing it in a more public manner, in the account we are to draw up next week. "I did not chuse to send M^r. Rittenhouse's original projection of the Transit, as it is a Society paper, to be inserted in our minutes, but I have enclosed an exact copy.

Pray desire him to take the sun's diameter again carefully, and examine the Micrometer by it.''
        With my Compliments to M⁰. Rittenhouse and family,
                I am, in great haste, Yours, &c.,
                                        WILLIAM SMITH.
To WILLIAM BARTON, Norriton, Pennᵃ.

From Mr. Rittenhouse to Dr. Smith.

                                NORRITON, July 18th, 1769.
    DEAR SIR: The inclosed is the best account I can give of the contacts, as I observed them, and of what I saw during the interval between them. I should be glad you would contract them, and also the other papers, into a smaller compass, as I would have done myself, if I had known how. I beg you would not copy anything merely because I have written it, but leave out what you think superfluous.
        I am, with great esteem and affection,
                        Yours, &c.,
                        DAVID RITTENHOUSE.
To REV. DR. SMITH.

    On the 20th of July, 1769, Dr. Smith, by direction, and in behalf, of his Committee—the Committee, I mean, which were to observe at Norriton—communicated to the Philosophical Society an account of the Transit, as observed at the place just named. It is thus:
                                PHILADELPHIA, July 19th, 1769.
    GENTLEMEN: Among the various public-spirited designs that have engaged the attention of this Society since its first institution, none does them more honor than their early resolution to appoint committees, of their own members, to take as many observations, in different places, of that rare phenomenon, the Transit of Venus over the sun's disc, as they had any probability of being able to defray the expense of, either from their own funds or the public assistance they expected.
    As the members of the Norriton Committee live at some distance from each other, I am, therefore, at their request, now to digest and lay before you in one view the whole of our observations in that place, distinguishing, however, the part of each observer, and going back to the first preparations. For I am persuaded that the dependence which the learned world may place on any particular Transit account will be in proportion to the previous and subsequent care, which is found to have been taken in a series of accurate and well-conducted observations, for ascertaining the *going* of the time-pieces, and fixing the latitude and longitude of the places of observation, &c.
    And I am the more desirous to be particular in these points, in order to do justice to Mr. Rittenhouse, one of our Committee, to whose

extraordinary skill and diligence is owing whatever advantage may be derived in these respects to our observation of the Transit itself. It is further presumed that astronomers, in distant countries, will be desirous to have not only the work and results belonging to each particular Transit Observation, but the materials also, that they may examine and conclude for themselves. And this may be more particularly requisite in a new observatory, such as Norriton, the name of which hath perhaps never before been heard of by distant astronomers; and therefore, its latitude and longitude are to be once fixed, from principles that may be satisfactory on the present as well as on any future occasion.

Our great discouragement, at our first appointment, was the want of proper apparatus, especially good Telescopes, with Micrometers. The generosity of our Provincial Assembly soon removed a great part of this discouragement, not only by their vote to purchase one of the best Reflecting Telescopes, with a Dollond's Micrometer, but likewise by their subsequent donation of £100, for erecting observatories, and defraying other incidental expenses. It was foreseen that on the arrival of this telescope, added to such private ones as might be procured in the city, together with fitting up the instruments belonging to the Honorable the Proprietaries of the Province, viz.: the equal Altitude and Transit instrument, and the large astronomical Sector, nothing would be wanting for the City Observatory in the State-House Square but a good time-piece, which was easily to be procured.

We remained however still at a loss how to furnish the Norriton Observatory. But even this difficulty gradually vanished. Early in September, 1768, soon after the nomination of our Committees, I received a letter from that worthy and honorable gentleman, Thomas Penn, Esq., one of the Proprietaries of this Province, which he wrote at the desire of the Rev. Mr. Maskelyne, Astronomer Royal, expressing their desire, "That we would exert ourselves in observing the Transit, for which our situation would be so favorable;" and enclosing some copies of Mr. Maskelyne's printed directions for that purpose.

This gave me an opportunity, which I immediately embraced, of acquainting Mr. Penn what preparations we had already made, and what encouragement the Assembly had given in voting £100 Sterling for the purchase of one Reflecting Telescope and Micrometer, for the City Observatory; but that we should be at a great loss for a telescope of the like construction for the Norriton Observatory, and requesting him to order a reflector of two, or two and a half feet, with Dollond's Micrometer, to be got ready as soon as possible in London. It was not long before I had the pleasure to hear that Mr. Penn had ordered such a telescope, which came to hand about the middle of May, with a most obliging letter, expressing the satisfaction he had in hearing of the spirit shown at Philadelphia for observing this curious phenomenon when it should happen; and concluding as follows:

I have sent, by Captain Sparks, a Reflecting Telescope, with Dollond's Micrometer, exact to your request, which I hope will come safe to hand. After making your observation with it, I desire you will present it, in my name, to the College—Messrs. Mason and Dixon tell me they never used a better than that which I formerly sent to the Library Company of Philadelphia, with which a good observation may be made, though it has no micrometer.

After giving all the calculations,* Dr. Smith thus concludes :

Thus, gentlemen, you have a faithful account of our whole work, which we could have wished to have reduced to less compass. Had our latitude and longitude been previously fixed, as they had been at Philadelphia by able mathematicians, a great part of our work might have been saved. But we thought it necessary (as hath been before hinted) to show that such pains were taken in these material articles that they may be depended on. And as we were happily favored at the transit with advantages of weather and other circumstances, which cannot have happened to the generality of observers in many parts of the world, it was thought we should be more readily excused by men of science for the insertion of things that might be superfluous, than the omission of the least article material in the account of a phenomenon that will never be observed again by any of the present generation of men.

I am,
Gentlemen, with great respect,
Your most obedient humble servant,
WILLIAM SMITH.

P. S.—As it is hoped that not only this Province in general, but likewise the Society who set on foot, and the honorable House of Assembly, who so liberally encouraged the design for observing the transit here, may derive some credit from the laudable spirit shown on that occasion, I shall add an extract of a letter from the Rev. Mr. Maskelyne, the Astronomer Royal, to show how well our labors have been received at home.

"At home"—We still and long after, so spoke of England. The extract just above referred to and addressed to Dr. Franklin, who, as we have said, was at this time in London as our Provincial Agent, was as follows:

GREENWICH, December 11, 1769.

Mr. Maskelyne presents his compliments to Dr. Franklin, and shall be obliged to him when he writes to Philadelphia for enquiring of Mr. Owen Biddle what is the bearing and what the absolute distance of Lewestown from the Stone on Fenwick's Isle in English miles ; or else what is the difference of latitude and departure in English miles ? He may also, if he pleases, acquaint Mr. Biddle that the latitude of the

---

* See them in the First Volume of the "Transactions of the Philosophical Society."

Middle Point between Fenwick's Isle and Chesapeake Bay, as found by Messrs. Mason and Dixon, is 38°, 27′, 34″; and the length of a degree of latitude, as measured by them, is 68,886 statute miles.

Mr. Maskelyne would also recommend it to Dr. Smith, and the other Norriton observers, to settle the bearing and distance in English miles between Norriton and the southernmost point of the city of Philadelphia, or else the State House square; as this will still further confirm the situation of the Norriton Observatory, by connecting it with Messrs. Mason and Dixon's Meridian line.

Mr. Maskelyne hopes the Pennsylvania observers will be so kind as to send us their observations of the transit of Mercury, which happened November 9th, if they were fortunate enough to see it; and any other observations they have made, which have not yet been sent here, tending to establish the difference of longitudes.

From Mr. Rittenhouse to Mr. William Barton.

(EXTRACT.)

NORRITON, July 26th, 1769.

I have done with astronomical observations and calculations for the present, and have sent copies of all my papers to Dr. Smith, who, I presume, has drawn up a complete account of our observations on the transit of Venus. This I hope you will see when you come to Philadelphia. I have delineated the transit, according to our observations, on a very large scale, made many calculations, and drawn all the conclusions I thought proper to attempt until some foreign observations came to hand to compare with ours; all of which have been or will be laid before the Philosophical Society. The Doctor has constantly seemed so desirous of doing me justice in the whole affair, that I suppose I must not think of transmitting any separate account to England.

At a meeting of the Philosophical Society, on the 18th of May, 1770, the following letter from the Rev. Nevil Maskelyne, B. D., F. R. S., Astronomer Royal, to Dr. Smith, acknowledging the receipt of the Norriton observations, and giving some account of the Hudson's Bay and other Northern observations of the same, was read:

GREENWICH, Dec. 26, 1769.

REV. SIR: I return you many thanks for the account of the valuable observations of the late transit of Venus, made at Norriton by yourself and two other gentlemen, which I have communicated to the Royal Society. It is ordered to be printed in the volume of their transactions for this year, and I will take care to see that it is printed correctly.

I sent to the Honorable Mr. Penn, a good while ago, my observations of the eclipses of Jupiter's first satellite made this year, desiring that he would communicate them to you, and I hope you have received them.*

Your measures of the nearest distances of the limbs of the Sun and Venus determine very well the nearest approach of Venus to the Sun's center, which was a very important observation, and could not be made here. If the appulses of the limbs of the Sun and Venus's center to the hairs of the equal altitude instrument should arrive in time, I will take care that they be inserted in the place left for them.

I see Mr. Rittenhouse, in making his projection, assumed 8″,65 for the Sun's horizontal parallax at the mean distance ; but, by the observations of the transit in 1761, Mr. Short and myself both found that to be the parallax on the day of the transit ; whence the Sun's mean horizontal parallax should be 8″,84. But what it will be as resulting from the observations of the late transit, cannot be known without a number of laborious calculations, which I have undertaken.

I could wish that difference of meridians of Norriton and Philadelphia, could be determined by some measures and bearings, within one-fiftieth or one-hundredth part of the whole ; in order to connect your observations with those made at Philadelphia and the Capes of Delaware, as also to connect your observations of the longitude of Norriton with those made by Messrs. Mason and Dixon, in the course of measuring the degree of latitude. I hope to be favored with an account of your observations of the late transit of Mercury, if you made any, and of the late eclipse of the moon. I shall be obliged to you for the continuance of your correspondence, and am, Sir, yours, &c.,

NEVIL MASKELYNE.

To REV. DR. SMITH.

William Alexander (Lord Stirling)† to Dr. Smith.

BASKENRIDGE, June 29th, 1770.

DEAR SIR : You have reason to think me negligent in not communicating (according to my promises to you) my Observations of the last Transit of Venus. I now send them, and you should have had them before, but I have been so much engaged in business the last twelve months, that I have had but little time to think of any thing else.

Last night, about ten o'clock, I discovered a New Star, about 78° distant from the pole. It would pass the meridian, I imagine, about

---

* " Here followed the observations." See " Transactions of the American Philosophical Society," Vol. I.

† William Alexander, son of James Alexander, a native of Scotland, who had taken part with the Pretender, and had come to America in 1716, was born in the city of New York in 1726. His father was quite a noted man in the Colonies, being Secretary of New York, Surveyor of New York and New Jersey, a lawyer, a man of science, and, with others, a founder of the American Philosophical Society. The father was presumptive heir to the Earldom of Stirling when he quitted Scotland. The son claimed the title, but did not succeed, although perhaps entitled to it.

midnight, and a little before Lyra. Its appearance was larger than a Star of the first magnitude, of a dull light, with a bright speck or nucleus, in the center. I take it to be a Comet, and that its tail is from us. But whether it be a Comet or not, will be determined in a few days; for as it changes its place, and the Earth moves on in its orbit, the position of the tail, with regard to the Earth, must be altered, and will then appear to encrease in length.

June 30th. Last night I again observed the new discovered Star. Its appearance was much as it was the night before, but I think rather larger. Its situation was about 70° from the pole, and it passed the meridian with Lyra almost half after eleven. I think I have its place so well marked, that in two or three evenings I shall be able to determine its course. What further observations I make before I have an opportunity of sending this, I will add hereto.

July 1st. The New Star, which, I no longer doubt, is a Comet, on his way to the Sun, passed the meridian last night about twelve o'clock, and nearly half an hour after Lyra, and was advanced to within 48° of the pole, being a little to the Northward of our Zenith. It seemed to me to be encreased in size, the shape rather more oval than circular, the nucleus no longer in the center, but advanced towards the northern part of the whole appearance.

July 2d. Last night at twelve o'clock, the Comet was nearly East from the pole Star, and about 8° distant from the pole.

July 4th. The night before last, being cloudy, the Comet was not visible; and last night (July 3d) although the sky was clear, the Stars bright, and myself on the watch for it till day light began to appear in the East, I could not discover any appearance of the Comet. It must now be gone to the region of light, and we shall not see it more until its return from the Sun.

The apparent velocity of this Comet, for the last three days of its appearance, has been prodigiously great, which, together with its apparent size, induces me to think that its real size is but small; and that its path lay at no very great distance from the Earth. But these matters may be better determined, if we have an opportunity of seeing the Comet again, in its return from the Sun.

I am, Dear Sir,
Your most humble Servant,
STIRLING.

On July 23d, 1770, at a meeting of the Philosophical Society, Owen Biddle, Esq., in his account to the Society, gave the following letter received by him from Dr. Smith. He says that it gives him "pleasure to find so little difference between the result of Charles Mason and Jeremiah Dixon's measurement and our own."

PHILAD., 23d July, 1770.

DEAR SIR: Since you finished your measurement from Newcastle Court-house to the Philadelphia Observatory in the State-house Square, the 58th vol. of Philos. Transactions has come to hand, containing the whole work of Messrs. Mason and Dixon in measuring a degree of latitude; and it is with great pleasure I find, that the longitude of the middle point of the peninsula (and consequently of your Observatory at Lewes) in respect to Philadelphia, will come out almost entirely the same from their work as from yours, altho' obtained by different* routs.

Longitude of the Middle Point, and of the Lewes Observatory West of the Philadelphia Observatory, agreeable to the Lines of Messrs. Mason and Dixon.

	Miles.	Chains.	Lin.
Observatory in the Forks of Brandywine West of the South point of the city of Philadelphia..................	31.	00.	00
Middle point of Peninsula East of Observatory in the Forks	2.	5.	49
The diff. gives the middle point of Penins. W. of S. point of Philad..	28.	74.	51
But S. point of Philad. is E. of Observatory in State-house Square..	0.	28.	75
The difference gives the *middle point* of Peninsula West of State-house Observatory...........................	28.	45.	76
But by your work the middle point is West of the Lewes Observatory 9286,3 perches.....................	29.	1.	57
The difference gives Lewes Observatory East of the State-house Observatory, from Mason and Dixon's Lines...	0.	35.	81
But by your measure to Newcastle the Lewes Obs. was East of the State-house Observatory 62,6 perches......	0.	15.	65
So that Mason and Dixon's lines give your Observatory more East that your own work, only...................	0.	20.	16

Thus, by their work, we get your Observatory not quite 2″, and by your own not quite 1″ East of the Observatory in the State-house Square.

---

* The result by Mr. Biddle's book is got, by going from the State-house Observatory to New-Castle Court-House, agreeable to his measurement; thence by the 12 m. radius and tangent line to the middle point. The result by Messrs. Mason and Dixon's work is got, by beginning at the south point of the city of Philadelphia (or the place of their Observatory,) on the north side of Cedar Street, between Front-Street and Delaware; thence to their Observatory in the Forks of Brandywine, which is 31 miles West, and 10″, 5 South of the southernmost point of the city; thence by the other lines of latitude and departure, wherewith they connect the Observatory in the Forks of Brandywine, with the middle point of the Peninsula. See their work in the volume of Transactions, quoted above.

Wherefore 1″ being taken as a mean, and applied to 5ʰ. 0′. 55″, the longitude of the State-house Observatory West of Greenwich; the longitude of the Lewes Observatory may be well depended on as stated from your own work, to be in time West of Greenwich   5ʰ. 0′. 34″

As British mariners generally take their departure from the land's end of England, and as by Mr. Bradley's observation of the late Transit of Venus the long. of the Lizard Point is now determined to be 5°. 15′ W. of Greenwich, if that be subtracted from 75°. 5′. 13″, 2, it will give:

The longitude of the Provincial Light-house near the $\Big\}$ 69°. 50′. 13″, 2
Capes West of Lizard Point.......................... $\Big\}$

If you think the above can be of any use, you may add it to the end of your account. I think there is no mistake in bringing out the different results; but if I can find leisure I will re-examine the work before the sheet is struck off.   I am, with great regard, yours, &c.

                                                              WILLIAM SMITH.

To MR. OWEN BIDDLE.

David Rittenhouse to Dr. Smith.

(EXTRACT.)

NORRITON, July 24ᵗʰ, 1770.

REVᴰ SIR: Herewith I send you the fruit of three or four days labour, during which I have covered many sheets, and literally drained my inkstand several times. It is an account, &c., of the Comet, which lately appeared, and I have no objection to its being made public. I might indeed have been a little more careful to have the precise time of my observations, as the near approach of this Comet required ten times the accuracy, that is necessary for computing the place of any planet. I am, however, quite satisfied that the situation I have given its orbit will be found very near the truth.

The circumstances most remarkable in this Comet were, its prodigious apparent velocity, the smallness of its size, and the shortness of the time it continued visible. Its velocity was at first surprisingly accelerated, and before it disappeared again retarded, from which its near approach to the earth may be inferred.

I did not see it till Monday the 25th of June; and, from its situation at that time, I expected it would have been visible for many weeks, if not months; and therefore did not prepare, with such expedition as I might have done, for observing its place with accuracy. But from the 27th to the 30th, the weather continuing fair, every evening about nine, I took the distance of the Comet from *Lucida Lyræ* and *Lucida Aquilæ*, with a common Hadley's Quadrant.

July the 1st, it was cloudy in the evening. At 10, however, I saw both *Lucida Lyræ* and the Comet through the clouds, and observed their distance; but the Comet was again hid before I could take its dis-

tance from the Pole star, which seemed to be about 5 or 6 degrees.
This evening it was distant from *Lucida Lyræ* 49° 17', whereas the
evening before it had been but 5° 42' from the same star at 9*h*. It had
therefore moved above 45° in the last 25 hours, and now appeared
much brighter than it had been before; there being also some appearance of a tail on the side opposite to the Sun. July the 2d it was cloudy
with rain in the evening; but in the morning of the 3d about 3*h*. I
observed its distance from the Pole star, from *Capella*, and from a star
of the second magnitude in *Cassiopeia*, which was the last time I saw
it.*   Ever yours,

                                        DAVID RITTENHOUSE.

On the 17th of August, 1770, Dr. Smith communicated to the
Philosophical Society the following account of the Terrestrial Meas-
urement of the difference of Longitude and Latitude between the
Observatories of Norriton and Philadelphia:

                              PHILADELPHIA, August 17th, 1770.

GENTLEMEN: Agreeable to the appointment you made (at the request
of the Astronomer Royal) Mr. Lukens, Mr. Rittenhouse and myself,
furnished with proper instruments, met at Norriton early on Monday,
July 2d, for the above service ; and took to our assistance two able and
experienced Surveyors, viz. : Mr. Archibald M'Clean and Mr. Jesse
Lukens. The first thing we did was accurately to ascertain the variation
of our Compass, which we found 3° 8', by Mr. Rittenhouse's Meridian
Line. We then carefully measured our chain, and adjusted it to the
exact standard of 66 feet. In the execution of the work, whenever the
instrument was duly set, each course was taken off, and entered down
separately, by three different persons, who likewise kept separate accounts
of all the distances, and superintended the stretching of every chain,
and the levelling and plumbing it, whenever there was any ascent or
descent in the road.

   July 4th. We finished the survey; and Mr. M'Clean, Mr. Jesse Lukens and myself, then agreed to bring out the difference of latitude and
departure separately on each course and distance to four or five decimal
places ; and there was so great an agreement in this part of the work,
when executed, that we had all the same results to a few links, and the
whole was at last brought to agree in every figure, by comparing the
few places where there was any difference, which scarce ever went farther
than the last decimal place. Mr. M'Clean and Mr. Lukens took the
trouble to bring out their work by multiplying each distance by the
natural Sine of the Course, to the Radius Unity, for the departure ; and

---

* Here follow the calculations, &c., which will be found in the 1st volume of the
transactions of the Philosophical Society.

by the Cosine for the latitude. Mine was done by Robertson's Tables. The whole follows, and we think it may be depended on for correctness.*

In bringing out the 52″ of time diff. of long. a degree of the equator was taken in proportion to Messrs. Mason and Dixon's deg. of the merid. in lat. 39″, 12, in the ratio of 60 to 59,7866 (agreeable to Mr. Simpson's table), which gave 365070 for a degree of the equator. By taking a degree of longitude as fixed at the middle point by Mr. Maskelyne in lat. 38° 27′ 35″, and saying as the cosine of that lat. is to cosine of mean latitude between Philadelphia and Norriton, so is the length of a degree of long. at the middle point (viz. 284869,5 feet) to the length of a deg. in mean lat. between Norriton and Philadelphia, the result was got 52″ 13; being only Thirteen hundredth parts of a second of time more.

The above account of the work was thought proper, that those who will take the trouble may examine and correct it, if in any part necessary.   WILLIAM SMITH.

Dr. Smith and others to the Philosophical Society.

To the American Philosophical Society, held at Philadelphia, for promoting useful knowledge.

November 16th, 1770.

GENTLEMEN: Agreeable to the order of the last Meeting, we have collected into one general and short view (from the last, or 59th volume of the Philosophical Transactions) the following Account of the different Observations of the late Transit of Venus made in Europe and other distant places; containing the Apparent Times of the contacts; the latitude and longitude of the places of observation, so far as known to us, with such other circumstances, as we judged proper for answering the end you had in view; namely the affording materials to persons of a curious and mathematical turn, who might be desirous of inquiring what Parallax of the Sun, may be deduced from a comparison of these distant Observations, with those made in this Province, by your appointment.   We are, &c.

WILLIAM SMITH,	HUGH WILLIAMSON,
JOHN EWING,	THOMAS COMBE,
OWEN BIDDLE,	D. RITTENHOUSE.

David Rittenhouse to Dr. Smith.

(EXTRACT.)

NORRITON, December 2d, 1770.

DEAR SIR: I was much pleased with a paragraph in the Gentleman's Magazine for *July*, 1770, by which it appears, that M. Messier discov-

---

* Here follow the calculations.

ered the last Comet in France 10 or 12 days sooner than we did here; because it affords another opportunity of comparing this Comet's motion with my theory.

According to M. Messier's observation, on the night between the 15th and 16th of June, the Comet's right ascension was 272° 57′ 37″ with 15° 55′ 24″ South declination. The hour of the night is not mentioned, but the place of the Comet was no doubt determined by its passing the meridian, which he says was about midnight, that is at Philadelphia June 15th, 7*h*.

It is remarkable of this Comet, that in any future returns, whilst it continues to move in the same orbit, it can never approach the earth nigher than it did this time. On the first of July, it was about one sixtieth part of the Sun's distance from us.

Ever yours,

DAVID RITTENHOUSE.

Dr. Smith to David Rittenhouse.

DEAR SIR: Though we were not lucky enough in America to discover the late Comet in its ascent from the Sun, yet I have the pleasure to acquaint you, that it was seen in England. I find, in the Gentleman's Magazine for *August*, that Mr. Six says, he had the unexpected pleasure (to you it would not have been unexpected) of seeing the Comet on its ascent from the sun towards its aphelion, and tho' not visible to the naked eye, yet with a Telescope magnifying 25 times, it appeared much like the Nebula in *Andromeda's* Girdle. Aug. 22d, half past two, *mane*, it had 106° 20′ right ascension, and 21° N. declin. The two succeeding days its longitude increased daily 1° 15′, but its latitude both days not more than 5′. Its apparent motion, he says, was nearly parallel to the ecliptic. If these subsequent observations agree as well, as Mr. Messier's previous observations, with your theory of this Comet, I think it will thereby be established past doubt.

I am yours, &c.

WILLIAM SMITH.

David Rittenhouse to Dr. Smith.

(EXTRACT.)

NORRITON, Dec. 26th, 1770.

REV^D SIR: I was favoured with your extract from the Gentleman's Magazine, for August, by which I find Mr. Six was lucky enough to discover the comet with his Telescope, after it had past its perihelion, though it was not visible to the naked eye. I have computed the comet's place to August 22^d, half-past two in the morning, and make its right ascension 108° 46′, with 21° 0′ north declination; agreeing with Mr. Six's observation entirely on declination; but differing from it about 2° in right ascension, which I cannot think material, unless I knew what method he took to determine the right ascension of a heavenly body, in our meridian.

Ever Yours,

DAVID RITTENHOUSE.

One would naturally suppose that such high topics as we have just shown that Dr. Smith much devoted himself to—taken in connexion with establishing a Corporation for the Relief of the Widows and Children of his clerical brethren; with the affairs of a college, the whole crowned by a sort of Episcopal supervision of the ecclesiastical affairs of the Province—were enough to engage his various powers, however various they were. He was not, however, himself of that opinion.

On the 2d of February, 1770, a letter was read before the Philosophical Society, from the Rev. Jonathan Odell, the well-known Rector of St. Mary's Church, Burlington, and for some time a Secretary of the Society, the purpose of which was to show the practicalness of making silk in America. A Society for the encouragement of the matter was formed; and Dr. Smith along with several other gentlemen elected managers. I am not able to see, however, that he, himself, ever deemed the thing very practicable. Nevertheless, he subscribed £3 to the enterprise; as much, perhaps, as an act of friendship to his reverend brother, Mr. Odell, for whom he entertained much esteem, as from any prospects of a gainful return. The Silk Society expired with the approaching war, and in 1782, the Philosophical Society succeeded to its properties and moneys, upon a pledge to re-deliver the same whenever called upon by a majority of its members.

CHAPTER XXXI.

WE now come back to matters when the reader will feel, perhaps, more at home: the College and Dr. Smith's letters on
subjects connected with the Church and the Clergy.

The College Commencement took place on the 5th of June.
Dr. Smith wrote and published *An Exercise* containing *A Dialogue
and two Odes,* there performed.   They were printed by Cruikshank
& Collins.

A more complete organization of the Medical Faculty having
been effected at the close of 1769, the session of 1769–70 may be
regarded as the commencement of greater vigor in the School.
The Faculty stood as follows:

Theory and Practice of Medicine,   JOHN MORGAN, M. D.
Anatomy, Surgery, and Midwifery,   WM. SHIPPEN, JR., M. D.
Materia Medica and Botany,   ADAM KUHN, M. D.
Chemistry,   BENJAMIN RUSH, M. D.
Clinical Medicine,   THOMAS BOND, M. D.

Additionally to the strictly medical courses, Dr. Smith delivered
lectures on Natural Philosophy to the Class.

Dr. Smith to the Secretary of the Propagation Society.

(EXTRACT.)

PHILADA., April 24th, 1770.

DEAR AND WORTHY SIR,

M^r. Ayres came in a very forward manner to solicit the Mission from
the people, but he had no encouragement from more than one or two

that I could hear of.   The Vestry will have nothing to do with him; & indeed he would not suit that place.   We thought considering his low parts and little education we did him a great favor to get him a place among some people in the Jersies who have not themselves much knowledge & whom we thought he might suit.   But he soon thought he deserved something higher & complained of his people to the last Meeting of our Clergy, but they did not approve his complaint as none of his people were present to answer; & we appointed M^r. Cook to enquire among the people and it seems they have given no cause for it, but perform their contract with M^r. Ayres to the utmost of their abilities.

With great affection and regard,

Worthy Sir, &^c.,

WILLIAM SMITH.

The Bishop of Oxford (Lowth) to Dr. Smith.

ARGYLE STREET, May 15th, 1770.

REV^D SIR: I have the honor of your letter, with your excellent Sermon before the Corporation for the Relief of Clergymen's Widows and Children, for which I beg of you to accept my best Thanks.*   I hope this very good design will meet with all the success that can be wished.   I should have been glad to have seen Mr. Coombe; but was unluckily from home when your Packett was delivered, and do not know where to enquire for him.   You may be assured I shall, at all times, be extremely glad of the favour of hearing from you; and God grant that for the future the situation of affairs on both sides of the Atlantic may afford more agreeable advices than I am afraid can be furnished from either at present.   I am, with the greatest regard, Revd Sir,

Your most Obedient and Humble Servant,

R. OXFORD.

We have now a letter of peculiar interest.†   It is one given by Dr. Peters, Dr. Smith and Mr. Duché, to the Bishop of London, recommending for orders two young gentlemen, the education of both of whom Dr. Smith had superintended.   One of them was Mr. William White, afterwards so eminent in the Church.

PHIL^A, September 24th, 1770.

MAY IT PLEASE YOUR LORDSHIP:

We return you our sincere Thanks for the kind regard your Lordship has always shown toward Persons recommended to you for Holy Orders. We hope we shall never write in favor of any but such as upon a

---

* See an extract from the Sermon, *supra*, p. 429–431.

† From the original draft in the MS. of Dr. Peters, in the possession of the Historical Society of Pennsylvania.

thorough examination will be found to be well qualified. It is upon this principle that we now beg Leave to introduce to your Lordship Mr. William White and Mr. Thomas Hopkinson, two young gentlemen who have gone through their studies in our College with Diligence and Applause, and in consequence have obtained the Degrees of Bachelor and Master of Arts. From their earliest years they have been under Religious Impressions. These have directed their studies, and we hope, as they have heretofore preserved unblemished Characters, they will, when admitted to the Profession they have so anxiously desired, they will prove usefull to Religion and be ornaments of the Church of England, with whose Doctrine and Discipline they are well acquainted, and which we trust they will be good Servants.

Your Lordship may remember that the names of these two young gentlemen were among those whom Dr. Smith mentioned to you some time since as then preparing themselves for the ministry. As they are not yet of sufficient age for Priests' orders, they are desirous of obtaining Deacons' orders, as soon as your Lordship may think convenient; and we do assure your Lordship that they cannot fail from their connections and the Esteem they have justly acquired of being provided for immediately upon their return to America in full orders.

We are now setting off to New York to the annual meeting of the Corporation for the Relief of the Widows and Children of Deceased Clergymen, where your Lordship's letter will be read and an answer returned. Your Lordship's present of Twenty Guineas to this fund has been long since paid to the Treasurer, and his receipt will be sent with the letter.   We are, &c.,

> RICHARD PETERS,
> WILLIAM SMITH,
> JACOB DUCHÉ.

Dr. Smith to the Secretary of the Propagation Society.

(EXTRACT.)

PHILADᴬ, 15ᵗʰ Octʳ, 1770.

REVᴰ AND WORTHY SIR:

The great bane of the Oxford Mission & the cause of the divisions I found among them was a lottery erected in Mʳ. Neill's time, which, instead of some hundred pounds which it ought to have cleared, never cleared thirty pounds that I can find any account of, & that part of the Congregation which were not in the management of the lottery accused the others of mismanagement, which laid the foundation of quarrels scarcely yet healed up, tho' I have endeavored to bring them to forget the Lottery & all that is past, as if it had never been.

Since Easter last the Congregation has been happy and flourishing, and I think will continue so. Its peace had been chiefly disturbed by one * * * * * *, a sort of Practitioner in Physic, who was bred an anabaptist, & who being turned out of that Society for seizing the elements at the sacrament by force, when the Minister had refused to admit him to the Communion, on account of some misconduct, he then turned to the Church, & was received by M^r. Neill, and came at last to be Churchwarden & wanted to govern everything in the same arbitrary way as he had attempted among the Baptists. For a year or two I kept him in the Oxford Vestry, hoping to reconcile all sides; but finding it could not be done, I let the people take their way last Easter & they turned him wholly out of all power, and then he left the Church, for which we have cause to rejoice, since they are now a *happy* and united people, & increasing in numbers daily, nor do I ever wish to see him in any office in that Church again while I have any care of it. I am told he and some of his family now join a strolling follower of Wesley's.

Thus I have given you the true and genuine state of the Oxford Church & the difficulties I had in it, which you will see are of such a nature that they are only fit to be mentioned in private, & are not for public view, lest they should widen those differences which I have been striving to close, & which, I thank God, I think I can now say are in a manner wholly closed.   *   *   *

I am, Rev^d and worthy Sir, &c.,

WM. SMITH.

Dr. Smith to the Secretary of the Propagation Society.

(EXTRACT.)

PHILAD^A, 14 Jan^y, 1771.

REV^D & WORTHY SIR:

    *   *   *   M^r. Griffith, who was appointed for Gloster Mission, New Jersey, has deserted it after staying about a month with them. He consulted none of us in this hasty step, but took his leave of the people last Sunday but one. D^r. Peters, M^r. Duché and myself endeavoured to persuade him to stay and wait the Society's pleasure for a removal. But he insisted on returning to New York, saying he only accepted of Gloster Mission by way of title to get ordained by, but not to stay with them. He complained that the People would do nothing for him, but in this he does them great injustice. They had subscribed £48 Pennsylvania money, about £30 Ster. They offered to give Bond for the payment of it, and also to hire a house and small Glebe. This was not only as much as they promised M^r. Griffith before he went to England, but likewise as much as they are really able to give, & more than is given by any Mission in this Province except one or two. It is true the Waterford Congregation did this without the Town of Gloster, as in the latter there never were more than 5 or 6 Church families, so that M^r. Griffith may have to say that one of his congregations would do nothing. The truth is, he did not stay to try whether they would do anything, and I have reason to think that the cause of his not settling

there was his intending to practice Physic and his not finding that it would answer any valuable purpose in the Gloster Mission.

Most obed' and obliged humble Serv',

WILLIAM SMITH.

In the midst of his *Episcopal* offices, as we may call them, Dr. Smith was still turning to the account of the College the transit of Venus, an operation the more agreeable to him as he was bringing Mr. Rittenhouse into closer connexion with himself and with it. He had induced that gentleman, whose reputation was now established, to leave Norriton, a country village, and come into the metropolis to reside. We have letters from both Dr. Peters and Dr. Smith on this topic. Dr. Peters, on the 22d of March, 1771, thus writes to Mr. Barton:

Dr. Smith has done wonders in favour of our friend Rittenhouse. His zeal has been very active; he has got enough to pay him for a second orrery, and the Assembly has given him £300. The Doctor, in his introductory lecture, was honoured with the principal men of all denominations, who swallowed every word he said with the pleasure that attends eating the choicest viands; and in the close, when he came to mention the orrery, he over-excelled his very self. . . . Your son will acquaint you with all the particulars respecting it. The lectures are crowded by such as think they can thereby be made capable of understanding that wonderful machine; whereas, after all, their eyes only give them the truth, from the figures, and motions, and places, and magnitudes of the heavenly bodies.

Dr. Smith to Mr. Barton.

(EXTRACT.)

PHILADELPHIA, 23d March, 1771.

DEAR SIR: I have been so busy these two months past that I could not find a moment's leisure to write. A good deal of time was to be given to the public lectures, the orrery, and the getting our dear friend Rittenhouse brought into as advantageous a light as possible, on his first entrance into this town as an inhabitant, all which has succeeded to our utmost wishes; and the notice taken of him by the Province is equally to his honor and theirs. The loss of his wife has greatly disconcerted him; but we will try to keep up his spirits under it.

Yours, &c.,

WILLIAM SMITH.

Dr. Smith to the Secretary of the Propagation Society.

(EXTRACT.)

PHILAD^A, May 3, 1771.

MY DEAR SIR: I have great pleasure in going to preach among them and in Summer particularly. My Country House where my Family resides is nearer Oxford Church than to Philadelphia, being about 2 miles from where M^r. Neill, the last Missionary, resided. The Congregation increases much since we got rid of one or two quarrelsome people. All the Swedish Families that are in that Neighborhood and were formerly a separate Congregation under the Swedish Missionaries, have joined Oxford Church and many of them are Communicants. We are this Summer about erecting a New Church about 5 miles from Oxford Church * for the better accommodating part of the Mission, & after preaching in the forenoon at Oxford, I go once a month in the afternoon to that place, and the Swedish Missionary from Philadelphia also goes once a month.

The people seem more desirous than ever of my continuance to officiate among them, & as it is at present a pleasure to me independent of some benefit it is of to my large family, I must rely on your goodness that there be no alteration made without the concurrence of the people & myself, a request which, from my long services to the Church in America, I hope the Society will think me entitled to make. Some of the people had heard that M^r. Thomas Hopkinson, one of the young Gentlemen I recommended to you in my last, and distantly related to the Bishop of Worcester, would apply for it, & there are several considerations that would make him very unfit for it, tho' he is a very valuable young man & only unhappy in his hesitation and manner of Speech. But I am well persuaded neither he nor his Friends would be so indelicate or ungrateful to me his old Master as to apply without my privity or knowledge for anything possessed by me; nor would the Society serve the meanest person in their service in that way, who did his duty with reputation and fidelity as I have done to that people amid all my other engagements.

I have written to the B^p of London to be on his guard against one Aiken, who was of the Presbyterian Preachers in this City & is forced out among them on acc^t of scandalous charges against him in respect to the Woman he is now said to have married. He applied to D^r. Peters and myself to be admitted among us but we refused him. However we hear that he has got some sort of papers signed in Maryland and is about taking a passage to England, on which D^r. Peters, M^r. Duché & myself wrote to him yesterday as follows:

SIR: As we understand you are about taking a Passage to England, we think it a piece of justice to inform you that if you continue your resolution of applying for holy

---

* White Marsh.

orders in our Church we must be obliged in duty to send such objections to the Bishop of London against receiving you as we are fully persuaded will render your application fruitless.

The man has so much assurance that I believe this will not stop him ; & therefore lest the letter I have sent to the Bishop of London (which goes by another Ship with our Governor) should not come to hand so soon as this, please to communicate to the Bishop as soon as possible what I have written about this M^r. Aiken or Aitken, for I know not exactly how he spells his name.

I am, Dear and Worthy Sir, &c.,
WM. SMITH.

Dr. Smith to Mr. Barton.

PHILADELPHIA, May 13th, 1771.

DEAR SIR : I never met with greater mortification than to find M^r. Rittenhouse had, in my absence, made a sort of agreement to let his orrery go to the Jersey College.   I had constantly told him that, if the Assembly did not take it, I would take it for our College, and would have paid the full sum should I have had to beg the money.   I thought I could depend, as much as upon any thing under the sun, that after M^r. Rittenhouse knew my intentions about it, he would not have listened to any proposal for disposing of it without advising me and giving our College the first opportunity to purchase.   I am surprised that M^r. Rittenhouse thinks so little of himself, as to suffer himself to be taken off his guard on this occasion.   This province is willing to honour him as her *own ;* and, believe me, many of his friends wondered at the newspaper article ; and regretted that he should think so little of his noble invention as to consent to let it go to a village ; unless he had first found on trial that his friends in this city had not the spirit to take it ; For if he would wish to be known by *this work*—and introduced to the best business and commissions for instruments, from all parts of the Continent—his orrery being placed in our College, where so many strangers would have an opportunity of seeing it, was the sure way to be serviceable to himself.   You will think by all this that I am offended with him, and that our friendship may hereby be interrupted.   Far from it.   I went to see him the day the newspapers announced the affair.   I soon found that I had little occasion to say any thing ; he was convinced before I saw him that he had gone too far.   But still, as no time was fixed for delivering the orrery, I was glad to find he had concluded that it should not be delivered till next winter ; against which time he said he could have a *second* one made, if this one staid by him for his hands to work by.   As I love M^r. Rittenhouse, and would not give a man of such delicate feelings a moment's uneasiness, I agreed to waive the *honour* of having the first orrery, and to take the second.

Yours, &c., in haste,
WILLIAM SMITH.

To REV. THOS. BARTON.

Cadwalaaer Colden to Dr. Smith.

NEW YORK, June 6th, 1771.

SIR: I did not know that you had done me the honour of choosing me a member of your Philosophical Society, till I saw my name in your printed Transactions.

Tho' I have spent many hours of my life in Physical enquiries, I now feel so many infirmities of age, that I can have little hope of being of use.

However, to shew that I am desirous, as far as in my power, to promote the useful purposes of your society, I enclose a paper for your inspection.

If the performance deserve examination, and meet with your approbation, perhaps I may be enabled to send you some other uncommon inferences from obvious phenomena. It is of no use to know the Author's name in examining the truth of his inferences, and he likes to be concealed.   I am, with great regard, Sir,

Your most obedient humble servant,

CADWALADER COLDEN.

Dr. Smith, it would seem, succeeded after all in the matter of the orrery. On the 7th of June, 1771, he thus writes to his friend, Mr. Barton:

Your and my friend, M^r. Rittenhouse, will be with you on Saturday. The Governor says the Orrery shall not go; he would rather pay for it himself. He has ordered a meeting of the Trustees on Tuesday next; and declares it as his opinion, that we ought to have the first orrery, and not the second—even if the second should be the best.

On the formation of the American Philosophical Society, Dr. Franklin was elected its president. Dr. Smith, who at the same time was elected one of its secretaries, now sends through him, as our Provincial Agent, copies of its works to Maskelyne and other men of science abroad. Franklin acknowledges them with a note, whose concluding words, if not its general tone, would indicate that no great cordiality towards Dr. Smith had yet arrived to him. Smith had not been brought up in a printing-office, nor served an apprenticeship at bookbinding.

Dr. Benjamin Franklin to Dr. Smith.

LONDON, July 4th, 1771.

REV^D SIR: I received the box containing eleven Copies of the Transactions sent me by order of the Society, and have already delivered most of them as directed. There should be more care taken by the Binder in collating the sheets, particularly of Books sent so far. The Book for the Society of Arts had one sheet twice over, and the Duplicate was return'd to me on a supposition that it might be wanting in some other volume. This I did not find. But the Book for D^r. Fothergill wanted a sheet in the Appendix to the Astronomical Papers, from p. 33 to 40 inclusive, and the other sheet would not supply the Defect. When the other Box arrives I shall take care to deliver and dispose of the Books agreeable to the Intentions of the Society.

I am, Sir, your humble Servant,

B. FRANKLIN.

REV'D DR. SMITH,
    at Phil^a.

Dr. Smith to the Secretary of the Propagation Society.

(EXTRACT.)

PHILADELPHIA, July 6th, 1771.

REV^D AND WORTHY SIR: * * There is indeed a good prospect opening for a large addition to the Mission where we are about to build the new church. They were a people that were like to fall in with the Methodists; and I think I can say without vanity that I have been a considerable means of shewing them how much better it is to join in a regular Congregation. Yet so it is that tho' I had been thus successful in preventing the Methodist Preachers from gaining any Settlement there, yet it had been said at New York that I had admitted some of their preachers to the pulpit of Oxford Church, but this was so far from being true that I never exchanged a word with one of their preachers nor was there ever one of them within Oxford Church, nor so much as asked by any of the people of that Church, who are far from having any inclination to follow such men.

The Box with the abstracts & some Prayer Books is come to hand, and I have delivered to M^r. Thomson, the library for Trenton, & have wrote to M^r. Magaw, as you directed me, informing him of the continuance of his £10. * * *

I am, Rev^d & worthy Sir, &^c.,

W^M. SMITH.

One of the remarkable institutions of *old* Philadelphia was its HAND-IN-HAND FIRE COMPANY, "for better preserving their own and their fellow-citizens' houses, goods and effects from fire." It was formed on the 1st day of March, 1741–2. Each member bound himself to provide four leathern buckets, one bag, and one convenient basket, which said bag, marked with the member's name and that of the company, should be kept ready at hand and

30

applied to no other use "than for preserving our own and our fellow-citizens' houses, goods and effects in case of fire." The articles further provided that, upon hearing of fire breaking out, each member would immediately repair to the same with his buckets, bag and basket, and there employ his best endeavors to preserve the goods and effects of such members of the company as should be in danger. "And to prevent as much as in us lies," said the articles, "suspicious persons from coming into or carrying away goods out of such houses as may be in danger, two of our members shall constantly attend at the doors, until all the goods and effects that can be saved are packed up and carried to some safe place, to be appointed by the owner or such of our company as shall be present, where one or more of us shall attend them till they can be conveniently delivered to or secured for the owner. And upon our first hearing the cry of fire in the night time, we will immediately cause two or more lights to be set up in our windows when it shall appear necessary, and such of the company whose houses may be thought in danger shall likewise place candles in every room to prevent confusion and that their friends may be the more able to give them the more speedy and effectual assistance."

There were no fire-engines in those days. No Fairmount, no fire-plugs, no hose, no hydrants. Pumps and leathern buckets were the apparatus. On arriving at the fire the members instantly formed themselves into two lines, one end of each line communicating with the nearest pumps, and the other end of each coming to the blazing or endangered house. Relays of members pumped water into the buckets, which, filled with water, were passed *up* one line with incredible celerity to the scene of danger and being emptied on the fire, were sent down with like rapidity to be refilled. The institution was a truly benevolent institution, and none in Philadelphia or out of it ever had a membership of more distinguished men.* On the 4th of October, 1771, Dr. Smith, now

---

* Between the years 1770 and 1805 the following eminent citizens were members of this company : Andrew Hamilton, Chief Justice Chew, Dr. John Morgan, Dr. Shippen, Dr. Thomas Bond, Thomas Willing, Joseph Sims, Samuel Rhoads, Alexander Stedman, Alexander Willcocks, John Lawrence, John Swift, Joseph Stamper, John Cadwalader, Samuel Powell, Robert Hare, William Bingham, George Mead, Samuel Meredith, John Swanwick, James Biddle, Tench Coxe, James Cramond, William Cramond, William Bradford, Esq., Francis Hopkinson, James Wilson, Benjamin Rush, George Clymer, Bishop White, Rev. Dr. Peters, Rev. J. Duché, Dr. Blackwell, Dr.

aged forty-four years, and in the vigor of manhood, became a contributing member; and on all occasions where his services were
needed—and they were not unfrequent in a city where wooden
buildings were numerous—was ever active with his fellow-firemen
in the work of beneficence. With the increase of fire companies,
brought about by the introduction of fire-engines and of hose, the
"Hand-in-Hand," which was very strictly limited to forty members, became in a large degree a Gentleman's Club; a club too of
a high order. I have understood that its clerical members—
including of course Dr. Smith, who was among the oldest of them
and whose social talents were pre-eminent—were ever welcomed
guests.

In the winter of 1771 Dr. Smith went to Charleston, whose
inhabitants were distinguished alike by wealth and liberality, to
ask contributions to the College. No other letter than this one,
that I know of, tells us of his journey.

Dr. Smith to Dr. Peters.

CHARLESTOWN, SOUTH CAROLINA,
December 2d, 1771.

DEAR SIR : As I have nothing to communicate to the President and
Trustees, but my own private Disasters, I must take the Benefit of Clergy
and do it through your Hands.

We were unfortunately detained six days at Reedy Island by cross
winds. I spent all the time in looking over and copying some scraps
and fragments of Evans's Poems to send by the Pilot boat to Mr. Duché,
and in copying a sermon or two of my own to send back to my wife, &
which my vanity made me wish to save—but I only got thro' two out of
six. Rising up from this copying-work after candles were brought in
the Evening before we sailed, viz.: Thursday, Nov. 14th, I was going
forward to the ship's Bow & perceived Rev^d M^r. Hart sitting where I
intended to go. "So, Brother Hart," said I, "you have got the Lee-
side. Well, I must turn over to the windward." Then crossing the
ship backwards and talking to him, I did not perceive the fore-scuttle
was open, till I fell down it with my whole weight and received a most

John Andrews, Dr. Samuel Magaw, Dr. J. Abercrombie, Dr. Pilmore, of the Episcopal
Church; Dr. Ashbel Green, Jared Ingersoll, Dr. Phineas Bond, Drs. John and Joseph
Redman, Dr. Adam Kuhn, Major William Jackson, Colonel Lambert Cadwalader,
Chief Justice Shippen, Chief Justice Tilghman, Horace Binney, Charles Chauncey,
John B. Wallace, William Meredith, Edward Burd, Nathaniel Chapman, M. D.,
Thomas Mayne Willing, George Willing, Daniel W. Coxe, Richard Peters, Jr., Charles
Willing Hare, Joseph Hopkinson, Hartman Kuhn, Thomas Cadwalader, Thomas W.
Francis, and other eminent persons in social and professional life.

violent Blow on my left Thigh. . . . I found that next day I could walk tolerably well, tho' I could not bear to lie in Bed on that side. I entirely neglected even to rub it with a little vinegar or spirit. But to my great surprise the ninth day after my Fall, just as we made the Land off Charlestown, the Pain became intense, I fell totally Lame in the space of two Hours, and upon examining the part found it swelled up to a great Hight and my whole Thigh, inside and outside, of a deep Purple color. This was alarming, especially as the weather was so rainy that the Pilot was doubtful whether he could carry us in that day, and standing out to sea, we might be beat off for a week. Had that been the case, the Doctor tells me I might have lost my Thigh altogether. But thanks to Providence, who ordered it otherwise, I got that night (Nov. 23^d) into the Hands of my worthy Friend and Physician, Dr. Garden, and tho' I have been obliged to bear the Surgeon's Knife & to have my Thigh laid open, yet I hope in a week more to be able to go about my Business. . . . D^r. Garden has given D^r. Phineas Bond an acc^t of my situation, so I need add no more on that head.

My great fear is that my Business here may suffer by my confinement. Gentlemen have Leisure to confirm each other in a Resolution they formerly made of suffering no more of their money to the support of foreign seminaries of Learning. They have a Bill before the Council for establishing a College on a grand Footing ; the money for the Buildings to be raised by subscription chiefly, the salaries for Professors to be established by Law and raised by public Tax. The Disputes between the Governor and Assembly they say cannot subsist long, and the College-Bill will be one of the first passed. They profess to love Phil^a as a place they have the chief connexion with on this continent. Had any misfortune happened to it by Fire or water ; had the college been *burnt* or *blown* down, we should find them, they say, some of the most benevolent of neighbours, but they do not see the propriety of giving away the money to another place which they want to apply for the same Purposes among themselves. I have not been out of my room—but these are the arguments which some few of my friends have hinted to me as tenderly as they could without distressing a sick man. How to answer these arguments or make a People *give* something against their own private Resolution I scarcely as yet know, yet I flatter myself I shall not return quite empty. I never saw a more polite People nor seemingly more humane. The Families of the first note, many to whom I had no Letters, and even Ladies, not a few have kindly visited me under my confinement— I hope to get a little of their money. I am sure of receiving their most respectful notice as soon as I can get out.

Lieu^t Govr Bull has been in the country ever since my arrival till yesterday, that he came to town to bury a Sister-in-law, so he has not yet had your Letter. There is one Circumstance wch will be unfavorable, and which we did not foresee, it being the Reverse of what happens in

all other Places. The greatest part of the gentlemen spend from 1ˢᵗ of
Novʳ to about 1ˢᵗ of May at their country Plantations, some 40, 50 to
100 miles Distance, the winter being their healthy & frolicking season.
From July to October they all crowd into Charlestown or escape to the
Northern Colonies. This will make it very difficult for me to meet with
half the Gentlemen I could wish to see. However, I shall do my best.

Pray take care that our Engagements to the People at Oxford be complied with. I hope Mʳ. Duché and you will receive Mʳ. Coombe on his
arrival with all that cordiality which his merit and his generous Partiality to his native place entitle him.

I have sent a large Packet to Dr. Alison and Mr. Kinnersley, relative
to Beresford & Oliphant, two Carolineans, from whom we shall incur
much Disgrace. They spend at the rate of between 2 and £300 sterling per annum, and can scarce be got to attend three Lectures in a
week. I beg the Trustees may interpose their Authority. You will see
by the Packet to Dr. Alison and Mr. Kinnersley what are Mr. Beresford's injunctions respecting his son, and surely you will not suffer yourselves to be trifled with by a Boy, but for the credit of our Discipline
see them complied with. Dr. Oliphant has sailed to Jamaica, and his
orders respecting his son sent to me by Capt. Blewer since I left Phila.,
but will find the letters in Mrs. Smith's hands, and Mr. Mayland has
also some Directions about them—I mean young Oliphant. I am quite
weak with the Loss of Blood, and my Head very giddy, so that I can
neither add more nor read over what I have written. And now, my
dear friend, you have my best Prayers, as I know I have yours, notwithstanding your infirm state and my present Distance. I have hopes we
may yet see one another in the land of the Living.

I am truly and affectionately yours,

Wm. Smith.

The Commencement Day of 1771 showed that Venus had not
made her transit in vain. The Commencement Day of 1769 numbered few graduates. The Commencement Day of the present
year more than doubled them. Among them was Samuel Armor.
This gentleman was a native of Pennsylvania. He was ordained
in the Episcopal Church by Bishop Seabury, in 1785. In 1783 he
had become Professor of Moral Philosophy and Logic in Washington College, and took charge of St. Luke's Church, Queen
Anne County, Maryland. In 1790 he had charge of Chester
Parish, Kent County, Maryland. In 1792 he returned to Pennsylvania, and died here, though I am unable to state in what year.
John McDowell, who was also one of the graduates, became Provost and Professor of Natural Philosophy in the University in A. D.
1806; posts which he held till 1810. He died in 1820.

We have already referred to the increased dignity of the medical faculty made at the session of 1769–70.

The Medical Commencement, on the 28th, was, on account of this, more than usually impressive. The Degree of Bachelor of Physic was conferred on Benjamin Alison, Jonathan Easton, John Kuhn, Frederick Kuhn, Bodo Otto, Robert Pottinger, and William Smith.

Messrs. Jonathan Elmer, of N. J.; Jonathan Potts, of Pottsgrove, Pa.; James Tilton, of Dover; and Nicholas Way, of Wilmington, then presented themselves, agreeably to the Rules of the College, to defend, in Latin, the Dissertations printed for the Degree of Doctor in Physic.

Mr. Elmer's Piece, "*De Causis et Remediis sitis in Febribus*," was impugned by Dr. Kuhn, Professor of Botany and Materia Medica.

Mr. Potts', "*De Febribus intermittentibus, potissimum tertianis*," was impugned by Dr. Morgan, Professor of the Theory and Practice of Physic.

Mr. Tilton's, "*De Hydrope*" was impugned by Dr. Shippen, Professor of Anatomy.

Mr. Way's, "*De Variolarum Insitione*" was impugned by Dr. Rush, Professor of Chemistry.

Each of the candidates having judiciously answered the objections made to some parts of their Dissertations, "the Provost conferred upon them the Degree of Doctor of Physic, with particular solemnity, as the highest mark of literary honor which they could receive in the profession."

Dr. Morgan then entered into a particular account of those branches of study which the medical gentlemen ought still to prosecute with unremitted diligence, if they wished to be eminent in their profession, laying down some useful rules for an honorable practice in the discharge of it. He observed that the "oath" which was prescribed by Hippocrates to his disciples had been generally adopted in universities and schools of physic on like occasions, and that laying aside the form of oaths, the College, which is of a free spirit, wished only to bind its sons and graduates by the ties of honor and gratitude; and that therefore he begged leave to impress upon those who had received the distinguished Degree of Doctor, that, as they were among the foremost sons of the institution, and as the birth-day of medical honors had arisen upon them with auspicious lustre, they would, in their practice, consult the safety of their patients, the good of the community, and the dignity of their profession, so that the seminary from which they derived their titles, might never have cause to be ashamed of them.

CHAPTER XXXII.

BIRTH OF A DAUGHTER, AFTERWARDS MRS. BLODGET—LETTER FROM DR. FRANK-
LIN TO DR. SMITH—DEATH OF THE REV. DR. SAMUEL JOHNSON, OF CONNECTI-
CUT—DEATH OF THOMAS GRÆME, M. D.—DR. SMITH PREACHES HIS FUNERAL
SERMON—DR. SMITH AND OTHERS TO THE SECRETARY OF THE PROPAGATION
SOCIETY—NATHANIEL EVANS—DR. SMITH MAKES A DISCOURSE BEFORE THE
AMERICAN PHILOSOPHICAL SOCIETY—COMMENCEMENT DAY, 1773—IMPROVES
HIS MANSION HOUSE AT THE FALLS OF SCHUYLKILL—DR. SMITH TO THE
BISHOP OF LONDON—HE AND DR. PETERS TO THE SAME—MR. OLIVER TO DR.
SMITH—DR. SMITH TO COLONEL JAMES BURD—WILLIAM SAMUEL JOHNSON TO
DR. SMITH—REV. THOMAS BARTON TO DR. SMITH—DR. SMITH TO THE
SECRETARY OF THE PROPAGATION SOCIETY—HE AND DR. PETERS TO THE
SAME.

ON the 11th of April, 1772, a second daughter was born to Dr. Smith. The good Doctor seems to have been observant of that hard old rubric of the English Church—one easily enough observed in the climates of Rome, from whose ritual I suppose it came, or in a church where baptism by midwives was encouraged, but not so practicable in the winters of the northern parts of northern America —that the baptism of the *nouveau-ne* should not be deferred longer than the first or second Sunday after the child's birth; so that if the little innocent came into being on Saturday night before 12 o'clock, he or she was to be taken to church, and at its door, in form, admitted on the following Sunday. The rubric which we speak of was retained in the " Proposed Book " of Dr. Smith, and, though largely disregarded, in the Book of Common Prayer as finally adopted. It was pretty strictly observed, however, in the case of this newly-arrived daughter. For, born on the 11th of April, she was carried on the 24th to Christ Church, where, under the name of Rebecca, she was duly made a member of the Christian fold by Dr. Peters, the sponsors being Miss Nancy Bond and Miss Nancy Harrison.

This daughter, of whom a lovely portrait by Gilbert Stuart attests the justice of the social judgment, was one of the most admired beauties that ever adorned the drawing-rooms of Philadelphia, and as much distinguished by sprightliness and wit as by personal comeliness. The portrait of her by Stuart has been universally acknowledged, I think, to be the finest female head that Stuart produced. Boston has some good heads of this sort, I know; but they are in Stuart's later style. That of this lady has a purity, an ethereal charm, which his pencil lost with the beginning of the nineteenth century. As a general thing Stuart's women were not successful. It seemed as if he required a male head, and one, moreover, of a high intellectual order, like that of the father, Dr. Smith, whom he painted; or Bishop White, or Robert Morris, or William Lewis, or Chief-Justice Shippen, or Thomas McKean—all of whom he painted—to bring out the full power of his wonderful pencil. He had to become *interested* in what he did, in order to do it well; but when the interest that he felt was that which beauty inspires, then, too, his pencil became inspired. It seemed as if the very angels guided it. This was the case in regard to the portrait of Mrs. Bingham, and of her sister—by some persons thought the handsomer person—Mrs. Major Jackson. It was as much so, or more, in regard to this beautiful daughter of Dr. Smith. Stuart's portrait was copied as a study of improvement by Sully, and was some years ago tastefully engraved by Cheney for an annual called " The Gift." It is a mere head: costume, or dress—" dry-goods," as Stuart used to call it —he left to " Tommy Lawrence." Sully's copy I own. This daughter of Dr. Smith became the wife of Mr. Samuel Blodget.

The College Commencement of this year gave to the bar of Philadelphia Mr. Moses Levy, for many years an active practitioner at it, and from 1802 to 1808 the recorder of the city, and afterwards, if I remember, president of its District Court.

We gave, a few pages back, a letter from Dr. Franklin, in which the great philosopher showed that he could sometimes be what is commonly in regard of manners called " dry." We are happy to give another which indicates a little more effusiveness.

LONDON, August 22d, 1772.

SIR: I received yours of May 16, with the Box of Books, and have already delivered and forwarded most of them as directed. I supply'd

Dr. Fothergill with the wanting sheet. I approve much of the Letter's being in English. I forwarded your Letter to Mr. White, son of *Taylor* White, Esqr, late Treasurer of the Foundling Hospital (now deceas'd), but he has not call'd for the Book. I am glad to hear of your success at South Carolina, and that the College flourishes. I send enclos'd a Pamphlet on a new discovery that makes some noise here. With my best wishes of Prosperity to the Society, and thanks of the number of Books they have sent me, which I shall endeavor to dispose of to their Credit, I am, Sir,

Your most obed^t hum^l Servant,

To Rev. William Smith.   B. Franklin.

The loss of early friends "by sudden blast, or slow decline," is that which happens to all men who live to see long years. Before Dr. Smith tasted of death he had not a little to lament in this way. But he began to have some evidences in this way even now.

On the 6th of January, 1772, he received intelligence of the death of a long honored and much loved early friend, Dr. Samuel Johnson, the first President of King's College (now Columbia), New York; one his superior much in years, to whose accurate learning he greatly deferred, and to whom he looked for sound judgment in all things relating to the Church. Dr. Johnson died at Stratford, Connecticut, and is buried in the chancel of Christ Church in that place. I find in the handwriting of Dr. Smith a copy of the inscription on his tomb; whether written by Dr. Smith, or only copied as a memento of a friend, equally worth giving to my reader.

M. S.

SAMUELIS JOHNSON, D. D.,

COLLEGII REGALIS NOVI EBORACI

PRÆSIDIS PRIMI

ET HUJUS ECCLESIÆ NUPER RECTORIS

NATUS DIE 14TO OCTOB., 1696,

OBIIT 6TO JAN., 1772.

A loss which affected him more sensibly happened soon afterwards. On the 4th of September, 1772, died his fellow-countryman and intimate personal friend, of Philadelphia, Thomas Græme, of Græme Park. "I was acquainted with him," says Dr. Smith, "almost twenty years; that is from the first day of my coming to Philadelphia, until the day of his death; and by a standing invitation spent every Sunday evening with him and his family, excepting in the Summer season, when they were at Græme Park, his family seat, about twenty-three miles from Philadelphia. At our meetings in the Winter season, I found him generally with five or six friends, besides the family, of congenial sentiments, and among others, the Rev. Dr. Peters, Rector of Christ Church and St. Peter's, Philadelphia."

This respectable man was of an ancient family, the GRÆMES of Bulgowan, where he was born, near Perth, in Scotland, the eldest branch of the noble family of Montrose. He was educated in the line of Physic, and came early into Pennsylvania, during the government of Sir William Keith, whose relation he married, and continued for many years a successful and highly respected Practitioner, in the line of his profession. As he advanced in years, a deafness to which he had been in part subject for many years, increased so much that it induced him to decline the practice of Physic, and to keep only a few medicines to be given away to such poor persons as, after examining their cases and circumstances, he thought wanted them. His understanding and mental faculties still remaining sound, the Penn family (with which he lived in great intimacy, when any of them visited or governed in person the Province) bestowed upon him a lucrative office in the customs, in which he conducted himself with such integrity and good manners as gave great satisfaction to the merchants, without any sacrifice of his duty to the government.

Dr. Græme had passed his 80th year when he died. At his funeral, on the 6th of September, Dr. Smith preached a sermon appropriate to the occasion; the text being that one, well-known, from the Proverbs, "*The hoary head is a Crown of Glory, if it be found in the way of Righteousness;*" to the choice of which he says that he was led by "the old age and venerable character of the man whose corpse now lies before us." How to render old age honorable in the eyes of others, and to render our hoary hairs a crown of glory to ourselves, is the subject of his sermon.

He says:

Old Age generally comes accompanied with many Infirmities both of body and mind; for the world hath no new hopes to flatter it with, and hath many fears to present to it, through its near approaches to the confines of another world. . . . But he who hath taken care to provide for all the former stages of a man's life, will surely not leave the last and most ripened stage of it, void of its share of Comforts; especially if it be found in the way he hath appointed—that is, in the Way of Righteousness.

If a proper foundation hath been laid in our early years—the fruits thereof will be our comfort in age. The irregularities of youth are the chief cause of an infirm and painful old age; loading our declining years with perplexities and distress, which a timely care and foresight might have prevented. . . . The reflection that we have long forgotten Him who can alone shew us any good, instead of comforting, will deprive us of all those calm and heartfelt joys, that ought to revive and warm our drooping frame, and will add to all our other growing pains, the terrible apprehensions of wrath and punishment to come.

Oh then! that those who are busy and employing all their cares to lay up some worldly provision, (as is indeed fit and proper) for the bodily support of their old age, would consider farther that all this care will avail them nothing, unless they lay up also some *spiritual* provision, a treasure of righteousness, in a life well spent; that they would provide, as more proper, a store of those home-felt, sweet and virtuous reflections, which will still grow upon enjoyment, and will never satiate or disgust us!

After speaking of the fault of Penuriousness and Avarice which so often creeps on old age, he says:

The golden rule for making the hoary head a Crown of Glory, is to preserve our place and rank in life, and in riper age with dignity; not shewing ourselves vainly attached to more of the world than our years and station require; and bestowing to *our own* where they need it, and to *others* where we can afford it, with a free, open and benevolent heart; shewing that it is our delight to make our nearest relatives and the whole world, as far as in our power, happy around us.

"Another fault of *old age*," he adds, "is too often a morose, suspicious and censorious temper, declining free converse with the world, and forbidding all approach, as it were, to its presence."

He proceeds:

Pain, sickness and infirmity lay some foundation, for this; but how gloriously would all these pains and infirmities be alleviated, how much more venerable would old age appear; if cheerfulness sat on its brow, if a glow of love and affection was shed over its whole countenance; if it were ready to make allowances for the frailties of mankind, and especially of youth; if it was ever ready to admonish with tenderness, and impart advice with a candid sincerity and complacency of heart?

Another way by which old age may render itself less respectable, is by quitting its rank, affecting to call back years that are flown, and mixing with the young in amusements which, though proper for one age, may be considered as levities in another.   A decent joining in the diversions of the young, if we suffer not our years and *gray hairs* to be thereby despised, is, on proper occasions, a mark of a candid and loving temper, and may give us an opportunity of doing them much good.   But to make this an excuse, to call off our thoughts from those nobler purposes of *being* to which the pursuits of the aged should be more particularly directed—this is not only contrary to Religion and Reason, but highly inconsistent with that seriousness and dignity of character, which become the hoary head, and render it a Crown of Glory.   Gray hairs at least, if nothing else, should warn a man, like the venerable Barzillai,* at a proper period of life, to withdraw himself from the follies, the vanities, and even the innocent and lawful amusements of the young and gay.

And having thus withdrawn ourselves, at a proper period of our age, from the strifes and vanities of the World, it is our duty to inquire what conduct will render our gray hairs a Crown of Glory?

And surely a more venerable spectacle cannot be beheld under the sun, than a man stricken in years, the father of a family, deserving and obtaining the love and esteem of all around him!

I am ravished with the thought, and my imagination presents to me the *good Old Man*, finishing his walk of life in the fear of God, and in good offices to Men.   No morning or evening passes over his head, without due praises and thanksgivings to his Almighty Maker, for all the benefits and mercies bestowed on him.   I behold him, like some ancient patriarch, (in the midst of his loving and beloved family) at once their Prophet, their Priest and their King—as their Prophet, counselling them with all the experience of years, and inspiration of Wisdom; as their Priest, offering up their prayers and pleading for their failings, at the throne of Grace; and as their King, ruling them with affection, and swaying them by the powerful example of his own goodness!

At one time, methinks I behold him tenderly interested in all their domestic concerns, and temporal happiness; at another time I see him retired from hurry and noise, resting his venerable limbs under some friendly shade; composing his soul to the exercises of private Devotion; reviewing in the field of calmer reason and religion, all the transactions of his former more busy and active years; bewailing the faults he hath committed, and taking sanctuary from their sting in the bosom of his Saviour, and his God!   And although rejoicing in the remembrance of his moments that were well spent, yet not even resting on his best works for salvation; but seeking it through the merits of Jesus Christ;

* 2 Samuel, ch. xix. ver. 32–37.

striving to humble and purify himself more and more, even as his Master, Christ, was humble and pure!

Methinks I behold him, at other times, comforting the afflicted, relieving where he can relieve; or, where that is not in his power, dropping at least the sympathetic tear, and wishing that the means of his bounty, were as enlarged as his heart to give. I hear him likewise giving ready counsel to all that ask; I behold him saving, or striving to save, some thoughtless youth from the snares of the world, pouring his balm into the wounded character and conscience, composing the strifes and contentions of jarring neighbours, and ever exerting himself to make a whole world happy; concealing and bearing with patience his own infirmities, and promoting religion, justice, peace and joy, to the farthest extent in his power.

None ever can approach such a man but with reverence! His gray hairs are indeed a crown of Glory! They strike even the giddy and profligate with awe.

Should a man who has acted such a dignified part as this, come at last to bear the greatest marks of decay, and even outlive all the active powers both of body and mind; yet still he will continue to be respected by all! Like some grand structure, tottering and crumbling beneath the hand of time, he will appear beautiful and majestic, although in ruins; and be still looked upon with reverence and awe! even by the giddy and the dissolute.

Notwithstanding, therefore, the common complaint, that old age is a thing not desirable; yet if it be such an old age as we have been describing, and which is in part copied from the life of the good man, whose breathless clay lies before us, it hath satisfactions more substantial than all the giddy and fantastic joys of former years. The autumn, and even the very winter of such a life, yield a calm sunshine of comfort, which the splendid spring and summer of life cannot yield to many who think themselves the most happy!

The following letter bears no more than a just tribute of praise to a gentleman long honored both in Bristol and in the neighboring city of Burlington; but whose name, though not a century has passed since he died, has largely faded from the remembrance of men.

Dr. Smith and others to the Secretary of the Propagation Society.

PHILADᴬ, Octʳ 14, 1772.

REVᴅ AND WORTHY SIR: This will be delivered to you by Dʳ. De Normandie, a worthy Member of the Church of England, as well as a Gentleman of Fortune, character & great public usefulness in this Province. Enclosed is an engagement for the support of a Missionary for the County of Bucks in this Province, a County in which there is not a single Clergyman of our Church, tho' there was formerly a Missionary there, and it is one of our interior Counties & a very great disposition in it, even among the Quakers, who are the most numerous body, to encourage the Church in preference to all other religious denominations except their own.

As D^r. DeNormandie will wait upon you in person, and can so fully give you an account of this County, & you may perfectly depend upon the truth of whatever he shall say to you on Church affairs, we have the less occasion to be particular. This is not properly opening a new Mission, but the restoring an old one which was discontinued on the ill conduct of one M^r. Lindsay, the last Missionary, & was occasionally supplied by M^r. Campbell, of Burlington, during his life, but his successor, M^r. Odell, has been excused from taking any charge of it. There is a prospect of a very flourishing Mission in this County. The People of Bristol, chiefly excited by D^r. DeNormandie's zeal, have enlarged their Church, which we have this Summer alternatively supplied for them, as there is in the Summer season a great resort of strangers of Distinction to that Town, on account of a mineral Spring & Bath there, and one or two more churches are soon intended to be built in the County, at such a distance as to be supplied by the same person who supplies Bristol.

If you will look into your list you will see how few Missionaries we have in this great & populous Province, which has more people in it than New York & New Jersey both. We hope then the Society will make such allowance as they are able for a Missionary in Bucks, & there is not the least doubt but the people, many of whom have both zeal & ability sufficient, will even do more than their present engagement & make the living for their Minister very respectable.

The Gentleman they have applied for is M^r. Hopkinson, who is known to them & has connexions among sundry of the most respectable members of the Church in that County, & we believe will be of great service among them. M^r. Hopkinson is also known to you, & has been recommended to the Bishop of London some years ago in conjunction with his class-mates, Messrs. Montgomery, Coombe & White, so that nothing need be added on that head. He is also in full orders, & wants nothing but the nomination of the Society, which we pray they may give him, agreeable to the request of the people, as Missionary for Bucks County, Pennsylvania.

We are, Rev^d & worthy Sir, &^c.,

RICHARD PETERS,
WILLIAM SMITH,
JACOB DUCHÉ.

Nothing is more striking in the character of Dr. Smith than the devotion with which he cherished literary merit and sought, within

the whole region where his influence extended, to do justice to its
possessor, whether that possessor was among the living or the
dead.   When it concerned his own pupils, it seems to have been
considered by him a sacred duty to cherish and perpetuate a
knowledge of it.

I have already spoken of the Rev. Nathaniel Evans, and in a
note made some reference to his history.   He died at an early age,
constrained by the love of Christ to devote all his powers to
preaching the gospel of salvation.   He was a favorite pupil of Dr.
Smith, who regarded him with great interest as likely to be useful
in the Church, an ornament to American letters, and a pride to his
family and friends.   But too soon for the interest of all these, and
for the pride and happiness of all with whom he was connected,
death took him from the world.   My father, Richard Penn Smith,
has left an account of him, whose insertion here by me I trust
that my readers will pardon to filial love and duty.   My father says:

If the rigid canons of criticism will not allow the name of Evans to
be inscribed among those of the inspired children of poesy and song,
yet the cause of virtue requires that there be some memorial of one, who
embodied in harmonious verse, the chaste conceptions and moral excellencies of a sound and well-regulated mind !   Apart from the merit
which might be claimed for him by his admirers, on account of the
supposed beauties which can be found in his writings, the demand of
justice is interposed, that there be rendered to his amiable character
and pure life the deserved tribute of esteem and honour.   Especially is
this called for, since circumstances, distinctly unfavourable at the time
of his brief career in life, have heretofore prevented an exhibition of the
claims which rest upon his countrymen for their admiration and respect.

The subject of this memoir was born in Philadelphia, on June 8th,
1742.   His father, who was a respectable merchant of the city, designed
him for the same pursuit, but, having ample means, determined to
afford his son the advantages of an education beyond the mere requisites
for commercial business.   He was accordingly entered in the College
of Philadelphia, and soon exhibited his fondness for classical learning,
and the wide range of polite literature.   He, in a brief time, endeared
himself to the faculty of that venerable institution by his close application and amiable temper; and the regard was reciprocated by our
young student in full measure.

Having continued in the college for six years, he was removed to the
counting-house of a merchant, with the view, on the part of his parent,
of qualifying him for a business which the former designed should be
pursued by his son.   The taste for literature, however, which he had

cherished in his academical course with so much delight and profit, made him regret that the duties of the counting-house interfered with pursuits so congenial with his mind's best wishes and inclination. On completing the term for which he was engaged at the desk, he immediately returned to the college, and resumed his studies with renewed vigour and devotion.

Perhaps there are few instances on record of greater progress in the pursuit of knowledge, or of a more ardent engagement in the occupations of the scholar, than that furnished by young Evans. Such was his great diligence in study that at the commencement, held on May 30th, 1765, a short time after his second matriculation, he was, by special mandate of the Trustees, upon the unanimous recommendation of the Board of Faculty, honoured with a diploma for the degree of Master of Arts; although he had not received the previous degree of Bachelor, on account of the interruption in his studies during the season which was spent in the counting-house.

Immediately subsequent to the commencement he embarked for England, favoured with the most honourable testimonials of respect and esteem for his great talents and virtues. The object of his visit to the mother country was the important one of receiving ordination in the Church of England, and the appointment of Missionary for Gloucester county, New Jersey, from the venerable " Society for Propagating the Gospel in Foreign Parts." If his acknowledged abilities were a qualification, in a literary point of view, for this sacred calling, his piety and the excellent virtues of his heart and life yielded the assurance of future usefulness. Upon the Society's nomination, he was admitted to orders by D^r. Terrick, Bishop of London, exercising provisional authority over the colonial churches. His examination gave the greatest satisfaction to the above prelate, particularly from the perusal of an elegant composition, which had been prepared in a few minutes, upon a theological subject, and upon which his views had been required.

On his return to Philadelphia, in 1765, he proceeded to his responsible charge in the neighbourhood, and settled himself in Haddonfield, N. J. With all that activity and great zeal, which were shown by him in every work to which his mind was directed, he entered upon the sacred duties of a Christian minister, and soon beheld the gratifying evidences of his acceptableness as a teacher in divine things. But he just lived long enough to show, by the excellent and amiable dispositions of his heart, the purity of his morals, the sublimity and soundness of his faith, and the warmth of his pulpit compositions, how well he was qualified for the sacred office to which he had wholly devoted himself. He died of consumption, October 29th, 1767, in the twenty-sixth year of his age, lamented by all who were favoured with his acquaintance, and none more deeply and affectionately mourned over a bereavement than the beloved people whom he had not yet served two years!

Not long before his death he committed his papers, which he had begun to prepare for the press, to the care of Dr. Smith and of a young lady in whom he felt an interest. The persons who were to encourage the publication of a volume of youthful poetry in that day were small. But the indefatigable Provost announced his purpose to publish them, and before very long procured no fewer than seven hundred and fifty-nine subscribers for the volume, among whom will be found the name of *Oliver Goldsmith*. Great at that time of day must have been the effort requisite to obtain so many patrons. But "he was my pupil," writes Dr. Smith, "and truly dear and affectionate to me in his whole demeanor." This was incentive enough for every effort. Having done this considerable work, Dr. Smith passed the list to a publisher in Philadelphia, Mr. John Dunlap, for £20, which sum, as we have already mentioned, Dr. Smith paid into the treasury of the then recently established corporation for the relief of the Widows and Children of the Clergy of the Church of England. The volume appeared in handsome style in the summer of 1772, with a preface by the editor. In an introduction he gives a piece by Mr. Evans himself in a short interval between a dangerous illness, which he had undergone, and a relapse which put an end to his life. The piece seems to have been intended as a *preface* to a contemplative volume of his own poems.

" Poetry has been accounted the most peculiar of all the liberal arts ; and it is the only One in the circle of literature, which a man of common capacity cannot, by mere dint of constant application, become master of. The most exalted prose writers that ever graced the learned world, have rendered themselves liable to ridicule in their addresses to the Muses."

" The great Cicero, not less famous for the elegance of his style, than for his universal knowledge, was a remarkable instance of the truth of this observation. And the wonder ceases, if what a celebrated Critic * says, be true, to wit: That to constitute a Poet, is required 'an elevation of soul, that depends not only on art and study, but must also be the Gift of Heaven.' I say, if this be the case, the riddle is immediately expounded, and we are at no loss to assign a reason, why some (comparatively speaking) illiterate men have been the sublimest poets of the age they lived in."

---

* Rapin.

31

"It is not strange, therefore, that those whom nature has thus distin-guished, should be looked on as a kind of prodigies in the world. For, according to Horace, it is not a trifling power the man is endued with—

————meum qui pectus inaniter angit,
Irritat, mulcet, falsis terroribus implet,
Ut MAGUS————   LIB. II. EPIST. I.

"There is a pleasing *Je ne scay quoi* in the productions of poetic genius, which is easier felt than described. It is the voice of nature in the Poet, operating like a charm on the soul of the reader. It is the marvellous conception, the noble wildness, the lofty sentiment, the fire and enthusiasm of spirit, the living imagery, the exquisite choice of words, the variety, the sweetness, the majesty of numbers, and the irresistible magic of expression.

The prose writer may indeed warm his Reader with a serene and steady fire ; he may keep up his attention with the energetic, the flowing period. But the Poet's it is, to wrap him in a flame—to dissolve him, as it were, in his own rapturous blaze ! The Poet's it is, to hurry him out of himself, with the same velocity, as though he were really mounted on a winged Pegasus—It is his to lift him up to Heaven, or plunge him into the gloom of Tartarus—It is his, to unveil to him the secrets of the deep, or to exhibit to his mind, all the novelty of this varied world—to carry him back into the darkness of antiquity, or waft him forwards into the vast sea of futurity—and finally, to inspire him with the patriot glow, or fire his soul with the heavenly ideas of Moral Beauty, and all the varied passions of Love, Fear, Terror, Compassion, &c., &c."

"Such is the genuine Poet, when improved by the Precepts of Art ; and the works of such have been the continual delight of mankind, as they afford the sublimest intellectual enjoyment. With such, to tread the flowery fields of imagination, and gather the rich fruits of knowl-edge, is Happiness indeed ! "

The preface concludes with this sentence unfinished, and "pro-phetic," says Dr. Smith, "of the author's own fate."

" But it is rare, that such Natural Geniuses are seen to arrive at this envied height. Some black obstacle still clogs their wings, and retards their progress.—Frequently those to whom Nature has been thus boun-tiful, have not leisure to attend to the cultivation of their talents—fre-quently, like the rose in the wilderness, they just bloom, and wither away in obscurity; and sometimes, alas ! the iron-hand of death cuts them suddenly off, as their beauties are just budding forth into existence, and leaves but the fair promises of future excellencies." . . .

"How far," continues Dr. Smith, "his Poems will answer the idea he had formed of poetic eminence, must be left for his readers to judge. Many of them are fragments, and unfinished ; and but few of them were revised by himself, with a view of being published. Some corrections have therefore been made, where there appeared anything materially faulty in respect to Grammar, the exactness of the rhymes, &c. But in these the Publisher has been sparing, and has taken care that the Author's sense should in no case be deviated from. The task he left to be performed was a mournful one ; but it has been executed with that fidelity, which the writer of this would wish might be extended to any performance of his own, that may be thought worthy of the public eye, by that true friend into whose hands it may fall, when he himself shall be no more!"

On the 22d January, 1773, Dr. Smith delivered an Oration before the American Philosophical Society. The Governor of the Province, the Speaker of the Assembly and other dignified persons were present. The oration was subsequently printed by order of the Society.

The Commencement at the College took place this year, as usual, in June. There were six graduates.

During the year, Dr. Smith built or greatly improved the Mansion-House at the Falls of Schuylkill, and removed his family thither. It was then a place eminent for the wild and picturesque character of its scenery. The hand of man has since sadly, in the artist's sense, though not in that of the banker, changed its aspect. Faint flashes only—caught here and there at points—remain of those ancient charms which attracted the poetic eye of Dr. Smith. Railways run at its very skirts. The steam-whistles of every sort of factory are heard in the early morning, at noon and at the curfew's toll.

We now resume our correspondence. It would be surprising to see by it, what numbers of disreputable people in colonial times sought to take holy orders, if we did not remember that for the most part they expected to come back with a fixed stipend as Missionaries of the Society for the Propagation of the Gospel.

Dr. Smith to the Lord Bishop of London.

(EXTRACT.)

PHILADELPHIA, October 13th, 1773.

MY LORD,

* * * It is with sorrow we are obliged humbly to represent to your Lordship that our Church has lately suffered greatly by several unworthy men who, by the recommendations of those who were not deserving the credit they have received, have found means to impose on your Lordship's goodness and have got into Holy Orders, some of whom have come to this place and some have gone to Maryland and Virginia.

M^r. *Illing*, whom your Lordship sent out, is as D^r. Peters represents him, a worthy man, but M^r. *Page* is every way the reverse.   The people in general, who subscribed and whose subscriptions he laid before your Lordship, believed him to be a Presbyterian and are chiefly of that persuasion.   He never meant to settle among them but only to get into Orders.   He knew none of us would recommend him.   Nay, he knew that we would write to your Lordship against him, if we had known of his intentions.   Despairing ever to obtain recommendations from any of the clergy here, as his conduct has been very exceptionable the short time he was in America, he applied, just before he embarked, for Letters from Father Harding, a worthy Jesuit in this Town, to the Bishop of Canada with a view to get ordained by him, and as he pretended he meant afterwards to recant his Errors and commence Preaching in our church.   Harding, who was always on good terms with us, discovered his Duplicity and want of Principle, & refused to have anything to do with him.   He then went among those People on our Frontiers, whom I have mentioned.   What other recommendations he produced to your Lordship we have not heard.   He never went near the people on Susquehannah, but on his arrival immediately set up as a separate Preacher in New York, without any Regard to Order or the Establishment there.

My Lord, your most dutiful Son and Servant,

WILLIAM SMITH.

Messrs. Smith and Peters to the Bishop of London.

(EXTRACT.)

PHILADELPHIA, October 29th, 1773.

MAY IT PLEASE YOUR LORDSHIP,

 *   *   *   But the principal thing we want to now inform your Lordship of is, that by a Letter received by D^r. Smith from M^r. Martin, Governor of North Carolina, we are made acquainted with the designs of a certain John Beard, who was educated in the College of that city and has taken orders among the Dissenters.   He has, as we are well informed, given offence and been called to account for want of Sobriety for his own people, and now wants to come over to the church.   Governor Martin is good enough to let it be known how M^r. Beard came to have his letters and countenance, & his Letter is enclosed, and we desire that if M^r. Beard attempts to make use of Governor Martin's or any other recommendations in order to gain admittance into Orders, that this, our letter, may be received as a caveat against such admission.

We always have been and ever shall be careful how we give any

Recommendations to people who offer themselves for Holy orders, and indeed in nothing are we, who are ever upon the spot, liable to be more imposed upon than those who apply on these occasions for our Recommendations. We are,

Your Lordship's most dutiful and
Obedient humble Servants,
WILLIAM SMITH,
RICHARD PETERS.

The letter from Massachusetts which follows and is signed "A. Oliver," might naturally be supposed to be from the Andrew Oliver, Lieutenant-Governor of Massachusetts, A. D. 1770–74, of whom mention is often made in our history, and whose name has so unenviable a notoriety in connection with Governor Hutchinson in the famous "Boston Letters," got, as is supposed, from Sir John Temple by Dr. Franklin in 1774 or thereabouts, and which were the subject of Mr. Wedderburne's celebrated but indecent invective. This, however, as we learn by the invaluable "Dictionary of Authors" of Dr. Austin Allibone, is not the case. The "A. Oliver" —Dr. Smith's correspondent—was a different person, a judge of the Court of Common Pleas of Essex, and an amateur of science. Dr. Allibone makes mention of his scientific papers, not numerous, but apparently somewhat esteemed.*

A. Oliver to Dr. Smith.

SALEM, 6ᵗʰ December, 1773.

REVᴰ, HONᴰ, & Dᴿ. SIR:

I received your very agreeable Per Mr. Mifflin, which he forwarded to me from Boston, but was not honoured with a visit from that gentleman at Salem, which your letter flattered me with the hopes of. Soon after his arrival at Boston, I made several journies myself into the country,

---

* It was objected by some critics, at the time when this truly great work of Dr. Allibone's appeared, that he made mention of far too many unimportant authors; men who had written little, or not with great ability. In nothing, in my opinion, is Dr. Allibone's work more truly useful or more to be commended than in exactly what it thus does. We have no difficulty in learning in a score of volumes everything concerning great authors—Dryden, Johnson, Burke, Webster, and others. We know not *where else* to look for many humble ones. I had looked in vain in several biographical dictionaries for mention of this "A. Oliver," as also of " Edward Antill," mentioned *infra*, on page 498, as a correspondent of Dr. Smith. But in vain. I open the volumes of this industrious and incomparable laborer, and I find about them both all that any one need desire to know.

whereby I missed of the pleasure of seeing, tho' I just heard of him at Providence and Newport.   I am very sorry that I had not an opportunity of shewing that respect which not only your recommendation entitled him to, but the united testimony of my friends at Boston, who had the happiness of an acquaintance with him, assured me was due to his merit.

I gratefully acknowledge the receipt of three copies of your oration, delivered before the American Philosophical Society of Philadelphia; one of which I sent to the Lieut.-Governor, as you desired, who returns you his respectful compliments, with thanks for the same.   He again enquired of me respecting his having been elected a member of the Society; I shewed him, as I had done before, your favor to me by Mr. Budd, wherein you informed me that I was "a member of the "Society by a *late* election, as the Lieut.-Governor is by a former "one."   But as he has received no certificate of such election, which he understands is customary, he is in doubt whether a correspondence as a member is expected from him, and of the propriety of it.

As you informed me that the Society had appointed a committee to examine the communications, and select the papers proper to be published in a Second Vol. of Transactions, I wrote some time since to Mr. Thos. Smith, desiring him to acquaint me what forwardness that Vol. was in, as I designed to expose myself by communicating to the committee some philosophical papers for their inspection.   In those papers I have endeavoured to frame a new theory, in order to account for the phenomena of lightning and thunder-storms, upon electrical principles; which, tho' different from any foregoing theories which have been erected for that purpose, is, I am persuaded, nearer the truth than any of them, and at least as well supported by experiments, not of my own, but which lie scattered throughout Dr. Priestley's History of Electricity, which I have been at no small pains to collect and compare together with that view.   I would send it herewith, but as I have just finished what I intended upon the Subject, I have put the papers into the hands of a philosophical friend for his examination, inspection, and correction, after which I purpose to transmit you a fair copy of them.

An ingenious clergyman in Boston, who is very curious in disquisitions of this kind, and to whom I communicated the first rough draught of the theory aforesaid, has promised me the sight of a theory of his own, respecting the *primary* and *immediate* causes of the ascent of vapors, upon which he thinks he can offer something that is new.   As this subject is nearly connected with that of lightning and thunder-storms, if I can be favoured with it in season, and can obtain liberty from the Author, I will communicate it with my own.

I sincerely wish success to the American Philosophical Society of Philadelphia; that under its auspices useful knowledge may be accumulated and propagated among mankind far and near; and shall esteem myself happy if ever it may be in my power to contribute towards that beneficent design.   I am,

Rev^d, Hon^d, and Dear Sir,

Your obliged and most obed^t humble serv^t,

A. OLIVER.

Dr. Smith to Col. James Burd, near Middletown.

PHILADELPHIA, Dec. 22nd, 1773.

DEAR SIR: Give me Leave to introduce to your Encouragement and Protection the Rev^d M^r. Illing*, ordained by the Bishop of London, and recommended to us by the Queen's German Chaplains.   He can preach both in German and English; and I hope the Lutherans, among whom he was bred, will allow him the occasional use of their Churches, as he will be strongly recommended by M^r. Muhlenberg.   He may be useful in your Parts.   He will shew you his Subscription List, and I beg you would give him your best advice, which will much oblige

Your Obedient Servant,

WILLIAM SMITH.

Favoured by the REV^D. M^R. ILLING.

The next letter refers to a question which long agitated the two States of Pennsylvania and Connecticut.   It was the question of title to a large part of Northern Pennsylvania, about where Susquehanna County now is; one portion of the people claiming under grants from Connecticut, and the other by grants from the Penns.   The matter led to great excitement, and after much litigation was, I believe, finally settled in the great case of *Van Horne's Lessee* v. *Dorance*, reported in one volume of Dallas's Reports.   Dr. Smith wrote an octavo pamphlet of about a hundred pages on it, in 1774, entitled, "An Examination of the Connecticut Claim to Lands in Pennsylvania; with an Appendix, containing Extracts of Original Papers."

William Saml. Johnson† to Dr. Smith.

STRATFORD, January 29th, 1774.

D^R S^R: I am extremely obliged to you for y^r favor of the 18th of Jan'ry, and the Pamphlet that accompanied it.   I rec'd it at Hartford, but so eager were those who are the most eager in the affair of the controverted Lands (of which I am not one) to see its contents, that I was

---

* Rev. *Frangott. Fred. Illing* was licensed to preach in 1772.

† Son of the Rev. Samuel Johnson, of Stratford, Connecticut, spoken of by us, *supra*, p. 473; born October 11th, 1727; died November 14th, 1819; aged 92 years.

not allowed to keep it in my hands an hour, and I have never been able to get a sight of it since. From the very cursory reading I gave it, I think it is well done, and states the proprietary arguments in support of their title, or rather those in derogation of the Connecticut Title, in a very advantageous point of light. I hope with you, if any answer is given to it, the like temper and candor will be observed, for to what purpose is checanery, scurrillity and abuse, but to dishonour those who make use of such infamous weapons. I shall not, I assure you, take up the Gauntlet, unless it should be enjoined upon me. I have an infinity of affairs of much more importance to me to attend to, which I cannot neglect. And of what use are these Appeals to the People? the appeal must finally be to Cæsar, or to a greater than Cæsar. On the part of the Proprietary, they may indeed be of some use to engage the People and Assembly of Pennsylvania to support the Cause, and I fancy the examination has had no small share in producing the resolves of y^r Assembly; something like which you told us they would come into, tho' others were clearly of opinion they would not meddle with the Controversy. Our Assembly (which I was obliged to leave before it had ended its deliberations upon this subject) have directed every preparation to be made for the Trial, and in the meantime desired the Governor to issue a Proclamation, prohibiting all Persons from entering upon any part of the contested Country. Among other things, they have directed the Latitudes to be taken, that we may not claim beyond our proper Limits, for which reason I wish I knew the price of Mr. Richenhous's Instrument, which you mentioned to us, for taking Latitudes, and how we could obtain one. They have also had in contemplation to erect a County there, and exercise Jurisdiction, at least over those settled under the Connecticut Claim. This, however, was not determined when I came from Hartford. Two reasons were urged for this measure, the one that the People there might have it in their power to exclude from among them, or bring to punishment, those who have escaped from justice in other Colonies, or may commit crimes there; the other to secure their possessions upon legal grounds. The last is founded upon a suspicion that you will endeavour to remove the settlers before the controversy is decided. But why should you do this? since if the controversy is determined in favor of the Prop^s, they must submit to them, and will become useful settlers under them, or at least, if they should then chuse to turn them off, will have cultivated a Country which they may sell at an advanced price to others. Why may you not let us know your intentions in this respect? The idea you mentioned to us at Frankfort, that there is good land enough for us beyond Pennsylvania, which we might take without offence to any body, I own made a strong impression upon me, as it has done upon several others to whom I have mentioned it. If so, why should we, at great expense and trouble, contest with you for this?

But will not the Crown give us as much trouble there as you will here, at least, it deserves to be considered of; but I am not yet sufficiently acquainted with the Geography, Quality, &c., of that country, to determine it, nor have I leisure to attend enough to it at present, but am, with compliments to all friends, and the most sincere esteem and respect,   Dear Sir,

Your Most Obedient humble Servant,

WM. SAML. JOHNSON.

P. S.—Some People, I find, are extremely wroth with our friend Ingersoll, for the assistance they imagine he has given to the proprietary Cause.

Rev. Thomas Barton to Dr. Smith.

LANCASTER, February 12th, 1774.

DEAR SIR: It has always been the wish of my family that Dr. Smith might be the Priest of Hymen; who should solemnize the first marriage in it.   But when we consider the unfavourableness of the weather, the distance between this place and Philadelphia, your many avocations, and the constant duties of your office, we find that we must either resign the pleasure which such an event would afford us, or infringe too far upon the rights of friendship by soliciting you, under the circumstances, to give us your company on Thursday the 3d of March next, which is fixed for my daughter's wedding-day.   Such is the Alternative before us.   How to act we know not.   Will you be kind enough to determine for us and to favor us with answer as soon as possible.   That in case you cannot indulge us, we might turn our eyes to some other gentleman whose attendance may not be interrupted by so many inconveniences. Let the result of your determination be what it will, I could not have concealed from *you* a matter of so much consequence to me.   You have often expressed and shown yourself interested in my happiness.   I should therefore wrong my heart, which will ever retain a pleasing remembrance of the confidence & friendly intimacy which have so long subsisted between us, if I did not drop you this intimation, which, you will however observe, is a la mode des Jesuites "tibi soli."

I am, my dear Sir,

Most cordially yours,

THOMAS BARTON.

REV. DR. SMITH.

P. S. Hetty, from her particular desire of receiving your benediction, begs me to add this Nota Bene to you.   If you set off on Wednesday, you may be back in Philadelphia on Saturday, so as to lose but *four* days in the whole.   But should you deny her this honor, be so good as to let us know whether Brother Thompson is at Charlestown, as he must come next in view.   I expect my son and two others from Philadelphia, who would be proud of your company.   Adieu.

A. Oliver to Dr. Smith.

SALEM, April 25th, 1774.

REV᷂ & HON᷂ SIR: I sent you by Capt. Goodhue an essay towards a new Theory of lightning and thunder storms, which I hope you have received. Without waiting to know the fate of that, I venture to expose myself further to your joint candor and criticism by sending you a few thoughts upon waterspouts, assuring you that I have not therein endeavoured to force the phenomena of nature into the service of a preconceived hypothesis, but to deduce a theory from the best accounts I could obtain of those phenomena. If they should not merit a place in the next volume of Transactions, they may possibly, by being on file, afford some hints to future speculators upon the subject.

I am, Rev᷂ & Hon᷂ Sir,

Your obliged & most

Humble Servant,

A. OLIVER.

To the REV᷂. WILLIAM SMITH, D.D.,
    Provost of the College at Philadelphia.

Dr. Smith to the Secretary of the Propagation Society.

(EXTRACT.)

PHILADELPHIA, May 2d, 1774.

REV᷂ AND WORTHY SIR: * * * I shall be more particular on the whole state of this Mission, as well as several other Missions in my next. We are still plagued and the Church hurt by irregular preachers that come out. One Rowland has just arrived here, of a very bad character, to whom we had refused recommendations & therefore he went to Wales, got recommended as a Curate, and was ordained Deacon by the Bishop of S᷂. Asaph, & Priest by the Bishop of Hereford ; and then immediately embarked for this Place. For God's sake, let him have no appointment ; for no Mission in this Province will receive him, and we must even write to our Brethren in other Provinces to make known his character. How long shall we groan under this hardship of bad people going from America and imposing on our Bishops, all of which might in a great measure be prevented if we had a Bishop here !

Worthy Sir, &᷂.,

WILLIAM SMITH.

The Same and Others to the Same.

(EXTRACT.)

PHILADELPHIA, May 17th, 1774.

REV᷂ SIR: * * * We are not yet clear that it would be a proper measure to erect the places he now supplies into a Mission, but as a person of his qualifications, capable of preaching both in German and English, would be truly useful on our Frontiers, and be the means of gathering many congregations, we would humbly propose to the Society to make some annual provision for M^r. Illing as an Itinerant in such parts of the Province as it may appear to the Episcopal Clergy here he can be most useful in, until we can more clearly see in what place he can be settled to the greatest advantage.

There is no Episcopal Clergyman in the whole County of Bucks. It might be made an important Mission. M^r. Hopkinson is now about to return to his native Country, & is willing to take the charge of that Mission for a time, where he will be acceptable to the people if the Society will be pleased to make a Provision for him such as the state of their Funds will admit.   Revd Sir, &^{c}.,

RICHARD PETERS,
WILLIAM SMITH,
JACOB DUCHÉ.

On Thursday, the 19th of May, 1774, Mr. Paul Revere—whose name both poets and historians have made familiar to all*—arrived in Philadelphia with a letter from the town of Boston, dated on the 13th, requesting the advice of the city of Philadelphia upon the occasion of the publication of the act of Parliament for shutting up the port of Boston. Notice was given to the public, and a meeting called to meet at the City Tavern† on the morrow.

---

* Paul Revere was an American patriot of Huguenot descent, a goldsmith by trade, born in Boston, January 1st, 1735, and died there May 10th, 1818. At twenty-one years of age he was a lieutenant in the Colonial army stationed at Fort Edward, near Lake George. After his term of office had expired he established himself as a goldsmith, and by his own unaided efforts learned the art of copperplate engraving, and at the breaking out of the Revolution was one of the four engravers then resident in America. He engraved the plates, made the press, and printed the bills of the paper money for the Provincial Congress of Massachusetts: was sent by that body to Philadelphia to learn the art of powder-making, and on his return he set up a mill. He was engaged in the destruction of the tea in Boston harbor in 1773, and was sent to New York and Philadelphia to carry the news of that event; and he again visited those cities to invoke their sympathy and co-operation when the decree closing the port of Boston was promulgated. The event that gave rise to Longfellow's "Paul Revere's Ride" was his escaping from Boston with the intelligence that General Gage, the British commander, had prepared an expedition to destroy the Colonial military stores at Concord. Revere rode by way of Charlestown, rousing the people on his route, until a little after midnight he reached Lexington, and communicated the news to Hancock and Adams. He became a lieutenant-colonel in the Massachusetts line, and, after the close of the Revolution, he embarked in the business of bell and cannon founding. The rolling works of the present Revere Copper Company at Canton, Massachusetts, were built by him.

† This was a large tavern on the west side of Second street, just above Walnut, sometimes called "Daniel Smith's Tavern." After a while it ceased to be kept as a tavern, and became "The Merchants' Coffee House." Its last occupation, I believe, was for an auction store.

On Friday, the 20th, between two and three hundred very respectable citizens met as requested at the City Tavern, and agreed as follows, viz.:

1st. That John Dickinson, Esq., William Smith, D. D.,
Edward Penington, Joseph Fox,
John Nixon, John Maxwell Nesbit,
Samuel Howell, Thomas Mifflin,
Joseph Reed, Thomas Wharton, Jr.,
Benjamin Marshall, Joseph Moulder,
Thomas Barclay, George Clymer,
Charles Thomson, Jeremiah Warden, Jr.,
John Cox, John Gibson,
Thomas Penrose,

Compose a Committee of Correspondence, until an alteration is made by a more general meeting of the Inhabitants.

2d. That the Committee shall write to the People of Boston assuring them that we truly feel for their unhappy situation; that we consider them as suffering in the general cause. That we recommend to them Firmness, Prudence and Moderation; that we shall continue to evince our Firmness to the cause of *American Liberty.*

3d. That the Committee shall transmit the foregoing Resolution to the other Colonies.

4th. That they shall apply to the Governor to call the Assembly of this Province.

5th. That they be authorized to call a meeting of the Inhabitants when necessary.*

On Saturday, May 21st, in pursuance of the above appointment, the following members, viz.: Dr. William Smith, John Nixon, Thomas Mifflin, Joseph Moulder, George Clymer, Jeremiah Warder, Jr., Edward Penington, Samuel Howell, Thomas Wharton, Jr., Thomas Barclay, Charles Thomson, John Cox, and John Gibson met at the City Tavern in the afternoon, when the following letter from the committee of the city of Philadelphia to the committee of the city of Boston, drawn up at the table by William Smith, was, after some debate and the addition of *one* sentence, unanimously agreed to by the committee:

PHILADELPHIA, May 21st, 1774.

GENTLEMEN: We have received your very interesting letter, together with a letter from the town of Boston, and the vote they have passed on

---

* The account here given of these two meetings of the 20th and 21st is taken from the original MS. of William Smith, D. D., in possession of John H. Brinton, M. D., of Philadelphia, endorsed "Notes and some papers on the commencement of the American Revolution."

the present alarming occasion ; and such measures have been pursued thereon as the shortness of the time would allow.   To collect the sense of this large city is difficult, and when their sense is obtained, they must not consider themselves as authorized to judge and act for this populous province in business so deeply interesting as the present is to all British America.   A very respectable number of the inhabitants of this city, however, assembled last evening to consult as to what was proper to be done, and, after reading the sundry papers which you transmitted to us, and also a letter from the committee of correspondence in New York, the inclosed resolves were passed, in which you may be assured we are sincere, and that you are considered as suffering in the general cause. But what further advice to offer you on this sad occasion is a matter of the greatest difficulty, which not only requires more mature deliberation, but also that we should take the necessary steps to obtain the general sentiment of our fellow-inhabitants of this province, as well as of the sister colonies.   If satisfying the East India Company for the damage they have sustained would put an end to this unhappy controversy and leave us on the footing of constitutional liberty for the future, it is presumed that neither you nor we could continue a moment in doubt what part to act ; for it is not the value of the tax, *but the indefeasible right of giving and granting our own money* (A RIGHT FROM WHICH WE CAN NEVER RECEDE), that is now the matter in consideration.   By what means the truly desirable circumstance of a reconciliation and future harmony with our mother country on constitutional grounds may be obtained is indeed a weighty question.   Whether by the methods you propose, of a general *non-importation and non-exportation* agreement, or by a *general congress* of deputies from the different colonies, clearly to state what we conceive to be our rights, and to make a claim or petition of them to his Majesty in firm but decent and dutiful terms (so as that we may know by what line to conduct ourselves in future), are now the great points to be determined.   The latter method we have reason to think would be most agreeable to the people of this province, and is the first step that ought to be taken.   The former may be reserved as our last resource, should the other fail, which we trust will not be the case, as many wise and good men in the mother country begin to see the necessity of a good understanding with the colonies upon the general plan of liberty as well as commerce.

We shall endeavor as soon as possible to collect the sentiment of the people of this province and of the neighboring colonies on these grand questions, and we should also be glad to know your sentiments thereon. In the mean time, with sincere fellow-feeling for your sufferings and great regard for your person, we are, &c.*

---

* This letter was only signed by the persons present at the meeting of the committee on the 21st. In regard to the rest—Dickinson, Fox, Nesbit, Reed, Marshall and Penrose—it was said that "their business and avocations prevented them from attending." (2 Hazard Register, p. 34.)

This letter being signed by the committee, Mr. Revere was despatched therewith to Boston, enclosing a copy of the above resolutions. Copies of the letter and resolutions were also forwarded to the colonies, who generally waited to know the proceedings at Philadelphia.

By the 28th of June public feeling in Philadelphia had somewhat declared itself, and "a very large and respectable meeting of the freeholders and freemen of the city and county of Philadelphia" was held on that day. Thomas Willing and John Dickinson, Esqs., were appointed chairmen.

It was resolved as follows:

I. That the act of parliament, for shutting up the port of Boston, is unconstitutional; oppressive to the inhabitants of that town; dangerous to the liberties of the British colonies; and that therefore, we consider our brethren, at Boston, as suffering in the common cause of America.

II. That a congress of deputies from the several colonies in North America, is the most probable and proper mode of procuring relief for our suffering brethren, obtaining redress of American grievances, securing our rights and liberties, and re-establishing peace and harmony between Great Britain and these colonies, on a constitutional foundation.

III. That a large and respectable committee be immediately appointed for the city and county of Philadelphia, to correspond with the sister colonies and with the several counties in this province, in order that all may unite in promoting and endeavoring to attain the great and valuable ends, mentioned in the foregoing resolution.

IV. That the committee nominated by this meeting shall consult together, and on mature deliberation determine, what is the most proper mode of collecting the sense of this province, and appointing deputies for the same, to attend a general congress; and having determined thereupon, shall take such measures, as by them shall be judged most expedient, for procuring this province to be represented at the said congress, in the best manner that can be devised for promoting the public welfare.

V. That the committee be instructed immediately to set on foot a subscription for the relief of such poor inhabitants of the town of Boston, as may be deprived of the means of subsistence by the operation of the act of parliament, commonly styled the *Boston port bill*. The money arising from such subscription to be laid out as the committee shall think will best answer the ends proposed.

VI. That the committee consist of forty-three persons, viz.: John Dickinson, Edward Penington, John Nixon, Thomas Willing, George Clymer, Samuel Howell, Joseph Reed, John Roberts (miller), Thomas Wharton, jun., Charles Thompson, Jacob Barge, Thomas Barclay, Wm.

Rush, Robert Smith (carpenter), Thomas Fitzsimons, George Roberts, Samuel Ervin, Thomas Mifflin, John Cox, George Gray, Robert Morris, Samuel Miles, John M. Nesbit, Peter Chevalier, Wm. Moulder, Joseph Moulder, Anthony Morris, jun., John Allen, Jeremiah Warder, jun., Rev. Dr. William Smith, Paul Engle, Thomas Penrose, James Mease, Benjamin Marshall, Reuben Haines, John Bayard, Jonathan B. Smith, Thomas Wharton, Isaac Howell, Michael Hillegas, Adam Hubley, Geo. Schlosser and Christopher Ludwick.

After the first reading of the resolutions and before they were put up separately, Dr. Smith made the following short address:

GENTLEMEN: The occasion of this meeting is fully known to you, and sundry propositions have been read, which are now to be separately offered for your approbation or disapprobation. But before you proceed to this business, it has been thought proper to submit a few things to your good judgment, with respect to the order and decorum necessary to be observed, in the discussion of every question.

It need not be repeated to you, that matters of the highest consequence to the happiness of this province, nay of all British America, depend upon your deliberations this day—perhaps nothing less than, whether the breach with the country from which we descended shall be irreparably widened, or whether ways and means upon constitutional grounds, may not yet be devised, for closing that breach, and restoring that harmony from which, in our better days, Great Britain and her colonies derived mutual strength and glory, and were exalted into an importance that, both in peace and war, made them the envy and terror of the neighbouring nations?

While subjects such as these are agitated before us, everything that may inflame and mislead the passions should be cast far behind us. A cause of such importance and magnitude as that now under our deliberation, is not to be conducted to its true issue by any heated or hasty resolves, nor by any bitterness and animosities among ourselves, nor even perhaps by too severe a recapitulation of past grievances; but require the temperate and enlightened zeal of the *patriot*, the prudence and experience of the *aged*, the strength of mind and vigour of those, who are in their prime of life; and, in short, the united wisdom and efforts of *all*, both high and low, joining hand in hand, and setting foot to foot, upon the firm ground of reason and the constitution.

Whenever party distinctions begin to operate, we shall give cause of triumph to those, who may be watchful as well as powerful to abridge us of our native right. There ought to be no party, no contention here, but who shall be firmest and foremost in the common cause of America. Every man's sentiments should be freely heard, and without prejudice.

While we contend for liberty with others, let us not refuse liberty to each other.

Whatever *vote* is known to be now passed, upon full deliberation, and by the unanimous voice of this great city and county, will not only be *respected* through all America, but will have such a weight as the proudest Minister in England may have reason to *respect*. But if it is known to be a *divided vote*, or adopted hastily on some angry day, it will only be injurious to our own cause.

What I have in charge to request of you is this—that if, on any point, we should have a difference of sentiments, every person may be allowed to speak his mind *freely*, and to conclude what he has to offer, without any such outward marks of approbation or disapprobation, as *clapping or hissing;* and that if a division should be necessary (which it is hoped may not be the case this day), such division may be made in the manner desired by the *chairmen*, with all possible order and decorum.

The following Circular Letter was sent by the Committee for the city and county of Philadelphia to the different counties in this province. The original now before me is in the handwriting of Dr. Smith, with alterations in that of John Dickinson.*

PHILADELPHIA, June 28th, 1774.

GENTLEMEN: The committee of correspondence for this city and county, beg leave to enclose you printed copies of the resolves, passed at a very large and respectable meeting of the Freeholders and Freemen in the State-house Square, on Saturday the 18th instant. By the 4th of those resolves, you will observe that it was left for the Committee "To determine on the most proper mode of collecting the sense of this province in the present critical situation of our affairs, and appointing Deputies to attend the *proposed Congress.*" In pursuance of this trust, we have, upon the maturest deliberation, determined upon the mode contained in the two following propositions, which we hope may meet with the approbation and concurrence of your respectable county, viz. :

1. That the Speaker of the Honourable House of Representatives be desired to write to the several members of Assembly in this province, requesting them to meet in this city as soon as possible, but not later than the 1st of August next, to take into their consideration our very alarming situation.

2. That letters be written to proper persons in each county, recommending it to them to get Committees appointed for their respective counties, and that the said Committees, or such number of them as may be thought proper, may meet in Philadelphia at the time the Represent-

---

* See *supra*, p. 492.

atives are convened, in order to consult and advise on the most expedient mode of appointing Deputies for the general congress, and to give their weight to such as may be appointed.

The Speaker of the Assembly, in a very obliging and ready manner, had agreed to comply with the request in the former of these propositions; but we are now informed that, on account of the Indian disturbances, the Governor has found it necessary to call the Assembly to meet in their legislative capacity on Monday, July 18th, being about the same time the Speaker would probably have invited them to a con ference or convention in their private capacity.

What we have therefore to request is, that if you approve of the mode expressed in the second proposition, the whole or part of the committee appointed, or to be appointed for your county, will meet the committees from the other counties at Philadelphia, on Friday the 15th of July, in order to assist in framing instructions, and preparing such matters as may be proper to recommend to our Representatives at their meeting the Monday following.

We trust no apology is necessary for the trouble we propose giving your committee, of attending at Philadelphia; as we are persuaded you are fully convinced of the necessity of the closest union among ourselves both in sentiment and action; nor can such union be obtained so well by any other method, as by a meeting of the county committees of each particular province, in one place, preparatory to a general congress.

We would not offer such an affront to the well-known public spirit of Pennsylvanians, as to question your zeal on the present occasion. Our very existence in the rank of Freemen, and the security of all that ought to be dear to us, evidently depend upon our conducting this great cause to its proper issue by firmness, wisdom and unanimity. We cannot therefore doubt your ready concurrence in every measure that may be conducive to the public good; and it is with pleasure we can assure you, that all the colonies, from South Carolina to New Hampshire, seem animated with one spirit in the common cause, and consider this as the proper crisis for having our differences with the Mother Country brought to some certain issue, and our liberties fixed upon a permanent foundation. This desirable end can only be accomplished by a free communion of sentiments, and a sincere fervent regard to the interests of our common country. We beg to be favoured with an answer to this and whether the Committee for your county can attend at Philadelphia at the time proposed.

(Signed by the Chairman.)

On the 15th of July a provincial meeting was held of the deputies chosen by the several counties in Pennsylvania to draft instructions to their representatives in assembly, Dr. Smith, John Dick-

32

inson, Joseph Reed, Thomas Mifflin and Charles Thomson "represented the city and county of Philadelphia." The following gentlemen were appointed a committee to bring in a draft of instructions :

John Dickinson, Joseph Reed, Elisha Price, James Smith, Daniel Brodhead, Dr. William Smith, John Kidd, William A. Atlee, James Wilson, John Okely and William Scull.

The instructions were presented to the members of the Assembly, and a resolution of thanks tendered to Mr. Dickinson for the same.

The letter which follows from Mr. Edward Antill, a wine-grower of New Jersey, is interesting as showing at how early a date the conviction was entertained that the making of Wine in our country would, in time, be a great benefit to it, and, as the author of the letter says, "to the mother country." To the former it has already become a great benefit; and with our largely increasing exports to Great Britain, it may "in time" become so to her also.

Mr. Edward Antill to Dr. Smith.

October 29th, 1774.

VERY REVEREND Sʀ. : Yesterday I was favoured with your very obliging Letter by the Reverend Mr. Cooke,* dated at New Brunswick the 14th of the present October.

Nothing can give greater pleasure to a lover of mankind, than to see Gentlemen of the first rank in knowledge as well as in fortune forming themselves into collective Bodies for the good and happiness of the world. An undertaking truely generous and noble, every way worthy of great and benevolent minds ! If the design be well and deeply laid, if it be founded upon the Rock of Wisdom ; if Virtue and true Religion be the leading Principles, and the real good and Happiness of Mankind be the end proposed and steadily pursued ; then if History may be depended upon, if Experience cannot deceive, and the Word of God be the Touchstone of Truth, such undertaking will prosper and succeed, and the Consequences must be greater than I can describe. But if Ostentation and Vain glory, if Party Zeal and the Spirit of opposition be at bottom or lurk within its Bowels, it must and will end in disorder and confusion, in Vanity and Smoke, and prove an inexpressible injury to the Community. What in the name of Heavens has Philosophy to do with Party, what have Arts and Sci-

---

* This, I suppose, was Mr. Samuel Cooke, Missionary of the Society for the Propagation of the Gospel, at Shrewsbury, N. J.

ences to do with Politicks, or Navigation, Agriculture and Manufactures
with great men in opposition? let these be the Objects of pursuit to
Ambition and Self Interest, or the Tinckling sounds to amuse and captivate the Vulgar.   But let Philosophy, let the Love of Mankind soar
above these foot-balls of Fortune, and generously unite in the discovery
of truth and of things profitable for the Ease and Happiness of Mankind.   I know you can bear with the Simplicity of an Old Man.   I am
sure I can freely venture to unload into your bosom, a mind affécted
with the Errors and Follies of a mistaken world, without the danger of
ridicule or of being despised ; it behooves me at this time of life to be
plain and sincere.

I am sensible of the Honour You in particular have done me, recommending me to so Respectable a Body of Gentlemen, and of the Obligation I am under to them for offering to receive me, in so kind and
generous a manner, as a member of the Body.   I blush to think of my
weakness and inabilities which must always sinck me below such distinction and Partiality.   It is some years since I have endeavoured to retire
from the World, in order to pursue such studies as are most fit for Old
Age ; and as the mind is fatigued by dwelling long on one set of Ideas,
I found it necessary to shift the scene, and to pursue others that were
innocently pleasing and entertaining ; of this kind, among others, was
the Vine, the culture and Benefit of Vineyards and the making of Wine ;
the knowledge of which I have endeavour'd to attain in Theory and
Practice, when I thought I had by a number of experiments become
master of the subject ; and being, as I thought, clearly of opinion, that
the making of wine would in time be a great benefit to this and the
Mother Country ; I drew up something for the Eye and Consideration
of the Publick : soon after which I writ a Letter to Dr. Sonmans upon
the same subject, he shewed it to the Society of which he is a member ;
this drew from me one or two letters more to him and Doctor Morgan,
upon which the Society was so very partial to these little performances,
that they were pleased to annex me as a Corresponding Member to their
Body in April last, and a Certificate of their having so done, was sent
me in a very polite and most indulgent letter from Doctor Morgan, all
which happened some time before I received your favour :   The Honour
done me by Doctor Morgan and the Worthy Society for promoting
useful knowledge, on this occasion, so far exceeds any merit in me, that
I have accepted of it with a suitable and grateful sense of the Obligation, and I do assure you and him that I shall, as a member of that
society, do everything in my power to promote the General Good of
Mankind.

I beg, S^r, you will render my most respectful salutations acceptable
to the Society of which you are a member, and assure them that I retain
a very grateful sense of the Honour they intended me, and altho' I am
precluded the advantage of being a member of their Respectable Body,

yet I shall most heartily, to the utmost of my power, endeavour to promote the general good Design, which I make no doubt both Societies
have in view.

I am, very Reverend S^r, with great Esteem and Respect,

Your most Obliged and most humble Servant,

EDWARD ANTILL.

To the VERY REVEREND DR. WM. SMITH.

CHAPTER XXXIII.

THE COLLEGE COMMENCEMENT OF THIS YEAR ATTENDED BY THE CONTINENTAL
CONGRESS—WILLIAM MOORE SMITH A GRADUATE—SKETCH OF HIM—LADY
JULIANA PENN TO DR. SMITH—DR. SMITH ELECTED PRESIDENT OF ST.
ANDREW'S SOCIETY—DR. SMITH'S POLITICAL VIEWS STATED IN CONNEXION
WITH THE TIMES—SERMON IN CHRIST CHURCH ON THE PRESENT SITUATION
OF AMERICAN AFFAIRS—GREAT IMPRESSION PRODUCED BY IT—EXTRACTS
FROM IT—FAVORABLE AND UNFAVORABLE OPINIONS ABOUT IT—THE PHILA-
DELPHIA CLERGY TO THE BISHOP OF LONDON—DR. SMITH TO HIM—DR.
SMITH TO THE SECRETARY OF THE PROPAGATION SOCIETY—SAME TO SAME.

WE are approaching to important times. The Continental Con-
gress of 1775 had just assembled in Philadelphia. It met on
Wednesday, May the 10th. The College proceeds undisturbed.
We have an account of the Commencement at it, which in this
year was on the 17th of May, in the *Pennsylvania Magazine* of
Robert Aitken.* I give an extract:

This day the public commencement for Graduates in the Arts was
held here, in the presence of the most illustrious assembly this seminary
ever beheld.

About half an hour after nine o'clock, agreeable to an invitation
previously given to them, the Honóurable Members of the Continental
Congress were pleased to proceed in a body from the State House to
the College, where they were received at the gate by the Provost, and
conducted to the places prepared for their reception in the Hall. As
soon as they were seated, the Trustees, with the Governor as President
at their head, followed by the Provost, Vice-Provost, Professors, Graduates and other Students, in their proper habits, entered the hall, and
took their places; the galleries and other parts of the house being filled
with as many of the respectable inhabitants of the city as could find
room.

---

* Vol. I., p. 235.

The business then proceeded in the following order, viz. :

1. Part of the church service, and an occasional prayer, by the Provost.

2. An Anthem, accompanied by the organ, and other instrumental music.

3. Latin Salutatory Oration, *de amicitia.* By Henry Ridgley.

4. On the Education of young Ladies. By Francis Brown Sappington.

5. Latin Syllogistic dispute, *Utrem detur sensus moralis?* Respondent, William Moore Smith; Opponents, Benjamin Chew and John Mifflin.

6. On Ancient Eloquence. By Thomas Ennals.

7. On Politeness. By John Mifflin.

8. The Fall of Empires. By William Moore Smith.

9. The degrees were then conferred as follows, viz. :

Bachelors of Arts.—Benjamin Chew, Townsend Eden,* Thomas Ennals,* John Farrel, John Mifflin, Henry Ridgley,* Francis Brown Sappington,* and William Moore Smith.

Masters of Arts.—Samuel Armor, John Park, and John Thomas.

Honorary Master of Arts.—James Ross.

10. A Dialogue and two Odes set to music.

11. Valedictory Oration. By Benjamin Chew.

12. Charge to the Graduates. By the Provost.

13. Concluding Prayer. By the Vice-Provost.

The reader will observe among the graduates of this year the name of William Moore Smith, the oldest son of Dr. Smith, and whose birth we recorded in the beginning of this volume.† He was my grandfather. At his graduation he delivered a speech on the Fall of Empires. It had probably been pre-arranged that the Continental Congress should be present. The purport of the speech is to show that empires are generally ruined by luxury; the imports from foreign climes. No allusion is made to the non-importation resolutions of the Congress of 1774; but the sentiments and arguments of the oration are all in support of them. Parts of the speech —the whole of which is given in the May number of the *Pennsylvania Magazine* of 1775‡—are quite eloquent. But our space forbids extracts. On leaving college, Mr. William Moore Smith studied law, and this profession was pursued by him with honor and profit, until the close of the last century, when he received an

---

* Those distinguished by this mark * are of Maryland, the others of Philadelphia.

† Page 214.   ‡ Page 215.

agency for the settlement of British claims in America, provided
for in the 6th article of Jay's Treaty. The duties of this appointment required his presence in England; and he accordingly
visited that country in 1803, successfully accomplishing the purpose for which his services had been engaged. On his return to
America, he retired from professional practice, to the family-seat
at the Falls of Schuylkill, where he continued to reside, engaged
in his favorite literary pursuits, until his death, which took place
on the 12th of March, 1821. He was a ripe scholar, as well
as an excellent jurist. His classical attainments were extensive, and he retained them in all their original freshness, by constant cultivation, to his death. He was remarkably studious; and
his acquisitions in knowledge of every kind, aided by a retentive
memory, made his mind a treasury of learning. He was a living
index to what had passed, as well as what was passing before him;
and his references were seldom marked by error. Notwithstanding his devotion to letters, he was not a voluminous writer. Being
without ambition to be observed of the world, or to win its renown, he could not be induced to give any work, which would
evidence the wealth which his mind had gained through a life
dedicated to study and contemplation. However, besides some
political pamphlets and essays, written for the special occasions
which called them forth, he published a volume of Poems in 1785,
and their merit procured a republication in London the following
year. He married, on the 3d of June, 1786, at the Trappe, in
Montgomery county, Pennsylvania, Ann, eldest daughter of Col.
Joseph Rudolph.*

We have now a letter from Lady Juliana Penn to Dr. Smith.†
As all our readers know, she was the wife of Thomas Penn, son of
William Penn, the Proprietor, by his second wife, Hannah Callow-
hill, and a daughter of Thomas Germon, first Earl of Pomfret.
As this letter shows, she was as much distinguished by elegance
of literary accomplishment, and apparently by goodness of heart
also, as she was by high descent and rank.

---

* The originator of the Rudolph family was a Swede, and came to America before
1682, and settled at the head of Elk, now Elktown.

† For this copy I am indebted to the courtesy of Mr. R. C. Davis, of Philadelphia,
in whose possession the original is.

STOKE, May 30, 1775.

SIR: I beg you to accept my thanks for the favor of y^r Packet delivered me by M^r. Hare on May 17th.* I had not before the pleasure of knowing him, but am obliged to you for procuring me that of his acquaintance. He did me the favor to dine with me just before I left London, by which I had an opportunity of Some Conversation with him. I am very glad to find you are likely to have him settled amongst you, as he must be a very agreeable acquisition to any society. I have not heard of M^r. Cox's arrival. If he does me the favor to call on me, I shall be very glad to shew him any civility in my power, and to any body from Phil^a you will mention to me, or is connected with you.

Your Packet for your Brother (in that directed to me) was delivered into his hand the same hour it came into mine. So I have the satisfaction to tell you it is safe.

I am much obliged to you for *Park's Map*, and will be careful to return it to you. I have shewn it to M^r. Baker & M^r. Wilmot. They had neither of them seen one before. When I wrote last I thought the Connecticut dispute would have been determined the first of May; it is now postponed to the 15th of June. As I spoke positively then, I am fearful of doing so now, or I should say it will then be decided. You are very obliging to have given me so exact answers to those questions I was desired to make you in mine of December last, and I hope soon to send you word they and your pamphlet have made the business very clear.

I must be obliged to M^r. Hare for conveying to you a Silver Medal, just struck, of the first Proprietor of Pennsylvania. I hope you will do me the favor to accept it; but I can send nothing from here but which some friend will take privately, which prevents me sending at the same time a print from a Painting of M^r. West's on the Subject of the Settlement of your Province, but shall take the first opportunity to send you one of them likewise. With wishing this to find you and your family in perfect health, I shall conclude, and am, Sir,

Your most obliged and very humble Servant,

JULIANA PENN.

In the year 1749 certain gentlemen—natives of Scotland—Dr. Thomas Græme, Charles Stedman, Thomas Cameron, John Wallace, Alexander Forbes, Annand Alexander, and a few others, whose names are not less ethnologically Scotch, met together in Philadelphia and established a benevolent association, known as THE ST. ANDREW'S SOCIETY. Its object was the excellent one of assisting with advice and money natives of Scotland coming to

---

* I suppose this to have been Mr. Robert Hare, of Philadelphia.

America and needing assistance of either kind. It has now existed for one hundred and thirty years, and with great credit and usefulness. It keeps its members in social relation, chiefly by a quarterly supper and by an annual dinner. General Hugh Mercer, the Rev. John Witherspoon, and many other eminent Scotchmen, have been among its members. Dr. Smith early became a member, and was soon chosen a Vice-President. On the death of his friend, Dr. Græme, who was its first President, he was elected to the place left vacant by the melancholy event, and long filled it with dignity and effect.

But we are now approaching grave events indeed. On Thursday, June 15th, 1775, George Washington is unanimously chosen General and Commander-in-Chief of the American Forces. On the next day he accepts the command. A person who had been so conspicuous as a public speaker, writer, and actor, as Dr. Smith had been for many years in Philadelphia, could not now, in times of need, shrink and disappear from the scene of public events. He was accordingly a speaker, writer, and actor in them both in 1775 and 1776.

It is important to define his views and course. So far back as 1765, and on the passage of the Stamp-Act, he had expressed himself to a British Dean* with distinctness as disapproving of the measure. He speaks of it as "contrary to the faith of charters and the inherent rights of Englishmen"—"a badge of disgrace"— the enforcement of which can, *perhaps*, by superior power, be made, but only "with such alienations of the affections of a loyal people, and such a stagnation of English consumption among them, that the experiment can never be worth the risque."

His expressions and course seem to have been equally plain from the year 1774. He was strong and constant in declaring openly that the measures of the British Parliament and Ministry were unconstitutional, unjust, and unwise. And, as we now discover by his letters lately brought out of the Archives of Lambeth and other ancient cartularies of England, he was just as strong and constant on this matter when addressing English Bishops and other people of importance in England as he was when speaking to our own people at home. I see no variableness nor shadow of

---

* Dean Tucker. See *supra*, p. 385.

turning in his expressions or his views on these matters anywhere. What he uttered was obviously the conviction of his understanding and the feeling of his heart. It was certain, therefore, to have consistency throughout.

He acted under a sense of moral responsibility in what he did. He felt the weight of Christ's commands upon him. He knew whence wars come. He knew that war was a tremendous evil; and that " the man who for any cause save the sacred cause of public security, which made all wars defensive—the man who for any cause but that—should promote or compel this final and terrible resort, assumed a responsibility second to none—nay, transcendently deeper and higher than any—which man can assume before his fellow-man, or in the presence of God, his Creator."

Dr. Smith did not consider the *only* question to be whether Independence should be had. Assuming that sooner or later it was to be fought for and would come, the questions with him were how it was to be brought about in the shortest time after the Declaration of it was made; how with the smallest measure of the horrors of war; how with the least overthrow of " national prosperity and individual happiness; " how, as least to overcome and destroy " the frugal, industrious, and virtuous habits of our people; " how without the suffering indescribable which in the unprepared way in which Pennsylvania entered the war, soon involved both her people and the army, and how without the bankruptcy universal which, as soon, became the calamity of the nation, and in millions of unpaid and still existing, but worthless notes, remains to this day, and will forever remain, among innumerable glories indeed, the dishonor of our Revolution.

Dr. Smith had heard before of worthless paper issued in times of war being made a legal tender for the payment of honest debts. He bethought him of his College, and saw in the visions of his prophetic mind that which shortly actually happened—the College ruined by scoundrel debtors paying their mortgages and redeemable ground-rents to it in the worthless issues which the precipitation of war at once brought upon the country.

But the contest between Great Britain and the Colonists would not be war. It would be revolution. Was the case of the Colonies then a case as yet for revolution? He says:

That was a question which it was not the province of the ministers of Christ, who had given us no rule in that matter, to decide. God, however, in his own government, never violated freedom; and the Scriptures did not belie his voice speaking in the hearts of men. Nor was continued submission to violence a tenet of our church.

The views, such as I have given above, were the views of Dr. Smith. He states to English and Americans alike, that we have many and great causes of complaint and remonstrance. He says to all alike that no gospel or epistle demands a life of servitude to any one; that revolution *may* become allowable. But whether that time has arrived, each man must judge for himself. And he ends with praying that God in mercy would restore good-will and enable Great Britain and her Colonies to live in perpetual friendship.

The Congress of 1775 does the same. In its address to George III., made so late as July 8th, 1775, it says:

Attached as we are to your majesty's person and government, with all the devotion that principle and affection can inspire, connected with Great Britain by the strongest ties which can unite societies, and deploring every event that tends in any degree to weaken them, we solemnly assure your majesty that we not only most ardently desire that the former happiness between her and these Colonies may be restored, but that a concord may be established between them upon so firm a basis as to perpetuate its blessings, uninterrupted by any future dissensions to succeeding generations in both countries, and to transmit your majesty's name to posterity, adorned with that signal and lasting glory that both attended the memory of those illustrious personages whose virtues and abilities have extricated States from dangerous convulsions, and by securing happiness to others have added the most noble and durable monuments to their own fame.

But after the Declaration had been made, and after it was plain to him that America would now listen to no terms of reconciliation but in Independence, Dr. Smith acquiesced in that condition of affairs. And when Independence was achieved and peace was made, he was ready to join with our citizens everywhere, to regard it as a national blessing, and perpetually in every year, to render thanks to Almighty God for it accordingly.

Of all men in America it became William Smith least to urge forward a rupture with Great Britain. He had been educated by her charity. Much that he was he owed to her, whether in childhood, in youth, or in maturer age. From her Sovereign, from her

Premier, from her Archbishops, from her Bishops, from her Church, from her Universities, from her people of every grade—the highest and the humble—had he not been receiving continually, for many years, acts of honor, and acts of kindness—acts of high honor, acts of solid kindness? Did it become *him* to be the first to kindle the flames of revolution? No one will assert that it did.

Reading Dr. Smith's sermons, speeches and letters, and contemplating his acts in the light of the observations just made, I see nothing in any of them to censure. Least of all, in any part of them do I see anything like a time-server. Contrariwise, I think that he acted the part of a brave though self-controlled man; of a man who disregarded rather than acted in reference to popular views or demands in either country, or to his temporal interests in either. And if it be wise in any case for the clergy to enter the arena of politics, or for any of them not in army chaplaincy to address bodies of armed men preparing for war, I do not see how any of them could do it in a manner more worthy of the Christian minister and the wise patriot than it was done by my own ancestor.

We revert to our historical narrative. We shall follow it with a special reference to the sermons of Dr. Smith preached in this year, and by his letters to the English clergy.

On the 23d of June, 1775, Dr. Smith preached in Christ Church a sermon, which attracted vast notice. It was entitled, "A Sermon on the Present Situation of American Affairs." It was preached at the request of the officers of the third battalion, volunteer militia, of the city of Philadelphia, and district of Southwark; commanded by Colonel John Cadwalader, afterwards the well-known General. The members of Congress were present; as also, by the report of Silas Deane, "a vast concourse of people."

The text was from Joshua, ch. xxii., v. 22:

The Lord God of gods—the Lord God of gods—He knoweth and Israel he shall know—if it be in Rebellion or in transgression against the Lord—save us not this day!

He begins by a history of the passage.

Two and a half tribes of Israel called Gileadites had chosen their inheritance, on the eastern side of Jordan, opposite to the other tribes of Israel. And although they knew that this situation would deprive them of some privileges which remained with their brethren on the other side, and particularly that great privilege of having the place of

the Altar and Tabernacle of God among them; yet, as the land of
Canaan was judged too small for all the twelve tribes, they were contented with the possession they had chosen.   These tribes, then, were
allowed to separate from the rest, and to dwell on the other side of
Jordan.   They were to assist their brethren in their necessary wars, and
to continue under one government with them—erecting no separate
Altar, but coming to perform their sacrifices at that one Altar of Shiloh,
where the Lord had vouchsafed to promise His special presence.   They
supported their brethren in their wars, " till there stood not a man of
" all their enemies before them."   No sooner had they entered their
own country, than in the fulness of gratitude they built an high Altar,
that it might remain an eternal monument of their being of one stock,
and entitled to the same civil and religious privileges with their brethren
of the other tribes.   But this their work of piety and love was misconstrued.   The zealots of that day scrupled not to declare them rebels
against the living God, in setting up an altar against his holy altar ; and
therefore the whole congregations of the brother-tribes, that dwelt in
Canaan, gathered themselves together, in a blind transport of unright-
eous zeal, to go up to war against their own flesh and blood, purposing
to extirpate them from the face of the earth as enemies to God and the
commonwealth of Israel !

In that awful moment some men there were whose zeal did not so far
transport them, but that, before they unsheathed the sword to plunge it
with unhallowed hand into the bowels of their brethren, they thought it
justice first to inquire into the truth of the charge against them.   And,
for the glory of Israel, this peaceable and prudent counsel prevailed.
A solemn embassy was prepared, at the head of which was a man
of sacred character, and venerable authority, breathing the dictates
of religion and humanity; Phinehas the son of Eleazer the high
Priest, accompanied with ten other Chiefs or Princes, one from
each of the nine tribes as well as from the remaining half tribe of Ma-
nasseh.   Great was the astonishment of the Gileadites on receiving this
embassy, and hearing the charge against them.   By a solemn appeal to
Heaven for the rectitude of their intentions, unpremeditated and vehement, in the words of the text, they disarm their brethren of every
suspicion.

After this astonishing appeal to the great God of Heaven and Earth,
they proceed to reason with their brethren ; and tell them that, so far
from intending a separation either in government or religion, this altar
was built with a direct contrary purpose—" that it might be a witness
" between us and you, and our generations after us ; that your children
" may not say to our children in time to come, ye have no part in the
" Lord."   We were afraid lest, in some future age, when our posterity
may cross Jordan to offer sacrifices in the place appointed, your posterity
may thrust them from the altar, and tell them that because they live not

in the land where the Lord's tabernacle dwelleth, they are none of his people, nor intitled to the Jewish privileges.

This noble defence wrought an immediate reconciliation among the discordant tribes. "The words pleased the children of Israel—they "blessed God together" for preventing the effusion of kindred blood, "and did not go up to destroy the land where their brethren dwelt."

The preacher now proceeds:

The whole History of the Bible cannot furnish a passage more instructive than this, to the members of a great empire whose dreadful misfortune it is to have the evil Demon of civil or religious Discord gone forth among them. And would to God, that the application I am now to make of it could be delivered in accents louder than Thunder, till they have pierced the ear of every Briton; and especially their ears who have meditated war and destruction against their brother-tribes in this our American Gilead. And let me add—would to God too that we, who this day consider ourselves in the place of those tribes, may, like them, be still able to lay our hands on our hearts in a solemn appeal to the God of Gods, for the rectitude of our intentions towards the whole commonwealth of our British Israel. For, called to this sacred place, on this great occasion, I know it is your wish that I should stand superior to all partial motives, and be found alike unbiassed by favour or by fear. And happy it is that the parallel, now to be drawn, requires not the least sacrifice either of truth or virtue?

Like the tribes of Reuben and Gad, we have chosen our inheritance, in a land separated from that of our fathers and brethren, not indeed by a small river, but an immense ocean. This inheritance we likewise hold by a plain original contract, entitling us to all the natural and improvable advantages of our situation, and to a community of privileges with our brethren, in every civil and religious respect; except in this, that the throne or seat of Empire, that great altar at which the men of this world bow, was to remain among them.

Regardless of this local inconvenience, uncankered by jealousy, undepressed by fear, and cemented by mutual love and mutual benefits, we trod the path of glory with our brethren for an hundred years and more —enjoying a length of felicity scarce ever experienced by any other people. Mindful of the hands that protected us in our youth, and submitting to every just regulation for appropriating to them the benefit of our trade—our wealth was poured in upon them from ten thousand channels, widening as they flowed, and making their poor to sing, and industry to smile, through every corner of their land. And as often as dangers threatened, and the voice of the British Israel called our brethren to the field, we left them not alone, but shared their toils, and fought by their side, "till there stood not a man of all their enemies "before them." Nay, they themselves testified on our behalf that in all things we not only did our part, but more than our part, for the common Good ; and they dismissed us home loaded with silver and with gold,* in recompense for our extraordinary services.

But what high altars have we built to alarm our British Israel ; and why have the congregations of our brethren gathered themselves together against us? why do their embattled hosts already cover our plains? will they not examine our case, and listen to our plea?

"The Lord God of Gods—he knows," and the whole surrounding world shall yet know, that whatever American altars we have built, far from intending to dishonour, have been raised with an express view to perpetuate the name and glory of that sacred altar, and seat of empire and liberty, which we left behind us, and wish to remain eternal, among our brethren, in the parent land !

Esteeming our relation to them our greatest felicity; adoring the Providence that gave us the same progenitors; glorying in this, that when the new world was to be portioned out among the kingdoms of the old, the most important part of this continent fell to the sons of a Protestant and Free nation; desirous of worshiping forever at the same altar with them; fond of their manners, even to excess; enthusiasts to that sacred plan of civil and religious happiness, for the preservation of which they have sacrificed from age to age; maintaining, and always ready to maintain, at the risque of every thing that is dear to us, the most unshaken fidelity to our common Sovereign, as the great center of our union, and guardian of our mutual rights;—I say, with these principles and these views, we thought it our duty to build up American Altars, or Constitutions, as nearly as we could, upon the great British model.

Having never sold our birth-right, we considered ourselves intitled to the privileges of our father's house—" to enjoy peace, liberty and safety;" to be governed, like our brethren, by our own laws, in all matters properly affecting ourselves, and to offer up our own sacrifices at the altar of British empire; contending that a forced Devotion is Idolatry, and that no power on earth has a right to come in between us and a gracious Sovereign, to measure forth our loyalty, or to grant our property, without our consent. These are the principles we inherited from Britons themselves.

The altars, therefore, which we have built, are not high or rival altars to create jealousy, but humble monuments of our union and love; intended to bring millions yet unborn, from every corner of this vast continent, to bend at the great parent-altar of British liberty; venerating the country from which they sprung, and pouring their gifts into her lap when their countless thousands shall far exceed hers.   *   *   *

---

* The parliamentary reimbursements for our exertions in the late war, similar to what Joshua gave the two tribes and a half on the close of his wars.

But it is said that we have of late departed from our former line of duty, and refused our homage at the great altar of British empire. And to this it has been replied that the very refusal is the strongest evidence of our veneration for the altar itself. Nay, it is contended by those charged with this breach of devotion that, when in the shape of unconstitutional exactions, violated rights and mutilated charters, they were called to worship idols, instead of the true divinity, it was in a transport of holy jealousy that they dashed them to pieces, or whelmed them to the bottom of the ocean.

This is, in brief, the state of the argument on each side. And hence, at this dreadful moment, ancient friends and brethren stand prepared for events of the most tragic nature.

The preacher now breaks forth:

Here the weight of my subject almost overcomes me; but think not that I am going to damp that noble ardor which at this instant glows in every bosom present. Nevertheless, as from an early acquaintance with many of you, I know that your principles are pure, and your humanity only equalled by your transcendent love of your country, I am sure you will indulge the passing tear, which a preacher of the Gospel of Love must now shed over the scenes that lie before us—Great and deep distress about to pervade every corner of our land! Millions to be called from their peaceful labours by "the sound of the trumpet, and the alarm of war! Garments rolled in blood," and even Victory itself only yielding an occasion to weep over friends and relatives slain! These are melancholy prospects; and therefore you will feel with me the difficulties I now labour under—forsaken by my text, and left to lament alone that, in the Parent-land, no Phinehas has prevailed; no Embassy* of great or good men has been raised, to stay the sword of destruction, to examine into the truth of our case, and save the effusion of kindred blood. I am left to lament that, in this sad instance, Jewish tenderness has put Christian benevolence to shame.

Is there no wisdom, no great and liberal plan of policy to re-unite its members, as the sole bulwark of Liberty and Protestantism, rather than by their deadly strife to encrease the importance of those states that are foes to freedom, truth and humanity? To devise such a plan, and to behold British colonies spreading over this immense continent, rejoicing in the common rights of Freemen, and imitating the Parent State in

---

* It is acknowledged with gratitude that many great and exalted characters have advocated the cause of America; and, previous to all coercive measures, advised an inquiry or hearing, similar to that for which Phinehas was appointed. What is here lamented, and will be long lamented, is that this council could not take place. If brethren could come together in such a temper as this, the issue could not fail to be for their mutual glory and mutual happiness.

every excellence—is more glory than to hold lawless dominion over all the nations on the face of the earth!

But the preacher here remembers that he is addressing a body of troops, armed to vindicate their country's freedom! He says:

But I will weary you no longer with fruitless lamentations concerning things that *might* be done. The question now is—since they are not done, must we tamely surrender any part of our birthright, or of that great charter of privileges, which we not only claim by inheritance, but by the express terms of our colonization? I say, God forbid! For here, in particular, I wish to speak so plain that neither my own principles, nor those of the church to which I belong, may be misunderstood.

Although, in the beginning of this great contest, we* thought it not our duty to be forward in widening the breach, or spreading discontent, although it be our fervent desire to heal the wounds of the public, and to shew by our temper that we seek not to distress, but to give the parent state an opportunity of saving themselves and saving us before it be too late; nevertheless, as we know that our civil and religious rights are linked together in one indissoluble bond, we neither have, nor seek to have, any interest separate from that of our country; nor can we advise a desertion of its cause. Religion and liberty must flourish or fall together in America! We pray that both may be perpetual!

A continued submission to violence is no tenet of our church. When her brightest luminaries, near a century past, were called to propagate the court doctrine of a dispensing Power, above Law—did they treacherously cry—"Peace, Peace," when there was no Peace? Did they not magnanimously set their foot upon the line of the constitution, and tell Majesty to its face that "they could not betray the public liberty," and that the monarch's only safety consisted "in governing according to the laws?" Did not their example, and consequent sufferings, kindle a flame that illuminated the land and introduced that noble system of public and personal liberty, secured by the revolution? Since that period, have not the avowed principles of our greatest divines been against raising the Church above the State; jealous of the national rights, resolute for the protestant succession, favourable to the reformed religion, and desirous to maintain the faith of Toleration? If exceptions have happened, let no society of Christians stand answerable for the deviations or corruptions of individuals.

The doctrine of absolute Non resistance has been fully exploded among every virtuous people. The free-born soul revolts against it, and must have been long debased, and have drank in the last dregs of

* Meaning here the clergy and members of the Church of England generally.

corruption, before it can brook the idea "that a whole people injured "may, in no case, recognise their trampled Majesty."

Now comes a fine passage:

But to draw the line, and say where Submission ends and Resistance begins, is not the province of the ministers of Christ, who has given no rule in this matter, but left it to the feelings and consciences of the injured. For when pressures and sufferings come, when the weight of power grows intolerable, a people will fly to the constitution for shelter; and, if able, will resume that power which they never surrendered, except so far as it might be exercised for the common safety. Pulpit-casuistry is too feeble to direct or controul here. God, in his own government of the world, never violates freedom; and his scriptures themselves would be disregarded, or considered as perverted, if brought to belie his voice, speaking in the hearts of men.

The application of these principles, my brethren, is now easy and must be left to your own consciences and feelings. You are now engaged in one of the grandest struggles, to which freemen can be called. You are contending for what you conceive to be your constitutional rights, and for a final settlement of the terms upon which this country may be perpetually united to the Parent State.

Look back, therefore, with reverence look back, to the times of ancient virtue and renown. Look back to the mighty purposes which your fathers had in view, when they traversed a vast ocean, and planted this land. Recall to your minds their labours, their toils, their perseverance, and let their divine spirit animate you in all your actions.

Look forward also to distant posterity. Figure to yourselves millions and millions to spring from your loins, who may be born freemen or slaves, as Heaven shall now approve or reject your councils. Think that on you it may depend, whether this great country, in ages hence, shall be filled and adorned with a virtuous and enlightened people, enjoying Liberty and all its concomitant blessings, together with the Religion of Jesus, as it flows uncorrupted from his holy Oracles; or covered with a race of men more contemptible than the savages that roam the wilderness, because they once knew the "things which "belonged to their happiness and peace, but suffered them to be hid "from their eyes."

And while you thus look back to the past, and forward to the future, fail not, I beseech you, to look up to "the God of Gods—the Rock of your Salvation. As the clay in the potter's hands," so are the nations of the earth in the hands of Him, the everlasting JEHOVAH! He lifteth up—and he casteth down—"He resisteth the proud, and giveth grace "to the humble—He will keep the feet of his saints—the wicked shall "be silent in darkness, and by strength shall no man prevail."

The bright prospects of the Gospel; a thorough veneration of the

33

Saviour of the world; a conscientious obedience to His divine laws; faith in His promises; and the stedfast hope of immortal life through Him—these only can support a man in all times of adversity as well as prosperity. You might more easily "strike fire out of ice," than stability or magnanimity out of crimes. But the good man, he who is at peace with the God of all Peace, will know no fear but that of offending Him, whose hand can cover the righteous; "so that he needs not fear " the arrow that fleeth by day, nor the destruction that wasteth at noon- " day; for a thousand shall fall beside him, and ten thousand at his " right hand, but it shall not come nigh to him; for He shall give His " angels charge over him to keep him in all his ways."

On the Omnipotent God, therefore, through his blessed Son, let your strong confidence be placed; but do not vainly expect that every day will be to you a day of prosperity or triumph. The ways of Providence lie through mazes, too intricate for human penetration. Mercies may often be held forth to us in the shape of sufferings; and the vicissitudes of our fortune in building up this American fabric of happiness and glory may be various and chequered.

But let not this discourage you. Yea rather let it animate you with a holy fervour—a divine enthusiasm—ever persuading yourselves that the cause of Virtue and Freedom is the Cause of God upon earth; and that the whole theatre of human nature does not exhibit a more august spectacle than a number of Freemen, in dependence upon Heaven, mutually binding themselves to encounter every difficulty and danger in support of their native and constitutional rights, and for transmitting them holy and unviolated to their posterity.

It was this principle that inspired the heroes of ancient times; that raised their names to the summit of renown, and filled all succeeding ages with their unspotted praise. It is this principle too that must animate your conduct, if you wish your names to reach future generations, conspicuous in the roll of glory; and so far as this principle leads you, be prepared to follow—whether to life or to death.

While you profess yourselves contending for Liberty, let it be with the temper and dignity of freemen, undaunted and firm, but without wrath or vengeance, so far as grace may be obtained to assist the weakness of nature. Consider it as a happy circumstance, if such a struggle must have happened, that God hath been pleased to postpone it to a period, when our country is adorned with men of enlightened zeal; when the arts and sciences are planted among us to secure a succession of such men; when our morals are not far tainted by luxury, profusion or dissipation; when the principles that withstood oppression, in the brightest æra of English history, are ours as it were by peculiar inheritance; and when we stand upon our own ground, with all that is dear around us, animating us to every patriotic exertion. Under such circumstances, and upon such principles, what wonders, what achievements of true glory, have not been performed!

For my part, I have long been possessed with a strong and even enthusiastic persuasion, that Heaven has great and gracious purposes towards this continent, which no human power or human device shall be able finally to frustrate. Illiberal or mistaken plans of policy may distress us for a while, and perhaps sorely check our growth ; but if we maintain our own virtue ; if we cultivate the spirit of Liberty among our children ; if we guard against the snares of luxury, venality and corruption ; the Genius of America will still rise triumphant, and that with a power at last too mighty for opposition. This country will be free— nay, for ages to come, a chosen seat of Freedom, Arts, and Heavenly Knowledge ; which are now either drooping or dead in most countries of the old world.

To conclude, since the strength of all public bodies, under God, consists in their Union ; bear with each other's infirmities, and even varieties of sentiments, in things not essential to the main point. The tempers of men are cast in various moulds. Some are quick and feelingly alive in all their mental operations, especially those which relate to their country's weal, and are therefore ready to burst forth into flame upon every alarm. Others again, with intentions alike pure, and a clear unquenchable love of their country, too stedfast to be damped by the mists of prejudice, or worked up into conflagration by the rude blasts of passion, think it their duty to weigh consequences, and to deliberate fully upon the probable means of obtaining public ends. Both these kinds of men should bear with each other ; for both are friends to their country.

One thing further let me add, that without order and just subordination there can be no union in public bodies. However much you may be equals on other occasions, yet all this must cease in an united and associated capacity ; and every individual is bound to keep the place and duty assigned him, by ties far more powerful over a man of virtue and honour, than all the other ties which human policy can contrive. It had been better never to have lifted a voice in your country's cause, than to betray it by want of Union ; or to leave worthy men, who have embarked their all for the common good, to suffer, or stand unassisted.

Lastly, by every method in your power, and in every possible case, support the laws of your country. In a contest for liberty, think what a crime it would be, to suffer one Freeman to be insulted, or wantonly injured in his liberty, so far as by your means it may be prevented.

Thus animated and thus acting—We may then sing with the prophet—

" Fear not, O land ! be glad and rejoice, for the Lord will do great things. Be not afraid, ye beasts of the field, for the pastures of the wilderness do spring—The tree beareth her fruit—the fig-tree and the vine yield their fruit."

Thus animated and thus acting—we may likewise pray with the prophet—

" O Lord, be gracious unto us—we have waited for thee. Be thou our arm every morning, our salvation also in time of trouble. Some trust in chariots and some in horses, but we will remember the name of the Lord our God—O thou hope of Israel, the Saviour thereof in time of need—thou art in the midst of us and we are called by thy name—Leave us not. Give us one heart and one way, that we may fear thee forever, for the good of ourselves and our children after us—We looked for peace, but no good came; and for a time of health, but behold we are in trouble—Yet will we trust in the Lord forever; for in the Lord Jehovah is everlasting strength—He will yet bind up the broken-hearted, and comfort those that mourn"—even so, oh our God do thou comfort and relieve them, that so the bones which thou hast broken may yet rejoice. Inspire us with a high and commanding sense of the value of our constitutional rights! may a spirit of wisdom and virtue be poured down upon us all; and may our representatives, those who are delegated to devise and appointed to execute public measures, be directed to such, as thou in thy sovereign goodness shall be pleased to render effectual for the salvation of a great empire, and re-uniting all its members in one sacred bond of harmony and public happiness! Grant this, oh Father, for thy Son Jesus Christ's sake; to whom, with thee and the holy Spirit, one God, be Glory, Honour and Power now and forever! Amen.

An attentive and logically-headed reader would perhaps say of this sermon that it resembled the final chapter of Raselas: in which we have a conclusion in which nothing is concluded; and to some extent this is true. The subject treated is not one for mathematics and logic; and no greater error could the preacher have made than to apply rules of those sciences to a subject incapable of being treated by them. He lays down general moral and political rules. The application it was not for *him* to make to either the bodies before him; to either the Congress or the army.

As for what he says on page 513 about the line, "where submission ends and resistance begins," * it is noteworthy that from just the same pulpit of Christ Church he had said just the same thing —only giving a little stronger accentuation to both parts of the case—so far back as June, 1755, when preaching against the doctrines of the Quakers, who would not allow of even defensive war in the then "present dangerous state of affairs," from the well-known text, 1 Peter ii. 17: "Love the Brotherhood, fear God, honour the King." He then said:

---

* Smith's Works, Vol. II., p. 36.

The doctri   of non-resistance is now sufficiently exploded. God
gave us freedom as a birthright, and in his own government he never
violates it. Nor can those be his vice-gerents who do. To say they are is
blaspheming his Holy Name and giving the lie to his righteous government. The love of mankind and the fear of God—those very principles
from which we trace the divine original of just government—would lead
us to resist every tyrant to destruction, who should attempt to enslave
the free-born soul and oppose the righteous will of God by defeating
the happiness of mankind.

This, however, is to be a last resort, and none but the majority of a
whole people, both in wisdom and force, can determine in what case
resistance is necessary. In the Scriptures, therefore, obedience is rightly
inculcated in general terms. For a people may sometimes imagine
grievances, which they do not feel; but will never miss to feel and
complain of them where they really are, unless their minds have been
gradually prepared for slavery by absurd tenets.

Putting the two sermons together, we have much the same ideas
presented by the great philosophic statesman, Mr. Burke, in his
reflections on the revolution in France :

The speculative line of demarkation where obedience ought to end
and resistance must begin is faint, obscure, and not easily definable.
It is not a single act or a single event which determines it. Governments must be abused and deranged indeed before it can be thought of;
and the prospect of the future must be as bad as the experience of the
past. When things are in that lamentable condition, the nature of the
disease is to indicate the remedy to those whom nature has qualified to
administer in extremities this critical, ambiguous and bitter potion to a
distempered state. Times, and occasions, and provocations will teach
their own lessons. The wise will determine from the gravity of the
case ; the irritable from sensibility to oppression ; the high-minded from
disdain and indignation at abusive power in unworthy hands ; the brave
and bold from love of honorable danger in a generous cause ; but with
or without right, a revolution will be the very last resource of the
thinking and the good.

The sermon produced a great public impression. Silas Deane
writes as follows:

It exceeded in style and sentiment anything I ever heard on the subject. As the Doctor has been called an high churchman, and one that
had a bishopric in expectation, I hope his thus publicly sounding the
pulpit alarm on the subject of liberty will be an example to the church

* Works, Boston edition, 1839, Vol. III., p. 49.

clergy elsewhere, and bring them off from the line of conduct which they have hitherto ingloriously pursued.

The battalion before which it was preached, in a note signed by Colonel Cadwalader, by their order, "agreed that Dr. Smith be thanked for his excellent sermon, preached at their request, and that he be requested to furnish a copy of the same for publication."

It was soon published, with a preface, in which Dr. Smith states that it was drawn up on a few days' notice, and without any view to the press, at the request of some of the author's worthy friends, to whom he could refuse nothing of this kind; and adds that at their request it was likewise submitted to the public, as it was preached, without varying or suppressing a single sentiment or material expression; and with the addition only of a few lines, and three or four explanatory notes.

The preface proceeds:

The author considered that, although he was called to this office by a particular body, yet he was to address a great and mixed assembly of his fellow-citizens, and a number of the first characters* in America, met in consultation, at a most alarming crisis.

Animated with the purest zeal for the mutual interests of Great Britain and the colonies; ardently panting for the return of those Halcyon-days of harmony, during which both countries so long flourished together, as the glory and wonder of the world; he thought it his duty, with the utmost impartiality, to attempt a state of the unhappy controversy which [then] rent the empire in pieces; and to shew, if peradventure he might be permitted to vouch for his fellow-citizens, so far as he had been conversant among them, that the idea of an independence upon the Parent-country, or the least licentious opposition to its just interests, was utterly foreign to their thoughts; that they contended only for the sanctity of charters and laws, together with the right of granting their own money; and that our rightful Sovereign had nowhere more loyal subjects, or more zealously attached to those principles of government, under which his family inherits the throne.

These, with a few things which seemed necessary respecting the clergy and church, whereof the author is a member, are the topics handled in the following Sermon. If the principles it contains are but thoroughly felt, the reader will not regret that the limits of a single discourse would not allow a particular application of them. They will lead to their own application; or, at least, that field is left open to succeeding preachers.

---

* The Continental Congress.

Upon the whole, if the kind expectations of the Author's friends can be in any degree answered ; if what he has delivered shall tend " to promote the cause of Liberty and Virtue ; " and particularly, if it may find its way to the closets, or rather to the hearts, of the Great, and (after all the arguments they have heard from others) can in the least induce them to juster and more benevolent sentiments concerning their American brethren—he will account it among the happiest circumstances of his life.

Enough has surely been attempted, by way of experiment, to convince our British Brethren that the people of this country know their rights, and will not consent to a passive surrender of them—It is, now at least, time to pursue another method, and to listen to some plan for averting the dreadful calamities which must attend a hostile prosecution of this unnatural contest. The Author's wishes for the accomplishment of such a plan, have been so frequently expressed, as to subject him, perhaps, to suspicions which he would not wish to merit. But still, if he could see such a plan of reconciliation take place upon a just and permanent foundation, he would be content, if it were required, to sing his ' *nunc dimittis,*' and to take a final leave of earthly concerns.

The fate of the sermon was rather remarkable. It became an object of notice and controversy, of praise and censure, in Great Britain as well as in America, according to the different principles of its readers, much more than from anything very marked in the sermon itself. Having in a few weeks run through several American editions, in Pennsylvania, Delaware, and some of the nearest neighboring States; Dr. Smith received a mark of displeasure from Governor Tryon, at New York, who told him that he had considered it as his duty to transmit a copy of it to the Bishop of London. Governor Tryon added that he did not doubt but that the Bishop would soon signify his highest disapprobation and severe censure of the preacher. Dr. Smith replied briskly that he had already sent a copy of the sermon, as well as of sundry other proceedings of the clergy, both in their civil and religious capacity, to the Bishop; that, as to himself (Dr. Smith), he had well weighed the principles contained in the sermon, before he submitted them to the public, either from the pulpit or the press; and that he must take his chance of the Bishop's pleasure or displeasure.

In England Dr. Priestly wrote to Dr. Franklin :

I thank you for Dr. Smith's excellent Sermon. If it be not impertinent, give him my most respectful compliments and thanks. I think to get it printed.

Dr. Price to the same person :

The chamberlain of London has just ordered ten thousand copies of Dr. Smith's Sermon to be printed at his expense, in so cheap a form as to be sold at two-pence each.

The Messrs. Dilly, besides a small edition printed at the expense of the chamberlain, published in a short time two elegant editions, in a large size, on their own account. Editions also were printed and published at Bristol and elsewhere in Great Britain and Ireland; and the polemical and political newspapers made it the subject of attention and controversy.

The authors of the *Monthly Review*, for August, 1775, gave the following favorable criticism on Dilly's second edition :

Our readers are not unacquainted with the abilities of this American orator ; whose volume of discourses preached on public occasions at Philadelphia, was recommended in the 21st volume of our review ; and again, on the appearance of a new edition, with additional sermons, in vol. 29th.

The reviewers then give some account of the occasion of the sermon, and proceed as follows :

It is left for us to add—what could not, with equal propriety, have come from the pen of the author—that his discourse is equally sensible and animated, and that his zeal for the cause of American Liberty, though warm enough to kindle the hearts of his hearers, never transports him beyond the bounds of that moderation, by which true Patriotism, on either side of the Atlantic, will ever be guided.

The authors of the *London Magazine*, for August, 1775, also give their judgment :

Dr. Smith, though an Episcopal Clergyman, appears to be as zealous a friend to the Liberties of America, and as warm against the measures of administration, as any person whatsoever.

Dr. Priestly, Dr. Price, and the authors of the *Monthly Review* and *London Magazine*, were Whig writers, or at least friends to the liberties of America. Another set of writers in pamphlets and newspapers spoke of the sermon in another strain.

The venerable John Wesley, now very old, said :

A sermon preached by Dr. Smith, in Philadelphia, has lately been re-printed here (in Bristol). It has been much admired, but proceeds

all along upon wrong suppositions. Dr. Smith supposes the Americans
have a right of granting their own money: that is, of being exempt
from taxation by the supreme power. If they contend for this right,
they contend for neither more nor less than Independency. That
they contend for the cause of liberty is another mistaken supposition.
They have no liberty, civil or religious, but what the Congress allows.
Vainly do they complain of Unconstitutional Exactions, Violated
Rights, and Mutilated Charters.

Junius now came to Dr. Smith's side. He says to Mr.
Wesley:

I have read your address to the Americans with much surprize and
concern. That a man, after a long life devoted to the awful concerns
of Religion, and of a rigidity of morals strikingly contrasted to the
times, should in his old age step forth a champion in a political controversy, is a paradox only to be solved by a reflection on the general
motives of such compositions. They exhibit a proof, Mr. Wesley,
that the most perfect men have hopes upon earth as well as in Heaven ;
and indeed you have the moderation and sincerity not to forbid us to
believe so. When you deliver your opinion you say you may be the
better believed, because unbiassed ; and then express yourself in this
unguarded language—I gain nothing by the Americans, nor by the
government, and *probably never shall.* This is not only an invitation
to the Minister to reward your pious labours, but a thorn in his foot if he
overlooks them. Had you said, *and positively never will,* I should
then (as I always have) believed you to be an honest and pious man.

And now, Mr. Wesley, I take my leave of you. You have forgot
the precept of your Master, that God and Mammon cannot be served
together. You have one eye upon a Pension and the other upon Heaven
—One hand stretched out to the King, and the other raised up to God.
I pray that the first may reward you, and the last forgive you.

It is not known what reward, if any, the Ministry gave Mr.
Wesley; but his pamphlet was given away gratis in London and
elsewhere, as an antidote to this sermon.

A writer in *The London Chronicle,* from September 2d to 5th,
1775, signing himself "A Friend to the Constitution," said:

The modern patriot, says he, may be described as a person who
despises Order, Decency, and all kind of human Authority. I have
been lately tempted to add, that he also despises divine Authority.
Some late publications, of a very extraordinary nature, have induced
me to mention this disagreeable subject. At the very instant, in which
our gracious Sovereign is attempting, by his proclamation, to extin-

guish the sparks of Sedition, our Patriots are blowing up the Coals, and our Presses are teeming with Rebellion and Treason.

Lest the venom should not be fitted to every palate, or be swallowed in sufficient potions, they have found the pious art of engaging the pulpit in their cause. The particular case I refer to is a seditious Sermon, just reprinted here. It was first preached about two months ago at Philadelphia, for the comfort and edification of the City-Volunteers —for the comfort too of the Continental Congress, which was then sitting there.

The Preacher is not satisfied with assailing the state, by proving from a very extraordinary passage of Scripture that the Americans ought to rebel; but he, with great effrontery, presses the doctrine of our Church into his service. Let us hear him speak on the subject.

Certainly this preacher would have us to understand, or else we must be void of understanding, that a continued submission to violence is now expected of the Americans, and that his present Majesty wishes the Ministers of peace should betray the public Liberty.

The author of this discourse is at the head of a College. We shall say nothing about the streams that may be expected from such a pure fountain, nor about the honour our Church derives from such a luminary. But we will venture to say that while such essays are reprinted and dispersed * with impunity, the mild voice of a Proclamation to suppress Rebellion will not be heard.

In the *Public Advertiser*, of September 14th, 1775, another writer, who signed himself "Unitas," inserted a piece against the sermon. He began thus, addressing himself to the printer of the *Public Advertiser:*

Pray, Mr. Woodfall, do you ever read sermons? A political one, or so, I suppose, now and then, *pour tuer les tems.* Well, if you have not seen Dr. Smith's on the present situation of American affairs, let me recommend it to you as a curiosity. It was preached and published at the instigation of ——, so you may be sure it is a good thing. —The business of the Sermon, as the Doctor assures us, is with the utmost impartiality (dele *im*) to attempt a state of the unhappy controversy (soft words for unnatural rebellion) that now rends the empire in pieces—and to say a few things which seemed necessary respecting the Church (his zeal for which is no less conspicuous than his loyalty to the king) at this time.—Should what he has delivered tend to promote the cause of Liberty and Virtue (he says) he would account it among the happiest circumstances of his life—and he might

---

* Alluding to the edition printed and distributed at the expense, and by the direction, of the chamberlain of London.

account it among the most extraordinary too; for he may as well expect to gather grapes of thorns and figs of thistles, as that the cause
of liberty and Virtue should be promoted by preaching Rebellion.
The Doctor concludes his preface by observing that enough has been
done to shew that the Americans are not passive, and therefore that it
is time for government to listen to some plan of accommodation, which
if he could see take place, on a just and permanent foundation, he
would be content, if it were required, to sing his *nunc dimittis*, and
take a final leave of earthly concerns.—Here Unitas exclaims—and
it is his most witty stroke—" What a heavenly Soul! It is a pity he
did not sing it before, instead of deferring it till after, Sermon."

   A notion prevailing that in America the clergy of the Church of
England are friends to government, and obedient subjects upon principle; the good Doctor, vexed at the heart to think their Religious
Usefulness among the people should be destroyed, and the Church
suffer through such an imputation, steps forth to vindicate both Church
and Clergy, and demonstrate that the charge is false.

   Dr. Smith now found himself—as David Hume said that by
force of Bishop Warburton's railing at his Essays, he found *himself*—"in very good company." He was really and more than
ever one of the famous men of two continents.

   On Monday, June 12th, 1775, the Continental Congress made
the following preamble and recommendation touching A FAST:

   As the great Governor of the World, by his supreme & universal
Providence, not only conducts the course of Nature, with unerring wisdom & rectitude, but frequently influences the minds of men to serve
the wise & gracious purposes of his Providential Government; and it
being at all times our indispensable duty devoutly to acknowledge his
superintending Providence, especially in times of public calamity, to
reverence and adore his immutable justice, as well as to implore his
merciful interposition for our deliverance—

   This Congress, therefore,—considering the present critical, alarming
& calamitous state of these Colonies,—do earnestly recommend that
Thursday, the 20th of July next, be observed by the inhabitants of all
the English Colonies on this Continent as a day of Public Humiliation,
Fasting & Prayer; that we may, with united hearts & voices, unfeign-
edly confess & deplore our many sins, and offer up our joint supplications to the All-wise, Omnipotent & Merciful Disposer of all events,
humbly beseeching him to forgive our iniquities, to remove our present
calamities, to avert those desolating judgments, with which we are
threatened, & to bless our rightful Sovereign, King George the Third,
& inspire him with wisdom to discern & pursue the true interest of his
subjects, that a speedy end may be put to the civil discord between
Great Britain and the American Colonies, without further effusion of

blood: And that the British nation may be influenced to regard the things that belong to her peace, before they are hid from her eyes: That these Colonies may ever be under the care and protection of a kind Providence, and be prospered in all their interests: That the divine blessing may descend and rest upon all our civil rulers, and upon the representatives of the people in their several Assemblies and Conventions, that they be directed to wise and effectual measures for preserving the union and securing the just rights and privileges of the Colonies: That virtue and true religion may revive and flourish throughout our land: And that all America may soon behold a gracious interposition of Heaven for the redress of her many grievances, the restoration of her invaded rights, a reconciliation with the parent state, on terms constitutional and honorable to both: And that her civil and religious privileges may be secured to the latest posterity.

And it is recommended to Christians of all denominations to assemble for public worship, and to abstain from servile labour and recreation on said day.

We now proceed to give different letters bearing on these troubled times; and especially to this Fast, " earnestly recommended," but not enjoined by the Congress.

The Philadelphia Clergy to the Bishop of London.

PHILADELPHIA, June 30th, 1775.

MY LORD :—We now sit down under deep affliction of mind to address your Lordship upon a subject, in which the very existence of our Church in America seems to be interested. It has long been our fervent prayer to Almighty God, that the unhappy controversy between the Parent Country and these Colonies might be terminated upon Principles honourable and advantageous to both, without proceeding to the extremities of civil war and the horrors of Bloodshed. We have long lamented that such a spirit of Wisdom and Love could not mutually prevail, as might devise some liberal Plan for this benevolent Purpose; and we have spared no means in our power for advancing such a spirit so far as our private Influence and advice could extend. But as to public advice we have hitherto thought it our duty to keep our Pulpits wholly clear from every thing bordering on this contest, and to pursue that line of Reason and Moderation which became our Characters; equally avoiding whatever might irritate the Tempers of the people, or create a suspicion that we were opposed to the Interest of the Country in which we live.

But the Time is now come, my Lord, when even our silence would be misconstrued, and when we are called upon to take a more public part. The Continental Congress have recommended the 20th of next month as a day of Fasting, Prayer & Humiliation thro' all the Colonies. Our Congregations too of all Ranks have associated themselves, determined never to submit to the Parliamentary claim of taxing them at pleasure ; and the Blood already spilt in maintaining this claim is unhappily alienating the affections of many from the Parent Country, and cementing them closer in the most fixed purpose of a Resistance, dreadful even in Contemplation.

Under these Circumstances our People call upon us, and think they have a right to our advice in the most public manner from the Pulpit. Should we refuse, our Principles would be misrepresented, and even our religious usefulness destroyed among our People. And our complying may perhaps be interpreted to our disadvantage in the Parent Country. Under these difficulties (which have been increased by the necessity some of our Brethren have apprehended themselves under of quitting their Charges), and being at a great distance from the advice of our Superiors, we had only our own Consciences and each other to consult, and have accordingly determined on that part, which the general good seem to require. We were the more willing to comply with the request of our Fellow Citizens, as we were sure their Respect for us was so great, that they did not even wish any thing from us inconsistent with our characters as Ministers of the Gospel of Peace.

Military Associations are no new Things in this Province where we never had any regular Militia Law. They subsisted during the different Alarms in the last War, and they now subsist under the special countenance of our own Assemblies, professing the most steady Loyalty to His Majesty, together with an earnest Desire of re-establishing our former harmony with the Mother Country, and submitting in all things agreeable to the ancient modes of Government among us.

Viewing matters in this Light, and considering not only that they were members of our own Congregations who called upon us, but that Sermons have heretofore been preached to such Bodies, we thought it advisable to take our Turn with the Ministers of other Denominations; and a Sermon was accordingly preached by Dr. Smith the 17th Instant, in which he thought it necessary to obviate any misrepresentations that might be made of the Principles of our Church.

Mr. Duché is likewise to preach on the 7th July, upon a similar Invitation; and all our Clergy throughout the Colonies, we believe, will preach on the Day recommended by the Continental Congress for a Fast. And God knows, that exclusive of such a Recommendation, there never was a Time when Prayer and Humiliation were more incumbent upon us.

Tho' it has of late been difficult for us to advise, or even correspond as usual, with our Brethren, the Clergy of New York, we find that they have likewise in their Turn officiated to their Provincial Congress now sitting there, as Mr. Duché did both this year & the last, at the opening of the Continental Congress.

Upon this fair and candid state of things, we hope your Lordship will think our conduct has been such as became us; and we pray that we may be considered as among His Majesty's most dutiful & loyal subjects in this and every other Transaction of our Lives. Would to God that we could become mediators for the Settlement of the unnatural Controversy that now distracts a once happy Empire. All that we can do is to pray for such a Settlement, and to pursue those Principles of Moderation and Reason which your Lordship has always recommended to us. We have neither Interest nor Consequence sufficient to take any Lead in the Affairs of this great Country. The People will feel and judge for themselves in matters affecting their own civil happiness; and were we capable of any attempt which might have the appearance of drawing them to what they think would be a Slavish Resignation of their Rights, it would be destructive to ourselves, as well as the Church of which we are Ministers. And it is but Justice to our Superiors, and your Lordship in particular, to declare that such a Conduct has never been required of us. Indeed, could it possibly be required, we are not backward to say that our Consciences would not permit us to injure the Rights of this Country. We are to leave our families in it, and cannot but consider its Inhabitants intitled, as well as their Brethren in England, to the Right of *granting their own money;* and that every attempt to deprive them of this Right will either be found abortive in the end, or attended with Evils which would infinitely outweigh all the Benefit to be obtained by it.

Such being our Persuasion, we must again declare it to be our constant Prayer, in which we are sure your Lordship joins, that the hearts of good and benevolent men in both Countries may be directed towards a Plan of Reconciliation, worthy of being offered by a great Nation, that have long been the Patrons of Freedom throughout the World; and not unworthy of being accepted by a People sprung from them, and by birth claiming a Participation of their Rights.

Our late worthy Governour, the Honble Richd Penn, Esqre, does us the favour to be the Bearer hereof, and has been pleased to say he will deliver it to your Lordship in Person. To him therefore we beg leave to refer your Lordship for the Truth of the Facts above set forth. At the ensuing Meeting of our Corporation for the Relief of Widows, &c., which will be the first week in October next, we shall have an Opportunity of seeing a Number of our Brethren together and consulting more generally with them upon the present state of our affairs and shall be happy on all occasions in the Continuance of your Lordship's paternal Advice and Protection.

(Signed)   RICHARD PETERS,
W^M. SMITH,
JACOB DUCHE,
THOMAS COOMBE,
WILLIAM STRINGER,
WILLIAM WHITE.

The preceding letter was enclosed, with a copy of Dr. Smith's recent Sermon on American Affairs, to the Bishop of London, in this one:

PHILADELPHIA, July 8th, 1775.

MY LORD,

The enclosed Letter signed by the Clergy of our Churches in this City was drawn up after frequent and serious Consultations with each other, and is dictated by Truth and a most dutiful regard to your Lordship as well as to the true Interest of the Mother Country.

The Sermon referred to in our joint Letter being now published is enclosed. No man has labored more earnestly than myself to avert the dreadful Calamity in which both Countries are now involved. God knows that my Endeavors to. promote conciliatory measures were so strong during the meeting of our provincial Convention last Summer, whereof I was a member, that I was considered as one willing to sacrifice essential liberty for temporary safety and even as an advocate for the measures of Administration respecting this country. I persevered however to recommend moderation till we finished those Instructions to our assembly which were generally approved in England as a rational plan of accommodating our differences. But the Continental Congress did not wholly adopt them. Tho' I thus took a part while matters were under deliberation, I have since that time wholly declined being of any new Committee or taking any public part in affairs, lamenting the Evils which I saw approaching (as I verily believed), for want of that benevolent spirit of Christianity, mutual good will and Zeal for the Good of the whole Empire, which if they could prevail might easily compromise this unnatural difference, and as Years are now growing upon me and the Bustle of the World is now very little my passion, Nothing could have called me forth but the joint advice of my Brethren and the reasons set forth in our joint Letter to your Lordship. But having once consented to appear again in public I would not violate my principles nor be cold to the Interests of America or of the Mother Country which are inseparably connected, nor could I suffer our Church or Clergy in America to be under Imputations which I am sure as far as I know them they do not merit.

It is undoubtedly the wish (indeed too openly avowed), of some in this Country to have the Church Clergy considered as Tools of Power, Slavish in their tenets and privately Enemies to the principles of the Revolution. Could this notion once prevail it would give a deadly wound to the Church in this Country. Indeed I question whether we should have the appearance of a Congregation in it. Thus, my Lord, I have with the utmost Candor and Humility stated my views in this sermon, the composition of which was one trying Incident in my Life. Permit me to entreat your Lordship's perusal of it with a view benevolent to the Times and circumstances. I hope then it may appear to have proceeded from the purest Intentions and to breathe that spirit of moderation and virtue wherewith I know your Lordship would wish those whom you honor with your protection to be distinguished. Neither the Church nor the credit of the Parent Country so far as we are considered to be its advocates can be promoted by any other conduct on our part.   I trust that this unhappy contest will yet be settled upon a plan of mutual Interest and that no retrospect to our conduct shall hurt our future religious usefulness, or that we shall ever stand justly chargeable with widening the Breach or encouraging Hostilities, by any Misrepresentations of Facts so far as we are necessarily called to take any public part.   I am, my Lord, your most

Dutiful Son and Servant,
WILLIAM SMITH.

P. S.—I have taken the Liberty to refer my good friend, D^r. Hind, to this Letter and to our joint address to your Lordship; the purport of which I have briefly mentioned to him.

It would seem that at the coming on of these times the Society for the Propagation of the Gospel addressed something like circular letters to their missionaries.   The gentlemen named in the second line of the letter below were in the Society's service:

Dr. Smith to the Secretary of the Propagation Society.

PHILADELPHIA, July 10th, 1775.

REV^D & WORTHY SIR:

The several letters which you have directed to my care by the last Ships, viz.: to Messrs. Tingly, Battwell, Curry, Murray, Craig, & Magaw are duly forwarded.   Their difficulties in their Missions are greatly increased by the present alarming state of things & never were men in a more trying or delicate situation.   We had hitherto with one consent and one mind kept our pulpits wholly free from everything bordering on the present unnatural controversy.   But now our people have all taken up Arms and entered into associations never to submit to the Parliamentary claim of taxing them at pleasure.   We see nothing in our Churches but men in their uniforms, & tho' they excuse us on Sundays yet they are now everywhere requesting occasional sermons on the present situation of things.   The case of the poor Missionaries is hard. To comply may offend their protectors and those that support them in the Parent Country.   To refuse would leave them without Congregations everywhere; and perhaps it is more the wish of some that they should refuse than comply.

We intended to have held a general meeting to consult together on these difficulties but found that it might involve us in new difficulties by having it suspected we met for purposes of another kind.   All these

difficulties encreased from the necessity some of our Brethren apprehended themselves in of quitting their charges and going to England. I
wish they could have stood their ground which I think might possibly
have been accomplished without any unworthy compliances on their
part; for when the Shepherds are out of the way the Flocks will be scattered.   Some of D^r. Chandler's Congregation whom I have seen, do insist that he would have been perfectly safe in staying; but of that matter
he and his family perhaps could only judge or at least in such a way as
to satisfy his own mind.   We have not been able of late to correspond
with our Brethren in New York so that I have not the particulars of D^r.
Cooper's case, but have heard that he was under an evident necessity
of retiring for a time.   It is a hard situation when such dangers arise
from endeavors to support order, &^{c}.   But we are told that these matters
do not belong to us or that we are not to be busy in them; or that the
submission we would enjoy amounts to slavery.   I hope & believe that
those of our Clergy who are now with you will shew themselves Friends
to America in the truest sense & yet convince their opponents that they
mistook their principles or suffered themselves to be imposed upon.
They have it now in their power to become mediators in this contest &
to be entitled to the blessing of thousands on their return.   I am about
writing to them & suggesting what I think they might do; but cannot
finish by this opportunity of which you will please to acquaint them
when you see them.   But to return from this digression.   If our Clergy
were generally to quit their people at this time I say we should not have
the appearance of a Church or people left.   A conduct, therefore, of the
most prudent nature is required from us.   We need not widen the breach
& yet we may wish well to (nay, in all decency and firmness contend
for) the just rights of America; & so far indulge our people as to convince them that the Clergy of our Church are as true Friends to liberty
& as much devoted to the constitutional & just rights of their Country,
as any other men in America, and upon this plan we have all judged it
our duty to prepare for keeping the fast recommended by the *Congress*
to be kept July 20th & also not to decline our turns of the occasional
service required of us by our people at other times; hoping our prudence
and consciences may lead us safely thro' the difficulties with which we
are beset; indeed, exclusive of the recommendation, never was fasting
and humiliation more our duties.

We have stated all these matters fully in a Letter to the Bishop of
London, an exact copy of which is enclosed.   The original is gone two
days ago by the Honorable Richard Penn, Esqr., our late Governor, who
is to deliver it in person as you will see by the copy.   I need not add
therefore that this copy is only sent to you in case of an accident which
I pray God to avert from a valuable man, vizt: that if the original should
not come to hand in any probable time after you receive this you will
then in our behalf deliver the copy.   For as M^r. Penn has undertaken

34

this business it would not be delicate to anticipate his kind intentions by delivering a copy before he may get up to London. I need say no more on this head, as your own prudence will direct the rest & lead you to make the proper use of the knowledge you will derive of our circumstances from these papers. I enclose you a copy of the Sermon referred to in the letter to the Bishop. I am sure you will read it with candour and a benevolent view to our situation at this time. M^r. Duché preached a similar Sermon last Friday. M^r. Coombe is next in turn. Our Missionaries are likewise preparing in their several Districts & M^r. Battwell and M^r. Barton, I hear, have preached to different bodies in their large Missions. M^r. Duché's Sermon is requested for the Press. How many more may be printed I cannot tell. I believe few of our Clergy are ambitious of that honor & seem willing the matter should rest as I have put it in my Sermon ; wherein I had lead the way & travelled in an untried path. No man has labored more earnestly than myself to avert the dreadful calamities in which both Countries are now involved. I wrote to you the motives of my conduct last year when I assisted in preparing instructions for our Assembly which were generally thought in England to contain the most reasonable plan of reconciliation yet proposed.* From that moment I declined any further public concern in affairs; lamenting in private the evils which I saw approaching as I verily believed for want of that benevolent spirit of Christianity, mutual temper & zeal for the good of the whole Empire, which ought to have drawn Brethren to consult together before blood was spilt & coercive measures pursued. Had this been the case, I still hoped a happy reconciliation, & till it becomes the case, the day of our felicity cannot dawn. My exhortations and wishes have been so frequent on this head that I have ever been considered as willing to sacrifice essential liberty to temporary safety, and as an advocate for the measures of administration against the Colonies. But I am above paying any regard to the opinions of heated times. Tho' I wish for peace I would not make an undue sacrifice to obtain it. Tho' I wish not to be forward or busy in speaking & tho' I could have wished our Pulpits to have been wholly left for the usual purposes of the Gospel, yet when unavoidably called to speak from thence I could not appear cold to the interests of this or the Parent Country which appear to me inseparably connected. I could not betray the cause of universal liberty ; nor suffer our Church or Clergy to labor under the imputation of departing from those principles which distinguished some of her brightest Luminaries near a century past. For my own heart not only dictates these principles ; but I am sure also that they

---

* This is in allusion to the meeting on July 15th, 1774. The credit of drafting the instructions was given to John Dickinson, as Chairman, and a resolution of thanks made to him. As we have already said (*supra*, p. 496), the original draft is in Dr. Smith's handwriting.

are the principles of all our Brethren in these parts; and were we to suffer the contrary notion to prevail (and some indeed wish it may prevail), namely that the Church Clergy are tools of power, slavish in their tenets and secret enemies to the principles of the Revolution, it would, as I said, give a deadly wound to the Church in America.

But to conclude this long letter. I leave the Sermon to your own candor. Some thousands have been disposed of here in a day or two. It was my desire that there might not be one intemperate expression in it, or one sentiment that does not tend to a happy reconciliation upon any plan that does not require an absolute submission, which would deprive us of every right by which Britons ought to be distinguished. The Preface has fully set forth the design of the composition; & I verily believe if I had not stepped forth on this occasion, we should all have been viewed in a light we would not wish to merit.

You see, my dear Sir, that this is a long and free letter. I have no copy of it, & your own prudence will tell you that it is intended for no public use but only to satisfy you and enable you to satisfy others of the motives of our conduct. Much hurt has happened to individuals in this Country from Letters, and therefore I now write but seldom. The letter to the Bishop, if his Lordship pleases, may be read to the Society; but we think with all humility it ought not to be made any other public use of. If you think any thing from this letter necessary you will please to take memorandums of them, should you have occasion to mention any thing about it to the Society.

Excuse these little anxieties, as they are a testimony of the most perfect confidence in your goodness and Friendship. I must conclude,

And am, dear & worthy Sir, &c.,

WILLIAM SMITH.

On the 20th of July, 1775, in pursuance of the recommendation of Congress which precedes, Dr. Smith preached a Fast Sermon, at All-Saints' Church, in Lower Dublin; a small church in the county of Philadelphia. This Fast was the first American Fast recommended by Congress. The Sermon was preceded by a Prayer composed by Dr. Smith. We give parts of it.

Father and Lord of all! Creator, Preserver and Judge of the world! Thou first and best of Beings! Glory, eternal glory, be ascribed to thee, who hast made us capable of knowing, seeking, and loving thee—calling us to fly to thy mercy, as children to a father, for aid and direction in all our undertakings, and for strength and deliverance in all our dangers.

When we contemplate thy Providence, we must confess that thou hast done wonderful things for us, and for our fathers of old! Thou gavest them a goodly heritage, and the power of thy goodness hath often supported them and us in the days of danger! But our thankfulness has not followed thy mercies, and our transgressions have multiplied against thy goodness. "Thou hast visited us for these things, but we have not learned righteousness; and justly might thy soul be avenged on such a nation as this."

But spare us, Lord most holy! O! God most merciful! cast us not wholly off. Although we have sinned against thee, yet still we will trust in thee—and we know in whom we trust! "Thy hand is not shortened that it cannot save, neither thine ear heavy that it cannot hear." "The bruised reed thou wilt not break, nor quench the smoking flax." Suffer us, therefore, O God, through the merits of Christ, to seek refuge at thy mercy-seat; humbled under thy chastisements; confessing and bewailing our manifold offences, and steadfastly purposing to amend our lives; and striving to revive (each in ourselves and in others, as far as our influence extends) a spirit of primitive piety, virtue, and integrity.

As the true foundation of this, inspire us with an awful reverence of thy glorious majesty, with a prevailing love and deep veneration of the pure religion of Jesus, and that genuine liberty, both spiritual and temporal, with which the Gospel makes us free. For the support of this liberty, and this only, may all our efforts, public and private, be directed. By the true spirit of it may we be guided; and, at its sacred uncorrupted call, may we follow, whether to life or to death!

In compassion to a bleeding land, and through the intercession of thy blessed Son, hear the fervent and sincere prayers this day offered, or to be offered, unto thee, for a speedy, just and happy termination of this unnatural strife of death among brethren—children of the same parentage and blood! May our hearts be again knit together in the mutual bands of love, virtue, and common good; and may our Gracious Sovereign, as the Father of all his people, be endued with wisdom from thee, to reconcile and establish their mutual rights upon the most permanent foundation; regarding all his subjects with an equal eye, considering their joint happiness as his greatest glory; and after thy divine example, placing his supreme delight in mercy, peace, truth, righteousness, and doing good!

May all who exercise subordinate authority, whether derived from prince or people, consider the account they must give to thee; seeking, above all things, the maintenance of religion as the true way of restoring our lost peace, preventing the further effusion of kindred blood, and healing our country's wounds, upon a true plan of constitutional liberty, which can only stand upon that just subordination to the parent state, which is for the mutual interest both of parent and children. May every licentious thought be removed from our hearts; and may we still consider that government is of the appointment of God, for the terror of evil-doers, and the praise of them that do well.

In mercy to a nation, that has long been thy peculiar care—in mercy to us their children too—grant that we may all regard the things that belong to our true peace and salvation, lest, for our offences, they should be finally, and forever, hid from our eyes! Hasten that happy time, when, in thy love and fear, we may all "sit quietly under our vine, and under our fig-tree, none making us afraid." May this day's humiliation before thee—our Godly sorrow and repentance, our tears, our prayers, our praises, be acceptable in thy sight, through the merits of Christ Jesus, in whose name we further pray—Our Father, &c.

The Text of the Sermon was from Isaiah lviii. 4, 5, 6, 7. The Sermon itself thus opens with political allusions:

In the present calamitous situation of public affairs, this day has been recommended, by those exercising the delegated authority of the people of these colonies, as a day of general fasting, humiliation and prayer.

Upon an occasion so interesting, when regular government is convulsed, and its branches or parts clashing together in dreadful conflict, I shall not seek to increase the general confusion or add to the distress, by any severe scrutiny, into the right of appointing special fasts for the church in general, or any particular church; especially as this day's fast is not authoritatively enjoined, but only recommended.

I know that the members of the Church of England, to which we belong, feel as much as others for the calamities and divisions of our citizens and country on both sides of the Atlantic, and are equally concerned for the preservation of our just rights; nor averse to lament every danger to which they may be exposed, and to put up fervent supplication to the Almighty, " that they may be preserved inviolate, and transmitted safe, to our latest posterity! "

From the first origin of this unhappy strife, it has been my unfeigned wish and prayer that, in the dreadful conflict wherein this country seems about to engage with the great nation from which we sprung, a deep and solemn pause might be made, on both sides, for serious meditation; and that all of us, in the first place, might turn our thoughts to God and his Providence; consider the gracious purposes for which he seems to have planted us in this land; search our own hearts narrowly, and discover how far we conspire with, or counteract his will and ways, in the dissemination of human wisdom and human happiness!

I could not, therefore, so ill reward the confidence which these congregations have so long placed in me, as to decline meeting you this day, in order to assist your meditations, lest I might leave you under the necessity of seeking that assistance from those who might not, perhaps, improve the present opportunity for leading your thoughts into that channel in which I would wish them to flow at this trying time. For although our temporal calamities have called us to the present duty, yet I propose to carry you beyond them, into a more extensive field.

Days of fasting have been in use among all nations professing a belief of God's overruling Providence.   The Scriptures abound in examples of fasts, for deprecating the righteous visitations and impending judgments of the Almighty.

The preacher then gives different instances recorded in the Old Testament of fasts and fasting, and explains the nature of a true fast.   " Even in an Old Testament Fast," he says, " all outward observances and ceremonies were only so far of any value before God, as they were the fruits of the spirit, the genuine mark of hearts loathing iniquity; striving to loose the strong bands of wickedness; ceasing from evil; learning to do well; and calling forth the soul in all actions of mercy, loving-kindness, and true benevolence."   "And our Saviour himself," he continues, " confirms the doctrine, telling us that our fasting should not be like that of the hypocrites, consisting only in sad countenances, and disfigured faces; but in godly sincerity, not regarding the applause of men; but fasting in the secrecy of heart, considering ourselves only as in his presence, ' who seeing in secret will reward openly all those who come to him with souls thus sincerely penitent.' " He proceeds:

You have, I hope, turned your thoughts to Almighty God. You have beheld His hand lifted up over this prostrate and afflicted land—afflicted with the worst of evils—the demon of discord and civil distraction— You are all ready to cry out—"who will shew us any good ? Lord, have mercy upon us, and deliver us—We repent of our sins, and seek Thy grace for reformation and amendment."

I would, therefore, cherish these good dispositions; and what may, peradventure, have begun through Fear, I would ripen into maturity by the more cheering beams of Love.   Instead of increasing your afflictions, I would convey a dawn of comfort to your souls; rather striving to woo and to win you to Religion and Happiness, from a consideration of what God hath promised to the Virtuous, than of what He hath denounced against the Wicked, both through Time and in Eternity.

It hath always been a favourite theme with me, in my public addresses, to dwell much upon those Prophecies, and portions of holy Scripture, which predict that, God's own government, in the hearts of men through the Gospel of Jesus Christ and the Grace of his Holy Spirit, shall be extended, among those that "sit in darkness and the shadow of death, even to the remotest ends of this habitable world;" and that although

God's gracious purposes may be counter-worked and stayed long, by the unworthiness of the instrument which he hath chosen—perverse Man—yet they cannot, finally, be frustrated !

I would now pursue this subject, and impress this strong hope, that notwithstanding the darkness that now hangs over us, the Lord (as the Prophet elsewhere expresses it) offers himself as "an everlasting Light to us"—that if we will obey His call, and follow where His divine Providence points our glorious way, our days of Mourning shall yet be turned into joy. " We shall yet become a righteous people and inherit "the land forever, as a branch of His planting, in which he may be "glorified—that a little one among us shall become a thousand, and a "small one a strong nation, and that He, the Lord, will hasten it in "his time." *

This ravishing hope, my Brethren, if duly cherished, will lead us, better than a thousand arguments founded in Fear, to improve the design of our present meeting, by a view of our own situation in this country, the designs for which God appears to have planted us in it, and the part which it is our duty to act in this day of trial ; so as neither to counteract our promised bliss by licentious Impatience, nor forfeit our hopes of it by unmanly Fears.

If we turn our thoughts to the ways of Providence, as recorded in history, profane as well as sacred, and consider the fate of Christian empires—how they have been alternately blessed with the enjoyment of Gospel-light, Liberty and Happiness, alternately lifted up and cast down, according to their due use, or corrupt abuse, of these blessings ; if we mark their progress through the old world ; and impartially examine the prophecies which relate to their gradual extension to the remotest habitations of the Gentiles ; we shall find rays of Hope darting in upon us, which may yet help to cheer us, amidst all the gloom that now broods over us.

Like the Sun, these mighty blessings (Gospel-light, Liberty and Happiness) have still pursued their western course, since the birth of Christianity, till, in meridian splendour, they reached the utmost verge, the *ultima Thule*, of the old world ; where they long illuminated the favoured land from which we sprung. And, while they shone in noontide glory there, their cheering rays extended with our ancestors across the vast Atlantic, dispelling the long, long, night of darkness in which these American regions lay involved ; and opening upon Us a radiant Morn, which gave the joyous earnest of a future resplendent day. That Morn is now overcast ; but our Sun, we trust, only hides his head from us for a time, and is not commanded, by an unappeasable Providence, to revert from his destined course, and measure back his former way.

If we make a due improvement of the present visitations of Heaven,

---

* Isaiah lx. 22.

the clouds will speedily disperse; our Sun will break forth with renewed vigour, and these " ends of the earth shall yet see the salvation of God." * * *

It is more than probable that 'the chief concern of the greatest part of us this day—the sentiment uppermost in our hearts—relates to our temporal salvation. This is not blameable, but only in the degree of our concern. Our temporal distress assembled us here, and has prostrated us at our Maker's feet; when, probably, had Prosperity surrounded us, we should have been forgetful of Him, and spending the precious moments in Vanity, and things of no Spiritual Profit.

Of this principle I will avail myself, therefore, in the first place. Would you be thought Patriots indeed? Do you profess yourselves, in good earnest, ready to sacrifice your blood and treasure for the temporal safety of your country? Have you lifted up your voices to God in fervent supplications, that he would strengthen your resolutions and prosper your endeavours? And in return for his expected deliverance, have you in his awful presence, deprecated your former sins, and (solemnly renouncing them) promised to devote yourselves to his will and ways, all the days of your lives? So far as you have done this, you have done well. So far you have kept a true Fast, considering it as something infinitely above all human Appointments.

But if any seeds of Ambition, Licentiousness or Revenge, are yet left to spring up in our hearts, to check those Fruits of Peace and Love, which the Gospel of Christ would cherish there; if we have brought to this solemn Fast any turbulent Desires, any secret views of fostering Party-Spirit, any Lust of unjust Dominion, any Impatience of lawful Government, or wish to weaken its bands, or intrench upon plighted Faith and the Sanctity of Laws—then let us be assured that we counterwork our own Salvation, not only in the next world, but in this. Our Fast, this day, is only a mockery of our almighty Creator!

If we come to God for a blessing on our temporal affairs, it must be with the conviction that all earthly happiness is derived from Him; that, in his sight, the best Christian is the best Patriot; that the Man who upholds the Purity and Majesty of Religion can best serve his country; and that where the Sense of Religion is once lost, the Sense of Liberty, and of everything else that is valuable in this world, must be immediately lost with it.

My Brethren, I am now upon a very serious subject, and in very serious times. I trust you will suffer and expect me to speak with the utmost freedom, as becomes one professing, from scripture, to speak the will and word of God among you.

If then we would seek true inducements for Heroism and Virtue in every time of danger, let us not consider this fruitful land which we possess, as given to us merely for advancing our own temporal interests; but also that we might be the means of diffusing the Knowledge and

.Practice of Religion, as well as of civil Liberty and Happiness, to the nations that sit in Darkness round us.

Nay, we ought to view this design—(the planting and raising an Empire of Christian Knowledge here) as the first and greatest work we have to do.

A temporal Empire, however favourite a notion, is a secondary work, which can only spring from, and be supported by, the former; without which, all other blessings of nature or industry—the happiness and fertility of soil, zeal and struggles for Liberty, will be totally vain.

That this whole continent shall one day become a happy seat of knowledge and freedom, arts and polished life, and whatever can exalt or adorn mankind; is a hope which, as I said before, the voice of Scripture and Prophecy leads us fondly to cherish in our breasts. It seems the mighty purpose of God, in many predispositions of his Providence, to enlighten the dark parts of this new world; and He will raise up proper instruments, if not in us, at least in others more worthy, should we neglect the advancement of His divine purposes.

It becomes us, therefore, impartially to examine our own hearts and ways; to consider how far we are striving to embrace the opportunities offered us of becoming instruments in the hands of Providence for spreading Religion and Virtue through this immense country.

With what reproach would our names be transmitted to posterity, should we act as if we had come into this land flowing with Milk and Honey, only to eat and enjoy the fruits thereof; to wrest from the former Lords of the soil the possessions which they have held from age to age; without striving, in return, to better their condition, by Example, by Precept, by every means in our power; diffusing among them all the blessings which a pure Religion and a temperate System of Laws can give.

In this view of things, and on this solemn occasion, let me therefore sum up all I have to say by entreating you, in the name of God and by the love you profess for your country, to regulate all your conduct by the principles of Truth, Justice and Righteousness. Keep in view the divine Work in which you are called to be Instruments, so far as we seem capable to comprehend the Promises and Revelations of the Almighty. Strive in the first place to preserve your spiritual Liberty, and to resist the Dominion of Sin, adorning your profession by the Purity of your Lives; and then you may hope for a blessing in every effort for the support of your civil Liberty—Let no Acts of Violence, Rashness, Intemperance, or Undutifulness to the country from whence we spring, ever disgrace our cause. And be assured, as I said before, that he is truly the greatest Patriot, and the best man, who, in all his ways, supports the majesty of Religion, reverences the laws of his country, and keeps a conscience void of offence towards God and towards man.

While you act within this line; while you can carry with you a true conviction that Religion, Justice, Laws divine and human, are on your side, in this great contest; the worst events will not appall you too much; nor the most prosperous elate you into forgetfulness of God. Your zeal will be enlightened, but temperate. The pulse of glory will beat high, but not with a Feverish heat.

May the almighty God, therefore, in this day of his visitation, direct you in all your ways, and speedily give you "Beauty instead of Sackcloth and Ashes, the Oil of Joy instead of Mourning, and the Garment of Praise instead of heaviness of Heart."

Amen.

Politically and ecclesiastically this was all unexceptionable so far as I see. It was, no doubt, *in generalibus.* But nothing else would in such times have been suited to the pulpit anywhere; either in England or America. Such a prayer as was made for our "Gracious Sovereign" was not enough to constitute a Loyalist. It was quite unlike the prayers of the Liturgy, and was almost as much an *exprobatio* as an *oratio.* It was made more than a year before the Declaration of Independence, when prayers for the King, etc., were continued as usual, in all our churches; and when the people of America, by their delegates in Congress, claimed only a redress of grievances; expressed nothing but their former attachment to the government of Great Britain, and sought nothing but reconciliation with the mother country and their brethren there, on the constitutional terms of a restoration to, and the continuance of, equal rights and privileges.

Dr. Smith to the Secretary of the Propagation Society.
(EXTRACT.)

PHILADELPHIA, 28th Aug^st, 1775.

REV^D AND WORTHY SIR,

* * *   The Americans continue firm in the measures they have adopted for opposing Parliamentary taxation and the Colony of Georgia has now joined the other twelve Colonies. Administration can expect nothing by hopes of disunion here. Would to God that a suspension of hostilities & a negotiation could take Place before either side have proceeded too far in measures so ruinous to both. For this I pray & for this I labor daily & in such a way perhaps as may subject me to the blame of the violent of both sides. But I look far beyond the present heated times. I know the dignity of the Parent state may be well supported without evading any essential right of the Colonies, & till a plan for this purpose is devised and executed we can never more expect a return of our former harmony. It was with a view to propa-

gate these principles that my Sermon was drawn up as I mentioned in my last. Whether it may be considered in that light on your side of the Atlantic I know not. But God knows my love is strong & my zeal ardent for the prosperity of both Countries.

Since I wrote you all our Clergy within my knowledge, two only excepted in four Provinces, have Preached on the fast of July 20th. Some of their Sermons are printed & more in the press. You will herewith receive two of Mr. Duché & one of Mr. Coombe's. Please to communicate them to the Lord Bishop of London. His Lordship will be pleased to peruse them. He will thereby be enabled to judge of us all as he has done that honor to mine; & the circumstances in which we are placed cannot be easily known by those who are at a distance. But we hope our present conduct will be justified from a recollection of that prudence and temper which we have endeavored to exercise on all former occasions; & the proper allowances for youth and riper years to be likewise made. I am more and more convinced that had our Clergy acted a different part on the late occasion we should have ruined the Church Interest here.

I am with great truth, Dear Sir, &c.,

WILLIAM SMITH.

CHAPTER XXXIV.

POPULAR IMPRESSION AS TO DR. SMITH'S SERMON ON AMERICAN AFFAIRS—SKETCH OF GENERAL RICHARD MONTGOMERY—ATTEMPT TO REDUCE THE CANADAS— GENERAL MONTGOMERY AND OTHER OFFICERS KILLED BEFORE QUEBEC—CONGRESS REQUESTS DR. SMITH TO PRONOUNCE A FUNERAL ORATION UPON THEM —HE PRONOUNCES IT—MUSICAL ACCESSORIES INTRODUCED IN IT—EXTRACTS FROM THE ORATION—JOHN ADAMS' CHARACTERIZATION OF IT—THEODORE SEDGWICK, BENJAMIN FRANKLIN AND ALEXANDER HAMILTON'S CHARACTERIZATION OF JOHN ADAMS—HIS CENSURES OF NO VALUE.

THE effect of Dr. Smith's sermon on American affairs was, in *popular impression,* to place him among those who, like the " violent spirits " of Boston, wished, by an " immediate rupture " with Great Britain, to involve all the other colonies in the condition in which their own Governor Hutchison and Lieutenant-Governor Oliver, by inciting the British ministry to illegal acts, had involved them. There was, however, nothing in the sermon which in good reason warranted or invited this idea. We have on previous pages stated its character fairly, and have made such extracts from it as would enable the reader to judge of its character for himself.

We come now to another sermon of Dr. Smith's which attracted great public notice; that on the death of General Richard Montgomery. Our readers will recall the main events in the life of this gallant officer.

He was the son of an Irish baronet, and born at Conway House, in Ireland, A. D. 1738. After receiving a liberal education, he entered the British army at the age of eighteen, and served in it and on this continent, in what we call the French and Indian War (the Seven Years' War) of 1756, between England on the one side, and France, with other European powers, on the other, and which involved the colonists in war with the people of the Canadas and the Indian tribes; that war in which for the second time we became possessed of Louisburg. At the conclusion of that war Montgomery returned to Europe, where he remained nine years, " a close observer of the aspect of the times." In 1772, resigning his commission in the British army, he came to America. He bought a farm at King's Bridge, near New York, and soon afterwards married a daughter of Robert R. Livingston, then a Judge of the King's Bench, after which he went to Rhinebeck, still pursuing agriculture. The events of the day brought him, in 1775, into the first Provincial Convention at New York; and in June, 1775, Congress appointed him a Brigadier-General in the Continental army. By this time—a year and more before the Declaration of Independence—it was deemed a plain measure of prudence that the Colonies should hold the Canadas in such a state, that in the event an effort for independence, and of consequent war with Great Britain, becoming necessary, we should not be exposed to the atrocities which would follow an alliance of the Canada or frontier Indians with the English, as, while supporting England, we had been exposed to them, some years before, when the Indians allied themselves with the French. Accordingly it was resolved to invade the Canadas. This was done by two routes; the one by way of the Kennebec, through Maine; the other by the river Sorel. The command of the invading force, in consequence of the illness of General Schuyler, fell on Montgomery. The campaign was a winter campaign, and marked by the dreadful exposures incident to such an expedition into such high latitudes. Montgomery had, of course, much sickness and great suffering in his camp. Notwithstanding which—while acting with the utmost humanity to his men—he steadily went on, reducing the fortresses of St. John's, Chamblee, and Montreal, and effecting a junction with the expedition (under Arnold) sent through Maine. The great matter to be effected was the capture of Quebec. This citadel was commanded by the brave, cautious, and accomplished General Guy Carleton. He had been the quartermaster of Wolfe. It could be neither invested nor taken by siege. If taken at all, it had to be by storm. On the last day of the last month of 1775, the movement of the troops commenced before daylight upon the Plains of Abraham. It was a night of terrific cold. Accumulated ice and snow blocked every passage; but the dauntless band pushed forward. When all was ready for the attack, " Men of New York," said Montgomery—waving in the air his sword, and beckoning for his men to come on—" follow where your General leads ! " There is a rush, a death-like pause, a surging to and fro of armed men; the plume of the gallant leader sweeps the snow of the battlefield; Montgomery falls, pierced with deadly wounds. He was an able and an accomplished soldier. " Of Washington's thirteen Generals, elected by the Continental Congress,* two only," says General Cullum, " Schuyler and Greene, could be compared to him, and neither of these was his superior in character, attainments, or military experience." By the order of General Carleton, his body was buried with all the honors of war within the walls of the city of Quebec.

Among those killed in that storming of Quebec which concluded this terrible expedition were two young men of Pennsylvania —one Captain John MacPherson—the first Philadelphian of any note killed in battle—the other Captain Henricks, from the interior of the State ; somewhere—though I know not exactly

---

* See " Washington and the Generals of the American Revolution," Vol. II., p. 187; an anonymous work, published A. D. 1847, by Carey & Hart, Philadelphia— quite a different book from one of Mr. Headley's with the same title. I use much of its language.

The person who desires to see a full and scientific account of Montgomery's expedition, and of him personally, will find it admirably presented by General G. W. Cullum, in a paper read at the great Centennial Commemoration of the Declaration of Independence, at the State-house in Philadelphia, July 2d, 1876, and now in print, and in an anonymous pamphlet printed in 1876, entitled, " Biographical Notes Concerning Richard Montgomery, together with hitherto unpublished letters."

where—upon the Susquehanna. He had gone through Maine with Arnold.

Captain MacPherson was the son of a gallant sailor, whose bravery in the older wars was conspicuous. The son had been educated partly at the College of Philadelphia and partly at that of Princeton. After being graduated, he studied law in Philadelphia with John Dickinson. A few days before his death he visited the spot where General Wolfe expired. As a reward for his services, he was appointed by the Congress a Major in a battalion to be raised in the Delaware counties; but at the time of his death, had received no account of this promotion. On the day before the assault on Quebec, he wrote to his father the following letter, intrusting it to General Schuyler, to be forwarded only in case of his death:

HEAD-QUARTERS BEFORE QUEBEC, 30th Dec., 1775.

MY DEAR FATHER:—If you receive this, it will be the last this hand shall ever write you. Orders are given for a general storm on Quebec this night; and Heaven only knows what may be my fate. But, whatever it may be, I cannot resist the inclination I feel to assure you that I experience no reluctance in this cause to venture a life which I consider as only lent, to be used when my country demands it.

In moments like these, such an assertion will not be thought a boast by any one—by my father I am sure it cannot. It is needless to tell that my prayers are for the happiness of the family and for their preservation in this general confusion. Should Providence, in its wisdom, call me from rendering the little assistance I might to my country, I could wish my brother did not continue in the service of her enemies.*

That the All-gracious Disposer of human events may shower on you, my mother, brothers and sisters, every blessing our nature can receive,

---

*The allusion, in Captain John MacPherson's letter, is to his brother, William MacPherson, who, before the commencement of hostilities, was an officer in the British army, and Adjutant of the Sixteenth Regiment of foot. This regiment was not then in service in the northern part of America. Captain MacPherson at that time presented his resignation, which was refused. When the regiment afterward arrived at New York, he again tendered his resignation to Sir Henry Clinton, declaring that he would never bear arms against his countrymen. It was then accepted, and in 1779 Captain William MacPherson joined the American army, and was made Major by brevet. After the Revolution he was a prominent citizen of Philadelphia, and commanded the fine legion called " MacPherson's Blues." It went in 1794 against the insurrection at Pittsburgh, known as " The Whiskey Insurrection." He married a daughter of Bishop White; a woman distinguished by dignity and sense. General MacPherson, as he had now become, resided at a place called Mount Pleasant, then described as being in the Northern Liberties, on the Schuylkill. It contained one hundred and twenty acres. It is now in the East Park.

is, and will be to the last moment of my life, the sincere prayer of your
dutiful and affectionate son,

JOHN MACPHERSON.

General Schuyler despatched this letter to Captain John Mac-
Pherson, the father, with the following missive from himself:

ALBANY, 14th June, 1776.

Permit me, sir, to mingle my tears with yours for the loss we have
sustained—you as a father, I as a friend.   My dear young friend fell by
the side of his General, as much lamented as he was beloved—and that,
I assure you, sir, was in an eminent degree.   This, and his falling like a
hero, will console, in some measure, a father who gave him the example
of bravery, which the son, in a short military life, improved to advantage.

General Montgomery and his corpse were both interred by General
Carleton with military honors.

Your most obedient and humble servant,

PH. SCHUYLER.

Of the death of Captain Henricks, Dr. Smith gives some interesting particulars.*

Captain Cheeseman, of New York, an associate and friend of
both these young men, was killed in the same assault.

On the 25th of January, 1776, the official report having come
from the army, the Congress

Resolved, That *Dr. Smith* be desired to prepare and deliver a FUNERAL
ORATION in honor of General MONTGOMERY, and of those *Officers* and
Soldiers who magnanimously fought and fell with him in maintaining
the principles of *American Liberty.*

Dr. Smith could not decline this invitation.   He was aware that
he would have to address as great and respectable an audience as
was ever assembled on this continent.   He foresaw the difficulties
incident to the undertaking.   The death of such an officer as Montgomery, and the loss of two conspicuous and gallant youths, both
from our own State, and of many privates belonging to it also, with
the mortifying failure of the expedition, had wrought up public
feeling to a great degree.   He could hardly say anything, not
breathing out threatenings and slaughter, which would satisfy the
rage of some.   Yet he did not mean to be either blown or drifted
from the anchorage of his own intelligently fixed principles.   He
had no great time to prepare a Funeral Oration.   The resolution

---

* *Infra,* p. 558.

asking for it could have hardly reached him before the 26th or 27th of January; and the oration was delivered on the 19th of February. The occasion was a military one. It was "a funeral oration," not a sermon, that he was about to deliver.

Dr. Smith had a great eye and ear for effects. Music, scenic decoration, dramatic art, pomp and circumstance—all entered largely into his ideas of what was requisite to give full impression to orations, commencement-days, the conferring of degrees, etc. An oration on a military hero and his brave associates presented of course a fine occasion for impressive accessories. The whole Congress, the Assembly of the Province, the Municipal Authorities, and whatever of the army had survived and was not in the field, away, would be there. Great preparations were made. The oration contained some poetical quotations. These, as the reverend orator began to quote them, would be taken up by the choir from his mouth, and a charming effect was, of course, produced.

In this connexion we must print a letter of Dr. Smith to his friend, Jasper Yeates, of Lancaster, which will give some idea of the trouble of such a celebration in those days.

Dr. Smith to Jasper Yeates.

PHILA, February 13th, 1776.

DEAR SIR: The Bearer * is sent express to request the favor of Eberhart Michael to set off immediately for Philadelphia to assist in the solemn music which is to accompany Gen. Montgomery's funeral oration on Monday next.

Messrs. Bremners, Peters, Beach, Hare, Hillegas, Franks, and all the gentlemen in Town, who are able, will assist in the music. But we shall want two violins, and have sent to New York for another. I write this by Direction of the Committee of Congress, who have the conduct of the solemnity, and Mr. Michael's declining would be thought *disrespectful to the cause* and to all of us who take our Part. I refer you to Mr. Barton's letter for some further account, & should be glad to see you here at the Performance. Let Mr. Michael set out with the Express on Thursday morning at farthest.

But we rather wish if he could that he might be here early on Friday. I beg a line by the bearer and am,

Affectionately yours,

WILLIAM SMITH.

To JASPER YEATES, Esq., Lancaster.

---

* This was Col. Timothy Matlack.

On Monday morning, February 14th, 1776, the persons who were to participate in the solemnities met at the State-house, from which place Congress, the Provincial Assembly, the City Corporation, the Mayor, the Committees of Inspection and of Safety, the four city battalions of Associators, and rifle companies, with the officers of the Pennsylvania Continental Battalions, moved in procession down Chestnut street to Fourth, and up Fourth on their way to the new German Calvinist Church, in Race street, below Fourth, where the oration was to be delivered. Dr. Smith joined them at the door of his own house, at the southwest corner of Fourth and Arch streets, with his brother clergy, and proceeded to the church, where he delivered the oration.

The opening part of the discourse was a grand review from classic poets and other authors, laying, in the customs of the Hebrews, Egyptians, Greeks, Romans, etc., a wide foundation for honors, after death, to heroes and statesmen; persons who might be said to live and to die not to themselves, but to others. This exordium is highly studied, and plainly could not have been first written for this oration. In welding it on and even in parts of the thing itself, it is a little turgid as we read it. It puts you in mind of one of David's large pictures in the Louvre, with lines of *tubicines* and long trumpets, of the Lictor and his *fasces*, of standards and S. P. Q. Rs and all old Rome in solemn procession. A fine dramatic manner, which Dr. Smith undoubtedly possessed, probably carried off well that which, differently delivered, would have seemed declamatory and have been flat. But all this exordium— and the musical part also of the body of the discourse—had, I apprehend, a purpose independently of exordium and musical sounds. The Provost was not preaching a sermon in Trinity Church, Oxford, nor at All Saints, Lower Dublin, where he could make his discourse just as long or as short as he pleased. He was bound to give the Congress a certain amount of oration; an hour or an hour and a half of discourse. He had been invited, perhaps, for the exact purpose of making him commit himself to some specific line of counsel. His task was very difficult. He would have to walk over burning plough-shares. No declaration of independence had yet been made. On the contrary, the same Congress had but a few months before expressed what might be called their abhorrence of the thought of independence.* But

35   * See *supra*, p. 506.

opinion was divided. Violent men were on both sides. And Dr. Smith could say nothing—if he said much—which would not greatly incense one party or the other, and almost while he yet stood in the pulpit raise cries of "Hosanna" from one side and "Crucifigatur" from the other. He knew all this as well as any one; better, probably. And I rather suppose that his large classical and poetical exordium—which has been criticised by some good judges as feeble and declamatory—and his musical interludes were made by way of "fending off" from the main topic, or rather from too much of the main topic. They were arts of the drama; availed of with great effect in the resources of the stage. The solemnity would be a fine affair. A grand funeral oration would have been delivered. But no more would be said than, in a moment where a word might provoke the whirlwind, was proper to be said. Everybody it was hoped would thus be satisfied. And so, as far as I can learn, nearly everybody was.

The orator, after his array of classic scenes and authors, thus comes down to his more immediate topic:

Having now, my respected countrymen—and I hope I do not weary you—laid a wide foundation upon the practice of the wisest nations—in support of the present solemnity, I shall add but little more concerning the public utility of the thing itself.

Circumstanced as we now are, and perhaps shall long be, in building up a fabric for future ages, it would be a wise institution if, in imitation of the Genoese *Feast of Union*, we should make at least an annual pause for a review of past incidents, and of the characters of those who have borne an illustrious share in them; thereby animating our virtue, and uniting ourselves more closely in the bonds of mutual friendship.

The world, in general, is more willing to imitate than to be taught, and examples of eminent characters have a stronger influence than written precepts. Men's actions are a more faithful mirror of their lives than their words. The former seldom deceive; but the latter often. The deeds of old contract a venerable authority over us, when sanctified by the voice of applauding ages; and, even in our own day, our hearts take an immediate part with those who have nobly triumphed or greatly suffered in our behalf.

But the more useful the display of such characters may be to the world, the more difficult is the work. And I am not to learn that, of all kinds of writing, panegyric requires the most delicate hand. Men seldom endure the praise of any actions but those which their self-love represents as possible to themselves. Whatever is held up as an example, if placed beyond the common reach of humanity, duly exalted by public spirit, will excite no emulation; and whatever is placed within the vulgar walks of life will attract no attention.

There is a further difficulty peculiar to certain times, particularly those of civil dissension, when the tempers of men are worked into ferment. Whence it happens, that they who have been the subjects of obloquy in one age, or in one state of party, have become the theme of praise in another. Such was Hampden—in the days of passive obedience, branded as a seditious disturber of his country's peace, and at the blessed æra of the revolution exalted into the first rank of *patriots*. Such was Sidney—condemned to a scaffold in the former period, and in the latter immortalized by the delegated voice of the nation!

What judgment posterity will form of the present mighty contest in which these United Colonies are engaged, I am at no loss to determine in my own mind. But, while the same actions are by one part of a great empire pronounced the most criminal resistance, and by another the most laudable efforts of self-preservation, no public character can be drawn alike acceptable to all. Nevertheless, as the faithful *historian* is the best panegyrist of true merit, he will not fashion himself to times and seasons, but exalt himself above them; and, conscious of his dignity as responsible to succeeding ages, will take eternal truth as his support, which can alone bear the impartial test of future examination. He knows that the divine colors of virtue, although they may give a temporary glare, will not blend or mellow into a ground-work of vice.

Whatever events, disastrous or happy, may lie before us, yet some degree of applause, even from an enemy, is certainly due to those illustrious men, who, led by conscience and a clear persuasion of duty, sacrifice their ease, their lives and fortunes to the public; and from their friends and country they are entitled to a deathless renown.

Perish that narrow pride, which will suffer men to acknowledge no virtue but among their own party. In this direful contest, the chief concern of a liberal mind will be that so much personal virtue as may be found on both sides, instead of being united in some great national object for the common good, should be dreadfully employed to the purpose of mutual destruction. And a man can as soon divest himself of his humanity as refuse the tribute of veneration due to actions truly magnanimous.

When once it becomes criminal to plead the cause of a suffering people, when their virtues can no longer be safely recorded—then tyranny has put the last hand to its barbarous work. All the valuable purposes of society are frustrated; and whatever other human fate remains will be wholly indifferent to the wise and good.

There are also many whose minds are so little that they can conceive nothing great, which does not court the eye in all the trappings of dress, titles, and external splendor. An *American-Patriot!* a *Blanket-*

Hero! a *General* from the *plough!* all these are terms of ridicule and reproach among many. Yet such was Cincinnatus, in the best days of Roman virtue; and a British poet, already quoted, hath boldly taught his countrymen this noble lesson—

> " Some, with whom compar'd, your insect-tribes
> Are but the beings of a summer's day,
> Have held the scale of empire, rul'd the storm
> Of mighty war; then, with unweary'd hand,
> Disdaining little delicacies, seiz'd
> The *plough*, and greatly independent liv'd."—THOMSON.

The same noble lesson is also taught by the well-known story of the two Spanish grandees, who were sent ambassadors to the Hague. Notwithstanding all the pride of their nation, they did not despise the Dutch deputies when they met them in a plain habit, and saw them on a journey sit down upon the grass to a frugal repast of bread and cheese out of their knapsacks. On the contrary, they cried out, " We shall never be able to conquer these people; we must even make peace with them."

Should ambassadors honour us with a visit upon a like occasion, let us be prepared to meet them in the same majestic simplicity of garb and manners. Let us convince them that public virtue is confined to no class of men; and that although it sometimes basks in the sunshine of courts, it frequently lies hid in the shades of obscurity, like the latent fire in flint, till called forth by the collisive hand of oppression.

Adversity is the season which shews the spirit of a man in its full vigor; and times of civil calamity never fail to strike forth lights, sometimes single, and sometimes whole constellations, mingling their kindred rays to warm and to illuminate the genius of their country.

The sacred flame, thus enkindled, is not fed by the fuel of faction or party, but by pure benevolence and love of the public. It, therefore, soon rises above the selfish principles, refines and brightens as it rises, and expands itself into heavenly dimensions. Being inextinguishable in its own nature, the blood of thousands, on the scaffold or in the field, is but as oil poured into a conflagration, increasing its vehemence, till it consumes all before it, burning still clearer and stronger unto the full day of peace and civil happiness.

Those who enjoy a true portion of this divine flame, duly called forth into exercise, stand in no need of further titles or distinctions, either by birth or grant. For what can the world present greater to the sight of mortals, or even immortals, than a man who knows and courts the blessings of peace, who wishes to breathe out his last in its arms; and, keeping it still as his object, is nevertheless roused by the first pang of his suffering country; gives his whole illustrious spirit to her relief; rises above all human allurements; never remits his zeal; fears nothing; regards nothing—but the sentiments which virtue and magnanimity inspire? What higher qualities can be required to entitle a man to the veneration and eulogies of his country? And these too will be his most durable monument.   * * *

But whither am I borne? to what heights have I ascended? I look down with astonishment and tremble at my situation! Oh! Let your friendly arms be extended to save me as I fall. For in the idea I have of my subject, I have undertaken to guide the chariot of the sun; and how shall I steer through the exalted tract that lies before me? Considering myself as honoured with this day's office by the delegated voice of some millions of people through a vast continent, upon an occasion wherein their gratitude, their dignity, their love of liberty, nay even their reputation in literature, are all in some degree concerned; what language shall I use, or how shall I accommodate myself to every circumstance in the arduous work?

Truth alone must guide the hand that delineates a character. So far will I strive to imitate *him,** who always animated himself with his subject, by thus accosting himself before he went forth to speak—

"Remember, thou art this day going to address men born in the arms of liberty, *Grecians, Athenians!*"—Let no thought enter thy heart—let no word fall from thy tongue—unworthy of such an audience.

As to that hero, whose memory we are now met to celebrate as a *Proto-Martyr*† to our rights—for through whatever fields I have strayed he has never escaped my view—as to him, I say, if any thing human could now reach his ear, nothing but the great concerns of virtue, liberty, truth and justice would be tolerable to him; for to these was his life devoted from his early years.

He had received a liberal education in Ireland, his native country, before he went into the army, and was indeed endued with talents which would have led him to eminence in any profession. His own he studied with a felicity which soon distinguished his military abilities. But war and conquest having no other charms to him than as the necessary means of peace and happiness to mankind, he still found leisure, in the midst of camps, to cultivate an excellent taste for philosophy and polite literature. To these he added a careful study of the arts of government, and the rights of mankind, looking forward to that time when he might return into the *still scenes* of private life, and give a full flow to the native and acquired virtues of a heart rich in moral excellence.

Above eighteen years ago he had attained the rank of captain in the 17th British regiment, under General Monckton, and stood full in the way of higher preferment, having borne a share in all the labours

---

* Pericles.

† The author did not intend to appropriate this term so as to forget the merit of Dr. Warren and other brave men, who fell before in the same cause.

of our American wars, and the reduction of Canada. Ill-fated region!
short-sighted mortals! Little did he foresee the scenes which that land
had still in reserve for him! Little did those generous Americans, who
then stood by his side, think that they were assisting to subdue a country which would one day be held up over us, as a greater scourge in the
hands of friends, than ever it was in the hands of enemies!

Had such a thought then entered their hearts, they would have started
with indignation from the deed of horror. Their heroism would have
appeared madness and parricide! The lifted steel would have dropped
from the warrior's arm! The axe and the hoe from the labourer's hand!
America would have weeped through all her forests; and her well-cultivated fields refused to yield farther sustenance to her degraded sons!

But far different were our thoughts at that time. We considered
ourselves as co-operating with our British brethren for the glory of the
empire; to enable them to secure our common peace and liberty; to
humanize, adorn, and dignify, with the privileges of freemen, a vast
continent; to become strong in our strength, happy in our happiness;
and to derive that from our affection, which no force can extort from a
free people; and which the miserable and oppressed cannot give!

And these, too, were the sentiments of our lamented hero; for he
had formed an early attachment, amounting even to an enthusiastic
love, to this country! The woodland and the plain; the face of
nature, grand, venerable, and yet rejoicing in her prime; our mighty
rivers, descending in vast torrents through wild and shaggy mountains,
or gliding in silent majesty through fertile vales; their numerous
branches and tributary springs; our romantic scenes of rural quiet; our
simplicity of manners, yet uncorrupted by luxury or flagrant vice; our
love of knowledge and ardor for liberty—all these served to convey the
idea of primæval felicity to a heart which he had taught to beat unison
with the harmony of Heaven!

He therefore chose America, as the field of his future usefulness; and
as soon as the blessings of peace were restored to his country, and duty
to his sovereign would permit, he took his leave of the army; and
having soon connected himself, by marriage, with an ancient and
honourable family, in the province of New York, he chose a delightful
retirement upon the banks of Hudson's river, at a distance from the
noise of the busy world! Having a heart distended with benevolence,
and panting to do good, he soon acquired, without courting it, from
his neighbours, that authority, which an opinion of superior talents and
inflexible integrity never fails to create.

In this most eligible of all situations, the life of a country gentleman,
deriving its most exquisite relish from reflection upon past dangers and
past services, he gave full scope to his philosophic spirit, and taste for
rural elegance.   Self-satisfied and raised above vulgar ambition, he
devoted his time to sweet domestic intercourse with the amiable partner

of his heart, friendly converse with men of worth, the study of useful books, and the improvement of his favoured villa. Nor from that happy spot did he wish to stray, until he should receive his last summons to happiness more than terrestrial.

But when the hand of power was stretched forth against the land of his residence, he had a heart too noble not to sympathize in its distress. From that fatal day—in which the first American blood was spilt by the hostile hands of British brethren, and the better genius of the empire, veiling her face in anguish, turned abhorrent from the strife of death among her children—I say, from that fatal day, he chose his part.

Although his liberal spirit placed him above local prejudices, and he considered himself as a member of the empire at large; yet America, struggling in the cause of Liberty, henceforth became his peculiar country;—and that country took full possession of his soul; lifting him above this earthly dross, and every private affection! Worth like his could be no longer hid in the shades of obscurity; nor permit him to be placed in that inferior station with which a mind, great in humility and self-denial, would have been contented. It was wisely considered that he who had so well learned to obey, was fittest to command; and therefore, being well assured of his own heart, he resigned himself to the public voice, nor hesitated a moment longer to accept the important commission freely offered to him; and with the firmness of another Regulus, to bid farewell to his peaceful retirement, and domestic endearments.

Here followed a scene of undissembled tenderness and distress, which all who hear me may, in some degree, conceive; but all cannot truly feel. You only who are husbands and fathers—whose hearts have been intimately blended with the partners of your bliss, and have known the pangs of separation, when launching into dangers, uncertain of your fate—You only would I now more directly address. Give a moment's pause for reflection! Recall your own former feelings, your inward struggles, your virtuous tears; even on a transient separation from a beloved family! Here bid them again freely flow while you listen to our hero's parting words—*

> Ye scenes where home-felt pleasures dwell,
> And thou, my dearer self, farewell!
> " Perhaps the cypress, only tree
> " Of all these groves, shall follow me "—†
> But still, to triumph or a tomb,
> Where Virtue calls, I come, I come.

---

* The choir then broke forth with the lines which follow in the text and which had been set to music; the orator at the last words, " I come, I come," advancing, and with all the impressiveness of a fine figure. well robed, taking the words from it and proceeding in his oration.—H. W. S.

† Hor. B. 2, Ode, 14. L. 22, 24.

"I COME, I come!" Nor were these the words of disappointed
ambition; nor dictated by any sudden start of party zeal. He had
weighed the contest well, was intimately acquainted with the unalienable rights of freemen, and ready to support them at every peril! He
had long foreseen and lamented the fatal issue to which things were
hastening. He knew that the sword of civil destruction, once drawn,
is not easily sheathed; that men, having their minds inflamed and the
weapons of defence in their hands, seldom know the just point where
to stop, even when they have it in their power; and often proceed to
actions, the bare contemplation of which would at first have astonished
them.

It was therefore his desire rather to soften than enflame violent
humours, wishing that America, in all her actions, might stand justified
in the sight of God and the world. He foresaw the horrid train of
evils which would be let loose by the stroke which should sever the
ancient bond of union between Great Britain and us. It was therefore
his wish that such a stroke should never proceed first from the hand of
America. Nor did it so proceed.

The resistance made at Lexington was not the traitorous act of men
conspiring against the supreme powers; nor directed by the councils
of any public body in America; but rose immediately out of the case,
and was dictated by self-preservation, the first great law of nature as
well as society. If there was any premeditated scheme here, it was
premeditated by those who created the dreadful necessity, either of resistance or ruin. For could it be expected that any people, possessing
the least remains of virtue and liberty, would tamely submit to destruction and ravage—to be disarmed as slaves; stripped of their property,
and left a naked prey even to the insults of surrounding savages?

Was this an experiment worthy of Great Britain? Where was the
wisdom of her counsellors? Had their justice, their moderation quite
forsaken them? Could they possibly expect obedience in such a case
as this? Would they themselves, in a similar case, even under a legislative authority of their own free choice, submit to laws which would
destroy the great end of all laws, self-preservation? Human nature
says, no. The genius of the English constitution says, no. The nation
itself hath heretofore said, no; and a great oracle * of its laws has
given his sanction to the verdict—"In cases of national oppression,"
says he, "the nation hath very justifiably risen as one man, to vindicate
"the original contract, subsisting between the king and the people."
And—"If the sovereign power threaten desolation to a state, mankind
"will not be reasoned out of the feelings of humanity, nor sacrifice
"liberty to a scrupulous adherence to political maxims."

If the case of America does not come within the above description,

---

* Blackstone.

there seems to be no equity left upon earth; and whatever is exacted by *force* must be yielded through *fear*. But if justice be anything more than a name, it is surely a solecism in politics to say, that one part of a free country has a right to command that which the other "cannot *obey* without being *slaves,* nor *resist* without being *rebels*." Yet to such a sad dilemma does the parliamentary claim of a "right to bind us in all cases whatsoever," reduce America; involving in it a total surrender of our liberties; superseding the use of our own legislatures, marking us with such a badge of servitude as no freeman can consent to wear; and subjecting us to burdens laid by those who are not only unacquainted with our circumstances, and bear no part of the weight, but ease themselves in proportion as they load us. If this be *law*, if it be *equity*, it has no example among any other people, possessing the least glimmerings of virtue or native freedom.

But although this claim be so repugnant to every idea of natural as well as legal justice, that the guilt of blood which it may occasion can be chargeable only on those who attempt to enforce it; yet I am well assured that when compelled at last by hard necessity, either to avert the dagger pointed at our breast or crouch to unconditional servitude, our hero's heart bled for the dreadful alternative.

His principles of loyalty to his sovereign (whom he had long served, and whose true glory consists in healing those streaming wounds) remained firm and unshaken. Love to our brethren whom we must oppose; the interchange of good offices, which had so intimately knit the bonds of friendship between them and us; the memory of those better days in which we fought and triumphed together; the vast fabric of mutual happiness raised by our union, and ready to be dissolved by our dissensions; the annihilation of those numerous plans of improvement in which we were engaged for the glory of the empire—all these considerations conspired to render this contest peculiarly abhorrent to him and every virtuous American, and could have been outweighed by nothing earthly, but the unquenchable love of liberty, and that sacred duty which we owe to ourselves and our posterity.

Hence, as appears from his papers, even in the full triumph of success, he most ardently joined his worthy friend * General Schuyler in praying that "Heaven may speedily re-unite us in every bond of affection and "interest; and that the British Empire may again become the envy and "admiration of the universe, and flourish" till the consummation of earthly things.

This part of his character I dwell upon with particular satisfaction; and indeed had he evidenced a contrary sentiment, or gone forth in the rage of conquest, instead of the spirit of reconciliation; not all his other virtues, nor yet the respect which I owe to the appointment wherewith

---

* In his letter of Nov. 8th.

I am now honoured, could have induced me to appear in this place, on this occasion.

God forbid that any of the profession to which I belong should ever forget their peculiar character, exercise a turbulent spirit, or prostitute their voice to enflame men's minds to the purposes of wild ambition or mutual destruction. * I am happy in knowing that nothing of this kind is wished from me; nay, that the delegated voice of the continent, as well as of this particular province, supports me in praying for a restoration " of the former harmony between Great Britain and these Colonies "upon so firm a basis as to perpetuate its blessings, uninterrupted by "any future dissensions, to succeeding generations in both countries." *

Indeed this matter rests in safe hands, and is clear in itself. If redress of grievances, essential liberty and security against future oppression can be obtained, according to our own desires; then neither consistency, dignity, nor a regard to our illustrious British friends, who have defended our cause, pledged themselves for our sincerity, and hope by our aid to restore and perpetuate the glory of the whole empire, can suffer us to hesitate. To say, let them look to their own safety, and we will look to ours, would be unworthy of the liberal soul of any American, truly animated in our present cause, and with the love of universal liberty.

But suppose these terms cannot be obtained? Why then, there will be no need of further arguments, much less of aggravations. Timid as my heart perhaps is, and ill-tuned as my ear may be to the din of arms and the clangor of the trumpet; yet, in that case, sounds which are a thousand times more harsh—" even the croaking of frogs in the uncul-"tivated fen," or the howling of wild beasts around the spot, where liberty dwells—would be " preferable to the nightingale's song," in vales of slavery, or the melting notes of Corelli in cities clanking their chains !

If this be a digression, pardon it as the last, and due to my own principles and consistency. I now hasten to attend our hero through the remainder of his career—short indeed ! but crowded with scenes of virtuous activity, which would have dignified the longest life ; and the best achievements of ancient renown.

The Canada expedition is one of those measures, which the enemies of American peace having first rendered necessary, will now strive to misconstrue into hostility and offence. But when authentic proofs were obtained that a people professing a religion, and subjected to laws, different from ours, together with numerous tribes of savages, were instigated and preparing to deluge our frontiers in blood, let God and the world judge whether it was an act of offence ; or rather, whether it was not mercy to them, to ourselves, to the whole British empire, to use the means in our power for frustrating the barbarous attempt.

Indeed there was benevolence in the whole plan of this expedition.

It was to be executed not so much by force as by persuasion; and appearing in the country with such a respectable strength, as might protect the inhabitants from the insults and vengeance of those who were striving to make them lift up their reluctant arm to the shedding fraternal blood.   It was further wished to kindle up the expiring lamp of liberty among them; to open their eyes to its divine effulgence; and enable them to raise their drooping head, and claim its blessings as their own.

This was a work, in all its parts, suited to the genius of a MONT-GOMERY.   He had a head and heart which equally pointed him out as a fit guide in such an undertaking; for he understood and could well explain the blessings of a free government.   Persuasion dwelt upon his tongue.   He had a soul, great, disinterested, affectionate, delighting to alleviate distress, and to diffuse happiness.   He had an industry not to be wearied out; a vigilance not to be imposed upon; and a courage, when necessary, equal to his other abilities.

But still, with a few new-raised men, of different colonies, and perhaps different tempers; ill supplied with arms and ammunition; worse disciplined; unaccustomed to look cannon in the face; to make or to mount a breach—in such circumstances, I say, and in the short space of an autumnal and winter campaign, in rigorous northern climes, to achieve a work which cost Great-Britain and the colonies the labour of several campaigns, and what was a sacrifice of infinitely more value— the life of the immortal Wolfe—this certainly required a degree of mag-nanimity beyond the ordinary reach, and the exertion of the highest abilities of every kind.

The command and conduct of an army, were but small parts of this undertaking.   The Indians were to be treated with restrained and kept in temper.   The Canadians were likewise to be managed, protected and supported: And even his own army in some degree to be formed, dis-ciplined, animated, accustomed to marches, encampments, dangers, fatigues, and the frequent want of necessaries.

Camps, of all worldly scenes, often exhibit the greatest pictures of dis-tress.   The sick and the wounded—the dying and the dead—as well as the wants and sufferings of the living—all these call forth the most tender feelings, and require of a general, that, to the courage of a soldier, he should unite the utmost benevolence of a man!

Our general possessed these united qualities in their highest lustre; of which there are numerous testimonies not only from his own army, but from the prisoners, English as well as Canadians, now amongst us.

When his men laboured under fatigue, wanted bread and other neces-saries, had their beds to make in snow or deep morasses, they were ashamed to complain, finding that he was willing to share in the execu-tion of whatever he commanded.   And the example which he thus set to others, did more to inspire patience, obedience, love of order and discipline, than the most rigid exercise of power could have done. The influence of this example was still stronger, as it did not appear to be the effect of constraint or political necessity; but the amiable expression of a sympathizing soul; leading him to condescend to all capacities; exact in his own duties, and great even in common things. His letters, confidential as well as official, are a full proof of this.

" Our encampment is so swampy, I feel," says he, " exceedingly for the troops; and provisions so scarce, it will require not only dispatch, but good fortune, to keep us from distress—Should things not go well, I tremble for the fate of the poor Canadians, who have ventured so much. What shall I do with them, should I be obliged to evacuate this country? I have assured them that the United Colonies will as soon give up Massachusetts to resentment as them."—

These sentiments were worthy of a heroic soul, and of the faith he had pledged to those people. Nor is he less to be venerated for his tender regard towards his own army—Instead of making a merit of his difficulties (which were indeed more than ought to be mentioned in this place) he often seeks to conceal them; ascribing any little faults or tardiness, in his young troops, to their want of experience in forming; to their hard duty, the constant succession of bad weather and the like —still encouraging them to nobler efforts in future. And if any impatience of discipline appeared, he nobly attributes it to " that spirit of freedom, which men accustomed to think for themselves, will even bring into camps with them."

His own superior military knowledge he has been known to sacrifice to the general voice, rather than interrupt that union on which success depended; and when a measure was once resolved upon by the majority, however much contrary to his own advice and judgment, he magnanimously supported it with his utmost vigor; disdaining that work of low ambition, which will strive to defeat in the execution, what it could not direct in planning.

His perseverance and conduct in gaining possession of St. John's and Montreal, have already been the theme of every tongue, and need not be mentioned in this place. His abilities in negotiation; the precision with which the various articles of treaties and capitulations are expressed; the generous applause he gives, not only to every worthy effort of his own officers, but to the commanding officer and garrison of St. John's; his noble declaration to the inhabitants of Montreal, " that the continental armies despise every act of oppression and violence, being come for the express purpose of giving liberty and security "—all these, I say, did honour to himself, and to that delegated body, under whose authority he acted. * * *

Having approached those plains which the blood of Wolfe hath consecrated to deathless fame, our hero seemed emulous of his glory, and animated with a kindred spirit. The situation of his army pressed dispatch ! snows and frost only quickened his motions.   He hoped by one successful stroke, before the arrival of succours to the garrison, to complete his plan, and save the future effusion of much blood.   He further flattered himself, that his success, if speedy, might have some influence upon parliament, in hastening a reconciliation.   He understood that maxim of Folard : "No obstacle should break our resolution, when "there is but a moment between a bad situation and a worse."   This sentiment he expresses in his last letter with a spirit of modesty, and a sense of duty, as well as the danger attending it, which ought to be forever recorded to his glory : "I shall be sorry to be reduced to this "mode of attack ; because I know the melancholy consequences.   But "the approaching severity of the season, the weakness of the garrison, "together with the nature of the works, point it out too strong to be "passed by.   Fortune often baffles the most sanguine expectations of "poor mortals—I am not intoxicated with the favours I have received "at her hands—But I think there is a fair prospect of success."

Poor mortals indeed, if nothing was to remain of them after death ; for while he was courting this success, and gloriously leading on his troops in the front of danger, he received the fatal stroke, which in an instant released his great spirit, to follow and join the immortal spirit of Wolfe !

O thou swift-winged messenger of destruction, how didst thou triumph in that moment ! the stroke that severed Montgomery from his army, deprived them of more than a member.   It reached the vitals, and struck the whole body with a temporary death.   As when the forked lightning, darting through the forest, amid the black tempests of night, rends some towering oak, and lays its honours in the dust, the inferior trees which it had long sheltered from the storm, stand mournful around, so stood the astonished bands over their fallen chieftain !

Dr. Smith now speaks of the Pennsylvania officers and of their brave companion-in-arms, young Cheeseman.

Here, ye Pennsylvanian youths, second to none in virtue, let a portion of your tears be sacred to the *manes* of Macpherson !   You remember his generous spirit in his early years, for he drank of the same springs of science with many of you now before me ; and we who reached the cup to your lip, rejoice that it contributed to invigorate both him and you into wisdom and public spirit.   Having finished his scholastic education, he studied the laws of his country, under a lawyer and patriot of distinguished name ; and animated by his example, as well as precepts, had become eminent in his profession, at an age when some have scarce begun to think of business.   The love of liberty being his ruling passion, he thought it his duty in the present struggle, to offer himself to the service of his country, and he had soon an opportunity of attaining that military pre-eminence, of which he was laudably ambitious.

Enjoying a hereditary bravery, joined to a well-cultivated understanding, and an active spirit, he soon became the bosom friend of General Montgomery, was his aid-de-camp, was entrusted with a share in the management of his most important negotiations, stood by his side in the attack upon Quebec, and being, as it were, animated by one common soul, and dear to each other in life—in death, they were not a moment divided !

Here, likewise, fell Captain Cheeseman, of the New-York forces, covered with honour, and lamented by all who knew him, as an active and gallant officer. His particular merits, as well as the merits of some others, who shared his fate, ought to be more fully commemorated on this occasion, if proper accounts of them could be collected.

I must not, however, omit the name of the brave Captain Hendricks, who commanded one of the Pennsylvania rifle-companies, and was known to me from his infancy. He was indeed prodigal of his life, and courted danger out of his tour of duty. The command of the guard belonged to him, on the morning of the attack ; but he solicited and obtained leave to take a more conspicuous post ; and having led his men through the barrier, where his commanding officer, General Arnold, was wounded, he long sustained the fire of the garrison with unshaken firmness, till at last, receiving a shot in his breast, he immediately expired.[*]

Such examples of magnanimity filled even *adversaries* with veneration and esteem. Forgetting the *foes* in the *heroes*, they gathered up their breathless remains, and committed them to kindred dust, with pious hands "and funeral honours meet." So may your own remains, and particularly thine, O ! Carlton, be honoured, should it ever be your fate to fall in hostile fields ! Or if, amid the various chances of war, your lot should be among the prisoners and the wounded, may you be distinguished with an ample return of that benevolence which you have shewn to others. Such offices of humanity, softening the savage scenes of war, will entitle you to an honour which all the pride of conquest cannot bestow—much less a conquest over fellow-subjects, contending for the common rights of freemen.

By such offices as these, you likewise give a gleam of comfort to those mourners, who mix their tears without our [†] Schuylkill and Susquehannah ; and to her [‡] especially, on Hudson's river, pre-eminent in woe !

---

[*] These particulars were certified by General Thompson and Colonel Magaw, his commanders in the Pennsylvania rifle-regiment, and they give me this further character of him in their letter, viz. : "No fatigues or duty ever discouraged him. . . . He paid the strictest attention to his company, and was ambitious that they should excel in discipline, sobriety and order. His social and domestic virtues you were well acquainted with."

[†] The rivers on which the parents of Major Macpherson and Captain Hendricks live.

[‡] Mrs. Montgomery.

Ye angels and ministers of grace, complete her consolations.   Tell her, in gentlest accents, what wreaths of glory you have entwined, to adorn the brows of those who die for their country ; and hovering for a while, on the *wing of pity*, listen to the mournful strain, flowing to a deceased husband.*

> Sweet ivy twin'd with myrtle, form a shade
> Around the tomb where brave *Montgomery's* laid !
> Beneath your boughs, shut from the beams of day,
> My ceaseless tears shall bathe the warrior's clay ;
> And injur'd " Freedom shall a while repair,
> To dwell, with me, a weeping hermit there."

The choir having sung with pathetic grace these lines—slightly altered from those well known of Collins—

> " Wind, gentle evergreen, to form a shade
> Around the tomb where Sophocles is laid "—

the orator concludes :

Having now paid the honors due to the memories of our departed friends, what need I add more?   Illustrious, though short, was their race !   " But old age is not that which standeth in length of time, nor is measured by number of years.   Wisdom is the gray hair to man, and an unspotted life is old age.''

To such men Rome in all her glory would have decreed honors ; and the resolve of Congress to transmit the memory of their virtues is worthy of that magnanimity which ought to characterize public bodies.   Jealous and arbitrary rulers are sparing of honors to those who serve them, lest their own should be thus eclipsed.   But your lustre, gentlemen, can suffer no diminution in this way, and the glory you justly bestow on others will only be reflected to increase your own.

Strange to say, this fine oration was not well received by that portion of the Congress led by John Adams and his more special friends.   " *Sink* or swim, survive or *perish*," *they* were determined on a rupture and a war.   From one of those letters written by this singular man, and left by him to be published when the persons whom he calumniated could not disprove his statements, he says : †

The oration was an insolent performance.   A motion was made [in Congress] to thank the orator and ask a copy ; but it was opposed with great spirit and vivacity from every part of the room, and at last withdrawn, lest it should be rejected, as it certainly would have been with

---

* The choir here, in pensive strains, broke in again.
† " Forces' Archives," Fourth Series, Vol. III.

great indignation.   The author then printed it himself, after leaving out and altering some offensive passages. . . . The appointment of him to make this oration was a great oversight and mistake.

There is no evidence known to me but this statement of Mr. Adams, that the oration was altered in any important parts of it. It could not, I should think, have been altered in any such parts without being recast.   There would have been a plain incongruity between its parts, which, as it stands, there is not.   Dr. Smith, in printing it, says expressly that two or three quotations have been transferred from the text to the margin; that a few alterations, chiefly *verbal*, have been made upon the recommendation of some friends, and a paragraph which was forgotten in the delivery is printed in its place.   The paragraph which is supposed to have offended Mr. Adams is one which in this volume is printed on page 554, near the upper part of the page, and is included between two stars.   It is a quotation from the petition made by the Congress of 1775—the very Congress which was sitting, and in which Mr. Adams was—on the 8th of July, 1775, to "the King's Most Excellent Majesty"—the last petition which had been made.*   Referring to that paragraph, which is found in the first as in all other editions of the oration, Dr. Smith says, that having it "either misrepresented or misunderstood by some, the author does not think himself at liberty to make the least alteration of it, even if he judged any to be necessary."
He says further and rightly:

The quotation from the last petition of Congress, as well as the reference made to the instructions of our assembly, both point to a past period; and the author cannot be considered, from thence, as taking upon him to make the least declaration concerning the present sentiments of either of these bodies ; nor is there a word which can preclude the taking into the terms of accommodation, so far as may be thought reasonable, the redress of whatever grievances or losses we may have sustained, since that period.   Upon the whole, it is presumed that a single sentiment is not to be found in the oration, which is not fully consonant to every declaration of Congress which has yet appeared.   And to impute to them, or even suspect, the least change of sentiment, before they themselves have declared it, would not only be indecent but very injurious to our cause.   The author is also consistent with himself, and

---

* See *supra*, p. 514.

if the same doctrines which he has been told were well received in his late
publication [Sermon on American Affairs] should now be disagreeable
to any, the fault is not his.

Upon the whole, the author hopes he has done justice to the memory
of those *brave* men who are the subjects of the oration ; and with respect
to those reflections upon public affairs which must rise out of public
characters, and are intimately connected with them, he is so far from
wishing them retrenched, that (on a careful review) he is willing to rest
upon them, whatever claim he may have to the appellation of a *good
Citizen*, or *friend to Liberty*, so long as it may be remembered that he
either lived or wrote in America.

There is another matter in the sermon which may have caused
a dissatisfaction. A part—commanded by a Colonel Enos—of
that division of the army which went with General Arnold—the
division that went through Maine—had not gone on. They were
popularly charged with desertion, and in the oration Dr. Smith
says : "About a third of the army of the latter—deserted shall I
say—or use the more courteous language—returned home." No
name was mentioned. In point of fact, at the time the oration was
delivered, an inquiry had been made into the reasons of the return
of this part of the army, and the commanding officer had been
acquitted. Dr. Smith was not aware of the fact, though in printing
his sermon he made every *amende*.

A great-grandson is not likely to be the most impartial judge
of his ancestor's acts. But so far as I can myself see in regard to
this one, the case is with Dr. Smith, and not with John Adams.

The truth is, as I have said, that if there was any mistake anywhere, it was in making discourses in times of high political and
military excitement, before political and military bodies of any
kind. The Rev. Mr. White—afterwards the well-known Bishop—
speaks of the matter, and mentions that " one of the warmest spirits
of the day," Colonel Timothy Matlack, " whose ardor in the American cause," he says, " cannot but be still remembered by many,"
invited *him* to preach before a battalion, but that he would not do
it. This, perhaps, was the wiser course. But Mr. White was
never in the least a popular orator, as Dr. Smith always was.
Neither had Mr. White ever entered upon the political questions
of the day, as Dr. Smith, by an instinctive disposition towards
public subjects, had more or less done from his first coming to
America. Mr. White could decline such invitations without an

36

inconsistency with his previous action. Dr. Smith hardly could. And his refusal might be misconstrued, and as he supposed·would immediately subject his College, dearer than himself, to wrong and injury. Moreover, an invitation by Colonel Matlack to preach before a battalion was a thing of a different sort of weight from an invitation by the Congress of America to deliver a funeral oration upon General Richard Montgomery and the brave companions who had died at his side. The former might be declined by Mr. White. The latter hardly could be by any one.

This sermon on General Montgomery and the other officers who fell at Quebec was printed in Philadelphia soon after its delivery. It was reprinted in Burlington, New Jersey, in the city of New York, and in London. I do not think that Mr. Adams' censure of it as "an insolent performance" was sustained by any intelligent class of readers. His statement is to be classed among those "wild and irregular starts"—as Mr. Theodore Sedgwick, of the Senate of the United States, called some of Mr. Adams' acts—" of a vain, jealous and *half-frantic* mind;" one of that sort which entitled him to the last trait of the character given of him by Dr. Franklin, "a man always honest, sometimes great, but often *mad;*" a character to the justness of which Alexander Hamilton said that *he* subscribed, "adding to the *first* trait of it this qualification—as far as a man excessively vain and jealous, and *ignobly* attached to *place*, can be!" *

CHAPTER XXXV.

COMMENCEMENT AT THE COLLEGE; THE LAST FOR SOME TIME—JAMES ABER-
CROMBIE, D. D.—THE REV. JAMES MADISON TO DR. SMITH—A DAUGHTER
BORN TO DR. SMITH—DR. SMITH BUYS LAND WHERE NORRISTOWN NOW IS—
OBSERVES A TRANSIT OF MERCURY IN 1776, AND AN ECLIPSE OF THE SUN IN
1777—THE COLLEGE EDIFICE AND GROUNDS OCCUPIED BY TROOPS—THE
FACULTY REMONSTRATE—DR. SMITH VISITED BY COLONEL DELANY—PASSAGE
IN BISHOP WHITE'S MEMOIRS EXPLAINED—SIR WILLIAM HOWE CAPTURES
PHILADELPHIA—DR. SMITH LEAVES THE FALLS OF SCHUYLKILL, AND GOES
WITH HIS FAMILY TO BARBADOES ISLAND, HIS PLANTATION IN THE SCHUYL-
KILL.

DARK days were soon to come upon the College of Philadelphia. Its halls were shortly to be occupied by our own soldiers;

---

* See "Hamilton's Works," Vol. V., p. 217; and Vol. VI., p. 448.

its charity schools disturbed, its teachers left without lodging-rooms, its grounds crowded with wagons and horses of the army. But we will not anticipate these sad times, nor those worse which soon followed, when the College was wholly closed to the purposes for which it was founded; when British troopers were desecrating its halls, and its Provost and its Professors sent exiles from their offices and homes.

It had yet *one* commencement. This took place in June, 1776. We give the names of all the graduates:

James Abercrombie, John Leeds Bosman, John Claxton, William Cock, Jacob Hall, Thomas Duncan Smith, William Thomas, Ralph Wiltshire. The graduate who became best known in Philadelphia is the one who, in alphabetical order, heads the list— *James Abercrombie.* This gentleman was born in Philadelphia, January 26th, 1758, and was the son of a Scotchman who had formerly been an officer of the British navy, who came to America in 1753, and was resident in Philadelphia. After his arrival here, he still adhered to his profession, and was lost in 1760 by shipwreck in the German ocean. His son James—at that time but two years of age—was brought up by his mother. He was instructed in the city at a private school kept by Dr. Gardiner, and afterwards was entered at the College. Shortly after being graduated, he began the study of divinity under the Rev. William White. After two years' attention his eyesight became so much affected that he was compelled to relinquish study. In 1780 he went into mercantile life, and in 1783 into partnership with the late John Miller, Jr. During this time he engaged in political life, and in 1792 was elected a member of Common Council of the city. In 1793 he resumed his theological studies, and was ordained deacon at St. Peter's, December 29th, 1793. In June, 1794, he was appointed one of the "ministers" of the united churches, of which St. Peter's was one; and so became junior minister, Dr. Robert Blackwell, who had been appointed in 1781, being the senior.* He was useful in other parishes, his services being frequently given to the rural churches in the neighborhood of the city—notably to Trinity, Oxford, and All-Saints', Lower Dublin, parishes in which Dr. Smith had pre-

---

* The ministers of the united churches of Christ Church and St. Peter's were popularly called Assistant Ministers. But their charter title is "Ministers;" the head of the corporation not being called a "minister" of any sort, but "the Rector."

ceded him.   Dr. Abercrombie preached at each once a month for three years.   His salary not being sufficient for his support, he founded, in 1800, the Philadelphia Academy, in connection with Rev. Dr. Magaw, of St. Paul's, and in 1803 became sole director of the institution.   In 1817 he resigned this charge.   He continued one of the ministers of the united churches until November, 1832; a space of more than thirty-eight years, and died June 26th, 1841, aged eighty-three years.   As we learn by Mr. Hildeburn's valuable book of epitaphs in St. Peter's church-yard, he is interred on the south side of that church, in which he so long ministered.   Dr. Rufus Wilmot Griswold, in his work called "The Republican Court," thus describes Dr. Abercrombie:

Educated for the liberal professions, he had been engaged in commerce in Philadelphia; and though in relinquishing a lucrative business for "the order of poverty," as well as by the general course of his life, he had given unquestionable proofs of his earnestness, a certain fondness for convivial pleasure, and a high tone both of ecclesiastical and political sentiment, caused his sincerity to be sometimes doubted by persons who looked no deeper than the surface of things.   Following the occasional practice of the English clergy of the last century, he had once or twice visited the theatre on "the author's night," which caused scandal among many who every day of their lives may have done something much worse.   Then his aversion to the infidel sentiments suspected to be held by Mr. Jefferson made him at a later period very reluctant to read the prayers for the President of the United States, prescribed in the Episcopal ritual; and when informed by his Diocesan that it was not a matter in the least discretionary with him, he comforted his Federal friends with the assurance that he had not "prayed," but only "read" them.   Not content with provoking the Democrats, he had, on more than one occasion, involved himself in trouble with the aristocracy of his parish, by his strict and manly adherence to what he deemed his duty, prescribed by the canons and rubrics of his church.   His celebration of the marriage of William Penn, an eccentric great-grandson of the founder of Pennsylvania, attracted a great deal of attention.   This gentleman took a fancy to address a woman celebrated for her beauty, but whose course of life, not less than her origin and associations, rendered it impossible for his friends of either sex to recognize her as his wife.   Almost any other of the clergy would have refused, on grounds of prudential regard to their own interests, to perform the marriage office under circumstances so peculiar; but Dr. Abercrombie, having used in vain all suitable endeavors to persuade Mr. Penn from so fatal a connection, and finding that there was no legal or canonical impediment, married them, considering himself bound as a Christian minister to do so. The excitement, however, became so great, and his popularity was so much in danger of being affected by it, that he was obliged to defend himself in a pamphlet—" Documents Relative to the Celebration of a Late Marriage "—to the principles of which Bishop White gave his entire approval. There can be no doubt, I think, that Dr. Abercrombie was right, and evinced that a sense of duty was the controlling influence of his conduct ; and the approval of what he had done by Bishop White is a fact worth recording, as the clergy are often called on to act in cases like that here referred to, though not often in quite as strong ones.

Bishop De Lancey, who succeeded him in officiating at St. Peter's, says of him, " that he was admired for his excellence as a reader of our liturgy, for his ability as a writer and eloquence as a speaker; and exhibited, in his long-continued, active, and steady discharge of ministerial duty, an unbroken attachment to the cause of Christ and of his church." Dr. Abercrombie was a great reader of the works of Dr. Samuel Johnson, and a correspondent of his biographer, as will be seen by a reference to Boswell's life of this great author.

We now approach the great—the eventful—4th of July. The last communication of Dr. Smith which I have found to any English correspondent is a note to Lady Juliana Penn. That bears date March 14th, 1776. In it he says:

The times are such that I have long declined correspondence with England ; but I propose soon to write, when I see what situation affairs are likely to be in upon the arrival of the Commissioners expected from England. God grant that they may have proper terms to offer, and reconciliation may yet take place. If the terms are otherwise, I need not say what will be the consequence.

The Provost Stillé calls attention to "the perfect harmony of tone" of this note with the reasons given in the Report of the Committee of the Assembly, of which Mr. Robert Morris was one, for releasing the Delegates of Pennsylvania in the Continental Congress from the instructions previously given to them to resist all measures looking to Independence. The Committee say:

The happiness of these Colonies has, during the whole course of this fatal controversy, been our first wish ; their reconciliation with Great Britain, the next. But if we must renounce the one or the other, our choice must be determined by the overruling law of self-preservation.

The following letter from James Madison, afterwards Bishop of Virginia, but at this time a Professor in William and Mary College, attests in part the respect with which the College at Philadelphia was held at the outbreak of the Revolution.

The Rev. James Madison to Dr. Smith.

WILLIAM & MARY COLLEGE, VIRGINIA, Sept. 25, 1776.

DEAR SIR: Agreeable to your request I have now ye Pleasure of sending you ye Extract from y^e *Recueil pour les Astronomes, par M. Jean Brêmoulli, Astronome Royal,* &^{c}. That I may do no Injustice to ye Author, I shall send you his own words; but as ye first Part contains little more than ye History of your Society,* I shall pass over it.

Lorsque la Société jugea avoir reçu un nombre suffisant de Mémoires pour former un Volume, elle nomma des commissaires pour assister les Secretaires dans le choix des meilleurs piéces. Ce sout celles-ci qui composent le volume dout il est question, & qui est divisé en les sections. La première consiste, pour la plupart, en mémoires astronomiques relatifs au passage de Venus en 1769. La Pènsylvanie étant un pays bien mieux situé pour observer ce phénomène que ne l'etoit l'Angleterre, la Société nomma des commissaires pour observer ce passage en differens endroits. Ils eurent bien de la peine à en venir a bout; ce n'étoit pas leur seul embarras de déterminer avec exactitude les longitudes & les latitudes; mais encore il falloit les instrumens nécessaires et principalement de bons telescopes. L'Assemblé Provinciale et M. Thomas Penn, supplièrent généreusement à ce defaut. Il'étoit impossible de répondre mieux à tout d'encouragements qu'ont fait ces Astronomes, qu'en considérant soit le soin & la diligence avec laquelle ils out entrepris leur Observations, soit la fidelité de leur recits, & la netteté & la justesse de leur raisonnements sur ce sujet ainsi curieux que difficile.

Les écrits de M. Rittenhouse et du Dr. Smith sout à cet egard bien de l'honneur à cette nouvelle société. Dans le relation de leur procédés les differentes commissions qui avoient été envoyées à Philadelphie à Norriton et aù Cap. Henlopen sont [part of the MS. gone] donner non seulement les resultats de leur observations, mais aussi les materiaux qui les out fournis, afin que d'autres puissent examiner et juger pour eux-mêmes; un exemple digne d'imitation pour ces Astronomes Européens, qui sont si retenus dans le détail et qui ne parlent de leurs instruments & de leurs observations qu'en termes généraux.

Outre les Mémoires sur le passage de Vénus il y a encore une rélation du passage de Mercure du 9 Novembre, 1769. Des Observations sur la Comète en Juin et Juillet en 1770; Une Amélioration de la Construction du Quartier de Godfrey (apellé communément l'Octave de Hadley) & une tres bonne méthode pour déduire le tems du passage du soleil, des hauteurs correspondantes, sans l'aide des Tables de correction relatives au changement du soleil en déclinaison.

Voila beaucoup d'éloges qu'on donne à nos Astronomes Américains, mais ils sont bien mérités.

What follows is mostly relative to ye dispute between Mr. Ludlam & Mr. Ewing, but as ye author has taken no part in it, it is scarcely worth transcribing.

---

* Meaning the American Philosophical Society.

Our worthy President, Mr. Page, had resolved to send you his Papers upon ye last Transit, which he observed at his seat, but ye hurry of Business at present prevents him from putting ye finishing hand to them.

You will find enclosed a few (MS. torn) of which you will best know how to dispose. I believe there is no doubt of y^e accuracy of y^e Observations upon y^e Longitude & Latitude of y^e places mentioned. I might add y^e Longitude of Williamsburg, which I have found by a Mean of several Observations $= 5° 6' 22''$.

There is nothing here of a Public nature worth sending you. The only Dangers that seem to threaten us with disagreeable consequences, are y^e Elements themselves, as it is thought, one-half of us must become Adamites thro' necessity; we have been improvident in laying up Winter Clothes. The approaching Assembly is to new-model our College. They w^d fain have it beneficial to ye Country, and I wish ye Means to obtain so desirable an End, may be weighed with that attention which they deserve. But there are many difficulties in ye way. Not only, perhaps ye want of a Revenue, but of a proper Plan, especially such a one as w^d suit this country the best. I had resolved to beg ye Favour of you, if it be not too troublesome to send me a Sketch of your's, as many here are fond of putting this upon your Plan, without knowing scarcely what it is; and if you will favour me also with the expected Time of Conjunction for Mercury in November, at Philadelphia, as soon as possible, I shall be much obliged.

I am, Dr Sir, with much respect,

Y^r most Obed^t Servt & Friend,

JAMES MADISON.

On the 26th of October, 1776, another daughter having been born to Dr. Smith, and Dr. Peters, who baptized some of his other children, having died on the 10th of July, 1776, she was baptized by the Rev. Mr. William White, with the name of Elizabeth; Miss Williamina Bond* and Miss Elizabeth Lynch being sponsors.

Four days after this, Dr. Smith bought of Colonel John Bull between five and six hundred acres of land, including a beautiful island in the Schuylkill, called Barbadoes Island, in what was then Philadelphia county, but is now called Montgomery. Norris-

---

* Miss Williamina Bond was the daughter of Dr. Phineas Bond, of Philadelphia. She was born in that city, February 26th, 1753, married to Gen. John Cadwalader (being his second wife) on the 30th of January, 1779. Two of their children reached maturity—Gen. Thomas Cadwalader, of Philadelphia, and Frances, who in the year 1800 married Lord David Montagu Erskine, of Restormel Castle, Cornwall county, England; she died, March 25th, 1843.

town is at present on the mainland thus purchased.*   It was upon
this tract, called the Norriton Manor, that David Rittenhouse was
living in 1769, when with him, Dr. Smith and Mr. Lukens observed
the Transit of Venus.   I have the original agreement of Colonel
Bull with Dr. Smith for the sale of the tract to him.   "Wm. White,"
afterwards the Bishop, is a witness to it.   It may serve as a variety
upon the topics largely treated of late, if I give it to my readers.

MEMORANDUM of an agreement had, fully made and agreed upon the
30th day of October, 1776, between the Rev. Dr. William Smith, of the
City of Philadelphia, of the one Part, and John Bull, of the County of
Philadelphia, Esquire, of the other Part, Witnesseth that it is mutually
agreed between the said parties to these presents in manner following,
viz.: the said John Bull for himself, his heirs, executors and administrators, doth covenant and agree to and with the said William Smith,
his heirs, executors, administrators and assigns, that the said John Bull,
his heirs, executors or administrators shall and will on or before the 5th
day of November next, for the consideration herein after mentioned,
grant and convey unto the said William Smith, in fee simple, all that
messuage or tenement, grist-mills, saw-mill, powder-mill and tract of
land situate in Norristown, in the County of Philadelphia aforesaid

---

* It was not until some time after the Revolution that Norristown became a place of
importance.   Immediately below the borough may be seen the place where the Americans, under Washington, on their way to Valley Forge, crossed the river Schuylkill.
Here also the earth was thrown up to secure their protection against the threatened
attack of the British.   The little stone tavern, which sheltered Washington on his
march to Valley Forge, still stands, and looks as strong as though it were built but yesterday.   Where now stands that beautiful and costly edifice, the Oakland Institute,
lived and died James Wilson, one of the signers both of the Declaration of Independence and of the Constitution of the United States; afterwards appointed by Washington a Judge of the Supreme Court of the United States.   Immediately to the east
of Norristown is Whitemarsh, where once lay the army of Washington, and where
works may be seen to this day that were thrown up by his men, to secure themselves
against a surprise from the enemy.   Away to the north lies Skippack; and right in
view, with her hills high above us, is the Valley Forge.   This celebrated place is
connected with the most gloomy period in the history of our country, when Conway
and his friends were plotting the destruction of Washington.   The sufferings our men
endured had well nigh driven them to despair; but Washington, undismayed, held
together, by his power and influence, the little band, and soon after achieved the independence of the nation.   The house which Washington made his head-quarters still
stands, and with the entrenchments and forts erected by the army may be seen to
this day.   It is most agreeable to me to add that through the efforts of the Ladies of
the Valley Forge Centennial Association, presided over by the amiable and engaging
Mrs. Anna Holstein, aided by the energetic and accomplished Mrs. Aubrey Smith, it
is likely that the Head-Quarters of Washington at the Valley Forge will be preserved forever as a monument of the nation's gratitude to the great and good commander.

(being the same premises which the said John Bull purchased of Mary Norris, widow), containing about six hundred acres, including *Barbados Island,* in the River Schuylkill (certain part thereof, containing between forty and sixty acres or thereabouts, which the said John Bull heretofore conveyed to a certain Josiah Wood, with a privilege of said mill and a foot-path to and from the same only excepted). Together with a lime-rock and kiln containing about one acre of land, and all the appurtenances unto the premises belonging. In consideration whereof he, the said William Smith, doth hereby promise to pay unto the said John Bull, his heirs, executors or administrators on that day when the said conveyance shall be completed, the sum of £6,000 lawful money of Pennsylvania aforesaid. The Title to be such as Counsel learned in the law shall approve. . . . And it is further agreed by and between the said parties to these presents, and the said John Bull doth hereby agree to accept of a lease from the said William Smith, his executors, administrators or assigns for all the remaining part of the premises not now under lease to Josiah Wood, along with the mill. For which he, the said John Bull, doth agree to pay to the said William Smith, his executors, administrators or assigns, the yearly rent of £160 for the term of three years and six months, to commence from the 6th day of November next, the rent of £130 for the grist-mill now under lease to the said Josiah Wood, to be paid unto the said William Smith, his executors, administrators or assigns, as it accrues and becomes due from the said 6th day of November next.

In Witness whereof the said parties to these presents have interchangeably set their hands and seals hereunto, dated the day and year first above written.

Sealed and delivered in the presence of us,
    PETER MILLER,
    JAMES RANKIN.   JNO. BULL. [L. S.]

Received the day of the date of the above Articles £500 in part of the consideration money above mentioned.

    Witness,   JOHN BULL.
PETER MILLER.

Received, November 2d, 1776, of the Rev. Dr. Smith the further sum of £2,300, in part of the consideration money mentioned in the foregoing article—which, with the preceding sum of £500, are included in the receipt on the Conveyance to the said William Smith.

    Witness,   JOHN BULL.
WM. WHITE.

On the 2d of November, 1776—undisturbed by the political and military events around him, and while our brave associators—Gen.

John Cadwalader, Col. John Bayard, Major William Bradford, Col. Clement Biddle and other well-known Philadelphians—were arming for the fields of Trenton and Princeton—so soon to become immortal—the Provost, at this time the Professor of Astronomy in his college, with his old friends of the Transit day in 1769, David Rittenhouse and John Lukens, were observing the Transit of Mercury over the sun, which took place at this time. Again on the 9th of January, 1777—Trenton and Princeton having been fought and gained—we find Dr. Smith, along with Mr. Rittenhouse, again engaged in the study of the celestial phenomena. He is now taking observations on an eclipse of the sun. A full account of these observations will be found in the Transactions of the Philosophical Society.

By the 23d of January, 1777, the College property and grounds had come under the calamities of war. We have on that day an application made by Dr. Smith and other members of the Faculty of Arts to the Council of Safety, for relief against all unnecessary invasion of the military force into precincts where they were so little in keeping with the proper duties of the place.

COLLEGE OF PHILADELPHIA,
January 23d, 1777.

GENTLEMEN: The Interruptions which we have met with in the important Business of Education committed to our Charge, compel us once more to make our earnest Application to you for Relief. This Seminary was founded, and has been hitherto supported (with scarce any public Assistance) by the private Benefactions of the Generous Friends of Literature, from various Parts of this Continent, as well as from Great Britain & Ireland. It can boast of having raised up Numbers of Youth who now, in the Day of Trial, fill many of the Highest Offices, Religious & Civil, as well as Military; a d who, by their public Spirit & distinguish'd Abilities, do Honor to their Country & the Place of their Education. These Considerations, we humbly hope, should entitle us to that Protection, and those Exemptions, which in all civilized States, are given to such Institutions, unless in Cases of the most clear and urgent Necessity.

But we have to complain that, as if it were intended particularly to distress us, contrary to the General Orders respecting Schools and Places of Worship; and without any Necessity which we could see, without any written Authority, without giving us a moment's previous Notice to remove Books, Papers or Furniture, or even allowing Time to send for the Keys, the Doors of the Schools, Lecture Rooms, and even Bed

Rooms have been forced open by some violent young Men calling themselves Deputies of the Barrack Master; and some Hundreds of Soldiers
quartered upon the College at a Time, who have burnt our Wood and
done other Damage, when we have offered to shew, and have actually
shewn, Empty Houses, where they could have been far better accommodated. This has been repeated upon us three or four Times within
so many Weeks, so that before we could well clear away the Dirt and
Filth left by one Set of Soldiers, and meet again in our Places, another
Set has been forced upon us; owing to which, we have scarce yet
been able to collect together a third Part of the former Number of our
Youth: And unless we can be placed upon some more certain Footing,
the Schools must either be wholly broken up, or removed to some other
Place.

This is a matter of very serious Concern to us, not only on account
of the present Set of Youth, who may be thereby deprived of their Opportunity of Education, but on our own Accounts also, whose Livings
depend on the Execution of our Duty, and cannot expect to be supported without Service done.

We are persuaded that none who know us, or the Gentlemen concerned in the Trust of this Seminary, will think that these Complaints
are groundless, or proceed from any Desire to retard the necessary public
Service. We only Pray that we may not be particularly distressed; that
if any Emergency shall arise, when we cannot have that Exemption
which is due to Seminaries of Religion and Learning, you yourselves
will judge of that Emergency, without leaving us every Moment at the
arbitrary Disposal of any Officers under you, or their Deputies; that
when any Requisition is to be made, you will be pleased to give us timely
Notice, laying no greater Burthen upon us than upon other Places in
Proportion; considering the College & its different Schools and Houses,
to be duly inhabited and furnished in the same Manner as other Houses
are, according to the Purposes for which it was intended and erected.
We request your speedy Consideration of the Premises, and are with
due Respect,

> Gentlemen,
> Your most obedient Humble Servants,
> > WILLIAM SMITH,
> > FRANCIS ALISON,
> > JAS. DAVIDSON,
> > JAMES CANNON.

P. S.—We are now actually incommoded with about one hundred
and fifty Soldiers; our Yard crowded with Horses & Wagons, the
Charity Schools disturbed, & the Schoolmistress forced out of her
Lodging Rooms.

On the 30th day of June, 1777, the College was closed.

On the 31st of August, 1777, Sir William Howe now advancing towards Philadelphia with a view of capturing it, the Supreme Executive Council, in pursuance of a recommendation of Congress that "all persons who have in their general conduct and conversation evinced a disposition inimical to the cause of America should be apprehended and secured," issued a general warrant "to secure the persons" of forty-one well-known citizens of Philadelphia by name, Dr. Smith being one of them. But expressing its wish "to treat men of reputation with as much tenderness as the security of their persons and papers will admit," it desired the officers who were to execute the warrant, in case the persons (with the exception of seven, Tories outright, I believe) "would promise in writing to remain in their dwellings ready to appear on demand of Council, and, meanwhile, to refrain from doing any act inimical to the United States of North America, by speaking, writing or otherwise, and from giving intelligence to the Commander-in-Chief of the British forces, or any other person concerning public affairs," to dismiss them from confinement of their persons. Twenty-six of the forty-one persons named—seventeen being Friends—refused to make the promise required or any promise equivalent to it, and were apprehended and confined in the Free Masons' Lodge; a large edifice used for oratorios, concerts, etc. A few days before the entry of Sir William Howe, the number of the prisoners being now reduced to twenty—seventeen being Friends—these twenty were sent to Winchester, in Virginia, and kept for some months, when they were liberated; no judicial accusation having ever been at any time made against them. As Dr. Smith was never taken into custody and was only asked to give parole—from which, on the evacuation of the city, he was discharged—it is probable that he gave the required promise, except as to keeping himself within his own house, which it would seem he did not give. His papers were examined by Col. Sharpe Delany, who was the officer detailed to wait upon him. But nothing was found that implicated him in offence, and nothing was taken away. He had taken the oath of allegiance several months before.

The battle of Brandywine, fought on the 11th of September, and the nearer approach of the British army to Philadelphia, soon made the Supreme Executive Council much more concerned about themselves than they were about Dr. Smith. He was now free to do what he pleased. He did not, however, communicate with the British army. On the contrary, disposing of some of his children with his relatives, and taking his wife and others with him, he went quietly to his Barbadoes Island, near to the American army; and there, close by the Valley Forge, remained during the occupation of the city.*

I am ignorant of any sufficient ground for this proceeding against Dr. Smith. I believe that on the 11th of March, 1776, that is to say, nearly four months prior to the day when the Declaration was ordered to be made, he printed a small pamphlet containing essays, signed Cato, showing the impolicy of separating ourselves from the mother country. In the opinion that to do so —and especially to do so before we were better prepared for war than Pennsylvania then was—would be impolitic, he was supported by the opinions of many of the most upright and intelligent men of the State—Robert Morris, James Wilson, Thomas Willing, John Dickinson, by a large part of the Congress of 1776 itself, and by almost the whole of old Philadelphia. But I have myself no knowledge of anything that he wrote after July 4th, seeking to show that the Declaration ought not to have been made, or to oppose the measures which it required to make it effective. He probably suffered to some extent in reputation as a *Patriot* by his family connexion. His father-in-law, William Moore, of Moore Hall, Chester county, now an old man, was indisposed in common with nearly every one in that county towards independence,

---

* His oldest son, William Moore Smith (my grandfather), was sent to his grandfather, William Moore's, at Moore Hall, in Chester county. His sister, Williamina, Dr. Smith's oldest daughter, then sixteen years old, was with her aunt, Mrs. Phineas Bond, who remained in Philadelphia during the occupation. Being a beautiful and sprightly girl, she soon attracted the notice of young British officers and especially of the accomplished André, who induced Mrs. Bond to let her figure as one of the ladies in the *Mischianza*. The matter produced an unpleasant feeling between Dr. Smith and Mrs. Bond. But young girls, in such circumstances—who could control them ? Mr. William Moore Smith, becoming acquainted with Michael Rudolph, an officer of our army at Valley Forge, used sometimes to accompany him on expeditions in search of grain and cattle for the suffering army. On one of these the two young gentlemen stopping at the house of Col. Joseph Rudolph, who had removed his family from Darby, Delaware county, to Skippack, Montgomery county, Mr. W. M. Smith became acquainted with a daughter of Col. Rudolph's—Miss Ann Rudolph. The acquaintance became one of attachment, and she became Mr. Smith's wife some years afterwards, June 3d, 1786.

war and separation.* His wife's nephew, Phineas Bond, was a Loyalist outright, who remained in the city during the occupation.

Moreover, there were two other William Smiths arrested with him, both of whom were sent off to Winchester. They were Tories undoubtedly. In a time of general civic alarm and confusion, when every kind of story is propagated and what is told at one place is distorted, magnified and even completely changed before it gets to another; it is not impossible—in view of the fact that nothing was done to Dr. Smith except to ask a parole from him—that acts or conversations of one or the other or of both of these gentlemen—Tories, undoubtedly, as I have said—may have been improperly attributed to him. This, however, is conjecture merely.

The charge of Dr. Smith's having been a Loyalist—that is, a supporter of British supremacy after the 4th of July, 1776—rests, I think, chiefly upon a misinterpretation of a passage in Bishop White's Memoirs of the Episcopal Church.† The Bishop is speaking of the Convention of 1785, at which a form of Common Prayer-Book, suited to our new and independent state, was to be considered; and he states that one of the matters before it came up on a motion for framing a service of thanksgiving to be used in each year upon the 4th of July. The Bishop, in the convention, opposed the introduction of such a service; and he says that he was greatly surprised that there was but one person beside—a gentleman who (like himself) had belonged to the Revolutionary side—that was opposed to introducing it; and that accordingly it was voted in by a large majority. He then says:

---

* Mr. S. W. Pennypacker, to whose agreeable narratives in his " History of Phœnix-ville," I have been often much indebted, gives the following anecdote about Mr. Justice Moore. He says: "At this time it was important that all tories should be deprived of arms. A party from the American army visited *Moore Hall* at a time when its high-spirited and haughty occupant was confined to his easy chair with the gout. They searched the house carefully, and among other things found, hidden away in a closet, a beautifully wrought sword. The blade was of finely tempered steel, and the handle was inlaid with gold and silver. The old man expressed much attachment for the weapon, which had probably been an heir-loom, and asked permission to examine it once more. To gratify him, they handed him the sword. No sooner was it in his possession than, in a twinkling, with his foot, upon the floor, he broke the blade from the handle. Then clenching tightly the hilt, he threw to them the useless blade, and with a gesture of contempt said, ' There, take that if you are anxious to fight, but you have no business to steal my *plate.*' "

† Pages 104, 105, 2d Edition. New York, 1836.

Bodies of men are more apt than individuals to calculate on an implicit submission to their determinations. The present was a striking instance of the remark. The members of the convention seem to have thought themselves so established in their station of ecclesiastical legislators, that they might expect of the many clergy who had been averse to the American Revolution, the adoption of this service; although, by the use of it, they must make an implied acknowledgment of their error in an address to Almighty God. What must further seem not a little extraordinary, the service was principally arranged, and the prayer alluded to was composed, by a reverend gentleman (Dr. Smith) who had written and acted against the *d*eclaration of *i*ndependence, and was unfavourably looked on by the supporters of it, during the whole revolutionary war. This conduct, in the present particular, was different from what might have been expected from his usual discernment; but he doubtless calculated on what the good of the Church seemed to him to require, in consequence of a change of circumstances; and he was not aware of the effect which would be produced by the retrospective property of the appointment. The greater stress is laid on this matter, because of the notorious fact, that the majority of the clergy could not have used the service without subjecting themselves to ridicule and censure. For the author's part, having no hindrance of this sort, he contented himself with having opposed the measure, and kept the day from respect to the requisition of the convention; *but could never hear of its being kept, in above two or three places besides Philadelphia.* He is thus particular in recording the incidents attached to the matter stated, with *the hope of rendering it a caution to ecclesiastical bodies, to avoid that danger into which human nature is so apt to fall, of governing too much.*

The Bishop did not mean to make any *charge* against Dr. Smith. The fact that he states about that gentleman, and which he assumes as a certain and known fact, is a mere incidental remark, tending to give a little more point to his general counsel to persons assembled in Ecclesiastical Conventions—of the folly of some of whom, at the time he was writing, he had seen a good deal—in thinking that because they were assembled in convention, they could force upon the people of the Church anything that they chose to put upon them. And this incidental fact which the Bishop assumes as undeniable, to wit, that Dr. Smith did write against the Declaration of Independence, is fully satisfied by the publication of the letters of Cato, on the 11th of March, 1776. Both the word " declaration" and the word "independence," in the Bishop's memoirs, are printed, at the beginning of them, not with capital letters, but with those which printers call lower case. And I infer that he means that at the time when we were considering whether we would or would not declare ourselves independent of Great Britain, Dr. Smith had both written and acted against our doing it. The Bishop is not speaking of the *document* which we call the Declaration of Independence, but of doing or not doing the thing, for the having done which that document sets forth to the world the reasons.

To oppose, prior to July 4th, 1776, the declaring of independence, was no fault of any kind.

To do it afterwards was treason against the government *de facto*, which became a government *de jure;* and exposed the party to the penalties of treason and to a public reproach. In addition to which, as, after July 4th, 1776, till his death, Dr Smith was living under the allegiance of the United States, and could, after the date named, have only written and acted covertly against the Government, it would imply double-dealing and falsehood. Bishop White was among the last men on earth—among the rearmost of the last—to leave a *charge* on the memory of any one, unless morally bound to leave it; least of all would he have left it on the memory of a venerable person deceased, under whose care as a preceptor he had been almost from infancy to manhood;—from the time that he was seven years old to the time when he was seventeen; with whom, in adult life, he had been connected as a trustee of the College, and to which he over and over again declared that high-handed wrong had been done in abrogating its charter; an abrogation made in part on the allegation that Dr. Smith had been disloyal to the State of Pennsylvania; an offence which could not have been committed prior to July 4th, 1776.

Indeed we have Bishop White's own declaration, when, in writing some account of the Church, he adverts to the fact that in " recording transactions in which the Rev. Dr. Smith bore a conspicuous part," there should be so little said in the narrative concerning his agency in them. The Bishop declares that it was because, in some matters connected with the Church, he had had " frequent collisions " with Dr. Smith, and therefore " ought not to claim the commendation of an impartial narrator."* The Bishop notes, however, that after these were over, their relations were " very amicable:" and that Dr. Smith had shown confidence in him by associating him with his brother† and Judge Yeates in a trusteeship of

---

* Wilson's Life of him, p. 19.

† The Hon. Thomas Smith, Judge of the Supreme Court of Pennsylvania.

lands conveyed for the benefit of his younger daughter, and by his last will had " bequeathed him a ring." It is impossible to suppose that Bishop White meant by the passage above spoken of to reproach the memory of his deceased brother; and as the only interpretation of the remark, which to some degree does not reproach it, is the one which refers to a writing and action before July 4th, 1776, it follows that that was what the Bishop meant.

While, therefore, we may admit all that Bishop White says, no such conclusion follows from it as some have sought to draw. The Bishop's statement is wanting in precision as to time, only because the whole matter is but an unimportant incident to his general purpose, and the time when was not important for the purpose for which he referred to the fact.

We here end our first volume. The College Academy and Charity Schools have been closed. The students and the scholars are scattered wide. The Provost is an exile from the halls of science. All that we need here add is the condition of the College at the time when these events occurred. This the Provost Stillé properly describes as follows:

The large fund collected by Dr. Smith in England had been increased by contributions in Jamaica, in Carolina, and in this city. The reputation of the institution had never been higher; the number of pupils in all the departments being in the year 1773 nearly three hundred. Its financial concerns were at last upon a sound footing, and their condition was constantly improving, one proof of which is found in the ability of the Corporation to erect in the year 1774 the large house still standing at the southwest corner of Fourth and Arch streets for the residence of the Provost. The high standing of the College was maintained by the instructions of Professors of well-established reputation throughout the Colonies, and of long experience in this particular institution. Dr. Smith gave lectures in the Mathematics, Natural Philosophy, Astronomy and Rhetoric; Dr. Alison, in Logic, Metaphysics and Moral Philosophy, besides having charge of the instruction in the higher Classics; Mr. Davidson was the Professor of Ancient Languages; Mr. Kinnersley, who for twenty years had been Professor of English and Oratory, had just resigned, and Mr. Paul Fooks was Professor of French and Spanish. Besides, there was a Medical School, even then giving promise of its future reputation, under Drs. Morgan, Shippen, Kuhn, Rush and Bond.

37

APPENDIX.

No. I.—Page 77.

The Rev. Thomas Barton.

THE REV. THOMAS BARTON was a native of Ireland, and a graduate of Trinity College, Dublin. After coming to this country he was employed as an assistant in the College of Philadelphia for more than two years. He married, in 1753, the sister of David Rittenhouse, the celebrated astronomer, and went in 1754 to England, where he received Holy Orders and was appointed a Missionary of the Church in the then frontier counties of York and Cumberland, by the Society for the Propagation of the Gospel. He resided in Reading township, near York, from 1755 to 1759, and was Chaplain to General Forbes's expedition against Fort Duquesne in 1758. He afterwards removed to Lancaster, where he resided as Rector until 1778. In consequence of his attachment to the Royal cause, and some allegations that he had been privy to a plan to destroy the public magazines at Lancaster, he was obliged to remove to New York, where he died, May 25th, 1780, aged 50 years.

William Barton, author of the "Life of Rittenhouse," and Benjamin Smith Barton, well known as a Botanist and as a Professor in the University of Pennsylvania, were his sons. During the French and Indian war upon our western frontiers, Mr. Barton rendered signal service to the people by his personal bravery. John Penn, the Proprietary of Pennsylvania, speaking in a letter of this part of his history, says:

He deserves the commendation of all lovers of their country. . . . Had others imitated his example, Cumberland county would not have wanted men enough to defend it. Nor has he done anything in the military way but what hath increased his character for piety, and that of a sincerely religious man and zealous minister. In short, he is a most worthy, active, and serviceable pastor and missionary; and as such please mention him to the Society.

Dr. William Smith writes, in 1755, of him to the Bishop of Oxford:

Poor Mr. Barton has stood it upwards of a year at the risk of his life; like a good soldier of Jesus Christ, sometimes heading his people in the character of a clergyman, and sometimes in that of a captain, being often obliged when they should go to church, to gird on their swords and go against the enemy. . . . I ventured out three weeks ago to visit him and some of our German schools in the neighborhood, and found him universally beloved of his people; but then love is the most they can give him in their present distressed state; and, therefore, I wish your Lordship would move the Honorable Society to make him some gratuity above his salary in these troublesome times. I am sure he both wants and deserves it.

The history of what he encountered in this way is told in a letter of his own to the Rev. Richard Peters, Rector of Christ Church:

HUNTINGTON, April 11th, 1758.

REV. DEAR SIR:

I have the misfortune to acquaint you that we are all confusion. Within twelve miles of my house, two families, consisting of eleven persons, were murdered and taken. And in the counties of Lancaster and Cumberland, the people are daily alarmed with fresh ravages and murders. The poor inhabitants are flying in numbers into the interior parts. I prevailed yesterday upon the inhabitants of Canawago and Bermudian to assemble themselves together, and forming themselves into companies, to guard the frontiers of this county, till we see what will be done by the troops, who are going upon the Western expedition. And I hope by this means we shall be able to keep these settlements from breaking up.

Mr. Alricks tells me that he is determined (provided he can obtain the Governor's permission) to go out to the Ohio a volunteer in defence of his King and country. As he is certainly a man of resolution and valor; a man who can undergo hardships and fatigues; and moreover, a man who has an interest with, and an influence upon the country people, and is as likely to raise a number of them as any man I know, I think he stands well entitled to a commission. And as I make no doubt but his honor the Governor will have these qualifications in view in the disposition of the commissions now to be given out, I hope this gentleman will not be forgot. I well know that the least representation from you in his favor, will do the business for him: and he and his friends will ever gratefully acknowledge your friendship upon this occasion.

I am, worthy Sir,
Your faithful and affectionate
Friend and servant,
THO. BARTON.

We give now one or two letters after his removal from the frontiers:

MR. BARTON TO THE SECRETARY OF THE PROPAGATION SOCIETY.

(EXTRACT.)

LANCASTER IN PENNSYLVANIA, January 23d, 1766.

REV. SIR,

I have the pleasure to assure you that the young people in my congregations show a seriousness and warmth in matters of religion not common in persons of their years— several of them came to the Lord's table at Christmas and *presented their souls and bodies* with so much devotion and contrition of heart as not only pleased but affected the whole congregation. Many more are now preparing to follow their example at

Easter. May I humbly desire the favor of the venerable society to encourage these good dispositions by granting them some of the tracts called the *Reasonable Communicant?*

Having so lately wrote to you by Mr. Wilson I shall take the liberty to defer sending you any particular accounts till after Easter. The churches at Whiteclay Creek and New London are now entering into subscriptions, etc., which I shall send you as soon as they come to my hands. They are a religious, good sort of people, and I make no doubt will exert their best endeavors to encourage and support a missionary.

Permit me to inform the venerable society that in the month of September last I paid a visit to Sir William Johnson in the Mohawk country, about 350 miles from this place. There I had an opportunity of making myself acquainted with the state of the Mohawk Indians; and of enquiring into the best methods of carrying the gospel into the Indian country in general. The Mohawks, I found, are very desirous to have an opportunity to receive instruction. There are several families still residing at their castles, one of which is on the Mohawk river and now called Fort Hunter, the other at Canajoheri. They complain that they have been much neglected since the removal of Mr. Ogilvie; and would be glad to be supplied with the means of knowledge. A society of gentlemen in New England have set up an *Indian School* under the direction of one Mr. Wheelock, a dissenting preacher. They send young men from their colleges received as *probationers* into the *woods*, where they stay till they have prevailed upon the Indians to send some of their children to this school with which they return; and then others are sent. I saw one of these missionaries at Sir William Johnson's, returning from the Indian country with five or six Indian boys. This appears to be the most plausible method to civilize these rude and barbarous creatures, and to prepare them for the reception of knowledge and religion, and is highly worthy of imitation. Sir William Johnson, who is a worthy member of the Church of England, and universally esteemed for his goodness of heart, seems desirous to interest himself in this good cause. * * *

I am sincerely concerned at the present turbulent and disturbed situation of the colonies. Every day presents us with indecent and inflammatory papers. It is hoped the mother country will be able to discover who the people are that first raised and encouraged these disturbances, that the innocent may not be involved with the guilty. But this is a subject on which it is not *safe* for a man who has not virtue enough to make him a martyr to speak or write freely here.

A paragraph has been lately published in our American papers that orders were sent to the agents of the colonies to remonstrate against the introduction of Episcopacy in America as a thing that would be highly disagreeable to the people in *general.* Suffer me to assure you, sir, that this is a report founded in falsehood. Certain I am that the introducing Episcopacy into America would not *at present* be disagreeable to any Protestant society in it except *one*, which one no doubt made use of this opportunity when they knew the minds of many were inflamed to propagate this report. I have often wished that *Keith's Presbyterian and independent churches brought to the test* could be sent over to every mission. Nothing but the good providence of God could preserve anything like the National Church here. For "many there be that would swallow it up." But in spite of every obstacle and discouragement thrown in its way, it gains ground, and will I hope one day be the great ornament and blessing of this immense continent.

Rev. Sir, etc.,

THOS. BARTON.

In the year 1767 Mr. Barton printed a Book of Family Prayers. Its title was as follows:

THE FAMILY PRAYER BOOK,

CONTAINING MORNING AND

EVENING PRAYERS,

For Families and Private Persons;

To which are annexed directions for a devout
and decent behavior in the Public
Worship of God.

More particularly in the use of the
COMMON PRAYER appointed
by the
CHURCH OF ENGLAND,
together with the
CHURCH CATECHISM.

Collected and published chiefly (of) the
Episcopal Congregations of
Lancaster, Pequea, Carnarvon,
Ephrata (printed), for
THOMAS BARTON,
1767.

MR. BARTON TO THE SECRETARY OF THE PROPAGATION SOCIETY.

LANCASTER IN PENNSYLVANIA, June 20th, 1771.

REV. AND VERY WORTHY SIR:

Mr. Stuart is most usefully employed at Fort Hunter. He has already made himself so far master of the Mohawk language, as to be able to read in church about half of the morning service; which he does every Sunday to the Indians. Besides this duty he officiates constantly in English to the white inhabitants. This gentleman, by all accounts, is a most zealous and faithful laborer in the vineyard. It is hoped that by his means under God an effectual door will at last be opened for the introduction of religion into the heathen country. Sir William Johnson, in a late letter to me, gives the testimony in his favor: "Mr. Stuart has been some time at his mission, where he is much esteemed not only by the Indians, but by the English and Dutch inhabitants who constantly resort to his church. I have great hopes from his appointment." . . .

Canada, it is true, "has not been totally neglected." I know there are three chaplains supported there by government. But these gentlemen, who are confined to particular regiments and garrisons, can be of little service in promoting the Protestant religion in that country. Mr. Delisle, chaplain to the garrison at Montreal, is very sensible of this, and has, I am told, constantly complained that some hardy and faithful missionaries of the Church of England have not been established in Canada. You have however sufficiently accounted for this *seeming* neglect with regard to the Society. The matter rests with the government, and wisdom will one day, and we trust ere long, point out the necessity of giving it due attention.

I am, Rev. and worthy Sir, &c.,

THOS. BARTON.

THE SAME TO THE SAME.

(EXTRACT.)

LANCASTER IN PENNSYLVANIA, July 1st, 1774.

REVEREND SIR: My mission gains such ground as to require greater duties than it is in the power of one person to perform. The churches are generally full. That at Pequea in particular is much increased. Besides the stated duties claimed by these churches, I am often obliged to itinerate to a considerable distance to serve others who are continually soliciting a share of my labors.

Your obed't, &c.,

THOS. BARTON.

No. II.—Page 81.

Henry Antes.

FOR the following account of Henry Antes, one of the testes whose name appears to the petition at the top of page 81, I am indebted to the Transactions of the Moravian Historical Society, published by the Moravian Society at Nazareth.

The name of Henry Antes is one of frequent occurrence in the meagre records come down to us, touching the state of religion among the early Pennsylvania Germans. As far as we have been able to ascertain, he emigrated with his father from Fraentzheim, in Rhenish Bavaria, prior to 1725, and settled in the region of country lying back of Pottstown, including the present townships of Hanover and Frederick (since 1784 in Montgomery county), then called Falckner's Swamp. Here he farmed and followed his trade, which was that of a wheelwright. In February, 1726, he was married to Catherine De Weesm, at White Marsh, by the Rev. J. Philip Boehm, an ordained clergyman of the German Reformed Church, of which the Anteses were members. Excepting this item, we know nothing of the man prior to 1736, in the spring of which year he became acquainted with Spangenberg, who was sojourning among the Schwenkfelders of Towamensing Township, in Skippack. Mr. Antes's subsequent intimate relations towards the Moravians date from this acquaintance. Deeply concerned about the religious destitution of his fellow-countrymen in the province, we need not be surprised at learning that, as he was a man of earnest piety, his Christian sympathy and activity were enlisted in their behalf. Although but a layman, he accordingly undertook to instruct them in the way of life, calling them together in their houses for singing, for prayer, for reading the Scriptures, and for exhortation. Thus we find him employed in the populous district of Oley, Berks county, as early as 1736. When, in that year, John Adam Gruber, of Germantown, sent out a call to his awakened countrymen in the eastern counties of Pennsylvania, to meet in convention for the purpose of ratifying a religious union or alliance on the basis of evangelical truths, Antes seconded the movement by issuing, in December of 1741, a circular which led to the formation of what was called the Synod of Pennsylvania, in which most of the denominations and sects in the province were duly represented. Next to Count Zinzendorf, Henry Antes was the most prominent member of this body. It met seven times in 1742, and subsequently. Through these meetings Antes was brought into closer relations with the brethren, and when their different elements one by one withdrew, leaving them exclusively under Moravian control, Antes felt moved to attend them as heretofore, and to attach himself to the people, with whose religious spirit his own was in sympathy. In June of 1745, accordingly, he became a resident of Bethlehem, and for five years rendered eminent services at that place and at the adjoining settlements—in superintending the temporal concerns of the Moravian Economy, the labors of its farms, and the erection of its mills. The grist mill at Bethlehem, that at Friedensthal, and the grist and saw mills at Gnadenhütten, were the works of Henry Antes. In October of 1749 he was made a *censenior civilis*—an officer to whom pertained the legal care of the community's estates and property. In the capacity of a justice of the peace in the county of Bucks, Mr. Antes furthermore did the Moravians many timely services. In September of 1750 he retired to his home in Frederick Township, and although he had been moved to this step in consequence of a disagreement with the brethren respecting their ritual, he approved himself their friend and counsellor to the end of his life. In August of 1752 he accompanied Bishop Spangenberg to Western North Carolina, the latter's errand being the selection of a tract of land for a projected settlement in that colony on the part of the Moravians. This was Mr. Antes's last act in the interest of the church to which he was strongly attached. He died on his farm on the morning of July 20th, 1755, and next day his remains were buried in the family graveyard, close by his father Frederic, who had preceded him to the eternal world on the 28th of November, 1746. Bishop Spangenberg delivered a consolatory address on the occasion, Abraham Reincke read the Moravian burial service, and ten pall-bearers from Bethlehem conveyed the remains of "the pious layman of Frederick Township" to their final resting-place. In June of 1854 this deserted place of sepulture was still discernible on the old Antes farm, then owned by a Mr. Reif; but saving fragments of soapstone, inscribed occasionally with a few letters, there was nothing to remind the visitor that the ground on which he stood was hallowed by the ashes of the dead.

Mr. Antes was the father of eleven children, six sons and five daughters. Ann Catharine was born November, 1726, and in 1809 was residing in Bethabara, N. C. Ann Margaret was born October, 1728, went to England and married —— La Trobe. She was the mother of the late B. H. La Trobe, Esq., C. E., of Baltimore. Died in London, in 1794. Philip Frederic was born July, 1730, and died in Lancaster, September, 1801. His daughter Catharine was the wife of Governor Simon Snyder. William was born November, 1731, and in 1809 was residing in Genesee county. Elizabeth was born February, 1734, and married Philip Dotter, of Oley. John Henry was born October, 1736, was some time sheriff of Northumberland county, and in 1804 resided at Nippenose, Lycoming county. Jacob was born September, 1738, and died in infancy. John was born March, 1740. He entered the service of the Moravian Church, became a missionary, and died at Bedford, England, in 1810. Mary Magdalene was born October, 1742, went to Germany, married Ebbing, and died at Hernhutt, April, 1811. Joseph was born January, 1745, died at Bethlehem, August, 1746. Benigna, born September, 1748, died at Bethlehem, December, 1760.

No. III.—Page 148.

Conrad Weiser.

CONRAD WEISER, whose name occurs continually during the middle of the last century, whenever the subject of our intercourse with the Indians is concerned, was of German origin. His father emigrated from that country to Schoharie county, N. Y., about the year 1712, under a proclamation of Queen Anne, which allowed settlers not only to take up land free of cost, but also to be exempted from taxes. The Queen's agent, Nicholas Bayard, afterwards coming to record the metes and bounds of the land which they had settled on, the settlers got alarmed and offered resistance. Strife ensued. Upon the invitation of Sir William Keith, Governor of Pennsylvania, Weiser came to this State with his family. Conrad early became an interpreter between the Indians and the whites. He acted as such in nearly every treaty effected in his time, and was regarded with great confidence by both sides. He became a Colonel in the French and Indian war of 1756. His residence was at Womelsdorf, a town situated between Reading and Harrisburg.

No. IV.—Page 165.

Ebenezer Kinnersley.

[By Hon. Horatio Gates Jones.]

THE Rev. Ebenezer Kinnersley, A. M., was born in the city of Gloscester, England, November 30th, 1711. His father, William Kinnersley, was a Baptist minister, who migrated to America in 1714, when his son was three years of age, and settled in Lower Dublin township, Philadelphia county, Pa., where he united himself with the Pennepek (now called the Lower Dublin) Baptist church, the first permanent society of the Baptists in Pennsylvania. On the 6th of September, 1735, about a year after his father's death, young Kinnersley was baptized, and united himself with the Pennepek church. About the year 1739 he became a resident of the city of Philadelphia, where there was also a Baptist church, with which he was accustomed to worship. His abilities as a man and his excellence as a speaker led the church to call him to the ministry, and he was ordained in 1743, but he never became a pastor. He was a conservative in his religious opinions, and hence did not approve of the measures of the celebrated Whitfield, nor did he hesitate to protest against them from the pulpit of the Baptist church. This he did, July 6th, 1740, and so great was the excitement produced that he was forbidden the privilege of communion by the church, and for some time afterwards attended the Episcopal church. The difficulty, however, was settled ere three years had elapsed, as he was ordained in 1743, and on May 5th, 1746, when the Philadelphia church was organized as a distinct church from that at Pennepek, Mr. Kinnersley was one of the members, and remained so until his death. Mr. Kinnersley is entitled to notice and received in his day great honor, because of his attainments as an electrician. He began in 1746 the study of the electric fluid, and was associated with Dr. Franklin in his experiments which finally led to the discovery of the lightning rod. His devotion to this subject was only equalled by that of Franklin, and he was the first person in America who publicly delivered lectures on Electricity, and illustrated the effects of that fluid by wonderful and ingenious experiments. The discoveries which he made and communicated to Dr. Franklin, and the knowledge which he attained, justly entitled him to be regarded as THE AMERICAN ELECTRICIAN.

In 1753 Mr. Kinnersley became head master of the English school connected with the College of Philadelphia (now the University of Pennsylvania), and in 1755 was chosen Professor of English and Oratory in the college. He held that position until October 17th, 1772, when failing health compelled him to resign it. In 1757 the trustees of the college conferred upon him the honorary degree of Master of Arts, and in 1769 he was elected a member of the American Philosophical Society. After his resignation as professor he visited the Bermudas on account of his health, and on his return removed to Lower Dublin, and there, amid the scenes of his youth, passed the few remaining years of his life. He died July 4th, 1778, aged 68 years.

His remains now lie in the burial ground of the Pennepek church, marked by a simple head and foot stone of marble.

Professor Kinnersley married, in 1739, Sarah Duffield, who died November 6th, 1801, aged 81 years. He left two children—a son, William, who graduated at the college of Philadelphia in 1761, studied medicine, settled himself in Northumberland county, Pennsylvania, and died, unmarried, in April, 1785. The other child was a daughter, Esther, who was married to Joseph Shewell, a merchant, and became the mother of three children.

Among the memorial windows in the University of Pennsylvania, in West Philadelphia, is one placed there by Alumni of the Institution, and others, to the honor of the subject of this notice.

No. V.—Page 344.

Protest Against the Appointment of Dr. Franklin as our Colonial Agent.

A. D. 1764.

WE whose names are hereunto subscribed do object and protest against the appointment of the person proposed as an agent of the Province for the following reasons:

First. Because we believe him to be the chief author of the measures pursued by the late Assembly, which have occasioned such uneasiness and distraction among the good people of this Province.

Secondly. Because we believe his fixed enmity to the proprietors will preclude all accommodation of our disputes with them, even on just and reasonable terms, so that for these two reasons we are filled with the most affecting apprehensions that the petitions lately transmitted to England will be made use of to produce a change of our Government, contrary to the intentions of the petitioners, the greater part of whom, we are persuaded, only designed thereby to obtain a compliance with some equitable demands. And thus, by such an appointment, we and a vast number of our most worthy constituents, are deprived of all hope of ever seeing an end put to the fatal dissensions of our country ; it being our firm opinion that any further prosecution of the measures for a change of our Government at this time will lay the foundation of unnecessary feuds, and all the miseries of confusion among the people we represent and their posterity. This step gives us the more lively affliction, as it is taken at the very moment when we are informed by a member of this House that the Governor has assured him of his having received instructions from the Proprietors, on their hearing of our late dispute, to give his assent to the taxation of their estates in the same manner that the estates of other persons are to be taxed, and also to confirm for the public use the several squares formerly claimed by the city, on which subjects we make no doubt the Government would have sent a message to the House if this had been the usual time of doing business, and he had not been necessarily absent to meet the Assembly of the lower counties. And therefore we cannot but anxiously regret that at a time when the Proprietors have shewed such a disposition, this House should not endeavor to cultivate the same, and obtain from them every reasonable demand that can be made on the part of the people, in vigorously insisting on which we would most earnestly unite with the rest of this House.

Thirdly. Because the gentleman proposed, as we are informed, is very unfavorably thought of by several of his Majesty's ministers, and we are humbly of opinion that it will be disrespectful to our Most Gracious Sovereign, and disadvantageous to ourselves and our constitution, to employ such a person as our agent.

Fourthly. Because the proposal of the person mentioned is so extremely disagreeable to a very great number of the most serious and reputable inhabitants of this Province, of all denominations and societies (one proof of which is, his having been rejected, both by this city and county, at the last election, though he had represented the former in Assembly for fourteen years), that we are convinced no measure this House can adopt will tend so much to inflame the resentments and embitter the divisions of the good people of this Province as his appointment to be our agent. And we cannot but sincerely lament that the peace and happiness of Pennsylvania should be sacrificed for the promotion of a man who cannot be advanced but by the convulsions of his country.

Fifthly. Because the unnecessary haste with which this House has acted in proceeding to this appointment (without making a small adjournment, though requested by many members to consult our constituents on the matters to be decided, and) even before their speaker has been presented to the King's representative, though we are informed that the Governor will be in town the beginning of next week, ... may subject us to the censures and very heavy displeasure of our most gracious sovereign and his ministers.

Sixthly. Because the gentleman proposed has heretofore ventured, contrary to an act of Assembly, to place the public money* in the stocks, whereby this Province suffered a loss of £6,000; and the sum added to £5,000 granted for his expenses, makes the whole cost of his former voyage to England amount to *Eleven Thousand Pounds;* which expensive kind of agency we do not choose to imitate, and burden the public with unnecessary loads of debt. For these and other reasons, we should think ourselves guilty of betraying the rights of Pennsylvania if we should presumptuously commit them to the direction of a man against whom so many and just objections present themselves.

Lastly. We being extremely desirous to avert the mischiefs apprehended from the intended appointment, and as much as in us lies to promote peace and unanimity among us and our constituents, do humbly propose to the House, that if they will agree regularly to appoint *any* gentleman of integrity, abilities, and knowledge, in England, to assist Mr. Jackson as our agent, under a restriction not to present the petitions for a change of our government, or any of them, to the King or his Ministers, unless an express order for that purpose be hereafter given by the Assembly of this Province, we will not give it any opposition. But if such an appointment should be made, we must insist (as we cannot think it a necessary one) that our constituents, already labouring under heavy debts, be not burthened with fresh impositions on that account; and therefore in condescension to the members, who think another agent

---

* The money here meant was a sum granted by Parliament as an indemnification for part of our expenses in the late war; which, by act of Assembly, was ordered, for its better security, to be placed in the bank.

necessary, we will concur with them, if they approve of this proposal, in paying such agent at our own expense.

October 26th, 1764.

JOHN DICKINSON,	WILLIAM ALLEN,
DAVID McCANAUGHY,	THOMAS WILLING,
JOHN MONTGOMERY,	GEORGE BRYAN,
ISAAC SAUNDERS,	AMOS STRETTELL,
GEORGE TAYLOR,	HENRY KEPPELE.

NOTE.—DR. JOHN FOTHERGILL, of London, was mentioned by the subscribers to this paper as a proper person to represent the Province.

Dr. Fothergill, in the years 1773, 1774 and 1775, so conspicuous for his excellent efforts to induce Great Britain to grant reasonable terms to the Colonies, was otherwise so excellent a character, that a short sketch of him will be in place.

He was born at Carr-End, the family estate in Wensleydale, Yorkshire, England, of a preceding generation, March 8th, 1712. His father was a member of the Society of Friends. His mother, of the family name of Hough, was a woman of fortune. Young Fothergill was put at school near Frodsham, in Cheshire, where he remained till he was twelve years old. He was then transferred to Ledburgh school, in Yorkshire, at that time and since, famous for classical literature and mathematics, and where he made great progress in his studies. About his sixteenth year he was placed with Benjamin Bartlett, an eminent apothecary at Bradford, Yorkshire. He soon afforded such instances of superior sagacity in this business as induced his intelligent master to permit him, at an early date, to visit and prescribe for patients. After his apprenticeship ended, he moved to Edinburgh to study physic in the colleges there, and was a pupil of the great anatomist Monro. In 1736 he was graduated and came to London, where he attended lectures in St. Thomas's Hospital. Before fixing himself in practice he visited the Continent. On his return, A. D. 1740, he established himself in practice in London, and soon became eminent not only in England and on the Continent, but in America also; and not only as a physician and as a writer on materia medica, and other branches of medical science, but as a good man and a benefactor of his race in every way and everywhere. His correspondents were very numerous. On Dr. Franklin's first going to England, he became acquainted with him, and an intimacy existed between the two persons for the residue of their common lives. He greatly interested himself in the concerns of our country, seeking to advance its interests; and in 1773, 1774 and 1775, when Dr. Franklin fell into bad favor with the British Ministry, he, with David Barclay, an eminent banker and merchant of London, was much with him, concerting measures to avert the coming revolution and the dismemberment of the then great British Empire of which the Colonies were so great and dignified a part. " Our excellent friend," says Dr. Franklin, speaking of him, "was always proposing something for the good of mankind. If we may estimate the goodness of a man by his disposition to do good, and success in doing it, I can hardly think of a better man." He died December 26th, 1780, in the summit of celebrity ; surrounded with the caresses of a numerous acquaintance ; deeply and universally regretted. Dr. Franklin thus wrote soon afterwards to David Barclay :

PASSY, Feb. 12th, 1781.

DEAR SIR :

I condole with you most sincerely on the loss of our dear friend, Dr. Fothergill. I hope that some one who knew him well will do justice to his memory, by an account of his life and character. He was a great doer of good. How much might have been done and how much mischief prevented if his, your or my joint endeavors in a certain melancholy affair had been attended to.

With great respect and esteem I am, &c.

B. FRANKLIN.

The "certain melancholy affair," referred to by Dr. Franklin, is the miscarriage of the effort of himself, David Barclay and Dr. Fothergill, to bring about a reconciliation between Great Britain and her Colonies, and to prevent the war for Independence, which subsequently took place.

No. VI.—Page 10.

THE history of Benjamin West is very well known in Pennsylvania, though somewhat less well, perhaps, elsewhere. He was born in the autumn of 1738, in Chester county. His family were Friends—among the strictest of that respectable society in the county just named, where scarce any other religious society prevailed. One of the first persons who encouraged him to paint and assisted him with some materials, was Mr. Penington, a well-known merchant of Philadelphia ; and Samuel Shoemaker, both, like the family of West himself, of the Society of Friends. His efforts, thus far, were confined to painting portraits, flowers, etc.

"Among those," says his biographer, John Galt, "who sent to him in this early stage of his career"—he being at this time, as I suppose, from twelve to fourteen years old—"was a person of the name of William Henry. Henry," says Galt, "was indeed in several respects an extraordinary man, and possessed the power generally attendant upon genius under all circumstances—that of interesting the imagination of those with whom he conversed. On examining the young artist's performance he observed to him that if *he* could paint as well, he would not waste his time on portraits, but would devote himself to historical subjects, and he mentioned the death of Socrates as affording one of the best topics for illustrating the moral effect of the art of painting. The painter knew nothing of the history of the philosopher, and upon confessing his ignorance, Mr. Henry went to his library, and, taking down a volume of the English translation of Plutarch, read to him the account given by that writer of this affecting story. The suggestion and description wrought upon the imagination of West, and induced him to make a drawing, which he showed to Mr. Henry, who commended it as a perspicuous delineation of the probable circumstances of the event, and requested him to paint it.* West said that he would be happy to undertake the task, but having hitherto painted only faces and men clothed, he should be unable to do justice to the figure of the slave who presented the poison, and which he thought ought to be naked. Henry had among his workmen a very handsome young man, and, without waiting to answer the objection, he sent for him into the room. On his entrance he pointed him out to West, and said, 'There is your model!' The appearance of the young man, whose arms and breast were naked, instantaneously convinced the artist that he had only to look into nature for the models which would impart grace and energy to his delineation of forms.''

"When the death of Socrates,"continues Mr. Galt, "was finished, it attracted much attention, and led to one of those fortunate acquaintances by which the subsequent career of the artist has been so happily facilitated. About this period the inhabitants of Lancaster had resolved to erect a public grammar school ; and Dr. Smith, the Provost of the College at Philadelphia, was invited by them to arrange the course of instruction, and to place the institution in the way best calculated to answer the intention of the founders. This gentleman was an excellent classical scholar, and combined with his knowledge and admiration of the merits of the ancients that liberality of respect for the endeavors of modern talent with which the same kind of feeling is but rarely found connected. After seeing the picture and conversing with the artist, he offered to

---

* The accuracy of this account—with a small exception of circumstance—is confirmed to me in conversation with Mr. John Jordan, the senior Vice-President of the Historical Society of Pennsylvania, a great-grandson of William Henry, spoken of in the text. The volume taken down from the shelves of Mr. Henry's library was not Plutarch's Lives, but Rollin's Ancient History. The engraving and young West's picture copying it, are yet preserved at Nazareth, by Mr. William Henry, another great-grandson of West's early patron; a cousin of course of Mr. Jordan.

undertake to make him to a certain degree acquainted with classical literature ; while at the same time he would give him such a sketch of the taste and character of the spirit of antiquity, as would have all the effect of the regular education requisite to a painter. When this liberal proposal was communicated to old Mr. West, he readily agreed that Benjamin should go for some time to Philadelphia, in order to take advantage of the Provost's instructions ; and, accordingly, after returning home for a few days, Benjamin went to the capital.''

"Provost Smith," continues the biographer, "introduced West, among other persons to four young men, pupils of his own, whom he particularly recommended to his acquaintance as possessing endowments of mind greatly superior to the common standard of mankind. One of these was Francis Hopkinson, who afterwards greatly distinguished himself in the early proceedings of the Congress of the United States. Thomas Godfrey, the second, died after having given the most promising indications of an elegant genius for pathetic and descriptive poetry. He was an apprentice to a watchmaker, and had secretly written a poem which he published anonymously in the Philadelphia newspaper, under the title of 'Temple of Fame.' The attention which it attracted, and the encomiums which the Provost in particular bestowed on it, induced West, who was in the poet's confidence, to mention to *him* who was the author. The information excited the alert benevolence of Smith, and he lost no time until he had procured the release of Godfrey from his indenture, and a respectable employment for him in the government of the State." *

"Provost Smith was himself possessed of a fluent vein of powerful eloquence ; and it happened that many of his pupils who distinguished themselves in the great struggle of their country appeared to have imbibed his talent ; but none of them more than Jacob Duché, another of the four youths whom he recommended to the 'artist.'

"There was something," Mr. Galt further proceeds, "so judicious in the plan of study which Provost Smith had formed for his pupil, that it deserves to be particularly considered. He regarded him as destined to be a painter, and on this account did not impose on him those grammatical exercises of language which are usually required from the young student of the classics ; but directed his attention to those incidents which were likely to interest his fancy, and to furnish him at some future time with subjects for the easel. He carried him immediately to those passages of ancient history which make the most lasting impression on the imagination of the regular bred scholar ; and described the pictur-

---

* See *supra*, pp. 187, 389.

esque circumstances of the transaction with a minuteness of detail which would have been superfluous to a general student."

This was all in the year 1754; before West had reached his sixteenth year. In 1756 West established himself as an artist in Philadelphia.

In October, 1757, as we have mentioned in the body of our book,* *The American Magazine* was established, Dr. Smith being made the editor. In the February number of 1758 we have among the Poetical Essays these—

VERSES UPON SEEING THE PORTRAIT OF MISS **———**, BY MR. WEST.

Since Guido's skilful hand, with mimic art,
  Could form and animate so sweet a face,
Can Nature still superior charms impart,
  Or warmest Fancy add a single grace?

The enlivened tints, in due proportion, rise;
  Her polished cheeks with deep vermilion glow;
The shining moisture swells into her eyes,
  And from such lips nectareous sweets must flow!

The easy attitude, the graceful dress,
  The soft expression of the perfect whole,
Both Guido's judgment and his skill confess,
  Informing canvas with a living soul.

How fixt, how steady, yet how *bright* a ray
  Of modest Lustre beams in every smile!
Such smiles as must resistless charms convey,
  Enlivened by a heart devoid of guile.

Yet sure his flattering pencil's unsincere;
  His Fancy takes the place of bashful Truth,
And warm Imagination pictures here
  The Pride of Beauty and the Bloom of Youth.

Thus had I said, and thus deluded, thought,
  Had lovely Stella still remained unseen,
Where grace and beauty to perfection brought,
  Make every imitative Art look mean.   LOVELACE.

PHILADELPHIA, Feb. 15th, 1758.

Dr. Smith, the editor, in introducing the verses, says: †

We are glad of this opportunity of making known to the world the name of so extraordinary a genius as Mr. West. He was born in Chester county, in this Province, and without the assistance of any master has acquired such a delicacy and correctness of expression in his paintings, joined to such a laudable thirst of improvement, that we are persuaded when he shall have obtained more experience and opportunities of viewing the productions of able masters, he will become truly eminent in his profession.

---

* See *supra*, p. 165.   † American Magazine, p. 238.

In another place, Mr. Smith says: *

We communicate the little poem upon one of Mr. West's portraits with particular pleasure, when we consider that the lady who sat, the painter who guided the pencil, and the poet who so well describes the whole, are all natives of this place, and all very young.

The whole world knows who "the painter who guided the pencil" was. Can any one upon the footstool tell us who was "the lady that sat?" or who "the poet who so well describes the whole?"

Of the particular portrait of West which I had the pleasure to present to the Historical Society, and for which there is a companion-piece of Mrs. Smith, *née* Moore, in the possession of one of my cousins, Mr. Galt gives this account. It will explain the several characters of the picture, and particular attitude of the subject of the portrait:

Among the pictures of Governor Hamilton was a St. Ignatius—a fine piece of Murillo—which had been found on board of a Spanish prize, and which Mr. West obtained leave to copy. The copy was greatly admired by his valuable friend, the Provost Smith, to whom it suggested the notion that portrait-painting might be raised to something greatly above the exhibition of a mere physical likeness; and he in consequence endeavored to impress upon the mind of his pupil that characteristic painting opened a new line of art only inferior in dignity to that of history; but requiring, perhaps, a nicer discriminative tact of mind.

The portrait in the Historical Society—a grateful offering from the artist to the Provost—was made in this idea.

---

* American Magazine, p. 237.

END OF VOLUME I.

LIFE AND CORRESPONDENCE

OF THE

REV. WILLIAM SMITH, D.D.

VOL. II.

Engraved by John Sartain, Phila.1880.

WILLIAM SMITH, D.D.

ÆTAT, 75.

From the original picture by Gilbert Stuart, painted 1800.
in the possession of his Great Grandson John H. Brinton, M.D.

LIFE AND CORRESPONDENCE

OF THE

REV. WILLIAM SMITH, D.D.,

First Provost of the College and Academy of Philadelphia.
First President of Washington College, Maryland. President of the St. Andrew's Society of Phila-
delphia. President of the Corporation for the Relief of the Widows and Children of
Clergymen in the Communion of the Church of England in America.
Secretary of the American Philosophical Society, etc., etc.

WITH COPIOUS EXTRACTS FROM HIS WRITINGS.

BY HIS GREAT-GRANDSON,

HORACE WEMYSS SMITH,

Member of the Historical Society of Pennsylvania.
Editor of the "Miscellaneous Works of Richard Penn Smith," of "The York-Town Orderly Book,"
"Andreana," etc., etc.

VOL. II.

PHILADELPHIA:
PUBLISHED BY FERGUSON BROS. & CO.,
15 NORTH SEVENTH STREET.
1880.

Entered according to Act of Congress, in the year 1878, by

S. A. GEORGE & CO.,

In the Office of the Librarian of Congress, at Washington, D. C.

FERGUSON BROS. & CO.,
PRINTERS AND ELECTROTYPERS,
PHILADELPHIA.

CONTENTS.

CHAPTER XXXVI.

(3)

4 *CONTENTS.*

CHAPTER XLVI.

CHAPTER XLVII.

CHAPTER XLVIII.

CHAPTER XLIX.

CHAPTER L.

CHAPTER LI.

CHAPTER LII.

CHAPTER LIII.

CHAPTER LIV.

CHAPTER LV.

CHAPTER LVI.

CHAPTER LVII.

CHAPTER LVIII.

CHAPTER LIX.

CHAPTER LX.

CHAPTER LXI.

CHAPTER LXII.

LIFE AND CORRESPONDENCE

OF THE

REV. WILLIAM SMITH, D. D.

CHAPTER XXXVI.

Dr. Smith Preaches in the Churches near the Valley Forge—His Cattle and Horses are taken for the Army, but Restitution or Compensation is Honorably made by Order of General Washington—Makes Observations, along with Rittenhouse and other Men of Science, on an Eclipse of the Sun—Preaches on St. John's Day, before Washington and the Society of Free Masons.

As the reader will remember, the last chapter of Volume I. of this work left the British in the possession of Philadelphia, and Dr. Smith and part of his family residing on Barbadoes Island, seventeen miles above the city, within an hour's ride of the Valley Forge. On some occasions during the winter he preached in the churches in the Valley and at Radnor; both churches, as all others in the State, having been vacated permanently or temporarily by their rectors. The Rev. Mr. White, afterwards the Bishop, who was chaplain of Congress at Yorktown, the Rev. Mr. Blackwell, afterwards the well-known Dr. Blackwell, who was chaplain to the First Pennsylvania Regiment and surgeon to one of the regiments at the Valley Forge, and my ancestor, Dr. Smith, were, at this time, I presume, the only three Episcopal clergymen in the State. Mr. Currie, in Chester county, had been for some time pretty much superannuated, and was now, I think, not in the Commonwealth. Mr. White was with the Congress, during the occupation, at Yorktown. Mr. Blackwell, in his double office of spiritual and bodily physician, was closely occupied on the hills and in the huts of the

9

Valley Forge. So that the only person who could perform anything like parochial duty was the subject of our biography.

I find but little of Dr. Smith's correspondence during the winter, and but little of his personal history of interest to the reader, except that Michael Rudulph and certain of the troops drove off some of Dr. Smith's cattle and his *best horse*, which was taken for the use of his friend, General Porter. However, upon an application to General Washington, his cattle were returned and he received pay for his horse.

On the 28th of March, Dr. Smith was present at a meeting of the people, held at Forty Fort, Wyoming, in regard to the claims of Connecticut to lands in Pennsylvania; a question which long and deeply agitated a portion of the State. Samuel Sutton was chairman, and Dr. Smith reported to the meeting that he and Dr. Ewing had succeeded in having the " Confirming Law" repealed.

On the 24th of June, assisted by his old scientific friends of the "Transit" day—Mr. Rittenhouse, Mr. Lukens, and Mr. Owen Biddle—he made for the Philosophical Society the observations of an eclipse of the sun. The result of these observations from the manuscript of Dr. Smith, is published entire in the Appendix of "Barton's Life of Rittenhouse."

On the 10th of July, 1778, Dr. Smith preached in Oxford Church, on the first opening of the churches after the evacuation of the city by the British.

From the 28th of June, 1777, to the 25th of September, 1778, there were no public meetings of the Board of Trustees of the College. The affairs of the institution during the occupation of the city by the British had a great advantage from a supervision of them by the Honorable Thomas Willing, one of the trustees, who remained in the city during that term; a gentleman whose patriotism was never questioned, although he voted steadily against the Declaration of Independence. His very high personal character saved him from any molestation by either side.

Ebenezer Kinnersley died on the 4th of July, in the year last mentioned; his health, which a residence of considerable length in the islands of the West Indies did not re-establish, having been for a good while before enfeebled. On the 15th of December of this same year, the minutes of the College tell us that " Dr. Smith informed the board that some years ago Mr. Kinnersley had made an offer to the College of his electrical apparatus and the several fixtures belonging to it, upon a valuation to be made by some proper judges; that the trustees were then disposed to accept of the proposal, but that through the disturbance of the times the business had not been completed; that Mr. Kinnersley being since deceased, the apparatus, by order of his executors, had been valued at about five hundred pounds, was now in complete order, and perhaps equal to any apparatus of the kind in the world, and, therefore, proper to be kept as it stands, for the use of the College."

"The trustees who are present," continued the minutes, "are of opinion that the said apparatus should be taken at the valuation set upon it for the use of the College, and that it be inserted in the notices to be given of next meeting; that money is proposed to be laid out in order to have a full authority for this purchase."

At the meeting thus called, and which was held December 23d, 1778, it was agreed "that the treasurer may pay Mrs. Kinnersley on account of the College for the electrical apparatus, as the same has been valued by Mr. Rittenhouse and Mr. Bringhurst, and that the inventory thereof be procured and inserted in the minutes."

On the 28th of December, 1778, the anniversary of St. John, the Evangelist, the grand and subordinate lodges of Masons determined to celebrate the day with a procession and sermon. They appointed a committee to wait upon the Grand Secretary, Dr. Smith, and request him to deliver the sermon, and to personally wait on "Brother George Washington, and request his excellency to attend the procession." Dr. Smith, having agreed to preach the sermon, waited upon the General, who courteously promised to take part in the procession. Accordingly, at nine o'clock in the morning of St. John's Day, nearly three hundred of the brethren assembled at the College, and at eleven o'clock went in regular procession thence to Christ Church to attend divine service.

The order of the procession was as follows, viz.:

1. The Sword Bearer.
2. Two Deacons, with blue wands tipt with gold.
3. The three orders, Dorick, Ionick and Corinthian, borne by three brethren.
4. The Holy Bible and Book of Constitutions, on two crimson velvet cushions, borne by the Grand Treasurer and Grand Secretary.
5. A reverend brother.

6. Four Deacons, bearing wands.

7. His Excellency the illustrious Brother GEORGE WASHINGTON, Esq., supported by the Grand Master and his Deputy.

8. The two Grand Wardens, bearing the proper pillars.

9. The Past Masters of the different lodges.

10. The present Masters of lodges.

11. The Senior Wardens, ⎫
12. The Junior Wardens, ⎬ of the different private lodges.
13. The Secretaries,   ⎪
14. The Treasurers,   ⎭

15. Brother Proctor's band of music.

16. Visiting brethren.

17. The members of different lodges, walking two and two, according to seniority.

The procession entered the church in the order of their march, and the brethren took their seats in the pews of the middle aisle, which were kept empty for their reception.   Prayers were read by the Rev. Mr. White, and the following anthem was sung in its proper place by sundry of the brethren, accompanied by the organ and other instrumental music, viz.:

A GRAND SYMPHONY.

CHORUS.

Behold now good and joyful a thing it is, brethren, to dwell together in unity.

SOLO.

I will give thanks unto Thee, O Lord! with my whole heart secretly among my brethren, and in the congregation will I praise Thee: I will speak the marvellous works of Thy hands, the Sun, the Moon, and the Stars, which Thou hast ordained.

SOLO.

The people that walked in darkness hath seen a great light, and on them that dwelt in the land of the shadow of death doth the glorious light of Jehovah shine.

SOLO.

Thou hast gathered us from the East, and from the West, from
the North, and from the South ; Thou hast made us
companions for the mighty upon earth, even
for princes of great nations.

TRIO.

O ! I am ! inspire us with wisdom and strength, to support
us in all our troubles, that we may worship Thee
in the beauty of holiness.

After which Dr. Smith preached a well-adapted sermon. The
text was taken from the 1st Epistle of Peter, 2d chapter, and 16th
verse. The brethren requested a copy of the sermon for publication, and the profits were applied to the use of the poor.

After divine service the procession returned to the College; the
musical bells belonging to the church and the band of music
playing proper Masonic tunes. The brethren being all "new
clothed," and the officers in the proper jewels of their respective
lodges, and their other badges of dignity, made, we are told, "a
genteel appearance."

The brethren afterwards departed to their respective lodges,
where they dined together. The sum of £400 was collected in
the church, among the brethren and others, for the relief of the
poor.

CHAPTER XXXVII.

On the Evacuation of Philadelphia by the British, Dr. Smith returns
to the City, and begins the Work of Re-establishing the College—
His Great Services of every sort, Literary, Fiscal and of Business
Generally, herein—The College Finances put upon as good a Foot
as Practicable in the Supremacy of Continental Paper—Instructors
brought back, and Degrees again Ordered to be Conferred.

Upon the evacuation of Philadelphia by the British forces, Dr.
Smith immediately returned to that city and began to make
arrangements to again open the College, Academy and Schools.
The opening took place early in January of this year. It at once
showed that the character and good fame which the institution
had acquired before the war began was still possessed by it.

" Pupils," says Dr. Stillé, " soon flocked to the schools; though the greater portion of them was in the lower departments."

Political spirit, of course, still ran high. Arnold was in command of the city, and under his permission the worst portion of a party, downright and profligately Tory, was insolently asserting itself. Such a nest brought discredit and insult from the common people to a very different class of persons, and, indeed, to some degree to all who had ever belonged to the ancient proprietary party. Any man who had not been *violent* in denouncing George III., and equally violent in approving of the Declaration of Independence, exactly as and when made, was a target for the arrows of every illiterate and malignant fellow. Dr. Smith came in for a good share. He had hardly got back to the city before an ignoramus, named Cress, who, as the *jurat* showed, was unable to write his name, published in the newspapers an affidavit as follows :

Deposition of Peter Cress.

Pennsylvania ss.

Before me, Plunket Fleeson, Esquire, one of the Justices of the Peace, &c., comes Peter Cress of the City of Philadelphia, Saddle and Harness maker, and being duly sworn, deposeth and saith, That on the day on which the attack was made by the Vigilant on the fortification at Mud island, Doctor William Smith, Provost of the college of Philadelphia, with a number of other people of the City of Philadelphia, was on the banks near the mouth of the river Schuylkill, viewing the attack with a large Spy-Glass or Telescope. That after the firing from the Round Tops of the Vigilant began and was returned from the fort, he, the said Peter Cress, was standing behind and very near the said Doctor Smith, and heard him, the said Doctor Smith, say, that " if they (the men in the Fort meaning) do not surrender they ought every man of them to be put to the Sword," or words to this effect. And further the deponent saith not.   his

PETER ⋈ CRESS.

mark

Sworn before me at Philadelphia this twentieth day of March, A. D. 1779.   PLUNKET FLEESON.

Dr. Smith replied to this by a publication in the same paper, in which he denied ever having spoken the words alleged against him, or that he had said anything that could be construed as meaning what they did. Of course nothing came of the matter except to show that " Peter Cress, of the City of Philadelphia, Saddle and Harness maker," was a super-serviceable ass.

We now were beginning to feel severely the calamity, which
Dr. Smith had foreseen, of entering on war before we were at all
prepared for it, and the consequent issue of paper money beyond
our ability to redeem it on demand. The crisis, indeed, had not
yet come. We were only on the swelling, or rather on the hugely
swollen tide of a paper money system. But this was worse than
the crisis which soon after did occur. The extravagant deprava-
tion of morals was frightful. Arnold was in command of the city,
and peculation, speculation, debauchery, and fraud of every kind
prevailed. It is set forth in a paper by Mr. F. D. Stone, read in May,
1879, before the Historical Society of Pennsylvania, entitled, " Philadelphia a Century Ago, or the Reign of Continental Money."*
The minutes of the Board of Trustees show that on the 25th of
March, 1779, both Dr. Smith and Dr. Alison represented to the
Board that their receiving, " in the present currency," only *double*
the nominal sums of their former salary was no way adequate to
the increased price of necessaries, and prayed that the fact might
be taken by the Trustees into consideration. The Board ordered
that in the notices of next meeting it should be inserted that the
disposition of money would be part of the business before it. At
this next meeting the salaries were raised.

The work of the College now goes on, though it is to some
degree the work of reconstruction. Dr. Smith and Dr. Alison, at
a meeting of May 4th, 1779, informed the Board that they had
examined one Mr. Cochran, who offered himself as an usher in
the Latin School at the rate of £400 per annum ; and that they
were of opinion that, though he had not for some time been
employed in teaching the classics, yet by diligent study he might
supply an usher's place. It was therefore ordered that he be
received on a quarter's trial.

Dr. Smith's *universal* usefulness exhibits itself now even above
what it did in earlier times. He was requested by the Board to
visit the tenants on the Perkasie Manor, and to report the state
of the farms ; to give the tenants notice that their leases being
expired they must come to Philadelphia and enter into new agreements for rents in wheat, or the price thereof as it may be at
Philadelphia, yearly, when the same becomes due. This, with an

---

* See The Pennsylvania Journal of Biography and History, Vol. 3., p. 361

authority " to employ some person to collect the *old rails* scattered
on the different parts of the Norriton Plantation, and enclose the
meadows as soon as possible to prevent them being damaged
further by cattle and swine," was rather strange business to put
upon the Provost of the College, he too a Reverend Doctor of
Divinity by diplomas of Oxford, Edinburgh, and Dublin. However, disdaining no office in life where he could be useful to
science and letters, Dr. Smith went at it all cheerfully and did it
all effectively.

A controversy arose with Colonel Bull about the lands which,
we have mentioned in our first volume, were sold by him to Dr.
Smith, at or near Norristown, and which Dr. Smith had transferred
to the College; Colonel Bull claiming certain small islands or
sand-banks, which he pretended had not passed by his grant to
Dr. Smith, while Dr. Smith and the College, on the strength of a
map which accompanied the deed, asserted that they had; and,
moreover, that as certain parts of the estate, undeniably granted,
were wholly useless and incapable of being in the least enjoyed,
unless the parts claimed by Colonel Bull passed also, that they
were absolutely appurtenant and had been well conveyed. Colonel Bull finally relinquished his claims.

He visited the farms belonging to the College in Perkasie
Manor, and, in the presence of witnesses whom he took with him,
Mr. John Heany and Colonel Smith, one of the members of
Assembly for Bucks county, received the proposals of the tenants
for new leases, and appointed them to attend the Board of Trustees
at a meeting to be held May 18th. The tenants accordingly
attended at the proper time, and, being called in one after another,
the terms of their future leases, for seven years from the 25th of
March, 1779, were settled with them severally, and leases were
ordered to be executed to them under the seal of the Corporation,
and the counterparts duly executed to be deposited with the
treasurer. With respect to the year, from 25th March, 1778, to
25th March, 1779, which they have severally held over their
former term, it was mutually agreed to take a note of hand from
each of them for the like payments in wheat or its value on the
15th of September next, as they were severally to pay for each
year of their new term. Certain trespassers—Clark, Painter, and
others—on the Woodlands on Rockhill, by making settlements

without leave, were ordered to move off in three months from the day of notice given them by Dr. Smith, and to remain accountable for the damages and waste they had committed. It was further ordered that no persons should be allowed, for the future, to settle on the said Woodlands, but that that portion of the estate be reserved for the supply of the other plantations* now leased, in such manner as the Trustees or their agents should direct. Lastly it was ordered that a power of attorney should be given to Mr. Heany, in whose neighborhood they were, to superintend the plantations now leased in order to prevent waste and breach of covenant.

The vigilant and effective agency of Dr. Smith extended itself over every part of the estates of the College. We find him at this same meeting acquainting the Board that part of the " New Build- ings " having been rented by him, at the desire of the Trustees, to one Mr. Dancer, at the rate of £30 per quarter, either party to have the liberty of giving the other a quarter's notice for dissolv- ing, and the value of money being now greatly altered, he had given notice to Mr. Dancer more than three months ago, that he could not continue at that rent; and that Mr. Dancer had never yet paid any rent. It was accordingly ordered that he be called upon for his past rent, and that he deliver up the house unless he comes to a new agreement for a larger rent.

How completely, indeed, every detail—even those of the most homely and unappropriate kind—were thrown upon the Provost in these days of war and desolation appears from the records of a meeting of the Trustees, held June 1st, 1777, when Mr. Dancer, having been ejected from the premises for which he would pay only in "bankruptcy" the rent that he had promised to pay in bullion, it was ordered that an inventory be taken of the *kitchen furniture*, and that *Dr. Smith* and Dr. Alison direct the same to be sold at public vendue, and these gentlemen were to agree with another person, one Monsieur Marie, for one quarter's rent of the house. However, in the midst of all these disgusting details, the care of which would have been better consigned to a real-estate agent—if, indeed, one who had the capacity, the zeal, the fidelity, and the humility of Dr. Smith could have been found—it is

----

* They were fourteen in number.

2

refreshing to discover an entry or two in the College minutes which show that the groves of the Academy still existed, and that masters and scholars sometimes could refresh themselves in its pleasing walks.

At a meeting of the 28th of June, 1779, "The Provost represented," say the minutes, "that the following gentlemen who have been educated in this Seminary and took their Bachelor of Arts degree with great approbation, had applied in due time and manner to be admitted to the degree of Master of Arts, for which they are of standing, and qualified according to the rules of the Institution, viz.: Messrs. Benjamin Chew, Jr., John Mifflin, William Moore Smith, James Abercrombie, Thomas Duncan Smith, and Jacob Hall." The names of these gentlemen were accordingly ordered to be inserted in the mandate for admission to the degree aforesaid.

The minutes of September 14th, 1779, show equally the zeal of the Trustees and the Provost in getting the College under its ancient and full course of usefulness. He is directed to "advertise for an English and Latin usher, and also to write to Newcastle to engage a gentleman who teaches a Latin school in that place and formerly offered his services as an usher."

CHAPTER XXXVIII.

The Abrogation of the College Charter by President Reed and the Legislature of Pennsylvania—A Truthful and Eloquent History of the Transaction by the Provost Stillé—The Transaction Characterized and Condemned—The Episcopal Academy Founded in Consequence of the Injustice done to the College—Dr. Smith left without means of living—Final Repeal in 1789 of the Act of Abrogation as Repugnant to Justice, Unconstitutional, and Dangerous to Chartered Rights.

WE come now to the history of a great event in the life of Dr. Smith, in the annals of the College, and, as we may add, of the State; the abrogation of the College charter by the President and Legislature of Pennsylvania in the year 1779, on the alleged ground of disloyalty to the new State of Pennsylvania, and of an undue devotion to the interests of the Church of England.

We have stated in our former volume,* upon Dr. Smith's own
authority, that, from private animosity towards Dr. Smith, and
political dislike of the Penns, who were liberal patrons of the College, Dr. Franklin, while in England, in 1764, had represented to
sundry dissenters that the College was "a narrow, bigoted institution," put into the hands of the Proprietary party as an engine of
government; that the dissenters had no influence in it—although,
as Dr. Smith observed, all the professors in it but himself were
Dissenters—that the College had no occasion to ask assistance
from abroad, and that the country and province would readily
support it if it were not for the things above stated; and that Dr.
Franklin, with virulence, had made many other representations
grievously reflecting upon the principal persons concerned in the
Institution.

I have shown how false and how much inspired by personal and
political animosities were these statements of the great philosopher.

Coming from a man so well known and regarded by so many
persons as one of impartiality, the statements were not without a
pernicious and, as we shall see, a lasting effect; one, indeed, as we
may admit, greatly beyond—both in the matter of duration and
effect—what Dr. Franklin himself—whose object was doubtless
confined to thwarting Dr. Smith and to injuring the Penns and
their friends in Philadelphia—at all designed or anticipated.

At the outbreak of the Revolution the Trustees of the College
were composed of a body of gentlemen, the very first in point of
birth, property, education, intelligence, integrity, and honor to be
found in the city of Philadelphia. While they were not hasty in
rushing into a revolution, they were just as far, as a whole, from
aiding, abetting, or approving the illegal acts or purposes of the
British ministry. And this same state of disposition, it may be
affirmed with truth, characterized the body of the best people of
Philadelphia.

But there was in Pennsylvania a violent party, distinguished by
a proscriptive policy, in the eyes of which every man who was not
ready to rush into revolution was a Tory, and which, to use the
language of Horace Binney, "implicated every such person in a
lesser or greater treason, like the *bye* and the *main* of Sir Walter
Raleigh and his friends."

---

* Vol. I., p. 336.

President Reed was one of this bitterly proscriptive party; none of the Trustees of the College were, and none of the professors; though most of both bodies were true patriots, distinguished by consistent fidelity, not less to the country and the country's cause than to every interest committed to their charge.

On the outbreak of the Revolution Dr. Smith was awake to the perils to which all institutions having property were subjected; and so early as 1776 and during the sittings of the First Republican Convention of the State, a meeting was held at his house of prominent gentlemen interested in maintaining the inviolability of the rights and possessions of religious and scientific corporations. Dr. Franklin, President of the American Philosophical Society, in which many members were suspected of Toryism, was among them, and promised to propose (as he afterwards did) to the Convention an article securing all chartered rights. It is probable enough that he thus sought to repair to the College the possible injury which his remarks on it in England were likely to do to it. The article was adopted by the Convention, and was an article of the Constitution subsisting at the time of which we are about to speak.

Three only of the twenty-four trustees which composed the College Board had refused to take the oath of allegiance to the new State of Pennsylvania; and different vacancies, which had occurred after the Declaration of Independence, were filled by such men as Robert Morris, Francis Hopkinson, Alexander Wilcocks, Edward Biddle, John Cadwalader, and James Wilson. Dr. Smith was the only member of the Church of England in the Faculty, and though a majority of the trustees belonged to that church, no undue preference had ever been shown to its members, nor the least effort to inculcate its doctrines.

It has been commonly supposed, I think, that the action of President Reed and of his political friends was aimed against Dr. Smith and the ancient trustees. The Provost Stillé, as we shall see, regards Dr. Smith as having been the chief object of attack. Bishop White, however, tells* us—and his authority, on every account, is of the highest value—that *his* opinion was, in the beginning, and so always remained, "that what principally gave

---

* Life by Wilson, p. 60—*note.*

offence was the political complexion of the trustees lately chosen. They were gentlemen," adds the Bishop, "prominent in the Revolution, but, in the politics of the State, opposed to those who governed it;" that is to say, opposed to President Reed and some of his friends. They were not of *that* "popular party" to which President Reed belonged; though they were Republicans and the faithful and uniform friends of Washington, which it would be hard to prove that President Reed himself ever was.*

The interests of the College were defended against this unjust attack with great ability, by James Wilson and William Lewis, two of the ablest and most upright lawyers whom the United States have produced.

But I forbear to give in my own words a particular account of this matter, since the history has been succinctly, fearlessly, truthfully, and well told by the Provost Stillé, in a recital of it which no man can improve. The Provost says:

On the 23d of February, 1779—more than two hundred pupils having already flocked to the Schools—the Assembly of the State passed the following resolution:

"Ordered that Mr. Clymer, Mr. Mark Bird, Mr. Hoge, Mr. Gardiner, and Mr. Knox, be a Committee to inquire into the present state of the College and Academy of Philadelphia, its rise, funds, etc., and report thereon to the House, and that they be empowered to send for persons and papers."

This Committee was met by a Committee of the Board of Trustees, who, on the 16th of March, 1779, delivered to them an elaborate statement prepared by Dr. Smith, containing a complete history of the College. It was designed to meet, and it did meet fully, every objection which had been made against the Institution by ill-disposed persons. On all points it seems to me most satisfactory, and, therefore, I have made free use of it in the present Memoir. This Committee of the Assembly, so far as I have been able to discover, never made a Report. The matter seems to have been allowed to sleep until July of the same year, when it was mentioned in the Board of Trustees that the President of the State, General Reed, had intimated that it would be improper to hold a public Commencement at that time, some of the Trustees, in the

---

* See his letter of 1776 to Charles Lee, in the dark days preceding the battle of Trenton (Lee's Memoirs, p. 178), and his letter to General Gates in the darker days of Conway's Cabal, of November, 1777, in the History of the Republic, by John C. Hamilton, Vol. I., p. 368. The latter letter, which, I think, was not in print until printed by Mr. Hamilton (after the Biography of President Reed by his grandson was published), is not given in the Biography. The former, which is, was in print before.

opinion of the Council, being under legal disqualifications. To this strange menace the Trustees made the very proper reply, that there was a very simple means of ascertaining whether any of them were disqualified, and if on that account the Board had lost its chartered rights, and that was, by a judicial inquiry, the matter being wholly out of the province of the President or his Council. The Trustees, however, thought it advisable "to defer to the Executive part of the Government," and no Commencement was held.* In September, a newly-elected Assembly met, and the President of the State, in his message of the 9th of that month, brought the subject of the College before them in the following terms:

> "The principal Institution of learning in this State, founded on the most free and catholic principles, raised and cherished by the hand of public bounty, appears by its Charter to have allied itself so closely to the Government of Britain by making the allegiance of its Governors to that State a pre-requisite to any official act, that it might well have been presumed they would have sought the aid of Government for an establishment consistent with the Revolution, and conformable to the great changes of policy and government. But whatever may have been the motives, we cannot think the good people of this State can, or ought to, rest satisfied, or the protection of Government be extended to an Institution framed with such manifest attachment to the British Government and conducted with a general inattention to the authority of the State. How far there has been any deviation from the liberal ground of its first establishment, and a pre-eminence given to some societies in prejudice to others equally meritorious, the former inquiries of your Honorable House will enable you to determine."

The subject was referred to a Committee of the House, and before the end of September a majority of the Committee (three out of five) made a report which was a mere echo of the message of the President. They conclude by recommending that a Bill should be brought in "effectually to provide suitable funds for the said College (remodelled), to secure to every denomination of Christians equal privileges, and establish said College on a liberal foundation, in which the interests of American liberty and independence will be advanced and promoted, and obedience and respect to the Constitution of the State preserved."

---

* The following was the Minute and resolve of the Trustees of the College:

"COLLEGE OF PHILADELPHIA, July 8th, 1779.

"As the President of the State has thought proper to inform this Board, through some of its members, that certain legal objections lay to the exercise of some of their rights under their charter, and to advise the not holding a commencement at the time appointed, the Board have, for the present, deferred holding the commencement from an expectation that some mode will be speedily adopted on the part of Government to draw such their rights into question in a legal way, when this board will take the proper steps to defend their charter according to law.

"*Resolved*, That Mr. Willing, Mr. Powell, and Mr. Hopkinson be a committee to communicate the sense of the Board on this subject to the President."

The minority of the Committee reported that "no evidence had arisen during the inquiry to support the same, but that much the contrary had appeared." The House refused a motion that the evidence upon which the report was founded should be laid before it, and also voted against taking the opinion of the Judges of the Supreme Court upon the legal questions involved, although they had been summoned for that purpose.

A Bill was accordingly brought in, and on the 27th of November, 1779, was enacted into a law, declaring the charter of 1755 void, dissolving the Board of Trustees and the Faculty, and vesting the College estates in a new Board of Trustees composed of certain State officials, of the senior Clergyman of each of the principal religious denominations in the City, and of sundry other persons who were conspicuous members of the political party which at that time controlled the State. The Act provided also that the Council should reserve for the use of the new Institution, which was called "The University of the State of Pennsylvania," £1500 a year from the proceeds of the confiscated estates.

As this Act of the Legislature was the severest blow which the higher interests of learning in this State ever received (as no one who has read the foregoing account of Dr. Smith's services, and who knows anything of the history of the Institution during the years which followed can doubt), and as it appears on its face to be a simple act of spoliation, transferring the property of one set of men to the pockets of another, we must examine somewhat minutely the reasons given for this extraordinary proceeding. Upon looking at the Preamble of the Act, we find the most frivolous and unfounded of all the pretexts which had been alleged in the report of the Committee and the message of the President as reasons for the abrogation of the Charter, made the basis of the Assembly's action. It is there stated that the Trustees by a vote or by-law adopted June 14, 1764, "departed in the management of the Institution from the free and unlimited Catholicism of its original founders." On turning to the by-law referred to we find that it was the fundamental Declaration adopted by the Trustees in regard to the use of the money then recently collected by Dr. Smith in England, the very object and intention of that Declaration, as has been before stated, being to perpetuate the "free and unlimited Catholicism" of the Founders of the College.* Anything more preposterous than such a reason for so grave an act (strangely ranked by the biographer of President Reed as a trophy of his administration of the government with the Act abolishing slavery in Pennsylvania) it would be difficult to conceive.

The only other cause of incapacity alleged in the Act against the Trustees was that provision in the Charter of 1755 which required them before entering upon 'their office to take certain oaths of allegiance.

---

* See Vol. I., pp. 350, 351.—H. W. S.

But these oaths were precisely the same which had been exacted of every one called to fill any civil office in the province prior to the Revolution, and their obligation was always understood to have ceased upon the establishment of a new government. The Trustees were therefore precisely in the same position as any one who had ever held office under the Crown. Test oaths, and oaths of allegiance, are, as we all know, favorite devices in revolutionary times. The Assembly, as a means most probably of discovering the disaffected, directed on the 13th of June, 1777, that every white person above the age of eighteen should take an oath of allegiance to the State, and by another act passed on the first of April, 1778, enacted that all Trustees, Provosts, Professors, and Masters (among others) should take the same oath before the first of June of that year, or forfeit their offices. The following is the form of the oath:

"I, A. B., do swear that I renounce and refuse all allegiance to George III., King of Great Britain, his heirs and successors, that I will be faithful and bear true allegiance to the Commonwealth of Pennsylvania, as a free and independent State, that I will not at any time do or cause to be done any matter or thing that will be prejudicial or injurious to the freedom and independence thereof as declared by Congress; and also that I will discover and make known to some one Justice of the Peace of said State all treasons or traitorous conspiracies which I now know or hereafter may know to be formed against this, or any other of the United States of America."

Twelve of the Trustees, the Provost, and all the Professors, took this oath as required by law, before June 1, 1778. By November, 1779, when the Charter was taken away, the Board was full, and twenty-one out of the twenty-four Trustees had previously taken the oath, the three who had not done so being Richard Penn, William Allen, and Dr. Bond. It is a little remarkable as showing how different were the real reasons for taking away the Charter from those which were assigned in the Act, that notwithstanding his alleged disqualification, Dr. Bond was named in it as a Trustee of the new corporation, as were also three others, who had not only never taken the oath to the State, but had just before taken it to the King, one of whom had served as Chaplain in the British Army while it occupied Philadelphia.

The grounds upon which the Assembly proceeded, as stated in the Act itself, being thus wholly without foundation, it is only necessary to add that the action it took was expressly forbidden by the provisions of the Constitution of the State, in regard to property held for the use of churches, colleges, and hospitals, by the well-known doctrine that, no misconduct of a Trustee can work a forfeiture of his trust, and by the equally well-settled rule that, alleged infractions of a Charter are to be determined by judicial proceedings, and not by the Legislature.

It has been sometimes said that, although the abrogation of the Charter was made without legal authority, yet that it may have been justifiable at that period of the Revolution for reasons of State policy. Before admitting such a plea as a safe criterion in this case, we must remember that the College Charter was in existence, and the College itself was in full operation at the time of the adoption of the Constitution, which was subsequent to the Declaration of Independence, and that the Convention, with a full knowledge of its organization, solemnly guaranteed the protection of its property and franchises. Nor had any change taken place since, either in the men who controlled it, or in the system of instruction, which could, in any way, be construed as unfavorable to the principles of the Revolution. The vacancies in the Board of Trustees since the Declaration of Independence had been filled by Robert Morris, Francis Hopkinson, Alexander Wilcocks, Edward Biddle, John Cadwalader and James Wilson, and no Pennsylvanian need be told that these were among the most eminent patriots of the Revolution. The system of instruction was also wholly unchanged, and as if nothing should be wanting to prove that the act was one of simple spoliation, that system, and every one of the Professors of the old College, in both Faculties, except Dr. Smith and Dr. Alison (who had died during the controversy), were transferred to the new institution.

We are, therefore, compelled to conclude that the conduct of the Assembly rested upon no legal authority, nor upon the broader ground of an overruling necessity; but that it is the most striking instance of the baneful effects of an unscrupulous party-spirit recorded in our State history. Its object was to strike down and disfranchise the purest and best men in the community, associated in an undertaking which had brought nothing but honor and advantage to the State. To conciliate the unthinking masses, and as some apology for the spoliation, a pretence was made of establishing a new Institution upon a broader basis than the old, and the cheap device was resorted to of endowing it with the proceeds of the confiscated estates. One of the complaints against the old College had been, that it had never applied to the State authorities for money, and it was thought that the prosperity of the new was certainly assured by the Legislative grant of £1500 a year. But it never prospered. The original taint of its birth seems to have poisoned all its sources of growth, so that on the 22d of August, 1791, just before its dissolution, when the College estates had been restored to their rightful owners, its debts are stated in a minute of that date to be £5187, nearly all due to the Professors for arrears of salary, while its resources from its income were: "Debts recoverable by next March, say £2000; due from the State, £375."

But there were other sources of decay, inherent in the scheme itself, and rapidly developed by the influences surrounding it, which must have soon proved fatal to it. Of all human institutions, it may be most truly said of Colleges and Universities, that they "are things that grow, and are not made." A popular error prevails that a large endowment, an extended *curriculum*, and an imposing array of Professors, are all that is necessary to insure the permanent success of a newly-founded College. Such an opinion is contradicted by universal experience. Both in Europe and in this country, institutions of learning which have gained reputation and success have all had their day of small things, and their present strength is only the natural development of a slow but steady and healthy growth. There have been thousands of failures, where the greatest zeal, aided by large endowments, has established Colleges. Defects in the most brilliant projects have been brought to light by experience, or the soil in which they were planted has not proved kindly to their nurture. Such was the case with the short-lived "University of the State of Pennsylvania."

He must indeed have been a bold and sanguine man who thought it possible to establish, with any chance of success, a new College in this State in the year 1779. In the very crisis of the Revolution, with the fortune of every man who had been engaged in trade ruined by the worthlessness of the currency, with the cost of living increased in the proportion of sixty to one, with every nerve strained to keep up the sinking fortunes of the war, with dissensions among the best men in the State more bitter than their hatred of the common enemy; with the belief among nearly all who had been real supporters of learning that the Charter had been taken away from party malice, and that the new institution would be managed in such a way as to subserve party ends; above all, with the ever-present consciousness that the money they were using did not belong to them in law or morals, it is not to be wondered at that the projectors of the new establishment soon found that they had been building upon the sand. There was certainly but one man living in this State, at that time, who could have carried even an old College successfully through the dangers which threatened the interests of learning during the Revolution, and for ten years afterwards, and that was the very man whom a blind party-zeal had driven from his post. When we consider what Dr. Smith did for those interests during the twenty-five years in which they had been in his special charge, we may form some estimate of the loss sustained, both by the College and the State, by the forced employment of the remaining twenty-five years of his life in other pursuits.

As the removal of Dr. Smith was, no doubt, the great object aimed at in the abrogation of the Charter, so he was the chief victim of that measure. He had to mourn not merely, in common with all his friends, that the work he had been so long painfully building up was in ruin, and that the pledges which he had given as to the management of the funds which he had collected were shamefully violated, but he was ejected from his office, and without the means of supporting his family. But it was not in the man's nature to despond. Feeling that he could hope for no redress in Pennsylvania, as its Government was then constituted, he went to Chestertown, in Maryland, and became Rector of a church there. He found at that place an Academy with a few pupils. He was made Principal of it, and in a short time one hundred and forty scholars were in attendance. He then applied to the Legislature of Maryland for a Charter, erecting this Academy into a College, modelled upon the plan of the College of Philadelphia, to be called "Washington College." The charter was granted in the spring of 1782, and within one year from that time this indefatigable man collected, principally from the planters of the Eastern Shore of Maryland, nearly ten thousand three hundred pounds towards its endowment. General Washington contributed fifty guineas, and General Cadwalader headed the Maryland subscriptions. This was, of course, before the close of the Revolutionary war, and it is very evident that these gentlemen did not hold the opinion entertained by the party in power in Pennsylvania in regard to Dr. Smith's disaffection to the American cause.

But that party ceased to reign in 1783, and Dr. Smith lost no time in seeking justice at the hand of those who took its place. At the September session, 1784, the Trustees and Dr. Smith presented their petition to the Assembly, asking that so much of the Act of 1779, which took away their estates and franchises, should be repealed. The Committee to whom the matter was referred made a report favoring the application, and brought in a bill granting it. But when the bill was about to pass, the minority left the House (in modern phrase, "*bolted*"), and thus dissolved the Assembly. The matter lingered for several years, and until March 6, 1789, when the Assembly passed the bill, the preamble to it stating as the reason for its action that the Act of 1779 was "repugnant to justice, a violation of the Constitution of this Commonwealth, and dangerous in its precedent to all incorporated bodies, and to the rights and franchises thereof."

But of all this I shall speak at the proper time.

The act of confiscation, which the Provost Stillé describes, has been justly considered a stigma upon the Revolutionary Legislature of Pennsylvania, and still more so upon the name—now much better remembered than are those of most in the Legislature—of General Joseph Reed, the President of the State. Along with his much-suspected disloyalty to his Commander-in-Chief, and his being charged by that patriotic man, General Cadwalader, in a printed pamphlet—of a disregard of truth, *that* offence which ends the character of a gentleman, and which, truly considering, was the *gist* of Cadwalader's accusation—this his conduct in regard to

the old College of Philadelphia conspired to bring about that condition of feeling towards him described by Mr. Binney in his
"Leaders of the Old Bar of Philadelphia,"* in which tract the
author, speaking of President Reed's inability to do to one of his
young *protégés* of the bar any great professional service, says:

President Reed's political ardor during his term of office, and an
embittered opposition to him which had been kindled among men of
business and of importance in Philadelphia, did not make his return to
the Bar in 1781 very easy or agreeable; nor, as I have heard Mr. Ingersoll say, did his mind return willingly to the pursuits of the law. The
patron, therefore, must have been more willing than able to assist him,
and in a short time Mr. Reed's health gave way, and after visiting
England, in 1783, he returned towards the close of 1784, and, without
attempting to resume his profession, died on the 5th of March, 1785.

While speaking thus of President Reed's malevolence towards
those politically opposed to him, and of the want of sincerity
which distinguished his character, I am not insensible to his many
endearing domestic traits, to his considerable abilities, and to his
not less considerable accomplishments. We may concede, too,
that both by wisdom in council and conduct in action he promoted
essentially the Revolution in America; and his want of success in
the great struggle of life, after much labor, many privations, and
many misfortunes, give, too, to his memory a title to our pathetic
regard. But with all this, and after all the efforts that his grandson and biographer has brought to redeem his reputation,† I look
upon the judgment of those who were among the most intelligent
of his contemporaries as true—that his talents were more than
equal to his integrity; and that in few acts of his life did this unenviable preponderance appear more manifest than in the transaction that the Provost Stillé above describes. Of few political
events of the Revolution did the late Bishop White speak with
more emphatic disapprobation. It roused the indignation of the
whole Episcopal Church, and was followed at once by the establishment of the Episcopal Academy; an institution still existing in
honor, after a century of useful labors. The biographer of the
President—one of his grandsons—while defending every act that

---

* Page 84.
† Life and Correspondence of President Reed, by his Grandson, William B. Reed,
2 vols., 8vo.   Phila., 1847.

was defensible in his ancestor's public life, and one which was
much the reverse, glosses over this, but defends it not; indeed,
while palliating, is compelled to condemn it.*   I do not, of course,
forget that the times in which President Reed chiefly figures were
times of revolution; that party-spirit had risen to a great height
and exhibited itself in scenes of violence; that in the very Congress
of the country there were, at this same date, men who, like Rush,
Conway, Gates, Lovell, and others, seemed to hate Washington
and his friends as fully as they did the common enemy.   The best
excuse for President Reed is found in his own language in the last
letter which he ever wrote, " I was thrown into turbulent times,
which did not leave me at liberty to speculate, was obliged to act,
and too often without time to consider or advice to guide me." †

CHAPTER XXXIX.

Dr. Smith interests himself in having General Washington made a Grand
   Master over all the Masonic Lodges formed or to be formed in the
   United States.

WE have noted in our former volume, as a feature of Dr.
Smith's mind, and one tending to prove its high order, that no
matter in what troubles he might be involved or in what exciting
scenes engaged, his mental faculties and his power to use them
seemed always undisturbed.   Even in such trials as we have described in the preceding chapter, when his very means of living
were taken or about to be taken from him, he interests himself
vividly in the affairs of the Masonic Society, and in an endeavor
to have General Washington elected a Grand Master over all the
Grand Lodges formed or to be formed in these United States.
We give some of his correspondence on this subject:

Dr. Smith to Joseph Webb, Esq.

PHILADELPHIA, August 19th, 1780.

SIR: I do myself the honor to address you, by order of the Grand
Lodge of Ancient York Masons, regularly constituted in the City of

---

* Life and Correspondence of President Reed, by his Grandson, William B. Reed.
Vol. II., pp. 169–172.
† *Id.* p. 417.

Philadelphia. This Grand Lodge has under its jurisdiction in Pennsylvania and the States adjacent, thirty-one different regular Lodges, containing in the whole more than one thousand brethren. Enclosed you have a printed abstract of some of our late proceedings, and by that of January 13th last, you will observe that we have, so far as depends on us, done that honor which we think due to our illustrious Brother, General Washington, viz., electing him Grand Master over all the Grand Lodges formed or to be formed in these United States, not doubting of the concurrence of all the Grand Lodges in America to make this election effectual.

We have been informed by Col. Palfrey that there is a Grand Lodge of Ancient York Masons in the State of Massachusetts, and that you are Grand Master thereof; as such, I am, therefore, to request that you will lay our proceedings before your Grand Lodge, and request their concurrent Voice in the appointment of General Washington, as set forth in the said Minute of January the 13th, which, as far as we have been able to learn, is a Measure highly approved by all the brethren, and that will do honor to the Craft.

I am, etc.,   WILLIAM SMITH, Grand Secretary.

To JOSEPH WEBB.

Reply to the Preceding Letter.

BOSTON, September 4th, 1780.

SIR: Your agreeable favor of the 19th ult., I duly received the 31st, covering a printed abstract of the proceedings of your Grand Lodge. I had received one before, near three months, from the Master of a travelling Lodge of the Connecticut line, but it not coming officially, did not lay it before the Grand Lodge, but the evening after I received yours, it being Grand Lodge; I laid it before them and had some debate on it, whereupon it was agreed to adjourn the Lodge for three weeks, to the 22d instant, likewise to write to all the Lodges under this jurisdiction to attend themselves if convenient by their Master and Wardens, and if not, to give instructions to their proxies here concerning their acquiescence in the proposal.

I am well assured that no one can have any objections to so illustrious a person as General Washington to preside as Grand Master of the United States, but at the same time it will be necessary to know from you his prerogative as such; whether he is to appoint sub-grand or Provincial Grand Masters of each State: if so, I am confident that the Grand Lodge of this State will never give up their right of electing their own Grand Masters and other officers annually. This induces me to write to you now, before the result of the Grand Lodge takes place, and must beg an answer by the first opportunity, that I may be enabled to lay the same before them. I have not heard of any State except yours and this that have proceeded as yet since the Independence to elect their officers, but have been hoping that they would.

I do not remember of more Grand Masters being appointed when we were under the British Government than South Carolina, North Carolina, Pennsylvania, New York, and Massachusetts, but now it may be necessary.

I have granted a Charter of Dispensation to New Hampshire till they shall appoint a Grand Master of their own, which suppose will not be very soon, as there is but one Lodge in their State. Inclosed I send you a list of the officers of our Grand Lodge, and have the honor to be, with great respect and esteem,

Your affectionate Brother and humble servant,

JOSEPH WEBB, Grand Master.

This communication was laid before the Grand Lodge of Pennsylvania, at a special Grand Communication on the 16th of October; and a committee, consisting of Dr. Smith and Colonel Palfrey, was appointed to prepare an answer, which was as follows:

William Smith, D. D., to Joseph Webb, Esq.

PHILADELPHIA, October 17th, 1780.

RESPECTED SIR AND R. W. BRO.: Your kind and interesting letters of the 14th and 19th, by some delay in the Post-office, came both to my hands together, and that not before the 10th inst. They were both read and maturely considered at a very full Grand Lodge last evening, and I have it in charge to thank you and all the worthy members of the Grand Lodge of Massachusetts for the brotherly notice they were pleased to take of the proposition communicated to you from the Grand Lodge of this State.

We are happy to find that you agree with us in the necessity of having one complete Masonic jurisdiction under some one Grand Head throughout the United States. It has been a measure long wished for among the brethren, especially in the army, and from them the request came originally to us, that we might improve the opportunity which our central situation gave us of setting this measure on foot. From these considerations, joined to an earnest desire of advancing and doing honor to Masonry, and not from any affectation of superiority or of dictating to any of our brethren, we put in nomination for Grand Master over all these States (and elected, so far as depended upon us) one of the most illustrious of our brethren, whose character does honor to the whole Fraternity, and who, we are therefore persuaded, would be wholly unexceptionable. When our proposition and nomination should be communicated to other Grand Lodges, and ratified by their concurrence, then, and not before, it was proposed to define the powers of such a Grand Master General, and to fix articles of Masonic union among all the Grand Lodges, by means of a convention of committees from the different Grand Lodges, to be held at such time and place as might be agreed upon. Such convention may also have power to notify the Grand Master General of his election, present him his diploma, badges of office, and instal with due form and solemnity.

To you who are so well learned in the Masonic Art, and acquainted with its history, it need not be observed that one Grand Master General over many Grand Lodges, having each their own Grand Masters, is no novel institution, even if the peculiar circumstances of the Grand Lodges in America, now separated from the jurisdiction from whence they first originated, did not render it necessary. We have also a very recent magnificent example of the same thing in Europe which may serve, in respect to the ceremonies of installation, as a model for us. I will copy the paragraph as dated at Stockholm, in Sweden, the 21st of March last, as you may not perhaps have seen it.

"The 19th of this month (March, 1780) will always be a memorable day to the Freemasons established in this kingdom, for on that day the Duke of Sundermania was installed Grand Master of all the Lodges throughout this kingdom, as well as those of St. Petersburg, Copenhagen, Brunswick, Hamburg, etc. The Lodge at St. Petersburg had sent a Deputy for this purpose, and others had intrusted the diploma of the instalment to Baron Leyonhrefrud, who had been last year to Copenhagen and in Germany on this negotiation. This instalment was attended with great pomp. The assembly was composed of more than four hundred members, and was honored with the presence of the king, who was pleased to grant a charter to the Lodge, taking it under his royal protection, at the same time investing the new Grand Master with an ermined cloak; after which he was placed upon a throne, clothed with the marks of his new dignity, and there received the compliments of all the members, who according to their rank were admitted to kiss the hand, sceptre, or cloak of the new Grand Master, and had delivered to them a silver medal, struck to perpetuate the memory of this solemnity, which passed in Exchange Hall. It is said the king will grant revenues for the Commanderies, and that this Royal Lodge will receive of each an annual tribute. This solemnity hath raised the Order of Freemasons from a kind of oblivion into which they were sunk."

What the particular authorities of the Grand Master of these United States were to be, we had not taken upon us to describe, but (as before hinted) had left them to be settled by a convention of Grand Lodges or their deputies. But this is certain, that we never intended the different Provincial or State Grand Masters should be deprived of the election of their own Grand Officers, or of any of their just Masonic rights and authorities over the different Lodges within the bounds of their jurisdiction.

But where new Lodges are to be erected beyond the bounds of any legal Grand Lodges now existing, such Lodges are to have their warrants from the Grand Master General, and when such Lodges become a number sufficient to be formed into one Grand Lodge, the bounds of such Grand Lodge are to be described, and the warrant to be granted by the Grand Master aforesaid, who may also call and preside in a convention of Grand Lodges when any matter of great and general importance to the whole United Fraternity of these States may require it. What other powers may be given to the Grand Master General, and how such powers are to be drawn up and expressed, will be the business of the convention proposed.

For want of some general Masonic authority over all these States, the Grand Lodge of Pennsylvania, *ex necessitate,* have granted warrants beyond its bounds to the Delaware and Maryland States, and you have found it expedient to do the same in New Hampshire, but we know that necessity alone can be a plea for this.

By what has been said above, you will see that our idea is to have a Grand Master General over all the United States, and each Lodge under him to preserve its own rights, jurisdiction, etc., under him as formerly under the Grand Lodge of Great Britain, from whence the Grand Lodges in America had their warrants, and to have this new Masonic constitution and the powers of the Grand Master General fixed by a convention of committees aforesaid.

Others we are told have proposed that there be one Grand Master over all these States, and that the other Masters of Grand Lodges, whether nominated by him or chosen by their own Grand Lodges, should be considered as his deputies. But we have the same objections to this that you have, and never had any idea of establishing such a plan as hath been suggested before.

This letter is now swelled to a great length. We have therefore only to submit two things to your deliberation :

First. Either whether it be best to make your election of a Grand Master General immediately, and then propose to us a time and place where a committee from your body could meet a committee from ours to fix his powers and proceed to instalment; or,

Second. Whether you will first appoint such a place of meeting and the powers of the proposed Grand Master, and then return home and proceed to the election, and afterwards meet anew for instalment. This last mode would seem to require too much time, and would not be so agreeable to our worthy brethren of the army, who are anxious to have this matter completed.

As you will probably choose the first mode, could not the place of our meeting be at or near the headquarters of the army, at or soon after St. John's day next? At any rate, you will not fix a place far northward on account of some brethren from Virginia who will attend, for we propose to advertise the business and the time and place of meeting in the public papers, that any regular Grand Lodges which we may not have heard of may have an opportunity of sending representatives.

Your answer as soon as possible is requested under cover to Peter Baynton, Esq., Postmaster in Philadelphia.

   I am, etc.,   WILLIAM SMITH, Grand Secretary.

To JOSEPH WEBB, ESQ., Grand Master of Massachusetts.

3

This effort of Dr. Smith's to establish a General American Head over all the Lodges in this country seems to have been the only one made in Pennsylvania; and when the project has been advocated by other Grand Bodies, the voice of the Grand Lodge of Pennsylvania has been invariably against it. From this action, in 1780, arose, undoubtedly, the widespread appellation of the title of General Grand Master to Washington—an historical error which has not yet been eradicated from the minds of all Masons.

CHAPTER XL.

Dr. Smith goes to Chestertown, Kent County, Maryland, and establishes his School, which finally became Washington College—Takes charge of a Parish there—Preaches a Thanksgiving Sermon for the Establishment of Peace and Independence, July 4th, 1780—Assembles the Church in Convention, November 9th, 1780—The First Church Convention in Maryland—Address of the Parishes to the General Assembly of the State—The Name "Protestant Episcopal Church" first given to the Church of England at this Convention.

As we have seen by the concluding part of our extract from the Provost Stillé's narrative of the Legislative attack on the College, the year 1780 found Dr. Smith in Philadelphia without any situation, with a young family depending upon his exertions for their daily bread, and with the opposition of the Presbyterian and "Constitutionalist" parties to contend with. The labors of twenty-six years of his life were laid in the dust, together with his official honors. But as the Provost whom we have just named truly says, he was not a man to be dismayed; he looked realities in the face; and at once left everything, and with his wife and children moved to Chestertown, Kent county, Maryland, to found and set in operation a village school or academy. He was here offered charge of the Parish, and was to receive as his compensation *no money*— but 600 bushels of wheat. Such, too, were the discouraging prospects of reward that it took one hundred and twenty-two persons to agree to contribute before this amount of wheat could be promised. His first sermon was a Thanksgiving Sermon for the Establishment of Peace and Independence in America. It was preached in Chestertown Church, July 4th, 1780, the text being from Isaiah lii. 10.

So vigorously did Dr. Smith set himself to work at his new enterprise that ere the close of the year he had also charge of the Kent County School, combining it with his own private class—a combination out of which grew Washington College, two years afterwards.

Immediately upon his going to Maryland he took a marked position and influence in regard to the whole Episcopal Church in that State. From Dr. Ethan Allen's invaluable history of the Church, we learn that before the year 1776, the Parishes numbered forty-four, each having its rector, and many of these his curate or assistant, of which there were ten or more. But before the 4th of July ensuing four of the clergy had abandoned their Parishes; it being no longer safe for them to remain, and had gone to England.

On the establishment of the State government in that year the Bill of Rights deprived the clergy of their legal support, which they had enjoyed for three generations, and left them without it. Not long after, followed an oath required of them, which, if they had taken it, would have been, says Dr. Allen, a violation of their ordination vows. Under these restrictions nine of them gave up their cures and went to England. Six went to Virginia; one (Dr. John Andrews) to Pennsylvania; one to Delaware; one to Elkton; one to his estate in Charles county; one to his seat in Prince George's; two to their estates elsewhere, and two or three to teaching. In the meanwhile about seven had died, and three new Parishes had come into existence under the Act of 1770.

In 1779 the General Assembly of Maryland had passed an Act for electing vestries in the existing Parishes, and, when elected, giving to such vestries, in fee simple, the glebes, places of worship and other church property, and the appointment of ministers for their respective Parishes, but making no provision for their support, saving what might be voluntary. This prompted the movement of the succeeding Conventions.

Such was the condition of the Church in Maryland when Dr. Smith went into that State.

The *Parishes*, however, were still numerous, and I suppose had never been legally destroyed: and in 1780 there were at least six clergymen, including Dr. Smith, in the State. Dr. Smith set himself at work immediately to assemble the churchmen of Maryland in convention and to raise up the Church from the ruin into which the Revolutionary war had laid it.

A Convention—the first, we may perhaps say, in the State of Maryland—was accordingly assembled at Chestertown, Kent county, November 9th, 1780.

There were present:
Rev. Samuel Keene, Rector of St. Luke's, Queen Anne's county.
Rev. William Smith, D. D., Rector of Chester Parish, Kent county.
Rev. James Jones Wilmer, Rector of Shrewsbury Parish, Kent county.
Col. Richard Lloyd, Vestryman of St. Paul's Parish, Kent county.
Mr. James Dunn,   "   "   "   "   "
Mr. John Page,   "   "   "   "   "
Mr. Richard Miller,   "   "   "   "   "
Mr. Simon Wickes,   "   "   "   "   "
Dr. John Scott, Vestryman of Chester Parish, Kent county.
Mr. John Bolton,   "   "   "   "   "
Mr. J. W. Tilden,   "   "   "   "   "
Mr. St. Leger Everett,   "   "   "   "
Mr. James Wroth,   "   "   "   "   "
Mr. John Kennard, Church Warden of Chester Parish, Kent county.
Mr. Sturgess,   "   "   "   "   "   "
Mr. Christopher Hall, Vestryman of Shrewsbury, S. Sassafras, Kent.
Mr. George Moffett,   "   "   "   "
Mr. William Keating,   "   "   "   "
Mr. C———, Church Warden,   "   "   "
Mr. John Brown, Vestryman of St. Luke's, Queen Anne's county.
Mr. Downs,   "   "   "   "   "
Dr. William Bordly.
Dr. Van Dyke.
Col. Isaac Perkins.
Mr. Charles Groom.
Mr. William Keene.
Mr. James Hackett.

Dr. Smith was appointed President of this Convention.

A petition to the General Assembly of Maryland for the support of public religion was read and approved, and ordered to be sent to each vestry in the State; and if by them approved, after obtaining signatures in their respective Parishes, it was carried up to the Legislature. The petition, which I presume was from the pen of Dr. Smith, was as follows:

To the Honorable the General Assembly of the State of Maryland:

The petition of the Vestry and Church Wardens of the Parish of
————, ———— county, humbly sheweth that it is manifest from reason
as well as the clear light of revelation, that the worship of the Almighty
Creator and Governor of the universe is the indispensable duty of his
dependent creatures, and the surest means of preserving their temporal
as well as eternal happiness, that where religion is left unsupported,
neither laws nor government can be duly administered; and as the experience of ages has shown the necessity of providing for supporting the
officers and ministers of government in all civil societies, so the like
experience shows the necessity of providing a support for the ordinances
and ministers of religion, because if either of them were left wholly dependent on the benevolence of individuals, such is the frailty of human
nature and the averseness of many to their best interests, that the sordid
and the selfish, the licentious and profane would avail themselves of
such liberty to shrink from their share of labor and expense, and thereby
render that which would be easy where borne by all, an intolerable burden to the few whose conscience and principles of justice would not
permit them in this or in any other case to swerve from their duties,
civil or religious.

That our pious ancestors, the worthy and respectable founders of this
State, convinced of the foregoing truths, and declaring that "in every
well-grounded commonwealth matters concerning religion ought in the
first place to be taken into consideration, countenanced and encouraged
as being not only most acceptable to God, but the best way and means
of obtaining his mercy and a blessing upon a people and country"
(having the promises of this life and of the life to come), did frame and
enact sundry laws for erecting churches and places of public worship, the
maintenance of an orthodox clergy, the support and advancement of religion, and the orderly administration of its divine and saving ordinances.

That the delegates of this State at the great era of our independence
in free and full convention assembled for the purpose of establishing a
new constitution and form of government upon the authority of the
people, appearing in their wisdom to have considered some parts of the
said laws as inconsistent with that religious liberty and equality of assessment, which they intended of their future government, did by the
33d section of the Declaration of Rights abrogate all such laws theretofore passed, as enabled any Courts on the application of Vestrymen and
Church Wardens to make assessments or levies for the support of the
religious establishments, but not with a view of being less attentive than
their pious ancestors had been to the interests of religion, learning and
good morals.   On the contrary, by the very same section, an express
recommendation and authority are given to future legislatures, "at their
discretion to lay a general and equal tax for the support of the Christian religion" agreeably to the said declaration.

That your petitioners are sensible of the many urgent civil concerns in which the honorable and worthy Legislatures of this State have been engaged since the great and trying period, and how much wisdom and deliberation are at all times necessary in framing equal laws for the support of religion and learning, and more especially amidst the horrors and confusion of an expensive and unrelenting war. But they are sensible at the same time (and persuaded the Honorable Assembly are equally sensible) that where religion is left to mourn and droop her head while her sacred ordinances are unsupported, and vice and immorality gain ground, even war itself will be but feebly carried on; patriotism will lose its animating principle; corruption will win its way from the lowest to the highest places; distress will soon pervade every public measure; our graveyards, the monuments of the piety of our ancestors, running into ruin, will become the reproach of their posterity. Nay, more, the great and glorious fabric of public happiness, which we are striving to build up and cement with an immensity of blood and treasure, might be in danger of tumbling into the dust as wanting the stronger cement of virtue and religion, or perhaps would fall an easy prey to some haughty invader.

Deeply impressed with these momentous considerations, and conceiving ourselves fully warranted by our constituents in this application to your honorable body, having advertised our design without any objection yet notified to us, your petitioners therefore most earnestly and humbly pray.

That an act may be passed agreeably to the aforesaid section of the Declaration of Rights, for the support of public religion by an equal assessment and laws, and also to enable the vestry and church wardens of this parish, by rates on the pews from time to time, or otherwise, as your wisdom shall think fit, to repair and uphold the church and chapel and the churchyard and burying-ground of the same. All which your petitioners conceive may be done not only for this parish, but at the same time, if thought best, for any other parish within this State (which it is believed earnestly desires the same), by a single law in a manner perfectly agreeable to the liberty and wishes of every denomination of men, which would be esteemed good Christians and faithful citizens of the State.

And your petitioners, as bound, shall ever pray, etc.

On motion, it was resolved that the church formerly known in the province as the Church of England, should now be called "the Protestant Episcopal Church."

Dr. Smith has had the credit of having given this name to the church; but if a statement made by the Rev. James Jones Wilmer be correct, it is apparently without sufficient foundation. In a letter dated May 6, 1810, from the Rev. Mr. Wilmer to Bishop Claggett, he writes: "I am one of the three who first organized the Episcopal Church during the Revolution, and am consequently one of the primary aids of its consolidation throughout the United States. The Rev. Dr. Smith, Dr. Keene and myself held the *first* convention at Chestertown, and I acted as secretary." He also states in this letter that "he moved that the Church of England as heretofore so known in the province be now called The Protestant Episcopal Church, and it was so adopted."—See Md. Archives.

CHAPTER XLI.

Dr. Smith Preaches a New Year's Sermon in St. Peter's Church, Philadelphia—Proposes General Washington as a Member of the American Philosophical Society—General Washington's Letter of Acceptance to Dr. Smith—Dr. Smith to Cæsar Rodney—Dr. Smith Preaches a Funeral Sermon at the Burial of Mrs. Coudon—Preaches, in May, 1781, a Fast Sermon in Chestertown, and in December of the same Year a Thanksgiving Sermon—Extracts from these Two Last—Death of John Wemyss—Extract from the Minutes of the Grand Lodge—The Ahiman Rezon.

NOTWITHSTANDING his new enterprises in Maryland, Dr. Smith maintained, in continuing strength, his old attachments in Philadelphia, and his diary tells us that on the 1st of January, 1781, he was in that city, by appointment, to preach a New Year's sermon in St. Peter's Church, the church of his consecration, as we may call it, and even beyond Christ Church of his special love. His text seems to have had a special suggestion from his own lately eventful history. It was in those striking verses in St. James' Epistle General:

"Go to now, ye that say to-day or to-morrow we will go into such a city, and continue there a year and buy and get gain; whereas, ye know not what shall be on the morrow. For what is your life? it is even a vapor, which appeareth for a little time, and then vanisheth away. For that ye ought to say, if the Lord will, we shall live and do this or that."*

---

* Chapter IV., verses 13, 14, 15.

While in Philadelphia, he attended a meeting of the American Philosophical Society, on January 19th, and proposed General George Washington as a member; the General was elected, and Dr. Smith was appointed to notify to him the fact. The General soon afterwards thus politely acknowledges the honor:

General Washington to Dr. Smith.

HEAD-QUARTERS, Passaic Falls.*

SIR: I am particularly indebted to you for the obliging manner in which you have executed the trust reposed in you by the American Philosophical Society. An excuse for the little delay that attended it could have only found a motive in your politeness.

All the circumstances of the Election are too flattering not to enhance the honor I feel in being distinguished by the fellowship of a Society so eminently respectable.

I warmly unite with you in the wish that the happy period may speedily arrive which will enable all the members to devote themselves to advancing the objects of this most useful institution.

I am, Sir, with very great respect,
Y^r Most Obedient Humble Servant,
GEO. WASHINGTON.

To REV^D. WILLIAM SMITH.

Returning in a short time to Maryland, we find Dr. Smith engaged in his work of corresponding, preaching and teaching.

Dr. Smith to Cæsar Rodney, President of the State of Delaware.

CHESTERTOWN, Maryland, Feb. 8th, 1781.

SIR: When I had last the honour to wait on your Excellency at New Castle, I informed you that I had left in the hands of Mr. Mc-William, Jr., the Draft of a Bill for the Wilmington Lottery. As Mr. Read, on whom we chiefly depend for getting this Bill forwarded, may be engaged in the House when the Post passes through New Castle, and not so easily found as your Excellency, I have taken the Liberty to request that if it be not too much trouble for yourself to inform me the State and Progress of the Bill by return of this Post. You will be pleased to desire or direct Mr. Booth to do me that favour.

I thank your Excellency for that gentlemanlike, liberal and candid regard which I am well informed you have been pleased to pay to my good name, when called in question by prejudiced or narrow-minded

* This letter, which is in the collection of Colonel Frank Etting, is not dated; but, as the election was on the 19th of January, 1781, the letter must have been written soon afterward.

men. I wish it may ever fall in my way to do any part of that justice to your public character which it so eminently merits. This little quiet town produces no news.

> I have the honour to be
> Your Excellency's Most Obedient Servant,
> WILLIAM SMITH.

To His Excellency Cæsar Rodney, Esq., New Castle.

On February 9th he preached a funeral sermon at Chestertown, Maryland, on the burial of Mrs. Rachel Coudon, wife of the Rev. Joseph Coudon, a clergyman of that diocese.*

A second convention of the church was held April 5th, 1781, at Chestertown. We have no journal of it. It was probably but a small assemblage, and its proceedings were perhaps but few. Its object apparently was to petition the General Assembly of the State to pass an Act for the maintenance of the Gospel agreeably to the new Constitution of Government.

In the beginning of the year 1781 the Congress of the United States recommended Thursday, May 23d, as a day of general Fasting, humiliation and prayer; and on the day appointed Dr. Smith preached a Fast sermon accordingly in Chester chapel. The text was from—

Isaiah lviii. 3: "Wherefore have we Fasted, say they, and thou seest not? Wherefore have we afflicted our soul, and thou takest no knowledge!"

---

* *Joseph Coudon, A. M.*, a native of Maryland, brought up in the Church—ordained 1781 by Bishop White, and became Rector of North Elk, Cecil, where he had been Lay Reader, and in charge of the Academy; in 1789 he added Augustine Parish, Cecil. He was a member of the General Convention and of the Standing Committee. He died in 1792, æt. 51.—*Allen's History.*

The *Rev. Ethan Allen, D. D.*, to whom I am indebted for the preceding sketch and for those various notices of the Maryland Clergy which I have used in this work, as well as for other most valuable information in every part of what relates to the Church in Maryland, is a native of Massachusetts. He was brought up a Congregationalist, but, coming into the Church, was ordained in 1819 by Bishop Kemp, and became Rector of St. John's Parish, Prince George county, Maryland, and in 1823 of Washington Parish, Washington City. In 1830 he removed to Ohio, and in 1847 returned to Maryland and became Rector of St. John's, in the valley—now Western Run Parish— Baltimore county, and in 1855 of St. Thomas Homestead, in the same county. In 1854 he was a member of the Ecclesiastical Court. In 1855 he preached the Convention sermon, and was put into the Standing Committee and became the Agent for Diocesan Missions. He was an editor of the "Theological Repertory," and has published seven sermons and addresses, "A History of St. Ann's Parish," "The Early History of Maryland," and some sixteen Biographical Memoirs. He enjoys deservedly the reputation of a learned and most amiable man.

We give some extracts from the discourse :

Frequent have been the days of humiliation and the fasts which our Rulers, in their Piety, have recommended during a few years past, and once at least every year (if not oftener) hath beheld the inhabitants of these States, in consequence of such recommendation, assembled and prostrated, before the Lord, in Prayer and Fasting : and now at length, through the impatience of our tempers, the deceitfulness of our hearts, and the weakness of our faith, we are ready, perhaps, to take up the complaint of the Jews, and in the language of despair, instead of the voice of Godly sorrow and repentance, to argue the matter with our great Creator, and to question his goodness and justice in the words of my text.

These questions in this text are awful questions, and which He only to whom they are addressed can answer. And therefore, since, by his holy prophet, he has vouchsafed an answer to these and such like questions, to the desponding Jews, in circumstances not unlike to our own ; we cannot better employ our time, on this solemn occasion, than by considering—

First—The answer given by the prophet to these questions of the Jews, and the reasons of the Almighty for the frequent rejecting of their fasts.

Secondly—How far our fasts may be chargeable with the like defects in the sight of a just and all-seeing God? And how, through His grace, our Prayers and Fastings, our Praises and Thanksgivings, may be rendered more acceptable to Him?

Although we have the Gospel in our hand, as the fulness of Divine Light and Knowledge, to which no addition can be made in our mortal state ; yet we are to adore that Providence which has given us the Old Testament also, wherein is contained an account of the dealings of the Almighty, in ancient times, with his own chosen people ; and from whence lessons are to be derived, that with profit may be applied to the instruction of mankind in all succeeding ages.

Let us then consider the situation of the Jews, after they had been first spoiled by the Assyrians, and afterwards by the Babylonians, as set forth in the forty-second chapter of this prophecy, now claiming attention. And truly melancholy and miserable it was.

"This people (saith the prophet) is robbed and spoiled. They are all of them snared in holes, and hid in prison-houses ; They are for a prey, and none delivereth ; for a spoil, and none saith, restore. Who among you will give ear to this? Who will hearken and hear? Who is there that, by the present judgments, will take warning, and strive to avert the like judgments in the time to come."

Think not that these judgments spring up from the dust, or have come upon you without a cause. "For who was it that gave Jacob for a spoil and Israel to the robbers? Did not the Lord? He against whom we have sinned?" And for what reason did the Lord thus deliver his people to be robbed and spoiled by their enemies? The prophet answers plainly—"Because they would not walk in his ways, nor be obedient unto his Laws—Therefore he hath poured upon them the fury of His anger, and the strength of battle—and it hath set him on fire round about, yet he knew it not"—That is, all the horrors and fury of war, and their very city and temple burnt to ashes by the Chaldean army, did not lead them to consider and turn again unto the Lord whom they had offended. They still continued in their sins, despised the Law of God, nor from all His visitations would they learn the righteousness.

'Tis true that so far as outward professions would go, so far as having the name of religion in their mouths, and claiming the privileges promised and covenanted by God to their Fathers for keeping the Law—so far as outward professions and claims of peculiar favour would go, they continued zealous before God—Nay, so far as days of solemn Fasting and Humiliation, on special visitations and calamities, might be thought a duty, they were not backward in the appointment and observation of them. But what sort of Fasts they were, we shall soon learn from the Sermon of the prophet, in the chapter from which my text is taken.

The first verse is an awful command to him to go among the people on the solemn Fast-day; and to warn them of their sins—"Cry aloud and spare not; lift up thy voice like a trumpet, and shew my people their transgressions, and the House of Jacob their sin." That is to say —In the boldest and most public manner, with all the freedom becoming a prophet and messenger of God, concealing nothing through Fear or Love, declare to the people their many transgressions, and especially their open hypocrisy, and "the iniquities of their Holy things."

For to all their offences they add this provoking aggravation, namely —high professions and shew of religion—"They seek me daily," or draw nigh to me in all outward ordinances, as a nation that would be thought to delight in knowing my ways and performing righteousness; and they ask of me the ordinances of justice, the rewards promised to holiness; and, wondering that they do not receive an immediate answer to their Prayers and Fastings, they cry out in the midst of every adversity—

"Wherefore have we Fasted, and thou seest not? Wherefore have we afflicted our soul, and thou takest no knowledge?"

Attend, therefore, Brethren, to the Prophet's answer to these most important questions! Astonished at their blindness to their own faults, and their expecting an immediate answer of favour from God, in all their religious approaches to Him; the Prophet reminds them that they are taught from their own scriptures, "that the sacrifices of the wicked are an abomination in God's sight; and that he will not hear sinners"

(though they call to Him in distress) without Repentance and Amendment of life.

"Behold, says the prophet, in the day of your Fast, you find pleasure and exact all your labours"—Amidst all your pretended Humiliations before me, you still find a way of gratifying your own Passions
and Covetousness, grieving and oppressing the Poor, and exacting
every labour of those over whom you rule—Nay, instead of fasting from
the Love and Fear of God—"Behold ye fast for strife and debate, and
to smite with the fist of wickedness." Your Fasts have only an outward appearance of devotion, while their true design is to promote some
selfish or party view, or to sanctify in the sight of men some enormous
wickedness; for such was the conduct of Jezebel, who, having determined to destroy Naboth, and rob him of his vineyard, ordered a fast
to be proclaimed, and to have him falsely arraigned and condemned of
blasphemy, as a part of that day's solemnity.

But, saith the Prophet, all this is abomination; and if you would
truly Fast, it shall not be as you Fast this day, to make your "Voice to
be heard on high," as if noise and outward vehemency could supply the
place of true humiliation of soul and inward piety—Instead of having
the fear and love of God reigning in your hearts; instead of bending in
humble adoration before his throne; purging away the dross of your
iniquity, and setting your whole affections, your hopes of relief and
deliverance, on the most High, "You Fast to appear righteous before
men, and to promote your own unjust views." But, continues the
prophet—"Is it such a Fast as this that the Lord has chosen—For a
man to bow down his head as a bulrush, and to spread sackcloth and
ashes under him? Wilt thou call this a Fast, and an acceptable Day
unto the Lord?" These are all vain pageantries and insignificant ceremonies of themselves, and no way tending to renew and purify the heart.

But, continues our sublime Prophet, would you know the true Fast
which the Lord hath chosen, is it not this?—

"To loose the bands of wickedness, to undo the heavy burdens; to
let the oppressed go free, and to break every yoke? Is it not to deal
thy bread to the hungry and that thou bring the poor that are out cast
to thy house? When thou seest the naked that thou cover him, and
that thou hide not thyself from thine own flesh."

Here is a glorious catalogue of Virtues, a divine frame of Soul to
bring with us in our humble approaches to God. For, without this
divine frame of Soul, what are all the Mortifications of the flesh; what
are all the penances inflicted on the Body, what is bowing down the
head to the earth, the prostrating ourselves on sackcloth, the wallowing
in ashes, or any outward rite or performance compared to this holy,
humble and benevolent frame of mind, and those deeds of Virtue,
Beneficence, Mercy and Justice which Isaiah prescribes as the true
Requisites of a fast?

As far as Heaven is exalted above the earth, so far the latter tran-
scends the former! and all Bodily Abstinences and Humiliations are of
no other value, than as they tend to Purify and Spiritualize the Inner
Man.

What would it avail us, on this solemn day, to have abstained from
our usual food and labours? What would it avail us to have humbled
ourselves and bewailed our sins, and to have prayed to God to avert
His anger from us, and to deliver us from the judgments with which we
are threatened, unless we resolve to "loose every band of wickedness;
and to do away every unjust burden which we can remove from our
fellow-creatures?" Of this we may be assured, that nothing but our
own sins can stand between us and the propitious smiles of Heaven.
When these are done away, through the mercies of Christ leading
us to repentance and amendment, we shall no longer "fast and the
Almighty not see—we shall no longer afflict our souls, and He take no
knowledge."

For what purpose God has thought fit to permit a continuance of our
present calamities, whether in judgment or mercy, or both, is a matter
which it becomes every man to consider in his own conscience. I hope
but few of the crying offences for which the Jews were reduced to the
extremest misery, and delivered over to the power of their enemies,
can be justly chargeable to the people of this land; nor can we poor
short-sighted mortals pretend to open the mysterious volumes of Providence and read its future purposes either of mercies or judgments
towards ourselves—Nor am I fond of ascribing every striking dispensation of Providence to any particular Interposition of its power. It is
sufficient for us that we consider ourselves always under its general
government—and that we look upon our own fortunes as suspended at
all times in the uplifted hand of the Almighty!

And therefore such questions as the following will never be improper
—viz. Whether an incorruptible spirit prevails in all our public
measures? Whether the cries of the Widow, the Orphan, the helpless,
never ascended, unpitied and unredressed, among us? Whether no
rapacious and extortionate men, lifted into power by us, have sought to
heap up wealth for themselves at the expense of their bleeding and
suffering country?—

But I forbear these and the like questions; because, as I believe, the
guilt of none of these things can be chargeable to any who now hear
me; so neither is the Redress of such evils so immediately in our power;
and a thorough Redress, there is reason to think, will be endeavoured by
the proper authorities—

What chiefly concerns us is, Repentance, accompanied with earnest
endeavours to amend our Lives, and fervent Prayers for Grace to enable
us to resist Temptation, "to overcome the world," and to turn from all
Iniquity. For this we may be assured of that nothing but our own

Sins and Unworthiness can come between us and the propitious smiles
of our merciful Creator. When these are done away, through the
Grace of God, leading us to Repentance and Amendment—"We shall
no longer Fast, and the Almighty not see—We shall no longer afflict
our souls, and He take no knowledge," or pity of our distress. We
shall be raised from Sorrow, and receive the blessing promised to the
Jews, on the like conduct—"Our light shall break forth as the morning,
our Health (or political salvation) shall spring forth speedily; our
Righteousness shall go before us, and the glory of the Lord shall be our
Rere-ward. We shall call, and the Lord shall answer: We shall cry,
and He shall say, Here I am! If thou take away from the midst of
Thee the Yoke, the putting forth of the Finger and speaking Vanity;
If thou draw out thy soul to the Hungry, and satisfy the afflicted Soul;
then shall thy Light rise in (or out of) obscurity, and thy darkness be
as the noon-day: The Lord shall guide thee continually, and satisfy
thy soul in drought, and make fat thy bones: Thou shalt be like
a watered Garden, and like a spring of water, whose waters fail not—
They that shall be of you (or remain of you, your reformed and happy
posterity) shall build the old waste places (that is, the Houses and
Cities, that have been destroyed and made desolate, shall again be built
up, and become the joyous dwellings of a happy people, by dependence
upon God and turning to the ways of his commandment, as warned by
his late visitation of you in judgment). Ye shall yet be raised up, as
the foundations of many generations—Millions shall spring from your
loins to possess an immense and happy country; and every Hero, every
Patriot, every Wise and Good Man who contributes his share towards
the promotion of the general welfare shall be called the Repairer of
the Breach, the Restorer of paths to dwell in."

Great and gracious God! Grant that by thus following the advice of
the Prophet to the Jews, for keeping a True Fast, and especially for
"hallowing the Sabbath Day, not doing our own ways, nor finding our
own pleasure, nor speaking our own words, but delighting in Thee, we
may receive the promised reward, and be fed with and preserved in the
Heritage of our Fathers;" and to Thy Name, with Thy blessed Son and
Holy Spirit, ONE GOD, Let the Glory and Praise be ascribed forever
and ever! Amen!

There may be, perhaps, nothing very remarkable in this discourse. It is in the good old-fashioned style of the Church of
England. It is certainly solid, serious and true. The topic being
one so very often well treated by others, I should not have made
so considerable extracts from it except to follow it by like extracts
from a sermon in contrast with it—a sermon preached in the same
Chester Chapel, Maryland, after the capture of Cornwallis, at

Yorktown, which was in fact the end of the Revolution, and when the Congress prescribed the 13th of December, 1781, as a day of general *Thanksgiving* and *Prayer* throughout the United States. This latter sermon, I think, is in one of Dr. Smith's best styles: a style, at all events, one of his most natural and easy.

The text was from Exodus xv. 1 :

"I will sing unto the Lord: for He hath triumphed gloriously."

After a few words *de circonstance* the preacher breaks forth:

Songs, or Hymns of praise and triumph, addressed to the great Creator of Heaven and earth (or to the Divinities considered by the nations that knew not the true God, as the supreme benefactors of mankind), were among the oldest and most exalted compositions of Poets, and other writers, inspired as well as uninspired.

There is something in Poetry and Music admirably suited to divine and lofty subjects; and it is natural for the soul of man, when struck with anything surprisingly great, good, or marvellously new, to break forth beyond the common modes of speech, into the most rapturous strains of expression, accompanied with correspondent Attitudes of Body and Modulations of Voice. Even the untutored savages around us furnish proofs of this!

Hence it arose, that Poetry and Music were originally appropriated and confined to the worship of the Supreme God, or the divinities of the nations, to whom He was not known; and the best and wisest men of all ages have had recourse to divine Hymns and Spiritual Songs in the effusions of the soul to the almighty Lord of heaven and earth.

Ere yet temples were built, or fixed hours of devotion set apart; when the voice of Conscience could be heard, and the busy scenes of Art had not seduced away the attention of Man from the grand scenes of Nature; the great Progenitors of our Race, and Patriarchs of Mankind, as they tended their flocks onward from pasture to pasture, as they beheld the refreshing Rains descend, and the Sun, in his turn, pour down his refulgent beams, to vivify and fertilize the earth, and to rejoice the heart of man and of every living creature; or when they were struck with any more surprising effect or manifestation of Almighty Power and Goodness, kindling their admiration and gratitude—that auspicious moment they embraced, as the Tongue or Organ of Praise for the whole Animal Creation on earth, and rapt into sacred extasy, poured forth their unpremeditated strains to that adorable God, the author of all this bounty, who formed the earth, the Sun and Moon which they beheld; that poised the clouds in air, that enriched their bosoms with treasure and bade them drop down in fatness, to rejoice herb, and beast, and man.

These divine emanations of the soul, in strains of praise and gratitude to heaven, are surely nothing less than the express inspirations of God himself, through the secret agency of his grace, and the power of his works, in the hearts of men, in those first ages of simplicity and love; and, as this was the first origin of Poetry, Music, and Songs of praise before God, it were to be wished that, among all our other improvements, we had not too much improved away this pure primitive intercourse with the Father of Light and Spirits! Yet still, we are to reflect that this is a world of imperfection; and that, as there are advantages, there are also inconveniences, to every stage of its progress, from original simplicity to its last stage of improvement and refinement.

But to proceed; some of the most beautiful pieces of divine poesy are left us by the eastern nations, and especially by the Hebrews; in whose compositions of this kind we are more directly concerned, as they are recorded for us in our Bibles. One of the most exalted of these is the Song of Moses, from which I have taken my text—composed in a transport of joy, admiration and gratitude, when he beheld the Mighty One of Israel divide the great deep before his people, and lead them through on dry ground; while the waters closed with irresistible fury behind them, and whelmed their proud pursuers in the bottom of the sea!

This was a subject marvellous indeed, and astonishing beyond a parallel! At the blast of the nostrils of the God of heaven, the course of Nature was controuled. A mighty ocean divided itself before the Lord. The waters left their channel in the heart of the sea. They were gathered up on either side, wave on wave, heap on heap, and stood arrested or congealed in liquid mountains at the nod of the Almighty! The children of Israel passed through on dry ground. Immediately the waters closed with irresistible fury; and the hosts of their proud pursuers were covered, overwhelmed, consumed—as a stone that sinks to the bottom.

"Thus the Lord saved Israel that day, out of the hand of the Egyptians, and Israel saw the Egyptians dead upon the sea-shore—

"Then sang Moses and the children of Israel this Song unto the Lord, saying—I will sing unto the Lord for he hath triumphed gloriously. The Lord is my strength and my Song; and he is become my salvation. He is my God and I will prepare Him an habitation; my father's God, and I will exalt him. The Lord is a man of war; the Lord is his name." *

In such strains as these did the raptured leader of Israel, and all his host of followers, celebrate the God of their fathers, on their deliverance from the rage of Pharaoh; leaving an example for all succeeding ages on the like grand occasions.

A like sacred example we have in the great festival sacrifice and

---

* Exodus, chapter xv.

thanksgiving of David, on receiving back the Ark of God, the great
pledge and deposition of the civil and religious privileges of his nation.
On that happy occasion * "He and all the Elders of the people, and
the Levites, and the Captains over thousands, appeared in solemn procession, with instruments of music, psalteries, and harps, and cymbals,
and the sound of the cornet and of the trumpet, and the lifting up the
voice with joy; and David himself came singing and dancing before
them, as a testimony of his true piety and gratitude; though Saul's
daughter, beholding out at a window, and not animated with the same
godly rapture, despised or laughed at him in her heart as guilty of
levity."

But why should I mention more examples? The same Reason that
calls us to humble ourselves before God, on the marks of his Displeasure, calls us to rejoice before Him, with Thanksgiving, on the
marks of his Favour. For a series of years past we have had many
days of weeping and sorrow and fasting; and the hardest heart must
bleed to recount the scenes of suffering and anguish and distress which
we have beheld. In every city, in every village, nay, in every private
house and family, long hath the voice of sorrow been heard, for heroes
slain in battle; kindred hands imbrued in kindred blood; fathers deprived of sons; sons of fathers; wives of husbands; brothers of brothers;
and friends of friends.

But we are this day called to express our gratitude to God on events
of a more pleasing nature, the Success of the allied armies of these
United States, almost in every quarter of our country, by land and by
Sea; the blessing the fruits of the earth, and giving us plentiful harvests; and, particularly, the capture of a General † of the first rank,
with his whole army, under the direction of our illustrious commander-
in-chief; yielding us the happy prospect of a speedy restoration of our
former peace and tranquillity, upon solid and lasting foundations.

Although we dare not call this deliverance a miracle in our favour, or
in any degree comparable to the miracle for which the song in our text
was offered to the God of Israel; yet when we reflect on the gloomy
prospect which lay before us a few months ago; when we expected the
war at our doors, and all its concomitant ravages and distress; when we
beheld our Fields waving with Plenty, and almost despaired of reaping
them in Peace, or enjoying their Fruits in Safety; can we forbear
praising the Lord of Hosts, the God of our salvation, for the deliverance he hath wrought for us, and the security we enjoy? Can we forbear to adore that Providence, which, by means almost unexpected to
us, "on the same day; nay almost at the same hour, brought Fleets
from the South, and Armies from the North, for our protection and
aid?" Can we cease to admire that magnanimity and steady perse-

---

* 1 Chronicles xv. 16, etc.   † Lord Cornwallis.

4

verance, which enabled our allied forces to accomplish this great deliverance; almost without any bloodshed of their Enemies; and to exercise all the Virtues of Moderation and Christian Heroism, even amidst the Triumphs of Victory?

This great event hath already been celebrated in Camps, in Cities, in Towns and Villages, by separate and voluntary marks of joy and gratitude—But we are this day called to join, with one voice, throughout all these United States, as a people connected in one great and common interest to celebrate this goodness of the Almighty; and the ministers of the altar, by their sacred office, are to stand as the mouth or organ of the people, to offer up and convey their public gratitude to the throne of the Omnipotent!

The joy of this day, therefore, Brethren, must not be that noisy and tumultuous joy, which consists in outward actions; the glare and pomp of victory; the display of the spoils of War and Enemies; Shouts of Triumph; Illuminations; Feastings, and carnal Mirth. It must be a Religious Joy; the Joy of the Heart before the Lord; mixt with a holy and reverential Fear. We are to rejoice in our prosperity, but yet chiefly as we consider it to be the means of Peace and Safety; and, therefore, while the final issue of things remain undetermined, although we may rejoice, we must rejoice with fear and trembling; lest our future Unworthiness should provoke the Almighty to withhold his promised blessings, and lengthen out the day of our visitation for the further correction of our sins, and the manifestation of his power and goodness.

Thus did Israel rejoice on their great deliverance, referred to in our text.

For, "Israel saw that great work, which the Lord did upon the Egyptians; and the people feared the Lord, and his servant Moses.— Who, said they, is like unto Thee, O Lord, amongst the Gods? who is like unto Thee; glorious in holiness, fearful in praises, doing wonders?"

In this spirit runs the proclamation for this day's solemnity, which has been recited above.

Let us therefore lift up our voices to God, who, for our deliverance, "hath triumphed gloriously. The horse and his rider hath he thrown into the sea. The Lord is our strength and salvation, and he shall be the subject of our song. He is our God and we will prepare Him an habitation; our father's God, and we will exalt Him. The right hand of the Lord is become glorious in power, and hath dashed in pieces the enemy. They said, we will pursue, we will overtake, we will divide the spoil."—But the weakness of God is stronger than the strength of proudest man—When his people were but few, and strangers in a foreign wilderness; when they went from nation to nation in search of a settlement for themselves and their unborn posterity, the Lord suffered no man to do them wrong; yea He reproved even Kings for their sake.

" Blessed be the Lord God of Israel, for ever and ever : and all the people said Amen, and praised the Lord ! "

Be these great examples of Praise and Thanksgiving followed by us this day; for surely whoever would be called a subject of these states, and is content to hold his Liberty and Property under their protection, could never desire to see their peace, however dear, established on Conquest or Force, by any power upon earth ; and therefore we must rejoice when the Almighty in his providence appears to blast and defeat the most powerful reiterated attempts for reducing a free People, to a Government at will, and unconditional Submission.

After the days of mourning which we have beheld, the short period of about nine months hath produced such a series of favourable events, for these infant states, as astonishes ourselves ; and, among our posterity, will scarcely be believed.   Had the incidents which have taken place been but proposed to our hopes a twelve-month ago, by any person living, we should have thought that he mocked our Credulity, or insulted our Distress.   But all things are possible with God ; and when the affairs of a People are at the worst, then is often the time when the mighty One of Israel is pleased to interpose, and therein to " triumph gloriously."

In such cases, it is our indispensable duty to mark the manifestations of his power with humble reverence ; and to rejoice before him exceedingly ; but still, as was said before, we must " rejoice with trembling," because the same almighty Power which raised us up in our low estate, can dash us to the ground again, if, like the proud Assyrian of old, we begin to boast ourselves, and say that our own Hand, or the strength of our own Arm, got us the victory.

Wherefore, Brethren ! let me, in conclusion, as is my duty, earnestly exhort you, in your best and most prosperous estate, to be clothed with Humility, and the Fear of God, in the fulness of his Love ; ascribing only to Him all power and glory and victory.

When we come to give Thanks unto God, for blessings received, or to Pray to Him for success in our undertakings, it must be with a conviction that all the Events of this world, and the fortune and fate of all the People and Nations in it, are in his supreme disposal !   Let us, therefore, be persuaded that the People and Nations, who most fervently and earnestly follow His holy Laws, and support the Purity and Majesty of that Divine Religion, which he hath made known to them, will most effectually serve their country, by obtaining His favour.

In the present moment of trial, all who profess to love their country, would certainly wish to shew that Love by their Courage and Heroism, when duly called upon to exercise them.   But these glorious qualities can stand upon no foundation but a Conscience at Peace with God, and a Conviction that we are engaged in His divine Cause.   I trust that we have long since satisfied our own Reason and Conscience, that the cause in which we are engaged is not grounded on the wicked passions of Ambition, Malice, Revenge, Cruelty, and the like; but that, in sight of Men and Angels, and of Him, who is above all the quires of Angels, we contend for the security of those sacred and unalienable Rights, which the good Providence of God called us to inherit.   These we are never to desert, but to strive for them, at every peril, with a holy and unquenchable Zeal; persevering, if need be, even unto Death.   Every People and Country have native and essential Rights, which neither in conscience, nor in duty to God and themselves, they can tamely surrender.   When Liberty is invaded, when Property is insecure, when Devastation, and Plunder, and all the Horrors of War, are around a People, it is their sacred Duty, by every brave and heroic Exertion, to repel such Iniquity; and to seek for the Re-establishment of Peace and Safety, by every means in their power, hostile or otherwise.   In such cases, Resistance is the voice of Nature, and of God.   We have resisted —and Resisted even unto Blood; and through the blessing of God, have repelled the danger, and opened the Prospect of future Safety— opened it so far indeed, that, as already observed, our present Hopes, compared with our former Fears, in the short period of about nine months, have converted a kind of temporary Despondency into a well-grounded Confidence, in the Strength of the Almighty. . . . . .

Lost, therefore, to every sentiment of religious Gratitude should we be, if we did not this day, adore that Providence which has accomplished such a mighty Salvation for our country!   And especially, let us remember, as I hinted before, to temper our Joy, with the consideration, that even the best Fruits of Victory are beset with thorns; and that what are days of Rejoicing to some, are but days of Mourning to others, whose dearest Relatives, have given their lives, as a sacrifice, in the Contest.   This world is a chequered scene, and we are to expect no pure Bliss in it.   But let us act the part of good Citizens, good Men and good Christians; and then we may safely trust the Issue to the Direction of that Almighty Being, who is supremely, just, wise, and holy!

Dr. Smith entertained for his family connections in general a warm regard, and in the event of their death, usually made some record of the fact.   I find in his "Diary" this entry, May 3d, 1781:

"John Wemyss died at this date, at Glasgow, Scotland.   He was a Lieutenant in the 42d Royal Highlanders, 2d Battalion, now 73d." *

---

* I infer that this John Wemyss was a relative of Dr. Smith's wife, as she (as will be seen hereafter) was connected with the family of the Earl of Wemyss.   Lieutenant John Wemyss had served in America with Bouquet, and had been an officer in Montgomery's Highlanders.   He had also furnished Dr. Smith with much of the matter out of which he compiled his account of the expedition against the Ohio Indians.   James Wemyss, who was an uncle to Dr. Smith's wife, was also with this expedition.   He was stationed in New York, but returned to Scotland and became the Fifth Earl of Wemyss.

During the year 1781 Dr. Smith, who had been elected Grand
Secretary of the Masonic Grand Lodge of Pennsylvania, was requested to prepare for the press a new edition, in an abridged form,
of the "Book of Constitutions." This he did, making also a Preface
to the work. The minutes of a meeting held November 22, 1781,
give us these records :

> The Abridgement of the Book of Constitutions being read, the same
> was unanimously approved of, and ordered to be printed; and also, that
> the Thanks of this Grand Lodge be given to our beloved Brother, the
> Reverend William Smith, D. D., Grand Secretary, for the great Care
> and Attention he has bestowed in revising and abridging the said Book
> of Constitutions.
>
> *Resolved*, That the Mason's Arms be engraved as a frontispiece for
> the book, and in case our beloved and illustrious brother Gen¹ Wash-
> ington permit it to be dedicated to him, that his Excellency's arms be
> engraved and prefixed to the dedication.

The Dedication to General Washington is found in the book.
It is thus :

> To his Excellency George Washington, Esq., General and Commander
> in Chief of the Armies of the United States of America:
> In Testimony, as well of his exalted Services to his Country, as of
> that noble Philanthropy which distinguishes him
> among Masons.
> The following Constitutions of the most ancient and honour-
> able Fraternity of Free and Accepted Masons, by
> Order and in Behalf of the Grand Lodge
> of Pennsylvania, &c., is
> dedicated,
> By his Excellency's most humble Servant,
> and faithful Brother,
> William Smith, Grand Secretary.
> *June* 24, 1782.

The Preface to the book, as we have said, is from Dr. Smith's
pen. It is curious as illustrating the range of his information and
interests. To those readers who take pleasure in the recondite
subject of Free Masonry, it will have perhaps attraction. For them
chiefly I give it here :

> The design of the following work (according to the appointment of
> the Grand Lodge) is only to extract, abridge and digest under distinct
> heads, the several parts of Ahiman Rezon, so as to be most intelligible

and useful to operative Masons in America. The officers of Lodges, and those members who wish to be more completely learned in the grand science and sublimer mysteries of Ancient Masonry, will think it their duty, as opportunities offer, to furnish themselves, or their Lodges, with at least one copy of all approved and duly authorised books of Masonry, which may be published by the learned Lodges, or illustrious brethren, in different languages and countries of the world, from time to time.

Upon this plan, therefore, it will not be necessary to detain the reader with any long account of the antiquity of the Royal Art. Certain it is, that when the first man was formed in the image of God, the principles of Masonry, as a divine gift from heaven, were stamped upon his heart by the great Architect of the universe. The same principles were after-wards renewed and placed upon everlasting foundations, by the wisdom of his glorious Son; and they are daily cultivated in every soul that delights in order, harmony, brotherly love, morality and religion, through the grace and goodness of his divine Spirit—thrice blessed Three, in one eternal God-head!

Thus instructed from above, the sublime operative and mechanic part of Masonry was practised by Adam in the bowers of Paradise, and propagated among chosen men of his posterity, in a lesser or greater degree of perfection, through the different nations of the world (as learned brethren have fully shewn), nor was the noble art lost by the Israelites either during their peregrination in Egypt, or journeyings in the deserts of Arabia. For there it pleased the supreme Architect to inspire those great Master Masons, Bezaleel and Aholiab, and to put "wisdom and understanding into their heart, and to teach them how to work all manner of work, for the service of the *Sanctuary, and erecting that most glorious Tent or Tabernacle, wherein the divine Shechinah vouchsafed to promise a special residence; which, although not of stone or brick, was framed by Geometry, a most beautiful piece of architecture (and afterwards the model of Solomon's Temple) accord-ing to the pattern that God had shewn to Moses in the Mount."

And thus Moses, a man supremely skill'd in all the Egyptian learn-ing, who, to his other titles, added that of King of Jesurun, being divinely taught in the art of building, became Grand Master-mason or Builder among the Israelites, "and often marshalled them into a regular and general Lodge, while in the wilderness; and gave them wise charges and orders, had they been but well observed."—But of this no more must be mentioned.

We pass on to speak more particularly of Solomon's Temple, at the building of which, under the divine direction, were displayed, in an

---

* Exodus xxxvi.

unparalleled degree, all the glory, beauty and sublimity of Masonry;
there being no fewer than * three thousand six hundred Master Masons,
eighty thousand Fellow Craftsmen, and seventy thousand Labourers,
employed in this magnificent and Heaven-conducted work.

But above all the rest, our Grand Master Hiram shone superlatively
great, as chief Director, and the most accomplished Mason upon earth.
For to this character of him the holy Scripture gives testimony, in the
recommendatory letter which Hiram, King of Tyre, sent with him to
King Solomon,—"And now I have sent a cunning man, endued with
understanding, the son of a woman of the daughters of Dan; and his
father was a man of Tyre, skilful to work in gold and in silver, in brass,
in iron, in stone and in timber, in purple, in blue and in fine linen, and
in crimson; also to grave any manner of graving, and to find out every
device which shall be put to him with thy cunning men and with the
cunning men of my Lord David, thy Father." †

Thus we see that our great Master Hiram was accomplished in almost
every art and science then known upon earth; as all those should aspire
to be, who wish to become useful Masons, the Masters of Lodges, and
the Rulers or Instructors of others. It is here further to be observed,
that so highly was this Chief of Masons honoured by his master the
King of Tyre, that in all probability he had called him Hiram, or
Huram, after his own royal name.

It would be foreign to our present design (as already hinted) to mention the illustrious Masons that in all ages, from the building of Solomon's Temple down to the ages of general darkness and barbarity, have
adorned the different countries of the world; as Syria, Mesopotamia,
Assyria, Chaldea, Babylonia, Media, Persia, Arabia, Africa, lesser Asia,
Grecia, Rome, &c., &c. The remains of temples, pyramids and mighty
towers, yet declare their builders' glory; and, even in Gothic ages, the
chief monuments of taste and grandeur are to be seen in the works of
Masonry and Architecture.

Seven hundred years ago, William, called the Conqueror, built the
Tower of London; his son, William Rufus, built Westminster Hall;
which, as one room or Lodge, is said to be the largest in the known
world;—which grand monuments of Gothic Architecture were all raised
in the taste and spirit, delivered down from those ancient Craftsmen
and learned Masons sent into England, at the request of the Saxon
Kings, by Charles Martell, King of France, more than one thousand
years ago.

But for the further instruction of the reader, concerning the foundation and antiquity of what is called York Masonry, the following record,
written in the reign of Edward IV. of England, viz., three hundred

---

* 1 Kings v. 15; 2 Chron. xi. 18.   † 2 Chron. ii. 13, 14.

years ago, is here inserted; which, with another famous record, published by the great Philosopher John Locke, Esq.; (and likewise herein
after inserted) will be enough on this subject.

"Although the ancient records of the brotherhood in England were
many of them destroyed or lost in the wars of the Saxons and Danes,
yet it is known that King Athelstan, the grandson of Alfred the Great,
who was a mighty architect, the first true King of England, and who
translated the holy Bible into the Saxon tongue, when he had brought
the land into rest and peace, built many great works, and encouraged
many Masons from France, who were appointed overseers thereof, and
brought with them the charges and regulations of the Lodges preserved
since the Roman times. These Masons likewise prevailed with the King
to improve the Constitution of the English Lodges according to the
foreign model, and to increase the wages of working Masons.

"The said King Athelstan's youngest son Edwin being taught
Masonry, and taking upon him the charges of a Master Mason, for the
love he had to the said craft, and the honourable principles whereon it
is grounded, purchased a free charter of his father; giving the Masons
a right of correction among themselves (as it was anciently expressed)
or a freedom and power to regulate themselves, to amend what might
happen amiss, and to hold an Yearly Communication, or General
Assembly.

"In virtue of this charter, Prince Edwin summoned all the Masons in
England to meet him in a congregation at York; who accordingly attended his summons, and composed a General Lodge, of which he was
Grand Master; and having brought with them and collected together
all the writings and records which were extant concerning Masonry
(some in Latin, some in French, and other languages) from the contents of the whole, that Assembly or grand Congregation did frame the
Constitution and Charges of the English or great ancient York Lodge;
and made a law to preserve and observe the same in all future time,
ordaining likewise good pay for working Masons.—And the said constitution, charges and laws, having been afterwards seen and perused by
Henry the VI. and by the Lords of his Council (most of whom were
Masons) were consented to and allowed to be right, good and reasonable to be holden, as they were thus drawn out and collected from the
records of ancient times." The great Philosopher, Mr. Locke, already
mentioned, likewise tells us that the famous manuscript, on the antiquity of Free Masonry, found in the Bodleian Library (herein after
published) is said to have been originally in the "hand-writing of the
same King Henry."

'Tis true, while this Prince was an infant, and his Parliament, it is
believed, not very wise (learning being then deemed a crime, and
Geometry passing for Conjuration), a law was passed which deprived
Masons of some of their ancient charter privileges, by forbidding them
"to confederate themselves into Chapters and Congregations."

"Whereas (says the law) by yearly Congregations and Confederacies, made by the Masons in their General Assemblies, the good course and effect of the statutes for labourers be openly violated and broken, in subversion of the law, and to the great damage of all the commons, our Sovereign Lord the King, willing in this case to provide a remedy, by the advice and assent aforesaid, and at the special request of the commons, hath ordained and established that such Chapters and Congregations shall not hereafter be holden; and if any such be made, that they cause such Chapters and Congregations to be assembled and holden, if they thereof be convict, shall be judged for felons, and that the other Masons that come to such Chapters and Congregations be punished by imprisonment of their bodies, and make fine and ransom at the King's will."—*Co. Inst.* 3.

But, as was said before, this Parliament does not seem to have been made up of many wise heads, and tradition informs us also that they were too much influenced by the ignorant Monks and illiterate Clergy (not like those of modern days, or of the early ages, who were many of them eminent Masons and friends to Masons) but a sett of men, who thought they had a right to know all men's secrets, by means of confession; and therefore hated the Masons, and represented them as dangerous to the state, because they kept their own secrets, and made no use of Confessors at all. But the King, when he came to man's estate, approved the Masonic Constitution, as above set forth, without any regard to the said Act of Parliament; which the great Lord Coke tells us is now of no effect—"For," says he, "all the Statutes concerning labourers, whereunto this act doth refer, are repealed by the Statute V. Eliz. Chap. IV.; whereby the cause and end of making this Act is taken away, and consequently this act is become of no force or effect; for *cessante ratione Legis, cessat ipsa Lex.* And the indictment of felony upon this Statute must contain, that those Chapters and Congregations were to the violating and breaking of the good course and effect of the Statutes of labourers; which now cannot be so alledged, because these Statutes be repealed." This quotation is thought to confirm the tradition that this most learned Judge really belonged to the ancient Lodge, and was a faithful Brother.

We read further, that Queen Elizabeth once entertained some considerable prejudices concerning the truly ancient and honourable body of Free Masons. We know it was part of this Queen's character, among all her rare and princely virtues, to be of a jealous temper, with a great curiosity to be Mistress of all secrets, and an enemy to all meetings or assemblies of her subjects, whose business she was not duly apprized of. Being told by some of her ignorant and busy meddling Courtiers, that the Masons had secrets that could not be revealed to her, and altho' as a woman, she could govern a Nation, yet she could not govern a Lodge, nor be made Grand Master (or Mistress) of Masons; she therefore sent an armed force to break up the annual Grand Lodge at York, on St. John's Day, December 27th, 1561. Sir Thomas Sackville, then Grand Master, instead of being dismayed at such an unexpected visit, gallantly told the officers that nothing could give him greater pleasure than seeing them in the Grand Lodge, as it would give him an opportunity of convincing them that Free Masonry was the most honourable institution that ever was founded, and truly consonant to Laws both divine and moral. The consequence was that he made the chief men Free Masons; who, on their return, made an honourable report to the Queen, so that she never more attempted to dislodge or disturb them, but esteemed them as a peculiar sort of men, that cultivated peace and friendship, arts and sciences, without meddling in the affairs of Church or State.

Thus hath Masonry flourished through different ages in the old world, and hath obtained a very noble and solid foundation in this new or American world. Were it necessary, we might proceed to shew that from this ancient Fraternity, "the Societies or Orders of Warlike Knights, and even some religious Orders and Societies, have borrowed many of their wisest institutions and most solemn usages. For none of them were better instituted, more decently installed, or did more sacredly observe their Laws and Charges, than the Free and Accepted Masons have done; and therefore their whole body, thus cemented, resembles a strong and well-built Arch, having as its members and parts, for time immemorial, Princes and Nobles, Gentlemen, Clergymen, learned Scholars and Artists of the first rank, in all countries."*

Three dozen of the books of the Constitutions were presented to Dr. Smith "for the great care and attention which he has had in revising the same." This "Ahiman Rezon" is still known as "Smith's." It has a beautifully engraved frontispiece, and is a book much valued by collectors. The preface to it has been the subject of eulogy in my hearing by the accomplished chairman of the Library Committee of the Grand Lodge of Pennsylvania, Mr. C. E. Meyer, for the skill with which it states matters long the subject of difference between certain Grand Lodges.

---

* The title page is thus: "AHIMAN REZON | abridged and digested: | as a | Help to all that are, or would be | Free and Accepted Masons. | To which is added | A SERMON, | Preached in Christ-Church, Philadelphia, | At a General Communication, | Celebrated, agreeable to the Constitutions, on | Monday, December 28, 1778, | as the Anniversary of St. John the Evangelist. | Published by order of | the Grand Lodge of Pennsylvania, | By William Smith, D. D. | Philadelphia: | Printed by Hall and Sellers. | M,DCC,LXXXIII."

CHAPTER XLII.

DR. SMITH PREACHES A FUNERAL DISCOURSE ON THE REV. HUGH NEILL, OF
WHOM SOME ACCOUNT IS GIVEN—DEATH OF MRS. BLACKWELL, WIFE OF THE
REV. MR. BLACKWELL—NOTICE AND ELEGIAC STANZAS UPON HER DEATH
ATTRIBUTED TO DR. SMITH--THE CONVENTION OF 1782 IN MARYLAND—
SUCCESS OF KENT COUNTY SCHOOL, AND DEVELOPMENT OF WASHINGTON
COLLEGE, MARYLAND—DEATH OF WILLIAM MOORE, ESQ., OF MOORE HALL.

IN the account which we have given in our former volume of
St. Paul's Church, in Third street, Philadelphia, the matrix of the
low-church parishes in Pennsylvania, we refer to the Rev. Hugh
Neill, one of the most respectable of the clergy of this Methodistical side of the Episcopal body.   Mr. Neill was born in New
Jersey, and had been bred a Presbyterian, and preached in that
sect in his native State until 1749, when he went to England and
took orders in the Church, and was licensed by the Bishop of
London for Pennsylvania, March 26th, 1750.   He was sent,
however, by the Society for the Propagation of the Gospel, to
Dover, in Delaware, which, indeed, then made a part of Pennsylvania, and here he remained until 1760, when he was transferred
to Trinity Church, Oxford, Pennsylvania, preaching on Sunday
evenings at Germantown.   In 1765 he officiated in Philadelphia at
St. Paul's, and in 1766, having received from Governor Sharpe, of
Maryland, an induction as rector of the parish of St. Paul's in
Queen Anne county, he left Philadelphia for that charge, having
refused to receive any pay for his services.   In order to show their
appreciation of this kindness, the vestry of St. Paul's, Philadelphia,
presented him with a piece of plate bearing the following
inscription:

The Gift of
St. Paul's Church in Philadelphia
to
the REV. HUGH NEILL,
in gratitude for his disinterested ministerial
services to that Church.
A. D. 1766.

In 1773, refusing to take the oath of allegiance to the new Government, he left his charge. He returned, however, in 1780. By his last will he left the above-mentioned piece of silver plate to St. Paul's Church. He ministered at St. Paul's, in Queen Anne county, Md., sixteen or seventeen years. Though he was, as I suppose, of the school of Wesley and Whitfield, and though Dr. Smith, according to Mr. Neill's own account, treated him, on one occasion at least, very roughly,* he had so many good qualities of personal character, that Dr. Smith came at last to entertain for him a sincere regard, and apparently did so even while he was in Philadelphia and connected with St. Paul's there, a parish in which Dr. Smith was no more a favorite than were any other regularly behaved clergy of the Church of England. After Dr. Smith went to Maryland, he met often his ancient acquaintance of Philadelphia, and at his death preached, January 23d, 1782, an affecting sermon at his funeral. Dr. Smith's text, from Genesis xv. 15—"Thou shalt go to my fathers in peace; thou shalt be buried in a good old age"—suggests that Mr. Neill at his death had attained to venerable years.

We have mentioned in our first volume the interest which Dr. Smith took while in Philadelphia in "the mission at Gloucester," as it was called; a mission in New Jersey, of the Society for the Propagation of the Gospel. With the mission at Burlington (N. J.), occupied by Dr. Smith's accomplished and much valued friend, Dr. Jonathan Odell, it was one of the important missionary stations of New Jersey, especially in its aspects to the Church in Philadelphia. The Rev. Nathaniel Evans, a favorite pupil of Dr. Smith, and a graduate of the College at Philadelphia, a young man of singular talents, accomplishment and piety, had been the first occupant of it, entering upon the mission in 1765, and dying there two years afterwards, in 1767, deeply lamented by all who knew him.† Dr. Smith edited his literary remains, thus showing his regard for him. Dr. Smith was thus a frequent visitor at Gloucester, where he became intimately acquainted with the most important families of the region, including more particularly among them that of Mr. Joseph and Ann Harrison. Dr. Smith took much pains to re-establish the missions after Mr.

* See Perry's Historical Collections of Pennsylvania, page 319.
† For a sketch of, see vol. 1st, pp. 434, 479.

Evans' death. The Rev. David Griffith, afterwards Bishop elect of Virginia, was in it; only, however, for a short time. The Rev. John Lyons also occupied it for a short time, but neither with effect. In 1772 the Rev. Robert Blackwell entered into charge— a young gentleman of high integrity, amiable disposition, sound sense, solid learning and unquestioned piety. These excellent qualities made him a favorite with all who knew him, and especially with Dr. White and Dr. Smith.* Mr. Blackwell remained at Gloucester until the mission was broken up by the Revolution, when, becoming a chaplain in the army, he went to the Valley Forge, and during the winter of 1777–78—which Dr. Smith passed close to him at Norristown—the two clergymen were, of course, in more or less consultation as to the exercises of their office; Dr. White being at Yorktown with the Congress, as we have already stated in an early part of this volume. In 1781 Mr. Blackwell became one of the ministers of the United Churches of Christ and St. Peter's, in Philadelphia, a post which he occupied with much dignity and usefulness for thirty years, and in which, as in the College of Philadelphia, of which he was afterwards a trustee, he was of necessity in frequent relations with Dr. Smith. While at Gloucester, he became attached to Miss Rebecca Harrison, a daughter of the family of which we have spoken, and for which Dr. Smith had cherished a high regard;—a young lady of unusual attractiveness and merit. She died on Monday, the 25th of February, 1782, a year or two after her marriage, in giving birth to a daughter, who survived. An obituary notice of her and some elegiac stanzas addressed to her sister, and attributed to Dr. Smith, may properly be here inserted as an illustration alike of his sympathetic heart and ever-ready and accomplished pen. Such things are indeed in one sense of no great value. Nevertheless, like a good deal that I have sought to preserve in my volumes, they show a refinedness of feeling in our early society, and an elegance in our early ephemeral literature which it would be well for our own day if they had descended in a more abundant measure to it.

Death of Mrs. Rebecca Blackwell.

On Monday morning last, the wife of the Rev. Mr. BLACKWELL, Assistant Minister of the United Churches, Philadelphia, was safely

* For a sketch of this respected gentleman, see Appendix No. I.

delivered of a daughter at his house in Gloucester to the great joy of his family and friends. But the pleasing hopes arising from the happy event were soon changed to the deepest sorrow on perceiving an alteration which indicated her approaching dissolution ; and, notwithstanding that the best medical assistance was procured, she expired about four o'clock the same afternoon.

Her remains were deposited on Thursday, attended by a great concourse of friends and acquaintances to pay the last melancholy offices to a character so deservedly esteemed and beloved.

Blessed by nature with a comprehensive understanding and most lively fancy, she had improved the one by an excellent education, and refined the other by a solidity of judgment uncommon to her sex. With the former she ever promoted the cause of virtue, and with the latter made folly ridiculous, and put vice out of countenance. Adorned with every social virtue, she felt the most exalted sentiments of friendship; and with a delicacy peculiar to herself, selected such to share her confidence as were capable of the same refined ideas, while the tenderness of her heart melted at the tale of woe, and from the child of want her face was never turned aside. When the voice of nature and of reason dictated a change of condition, she did not place her affections on pomp or wealth, but bestowed them on one whose propriety of sentiment and purity of morals were consonant to her own. And the happiness of both was such as might be expected from a union where kindred merits and mutual esteem had ripened friendship into love. Thus, though in possession, yet from a conviction of the instability of human happiness, she had remembered her Creator in the days of her youth, and devoted herself to the practice of those essential duties of religion without the performance of which no true felicity can be enjoyed here, or a happy immortality be hoped for hereafter. Thus living and thus beloved, by a stroke unexpected to her friends, but not sudden to herself, whose lamp was always burning, on the 25th of February, 1782, and in the 25th year of her age, was this amiable pattern of Christian virtues, to the unspeakable grief of her relations, and the irreparable loss of her husband, removed from this transitory scene.

Not to be affected with and lament a blow so severe, would discover a want of those feelings which constitute the dignity of human nature.

TO STELLA.*

UPON A LATE MELANCHOLY BEREAVEMENT.

No more my fancy charms, ye dreams
Of earthly bliss :   More awful themes
　　Demand a serious strain.
Your grief sublimer thoughts inspire
Than trifling mirth or vain desires,
　　Or pleasure's gayest scenes.

---

* Miss Sarah Harrison, I suppose; sister to Mrs. Blackwell.—H. W. S.

The solemn spectacle is o'er,
Yet, bowed with grief, you still deplore,
   With pining anguish, mourn.
Forever flow your streaming eyes,
Your bosom heaves, with deepest sighs,
   For her who can't return.

She is no more !   The fatal blow
Filled every breast with poignant woe.
   Then what must Stella feel !
Whose heart, by strong affection swayed,
With fond affection was repaid,
   And friendship's warmest zeal.

On her was every grace bestowed,
Soft from her lips persuasion flowed,
   And charmed each listening ear.
Like music through the veins it thrilled,
Each breast with sweetest rapture filled,
   And smoothed the brow of care.

But now to parent earth consigned,
Oh ! where shall we her equal find,
   The joys of life to crown !
Her loved remains in dust reposed,
Her radiant eyes forever closed,
   Where mildest influence shone.

Oh, could the grateful *Muse's* strain
Console the grief, assuage the pain,
   Which fills your tender breast—
From sorrow could she draw a smile,
Or keen affection's pangs beguile,
   The thought would make her blest !

Yet can, dear maid, RELIGION charm
Death of its sting, despair disarm:
   TO THAT RESOURCE APPLY.
RELIGION calms the pangs of grief,
In HER alone we find relief,
   When all we value die.

But turn, oh, turn your weeping eyes
To where her lovely infant lies
   That claims a mother's care !
A mother's care she'll never know,
But Stella will that love bestow,
   And guard her infant years.

Sweet, smiling babe !   Oh, may thy breast
With peace and harmony be blest !
And may thy Friend, thy parent see
Thy mother's graces bloom in thee,
   And all HER virtues share.*

---

* This prayer was abundantly granted.   The child, who survived, became, somewhere I suppose about the year 1800, the wife of Mr. George Willing, and lived till
the year 1852, I think; honored and beloved by as many as ever knew her.- -H. W. S.

Not long after this event, on the 30th of May, 1782, died Dr.
Smith's own relative—his father-in-law—William Moore, Esq., of
Moore Hall, Chester county, Pennsylvania. I have spoken of
him, and described some incidents in his life, in my former volume.* He belonged to a class of men in Pennsylvania who constituted the most thorough gentry that the Province or State ever
had, but whose fame, and indeed whose very names, have almost
wholly disappeared from its popular history. Their biographies,
however, have been written—written only, however, in that kind
of ink called "invisible." It is an ink not more legible than water
when first put to paper. It lasts, however; and when that sort of
fluid, which gave at once its full black force to the eye, has grown
dim and finally faded quite away, *it* will, I think, grow more and
more bright and strong, and present a history full of interest. I
venture to offer, in an Appendix,† the embryo of a chapter to
whomsoever shall be the future collector of these annals of our
ancient gentility.

In April, 1782, a third Convention of the Church in Maryland
was held. This one was held in Baltimore. We do not learn—
there not having been a journal—who were present. We know
only that the Rev. Dr. West, of St. Paul's, and the Rev. Mr. John
Andrews, of St. Thomas and St. John's, Baltimore county, a clergyman well known of former days in Pennsylvania, were *added* to
the number before present. The presence of Mr. Andrews, however, shows that it must have been after his return to Maryland,
in April of 1782, from Pennsylvania. From his general activity
in affairs of the Church, and especially from his capacity in its
councils, we can hardly doubt that Dr. Smith was present. If so,
he probably presided.

Such had been the success of Dr. Smith in the charge of the
Kent County School, at Chestertown, that there were now one
hundred and forty students, with prospects of increase. The visitors, therefore, asked the Legislature that the School might be
incorporated a College. This was granted, and the name given
it of Washington College, at the April session, in honorable and
perpetual memory of his Excellency the Commander-in-Chief of
the Army.

---

* See pages 168–174, 194, 574, *n.*   † See Appendix, No. II.

The College was soon organized, with Dr. Smith as President; Colin Ferguson, A. M., Vice-President; Samuel Armer, A. M., Professor of Natural Philosophy and Logic; together with two Tutors, a French teacher and others; one of whom was Mr. Coudon, the former head of the school. Two of these gentlemen, Mr. Coudon and Mr. Ferguson, immediately became lay readers in vacant parishes, and in due time, with a third, entered into Holy Orders.

It was still a time of *revolution*, of desolating war. The population of the State had decreased 80,000. Money had become exceedingly scarce, £200,000 only being the estima ed amount in circulation in the State; yet on the Eastern Shore £10,300 were contributed for the College, and a brick building had been erected for it, 160 feet long and three and a half stories high, capable of containing 200 students. The names of its trustees showed the high standard it aspired to. General Washington headed the list, and then follow those of the Hon. John Henry, the Hon. Samuel Chase, Governor Paca, Rev. Dr. Smith, Rev. Samuel Keene, Rev. William Thomson, Robert Goldsborough, William Perry, Nicholson, Scott, Bordley, Perkins, Gale, and seven others, all of whom were churchmen, prominent and leading men, liberal donors to its funds, and pledged to its interests.

In our next chapter we give a more particular account of this College.

CHAPTER XLIII.

DR. SMITH'S ACCOUNT OF WASHINGTON COLLEGE—ADDRESS TO THE INHABITANTS OF MARYLAND IN REGARD TO THE COLLEGE—LIST OF THE SUBSCRIPTIONS—DR. SMITH AND PEREGRIN LETHBURY TO THE ASSEMBLY OF MARYLAND—ADDRESS OF THE VISITORS TO THE ASSEMBLY—DR. SMITH IN BEHALF OF THE VISITORS TO GENERAL WASHINGTON—GENERAL WASHINGTON TO DR. SMITH IN REPLY—PROCEEDINGS OF THE ASSEMBLY OF MARYLAND.

THE following account of the College is from the pen of Dr. Smith. We append to the account such documents and letters as assist in giving a true impression of an institution founded under circumstances, as will be seen from what we have stated at the close of our last chapter, of a most unusual kind.

Dr. Smith's Account, etc.

In that extent of territory which, through the Providence of God, is

5

now the sovereign Domain of the UNITED STATES OF AMERICA, an attentive observer cannot but behold the foundations of an EMPIRE laid, which promises to enlarge itself to vast dimensions, and to become the happy means of diffusing *Knowledge, Liberty* and *Happiness,* through every other part of this American continent.

In a *commercial view,* it is almost needless to mention the great and growing importance of these states; on account of their rich variety of soil and produce, their length of sea-coast and other conveniences of navigation, both internal and external.   From this variety springs likewise one of the first of earthly blessings—a blessing, perhaps, not known in an equal degree by any other people, living in the same community or fœderal union, throughout the globe—We have the staff of life —BREAD in abundance, not only for ourselves, and the immense number of industrious settlers, constantly flowing in among us from different parts of the old world ; but likewise for exportation to supply the wants of others, and to multiply the sources and channels of our trade.   Nor is there a probability, under the favour of Heaven, and a due exertion of our skill and industry (as the experience of near two hundred years can tell us) that we shall ever suffer, through scarcity or want.   For, in such an extended country, and with such variety of soil and climate, if the productions of one kind, or of one part of the country should fail, there will remain a sufficiency of the other kinds, and those the far greater part, unless (thro' the direction of Providence for its own wise purposes) a revolution of seasons should take place, whereof neither past experience or memory can suggest any example or precedent.

Nor are the soil and climate thus favourable to the productions of the earth only ; but likewise to all the best powers, both of body and mind, in the human species ; nursing up a race of bold and hardy men ; who in the vindication and establishment of their native rights and independence, have given the most illustrious proofs of their wisdom, valour and magnanimity during a long and arduous contest with one of the most powerful nations upon earth.   And with the like exertions of virtue and public spirit, looking up to God as our protector and Guide, we need have but little to fear from any future wars of the old world or the new—should WAR, in ages hence, continue to be the unchristian mode of arbitrating the differences of Christian nations !

But, we may trust, the time is not distant when " Violence shall no more be heard upon earth ; when nation shall not lift up sword against nation, neither shall they learn *war* any more."   As a prelude to that happy period, which (we are assured) shall yet come, may not these American States, even now, " beat their swords into plough-shares, and their spears into pruning-hooks ? "   Remote as we are in situation, may we not keep ourselves alike remote in our inclination, from the intrigues, the ambition and the quarrels of the other powers of the world ; yielding as great a proof of moderation in peace as of magnanimity in war ?

The idea is truly animating, and in the hope of its being realized, a friend to mankind cannot but adore that Providence which (in portioning out the countries of the new world among the nations of the old) gave that part of America, which seems ordained to preheminence of improvement above the rest, to an enlightened and civilized people— professing themselves the votaries of KNOWLEDGE and FREEDOM in their purest and most improved state. For however flattering it may be to consider the growth of these rising States as tending to increase the wealth and commerce of the world ; they are to be considered in another more serious view, as ordained to enlarge the sphere of HUMANITY. In that view the great interests of civil LIBERTY, the parent of every other social blessing, will not be forgotten; but every true citizen of the States will consider himself as a chosen instrument for supporting her cause in the *new* world, at a time when drooping or decaying in the *old;* and will accordingly rejoice to water the tender plant that hath taken root among us, and to rear and shelter it from the *storm*, till it shoot up into a *great tree*, " sending forth its boughs unto the ocean, and its branches to the utmost rivers." But in this great work, we are not to trust to the most successful struggles either against foreign or domestic enemies, nor yet to the best constituted forms of government for the preservation of our civil or religious *rights*. We must strive to maintain our own virtue—We must avoid the snares of luxury, venality and corruption among ourselves. We must regard the great concerns of religion and another world. We must attend to the rising generation. The souls of our youth must be nursed up to the love of LIBERTY and KNOWLEDGE; and their bosoms warmed with a sacred and enlightened zeal for everything that can bless or dignify their species.

In short, lasting provisions must be made by GOOD EDUCATION, for training up a succession of Patriots, Lawgivers, Sages and Divines ; for LIBERTY will not deign to dwell, but where her fair companion KNOWLEDGE flourishes by her side ; nor can GOVERNMENT be duly administered but where the principles of Religion, Justice, Virtue, Sobriety, and Obedience for CONSCIENCE-SAKE, are upheld.

Every well-regulated Seminary of Learning, therefore, that promises to exalt the genius of our country, and to become the means of diffusing useful knowledge still further and wider over this great continent, should be an object of general regard, wheresoever it is founded ; for in this respect, we have but one common interest to pursue.

It is hoped, then, that we may now have leave to mention " Washington-College in the State of Maryland," as an institution of this kind, well worthy of the encouragement of the public in its present infant-state, and more especially of the inhabitants of the Peninsula for whose more immediate advantage it is founded.

Altho' some considerable provision had been made by former Legislatures of Maryland for the rudiments of learning in county schools, yet the State had been long without any public seminary of universal learning for the benefit of youth, as is set forth more at large in the act for founding this College ; a copy of which follows, viz. :

AN ACT FOR FOUNDING A COLLEGE AT CHESTER, IN MARYLAND.*

WHEREAS Institutions for the liberal education of youth in the principles of virtue, knowledge, and useful literature, are of the highest benefit to society, in order to raise up and perpetuate a succession of able and honest men for discharging the various offices and duties of the community, both civil and religious, with usefulness and reputation ; and such institutions of learning have accordingly merited and received the attention and encouragement of the wisest and best regulated States.

AND WHEREAS former legislatures of this State have, according to their best abilities, laid a considerable foundation in this good work, in sundry laws for the establishment and encouragement of county schools, for the study of " Latin, Greek, Writing, and the like ;" intending, as their future circumstances might permit, to engraft or raise, on the foundation of said schools, more extensive seminaries of learning, by erecting one or more Colleges or places of universal study, not only in the learned languages, but in philosophy, divinity, law, physic, and other useful and ornamental arts and sciences.

AND WHEREAS this great and laudable undertaking hath been retarded by sundry incidents of a public nature, but chiefly by the great difficulty of fixing a situation on either shore of this State, for a seminary of universal learning, which might be of equal benefit and convenience to the youth of both shores ; and it having been represented to this General Assembly, that it would probably tend most to the immediate advancement of literature in this State, if the inhabitants of each shore should be left to consult their own convenience, in founding and freely endowing a College or seminary of general learning each for themselves, under the sanction of law ; which two Colleges or seminaries, if thought most conducive to the advancement of learning, religion and good government, may afterwards, by common consent, when duly founded and endowed, be united under one supreme legislative and visitatorial jurisdiction, as distinct branches or members of the same State University, notwithstanding their distance of situation.

AND WHEREAS Joseph Nicholson, James Anderson, John Scott, William Bordley, and Peregrine Lethbury, Esquires, William Smith, Doctor in Divinity, and Benjamin Chambers, Esquire, the present Visitors of Kent county school, in the town of Chester, have represented

* The important features of this Statute were no doubt suggested by Dr. Smith ; and probably its exact language.—H. W. S.

to this General Assembly, " That the said school hath of late increased greatly by an accession of students and scholars, from various parts of the Eastern Shore of this State, and the neighbouring Delaware State; there being now about one hundred and forty students and scholars in the said school, and the number expected soon to increase to at least two hundred,—and that the Latin and Greek languages, English, French, Writing, merchants' accounts, and the different branches of Mathematics are taught in the same, under a sufficient number of able and approved Masters; that sundry of the students are preparing, and desirous, to enter upon a course of philosophy, and must repair to some other State, at a very grievous and inconvenient expence, to finish their education, unless they, the said Visitors, are enabled to enlarge the plan of the said school, by engrafting thereon, a system of liberal education in the arts and sciences, and providing necessary books and apparatus, with an additional number of Masters and Professors." And the said Visitors have further expressed their assurance, that if they were made capable in law of erecting the said school into a College or general seminary of learning, for the Eastern Shore or Peninsula between the bays of Chesapeake and Delaware, (maintaining the original design of the said school, as a foundation not to be violated) very considerable sums could be raised in a few years within the said Peninsula, by free and voluntary contributions, for the establishment and support of such seminary. And have accordingly prayed, that a law may be passed to enable them, the said Visitors, to enlarge and improve the said school into a College, or place of universal learning, with the usual privileges.

Now this General Assembly taking the said petition into their serious consideration, and being desirous to encourage and promote knowledge within this State, have agreed to enact, and be it enacted by the General Assembly of Maryland, That the said Joseph Nicholson, James Anderson, John Scott, William Bordley, Peregrine Lethbury, William Smith, and Benjamin Chambers, the present Visitors of Kent county school, and their successors, shall have full power and authority to erect the said school into a College or Seminary of universal learning, and to increase the number of Visitors and Governors thereof to twenty-four, in manner following; that is to say,

First. The said Visitors of Kent county school, and their successors, for and during the term of five years next after the passing of this act, are hereby empowered and made capable to receive contributions and subscriptions for the said intended College or Seminary of universal learning, of any person or persons who may be willing to promote so good a design; and in case any number or denomination of contributors in any county of the Eastern Shore of this State, or of the Peninsula aforesaid, in the neighbouring States, shall subscribe and engage to pay towards the founding and supporting the said intended

College, any sum not less than £500 current money, payable in Spanish milled dollars, or the value thereof, as the same may be at the times of payment, in good merchantable wheat or tobacco, the said Visitors and their successors, may covenant and agree with such subscribers and contributors, that there shall be one Visitor and Governor of the said College, chosen for ever out of such county, for every £500 of specie so subscribed and paid, or secured to be paid, towards founding and supporting the said College, and that the first election of every such county Visitor and Governor of the said College, shall be made by the subscribers and contributors in the county, within three months after the sum of £500, or the value thereof, shall be subscribed and paid, or secured to be paid as aforesaid; and due notice of the time and place of election shall be given to the subscribers and contributors in every county, in such form and manner as shall be agreed upon by the Visitors of Kent county school, and set forth in the preamble of the subscription papers, which the said Visitors shall send into the several counties for obtaining subscriptions towards founding and a supporting the said College.

Secondly. If the Visitors of any county school on the said Eastern Shore, for the more effectual advancement of useful knowledge, and the better promoting the good purposes for which such county schools were originally founded, shall be desirous to engraft and consolidate the funds and estate of such county school, or any part or parts of the same with the funds and estate of the said intended College, the Visitors of Kent county school, for and during the term of five years next after passing this act, (unless the said College is sooner established agreeably to the tenor hereof) and the Visitors and Governors of the College, at any time after the same shall be so established, shall have full power and authority to treat and agree with the Visitors of such county school, and to allow one Visitor and Governor of the College, to be for ever chosen from among the inhabitants of such county, for every £500 which any such county schools may contribute towards founding and supporting the said College, the first choice to be in the Visitors of such county school; or in consideration of the said £500 contribution, or of any sum or estate of greater or less value, that may be thus given by any county school, towards the said College; any other privileges and advantages, in respect to the education of the youth of such county in the College, may be fixed and agreed upon, as shall be judged reasonable between the Visitors and Governors of the College, and the Visitors of such county school, instead of fixing any Visitor and Governor to be for ever chosen from the said county. And all contracts and agreements truly and fairly made for founding and supporting the said College as above set forth, shall be good and effectual in law, according to the plain intent, and the true and legal construction of the same ; Provided always, That the whole number of Visitors and Governors of the said College, shall never be more than twenty-four at one time, nor under seventeen ; and that not less than seven of them shall have their usual residence in Kent county, and within seven miles of the town of Chester, aforesaid.

Thirdly. When any of the first Visitors and Governors of the said College chosen as aforesaid on the part of any county, or any of the Visitors and Governors in general, shall die, or remove out of the county for which he was chosen, or absent himself from four succeeding quarterly meetings, without such excuse or plea of necessary absence as shall be deemed reasonable by a legal and just quorum of the said Visitors and Governors, duly assembled at a quarterly visitation of the said College, such quorum so assembled, shall proceed by a new election to fill up the seat and place of such deceased, removed or absenting member ; having special regard that in the room of a deceased, removed or absenting Visitor and Governor, from any particular county, another of the same county be always chosen in his room and stead.

AND BE IT ENACTED, That when ten Visitors and Governors of the said intended College shall be chosen as aforesaid, in addition to the seven Visitors of Kent county school for the time being, and when the said seventeen Visitors and Governors shall, by an instrument of writing under their hands, to the General Assembly of this State, directed and duly delivered, declare, that they are willing and desirous to take upon them, and to discharge, the trust of Visitors and Governors of the said intended College, and that an estate, or sum and sums of money, not less than £5000 current money, or the just value thereof (including the estate of the said Kent county school) is in their hands, or so secured to be paid to them that they will answer for the value thereof, and the application of the same towards founding, endowing, and supporting the said intended College, according to their best judgment, and the tenor of this act ; Provided always, That such instrument of writing be lodged with the General Assembly as aforesaid, within five years after the passing of this act ; that then and in such case, the said seventeen Visitors and Governors, and such other person and persons as they shall choose to make up and perpetuate the number of twenty-four, agreeable to the tenor hereof, shall be, and are hereby declared to be, one community, corporation and body politic, to have continuance forever, by the name of "The Visitors and Governors of Washington College, in the State of Maryland," in honourable and perpetual memory of his excellency General Washington, the illustrious and virtuous commander-in-chief of the armies of the United States ; and by the same name they shall have perpetual succession ; provided nevertheless, that seventeen of the said Visitors and Governors, shall always be residents on the Eastern Shore of this State, but that, the seven additional Visitors and Governors (to make up and perpetuate the number of twenty-four) may be chosen from this, or any part of the adjacent States, if they are such persons as can reasonably undertake to attend the quarterly visitations, and are thought capable, by their particular learning, weight and character, to advance the interest and reputation of the said Seminary.

AND BE IT ENACTED, That the said Visitors and Governors, and their successors, by the same name, shall be able and capable in law, to purchase, have and enjoy to them and their successors in fee, or for any other lesser estate or estates, any lands, tenements, rents, annuities, pensions or other hereditaments, within this State, by the gift, grant, bargain, sale, alienation, enfeoffment, release, confirmation or devise of any person or persons, bodies politic or corporate, capable to make the same; and such lands, tenements, rents, annuities, pensions or other hereditaments, or any lesser estates, rights or interests of or in the same, (excepting the estate of the said Kent county school) at their pleasure to grant, alien, sell and transfer, in such manner and form, as they shall think meet and convenient for the furtherance of the said College; and also that they may take and receive any sum or sums of money, and any kind, manner or portion of goods and chattels that shall be given, sold or bequeathed to them, by any person or persons, bodies politic or corporate, capable to make a gift, sale or bequest thereof, and employ the same towards erecting, setting up and maintaining the said College, in such manner as they shall judge most necessary and convenient for the instruction, improvement and education of youth, in the vernacular and learned languages, and generally in any kind of literature, arts and sciences, which they shall think proper to be taught for training up good, useful and accomplished men, for the service of their country in Church and State; and youth of all religious denominations and persuasions, shall be freely and liberally admitted to equal privileges and advantages of education, and to all the literary honors of the College, according to their merit, and the standing rules of the Seminary, without requiring or enforcing any religious or civil test whatsoever upon any student, scholar or member of the said College, other than such oath of fidelity to the State as the laws thereof may require of the Visitors, Governors, Masters, Professors and Teachers in schools and seminaries of learning in general; nor shall any preference be given in the choice of any Visitor and Governor of the said College, or of the Principal, Vice-Principal or any Professor or Master, on account of his religious persuasion, but merely on account of his literary and other necessary qualifications to fill the place for which he is chosen.

AND BE IT ENACTED, That the said Visitors and Governors, and their successors, by the name aforesaid, shall be able in law, to sue and be sued, plead and be impleaded, in any court or courts, before any judge, judges or justices within this State and elsewhere, in all and all manner of suits, complaints, pleas, causes, matters and demands, of whatsoever kind, nature or form they be ; and all and every other matter and thing therein to do in as full and effectual a manner as any other person or persons, bodies politic or corporate within this State, or any of the United States of America, in like cases, may or can do.

AND BE IT ENACTED, That the said Visitors and Governors, and their successors, shall have full power and authority to have, make, and use one common and public seal, and likewise one privy seal, with such devices and inscriptions as they shall think proper, and to ascertain, fix and regulate the uses of both seals by their own laws, and the same seals, or either of them, to change, break, alter, and renew at their pleasure.

AND BE IT ENACTED, That the said Visitors and Governors, and their successors, from time to time, and at all times hereafter forever, shall have full power and authority to constitute and appoint, in such manner as they shall think best and most convenient, a *Principal* and *Vice-Principal* of the said College, and Professors, with proper Tutors and Assistants, for instructing the students and scholars of the said Seminary, in all the liberal arts and sciences, and in the ancient and modern tongues and languages ; who shall be severally styled Professors of such arts, sciences, languages, or tongues as they shall be nominated and appointed for, according to each particular nomination and appointment ; and the said Principal, Vice-Principal, and Professors so constituted and appointed from time to time, shall be known and distinguished forever as one learned body or faculty, by the name of " The Principal, Vice-Principal and Professors of Washington College, in the State of Maryland," and by that name shall be capable of exercising such powers and authorities as the Visitors and Governors of the said College, and their successors, shall, by their ordinances, think necessary to delegate to them for the instruction, discipline and government of the said Seminary, and of all the students, scholars, ministers and servants belonging to the same ; and the said Principal and Vice-Principal, Professors, students, scholars, and such necessary ministers and servants as give constant attendance upon the business of the College, shall be exempted from all rates and taxes on their salaries, and from all military duties, except in the case of an actual invasion of the State, and when general military law is declared.

AND BE IT ENACTED, That the clear yearly value of the messuages, houses, lands, tenements, rents, annuities or other hereditaments and real estate of the said College and corporation, shall not exceed six thousand pounds current money, to be reckoned in Spanish milled dollars, at the present rate and weight ; and all gifts, grants and bequests to the said College and corporation, after the yearly value of their estates shall amount to six thousand pounds as aforesaid, and all bargains and purchases to be made by the said corporation, which may increase the yearly value of said estate, above or beyond the sum aforesaid, shall be absolutely void and of none effect.

AND BE IT ENACTED, That the said Visitors and Governors, and their successors, shall meet at least four times in every year, in stated quarterly meetings, to be appointed by their own ordinances, and at such other times as by their said ordinances they may direct, in order to examine the progress of the students and scholars in literature, to hear and determine on all complaints and appeals, and upon all matters touching the discipline of the Seminary, and the good and wholesome execution of their ordinances ; in all which examinations, meetings and determinations, such number of the said Visitors and Governors, duly met, (provided they be not less than seven) shall be a quorum, as the fundamental ordinances at first, or any time afterwards duly enacted by a majority of the whole Visitors, shall fix and determine.

AND BE IT ENACTED, That a majority of the said Visitors and Governors for the time being, when duly assembled at any quarterly, or other meeting, upon due notice given to the whole body of Visitors and Governors, shall have full power and authority to make fundamental ordinances for the government of the said College, and the instruction of the youth as aforesaid, and by these ordinances to appoint such a number of their own body not less than seven, as they may think proper to be a quorum for transacting all general and necessary business of the said Seminary, and making temporary rules for the government of the same ; and also by the said fundamental ordinances, to delegate to the Principal, Vice-Principal and Professors, such powers and authorities as they may think best for the standing government of the said Seminary, and the execution of the ordinances and rules of the same ; provided always, that they be not repugnant to the form of government, or any law of this State.

And for animating and encouraging the students of the said College to a laudable diligence, industry and progress in useful literature and science, be it enacted, that the said Visitors and Governors, and their successors, shall by a written mandate, under their privy seal, and the hand of some one of the Visitors and Governors to be chosen annually as their President, according to the ordinance to be made for that purpose, have full power and authority to direct the Principal, Vice-Principal and Professors, to hold public commencements, either on stated annual days, or occasionally as the future ordinances of the said Seminary may direct ; and at such commencements to admit any of the students in the said College, or any other persons meriting the same (whose names shall be severally inserted in the said mandate) to any degree or degrees in any of the faculties, arts and sciences, and liberal

professions to which persons are usually admitted in other Colleges or
Universities in America or Europe; and it is hereby enacted that the
Principal, or in case of his death or absence, the Vice-Principal, and in
case of the death or absence of both, the senior Professor who may be
present, shall make out and sign with his name, Diplomas or certificates
of the admission to such degree or degrees, which shall be sealed with
the public or greater seal of the said corporation or College, and delivered to the graduates as honorable and perpetual testimonials of such
admission; which diplomas, if thought necessary for doing greater
honor to such graduates, shall also be signed with the names of the
different Professors, or as many of them as can conveniently sign the
same; provided always, that no student or students within the said College, shall ever be admitted to any such degree or degrees, nor have
their name inserted in any mandate for a degree, until such student or
students have been first duly examined and thought worthy of the same,
at a public examination of candidates, to be held one whole month previous to the day of commencement in the said College, by and in the
preference of the said Visitors and Governors, or of such quorum of
them, not less than seven, as the ordinances of the College may
authorize for that purpose, and in the presence of any other persons
choosing to attend the same; and provided further, that no person or
persons, excepting the students belonging to the said Seminary, shall
ever be admitted to any honorary or other degree or degrees in the
same, unless thirteen of the Visitors and Governors (of whom the President shall be one) by a mandate under their privy seal, and signed by
the hands of the whole thirteen, to the Principal, Vice-Principal and
Professors directed, have signified their approbation and authority for
the particular admission of such person to said degree or degrees.

AND BE IT ENACTED, That the Visitors of Kent county school may
set aside and appropriate ten acres of the land belonging to the said
school, where they shall think most convenient, for erecting necessary
buildings for carrying on the said College, and laying out gardens and
grounds for the recreation and refreshment of the youth, and other
suitable exercises. And the remainder of the grounds belonging to the
said Kent county school, may and shall be leased out by the Visitors of
the said school for the time being, and by the Visitors and Governors
of the said College, after the same shall be established, in leases for
lives, or ninety-nine years, or on any other leases that may be judged
most beneficial for advancing the cause of learning, and promoting the
said College agreeable to the original design for which the said Kent
county school was founded, and for which the said school-lands were
purchased.

AND BE IT ENACTED, That the ordinances which shall be from time
to time made by the Visitors and Governors of the said College, and

their successors, with an account of their other proceedings, and of the management of the estate and monies committed to their trust, shall, when required, be laid before the General Assembly of Maryland, for their inspection and examination ; but in case at any time hereafter, through oversight or otherwise, through misapprehensions and mistaken constructions of the powers, liberties and franchises in this charter or act of incorporation granted or intended to be granted, any ordinances should be made by the said corporation of Visitors and Governors, or any matters done and transacted by the corporation contrary to the tenor thereof, IT IS ENACTED, That although all such ordinances, acts and doings, shall in themselves be null and void ; yet they shall not, however, in any courts of law, or by the General Assembly, be deemed, taken, interpreted or adjudged into an avoidance or forfeiture of this charter and act of incorporation, but the same shall be, and remain unhurt, inviolate and entire unto the said corporation of Visitors and Governors, in perpetual succession ; and all their acts conformable to the powers, true intent and meaning hereof, shall be, and remain in full force and validity, the nullity and avoidance of such illegal acts to the contrary in any wise notwithstanding.

AND BE IT ENACTED AND DECLARED, That this charter and act of incorporation, and every part thereof, shall be good and available in all things in the law, according to the true intent and meaning thereof, and shall be construed, reputed and adjudged in all cases most favorably on the behalf, and for the best benefit and behoof of the said Visitors and Governors, and their successors, so as most effectually to answer the valuable ends of this act of incorporation, towards the general advancement and promotion of useful knowledge, science and virtue.

AND BE IT ENACTED, That no person shall act as Visitor and Governor, or as Principal or Vice-Principal, or as Professor in the said College, before he shall take the oath of fidelity and support to this State required by the constitution, or by the laws of this State.

The foregoing Charter or Act of Incorporation having duly passed the General Assembly, at their Spring-sessions, 1782, a meeting of the seven Visitors and Governors named in it was held, and the Rev. Dr. Smith, their President, at the request and by the appointment of the Board, undertook to visit the different counties on the Eastern shore, in order to open the subscriptions for founding the Seminary, agreeably to the tenor of the law. On his own horse, he went from country-seat to country-seat, and almost from farm to farm, seeking personally the means of building the new seminary. The following was the preamble to the different subscription-papers:

To the Inhabitants of the Eastern Shore of Maryland, &c.

GENTLEMEN :—By the foregoing Act for founding a COLLEGE on this Shore, an Opportunity is offered, which good and wise men have long wished for, of making a provision for the future education of your Youth, in the liberal Arts and Sciences, and all the branches of useful and ornamental Knowledge.

Colleges and Schools of general learning have, long since, been founded in most of the Sister-States, and the advantages which our Youth have derived from them, have been manifested in all the late and former trials of the wisdom, virtue and magnanimity of America. The Youth of Maryland have been particularly distinguished among the rest; but have been obliged, at a very grievous and unequal expence, to prepare themselves for public life by repairing, for their education, either to Great Britain, or to some of the neighboring American States.

The inhabitants of this Shore and Peninsula, for whose benefit this Foundation is more immediately designed, are descended from some of the most ancient families and settlers in America, and would undoubtedly wish, by good education, to support the rank of their posterity, and to give them their full consequence in this rising EMPIRE,—Further arguments would be needless.

The Visitors of Kent County School wish to discharge the important trust committed to them by the foregoing Act, with zeal and integrity, according to their best abilities. The school and valuable estate under their care, want only a little public assistance and countenance, to place them on a footing with the most respectable Colleges or Universities in America, being little inferior to any of them in the present number of scholars and students.

The distance of the town of Chester from alarms in time of war, its healthful situation, and convenience of accommodation for Youth, have, by general agreement, pointed it out as the best place for a Seminary of universal Learning on this Shore.

Being persuaded, therefore, that the present opportunity, which hath been so long desired, will be cheerfully embraced, for founding a College on this Shore, under the auspicious name with which the Legislature have dignified it; We, the Visitors aforesaid, in execution of the trust and duties committed to us, by the said act, propose the following—

ARTICLES to be mutually binding on the Visitors of Kent County School, and the Subscribers and Contributors towards founding and supporting "WASHINGTON COLLEGE, in the State of Maryland."

I. Every subscription shall be made in specie of gold and silver, and payable (as the Act directs) in Spanish milled Dollars of the usual weight, or the value thereof, as the same may be at the times of payment, in good merchantable Wheat or Tobacco.

II. For the greater ease of the Subscribers, the payments shall be made in three equal parts ; one-third part on the first Monday in January, 1783; another third part on the first Monday in January, 1784; and the remaining third on the first Monday in January, 1785 ; which several payments shall be made to the Treasurer of Kent County School, till the College is established according to law, and afterwards to the Treasurer of the College, as nominated by the Visitors and Governors thereof; and the hand-writing of every particular subscriber shall be binding in law on himself, his heirs, executors and administrators, for the sum subscribed, or the value thereof, with legal interest, if not paid when due ; and the receipt of the Treasurer aforesaid shall be a sufficient discharge for all subscriptions and contributions.

Within three months after the sum of £500 shall be subscribed by any number of contributors or persons in any county, or district of a county, in sums not less than £9 or £3 per annum for three years, by single subscribers or contributors, and the same shall be notified by any three of the subscribers to the Visitors of Kent County School, accompanied with an authentic list of the subscribers, the said Visitors, agreeable to the foregoing Act, will fix a convenient time and place for such subscribers and contributors of £9 and upwards, to meet within the county, for electing one person as a Visitor and Governor of the College for such county, or district of the county ; and will cause written or printed notices of the time and place of election, to be fixed up at the Court-House and different Parish Churches within such county, at least ten days before the day of election, that all persons concerned may duly attend.

In less than three months the subscription-papers were filled up by subscriptions in the different counties on the Eastern Shore, and on the 26th of November, 1782, were delivered to the General Assembly, agreeably to the Charter or Incorporating Act of the College. They were thus:

Subscriptions, &c.

	£.	s.	d.
His Excellency George Washington, Esq., General and Commander in Chief of the Armies of the United States, as an Earnest of his Good-will, Fifty Guineas	£87	10	0
KENT COUNTY.			
John Cadwalader	50	0	0
William Slubey	55	7	10
Amount carried forward	£192	17	10

	£.	s.	d.
Amount brought up	192	17	10
John Page	25	0	0
John Lambert Wilmer	30	0	0
Richard Graves	30	0	0
Robert Buchanan	20	0	0
Thomas Smyth	30	0	0
William Dunn	9	0	0
Simon Wickes	9	0	0
James Claypoole	9	0	0
Amount carried forward	£354	17	10

	£.	s.	d.		£.	s.	d.
Amount brought over	354	17	10	Amount brought up	1046	14	5
Thomas Van Dyke	11	5	0	William Wilmer	9	0	0
Horatio Belt	9	0	0	Arthur Miller	24	0	0
William Houston	9	0	0	William Ringgold, jun.	10	0	0
Thomas Kemp	9	0	0	Joseph Wickes	9	0	0
Robert Blake	9	0	0	Simon Wickes, jun.	12	0	0
John Wickes	9	0	0	Richard Hinson	9	0	0
John Harragan	9	0	0	Morgan Brown	9	0	0
Joseph Forman	30	0	0	John Sutton	9	0	0
Isaac Perkins	20	0	0	Richard Spencer	15	0	0
William Bordley	18	0	0	Charles Tilden	16	0	0
Robert Anderson	15	0	0	Marmaduke Tilden, jun.	9	0	0
John Lorrain	15	0	0	James Frisby	10	0	0
Joseph Williams	9	0	0	John Moore, jun.	9	0	0
Philip Brooks	9	0	0	James Williamson	9	0	0
Richard G. Smyth	30	0	0	Jere Nichols	15	0	0
Joseph Nicholson	18	0	0	Richard Ricaud	12	0	0
James Anderson	30	0	0	Richard Miller	9	0	0
William Smith	18	0	0	William Gale	10	0	0
Benjamin Chambers	18	0	0	Arthur Bryan	5	5	0
John Scott	18	0	0	James Dunn	15	0	0
James M. Anderson	9	0	0	James Hodges	9	0	0
Barney Corse	9	0	0	John Williamson	15	0	0
Edward Wright	9	0	0	Joseph Brown	9	0	0
Simon Wilmer	15	0	0	Morgan Hurt	9	0	0
Edward Worrel	9	0	0	Robert Dunn	12	0	0
John Sturgis	9	0	0	John Carvil Hinson	9	0	0
Peregrine Lethrbury	9	0	0	Samuel Gott	9	0	0
Josias Ringgold	15	0	0	William Frisby	9	0	0
John Bolton	9	0	0	John Day	9	0	0
James Piper	9	0	0	William Maxwell, jun.	15	0	0
Anne Deane	15	0	0	James Pearce	15	0	0
Anthony Banning	15	0	0	Isaac Freeman	12	0	0
Emory Sudler	18	0	0	Nathaniel Comegys	12	0	0
St. Leger Everett	10	0	0	Isaac Spencer	12	0	0
Charles Groom	9	0	0	John Wallis (Morgan's Creek)	10	0	0
William Embleton	10	0	0	John Brooks	9	0	0
John Kennerd	10	0	0	William Hanson	9	0	0
James Smith	9	0	0	Malachi Ambrose	10	0	0
Marmaduke Medford	11	5	0	Samuel Davis	15	0	0
James M'Clean	25	6	7	James Hinson, jun.	9	0	0
Luke Griffith	9	0	0	Alexander Baird	15	0	0
Rasin Gale	9	0	0	John Gleaves	10	0	0
Thomas Smith, jun.	18	0	0	William Geddes	30	0	0
John Blakeway	9	0	0	William Wilson	9	0	0
Edward Scanlan	9	0	0	Ebenezer Massy	9	0	0
Daniel Matzler	10	0	0	Thomas Boyer	9	0	0
John Wilson, jun.	15	0	0	George Wilson	15	0	0
Thomas Medford	10	0	0	Robert Roberts	9	0	0
Robert Constable	10	0	0	Nathaniel Kennard, jun	9	0	0
Robert Cruckshank	10	0	0	Marmaduke Tilden	15	0	0
Richard Lloyd	20	0	0				
James Lloyd	15	0	0	Total Amount of Kent			
				County at the Elections,	£1599	19	5
Amount carried forward £	1046	14	5	October, 1782			

NOTE.—The subscriptions, of course, in pounds, shillings and pence are not sterling money, but money of Maryland.

QUEEN ANNE'S COUNTY.	£.	s.	d.		£.	s.	d.
				Amount brought up	990	0	0
William Paca	50	0	0	John Foreman	10	0	0
Edward Tilghman	50	0	0	Richard B. Lloyd	50	0	0
William Hemsley	50	0	0				
J. Beale Bordley	50	0	0	Total Amount of Queen			
Edward Coursey	32	10	0	Anne's County at the			
Richard B. Carmichael	20	0	0	Election of two Visit-	£1050	0	0
Alexander Lawson	20	0	0	ors, October, 1782.			
Robert Dawson	9	0	0				
Richard S. Earle	30	0	0	TALBOT COUNTY.			
Walter Jackson	18	0	0		£.	s.	d.
Joseph Nicholson, jun.	30	0	0	Edward Lloyd	60	0	0
C. J. Wederstrandt	9	0	0	Robert Goldsborough, jun.	30	0	0
James Earle	15	0	0	Howes Goldsborough	18	0	0
William Bruff	12	0	0	William Frazier	15	0	0
S. Clayton	9	0	0	William Marsh Catrup	9	0	0
Thomas Wright	32	10	0	John Roberts	12	0	0
Arthur Emory, jun.	22	10	0	Richard Grason	9	0	0
Thos. Emory of Arthur	10	0	0	Peregrine Tilghman	20	0	0
Edward Downes	9	0	0	Richard Tilghman, jun.	20	0	0
William Hacket	9	0	0	Matthew Tilghman	30	0	0
James Clayland	9	0	0	William Hindman	11	5	0
William Wright	12	10	0	Alexander M'Callum	12	0	0
Turbutt Wright	30	0	0	W. Goldsborough, jun.	12	0	0
Richard Emory	9	0	0	William Tilghman	20	0	0
Robert Wilson	9	0	0	William Bordley	17	10	0
James Seth	10	0	0	Joseph Bruff	12	0	0
Clement Sewell	18	0	0	William Goldsborough	35	0	0
Richard Tilghman	18	0	0	Thomas Gordon	10	0	0
William Ringgold	9	0	0	James Hindman	15	0	0
Thomas Marsh Forman	18	0	0	John Bracco	15	0	0
J. W. Clayton	9	0	0	Samuel Lloyd Chamberlaine	27	0	0
William Thompson	10	0	0	William Hayward	21	0	0
Charles Troup, a Certificate				William Perry	20	0	0
for £200, valued at	60	0	0	Rev. John Bowie	15	0	0
John Brown	15	0	0	Robert Lloyd Nichols	15	0	0
Samuel Ridgeway	18	0	0	Rev. John Gordon	9	0	0
James Bordley	15	0	0	John Coates	9	0	0
Jacob Ringgold	9	0	0	John Troup	9	0	0
William Smyth	9	0	0	Charles Gardiner	9	0	0
Vachel Downes	9	0	0	Richard Skinner	9	0	0
James O'Bryan	15	0	0	John Needles	10	0	0
John Fisher	9	0	0	Isaac Gilpin	9	0	0
James Hacket	9	0	0	Charles Crookshanks	18	0	0
Samuel Thompson	15	0	0	Nicholas Cox	9	0	0
John Thompson	20	0	0	The Visitors of Talbot free			
M. Hawkins	9	0	0	School	400	0	0
Griffin Fount Le Roy	18	0	0				
Robert Walters	20	0	0	Total Amount of Talbot			
Joshua Seney	13	0	0	County	£971	15	0
Robert Wright	30	0	0				
James Kent	9	0	0	DORCHESTER COUNTY.			
John Dames	9	0	0		£.	s.	d.
James Gould	9	0	0	Robert Goldsborough	100	0	0
Samuel Seney	9	0	0	William Ennalls	60	0	0
Elijah Bishop	12	0	0	Henry Ennalls, jun.	75	0	0
Amount carried forward	£990	0	0	Amount carried forward	£235	0	0

	£.	s.	d.
Amount brought over	235	0	0
James Murray	50	0	0
Rev. Samuel Keene	30	0	0
Henry Hooper	15	0	0
John Dickinson	9	0	0
Joseph Daffin	30	0	0
Henry Ennalls	9	0	0
John Stevens	9	0	0
Wm. Ennalls Hooper	9	0	0
Levin Kirkman	15	0	0
Willis Newton	9	0	0
James Shaw	20	0	0
John Smoot	20	0	0
James Sullivan	30	0	0
Archibald Patison	40	0	0
Joseph Richardson	15	0	0
John Marshal	9	0	0
Thomas Bourke	9	0	0
Robinson Stevens	15	0	0
Henry Murray	36	0	0
Henry Maynadier	15	0	0
Henry Waggaman	12	0	0
Gustavus Scott	22	0	0
Bartholomew Ennalls, jun.	9	0	0
James Gordon	9	0	0
William Wheland	9	0	0
Richard Stanford	9	0	0
John Hooper	9	0	0
William E. Hicks	9	0	0
Alexander Smith	9	0	0
Levin Travers	9	0	0
Bartholomew Ennalls	9	0	0
Tho. Ennalls (*Blackwater*)	9	0	0
George Bonwill	9	0	0
John M. Anderson	12	0	0
Robert Ewing	9	0	0
Thomas Jones	9	0	0
Anne Muse	30	0	0
Elizabeth Ennalls	30	0	0
John Goldsborough	20	0	0
John Le Compte	15	0	0
Moses Allen	15	0	0
Pritchet Willey	9	0	0
John Owens	9	0	0
Anne Steel	15	0	0
Levin Woolford	9	0	0
Thomas Lockerman	9	0	0
Robert Griffith	9	0	0
John Keene	9	0	0
Arthur Whiteley	30	0	0
Stanley Byus	15	0	0
James Steel	15	0	0
Total Amount of Dorchester County }	£1021	0	0

SOMERSET COUNTY.

	£.	s.	d.
John Henry	50	0	0
Francis Jenkins Henry	9	0	0
Levin Gale	50	0	0
Henry Jackson	25	0	0
Samuel King	20	0	0
John Denwood	9	0	0
Nehemiah King	37	0	0
Lambert Hyland	9	0	0
John Dashiell	9	0	0
R. Waters	10	0	0
Ez. Gillis	9	0	0
John Winder	9	0	0
Thomas Sloss	20	0	0
George Dashiell	25	0	0
William Davis Allen	15	0	0
John Done	9	0	0
Thomas Maddux, jun.	9	0	0
John Stewart	25	0	0
Esme Bayly	9	0	0
Henry Handy	9	0	0
William Horsey	9	0	0
William M'Bryde	9	0	0
George Day Scott	20	0	0
William Winder	15	0	0
James Houston	9	0	0
George Handy	9	0	0
Ebenezer Waller	9	0	0
Gilliss Polk	9	0	0
William Adams	25	0	0
John Adams	25	0	0
Henry Lowes	40	0	0
John Waters	15	0	0
Hamilton Bell, jun.	9	0	0
Wm. Dashiell, sen.	9	0	0
A. Cheney	10	0	0
John Evans (of *Nicholas*)	9	0	0
Alexander Roberts	9	0	0
Thomas Bruff	9	0	0
Total Amount of Somerset County }	£616	0	0

WORCESTER COUNTY.*

	£.	s.	d.
Joseph Dashiell	25	0	0
Peter Chaille	25	0	0
Benjamin Burnell (of *Matthew*)	15	0	0
Charles Bennet	9	0	0
Solomon Long	18	0	0
Philip Quinton	10	0	0
William Purnell	25	0	0
Robert Done	15	0	0
Amount carried forward	£142	0	0

* The original manuscript of this subscription is now in the collection of Wm. Kent Gilbert, M. D.

6

	£.	s.	d.		£.	s.	d.
Amount brought over	142	0	0	Amount brought up	150	0	0
William Selby	10	0	0	Michael Earle	20	0	0
James Quinton	9	0	0	John Miller	15	0	0
John Martin, jun.	9	0	0	Rev. John Lewis	9	0	0
George Fruitt, jun.	15	0	0	Sidney George	20	0	0
Dr. Bishop	15	0	0	John Leach Knight	20	0	0
Thomas Martin	12	0	0	John Carnan	9	0	0
Jethro Bowin	9	0	0	Daniel Charles Heath	60	0	0
John Parramore	10	0	0	Henry Ward Pearce	50	0	0
William Holland	10	0	0	Joshua George	20	0	0
Levin Davis	10	0	0	Perry Ward	18	0	0
Levin Blake	15	0	0	John Ward Veazey	10	0	0
Levin Hill	9	0	0	James Louttit	20	0	0
M. Downes	9	0	0	John Ward (Son of Perry)	9	0	0
Henry Ayres	9	0	0	John Cox	20	0	0
John Ayres	9	0	0	John Hall	9	0	0
Joshua Townsend (Indian				William Rumsey	15	0	0
Town)	15	0	0	John Rumsey	12	0	0
William Handy	12	0	0	William Ward	10	0	0
John Selby	15	0	0	John Ward	9	0	0
John Warner	12	0	0	Thomas B. Veazey	9	0	0
John Neill	9	0	0	John Dochery Thomson	12	0	0
Moses Chaille	9	0	0	William Matthews	15	0	0
James Martin	9	0	0				
Isaac Houston	9	0	0	Total Amount of Cœcil County	£541	0	0
Parker Selby (of Parker)	9	0	0				
William Allen	30	0	0				
Henry Dennis	50	0	0	CAROLINE COUNTY.			
Robert Dennis	9	0	0		£.	s.	d.
Thomas Purnell, sen.	25	0	0	Mathew Driver	30	0	0
William Morris	15	0	0	Charles Daffin	30	0	0
Zadock Purnell, sen.	45	0	0	William Hopper	35	0	0
Samuel Handy	18	0	0				
John Pope Mitchell	15	0	0		£95	0	0
Thomas Purnell (W. N.)	18	0	0				
Total Amount of Worcester County	£626	0	0	ACCOMACK COUNTY.			
				(Virginia.)			
CŒCIL COUNTY.					£.	s.	d.
				George Corbin	30	0	0
	£.	s.	d.	George Stewart	20	0	0
The Visitors of the free School	150	0	0	Skinner Wallop	10	0	0
				Virginia Money	£60	0	0
Amount carried forward	£150	0	0				

N. B. The Subscriptions in Caroline County, and in Accomack and Northampton Counties, in Virginia, as well as the upper Part of Cœcil County, are yet left to be completed, together with the additional Subscriptions proposed to be opened in the other Counties of the Eastern Shore.*

---

* These subscriptions I am not able to give from any memoranda of Dr. Smith's just now accessible to me. They are supposed, however, to have been considerable; although those above given show Dr. Smith's wonderful services in the cause of letters.
—H. W. S.

The Instrument of Trust.

To the Honorable the GENERAL ASSEMBLY of Maryland.

We, the subscribers, agreeable to our appointment by "the Visitors and Governors of Washington College, in the State of Maryland," and on their behalf, beg leave to present and deliver to the General Assembly, the instrument of writing, or declaration of trust, required by law, as the condition upon which the operation of their charter is to commence.

The very numerous and liberal subscriptions which have been obtained towards founding and supporting this College, in·the different counties to which our applications were directed, are a proof of the zeal of the subscribers for the advancement of knowledge, virtue and public spirit.   By that zeal, the Visitors of Kent county school have been enabled to give existence to a Corporation for the advancement of literature, in less than five months, for which they were allowed five years by the indulgence of law.   We trust, and are assured, that such exertions of individuals, for the public emolument, do not only merit, but will receive the most public approbation, as well as future protection and encouragement of the Legislature.   Together with the Declaration of Trust, and list of subscriptions, we beg leave to present to the General Assembly, copies of a letter from the Visitors of Kent county school to his Excellency, the illustrious Commander in Chief of our armies, on the subject of this College, and of the answer which they had the honor to receive from him.   The exalted and patriotic sentiments which it contains can only be truly conveyed to the public by the letter itself.

We would further humbly pray the General Assembly, that the several papers and subscription lists herewith presented may be preserved among their journals and printed with the same ; that the names of the first founders, benefactors and patrons of this seminary may remain on PERPETUAL RECORD.   The names of future benefactors will be reported and recorded as occasion may require.

WILLIAM SMITH.
PERE. LETHBURY.

November 26, 1782.

Declaration of the Visitors and Governors.

To the Honorable the GENERAL ASSEMBLY of Maryland.

We, the subscribers, " Visitors and Governors of Washington College, in the State of Maryland," beg leave to declare, that, agreeable to the act, whereby we are incorporated, entitled, "An Act for founding a College at Chester Town," there are ten visitors and governors duly chosen in different counties of this shore, upon subscriptions of £500 each, in addition to the seven visitors of Kent County School ; and that "we are willing and desirous to take upon us and discharge the trust of visitors and governors of the said College, and that an estate or sum and sums not less than Five Thousand Pounds current money (including the estate of Kent county school) is so secured to be paid to us, that we will answer for the value thereof, and the application of the same, towards founding, endowing and supporting the said College, according to our best judgment and the tenor of the said act," which is our CHARTER.   And we further declare that a sum of money, exceeding £5,000, (exclusive of the estate of Kent county school) and amounting to £5,992 14s. 5d.,* is subscribed towards the said College, as will appear by the subscription lists herewith delivered ; and that we will use our best endeavors, and have no doubt to obtain a due collection of the whole of the said subscriptions, and will faithfully apply the same, as far as obtained, towards founding, endowing, and supporting the said College ; and also all future benefactions, subscriptions, and contributions that may come into our management and power—

This we declare this 15th of Oct., 1782, under our hands, having first taken the oaths of fidelity and support to this State, according to the direction of our said charter of incorporation.

Oct. 15th.
- William Smith, President.
- Jos. Nicholson,
- James Anderson,
- John Scott,
- William Bordley,
- Pere. Lethbury,
- Benjamin Chambers,
- John Page,
- Robert Goldsborough,
- Wm. Perry,
- Peter Chaille,
- James Lloyd,
- Joshua Seney.

Oct. 22d.   Thomas Smyth, jun.
Nov. 8th.   Samuel Keene.
Nov. 13th.   Wm. Paca.
Nov. 19th.   Wm. Thomson.

The following correspondence makes a proper part of the narrative:

---

* This was the Amount at the Time of delivering the List of Subscribers to the General Assembly.   But as the List stands above, added to what was produced by the Sale of Leases of Ninety-nine Years for Sixty-three Lots of Ground, hereinafter mentioned, the whole Capital raised for the founding this Seminary of Learning from the Time of passing the Charter in May, 1782, to the first Commencement in May, 1783, was about £10,300.   Considerable Benefactions have been since received, and a much larger Number soon expected, which will be laid before the World, in a future Publication.   (Original note by Dr. Smith.—H. W. S.)

The Visitors of Kent County School, to General Washington.

CHESTER IN KENT COUNTY, MARYLAND, July 8, 1782.

May it please your Excellency,

By order and in behalf of the Visitors of Kent County school, I have the honor to enclose to your Excellency, an act of the General Assembly of Maryland, for erecting a COLLEGE at Chester, for the benefit of the Eastern Shore, or Peninsula between Chesapeak and Delaware Bays, which they have dignified with the auspicious name of " WASHINGTON COLLEGE, in the State of Maryland, in honorable and perpetual memory of his Excellency General Washington, the illustrious and virtuous Commander in Chief of the armies of the United States."

In every possible way, your country wishes to erect public monuments to you, even while living, and posterity, without doubt, will greatly increase the number; but none, it is believed, can be more acceptable to you, than a seminary of universal learning expressly dedicated to your name, with a view of instructing and animating the youth of many future generations to admire and to imitate these public virtues and patriot-labours, which have created a private monument for you in the heart of every good citizen.

As this College is to be instituted upon the foundation of Kent county school, the Visitors of the said school are by law honored with the great trust of carrying the design into execution. They have already been favoured with very liberal subscriptions, under the auspices of your name; and have no doubt of speedily receiving such farther subscriptions, payable in three equal yearly payments, as will amount to the estimate in the law, and enable them, the next spring, to build the necessary school rooms for lectures in the sciences, and to furnish them with books and philosophical apparatus.

The Visitors hope to obtain your Excellency's permission to place your name at the head of the seven additional Visitors and Governors of the College, which the law allows to be chosen from any of the neighbouring States, to make up the number twenty-four, as you will observe in the perusal thereof. They further hope, that the time is not very remote, in which this infant seminary may salute you in person, and, like a dutiful child, as one of its first works, present the olive wreath and other emblems of peace to its father, guardian and protector.

I have the honor to be, in behalf and by order of the Visitors of Kent county school, your Excellency's most obedient and most humble servant,   WILLIAM SMITH.

General Washington's Answer.

HEADQUARTERS, NEWBURGH, 18th August, 1782.

I have had the honor to receive your favour of the 8th ult. by Colonel Tilghman, who arrived here about ten days ago, and to whom I have committed the charge of forwarding this answer.

To the gentlemen who moved the matter, and to the Assembly for adopting it, I am much indebted for the honor conferred on me, by giving my name to the College at Chester. At the same time that I acknowledge the honor, I feel a grateful sensibility for the manner of bestowing it ; which, as it will remain a monument of their esteem, cannot but make a deep impression on my mind, only to be exceeded by the flattering assurance of the lasting and extensive usefulness of the Seminary.

If the trifling sum of Fifty Guineas will be considered as an Earnest of my wishes for the prosperity of this Seminary, I shall be ready to pay that sum to the order of the Visitors, whenever it is their pleasure to call for it—It is too trifling to stand in any other point of view—nor would I wish it to do so.

With much pleasure should I consent to have my name enrolled among the worthy Visitors and Governors of this College; but convinced as I am that it will never be in my power to give the attendance which by law is required, my name could only be inserted to the exclusion of some other, whose abilities and proximity might enable him to become a more useful member.

When that period shall arrive when we can hail the blest return of peace, it will add to my pleasure, to see this infant seat of learning rising into consistency and proficiency in the sciences, under the nurturing hands of its founders.

I have the honor to be, Reverend Sir,

Your most obedient Servant,

GEORGE WASHINGTON.

To the Rev. Dr. Smith, at Chester, in Kent County, Maryland.

The following proceedings in the House of Delegates, of Maryland, November 27th, 1782, will conclude our narrative of the establishment by Dr. Smith of Washington College; a narrative somewhat long we fear, but necessary fully to exhibit the abilities of Dr. Smith and his undisturbed equanimity and courage under trials and adversities, which would have driven most men into despondency or recklessness:

The Address in behalf of the Visitors and Governors of Washington College and their Declaration of Trust, with the list of subscriptions towards founding and supporting the said College, and copies of the letter from the Visitors of Kent County School, to his Excellency General Washington, and his answer, being read.

Resolved, That the Visitors of Kent County School have exerted themselves with a laudable diligence and address in the execution of the trust committed to them for founding the said College.

Resolved, That the numerous subscribers towards founding this College have given an exemplary proof of their zeal for the honor and interest of their country, by contributing so freely and liberally toward the establishment of a general Seminary, for the advancement of knowledge, virtue and public spirit.

Resolved, That the Declaration of Trust by the Visitors and Governors of the said College is an acceptable pledge and assurance that they will continue to exert the utmost zeal and abilities to carry on and completing the establishment of a Seminary so successfully begun, and which promises to be of public utility to the present and future generations.

Resolved, That their exertions merit the approbation of the Legislature, and (when circumstances will permit) ought to receive their public encouragement and assistance.

Resolved, That the exalted and patriotic sentiments contained in the letter of his Excellency General Washington, in answer to the letter of the Visitors of Kent County School, and the polite manner in which he hath been pleased to accept the honorable intentions of the General Assembly, in dignifying the College with his name, are proofs of that goodness and greatness of soul by which he is actuated in all his conduct.

Resolved, That the several papers upon which these resolutions are founded be entered on the journals of the Assembly, and be published with the same, in honor of the first founders, benefactors and patrons of this Seminary.

CHAPTER XLIV.

First Commencement of Washington College, May 14, 1783—List of Graduates—Corner-Stone Laid—Convention at Chestertown, May 12, 1783—Petition the Assembly—Dr. Smith to Rev. Dr. White—Convention at Annapolis, August 13, 1783—Petitions to the General Assembly of Maryland—Declaration of Rights—Notice of Rev. Thomas Gates—Dr. Smith Chosen for Bishop of Maryland—Clergy of Maryland Give Recommendation of Him for Consecration to the Bishop of London—Notices of the Rev. Dr. Gordon and of the Rev. Dr. West—Marriage of Dr. Smith's Eldest Daughter.

On Wednesday, the 14th of May, 1783, was held the First Commencement in *Washington College* for Degrees in the Arts and Sciences. The scene was new and interesting, not only to the inhabitants of Chestertown, but to those of the State in general.

We have the following contemporary account of the event:

At ten in the forenoon, a procession was formed from the place where the schools were kept, to the Church, in the following order, viz. :

1st. The body of Scholars and Students, two by two.

2d. The Candidates for Degrees, in the like order.

3d. The Faculty of Professors, with the REV. WILLIAM SMITH, D. D., President of the Visitors and Governors, who acted, by appointment, as PRINCIPAL pro Tempore, at their head.

4th. The corporation of Visitors and Governors, his Excellency WILLIAM PACA, Esq. ; Governor of the State, and one of the said Visitors and Governors, at their head.

When the procession arrived at the Church door, the scholars, students and candidates for degrees filed off to the right and left, forming a lane through which the Faculty and Corporation of Visitors and Governors marched into the Church, followed by the candidates, and then the students and scholars according to their classes and seniority.

The company being seated, the PRINCIPAL pro Tempore (Dr. SMITH) opened the business of the day with a solemn PRAYER and ADDRESS to the SUPREME BEING; and afterwards a short Latin oration to the learned and collegiate part of the audience, as custom seems to require. The candidates then proceeded with the public exercises as follows, viz.:

1. A Latin SALUTATORY ORATION, by Mr. JOHN SCOTT.

2. An oration in French, by Mr. JAMES SCOTT.

3. A Latin SYLLOGISTIC DISPUTE—"*Num Æternitas Pœnarum contradicit divinis Attributis ?*"   Respondent Mr. CHARLES SMITH;* Opponents Messrs. WILLIAM BARROL and WILLIAM BORDLEY.

4. An English FORENSIC DISPUTE,—" Whether the state of nature be a state of war?" The speakers were Messrs. John Scott, William Barrol, William Bordley and James Scott.

5. The Degrees were conferred by the PRINCIPAL as follows:

Messrs. { Charles Smith, James Scott, John Scott, William Barrol, William Bordley, } Bachelors of Arts.

Mr. Samuel Kerr, Honorary Bachelor of Arts.

Mr. Colin Ferguson, Master of Arts.

Mr. Samuel Armor, Master of Arts of the College of Philadelphia, admitted *ad eundem.*†

6. An English Valedictory Oration, which concluded with a striking and prophetic copy of verses on the progress of the sciences and the growing glory of America—By Mr. Charles Smith.

---

* This Charles Smith was the third son of Dr. Smith. He was born in Philadelphia, March 4th, 1765, and baptized in Christ Church in that city by the Rev. Mr. Sturgeon on the 21st of August of the same year, John Moore, Esq., and Charles Smith, his uncles, being sponsors. He was President Judge of the Court of Common Pleas of Franklin and Cumberland counties, and afterwards, when the District Court of Lancaster was created, he became its first President Judge, and the author of a valuable annotated edition of the Laws of Pennsylvania.

† The last two gentlemen were the senior or chief Professors in the Arts and Sciences, and Mr. Kerr one of the Masters in the Grammar School.

7. The PRINCIPAL then closed the business of the Commencement, with an affectionate and pathetic CHARGE to the GRADUATES, respecting their future conduct in life ; and what was to be expected from them, as the first or eldest sons of this rising seminary !—

The different speakers were honored with the justest applause of the audience, for the propriety of their delivery and many masterly strokes of eloquence in the different languages which they spoke, viz. : Latin, French and English.—The Valedictory Oration in particular, from the nature of the subject, as well as beauty of the delivery, had a very striking effect upon all who were present.—

In the evening of the same day, Dr. YOUNG'S TRAGEDY OF THE BROTHERS, notwithstanding the difficulty of the composition, was acted with the greatest applause before a vastly crowded and discerning audience, by the graduates and some others of the students. Messrs. Charles Smith and John Scott, who had before distinguished themselves in Tamerlane and Bajazet, as well as in some principal characters in other performances, during the last years of their education, concluded their scholastic labours in this way, by shining in the characters of the Two Brothers !

The day following (viz. : on Thursday, May 15th) the Visitors and Governors, the Masters, Students and Scholars, accompanied by a great number of gentlemen from the neighboring counties, went in procession to the hill where the new College is to be built ; and after PRAYER by the Rev. Dr. SMITH, the FOUNDATION STONE was laid, with the proper ceremony, by his Excellency, GOVERNOR PACA, who was saluted on the occasion by thirteen discharges of cannon. Orations in French were delivered by Messrs. Thomas Worral and Ebenezer Perkins ; and a Pastoral Dialogue was spoken by three of the younger scholars, in shepherds' dresses, viz.: Messrs. Richard Smith,* Robert Buchanan and Joseph Nicholson. The performance being too long, perhaps, to insert at large, we give a few lines from the beginning and conclusion—

" When Athens flourish'd with the Grecian reign,
And Chiefs and Heroes liv'd—a God-like Train !
When by her Arms each neighbouring State was sway'd,
And Kings an Homage to her Warriors paid—
Ev'n then those Chiefs, who all the World subdu'd,
Lower'd their proud Faces to the Learn'd and Good :
Nor with less Glory in the Rolls of Fame
Shines every SAGE'S, than each Hero's Name."

This happy Day we glory in a Scene,
Which Athens Self enraptur'd would have seen ;
Science triumphant and a Land refin'd,
Where once rude Ignorance sway'd th' untutor'd Mind ;

* Dr. Smith's youngest son.

The Wise, the Good, the FATHERS OF THE STATE,
Conven'd with Joy to fix the MUSE's Seat ;
To lay a fast FOUNDATION-STONE, which shall
Be only mov'd when sinks this Earthly Ball !
Auspicious Day ! no more the Muses mourn,
But hail their Parent PEACE on her Return—
Heav'n gives the Word, and bids Mankind repose,
Contending Nations blush that they were Foes ;
Old Warriors now shall glow with Rage no more,
But reap the Fields their Valour sav'd before.
Hail Goddess PEACE ! in thy celestial Mien
Sweet Happiness and ev'ry Grace are seen ;
O'er thy smooth Brow no rugged Helmet frowns,
An Olive Wreath thy shining Temple crowns.
Let now the Muses hasten to explore
The tawny Chief on ERIE's distant Shore,
Or trace his Steps among the Forests wide,
That deep imbrown the vast ONTARIO's Side ;
And bid him quick his deadly Bow unbend,
For now destructive WAR is at an End ;
Let mighty MISSISSIPPI, as he runs,
Proclaim aloud to all his swarthy Sons,
That to Earth's Ends fair Science shall encrease,
And form one Reign of LEARNING and of PEACE !

The rapid and great success of Washington College, not less than his own commanding powers as an orator, writer and executive agent in every department, had by the year 1783 made Dr. Smith a conspicuous and influential person of the Church in Maryland. And as he abated nothing of his more youthful activity in ecclesiastical affairs, his agency soon began to show itself in that new State of his residence, with obvious results.

The effect of the Declaration of Independence on the 4th of July, 1776, and of different Acts of the Legislature of the State passed about the same time, left in an uncertain and precarious condition the property of the different parishes of the Church of England in the new commonwealth. Soon after going to Maryland, therefore, and even during the war, Dr. Smith prepared and caused to be signed by laymen of several parishes and by those few of the clergy who then remained, a petition to the General Assembly of the State seeking to have the matter of church-rights established. The document was thus :

To the Honourable the General Assembly of the State of Maryland, the Petition of the Vestry and Church-Wardens of the Parish of ———, ——— County,

Humbly Sheweth, That it is manifest from Reason, as well as the clearer Light of Revelation, that the Worship of the Almighty Creator and Governor of the Universe, is the indispensable duty of his dependent Creatures, and the surest means of procuring their temporal as well as eternal Happiness: That, where Religion is left unsupported, neither Laws nor Government can be duly administered; And, as the experience of ages has shewn the necessity of a provision for supporting the Officers and Ministers of Government, in all civil Societies; so the like experience shews the necessity of providing a support for the Ordinances and Ministers of Religion—because if either Religion or Government were left wholly dependent on the benevolence of individuals, such is the frailty of human nature, and the averseness of many to their best Interests, that the Sordid and Selfish, the Licentious, and Prophane, would avail themselves of such Liberty to shrink from their share of labour and expense, and thereby render that, which would be easy when borne by All, an intolerable burden to the Few, whose conscience and principles of Justice would not permit them in this, or any other case, to swerve from their Duties, Civil or Religious.

That our pious ancestors, the worthy and respectable Founders of this State, convinced of the foregoing Truths, and declaring that, "In every well-grounded Commonwealth, matters concerning Religion ought, in the first place, to be taken into consideration, countenanced and encouraged; as being not only most acceptable to God, but the best Way and Means of obtaining His Mercy, and a Blessing upon a People and Country," (having the Promises of this Life and of the Life to come) did frame and enact sundry Laws for erecting Churches and Places of Public Worship, the maintenance of an orthodox Clergy, the Support and advancement of Religion, and the orderly Administration of its divine and saving Ordinances.

That the Delegates of this State, at the great Æra of our Independence, in free and full Convention assembled, for the purpose of establishing a new Constitution and Form of Government, upon the authority of the People, appearing in their Wisdom to have considered some parts of the said laws as inconsistent with that Religious Liberty and Equality of Assessment, which they intended as the basis of their future Government, did, by the 33d Section of the Declaration of Rights, abrogate all such Laws theretofore passed, as enabled any County Courts, on the Application of Vestrymen and Church-Wardens, to make Assessments or Levies for Support of the Religious Establishment; but not with a View of being less attentive than their pious Ancestors had been, to the Interests of Religion, Learning, and Good Morals. On the contrary, by the very same Section, an express Recommendation and Authority are given to future Legislatures, "At their discretion, to lay a general and equal Tax, for the support of the Christian Religion," agreeably to the said Declaration.

That your Petitioners are sensible of the many urgent civil concerns, in which the honorable and worthy Legislatures of this State have been engaged, since the commencement of the present great and trying period; and how much wisdom and deliberation are at all times necessary in framing equal laws for the Support of Religion and Learning, and more especially amidst the horrors and confusions of an expensive, cruel, and unrelenting War. But they are sensible, at the same Time (and persuaded the honorable Assembly are equally sensible), that where Religion is left to mourn and droop her head, while her sacred Ordinances are unsupported, and Vice and Immorality gain Ground, even War itself will be but feebly carried on, Patriotism will lose its most animating Principle, Corruption will win its Way from the lowest to the highest Places, Distress will soon pervade every public Measure; our Churches, our Grave-Yards—the Monuments of the Piety of our Ancestors, running into Ruin, will become the Reproach of their Posterity; nay more, the great and glorious Fabric of public Happiness which we are striving to build up, and cement with an Immensity of Blood and Treasure, might be in Danger of tumbling into the Dust, as wanting the stronger Cement of Virtue and Religion, or perhaps would fall an easy Prey to some haughty Invader!

Deeply impressed with these momentous Considerations, and conceiving ourselves fully warranted by our Constituents, in this Application to your honorable Body, having duly advertized our design without any objections yet notified to us—your Petitioners, therefore, most earnestly and humbly pray that an Act may be passed, agreeably to the aforesaid Section of the Declaration of Rights, for the Support of public Religion, by an equal assessment and tax, and also to enable the Vestry and Church-Wardens of this Parish, by rates on the Pews, from time to time, or otherwise, as in your Wisdom you shall think fit, to repair and uphold the Church and Chapel, and the Church-Yards and Burying-Grounds of the same; all which, your Petitioners conceive, may be done, not only for this Parish, but at the same time, if thought best, for every other Parish within this State (which, it is believed, earnestly desires the same) by a single Law, in a manner perfectly agreeable to the Liberty and Wishes of every denomination of Men, who would be deemed good Christians and faithful Citizens of this State. And your Petitioners, as bound, shall ever pray, &c.

In the foregoing Petition, as my readers will have observed, no exclusive privilege was prayed for; but only "that a law may be passed agreeably to the Bill of Rights, and to the liberty and wishes of every denomination of men, who would be deemed good Christians and faithful citizens of this State." However, some of the vestries that presented the petitions, finding the public difficulties increasing, were apprehensive that injury might be done to the Church by pressing the petition, and soon afterwards signified their desire to the General Assembly that further consideration of the matter might be postponed to a time of less distress and danger.

On the establishment of peace, Governor Paca, who had been a pupil of Dr. Smith's (a graduate in the year 1759 of the College at Philadelphia), and between whom and the Provost there ever subsisted a warm attachment, with a paternal and pious care for the concerns of religion, as inseparably connected with the interest of the State, was pleased, May 6th, 1783, to revive the business, in an address to the General Assembly. He said, speaking for himself and his council:

" It is far from our Intentions to embarrass your deliberations with a variety of objects ; but we cannot pass over Matters of so high Concernment as RELIGION and LEARNING. The Sufferings of the Ministers of the Gospel of all Denominations, during the War, have been very considerable ; and the Perseverance and Firmness of those, who discharged their sacred Functions under many discouraging Circumstances, claim our Acknowledgments and Thanks. The Bill of Rights and Form of Government recognize the principle of public Support for the Ministers of the Gospel, and ascertain the Mode. Anxiously solicitous for the Blessings of Government, and the Welfare and Happiness of our Citizens, and thoroughly convinced of the powerful Influence of Religion, when diffused by its respectable Teachers, we beg leave most seriously and warmly to recommend, among the first Objects of your Attention, on the return of Peace, the making such Provision, as the Constitution, in this case, authorizes and approves."

A copy of this address, about a week after it was delivered to the Assembly, came into the hands of Dr. Smith and others of the Episcopal Clergy of Maryland, most of whom were assembled at the commencement in Washington College in May, 1783, of which we have already spoken. Dr. Smith, finding the concerns of religion so strongly recommended by the executive to the legislative part of government, thought it wise that there should be a council or consultation of clergy held immediately for the purpose of considering " What alterations might be necessary in our liturgy and service; and how our church might be organized and a succession in the ministry kept up, so as to be an object of public notice and support, in common with other Christian churches under the Revolution." A convention accordingly assembled in the hall of Washington College, May 12–15, 1783; Dr. Smith presided.

It was considered by this convention that some legislative interposition or sanction might probably be necessary in the course of this business; for as our church derived her liturgy from the Church of England, and was formerly dependent on the same church for a succession in her ministry, and had certain property reserved to her by the constitution of Maryland, under the name of the Church of England, it became a question whether, if any alterations should be made in the liturgy, or in the mode of succession in the ministry, she could any longer be considered as the church described in the constitution of this State, or entitled to the perpetual use of the property aforesaid. An incorporating act, or charter, was also deemed necessary to enable the clergy, or some representative body of the church, to raise and manage a fund for certain charitable and pious purposes; such charters having been granted to Christian societies of every denomination in other of the neighboring States, wherever they had been prayed for.

Dr. Smith, who, with the Rev. Mr. Thomas Gates,* had been appointed a committee, with extensive powers, accordingly now prepared another petition. It was thus:

To the Honourable the General Assembly of the State of Maryland, the Memorial and Petition of the Subscribers in Behalf of Themselves and others, the Clergy of the Episcopal Churches,

Sheweth—That the happy termination of War, the establishment of Peace, and the final recognition and acknowledgment of the Sovereignty and Independence of these United States among the Powers of

---

* Thomas Gates, D. D.—a native of England; brought up in the church. He was ordained in England. In 1781 he became rector of St. Ann's, Annapolis; in 1785, of St. Peter's, Talbot, a member of the Standing Committee. In 1789 he removed to South Carolina, and there continued till his death in 1832. (Allen's History.)

the World, yield a favourable occasion (which this State in particular
hath long desired) of making some permanent Provision, agreeably to
the Constitution, for "the Ministers of Religion," and the advancement of useful Knowledge and Literature, through this rising American
Empire.

That, in respect to the Episcopal Churches in this State (to the
Communion of which so large a proportion of the good people of
Maryland belongs) the following things are absolutely necessary, viz.:

1st. That some alterations should be made in the Liturgy and Service,
in order to adapt the same to the Revolution, and for other purposes of
Uniformity, Concord and Subordination to the State.

2d. That a plan for educating, ordaining, and keeping up a succession of able and fit Ministers or Pastors, for the service of said churches
agreeably to ancient practice and their professed Principles, as well as
that universal Toleration, established by the Constitution, be speedily
determined upon and fixed, under the public authority of the State, and
with the Advice and Consent of the Clergy of the said Churches, after
due Consultation had thereupon.

Your Petitioners, therefore, humbly pray—

That the said Clergy may have leave to consult, prepare and offer to
the General Assembly, the Draft of a Bill, for the good Purposes
aforesaid—and your Petitioners, as in Duty bound, shall pray, &c.

WILLIAM SMITH.
THOMAS GATES.

The prayer of the foregoing petition was granted.

A convention of the clergy was now accordingly called to be
held at Annapolis on the 13th of August, 1783. Prior to this
convention being assembled, we have the following interesting
letter from

Dr. Smith to Dr. White.

CHESTER, August 4th, 1783.

DEAR SIR: The Clergy in Maryland are to meet (in pursuance of the
sanction obtained from the Grand Assembly) on the 13th of this month:
but as M^r. Gates and myself were to call this meeting we found upon
consulting our nearest brethren that they did not think it proper, nor
that we were authorized to call any Clergy to our assistance from the
neighboring States; that the Episcopal Clergy of Maryland were in
some respects peculiarly circumstanced, and ought in the first instance
to have a preparatory convention or conference to consider and frame
a Declaration of their own Rights as one of the Churches of a separate
and independent State; to agree upon some articles of Government and
unity among themselves; to fix some future time of meeting by adjourn-

ment; to appoint a committee to bring in a plan of some few alterations that may be found necessary in the Liturgy and Service of the
Church; and by the authority of this first meeting to open a correspondence on the subject with the clergy of the neighboring States, and to
have some speedy future and more general meeting with the clergy of
these States, or Committees from them, to unite if possible in the alterations to be made which many among us think cannot have a full Church
Ratification till we have decided on some plan or another; the three
orders of Bishops, Priests, and Deacons to concur in same. What State
or civic ratification may be necessary, or whether any, is a question yet
to be determined. In Maryland I presume a few words of a Declaratory Act that a Clergy ordained in such a form, and using a Liturgy
with such alterations as may be agreed upon, are to be considered as
entitled to the Glebes, Churches and other property declared by the
Constitution to belong to the Church of England for ever. I say such
a short act as this, or the opinion of the Judges that such act is not
necessary, is, I conceive, all that will be wanted.

I am, &c.,

WILLIAM SMITH.

To Rev'd Dr. White.

One part of the proceedings of this Convention of August 13th,
1783, held at Annapolis, was to nominate a committee " To prepare
the draft of an Act or Charter of Incorporation, to enable the
Episcopal Church of this State, as a body corporate, to hold
goods, lands and chattels, by deed, gift, devise, etc., to the amount
of —— per annum, as a fund for providing small annuities to the
widows of clergymen, and for the education of their children, or
any poor children in general, who may be found of promising
genius and disposition, for a supply of ministers in the said church,
and for other pious and charitable uses."

We here see Dr. Smith's hand again. This was with him an old
scheme introduced nearly fifteen years before into Pennsylvania,
New York, and New Jersey, and still beneficially existing in all
these States, but in Pennsylvania especially.* He now applied it
to Maryland, where, we believe, it still exists with valuable results.

Other business of this Convention was to deliberate concerning
the mode of obtaining a succession in the ministry, the choice of
fit persons for the different orders of the same, and some fundamental articles for future uniformity, concord, and good govern-

---

* Described by us, Vol. I., page 423.

ment, for which purpose the following were unanimously agreed upon and subscribed, viz.:

A Declaration of certain fundamental Rights and Liberties of the Protestant Episcopal Church of Maryland, drawn up and subscribed, viz.

Whereas by the Constitution and Form of Government of this State —"All persons professing the Christian Religion are equally entitled to protection in their Religious Liberty, and no person, by any Law, or otherwise, ought to be molested in his person or estate, on account of his Religious Persuasion or Profession, or for his Religious Practice; unless, under colour of Religion, any man shall disturb the good Order, Peace, or Safety of the State, or shall infringe the Laws of Morality, or injure others in their Natural, Civil, or Religious Rights:" And whereas the Ecclesiastical and Spiritual Independence of the different Religious Denominations, Societies, Congregations, and Churches of Christians in this State, necessarily follows from, or is included in, their Civil Independence.

Wherefore we, the Clergy of the Protestant Episcopal Church of Maryland (heretofore denominated the Church of England, as by Law established) with all duty to the civil authority of the State, and with all Love and Good-will to our Fellow-Christians of every other Religious denomination, do hereby declare, make known, and claim, the following, as certain of the Fundamental Rights and Liberties inherent in and belonging to the said Episcopal Church, not only of common Right, but agreeably to the express Words, Spirit and Design of the Constitution and Form of Government aforesaid, viz.,

I. We consider it as the undoubted Right of the said Protestant Episcopal Church, in common with other Christian Churches under the American Revolution, to complete and preserve herself as an entire Church, agreeably to her ancient Usages and Profession, and to have the full enjoyment and free exercise of those purely Spiritual Powers, which are essential to the being of every Church or Congregation of the faithful, and which, being derived only from Christ and his Apostles, are to be maintained independent of every foreign or other Jurisdiction, so far as may be consistent with the civil Rights of Society.

II. That ever since the Reformation, it hath been the received Doctrine of the Church whereof we are Members (and which by the Constitution of this State is entitled to the perpetual Enjoyment of certain Property and Rights under the denomination of the Church of England) "That there be these three Orders of Ministers in CHRIST's CHURCH: BISHOPS, PRIESTS, and DEACONS," and that an *Episcopal Ordination and Commission are necessary to the valid Administration of the Sacraments, and the due Exercise of the Ministerial Functions in the said Church.*

7

III. That, without calling in Question the Rights, Modes, and Forms of any other Christian Churches or Societies, or wishing the least Contest with them on that subject, we consider and declare it to be an essential Right of the said Protestant Episcopal Church to have and enjoy the Continuance of the said three Orders of Ministers forever, so far as concerns Matters purely spiritual; and that no Persons, in the Character of Ministers, except such as are in the Communion of the said Church, and duly called to the Ministry by regular Episcopal Ordination, can or ought to be admitted into, or enjoy any of the " Churches, Chapels, Glebes, or other Property," formerly belonging to the Church of England in this State, and which, by the Constitution and Form of Government, is secured to the said Church forever, by whatsoever Name, she the said Church, or her superior order of Ministers, may in future be denominated.

IV. That as it is the Right, so it will be the Duty, of the said Church, when duly organized, constituted, and represented in a Synod or Convention of the different Orders of her Ministry and People, to revise her Liturgy, Forms of Prayer, and public Worship, in order to adapt the same to the late Revolution and other local Circumstances of America; which it is humbly conceived, may and will be done, without any other or farther Departure from the venerable Order and beautiful Forms of Worship of the Church from whence we sprung, than may be found expedient in the Change of our Situation from a DAUGHTER to a SISTER-CHURCH.

August 13th, 1783.

WILLIAM SMITH, President, St. Paul's & Chester Parishes, Kent County.

JOHN GORDON, Rector of St. Michael's, Talbot.

JOHN M'PHERSON, Rector of William and Mary Parish, Charles County.

SAMUEL KEENE, Rector of Dorchester Parish, Dorchester County.

WILLIAM WEST, Rector of St. Paul's Parish, Baltimore.

WILLIAM THOMSON, Rector of St. Stephen's, Cœcil County.

WALTER MAGOWAN, Rector of St. James's Parish, Ann-Arundel County.

JOHN STEPHEN, Rector of All-Faith Parish, St. Mary's County.

THOMAS JOHN CLAGGETT, Rector of St. Paul's Parish, Prince George's County.

GEORGE GOLDIE, Rector of King and Queen, St. Mary's County.

JOSEPH MESSENGER, Rector of St. Andrew's Parish, St. Mary's County.

JOHN BOWIE, Rector of St. Peter's Parish, Talbot County.

WALTER HARRISON, Rector of Durham Parish, Charles County.

WILLIAM HANNA, Rector of St. Margaret's, Westminster Parish, Ann-Arundel County.

THOMAS GATES, Rector of St. Ann's, Annapolis.

JOHN ANDREWS, Rector of St. Thomas's Parish, Balti-

more County.

HAMILTON BELL, Rector of Stephney Parish, Somerset County.

FRANCIS WALKER, Rector of Shrewsbury Parish, Kent County.

Signed
June 23d,
1784.

The foregoing declaration of rights being made and subscribed, a copy of the same was presented to his Excellency the Governor, with the following address, prepared, undoubtedly, like most or all of the other documents in the case, by Dr. Smith:

To HIS EXCELLENCY WILLIAM PACA, ESQ., GOVERNOR AND COMMANDER-IN-CHIEF, &c., &c., OF THE STATE OF MARYLAND.

We the Protestant Episcopal Clergy of the said State, at a Meeting or Convention held at Annapolis this 13th August, 1783 (in pursuance of a Vote of the House of Delegates passed at their last Session), in order to consider, make known and declare those fundamental Christian Rights, to which we conceive ourselves entitled, in common with other Christian Churches; Do hereby, in the first Place, return your Excellency our most sincere and hearty Thanks for your great Concern and Attention manifested for the Christian Church in general and her suffering Clergy of all Denominations. We trust and pray that your Excellency will continue your powerful Intercession till some Law is passed for their future Support and Encouragement, agreeably to the Constitution.

We herewith lay before your Excellency an authentic Copy of a Declaration of certain Rights, to which, according to our best knowledge of the Laws and Constitution of our Country, we think ourselves entitled, in common with other Churches. Should your Excellency, from your superior knowledge of both, think that the Declaration we have made stands in need of any further Sanction, Legislative or otherwise, we are well persuaded that a Continuance of the same Zeal and Regard which you have formerly shown, will at Length produce the happy Effect which you so anxiously desire.

Praying for a continued Encrease of your Excellency's public Usefulness, and that you meet the reward thereof in the World to come,

We are, &c.

[Signed by all the Members, as the above Declaration of Rights was signed.]

To this Governor Paca was pleased to return the following answer, viz.:

GENTLEMEN :—I have attentively considered the paper intitled "A declaration of certain Fundamental Rights and Liberties of the Protestant Episcopal Church of Maryland." And as every denomination of Clergy are to be deemed adequate Judges of their own Spiritual Rights, and of the Ministerial commission and authority necessary to the due administration of the Ordinances of Religion among themselves, it would be a very partial and unjust distinction to deny that Right to the respectable and learned Body of the Episcopal Clergy in this State; and it will give me the highest happiness and satisfaction, if, either in my individual capacity, or in the public character which I now have the honour to sustain, I can be instrumental in advancing the interests of Religion in general, alleviating the Sufferings of any of her Ministers, and placing every branch of the Christian Church in this State, upon the most equal and respectable footing.

I am,

GENTLEMEN,

Your most obd't, humble Servant,

WILLIAM PACA.

In due time every concession needed from the State was obtained. Some, at first thought needful, were declared by sufficient authority to be unnecessary; and the Protestant Episcopal Church in Maryland succeeded to every desirable right of the old Church of England in the Province.

In all these operations Dr. Smith was not only the main-spring but the machinery and regulator also. It is impossible, I think, to look at his efforts in re-establishing the church in Maryland, after it had been laid in ruins by the war of the Revolution, without a lively feeling of gratitude to his memory.

One of the memorable acts of this convention was the election of Dr. Smith to the office of Bishop of Maryland. He moved into the place by the force of gravitation; by the power which moves all inferior men to look up to and respect one of abilities entirely transcending their own. He was directed to proceed to England for consecration, the convention recommending that the various parishes should take up collections for the purpose of paying his expenses.

The following is a copy of his testimonial* intended to be given to the Bishop of London, if the Bishop-elect should think fit to ask for consecration :

---

* Manuscript in Dr. Smith's papers.

ANNAPOLIS, MARYLAND, August 16, 1783.

My Lord:—Whereas the good people of this State, and in connection with the Church of England, have long labored, and do still labor, under great difficulties, through the want of a regular clergy to supply the many poor parishes that have for a considerable time been vacant.

To prevent, therefore, and guard against such an unhappy situation for the future, we, the Convention, in meeting of the Clergy of the Church of England, have made choice of, and do recommend, our brother, the Rev. Dr. William Smith, as a fit and proper person, and every way well qualified to be invested with the sacred office of a Bishop, in order to perpetuate a regular succession of clergy among us. We do with great confidence present unto your Lordship this godly and well-learned man to be ordained and consecrated Bishop, being perfectly satisfied that he will duly execute the office whereunto he is called, to the edifying of the Church and to the glory of God.

Your Lordship's well-known zeal for the Church and propagation of the Christian religion induces us to trust that your Lordship will compassionate the case of a remote and distressed people, and comply with our earnest request in this matter. For without such a remedy, the Church in this country is in imminent danger of becoming extinct. That your Lordship may long continue an ornament to the Church is the hearty prayer of, my Lord, your very dutiful and most obedient servants,

*1745. JOHN GORDON, St. Michael's, Talbot county.
1751. JOHN MACPHERSON, William and Mary Parish, Charles co.
1750. WM. THOMSON, St. Stephen's, N. Sassafras Parish, Cecil.
1760. SAMUEL KEENE,† Dorchester and Great Choptank Parishes, Dorchester.
1761. WILLIAM WEST,† St. Paul's Parish, Baltimore.
1766. GEORGE GOLDIE, King and Queen, St. Mary's.
1770. JOHN BOWIE,† St. Peter's, Talbot.
1748. WALTER MAGOWAN, St. James' Parish, Ann Arundel county.
1764. JOHN STEPHEN, All Faith, St. Mary's.
1774. WALTER H. HARRISON,† Durham Parish, Charles.
1772. WM. HANNA,† St. Margaret's Westminster, Ann Arundel co.
1772. JOSEPH MESSENGER, St. Andrew's Parish, St. Mary's county.
1767. THOMAS JOHN CLAGGETT,† St. Paul's Parish, Prince Geo. co.
THOMAS GATES, St. Ann's, Annapolis.
1767. JOHN ANDREWS,† St. Thomas', Baltimore county.
1773. FRANCIS WALKER, Kent Island, Queen Anne county.

---

* These are the dates of the respective ordinations of the clergy.
† Natives of the States—two natives of Virginia and three of New York.

1774. HAMILTON BELL,* Stepney Parish, Somerset county.
1763. LEONARD CUTTING, All Hallows', Worcester county.
WILL SMITH, Stepney Parish, Worcester county.
1774. RALPH HIGINBOTHAM, St. Ann's, Ann Arundel county.
1784. EDWARD GANTT,* Christ Church, Calvert.
1785. HATCH DENT,* Trinity, Charles county.

The Convention agreed that until a regular ordination of clergy could be obtained, there should be three clergymen appointed on each Shore, in order to examine such young gentlemen as might offer themselves candidates for Holy Orders in our churches; such examiners to report their moral character, their knowledge in the learned languages and divinity, and their attachment to the doctrines of the Christian religion as professed and taught in our Church; and to recommend such candidates as upon examination might be thought worthy to serve as readers in any parish that might think proper to employ them, leaving such parishes, as to the administration of the sacraments and other proper functions of the clerical character, to the more immediate direction of such neighboring clergymen as might agree to visit them occasionally for the purpose.

Dr. Smith, the Rev. Dr. Gordon,† and Dr. Samuel Keene were appointed for the Eastern Shore, and the Rev. Dr. West,‡ Dr. Thomas John Claggett, and Dr. Thomas Gates, for the Western.

On the 15th of May of this year an important event took place in the domestic affairs of Dr. Smith: his eldest daughter, Williamina,§ was married to Charles Goldsborough, Esq., of Horn's

---

* Natives of the States—two natives of Virginia and three of New York.

† JOHN GORDON, D. D., a native of Scotland, brought up in the Church, ordained in 1745. On coming to Maryland became the incumbent of St. Ann's, Annapolis; in 1750, of St. Michael's, Talbot; a Whig of the Revolution; after 1776 had a school at his residence; published three sermons; died in 1790, aged upwards of 70.—ALLEN.

‡ WILLIAM WEST, D. D., a native of Virginia, brought up in the Church, ordained in 1761. Coming from Virginia in 1763, he became the incumbent of Westminster Parish, Ann Arundel county; in 1767 of St. Andrew's, St. Mary's; in 1772 of St. George's, Hartford, and in 1779 Rector of St. Paul's, Baltimore. A Whig of the Revolution; successively Secretary and President of the Maryland Convention, and member of the examining, superintending, and standing committees, and delegate to the General Convention. He died 1791, æt 54.—ALLEN.

§ The portrait of this lady (which accompanies this volume) is taken from a miniature in a ring, which tradition says was painted by the unfortunate Major André, at the time of the Meschianza, in which she participated. The ring is now the property of Thos. P. Cradock, Esq., of Maryland, to whom I am indebted for its use.—H. W. S.

WILLIAMINA SMITH.

ÆT: 16.

Point, Dorchester county, Maryland. The ceremony was performed in the homestead at Chestertown, by the Rev. Samuel Keene, in the presence of Governor Paca, and a large assembly of the first people of the State, who had been called together by the laying of the corner-stone of Washington College, and the Convention of the Church. Mr. Goldsborough was the son of Robert Goldsborough, Barrister-at-Law ; had been brought up a lawyer; born Nov. 21st, 1761, died June 22d, 1801.

CHAPTER XLV.

Dr. White, Dr. Blackwell of Pennsylvania and Dr. Beach of New Jersey Desirous of a Continental Convention — Dr. Smith in Maryland Assists the Project — Dr. Smith to Dr. White — A Church Conference is Made at a Meeting of the Clergy to Re-establish the Corporation for the Relief of the Widows and Children of the Clergy, Founded, 1769 — Ecclesiastical Convention of Pennsylvania, May 25th, 1784 — Declaration by it of Principles — Ecclesiastical Convention of Maryland, June 22d, 1784 — Dr. Smith's Sermon at it — Declaration by it of Principles Sufficiently Harmonious with those of the Pennsylvania Convention — Convention of Several States in New York, October 6th, 1784 — Dr. Smith Presides — Fundamental Principles Declared by it, and Proceedings End — Dr. Smith Chairman of Committee to Frame an Ecclesiastical Constitution and to Frame and Propose a Proper Substitute for the State Prayers — Dr. Smith Elected President of the Corporation for the Relief of the Widows, etc.

While Dr. Smith was thus actively engaged in the work of education in Maryland and in re-establishing the church in that State, his brethren in Pennsylvania, Dr. White and Dr. Blackwell, were equally active not only in re-establishing the Church in Pennsylvania, but also in the further work of endeavoring to assemble the clergy of *all* the States in what was called a " *Continental* Convention." The efforts of the respective parties—originated probably by the Reverend Abraham Beach, D. D., at one time a minister of Trinity Church, New York, but more lately resident in Brunswick, N. J.—were natural to their positions.

Dr. Smith had been driven from Pennsylvania by an embittered and proscriptive political faction, and found in the quiet shades of Chestertown a retreat from their gross and exasperating injustice. *Maryland,* he supposed it probable, might thenceforth become *his* home; and *there* the scene of whatever usefulness, in the order of Providence, it might be allotted to him to be the means of. White, on the other hand, as chaplain of the Congress, and Blackwell as chaplain in the main army, for some time close to the Congress, were brought into intimate relations with the representatives of the church from all parts of the country, and like most of the men by whom the liberties of the country were achieved on the field, were ever in favor of UNION; of a *corporate* dignity—both in the State and in the Church. Though now in Pennsylvania, Blackwell's family—an influential one—was of New York, while his first ministerial duties had been in New Jersey, over the *whole* of which province he had received a license from the Bishop of London in 1772 to act. These men therefore naturally extended their views over all the States, and were desirous of having a *General* Convention.* But a General Convention was a hard thing to accomplish. Fears, by some, of what might be resolved on in such a body—the ambitions, probably, of others who, in the church, as was afterwards the case with some in political affairs, knew that their purposes could best be accomplished, and their views best carried out, by the supremacy of State organization— put obstacles in the way.

White, Smith, Blackwell, Magaw, Beach, Frazer, Provost, Moore, Wharton, and indeed most of the clergy, so far as I know, of New York, Pennsylvania, New Jersey, Delaware and Maryland, while clear upon the necessity of dioceses, of which the States would in that day be the natural limit, were equally desirous of a' " Federal Union," as we may call it; a union by which the church should be made one in organization as it was one in faith. The first efforts at a general convention came from New Jersey, operating upon Pennsylvania and New York; and a representation from even so many States was brought about, not by any announcement that the affairs of the *church* were to be considered, but by a call upon the clergy and laity who were the trustees of that useful

---

* I ought probably to include with the names of White and Blackwell that of the Rev. Dr. Samuel Magaw, of Philadelphia. But while everything which I ever heard of him is to his honor, we have so little biographical account of him, that I am not able to say with confidence much about him. He was undoubtedly the personal friend of White and of Blackwell, and I believe, generally speaking, a coadjutor with both in most that relates to the church. A biography of him is much needed.

and now opulent corporation for the relief of the widows and children of clergymen—which we have described much at large in our
former volume,* and which was a corporation, it will be remembered, of the three States just named—to assemble at New Brunswick, in New Jersey, to consider the best means to save its
property, which had been much endangered by different fiscal
operations of the Congress and the States, from further peril, and
to put the institution again into active and stable operation.

This call brought together certain gentlemen of the clergy, to
wit :

> From PENNSYLVANIA, Dr. White, Dr. Magaw and Mr. Black-
> well.
> "   NEW JERSEY,   The Rev. Messrs. Beach, Frazer and
> Ogden.
> "   NEW YORK,   The Rev. Messrs. Bloomer, Benjamin
> Moore and Thomas Moore.

The affairs of the church in the lately British Provinces generally was a natural subject of consideration ; and there happening
to be at the time in New Brunswick—though there by public
business of a civil kind—some gentlemen of the laity from New
York and New Jersey, who were represented by the clergy from
those States as taking an interest in the welfare of the church, *they*
were requested to join the meeting of the clergy. These gentlemen of the laity were John Stevens, Richard Stevens, John
Dennis, James Parker, Colonel Hoyt and Colonel Furman. And
thus was formed, of clergy and laity, the embryo of the General
Convention of the church in America. Dr. Smith was not present at this meeting. The corporation for the relief of the widows,
etc., in behalf of which the meeting was called—a Pre-Revolution-
ary Corporation—was not a corporation of Maryland, although
after going there in 1780, Dr. Smith originated and caused to be
there established a similar organization. His name therefore does
not appear in any way in this first convention; if the accidental
meeting is to be called " a convention " in any sense in which
the word, in connection with the church, is now commonly used.
Dr. White presided at this meeting ; and opened it with a sermon.

---

* Pages 423–432.

Beyond discussing principles of ecclesiastical union little was done here. But before the clergy parted, it was agreed to procure as general a meeting as might be, of representatives of the clergy and laity of the different States, to be held in the city of New York, on the 6th of October following; that is to say, the 6th of October, 1784. The gentlemen of New York were to give notice to their brethren eastward, and those of Philadelphia were to do the same by their brethren southward. Dr. Smith had been apparently informed during the session of this meeting of its general purpose; and though as we have already seen* he was desirous not to have the identity or separate existence of Maryland, ecclesiastically obliterated, we find him immediately doing what he could to advance the matter of a general or a "continental convention," and a combined organization of the church throughout the whole country. The following is a letter addressed by him to influential members of Trinity Church, Oxford, Philadelphia—the parish where he had once served while a resident of Pennsylvania, under the appointment of the Society for the Propagation of the Gospel.

Dr. Smith to Messrs. Cotman and Johnson.

CHESTERTOWN, MARYLAND, May 23d, 1784.

To Messrs. BENJ. COTMAN and BENJ. JOHNSON.

I know not what can be done at your meeting of vestries. This, at least, I wish, that a clergyman or two, and about two vestrymen may be appointed a committee to meet committees from the neighboring States at some convenient place, about next October, to fix a general plan for all our Churches, both in respect to Discipline and our Church service. Something fundamental ought also to be agreed upon respecting ordination, &c., similar to what was done in Maryland, a copy of which I gave to Dr. Magaw, declaring that Episcopal ordination is an indispensable qualification for every person who may be desirous to hold any living in our Church. Certainly none else can hold any of the Churches heretofore established or built under the Society for the Propagating of the Gospel, nor the Glebes, where any are. There will be committees from several of the Southern States, especially Maryland and Virginia, but they can hardly be got together till toward the end of September. I hope they may be induced to meet as far North as conveniently may be; perhaps at Philadelphia, or Brunswick, or Wilmington, in Delaware State.   WILLIAM SMITH.

---

* Supra page 95, Letter to the Rev'd Dr. White.

This letter as appears from an indorsement on the original, yet preserved, was read by Dr. White before the committee at their meeting in Christ Church, Philadelphia, May 25th, 1784.

Bishop White, in his Memoirs,* says of this meeting (May 25th, 1784,) at New Brunswick, "that notwithstanding the good humor which prevailed at it, the more Northern clergymen were under apprehensions of there being a disposition on the part of the more Southern to make material deviation from the ecclesiastical system of England in the article of Church government." He adds, for his own part, that "at the same time he wondered that any sensible and well-informed persons should overlook the propriety of accommodating that system, in some respects, to the prevailing sentiments and habits of this country, now become an independent and combined commonwealth."

The clergy of Pennsylvania—doubtless in view, alike of quieting the alarms of the Northern churchmen and of guarding against the adoption of some of the very low church principles, or rather, the no church principles, at all, that had a certain prevalence in Virginia and South Carolina—met with lay representatives in convention in Christ Church, Philadelphia, May 24th, 1784, and agreed upon certain matters of the fundamental sort; which, as "instructions" should bind a standing committee, which the convention appointed with power to correspond and confer with representatives from the Episcopal Church in other States, or any of them, to assist in framing an Ecclesiastical Government. The fundamental principles as then declared in Pennsylvania were these:†

First. That the Episcopal Church of these States is, and ought to be, independent of all foreign Authority, ecclesiastical or civil.

Secondly. That it hath, and ought to have, in common with all other religious societies, full and exclusive Powers to regulate the Concerns of its own Communion.

Thirdly. That the Doctrines of the Gospel be maintained as now professed by the Church of England; and Uniformity of Worship be continued as near as may be to the Liturgy of the said Church.

Fourthly. That the Succession of the Ministry be agreeable to the Usage which requireth the three Orders of Bishops, Priests and

* Second Edition. New York, 1836. Page 79.
† Wilson's Life of Bishop White, page 100.

Deacons; that the Rights and Powers of the same respectively be ascertained; and that they be exercised according to reasonable Laws, to be duly made.

Fifthly. That to make Canons or Laws, there be no other Authority than that of a representative Body of the Clergy and Laity conjointly.

Sixthly. That no Powers be delegated to a general ecclesiastical Government, except such as cannot conveniently be exercised by the Clergy and Laity in their respective Congregations.

Soon after this convention of the clergy and laity of Pennsylvania had taken place, Dr. Smith invited a convention of the clergy and laity in Maryland. He was in Philadelphia so late as the 18th of June, and probably present, though not as a delegate, at the convention on the 24th of May. It is obvious that between him and Dr. White there was a good understanding, and that the two persons were acting as co-workers to one end.

The Convention of Maryland met in that State, at Annapolis, on the 22d of June, 1784, and declared among other things:

According to what we conceive to be of true Apostolic Institution, the duty and office of a Bishop differs in nothing from that of other Priests, except in the Power of Ordination and Confirmation, and in the right of precedency in Ecclesiastical meetings or synods. And if any further distinctions and regulations in the different orders of the ministry should afterwards be found necessary for the good government of the Church, the same shall be made and established by the joint voice and authority of a representative body of the Clergy and Laity at future Ecclesiastical Synods and Conventions.

Ecclesiastical State Conventions of Synods of this Church shall consist of the Clergy and one *Lay Delegate* or Representative from each Vestry or Parish, or a majority of the same.

There was thus a general accord between the churches in the two important States of Pennsylvania and Maryland. And this was an important fact. These two churches made, in terms generally similar, and in moderate but yet firm pretensions, a great and fixed class of principles to which the very *low* churches south of Mayland, and the quite *high* ones north and east of Pennsylvania, could perhaps find something on the respective sides to attach themselves to, and so make one and a connected body; though there would be confessedly a considerable difference in the aspect of one extremity of it from the aspect of the opposite extremity.

At the Convention of June 22d, 1784, in Maryland, Dr. Smith presided, and preached the opening sermon. The text was those well-known verses from the Second Epistle of Timothy, chapter i., verses 13, 14; chapter iv., verses 3, 4.

Hold fast the form of sound words which thou hast heard of me in faith and love which is in Christ Jesus—that good thing which was committed unto thee, keep by the Holy Ghost which dwelleth in us.

For the time will come when they will not endure sound doctrine, but after their own lusts shall heap to themselves teachers, having itching ears, and they shall turn away their ears from the truth, and shall be turned unto fables.

The preacher's mode of treating the text shows the heats of which there was danger, in the discussion of those matters which the times demanded should be considered both in State conventions and in conventions at large. He opens the discourse in a vein of sarcasm, in which he not unfrequently indulged in political discussion or conversation, and in which he there found a powerful weapon, but which his high sense, both of dignity and consistency, prevented much use of in the pulpit. He was here, however, speaking as he was to the Convention of Maryland, *at home* and *inter suos*—more at liberty; and it was perhaps the most effective way to cure some among them affected with stiffness in their cervical *vertebræ*. Thus the Bishop-elect begins:

In this very adventurous and inquisitive Day, when men spurning their kindred-earth, on which they were born to tread, will dare, on airy wing to soar into the regions of the sky; were it the pleasure of our Almighty Creator to purge any of us mortals of our terrestrial dross, and to place us, in good earnest, upon some distant orb, from which with clear and serene view, corporeal as well as intellectual, we could survey this world of ours—what a strange scene would it appear? Itself in the rank of worlds, dwindled into a small mole-hill; and men, the little emmets upon it, bustling and driving and crossing each other, as if there were no settled walk of life, no common tie, or " Form of sound words to be held fast of all, in faith and love which is in Christ Jesus ? "

In our intellectual view, from this eminence of station, we should behold one set of men, who boast of the all-sufficient and transcendent power of Reason, as their rule and guide; but yet all wandering through different tracts, although in the same pursuits of Happiness and Peace ! Another set of men would be seen who call themselves the Special Favourites of Heaven, and say they are guided by a glorious Inward Light, communicated immediately from the everlasting Fountain of all Light! yet we should not see them walking together in unity, or pursuing any common path or way; but fiercely contending concerning their Inward Light; some calling their's the good Old-Light, and others calling their's the true New-Light. To whom an old divine of our church, (the venerable Bishop Andrewes,) were he now living, would say—"There is no Light among you—the Devil hath blinded you all."

But, Thirdly, we should find another set of men, and those of truly respectable and venerable name, professing themselves guided only by a sure and written Form of Sound Words, revealed and given to them for their Instruction, their Guide, and their Salvation, by their Almighty Creator himself—Yet, alas! they would be seen, perhaps, almost as irregular and eccentric in all their motions as the rest!

This is a sad view of things—and as the Poet says—

> "In Pride, in reasoning Pride, the error lies,
> All quit their sphere, and rush into the skies!"

And would to God, therefore, that, in all Religions and in all Sciences, this accursed root of Bitterness and Contrariety could be wholly plucked out of the Christian world. For until Humanity and divine Charity can have their sway, until our Faith is exercised in Love, and the Truths of God are held in Righteousness of Life, there will never be a total harmony among men!

However strong our Reason, however enlightened our Souls, however ardent our Faith; unless that spirit of Love and Humility be in us, which was in Christ Jesus, all besides will be of little value.

With good reason, therefore, does St. Paul admonish his beloved Timothy to let his Faith be exercised in Love, and "to hold fast the Form of sound Words which he had heard of him;" for even in those early days, some had begun to depart from the foundation laid by Christ and his Apostles; following "vain babblings," being like withered leaves, sticking to the tree, only to be blown away by the first wind of doctrine; still desiring to hear some new thing; led by the ear and not by the heart, or as it is strongly expressed in my text, "heaping to themselves Teachers, having itching Ears," &c. . . . . All other marks of our faith, therefore, are vain and delusive, unless we have that Scripture mark of hearts glowing with Love—a transcendent Love, flowing forth in fervent Piety towards God, and universal goodwill towards Man!

Faith, therefore, according to my text, cannot be a mere empty assent to truth, but the holding of truth in love. It is love that shews the true nature of faith. By this it must work; and by this only can God be pleased. For love flowing from faith is the hand-writing of God on the heart. Whatever proceeds from it thus, will bear His

image and superscription. He will know it as His own, and at the last
day openly acknowledge it as such before men and angels—This fruit
of Love is the mark which our Apostle everywhere gives for the trial of
faith and of spirits. The fruits of the spirit are "Love, Joy, Peace,
Long-suffering, Gentleness, Goodness, Meekness, Temperance, and the
like."

He thus speaks of the so-called "evangelical party," whom
Whitefield had raised up to disturb the peace of Zion; part of which
apostatized into Methodists, and part of which, while abandoning
the *principles* of the Church, still remain ostensibly within its pale.

Too many, letting go their hold of the form of sound words, and
substituting, or mistaking, mere mechanical motions—the fervours of
heated imagination—for the true and active signs of Grace, those living
impulses of God on the soul, are often carried into the wildest extrava-
gances. Fetching the marks of their religion from the notions of
visionary or mystical men, instead of looking for them in the life and
Gospel of Christ, they set their passions to work, and at length
persuade or terrify themselves into all those experiences and feelings,
which pass, in their Creed, as the evidences of Salvation.
Buoyed up by such strong delusions, they think "they have built
their mansions among the Stars, have ascended above the Moon, and
left the Sun under their feet;" while they are still but like their
Kindred Meteors which, having scarce mounted to the middle regions,
are precipitated downwards again by their own gross and earthly
particles! A devotion worked up by fervour, whatever proceeds from
the mere force of animal spirits, is of the Earth, earthy; in no manner
like to that true Spirit of Regeneration which is of the Lord from
Heaven, and begets the divine life in the souls of men. This true
celestial warmth will never be extinguished, being of an immortal
nature; and when once vitally seated in the heart, it does not work by
fits and starts, but expands itself more and more, regulating, purifying
and exalting the whole inward man!

But he deals equally with the mere formal observers of religion.

Although it is of great importance, that we adhere to the Form of
sound words, as our text directs us; yet we must not halt at Forms, or
fundamental Principles and Doctrines; but we must strive, with all our
might and zeal, through the grace given us, "to go on to Perfection."
Our Faith must not be a mere empty assent to the truth, but the Holding the Truth in Love. It is Love that shews our Faith to be genuine.
By this it must work, and by this only can God be well pleased. For
Love flowing from Faith is the Hand-writing of God on the heart.

Whatever proceeds from it will bear his Image and Superscription.   He will know it as his own, and openly acknowledge it as such, before Men and Angels, at the last day.

This Fruit of Love is what St. Paul everywhere holds up for the trial of our Faith and Spirits—"The Fruits of the Spirit are Love, Joy, Peace, Long-Suffering, Gentleness, Goodness, Meekness, Temperance, and the like." All other marks of the Soundness of our Faith, except these Gospel-marks, namely, the Fruits of the Spirit, are only a dangerous ministration of fuel for inflammable tempers, or of despair to those of a contrary frame.

Come we now to his immediate subject.   He continues:

Why need I spend more of your time in applying the doctrine of my Text to the present occasion of our meeting?—an occasion (I will only add) on which if you could be indulged to hear the voice of an Apostle or Angel from God, he would preach to you Love and Unity.

Consider that you are members of a Church, which is acknowledged by all the Christian World to teach the doctrine of the Gospel, and to hold fast the Form of sound Words, the Faith once delivered to the Saints—a Church which has given to the world a long and illustrious list of eminent Divines, pious Preachers, and even glorious Confessors and Martyrs for the Truth, as it is in Jesus.

But in this country at present, such is her state that she calls for the pious assistance and united support of all her true Sons, and of the friends of Christianity in general.   Besides a famine of the preached word, her sound Doctrines are deserted by many, who "turn away their ears from the Truth," as taught by her, and heap to themselves Teachers as described in the Text. . . . . Too many more are spoiled or staggered in their Faith by what is called the Free and Philosophic, but more truly, the loose and libertine principles of the present day.* Many others, from a selfish and niggardly spirit, or from a dissipation of their substance in luxury and intemperance, will not, or cannot, yield the mite which is necessary for supporting the Ordinances of Religion.   Thus they become ashamed to appear in the place of God's Worship, leaving the burden of all upon a few, whose conscience and the awful dread of an account to be given hereafter, will not suffer them to desert their Master's Gospel, to renounce their Baptism, and trample under foot the Blood of the Covenant wherewith they are sanctified.

Hence religion mourns, and the houses and altars of God, erected by the piety of our Forefathers, are deserted and running into ruin.   The tempests beat and the winds howl through the shattered roofs and moul-

---

* Even in 1784 the pernicious infidelity of the French Revolution was beginning to show itself.—H. W. S.

dering walls of our places of Worship; while our Burying-grounds and
Church-yards, the graves, the monuments, and the bones of our Fathers,
Mothers, Brothers, Sisters, Children and Friends, are left open and unprotected from the Beasts of the field; as if all our care was only to
succeed to the honours, the estates and places of emolument which
belonged to our Friends and Ancestors, without any regard to their
Memories or venerable Ashes!

In the late times of war, distress and confusion, there might be some
plea for this reproach of our Christian name; but now, with the blessed
prospects of Peace, Liberty, Safety and future Prosperity before us, I
trust this reproach will be speedily done away; to which nothing can
so eminently contribute as Love and Union among ourselves, joined to
a rational and enlightened Zeal and public Spirit.   For, in all our pursuits, we must rest at plain and practical points at last, which are few in
number, and in Religion come to little more than Solomon declared,
viz. that "the Fear of God and keeping his Commandments is the
whole duty of Man;" or, in all the Sciences, what another wise man
declared to be the Sum of all his inquiries—that

> TEMPERANCE is the best PHYSIC,
> PATIENCE the best LAW,
> CHARITY the best DIVINITY!

O Heaven-born Charity! what excellent things are spoken of thee!
What a transcendent rank was assigned thee, when the Saviour of the
World gave thee as the badge of his holy Religion; and his inspired
Apostles enthroned thee as the Queen of all Evangelic Graces and Virtues!   Could the tongues of men or of angels exalt thee more than
this—declaring—"That neither the Martyr's Zeal, the Self-denial of
the Saint, nor all Knowledge, nor any Virtue besides, can profit or
adorn the Man, who is unadorned with thy sweet celestial Garb!   But
he who is thus adorned is the most august human spectacle upon earth—
whom even Angels behold with delight, as clothed in that peculiar
Garb which Christ vouchsafed to wear here below, and which shall not
need to be put off above: and therefore, if on every slight occasion, or
indeed on any occasion, we cast off this Garb, we are none his true
Disciples!

Wherefore then, Brethren, put on this most excellent gift of Charity.
Try the Faith that is in you by this great Test—Hold fast the Form of
sound Words, the holy Scriptures, the pure Doctrines, the excellent
Forms of Prayer, Praise and Thanksgiving, drawn from Scripture by
our Church—Hold them fast in Faith working by Love.   Take them
for your perfect rule and guide—They will make you wise unto Salvation—Whatever is imagined more, or beyond Scripture—all that is
beside final Perfection and Salvation, count it vain and superfluous.

8

Seek not to be *wise above what is written*, nor establish any vain imaginations of your own for the sure Form of sound Words. What you
have received, hold fast with a fervent and enlightened, but with a holy
and charitable, Zeal. Add nothing, diminish nothing; but let this
Lamp of God shine among you till the Day Dawn, till the Morning of
the Resurrection; and walk ye in the Light of it, not kindling any
Sparkles of your own to mix with its pure and hallowed Lustre.

Let not your best State too much elevate, nor your worst too much
depress, you. Whereunto you have attained, walk; yet sit not down
with attainments, but forgetting what is behind, press still forward,
having perfect Holiness in your eye and purpose.

"Remember that Faith without Works is dead. Remember that God
commands Works, Grace establishes them, Christ died to confirm
them, the Spirit is given to influence them; and that, without a holy,
humble and peaceable Life, we annul the Law, abuse the Gospel, trample upon Grace, frustrate the end of Christ's Death, grieve the Spirit,
dishonour God, and give the lie to our holy Profession." If one coming as an Apostle or as an Angel from Heaven, were to preach to you
any other Gospel than you have received, I trust, you would say, let
him not be believed.

Thus, with the Truth in our Heads and Love in our Hearts; with
Zeal and public Spirit; with a concern for Liberty, Civil and Religious;
with Industry and Economy; with a strict care for the Education of
Youth, and their nurture and admonition in the Fear of the Lord; this
American land shall become a great and glorious Empire!—

Hasten, O blessed God, hasten this glorious period of thy Son's
Kingdom, which we know shall yet come! And, O ye, who now enjoy
the blessed opportunity, be ye the happy means of hastening it. Adorn
by your lives the Divine doctrines which you profess with your lips;
that the Heathen and Unbeliever, seeing your good Works may be the
sooner led to glorify your Father who is in Heaven!*

Bishop White, in a passage of his memoirs, which we quote
here, often speaks of the great service done to the church by the
last two conventions in Maryland, to which we have referred, and
which he rightly says " were chiefly originated and conducted by
Dr. Smith."

---

* This sermon was published at the time with the following dedication:

To his Excellency | William Paca, Esquire, | Governor and Commander in Chief
of the State of | Maryland, &c. | The following Sermon | is inscribed, | in sincere
testimony and acknowledgment, | as well of his public zeal and regard | for the | in-
terests of Religion and Learning, | as of | the private friendship and esteem, | with
which, | from an early period of his life, | hath subsisted between him, | and his most
affectionate, | old preceptor, | and obedient servant, | the Author. |

The churches of Maryland and Pennsylvania being now, as we have said, in sufficient accord, and their principles such, in the main, as churchmen could generally admit, the general convention, which the clergy and laymen who had been at New Brunswick in May had recommended should take place at New York, on the 6th of October, 1784, now took place. There came to this Convention

From MASSACHUSETTS and RHODE ISLAND,   The Rev. Samuel Parker.

"   CONNECTICUT,   The Rev. J. R. Marshall.

"   NEW YORK,   The Rev. Messrs. Samuel Provoost, Abraham Beach, Benjamin Moore, Joshua Bloomer, Leonard Cutting, and Thomas Moore, with the Hon. James Duane and Marinus Millet and John Alsop, Esquires.

"   PENNSYLVANIA,   The Rev. Drs. White and Magaw, the Rev. Mr. Joseph Hutchins, with Mathew Clarkson, Richard Willing, Samuel Powel and Richard Peters, Esquires.

NEW JERSEY,   The Rev. Uzal Ogden, John De Hart, Esq., John Chetwood, Esq., with Mr. Samuel Spragg.

"   DELAWARE,   The Revs. Sydenham Thorn and Charles Henry Wharton, with Mr. Robert Clay.

"   MARYLAND,   The Rev. Dr. William Smith.

The Rev. David Griffith (afterwards Bishop-elect of Virginia) was present by permission, but not as a delegate—the clergy of Virginia, by laws of that State then in force, being restricted from sending delegates.

Of this body, Dr. Smith was chosen President; the Rev. Benjamin Moore, afterwards the excellent and honored Bishop of New York, being the secretary.

The body recommended to the clergy and congregations of their communion in the States represented as above, and proposed to those of the other States not represented, that as soon as they should have organized themselves in the States to which they respectively belonged, agreeably to such rules as they should

think proper, they should unite in a GENERAL ECCLESIASTICAL
CONSTITUTION on the following fundamental principles :

I. That there shall be a General Convention of the Episcopal Church
in the United States of America.

II. That the Episcopal Church in each State send Deputies to the
Convention, consisting of Clergy and Laity.

III. That associated Congregations in two or more States may send
Deputies jointly.

IV. That the said church shall maintain the Doctrines of the Gospel
as now held by the Church of England, and shall adhere to the Liturgy
of the said Church as far as shall be consistent with the American
Revolution and the Constitutions of the respective States.

V. That every State where there shall be a Bishop duly consecrated
and settled, he shall be considered as a member of the Convention,
ex-officio.

VI. That the Clergy and Laity assembled in Convention, shall deliberate in one Body, but shall vote separately ; and the concurrence of
both shall be necessary to give validity to every measure.

VII. That the first meeting of the Convention shall be at Philadelphia, the Tuesday before the Feast of St. Michael next; to which it is
hoped, and earnestly desired, that the Episcopal Churches in their
respective States will send their clerical and lay Deputies herein
proposed for their Deliberation.

A committee was appointed to essay the fundamental principles
of a general constitution.

The following gentlemen were appointed: The Rev. Dr. Smith,
Rev. Dr. White, Rev. Mr. Parker, Rev. Mr. Provoost, Mr. Clarkson,
Mr. De Hart, Mr. Clay, Mr. Duane; and they were likewise
desired *to frame and propose to the Convention a proper substitute
for the State prayers* in the liturgy, to be used for the sake of
uniformity, till a further review should be undertaken by general
authority and consent of the Church—Dr. Smith was chairman of
this important Committee.

While at this Convention of the Church, in October, 1784, Dr.
Smith, with its other trustees, continued the good work, which
had been begun in May of the same year, of re-establishing the
corporation for the relief of the widows and children of the clergy.
The historian of the corporation says :*

* John William Wallace, LL. D., in "A Century of Beneficence—1769–1869."
Philadelphia, 1869, pp. 41, 42, 43.

"The late president, Dr. Peters, having died July 10th, 1776, and it being now proposed to appoint a chairman to open business, Dr. Smith was chosen for that purpose. The Rev. Benjamin Moore, afterwards the venerable Bishop Moore, of New York, acted as the secretary. The first thing was the appointment of a committee of three clerical and three lay members—Drs. Smith, White and Provoost, being appointed from the former, and Messrs. Duane, Peters and Livingston, from the latter—'to examine into the affairs of this Corporation since the last meeting at Philadelphia, on Tuesday after the feast of St. Michael, in the year 1775, and to report thereon as soon as may be.' Having adjourned to attend divine service at St. Paul's Church, New York, on Wednesday the 6th, where the annual sermon was preached by Dr. Magaw, the Rector of St. Paul's Church, Philadelphia, the Corporation then afterwards proceeded to ballot for twenty-nine new members. Their names appear upon the roll of corporators, under the date of 1784. It is interesting to note the names of General Alexander Hamilton, then in his 27th year, and of John Jay, among those from New York, and of both Robert and Gouverneur Morris, among those from Pennsylvania. Officers were also elected; Dr. Smith, now venerable for his years, and deserving such honor from his long and great service to the Society, was appointed president; and the Rev. Benjamin Moore, already mentioned, secretary. The treasurers were, for New York, John Alsop; for New Jersey, Joshua Maddox Wallace; and for Pennsylvania, Samuel Powel—this last reappointed. Standing committees of correspondence, and for obtaining an alteration and confirmation of the charter, were also elected—Dr. White and Mr. Peters, for Pennsylvania; Messrs. John Stevens and J. M. Wallace, for New Jersey; and Messrs. Duane, Robert R. Livingston, with the Rev. Mr. Provoost, for New York—the first and second named gentlemen in regard to the charter, and the first and third as a standing committee.

"Dr. Smith, after the adjournment of the meeting at New York, remained behind in that city to preach there on the following Sunday, both morning and afternoon, which he did with so good effect as to have added £112 19*s.* 10*d.* to the corporate moneys."

CHAPTER XLVI.

Convention of the Church in Seven States, held a. d. 1785, at Christ
  Church in Philadelphia—Dr. Smith Chairman of a Committee to make
  a Review of and Further Alterations, with Additions to the Liturgy—The Thirty-nine Articles Presented in a Condensed Form—
  The Alterations, Additions and Condensation Adopted by the Convention—The Whole Ordered to be Printed in a Book—The Proposed
  Book—Dr. Smith Requested to Preach a Sermon at the Close of the
  Convention suited to the Solemn Occasion—He does so—Extracts
  from the Sermon—Dr. White, Dr. Smith and the Rev. Mr. C. H.
  Wharton, at this time of New Castle, Delaware, but better known
  afterwards as Dr. Wharton, of Burlington, N. J., appointed a Committee to see the Proposed Book through the Press.

As will have been observed by the reader, the fourth fundamental article adopted by the Convention of 1784* laid down as
a principle that the church in America should adhere to the liturgy
of the Church of England, so far as should be consistent with
the American Revolution and the constitutions of the respective
States; and the power entrusted by the same Convention, to the
committee of which Dr. Smith was chairman, was confined, of
course, to framing and proposing a proper substitute for the *State*
prayers, to be used for the sake of uniformity till a further review
should be undertaken by general authority and consent of the
church.

Dr. Smith, I think it probable, was the person chiefly desirous
of a further considerable review, and the person chiefly active in
bringing on a discussion concerning the change, and in suggesting
and introducing the particulars of it. The prospect which was
held out, in the language by which the committee was constituted,
led, no doubt, after the adjournment of the Convention of New
York, October 6th and 7th, 1784, to a good deal of consideration
and conversation upon the subject by churchmen who were present and assisted at that convention, before the next convention
was held; that is to say, before the 27th of September, 1785, when
this next convention met in Philadelphia.

---

* See *supra*, p. 107.

This Philadelphia Convention of 1785 appointed a committee, of which Dr. Smith was again the chairman, "to consider of and report such alterations in the liturgy as shall render it consistent with the American Revolution and the constitutions of the respective States, *and such further alterations in the liturgy as it may be advisable for this Convention to recommend.*"

This committee, which was in part clerical, and in part lay, was thus composed :

For NEW YORK,	The Rev. Mr. Provoost and the Hon. Mr. Duane.
" NEW JERSEY,	The Rev. Mr. Beach and Mr. Dennis.
" PENNSYLVANIA,	The Rev. Dr. White and Mr. Peters.
" DELAWARE,	The Rev. Dr. Wharton and Mr. Sykes.
" MARYLAND,	The Rev. Dr. Smith and Dr. Cradock.
" VIRGINIA,	The Rev. Mr. Griffith and Mr. Page.
" SOUTH CAROLINA,	The Rev. Dr. Purcell and the Hon. Mr. Read.

This committee made frequent reports. It having been resolved by this Convention that the 4th of July should be forever observed as a day of Thanksgiving to Almighty God for the inestimable blessings of Religious and Civil Liberty vouchsafed to the United States of America, a committee, consisting of the Rev. Dr. Smith, the Rev. Dr. Magaw, the Rev. Dr. Wharton and the Rev. Mr. Campbell, were appointed to prepare the proper form of prayer and thanksgiving.

The alterations which, according to a record left us by Bishop White in his Memoirs,* were *resolved on*, and the alteration *proposed* and *recommended* by the General Convention of 1785— General we call it, though no churches from the New England States were represented—were these. They were made after reports from the committee :

I. *Alterations agreed on and confirmed in Convention, for rendering the Liturgy conformable to the principles of the American Revolution, and the constitutions of the several States.*

---

* Second Edition. New York, 1836, page 363.

1st. That in the suffrages after the Creed, instead of

O Lord, save the King,

be said :

O Lord, bless and preserve these United States.

2d. That the prayer for the Royal family, in the morning and evening service, be omitted.

3d. That in the Litany the 15th, 16th, 17th and 18th petitions be omitted, and that instead of the 20th and 21st petitions, be substituted the following :

That it may please Thee to endue the Congress of these United States, and all others in authority, legislative, executive, and judicial, with grace, wisdom and understanding, to execute justice and to maintain truth.

4th. That when the Litany is not said, the prayer for the high court of Parliament be thus altered:

Most gracious God, we humbly beseech Thee, as for these United States in general, so especially for their delegates in Congress, that thou wouldest be pleased to direct and prosper all their consultations to the advancement of thy glory, the good of thy Church, the safety, honour, and welfare of thy people, that all things may be so ordered and settled by their endeavors upon the best and surest foundations, that peace and happiness, truth and justice, religion and piety, may be established among us for all generations, &c., to the end.

And the prayer for the king's majesty, altered as follows, viz.:

O Lord, our heavenly Father, the high and mighty Ruler of the universe, who dost from thy Throne behold all the Dwellers upon Earth; we most heartily beseech thee, with thy Favour to behold all in Authority, legislative, executive and judicial in these United States; and so replenish them with the Grace of thy holy Spirit, that they may alway incline to thy will and walk in thy way. Endue them plenteously with heavenly Gifts, grant them in Health and Wealth long to live and, that after this Life, they may attain everlasting Joy and Felicity, through Jesus Christ our Lord.   Amen.

5th. That the 1st Collect for the King in the Communion Service be omitted : and that the second be altered as follows—instead of

The hearts of Kings are in thy rule and governance,

be said :

That the hearts of all Rulers are in thy governance, &c. ;

and instead of the words

heart of George thy servant,

insert,

so to direct the Rulers of these States, that in all their thoughts, &c.—

changing the singular pronouns to the plural.

6th. That in the answer in the Catechism to the question,

What is thy duty towards thy neighbour?

for,

to honour and obey the king,

be substituted

to honour and obey my civil rulers, to submit myself, &c.

7th. That in the Forms of Prayer to be used at Sea, in the Prayer "O eternal God, &c.," instead of these Words,

unto our most gracious Sovereign Lord King George and his Kingdoms,

be inserted the Words,

to the United States of America;

and that instead of the Word "Island" be inserted the Word "Country;" and in the collect "O Almighty God, the Sovereign Commander," be omitted the Words, "the Honour of our Sovereign," and the Words "the Honour of our Country" inserted.

8th. That instead of the observation of the 5th of November, the 30th of January, the 29th of May, and the 25th of October, the following service be used on the 4th of July, being the Anniversary of Independence.

Service for the 4th of July.

WITH THE SENTENCES BEFORE MORNING AND EVENING PRAYER.

The Lord hath been mindful of us, and he shall bless us, he shall bless them that fear him, both small and great. O that men would therefore praise the Lord, for his goodness, and declare the wonders that he doeth for the children of men.

HYMN INSTEAD OF THE VENITE.

My song shall be alway of the loving kindness of the Lord: with my mouth will I ever be showing forth his truth from one generation to another. Psal. lxxxix. 1.

The merciful and gracious Lord hath so done his marvellous works: that they ought to be had in remembrance. Psal. cxi. 4.

Who can express the noble acts of the Lord: or show forth all his praise. Psal. cvi. 2.

The works of the Lord are great: sought out of all them that have pleasure therein. Psal. cxi. 2.

For he will not alway be chiding: neither keepeth he his anger forever. Psal. ciii. 9.

He hath not dealt with us after our sins: nor rewarded us according to our wickedness. Verse 10.

For look how high the heaven is in comparison of the earth; so great is his mercy toward them that fear him. Verse 11.

Yea, like as a father pitieth his own children: even so is the Lord merciful unto them that fear him. Verse 11.

Thou, O God, hast proved us: thou also hast tried us, like as silver is tried. Psal. lxvi. 9.

Thou didst remember us in our low estate, and redeem us from our enemies: for thy mercy endureth forever. Psal. cxxxvi. 23, 24.

Proper Psalms, cxviii. except v. 10, 11, 12, 13, 22, 23, and to conclude with v. 24. 1. *Lesson*, Deut. viii. 2. *Lesson*, Thess. v. verses 12–23 both inclusive.

COLLECT FOR THE DAY.

Almighty God, who hast in all ages showed forth thy power and mercy in the wonderful preservation of thy church, and in the protection of every nation and people professing thy holy and eternal truth, and putting their sure trust in thee; we yield thee our unfeigned thanks and praise for all thy public mercies, and more especially for that signal and wonderful manifestation of thy providence which we commemorate this day; wherefore not unto us, O Lord, not unto us, but unto thy Name be ascribed all honour and glory, in all churches of the Saints, from generation to generation, through Jesus Christ our Lord. Amen.

A THANKSGIVING FOR THE DAY, TO BE SAID AFTER THE GENERAL THANKSGIVING.

O God, whose name is excellent in all the earth, and thy glory above the heavens; who as on this day didst inspire and direct the hearts of our delegates in Congress, to lay the perpetual foundations of peace, liberty, and safety; we bless and adore thy glorious Majesty, for this thy loving kindness and providence. And we humbly pray that the devout sense of this signal mercy may renew and increase in us a spirit of love and thankfulness to thee its only Author, a spirit of peaceable submission to the laws and government of our country, and a spirit of fervent zeal for our holy religion, which thou hast preserved and secured to us and our posterity. May we improve these inestimable blessings for the advancement of religion, liberty and science throughout this land, till the wilderness and solitary place be made glad through us, and the desert rejoice and blossom as the rose. This we beg through the merits of Jesus Christ our Saviour. Amen.*

II. *Alterations in the Book of Common Prayer and Administration of the Sacraments, and other Rites and Ceremonies of the Church, according to the use of the Church of England, proposed and recommended to the Protestant Episcopal Church in the United States of America.*

In the Order for Morning and Evening, service Daily throughout the Year.

1st. The following Sentences of Scripture are ordered to be prefixed to the usual Sentences, viz.:

The Lord is in his Holy Temple; let all the Earth keep Silence before him. Hab. ii. 20.

---

* The Epistle and the Gospel were added by the Committee, after the Convention had adjourned, agreeably to an authority which they conceived to be vested in them, in the appointment made by the Convention of them to see the proposed book through the press.

From the Rising of the Sun even unto the going down of the Same, my Name shall be great among the Gentiles; and in every Place Incense shall be offered unto my Name, and a pure Offering: for my Name shall be great among the Heathen, saith the Lord of Hosts.   Mal. i. 11.

Let the words of my Mouth, and the meditation of my Heart, be alway acceptable in thy sight, O Lord, my Strength and my Redeemer.   Psal. xix. 14.

2d. That the Rubric preceding the Absolution be altered thus:

A declaration to be made by the Minister alone, standing, concerning the forgiveness of sins.

3d. That in the Lord's prayer, the word "who" be substituted in lieu of "which;" and that "those who trespass" stand instead of "them that trespass."

4th. That the "Gloria Patri" be omitted after the "O come let us sing, &c.," and in every other place, where, by the present Rubric, it is ordered to be inserted, to "the end of the" reading psalms; when shall be said or sung "Gloria Patri, &c.," or, "Glory be to God on high, and in earth peace and good will towards men, &c.," at the discretion of the Minister.

5th. That in the "Te Deum" instead of

honourable

it be

adorable, true, and only Son,

and instead of

didst not abhor the Virgin's womb,

it be

didst humble thyself to be born of a pure Virgin.

6th. That until a proper selection of Psalms be made, each Minister be allowed to use such as he may choose.

7th. That the same liberty be allowed, respecting the lessons.

8th. That the article in the Apostles' creed " He descended into hell" be omitted.

9th. That the Athanasian and the Nicene creeds be entirely omitted.

10th. That after the response "and with thy spirit," all be omitted to the words "O Lord show thy mercy upon us;" which the Minister shall pronounce, still kneeling.

11th. That in the suffrage "make thy chosen people joyful," the word "chosen" be omitted; and also the following suffrages, to "O God, make clean our hearts within us."

12th. That the Rubric after these words "and take not thy Holy Spirit from us," be omitted.   Then the two collects to be said : in the collect for grace, the words "be ordered," to be omitted; and the word "be" inserted, instead of "to do alway that is."

13th. In the collect "for the Clergy and People," read—

Almighty and everlasting God, send down upon all Bishops and other Pastors, and the Congregations committee, &c., to the end.

14th.*

15th. That the Lord's prayer after the Litany, and the subsequent Rubric be omitted.

16th. That the short Litany be read as follows:

Son of God, we beseech thee to hear us. Son of God, we beseech thee to hear us. O Lamb of God, that takest away the sins of the world, Grant us thy peace. O Christ, hear us. Lord, have mercy upon us and deal not with us according to our sins, neither reward us according to our iniquities.

After which, omit the words—"Let us pray."

17th. That the "Gloria Patri," after "O Lord arise, &c.," be omitted; as also "Let us pray," after "we put our trust in thee."

18th. That in the following prayer, instead of

righteously have deserved,

it be

justly have deserved.

19th. That in the 1st warning for the Communion, the word "damnation," following these words "increase your, &c.," be read "condemnation;" and the two paragraphs after these words "or else come not to that holy table," be omitted; and the following one be read:

and if there be any of you, who by these means, cannot quiet their conscience, &c.

The words "learned and discreet," epithets given to the ministers, to be also omitted.

20th. In the exhortation to the communion, let it run thus:

For as the benefit is great, &c., to drink his blood, so is the danger great, if we receive the same unworthily. Judge therefore yourselves, &c.

21st. That in the rubric preceding the absolution, instead of

pronounce this absolution,

it be
Then shall the minister stand up, and turning to the people say, &c.

22d. That in the baptism of infants, parents may be admitted as sponsors.

23d. That the minister, in speaking to the sponsors, after these words

---

* Here is an erasure from the manuscript: the article being found a repetition of part of the 4th. *Vide* White's Memoirs, p. 367, where "13th" is a misprint for "4th."

"vouchsafe to release him," say, "release him from sin." In the second prayer, instead of

remission of his sins,

read

remission of sin.

24th. That in the questions addressed to the sponsors, and the answers, instead of the present Form, it b: as follows:

the sinful desires of the flesh.

25th.

Dost thou believe the articles of the Christian faith, as contained in the Apostles' creed, and wilt thou endeavour to have this child instructed accordingly? Answer: I do believe them, and, by God's help, will endeavour so to do.

Wilt thou endeavour to have him brought up in the fear of God, and to obey God's holy will and commandments? Answer: I will, by God's assistance.

26th. That the sign of the cross may be omitted, if particularly desired by the Sponsors or Parents, and the prayer to be thus altered (by the direction of a short rubric):

We receive this child into the congregation of Christ's flock; and pray that hereafter he may never be ashamed, &c., to the end.

27th. That the address, "seeing now dearly beloved, &c.," be omitted.

28th. That the prayer after the Lord's prayer be thus changed:

We yield thee hearty thanks, &c.,

to

receive this Infant as thine own child by baptism, and to incorporate him, &c.

29th. That in the following exhortation, the words "to renounce the devil and all his works," and in the charge to the sponsors, the words "vulgar tongue" be omitted.

30th. That the forms of private baptism and of confirmation be made conformable to these alterations.

31st. That in the exhortation before matrimony, all between these words "holy matrimony," and "therefore if any man, &c.," be omitted.

32d. That the words "I plight thee my troth" be omitted in both places; and also the words "with my body I thee worship;" and also "pledged their troth either to other."

33d. That all after the blessing be omitted.

34th. In the burial service, instead of the two Psalms, take the following verses of both, viz.: Psalm xxxix., verses 6, 7, 8, 9, 12, 13, and Psalm xc., to verse 13. In the rubric, the words "unbaptized or" to be omitted.

For the Declaration and form of interment, beginning "Forasmuch as, &c.," insert the following, viz. :

Forasmuch as it hath pleased Almighty God, in his wise Providence, to take out of this world the soul of our deceased brother (sister) lying now before us; We therefore commit his (her) body to the ground, earth to earth, ashes to ashes, dust to dust; (thus at sea—to the deep to be turned into corruption) looking for the general resurrection in the last day, and the life of the world to come, thro' our Lord Jesus Christ; at whose second coming in glorious Majesty, to judge the world, the earth and the sea shall give up their dead; and the corruptible bodies of those who sleep in him shall be changed, and made like unto his own glorious body, according to the mighty working, whereby he is able to subdue all things unto Himself.

In the sentence "I heard a voice, &c.," insert "who" for "which."

The prayer following the Lord's prayer to be omitted. In the next collect, leave out the words "as our hope is, this our brother doth." For "them that," insert "those who."

35th. In the visitation of the sick, instead of the absolution as it now stands, insert the declaration of forgiveness which is appointed for the communion service; or either of the collects, which are taken from the Commination office, and appropriated to Ash Wednesday, may be used.

In the Psalm, omit the 3d, 6th, 8th, 9th, and 11th verses. In the Commendatory prayer, for "miserable and naughty," say "vain and miserable." Strike out the word "purged."

In the prayer "for persons troubled in mind," omit all that stands between the words "afflicted servant," and "his soul is full, &c.," and instead thereof say "afflicted servant, whose soul is full of trouble," and strike out the particle "but," and proceed, "O merciful God, &c."

36th. A form of Prayer and visitation of Prisoners for notorious crimes, and especially persons under sentence of death, being much wanted, the form entitled "Prayers for persons under sentence of death, agreed upon in a Synod of the archbishops and bishops, and the rest of the clergy of Ireland, at Dublin, in the year 1711," as it now stands in the book of Common Prayer of the Church of Ireland, is agreed upon, and ordered to be adopted, with the following alterations, viz. :

For the absolution, take the same declaration of forgiveness, or either of the collects above directed for the visitation of the sick. The short collect "O Saviour of the world, &c.," to be left out; and for the word "frailness," say "frailty."

37th. In the Catechism, besides the alteration respecting the civil Powers, alter as follows, viz. :

Q.—What is your name ?
A.—N. M.
Q.—When did you receive this name?
A.—I received it in Baptism, whereby I became a member of the Christian church.

Q.—What was promised for you in Baptism?

A.—That I should be instructed to believe the Christian faith, as contained in the Apostles' Creed, and to obey God's holy will, and keep his commandments.

Q.—Dost thou think thou art bound to believe all the articles of the Christian faith, as contained in this creed, and to obey God's holy will and keep his commandments?

A.—Yes, verily, &c.

Instead of the words "verily, and indeed taken," say—"spiritually taken."

Answer to Question "How many sacraments?" "Two, Baptism and the Lord's Supper."

38th. Instead of a particular Service for the churching of women and psalms, the following special prayer is to be introduced, after the General Thanksgiving, viz.: This to be said, when any woman desires to return thanks, &c.

O Almighty God, we give thee most humble and hearty thanks, for that thou hast been graciously pleased to preserve this woman, thy servant, through the great pains and perils of childbirth. Incline her, we beseech thee, to show forth her thankfulness, for this thy great mercy, not only with her lips, but by a holy and virtuous life. Be pleased, O God, so to establish her health, that she may lead the remainder of he days to thy honour and glory, through Jesus Christ our Lord. *Amen.*

39th. The Commination office for Ash Wednesday to be discontinued, and therefore the three collects, the first beginning—"O Lord, we beseech thee,"—2d, "O most mighty God,"—3d, "Turn us, O Good Lord," shall be continued among the occasional prayers; and used after the collect on Ash Wednesday, and on such other occasions as the minister shall think fit.

III. Articles of Religion.

1. Of Faith in the Holy Trinity.

There is but one living, true, and eternal God, the Father Almighty; without body, parts or passions; of infinite power, wisdom and goodness; the maker and preserver of all things both visible and invisible: and one Lord Jesus Christ, Son of God, begotten of the Father before all worlds, very and true God; who came down from heaven, took man's nature in the womb of the Blessed Virgin of her substance, and was God and man in one person, whereof is one Christ; who truly suffered, was crucified, dead and buried, to reconcile his Father to us, and to be a sacrifice for the sins of all men; He rose again from death, ascended into heaven, and there sitteth until he shall return to judge the world at the last day: and one Holy Spirit, the Lord and giver of life, of the same divine nature with the Father and the Son.

2. Of the Sufficiency of the Holy Scriptures for Salvation.

Holy Scripture containeth all things necessary to salvation: so that whatsoever is not read therein: nor may be proved thereby, is not to be required of any man, that it should be believed as an article of the Faith, or be thought requisite or necessary to salvation. In the name of the Holy Scriptures we do understand the canonical books of the Old and New Testament.

Of the names and numbers of the canonical Books.

Genesis, Exodus, Leviticus, Numbers, Deuteronomy, Joshua, Judges, Ruth, The 1st Book of Samuel, The 2d Book of Samuel, The 1st Book of Kings, The 2d Book of Kings, The 1st Book of Chronicles, The 2d Book of Chronicles, The 1st Book of Esdras, The 2d Book of Esdras, The Book of Hester, The Book of Job, The Psalms, The Proverbs, Ecclesiastes or Preacher, Cantica or Songs of Solomon, Four Prophets the greater, Twelve Prophets the less.

And the other books the Church doth read for example of life, and instruction of manners; but yet doth it not apply them to establish any doctrine; such are these following:

The 3d Book of Esdras, The 4th Book of Esdras, The Book of Tobias, The Book of Judith, The rest of the Book of Hester, The Book of Wisdom, Jesus the Son of Sirach, Baruch the Prophet, The Song of the three Children, The Story of Susanna, Of Bell and the Dragon, The Prayer of Manasses, The 1st Book of Maccabees, The 2d Book of Maccabees.

All the books of the New Testament, as they are commonly received, we do receive and account them canonical.

3. OF THE OLD AND NEW TESTAMENT.

There is a perfect harmony and agreement between the Old Testament and the New; for in both, everlasting life is offered to mankind by Christ, who is the only mediator between God and man; being both God and man: and altho' the law given by Moses, as to ceremonies and the civil precepts of it, doth not bind Christians: yet all such are obliged to observe the moral commandments which he delivered.

4. OF CREEDS.

The creed, commonly called the Apostles' creed, ought to be received and believed: because it may be proved by the Holy Scripture.

5. OF ORIGINAL SIN.

By the fall of Adam, the nature of man is become so corrupt, as to be greatly depraved, having departed from its primitive innocence, and that original righteousness in which it was at first created by God. For we are now so naturally inclined to do evil that the flesh is continually striving to act contrary to the Spirit of God, which corrupt inclination still remains even in the regenerate. But tho' there is no man living who sinneth not; yet we must use our sincere endeavors to keep the whole law of God, so far as we possibly can.

6. Of Free-Will.

The Condition of man after the fall of Adam, is such that he cannot turn and prepare himself by his own natural strength and good works to faith and calling upon God: Wherefore we have no power to do good works, pleasing and acceptable to God, without the grace of God by Christ giving us a good will, and working with us, when we have that good will.

7. Of the Justification of Man.

We are accounted righteous before God only for the merit of our Lord and Saviour Jesus Christ by faith, and not for our own works, or deservings. Wherefore that we are justified by faith only, is a most wholesome doctrine, and very full of comfort.

8. Of Good Works.

Albeit that good works, which are the fruits of Faith and follow after Justification, cannot put away our sins, and endure the severity of God's judgment; yet are they pleasing and acceptable to God in Christ, and do spring out necessarily of a true and lively faith, insomuch that by them a lively faith may be as evidently known, as a Tree discerned by the Fruit.

9. Of Christ alone without Sin.

Christ, by taking human nature on him, was made like unto us in all things, sin only excepted. He was a lamb without spot, and by the sacrifice of himself once offered, made atonement and propitiation for the sins of the world; and sin was not in him. But all mankind besides, tho' baptized and born again in Christ, do offend in many things. For if we say we have no sin, we deceive ourselves, and the truth is not in us.

10. Of Sin after Baptism.

They who fall into sin after baptism may be renewed by repentance : for tho' after we have received God's grace, we may depart from it by falling into sin; yet thro' the assistance of his Holy Spirit, we may by repentance and the amendment of our lives, be restored again to his favour. God will not deny repentance of sins to those who truly repent, and do that which is lawful and right ; but all such thro' his mercy in Christ Jesus, shall save their souls alive.

11. Of Predestination.

Predestination to Life, with respect to every man's salvation, is the everlasting purpose of God, secret to us: and the right knowledge of what is revealed concerning it, is full of comfort to such truly religious Christians, as feel in themselves the Spirit of Christ, mortifying the

9

works of their flesh, and their earthly affections, and raising their minds to heavenly things. But we must receive God's promises as they be generally declared in Holy Scripture, and do his will, as therein is expressly directed; for without Holiness of Life no man shall be saved.

12. Of Obtaining Eternal Salvation only by the Name of Christ.

They are to be accounted presumptuous, who say, that every man shall be saved by the Law or Sect which he professeth, so that he be diligent to frame his life according to that law, and the light of nature. For Holy Scripture doth set out unto us only the Name of Jesus Christ, whereby men must be saved.

13. Of the Church and its Authority.

The visible Church of Christ is a congregation of faithful men, wherein the pure word of God is preached, and the sacraments are duly administered, according to Christ's ordinance in all things necessary and requisite: And every Church hath power to ordain, change and abolish rites and ceremonies, for the more decent order and good government thereof, so that all things be done to edifying. But it is not lawful for the Church to ordain anything contrary to God's word; nor so to expound the Scripture, as to make one part seem repugnant to another; nor to decree or enforce anything to be believed as necessary to salvation, that is contrary to God's holy word. General Councils and Churches are liable to err, and have erred, even in matters of Faith and Doctrine, as well as in their ceremonies.

14. Of Ministering in the Congregation.

It is not lawful for any man to take upon him the office of public preaching, or ministering the Sacraments in the Congregation, before he be lawfully called, and sent to execute the same. And those we ought to judge lawfully called and sent, who are chosen and called to this work by men who have public authority given unto them in the congregation, to call and send Ministers into the Lord's vineyard.

15. Of the Sacraments.

Sacraments ordained of Christ, be not only badges or tokens of Christian men's profession: but rather they be certain sure witnesses, and effectual signs of Grace, and God's good will towards us, by the which he doth work invisibly in us, and doth not only quicken, but also strengthen and confirm our Faith in him.

There are Two Sacraments ordained of Christ our Lord in the Gospel, that is to say, Baptism and the Supper of the Lord.

16. Of Baptism.

Baptism is not only a Sign of profession and mark of difference, whereby Christian men are discerned from others that be not Christened; but it is also a sign of regeneration or new Birth, whereby as by an Instrument, they that receive Baptism rightly, are grafted into the Church; the promises of the forgiveness of sin, and of our Adoption to be the Sons of God, by the Holy Ghost, are visibly sign'd and sealed; Faith is confirm'd, and Grace increas'd by virtue of prayer unto God. The Baptism of young Children is in any wise to be retained in the Church, as most agreeable with the Institution of Christ.

17. Of the Lord's Supper.

The Supper of the Lord is not only a Sign of the Love that Christians ought to have among themselves one to another; but rather is a Sacrament of our redemption by Christ's death : Insomuch that to such as rightly, worthily and with faith receive the same, the Bread which we break, is a partaking of the Body of Christ: and likewise the Cup of Blessing, is a partaking of the Blood of Christ.

Transubstantiation (or the change of the substance of Bread and Wine) in the Supper of the Lord cannot be proved by Holy Writ; but is repugnant to the plain words of Scripture, overthroweth the nature of a Sacrament, and hath given occasion to many superstitions.

The Body of Christ is given, taken and eaten in the Supper of the Lord only after an heavenly and spiritual manner. And the mean whereby the Body of Christ is received and eaten in the Supper is Faith.

18. Of the one Oblation of Christ upon the Cross.

The offering of Christ once made, is that perfect redemption, propitiation and satisfaction for all the sins of the whole world, both original and actual; and there is none other satisfaction for sin, but that alone.

19. Of Bishops and Ministers.

The Book of Consecration of Bishops and Ordering of Priests and Deacons; excepting such part as requires any oaths or subscriptions inconsistent with the American Revolution, is to be adopted as containing all things necessary to such consecration and ordering.

20. Of a Christian Man's Oath.

The Christian Religion doth not prohibit any man from taking an oath, when required by the Magistrate in testimony of Truth; But all vain and rash swearing is forbidden by the Holy Scriptures.*

---

* These articles, though now superceded by the original thirty-nine articles of the Church of England, adopted by us in 1789, may still, *perhaps*, I rather take it, be referred to as explaining these last when not clear.—H. W. S.

IV. The Table of Holy Days.

The following Days are to be kept Holy by this Church, viz. :

All the Sundays in the year in the Order enumerated in the Table of Proper Lessons with their respective Services.
Christmas.
Circumcision.
Epiphany.
Easter Day, Monday and Tuesday.
Ascension Day.
Whit-Sunday, Monday and Tuesday.

The following Days are to be observed as Days of Fasting, viz. :

Good Friday and Ash Wednesday.

The following Days are to be observed as Days of Thanksgiving, viz. :

The 4th of July, in commemoration of American Independence.
The First Thursday in November as a Day of General Thanksgiving.

After the alterations, abridgments, additions and modifications in the Liturgy which we have spoken of above, under our Head II, had been agreed to by the Convention, they were proposed and recommended to the Church in those States from which there were deputies to the Convention; and the Articles of Religion as presented in their new form were recommended to the Church to be by them adopted in the next General Convention. Nothing as yet was in print; but the new Liturgy being transcribed and having been read, Divine Service according to it was held in Christ Church, Dr. White saying the prayers and the Rev. Dr. Smith preaching a sermon, as he had been requested by the Convention to do, " suited to the solemn occasion of the Convention." This proceeding took place October 7th, 1785. The text is from St. Luke, chap. xiv., ver. 23 :

And the Lord said unto the servant, Go out into the highways and hedges, and compel them to come in, that my house may be filled.

The earlier part of the discourse probably had not been written for this special occasion, and may have been used merely as a suitable introduction for more particular matter. The preacher begins :

In the parable, of which the words of my text are a part, the unspeakable happiness of the kingdom of God, as begun in the hearts of believers in this world, and to be consummated in the world to come, is represented under the figure of a great Feast, or Supper, to which multitudes were bidden; and the excuses, which they offer for not coming, strongly describe the various obstructions which the Gospel would meet with in its reception among men; from the time of its first promulgation, to that blessed period when the dispersed among the highways and hedges of remotest nations shall hear its Divine call, and " all the kingdoms of this world become the kingdoms of our Lord, and of his Christ ! "

After speaking of certain methods of bringing men to the Heavenly Feast, which the Gospel will not justify—such as external compulsion, or what was as unscriptural, the dressing out the pure religion of the Gospel in a way that offers salvation without obedience to its moral precepts, and strives to persuade men that they may become Christians on easier terms than Christ hath appointed, the preacher, coming to the more joyous branch of his subject, says: "The consideration of those methods which the Scriptures not only justifies but commands; whereby all, both clergy and laity, may be instrumental, through the help of God, in compelling others to the profession of the Gospel, and the practice of its Divine precepts." "This," he says, "we may do—

" 1st. By special instruction and exhortation;

" 2dly. By living example; and

" 3dly. By the decency, devotion, fervency and solemnity of our forms of public worship, and by embracing every opportunity of their further improvement."

Having treated, in a forcible way, the first two modes above mentioned, he comes to the one which prompted the discourse. He says:

This brings me to my third and chief head on this great occasion; which was to show that another powerful method of compelling men to come in, is by the decency, devotion, fervency and solemnity of our forms of Public Worship; using every endeavour in our power for their further improvement. For this good purpose, the representative body of our Church, from a number of these United States, are now assembled or convened.

Arduous was the work that lay before us. When we took up our Liturgy with a view to certain necessary alterations, we were struck with the utmost diffidence. We contemplated our Church service as an august and beautiful fabric—venerable for its antiquity—venerable from the memory of those glorious, and now glorified, Luminaries, Saints and Martyrs, who laid the foundations of our Church on the rock of ages. We stood arrested, as it were, at an awful distance—It appeared almost sacrilege to approach the porch, or lift a hand to touch a single part, to polish a single corner, or to clear it from its rust of years.

When, on the one hand, we looked back to the days of the first reformation in Religion, the progressive steps by which those pious worthies broke down the enormous pile of rubbish and error, which for ages had been built up to obscure the ancient foundations laid by Christ and his Apostles; when we considered the difficulties which they had to encounter—the powers of this world combined against them—the strength of ancient habits and prejudices—the ignorance of the age (learning and philosophy being then at a low ebb, and chiefly engrossed by those whose interest it was to support the former error;) when we considered these things, we were rather astonished that they had gone so far than that they went no farther—but, we were encouraged to proceed, by considering, on the other hand, that we had none of those difficulties to deter us.

Blessed be God, we live in a liberal and enlightened age, when Religion, if not so generally practised as it ought, is never eless generally better understood; and when nothing can be considered as deserving the name of Religion, which is not rational, solid, serious, charitable, and worthy of the nature and perfections of God to receive and of free and reasonable creatures to perform—Nor had we to contend against, nor suffer from, the rulers of this world. Blessed be God again, they yield us that best protection and assistance which Religion can receive from earthly powers—perfect and equal liberty to worship God according to that sense of holy Scripture which our reason and conscience approve; and to make such alterations and improvements in points of decency, order, government and edification, as the general body of the Church, from time to time, may judge most expedient.

Favourable to our wishes, therefore, was the present æra. Through the wise ordering of Providence, we had just become a sovereign and separate people among the nations of the earth; independent of all foreign jurisdiction, in matters ecclesiastical as well as civil. With vast labour and application our forms and constitutions of civil government had been built up and established upon the purest principles of political wisdom and liberty; in consequence of which, certain changes in our ecclesiastical constitutions became necessary, as well as in our forms of Prayer for the "powers that be;" considering them "as ordained of God."

These alterations being once made, an occasion was offered (such as few Churches before us have ever enjoyed) of taking up our Liturgy or public Service, for a Review, where our former venerable reformers had been obliged to leave it; and of proposing to the Church at large, such further alterations and improvements, as the length of time, the progress in manners and civilization, the increase and diffusion of

charity and .toleration among all Christian denominations, and other
circumstances (some of them peculiar to our situation among the highways and hedges of this new world) seem to have rendered absolutely
necessary.

Ardent, and of long continuance, have been the wishes of many of
the greatest, wisest and best Divines of our Church, for some alterations
and improvements of this kind. Among these we have a Whitby,*

---

* The judgment and wishes of some of those great Divines, which could not so conveniently be delivered in a Sermon, I have collected into the following notes, for the
further information of the reader:

"If our rulers (says Dr. Whitby) would be pleased to change the present Liturgy as
much from what it is, as it is altered from what it was, in the days of Edward the VIth,
I verily believe that alteration would render it acceptable to many, who do now refuse
submission to it. The Church of Christ hath judged it fit to alter many things which
were first instituted by the blessed Apostles themselves, or by the primitive age of the
Church [namely the kiss of charity and some other usages;] yet I hope this tempteth
no man to suspect the wisdom of the Apostles of our Lord, or of the primitive professors of Christianity. Why, therefore, should a like practice tempt any to suspect the
wisdom of our first reformers? We have already altered many things, which were
allowed and done by them. They at first retained chrism, prayer for the dead, baptism by women; and many other things of a like nature. And if these things might
be reformed, without reflection on their wisdom, why may not other things be so?"

"The serious and speedy review of the Liturgy," says Bishop Gauden (in the year
1661), "much desired by some, and not much opposed by others, may be of good use
for explaining some words and phrases which are now much antiquated, obscure and
out of vulgar understanding; which is no news after an hundred years, in which, language, as well as all things under heaven change. This work, once well and wisely
done, may, by God's blessing, much tend to the satisfaction of all sober Christians;—
for as one day teacheth another, so there may be (as in all outward forms of Divine
Worship) both harmless additions, and innocent variations; yea, and sometimes inoffensive defalcations of some redundancies, according as men and times, and words
and manners and customs, vary."

Bishop Sanderson (in a visitation Sermon, 1641), speaking of our reformation, although he says "he had a great esteem for the moderation of it, and a great veneration
for the instruments employed by God in it, and a great love of that wholesome way
of doctrine, life, devotion and government; yet he was not such a formalist, but that he
wished for alterations, though he judged that all alterations, in such grand and established concerns as Religion, should be done by the public spirit, counsel and consent
of the Prophets, Prince and People."

"Nothing," says Bishop Beveridge, "was anciently more usual with the Churches
of God, than when times and necessity required it, to change the laws made by themselves; to abrogate old ones, and substitute others and perhaps different ones, in their
stead." "And," says Bishop Kennet, "let us hope and pray that whatever addition
can be made to our happiness, God in his time will add those things unto us. In the
Churches of Corinth and Crete, planted by an Apostle, there were some things wanting, to be afterward set in order."

Bishop Burnet "wishes some things may be taken away, and others softened and
explained. Many things were retained at the reformation, to draw the people the
more entirely into it; which was at that time a lawful consideration, but is now at an
end," &c.

Tillotson, Saunderson, Stillingfleet, Burnet, Beveridge, Wake, Tennison, Hales, and innumerable others of venerable name among the Clergy; and among the Laity a multitude more, at the head of whom may be placed the great Lord Bacon, the father of almost all reformation and improvement in modern philosophy and science.

Eight different times, from the days of Edward the sixth, when our Liturgy was first framed, to the year 1661, has it been revised and altered by public authority. And, says Archbishop Tennison, some who have well considered all the alterations and amendments which were then made (viz. in 1661), and which amount to the number of six hundred, are sufficiently convinced that if there was reason for those changes at that time, there is equal, if not greater reason, for some further improvements now.

Our Church, in the preface to our common prayer, allows the expediency and necessity of such alterations from time to time. Even our language itself is fluctuating, and receiving frequent improvements; and in what concerns Religion, and its various forms, rites and ceremonies, no Church on earth can claim perfection. This belongs only to the Church of the first born in Heaven!

But the greatest and most important alterations and amendments were proposed at the Revolution, that great æra of liberty, when in 1689,* commissioners were appointed, among whom were many of the great divines already mentioned; of whom, and of those who were nominated for the like great work before the revolution, Archbishop Wake says—"They were a set of men, than whom this church was never, at

---

* The preamble to the commission in 1689, was as follows, strongly setting forth the need of alterations from time to time, viz.:

"Whereas the particular forms of divine worship, and the rites and ceremonies appointed to be used therein, are things in their own nature indifferent and alterable and so acknowledged; it is but reasonable that, upon weighty and important considerations, according to the various exigencies of times and occasions, such changes and alterations should be made therein as to those that are in place and authority should from time to time seem either necessary or expedient."

Archbishop Wake, lamenting the miscarriage of the great and good design of this commission, declares it to have been as follows, and makes some other strong remarks upon the whole proceedings, with which I shall close these notes.

"The design," says he, "was in short to improve, and, if possible, to enforce our discipline, to review and enlarge our liturgy, by correcting of some things, by adding of others, by leaving some few ceremonies, confessed to be indifferent in their nature, as indifferent in their usage. No alterations were intended, but in things declared alterable by the church itself. And if things alterable, be altered upon the grounds of prudence and charity; and things defective be supplied; and things abused be restored to their proper use; and things of a more ordinary composition be revised and improved, while the doctrine, government and worship of the church, remain entire in all the substantial parts of them; we have all reason to believe that this will be so far from injuring the church, that on the contrary, it shall receive a very great benefit thereby."—SPEECH ON SACHEVERELL'S TRIAL.

any one time, blessed with either wiser or better, since it was a church."
They set earnestly about the great work committed to them; making
many important and necessary alterations in the morning and evening
service; revising the various collects throughout the year, and rendering them more suitable to the epistles and gospels; striking out unnecessary repetitions in the service, and also such psalms and lessons of
the Old Testament, as appeared less suitable to the worship of a Christian church; altering and amending the offices of baptism, confirmation, matrimony, visitation of the sick, and burial of the dead, in all
things justly exceptionable; so that the whole service might thus become
more connected, solemn and affecting.

This great reformation was, however, lost through the heats and
divisions which immediately followed, both in church and state, under
King William; and such hath been the situation of things that it
hath never since been resumed in the mother church, by any public
authority.

But singularly to be admired and adored are the ways of Providence! At the commencement of a new æra in the civil and religious
condition of mankind in this new world, and upon another great
Revolution about an hundred years after the former, all those proposed
alterations and amendments were in our hands; and we had it in
our power to adopt and even to improve them, as might best suit our
circumstances in that part of our church, which the Lord hath planted
and permitted to flourish among the highways and hedges of this immense continent!

To embrace such an occasion, we are certain that multitudes in the
mother church would rejoice! And for us, not to have embraced it,
would have been ungrateful to our God, unjust to ourselves and our
holy religion, and unpardonable by our posterity. It hath been
embraced!—And, in such a manner, we trust, as will carry our Church
through all the shoals of controversy, and conduct her into a safe and
quiet harbour!

What glories will shine upon the heads of our Clergy whom God
hath made instrumental in this good work! How much shall our laity
be venerated for the candor, liberality, and abilities, which they have
manifested on this great occasion. Looking back upon the wonderful
things which God hath of late done for them, and forward upon the
long tract of glory which is opening before them as a people; they
could not but consider that, after all their illustrious toils for the civil
happiness of their country, they had done but little for their posterity
if the great concerns of Religion were neglected; knowing that righteousness only exalteth a nation, and that empires and kingdoms can
rise and flourish upon no other foundation, than Religion and Virtue.

What now remains, lies with the body of our Church at large;

namely, to receive, with the like temper of liberality, gravity and seriousness, as in the sight of Almighty God, what is now offered to their acceptance and use by their Church representatives or deputies. One part of the service you have just heard, and have devoutly joined in it. Here the alterations are but few, and those, it is hoped, such as tend to render it more solemn, beautiful and affecting! The chief alterations and amendments are proposed in the various offices, viz.: of Baptism, &c., as hath been observed to you before, with the addition of some new services or offices; namely, for the 4th day of July, commemorative of the blessings of Civil and Religious Liberty; the first Thursday of November as a Thanksgiving for the fruits of the earth; and an office for the visitation of persons under the sentence of death; of all which you can only form a true judgment, when they shall be published and proposed to you in the new prayer book.

Brethren! I am not a stranger to you in this pulpit! But some years have elapsed since I have addressed you from hence; and a few years more will close my lips forever! This may possibly be my last Sermon to you; and, therefore, I would exhort you again to receive, and examine, with a meek, candid, teachable and charitable temper of mind, what is proposed to you on this solemn occasion; as a work intended holy for the advancement of Religion and the maintenance of Peace and Unity in our Church to latest posterity. Let all prejudices and prepossessions be laid aside. Consider seriously what Christianity is! What the truths of the Gospel are! And how much it is our duty to have them set forth and promulgated to the Christian world, and also the Heathen world around us, in the clearest, plainest, most affecting and majestic manner! Let them never be obscured by dark and mysterious sentences and definitions; nor refined away by cunningly devised fables, or the visionary glosses of men, thinking themselves wise above what is written. Were our blessed Saviour now upon earth, he would not narrow the terms of communion, by such ways as these; and it is our duty, as it hath been our great endeavour in all the alterations proposed, to make the consciences of those easy who believe in the true principles of Christianity in general, and who, could they be made easy in certain points no way essential to Christianity itself, would rather become worshippers as well as labourers, in that part of Christ's vineyard, in which we profess to worship and to labour, than in any other. And what good man or Christian, either of the Clergy or Laity, can object to this? If we are Christians, indeed; if the love of truth and of one another, the true signs of the peace of Christ, prevail in our hearts; there will be no disputing or gainsaying, in matters of this kind. In all things, fundamental and necessary to salvation, we 'shall speedily find a decision in the word of God;' and as to things speculative and unnecessary, 'not finding them written there,' we will seek for their decision, by suffering them to glide smoothly down the stream of mutual forbearance, till at length they be discharged into the unbounded ocean of Christian love, and be there swallowed up and lost forever !

Let us not, therefore, repeat former errors; nor let the advantages now in our hands slip from us. If we become slack or indifferent in the concerns of Religion; if we discourage every endeavour for reformation,* "not only departing from the Law but corrupting the covenant of Levi, so as to make men stumble at the Law; the Lord our God hath said that he will make us base and contemptible among the people, and all our flock shall be scattered." God will be provoked to remove his candle from us, that glorious light which he hath revealed to us; and we shall fall back again into the former grossness and superstition!

If, Brethren, in the present work any thing be offered or done, with less clearness, precision, purity, or elevation of thought and expression, let it be considered calmly, judged of by Christian methods, and proposed for future amendment with singleness of heart; imitating the meekness and love of our master Jesus ! Thus shall we approve ourselves his disciples; and be justified in our endeavours for the purity of our Religion, not only in the sight of men and angels, but of Him especially, who will be our sovereign Judge, and sits enthroned above all the choirs of angels.

Thus also shall men be compelled to join in our worship, and our Sabbaths become more and more sanctified. Our very hearts and flesh will long for the courts of God's house—for the return of every Sabbath, as a blessed remainder, yet left us, of our original bliss in paradise, and a happy foretaste of our future bliss in the paradise that is above—a day of grace whereon our heavenly King lays open the courts of his palace, and invites us to a more immediate communion with himself! . . . .

Wherefore, then, Brethren, let our Sabbaths be remembered, and more and more sanctified. The Scriptures encourage us to look for a time when there shall be an universal diffusion of the gospel throughout this land ; when they who dwell in the Wilderness shall bow down before the Lord, when among the highways and hedges to the remotest part of the Continent decent places of worship shall be erected—villages, towns and great cities arise—and the service and worship of our church as we have introduced it, be not only adopted, but through the blessings of God, become happily instrumental in compelling the fulness of the Gentile world to come in.

O Time, may thy wheels move quickly round, until the approach of the blessed æra, till there be a fulness of spiritual food through every part of this new world ; and all nations, kindreds and tongues have

---

* Mal. Ch. II. ver. 8, 9.

access with us unto ONE GOD, and be sealed with us unto the day of Redemption, through Jesus Christ our Lord and Saviour, Amen.

As we have already said, nothing was yet in print. Certain of the alterations—those not rendered necessary by the Revolution—had been agreed on, proposed, and recommended, but all the alterations alike—as well those *resolved* on as those *proposed* and *recommended*—were yet on the journal and in manuscript, and without much shape or finish. Dr. White, the President of the Convention, Dr. Smith and Dr. Wharton were now appointed " to *publish* a Book of Common Prayer, with the alterations, as well those now ratified in order to render the Liturgy consistent with the American revolution and the constitutions of the respective States, as the alterations and new offices *recommended* to this Church," and it was resolved "that the book be accompanied with a proper Preface or Address, setting forth the reason and expediency of the alterations ; and that the Committee have the liberty to make verbal and grammatical corrections ; but in such a manner as that nothing in form or substance be altered."

It was also resolved that the same Committee be authorized to publish, with the Book of Common Prayer, such of the reading and singing Psalms, and such a calendar of proper lessons for the different Sundays and holidays throughout the year, as they might think proper.

It was further *ordered* that the said Committee be authorized to dispose of the copies of the Common Prayer when printed ; and that after defraying all expenses incurred therein, they remit the neat profits to the treasurers of the several corporations and societies for the relief of the widows and children of deceased clergymen in the States represented in this Convention—the profits to be equally divided among the said societies and corporations.

It was agreed by the Committee that the " Proposed Book," as it was now called, should be printed at *Philadelphia ;* and by Hall and Sellers. Dr. White was to see the proofs, and to send them to Dr. Smith, who would communicate with Dr. Wharton, who was residing in Delaware, the rector of Emanuel Church, Newcastle. This led to a good deal of correspondence between Dr. White and Dr. Smith, with occasional letters to and from Dr. Wharton. We give the most of this correspondence. It will be seen that the Committee construed liberally the leave given them to make verbal and grammatical alterations—more liberally than Dr. White himself quite approved.*

CHAPTER XLVII.

CORRESPONDENCE BETWEEN DR. SMITH AND DR. WHITE, WITH A LETTER FROM DR. WHARTON TO THE LATTER WHILE THE COPY OF THE "PROPOSED BOOK" WAS GOING THROUGH THE PRESS, INCLUDING DR. WHITE'S "HINTS FOR A PREFACE," AND DR. SMITH'S PREFACE—DR. SMITH TO THE REV. SAMUEL PARKER.

WE proceed to give the correspondence referred to in our last chapter relating to the publication of the Proposed Book. For the preservation of it, we are indebted, in former years, to Bishop White and Dr. Smith, in later ones to the excellent archæologist of our church, Dr. Perry, now Bishop of Iowa, who first gave it to the public.†

The Rev. Dr. White to the Rev. Dr. Smith.

PHILADELPHIA, October 19, 1785.

DEAR SIR: The first proof-sheet will accompany this and I expect to send you another by Saturday's post to Baltimore. I think we have fallen into an error, which Mr. Hall says we can easily correct, and our brethren here join with me in wishing it corrected. It is the making the Litany a necessary part of the Morning Service. The way I would propose to correct it is thus : In the rubric let it be "The Litany, etc., to be used on Sundays and other holidays, appointed to be observed by this Church." After the prayer, "We humbly beseech thee, O Father, etc.," let there be this rubric, "But when the Litany is not used, the three following prayers shall be said instead thereof;" then insert the

---

* Bishop White, in his Memoirs (Second edition, p. 109), referring to the fact that the Committee had been authorized to make verbal alterations, but were restrained from departing in either form or substance from what had been agreed on by the Convention, says that "the imperfections evidently remaining on some points by reason of haste [in the Convention], and which could have been remedied had they been attended to, and, added to this, the importunities of some of the clergy who pressed the Committee to extend their powers pretty far, in full confidence that the liberty would be acceptable to all, were such that, in the end, they were drawn on to take a greater latitude than ought to be allowed in such a work."

† In presenting it, in print, in this volume, I have avoided the contractions in orthography, which Bishop White, following a custom of his youth, continued through his life.

prayers "for the Congress," "for other civil rulers," and "for all conditions;" then let there follow the General Thanksgiving, St. Chrysostom's Prayer and the Benediction. To prevent repetition in the Evening Service, insert after the prayer against the dangers of the night, the following rubric:

Then shall be said the prayer for the Congress and the other prayers which follow it in the Morning Service to the end thereof.

There will be occasion for a rubric at the head of the Collects, Gospels and Epistles, directing the use of the Collects for each Sunday and holiday until the next Sunday or holiday; after the suffrages, at morning prayer when the communion service is not said; and always at evening prayer.

Quære.—Will it not be best to place the two invitations to the communion at the end of that service? At present they make an awkward break.

Please to mention these matters to Dr. Wharton, to whom I desire my affectionate remembrances.

I am, your affectionate humble servant,

WM. WHITE.

Rev. Dr. Smith to Rev. Dr. White.

October, 1785.

DEAR SIR: I am favored with yours of the 19th, enclosing the first sheet of the Prayer Book, and shall expect a second sheet at Baltimore on Tuesday. . . . .

On Wednesday last Dr. Wharton came to my house in Chester. Thursday being a storm, we sat down in the morning, and devoted the whole day to those parts of the Prayer Book, yet left to be prepared for the press.

1st. As to the office of Thanksgiving for the Fruits of the Earth, we wish to change one of the lessons, and also to make some additions to the Thanksgiving prayer, which will give it a little more animation; by taking something from prayers on the same subject, which Dr. Wharton thinks are to be found as well in the Roman Missal, as in the works of Bishop Wilson, of Sodor and Man—both which he will consult on his return to New Castle, in sufficient time for the press.

But our great business on Thursday was to read over the Psalms, taking, as we went along, your very judicious selection or rather rejection of particular Psalms and parts of Psalms. We propose rejecting some parts more, which may have escaped your notice, and retaining some few passages which you have proposed to reject; for by taking the Bible translation some of these passages are truly beautiful; and therefore in going over the work, we constantly compared the Bible translation with that of the Prayer Book, and find that out of both, sometimes using

the one and sometimes the other, sometimes in whole Psalms, and sometimes in particular verses, we shall greatly improve the reading Psalms
in general; but by our plan there will not so many be retained upon
the whole, as you have left standing. On my return from Baltimore,
I shall send you, or more probably bring to Philadelphia this part of the
work; and then by counting up the whole number of verses retained
and dividing them by thirty, we can average the number of verses (a
few over or under as the sense may require) which we shall have for
daily service. Out of the reading Psalms to be retained in our book,
it will be easy to make a selection of the best metre translations, of the
best Psalms, to which there may be an addition of some of Watts' best
Psalms, and hymns for the festivals and other occasions, which may be
got from sundry authors—I hope some may be offered by members of
our own Church in America, who are distinguished for their poetical
talents, and not ashamed to exert them on the lofty themes of religion.
But I am wandering and have no time to write what I wish on this particular topic.

Dr. Wharton left me on Friday, crossed over to Annapolis, and by
the good offices of Governor Paca and Mr. Chase, settled all his private
concerns with the intendant, and returned time enough to preach for
me in Chester this afternoon. He leaves me to-morrow, but I expect
a day from him on his return from Talbot, when we shall take up the
calendar, in which I believe you have not left us much to do.

I now proceed to answer your letter, respecting the first proof-sheet.

I do not think it an error, that the Litany is made a part of the
Morning Service. I think that service would be very incomplete in
the essential parts of prayer, and would lose much of its beauty if left
without the Litany. Although it is directed to be used every morning,
yet the use of it is not made so necessary, but that, where a clergyman
is weak in body, the weather severe, or for any other good reason, it
may not be omitted.

But I submit to your consideration, whether as you propose to alter
the rubric, viz., "The Litany to be used on Sundays and other holidays"—Wednesdays and Fridays will be considered as holidays. And
surely in large towns and cities (of which America will have many in a
hundred years more) the good old custom of week-day prayers will not
be laid aside. But, without the Litany, Wednesday and Friday prayers
(there being no sermon), would not draw many to church. Let not our
abridgments be too great, at least till we see how what hath been done
will be received. I think, then, there will be no harm in leaving the
rubric before the Litany, as it now is; only striking out the word
"every"—and after the prayer, "We humbly beseech thee, etc.," you
may add the rubric which you propose, viz : *"But when the Litany
is not used, the three following prayers shall be said instead thereof"*—

which (as the latter rubric may be supposed to explain the former) will at least imply a discretionary power in the minister to omit the Litany even in Morning Service, when in his discretion he thinks it necessary.

If the place of the two exhortations to the communion is to be altered, Dr. Wharton and myself are of opinion that they should not be placed at the end of the Communion Service (for it would appear very awkward to have an exhortation to an act of worship, standing after the act itself) but at the beginning, viz., before the prayer, *"Almighty God unto whom all hearts be open,"* etc., with a rubric separating them from the Communion Service, and directing that they be read when the notice is given, viz., on the Sunday or some holiday before the communion.

The proof-sheet is returned. You will see the corrections proposed by Dr. Wharton and myself on the margin; and the reasons will be obvious. Thus in the Litany—*"In all time of our tribulation:"* a semi-colon—yet it is connected with *"Good Lord deliver us"*—but at the end of the sentence, after the words *"Day of Judgment"* there is only a comma, and so in all the preceding sentences, each of which should have a semi-colon at the end of the sentence, as well as in the previous division of the different members of the sentence.

After a proof-sheet or two more, I would not wish to give you the trouble of sending the remainder to me, unless you have any alteration to propose; in which we must be very delicate, in consideration of the great trust committed to us. Dr. Wharton's best compliments. He sits by me while I subscribe myself,

Yours, etc.,

WM. SMITH.

Rev. Dr. White to Rev. Dr. Smith.

PHILADELPHIA, October 21, 1785.

DEAR SIR: I expect to send you by this opportunity the two first proof-sheets.

Lest you may have left Chester before the return of Wednesday post, I must repeat the substance of my former letter.

We are all here of opinion that the Litany ought not to be a necessary part of the Morning Prayer. The alteration, if you approve of it, may be made as follows: let the rubric before the Litany say, " to be used on Sundays and other holidays appointed by this Church." After the Litany with its attendant Prayers, insert this rubric—"And when the Litany is not said, the three following Prayers shall be used instead thereof," setting down the prayers for the Congress, for the other rulers, and for all conditions. Then set down the General Thanksgiving, etc. In the Evening Service, after the Prayer for Protection during the Night, let there be a reference to the Morning Prayer for the residue.

There is wanting a rubric at the head of the Collects, Epistles and Gospels, enjoining the use of the proper Collect in the Morning Prayer when used separate from the Communion Service, and always in the Evening Prayer.

Quære. Will not the two Exhortations in the Communion Service stand better either in the beginning or the end? At present they make an awkward break.

Quære, the propriety of introducing a rubric before the Prayer for our Rulers, in the Communion Service, specifying that the same is to be said, when that service is not used with the Morning Prayer. The clergy here wish for it; and many of our hearers wish that we had been as tender of repetition here, as in the case of the Lord's Prayer.

I hope to hear from you by return of the post, and am

Yours, etc.,

WM. WHITE.

P. S.—I observe that the second proof-sheet has a rubric, expressing that the Prayer for Congress, etc., shall be said in the evening and at other times when the Litany is not said; this removes my objection in part, but the two rubrics are contradictory. I think you will prefer the arrangement I have proposed.

I hope you have attended to the Psalms and Lessons. I recollect in the case of the Venite, we agreed to strike out the Latin; accordingly I have done it in the proof-sheet to the other Latin introductions. For the same reason (*i. e.*, its being agreed on in the case of the Venite) I have erased the unnecessary provisions against repetition.

Mr. Hall keeps the second proof-sheet so long on its second coming from the press, that I have no time to review it; and indeed I have reviewed the other but imperfectly. I hope your accuracy will render another reading unnecessary.

Rev. Dr. White to Rev. Dr. Smith.

PHILADELPHIA, October 23, 1785.

DEAR SIR: Similar proof-sheets to the enclosed were to have been sent by Saturday's post; but owing to the press, they were a few minutes too late, and are now in the office with my letter. I determined to take the chance of the stage, but knowing the uncertainty as to the delivery of letters, shall let mine remain with the sheets in the post-office.

Yours, etc.,

WM. WHITE.

P. S.—I have altered the arrangement in this proof-sheet according to the plan proposed in my letter—merely for your inspection.

10

Rev. Dr. White to Rev. Dr. Smith.

PHILADELPHIA, October 25, 1785.

DEAR SIR: Owing to the press, I was a few minutes too late for the last post. I sent proof-sheets by the wagon, which I consider as an uncertain mode of conveyance.

In the letter which encloses the proof-sheets by this opportunity, instead of three prayers read four; I wrote from memory and forgot that for the clergy.

I enclose you extracts from the constitution; to prevent errors of the transcriber you will compare it with the originals; I would do it now, but am in great haste.

Please to express at the head of the letter to the Bishops, that the original goes by the " Harmony," Captain Willet, from Philadelphia.

. . . .

I wish my affectionate respects to such of our brethren at the Convention as I have the pleasure of being acquainted with.

I am

Yours, etc.,

WM. WHITE.

REV. DR. SMITH.

Rev. Dr. Smith to Rev. Dr. White.

BALTIMORE, October 28, 1785.

DEAR SIR: I gave you my thoughts so fully in my letter from Chester last post concerning the alteration of rubric before the Litany, that I need not add anything further on that head. As the number of country congregations in America exceed those in towns, I may say fifty to one, and cannot have the Litany but as part of the Morning Service (and which, with the abridgments now proposed, would appear very short and incomplete without the Litany), and as for these reasons the Convention agreed that the Litany should be printed *in*, and as a part *of*, the Morning Service, it would not be proper for us to make so material an alteration as to put four prayers just after the Litany, as a substitute for the same, and which will be considered as an invitation to indolent or lukewarm readers of prayers to cut the people generally out of their general supplication. Of these sentiments are the Convention here, whom I consulted on this point, but without intimating to them that any such change was proposed by us of the Committee, but that it had been mentioned by some as a matter worthy of consideration at some future general convention.

The four prayers stand very properly where they now stand as an essential part of the Evening Service at all times, and would not stand so properly in the Morning Service, where they are only proposed as a conditional part; that is when the Litany is not used, and when that condition takes place it is very easy to turn forward one leaf to read them. Besides this the Evening Service would appear quite naked without them. But I need not have written half so much to you on this subject, only from a desire that we should by a candid exchange of sentiments go through the great work committed to us, with the same prefect agreement with which it hath hitherto been conducted ; and I know you will make no change from what was done in Convention ; unless in the exercise of the discretionary power given us, we can all, as a Committee, agree upon the expediency of such change.

As I said in my former letter, then, let the word "every" be struck out of the rubric before the Litany, and let the rest of the rubric stand as it is printed in the enclosed proof; and let the four prayers, and indeed the whole Evening Service, stand also just as they are in the same enclosed proof; with their several rubrics as they are, and there will be sufficient latitude for any minister when necessary to omit the Litany, and supply its place from the Evening Service; which last Service will look much better in this form. You will be pleased to attend to such corrections as I have made, and particularly in the prayer for "all sorts and conditions of men." The words "good estate of the Catholic Church" have been objected to by our Convention here, 1st, because "good estate" may be considered in a worldly sense, and if taken in any other is but an awkward or antiquated expression ; and 2dly, the word "Catholic" although intelligible enough to many, yet it is not approved of by many others, on account of the vulgar application of it to one particular Church. Now as this prayer for "all sorts and conditions" is a general prayer, never to be used when the Litany is used, why may not the Church be prayed for in the same words here as in the Litany, viz.: "thy holy Church universal?" And then the prayer will be, "more especially we pray for thy holy Church universal, that it may be guided," etc. Or if you think it will run better—"more especially we pray that thy holy Church universal may be so guided," etc.

One or the other of these corrections is desired by our Convention, and I have given you their reasons, and if you will agree to the alteration, I heartily concur with you, and think it will be approved by all our body.

I expect to hear from you by next week's post. Direct to me at Chester by the Eastern Shore post. I have a great many people talking round me, and write in haste.

Yours,

WM. SMITH.

REV. DR. WHITE.

P. S.—Your two packets by post have just come to my hand. What you propose as a rubric for the use of the Collects is proper. The other parts of your letters are either answered in this and my former letter, or shall be on my return to Chester, for which place I am just setting off, *via* Annapolis. I say no more about the Litany. Dr. West, etc., and some more clergy, Mr. Cutting in particular, who have come here since our Convention adjourned, and who are now with me, all concur in this letter, and that no alterations be made respecting the use of the Litany, which they all say must continue a necessary part of the Morning Service, unless dispensed with by any minister in his discretion, for want of health, shortness of time, such as riding ten or twelve miles to read prayers and preach twice in the same day. A future Convention may consider further upon the whole, in the mean time we do our duty in letting it remain as agreed upon by the body from which we derive our power as a committee.

Dr. West and a few more are about raising the money from this State for the book, but wish to have at least one thousand copies for Maryland alone, so that Mr. Hall, if not too late, should be told that four thousand copies will be too few. He may venture on five or six thousand, if he has paper enough ready.

Rev. Dr. White to Rev. Dr. Smith.

PHILADELPHIA, October 29, 1785.

. DEAR SIR : I expected to have sent you the third half sheet by this post, but it will be not quite ready. Mr. Hall intends to proceed quicker hereafter.

We expect the paper this evening ; on receiving the proof-sheets from you (which I suppose will be on Monday), we shall have one sheet ready for the last impression.

I say the less as I consider it uncertain whether this will reach you in Baltimore.   Yours, etc.,

WM. WHITE

REV. DR. SMITH.

Dr. Smith to Dr. White.

CHESTER, October 30, 1785.

I have just got back to Chester from Baltimore by the way of Annapolis, which last place I left yesterday afternoon. By the date you will perceive that I write on Sunday, a rainy morning, service put off till the afternoon. As soon as service is over, I must go to Dorset, to attend the baptism of my grandson, and bring Mrs. Smith home, who has been waiting for me more than a week past. My present letter will therefore be short ; nor is there occasion for a long one. Mr. Bryson writes me that he delivered to you my letter from Chester by last week's post. To both your letters which I received at Baltimore, I left an answer to go by yesterday's post, which I hope you will receive to-morrow, containing the general sentiments of the clergy of our late Convention, agreeing with what I wrote you from Chester and have repeated from Baltimore, concerning the Litany, etc.

By your last letter you seem to have attended to the rubric before the prayer for Congress, which in my first letter (not received by you at the time of writing) I wished you to notice, as it would remove your objections, etc. You say it has removed them in part, but leaves a contradiction between the two rubrics. This too you will find removed by striking out the word "every" before the word "morning" in the rubric prefixed to the Litany, so that comparing the two rubrics together, sufficient latitude will be left, without either disbanding the Litany, or putting a rubric and substitution of prayers after it, which would stand as an invitation to the lukewarm or lazy, always to pass over the Litany, which in the idea of all the clergy I have seen was considered by the Convention as a part of the Morning Service, indispensable except for some good reasons, and it hurts their feelings to think the use of the Litany should be thought a burden, or that our service could be complete without this excellent part. Of all this I have written fully, candidly and more than enough, and only repeat lest my Baltimore packet miscarry. All things will stand well, at least in this first edition of our book, and till next Convention, in the order in which we fixed them at Philadelphia, and as they are in the proof-sheets you have sent me, only striking out the single word "every" in the rubric before the Litany.

. I have no time to read critically the proofs, farther than I did in a few minutes at Baltimore. They will be very safe in your hands, with one or two readings. Let them be worked off as fast as possible, and a thousand copies or two more than we thought of at first (which I think was four thousand) if paper can be got. The book will be in great.*
. . . . . Baltimore alone a subscription is on foot; and Dr. West will speedily remit a large part of the $100, if not more than the whole, to which I shall add considerably from this shore, as soon as I return from Dorset, which I hope will be in three or four days at farthest.

If my letter from Baltimore is not come to your hand, you will attend to the following corrections which I made in the proofs of the second sheet enclosed therein.

At the end of morning and evening prayer, viz., " Here endeth the order of morning [evening] prayer"—Dele words "order of"—lest it should be implied that something might yet be prayed which is disorderly—prayer for clergy, instead of "*all* bishops and other ministers, and all congregations" insert "the congregations," to avoid a repetition of the word *all* so near the first *all*. But I think the whole sentence might be better altered thus—" send down upon the bishops and ministers of thy church and all congregations," etc.

---

* Manuscript imperfect.

In the end of the rubric entitled "Prayers and Thanksgivings upon several occasions"—to avoid the words "prayers" and "prayer," occurring in the space of one line, let the word "service" be put for the word "prayer" and read "two final prayers of morning and evening service."

In the prayer for "all sorts and conditions" please to make the correction proposed by the Baltimore Convention, as in my said letter from thence, and read thus: "More especially we pray for thy holy church universal, that it may be so guided," etc. Or, "We pray that thy holy church universal may be so guided." This will agree with the prayer for the church as in the Litany, instead of which this is to be used, and rids us of the exceptionable word too many, viz., "Catholic," and also the awkward words "good estate of the church," by which some will say we mean good Glebes and salaries or estate merely temporal. These little alterations are in our power, and not improper when desired by any respectable number of our brethren.

Our Convention read over with general approbation the proposed improvements and alterations; but stormy weather and that bay which often renders business precarious, made our meeting thin, and we adjourned to meet at Annapolis in April, or sooner if called by me as President.

.   .   .   .

Next week my copy of the Address to the Archbishops, etc., will go by a ship from Baltimore or Annapolis. I wish the sentence, "That these States should become *free*, sovereign," etc., had been expressed "separate Empires, States or Governments." It seems to *insult*, or at least to *renew* old complaints that we were not *free* before. Can an alteration be made in the other copies? I could yet have it made in mine by a letter to London per packet New York. I beg another copy of said Address, for I was obliged to send mine, on an hour's notice, without taking a copy. Governor Paca and our other friends in Annapolis, except as above, approve the address, and it will be easy to get a certificate from the Executive of the State that granting the prayer of it can give no offence, but is perfectly consonant to the Constitution. I shall be at Philadelphia time enough for the Psalms, Lessons, Calendar, Preface, etc., to save this voluminous writing, for I find I cannot make my letters short. In two or three weeks, perhaps sooner if the bank will assist us, I shall see you.

Yours,

W. SMITH.

Rev. Dr. White to Rev. Dr. Smith.

PHILADELPHIA, November 2, 1785.

DEAR SIR: I have received yours of the 28th, which I have sent to the press in the manner you approve of, having first reviewed and compared the pointing of it with an Oxford edition of the Prayer Book printed in 1775, and adjusted it accordingly. This I think you cannot but approve of, as the said edition appears to have been made on great deliberation in that seat of letters. I observed that wherever you had altered the pointing in the proof-sheet, you had done it conformably to the same book. I intend to bestow the same pains on all I shall send to the press.

I expect to send by this opportunity a proof-sheet, containing the greater part of the Communion Service, which will come to me the second time from the press; another is also in hand. I mentioned to you in a letter which I sent with the Sermons by Thursday's stage (and which do not appear to have come to hand when you were setting out for Annapolis) that some of our brethren, supported by remarks of the people, thought the prayer for the civil rulers an unnecessary repetition in the Communion Service; and that the evil might be avoided by a rubric dispensing with it, provided the Morning Service had been used immediately before. I told them I doubted of our right to alter it, and therefore merely mention it to you as information.

Mr. Provost has enclosed to me a copy of a letter from the President of Congress to the Minister at the Court of Great Britain. After stating our late proceedings and the political hindrances on a former occasion, he says, that if our application to the bishops should come before the King and Ministry, it is the wish of "the Church of England Members of Congress," that Mr. Adams may assure them of our right to take the said step and that the granting our petition would not be an intermeddling in the affairs of these States.

You give me leave to go on with the press alone, after the first sheet or two. But it is a liberty I shall never use, unless the press should be like to stop without it; which is not a probable case. At any rate, I shall not venture on any alterations without consent.

I am,

Yours, etc.,

W. WHITE.

REV. DR. SMITH.

I shall direct three thousand copies.

Rev. Dr. White to Rev. Dr. Smith.

PHILADELPHIA, November 2, 1785.

DEAR SIR: I have received yours from Chester, and indeed all which you mention to have written hitherto.

I shall attend to the alterations you propose; all which I approve, except the word Ministers for Pastors in the prayer for the clergy, which you only seem to throw out for consideration.

The latter word is used in all the other places and was that approved of by the Convention.

I am sorry I made it necessary for you to write so much about the Litany; it is fixed to your mind and I am satisfied.

I shall do all you desire in respect to advertising, etc., except that it cannot be in this day's paper, which came to my house before your letter.

What you propose respecting the letter to the bishops is too late ; or I should not object to the alteration. The original is gone by Willet, and I suppose the other copy goes to-day from New York by the packet, and will probably (as the packets sail fast) be delivered before any subsequent letter can reach England. I will send you another copy, but cannot transcribe it for this day's post.

.   .   .   .

I am, in haste,

Yours, etc.,

W. WHITE.

COMMUNION SERVICE.

Quære, the insertion in the rubric before the exhortation, the words " or so much thereof as he may think convenient." I have taken the liberty but can easily expunge.

Quære, the leaving out these words in the rubric before the collect " so that the ordinary, etc." Probably it will be thought the ordinary need have nothing to do, without complaint from the person forbidden.

In the sentences, quære the propriety of inserting those which relate to the support of the ministers of the gospel, it is expressly said the money shall be given to the poor.

Rev. Dr. White to Rev. Dr. Smith.

PHILADELPHIA, November 16, 1785.

DEAR SIR: After you left me, I thought it best to continue the consideration of the subject which had been before us. Accordingly I corrected, in the way of private memorandum, to the end of the Psalms. Afterwards, finding that the Psalms contained 2,498 verses, and that they would be reduced about one-third by our review, I made my division ; in which I have taken care to make the portions as equal as the analogy of the subjects, and sometimes the extraordinary length of single Psalms permitted. In some places I have omitted a few verses of what we had retained, as not suiting the preceding and following. I send you the fruit of my labor, hoping you will review it and send me such alterations as may occur to you ; which you may easily do (as I have with me a copy) by merely alluding to my subdivisions. I will then fairly fix the book, pasting from an old Bible such verses as we prefer of that translation.

The press began on Monday, and Mr. Hall assures me it shall work constantly; and that when the assembly shall rise, he will set two presses agoing.

I am, yours, etc.,

W. WHITE.

DR. SMITH.

I suppose it will be best in the Ash Wednesday Service to omit the Commination Psalm, which may be read on that occasion in the proper place; and to introduce the prayer immediately after the collect, with a rubric, directing the reading of them after the Litany and immediately before the General Thanksgiving.

Rev. Dr. White to Rev. Dr. Smith.

PHILADELPHIA, November 23, 1785.

DEAR SIR: No letter came to hand from you to-day, which I suppose is owing to your visit to Annapolis; and that on your return you will carefully revise the Psalms and examine the division I have proposed.

On looking over the offices as they stand prepared in the Prayer Book, I determined to propose the following matters to your consideration:

1. In the Baptismal Service, will it not be best to omit the command to kneel at the latter part of it, this being often inconvenient, especially in private houses? As we have shortened the printing of the private baptism, by referring to the public for all that follows the declaration, "We receive this child," etc., may it not be further shortened by reference as follows? viz.: after the address, "I certify you," etc., insert this rubric—

Then shall follow the gospel from St. Mark x. 13, with the exhortation and prayer following the same, as in the form of Public Baptism.

2. In the beginning of the Marriage Service, we have changed the word congregation into the word company. Quære, is not either word improper, as there used, if it be in a private room, and will it not be better to speak only of our being in the sight of God?

3dly. In the Burial Service, this verse was struck out, " Lord, let me know my end," etc. But as it stands in the Burial Service is it not unexceptionable, and will it not be the best introduction of the Psalm?

4thly. In the Forms at Sea, there are two Thanksgiving Psalms. I think one (viz.: the last) will be sufficient.

I was in hopes of having for you the fifth form from the press, but am disappointed. The two enclosed forms will be finally struck off this week.

I am, yours, etc.,

W. WHITE.

REV. DR. SMITH.

Rev. Dr. White to Rev. Dr. Smith.

PHILADELPHIA, November 30, 1785.

DEAR SIR: I suppose you have not returned from the Western shore, from my not hearing by this day's post. . . .

The fifth form was sent to me on Saturday, and is now working. The sixth is not ready. I regret, however, your not seeing them in proof; the less however as it is plain sailing and there can be no errors, unless typographical, which I shall endeavour to prevent.

I am, yours, etc.,

WM. WHITE.

REV. DR. SMITH.

Rev. Dr. Wharton to Rev. Dr. White.

NEW CASTLE, November 29, 1785.—At night.

DEAR SIR: . . . . I have looked over the lessons which you have retained or adopted—can see no objection to any of them, unless you should deem it more proper to adopt some of the exhortations to repentance from the Prophets, instead of the lessons from Genesis for the Lent Sundays. Perhaps the prophecy of Daniel would be no improper lesson or lessons as preparatory to the completion of the Christian sacrifice. Your idea of suiting the lessons to the several seasons of the Ecclesiastical year agrees perfectly with mine. The selection which you have made, I think, meets this idea. I observe but one lesson from Daniel, nineteenth Sunday after Trinity, cap. three. Now I conceive the seventh, eighth and ninth chapters, containing the prophetic history of the four great Empires and of the coming of Christ, to be very interesting. As I observed before, they would suit well the season of Lent, at least the ninth chapter. As to the general calendar, I apprehend the committee has power to alter it, as the Convention judged proper to omit the Saints' days. I would be for retaining, however, the names of a few such as Lady-day, Michælmas, All Saints', with the Apostles' days—St. Stephen and Innocents. These last three, being Scripture festivals, should not be omitted—I mean a commemoration of Scriptural persons and martyrs. All Saints' days of more modern date should be expunged. No mention, I suppose, will be made of fast or abstinence days.

Yours entirely,

C. H. WHARTON.

Rev. Dr. White to Rev. Dr. Smith.

PHILADELPHIA, December 6, 1785.

DEAR SIR: My last three letters, lately written to you and which you had not seen when we parted, contain so much matter for your consideration that I ought not perhaps to burden you with more until those points

are settled. But thinking you may possibly wish to have the Table
of Lessons before you at the same time, I herewith send it, together
with a proposed rubric for the Psalms. I wish you to attend particularly to the note written lengthwise of the paper on the Table of Lessons
and containing a new arrangement which I have proposed in consequence of an observation of Dr. Wharton's after examining the said
table here enclosed; which he says he approves of after an attentive
consideration.

I am, yours, etc.,

WM. WHITE.

REV. DR. SMITH.

P. S.—Since writing the above, it came into my head to draw up a
few hints towards a preface. If you think they will be not useful
towards that purpose, throw them into the fire.

HINTS TOWARDS A PREFACE.

This Church, following the example of the Church of England in
times past, as is set forth in the preface to the Book of Common Prayer,
hath upon weighty considerations made such alterations in the form of
divine worship, as seem at this time either necessary or expedient.

The alterations, to which her attention was in the first place drawn,
were such as had become necessary in the prayers for our civil rulers.
These have been accommodated to the Revolution, which, in the course
of divine Providence, has taken place in the United States; and the
principal care herein has been to make them conformable to the proper
end of all such addresses, "That we may lead quiet and peaceable lives
in all godliness and honesty." And whereas it has been the practice
of the Church of England to set apart certain days for the rendering
of thanks to the Supreme Ruler of the Universe for signal mercies
vouchsafed to that Church and Kingdom, it has in like manner been
now thought to tend to godliness, that there should be two annual
solemn days of prayer and thanksgiving to Almighty God for the distinguished blessings of the land in which we live; in order that we may
be thus moved to gratitude for these mercies of his good Providence,
which might otherwise be the occasions of licentiousness.

The alterations of the Morning and Evening Prayer are chiefly,
either for the avoiding of repetition, or for the disuse of such words as
have varied from their former meaning, or for the arranging of the
prayers in a method more easy for the worshipper. In the Apostles'
Creed, one clause of uncertain meaning, which was introduced into the
Church by the Council of Aquileia about 400 years after Christ, is
omitted.

As the Psalms are a considerable part of the Morning and Evening
Prayer, it may be proper to mention in this place the reason of their
being so considerably shortened. "All Scripture is given for doctrine

and instruction in righteousness." Yet it is supposed that all parts thereof were not indited for Christian worship; and that the Church hath a latitude to select such parts as she shall judge best suited thereto. Therefore such portions only of the Psalms are retained as were thought the most beautiful and affecting. In order to add to the propriety and sublimity of the psalter, the translation in the Bible has been preferred, where it was thought to have a stronger tendency than the other to raise devotion. A new division became necessary in consequence of the preceding changes; and it was supposed that the excellence of this part of the service would be still more increased, by the permission to combine it with that ancient doxology somewhat shortened—the Gloria in Excelsis.

In regard to the reading of the Holy Scripture at Morning and Evening Prayer, the same reasons which occasioned a select Table of First Lessons for Sundays and other holy-days seemed to extend in favor of the making a table of Second Lessons also; which is accordingly done. Those for the morning are intended to suit the several seasons; and yet without a repetition of the portions of the Gospel included in the Communion Service; and those for the evening are selected in the order of the sacred Books. Besides this, the Table of First Lessons has been reviewed; a few new chapters are introduced from the supposition of their being more edifying than the old; and transpositions have been made where they seemed to suit the lessons more to the season of the year. It has been thought that a calendar is unnecessary; and that the managing the lessons for the ordinary days agreeably to the civil year is not so expedient as the making them correspond, like the others, with the ecclesiastical year. Accordingly the minister is left to his discretion in the choice of lessons for the intermediate days, with the expectation that such will be taken as the most nearly suit those selected for the Sundays and other holy-days.

The Offices for Baptism have undergone some change. The requiring other godfathers and godmothers than the parents is dispensed with, if the same be desired; and thus regard is still maintained for an ancient and useful institution; and yet the complaint avoided, that in some cases, especially among the poor, it is difficult to provide sponsors, unless such as will most probably neglect the duties of that relation, to the great hazard of their own souls. The sponsors, instead of answering in the name and person of the infant, now answer for their own discharge of the obligation they have come under. The sign of the cross is retained, from a conviction of its having been used in the earliest ages of the Church as expressive of the being devoted to the service of Christ, who for our sake, " endured the cross, despising the shame." Nevertheless in tenderness to those who may entertain conscientious scruples concerning the use of this venerable rite, the minister is to dispense with it, when desired, by the sponsors.

The alterations made in the Catechism and the Service for Confirmation are such as became necessary to make those offices correspond with the Forms for Baptism; except the change of a few words of the service which was thought to be not sufficiently clear, in that part of the Catechism which relates to the Holy Communion.

It was thought that the Office for Matrimony could bear considerable shortening; which is accordingly done.

The Visitation of the Sick is nearly as in the old service. But a few verses in the Psalm have been omitted, as not appearing altogether applicable to the occasion; and the absolution has given way to what was conceived to be the more scriptural form used in the Communion Service.

In the Burial Service it was thought proper to omit some inapplicable verses in the Psalms; such expressions as seem to pronounce too positively concerning the state of the deceased; and the thanking of God for an event in which resignation only is required.

None of the Form for "the Churching of Women" is retained, except the Thanksgiving Prayer, which is placed among the other occasional Thanksgivings: it being supposed that many parts of the daily service are equally applicable to that occasion with what is omitted.

Such parts of the Commination Service, as were thought calculated to produce Christian penitence, are inserted after the Collect for Ash-Wednesday; except the Psalm, which is appointed to be read for the day.

The Forms to be used at Sea have undergone very little change, other than what arose from adapting it to the Revolution.

The case of such unhappy persons as have forfeited their lives to the laws of their country claimed the consideration of this Church: which has therefore adopted into her Liturgy the Form for Visitation of Prisoners under Sentence of Death—passed by the Convocation and Parliament of Ireland.

The Articles of Religion have been reduced in number. Yet it is humbly conceived, that the doctrines of the Church of England are preserved in their full extent; as being thought agreeable to the Gospel. It is therefore foreign to the intention of this Church to alter anything which appeared to be essential to the true sense and meaning of the Thirty-nine Articles; nevertheless, some variation has been made in the expression; and such parts omitted as were evidently adapted either to the time when the Articles were composed, or to the political constitution of England.

From the Psalms translated in metre by N. Brady amd N. Tate, there have been selected only such a number as were thought to make a sufficient variety for divine worship, and the parts selected are arranged under heads, agreeing with the subjects of them respectively: which it was thought would tend to the judicious use of them both in public and in private.

This Church, therefore, having gone through the important work of accommodating her Service to her new situation; it is hoped that the divine blessing will attend the same to the promoting of Piety in her children, and to the influencing them to live in peace and love with all Mankind.

The above "hints" are endorsed in the handwriting of the Rev. Dr. Smith, as follows:

PROPOSED BY DR. WHITE.

N. B.—The Preface has been composed upon another plan by W. S., who has made use of some of the within "hints."

Dr. Smith's Preface as finally made, after a few suggestions as to small matters from Dr. White,* came forth in the following form. Dr. White, it is agreeable to know, liked this Preface both in plan and execution. He could hardly do otherwise. It is undoubtedly a grand document, in point, alike, of strong common sense, of argumentative force, of the presentation of authorities, and of literary elegance and effect:

The Preface.

It is a most invaluable part of that blessed "liberty wherewith Christ hath made us free"—that, in his worship, different forms and usages may without offence be allowed, provided the substance of the faith be kept entire; and that, in every church, what cannot be clearly determined to belong to *doctrine* must be referred to *discipline;* and, therefore, by common consent and authority may be altered, abridged, enlarged, amended, or otherwise disposed of, as may seem most convenient for the edification of the people, "according to the various exigencies of times and occasions."

The Church of England, to which the Protestant Episcopal Church in these States is indebted, under God, for her first foundation and a long continuance of nursing care and protection, hath in the preface of her book of common prayer laid it down as a rule, that—" The particular forms of divine worship, and the rites and ceremonies appointed to be used therein, being things in their own nature indifferent and alterable, and so acknowledged, it is but reasonable that, upon weighty and important considerations, according to the various exigencies of times and occasions, such changes and alterations should be made therein, as to those who are in place of authority should, from time to time, seem either necessary or expedient."

---

* See *infra*, page 179 and 181.

This is not only the doctrine of the Church of England, and other Protestant Churches, but likewise of the Church of Rome ; which hath declared, by the Council of Trent*—"That the Church always had a power of making such constitutions and alterations in the dispensation of the Sacraments, provided their substance be preserved entire, as, with regard to the variety of circumstances and places, she should judge to be most expedient for the salvation of the receivers, or the veneration of the Sacraments themselves."

The Church of England has, not only in her preface, but likewise in her articles† and homilies,‡ declared the necessity and expediency of occasional alterations and amendments in her forms of public worship ; and we find accordingly, that seeking to "keep the happy mean between too much stiffness in refusing and too much easiness in admitting variations in things once advisedly established, she hath, in the reign of several§ princes, since the first compiling of her liturgy in the time of Edward the VIth, upon just and weighty considerations her thereunto moving, yielded to make such alterations in some particulars, as in their respective times were thought convenient: yet so as the main body and essential parts of the same (as well in the chiefest materials, as in the frame and order thereof) have still been continued firm and unshaken."

"Her general aim in these different reviews and alterations hath been (as she further declares in her said preface) to do that which, according to her best understanding, might most tend to the preservation of peace and unity in the Church ; the procuring of reverence, and the exciting of piety and devotion in the worship of God ; and (finally) the cutting

---

* Declarat (sancta synodus) hanc potestatem perpetuo in ecclesia fuisse; ut in sacramentorum dispensatione, salva illorum substantia, ea statueret vel mutaret quæ suscipientium saluti, seu ipsorum sacramentorum venerationi, pro rerum, temporum et locorum varietate, magis expedire judicaverit.—Sess. 21, cap. 2, Concil. Trident. And agreeably to this, their Breviary and Missal have been frequently reviewed; the Breviary heretofore three times in the short space of sixteen years only.

† "It is not necessary that traditions and ceremonies be in all places one, or utterly alike, for at all times they have been divers, and may be changed according to the diversity of countries, times and manners; so that nothing be ordained against God's word; [And therefore] every particular or national Church hath authority to ordain, change and abolish ceremonies or rites of the Church, ordained only by man's authority; so that all things be done to edifying."—*Art.* 34.

‡ "God's Church ought not, neither can it be so tied to any orders now made, or hereafter to be made and devised, by the authority of man, but that it may, for just causes, alter, change or mitigate—yea recede wholly from, and also break them," etc. And again—"The Church is not bound to observe any order, law or decree made by man to prescribe a form of *religion;* but hath full power and authority from God to change and alter the same, when need shall require."—*Homily on Fasting, Part I.*

§ The liturgy, in sundry particulars, hath been reviewed, altered and amended about eight different times, from its first publication, according to act of parliament in 1594; and its last review was in 1661, as it now stands, according to the Act of Uniformity.

off occasion, from them that seek occasion, of cavil or quarrel against her liturgy.'' And the necessity and expediency of the several variations made from time to time (whether by alteration, addition, or otherwise) she states chiefly under the following heads, viz. :

1st. For the better direction of them that are to officiate in any part of divine service; which is chiefly done in the *Calendars* and *Rubrics*.

2d. For the more proper expressing of some words or phrases of ancient usage in terms more suitable to the language of the present times; and the clearer explanation of some other words and phrases that were of a doubtful signification, or otherwise liable to misconstruction ; or

3d. For a more perfect *rendering* (or translation) of such portions of holy Scripture as are inserted into the liturgy (and made a part of the daily service); with the addition of some *Offices, Prayers and Thanksgivings,* fitted to special occasions.

If, therefore, from the reasons above set forth (namely the change of times and circumstances, and the fluctuation of our language itself), so many different reviews, alterations and amendments, were found necessary in the first hundred and twelve years after the Reformation ; it could not be expected, but (the same causes and reasons still operating) some subsequent reviews, alterations and amendments would not only be found necessary, but be earnestly desired by many true members of the Church, in the course of at least one hundred and twenty years more. And we accordingly find that in less than thirty years after the last review in 1661 (viz., on the 13th of September, 1689), a commission for a further review of the liturgy and canons, etc., was issued out to a number of bishops and other divines; "than whom (it hath been truly acknowledged) the Church of England was never, at any one time, blessed with either wiser or better, since it was a Church.''

The chief matters proposed for a review at that time, and which have been since repeatedly proposed and stated under the decent and modest form of quæries, are included under the following heads :

1st. Whether the public service on Sunday mornings be not of too great length, and tends rather to diminish than increase devotion, especially among the lukewarm and negligent?

2d. Whether it might not be conveniently contracted, by omitting all unnecessary repetitions of the same prayers or subject-matter; and whether a better adjustment of the necessary parts of the three different services, usually read every Sunday morning in the Church, would not render the whole frame of the service more uniform, animated and complete?

3d. Whether the old and new translations of the Psalms ought not to be compared, in order to render both more agreeable to each other and to their divine original; so as to have but one translation, and that as complete as possible?

4th. Whether all the Psalms of David are applicable to the state and condition of Christian societies, and ought to be read promiscuously as they now are; and whether some other method of reading them might not be appointed, including a choice of psalms and hymns, as well for ordinary use, as for the festivals and fasts, and other special occasions of public worship?

5th. Whether the subject-matter of our psalmody or singing psalms should not be extended beyond those of David, which include but a few heads of Christian worship, and whether much excellent matter might not be taken from the New Testament, as well as some parts of the Old Testament, especially the Prophets; so as to introduce a greater variety of anthems and hymns, suited to the different festivals and other occasions of daily worship, private as well as public?

6th. Whether, in particular, a psalm or anthem should not be adapted to, and sung at, the celebration of the Eucharist, as was the primitive practice, and that recommended in our first Liturgy?

7th. Whether all the lessons which are appointed to be read in the ordinary course are well chosen; and whether many of them may not be subject to one or more of the following objections, viz.: 1. Either inexpedient to be read in mixt assemblies; or, 2. Containing genealogies and passages either obscure, or of little benefit to be read in our congregations; or, 3. Improperly divided; sometimes abrupt and unconnected in their beginning, as having respect to something that hath gone before; and sometimes either too short or too long, and apocryphal lessons included among the number?

8th. Whether our epistles and gospels are all of them well selected; and whether after so many other portions of Scripture they are necessary, especially unless the first design of inserting them, viz.: as introductory to the Communion, should be more regarded, and the Communion be again made a daily part of the service of the Church?

9th. Whether our collects, which in the main are excellent, are always suited to the epistles and gospels; and whether too many of them are not of one sort, consisting of the same kind of substance? And whether there is any occasion of using the collect for the day twice in the same service?

10th. Whether the Athanasian creed may not, consistently with piety, faith and charity, be either wholly omitted, or left indifferent in itself?

11th. Whether our catechism may not require illustration in some points and enlargement in others; so that it may not only be rendered fit for children, but a help to those who become candidates for confirmation? And whether all the other offices, viz.: the litany, the communion office, the offices of confirmation, matrimony, visitation of the sick, churching of women, and more especially those of baptism, burial.

and communion, do not call for a review and amendment in sundry particulars?

12th. Whether the calendars and rubrics do not demand a review and better adjustment; and whether any words and phrases in our common prayer, which are now less intelligible or common, or any way changed in their present acceptation from their original sense, should be retained? And whether others should not be substituted which are more modern, intelligible, and less liable to any misapprehension or misconstruction?

13th. Whether the Articles of Religion may not deserve a review; and the subscription to them and the common prayer be contrived after some other manner, less exceptionable than at present?

These are the principal matters which have been long held up for public consideration, as still requiring a review in the book of common prayer; and although in the judgment of the Church, there be nothing in it "contrary to the word of God, or to sound doctrine, or which a godly man may not submit unto, or which is not fairly defensible, if allowed such just and favorable construction as in common equity ought to be allowed to all human compositions;" yet, upon the principles already laid down, (namely, "the promoting of peace and unity in the church, the exciting of piety and devoti n, and the removing, as far as possible, of all occasion of cavil or quarrel against the liturgy,") the pious and excellent divines who were commissioned in 1689, proceeded to the execution of the great work assigned them. They had before them all the exceptions which had, since the act of uniformity, been at any time made against any parts of the church service, which are chiefly set forth in the foregoing queries. They had likewise many propositions and advices, which had been offered at several times by some of the most eminent bishops and divines upon the different heads in question. Matters were well considered, freely and calmly debated; and all was digested into one entire* correction of everything that seemed liable to

---

* It will, without doubt, be agreeable to the members of our Church, and those who esteem our liturgy and public service, to have at least a general account of the alterations and amendments which were desired and designed by such great and good men as Archbishop Tillotson and others, whose names are in the following account taken from Bishop Burnet, who was also in the commission, and from Dr. Nichols:

"They began with reviewing the liturgy; and first they examined the calendar; in which, in the room of the *apocryphal* lessons, they ordered certain chapters of canonical Scripture to be read, that were more for the people's edification. The *Athanasian* creed being disliked by many persons on account of the damnatory clause, it was left at the minister's choice to use or change it for the Apostles' creed. New collects were drawn up more agreeable to the epistles and gospels, for the whole course of the year, and with a force and beauty of expression capable of affecting and raising the mind in the strongest manner. The first draught was by Dr. Patrick, who was esteemed to have a peculiar talent for composing prayers. Dr. Burnet added to them yet further force and spirit. Dr. Stillingfleet then examined every word in them with the exact-

any just objection.   But this great and good work miscarried at that time, and the civil authority in Great Britain hath not since thought it proper to revive it by any new commission.

But when, in the course of divine providence, these American States became *independent* with respect to civil government, their *ecclesiastical independence* was necessarily included; and the different religious denominations of Christians in these States were left at full and equal liberty to model and organize their respective churches and forms of worship and discipline, in such manner as they might judge most convenient for their future prosperity, consistently with the constitution and laws of their country.

The attention of this Church was, in the first place, drawn to those alterations in the liturgy which became necessary in the prayers for our civil rulers, in consequence of the revolution; and the principal care herein was to make them conformable to what ought to be the proper end of all such prayers, namely, that "rulers may have grace, wisdom and understanding to execute justice and to maintain truth; and that the people may lead quiet and peaceable lives, in all godliness and honesty."

But while these alterations were in review before the late Convention, they could not but, with gratitude to God, embrace the happy occasion which was offered to them (uninfluenced and unrestrained by any worldly authority whatsoever) to take a further review of the public service, and to propose to the Church at large such other alterations and amendments therein as might be deemed expedient; whether consisting of those which have been heretofore so long desired by many, or those which the late change of our circumstances might require, in our religious as well as civil capacity.

By comparing the following book, as now offered to the Church, with

---

est judgment.   Dr. Tillotson gave them the last hand, by the free and masterly touches of his flowing eloquence.   Dr. Kidder, who was well versed in the oriental languages, made a new translation of the Psalms, more conformable to the original.   Dr. Tennison, having collected the words and expressions throughout the liturgy, which had been excepted against, proposed others in their room, which were more clear and plain. Other things were likewise proposed, as that the cross in baptism might be either used or omitted at the choice of the parents; and it is further added from other certain accounts, "that if any refused or scrupled to receive the Lord's Supper kneeling, it may be administered to them in their pews; that a rubric be made, declaring the intention of the Lent fasts to consist only in extraordinary acts of devotion, not in distinction of meats; that the absolution may be read by a deacon; the word *priest* to be changed into *minister;* the *Gloria Patri* not to be repeated at the end of every psalm, but of all appointed for morning and evening; that the words in the *Te Deum, Thine honorable, true and only Son,* be changed into *Thine only begotten Son;* that the *Benedicite* be changed into the 128th Psalm, and other psalms appointed for the *Benedictus* and *Nunc Dimittis;* that if any desire to have godfathers and godmothers omitted, their children may be presented in their own names," etc.

this preface and the notes annexed, it will appear that most of the amendments or alterations, which had the sanction of the great divines of 1689, have been adopted, with such others as are thought reasonable and expedient.

The service is arranged so as to stand as nearly as possible in the order in which it is to be read. A selection is made both of the reading and singing psalms, commonly so called. Wherever the Bible-translation of the former appeared preferable to the old translation, it hath been adopted; and in consequence of the new selection, a new division and considerable abridgment of the daily portions to be read became necessary; and as the "Glory be to the Father," etc., is one said or sung before the reading of the psalms in Morning and Evening prayer, it was conceived that, in order to avoid repetition, the solemnity would be increased by allowing the minister to conclude the portion of the psalms which is at any time read, with that excellent doxology somewhat shortened, "Glory to God on high," etc., especially when it can be properly sung. With respect to the psalmody or singing psalms, for the greater ease of choosing such as are suited to particular subjects and occasions, they are disposed under the several metres and the few general heads to which they can be referred; and a collection of hymns are added, upon those evangelical subjects and other heads of Christian worship, to which the Psalms of David are less adapted, or do not generally extend.

It seems unnecessary to enumerate particularly all the different alterations and amendments which are proposed. They will readily appear, and it is hoped the reason of them also, upon a comparison of this with the former book. The calendar and rubrics have been altered where it appeared necessary, and the same reasons, which occasioned a table of first lessons for Sundays and other holy-days, seemed to require the making of a table of second lessons also, which is accordingly done. Those for the morning are intended to suit the several seasons, without any material repetition of the epistles and gospels for the same seasons; and those for the evening are selected in the order of the sacred Books. Besides this, the table of first lessons has been reviewed; and some new chapters are introduced on the supposition of their being more edifying; and some transpositions of lessons have been made, the better to suit the seasons.

And whereas it hath been the practice of the Church of England to set apart certain days of thanksgiving to Almighty God for signal mercies vouchsafed to that Church and nation, it hath here also been considered as conducive to godliness that there should be two annual solemn days of prayer and thanksgiving to Almighty God set apart, viz.: the fourth day of July, commemorative of the blessings of civil and religious liberty in the land wherein we live; and the first Thursday of November for the fruits of the earth : in order that we may be thereby stirred up to a more particular remembrance of the signal mercies of God towards us ; the neglect of which might otherwise be the occasion of licentiousness, civil miseries and punishments.

The case of such unhappy persons as may be imprisoned for debt or crimes claimed the attention of this Church ; which hath accordingly adopted into her liturgy the form for the visitation of prisoners in use in the Church of Ireland.

In the creed commonly called the Apostles' creed, one clause* is omitted, as being of uncertain meaning ; and the Articles of Religion have been reduced in number ; yet it is humbly conceived that the doctrines of the Church of England are preserved entire, as being judged perfectly agreeable to the gospel.

It is far from the intention of this Church to depart from the Church of England any farther than local circumstances require, or to deviate in any thing essential to the true meaning of the Thirty-nine Articles ; although the number of them be abridged by some variations in the mode of expression, and the omission of such articles as were more evidently adapted to the times when they were first framed and to the political constitution of England.

And now, this important work being brought to a conclusion, it is hoped the whole will be received and examined, by every true member of our Church and every sincere Christian, with a meek, candid and charitable frame of mind, without prejudice or prepossessions ; seriously considering what Christianity is, and what the truths of the Gospel are; and earnestly beseeching Almighty God to accompany with his blessing every endeavor for promulgating them to mankind in the clearest, plainest, most affecting and majestic manner, for the sake of Jesus Christ, our blessed Lord and Saviour.

We now resume the correspondence.

The Rev. Dr. White to the Rev. Dr. Smith.

PHILADELPHIA, January 4, 1786.

DEAR SIR : I send you the sheets as far as finished, and have corrected the proofs as far as to the beginning of the Burial Service.

I have just now delivered to Mr. Hall the offices of the Fourth of July and for November; as they will be gone on with to-morrow. I kept

---

* The clause meant is "Christ's descent into hell," which, as Bishop Burnett, Bishop Pearson, and other writers inform us, is found in no creed, nor mentioned by any writer, until about the beginning of the fifth century; and in the first creeds that have this clause or article, that of Christ's burial not being mentioned in them, it follows that they understood the descent into hell only of his burial or descent into the grave, as the word is otherwise translated in the Bible. The Nicene creed hath only the burial, and the Athanasian only the descent into hell.

them to the last with the hope of hearing from you, but there was no post this week.

In preparing said offices for the press, it occurred to me that their wanting gospels and epistles made them not harmonize with the rest of our service. Our brethren here were unanimous in advising me to add them ; and I was the more encouraged by Dr. Magaw's saying that it was not thought of in the committee. The passages chosen are Philippians iv. 4–8, with St. John viii. 31–37 ; and St. James i. 16, with St. Matthew v. 43. The lessons, taken by the same advice for the first Thursday in November, are Deuteronomy xxviii. to verse 15, and St. Matthew vii. 7.

I am sorry that I have been obliged to do these things without waiting for your approbation ; but I hope they will still merit it.

The post is just going, so that I can only write myself,

Yours, etc.,   · W. WHITE.

DR. SMITH.

Rev. Dr. White to Rev. Dr. Smith.

PHILADELPHIA, January 17, 1786.

DEAR SIR : I have lost no time in making provision for inserting a few tunes in the prayer book. We have selected some which I send you the names of on an enclosed paper. Mr. Hopkinson* is beginning to copy them for the engraver, and I expect they will be done with sufficient speed.

It was natural for me, when on this subject with a gentleman of Mr. Hopkinson's taste, to communicate to him our arrangement respecting the psalms. He objected, as indeed has almost every one to whom I have mentioned it, to the running the psalms into one another. The issue of the conference with Mr. Hopkinson was his suggesting a plan of which I give you a sketch on an enclosed paper, and which I think on the whole will be the simplest and most elegant. Unless you disapprove, I will execute it on this plan, although I shall have lost some labor of transcribing ; in doing of which, however, I became more and more dissatisfied with the running of psalms into one another ; and indeed in this way, I find that many fine passages must be lost, or else such a repetition made as in the same psalm would be improper and disgusting. I expect your draft of a preface by next post and am

Yours, etc.,   WM. WHITE.

REV. DR. SMITH.

P. S.—On Mr. Hopkinson's plan, the insertion of the term chapter will be unnecessary.

---

* The Hon. Francis Hopkinson, one of the signers of the Declaration of Independence, judge of the Admiralty Court of Pennsylvania, and appointed by Washington judge of the District Court of the United States for Pennsylvania and New Jersey. See the Pennsylvania Magazine of History and Biography, Vol. II., page 314.

Rev. Dr. Smith to Rev. Dr. White.

Sunday night or Monday morning, January 23, 1786.

I received your last letter of 17th of January, and observe what you say concerning the objections which have occurred as to running our collection or selection of singing psalms into one another. You know this arrangement was proposed for the convenience of clerks and of the people for finding any proposed sum. We could not then think of any better mode. I have no attachment to any particular arrangement that appears best. But I could see no impropriety, nor can yet see any in making one chapter or psalm of all those different parts of different psalms which are selected on the same subject and in the psalm metre ; for except in metre 1st, and in psalms of praise, etc., none of them would be very long in this way ; and I know not how you can make your breaks in the same metre, so as to close the service without running many of them into one another. For of some psalms only a verse or two are taken, and surely so small a portion cannot stand by itself. All the reading psalms for a morning or evening service, although not arranged under different heads as the singing psalms, are nevertheless run into one another, without inconvenience. On the contrary it appears a beauty. The same has been done in choosing psalms for particular services even by our Mother Church.

But I have no objection to the method now proposed. As far as I can understand it from your short scrip, it was what we first proposed, although some difficulties then occurred. Mr. Hopkinson's judgment will always have great weight with me, especially on a subject of elegance and taste. I am happy that he has agreed to devote a few hours to the psalmody. Under his hand it will become a most acceptable addition to the Prayer Book, and with the hymns to be annexed will recommend the purchase of it to many, and I hope greatly increase their love both of public and private devotion.

With the assistance of our organist Mr. Limburner, our clerk, and some other gentlemen of this town, I have examined the tunes which are to be engraved and we generally approve of them ; except Canterbury, which is too flat and inanimate. St. Anne's, though good, is too difficult for singers in general. These two might be exchanged for some more popular tunes, which you have omitted, such as Brunswick and Stroud tunes. We also wish to have in the collection the tune . . . . and St. Peters is adapted to that noble hymn . . . . published among the collection of hymns—

When all thy mercies, O my God, etc.

In addition to the tunes which are proposed in your list, we would offer the six which are enclosed, or such of them as you think may vary most from those of the same metre which you retain. I should wish to see the first proof-sheet of the singing psalms before it is worked off. I hope Mr. Hall is now upon it, and I wish not to delay him.

I enclose you a collection of hymns to follow the psalms, and which I have every reason to believe will be a great recommendation of our Prayer Book to multitudes of our most serious and religious members. The Methodists captivate many by their attention to Church music, and by their hymns and doxologies, which, when rationally and devoutly introduced, are sublime parts of public and private worship. I have arranged the hymns under proper heads, have chosen the best I could possibly find, and have spent several whole nights this last week in copying them for the press, abridging them where it could be done, and correcting some of them in a few places. I shall be happy if they meet with your approbation and save you some trouble in this part, as you have had far more than your share in other parts, which it was not in my power to ease you from, on account of my many late calls from home.

The number of hymns is more than I expected when I sat down to collect them; but I see none that I could wish to leave out. On the great festivals of the Church, there should be some variety, at least three or four, and of different metres, to complete the psalmody of the day.

There are about eight hymns yet wanting, which I hope to send you next post, viz.: Hymns or Psalms for a Public Fast, Meditational Hymns on Death, Funeral Hymns, a Hymn on the Last Judgment, and a Hymn on Immortality, exhibiting a Glimpse of the Kingdom of Glory. But on these last two awful and exalted subjects, I know not where to choose. They far transcend the power of our common class of poets, and those of the greatest genius have left them unsung, at least in that kind of verse which is proper for psalmody . . . . . . singing psalms, that those portions of them . . . . . . of hymns, are adapted to particular occasions of service, thanksgiving, etc., as July 4th, the first Thursday in November, etc., are not to be printed in their place with the other psalms, which are selected for common use. Should any of them be chosen on any other occasion than those to which they are adapted among the hymns, the clerk and congregation can turn to them where they stand. The hymns and psalmody both together will not be near so long as the former psalmody by this plan, unless your new arrangement should lengthen them somewhat. The hymns will not require two half sheets, but were it more, they will pay for themselves in the sale of the book and in the satisfaction which Christians in general will derive. Few will grudge a dollar if, with the addition of hymns and tunes, etc., we think that should be the price. You will not forget to take Addison's 23d Ps. from Spectator No. 441—his nineteenth from No. 465, to be inserted among the psalms under their proper metres.

You will also take his hymn, on Gratitude, from No. 453 to be inserted among the hymns where I left a blank in copying, for want of time.

As I do not know in what order you have arranged the metres in publishing the singing psalms, I must beg you to fill up the blanks I have left for the metres of the *Gloria Patri*, so as to answer to our select psalms, for it will not do to say as formerly—such a metre as Ps. 25, Ps. 123, Ps. 148, etc., as our psalms and metres will not now answer to those numbers, but to metre first, second, third, etc., as you may place. I believe I said before (but have not time to look back) that I beg to see the first proof-sheet of the singing psalms before it goes to the press, I hope by next post—I will try by that time to send you the preface or address nearly upon the plan you have sketched. You speak in some former letter of collecting for the feasts and fasts some passages of psalms to supply the place of the *Venite* on different festivals. Will not this take too much from the reading psalms of those days? Might . . . . . of Scripture in the Old and New Testament . . . . . . Easter Day the substitute for the *Venite* is wholly so . . . such a choice as this may interfere with the lessons, and the epistles and gospels of the day. There are difficulties both ways, I leave to your own judgment. And where anything we had before (as the old *Venite* a little altered) will do, I would not introduce, for the present at least, any very great alterations. All the hymns, etc., except a few from Watts and Addison, have long been in use in the Church in the supplement to Tate and Brady's Psalms and other collections, printed with different prayer books, by religious societies, etc. The hymns, therefore, are only a more copious collection, arranged more properly, of such as have been long in use, for even some of Watts's are not new in our Church, and you know Dr. Johnson gives them a high name in his "Lives of the Poets." I wish I could have found more than about six or eight of Watts's to introduce, or that I could glean from him what is yet wanted on the last Judgment and the Kingdom of Glory. I know not where else to look. If you know of any on those subjects, I wish you to point them out. I have got two or three funeral hymns to be copied out in my next, and also hymns proper for the service of the Church at Sea and after Storms, etc., etc.

It is now four o'clock in the morning. I am drowsy and half-blind—cannot stay to read what I have written—believe I have forgot nothing material. I shall be ruined if the packet does not come safe to your hand. I have no copy, nor even a list or table of the hymns which I intend should be added at the end, after we know the pages to which we must refer. This may be done by the printer. You will therefore not fail to acknowledge the receipt of them by the return of post. If I have no letter, I shall conclude you have not received them, and be very unhappy till I hear that you have.

Yours, with great regard,   WM. SMITH.

The hymns must be printed in a smaller letter, as many of the metres are long.   Attend well to the note at bottom of page 38.

Rev. Dr. White to Rev. Dr. Smith.

PHILADELPHIA, January 25th, 1786.

DEAR SIR: I have received your letter with the enclosed hymns; of which the time admits my saying no more at present, but that I make no doubt of their being unexceptionable.   If I have any remarks to make, you shall have them in my next.

As you have no objections to the method last proposed respecting the psalms, I shall do whatever on a re-examination appears to our friends here the best.

I am afraid your proposals, concerning the tunes, are too late to be accomplished without either spoiling what has been done or making an addition in this article; which, by-the-by, will be much more expensive than you imagined.   However I shall accommodate it to your ideas, as much as I should think you would yourself, were you on the spot.

I expect we shall finish the reading psalms this week, and that we shall have the first sheet of the singing psalms ready for next post. The waiting for it can be no injury in regard to the composing part, but for the press work (which Mr. Hall considers as the principal), it may put us back a little.

In regard to the selections, instead of the *Venite,* I believe they had better stand as they are.   You know the design is to introduce such portions respecting the Messiah as could not be agreeably retained in their old places; now the including some Scriptural sentences must either supersede some of said portions or make this part of the service too long; at least this would be the case on Good Friday and Christmas day.   With regard to the reading psalms of those days I mentioned to you, and requested you to look at them, that I had in a rubric at the end referred to one portion of the Psalter to be read on all these festivals at morning prayer, another at evening prayer, another for the morning of the fast days, and another for the evening of the same.

I have been considering the daily calendar; and do not find that we have any power given us on this head.   Nevertheless the reading the Apocrypha has been so old an objection to our Church, that I believe it would be taken well if we were to substitute others.   My plan for this is to divide so many of the longer chapters as will make up for the number to be expunged, which I find on examination may easily be done.   Perhaps, too, it might be well to divide as many chapters of the Gospels and Acts as may be suited to the reading them over twice instead of thrice in the year.   Those from the Epistles may very well stand as they are.   I must request your opinion on this head.

On another review of my plan of proper lessons I am fully satisfied with it.

I know of no suitable hymns on the subjects you have named.

I do not think it will be necessary to print the hymns in a smaller type than the rest, and if not necessary, you will agree with me that it will not look so well.

I am, yours respectfully and affectionately,

WM. WHITE.

REV. DR. W. SMITH.

P. S.—I hope to send you per next post the Psalter complete.

Rev. Dr. Smith to Rev. Dr. White.

January 30th, 1786.

I enclose the remaining hymns. The Psalms of David, unless where tortured by versifiers, have but few evangelical subjects, and stood much in need of a supplement, which our Church has allowed from time to time and we have full power to offer, as neither the psalms which we have selected nor this supplement of hymns are more than an exercise of our best discretion in the work committed to us, and not an essential part of our reformed liturgy.

You will find the hymns all upon evangelical subjects and practical Christianity, viz. : On the Nativity, on the Passion, Resurrection, Ascension, Gift of the Holy Ghost, The Holy Communion, Time, Life, Death, Hymns at Sea and various Occasions of Life, in Sickness, in Time of Public Calamity, Thanksgivings for Mercies received, On State Days, as July 4th, November 1st, Thursday, etc., concluding with Christ's commission to preach the Gospel, two hymns which, when we have ordination of ministers at home, may be properly sung in time of public worship. The subjects you see are numerous, and not more than two or three hymns at most on any subject. The hymns are generally short, too. Should you think that any of them might be left out, I could wish to know which of them. There is the greatest number for the Nativity and for Funerals, but here we ought not to be too sparing. In the enclosed collection, Hymns 36, 39, 40–43 are particularly and beautifully applicable to their subjects. In short, I have taken great pains to collect and adapt them, giving nothing of my own, and I think the number, as they are generally short (although amounting to fifty), is not too great, as the Psalms of David are greatly abridged, and many of them taken out of the places where they stood promiscuously with other psalms, and placed as hymns under the heads to which they belong, so that you will take care not to print these particular passages of the psalms with the singing psalms. Let me hear particularly from you next post on this whole subject. I am more and more pleased with the arrangement of the singing psalms under the different heads to which they will apply, which are but four or five, and finding hymns founded on other Scriptures, as we . . . . worship. Clergy and laity here are greatly . . . . to purchase books.

You will please to put the proper numbers to the pages of the enclosed hymns, as I have forgot at what my last week's copy closed, and therefore have marked or paged them A, B, C, etc., which you will expunge when you put the numbers. Please to put Hymn 25 on *Recovery from Sickness* in the former copy next after Hymn 40 of this enclosed copy, being on the same subject ; and alter the numbers of the hymns accordingly from No. 25 to No. 40, inclusive.

Next post shall answer all the unanswered parts of your former letters, send you the preface, and conclude this business, with great thankfulness to God who hath enabled us to carry it forward, with so great harmony and satisfaction to ourselves, and I trust it will be to the full satisfaction of our constituents and the public. Write me fully this week, as I am to cross the bay next Sunday evening.

Yours,
Wm. Smith.

Rev. Dr. White to Rev. Dr. Smith.

Philadelphia, February 1st, 1786.

Dear Sir : I have received yours by this day's post ; and, agreeably to your desire, sit down to write to you particularly on the subjects of it.

I send you (with the Psalter) the first proof-sheet of the psalms. You will see that I have divided them. You objected to this in your former letter that it will become necessary to leave out parts of psalms for want of enough to make one division. I answer that it will not happen if we allow that to be enough which may suffice for one time of the clerk's singing. You also took notice that the other plan was adopted in respect to the reading psalms. I answer that the same reason does not hold in the singing psalms, viz. : their being used together. Our brethren here are clear for dividing them and authorize me to say so, and Mr. Hopkinson thinks the other plan very exceptionable. I beg you to weigh the matter once more ; and if after all you should continue in your present mind I will execute it accordingly, provided you will take your pen and set down precisely what psalms shall follow one another, so as to be a guide to the printer. In doing this you will probably (like myself) be tired of the idea of running them into one another : if not, I will perform my promise. You will observe that I have put the rubric mark. I thought this proper to make it harmonize with the other parts of the liturgy, and to show with what view the psalms are introduced. In the old book they were no part of the common prayer, but were only used by the royal permission. With us, as I conceive, they are to be part of the liturgy.

In regard to the form of the hymns I have to remark that I think they should be introduced like the psalms, with the rubric mark before them, with a similar direction in regard to the discretion of the minister, leaving out the word "Supplement," because they will be nearly, if not quite, as large as the collection of psalms.   I would change the Latin *Gloria Patri* to English and call it Hymn 1.

In the collection sent up last week (I do not think the other admits the same criticism) there are some lines which I wish for your consent to alter, under the condition of Mr. Hopkinson's joint approbation.

> Well may the sun as hell be black.

I wish for a substitute for this.

> See streaming from th' accursed tree,

may be thus altered,

> Behold, fast streaming from the tree, etc., etc.

Mr. Hopkinson thinks, with me, that it is altogether improper to transfer psalms to the head of hymns, merely to change their names; and we think that they may very well stand in their proper places to be applied discretionately, except where some considerable changes in the composition to accommodate it to the occasion may apologize for the transposition; or else a collection be made from different psalms.

The psalms applied to the Ascension must be taken in so strained a sense as not to consist with the liberty allowable in composing a hymn. The two hymns which conclude your second collection, and which refer to Christ's command to preach the Gospel, would suit admirably well for this festival.

I enclose you a little essay of Mr. Hopkinson for the Fourth of July and the first Thursday in November.   He desires me to mention that he is conscious of having left out in the latter some fine portions of the second psalm from which it is taken; but it was to make it a reasonable portion for singing at one time.   He thinks one for each occasion sufficient, and that for the other time of singing, a portion might be taken at discretion from the psalms.   But if you choose two for each occasion, you have got one for November against which there can be no objection unless that the sentiments are the same with those of Psalm 65.   As to the very fine parts of Psalm 68, I foresee many objections to the making it a stated part of our service for the day.   Besides the delicacy of our situation, as well as on account of the prejudice of our brethren at our present application to England, it may well be questioned whether the use of such expressions be not inconsistent with the sentiments which should take place with peace, however proper "flagranti Bello."   Even the line,

> Their proud oppressors' righteous doom,

in (perhaps) the best verse of the psalm is rather too strong. I would prefer something from Psalms 89 and 18, of which I shall send you a sketch on a piece of paper.

I forgot to mention when writing of the psalms, the order in which I had arranged them. You know the four general heads we fixed on were, Psalms of Praise, etc.; Psalms of Prayer, etc.; Psalms of Thanksgiving, etc.; and Psalms of Instruction, etc. I found all would range under these heads except a few, which I have thought best to put at the end under· these two heads: Prophetical Psalms, applied in the New Testament to the character of the Messiah—and psalms composed during the want of an opportunity of the public worship of God. If you propose any alteration of this order, you will be pleased to set down minutely, the psalms that suit any new heads you may propose. Notwithstanding the impatience of the public (and I may add my own desire of having this business out of hand) I very willingly stop the press this week, to comply with your desire of seeing the first sheet of the psalms, before it be worked off. Mr. Hall says it will be to no purpose to go on composing, as the preparing a sheet will not take him half the time of working it off. The week, however, will not be wholly lost; as to prevent it, I have given him the tables for finding the holy days; which take up just a form. The Table for Easter I have adjusted to two Cycles of the moon, adding the Epacts, Golden Numbers and Dominical Letters; the present year begins a Cycle and the second ends at 1823. This space makes a convenient page with our letter. I have omitted in this table all the holy days besides Easter; because that being known, the next table shows the others. In all other respects I shall print the said tables, agreeably to Dr. Franklin's book,* which has them in the neatest way of any I have seen. This form will be our week's work.

---

* The title of the book is as follows:

"Abridgment of the Book of Common Prayer, and Administration of the Sacraments, and other Rites and Ceremonies of the Church, according to the use of the Church of England, together with the Psalter or Psalms of David. Pointed as they are to be sung or said in Churches. London, Printed in the Year MDCCLXXIII."

Dr. Franklin, in replying to Mr. Granville Sharp, who had written to him making some inquiry as to the character of this book, thus writes:

PASSY, July 5, 1785.

"DEAR SIR: .... The liturgy you mention was an abridgment of the prayers, made by a noble lord of my acquaintance, who requested me to assist him by taking the rest of the book, viz., the Catechism and the reading and singing psalms. Those I abridged, by retaining of the Catechism only the two questions, *What is your duty to God? What is your duty to your neighbor?* with their answers. The psalms were much contracted, by leaving out the repetitions (of which I found more than I could have imagined), and the imprecations, which appeared not to suit well the Christian doctrine of forgiveness of injuries, and doing good to enemies. The book was printed for Wilkie, in Paul's Churchyard, but never much noticed. Some were given away, very few sold, and I suppose the bulk became waste paper. In the prayers so much

I have the table of proper lessons ready; and have taken more pains with this than with any part of the book.

As to the Calendar with the table of common lessons, I believe all we can do with it is so to divide the long lessons as to afford the expunging of the Apocrypha. I have minuted the lessons which may be so divided; omitting in my way a very few lessons, the public reading of which appears indecent: and more than a few we cannot dispense with, without spoiling the design of having the Bible read through in the course of the year.

I rejoice with you on our having so nearly finished the business with so·much harmony, and am

Yours, affectionately,

WM. WHITE.

Pray do not cross the Bay without writing to me particularly. I have written you a very disorderly and I suppose incorrect letter; but I write in haste and yet wish to be full.

Respecting the tunes.

I have contrived to substitute *Brunswick* for *St. Ann's.*

The hymn tune and those you sent up would take up very considerable room and therefore I mention what follows.

Mr. Hopkinson had so fitted his tunes as to occupy an half sheet on both sides; besides which, he is desirous of inserting a page of chants; and if I comply with this, it will be to gratify him, as he has taken so much trouble in the matter. Now the half sheet only will be a very expensive matter. The ruling press alone (if Mr. Leacok's proposals are reasonable, and he says he has made them lower than he would for any but a charitable purpose—however I shall consult judges) will be a demand on us for £62 10s. When the book comes out it will be some time before remittances of cash are made from the other States, and in the mean time I shall have to settle with the printer, bank, etc. Matters being thus circumstanced, I wish to add no more to the music. You know tunes may be sung besides those printed. For my part, I am convinced, that no one circumstance impedes singing in our churches so much as great diversity of tunes.

N. B.—Mr. Hopkinson thinks the tunes sent up very bad and destitute of melody.

---

was retrenched, that approbation could hardly be expected; but I think with you, a moderate abridgment might not only be useful, but generally acceptable.

"I am, dear Sir, etc., etc.,

"B. FRANKLIN."

Rev. Dr. Smith to Rev. Dr. White.

CHESTER, February 6, 1786.

I hope, as you have ordered matters, there will be no great delay at the press. I received by your sending me these proofs, the psalmody. It was only that I might have a specimen with me across the Bay as far as the book is printed. If you have attended fully to what I wrote in my former letter, I think I left you at liberty to follow the arrangement you have made of the psalms, provided enough could be had from every one psalm, for a short portion to sing, which from memory I did not apprehend would be the case, as from some of the reading psalms but one or two verses were retained ; and these I thought must either be rejected in the singing psalms or joined with some other psalms. After all I see no difference in this mode, for all that comes under the first metre, on praise and adoration, stands exactly in the same order it would have done in the other mode, and would have made but thirty-five verses as one chapter or psalm. But I am very well satisfied as it is: only as in the rubric prefixed, all of them are said to be "selected from the Psalms of David"—the name of David need stand at the head of each particular new psalm or selection. Might it not be Psalm 1 [from 8th,] and yet it seems as well as you have it—so I have no more to say on this head.

I think the substitutes for *O come let us sing, etc.*, on Christmas, Ash Wednesday, etc., Good Friday, etc., as well as the old one for Easter, in all future editions, had better be inserted with their proper titles in the place where they are to be read, that is just after the daily *Venite* or *O come, etc.*, to save the trouble of turning the book and to be consistent with the rest of our arrangements. There is a precedent for this in the Communion Service, where all the *Prefaces* for these particular days are collected into the place where they are to be said or sung. If you approve this, it is easy to alter the rubric prefixed to these new *Venites* accordingly. That for Ascension Day might have concluded with the eighth verse. The following verses, especially from Psalm 2, might have better been for Whit-Sunday with some other verses which are now set apart for it. But I do not now wish to alter the press, except in the rubric aforesaid, if you approve the transposition of all the substitutes into one place with the daily *Venite* in future editions.

The line "See streaming from th' *accursed* tree"—is by taking it from the original author, Watts. 'Tis altered thus in the Magdalen Collection from which you recommended in your note :

See, streaming from the *fatal* tree—

And the other line—

Thou sun as *deepest night* be black.

I can see no more impropriety in transferring the singing psalms into

hymns under the heads to which they apply, than in the method we
have taken to transfer them under the three proper heads of praise, etc.,
as now to be published.   The few passages that relate to the Crucifixion, to the Ascension, etc., can stand no where so well as among the
hymns under those heads.   They would . . . . . psalms, or under any
of the few heads which the . . . . . taken by Tate and Brady in versi-
fying the psalms and the composition of some other parts of Scripture.
I pay great regard to the judgment of Mr. Hopkinson and my other
respected friends, the clergy of your city; but we have clergy of some
judgment here whom I consult also, and in this arrangement and collection of hymns, something of which kind has been long wished.   I
have some dependence on my own judgment also, and should be happy
if you and the other gentlemen could agree to have the specimen of
hymns offered to the public with as few deviations as possible from the
plan which upon great deliberation I have submitted to you, and Dr.
Wharton, if he can be consulted.

I cannot conceive for what reason you say the psalms applied as
hymns for the Ascension must be taken in strained sense to apply to that
occasion.   Are they not the 24th and 47th, the very same which you
have applied instead of the *Venite* for that day?   The two hymns in
the conclusion do not apply better to the Ascension than to Whitsunday, or some other days.   Christ's commission was delivered to his
Apostles while on earth, and the gifts which he sent from on high to
enable them to go forth in his name were not on the Day of Ascension.
They seem to stand very well where they are either to be used on the
occasion as suggested, or any other to which they will apply.   I think
less than *two* hymns for any one festival or occasion would not do.
You have forgot to enclose Mr. Hopkinson's psalm or hymn for July
4th.   What you propose may, if you will, be added to July 4th, but
the few verses I have taken of Psalm 68, I think might stand.   The
words *proud oppressor* you may alter, and the five lines which I hinted
at in my note and which are in the following part of the psalm, you
know I never intended to be made part of our stated service for the
present at least.

Please to finish the calendar as you propose.   You have taken so much
pains with it that unless I could find time to take equal pains in the
examination it would be wrong to interfere.   I think your plan good,
only do not make any of the lessons unreasonably long, and contrive
the introductions and breaks suitably.

Enclosed you have my essay of a preface; the post is just setting off.
The preface or address which was a matter particularly entrusted to the
committee I have ever considered as a matter of great importance, as
the first impressions on the introduction of the book may be of serious
concern.   Of this the Church was sensible in Charles 2d's time, on the

12

last review, when they wrote their several prefaces, giving a full account of the reasons of all the alterations, the abolition of Ceremonies, etc. I have therefore interwoven much of that preface, and rather than to set forth what we have done ourselves, which indeed is but little, have given an account of what the wisest and best members of the Church of England have long wished to have done, in order to show that we are not pretending to be leaders in reformation, but follow them and remain connected with them. This will state our work quite in a light, wherein few consider it, and give a historical information with which the people in general of our communion will be pleased, and be made able to give an answer to gainsayers.

I have also interwoven the chief part of your preface; but found it unnecessary to give the reason of every particular alteration, but rather following the example of the old preface, to pay the necessary mark of complaisance to the reader by observing that a comparison of the old book with the new would sufficiently [show] both the alterations and the reason of them. The preface should be set in a small and handsome letter. It will not altogether be so long as the old preface to our common prayer, the treatise and ceremonies and other notifications which were found necessary to preface to that book ; and our reasons for being particular are at least as strong as the Church of England in 1662. Many will strive to make the people believe we are wholly departing from the Church of England—nay treating her as a corrupt and erroneous church, by setting up a reformation of our own. But I hope this preface will obviate and confute these and all such like misrepresentations, especially, when it has undergone your judicious and sober revisal. You must not, *i. e.*, I hope you will not, regard a few pages or sentences more or less in the length of this important part, nor the little additional expense of the psalms. The book will sell as readily at 7*s.* 6*d.* as at 5*s.*

.   .   .   .

You apprehended some haste and incoherence in your last to me. You have all that in this letter, the last part of which has been written in the office while the mail was closing, having been very late this morning before I got the preface concluded. I hope now we have nearly done, and so without more *prefaces* or *conclusions*,

I remain, etc.,

Yours affectionately,

Wm. Smith.

Rev. Dr. White to Rev. Dr. Smith.

Philadelphia, February 10, 1786.

Dear Sir: I received yours of the 6th with the preface. As you seem not fully satisfied as to the propriety of leaving out the words "of David" I have left them stand. Your criticism respecting part of the

2d Psalm was so evidently just, that I have given Mr. Hall the trouble of transposing the verses from the end of Ascension Day to the beginning of Whitsunday. The transposing of the substitutes for the *Venite* to the Morning Prayer seems to me not quite so proper, as the placing them as we have done in the case of the 4th of July, etc., and the collects for Ash Wednesday, to services appropriate to the respective days; besides which, it would make a break in the Morning Prayer, which at present stands just as it is to be read. The prefaces in the communion being continuations and part of the sentence of what precedes them, could not have been otherwise placed without confusing the officiating minister. You do not lay stress on this, and it stands as before.

I give up my sentiment respecting the hymnifying the psalms; and shall only observe, that in mentioning the opinion of our brethren of this city, my intention was not to undervalue yours, or that of our brethren whom you have an opportunity of consulting; but only to be a counterpoise to that deference I entertain for your judgment which might otherwise have made me sacrifice my sense of the matter rather more easily than my duty in the present business would warrant.

I enclose you Mr. Hopkinson's hymns of which I request your opinion. I intend executing this matter agreeably to your desires. You seem to have left a little liberty with regard to verbal alterations: If I am wrong you will correct me. I wish you could get rid of "the Spoil of Armies once their dread," as applied to Ascension Day.

I shall be attentive to the Calendar. It is not within our appointment; and yet I believe we shall be thanked for so dividing the lessons as to serve the triple purpose of shortening the service, expunging the Apocryphal chapters, and getting rid of some the public reading of which may seem immodest. I fear we must let the New Testament lessons stand as at present: and yet the Gospels and Acts might be very well worded so as to be read twice instead of thrice in the year. As to the table of proper lessons, I have taken great pains with it and hope it will meet your approbation.

I like your preface both in plan and in execution. The particularities in mine are rendered unnecessary by the articles you have inserted as proposed at the Revolution. A few observations that occurred to me in the reading I have noted in a separate paper and will enclose.

You seem to have applied what I said on the article of expense to the printer's business instead of the psalmody. I approved highly of your proposal in this respect; but should begrudge the money, if much were to be inserted. You seem to have been as little versed as myself in the costs of this business.

You speak of $1 for the book. I thought of the same; but find some are of opinion, that it will be considered as *forcing* money for our funds. It is an objection that should have no weight, but for our reading psalms, which will make the purchasing of new books indispensably necessary to the joining in our service: and we might have some regard to those of middling condition who would wish a Prayer Book to be in the hands of every member of their families.

On the other hand, it is natural for us to wish to see our labors in this business productive of some fruit to the widows and the orphans.

I only throw out the above for your consideration, and am

Your affectionate humble servant,

W. White.

P. S.—I request you to consider whether it will not be best to bring in Addison's Translations "*The Lord my pasture shall prepare*," and "*The spacious firmament, etc.*," among the hymns. They are not strict translations. The latter at least can come in no other way as it is in the same metre with Tate and Brady's Translations of the 19th Psalm. It will not be too late to decipher this by return of post.

P. S.—The December packet informs of Willet's arrival: by whom went the original letter to the bishops.

Some Quæries on the Preface to the Common Prayer. (Dr. White.*)

Page 2d. Quære the propriety of saying anything about the Church of Rome.

Page 10. *Protestant Episcopal Churches.* Would it not be better in the singular number—at least it should be so when we speak of the acts of the late Convention, in order to harmonise with the phraseology of the Constitution.

Page 12. The apology for not reviewing the collects, etc., appears to me exceptionable. 1st, because the pleading the want of time seems an improper excuse in business of this magnitude and holds out the expediency of another review; 2dly, because we do not know that the Convention would not have given the necessary powers to the committee as is insinuated, and 3dly, because there are other alterations alluded to which we have not adopted. I wish the expression to be more general; thus—"it will appear that almost every amendment, etc." Ibid. It is said, that the service is so arranged as that we need not turn backwards and forwards. This being not exactly true, I wish the explanation modified.

---

* The *Quæries* of Dr. White are, of course, upon the preface by Dr. Smith, as originally *written.* Dr. Smith adopted some of the suggestions and not others. The force of Dr. White's suggestions, of course, do not so clearly appear in the case of those adopted; since, in the preface as given *supra*, (pp. 158–165), the original language of Dr. Smith disappears in the new words adopted.—H. W. S.

For Dr. Smith's views upon Dr. White's *Quæries*, see *infra*, pp. 188–190.

Page 13. "For the greater ease of the clerks, etc." This rubric says they are to be sung at the discretion of the minister. It may be corrected by putting the words "of choosing" instead of "of the clerks."

Page 14, in the note. I have here two remarks to make. 1. It seems hardly worth while to quote Bishop Burnet for what is to be found in so many writers. 2dly. The explanation will militate against the whimsical ideas of some persons grounded as they conceive on holy writ. We should avoid touching of principle as much as possible; and the footing on which (I think) we should rest the omission of the clause with the persons alluded to, is that even supposing their opinion true, yet, being grounded on a few controverted passages, it ought not to be made part of so very concise and general a confession of our faith.

Page 15. "*Son* of the Church"—say "*Member*," lest we may seem to deny the right of female judgment.

Quære. Ought not some reason to be given for omitting the creeds? The reason might be that we did not judge the Athanasian to tend to edification, and that the Nicene was a repetition.

And ought not a reason to be briefly given for "the Visitation of Prisoners?" if it were only to make an honest acknowledgment of our debt to the Church of Ireland.

Rev. Dr. White to Rev. Dr. Smith.

PHILADELPHIA, February 6, 1786.

DEAR SIR: I had written you a long letter, to send by the Western Shore post: but missed the opportunity from not knowing that the office had changed the days. Another post goes to-morrow morning, but as you may have left Annapolis, I have thought it best to reserve it for the Eastern Shore on Wednesday. If, however, I should have a line from you at Ann's informing of your stay there this week, I will repeat the substance of what I have written, although there is nothing requiring an immediate answer.

So I shall say no more at present, except to acknowledge the receipt of the preface, and to express my approbation of it, and that

I am, yours affectionately,

W. WHITE.

REV. DR. SMITH.

Rev. Dr. Smith to Rev. Dr. White.

BALTIMORE, February 25, 1786.

DEAR SIR: As Mr. Green, by his newspaper, knew the different places where I was to be every day during my late tour for holding the election of Visitors and Governors of St. John's College, he forwarded your short letter of February 12th to Upper Marlboro' where it met me the 22d instant on my way to this town; and gave me the great satisfaction of hearing that you had received the preface, and that it hath met with your approbation. By our appointment, among other things, we were directed to "accompany the Prayer Book with a proper *Preface* or *Address*, setting forth the reason and expediency of the alterations, etc." This, therefore, was a very important part of the great trust committed to us, and I was exceedingly anxious that it should be discharged in the fullest and yet least ostentatious manner possible, holding forth this leading idea through the whole, that we were not attempting any *novel* reformations or the least departure from what has been the general sense of the greatest and best men in our Church for a century past. If our address has the effect intended, it will procure a ready acceptance of the book, and that not upon the mere authority of the Convention, but upon principles carrying conviction to every rational mind, and enabling them as I hinted in my last to give a reason, etc., to all who may call in question any part of the alterations or improvements, which are offered. In this view, the preface is a necessary and essential part of our work, and I hope will not be thought too long as I cannot see in what part it could well be abridged without injury. I speak this from my own wish to have had it shorter: for you do not seem to make any objection to its length, or to anything else in it, which as I said before gives me great satisfaction. I think I mentioned in my last letter that if printed in a smaller letter it will not take more room than the different prefaces before the old Prayer Book, which are three or four (exclusive of the Act of Uniformity), viz.: 1st. The General Preface; 2d. Concerning the Service of the Church; 3d. Of Ceremonies, etc.; 4th. How the Psalter and Scripture are to be read. I beg your attention to the punctuation, both of the hymns and preface, as I never read them over with a view to punctuation, and you have only such stops or points as fell from my pen in a hasty transcription.

Please to direct the bookbinder to prepare half a dozen copies of the best and first binding in his power for my use, as I have engaged them to some persons of distinction, friends and patrons of our great undertaking.

Our Convention meets the 4th of April. I hope we shall not be disappointed in our five hundred books; some of which ought to be distributed in the different parishes before that time. You will give all dispatch possible. Dr. West gives you his best compliments. He is just elected by Baltimore Town, a Visitor and Governor of St. John's College. We meet for the first time, as a body corporate at Annapolis on Tuesday next; and on Wednesday, March 1st, I hope to cross the Bay to Chester and to receive your several letters which may wait for me there. . . . . . Have you yet heard anything from England?

Yours, etc.,

WM. SMITH.

Rev. Dr. Smith to Rev. Dr. White.

March 17th, 1786.

DEAR SIR : Yours of the 15th does not require a long answer. I have hastily, since my last, run over the metre psalms; but except some corrections in the punctuation, which I think might be made to advantage in sundry passages, I see little that needs alteration; and even these are too insignificant, to require a table of *Errata.* A candid reader will easily see they are but little oversights, and I have seen no impression of the psalms or indeed of the Prayer Book in general, more free from typographical errors, for which we are indebted to your indefatigable attention to the sheets, joined I am persuaded to some considerable care and attention in Messrs. Hall and Sellers.

In the hymns enclosed to me in your last are a few lines I could have wished to amend, but hope they are now printed off, and so they must stand as they are at present. You objected in your letter of February 1st upon receiving the copies of the hymns, to a line in the 4th hymn (viz., for Good Friday), "*Well may the sun as hell be black,*" also in your letter of February 16th you objected to the expression, "*Spoil of armies once their dread,*" in the 2d Hymn for the Ascension, being Hymn X. I thought both your objections well grounded, and readily proposed substitutes; the last of which on Ascension Day (as I wrote you) I considered as a great improvement; but as I had not kept copies of the original hymns which I transmitted to you, I made the alterations or substitutions, from what my memory retained of them and in both cases changed the person, viz., putting the second person for the third; instead of

" Thou sun as darkest night be black,"

It should be "*The sun, etc.,*" and perhaps "*deepest night*" for "*darkest night.*"

Again in Hymn X, the second for the Ascension, in stanzas 5 and 6, the second person should be everywhere changed into the third person, not only on account of the rhyme in the 5th stanza, as "Thou" does not rhyme to "captivity," but also on account of the sense and beauty of connection, which, as I said before, I could not so well perceive in offering the amendment from memory. The hymn is in double rhymes, and the two stanzas, viz., 5th and 6th, should run thus:

5 Ascending high, in triumph, HE
   Hath gifts receiv'd for sinful men ;
   And captive led captivity,
     That God may dwell on earth again.

6 Ev'n Rebels shall partake HIS grace
   And humble proselytes repair,
  To worship at HIS dwelling-place,
    And all the world pay homage there.

And in Hymn IX (the first for the Ascension) which I consider as one of the most beautiful and animated in the whole collection—nay, even sublime—the first and second verses taken from Psalm xxiv, and connected with verses that follow, which follow in *double rhymes*, should for uniformity, had it been attended to in due season, have been changed into double rhymes also, which might easily have been done as follows, viz., for the words "*eternal gates*," in the first line, putting "*eternal domes*," and for the words "*his foes*" in the third line of verse second putting "*his foe*," which would have been much stronger in the singular number than the plural, in making it applicable to the *one great foe*, whom Christ came to subdue. As the hymns are of different metres, they might have been marked as such; but being all I think of the first and second metre, the clerks cannot well mistake them. I would observe too that in singing or metre psalms, instead of putting the numbers of the psalms, as the running title at the top of each page, the top of the page, or running title, had perhaps better have been the subjects or heads under which they are classed, as "*Psalms of Praise and Ador ation*," "*Psalms of Prayer*," etc. Thus at every opening of the book, the clerks or ministers would know the subject, without turning back to the title or heads at the beginning of each class or set of psalms; and these titles would have stood in as little room at the top of each page as "Psalms II. III.—Psalms V. VI.," which are of little use on the *top*, as a glance of the eye shows the number, in the *body* of the pages. But all these little amendments (the last of which is an afterthought) are too late for the present, even if they should be deemed amendments.

In that part of the preface which speaks of the failure of the great work of the review at the Revolution in 1689, I would have wished to have said a little more concerning the reasons of that unhappy failure; and that in the words of Dr. Warner, from the preface to his commentary on the Common Prayer, a very excellent and judicious work to which I had not attended when I drew up the preface to our book. It might yet be added in a note upon the word "*miscarried*" in the following paragraph of the preface, which you can easily find. In my rough copy it runs thus, which is all that is said, viz.:

But this great and good work miscarried at that time; and the civil authority of Great Britain hath not since thought proper to revive it by any new commission.

The note on the foregoing is as follows, or it might have been interwoven with the text, or stood altogether instead of the paragraph just quoted, viz.:

After giving an account of the alterations intended at the Revolution, much as I have stated them from the same authors, as he had to follow, he concludes thus:

But while this important affair was carrying on, the party which was now at work for the *abdicated King*, took hold on this occasion to inflame men's minds. It was pretended that the Church was to be demolished, and Presbytery set up. The trumpet of sedition was sounded as usual from the pulpits. The Universities took fire, and began to declare against the commission and against all who promoted it, as men who intended to undermine the Church. So that it was very visible that the temper of men was not cool or calm enough to encourage the further prosecution of this great and good design, which would have been so much to the improvement of our public worship, to the interest of the Protestant religion, and to the honor of the Church of England: and thus it was defeated by the turbulency and restless spirit of ignorant and factious and evil-minded men. Why it has not been resumed in the days of more knowledge, more candor and Christian charity, is a question which many good men have often asked with seriousness and zeal, but which no great men, upon which it lies to do it, I believe, have ever answered.

I say that if I had adverted to this paragraph in time, I should probably have inserted it at large instead of the few general lines which I have quoted in the two last lines of the foregoing page, and the first line of this; or have thrown it in a note at the bottom as now proposed. Had it stood in the body of the preface, it would come in very well; for after Dr. Warner's words, "which no great men, upon whom it lies to do it, I believe, have ever answered," the next paragraph of our preface beginning, *"But when in course of his divine Providence, etc.,"* would just as well have followed, as it does the few words I have said on the subject. But I submit wholly to you, whether it may be proper now to insert it by way of note, or in the body, or to leave the preface just as it is without entering more particularly into the reasons of the miscarriage at the Revolution in England. I would not wish to draw any opposition to what has been done in our Church; and yet I fear the quotation above from Dr. Warner will yet be necessary (though it may be left out for the present,) to show, if any opposition arises among us, it will be from the same principles as that in England, a dislike to our American Revolution. I would not ascribe the opposition or rather disapprobation which I find in some of my friends to this principle, because I believe they are well satisfied with what Providence has permitted to take place respecting American independency; but they object strongly to setting the State so much above the Church, for which you bear much of the blame on account of your old pamphlet,* and

---

* " The Case of the Episcopal Churches in the United States considered, etc.," a tract misunderstood at the time and very unjustifiably used by certain low Churchmen since. Dr. White took pains in a note to his charge of 1807, to put himself right by showing that at the time he wrote the tract the Episcopal Church in Pennsylvania—so far as the events of the Revolutionary War could be anticipated—was in danger of annihilation, if we had to wait for consecration by the English Bishops. The moment that there came a prospect of peace he called in and destroyed all copies of the tract that he could easily procure. He also left a manuscript produced, in fac simile quite lately, by his great-grandson, Mr. T. H. Montgomery—a gentleman, I may add, to whom our Church is much indebted for illustrations of its history—in which he again vindicates himself against the ideas which some low churchman, by reprinting his tract, sought

strenuous efforts at our last general Convention to bring that clause forward respecting the control of the laity over the appointment of bishops, and which may be made a handle of to prejudice many against other parts of our proceedings.

My learned but zealous high church little friend and relation (as he says), Mr. Smith, of Somerset, writes me as follows—which perhaps he did not yet wish me to communicate to you, although I believe he cares not who sees what he writes, yet you will keep it to yourself till I can see him, which will be in two weeks—but I lose the thread of my discourse—I say Mr. Smith, who says he has just received a long letter from Bishop Seabury on the same subject, with an account of their Connecticut Constitution, writes thus:

I have been looking all this while for a sight of the Prayer Book *altered*, and by a letter from Dr. White I understand it is hurrying on. A passage in that letter I did not and do not now perceive the propriety of—it is this—" I suppose you have heard of our application to the English Bishops, the Convention was far from wishing to show any disrespect to the Scots Episcopacy, etc."

And so he gives me a long extract of your letter, and then writes as follows :

These modes of proceeding may be consentaneous with the wisdom of this world, but Ill accords with that wisdom, who hath said—*My kingdom is not of this world— Ye are not of the world, etc.* To the account the Dr. (White) gives of Bishop Seabury's failure (as he is pleased to call it) I shall only say thus much. That the case of the Church in all the States, or in any individual one at present, is perfectly as a single diocese without a centre of unity, the presbyters of which have an unquestionable right to nominate a bishop, without the interference of any diocese having a bishop or not having one. Bishop Seabury's failure then, on ecclesiastical principles, is not owing to his being sent by presbyters acting in their private capacity—*Certificates* from the ruling powers is without a precedent in any Christian Church in the universe. This is fixing the Church under the power of the State for ever and ever with a witness. It is making Jesus Christ make obeisance to Cæsar!!! Reigning powers granting certificates! Tell it not in Gath! publish it not to the world lest we publish our own infamy. The Church in America to derive her power, nay her existence from temporal authority—perish the idea! Her charter from the hands of the eternal runs thus: "*As my Father hath sent me, etc.*" "*All power is given to me in Heaven.*" Let us render unto Cæsar, etc. The Church and the State are by God constituted separate, and let no man join what he hath separated. The sword of the Cherubim and Cæsar's are of different metals, the one pointing to the victim which should prevent the effusion of human blood by his own, the other occasioning multitudes of garments rolled in blood and the infinite number of the slain. " May the Church rest always on its own true foundation Jesus Christ, and the throne of Empire on its proper basis—Mercy. Adieu. May God direct you and those who sit in Moses' seat, etc."

---

to put upon him. His plan acknowledged the necessity of Episcopal ordination in every case where it could be obtained; but until it could be, proposed to follow its form, awaiting the consummation of the substance. Dr. Smith, it is certain, held to the same ideas that Dr. White did on the subject of ordination. See my former volume, page 402. And it is equally certain that those views can be justified by some of the most authoritative writers of the Church of England. See Appendix, No. IV.—H. W. S.

You will meditate on all this and do with the proposed addition in the preface as you think best, only do not delay it for sending me proofs. . . . . In the paragraph of the preface beginning "When in the course of divine Providence, it pleased Almighty God that these *American States*, etc.," a few lines afterwards you have the words "these States" a second time, dele the repetition of "these States." You will supply all the omissions of words, etc., in this letter, for as usual I put off sitting down to write you till within an hour of the post going of. . . . . .

Yours, etc.,

WM. SMITH.

Rev. Dr. Smith to Rev. Dr. White.

CHESTER, March, 1786.

. . . .

With respect to our friend Mr. Hopkinson's hymns, that for first Thursday in November is only another arrangement of some of the verses of the same psalms which stand in my collection for the same day, and whether for the better or worse, you only can tell, as I have no copy of those I sent you before, and to which you have given your general approbation. If this hymn of Mr. Hopkinson's collection is all he intends for first Thursday of November, it is very defective, or at least, as there will be psalmody twice if not oftener on that day, we should have more than one hymn; and I leave the matter wholly with you, if the business is not already finished, being persuaded that you will not break in upon the arrangement I had (with great application) made without some good purpose in view.

As to the Fourth of July. The hymn offered by Mr. Hopkinson is in many parts far too flat for the great occasion, and no way equal to what I have taken from Psalms 81 and 68. Thus—War *darkening* all the land—God brings nations to *decay*—Willing mercy *flew*—How *good* the Lord has been—and also in the hymn for November—"Grass for our cattle to *devour*"—although taken from Tate and Brady, does not read clever: it represents the poor animals as ravenous and dying of hunger, so as to *devour* all before them, instead of *feeding happily* and *contentedly* upon plenty.

The lines from Psalm 81 (for July 4th), which are in the collection I sent you, ending thus—

> Your *Ancestors* with *wrongs oppress'd*,
> To me for aid did call,
> With pity I their Sufferings saw—
> And set them FREE FROM ALL—

have far more in them than all that is proposed in their room (if it is to be in their room) or if to be added, would be superfluity. There can be no objection to the words " *with wrongs oppress'd* "—for it is stronger still in Mr. Hopkinson's, viz.: *"to rescue from oppressive rage"*—and in the former, the beautiful reference to "Ancestors" will ages hence continue to be used with a noble propriety. However, if these hymns can come in without tearing the whole texture of the others, and if it be Mr. Hopkinson's wish to have them, I am satisfied, for unless I had the whole before me, as proposed to be altered, I cannot take upon me to judge properly, and must leave that to you. Only I wish you to save an exact copy, or the whole originals of the hymns as I sent them to you.

As we have kept the collects, epistles and gospels, for about twenty-two holy days, beginning with St. Andrew, and ending with All Saints', it will be necessary to mark in the calendar, as heretofore, the days of the month, on which these holy days fall, and to retain the table of lessons for those days, as the churches which think it proper will still be as ready to observe those days, or some of them, as occasion may require.

I know you have taken great pains with the table of lessons, and I am persuaded I shall have much reason to approve of what you have done; which will be best considered when the whole is taken together; and it would be wrong to judge by piece-meal, of anything which the necessity of the case has made the work of one alone, and on which his particular attention hath been bestowed, taking the whole in one large and consistent view.

The same is the case with respect to the preface, on which, as a most material part of our trust and commission, I had determined from the beginning to bestow every convenient and possible attention, and it gives me the highest satisfaction that you "like it both in the plan and execution." I have no exact copy of it, only notes and sketches of the principal parts, so that I can make no use of your reference to pages in your remarks; but still can answer them in substance, so as to enable you to correct it, if not too late for the press. In my last from Balti-more I wished you to attend to punctuation, etc., both in the hymns and preface, as I had not read either of them over with a view either to the niceties of language, grammar or stops. I proceed to your remarks.*

1. I think the little quotation from the Council of Trent, exceeding proper to show that all churches agree with the Church of England in the doctrine of her prefaces, respecting the necessity of alterations, according to times and exigencies. In Maryland we have many Roman Catholics, who are even already questioning some of our weak members, and charging us with novelties, and still further departures from the Catholic faith. The answer is ready in the quotation from a Council of their own Church, especially that of Trent.

---

* See these, *supra*, pp. 180–181.

2d. *Protestant Episcopal Churches* should be in the singular number; and yet if all our New England brethren should not join us,
they may say we take too much on us to call seven or eight States
the whole *Protestant Episcopal Church* of America.   I do not remember the connection of the paragraph; but if it be *churches*, in the
plural, some such idea must have been in my head; or it is a mistake
of the pen.   Make this and other like things consistent according to
your best judgment; for I know you will not *Aitkenise** anything,
being too judicious to put a *patch* that would not consort with the *garment* at large.

3d. Page 12. The apology for not revising the Collects may be
omitted in this preface.   Yet not for fear of hinting the probability of
further reviews, but because there were other things besides the Collects
which the Church of England at and before the Revolution had in contemplation to review, and which we have not yet touched upon; and
therefore every reader may be left to his own conclusion, as to the
necessity of future reviews, by a comparison of our book on the whole,
with the intended alterations at the Revolution, and I think the credit
of our work will rise on the comparison.

Ibid—You may say "The service is arranged so as to stand as nearly
as possible in the order wherein it is appointed to be read, without the
necessity of turning backwards and forwards, etc."

Page 13. Say "for the greater facility of choosing Psalms adapted to
particular subjects and occasions of divine worship;" or some such
amendment.

Page 14—in the note—Bishop Burnet, being a great name, and the
expositor of the articles, seems to me very proper to be mentioned, and
I should think, it being only a *note*, there is no need of leaving it out.
There is no alteration made in the whole book, which is like to create
so much difficulty as the omission of the *descent into hell;* and yet wherever I have had occasion to explain the matter as in the note alluded
to, it seems to have given content.   I would not give any reasons for
omitting the two other creeds.   The Athanasian seems freely to be parted
with on all hands, and as to the Nicene I would say nothing concerning
it in this edition of the Prayer Book; because I believe some whole
States will agree with the three New England States, in having it inserted
at their next Convention, and left optional either to be used, or to use the
Apostles' Creed, although not both in the same Morning or Evening Service; while others (I fear much from Virginia) will be for no creeds at all,
and also for striking out the Trinitarian introduction to the Litany.   Yet,
I hope, calmness and sound argument, through the blessing of God, may
reconcile all, and preserve the unity of the faith in the bond of peace.

---

* A reference, doubtless, to Robert Aitken, a Philadelphia printer of some note at
that time.

Page 15. "Son" of the Church may be made "member," and I had no more idea of excluding the "daughters" of the Church, than I have every Sunday, when I say "*Dearly beloved brethren.*" Something may be added, in a few words, in acknowledgment to the Church of Ireland, for the office adopted from her. You will know where to insert it.

I hope, now, my good Sir, we have wholly done; and it will ever give me pleasure to testify the great satisfaction I have had in the progress of this laborious work, and how much it hath been made easy to me (amidst the avocations I have had, and my distance from the press) by the candor and judgment which you have shown, the punctuality of your correspondence, and the great pains you have taken in digesting, transcribing, examining, correcting the press, etc., etc.

I wish to know whether Mr. Hall's calculation of the price of his work and paper was not on twenty sheets, and whether there will be any addition to the price on his account? Or on the bookbinder's? If none the only additional price will be the engraving and printing the tunes. You know it is part of our appointment to fix the price of the book, direct the distribution thereof, take care that it be sold only for money and the profits applied to the widows and fatherless. I cannot think a dollar will be too much. Had we suffered any printer here to do it on his own account, he would have asked a much greater price. You know what they charged for small imported Prayer Books, and the very smallest School Books. Yet for the reasons you suggest, I wish it to be as cheap as possible, so as to have some savings; for you may be assured that there will be money lost, or with great difficulty collected out of the hands of some to whom the books may be sent for distribution or sale.

I had almost forgotten your objection to—

"The spoil of armies once their dread,"

as applied to the *Ascension.* You know it is Tate and Brady's, and hath long stood among our psalms, but is easily altered thus, which I think will bring it nearer to the evangelical sense as well as sublimity of the original, which is Psalm 68, v. 18:

> In triumph, Thou, ascending high,
>   Hast *gifts* received for sinful men,
> And captive led captivity,
>   That God may dwell on earth again!

This I think will be very proper for the Ascension.

I have preserved and endorsed all your letters, and wish you to do the same with mine. They may refresh our memories at some future

day, or show our children after us what honest and conscientious labor
we bestowed on the work committed to us.

Yours,

WM. SMITH.

Rev. Dr. White to Rev. Dr. Smith.

PHILADELPHIA, March 8, 1786.

DEAR SIR: . . . . I send you the sheets finished; besides which there
is another form prepared for press containing the residue of the psalms
and the first Nativity Hymn: besides which other hymns are prepared
in a detached way, but cannot be put in form for want of quadrats remaining in the preceding forms; as these latter cannot be broken until
the receipt of some paper hourly expected from mill. We have not
yet suffered for want of it.   I lament our delays but cannot help them.
I will review the hymns to which your remarks or Mr. Hopkinson's
relate and endeavor to settle them to your satisfaction.   The only
liberty (so far as I recollect) that I have taken with the others is the
leaving out some verses in one of the hymns at sea respecting the blaspheming after a storm which appeared to me too much like the language
—*"I am not as this Publican."*   If you dislike this omission, I can still
retain the verses.   I have also put the Glory be to the Father, etc.,
immediately after the psalms before the notification that the hymns
begin: as it is meant to be a part of a psalm to convert it into a Christian hymn, but not itself commonly known under the term hymn.

The paper I have prepared for the press relative to the holy days has
the extra holidays just as you desire.   You have omitted answering me
on a very important question respecting the calendar lessons.   On the
one hand I find that by our taking it in hand, these three important
points may be gained: the shortening of the daily service, the getting
rid of the Apocrypha, and the omitting two or three lessons very offensive (in public reading) to modest ears.   On the other hand it is not
within the letter of our appointment, so that I should not like to accomplish what I think best on this subject without your concurrence.

I shall continue the preface to your satisfaction.   As to the punctuation of this and the hymns, I had presumed from a general glance over
the points that you had attended to them; but if any appear improper
in the proof-sheets I will correct them.

It gives me great pleasure that you are satisfied with the execution
of my part of the trust on this occasion; especially as I can with great
sincerity make a similar acknowledgment; and as I shall alway allow
you more credit on the score of *judgment* than you ought to allow me,
so also there is nothing you can say on that of candor and temper which
I shall not as freely and fully say of you.

You are right as to Mr. Hall's estimate of sheets, and as to the price
of binding nothing more has past.   Mr. Woodhouse has half the number prepared for the covers and is impatient to begin.

If you are clear as to the proposed price I have no objection.

It now becomes a matter of serious consideration, whether we shall avail ourselves of the copyright, for which (as I am told by a gentleman interested on these subjects) there are laws lately passed in other States, making ten States in all. I think the mode of doing it should be for Messrs. Hall and Sellers to enter it in their names, first executing to us an acknowledgment of trust, and so leaving the matter to the next Convention, which may order a conveyance of the right to the several corporations for widows, etc.

I will send you by the next post my opinion of the manner in which we should proceed in regard to the sale of the books; and shall only at present say on that head, that as the Maryland Convention is the first, all the copies that can be got ready for their use shall be devoted to them in preference to any demands on the spot.

I am, yours, etc.,

WM. WHITE.

REV. DR. SMITH.

P. S.—I shall carefully and with pleasure observe your desire respecting preserving your letters; but had I foreseen you would have bestowed the same attention on mine, I should not have sent you such hasty scrawls.

Rev. Dr. Smith to Rev. Dr. White.

DEAR SIR: I am happy to find that yours of the 8th instant leaves me nothing to write by this post, except to repeat my solicitations that the printers may be pressed to use all the dispatch possible with the remainder of the book; otherwise it will come too late for our Maryland Convention; and it is of considerable consequence that it should have a ready reception, with the sanction of the Church at large in this State upon its first appearance. Send me by this post as many of the remaining sheets and proofs, as you can get from the press.

I imagined that in my last I had given what you would consider as a sufficient answer to your "important questions" concerning the calendar, on which subject you had also written in some former letters. The arranging the calendar in the manner you mention, and which I had approved of when I saw you last in Philadelphia, is a work of great labor, requiring the reading over almost the whole Bible, and many collations and comparisons of different portions thereof. You had taken that labor upon you and I am assured have bestowed much attention and judgment upon it, while I have been either engaged in some other parts of the work, or called from home, as I have been for the greatest part of the past winter. Unless, therefore, I could have time to read all the proposed portions of Scripture, with the same attention which you have bestowed (for which time is not left, even if I had an exact copy of the calendar as proposed) it would be wrong for the reasons given in my last letter to interpose, lest by judging of that by parts, which you had under review in the whole, I should injure the texture, etc.   These sentiments I wished you to consider as an answer to your question concerning the calendar; being sensible also that you must have been possessed of the same way of judging and giving your approbation to some parts which fell to my share in carrying on our work.   By just hinting to you not to forget the place of the Apostles', etc., or extra holy days, I imagined that you would conclude . . . . . that I could depend fully on your execution of . . . . . part, viz., the . . . . . of lessons, as you have bestowed so much attention upon them.   Yet, still I apprehend that I have not with sufficient clearness, expressed what I wished about inserting in the calendar the days to which I referred in my last.   I did not mean that they should stand in a separate table or paper, but in the monthly calendar, as they now stand.   Thus in January, the Circumcision is 1st day, Epiphany 6th, Conversion of St. Paul the 25th.   These are all which should stand for that month.   The rest, as Lucian P., Hilary Bishop, Prisca V., and other legendaries, Fabian, Agnes, Vincent, and even King Charles Martyr, all expunged, and thirty of the rest, of the other months, in order that when the minister casts his eye on the monthly calendars, he may be reminded when any of those days happen on Sunday, or on Prayer Days, that he may take the Collects and Lessons, with the Epistles and Gospels accordingly; if *he thinks it proper* or *desired by his hearers*, especially the female part, on Wednesdays and Fridays.   I think we must not make our service too naked, nor will these days, viz., St. Paul, the Johns, Andrew, etc., be parted with all at once nor does it seem necessary.   A proper use of those days tends to edification, and gives some further knowledge of the History of the Bible.

On casting my eye on the singing psalms, I perceive some typographical errors.   Psalm 28, v. 2.

> When *thou* to seek thy glorious face
> *Thou* kindly, etc.

The first *"thou"* is *"us"* in the original, and would be better *"me."* As it now stands, the first *thou* makes nonsense.   Again, Psalm 38, v. 1st, line third wants a *foot*, viz., the word *"the"* before cherubs.   How many little *errors typographical* of this kind may be, I have not examined; but will spend a few hours in looking over the whole book, that if the errors be of any consideration, we may put a little table of corrections at the end.   Psalm 21 does not seem to stand under any metre at all.   I see some parts of the psalms appropriated for particular days as hymns, as 104—also some verses applicable only to the crucifixion, are in the general collection—which will make some repetitions; but as they are but a few verses I would not have anything omitted in

13

the hymn on this account. I will this week if possible. look further at the calendar, but do not delay anything on that account. I know I shall approve what you have done, as will the . . . . . not exactly within the letter of our authority.

N. B.—The first lesson for the first Sunday in Lent, on reading it, appeared to hurt me in some parts the Sunday before last. It is an instructive lesson on the whole, if we could leave out part of a chapter, or pass over verses, viz., where Lot offers his *virgin daughters* to the *men* to do with them as they pleased. If the calendar is in proof, pray send it, but still I beg no stop on my account.

I must conclude hastily and am as ever,

Yours,

WM. SMITH.

P. S.—My letters have been as much scrawled in haste as yours; but both of us may review and correct any hasty escapes of the pen, etc.

Rev. Dr. White to Rev. Dr. Smith.

PHILADELPHIA, March 15th, 1786.

To the best of my recollection the inclosed are the proper continuation of the sheets: if not, and there be a chasm, you will inform me and I will supply it by next post.

Besides these, I have corrected two proof-sheets for the press, so that I expect we shall have the hymns fully composed some time to-morrow.

Then going backwards from the Morning Prayer, we have a form composed containing the tables for finding the holy days. Two more forms will be taken up with the Tables of Feasts and Fasts, of proper lessons, and of the lessons according to the calendar. The preface will occupy another form, besides part of it being thrown forward to be on the same form or part of form with the Title Page. In short, by this day week, I hope to have the whole composed: which being done, they may finish at their leisure the press work of these few remaining forms, only striking off some for the bookbinder to begin.

There is nothing you mention as you wish (in yours of this day) concerning the calendar, but what is prepared agreeably to it. I should not have troubled you further on this subject, but that I understood what you had before written, as applying to the proper lessons only. But the chapter you mention, I have thought best to omit wholly.

I am sorry for the typographical errors and hope you will perform your promise of going over the whole book. Such slips will easier attract your eye than mine, which has already run over these sheets, both in the preparation and in the execution.

I am yours, etc.,

WM. WHITE.

DR. SMITH.

P. S.—I have not yet heard a word from England, but hope that the January packet will bring some information.

Rev. Dr. White to Rev. Dr. Smith.

PHILADELPHIA, April 1, 1786.

DEAR SIR: Mr. Woodhouse will send you by this opportunity six setts of the Proposed Book including (as I expect) all except the reviewed forms. The preface will not be in its proper form; but as I intend sending by the next post the sheets necessary to complete the book, you will please to leave directions at Annapolis concerning them, if you should leave it before their arrival.

I beg my affectionate compliments to such of our brethren at the Convention as I have the pleasure of knowing, and am

Yours, affectionately,

WM. WHITE.

Rev. Dr. Smith to Rev. Dr. White.

CHESTER, MARYLAND, April 3, 1786.

DEAR SIR: . . . . On the other sheet you have some corrections, which I wish in the preface and which I think will appear to you for the better, if you can make out to read them. Send me title page, calendar, preface, etc., by this post. The printers need only work a few of the titles and prefaces, till you hear from me next week. A few will keep the bookbinder at work.

I am yours, etc.,

WM. SMITH.

CORRECTIONS. . . . PREFACE.

Paragraph 1st. For the words "whatever cannot be clearly *determined*," say "*what cannot*, etc."

Paragraph 2d. For "laid down as a rule" say "laid *it* down, etc."

Paragraph 4th. After the words "too much stiffness in refusing," insert, "and" so as to read, "too much stiffness in refusing *and* too much easiness in admitting, etc."

In the paragraph beginning "3d. For a more perfect *rendering*," after the word "*liturgy*" and before the word "*made*" in the parenthesis insert "*and*," so as to read "are inserted into the liturgy (and made a part of the daily service)."

In the 6th quære. Beginning "Whether in particular a psalm or anthem should not be adapted and sung, etc.," insert the word "*to*" after adapted, and read "adapted to, and sung at the celebration, etc."

In the 8th quære. Relating to the Epistles and Gospels, after the word "*especially*" strike out the word "*as*" and insert "*unless*," and it will read "especially unless the first design of inserting this, viz., as introductory to the communion, etc.," putting a comma after the word communion.

In the 11th quære. The word *"Baptism"* should not be distinguished by italics from the other offices which are printed in Roman.

There are several other things of this kind, which neither the printer nor we perhaps have now time to notice.

In the paragraph beginning "But while these alterations, etc.," alter the whole so as to read thus:

> But while these alterations were in *review* before the late Convention, they could not but with gratitude to God, embrace the happy occasion which was offered to them (uninfluenced and unrestrained by any worldly authority whatsoever) to take a further review of the *public service*, and to propose to the Church at large such other alterations and amendments *therein* as might be deemed expedient, whether consisting, etc. (as it now stands).

In the next paragraph—in the last line—strike out the words *"at that time"* and read *"thought reasonable and expedient."* In the following paragraph, "speaking of the 'Glory to God on high'" after the *"etc."* insert *"which may be said,* unless" before the words "when it can be properly sung," the whole to read thus, "Glory to God on high, etc., which may be said, unless when it can be properly sung." In the paragraph which speaks of July 4th, for *"Blessing"* insert *"Blessings* of civil and religious liberty."

In the last paragraph, strike out so as to make it read "be received and examined, etc.," as it now stands, to the end.

Rev. Dr. White to Rev. Dr. Smith.

PHILADELPHIA, April 5, 1786.

DEAR SIR : . . . . . Several of the corrections which you propose in the preface, I had previously made! The rest shall also be made.

I hope you will not think of altering the title page, after some are binding. It will be attended with the following inconveniences: 1st. Mr. Smith must give two certificates different from each other, for the act requires the title to appear in the certificate.* 2d. Several will have gone (before the change) into quarters, where you will not wish such inconsistency to appear—to Boston for instance where the Convention of Massachusetts and Rhode Island meet on the 27th instant—and wish to have the whole before them. 3d. The persons who shall purchase the first copies will think themselves defrauded. And after all, there is nothing that can be so easily amended in future editions, the very nature of the present making a peculiarity necessary in the title.

I expect to have this evening the second page, with Mr. Smith's

---

* Dr. White here refers to the certificate of copyright by J. B. Smith, prefixed to the Proposed Book.

certificate and the table of contents, and to-morrow morning the re-
viewed forms.   The intervention of the newspaper has delayed them.
I am yours, etc.
WM. WHITE.

REV. DR. SMITH.

Rev. Dr. Smith to Rev. Dr. White.

CHESTER, April 9, 1786.

DEAR SIR: . . . . . We had a considerable majority of all our
clergy (not many of the laity) at our Convention, and have agreed to
receive and recommend to public use the new book, as far as the power
of our State Church may be supposed to extend in our present unorgan-
ized State.   A few alterations are proposed to be offered to the next
Convention.   The Nicene Creed to follow the Apostles', with an *"or
this."*   A little alteration, or rather discretionary power in the administration of baptism, where the minister may have great numbers to
baptize together, and an addition to the consecration prayer at the holy
sacrament, for a blessing on the elements, which being only a few
words, and those extremely proper, and agreeable to the practice of all
other Protestant Churches, as well as what was in the first liturgy of
Edward VI. hath perfectly reconciled Mr. Smith* to our service and
will prevent any further division between us and the numbers of clergy
coming among us from Bishop Seabury and the Scots' Church.

In the Scots' and Edward VI's liturgy the prayer was exceptionable
and leaning much to transubstantiation in these words : "Vouchsafe to
bless and sanctify these thy creatures of bread and wine, that they may
be unto us the *body* and *blood*, etc."   The Scots' still stronger, viz.,
"that they may *become* unto us the *body* and *blood*."   The alteration as
we propose it is thus, beginning at the words in the consecration prayer,
"Hear us, O merciful Father, we most humbly beseech Thee, and
vouchsafe so to *bless* and *sanctify* these thy creatures of bread and wine,
that we receiving them according to thy Son our Saviour Jesus Christ's
holy institution, in remembrance, etc.," as it now stands.   This reads
as well as before, pleases all sides, and is certainly an improvement, as
there was before no invocation of a blessing on the sacred elements.
When you send the book to Mr. Parker, of Boston, before their ensuing
Convention, send him as from me, with the compliments of the Maryland Convention, the foregoing proposed addition in the consecration
prayer, and also notify our agreement with our New England brethren
in the restitution of the Nicene Creed.

I beg by post at least one complete book.   I have none at present.
The title I have not seen, and do not wish to alter, but it should cor-

---

* The Rev. William Smith, of Stepney Parish, Somerset county, alluded to, *supra*,
page 186.   See a sketch of him, by an able hand, *infra*, page 274.

respond also with the title in the eleventh page of the journal of Convention. When shall we have books? Our clergy and laity complained much that they should have been obliged to judge of the book on a hasty reading, during the sitting of a Convention.

Yours,   WM. SMITH.

Rev. Dr. White to Rev. Dr. Smith.

PHILADELPHIA, April 12, 1786.

DEAR SIR: . . . . . I think the proposed alterations of your Convention will render our service more complete.

With this I shall send you the sheets that were wanting when you went down. Mr. W—— will furnish a parcel this week. As there is a vessel soon to sail for Charlestown, you will approve sending to the most distant States first. Be assured, you shall have a parcel, before a single book is sold here.

I am yours, etc.,

WM. WHITE.

DR. SMITH.

Rev. Dr. Smith to Rev. Dr. White.

CHESTER, April 17, 1786.

DEAR SIR: . . . . . In the preface at the bottom of page 4, there is an error, viz., "construction" for "misconstruction." It is the last word of the page, and is a capital mistake indeed! I think it could not have been in the copy. In the last page of the preface, second paragraph, "Visitation of *prisons*," should be "*prisoners*." I believe there is little else to be observed in the preface, although I cannot say I have read it critically, yet it seems to read sufficiently correct for the present. I shall before June next take the whole book, and make every correction which I think may be necessary in future editions, and lay them before the Convention.* I hope you and perhaps others of our brethren will do the same.

I wish you had taken my advice respecting David's 114th Psalm, which stood before as our 21st, and only have made a note at the end of the book that the psalm was misplaced, and ought in future editions to come in under its proper metre, as Psalm 16, and that the metres of 148 and 149 should be exchanged if such correction be necessary; for it is merely arbitrary which we call 5th and which the 6th metres, if the Gloria Patri's be arranged accordingly.

As you have taken our 24th Psalm or David's 149th from the sheet Gg and placed it Ff, the mere reprinting that one sheet Ff (which you

---

* Dr. Smith's own copy of the Proposed Book, with the manuscript corrections referred to in this letter, is now in the library of the Right Rev. William Bacon Stevens, D. D., of Philadelphia, to whom it was given by the present writer.—H. W. S.

have sent me), will not complete the book. You will have the first leaf of the sheet Gg to reprint, or else the whole sheet, if the book-binder does not choose the trouble to cut out a leaf in every sheet and paste it in the book which is immense trouble, and will occasion much delay. For you will observe, that after the sheet Ff (which is reprinted) the 4th, 5th, 6th, 7th, etc., verses of David's 148th Psalm must come in the sheet Gg, where his 149th now stands, and the beginning of his 96th or our 25th. This, as I said, will be great trouble and delay, which I am sorry for, as the people are become exceedingly impatient for copies of the book, and the more so as they have more experience of its use. My congregations were exceedingly pleased with the two Good Friday hymns, which, as they had not books, were first read and then sung, and also the two Easter hymns, No. VII and No. VIII, but what above all seemed to make the greatest impression was the two Communion hymns, viz., No. XVII, beginning *"My God, and is thy table spread,"* sung after sermon as an invitation to the Sacrament, and No. XVIII, beginning *"And are we now brought near to God, etc.,"* sung after the communion. It adds a solemnity which they confessed they had not experienced before. The hymns are indeed beautiful and every line of them applicable to the blessed occasion. Have you yet introduced them in this way? When you do you will find it of use to read them for the first time yourself, from the place where you are, the desk or communion table. Every communicant will, before another day, have them by heart as I believe was the case here, between Good Friday and Easter Sunday, as the book was sent for and sundry copies taken in writing, I mean of Hymns 17 and 18. I beg I may have at least one complete book this post. I gave all away at Annapolis, except the loose sheets which I had from time to time as proofs. You will take care to have receipts from the stage masters, skippers, etc., to whom you deliver books for distant places making them accountable for the number, and make the clergy to whom you address them accountable for the price—one dollar.

W. S.

Rev. Dr. Smith to Rev. Dr. White.

CHESTER, MD., April 24, 1786.

DEAR SIR: I am favored with your short note by last post, in which you just mention the receipt of mine by last post; but as it appears had not time to notice its contents. The two corrections in the preface, and a proper adjustment respecting the sheets in the singing psalms which you have thought necessary to reprint, have not, I trust, escaped your notice, as it will be a conclusion of the great attention and labor which the press has cost you. The post rider, I imagine, called on you to have some prayer books for his own disposal, on commission from sundry of his subscribers. But unless he gets them from booksellers in

Philadelphia who may be some time hence intrusted with the sale of copies, it will occur to you that neither he nor any other person from the neighboring States can have any copies at present. The proportion for each State must be sent, agreeably to our plan, to some one or more of the clergy in each State, who are to be responsible for the money arising from the copies, as well as an equal distribution of the books in the proportions agreed upon in their several Conventions. In Maryland we have fixed on three copies out of every five for the Western Shore; and two copies for the Eastern, the former to Dr. West's care, the latter to mine. And you will yet have the trouble to take receipts for the books of the post or stage carriers, or skippers, etc., obliging themselves to deliver parcels or boxes as directed. The expense of package, and carriage, etc., to be paid out of the profits of the sale, to make the price equal in all places, for Philadelphia should have no superior advantage in the price, by lying near the press. The book should be $1 to a purchaser in Philadelphia as well as in Charlestown, Carolina; and the stages, where they go by stage, will not take them without the pay advanced, though if they could be got to take them and be paid on the delivery at New York, Baltimore, Alexandria, etc., giving their receipt to you, it would perhaps insure their care of the parcels the better, not to have the money till the service was done. Your *local* situation will still throw all this care and trouble upon you, but I know you will not decline it, any more than you have heretofore in the prosecution of this work. The bookbinder should get all the help he can. I hope Mr. Marshal,* of Boston, has a few complete copies including the preface, calendar, etc. If he had them not in a bound book they should be sent in sheets, that they may have the whole before them, and especially the preface giving them what I hope will be a satisfactory account of the reasons, and expediency, etc., of all the proposed alterations.

Of the first five hundred copies for Maryland, let Mr. West have three hundred, which may go twice, viz.: one hundred and fifty in a box not to risk all at once, and to make it more convenient, for the binder. I should be glad of about twenty copies this week by our post, and if I cannot agree with him for a reasonable price for the remainder, I will order them by water to Duck Creek, and send for them from thence.

.   .   .   .

I am affectionately yours,

WM. SMITH.

---

* Doubtless a clerical error for "Parker," the Rector of Trinity Church, Boston. The Rev. John R. Marshall, A. M., of Connecticut, attended the primary meeting in New York in 1784, but his name is not found in connection with any subsequent proceedings.

Rev. Dr. Smith to Rev. Dr. White.

CHESTER, April 29, 1786.

DEAR SIR: I have received twenty-two copies (two in morocco) of the Prayer Book. I had to pay at the rate of five shillings per dozen carriage to the post, which will not do in future. There is a stage now set up from Philadelphia to this town, an acquaintance of mine of Newcastle, a Colonel Derby, at the head of it. I expect him here by next Wednesday's stage, which will be the second trip, and shall agree with him to bring the books and to do other business for me, as he has also a stage boat to Newcastle from Philadelphia and he will have a sufficient authority from me to produce to you when he calls for the remainder of our Eastern Shore complement of books, which I hope may be ready next week, as the few we have has only increased the demand of many, while some *old persons* do not show much desire to exchange the old for the new book. But all I hope in good time, and without much uneasiness, especially if there be no appearance of authority or compulsion in the case.

I wish there could be a little note of the principal errata pasted on the blank leaf at the end. They are not many; but "construction" for "*mis*construction" is one of some consequence, and yet a candid reader need hardly be told of it.

I am yours,

WM. SMITH.

Rev. Dr. White to Rev. Dr. Smith.

PHILADELPHIA, May 6, 1786.

DEAR SIR: . . . . . I received your note directing the books by the Newcastle stage: in consequence of which I now send you fifty, two of which are morocco; and these are the most that can be spared at present, consistently with our duty to the other States, none of which (I am sure) you would choose to have neglected. The Eastern Shore proportion of the whole is (as I understand) eight in the hundred; and you may rely on that proportion being always ready.

Perhaps on consideration you will not think it proper to print a table of errata at present, for these two reasons: 1st, because so many of the books are already out; and 2dly, because it is probable more errata may appear, which will seem intended, because not included in the table. The errors you allude to are so evidently typographical, that they cannot be otherwise taken.

.   .   .   .

I am yours, etc.,

WM. WHITE.

REV. DR. SMITH.

This ends the correspondence between Dr. White and Dr. Smith on the subject of giving the alterations, etc., in the old Prayer Book, ordered by the Convention of 1785, such form in print as should best carry out the general purpose of that body.

A single letter additional of Dr. Smith to a gentleman who, as Bishop of Massachusetts, subsequently became eminent, though he died within three months after his consecration, shall conclude what I have of my ancestor's correspondence on the Proposed Book, while it was yet going through the press.*

Dr. Smith to the Rev. Samuel Parker.

CHESTER, KENT COUNTY, MARYLAND, April 17, 1786.

DEAR SIR: Dr. White having a more ready communication with you than I could have, he has at the desire of our committee for the press, sent you the sheets of our revised Prayer Book, and I hope you will have the whole complete by the meeting of your Convention, which Dr. White writes me is to be about the end of this month. I trust that after a serious and candid consideration of what we have done, it will have the approbation of the worthy body, clergy as well as laity, who are to meet you in convention; or that if there be some things, which you may judge could have been done otherwise, or better, we can in future editions come to an easy agreement on this head, as would certainly have been the case had we been so happy as to have had your advice and assistance as we expected at the last Convention. I think there are few alterations which you did not wish. As chairman of the grand committee for revising, etc., I had the alterations which you had proposed in your last meeting, put into my hands the first day of our sitting, and you will see that I paid a full attention to them, and that we have agreed with you almost in every matter, except only respecting the Nicene Creed, and our Convention in Maryland which met last week have recommended the restoring that creed also, so that either it or the Apostles' may be read at discretion, provided both be not used in one service. The Maryland Convention have proposed also an addition in the consecration prayer in the holy communion, something analogous to that of the liturgy of Edward VIth and the Scots' liturgy, *invoking* a blessing on the elements of bread and wine, which was left out at the first review of the English liturgy, it is said, at the instance of *Bucer*, and otherwise because the invocation favored the doctrine of transubstantiation and it does now in the Scots' liturgy praying to bless and sanctify the elements that they may *become the body and blood, etc.*

---

* The Rev. Samuel Parker, consecrated Bishop (for Massachusetts) September 14th, 1804, died December 6th, 1804.

We have proposed to retain the prayer and yet avoid the exceptionable part, and it will run thus:

Hear us, O Merciful Father, we most humbly beseech thee, and with thy word and Holy Spirit vouchsafe so to bless and sanctify these thy creatures of bread and wine, that we receiving the same, according to thy Son our Saviour, Jesus Christ's holy institution, etc.

This I think will be a proper amendment, and it perfectly satisfies such of our clergy and people as were attached to the Scots' and other ancient liturgies, all of which have an invocation of a blessing on the elements, as is indeed most reasonable and proper.

I am anxious to write you by this post to have a chance of your receiving this before the meeting of your Convention. I have therefore no time to be more particular. Where we have gone further than was hinted in the alterations you formerly sent us, viz., in the arrangement of the reading and singing psalms, the calendars and rubrics, the collection of hymns on evangelical subjects as a supplement to the deficiencies of David's Psalms and other matters, which we have set forth in the preface, I say in all this I know you will exercise a candid and liberal judgment, and let me hear from you. We can only in the different States receive the book for temporary use, till our churches are organized, and the book comes again under review of conventions having their bishops, etc., as the primitive rules of Episcopacy require.

Excuse this hasty scrawl from

Your affectionate brother, etc.,

WM. SMITH.

P. S.—I shall write to Bishop Seabury next post.

CHAPTER XLVIII.

THE "PROPOSED BOOK"—ABSURD PRETENSIONS OF THE SO-CALLED "REFORMED EPISCOPAL CHURCH," THAT THE SCHISM OF THEIR SECT FOUND SUPPORT IN IT—HISTORY OF THE FORMATION OF THE BOOK—DR. SMITH CHIEFLY ENTITLED TO THE CREDIT OF IT—SOME DESCRIPTION OF THE RESPECTIVE ECCLESIOLOGICAL CHARACTERS AND TASTES OF DR. SMITH, DR. WHITE AND DR. WHARTON, AS APPLIED TO THIS SUBJECT—DR. SMITH'S SERVICES IN PROCURING THE EPISCOPAL SUCCESSION—ADJOURNED GENERAL CONVENTION OF 1786 AT WILMINGTON—A PARTIAL COMPLIANCE WITH THE SUGGESTIONS OF THE ENGLISH ARCHBISHOPS—DR. WHITE, DR. PROVOST AND DR. GRIFFITH RECOMMENDED TO THE ENGLISH BISHOPS FOR CONSECRATION—MARYLAND CONVENTION OF 1786—ATTESTATION BY HIS PARISH OFFICERS IN MARYLAND OF DR. SMITH'S FITNESS FOR CONSECRATION.

THE correspondence in the last chapter runs through two years (1785–86); therefore this chapter does the same.

I have already observed * that a religious consociation, calling itself the *Reformed Episcopal Church*, upon its first departure from the Protestant Episcopal Church in the United States, adopted temporarily as its liturgy the Proposed Book of 1785. It made omissions from it; which, if not made, would have struck a fatal blow to some of the new sect's grounds of schism, and it made at once an announcement of its purpose to subject the book to revision in its portions left; a revision to be made in accordance with certain principles which the "General Council" of the seceders set forth, and which, in fact, were at variance not only with the spirit of the Proposed Book, but with some of its letter also.† This schismatical party soon found that the Proposed Book—which indeed itself declared in terms, that it was "far" from the intention of the Church which promulged it to depart from the Church of England any further than *local* circumstances required—could not be managed by them at all; and sailing on the broad and uncharted sea of their own ignorance, audacity and error, before long threw the Proposed Book bodily overboard. Disregarding, however, the fact that no point of doctrine in the Church of England was denied by the new book, they have sought, by praising it, to convey the idea that the book justified their schism; and during the time that their conventicles did use it, they spoke of it —as they have also done since—by way of giving to it a weight which they could not give to it themselves, as *"Bishop White's Prayer Book;"*‡ a mode of speaking of it which I have already

---

* *Supra.*

† See the edition of the Proposed Book reprinted in 1873, under the authority of George David Cummins.   The Order for the Visitation of the Sick which is found in the original Proposed Book is wholly omitted from the reprint; and if the ideas of the so-called Reformed Church were well based were omitted with reason, since that order retains the English rubric directing that the sick person shall be "moved," *i. e.*, shall be recommended, urged or prevailed on, "to make a *special confession* of his sins, if he feel his conscience troubles him with any weighty matter," after which confession a declaration of absolution is to be made to him.

‡ Bishop Nicholson, in his "Reasons why I became a Reformed Episcopalian," says, in speaking (p. 26) of the service book of the new sect :

"It is in most things essentially the same as that known as Bishop White's Prayer Book, in the making of which were associated with the Bishop such men as Wharton, and Smith, and Provost, and Washington, and Jay."

Was ignorance ever more audacious than this ?   As will sufficiently appear hereafter, Dr. White never cordially liked the new book.   Washington had nothing under heaven to do with it, and Mr. Jay no more.   Jay was not a member of the Convention of Sept. 1785, which made the book, any more than was Washington.

called "audacious" and which undoubtedly, so far as it conveyed an assertion of exclusive authorship or compilation by that eminent person, had no foundation in fact.

It is not easy for me at this late day clearly to show to whom, in its particular composition, we principally owe the Proposed Book; a volume having some deficiencies no doubt, having some excellent points too, and entitled, under any circumstances, to the admiration of the people of America, as the basis on which was in part constructed the Book of Common Prayer set forth and ratified in 1789; a work nearly perfect, and one which, in view of the difficulties under which the Church in America—after our severance of obligation to the King of England, as the temporal head of the Church; to the Bishop of London as diocesan of our colonies, and to the Society for the Propagation of the Gospel as the source of support to many country churches—was placed by the independency, in law, of every parish of every other, and of every common superior, must be contemplated with gratitude and praise. The journal of the Convention of 1785 shows nothing particular of importance on the subject of the respective authors or makers of the book. Bishop Perry* rightly says that "a more guarded and incommunicative record could hardly be found," and we can learn from it neither the reasons for the changes proposed by the committee nor the reception that they met with from the members of the Convention. I think, however, that to Dr. Smith more than to any one else the formation of the book is due.

It is sometimes popularly supposed from the fact that Dr. White, Dr. Smith and Dr. Wharton were the persons by whom the *copy* for the Proposed Book was fitted for the press and published—that those three gentlemen were the persons who composed or framed it. This is a great mistake. What we find in

---

Another of these Reformed gentlemen—the Rev. Benjamin Johnson (Correspondence with the Rt. Rev. Dr. Beckwith, Bishop of Georgia, p. 21)—asks with similar ignorance:

"Would Bishop White, *whose recovered Prayer Book* so clearly exposes, etc."

The Rev. Mason Gallagher, in like style in "The Book of Common Prayer, Revision a Duty and Necessity," p. 54, says:

"The revision of *Bishop White* was in use but four years."

The book referred to was not the revision of Bishop White, and it was never in any general use at all.

* "Half Century of Legislation," Vol. III., page 100.

the Proposed Book was made, in its substance, and in its main form also, in and by the Convention of 1785; and the service as set forth in the book had been actually used at the conclusion of that Convention before the book was itself in print at all. It had been all brought into the Convention by a committee, the names of whose members we have already given;* men who, both as respects the clerical and the lay part of it, were men who, in general, thought and acted for themselves, though a spirit of conciliation towards each other, no doubt, on this occasion, largely prevailed among them. It is impossible, therefore, to say that the book was the work of any one man or of any three men. All that the committee, consisting of Dr. White, Dr. Smith and Mr. Wharton, did—so far as we know with certainty—was to carry out, with a liberal interpretation of their powers, the business of fitting the work for the press. Nevertheless, I do, as I have said, suppose that to my ancestor, Dr. Smith, as chairman of the committee intrusted with the work of the alterations, and as the person who reported them to the Convention, is due much of the frame-work of that book. Dr. White was President of the Convention and took no part in debate there upon the book except on a single occasion; which was to oppose the introduction of one feature—a service of thanksgiving for the 4th of July.† The work of the large committee appointed by the Convention was done in a sub-committee, of which Dr. White was not a member. The work of the sub-committee was not debated in the full committee, nor much in the Convention.‡

From the first coming of Dr. Smith to this continent he had a profound conviction of its great destinies; and he expressed, early and often, these convictions both in poetry and prose. At a later day, 1790, embodying some of them, he writes:

In my expanded view these United States rise in all their ripened glory before me. I look through and beyond every yet peopled region of the New World, and behold period still brightening upon period. Where one continuous depth of gloomy wilderness now shuts out even the beams of day, I see new States and Empires, new seats of wisdom and knowledge, new religious domes spreading around in places now

---

* *Supra*, page 119.
† " White's Memoirs."   Second Edition, pp. 104-105.
‡ *Id.*, 103.

untrod by any but savage beasts or man as savage as they.   I hear the voice of happy labor and behold towery cities growing into the skies.

How remarkable, too, is that passage in a letter of his, written A. D. 1785, nearly a century ago:

Surely in large towns and cities (of which America will have many in a hundred years more) the good old custom of week-day prayers will not be laid aside.

Did he foresee Chicago?   Was De Koven, the Rector of Racine, revealed to him?   Thank God, the day which he waited for—though he died without the sight—has arrived; and from churches everywhere in our land, and most of all from the very church which he dedicated,* and that elder one in which he oftener preached,† the voice of confession, and prayer, and thanksgiving, and praise now ascend every morning and evening daily throughout the year.

So soon, therefore, as the Church in America became independent of the Church in England, which—since and so long as that latter Church was a part of the State and under the control more or less of a British Parliament and British statutes—deprived of its independence—its wings clipped and its limbs manacled—our said Church in America necessarily did become—Dr. Smith contemplated it "in all its ripened glory" before him!   He saw the Protestant Episcopal Church in the United States of America spread over the whole continent; half of Mexico already annexed, and all of Canada soon to be.   What were the English bishops— lords of parliament though they were—to that consecrated host which assembles in *our* upper ecclesiastical house?   What the English laymen—in no office whatever, ecclesiastically speaking— to our body of lay representatives in General Convention with clergy triennially assembled?   Dr. Smith had no idea of subjecting the Church in this New World to a liturgy, to orders of service, or to articles which had been made in England only under the greatest difficulties; which were a temporary compromise between extreme parties on opposite sides; which had never proved satis-

---

* St. Peter's, Philadelphia, in which, by the efforts of the then youthful Odenheimer (now with God), the daily service and frequent communions were established.

† Christ Church, Philadelphia.   Indeed through the zealous work of the present Rector, Dr. Foggo, that church is now open all through the day for either public or private prayer.

factory to all of either the Church's clergy or its laity in England, and which would have been long before reformed and altered in England itself but for political heats and for the accidents of the day. *He* meant, therefore, to have the Church in America have its own Book of Common Prayer; one founded on Scriptural usage and compiled from primitive liturgies, so much as might be; leaving the Church in the little and vanquished isles of Great Britain to imitate and adopt it when she saw fit.

Notwithstanding that the United States declared themselves independent of Great Britain in 1776, and were acknowledged by her in 1783 to be so, it was a long while before, in many respects, we ceased to be colonies and to be really independent. We are so indeed only since the suppression, by the Federal arms, of the late Rebellion, and the complete success of our Great Exhibition of 1876. The leaders of the Federal party—men like Hamilton, Gouverneur Morris, Marshall, and some others—would at once have made us truly a nation of the earth, but some of the men of New England, and even those further south, were not able, for years, wholly to emancipate themselves; while the Democratic party, under the lead of Jefferson, Monroe, Gerry, and others, went at once into a state of absolute vassalage to France; a vassalage which continued pretty steadily to the time of Napoleon the bastard, sometimes called Napoleon III.; when we saw in him the Iago of the plot of our late rebellion, and were disenchanted. Dr. Smith, so soon as our political independence was acknowledged —indeed so soon as he saw that it was achieved—comprehended the whole situation. He saw at once, and with the glance of intuition, what many men did not see for about a century—indeed hardly see now, some of them—and he meant to make independence, *at once*, a fact, instead of a dream. Even in 1785, as we have seen,* on the first motion of a review of the Prayer Book, he hopes that hymns for the festivals and other occasions " may be offered by members of our own Church in America, who are distinguished for their poetical talents." He anticipated by half a century a hymnal which includes the strains of Muhlenburgh, of Henry Ustick Onderdonk, and of the elder Doane.

With what zeal he entered upon the subject of the alterations

---

* *Supra,* p. 143.

in the liturgy, and to what extent they were agreeable to *him*, may be inferred, not only from the already quoted sermon before the Convention of 1785, but from the ably written Preface to the Proposed Book which contains the alterations, and in which, as in notes to the sermon, he shows how necessary some alterations really were; how long they had been considered necessary in England by many of its soundest divines, and how especially desirable it was that any changes in the liturgy of the Church in America should be made *now* when—uninfluenced and unrestrained by any worldly authority whatsoever—they could so be made as to promulgate to mankind Christianity and the truths of the Gospel in the clearest, plainest, most affecting and majestic manner.

Dr. Smith, it must be remembered, was a Scotsman, not an Englishman. He was not a parochial minister who had been reading daily all his life the morning and evening prayers of the English Church, but was the head of a college where all the rest of the faculty were dissenters, and several of them dissenting clergymen, and where probably he was continually urged and sometimes compelled to use forms not to be found in the book of common prayer. He was, moreover, frequently called upon as a preacher for public occasions and ceremonies where religious services were used, but where neither the order for daily morning prayer, nor the order for daily evening prayer, of the book of common prayer could be used without modifications. Neither his education nor profession, therefore, gave him blind prepossessions or prejudices in favor of the liturgy of the Church of England, as adopted in 1660; only one of five forms which that Church had been using in the short term of about one century. Independently of all this, his mind was rich and imaginative. His conceptions of what best produced effect were somewhat theatrical. His own style of oratory was high and orotund; occasionally perhaps a little turgid, but oftener grand and sometimes even majestic.

Detesting, as matter of taste and of divinity also, we may believe, "the way of Romaine," and all the sweetened mud of the Methodist preachers of his day*—corresponding largely to

* See Vol. I., page 423.

"the low church" of a later and of ours—he yet wanted a body of hymns introduced into our prayer book ; writing to Dr. White that "the Methodists captivate many by their attention to church music and by their hymns and doxologies," which, as he says, "when rationally and devoutly introduced, are sublime parts of public and private worship," and again writing,

The Psalms of David, unless where tortured by versifiers, have but few evangelical subjects.

And writing again when Dr. White desired to leave the Litany a part of the service separable from the order for daily morning prayer :

Let not our abridgments be too great.   Without the Litany, Wednesday and Friday prayers would not draw many to church.

And again as to certain prayers :

The service would appear quite *naked* without them.*

A hymn, suggested by Dr. White, composed by Francis Hopkinson, a signer of the Declaration of Independence, Dr. Smith finds "too *flat* for the great occasion."

We can readily conceive that the simplicity in the style of parts of the English liturgy—its pure and little sonorous Saxon, and its merely self-abasing terms with which its liturgy opens—did not quite come up to the grandeur of thought, and the *sonorité* of utterance, and the impressiveness of spectacle, which the mind and eye and ear of Dr. Smith affected and indeed required.

To illustrate what I mean :

The Church of England begins her service with sentences purely penitential, and inviting to confession of sin, and the Exhortation which adverts to these "sundry places" thus put before the people in which the Scripture moveth them to confess their manifold sins and wickedness and assures them of the forgiveness of the same, if those sins and wickednesses are rightly confessed, we shall, by God's infinite goodness and mercy, obtain.   But there was no asceticism nor any vast humility in Dr. Smith's composition ; while there was always an awful sense of God's presence and greatness.   To Dr. Smith, therefore, have been generally

---

* See *supra*, pp. 143, 147, 168, 171.

ascribed and I presume rightly those two grand verses first found in the Proposed Book.

The Lord is in his holy temple: let all the earth keep silence before him.—Hab. ii. 20.

From the rising of the sun even unto the going down of the same, my name shall be great among the Gentiles; and in every place incense shall be offered unto my name, and a pure offering: for my name shall be great among the heathen, saith the Lord of hosts.—Mal. i. 11.

And this third one—meant to have been put there, though from accident apparently omitted—very appropriate to a person coming into God's house, but not a penitential sentence:

Let the words of my mouth, and the meditation of my heart, be alway acceptable in thy sight, O Lord, my strength and my Redeemer.* —Psalm xix. 14, 15.

I suppose too that to Dr. Smith's liking of an enriched ritual, and to the fact that he habitually used the communion service as one separate from the morning prayer, we owe that fine introduction from the communion into the daily service, as an anthem, of the *Gloria in Excelsis Deo,* instead of the *Gloria Patri;* and some other changes of a like kind.

In addition to this rich and decorated style of taste which characterized the subject of our memoir, we may observe that there was nothing *archaic* in his literary tastes. Paying to them great respect, and sometimes quoting them, he was never enamored of the old divines of the Church of England, nor of any antique expressions in them. Indeed, he mentions what we can well understand, that "in his situation" his reading had only been a dipping into books as occasion required and time would permit, "and that he did not remember" his ever having read any regularly through without skipping from place to place, except, perhaps, Robinson

---

* These sentences are so grand and impressive that they are retained in our present Book of Common Prayer, notwithstanding the penitential character of all those that succeed, and with the reference to *them only,* in the exhortation of the minister, which follows. If Dr. Smith could have given perfection to his idea, I rather apprehend that he would have considered his three verses as something apart from and preceding the order of daily morning service, and in the way in which the metre psalms and hymns are now allowed to be sung *in* (not *by*) all congregations *before* morning and evening prayer. What a grand *Processional* the three verses would make! What a παρασκευη, or preparation for confession of sins and absolution of them in the holy temple of the Lord! The Prayer Book of the "Reformed Church of England" does, indeed, somewhat thus use the first of these three verses.

Crusoe, Thomson's Seasons, and Young's Night Thoughts, at a time, as they appeared."* It is, therefore, under Dr. Smith's suggestion that those old words, "the good estate of the Catholic Church," which, in these days when old furniture has been hauled out of garrets to decorate the parlors, enchant our ecclesiologists, disappear. The churchmen in Maryland, he feared, would see in them the likeness of " glebes," and of a three-fold crown.† From this same wish to make the book acceptable to the people, Dr. Smith made and was energetic in introducing the form of thanksgiving for the 4th of July; a service which as the people of the United States valued their independence of Great Britain, and if they did *really* value it, he felt no doubt was not only proper for *them* but obligatory on them to use; however little it might be appropriate to such of the clergy and to such of the congregations committed to their charge as had been loyal in act or feeling to Great Britain; a class of persons, he well knew, not numerous in 1785, daily growing smaller and in a few years certain to disappear altogether. To Dr. Smith and to his distastes for all unnecessary polemical and conjectural divinity—that light bread which satisfieth not—we apparently owe the Articles of Religion as given, *supra*, pages 127–131, and the omission of such metaphysical dogmas as are contained in them as found in the old Prayer Book of the Church of England, and as have been reinstated in our own of 1789. They were not, however, in their new form, Dr. Smith's own work, but were taken for the most part from a book of an anonymous English Church Reformer.

It is quite certain that the articles in their present form, like some parts of the English liturgy, are put in with such " cunning " language as to mean things almost directly opposite, according as you read them with a point or without a point, or as the hearer or reader may choose to listen to them or fancy that they are read. They are the "*Ibis Peribis non Redibis*," given as answer by the old oracles, to the inquirer, who sought to know if he might safely go to the wars; an answer which, if the pause was made after the second word, meant that he should be slain; but, if after the third, meant the opposite, and that he should return in safety. These passages of the old Prayer Book are " the dark and mys-

---

* Dr. Smith's Works. Maxwell's Edition. Vol. II., page 487—note.
† See *supra*, page 150.

terious sentences," which Dr. Smith in the sermon that we have
already referred to, preached before the Convention of 1785, hopes
that "the truths of the Gospel may never be obscured by." The
purpose of this cunning device of the Church of England was no
doubt good. It was to keep within that Church those who were
nearly Puritans and those who were nearly Papists; but were not
wholly either. The Reformed Episcopal Church—a body of
schismatics existing now both in England and America—and the
defection to Rome of such men as Wilberforce, Manning and
Newman—with the unseceded body of so-called " Ritualists "—a
mild form, in their more advanced developments, of Romanists—
show that complete success has not attended the well-meant effort.
And what food have not such expressions with the very subtle
distinctions of some of the Church of England articles, not ministered for most learned and most curious disputations; dividing
the Church into parties to-day, and never thought of when the
day had gone. Where are now the two volumes, engendered in
the Church by the 17th article, of *"Comparative Views of the Con
troversy between the Calvinists and the Arminians, by William White,
D. D., Bishop of the Protestant Episcopal Church in the Commonwealth of Pennsylvania,"* published so late as 1817; one of the
most laborious and learned, one of the strongest and most acute,
one of the most logical and dispassionate controversial works ever
written, and till lately a text-book in the general Theological
Seminary of the Church? Gone—gone—almost as much as the
years beyond the flood. Where *will be* in less than half the time
that has elapsed since 1817 the fiery feuds in England and America, and the heated proceedings of some of our late Church Conventions, on the subject of the Eucharistic and Sacerdotal party
that we have just spoken of and called (improperly enough) the
Ritualists? Gone—gone—to follow them. Both I am ready to
concede likely to come back in the encyclicity of those parties,
whom our articles and liturgy in their present shape will ever keep
alive, but which Dr. Smith, by the Proposed Book, sought to send
away for ever from the Church. And by the rejection of a stum-
bling-block in the ministration of baptism—a word which though
explained by a general Convention, was still a terror to those once
thoroughly affrighted—he would, *perhaps*, have saved from apostacy
a portion of the Church which can argue with some plausibility—

though not at all with truth—that it carried away in its schism, that high portion of its orders which the Wesleys and Coke had never been able to detach.   He explains his purposes and hopes when he says, in the sermon of 1785 already quoted:

> Were our blessed Saviour now upon earth, he would not narrow the terms of communion, by such ways as these; and it is our duty, as it hath been our great endeavor in all the alterations proposed, to make the consciences of those easy *who believe in the true principles of Christianity in general,* and who, could they be made easy in certain points no way essential to Christianity itself, would rather become worshippers as well as laborers, in that part of Christ's vineyard, in which we profess to worship and to labor, than in any other.

Dr. Smith had already declared "that ever since the Reformation it had been a received doctrine of the Church," of which he was a member, "that there be these *three* orders of ministers in Christ's Church—Bishops, Priests and Deacons—and that an *Episcopal* Ordination and Commission are *necessary* to the valid administration of the Sacraments and the due exercise of ministerial functions in the said Church." *   This, we may infer, he would have regarded as among "the true principles of Christianity in general," and not in any way or ever to be surrendered.   These are different ideas from those of the apostate " Reformed Episcopal Church," and indeed from what we *now* call " low churchmen;" men still *in* the Church.   Such, I say, were Dr. Smith's ideas and purposes.   A clear and deep conception of what the Church was, lay, no doubt, at the base of all his plans and all his work.   But artificial, complicated and metaphysical formularies, articles or rites, however venerable or however wonderful, he looked upon as essentially of human elaboration and structure, and the more perfectly they were worked out in theological operation and detail, the more plainly did he see man's work and man's character stamped upon them.   His mind, in its natural structure, rejoiced in "that elder, wider and wiser view which contemplates Revelation only, as the fullness of and assurance of a grace previously developed in natural religion—a view which shuts not out, but rather gathers in the glory of the open universe;" though, of course, he considered too, that without the Church's interpretation, the refining beauty of

---

* See *supra,* page 97.

this beneficent nature could never be unsphered to us ; and through
that Church's mighty and long enduring ministration he sought,
therefore, to reveal the iris-lustre inherent in the common day,
but there invisible.*

That the purposes of Dr. Smith in his Proposed Book were
good is undeniable. That the book itself—unlike the book of the
so-called " Reformed Episcopal Church "—did not carry the review of the English Book of Common Prayer " into essential
points of doctrine," has been uniformly admitted both by the English and the American bishops and other clergy. How far the
plan of the Proposed Book would have secured the purpose which
it had in view—since the book was never adopted as the liturgy
of the Church in America—no man in this day can do more than
conjecture.

To Dr. Smith, too, aided considerably by Dr. Wharton, we owe
the system adopted in the Proposed Book, of leaving out psalms now
in the Psalter, or verses of particular psalms that are inappropriate
for public service ; and of joining parts or verses of one psalm to
those of another so as to make a uniformity of thought and feeling, and then of dividing the whole into parts of suitable length.†
Both of these gentlemen—Dr. Smith being, doubtless, the more
operative agent—could not but see the inappropriateness of people
reading in the public worship psalms and verses, some of which
—unless before they came to church they had read an Exposition
of the Psalter—were wholly unintelligible ; and others of which,
even if they did understand them, were entirely inappropriate ;
expressing sometimes high states of exultation, and at others
deep despondency—feelings, which—as common to them all, and
whether one or the other—could hardly exist in any congregation
of worshippers whatsoever.

The plan—though executed in the Proposed Book with great
skill and great good taste—was subject, no doubt, to objections
of more sorts than one. And the *"Selection* of Psalms," as made
in our present book and than which no arrangement or use of the

* See " Art and Scenery in Europe," by the late Horace Binney Wallace, of Philadelphia ; Second Edition, page 78 ; some of whose language I here quote.

† This plan has been adopted in his " Family and Private Prayer "—a beautifnl
manual of family worship—by the late Rev. William Berrian, D. D., Rector of Trinity
Church, New York.

Psalter can be more beautiful or appropriate, is, in my own opinion, the better plan; *if our clergy would only use the selections.* But unless they purpose to deliver a longer sermon than usual, or happen to be pressed for time, when they sometimes give us the Sixth Selection—a very short one—they rarely do use the selections; and we are left by the present book exactly where we were by the Church of England, whose use of the whole Psalter, we meant to decline as, in parts, inappropriate for public worship.

To Dr. Smith, exclusively or nearly so, I assume, that we owe the hymns in the Proposed Book, fifty-one in number, which are the basis of the great variety of hymns now in use; and he proposed to add more. In fact, as will be seen by his letter to Dr. White, he had anticipated the Hymnal of the Christian year and of our modern service, and adds that:

On the great festivals of the Church there should be some variety; at least three or four and of different metres, to complete the Psalmody of the day.*

He sought, it is evident, through the hymns, to make the Church a Holy Catholic Church—a holy Church universal—and to make its liturgy a book of prayer for all people, as its temples were houses of prayer for them also. He writes to Dr. White in April, 1786:

My congregations were exceedingly pleased with the two Good Friday Hymns, and also the two Easter Hymns, but what above all seemed to make the greatest impression was the two Communion Hymns, No. XVII beginning,

My God, and is thy table spread?

sung after the sermon as an invitation to the Sacrament, and No. XVIII beginning,

And are we now brought near to God?

as sung after the Communion. It adds a solemnity which they confessed they had not experienced before. The hymns are indeed beautiful, and every line of them applicable to the blessed occasion. Have *you* yet introduced them in this way?† . . . . Every communicant will, before another day, have them by heart.

---

* *Supra*, page 168.

† Of course the Proposed Book did not contain a rubric, such as is found in the Book of Common Prayer, which introduces a hymn, or a part of a hymn as a portion of the Eucharistic service. And as a matter of taste I think that the hymns had better have been left as the Proposed Book left them.

Dr. White was a person quite different in most respects from Dr. Smith. Indeed, between the two men we may say that there was an absolute contrast. Dr. White had been bred by pious parents in childhood in the Church; and every recollection of his earliest life must have been associated with the very words of all its liturgy.* We have no reason to think that if he could himself have controlled the thing he would have had the Convention of 1785 make any considerable departures from the old service books of the mother Church, but those required by the Revolution, and by that moderate review in some of its offices suggested by an obvious propriety.

As to any further review, he desired it, so far as he desired it at all, in order to satisfy weak brethren, who, he thought, might otherwise at some future day triumph in numbers and make alterations dangerous or heterodox. He foresaw even at that day what two different parties in the Church are now doing: both remaining in the fold, but both in different ways misrepresenting its doctrines, violating its rubrics, and departing from or corrupting its practices; one, in a disregard of services appointed for her saints, and holy days; in a substitution for hers of irregular prayers; in the constant violation, year after year, of a plain and positive rubric, which makes it the duty of the minister of *every* parish *diligently*, upon Sundays, holy days, or other convenient occasions, openly in the Church, to catechise children sent to him in the *Church's* catechism; in the low views of her great Eucharistic service; in the obliteration in all discourses from the pulpit of the Church's distinctive character and high office—and in other mat-

---

* The Bishop alludes to this affectingly in an address at the Consecration on the 25th of October, 1827, in Christ Church, of Bishop H. U. Onderdonk:

"He feels the full weight of an occasion, reminding him of his near approach to the end of the ministry in which he has been so long a laborer; and when during the transaction in which we have been engaged, he occasionally permitted his eye to rest on the spot [his paternal pew, now his own] and within the distance of a few feet, where, in the days of his boyhood, he joined in religious services within these walls; when from that spot his attention was transferred to the pulpit at his elbow, from which, though not unfavored by domestic instruction and encouragement, there sunk into his youthful mind the truths of the ever-blessed Gospel, and from which, for the space of fifty-five years, he has been proclaiming the same truths—with what effect will not be known until the day which shall try every man's work of what sort it is, but certainly with effect far short of his wishes and of his prayers—there results from these recollections and from others, a most weighty sense of the responsibility on which he has been so long acting."

ters also reducing that Church to a Methodist level; and the other
by a disregard of the rubrics just as blameworthy as that practised by the Methodistical party in our Church, and by constrained
and unjustifiable interpretations of our present prayer book, or by
a professed adherence to the usages of the Church of England, as
set forth in some of her earlier service books,* betraying her children by every insidious way into the hands of that "Bishop of
Rome," whose unscriptural observances our Church departed from
at the Reformation, and from whose "tyranny," and whose "detestable enormities," the litanies of those same earlier service books
prayed that the good Lord would deliver us.

Speaking of the Convention of 1785, Bishop White says:†

When the members of the Convention first came together very few,
or rather it is believed none of them, entertained thoughts of altering
the liturgy any further than to accommodate it to the Revolution.‡

And Bishop White assigned a reason, which, with his nice
sense of honor, would have been potential why none should be
made, a reason which applied to delegates from all the States
except Virginia. It is thus expressed by him:

---

* The books of King Edward VI.

† Memoirs, page 102.

‡ Dr. Stevens Perry, after quoting not quite fully the passage from Bishop White's
Memoirs, to which I refer, and after giving some proofs which he thinks sufficient, has
concluded that this idea of the Bishop was unfounded. I have the greatest respect for
the judgments, as also for the historical learning of the present Bishop of Iowa.
Nevertheless, I must think that Bishop White was likely to know from their own mouths
and from other testimonies, what thoughts the members of the Convention of 1785
entertained about altering the old liturgy; more likely even than Dr. Stevens Perry or
any man whatever now living is upon the same topics. Are not Dr. Perry's evidences
after all but letters addressed chiefly to Bishop White himself, and letters from persons
in States not represented in the Convention of 1785 at all? At any rate Bishop White
knew what thoughts *he* himself entertained on the matter, and when he says that it is
believed that "none" of the members "entertained thoughts of altering the liturgy
any further than to accommodate it to the Revolution," it would seem certain that *he*
did not. I am quite aware that at a later date, as is shown by the journals of the Conventions of 1826, and by his own memoirs, Bishop White, yielding, perhaps, to the
views of Bishop Hobart, did desire that the Morning Service might be shortened by
making the use of the Litany optional except in seasons or on days specially penitential. But even here, I am not certain that so far as his own particular views were concerned he would have so had it. (See "Bishop White's Memoirs," pages 52, 53, 251,
259.) It is absolutely certain that he never varied from the observance of what was
prescribed by rubrics; those, with his honorable integrity, he would have observed,
however little he might have either liked or approved what they enjoined.

There being no express authority to the purpose,* the contrary was implied in the sending of Deputies on the ground of the recommendation from New York, which presumed that the book, with the above exception, should remain entire.†

He proceeds, a little further on:

Every one, so far as is here known, *wished* for alterations in the *different offices*. But it was thought at New York, in the preceding year, that such an enterprise could not be undertaken until the Church should be consolidated and organized. *Perhaps it would have been better if the same opinion had been continued and acted on.*

The Bishop afterwards goes on showing how little hand he himself had in making the book in its substance. He says:

The alterations were prepared by another sub-division of the General Committee than that to which the author belonged. When brought into the committee they were not reconsidered, because the ground would have been to go over again in the Convention. *Accordingly he cannot give an account of any arguments arising in the preparatory state of the business.* Even in the Convention there were but few points canvassed with any material difference of principle.

The Bishop notices these few points. The only ones where a change in the old book was made, and the only ones important therefore to be here noticed, are these:

One about a form of Thanksgiving for the 4th of July, the introduction of which was displeasing to him, the Bishop tells us; and to oppose which he availed himself of a privilege which he had reserved on his acceptance of the Presidency of the Convention, to deliver his opinion.

A second, the alteration of the old 17th Article, about Predestination. The Bishop says about this:

Some wished to get rid of the new article introduced concerning Predestination without stating anything in its place. This, it is probable, would have been better than the proposed article which professes to say something on the subject, yet, in reality, says nothing. . . . . Although no one professed scruples against what is there affirmed, yet there seemed a difficulty in discovering for what purpose it was introduced. The author never met with any who were satisfied with it.

---

* Given by the different State Conventions to the Delegates, I suppose the Bishop to mean.

† See the recommendation referred to by the Bishop, *supra*, page 116.

He continues:

Less prominent debates on the articles are not here noticed. Whatever is novel in them was taken from a book in the possession of the Rev. Dr. Smith. The book was anonymous, and was one of the publications which have abounded in England, projecting changes in the established articles.

It might, too, on other grounds, be set down almost for certain that Dr. White did not like some of the alterations themselves. He was, no doubt, as I have already intimated, a theologian distinguished by acuteness as much as by solidity of mind. But he was nothing of a rhetorician. His style, though perfectly accurate, and often in the expression of feeling deeply affecting, is to the general reader, frequently, at first reading, obscure, and sometimes, until thoroughly comprehended, rather ineffective. As for what we call *elegance*, or richness of thought or diction, he had little of either; and so far as effects *merely* decorative constitute a part of worship, he had but a slight perception of them, if indeed he had any at all. He rather abhorred them as not fit agencies of the sanctuary. I am not meaning to say that he was not deeply imbued, in religious worship, with a sense of the true, the appropriate and the becoming. Undoubtedly he was deeply imbued with them all. But his conceptions and his expressions tended to plain and simple forms, rather than to rich and decorated ones. The same thing, I think, was true in regard to that part of public worship which engaged Dr. Smith's feelings so largely; the part so much assisted by music. We have, in historical collections of music, some compositions which we know that Dr. White liked. But my impression is that scientific musicians have not admired them highly. As for "captivating people by the art of Psalm-singing," Dr. White would have, I doubt not, resiled, with something like horror, from the idea. He never himself gave out more than two, or at most *three*, verses of a metrical psalm. And as for hymns—except perhaps at Christmas—one might defy the oldest parishioner of the United Churches to cite an occasion where he ever gave out one, unless where, as in communion, the rubric obliged him to do so.* Could he have regulated absolutely the subject of singing the metrical psalms, he would have affixed

---

* See "White's Memoirs," 2d edition, p. 256.—Note N. N

a tune to each psalm; the same tune always to be sung to that psalm; and not more than from twelve to twenty tunes to be ever heard in the Church.*

Undoubtedly he was extremely averse to changes in the church music or to any *exhibitions* from the organ loft. He had two of the finest musicians, Raynor Taylor and Benjamin Carr, both Englishmen, bred in the cathedral style, that ever graced the musical science of Philadelphia, in one of his own churches, St. Peter's; but he kept its music, as he did that of Christ Church, and of St. James' after it was built and became one of the United Churches, down to a plain, old-fashioned Church of England standard; and even had a book prepared whose tendency was to limit the chants and tunes for the metrical psalm or hymn to the comparatively small number already stated, and these of a simple kind—*Mear, Wells, Philadelphia,*† *Old Hundred, St. Martin's, St. Michael's,* and other ancient English airs. Pergolesi, Palestrina, and the Italian school generally, found no favor in his ears. Little of this was after the ideas of Dr. Smith, whose taste in music was high and artificial. I ought, perhaps, to add, while I say what I do, that I make no doubt that such compositions as Bishop White did deem appropriate, he would

---

* See his "Thoughts on the Singing of Psalms and Anthems," printed A. D. 1808. One of the ministers of the United Churches, Dr. Abercrombie, was fond of hymns, particularly of the hymn, not then in our collection,

" Jesu, Saviour of my soul ! "

And on ending a sermon on one occasion began with that line, letting the choir— under a prearrangement, of course—take it from his mouth and proceed with the rest of the hymn. This was rather effective, and would probably have been after Dr. Smith's taste. Bishop White, the Rector, desired that such a thing might not be repeated, and it never was in his presence. The doctor, who was not easily controlled, defended his action, and the necessity.of hymns, and the beauty of this hymn. "As for me," said the Bishop, "whatever thoughts or feelings I want to express, whether of praise, of gratitude, of penitence, or of joy, I can find them all in the Psalms of David." Dr. Abercrombie answered that the new dispensation rendered necessary something more than the Psalms of David would give us. "What, sir," replied Bishop White, "do you make of the inspiration and the prophetic character of David? And as for the hymn which you specially admire, I must say, Dr. Abercrombie, that its expressions of devotion are not expressions of that sort of devotion which our Church approves." It is noteworthy that in the correspondence, already given in the body of this book, when Dr. Smith asks Dr. White if he knows of any suitable hymns on the Last Judgment and the Kingdom of Glory, Dr. White replies that he knows of none (*supra*, p. 171.) I am quite aware of course of what Bishop Doane, of New Jersey, states of the Bishop's last hours, and of the two hymns then read to him.

† A tune, by his friend, Mr. Hopkinson.

have had richly performed. I never heard of his objecting to music as he heard it in the cathedrals, chapels-royal and collegiate churches of England. On the contrary, he tells us himself that at Magdalen College, Oxford, where he was invited to go to hear the music—which appears to have been especially fine at that college—"the music was as delightful as can be imagined." No doubt he would have had music just like it if he could have had it in our own larger churches; and would have said:

> "There let the pealing organ blow
> To the full-voiced quire below,
> In service high and anthems clear
> As may with sweetness through mine ear
> Dissolve me into ecstasies
> And bring all Heaven before mine eyes."

What he abhorred were the attempts so common in our churches to perform, with means wholly incompetent to produce them, great concerted pieces that only made the organ-loft sometimes ridiculous, sometimes disgusting, and sometimes distressing, and which tended almost of necessity to such indecent and irreverent performance as profaned the service of the sanctuary.

Indeed, while, no doubt, Dr. White ardently desired the extension of the Church, his means of extending it were never of any very popular sort. The Church, though it grew surely and fairly well, did not grow rapidly in his day. I think that he considered "that what made our Church so slow of growth was in its favor, and that what accommodates so many in the Roman, Methodist and other dissenting churches, was not in favor of theirs." No greater mistake has been made by the low churchmen of this day than to suppose that because his temper was sweet and his manners and character lovely, and because in matters of mere taste or feeling he was always ready to give way, rather than to create a disturbance, therefore he was a man of accommodating tempers in the larger and more important concerns of the Church. Like the great Chatham, in all that concerned great principles, either of religion, or morals, or public polity, he was as *un*accommodating as he was original, and we might add that the features of his mind had "the hardihood of antiquity."

The character of Dr. White has been described by the late Dr.

Rufus Wilmot Griswold in his "Republican Court; or, American Society in the Days of Washington." The description, in my opinion, is, in the main, so just that, though in part it has slight relation to our immediate subject, I here present it entire. He is speaking now of Philadelphia, and says:

At the head of the clergy stood Dr. White, as he was commonly called, the well-known first Bishop of the Episcopal Church in Pennsylvania. His ecclesiastical character has, in recent times, been greatly mistaken by both the extreme High and the extreme Low divisions of his own denomination. He was what in England would be called a historical low-churchman as distinguished from the ultra school of Laud and Philpotts, but was very far removed from what have been called low-churchmen in this country. Even in his day, when the Episcopal Church was extremely feeble, and concessions and compromises with other denominations were matters to which the temptations were extreme, Bishop White defined what he regarded as the just limits of both with a distinctness and precision which have made them their safest limits since. To him and to his moderate views and conciliatory temper we must ascribe the fact that, while the ecclesiastical establishment of England and the very name of Bishop had become odious in this country, the Protestant Episcopal Church departed so very little in form, while not departing at all in doctrine, from the Established Church of England. As a preacher he was earnest and persuasive, but he seldom fulminated threats or judgments, and had very decided views of the limits of clerical responsibility. He shrank from no proper responsibility, but he had too high a sense of courtesy and too just a regard for even the most delicate of rights to invade with freedom the atmosphere which every gentleman feels and acknowledges as a proper circle for himself and others. He was the man of his time for his position. His prudence saved what the zeal of others might have lost; and in the midst of political and ecclesiastical difficulties of the most discouraging kind, he founded that establishment which has grown to be one of the most majestic structures of the religion of the republic. His character will grow larger as the perspective becomes more truly fixed by time, and if it were separated from religious parties, posterity would probably place his name after the names of Washington, Marshall and Hamilton alone. He belonged to the same order of men, differing but in the sphere of his action from either.

It might be inferred from the correspondence between Dr. White and Dr. Smith, already given, that Dr. White in all respects approved of the book. I understand only that, being placed by the convention of 1785 upon the committee to put the book into form

for the press and to publish it, he gave his hearty effort to this
object, rendering an almost exclusive work in what was done in
the alterations in Calendar and some assistance also in the adapta-
tion of the Psalter, in the way preferred by Dr. Smith and Dr.
Wharton, to popular reading in the churches, by rejecting psalms
or parts of psalms incomprehensible to any reader, clerical or lay,
except after he had sought information of the circumstances under
which the psalm was written—and dividing them so as to shorten
that part of the service. But he did not, as we know from his
"Memoirs," himself approve of this plan. His poaposal was to
take the whole psalms, select such as fall in with the general
subjects of divine worship, and leave the officiating minister his
choice among those which should be selected. The plan finally
adopted by the majority of the committee, and in executing which
Dr. White, after it was fixed against his view, co-operated cordially,
will hereafter appear. Dr. White's liking of all parts of the book,
or of it in the main, is not to be inferred from his endeavors to
make it throughout as effective as possible. He disliked, and
strongly disliked, the service for the 4th of July. Yet by select-
ing appropriate lessons, etc., he made it more effective than the
convention and Dr. Smith had left it.* It was enough for him
that the *convention* liked the book, and he carried out, with absolute honesty, the purpose which the convention had in appointing
him, with Drs. Smith and Wharton, a committee to get it impres-
sively before the churches for adoption, if they liked it. With his
perfect candor and perfect integrity of nature, he could not have
done otherwise. But it is quite plain that he desired the book to
be considered at first only as a *proposed* book; and that if it ever
should become the Liturgy of the Church in the United States, it
should become so only upon full consent of all the churches deliberately and authentically expressed.

The key to what I suppose were Dr. White's feelings and action
about the alterations, so far as they were now made, are to be
found in his desire to make what—adopting terms from our political
system—we may call a Federal Church as distinguished from a
variety of *State churches.* He writes to the Rev. Mr. Parker,
August 6th, 1787 :†

---

* See *supra*, page 166.
† Perry's "Half Century of Legislation." Vol. I., pp. 35, 36.

I am most sincerely desirous of seeing our Church throughout these States united in *one* Ecclesiastical Legislature, and I think that any difficulties which have hitherto seemed in the way might be removed by mutual forbearance. If there are any further difficulties than those I allude to, of difference in opinion, they do not exist with me : and I shall be always ready to do what lies in my power to bring all to an agreement.

In the great opportunities for observation which his chaplaincy to the Congress had given him, he had seen the immense injury which the nation suffered prior to 1789 from the want of an effective general government, and he had seen, too, the immense difficulties, arising from local aims and jealousies, of effecting such a government. He saw the same exact two things in the Church, and therefore, in his mind, the first thing to be accomplished, and this even before the consecration of *any* bishop, was an UNION of all the churches.

He has explained the matter himself.* "Certainly," says he, "the different Episcopalian congregations knew of no union before the Revolution except what was the result of the connection which they had in common with the Bishop of London," and he adds :

The authority of that Bishop being withdrawn, what right had the Episcopalians in any State, or in any part of it, to choose a Bishop for those in any other? And till an union was effected, what is there in Christianity generally, or in the principles of this Church in particular, to hinder them from taking different courses in different places as to all things not necessary to salvation? which might have produced different liturgies, different articles, episcopacy from different sources, and, in short, very many churches, instead of one extending over the United States ; and this without any ground for schism, or of the invasion of one another's rights.

When Dr. White looked at South Carolina, he saw a church called Episcopal with what he rightly calls "an opposition to the very principle of episcopacy," and which made it a condition of coming into the church convention of 1785 that no Bishop should be settled in that State.† When he looked at Virginia, he saw a commonwealth whose House of Burgesses, most of whose members professed to be churchmen, not long before the Revolution thanking different writers who sought to prevent the consecration

---

* Memoirs, page 98, 2d edition.   † White's Memoirs, pp. 95, 96.

15

of a Bishop for any part of America—"for the wise and well-timed opposition they had made to the pernicious project for introducing an American Bishop."* In Maryland was my ancestor, Dr. Smith, a man of strong individual views, a man who could hardly be expected to submit his great powers and large experience to one twenty years his junior, whom he remembered as his pupil at the age of seven years and till his adolescence, and who, in his recent tract of the " Episcopal Churches Considered," had himself, from accidental circumstances, been *much* misunderstood, and was supposed by some to be endangering that Episcopal government, which *we* well know that it was one of the greatest desires of his life to save and perpetuate. In New Jersey was the Rev. Uzal Ogden, an ambitious, troublesome man; never a churchman but in profession, and who at last, ceasing even a profession, became a Presbyterian outright; while close beside him, in the same State, the Rev. Thomas Bradbury Chandler, who had declined a Bishopric from Great Britain, a churchman as high as Laud, and with quite as much zeal and far more abilities than that diminutive Archbishop of Canterbury ever possessed. Finally, in Connecticut was " Samuel," soon to be " Samuel, Bishop of Connecticut," with his mitre and all the accessories of an English prelate—a glorious specimen, indeed, of a churchman—but no doubt, as Mr. Burke said of Admiral Keppel, "though never shewn in insult to any human being, *something high*," with ideas that the whole South would scout at and rebel against. How was the sober sense and faithful allegiance to his views of Benjamin Moore, in New York, and Abraham Beach and William Frazer, in New Jersey, and of Robert Blackwell and Samuel Magaw, in Pennsylvania, to solve and make mingle these elements apparently so immiscible? Dr. White, therefore, was ready to give up any mere forms, however much he liked them, to any one, if thereby *union* among all the churches could be attained. He was ready to retain any forms possible to be retained, if thereby that same result could be secured. It was with White and the Church as it was with Lincoln and the Union. The martyr President would continue slavery if it kept us one nation. He would declare emancipation if *that* secured the blessed end.† Hence when " Samuel, Bishop of Con-

---

* See Vol. I., page 388.

† The same heavenly temper was exhibited by the Bishop in 1836 on another

necticut" writes to Bishop White, in 1787, "proposing a personal interview with him and Bishop Provoost previously to any decided steps being taken respecting the Liturgy and Government of the Church, and mentioning the old Liturgy as the most likely bond of union," Bishop White, May 21st, 1787, with a foresight that in his day seems prophetic, replies:

There is nothing I have more at heart than to see the members of our communion, throughout the United States, connected in *one system* of Ecclesiastical government; and if my meeting of you, in concurrence with Bishop Provoost, can do anything towards the accomplishment of this great object, my very numerous engagements shall not hinder me from taking a journey for the purpose. . . . . .

If it should be thought advisable by the general body of our Church to adhere to the English Book of Common Prayer (the political parts excepted) I shall be one of the first, after the appearance of such a disposition, to comply with it *most punctually.*

Further than this, if it should seem the most probable way of maintaining an agreement among ourselves, *I shall use my best endeavors to effect it.* At the same time, I must candidly express my opinion, that the review of the liturgy would tend very much to the satisfaction of most of the members of our communion, and to its future success and prosperity. The worst evil which I apprehend from a refusal to review is this, that it will give a great advantage to those who wish to carry

---

occasion. A young man, the Rev. John Waller James—burning with apostolic zeal— had lately been invited to become Assistant Minister in Christ Church. The church was an ancient church, with high, old-fashioned square pews, and the congregation was composed of the aristocracy of Philadelphia. Mr. James had never ministered in any large city. In Christ Church, Meadville, where he had been before, was a young, very active, enthusiastic congregation. Mr. James was rather disappointed not to find exactly the same sort of spirit in the venerable cote of which he was now to take charge. He attributed what he thought a lack of zeal in part to the great high, old-fashioned pews of which we speak. At any rate, he thought them unsuited to modern necessities, and was earnestly desirous to change them to those common in the present day. A considerable portion of the congregation were of his inclination. He proposed to remodel the interior of the church. We can well conceive, after reading the passage which we have quoted (*supra*, page 217—note), describing his early connections with the pews and pulpit of this church, how such a proposition must have affected the venerable Bishop. But he made no opposition to the change. If it was thought by those around him to promote the spiritual interests of the congregation, he was ready to make it, however painful to his own feelings. The alterations were begun in the summer of 1836, but during their progress both Bishop White and Mr. James died. Neither ever saw the completion of them. As it turned out, the alterations did nothing to change the condition of the parish. Under such a man as Mr. James any parish, sooner or later, would have prospered, irrespectively of whether the parishioners sat in pews with high backs or pews with low ones

the alteration into essential points of doctrine.* Reviewed it will unquestionably be in some places, and the only way to prevent its being
done by men of the above description is the taking it up as a general
business.† I have been informed that you, sir, and our brethren in
Connecticut think a review expedient, although you wish not to be in
haste in the matter. Our brethren in Massachusetts have already done
it. The Churches in the States southward of you have sufficiently declared their sentiments; for even those which have delayed permitting

---

* This sort of alteration is exactly the sort which the authors of the so-called "Reformed Episcopal Church" who vouch Bishop White as authority for their liturgy,
have made in their service-book as last adopted. Of what pertinence to their case,
then, would it be—were it true, which it is not—that the Proposed Book was the
work of Bishop White solely or chiefly; that book, by universal concession, never having carried the alterations into any such points; and, on that account, having been
abandoned by the so-called "Reformed Episcopal Church."

What Bishop White would have thought of the *Episcopate* of the said "Church"
may be inferred from a passage in that great charge of his, "On the Sustaining of the
Unity of the Church, in Contrariety to Disorder, Disunion and Division," page 13. It
was delivered in 1831, in his sunset of life, when mystical lore enabled him fully to
see those coming events which, even then, cast their shadows before. He says:

"There is sometimes, in conversation, proposed the question whether in the event
of a consecration performed by one bishop only, the act would be valid? That with
us, such a bishop would do what is contrary to the obligations under which he has
placed himself in a solemn appeal to God for his sincerity and in a pledge given for
the same publicly to the Church, *and that the recipient of what is supposed to be of the
character conveyed is a partaker of the crime, is obvious.*

"Still there may be thought to remain the question of validity, and may be anticipated with apprehension as what, at some future time, may be found an easy expedient
for the introducing of division into the Church.

"Although the enormity has not been practised by any bishop of this Church, yet
there cannot be denied the possibility that it may occur hereafter, either with the
avowed abandonment of religious and moral principle *or by the operation of that sort
of professed piety which, in pursuance of what is supposed to be a righteous end, considers it as superseding the claims of integrity and truth.* What would be the effect,
then, of the form of consecration? In answer, the opinion is confidently expressed
that it would be A NULLITY.

. . . . "In certain supposable circumstances, the act of consecration by a single
bishop, disengaged from provisions not in themselves essential, is valid. But if a
bishop of our Church, which requires the concurrence of two of his brethren, should
set the requisition at defiance, in violation of his promise, pledged with an invocation
of the notice of the all-seeing eye of God, there is no hesitation in expressing the
opinion that the only effect would be THE GUILT attached to it."

† Exactly the same views were expressed by the Bishop forty-five years later. (See
his charge of 1831, "On the Sustaining of the Unity of the Church in Contrariety to
Disorder, Disunion and Division," p. 18.)

"It is also probable that extreme tenaciousness and reluctance to moderate alteration
will give vigor to the opposite extreme of ill-digested projects for reform without
measure and without end. We may foresee that if such a spirit should be dominant
in our Church it will be promotive of confusion and of every evil work. It should,

the use of the new book, did it merely on the principles of the want of Episcopal order among them.*

We thus see the relations of Dr. White to the matter of alterations in the liturgy.   The only part of the Proposed Book which we know that he *actively* opposed was, as we have already said, the introduction of a form of Thanksgiving for civil and religious liberty, to be used on the 4th of July.   And this apparently on a moral ground, because that service put some of the clergy, who had conscientiously opposed the Revolution, into an attitude which compelled them to utter sentiments which they did not feel.   We have quoted in our former volume † what he has recorded on that topic.   At the same time we know that he speaks of his "frequent collisions" with Dr. Smith, ‡ which, as their general relations were apparently harmonious and even affectionate, we must rather infer had relation to Dr. Smith's urgency for alterations in the Liturgy, and to his modes of effecting them, and of getting them introduced into the churches.

Mr. Charles Henry Wharton—the committee's third member— so well known now as Dr. Wharton, of Burlington, N. J., was a person different every way from either Dr. Smith or Dr. White. He was born in Maryland, of a family distinguished in the Church of Rome, and was educated at St. Omer's, in France, for the Romish priesthood, into which he was ordained and for some time officiated.   He was converted to the Protestant faith, as his Romish enemies alleged, by a beautiful woman, whom he afterwards married.§   He had no *special* affinities nor tastes for the liturgy of the Church of England.   He says in one letter: ‖

I think the simplifying of the liturgy should be among the first objects of the Convention.   Whatever was left with a view of reconciling parties at the period of the Reformation, or retained as suitable to

---

therefore, be guarded against not only by the vigilance and the discountenance, but also by the moderation of all who take pleasure in the peace and prosperity of our Zion."

* Perry's "Half Century of Legislation," Vol. I., pages 346, 347.

† Page 575.

‡ See Wilson's "Life of White," page 20.

§ This lady, who is buried in the grounds of St. Peter's Church, became insane; a judgment the papists—who dealt damnation round the land, on each they judged *their* foe—alleged for his apostacy from Rome.   His *arguments* they left unanswered.

‖ Perry's "Half Century of Legislation," Vol. I., page 107.

Cathedral service, may safely be omitted by the American Church.   Perhaps such an opportunity never occurred since the days of the Apostles of setting a rational, unexceptionable mode of worship.

He adds in another : *

If no alterations in the liturgy are to be made but such as the Revolution requires, there is little need to think much upon the subject, unless, perhaps, omissions be not deemed alterations.   My decided opinion is that our prayers are too numerous as well as the repetitions.   I shall draw up a motion on this head which I mean to make at the Convention, if you should approve it.

However, though a sound thinker in the main ; a very finished scholar, a true and elegant gentleman, and an able controversial *writer*, Dr. Wharton was no debater at all, nor, unless provoked, was his spirit in the least militant.   The habits of the cloister clung somewhat about him all his life, and his part in the Convention I do not suppose to have been very active.†

We hardly pardon him—who lived long at Worcester, England, and must have often enjoyed the service at its fine Cathedral—writing :

Whatever was retained (in the English liturgy) as suitable to Cathedral may safely be omitted by the American Church.

Why? were not services exactly those of the Cathedral and differing from the humblest parish church only in their choirs, to be performed in America?   And were not Cathedrals themselves —the Bishop's Church—soon to be demanded by the voice of the Church throughout our dioceses ? ‡

---

* Perry's " Half Century of Legislation," Vol. I., page 108.

† See Sprague's " Annals of the American Pulpit," Vol. V., page 335.

‡ On this very 26th of May, 1879, as I write, I open the *Living Church*, a journal of Illinois, and read from the *Western Church*, a journal of Chicago, this passage :

" The American Church longs for the constitutional fatherly government of its Fathers in God.   In manifold ways the heart of the Church demands it.   It wants a true Bishop's Church in the See city, in which the educational, charitable and missionary work of the See is to centre.   It needs for its cathedral chapter, a body in which every diocesan interest shall be represented, the diocese at large, the institutions, the missionary work, the city parishes, the cathedral clergy, the laity as well as the clergy. It needs the Bishop at the head of the chapter, the informing factor, the guiding principle, the Father of his Flock, the Bishop in the truly ordered See."

This would have been the language of Dr. Smith ; and *his* pen, I should think, would never have stricken out that ancient rubric of our mother Church—

" In choirs and places where they sing, here followeth the anthem."

Nevertheless, he was not inclined to see the old Prayer Book reduced to the dead level of modern American low churchmen. By an accident apparently, the Convention had obliterated all the Saints' days. In writing to Dr. White, he says:

Your idea of suiting the lessons to the several seasons of the ecclesiastical year agrees perfectly with mine. . . . As to the general Calendar I apprehend the Committee has power to alter it as the Convention judged proper to omit the Saints' days. I would be for retaining, however, the names of a few, such as *Lady Day, Michaelmas, All Saints*, with the *Apostles' Days, St. Stephen's* and *Innocents*. These three last being Scripture festivals should not be omitted, I mean a commemoration of Scriptural persons and martyrs. All Saints of more modern date should be expunged."

I have gone thus at large into the history of the Proposed Book and of the parts which different people had in its composition, because of the great ignorance prevailing and of the gross misrepresentations made on the subject. How completely all the great, essential doctrines of the Church of England are presented in it, and how little ground the preachers of the so-styled *Reformed Episcopal Church*, who have referred to it as justifying their schism, have had for their reference to it, will appear sufficiently in these pages.

In addition to his great labor in the matter of the Proposed Book, Dr. Smith was chairman of the two other principal committees appointed by the convention of 1785; one of them being to prepare a draft, the form of an Ecclesiastical Constitution for the Protestant Episcopal Church in the United States of America; the other for preparing and reporting a plan for obtaining the consecration of Bishops, together with an Address to the Most Reverend the Archbishops and the Right Reverend the Bishops of the Church of England for that purpose.

We may reasonably infer, too, that, perhaps, with some reduction of force, it might have, expressed the views of Bishop White, who, in his charge of 1831, after saying that, in his view, a Bishop should not be made to take full charge of any parish, and that a third part of the parochial duty of any church of which a Bishop was Rector should be performed by an assistant, says:

" But when there are taken into the account our rapidly increasing population with which we may hope for a proportionate increase of our Church, it cannot be useless to keep in view *a matured system of a higher grade than our present provisions, and to be accomplished by degrees*, although the *full* accomplishment be so distant that the youngest among us may not be expected to witness it, while they may subserve it by incipient measures."

Though the labor of preparing and drafting the Ecclesiastical Constitution did not fall largely upon Dr. Smith, he was bound, of course, as chairman of his committee, to give to it his intelligent thought and care; and though, in the other committee, a large, perhaps the larger, share of labor was borne by others, we have, in petitions drafted by his own pen, the record of his work. The first address to the English Bishops was drawn by Dr. White. Its date is October 5th, 1785. The Proposed Book had not yet been seen by the English Bishops, and reports had got abroad exaggerating the alterations that had been made and misstating some matters of importance. The English Bishops, in a communication to the clerical and lay members, dated London, February 24th, 1786, and filled with expressions of kindness, stated that, while they were disposed to make every allowance for the difficulties which embarrassed the Convention of 1785, they could not help being afraid that in the proceedings of that convention some alterations in the Liturgy had been adopted or intended which those difficulties did not seem to justify. They proceed:

Those alterations are not mentioned in your address; and as our knowledge of them is no more than what has reached us through private and less certain channels, we hope you will think it just both to you and to ourselves if we wait for an explanation. For while we are anxious to give every proof not only of our brotherly affection, but of our facility in forwarding your wishes, we cannot but be extremely cautious least we should be the instruments of establishing an ecclesiastical system which will be called a branch of the Church of England, but afterwards may possibly appear to have departed from it essentially either in doctrine or in discipline.

Dr. Smith drafted a reply, although before being sent it was considerably modified by Mr. Jay, one of the convention, never much of a churchman, we may add, and of a disposition possibly somewhat jealous,* who thought its terms rather obsequious.

---

* See Mr. Jay's Remarks on "Induction"—"Life of John Jay," vol. I., pp. 434–442; and his correspondence with Judge Peters on the subject of Hamilton's relations to the formation of Washington's Farewell Address. Nothing, I think, but some latent jealousy of the great first Secretary of the Treasury could have induced so unfortunate an argument as that contained in Mr. Jay's letter to Judge Peters of March 29th, 1811—an argument completely demolished by the great paper of Horace Binney on the formation of the Farewell Address. See "Memoirs of the Historical Society of Pennsylvania," vol. I., page 249, and Mr. Binney's Essay.

The body of its ideas were retained. We give it here, more especially as it shows that Dr. Smith was not obstinately set in favor of his new book, but was ready to receive, as he afterwards did receive, and at once adopt many suggestions for its improvement.

To the Most Reverend and Right Reverend Fathers in GOD, the Archbishops and Bishops of the Church of England:

MOST WORTHY AND VENERABLE PRELATES!
The clerical and lay deputies of the Protestant Episcopal Church in the States of New York, New Jersey, Pennsylvania, Delaware, Maryland, Virginia and South Carolina, this day assembled in Convention in Christ Church, Philadelphia, had the honour to receive your letter dated London, February 24th, 1786, in answer to their address of October 5th, 1785.

Your Christian condescension and goodness, on this occasion, have filled our hearts with the most lively sentiments of gratitude; and we desire to offer our thankful acknowledgments to your venerable Body, for having taken the earliest opportunity of attending to our address, with that true and affectionate regard which you have always shown to that branch of the Episcopal Church planted by your great and pious Predecessors in America. We are, moreover, greatly encouraged by the fatherly assurance you give us that "nothing is nearer your heart than the wish to promote our spiritual welfare; to be instrumental in procuring for us the complete exercise of our holy religion, and the enjoyment of that ecclesiastical constitution which we sincerely believe to be truly apostolical, and for which (we trust) the most unreserved veneration will ever be maintained by our Church in America." We are also happy to be further assured that, on your " parts, you will use your best endeavours (which you give us hopes will be successful) to acquire a legal capacity of complying with the prayer of our address."

The Joy which we feel on this occasion would therefore be complete, were it not for the apprehensions you, our venerable Fathers, have suggested to us, "that in the proceedings of our last convention some alterations may have been adopted or intended which the difficulties of our situation do not seem to justify;" but we are greatly comforted, at the same time, by the kind assurance which you give us, and our firm dependence on your goodness, "that you are disposed to make every allowance which candor can suggest for those difficulties; and that you think it just, both to yourselves and to us, to wait for an explanation."

Nevertheless, while we regret that any difficulties have arisen from misrepresentations of our proceedings through any private or uncertain channels; we are, at the same time, greatly edified with the caution exhibited to us, by those whom we revere as the chief Guardians and

Depositories, under GOD, of the doctrines of the Church, whereof we profess ourselves members.

From those doctrines no essential deviations were intended by the convention, and we are confident it will appear that none have been made in the book which hath been proposed, and which we thought it but just and candid to publish to the world, and particularly to have it presented to your Lordships before any Clergyman nominated to the office of a Bishop among us should be sent to you for consecration. In the meantime it was to be our endeavour to remove as far as possible every objection that might remain or be apprehended among our Civil Rulers; to which we believe nothing could more contribute than an open and candid publication of the Alterations which seemed necessary or expedient, either in a civil or religious view. We conceived, moreover, that this declaration of our doctrines and public worship would contribute effectually to do away any prejudices against our Church, which may still be found among our fellow-citizens at large; these prejudices, we are persuaded, are few and inconsiderable. For some time past they have happily been subsiding, and your Lordships will undoubtedly approve of every measure which a sister Church can adopt towards completing the circle of Christian Charity and forbearance.

Some alterations became necessary upon the principles set forth in the preface to the proposed Book of Common Prayer; but we apprehend that there are none such as can induce your venerable Body to consider us as having adopted "an ecclesiastical system which will be called a branch of the Church of England, but which may appear to have departed from it essentially either in doctrine or discipline." We have already expressed our hope that there is no such departure, or, should it appear to your Lordships that there is any, we shall be happy to have it pointed out to us.

Our book is only a proposal, although we must say it is a very acceptable one to those of our Church who have had the greatest opportunity of being made acquainted with it. But we have not established it, nor do we consider ourselves as having authority so to do in the Churches of any of these States till they are fully organized and have their Bishops in Council and Government with them. When those shall be sent for consecration to the Church of England, they will be informed in what points, if any, there may appear to be essential deviations either in doctrine or discipline; and they, as well as the Conventions in the different States, will undoubtedly pay all that deference to your exalted characters which we know to be necessary for maintaining a perpetual harmony and union with the Church of England in all essentials.

We therefore Pray, That as our Church, in sundry States, hath already proceeded with nominations of Bishops and in others may soon proceed with the same; you will be pleased to give us as speedy an answer to this, our second address, as in your fatherly regard you were pleased to give to our former one; as it is our wish that some at least of the persons nominated should embark for England, so as to put themselves under your protection and patronage, against the meeting of Parliament next winter.   We are with great and sincere Respect

Most worthy and venerable Prelates.

It is no part of our purpose to give an ecclesiastical history of the day further than as Dr. Smith was connected with it. Suffice it, therefore, to say that when the Proposed Book was received in England—while the Bishops expressed their regret at several verbal alterations of the necessity or propriety of which they were not satisfied, and saw with grief that the Nicene and Athanasian creeds had been omitted—they did not deny that the essential doctrines of the faith, common to the two churches, had been retained. Strange to add, the principal thing faulted apparently by the Bishops was the omission of the passage in the Apostles' Creed which affirms the descent of Christ into Hell—an affirmation confessedly inserted but as a contradiction of an early heresy and without Scriptural authority beyond the passage in the First Epistle of St. Peter iii. 19, 20, speaking of Christ's preaching unto the spirits in prison; a passage considerably involved in obscurity, as all will agree. It subsequently appeared, moreover, that even this ground of objection was much urged apparently by no one but the Bishop of Bath and Wells; a venerable prelate, we may indeed admit, eminent as well for his theological learning as for his exemplary life and conversation; but not one who should have had power to enforce an objection, the least weighty of several, none of which were very weighty, that might have been made.

The changes chiefly desired by the English Bishops (except an adoption of the Athanasian Creed) were made by the convention almost *suâ sponte* upon the suggestion of them, and our Bishops were consecrated while the Proposed Book thus altered was before the Church for adoption, if the respective dioceses liked it.

While Dr. Smith was at Huntingdon, Pennsylvania, where he owned a large body of lands which he had gone to look after, Dr. White received from England communications from the two Archbishops expressing the regrets above mentioned, but withal giving a general assurance that the desired consecration would be given; expressing their hope that a change on the subject above mentioned as unsatisfactory would be made.

Dr. White immediately by letter informed Dr. Smith of the communications received from the two Archbishops, and that the Committee of Correspondence, to whom power had been given to call a General Convention, had called it to meet at Wilmington, in Delaware, on the 10th of October, 1786. Dr. Smith replies as follows :

Rev. Dr. Smith to Rev. Dr. White.

LANCASTER, August 18th, 1786, 4 o'clock P. M.

DEAR SIR : At Carlisle, on my return from Juniata, on the 15th instant, I received your letter giving me an account of the last communications from the two Archbishops of England. I had never any doubt but that on seeing our Book, such great and liberal Prelates as they are known to be would take a pleasure to protect and patronize our Church, as a great and growing branch of their own.

I presume any advice I could give concerning the calling of the Convention would be now too late, as a majority of the Committee have approved the measure. If that be the case, I can have no objection either to the time or place of meeting. But I can see little use in giving the Convention the trouble to meet in pursuance of anything which you have mentioned to me from the letter of the Archbishops. There can be no doubt of a general compliance with the alterations they recommend (the Athanasian creed excepted) whenever any new edition of the Prayer Book shall be directed by a convention having ecclesiastical and spiritual authority to ratify a book for our Church. And till such convention can be had (which certainly will not be next October) we have already determined not to enter upon the consideration of any amendments or alterations whatever. Should we take up those hinted by the Archbishops, how shall we refuse to go upon those also which have been proposed by different State Conventions? And may we not then at the end of next Convention, at Wilmington (could we possibly get *seven* States together in October), leave our Book in a far more exceptionable point of view with those Prelates, and many of our own Church, than it now is? For I think it stands now with as few objections to it both in America, and for what appears, in England, as ever it will. There are also some things proposed or recommended by the Archbishops which cannot be complied with by some States at all, or at least not without calling their conventions, and perhaps altering some part of their ecclesiastical constitutions, all which would require more time than to October, and probably would be productive of much confusion.

However, you and the other members of the Committee will find me ready to meet every difficulty, and to do my utmost for the general good of the Church, but I think we have no difficulties left unless we create them among ourselves.

Much do we owe to the two worthy Archbishops. I need not write more. I am pushing to be home on Sunday, and will strive to be at Philadelphia about Wednesday next, the 23d instant.   .   .   .   .

In haste, yours,   WM. SMITH.

REV. DR. WHITE.

After receiving intelligence from Dr. White of the letter from the Archbishops, two letters came by the same packet: one to Dr. White and one to Dr. Smith, from the Rev. *Alexander Murray,* prior to the Revolution a missionary of the S. P. G., and who, though returning to England on the Declaration of Independence, ever felt a warm interest in the ecclesiastical welfare of the colonies. Both letters were under cover to Dr. Smith. The one to Dr. White, and a letter from Dr. Smith to Dr. Wharton enclosing it, here follow:

Rev. Dr. Murray to the Rev. Dr. White.

LONDON, July 28, 1786.

DEAR SIR: Your favor of 4th April I received the 5th instant, *viâ* Liverpool, with the remaining parts of your liturgy; but I had before then, just as the June packet was ready to sail for New York, taken the liberty to remind the Archbishop of your Church concerns, and he wrote you accordingly by that opportunity which made it unnecessary for me also to advise you that your consecration bill had at last been passed, though late, owing to your own delays. This you had besides announced in all our newspapers by the packet. I waited then to send you the act printed. I pressed it twice a week, and with some threats. In the end I expect it in a few days. But as the " Mediator," for your port, is to sail to-morrow I thought it proper in the meantime to give you the material parts of the act, which is that it gives authority to either of our Archbishops to consecrate Bishops for foreign nations, "who profess the worship of Almighty God according to the *principles* of the Church of England, they having the good learning, soundness of faith, and purity of manners of the candidates ascertained to them," (the Bishops.) The other parts of the act are much the same with that for consecrating priests, which I sent you. I need hardly remark the liberal catholic spirit the act is stamped with. It leaves room for admitting local differences in lesser matters which affect not the vitals of our holy religion and the constitution of our Apostolic Episcopal Church.

.   .   .   .

Yours affectionately,
ALEXANDER MURRAY.*

REV. DR. WHITE.

---

* For a sketch of this minister of our Colonial Church, see Appendix No. III.

Rev. Dr. Smith to Rev. Dr. White.

CHESTER, September 11, 1786.

DEAR SIR: The enclosed is from Dr. Murray, but I suppose can contain nothing new, as mine which accompanied it is of an older date than our last from the Archbishop of Canterbury. If you have anything further of importance to communicate, or when you have I shall expect to hear from you. I shall go over to Annapolis next week, which, being at the election of the Senate, will give me an opportunity of doing some necessary business with gentlemen whom I could not otherwise meet till November. ' I would wish to have a little time before the General Convention to think of what may be proper to be done, or can with propriety be done, respecting the requisitions of the English Bishops. You know my apprehensions, etc. I hope you will bestow your serious thoughts upon the business, viewing it in proper lights.

Yours,   WILLIAM SMITH.

REV. DR. WHITE,
   Rector of Christ Church, Philadelphia.

The Convention called for Wilmington, assembled there, as invited, on the 10th of October, 1786. It lasted but two days. The letters of the English Archbishops being taken into consideration, *The Descent into Hell*—the expression of a belief in which had been omitted from the Apostles' Creed as given in the Proposed Book—was restored by a majority, to the liturgy. The Nicene Creed was restored by unanimous vote. The Athanasian was voted against—seventeen votes to three. The States were rather curiously divided on the subject of the admission of this last creed. In New Jersey the only persons favoring its readmission were laymen, Henry Waddell and Joshua Maddox Wallace, Esqs., voting for its admission against the clergy of the State— Mr. Uzal Ogden and the excellent William Frazier, of Amwell. In Delaware its support came from one clergyman, the Rev. Sydenham Thorne; he voting against the laity and the Rev. Dr. Wharton. The vote of Pennsylvania, clergy and laity alike, went solidly against the restoration. Maryland took no part in any of these questions from the fact of not being represented in this Convention.

In this Convention, Dr. White, Dr. Provoost and Dr. Griffith were recommended to the English Bishops by the members of this Convention for consecration to the Episcopal orders. Little or no mention is made of Dr. Smith in the proceedings of this short assembly, beyond his appointment (after Dr. Provoost, who was President of the Convention) on a committee, a majority of which had power to call a General Convention to meet in Philadelphia, and beyond what is disclosed in the following extract from the minutes themselves :

It was moved and seconded, that a Committee be appointed to draft a letter from this Convention, to the Archbishops of England, in answer to their late letters.

And the following gentlemen were appointed accordingly—Dr. Smith, Dr. White and Dr. Wharton.

This Committee retired, and after some time returned and reported a letter, which, after a few amendments, was agreed to as follows :

TO THE ARCHBISHOPS OF CANTERBURY AND YORK.

MOST WORTHY AND VENERABLE PRELATES:

In pursuance of your Graces' communications to the Standing Committee of our Church, received by the June packet, and the letter of his Grace the Archbishop of Canterbury of July the 4th, enclosing the Act of Parliament "to empower the Archbishop of Canterbury, or the Archbishop of York, for the time being, to consecrate to the office of a Bishop, persons being subjects or citizens of countries out of his Majesty's dominions," a General Convention, now sitting, have the honor of offering their unanimous and hearty thanks for the continuance of your Christian attention to this Church, and particularly for your having so speedily acquired a legal capacity of complying with the prayer of our former addresses.

We have taken into our most serious and deliberate consideration the several matters so affectionately recommended to us in those communications, and whatever could be done towards a compliance with your fatherly wishes and advice, consistently with our local circumstances, and the peace and unity of our Church, hath been agreed to, as, we trust, will appear from the enclosed Act of our Convention, which we have the honor to transmit to you, together with the Journal of our proceedings.

We are, with great and sincere respect,

Most worthy and venerable prelates,

Your obedient and very humble servants,

(By order)   SAMUEL PROVOOST, *President.*

IN GENERAL CONVENTION:

At Wilmington, in the State of Delaware,
          October 11, 1786.

What I suppose to be the original draft of this document thus signed, which is before me, is in the handwriting of Dr. Smith, Chairman of the Committee.

On the 24th of October, 1786, a Convention of the Protestant Episcopal Church in Maryland met at Annapolis, in that State, and chose Dr. Smith its President. The following instrument of writing was laid before the Convention, and is entered among its proceedings, viz. :

STATE OF MARYLAND, CHESTER PARISH, KENT COUNTY,
In Vestry, 19th of October, 1786.

TO WHOM IT MAY CONCERN:

Whereas, the Rev. WILLIAM SMITH, D. D., rector or minister of this Parish, and Principal of Washington College, in the same, hath communicated to us an instrument of writing certifying his nomination or election to the office of Bishop by his brethren, the Protestant Episcopal clergy of this State, in Convention met, and due notice hath been given of the same in our Parish Church, immediately after Divine Service on the Lord's Day, to the intent that if any notable cause or impediment, touching his sufficiency in learning, soundness in the faith and purity of manners, could be shown why he should not be consecrated to that sacred office, the same might be made known to us. Now we do think it our duty, in the most solemn manner, hereby to declare and testify that no such cause or impediment hath been made known to us: and further, that the said William Smith hath for six years last past been personally and intimately known to us as the minister of this parish, during which time he hath been regarded and distinguished among us as an orthodox, learned and truly evangelical preacher, yielding us both satisfaction and edification by his ministry, doctrine and conversation. We further testify that during that period he hath also acquitted himself with such zeal and abilities in the general service of the Church, and in laying permanent foundations for the advancement and support of religion and learning in this State, that we consider him as a benefactor to our country and worthy of its regard and esteem.

JOHN SCOTT,
R. BUCHANAN,
JERE. NICHOLS,
ST. LEGER EVERITT,   *Vestry.*
SIMON WILMER,
JNO. TILDEN KENNARD,
MARMADUKE TILDEN.
JOHN STURGES, *Church-Warden.*

The Convention then adjourned to meet at Chestertown, on the fourth Tuesday in May, 1787.

CHAPTER XLIX.

NOT to interrupt the unity of a narrative of some length about the General Conventions, Proposed Book, etc., we have comprehended two or three years in the last preceding chapters, without much reference to other matters. But with Dr. Smith's active mind and active hands and active frame, there were always works collateral to his main work, and these, operating on the sides of his *opus magnum*, whatever this last might be, he was always carrying on as steadily as he was the great work itself.

To a few of these in the years 1784, 1785 and 1786 we will now advert. On the 26th of October, 1784, a Convention of the Clergy and Lay Delegates of the Episcopal Church in Maryland was held at Chestertown, in Maryland. Dr. Smith presided, and the Rev. William West acted as secretary. The Rev. Messrs. Andrews, Keene, Thompson and McPherson were present. The following additional Constitutions respecting the future discipline and government of the Church in Annual or General Conventions were agreed upon, viz.:

I. General Conventions of this Church, consisting of the different

16

orders of clergy and laity duly represented (agreeably to the *Fourth Constitution* aforesaid) shall have the general cognizance of all affairs, necessary to the discipline and good government of this Church, including particularly the following matters, viz. : The power and authority necessary for receiving, or excluding from Church privileges, scandalous members, whether lay or clerical, and all jurisdiction with regard to offenders ; the power of suspending or dismissing clergymen from the exercise of their ministry in this Church ; the framing, approving of, or confirming all canons, or laws, for Church government; and such alterations, or reforms, in the Church service, liturgy, or points of doctrine, as may be afterwards found necessary or expedient, by our Church in this State, or of the United States in General Convention. And in all matters that shall come before the Convention, the clergy and laity shall deliberate in one body; but if any vote shall be found necessary, or be called for by any two members, they shall vote separately; that is to say, the clergy in their different orders, according to their own rules, shall have one vote ; and the laity, according to their rules, shall have another vote ; and the *concurrence* of both shall be necessary to give validity to any measure.

II. Future Conventions shall frame and establish rules, or canons, for receiving complaints; and shall annually appoint a committee, consisting of an equal number of clergy and laity (including the bishop, when there shall be one duly consecrated, among the number of the clergy), which committee shall have standing authority, government, and jurisdiction, agreeably to such rules as may be given them for that purpose, in all matters respecting the discipline and government of the Church, that may arise or be necessary to be proceeded upon, during the recess or adjournment of General Conventions: all which rules shall be framed, and jurisdiction exercised in conformity to the Constitution and Laws of this State for the time being.*

The reader will have already noted how broad and comprehensive was the cast of Dr. Smith's churchmanship. We have seen in our first volume † that he was inclined to bring into the Church —if the Bishop of London approved of the idea—the whole of the Lutheran clergy in Pennsylvania. He was equally desirous, and

---

* In the copy of these additional constitutions in the collection of early journals in the possession of the present Bishop of Iowa—Dr. Perry—which, though evidently inserted after the rest of the pamphlet was printed, is continuously paged with the preceding sheets, the words " or general " in the heading, and " the following matters, viz.," in paragraph I. are omitted ; the parenthetical clause " (of all orders) " is added to the assertion of "the power of suspending or dismissing clergymen; " and the words " or rule " appended at the close of the paragraph. There are several variations in typography, which, as they do not at all affect the sense, it is hardly important to notice.
  † Page 403.

even more so, to prevent the divisions made by the Wesleys from becoming permanent. While he could not see in the state of the English Church even in the days of those zealous souls, any justification or even any excuse for their conduct, and although no schism was then yet contemplated, he could not fail to discern how that the then existing state might naturally enough induce such "experience and practice" as they had brought about. And as America seemed the field on which the Wesleys, Whitefield, Coke, and Asbury were likely to reach their greatest success, and as our untutored thousands—black and white—were a class in more danger of being captivated than the better instructed, even if too much neglected, people of England—Dr. Smith watched, with the most lively attention, all that the leaders of this sect were doing, and earnestly sought to effect a return to a state of juncture with them; if, without a sacrifice of the great principles of the Church, such a return could be accomplished. The following letter illustrates his interest in the matter. Its writer was the Rev. John Andrews,* a native of Maryland, but who graduated at the College of Philadelphia under Dr. Smith, was afterwards a tutor in the grammar school of the institution, and was now the worthy rector of St. Thomas' parish, Baltimore county, in the State of Maryland.

The Rev. John Andrews to Dr. Smith.

BALTIMORE, December 31, 1784.

DEAR SIR: I promised to give you some account of what should pass at our proposed conference with Dr. Coke. It is an account, however, which I fear will be no ways interesting, and from which at any rate you can derive little satisfaction.

At the appointed hour, which was six in the evening, he did not fail to attend us; and brought with him Mr. Goff and Mr. Asbury. We drank tea, and conversed on indifferent subjects. The doctor was full of vivacity and entertained us with a number of little anecdotes not disagreeably. At length I took occasion to observe, that we had seen Mr. Wesley's letter of September last addressed to Dr. Coke and Mr.

---

* In the year 1785, having received the degree of a Doctor of Divinity from his old master's new college—Washington—at Chestertown, Dr. Andrews returned to Philadelphia, where, at a later date, he was made at first (A. D. 1789) a Professor in the University of Pennsylvania, afterwards (A. D. 1791) Vice-Provost, and finally (A. D. 1810) Provost of the same. He continued in that office till February, 1813. He died on the 29th of the following month.

Asbury; as also a book entitled, "The Sunday Service of the Methodists:" that we were happy to find from these publications that the
people called Methodists were hereafter to use the same liturgy that we
make use of, to adhere to the same articles, and to keep up the same *three
orders of the clergy;* that these circumstances had induced us to hope,
that the breach which had so long subsisted in our Church might at
length, in America at least, be happily closed : that we could not think
so unfavorably of the gentlemen who were at the head of that society,
as to suppose they could persist in *separating* from us, merely for the
sake of *separating;* or cherish in their breasts so unkind a spirit, as
would not suffer them even in doing of the very same things that we do,
to have any satisfaction without doing them in a different manner; with
such variations in point of form and other circumstances, as may create
an invidious distinction where there is no real difference : that the plan
of Church government which we had instituted in this State, was a very
simple, and, as we trusted, a very rational plan : that it was to be exercised by a convention consisting of an equal number of laity and clergy;
and having for their president a bishop elected by the whole body of
the clergy : that this bishop was to differ from a common presbyter in
nothing else than in the right of presiding in the Convention, of ordaining ministers, and administering confirmation after baptism to as
many as desired it : that such an episcopacy, at the same time that it
possessed all the powers requisite for spiritual purposes, would not upon
any occasion or to any person be either dangerous or burdensome. It
could not be said to *entangle* men more than Mr. Wesley's episcopacy
entangled them. What occasion then could there be for a separation
from us on the score of government? And as to articles of faith and
form of worship, they already agreed with us. If it would not be so
grateful to them to have their preachers ordained by a presbyter taken
from among us and *consecrated a bishop,* what hindered but that Dr.
Coke might be so *consecrated?* We could see no impropriety in having
two bishops in one State, one of which might always be elected from
among the people called Methodists, so long as that distinction should
be kept up among us.

To all this Dr. Coke made the following reply : That indeed he scarce
knew what answer to give us; as such an address had neither been foreseen nor expected : that any propositions, however, that we should
think proper to make on the subject he could transmit to Mr. Wesley.
Perhaps we were strangers to their itinerant and circuitous maxims : that
it was not proposed that any of their ministers should ever have a fixed
residence : and that for his own part he was inclined to think that our
two churches might not improperly be compared to a couple of earthen
basins set afloat in a current of water, which, so long as they should
continue to float in two parallel lines, would float securely : but the moment they began to converge were in danger of destroying each other.

Mr. Asbury was pleased to add—that the difference between us lay not so much in doctrines and forms of worship as in experience and practice. He complained that the Methodists had always been treated by us with abundance of contempt ; and that for his own part, though he had travelled over all parts of this continent, there were but four clergymen of our Church, from whom he had received any civilities. In expressing these sentiments, however, he did not mean to throw any reflection upon Mr. West and myself, whom, from the accounts he had received concerning us, he regarded as worthy characters.

Mr. West begged it might be well understood, that in holding this discourse with them, we acted altogether in a private capacity, *wholly unauthorized so to do by the Church to which we belonged;* and that in his opinion, the only material point to which it concerned us at present to enquire into was simply this—*Was the plan upon which the Methodists were now proceeding to act, irrevocably fixed?* Dr. Coke answered, *that there was no person who took more time than Mr. Wesley to deliberate upon his plans, and none who after he had deliberated upon them was more prompt and decided in the execution of them.*

Upon this the subject was dropped, and in a short time after they took their leave of us.

A day or two after I took the liberty to wait on Dr. Coke at his lodgings. I expressed a wish, that they could be induced to give rise to their orders in a regular manner; and this I observed they might do, and yet still continue to manage their own affairs, and remain as distinct a body from us as they might think proper. If they did not esteem it unlawful to *connect the succession,* I contended, that it was their duty *to connect it,* from motives of charity and of policy. By such compliance their departure from their brethren would be less considerable, and they would have fewer prejudices to encounter with.

Dr. Coke did not hesitate to acknowledge, *that it would be more consistent indeed, and more regular to connect the succession;* and that the time was when the Methodists might have been gained by a little condescension. But it was now too late to think of these things, when their plans were already adopted and in part even executed ; that he himself had received ordination agreeably to this *new system,* and conferred it on others. He set forth in his turn the great contempt and aversion with which the Methodists had always been treated in England, by the generality of the bishops, as well as by the laity and clergy; that when one of their preachers had an inclination to come over to this country with Lord Cornwallis' army under the character of a chaplain, Mr. Wesley could not prevail on the Bishop of London to ordain him ; that some clergymen of the Church of England, who had ventured to perform service in the Countess of Huntingdon's chapel had been prosecuted in the Court of Arches; that Bishop Newton in his last dying charge to his clergy solemnly enjoined them, that they should never cease to

oppose the Methodists: and upon the whole that such was the temper
of the English prelates, that they would much rather choose that the
whole body of the Methodists in England, though so very numerous,
should be lost to the Church by a total separation, than that they should
continue any longer with it.

To those particulars I made the best reply that I was able, apologized
for the great trouble I had given them, and then took my leave of them
in the most friendly and affectionate manner.

Thus ended our negotiation which served no other purpose than to
discover to us, that the minds of *these gentlemen are not wholly free from
resentment*, and it is a point which among them is indispensably necessary *that Mr. Wesley be the first link of the chain upon which their Church
is suspended.*

Although, as Dr. Andrews observes, Dr. Smith could not derive
much satisfaction from a letter which revealed nothing so much
as the fact that the estrangement of Coke from the Church was
likely to become a schism,—one, too, founded on the *spretæ injuria
formæ* much more than on an earnest contention for any faith ever
delivered to the saints—this effort at reunion was not without results of a permanently historic kind. The feelings of these gentlemen—whose separation was so much animated by "personal resentment"—came under the influence of that great physician Time.
Before many years they were "pricked in their hearts" and went
to a friend of Smith to inquire "what they should do."

The following letter (of 1791) of Mr. Coke to Bishop White, is
a memorable document indeed; its confessions and aspirations but
the *sequelæ* of the efforts made in 1784 and narrated as above, by
the Rev. Mr. Andrews:

RICHMOND, April 24, 1791.

RIGHT REVEREND SIR: Permit me to intrude a little on your time
upon a subject of great importance.

You, I believe, are conscious that I was brought up in the Church of
England, and have been ordained a presbyter of that Church. For
many years I was prejudiced, even I think, to bigotry in favor of it: but
through a variety of causes and incidents, to mention which would be
tedious and useless, my mind was exceedingly biassed on the other side
of the question. In consequence of this, I am not sure but I went
further *in the separation* of our Church in America than Mr. Wesley,
from whom I had received my commission, did intend. He did indeed
solemnly invest me, *as far as he had a right so to do*, with Episcopal
authority, but did not intend, I think, that our entire separation should

take place.   He being pressed by our friends on this side the water for ministers to administer the sacraments to them (there being very few clergy of the Church of England then in the States), *he went farther, I am sure, than he would have gone if he had foreseen some events which followed.*   And this I am certain of—*that he is now sorry for the separation.*

But what can be done for a re-union, which I wish for; and to accomplish which Mr. Wesley, I have no doubt, would use his influence to the utmost?   The affection of a very considerable number of the preachers and most of the people is very strong towards him, notwithstanding *the excessive ill usage he received from a few.*   My interest also is not small; and both his and mine would readily and to the utmost be used to accomplish that (to us) very desirable object; if a readiness were shown by the bishops of the Protestant Episcopal Church to re-unite.

. . . . . .   But there are many hindrances in the way.   Can they be removed?

1.   Our ordained ministers will not—ought not to—give up their right of administering the sacraments.   I do not think that the generality of them, perhaps none of them, would refuse to submit to a re-ordination if other hindrances were removed out of the way.   I must here observe that between sixty and seventy out of the two hundred and fifty have been ordained presbyters, and about sixty deacons only.   The presbyters are the choicest of the whole.

2.   The other preachers would hardly submit to a re-union if the possibility of their rising up to ordination depended on the present bishops of America.   Because though they are *all*, I may say, zealous, pious and very useful men, yet they are not acquainted with the learned languages. Besides, they would argue, If the present bishops would waive the article of the learned languages, yet their successors might not.

My desire of a re-union is so sincere and earnest that these difficulties almost make me tremble, and yet something must be done before the death of Mr. Wesley, otherwise I shall despair of success; for though my influence among the Methodists in these States, as well as in Europe, is increasing, yet Mr. Asbury, whose influence is very capital, will not easily comply—nay, I know he will be exceedingly averse to it.

In Europe, where some steps had been taken tending to a separation, all is at an end.   Mr. Wesley is a determined enemy of it, and I have lately borne an open and successful testimony against it.

Shall I be favored with a private interview with you in Philadelphia? I shall be there, God willing, on Tuesday, the 17th of May. . . .

In the meantime permit me with great respect to subscribe myself,

Right Reverend Sir,

Your very humble servant in Christ,

THOMAS COKE.

RIGHT REV. FATHER IN GOD, BISHOP WHITE.

On the 28th of April, 1785, the second commencement of Washington College was held. GEORGE WASHINGTON was present at it. The degree of A. B. was conferred upon the following gentlemen:

LAWSON ALEXANDER,   DANIEL MCCURTIN,
WILLIAM HEMSLEY,   SAMUEL KEENE, JR.,
EBEN. PERKINS,   ROBT. GOLDSBOROUGH,
                 THOMAS WORREL.

The second degree, that of A. M., was conferred upon

CHARLES SMITH,   JOHN SCOTT,
WILLIAM BORDLEY,   WILLIAM BANOLL,
                 REV. JOHN BOWIE.

The degree of D. D. was conferred upon

REV. JOHN GORDON,   REV. WILLIAM THOMSON,
REV. SAMUEL KEENE,   REV. JOHN CARROLL,*
REV. THOS. J. CLAGGETT, REV. JOHN ANDREWS,
REV. WILLIAM WEST,   REV. CHAS. HENRY WHARTON,
                 REV. PATRICK ALLISON.

The salutatory of this year was published with this title:

ORATIO SALUTATORIA

SUFFR. AMPLISS. FACULT PHILOS.

PRÆSIDE VIRO CELEBER,

DOMINO GULIEMO SMITH.

HABITA

IN ALMA ACAD., WASH.,

DIE DECIMO QUARTO MAII.

ANNO DOM. M.DCC.LXXXIII.

WILMINGTONI:

IMPRESSA A JACOBO ADAMS.

M.DCC.LXXXV.

While giving honors of the College, Dr. Smith was active in laying a strong basis for his distinctions in a college well endowed. We give a letter not dated—as it comes to us—but apparently of about this epoch.

---

* This gentleman was subsequently Archbishop of Baltimore.

Dr. Smith to Dr. West.

MY DEAR AND REV. SIR: Mr. Bowly will shew you the Baltimore Subscription Paper, begun here for the college. Yourself, the Rev. Mr. Sewell and Daniel Bowly, Thomas Yates, Thomas Russell, Luther Martin and David McMechin, Esqs., are nominated to take subscriptions and depute others in your town and county, in conjunction with Dr. Allison and Mr. Sterret, who are two of the agents, and have a right to open subscriptions themselves and to add any other persons they may think proper to those already named. The form of deputation Dr. Allison will see at the end of the subscription paper already began, and signed by Richard Ridgely, Daniel Bowly, Luther Martin, Thomas Yates. Mr. McMechin has subscribed the paper which was signed in the Senate and House of Delegates. Near *two thousand* pounds are subscribed in this town in twenty-four hours. Baltimore, no doubt, will far exceed any other place, nay, perhaps half this shore.

Considerable alterations were made in the plan first settled by Mr. Carroll, Dr. Allison and myself, respecting the *nice* provisos amongst different denominations in proportion to their *subscriptions*. The paper was printed off before I came over. But I was told by Carroll of Carrollton, Mr. Sprigg, etc., that the alterations were made in concert with Dr. Allison. I am satisfied, as I hope all our society will be, with the plan as it now is, and as I would have agreed it should originally have been, as I know that a *few grains* of mutual confidence and benevolence among different denominations of Christians will be better than splitting and torturing a design of this kind with all the provisos possible. Christian good will is not to be weighed out by *drams and scruples*. It should be *unconfined and universal.*

Please to deliver two of the blank subscriptions to Dr. Allison, and as Mr. Bowly is setting off, give the Doctor the *perusal* of this letter, as I cannot find time to write to him myself. Give the Rev. Mr. Sewell a subscription paper. Tell him that Mr. Digges will write to him, I believe, by Mr. Sprigg to-morrow, as I shall to Rev. Mr. Andrews. Carroll of Carrollton, Mr. Digges, etc., have subscribed liberally, as it is expected the rest of that society will do. I am, in haste,

Your affectionate brother,

WILLIAM SMITH.

REV. DR. WM. WEST.

On May 5th, 1785, Dr. Smith mentions in his diary his having attended the funeral of his old friend, Christian Frederick Post, at Germantown; returning to the city with Dr. White in his chair.*

---

* This reverend man, the most adventurous of Moravian missionaries employed among the North American Indians, was born at Conitz, Polish Prussia, in 1710. He emigrated to this country in June, 1742. Between 1743 and 1749 he was a mission-

We have now a letter from an old friend remaining in Pennsylvania:

Dr. Muhlenberg to Dr. Smith.

NEW PROVIDENCE, PENNA., May 7th, 1785.

VIRO MAXIME REVERENDO,
DOCTORI SMIDIO, FAUTORI SUO HONORATISSIMO,
   S. Pl. D. H. M. P. T. Candidatus Mortis.

To my comfort, your worthy son, *Juris Consultus, isque nobilissimus*, condescended to see me at my journey's end, being no more fit to converse with learned gentlemen, because I have almost lost the *organa sensoria* and *spiritus vitalis*. I am glad to understand that your noble son intends to reside here in our neighborhood, since it may, as often I shall see him, revive my memory with gratitude to remember the benevolence of his honorable parents towards me in times past.

In the month of October last I received a letter from the Rev. Dr. Wrangel, dated at Sahle in Sweden, in which he demandeth of me as follows :

If the Rev. Dr. Smith liveth, present my best compliments to him. I have wrote to him several times. I translated his sermon into Swedish on the beginning of the war, and presented it to His Majesty the King, who read it with much pleasure and called it a masterpiece, nicely handled.*

---

ary to the Moravian Indians in New York and Connecticut. He first married Rachel, an Indian of the Wampanoag tribe, and after her death, Agnes, a Delaware. Having become a widower a second time, he in 1751 returned to Europe. Hence he sailed for Labrador in 1752, engaging in an unsuccessful attempt to bring the Gospel to the Esquimaux. Having returned to Bethlehem in 1754, he was sent to Wyoming, where he preached to the Indians until in November of 1755. In the summer of 1758 Post undertook an embassy in behalf of Government to the Delawares and Shawanese of the Ohio country, which resulted in the evacuation of Fort Du Quesne by the French, and the restoration of peace. In September of 1761 he engaged in an independent mission to the Indians of that distant region, and built him a hut on the Tuscarawas, near Bolivar, in Stark county, Ohio. John Heckewelder joined him in the spring of 1762. But the Pontiac war drove the missionaries back to the settlements, and the project was abandoned. Impelled by his ruling passion, Post now sought a new field of activity in the southern part of the Continent, and in January of 1764 sailed from Charleston, via Jamaica, for the Mosquito coast. Here he preached to the natives for upwards of two years. He visited Bethlehem in July of 1767, returned to Mosquito, and was in Bethlehem, for the last time, in 1784. At this date he was residing with his third wife, who was an Episcopalian, in Germantown. Here he died May 1st, 1785. On the 5th of May his remains were interred in the Lower Graveyard of that place, Rev. William White, D. D., of Christ Church, saying the funeral service. The following inscription is upon his tombstone :

"In Memory of | the Rev. Christian Frederick Post, | Missionary for Propagating | the Gospel among the Indians | in the Western Country, on the Ohio, | at Labrador and the Mosquito | Shore in North America. | After laboring in the Gospel forty-five years | with distinguished Zeal, Prudence and Fidelity, | He departed this Life | on the first day of May, 1785, | Aged 75 years."

* Dr. Muhlenberg here refers to the sermon of 1775 on "The Present Situation of American Affairs," of which we have given a full account on pages 507-523 of Vol. I.

So you see, dear sir, on one side you are beloved and praised, and on the other side hated and envied, in order to keep and preserve your head and heart straight and upright—*Veritas odium parit.* In mine answer to Dr. Wrangel I enclosed all your printed proceedings in Maryland, etc., which I had collected, especially the Apostolic-spirited sermon, etc., and did send them along with due respects and esteem to your whole honorable house. I remain,

Reverend Sir, your most humble servant,

MUHLENBERG.

To the REV. DR. WILLIAM SMITH, in the State of Delaware.

On the 14th of November, 1784, the Rev. Samuel Seabury was consecrated Bishop for the Episcopal Church in Connecticut, the first bishop in America since the Declaration of Independence.* On the 3d of August, 1785, having returned to America, he was received by the clergy of Connecticut in convocation, and held the *first* ordination of the Protestant Episcopal Church on this Continent; the candidate—who was a son of Mr. Colin Ferguson, Vice-President of Dr. Smith's new college—having been a student of Dr. Smith's and prepared for Holy Orders under the direction of that gentleman and by him recommended for them. In a letter to Dr. Smith from Bishop Seabury, soon after the ordination, the Bishop says:

I cannot omit to mention the particular satisfaction Mr. Ferguson gave, not only to me but to all our clergy.

I can find no evidence of any Convention of the Episcopal Church of Maryland being held in the spring of 1785, and there may have been none; but Dr. Smith leaves a note of being at the 2d Annual Convention of the Church in Maryland on the 25th of October, 1785, and of there being present the following persons: Dr. Thomas Cradock, Samuel Johnson, Thomas Bond, Nicholas Merryman, Richard Wilmott, and Francis Holland, Esqs.

On the 28th of November, 1785, Dr. Smith preached at the

---

* As the Rev. George Morgan Hills, D. D., Rector of St. Mary's Church, Burlington, N. J., has made an interesting argument to show, there was at least one Bishop in America before Bishop Seabury, namely, *John Talbot*, Rector of St. Mary's Church, Burlington, N. J., a saintly man, consecrated by a non-juring Bishop, in or about the year 1722. A monument, with a *fac simile* of his Episcopal seal, is erected to his memory in *old* St. Mary's Church, Burlington. See "The Pennsylvania Magazine of Biography and History," Vol. III., page 32.

funeral of his brother-in-law, Dr. Charles Ridgely,* who had died on the 25th instant. He was buried at Dover, Delaware.

On the 5th of December of this same year Dr. Smith's diary says :

Received a letter from John M. Langguth at Bethlehem, in regard to the establishment of a school for the education of the German youth, such a plan having originated years ago by Dr. Muhlenberg and myself. I sent him all the plans as proposed at that time.†

---

* The following account of Dr. Ridgely is taken from an old Bible belonging to the family :

"Charles Greenberry Ridgely was born near Salem, N. J., January 26th, 1738. He was baptized by Mr. John Peirson; godfathers, Dr. Philip Chetwood and William Frazer, Esq. At his becoming of age he omitted the Greenberry, and wrote his name Charles Ridgely. He was an eminent physician. He acquired his classical and medical education at Philadelphia, practised his profession in Dover, Delaware, with great success and reputation, and deservedly obtained the esteem and confidence of his countrymen. He was many years a member of the Legislature, before the Revolution, and during the whole period of the contest, and a short time after its termination he was a member of the Convention of the State of Delaware which framed the Constitution of 1776. He departed this life Friday, November 25th, 1785, aged 47 years. He was buried on the 28th of the same month, in the Church burying-ground at Dover. His funeral sermon was preached by his brother-in-law, the Rev. Dr. William Smith."

† This interesting man was the son of a Lutheran clergyman settled at Walschleben, and born there in October of 1718. While at Jena he acted as tutor to young Zinzendorf. In 1739 he united himself to the Brethren at Herrnhaag. In 1745 he was adopted by Frederic, Baron of Watteville, a friend of Zinzendorf, into his family, and soon after received Imperial letters patent of nobility. Among the Brethren he was known as " Brother Johannes." In 1746 he married Benigna von Zinzendorf. Prior to his visitation of the Brethren's settlements and missions in North America, he was, in June of 1747, ordained a Bishop. He arrived at Bethlehem in September of 1748; thence he visited the Indian missions in Pennsylvania, New York and Connecticut. In April of 1749 he sailed for St. Thomas. Soon after his return to the Provinces, in July of that year, he repaired to Philadelphia to hold an interview with heads and deputies of the Six Nations, on which occasion he renewed a covenant of amity, which his father-in-law had ratified with that confederation, in August of 1742. He sailed for Europe in October, 1749. During this visitation, Bishop de Watteville presided at three Synods of the Church, baptized a number of Indians, laid the corner-stone of a church at Gnadenhütten on the Mahoning (Lehighton, Carbon county, Pa.), and reorganized a number of Moravian congregations.

After Zinzendorf's decease, in May of 1760, his son-in-law for a time directed the affairs of the Church. In 1764 de Watteville was elected to the Directory, and in 1769 to the Unity's Elder's Conference. While a member of this body he visited North America a second time, inspecting the Brethren's settlements and churches, both North and South, in the interval between June of 1784 and June of 1787. By authority of the above-mentioned board, he sanctioned the transforming of Nazareth Hall into a Boarding School for boys and the erection of a Boarding School for girls at Bethlehem in October of 1785.

Bishop de Watteville died at Gnadenfrey, Prussia, in October, 1788.

On February 11th General John Cadwalader died at his seat in Kent county, Maryland, in the 44th year of his age. He was sincerely valued by Dr. Smith, to whose splendid abilities he in turn looked up with admiration. Dr. Smith followed his remains to the old Parish Church at Shrewsbury, at which place he was buried; and here the Doctor preached a funeral discourse upon him. It is a matter which I much regret that the manuscript has not come down to my hands. The following inscription is upon General Cadwalader's tomb:

In Memory of
GENERAL JOHN CADWALADER,
Who departed this life the 11th of February, 1786, aged 44
Years, 1 month and 1 day.

The following character was given him by Thomas Paine, who, during his life-time, had been his violent political enemy:

" His early affectionate patriotism will endear
His memory to all the true friends of the American
Revolution. It may with the strictest justice be
Said of him that he possessed a heart incapable
Of deceiving. His manners were formed on the
Nicest sense of honor, and the whole tenor of his
Life was governed by this principle—the companions
Of his youth were the companions of his manhood.
He never lost a friend by insincerity nor made
One by deception. His domestic virtues were truly
Exemplary, and while they serve to endear the
Remembrance, they embitter the loss of him to all
His numerous friends and connections."

This stone is placed by his affectionate children to mark
The spot where his remains are deposited.

We are rendering our volume perhaps too much of a family diary by the insertion of facts and letters relating chiefly to domestic events. But such letters bring us into the best portion of a great man's life, and the letter which follows, from the wife of Dr. Smith to their son, may, I trust, be inserted without more apology, referring as it does to the two distinguished persons whose deaths I have so recently chronicled.

Mrs. Smith to her son Charles.

CHESTERTOWN, MD., March 12, 1786.

My Dear Son: . . . . . I have had a melancholy time since last I saw you. Our dear Mrs. Cadwalader, since July last, has buried two sons; but had that been all, a surviving son and daughter, as lovely children as ever were born, would have enabled her to bear the loss with patient resignation. A much severer blow was to be submitted to—her worthy husband departed this life the 10th of last month. At all these scenes I was a sorrowing witness.

Your poor Aunt Ridgely too has lost a most tender and indulgent husband. But in his children she is blessed. Nicholas practices the law at Dover and pays her every attention; and Charles lives with her.

Your dear Aunt Bond is really a woman of sorrow. This last stroke must be almost too much for her to bear. My heart bleeds for her. Do, my dear son, if anything is in your power, relating to her affairs, do for her as I am sure you would do for me; and depend upon it a blessing will attend your righteous endeavor. Cruel fate has separated her from the only son.* She was ever a mother to him; and such a son, oh my dear child, when I think of him I offer up my ardent prayers to the throne of mercy, and as one of the greatest blessings ask that *you* may prove, what I ever thought him.

Say for me to your dear wife, to her sweet little ones, and to your ever worthy uncle (Judge Thomas Smith) that while I have life they will be remembered with affection by their ever most tender and anxious friend,

Your mother,

REBECCA SMITH.

To CHARLES SMITH,
     Student at Law, Carlisle.

On the 27th of May, 1787, another Convention of the Church in Maryland was held at Chestertown, Dr. Smith being chosen to preside. Seven of the clergy and five laymen assisted. Beyond the appointment of Dr. Smith as a clerical deputy to attend the next General Convention—the one held at Philadelphia in 1789—I know of nothing worthy of special record. Two months afterwards his diary contains this record:

July —. My dear wife's kinsman, Richard Channing Moore, was this day ordained by Bishop Provoost, of New York.

This gentleman was the person afterwards well known as Bishop Moore, of Virginia.

I find no very various evidences of Dr. Smith's activity during

---

* Phineas Bond, afterwards British Consul at Philadelphia.

the year 1788. The violent party by which the charter of the old College of Philadelphia had been taken away, had itself now, after a life not long, come to a sudden and complete and rather ignominious end; and Dr. Smith devoted no small portion of his time and labor to having a repeal of the unjust enactments by which the chartered rights of the institution which he had founded and built, were so unjustly taken away by it in 1789; "a repeal," says Bishop White, in speaking of Dr. Smith, "which but for his labors and perseverance would probably never have been effected, notwithstanding the justice of the case." *   Much of Dr. Smith's time therefore was spent in Philadelphia; and he published in that city in 1788, by the respectable firm of Robert Aitken & Son, "An Address to the General Assembly of Pennsylvania, in the Case of the Violated Charter of the College, etc., of Philadelphia;" a powerful document, which I regret that my space prevents my here inserting.

But his Masonic friends at home were not forgotten. On the 29th of August, it being the feast of St. John the Baptist, he preached in the hall of Washington College, at the desire of the Grand Communication of the Maryland lodges.

The following letter has reference to the rights of St. John's College and of the Maryland churches. I am not able to explain it particularly from other sources, and therefore leave it to explain itself:

Rev. Dr. Smith to the Rev. Dr. West.

ANNAPOLIS, December 11, 1788.

DEAR SIR: I should have been much pleased if you had pursued your journey to Annapolis, as Mr. Hanson and the other gentlemen visitors of St. John's College are exceedingly desirous of a meeting, or a conference at least of as many of their Board as possible, but neither Clagget, Baines or Thomas have yet appeared, and Mr. Chase and myself are left to act by ourselves in behalf of our Church also, but we shall be sufficient, as we have drawn up a clause, preserving all our former rights, and under the vestry laws, and entitling our vestries, on the footing of equal liberty, to the like extension of their property, viz., 4000 bushels of wheat per annum, and to take by *deed*, gift, devise, etc., as other vestries, with a new clause also, viz.: that if by neglect or failure of an election on any Easter Monday, a vestry has

---

* "Wilson's Life of White," page 19.

heretofore, or shall hereafter expire, or be in danger thereof, the minister may call a meeting on the first Monday of any month follow
[sic], ar. l hold a new election to revive and continue the vestry and the
minister to be a member as heretofore. Dr. Carroll and Dr. Allison
went with me into the Senate and delivered the clause, declaring that
on the insertion thereof, we were all agreed to the bill.

I have done the best with Mr. Chase's usual good offices and the bill
will be taken care of in its passage through the House of Delegates by
Chase, W. Tilghman, and other members of our Church, but I cannot
return the minutes of our Convention by the bearer, as they are necessary to Mr. Chase and myself to show our authority. I shall take care
of them till next Convention, and am in haste,

Yours,   WILLIAM SMITH.

P. S.—To-morrow I shall hope to return to Chester and would wish
to hear from you as often as convenient.

The bill thus spoken of passed the Senate and was reported to
the House, but there it failed to be acted upon and for the time the
matter dropped.

CHAPTER L.

THE PROPOSED BOOK NOT SO WELL RECEIVED AS MIGHT HAVE BEEN REASONABLY
EXPECTED—THE CAUSE OF THIS THUS EXPLAINED—PROPOSED BY A CONVEN-
TION BEFORE THE CHURCH WAS PROPERLY ORGANIZED BY THE PRESENCE OF
THE EPISCOPAL ORDER—THE NEW ENGLAND CLERGY ALARMED BY A WRONG
IMPRESSION OF THE PURPOSE OF DR. WHITE'S "CASE OF THE EPISCOPAL
CHURCHES IN THE UNITED STATES CONSIDERED"—THE ALTERATIONS NOT
AGREEABLE TO ALL—BISHOP SEABURY'S STATEMENT OF SOME OF THE GROUNDS
OF DISLIKE—STATE PRIDE AND JEALOUSY AS MUCH A CAUSE FOR THE NON-
RECEPTION AS ANY BETTER REASONS—THE WORK TOO HASTILY DONE—LET-
TER TO DR. WEST.

ALTHOUGH, as we have said, the "Proposed Book" was universally admitted to contain no doctrines not those of the Church of
England, and to promulge in form more or less explicit all that
were clearly expressed in the old book as undeniably hers, and in
several respects to make valuable improvements upon this old
book, the volume did not give general satisfaction.

The New England Churches—under the guidance of the able,
upright and fearless Seabury—had some notions of churchmanship
that were perhaps rather too tightly drawn to be universally acknowledged as the only view allowed by the Church of England.

Those churches were disinclined to have the laity have any vote in
the councils of the Church; and as for any conventions in which
the Episcopal order was not represented, undertaking to remodel
and to settle anew its *liturgy*—in many cases the exponents of its
doctrines—even though at the time the Episcopal order did not
exist among us, and it was uncertain how soon exactly we would
get it—the idea struck them as only short of impious. They considered that in attempting to organize the Church before a head
had been obtained, the Convention of 1784 had begun and those
of 1785 and 1786 had been working at the wrong end; that without a Bishop the churches resembled the scattered limbs of a
body without any common centre of union or principle to animate
the whole. An Episcopate according to their idea was necessary
to direct their motions and by a delegated authority to claim
their assent. They held to the constant application and under
every circumstance, of the maxim—true no doubt in the abstract
and the general—*Sine Episcopo, nulla est Ecclesia.*

However unexceptional in itself, then, the Proposed Book might
have been regarded by them, they resiled from it as coming from
a wrong source; just as they would from the Prayer Book made
by a heretic or an infidel. An eccentric English nobleman, assisted
by Dr. Franklin, had in fact made a Prayer Book—which in
some respects the Proposed Book followed, and which some
persons professed to like exceedingly. But would THE CHURCH
accept a liturgy from such a source? Assuredly not. There
were laymen in the Conventions of 1784, 1785 and 1786, whose
faith in particular parts of the Church's teaching was as questionable as was Dr. Franklin's in those points and in many more of it.
The Church was then to be governed only as it was governed
in ancient times; by its clergy, the *Episcopi* being in the highest
seats, and where they could overlook the whole. And this view
—which had great force in it—was not the view of the New England clergy alone. It had advocates, in the Middle States, and
nowhere a more sincere and powerful advocate than in New
Jersey, where Thomas Bradbury Chandler, D. D., who, long before
the Revolution, had been endeavoring to have an Episcopate in
America, and had been battling in opposition to the great Presbyterian, Dr. Chauncy, was acting only in consistency with his
long maintained view. No doubt, too, the pamphlet of Dr.

17

White, the President of the Convention of 1785, which had framed the Proposed Book, did greatly alarm even those who could be called no more than conservative churchmen.* Our means of intercourse in that day were few, and information traveled slowly. As the true history of the publication became known, the fears, so far as they arose from any views of Bishop White—than whom the land never had any truer churchman, if we may take Hooker as an exponent of what a churchman is— departed.

The Proposed Book was, however, open to some objections in their nature intrinsical. While no heterodoxy was alleged against the book it is perhaps the fact that some true doctrines were left rather unguarded, and that some of the offices were so far lowered as that, in a measure, they would lose their influence. The omissions of particular psalms or parts of psalms as undesirable to be read was regarded by some as treating the Scriptures irreverently; and the uniting of different psalms into one portion for each daily

---

* "The Case of the Episcopal Churches in the United States Considered." Dr. Stevens Perry—to whose labors in advance of me, in the department of our Church history, I have already, as I must here again, express my acknowledgments for much that constitutes the value of my book, and to whose gracious and real aid many authors besides myself, as I know, acknowledge their obligations—has reprinted this pamphlet in the third volume of his truly useful " Half Century of the Legislation of the American Church." Having made in that work many explanations of things in the volume by reprinting large passages from Bishop White's writings, he has made, in my opinion, an omission (unavoidable, perhaps, from the size and cost of his book) and done injustice (unintentional, I am sure, if it does do injustice) to Bishop White, in not reprinting after or before " The Case of the Episcopal Churches," etc., the Bishop's history of the circumstances under which that pamphlet was issued, a history to which we have already alluded (see *supra*, pages 185, 186) as twice—we might have said thrice—made by the Bishop, with an emphasis—brought about by the misrepresentations of low churchmen in regard to his opinions—which disarms it of harm as any expression of opinion on Church polity; a harm which Dr. Perry's publication in an unexplained form perhaps tends and will assist to perpetuate. I assume, of course, that so learned a writer upon the history of the American Church and who seems to have been in close intimacy with the present diocesan of Pennsylvania, was not ignorant of the Appendix to Bishop White's charge of 1807 to the clergy of Pennsylvania; though in this I may be mistaken. Bishop White—who was the most modest of men, and as little as any man who ever lived, thought of his own fame either during life or posthumously—took no pains to preserve for consultation, by either his contemporaries or those who should come after him, his own sermons and fugitive pieces. The Philadelphia Library Company—where most Philadelphians deposit their own writings, at least—has scarce any of these pieces. The charge of 1807 is what Bibliophiles call " rare," and possibly may be absent from even the large and, as I suppose, generally complete collections of Dr. Perry. See Appendix No. IV.

service, was objected to as calculated to break their connection, especially of such as were prophetical. Some thought the verbal alterations too numerous; and there were not a few, to whom nearly every word in the book was endeared by so many affecting associations that they desired no change whatever, but what the Revolution made imperative, and what in regard to a very few passages a change in modes of speaking seemed to make decorous.

This part of the matter is set forth with so much force in a letter of Bishop Seabury to Bishop White, written in June, 1789, that I cannot forbear to quote it at large:*

Was it not that it would run this letter to an unreasonable length, I would take the liberty to mention at large the objections that have been here made to the Prayer Book published at Philadelphia. I will confine myself to a few, and even these I should not mention but from a hope they will be obviated by your Convention.

The mutilating the psalms is supposed to be an unwarrantable liberty, and such as was never before taken with Holy Scriptures by any Church. It destroys that beautiful chain of prophecy that runs through them, and turns their application from Messiah and the Church to the temporal state and concerns of individuals.

By discarding the word *Absolution*, and making no mention of Regeneration in Baptism, you appear to give up those points, and to open the door to error and delusion.

The excluding of the Nicene and Athanasian Creed has alarmed the steady friends of our Church, lest the doctrine of Christ's divinity should go out with them. If the doctrine of those creeds be offensive, we are sorry for it, and shall hold ourselves so much the more bound to retain them. If what are called the damnatory clauses in the latter be the objection, cannot these clauses be supported by Scripture? Whether they can or cannot, why not discard those clauses, and retain the doctrinal part of the creed?

The leaving out *the descent into Hell* from the Apostles' Creed seems to be of dangerous consequence. Have we a right to alter the analogy of faith handed down to us by the Holy Catholic Church? And if we do alter it, how will it appear that we are the same Church which subsisted in primitive times? The article of the *descent*, I suppose, was put into the Creed to ascertain Christ's perfect humanity, that he has a human soul, in opposition to those heretics who denied it, and affirmed that his body was actuated by the divinity. For if when he died, and his body was laid in the grave his soul went to the receptacle of departed spirits, then he had a human soul as well as body, and was very and perfect man.

The Apostles' Creed seems to have been the Creed of the Western Church; the Nicene of the Eastern; and the Athanasian, to be designed to ascertain the Catholic doctrine of the Trinity, against all opposers. And it always appeared to me, that the design of the Church of England, in retaining the three Creeds, was to show that she did retain the analogy of the Catholic faith, in common with the Eastern and Western Church, and in opposition to those who denied the Trinity of persons in the Unity of the Divine Essence. Why any departure should be made from this good and pious example I am yet to seek.

There seems in your book a dissonance between the offices of Baptism and Confirmation. In the latter there is a renewal of a vow, which in the former does not appear to have been explicitly made. Something of the same discordance appears in the Catechism.

Our regard for primitive practice makes us exceedingly grieved that you have not absolutely retained the sign of the cross in Baptism. When I consider the practice of the ancient Church, before Popery had a being, I cannot think the Church of England justifiable in giving up the sign of the cross, where it was retained by the first Prayer Book of Edward the VI. Her motive may have been good; but good motives will not justify wrong actions. The concessions she has made in giving up several primitive, and I suppose apostolical usages, to gratify the humors of fault-finding men, shows the inefficacy of such conduct. She has learned wisdom from her experiences. Why should not we also take a lesson in her school? If the humor be pursued of giving up points on every demand, in fifty years we shall scarce have the name of Christianity left. For God's sake, my dear sir, let us remember that it is the particular business of the Bishops of Christ's Church to preserve it pure and undefiled, in faith and practice, according to the model left by apostolic practice. And may God give you grace and courage to act accordingly!

In your burial office, the hope of a future resurrection to eternal life is too faintly expressed, and the acknowledgment of an intermediate state, between death and the resurrection, seems to be entirely thrown out; though, that this was a Catholic, primitive and apostolical doctrine, will be denied by none who attend to this point.

The Articles seem to be altered to little purpose. The doctrines are neither more clearly expressed nor better guarded; nor are the objections to the old articles obviated. And, indeed, this seems to have been the case with several other alterations; they appear to have been made for alteration's sake, and at least have not mended the matter they aimed at.

That the most exceptionable part of the English book is the Communion office may be proved by a number of very respectable names among her clergy. The grand fault in that office is the deficiency of a more formal oblation of the elements, and of the invocation of the Holy

Ghost to sanctify and bless them. The Consecration is made to consist
merely in the priest's laying his hands on the elements and pronouncing,
"*This is my body*," etc., which words are not consecration at all, nor
were they addressed by Christ to the Father, but were declarative to
the Apostles.   This is so exactly symbolizing with the Church of Rome
in an error; an error, too, on which the absurdity of transubstantiation
is built, that nothing but having fallen into the same error themselves,
could have prevented the enemies of the Church from casting it in her
teeth.   The efficacy of Baptism, of Confirmation, of Orders, is ascribed
to the Holy Ghost, and His energy is implored for that purpose; and
why He should not be invoked in the consecration of the Eucharist,
especially as all the old liturgies are full to the point, I cannot conceive.
It is much easier to account for the alterations of the first liturgy of
Edward the VI., than to justify them; and as I have been told there is
a vote on the minutes of your Convention, anno. 1786, I believe, for
the revision of this matter, I hope it will be taken up, and that God
will raise up some able and worthy advocate for this primitive practice,
and make you and the Convention the instruments of restoring it to
His Church in America.   It would do you more honor in the world,
and contribute more to the union of the Churches than any other alterations you can make, and would restore the Holy Eucharist to its ancient dignity and efficacy.

In addition, one of the "fundamental principles" set forth in the
Convention of 1784, inviting a General Convention of the Episcopal
Church in the United States of America, was:

IV. That the said Church shall maintain the doctrines of the Gospel
as now held by the Church of England, and *shall adhere to the Liturgy
of the said Church as far as shall be consistent with the American Revolution* and the Constitutions of the respective States.

It could therefore fairly be argued that the alterations suggested
in the Proposed Book were an implied violation of the call by
which the Convention of 1785 which suggested them was assembled;
and as made *ultra vires* of the Body making them, were absolutely
of no authority.

But with all this, the opposition with some was more perhaps of
a personal kind than from considerations better entitled to weight.
In the Church as in the Congress and country the fault and corruption of the nature of every State engendered of its supposed
original independence—an independence which never existed in
fact—by the extremes of the doctrine of "State Rights"—a doctrine wholesome within proper limits—was of its nature inclined to

evil; so that the infection remained, yea, even when the regeneration of a UNION was sought for; personal interest lusting always
contrary to the general good, and not subject any more than original sin either to the law of common sense or to the law of God.

The State Conventions were jealous of the authority of a General
Convention. A mere proposition to them—a *simple recommendation*—they would tolerate; and would probably adopt. Anything
that had the semblance of going beyond alarmed them, and set
them at once into a state of militancy. The matter is set forth
with perfect intelligibility by Bishop White in his Memoirs. He
says :*

> The Convention (of 1785) seems to have fallen into two capital errors,
> independently on the merits of the Book.
> The first error was the ordering of the printing of a large edition of
> the Book, which did not well consist with the principle of a mere pro-
> posal. Perhaps much of the opposition to it arose from this very thing,
> which seemed a stretch of power designed to effect the introduction of
> the book to actual use in order to prevent a discussion of its merits.
> The other error was the ordering of the use of it in Christ Church,
> Philadelphia, on the occasion of Dr. Smith's sermon at the conclusion
> of the session of the Convention. This helped to confirm the opinion
> of its being introduced with a high hand.

The Bishop tells us further that the Book was used by the
Philadelphia clergy on assurances given to them by gentlemen
from other places that *they* would begin it in their respective
churches immediately on their return; a thing which the greater
number of them never did; some being prevented because some
influential members of their congregations were dissatisfied with
some one of the alterations; "a fact," says the Bishop, " which shows
very strongly how much weight of character is necessary to such
changes as may be thought questionable." The Bishop, it is plain,
had he been left to his own course would not have had the book
printed for any general use at all, until the alterations had been
received and approved in the different States.

But in the nature of things how could a work done in a public
assembly, so hastily and with comparatively small consideration,
fail to require further consideration? The Convention of 1785 met
on Tuesday, the 27th of September, and adjourned on Friday, the

---

* Memoirs, 2d edition, page 107.

7th of October, ten working days; and it had other important subjects to attend to besides this work of revising the Liturgy. No such review could give satisfaction to all, nor, perhaps, on reflection, entirely to any one. It was not expected that it would; nor was more expected than that which Dr. Smith expressed when he expressed in behalf of the Convention the hope that it would be "received and examined by every true member of our Church and every sincere Christian with a meek, candid and charitable frame of mind; without prejudice or prepossessions; seriously considering what Christianity is and what the truths of the Gospel are."

In the nature of things, the subject would come further before the Church in the next Convention—that of 1789; a General Convention for all the States where the Church existed, as it proved to be, and competent therefore to speak with a wiser and more impressive authority.

Indeed, it is remarkable—considering how much Dr. Smith had had to do with the making as I suppose of the Proposed Book, how much time he bestowed upon fitting it for the press, and how desirous apparently he was of seeing it introduced into general use, that so soon as he perceived that it was not universally acceptable, he went right to work, without the least *amour propre d'auteur*, or the least tenacity to preconceived wishes, to make such a work as would be acceptable to all. He thus writes to Dr. West, one of the clergy of his own State, who obviously had not been well satisfied with the Book. It tends to disprove the allegation which in his lifetime was sometimes made against him that he was unreasonable and dictatorial, and impatient of any opposition to his views or wishes. It is quite true that he did not "suffer *fools* gladly" even though he himself was wise. But where he was dealing with men of sense no one was more patient or more open to conviction. The following is the letter to Dr. West:

Dr. Smith to Dr. West.

CHESTER, KENT COUNTY, June 16, 1789.

DEAR SIR: I beg that you may not forget to give me your whole and unreserved sentiments and. advice respecting our Church affairs, and every alteration, amendment or reservation respecting our Prayer Book, which you judge will tend most towards peace and uniformity, and a general acquiescence—nay, a cordial and pious acceptance and use of the book.   Yours, etc.,   WILLIAM SMITH.

The REV. DR. WEST.

CHAPTER LI.

THE CONVENTION OF 1789, A GREAT ECCLESIASTICAL COUNCIL—DR. SMITH IS
CALLED ON UNEXPECTEDLY TO PREACH ON ITS OPENING, AND SOON AFTERWARDS
ON THE SUDDEN DEATH OF DR GRIFFITH, BISHOP-ELECT OF VIRGINIA—A
MEMOIR OF DR. GRIFFITH—THE CONVENTION DELICATELY SITUATED IN RE-
GARD TO BISHOP SEABURY—BISHOP PROVOOST'S SOMEWHAT ECCENTRIC COURSE
IN REGARD TO THIS EMINENT AND PIOUS PRELATE—DIGNIFIED COURSE OF
BISHOP SEABURY—DR. SMITH, ALONG WITH BISHOP WHITE, ACCOMMODATE
MATTERS BETWEEN BISHOP SEABURY AND THE CONVENTION—THE VALIDITY
OF BISHOP SEABURY'S EPISCOPAL ORDERS, ON MOTION OF DR. SMITH, FULLY
RECOGNIZED BY THE CONVENTION—THE CONVENTION TEMPORARILY ADJOURNS
IN ORDER TO GIVE TIME FOR FURTHER CONSULTATION—CORRESPONDENCE BE-
TWEEN DR. SMITH AND BISHOP SEABURY—THE LATTER, WITH REPRESENTA-
TIVES FROM NEW HAMPSHIRE AND MAINE, COMES INTO THE ADJOURNED
CONVENTION—A GENERAL UNION EFFECTED A. D. 1789, IN PHILADELPHIA, IN
THE SAME ROOM IN THE STATE HOUSE WHERE INDEPENDENCE WAS DECLARED
IN 1776, AND THE CONSTITUTION OF THE UNITED STATES SIGNED IN 1787—
HAPPY CONCLUSION OF MUCH LABOR AND OF MANY SOLICITUDES.

THE year 1789 makes an epoch in the history of the American
nation. It was the year in which an United Church was constituted out of separated and somewhat discordant ecclesiastical
bodies; as well as the year 'in which "the United States of
America" gave to us from differing States that unity of government which constitutes us one people. Nor was there much less
difficulty in effecting an unity in the Church than there was in
effecting an unity in the nation. We shall speak of these matters
further on.

Since the Convention of 1786, Dr. White and Dr. Provoost had
been consecrated Bishops. But Dr. Provoost was indisposed, and
did not come to this Convention of 1789. Bishop Seabury had
not, as yet, in any way united himself to his Southern brethren.
The Convention met—all orders of the clergy and the laity—as
one body; Bishop White presiding. At the opening of the Convention, Dr. Smith was called upon by it, in a way which put to
proof his ready powers and his amiable disposition; and which
manifested equally the reliance which was had by the members of
the body upon both.

On the adjournment of the Convention of 1786, Dr. Provoost
had been requested to preach before the Convention of 1789. It
assembled July 26th of that year. But Bishop Provoost was not
there. Dr. Smith, upon one day's notice, was requested to preach
instead. He did so. He had hardly delivered this sermon before
he was called on for another. The Rev. David Griffith, who had
been elected Bishop of Virginia and was now attending the Convention, died suddenly at the house of Bishop White, on Monday,
the 3d of August. Dr. Smith was at the same short notice of a
single day requested to preach a funeral sermon. Both sermons
are good productions; the former,—which, for some reason not
known to me, was not included in the edition of Dr. Smith's
Works, begun by Maxwell of Philadelphia, A. D. 1803—was one,
I should say, of the best of his sermons which we have. It was
published however at the time at the request of the Convention,
and from it I make a single extract. The topic of the sermon is
Christian Perfection; the opening passage of the text,—which
embraces the first twelve verses from the 6th chapter of the Epistle
to the Hebrews—"Therefore, leaving the principles of the doctrine of Christ, let us go on unto perfection." Having developed
this fine theme in the true spirit of the Gospel, the preacher
concludes :

Above all, my brethren, in the great work now before us, where the
honor of our Church, the purity of our worship, true vital religion, and
the consequent happiness and salvation of millions, perhaps yet unborn,
are the awful and important subjects of deliberation—let us proceed with
candour and care, keeping the venerable sanction of antiquity and the
infallible word of God always in our view; not lightly given to change,
nor too rigidly stiff in matters unessential to the true substance of the
"faith once delivered unto the saints." In all our proceedings, however
much we may desire the wisdom of the serpent, let us also in a special
manner seek the harmlessness of the dove also;—adorning every other
acquisition with the clothing of humility and that excellent gift of charity.
But I will detain you no longer. Having put on that most excellent gift; trying the faith that is in us by tests and marks already laid
down and laboring daily after greater attainments in holiness, we shall
at length arrive to that state of spiritual health and perfection which is
the end of all the outward and visible ordinances of Religion; even that
"love of God which fulfilleth all things in us through Christ Jesus,
giving us to eat of spiritual meat and drink of the waters of health and
life everlasting freely."

Feed as then, O blessed God, we pray; feed us and nourish us more and more, with this heavenly meat and drink daily! and bring us at last to feed and live upon it eternally! And now, etc.

Better counsel, more necessary prayer, could no man offer, at the opening of this the greatest council that the American Church has held!

Dr. Griffith, on whom the other sermon was preached, was a native of New York and born A. D. 1742. He was educated chiefly in England and graduated in London as a student of medicine; a profession which, returning to America, he practised for some time in the province of New York. In 1770 he entered the ministry, being ordained by Bishop Terrick, then Bishop of London. After a short residence in Gloucester, New Jersey, as Missionary of the Society for the Propagation of the Gospel— where he succeeded the gifted young Nathaniel Evans, of whom we have spoken so much in our former volume—he went to Virginia; and being highly recommended by the Governor of that State, took charge of Shelburne Parish, Loudon county, Virginia. Here he continued till May, 1776, when he entered the army as Chaplain to the Third Virginia Regiment, and was at the battle of Monmouth and I suppose at other battles. He remained in the army till 1779. In 1780 he entered into the rectorship of Christ Church, Alexandria, a church which is known as the one in which Washington worshipped. This illustrious man was his parishioner. In May, 1786, he was elected by the Convention of Virginia to be Bishop of the Church of that State, and his testimonials having been signed by the General Convention at Wilmington, Delaware, of the same year, it was expected both by the English Bishops, and by Doctors White and Provoost that he would proceed to England and be there consecrated; so that there should be three bishops in America deriving consecration through the Anglican line. This, however, he was unable to do, and, soon after, he resigned to the Virginia Convention the honor proffered to him. He was a man of sincere piety, and of much usefulness in the Church, and was in the General Conventions (as we may call them to distinguish them from those of Virginia) of 1784, 1785, and 1786. He received his doctorate from the University of Pennsylvania in the last-named year. He died, as we have already said, in Philadelphia while attending the Convention of

1789. His funeral proceeded from the house of Bishop White to Christ Church; the clergy of all denominations in Philadelphia being invited to attend it.   The senior clerg; men of the deputation of each State attended as pall-bearers; Bishop White and Mr. Robert Andrews, lay deputy from Virginia, walking as chief mourners and the other members of the Convention as mourners.

The sermon was from those well-known verses of the 5th chapter of the 2d Epistle of Corinthians :

1. For we know, that, if our earthly house of *this* tabernacle were dissolved, we have a building of God, an house not made with hands, eternal in the heavens.

2. For in this we groan, earnestly desiring to be clothed upon with our house which is from heaven.

3. If so be that being clothed, we shall not be found naked.

4. For we that are in *this* tabernacle do groan, being burdened; not for that we would be unclothed, but clothed upon, that mortality might be swallowed up of life.

Dr. Smith thus opens his discourse:

BRETHREN: Upon this sad and solemn occasion, which hath assembled us at this place and time ; gloomy indeed would be our reflections, and inconsolable our condition, were it not for the joyful assurance which our text holds up for the renovation and support of our sickly faith.

Behold, in full view before us, that yawning grave !   On its brink, is deposited the breathless clay, the earthly house, of a venerable brother, a servant and minister of Christ !   It is for a moment deposited, to give us pause for reflection, and vent for the tribute due to the memory of virtue and worth.   That pause ended, the steadfast *grave* will do its part; and embracing, in firm hold, what we commit to its keeping, would leave the awakened tear to flow forever, sorrowing over our mortality, did not St. Paul come to our aid ; teaching us to wipe that tear away, and to console ourselves with the joyful assurance, that the earthly deposit before us, from a tabernacle of clay, shall yet rise up a building of God, a house not made with hands, capacious of immortal glory, honor and immortality !

Unprepared and disinclined, on the present sudden and interesting occasion, to enter upon a critical explication of this difficult, yet comfortable, text (in whatsoever sense considered), I shall not detain you to enquire from it.   Whether the body or earthly house of our present mortal tabernacle shall, upon its divorce from the soul by death, be immediately clothed upon with some other more celestial and incorruptible body; or whether it shall continue naked and unclothed upon, till the morning of the resurrection.

It was the doctrine of the illustrious Plato, who (without the external and revealed light of Christianity) reasoned so well concerning immortality and a world to come, that the soul, or heavenly spark within us, could not subsist of itself, nor act without some kind of body or vehicle ; and therefore the followers of his doctrine contend for an intermediate state between death and the resurrection, and think that the body, upon its dissolution by death, is immediately clothed upon, or changed into some other fit vehicle for the soul.

St. Paul, however, gives no countenance to this doctrine, in the text. The celestial clothing, which he speaks of, is something peculiar to the saints who shall be with the Lord ; and not to be looked for till after the redemption of the body, and that blessed period of the resurrection, "when this mortality shall be swallowed up of life;—when the trumpet shall sound, and the dead shall be raised, and this corruptible must put on incorruption, and this mortal must put on immortality."

Most comfortable to us, when we go to the house of mourning, is either of those doctrines; but we are to understand St. Paul in the latter sense, and then by the due use of reason, enlightened by the blessed considerations and doctrines of our text, after the example of the apostles and saints, and pure professors of Christianity in every age; death might be disarmed of his sting and spoiled of his victories. For, however terrible death may appear to the *sinner* with all his engines of destruction about him ; yet to those who have sought and found an interest in Christ Jesus, death hath lost his mighty terrors: and although the grave itself, which (considered as the door of another world, the entrance into eternity) appears so gloomy and awful to mere flesh and blood; yet to the just,—to those who live by faith, earnestly longing and groaning to be clothed upon with their heavenly house, the grave appears more beautiful than the gates of paradise itself; for at the gates of paradise, upon the banishment of our guilty first parents, the angry cherubim, with his flaming sword, was placed to forbid all future entrance to any of mortal race ; but angels of peace and love stand round the graves of the just, to shield them from harm and conduct them to glory. . . .

We are now assembled to pay the last funeral honors to a minister of the altar, who has for many years been conspicuous in his station, both in public and in private life; and much might be said as applicable to the sudden and melancholy occasion of his death. And though the suspicion of flattery too often accompanies the funeral characters of the present day, yet it is for the interest of virtue and mankind that they should not be brought wholly into disuse. The tribute of our praise and thankfulness to God is due for those who have, in some degree, been of benefit to the world, either in a civil or religious capacity, and who may be truly said not to have "lived to themselves but for their country— her rights, her laws, and her liberties, religious and civil; and, therefore, at whatever stage of life they have died, they have died unto the Lord." They have died for us also, so far as we may improve their

death to the great public and pious purposes, for which such holy
solemnities, as the present, were first appointed by the wisest nations.
For—

1st. They were appointed for the express purpose of commemorating
the public virtues of the dead, nay even their crimes; for if they have
been injurious to mankind, they may be held up to censure, with the
great intent of leading mankind to imitate the former, and to abhor and
shun the latter.

2dly. Such solemnities are intended to bring us into a proper familiarity with ourselves and our mortal condition; that we may be preparing for death, and enabled, through the grace offered us, to overcome
his terrors!

Upon each of these heads, I shall beg leave seriously to address you
on the present occasion.

After having expressed himself fully on the first head, the
orator coming to the second, proceeds:

I come now more particularly to speak of commemorating the virtues
of the *dead*, for the example and benefit of the *living*. This is an advantage, as I said before, which in these days is seldom improved.

The ancient Christians, besides the solemnity of their funerals, were
wont to meet at the graves of their martyrs and saints and holy men, to
recite the history of their sufferings and triumphs, and to bless God for
their holy lives and happy deaths, offering up also their prayers for
grace to follow their good example. And for this they seem to have
had St. Paul's express authority, and especially respecting the preachers
and teachers of the word of God. For he exhorts the Hebrews to
"remember them who had spoken unto them the word of God, whose
faith follow, considering the end of their conversation."

In this important light, we must long remember our worthy and
venerable brother, who hath been called suddenly (but, we have every
ground to believe, not wholly unprepared) to exchange his pulpit for a
coffin, his eloquence for silence, and his eminent abilities in doing good
for darkness and the grave.

In the service of his country, during our late contest for Liberty and
Independence, he was near and dear to our illustrious commander-in-
chief—he was also his neighbor, and honored and cherished by him as
a pastor and friend.* When, on the conclusion of the war, he returned
to his pastoral charge, and our church in these States, in the course of
divine Providence, were called to organize themselves, as independent
of all foreign authority, civil and ecclesiastical, he was from the beginning elected the chief clerical member to represent the numerous

---

* At Alexandria in Virginia.

churches of Virginia in our General Conventions; and highly estimable he was amongst us. He was a sound and able divine, a true son, and afterwards a father, as a bishop-elect, of our church; with his voice always, with his pen occasionally, supporting and maintaining her just rights, and yielding his constant and zealous aid in carrying on the great work for which we are assembled at this time.

Full of a devout desire for the final accomplishment of this work at the present time, he came to this city; but it hath pleased the sovereign goodness otherwise to dispose of him, and to call him, as we trust, to become a member of the church triumphant in Heaven.

With Christian patience and fortitude, though at a distance from his family and his nearest relatives and friends, he sustained his short but severe illness. Friends, nevertheless, closed his eyes. Friends and brethren now accompany him to the grave, mournful as to the flesh, but joyful and thankful to God in soul and spirit for his past usefulness and example. . . .

Let us not question the dispensations of Providence, nor murmuring, ask, Whether it were not to be desired, that men endued with eminent talents to serve their country and families, should be long preserved in health of body and vigor of mind; and that the hour of their death should be protracted to the latest period of old age? Say we not so. For the commander of an army best knows when to call the sentinel from his post. Every man in this world hath his office and station assigned by Heaven, and continueth therein so long as it pleaseth the supreme Ruler; and he that performeth his part best and liveth well, may be said to live longest.

Seeing, then, my brethren, that, by the faithful discharge of our civil and religious duties, we may overcome death, be prepared for eternity, and leave our names sweet to the world behind us; let us take for our example the virtue and goodness of our departed friends, and be persuaded that there is no honor, no happiness to be acquired here on earth, equal to that which we derive from acting our part with dignity; steadfast in the practice, as well as profession, of our holy religion; zealous for the happiness of our country and mankind, and always delighting in acts of love and goodness. The regard which is paid to such characters as these, will grow with their growing years; and when they come at last to take leave of this world, whether at an earlier or later period of years, as they have lived the life of the righteous, their latter end will be like his. . . .

It is a grand description which is given of the angel in the book of Revelation, who came down from Heaven to proclaim destruction to time. "He had in his hand a little book open: and he set his right foot upon the sea, and his left foot on the earth, and cried with a loud voice, as when a lion roareth: and when he had cried, seven thunders uttered their voices. And when the seven thunders had uttered their voices, I was about to write; and I heard a voice from Heaven saying unto me, Seal up those things which the seven thunders uttered and write them not. And the angel, which I saw stand upon the sea and upon the earth, lifted up his hand to Heaven, and sware by him that liveth forever and ever, who created Heaven, and the things that therein are, and the earth, and the things that therein are, and the sea, and the things which are therein, *that there should be time no longer.*" But far greater is the true Christian in the act of death. He sets one foot in the grave, and the other in the very porch of Heaven; being enabled, through Christ, to proclaim destruction to death and the grave. "Oh, death, I will be thy plagues; oh, grave, I will be thy destruction. Oh, death, where is now thy sting! Oh, grave, where is now thy victory!"

Then, too, can he add, without fear, "Farewell, my body, my mortal part! Why shouldst thou, my soul, be loth to part with thine old companion, to leave thy clay cottage, and to be without a body? Behold, thy Maker, and the spiritual and heavenly inhabitants, have no gross bodies such as thine! Hast thou ever seen a prisoner, when his jail doors were broke open, and himself manumitted and set loose at liberty?—and have you then heard him complain to take leave of his prison-house, and refuse to forego his fetters? Or, hast thou seen a wave-worn mariner, who has long been tossed and troubled on his stormy voyage, when arrived in sight of his native port, refuse to strike sail and enter in; choosing rather to launch back again into the perilous main? Why then, my soul, shouldst thou be thus fear-stricken and discomforted, at parting from this mortal bride, thy body? It is but for a time, and such a time as the body shall feel no need of thee, nor thou of her; and thou shalt again receive her back more goodly and beautiful, purified and perfected by absence, like unto that crystal which after the revolution of some ages, is said to be turned into the purest diamond; now, unto him who by his apostle, hath assured us after " our earthly house of this tabernacle shall be dissolved" and moulder into dust, we have a building of God, an house not made with hands, "eternal in the heavens,"— unto Him be glory and dominion and praise forever! Amen.

In the Convention it was

Resolved, That the thanks of this Convention be given to the Rev. Dr. Smith for his sermon preached at the funeral of the Rev. Dr. Griffith, and that he be requested to furnish the Convention with a copy for publication.

We have said that one United Church was first constituted out of the separated ecclesiastical bodies in the States in 1789: and that to effect this happy state of unity was a work of difficulty. The Proposed Book, Dr. White's tract, "The State of the Epis-

copal Churches in the United States Considered," the presence
of the laity voting in councils of the Church, and especially the
introducing them into trials of an ecclesiastic—which it was
wrongly supposed by some that it was the purpose of Bishop
White and Dr. Smith to do—with some things done in the Conventions of 1784, 1785 and 1786, had caused dissatisfaction and
anxiety with the northern clergy, and some estrangement.

But there was another matter of importance. Bishop Seabury
had been consecrated by Bishops of the Church in Scotland; the
English Bishops having declined to consecrate him from reasons
of political prudence only. His personal fitness—indeed his eminent personal fitness—even for the high and sacred office of a
Bishop, no one that I have heard of, ever disputed. He stands
forth and will always stand forth as one of the great, the heroic
characters of the Church in America.

No man was more able to appreciate the value of this great
churchman and bishop than Dr. Smith ; none more able to vindicate his right to the high orders which he claimed. As a Scotsman, too, and a churchman alike, he felt a pride in doing so.
Accordingly, immediately after the arrival in America of Bishop
Seabury, with whom he had long maintained an intercourse of a
free and friendly character, he wrote to him informing him of what
had been doing in Maryland in his absence, etc., and receiving
from him the following interesting and authoritative statement
of the reasons why he had accepted Scottish orders rather than
English. Bishop Seabury, writing to him on the 15th of August,
1785, says as follows:

The grand difficulty that defeated my application for consecration in
England appeared to me to be the want of an application from the
State of Connecticut. Other objections were made, viz. : that there was
no precise diocese marked out by the civil authority, nor a stated
revenue appointed for the Bishop's support. But those were removed.
The other remained—for the civil authority in Connecticut is Presbyterian, and therefore could not be supposed would petition for a bishop.
And had this been removed, I am not sure another would not have
started up : for this happened to me several times. I waited, and procured a copy of an Act of the Legislature of Connecticut, which puts
all denominations of Christians on a footing of equality (except the
Roman Catholics, and to them it gives a free toleration), certified by
the Secretary of State; for to Connecticut all my negotiations were

confined. The Archbishop of Canterbury wished it had been fuller, but thought it afforded ground on which to proceed. Yet he afterwards said it would not do; and that the Minister, without a formal requisition from the State, would not suffer the Bill, enabling the Bishop of London to ordain foreign candidates without their taking the oaths, to pass the Commons, if it contained a clause for consecrating American Bishops. And as his Grace did not choose to proceed without parliamentary authority—though if I understood him right, a majority of the Judges and Crown Lawyers were of opinion he might safely do it—I turned my attention to the remains of the old Scots Episcopal Church, whose consecrations I knew were derived from England, and their authority in an ecclesiastical sense, fully equal to the English Bishops.

But the succession through the English line was preferred by most churchmen in America; and in the establishment of the Church on this great continent all the clergy of the Middle and Southern States were desirous to have it if it could be had. When Dr. White and Dr. Provoost sailed for England to receive consecration it was expected, as we have already said, that Dr. Griffith, of Virginia, would accompany them, so that we should then have three Bishops; the number required by a rule of the Church of England—and thought wise by ourselves—to perform any new act of Episcopal consecration; and all three coming through the Church just named. But as we have also said circumstances prevented Dr. Griffith going to England, and he then or afterwards finally resigned his honors to the Convention of Virginia.

When, however, Bishops White and Provoost received their consecrations it was understood, though never in terms, that I know of, agreed on, by the English Bishops and by the two persons then consecrated, that before any acts of consecration should be performed by these two, Dr. Griffith or some other third person would come from America and be consecrated in England by the English Bishops; so that any new Bishop consecrated *in* America should have as consecrators *three* Bishops deriving their Episcopal orders through the Anglican line. Indeed in the Convention of 1786 the body was barely organized when Dr. Robert Smith, of South Carolina, moved:

That the clergy present produce their letters of orders or declare by whom they were ordained.

This motion was aimed at the Rev. Joseph Pilmore, a native of

18

Scotland (long the venerable Rector of St. Paul's Church, Philadelphia), who had received orders from Bishop Seabury, and at
the Rev. William Smith, of Stepney Parish, Somerset county,
Maryland, who had been ordained in Scotland,* by a Bishop of
the Church from whence Seabury had obtained consecration.
The application of the previous question moved by my ancestor,
Dr. Smith, and seconded by Dr. White, precluded the discussion
which it was anticipated would grow out of this motion, and the
resolution itself was lost.

Dr. Provoost, not satisfied with this expression of the will of
the Convention, then moved directly:

That this Convention will resolve to do no act that shall imply the
validity of ordinations made by Dr. Seabury.

Again the previous question cut off discussion and the main
question was determined in the negative; New York, New Jersey
and South Carolina alone supporting it. But Bishop Provoost
would not let the matter drop. In a Convention of New York,
held November 5th, 1788, and in view of the General Convention
of 1789 now at hand, it was resolved:

---

* The Rev. Thomas F. Davies, originally of the State of Connecticut, but long and
now the honored Rector of St. Peter's Church, Philadelphia, well known in that city,
not only as one of its ablest theologians, but also as among its most learned ecclesiastical historians, responding to my solicitations has been kind enough to give me, in a
friendly note, the following sketch of this eminent divine, already referred to by me,
supra, pages 186, 197:

"The younger Dr. William Smith was a fellow-countryman and townsman of your
distinguished ancestor, and was born at Aberdeen in 1754. He came to this country
in 1785, after his admission to Holy Orders, and was for two years minister of Stepney
Parish, Maryland. Most of his ministerial life, however, was passed in New England,
where he was successively Rector of St. Paul's, Narragansett; of Trinity Church,
Newport, R. I., and of St. Paul's, Norwalk, Connecticut. He was subsequently appointed Principal of the Episcopal Academy, Cheshire. He is remembered in the
Church as the compiler of the Institution Office, which was approved by the General
Convention in 1804, and was again set forth with some slight modifications in 1808,
and also as the author of a work which attracted much attention in its day, on Church
Music, Chanting and Metrical Psalmody.

"He preached the sermon at the consecration of Bishop Jarvis in 1797, a copy of
which is preserved in the library of St. Peter's Church.

"He was a man of eminent and versatile talents, of extensive learning, of soundness
in the faith, and of most exemplary life. Had his knowledge of mankind been in any
way equal to his scholastic attainments, his usefulness had been greater and his fame
more lasting. He passed the evening of his days in retirement at Norwalk, and died
in New York in 1821, in the 69th year of his age."

That it is highly necessary in the opinion of this Convention that measures should be pursued to preserve the Episcopal succession in the English line.

That the union of the Protestant Episcopal Church in the United States of America is of great importance and much to be desired, and that the delegates of this State, in the next General Convention, be instructed to promote that union by every prudent measure, consistent with the constitution of the Church and the continuance of the Episcopal succession in the *English* line.

These resolutions it appears were worded at the *particular request* of Bishop Provoost. Though a man of true Christian character, Bishop Seabury was one also of high spirit and could not but feel such resentments as were allowable to a Christian and a gentleman. He held himself off from any organization in which Bishop Provoost was to be a leader or very potential person; if any such organization there was to be. He writes, June 20th, 1789, to Bishop White, who had written to him to urge his coming to the Convention:

For my own part gladly would I contribute to the uniformity of all our Churches; but while Bishop Provoost disputes the validity of my consecration, I can take no steps towards the accomplishment of so great and desirable an object. The point, I take it, is now in such a state that it must be settled either by your Convention or by an appeal to the Christian world. But as this is a subject in which I am personally concerned, I shall refrain from any remarks upon it; hoping that the candor and good sense of the Convention will render the further mention altogether unnecessary.

The matter was the more important since as Bishop Seabury went so would go not only Connecticut but other, perhaps, of the New England States. The case required both vigor and circumspection. To counteract this dangerous conduct and motions of Bishop Provoost, Dr. Smith wrote to Bishop Seabury just before the Convention assembled urging him, as Bishop White had done, to come to the Convention; Dr. Smith offering to him the hospitality of his house.

Bishop Seabury replies to Dr. Smith.

NEW LONDON, July 23, 1789.

. . . . The wish of my heart, and the wish of the clergy and of the Church people of this State, would certainly have carried me, and some of the clergy, to your General Convention, had we conceived we could have done it with propriety. The ground on which Bishop Provoost disputes the validity of the Scotch Episcopal succession can best be explained by himself: I know not what it is. And the ground on which the letters of orders were called for from every clergyman, in a former Convention at Philadelphia—if I have been rightly informed—in order to make a distinction between English and Scotch ordinations, they can best explain who were concerned in it. As I know not precisely how this matter ended, I shall say no more about it. But while this matter stands as it does, and there is a resolve on the minutes of the New York Convention strongly reflecting on Bishop Seabury's Episcopal character —while by your own constitution no representation of clergymen can be admitted without lay delegates, and no church can be taken into your union without adopting your whole plan, I leave you to say whether it would be right for me, or for my clergy, to offer ourselves at a Convention where we could be admitted only in courtesy? Should we feel ourselves at home? or, as being on an equal footing with the other ministers?

The necessity of a union of all the Churches, and the disadvantages of the present disunion, we feel and lament equally with you: and I agree with you, that there may be a strong and efficacious union between Churches where the usages are different. I see not why it may not be so in this case, as soon as you have removed those obstructions which, while they remain, must prevent all possibility of uniting.

My joining with Bishops White and Provoost in consecrating a fourth Bishop was some time ago proposed to Bishop White, and by him declined. His noncompliance has had a bad effect here. It has raised a jealousy of attempting an undue superiority over the Church of Connecticut, which, as it at present consists of nineteen clergymen, in full orders, and more than twenty thousand people, they suppose as respectable as the Church in any State in the Union.

Before I wrote to Bishop White I took the most deliberate pains to obtain the sentiments of both clergy and laity; and I should not now think myself at liberty to act contrary to their sentiments, even did not my own coincide with theirs. I have, however, the strongest hope that all difficulties will be removed by your Convention—that the Connecticut Episcopacy will be explicitly acknowledged, and that Church enabled to join in union with you, without giving up her own independency.

A great deal, my dear sir, will depend on the part you now act. The dread of alterations in the liturgy here arises from the observation, that every review of the liturgy has set the offices of the Church lower, and departed further from primitive practice and simplicity. The book you published was a remarkable instance of depreciating the offices, and we hope to see it remedied. To enter into particulars after what I have

written to Bishop White will be useless.   But if a uniformity of worship
be aimed at, I know of no other method besides the one I mentioned
to Bishop White—to leave the matter to the bishops and the clergy.   It
is their business; and if your laity will not consent to it, they interfere
out of their sphere. . . . .*

Dr. Smith, now in the Convention, on the application which had
been made by the clergy of Massachusetts and New Hampshire
for the consecration of the Rev. Mr. Bass, as their Bishop, offered
to the Convention, which had then resolved itself into a Committee of the Whole the following resolves:

1st. That a complete order of Bishops, derived as well under the
English as the Scots line of Episcopacy, doth now subsist within the
United States of America, in the persons of the Right Rev. William
White, D. D., Bishop of the Protestant Episcopal Church in the State
of Pennsylvania, the Right Rev. Samuel Provoost, D. D., Bishop of
the said Church in the State of New York, and the Right Rev. Samuel
Seabury, D. D., Bishop of the said Church in the State of Connecticut.

2d. That the said three Bishops are fully competent to every proper
act and duty of the Episcopal office and character in these United
States, as well in respect to the consecration of other Bishops, and the
ordering of priests and deacons, as for the government of the Church,
according to such rules, canons and institutions, as now are, or hereafter
may be duly made and ordained by the Church in that case.

3d. That in Christian charity, as well as of duty, necessity and expediency, the churches represented in this Convention ought to contribute, in every manner in their power, towards supplying the wants,
and granting every just and reasonable request of their sister churches
in these States; and, therefore,

4th. That the Right Rev. Dr. White and the Right Rev. Dr. Provoost be, and they hereby are, requested to join with the Right Rev.
Dr. Seabury, in complying with the prayer of the clergy of the States
of Massachusetts and New Hampshire, for the consecration of the Rev.
Edward Bass, Bishop-elect of the churches in the said States; but that,
before the said Bishops comply with the request aforesaid, it be proposed to the churches in the New England States to meet the churches
of these States, with the said three Bishops, in an adjourned Convention,
to settle certain articles of union and discipline among all the churches,
previous to such consecration.

5th. That if any difficulty or delicacy, in respect to the Archbishops

---

* From the original MS. preserved among the Bishop White papers.   As this letter
is mutilated more or less on every page, omissions have been supplied from the first
draft contained in Bishop Seabury's Letter Book.

and Bishops of England, shall remain with the Right Rev. Drs. White and Provoost, or either of them, concerning their compliance with the above request, this Convention will address the Archbishops and Bishops, and hope thereby to remove the difficulty.*

These resolves were unanimously agreed to, as the report of the Committee.

The Committee, having finished the business committed to them, rose and reported to the Convention the above resolves.

On motion of Dr. Smith, seconded by Mr. Andrews, this report was unanimously agreed to.

Soon after this the Convention was adjourned till the 29th of September, in order to allow an opportunity to Bishop Seabury to assist in effecting a complete union. Dr. Smith now immediately wrote to Bishop Seabury; sending at the same time a letter drafted by him (Dr. Smith), and signed by a most respectable committee. We give both from original drafts in Dr. Smith's handwriting:

Rev. Dr. Smith to Bishop Seabury.

August 16, 1789.

RIGHT REVEREND AND DEAR SIR: I was happy to receive your letter of 23d July, in answer to mine of the 13th, from New York, which came to hand at a very critical moment, viz.: the first day of our Convention, and enabled me to be more effectually instrumental in projecting and prosecuting, I trust, to a nobler issue, the plan of an *union* of all our churches, than your letter of a prior date to Bishop White, gave us room to hope. The *healing* and *charitable idea* of "an efficacious union and communion in all essentials of doctrine, as well as discipline, notwithstanding some differences in the usages of churches," in which your letter as well as mine agreed, and which was at the same time strongly held up in the address of the Churches of Massachusetts and New Hampshire, and also in Dr. Parker's letter, gave an opening at last, as well by a new clause, viz., the second in our ecclesiastical constitution, as by five resolves unanimously passed, to lay the foundation of an union, whereon a superstructure may be raised, against which even the gates of Hell shall never prevail.

The fourth of those resolves, inviting you through the door so widely opened, to meet us in the Convention at Philadelphia, adjourned for

---

* This resolution had reference to the fact already mentioned in the text, that when Dr. White and Dr. Provoost were consecrated at Lambeth, the English Bishops were told that Dr. Griffith would follow them, and the English Bishops, as well as our own then consecrated, expected that he would, and so that there would be three Bishops in America under the Anglican title.

that end to September 29th, is the preliminary article of this union; and I scarce entertain a doubt but that the great Head of the Church will by His blessed Spirit, so replenish our hearts with love, and so bless our joint councils, that we shall attain a *perfect uniformity* in all our churches: or, what is, perhaps, alike lovely in the sight of God, a perfect harmony and brotherly agreement wherever, through local circumstances and use, smaller differences may prevail.

You will see from our printed journal herein enclosed, that, in a committee of the whole, the business of the Eastern Churches engaged our attention for the first five days of our sitting, and though a desire of union was everywhere evident among the members, yet much difficulty and variety of sentiment and apprehension prevailed as to the means, in so far that there appeared more than a probability of coming to no conclusion. In this stage of the business, I requested a postponement for one night, on the promise of proposing something against next morning which might meet the apprehensions of all; as we all had but one great object of union in view: and I shall ever rejoice in it as the happiest incident of my life, and the best service I have ever been able to render to our Church, that the resolves which were offered the next morning were unanimously and almost instantly adopted, as reconciling every sentiment, and removing every difficulty which had before appeared to obstruct a general union.

Bishop White, whom I consulted in framing the resolves, and Dr. Moore, of New York, and Mr. (now Dr.) Smith, of South Carolina, were particularly zealous in whatever tended to promote this good work; and I am well assured that you are in some mistake respecting Bishop White's having declined a "proposal" for your joining with him and Bishop Provoost in consecrating a fourth Bishop. He has assured me and also declared in Convention, that no such proposal was ever made to him; and I believe he has written, or will write to you on this subject. His whole conduct, wherever your name and Episcopate have been mentioned, does him honor, and is perfectly agreeable to his well-known excellent temper, and zeal for the peace and unity of the Church. It was Dr. White who seconded, on a former occasion, my motion for not suffering any question in Convention, which might imply even a doubt of the validity of your consecration, and that at a time when admitting a doubt of that kind was considered by some as a good means of forwarding his own and Dr. Provoost's consecration.

Now, I cannot have the least doubt of your attending the adjourned Convention, according to the truly respectable invitation given you. I must again repeat the invitation, that you will make my house your home, or place of residence, during your stay in Philadelphia. The Rev. Dr. Moore, of New York, will be my other and only guest, in the chamber adjoining yours, and he will accompany you from New York or Elizabeth to my house in Philadelphia, as you may agree: and I trust you will be with us a day or two before the 29th of September, rather than a day after, as we shall be pressed in respect of time. . . .

The College of Philadelphia have, on Dr. White's recommendation and mine, granted the degree of D. D. to the Rev. Mr. Bass and Mr. Parker, which we thought a proper compliment to the New England Churches. We are sorry we forgot to pay the same compliment to the venerable old Mr. Leaming, of the Connecticut Church. I hope he will accompany you to Philadelphia and receive that compliment from us in person, if he has nowhere else received it before.

I remain, Right Reverend and Dear Sir,

Yours, etc.,

WILLIAM SMITH.

The Committee to Bishop Seabury.

PHILADELPHIA, August 16, 1789.

RIGHT REVEREND SIR: Your letter to the Right Rev. Bishop White, and also yours of a posterior date to the Rev. Dr. Smith, were laid before the General Convention of our Churches, and read with that deference and regard which are due to the communications of the Bishop and Pastor of a respectable sister Church.

As we "feel equally with you the necessity of a general union of all our Churches in the United States, and lament whatever may occur as tending towards the continuance of disunion," those parts of your letters which had any reference to this important point became the immediate subject of the most affectionate, candid and serious discussion; leaving every other part, either to future joint deliberations or to be noticed in the answers of the gentlemen to whom your letters were, in part, personally addressed.

As a committee appointed for that purpose, we herewith transmit to you the printed proceedings of our Convention, and also a copy of our Address to the Archbishops and Bishops of England. By those documents you will readily perceive, that nothing hath been left unattempted on our part, which we conceived to be conducive, either towards the basis or superstructure of an union, so seemly and needful in itself, and so ardently desired by all.

By the *second* Article of our printed Constitution (as now amended) you will observe that your first and chief difficulty respecting lay representation is wholly removed, upon the good and wise principles admitted by you as well as by us, viz.: "That there may be a strong and efficacious union between churches, where the usages are in some respects different." It was long so in the different dioceses of England.

By the Article of our Constitution above mentioned, the admission of yours and the other Eastern Churches is provided for upon *your own*

principles of representation; while our Churches are not required to
make any sacrifice of theirs; it being declared

> That the Church in each State shall be *entitled* to a representation either of clergy,
> or laity, or of both. And in case the Convention [or Church] of any State should
> neglect or decline to appoint their deputies of either order, or if it should be their rule
> to appoint only out of one order; or if any of those appointed should neglect to at-
> tend, or be prevented by sickness, or any other accident, the Church in such State
> [district or diocese] shall, nevertheless, be considered as duly represented by such
> deputy or deputies as may attend, of either order.

Here, then, every case is intended to be provided for, and experience
will either demonstrate that *an efficacious union* may be had upon these
principles; or mutual good will, and a further reciprocation of sentiments will eventually lead to a more perfect uniformity of discipline as
well as of doctrine.

The representation in those States where the Church appoints clerical
deputies only, or chooses to be wholly represented by its Bishop, will
be considered as complete; and as it cannot be supposed that the clergy
will ever neglect to avail themselves of their voice and negative, in
every ecclesiastical decision, so neither can the laity complain in those
States where they claim no representation, and still less where they are
declared to have a voice, and claim a representation, but neglect to
avail themselves of their claim; which latter is too likely to be the case
in some of the States within our present union, where it is difficult to
procure any lay representation, although earnestly solicited by some of
the clergy, who are fully sensible of the advantages derived to our former Conventions, from the wise and temperate counsels, and the respectable countenance and assistance of our lay members.

As to the second point, respecting your own *consecration* and the *Scots
Episcopacy*, we are persuaded that you have fallen into some misapprehension concerning an entry made in the Journal of a former Convention, or have been misinformed of the circumstances attending it.
Nothing was ever agitated in that Convention concerning the Scots
Episcopacy, but the contrary. You may perceive by the Journal, that
the Convention refused to come to any resolution which would imply
even a doubt of the validity of your consecration; and the proceedings
of the present Convention upon that subject, we are persuaded, will be
more than sufficient to remove every obstacle of our future *union*, which
might have been apprehended on that score.

As the last and greatest proof which we could give of respect for our
sister Churches, and our desire of their assistance in the completion of
our ecclesiastical system, we have postponed everything except what was
intended immediately to open the door of union: and have adjourned
our Convention till the 29th day of September, in the full confidence
of then meeting a representation from all the Churches of the Eastern

States, for the purpose of devising and executing such measures as, through the blessing of God, may concentre all our future labors in the promotion of truth and righteousness, and for preserving our Church in the unity of the Spirit, and the bond of peace.

We hope that the time to which the Convention had adjourned may be found convenient to you and to your Churches. An early day was necessary, as the members from some of the Southern States could neither be detained long from home, nor return to their respective charges, with any prospect of attending at any more remote day, during the present year.

The day to which the adjournment was made, viz., Tuesday, September 29th, falls one week before the annual meeting of the Corporation for the Relief of the Widows and Children of the Clergy, for the States of New York, New Jersey and Pennsylvania, of which you are a member; and the very existence of that pious and charitable institution depends upon our obtaining a full board for the explaining and amending some of the fundamental laws. It was, therefore, proper to make the adjournment of the Convention a week earlier than the meeting of the Corporation, that the business of both might be better transacted without interference: and the City of Philadelphia is the place where, according to *Charter*, the Corporation is to meet this present year, and, exclusive of this consideration, Philadelphia was considered as more central and convenient, as well as less expensive, perhaps, to the members, than New York during the sessions of Congress, and the present concourse of strangers to that city.

We have now only to request your acknowledgment of the receipt of this Address as soon as convenient after it comes to your hand, with which we doubt not to have the agreeable assurance of meeting you (and such representation of your Church as your own rules may provide) in our adjourned Convention at Philadelphia, on the said 29th of September next.   We are, with all respect,

Your affectionate brethren and humble servants,

WILLIAM WHITE,
WILLIAM SMITH,
SAMUEL MAGAW,
FRANCIS HOPKINSON,
TENCH COXE.

Letters so evincive of a Christian spirit found a ready response in the noble Seabury's heart. He writes, at once:

I will, God permitting, most willingly join you at your adjourned Convention on the 29th of September next.

The adjourned meeting of the Convention assembled in Christ Church September 30th, 1789. The minutes say:

The Right Rev. Dr. Samuel Seabury, Bishop of the Protestant Episcopal Church in Connecticut, attended, to confer with the Convention,
agreeable to the invitation given him, in consequence of a resolve
passed at their late session; and the Rev. Dr. Samuel Parker, Deputy
from the Churches in Massachusetts and New Hampshire, and the Rev.
Mr. Bela Hubbard and the Rev. Mr. Abraham Jarvis, Deputies from
the Church in Connecticut, produced testimonials of their appointment
to confer with the Convention, in consequence of a similar invitation.

On the next day a Committee, of which Dr. Smith was the
Chairman, was appointed to confer with the Deputies from the
Eastern Churches on the subject of a proposed union with those
Churches.

The reader will remember that one principal ground of opposition by Bishop Seabury and his friends to a union was the provision in the General Ecclesiastical Constitution made by the Convention of 1785, which made the Convention consist of but a single House or Chamber, and made a Bishop but a member of a
Deputation sent from his State. Bishop Seabury and his friends
desired that the Bishops should form an independent House with
power completely to negative the action of the laity, if laymen were
to vote in the councils of the Church at all, as the churches in
Pennsylvania and elsewhere South absolutely insisted that they
should do.

The negotiation required great self-control, firmness and insinua-
tion, with dispositions to conciliate, and readiness to yield in all matters where concessions could be safely made. Dr. Smith, if old
John Adams' account of him, already quoted by us, be correct, was
eminently suited for the diplomatist of the Convention.*   He met
the Right Reverend and the Reverend gentlemen of the North,
and things were made harmonious. On Friday, October 2d, 1789,
he reported as follows:

That they have had a full, free and friendly conference with the deputies
of the said Churches, who, on behalf of the Church in their several
States, and by virtue of sufficient authority from them, have signified
that they do not object to the Constitution which was approved at the
former session of this Convention, if the third article of that Constitution may be so modified as to declare explicitly the right of the Bishops,

---

* See our Vol. I., p. 334. Adams characterizes him as "soft, polite, insinuating,
adulating, sensible, learned, industrious, indefatigable."

when sitting in a separate House, to originate and propose acts for the concurrence of the other House of Convention, *and to negative such acts proposed by the other House as they may disapprove.*

Your Committee conceiving this alteration to be desirable in itself, as having a tendency to give greater stability to the Constitution, without diminishing any security that is now possessed by the clergy or laity; and being sincerely impressed with the importance of an union to the future prosperity of the Church, do therefore recommend to the Convention a compliance with the wishes of their brethren, and that the third article of the Constitution may be altered accordingly. Upon such alteration being made, it is declared by the Deputies from the churches in the Eastern States that they will subscribe the Constitution, and become members of this General Convention.

This report was accepted by the Convention with a single modification to the effect that though the Bishops, when there should be three or more, should form a separate House with a right to originate and propose acts for the concurrence of the House of Deputies composed of clergy or laity, and that when any proposed act should have passed the House of Deputies, the same should be transmitted to the House of Bishops, the House of Deputies should have a negative thereupon, provided that the proposed act should not be negatived by the Bishops *if adhered to by four-fifths of the other House.*

As the States which had been in the Convention up to this time were but seven,* and as those that now desired an absolute right in the House of Bishops to negative any proceedings were three,† it was practically impossible to have *four-fifths* of the House of the Deputies carry any measure without the concurrence of these three. The qualification made in the amendment of the Report presented by Dr. Smith was probably made to "let down" in as easy a manner as possible some of the very low churchmen of the South, and it was disarmed of the last remnants of danger to the views of Bishop Seabury and his friends,—which in reality were the views also of Bishop White and Dr. Smith—by a resolution in these words:

That it be made known to the several State Conventions that it is proposed to consider and determine in the next General Convention on

---

* New York, New Jersey, Pennsylvania, Delaware, Maryland, Virginia and South Carolina.

† Connecticut, Massachusetts and New Hampshire.

the propriety of investing the House of Bishops with a full negative upon the proceedings of the other House.*

The minutes of the Convention go on to tell us that the General Constitution of the Protestant Episcopal Church, as now altered and amended, was laid before Bishop Seabury and the Deputies from the Churches in the Eastern States for their approbation and consent, and that after a short time they delivered the following testimony of their assent to the same:

October 2, 1789.

We do hereby agree to the Constitution of the Church, as modified this day in Convention.

> SAMUEL SEABURY, D. D., Bishop of the Episcopal Church in Connecticut.
>
> ABRAHAM JARVIS, A. M., Rector of Christ Church, Middletown.
>
> BELA HUBBARD, A. M., Rector of Trinity Church, New Haven.
>
> STATE OF CONNECTICUT.
>
> SAMUEL PARKER, D. D., Rector of Trinity Church, Boston, and Clerical Deputy for Massachusetts and New Hampshire.

The minutes add:

After subscribing as above, the Right Rev. Bishop Seabury, and the Clerical Deputies aforesaid, took their seats as members of the Convention.

Thus was the UNION OF THE CHURCH in America, through the good efforts of Bishop White and Dr. Smith, achieved! For this inestimable service, even more than for their other great services to her, their names should ever be honored by the children of the Church.

It is a remarkable fact that this great act of what we may call national ecclesiastical independence, and of a more perfect ecclesiastical union was achieved in that very Hall where, on the Fourth of July, 1776,—John Hancock placing his bold signature in the front,—was made our national political independence; that same Hall where, on the 17th day of September, 1787,—"George Wash-

---

* With this full negative the House of Bishops was invested by the Convention of 1808.

ington, President and Deputy of Virginia," leading the illustrious band,—was signed the Constitution of the United States of America. Inviolable remain forever and separated from all common uses the spot thus politically and ecclesiastically consecrated! *

The Convention of 1789, as I have mentioned in the text, first met in Christ Church, and sat there during the whole of the original session, and our General Conventions have usually sat in a church as do almost always our Diocesan Conventions.

But in the case of the Convention of 1789, on the 1st of October, the day before the union was effected, the minutes say :

> The meeting in Christ Church being found inconvenient to the members in several respects, it was resolved that the Rev. Dr. William Smith and the Hon. Mr. Secretary Hopkinson be appointed to wait upon his Excellency Thomas Mifflin, Esquire, the President of the State, and request leave for the Convention to hold their meeting in some convenient apartment in the State House.

At a later hour of the same day the entry is :

> The Rev. Dr. William Smith and Hon. Mr. Hopkinson reported that .the President of the State had very politely given permission to the Convention to hold their meetings at the State House in the apartments *of the General Assembly* until they shall be wanted for the public service.
>
> Adjourned to meet at the State House to-morrow morning.

---

* I am quite aware that the Carpenters' Company have, *lately*, pretended—for it is only within a few years that any such pretension has been made—that the Federal Convention of 1787 sat in their Hall. The pretension is the result of ignorance and assumption. The Official Journal of the Federal Convention, Chief Justice Yates's private minutes, contemporary newspapers, the motion of Dr. Franklin for prayers, June 28th, 1787, and his remarks at the close of the Convention about the rising and the setting sun on the back of the Speaker's chair, all show that the Federal Convention was held in the State House, just as a tablet in that edifice records; and the remarks of Dr. Franklin, on his motion for prayers, when read in the light of contemporary historical facts, show also (as indeed probably do his remarks about the rising and the setting sun on the back of the Speaker's chair) the very room; to wit, the Hall of Independence. Equally unfounded is the legend on one of the walls of the Hall that the eloquence of Adams, *Hancock* and Henry there inspired the patriots of the Revolution. The only Congress that sat in Carpenters' Hall was that of 1774, and Hancock was not in it. And both these pretensions are as void of truth as the one put forth by the orator of the Hall (Mr. Betts) to the Governors of the nine States, assembled there October 18th, 1879, on their way to Yorktown, that the Supreme Court of the United States sat there during the time that Philadelphia was the seat of the Federal Government. The minute-books of that Court, all preserved at Washington, show that the Court sat in the still-existing handsome south room (obviously made for a court-room) in the second story of the City Hall, at the southwest corner of Chestnut and Fifth streets, with one or two exceptions, when it sat in the State House or in the Council Chamber.

CHAPTER LII.

ON the union of the Churches in the New England States with
those in the Middle and Southern by which the Bishops thus far
consecrated for America (Seabury, White and Provoost) were
made members of the Convention, the Convention divided itself
into two chambers: that of the House of Bishops and that of the
House of Clerical and Lay Deputies. The Bishops, we are told
in the Journals, "withdrew." They retired, I presume, to the
room in the upper part of the State House, which was long used
by the Governor and Council; while the Clerical and Lay Deputies remained on the ground floor, in that chamber, on the east
side of the edifice, formerly known as the Assembly Room of the
Province, and since as the Chamber of Independence.

Immediately on the retirement of the Bishops, Dr. Smith was
elected President of the House of Clerical and Lay Deputies, and
was conducted, no doubt, to that same historic chair occupied, for
some years before the Revolution, by the Speakers of the Colonial Assembly, in 1776 by John Hancock, and in 1787 by George
Washington. Dr. Smith was not a vain-glorious, nor a self-elating
man; but I should suppose that in such a moment—called on as
he now was, to preside over an ecclesiastical assembly which might
fairly be called august—seated in that chair which the Speakers of
the old Quaker Legislature had once so self-complacently filled, he

could not have done other than recall the scene in that identical room some thirty years before, when, summoned before the Legislature of Friends—then the dominant power of Pennsylvania—for what *they* called a libel on the Government, he was insulted by these Broadbrims, and with contempt for his ecclesiastical orders and his academic distinctions alike, was convicted without evidence; and by a sentence unwarranted by the charge made against him, sent to the cells of the gaol at Walnut and Fifth streets.

We have mentioned elsewhere, that Smith's life seems filled with dramatic incidents. This, perhaps, is one of them. So does the whirligig of time bring about its revenges. Well does it behoove every man in power to remember the poet's precept:

> Æquam memento in rebus arduis
> Servare mentem, non secus in bonis
> Ab insolenti temperatam
> Lætitiâ, moriture Delli!

But Dr. Smith had not much time just now for meditation and moralizing. He had to go to work at once with important business.

The Proposed Book had not been adopted; and a review of "The Book of Common Prayer and administrations of the Sacraments and other rites and ceremonies of the Church, according to the use of the Church of England," was now, of course, in order.

Instead of appointing one large committee to do the work of review and alteration for the whole book—the plan adopted in the Convention of 1785 for the Proposed Book—the work of alteration and review in the Convention of 1789 was parcelled out among several committees—some of the committees being appointed in the House of Bishops and some in the House of Clerical and Lay Deputies.

Those appointed in the latter House, and, as I suppose, by the President, Dr. Smith, were these: one to which was given the preparation of a morning and evening service; a second, to which was given the preparation of the Litany, with occasional prayers and thanksgivings; a third, to which was given the preparation of a Calendar and Table of Lessons for Morning and Evening Prayer throughout the year; a fourth, to which was given the preparation of an order for the administration of the Holy Communion; a fifth, to which was given the duty of reporting in what

manner the Psalms should be used. Other parts of the Prayer
Book were taken in hand in the House of Bishops—we can hardly
say were placed in charge of committees, since the House consisted of but two persons, one of whom, Bishop Seabury, presided,
and the other, Bishop White, constituted the body, where motions
were made, seconded and carried; he being the "be-all" and
"end-all" of everything outside of the Bishop presiding.* Bishop
Provoost kept himself away from the Convention. He had been
"indisposed"—indisposed, perhaps, to come to it—at the original
Convention. He became more and more "indisposed" with the
prospects of "Dr. Cebra's" presidency and powers, and almost
threatened a secession, which, however, he never executed prior
to 1801, when he sought to resign his Episcopate, a resignation
which was not deemed admissible nor accepted.†

The Bishops in their "House" renewed, if I remember, the service for the Public Baptism of Infants; made alterations in the
English form of the solemnization of Matrimony, in the Order for
the Visitation of the Sick, in the Order for the Communion of the
Sick, in the form for the Visitation of Prisoners, in the Order for
the Burial of the Dead, alterations in the Catechism and in the

---

* While the Convention sat in Christ Church, the "House of Bishops" sat in its
"Vestry Room," a small place on the north of the pulpit, and about seven feet wide by
twelve long. The "House" was a very small one, no doubt, but still large enough
for the two persons who composed it, and their Secretary, the Rev. Mr. Clarkson.

† The feeling between Bishop Seabury and Bishop Provoost threatened at one time
serious results. Bishop Provoost did not even call upon his Right Reverend Brother
while the latter was in New York. He openly denied the validity of the Bishop of
Connecticut's Episcopal orders, and in private letters wrote of him as "Bishop *Cebra*,"
an inexcusable impropriety if meant for an indignity, though lessened by the fact that
there was a family on Long Island where Bishop Seabury had once been that thus
wrote their name. The fact was that Bishop Seabury had been an avowed Tory—a
Chaplain, during the war, in a British regiment, and after the war a recipient of half-
pay. Bishop Provoost had been a strong Whig from the beginning, and is said, on the
occasion of a sudden attack by the British, to have himself taken up arms. Dr. Smith,
seeing the dangerous consequences which such a state of relations between two Bishops—from whatever cause arising—threatened to the infant Church, sought at the
earliest date to bring the two gentlemen into harmonious intercourse. He spoke on
the subject to Bishop White, who responded to all his anxieties and wishes. Other
common friends were brought into council, and Dr. Smith suggested that Bishop Seabury should make a visit to Bishop Provoost, the latter agreeing to be at home to receive it. Bishop Seabury agreed to make the visit. Bishop Provoost received the
visit cordially, and asked Bishop Seabury to dine with him on the same day, inviting
Bishop White, Dr. Smith and others to meet him. The invitation was accepted, and
from that time relations of harmony were restored. His efforts to bring about this happy
reconciliation Dr. Smith considered among the good acts of his life.

Order of Confirmation. This House, too, prepared a Form of Family Prayer, the form and the manner of setting forth the Psalms in metre, a Ratification of the Thirty-nine Articles, with the exception of the 36th and 37th, and put other parts of the Book into shape.

The Prayer Book, as now used in the American Church, was thus very completely the joint work of the two Houses, each House doing its full share; each acting freely upon the work of the other, but each with perfect respect, good-will and good manners toward that other, although we know that the House of Bishops did not fully approve all that was finally agreed on; it agreeing to all, however, as in nothing essentially wrong. Dr. Smith's preface to the old Proposed Book, shortened and slightly altered—but with its essential thoughts and much of its exact language retained—made the preface to the new volume.

I ought not here perhaps to omit a little anecdote, illustrative of what I state just above, and which comes to me in a private letter from that well-known and much-honored divine of our Church, the Rev. Thomas W. Coit, D. D., derived by him from the lips of the late Dr. Samuel Farmar Jarvis, and given to Dr. Coit as Dr. Coit himself says, with that gentleman's characteristic interest when relating anything of vital consequence pertaining to the history of our American Prayer Book. "I presume," says Dr. Coit, "that Dr. Jarvis had it from his father, who may have been on the spot at the time of its occurrence." Dr. Coit continues:

Bishops Seabury and White constituted the House of Bishops when our present Communion Office was about to be proposed to the House of Deputies for their adoption. The two Bishops preferred the *Scotch* Communion Service to the English, and after they had sent *it* to the House of Deputies felt anxious and timid about the result; and well they might, when the Athanasian Creed had been ignored, the Nicene treated with ominous neglect, and even the simple Creed of the Apostles submitted to tinkering—a blemish inflicted on it which, even to this late day, our Church has not had the courage to erase!

The Bishops sent for Dr. Smith, then President of the House of Deputies, for a private conference. They frankly admitted that they had gone to the Scotch Communion Office for a material portion of their labors. But as Dr. Smith was a born Scotchman, this was a compliment to his country, which subdued his prejudices, if he had any. He agreed to introduce the new office to the House of Deputies and recommend it for adoption. The next day he informed the House of the document entrusted to him, and of its variations from the better known office of the Church of England. A storm began to brew, and hoarse whispers about popery reached his ears. He rose in his place, and, exclaiming, "Hear—[pronouncing it *Heyre*]—before ye judge," began to read. Dr. Smith was a superb reader and withal had just enough of a Scotch brogue to make his tones more musical and his emphasis more thrilling. He soon caught attention, and read his paper through without a single interruption, his hearers becoming more and more absorbed and charmed. When he had finished, the new office was accepted with acclamations. Wherefore, if there is anything in our Communion Office which Churchmen of the present day delight in, not to say glory in, they should hold the memory of Dr. William Smith in cherished admiration. If he had not read the office into the acceptance of the House over which he presided, a cold, hard vote might have consigned it, with the Athanasian symbol, into what the Orientals used to call "The Castle of Oblivion." *

The whole book was finally ratified by both Houses; and a committee, consisting of Dr. Smith, Dr. Magaw, Dr. Blackwell of the clergy, with Francis Hopkinson and Tench Coxe of the laity (Bishop White, of the House of Bishops, consenting to advise with the committee), were appointed to superintend the printing of the new book, either in octavo or in folio, or in both, and also to have an edition published "to contain only the parts in general use and the Collects of the day with references to the Epistles and Gospels."

The preparation of a SELECTION OF PSALMS, to be used instead of the Psalms for the day, at the discretion of the minister, originated in the House of Clerical and Lay Deputies; and, I presume, was suggested by Dr. Smith, who, knowing that the Psalter as arranged in the Proposed Book was not acceptable to Bishop Seabury, Dr. Chandler and some other persons—and adhering to his own opinion that the Psalms for the day as fixed in the Psalter were confessedly not always appropriate for a mixed assembly—

---

* This anecdote, in substantial form if not in circumstantial variety, receives confirmation—if, indeed, coming to me from the source which it does, it needs any confirmation—in what Bishop White tells us. He states that "the great change made in restoring to the consecration prayer the oblatory words and the invocation of the Holy Spirit, left out in King Edward's reign;" met, in the House of Clerical and Lay Deputies, with the disposition, in a few gentlemen, to oppose it, "which was counteracted by some pertinent remarks of the President." (Memoirs, 2d edition, page 154.)

fell on this happy idea, a happy one I must myself call it; although I am aware that in so far as it makes selections of verses from Psalms instead of selections of Psalms from the Psalter—which it does in the case of about one-third of the Psalms selected—it is open, to a certain, though far inferior degree, to the objections made to the Psalter as given in the Proposed Book. No doubt some beautiful Psalms are not in the selections. But the Psalms of the regular Psalter for many days are free from objection. So the omission of certain verses in certain Psalms—except that brevity was sought for—may be called, as it has been called, capricious; the verses omitted being in themselves as appropriate nearly or quite as others left. But brevity was one object of the Selections. The seventh and eighth Selections were suggested by Bishop White. Certainly—with all that may be suggested against them—the Selections are distinguished by great beauty. The choice and the arrangement are indicative alike of a knowledge of the Psalter and of rich and exquisite taste. I have already expressed my great surprise that the clergy so seldom use these selections—which if they object to any omission of any verse in any Psalm they can still do, for some of the selections are of Psalms in their entirety; but on the contrary, with a dull formality, worthy of the compilers of an almanac, stick doggedly to "days of the month," and force upon their parishioners as "Psalms of David" compositions some of which are not David's Psalms at all; and others of which, whether so or not, are certainly incomprehensible to the common readers, even when understood—which they are not always—by the minister. I find no fault with the clergy; but only with their forcing upon mixed congregations certain Psalms which they should never make a mixed congregation read anywhere but in their own closets, and with the commentaries of Bishop Horne and the more ponderous and partnership volumes of Drs. Neale and Littledale as expositions.

I am not disposed to institute any comparisons between the Proposed Book and the Book of Common Prayer as now in use in the United States. In *some particular respects* I prefer, and I think that churchmen in this day generally would prefer, what we find in the former book. In its abbreviation of the beautiful, tender and sublime conclusion of the *Benedictus* (St. Luke ii. 68) I think the Convention of 1789 made a great mistake. What can be more beautiful than the eight verses in the Proposed Book in sequence to the four in our present book from which they are cut off? What more beautiful especially than these concluding ones:

And thou, Child, shalt be called the Prophet of the Highest: for thou shalt go before the face of the Lord to prepare his ways;
To give knowledge of salvation unto his people: for the remission of their sins.
Through the tender mercy of our God: whereby the Day-spring from on high hath visited us;
To give light to them that sit in darkness, and in the shadow of death: and to guide our feet into the way of peace.

I think that the Convention of 1789 made as bad mistakes or worse in supplying the *Magnificat* and the *Nunc Demittis* of the early Church and retained in the Proposed Book, by anything whatsoever: I think that the same Convention made an equal mistake in making as part of the Litany or penitential *supplication*, a general Thanksgiving with the prayer of St. Chrysostom and the minor Benediction, accompanied by a right to the minister officiating to introduce one, two, or any number of special prayers and special Thanksgivings, and leaving it discretionary with him to omit some of the grandest and most affecting parts of the true and real Litany; down, I mean, to the prayer, "*We humbly beseech thee.*" I think that in taking away the exhortations to the Communion from the place where, acting by Dr. Smith's suggestion, the committee in charge of the Proposed Book put them—that is to say, at the *very beginning* of "The Communion"—and restoring them to the place where they now are, after the prayer for Christ Church militant—and so dividing the service (one service rightly viewed) into the "ante-Communion" and "the Communion,"—the term "ante-Communion," a term not found, I think, in the Prayer Book—thus *encouraging* the departure of the parishioners from the great service of the Church—they have lowered that office to such a degree that in a measure it loses its proper influence.*

---

* Led on by this error—I speak it reverently—of the Convention of 1789, some of our low-Church clergy—after having got, from those who do not communicate, their money, which, *if there is a communion*, the Church contemplates should be the offering of those who do—that is to say of all adults present—persons whom the Church supposes are baptized and confirmed—pronounce, with no authority whatsoever, the minor Benediction in the midst of the Communion; so, in fact, dismissing the whole

And I do not know that on the whole, in and by and for itself, the Prayer Book, as set forth by the Convention of 1789, has given more satisfaction than would have been given by the Proposed Book.

We know, at least, that at all times, many of the low-church clergy have taken pretty much what liberties—in one direction— they liked with it; violating its express rubrics, omitting of it what they disliked, inserting, of their own, what they liked better, and sometimes exhibiting a manifest disrelish for the whole Prayer-Book by meetings, morning and evening, for prayer, where the orders for morning and evening prayer, daily throughout the year, were completely set aside. We know, too, that animated and encouraged by the example set by this low-church party, and

congregation; first, however, some of these clergy at least, interpositing in a way the most unauthorized, an address of their own, telling the people whom they are about to dismiss, with the grace of the Lord, that "our Church invites everybody who loves the blessed Saviour—of whatever Christian denomination—to draw nigh and unite in the Holy Communion:" an invitation which is unwarranted by any rubric in the service, which is directly in the face of that one appended to the order of Confirmation declaring that "there shall be *none* admitted to the Holy Communion" until such time as he be confirmed or be ready and desirous to be confirmed; which is discountenanced by the first rubric in the ministration of baptism of those of riper years, and which proceeds, I presume, on a misconception of what the Church means in the priest's address to those who come to receive the Holy Communion. Do the clergy who interpolate the Holy Office with such addresses of their own, regard it as any part of "God's commandments" that people should be baptized, or be certified by the laying on of hands, of God's favor and gracious goodness towards them?

Suppose some respectable person, educated in the Society of Friends—a Friend still in reality, though not attending "Meeting" much, nor liking the total disregard of forms which the sect imposes on its members, but still undoubtedly as he or she believes "loving the blessed Saviour" and looking upon a participation in the Communion as an affecting ceremony—a very proper way of testifying publicly that love—but looking on it in no other way and not at all as a means of grace—were to come to the Communion habitually, in a church where such a speech as I have mentioned is habitually made. The minister would, in due time, I suppose, call on the person, inquire if he or she had been confirmed, or was ready and desirous to be so. The answer would be, "No, I do not believe in Confirmation. Besides, I have never been baptized in thy way. I do not believe in water-baptism. I never mean to be baptized with water. With the Spirit I trust I have been baptized." The clergyman, if he did his duty, would reply: "Sir, or Madame, or Miss, if such are your views and such your purposes, I am bound to let you know that a rubric of the Church declares that you shall not be admitted to the Communion." The replication would be, "Ah, indeed, that's new to me! I thought that thou saidst at thy Chancel, that thy Church cordially invited all who loved the blessed Saviour—of whatever name or sect—to come." What would be the rejoinder of this priest? The Church, assuredly, never disparaged its sacrament of Baptism and its holy rite of Confirmation, as these of its clergy, by their unauthorized interpolations into its most solemn office, make her do.

"bettering the example,"—so far as making a worse result is consistent with the meaning of the phrase—an opposite class in the Church have committed pretty much the same violence on the Book; fraudulently embellishing *their* proceedings with various sorts of Romish ceremonial and infusing through the whole so considerable a quantity of Romish doctrine and discipline, that if Rip Van Winkle was a Churchman, and, after his long sleep, happened to go into some of the Protestant Episcopal Churches of New York called " Ritualistic," he certainly would never believe in what sort of a Church he was. He would look amazed, indeed, when he was told that this was the exact Church of Samuel Provoost, and Benjamin Moore, and John Henry Hobart, and Benjamin Tredwell Onderdonk, and Jonathan Mayhew Wainright; and be very apt to doubt when he was really yet awake and in his right senses at all.

Then to come to people very different indeed from the two parties, one of whom would carry the Church to the Methodists and the other to Rome, did not the House of Bishops itself, in the General Convention of 1826, almost, if not altogether, unanimously agree to reform the Book in a most sweeping way—to leave out on all days, but on those especially appointed for humiliation, the whole Litany; to allow two alterations in the office for Confirmation; to allow alteration, at the minister's discretion, upon what are called "prayer days" in the lessons; to give to the minister on all days a permission, both in the morning and evening services, to exercise discretion as to the number of Psalms and to the portions of lessons; *provided only* in regard to each lesson that there be at least fifteen verses. This was bringing things back again in some respects to the Proposed Book ; and if we may credit, as I rather think we may, the statement made in that entertaining and instructive " Life of the First Bishop of Vermont" (at the time that I am speaking Rector of Trinity Church, Pittsburgh, Pennsylvania), by his son, the Rev. John Henry Hopkins, it was only through the ready powers of debate of that remarkable first-named person—in whom legal knowledge, powers of argument and the resources of sarcasm were united in a high degree as in a rare conjunction—that the thing was defeated by the negative of the House of Clerical and Lay Deputies.

Still, I am not insensible to the great value of the Prayer Book

of 1789; nor, taken as a whole, do I deny its superiority to the
"Proposed Book." The length of the Morning Service and some
few matters *quas incuria fudit,** are the greatest objections that I
think of to it. I am certainly ready to admit that in so far as
in its weight and body, the new liturgy comes nearer to the Book
of Common Prayer of the Church of England, than did the Proposed Book, a great point for the future is gained. The Church
in America and the Church in Great Britain and Ireland, and over
the vast colonial possessions of the latter nation are made by it
really one. United in doctrine it is most desirable that they be
united in that which largely with most people, and with many,
entirely, both explains and preserves doctrine. The present
"Common Prayers" of the Church of England and of our Church
—each having the same articles of religion—do, in the main,
unite the two churches. Perhaps each would do well never to
seek to make an union more complete. The subject assuredly
ought never to be thrown open to motions and debate in any large
bodies, nor to be agitated by newspaper or other form of popular
and prolonged discussions, nor in any form calculated to be a
dangerous one. The remarks of a well-known representative in
the Legislature of Pennsylvania,† A. D. 1834, when it was proposed to review the then very good Constitution of the State,
apply with force to the subject which we are now considering.

The right of the people to alter their government in such a manner
as they may think proper, is a right not to be questioned. But it is a
right which a people having a government under which they enjoy great
happiness and great prosperity, ought to call into exercise with extreme
caution. No system of government will be satisfactory to all; and

---

* I need not refer to that almost shocking one in the administration of the Lord's
Supper, by which, through the interposition of a word or two in the part of our " Invocation," imported from the " Prayer of Consecration," used by the Church of Scotland—the latter of which reads, " beseeching thee that *whosoever* shall be partakers
of this Holy Communion," while ours is, " beseeching thee that we and all others
who shall be partakers of this Holy Communion "—makes us, by adhering literally
to the rest of the prayer of the Church of Scotland, *exclude* the parties offering the
prayer from the benefits meant to be invoked! The omission in the Prayer Book of
1789 of the directions contained in the rubric of the English Book, how, in the Morning
Service, the First Lesson is to be read,—" distinctly, with an audible voice; he that read-
eth so standing and turning himself as best to be heard by all present "—makes senseless the rubric in our book, that the Second Lesson is to be read " in like manner."

† The late John Bradford Wallace, Esq., of Philadelphia, representing at the time
the county of Crawford, in the northwestern part of Pennsylvania.

when we begin to change it who shall say where the changes shall end? Sound wisdom has therefore adopted it as a maxim that it is better to endure some small defects in a good system, than to endanger the system by throwing it open to change. If it could be practically required that every point upon which a change was desired should be acknowledged by a majority of the people to be an evil, and a concurrence of the same majority in establishing a remedy, there would be no great danger in attempting the alteration. But the danger is this: One man is dissatisfied with a particular provision in the constitution. A second is content with that, but dislikes another. A third person approves both those provisions; but thinks some other very objectionable, and so on to a great extent. Each prefers the constitution to stand as it is, with the exception of only the particular part which he objects to. Passions are excited, prejudices are strengthened: and eventually all make common cause, and each to obtain his own alteration, unites with the others to obtain theirs: And thus a majority is obtained for many alterations, when the judgment of the same majority is opposed to the adoption of any one, and, of course, of every one of them.

Still, the eye of hopeful anticipation cannot but sometimes fancy that it sees a pleasing sight in future days. The Church of Great Britain and the Church in America have come of late years into an intercourse both close and frequent. Our Bishops will soon outnumber the English Bishops. Perhaps they do so now. In the writings of such men as Seabury, White, Dehon, Hobart, H. U. Onderdonk, Ravenscroft, Hopkins, Doane, DeLancey, Whittingham and Odenheimer among the Bishops, and of Dr. Chandler, Dr. Smith, Dr. S. F. Jarvis, Dr. S. H. Turner, Dr. Coit, Dr. Bowden, Dr. Chapman, Dr. Dorr, and many others, probably, not known to me, in the lower orders of the ministry, we have made contributions to a common theology which recall the days of Sherlock and Horseley and Secker and Porteus. Our Bishops are constantly visiting England and deriving new inspirations from what they see in that ancient land. The mitred lords of England are coming often here, and, seated in honor in our Conventions, are gaining for themselves and their Church hardly less than we have got from England.

I look forward to the day when the Church in England shall be disestablished and relieved from that onerous tribute which she now pays to the State. When that occurs—and each church is an ecclesiastical body alone—we shall surely come more closely together. Even as things are, we could perhaps do so; and possibly—in what is purely ecclesiastical—practically and in fact, be the same.   If our Liturgy is ever reviewed again, let it be done by a committee of our own Bishops and clergy in conjunction with Bishops and clergy of the Church of England, and then submitted and adopted or rejected by our Convention and their Convocation or Parliament, without debate.   I see no reason why, except in the matter of the State Prayers, the services should not be wholly consentaneous.   Indeed, if the Preface of our Books—that of the Proposed Book and that of the Book of 1789 alike—correctly say—as I think they do say correctly—that the " proper end of all prayers for civil rulers should be that they may have grace, wisdom and understanding to execute justice and to maintain truth, and that the people may lead quiet and peaceable lives in all godliness and honesty "—why shall not the Prayer Books of England and America be absolutely identical ?   Some things which America prefers, as the *Bonum est Confiteri* and the *Benedic, Anima Mea*, to be retained along with the English originals of the *Magnificat* and *Nunc Dimittis*, with an option for the minister to take any one of the three songs, anthems, or whatever else they may be, instead of either of two.   And so generally; giving what each nation prefers, and a liberty of choice.   Rome's boast that the voices of her ministers alone are heard ever ascending in the language of one Liturgy from the whole circle of the round world —a boast never founded in fact—could no longer be made.   " The Church of England," " The Protestant Episcopal Church in the United States in America," one and the same body,—" The Catholic Church Reformed "—with but diversity in name, would henceforth in the people's estimation, as in the gospel's truths they now are, be the Catholic Church of Christ.   Hasten, O God, if it be thy good will, this happy day ! that as we have one Lord, one faith and one baptism, we may, under one shepherd, be more completely than ever, *one*, thy own blessed Fold !

Among the early acts of the Convention which was still sitting in the form of a single Convention was the appointment of Dr. Smith, the Rev. Benjamin Moore, D. D., and the Rev. Uzal Ogden, to prepare an address to the President, George Washington, who, a few months before, had entered upon the untried duty of Chief Magistrate of the United States.   And Dr. Smith, the Rev. Abraham Beach, D. D., and Robert Andrews, Esq., were appointed a

Committee to prepare an address of thanks to the Most Reverend
the Archbishops of Canterbury and York for their good offices in
procuring the consecration of the American Bishops.

The actual work of preparing the addresses fell to Dr. Smith,
and before the Convention finally adjourned both documents were
ready for the signatures of the members, and were signed. We
now give both documents as Numbers I. and II. To the former—
which Bishop Provoost, Dr. Smith and certain other gentlemen
were requested to present to the President, we append the President's answer. Bishop White, Dr. Smith and other gentlemen
were appointed to forward the address to the Archbishops, which,
no doubt, they did.

Address No. I.

To the President of the United States.

Sir :—We, the Bishops, Clergy, and Laity of the Protestant Episcopal
Church in the States of New York, New Jersey, Pennsylvania, Delaware,
Maryland, Virginia, and South Carolina, in General Convention assembled, beg leave, with the highest veneration, and the most animating national considerations, at the earliest moment in our power, to express our
cordial joy on your election to the chief magistracy of the United States.

When we contemplate the short but eventful history of our nation ;
when we recollect the series of essential services performed by you in the
course of the Revolution ; the temperate yet efficient exertion of the
mighty powers with which the nature of the contest made it necessary to
invest you ; and especially when we remember the voluntary and magnanimous relinquishment of those high authorities at the moment of
peace ; we anticipate the happiness of our country under your future
administration.

But it was not alone from a successful and virtuous use of those extraordinary powers, that you were called from your honorable retirement to
the first dignities of our government. An affectionate admiration of
your private character, the impartiality, the persevering fortitude, and
the energy with which your public duties have been invariably performed,
and the paternal solicitude for the happiness of the American people, together with the wisdom and consummate knowledge of our affairs, manifested in your last military communication, have directed to your name
the universal wish, and have produced, for the first time in the history
of mankind, an example of unanimous consent in the appointment of the
governor of a free and enlightened nation.

To these considerations, inspiring us with the most pleasing expectations as private citizens, permit us to add, that, as the representatives of

a numerous and extended Church, we most thankfully rejoice in the election of a civil ruler, deservedly beloved, and eminently distinguished
among the friends of genuine religion—who has happily united a tender
regard for other churches with an inviolable attachment to his own.

With unfeigned satisfaction we congratulate you on the establishment
of the new Constitution of government of the United States, the mild
yet efficient operations of which, we confidently trust, will remove every
remaining apprehension of those with whose opinions it may not entirely
coincide, and will confirm the hopes of its numerous friends. Nor do
these expectations appear too sanguine, when the moderation, patriotism
and wisdom of the honorable members of the Federal legislature are duly
considered. From a body thus eminently qualified, harmoniously co-
operating with the Executive authority in constitutional concert, we confidently hope for the restoration of order and of our ancient virtues,—
the extension of genuine religion,—and the consequent advancement of
our respectability abroad, and of our substantial happiness at home.

We devoutly implore the Supreme Ruler of the Universe to preserve
you long in health and prosperity,—an animating example of all public
and private virtues,—the friend and guardian of a free, enlightened, and
grateful people,—and that you may finally receive the reward which will
be given to those whose lives have been spent in promoting the happiness
of mankind.

The President's Answer.

*To the Bishops, Clergy, and Laity of the Protestant Episcopal Church in
the States of New York, New Jersey, Pennsylvania, Delaware, Maryland, Virginia, and South Carolina, in General Convention assembled.*

GENTLEMEN : I sincerely thank you for your affectionate congratulation on my election to the chief magistracy of the United States.

After having received from my fellow-citizens in general the most liberal treatment—after having found them disposed to contemplate, in the
most flattering point of view, the performance of my military services,
and the manner of my retirement at the close of the war—I feel that I
have a right to console myself, in my present arduous undertaking, with
a hope that they will still be inclined to put the most favorable construction on the motives which may influence me in my future public transactions.

The satisfaction arising from the indulgent opinion entertained by the
American people, of my conduct, will, I trust, be some security for preventing me from doing anything, which might justly incur the forfeiture
of that opinion. And the consideration that human happiness and moral
duty are inseparably connected, will always continue to prompt me to
promote the progress of the former, by inculcating the practice of the
latter.

On this occasion it would ill become me to conceal the joy I have felt in perceiving the fraternal affection which appears to increase every day among the friends of genuine religion.   It affords edifying prospects indeed, to see Christians of different denominations dwell together in more charity, and conduct themselves, in respect to each other, with a more Christian-like spirit than ever they have done in any former age, or in any other nation.

I receive, with the greatest satisfaction, your congratulations on the establishment of the New Constitution of Government; because I believe its mild, yet efficient, operations will tend to remove every remaining apprehension of those, with whose opinions it may not entirely coincide, as well as to confirm the hopes of its numerous friends; and because the moderation, patriotism, and wisdom of the present Federal Legislature seem to promise the restoration of order and our ancient virtues—the extension of genuine religion—and the consequent advancement of our respectability abroad, and of our substantial happiness at home.

I request, Most Reverend and respectable Gentlemen, that you will accept my cordial thanks for your devout supplications, to the Supreme Ruler of the Universe in behalf of me.   May you, and the people whom you represent, be the happy subjects of Divine Benediction both here and hereafter !

GEORGE WASHINGTON.

August 19, 1789.

Address No. II.

An Address to the Most Reverend the Archbishops of Canterbury and York.

Most Venerable and Illustrious Fathers and Prelates :

We, the Bishops, Clergy, and Laity of the Protestant Episcopal Church in the States of New York, New Jersey, Pennsylvania, Delaware, Maryland, Virginia, and South Carolina, impressed with every sentiment of love and veneration, beg leave to embrace this earliest occasion, in General Convention, to offer our warmest, most sincere, and grateful acknowledgments to you, and (by your means) to all the venerable Bishops of the Church over which you preside, for the manifold instances of your former condescension to us, and solicitude for our spiritual welfare.   But we are more especially called to express our thankfulness for that particular act of your fatherly goodness, whereby we derive, under you, a pure Episcopacy and succession of the ancient Order of Bishops, and are now assembled, through the blessing of God, as a Church duly constituted and organized, with the happy prospect before us of a future full and undisturbed exercise of our holy religion, and its extension to the utmost bounds of this continent, under an ecclesiastical constitution, and a form of worship, which we believe to be truly apostolical.

The growing prospect of this happy diffusion of Christianity, and the assurance we can give you, that our churches are spreading and flourishing throughout these United States, we know, will yield you more solid joy, and be considered as a more ample reward of your goodness to us, than all the praises and expressions of gratitude which the tongues of men can bestow.

It gives us pleasure to assure you, that, during the present sitting of our Convention, the utmost harmony has prevailed through all our deliberations; that we continue, as heretofore, most sincerely attached to the faith and doctrine of the Church of England, and that not a wish appears to prevail, either among our Clergy or Laity, of ever departing from that Church in any essential article.

The business of most material consequence which hath come before us, at our present meeting, hath been, an application from our sister churches in the Eastern States, expressing their earnest desire of a general union of the whole Episcopal Church in the United States, both in doctrine and discipline; and, as a primary means of such union, praying the assistance of our Bishops in the consecration of a Bishop elect for the States of Massachusetts and New Hampshire. We therefore judge it necessary to accompany this address with the papers which have come before us on that very interesting subject, and of the proceedings we have had thereupon, by which you will be enabled to judge concerning the particular delicacy of our situation, and, probably, to relieve us from any difficulties which may be found therein.

The application from the Church in the States of Massachusetts and New Hampshire is in the following words, viz. :

The good providence of Almighty God, the fountain of all goodness, having lately blessed the Protestant Episcopal Church in the United States of America, by supplying it with a complete and entire ministry, and affording to many of her communion the benefit of the labors, advice and government of the successors of the Apostles :

We, Presbyters of said Church in the States of Massachusetts and New Hampshire, deeply impressed with the most lively gratitude to the Supreme Governor of the universe, for his goodness in this respect, and with the most ardent love to his Church, and concern for the interest of her sons, that they may enjoy all the means that Christ, the great Shepherd and Bishop of souls, has instituted for leading his followers into the ways of truth and holiness, and preserving his Church in the unity of the spirit and the bond of peace, to the end that the people committed to our respective charges may enjoy the benefit and advantage of those offices, the administration of which belongs to the highest order of the ministry, and to encourage and promote, as far as in us lies, a union of the whole Episcopal Church in these States, and to perfect and compact this mystical body of Christ, do hereby nominate, elect and appoint, the Rev. Edward Bass, a Presbyter of the said Church, and Rector of St. Paul's in Newburyport, to be our Bishop; and we do promise and engage to receive him as such when canonically consecrated, and invested with the apostolic office and powers by the Right Reverend the Bishops hereafter named, and to render him all that canonical obedience and submission which, by the laws of Christ, and the Constitution of our Church, is due to so important an office.

And we now address the Right Reverend the Bishops in the States of Connecticut, New York and Pennsylvania, praying their united assistance in consecrating our said brother, and canonically investing him with the apostolic office and powers. This request we are induced to make from a long acquaintance with him, and from a perfect knowledge of his being possessed of that love to God and benevolence to men, that piety, learning, and good morals, that prudence and discretion, requisite to so exalted a station, as well as that personal respect and attachment to the communion at large in these States, which will make him a valuable acquisition to the Order, and, we trust, a rich blessing to the Church.

Done at a meeting of the Presbyters whose names are underwritten, held at Salem, in the County of Essex, and Commonwealth of Massachusetts, the fourth day of June, Anno Salutis, 1789.

SAMUEL PARKER, Rector of Trinity Church, Boston.

T. FITCH OLIVER, Rector of St. Michael's Church, Marblehead.

JOHN COUSENS OGDEN, Rector of Queen's Chapel, Portsmouth, New Hampshire.

WILLIAM MONTAGUE, Minister of Christ Church, Boston.

TILLOTSON BRUNSON, Assistant Minister of Christ Church, Boston.

A true copy.

Attest: SAMUEL PARKER.

At the meeting aforesaid,

Voted,—That the Rev. Samuel Parker be authorized and empowered to transmit copies of the foregoing Act, to be by him attested, to the Right Reverend the Bishops in Connecticut, New York, and Pennsylvania; and that he be appointed our agent, to appear at any Convocation to be holden at Pennsylvania or New York, and to treat upon any measures that may tend to promote an union of the Episcopal Church throughout the United States of America, or that may prove advantageous to the interests of the said Church.   EDWARD BASS, *Chairman.*

A true copy.

Attest: SAMUEL PARKER.

This was accompanied with a letter from the Rev. Samuel Parker, the worthy Rector of Trinity Church, Boston, to the Right Rev. Bishop White, dated June 21st, 1789, of which the following is an extract:

The Clergy here have appointed me their agent, to appear at any Convocation to be held at New York or Pennsylvania; but I fear the situation of my family and parish will not admit of my being absent so long as a journey to Philadelphia would take. When I gave you encouragement that I should attend, I was in expectation of having my parish supplied by some gentlemen from Nova Scotia, but I am now informed they will not be here till some time in August. Having, therefore, no prospect of attending in person at your General Convention next month, I am requested to transmit you an attested copy of an act of the Clergy of this and the State of New Hampshire, electing the Rev. Edward Bass our Bishop, and requesting the united assistance of the Right Reverend Bishops of Pennsylvania, New York, and Connecticut, to invest him with apostolic powers. This act I have now the honor of enclosing, and hope it will reach you before the meeting of your General Convention in July.

The clergy of this State are very desirous of seeing an union of the whole Episcopal Church in the United States take place; and it will remain with our brethren at the southward to say, whether this shall be the case or not—whether we shall be an united or divided church. Some little difference in government may exist in different States, without affecting the essential points of union and communion.

In like spirit, the Right Rev. Dr. Seabury, Bishop of the Church in Connecticut, in his letter to the Rev. Dr. Smith, dated July 23d, writes on the subject of union, etc., as followeth:

The wish of my heart, and the wish of the Clergy and of the Church people of this State, would certainly have carried me and some of the Clergy to your General Convention, had we conceived we could have attended with propriety. The necessity of an union of all the Churches, and the disadvantages of our present dis-union, we feel and lament equally with you; and I agree with you, that there may be a strong and efficacious union between churches, where the usages are different. I see not why it may not be so in the present case, as soon as you have removed those obstructions which, while they remain, must prevent all possibility of uniting. The Church of Connecticut consists, at present, of nineteen clergymen in full orders, and more than twenty thousand people they suppose, as respectable as the Church in any State in the union.

After the most serious deliberation upon this important business, and cordially joining with our brethren of the eastern or New England Churches in the desire of union, the following resolves were unanimously adopted in Convention, viz.:

Resolved,—1st. That a complete Order of Bishops, derived as well under the English as the Scots line of succession, doth now subsist within the United States of America, in the persons of the Right Rev. William White, D. D., Bishop of the Protestant Episcopal Church in the State of Pennsylvania; the Right Rev. Samuel Provoost, D. D., Bishop of the said Church in the State of New York; and the Right Rev. Samuel Seabury, D. D., Bishop of the said Church in the State of Connecticut.

2d. That the said three Bishops are fully competent to every proper act and duty of the Episcopal office and character in these United States; as well in respect to the consecration of other bishops, and the ordering of Priests and Deacons, as for the government of the Church, according to such Canons, Rules, and institutions as now are, or hereafter may be, duly made and ordained by the Church in that case.

3d. That in Christian charity as well as of duty, necessity, and expediency, the Churches represented in this Convention ought to contribute, in every manner in their power, towards supplying the wants, and granting every just and reasonable request of their sister churches in these States; and therefore resolved,—

4th. That the Right Rev. Dr. White and the Right Rev. Dr. Provoost be, and they hereby are requested to join with the Right Rev. Dr. Seabury in complying with the prayer of the Clergy of the States of Massachusetts and New Hampshire, for the consecration of the Rev. Edward Bass, Bishop elect of the churches in the said States; but that, before the said Bishops comply with the request aforesaid, it be proposed to the churches in the New England States to meet the Churches of these States, with the said three Bishops, in an adjourned Convention, to settle certain articles of union and discipline among all the churches, previous to such consecration.

5th. That if any difficulty or delicacy, in respect to the Archbishops and Bishops of England, shall remain with the Right Rev. Drs. White and Provoost, or either of them, concerning their compliance with the above request, this Convention will address the Archbishops and Bishops, and hope thereby to remove the difficulty.

We have now, most venerable Fathers, submitted to your consideration whatever relates to this important business of union among all our

churches in these United States. It was our original and sincere intention to have obtained three bishops, at least, immediately consecrated by
the Bishops of England, for the seven States comprehended within our
present union. But that intention being frustrated through unforeseen
circumstances, we could not wish to deny any present assistance, which
may be found in our power to give to any of our sister churches, in that
way which may be most acceptable to them, and in itself legal and
expedient.

We ardently pray for the continuance of your favor and blessing, and
that, as soon as the urgency of other weighty concerns of the Church
will allow, we may be favored with that fatherly advice and direction,
which to you may appear most for the glory of God and the prosperity
of our Churches, upon the consideration of the foregoing documents and
papers

Done in Convention this eighth day of August, 1789, and directed to
be signed by all the members as the act of their body, and by the President officially.

CHAPTER LIII.

RESTORATION BY THE STATE OF PENNSYLVANIA OF THE CHARTER OF THE COL-
LEGE OF PHILADELPHIA, UNJUSTLY TAKEN AWAY IN 1779—AN ANECDOTE
ILLUSTRATIVE OF DR. SMITH'S READY HUMOR—HE TAKES LEAVE OF THE
CONVENTION IN MARYLAND—BISHOP WHITE'S TRIBUTE TO HIS SERVICES
TO THE CHURCH AND OTHERWISE IN THAT STATE—DR. WROTH'S ACCOUNT
OF WASHINGTON COLLEGE—DR. SMITH'S RETURN TO PHILADELPHIA, JULY
1ST, 1789—PROPOSED INSCRIPTION UPON HIS COLLEGE—PROCEEDINGS IN THE
DIFFERENT BRANCHES OF THE RECONSTRUCTION—FIRST COMMENCEMENTS,
MEDICAL, AND IN THE DEPARTMENTS OF ARTS, SINCE THE RESTORATION—
UNION OF THE COLLEGE OF PHILADELPHIA WITH THE UNIVERSITY OF THE
STATE OF PENNSYLVANIA UNDER THE NAME OF THE UNIVERSITY OF PENN-
SYLVANIA—THE REV. JOHN EWING ELECTED PROVOST—THE NEW INSTITU-
TION LANGUISHED AND CONTINUED TO LANGUISH FOR MANY YEARS, AND UNTIL
THE PROVOSTSHIP OF DR. STILLE—DR. SMITH PREACHES BEFORE THE CIN-
CINNATI, JULY 4TH, 1790—ENGAGEMENT AND MARRIAGE OF HIS SON CHARLES
WITH MISS YEATES—DEATH OF HIS DAUGHTER, MRS. GOLDSBOROUGH—
BEAUTIFUL INSCRIPTION ON HER TOMB—LETTERS IN CONNECTION WITH HER
DEATH.

THE last chapter ends Dr. Smith's ecclesiastical history for the
year 1789. But for the year he had in addition one which was
collegiate and personal. He had labored so perseveringly and
with so much ability to have the old College of Philadelphia restored to its rights that in the end he succeeded; and on the 6th
of March, 1789, the Assembly of Pennsylvania, declaring the Act

20

of 1779 repugnant to justice and in violation to the Constitution of the State, restored the ancient charter, with all its privileges. His position as Provost, if he chose to occupy again the place, which for the mere vindication of his honor it was supposed that he would, was at his command.

In connection with his efforts to procure the passage of the repealing act we may mention a piece of the Provost's ready wit. On the morning of passing this Act, while the members were collecting themselves, and before the Speaker took the chair, Dr. H——, a good-natured man, but a great politician and of abdominal dimensions more than aldermanic, came into the Committee Room, and offered to a member a paper by way of a *Rider* to the engrossed Bill, requesting him to present the same to the House. The member handed it to Dr. Smith, who happened to be near. Dr. Smith hastily looked over it, and finding its purport was to indemnify what was called the University from any particular account of their expenditure of the College stock and property during their usurpation of eight years and upwards, returned it to the member, who went into the House, and Dr. H—— after him. Dr. Smith got a piece of paper and wrote *extempore* as follows:

The Rider.

1.

"On mischief bent, by Ewing sent,*
    With *Rider* in his hands,
Comes Doctor GUTS, with mighty struts,
    And thus of Smith demands:

2.

" ' This Rider, sir, to save all stir,
    By Master Ewing's will,
I bring in haste, pray get some paste,
    And tack it to your Bill.'

3.

" Smith lifts his eyes—' Hoot ! mon,' he cries,
    ' Take back your stupid stuff,
Our answer's brief, the crafty thief
    Has *ridden* lang enuff.' ''

---

* Dr. Ewing, the Provost of the University of Pennsylvania who had supplanted Dr. Smith, was a Presbyterian.

This being privately thrown on the table of the Speaker, who was a man of humor, it was soon handed to some of the nearest members, and spread through the House with a laugh which did more to smother the poor *Rider* IN CUNABULIS than many long speeches could have done.

On the 2d of June the Sixth Annual Convention of the Episcopal Church of Maryland was held in Baltimore. Dr. Smith was elected President.

Before it finally adjourned he made known to it that he was about to retire from the State and return to Pennsylvania. The Convention was deeply affected by the intelligence, and directed its Secretary to assure him that "their minds were strongly impressed with a grateful sense of the services he had rendered to learning and religion by his attention to those important concerns and to return to him their sincere thanks."

We need not specify the great services which Dr. Smith did to both the Church and to literature in Maryland during his residence there. Bishop White, after speaking of the perils to which the Church in that State had been exposed by the Legislature, which, though consisting of men of various denominations, " took up," he says, " the subject of organizing the Church, and particularly of appointing ordainers to the ministry,"—and of the two Church Conventions of August, 1783, and June, 1784, by which they were counteracted, says :*

The proceedings of these conventions, with measures taken at other times and in other matters by the clergy of that State, were chiefly originated by the Rev. Dr. Smith, who in his residence there, during the seizure of the charter-rights of the College of Philadelphia, exerted his excellent talents in these and in other public works.

In every state of life to which God was pleased to call him, he learned not only to be content, but at once was highly useful.

We may say, indeed, with some confidence, that but for the activity and executive powers of Dr. Smith, it would have been impossible to have got the Church in the Southern States into a right condition for the great work of UNION, which through his, Bishop White's and Bishop Seabury's united efforts—and in the face of

---

* White's Memoirs, p. 92. Second Edition.

some inexplicable conduct of Bishop Provoost's, took place in 1789.*

It was with feelings of a touching kind that Dr. Smith took leave of his affectionate parish and devoted College at Chestertown. He left the former in the possession of the Rev. Mr. Robinson, of Virginia, as Rector, and the latter in that of the Rev. Colin Ferguson as President. Both parish and college were left in good hands, but neither in hands like those which now surrendered the possession.

I may here perhaps insert a letter giving some facts in regard to Washington College before I finally take leave of the subject. It is from the venerable Peregrine Wroth, M. D., a well-known physician of Maryland:

EASTON, TALBOT Co., October 23d, 1872.

HORACE WEMYSS SMITH, ESQ.

DEAR SIR: . . . . I send you a view of the old College, the one burnt down in 1827. It was rebuilt in 1846 in three separate buildings —all of which are not equal in size to the old College.

I should not forget to add that to the back of the common hall was built (to the old College) a chapel sixty feet square, joined to the common hall and to the two wings—the whole building in front about one hundred and twenty feet from end to end, and sixty feet wide. The endowment was £1,250 annually. And it was thus—about 1798-99— the State Legislature took away £750 of the fund, and in 1800 or 1801 the whole balance, leaving us to the *tuition* money of the students as our only support. We at once were obliged to dismiss all our Professors but one, and when the College was burnt we rented a house in town and kept up the school there in name, but greatly fallen off. When the fund was first lessened by our State Legislature, Mr. Daniel McCurtin, Professor of the Dead Languages, one day gave my class, then the head class in his department, a history of the endowment of the College. Before the Revolution, when Lord Baltimore was Lord Proprietor, he

---

* Bishop Seabury, with whom Dr. Smith's relations, as we have already said, were then friendly, thought, indeed, that in defining the office and duties of a Bishop (see *supra*, p. 108) as St. Jerom defined them, my venerable ancestor had rather too much lowered them. But Dr. Smith knew the churchmen of Maryland better than did Dr. Seabury. He raised them to as high a point as it was at that time possible to raise them, and had he attempted to force Dr. Seabury's high views upon them, there would have been an utter collapse and break down in his beneficent efforts. He laid a foundation strong enough for the best superstructure; one which has sustained a church in which Claggett and Kemp and Stone and WHITTINGHAM have filled the highest office.

gave the Legislature £40,000 on condition that they would pay £3,000 annually to two Colleges—should such be built—*one* at Annapolis, the metropolis of the State, and the other at Chestertown, on the eastern side of Chesapeake Bay—£1,750 to that on the western shore and £1,250 to that at Chestertown, on the eastern shore. During the war (of the Revolution) the money was used by the State, and when, by the great exertions of the Rev. William Smith, who travelled through the whole eastern shore on *horseback* for that purpose, the necessary fund for building the College was raised, the Legislature imposed a tax on "Hawkers and Pedlars and Marriage Licenses," and paid to Washington College £1,250, founded in 1782, and to St. John's College, at Annapolis, built about 1783 or 1784, the annual sum of £1,750. It was made by Act of Legislature a perpetual endowment! How they could have a right to take it away afterwards is a question.

The above statement, spoken of afterwards so often by my class and others, was indelibly impressed on my mind, and, I believe, every word of it. But I confess that though I made many efforts years ago to verify it, I have not succeeded.

Before the College was founded, Dr. Smith, as you are probably aware, was principal of a large and fine school in Chestertown, and Rector of the parish of I. U., built in 1767 in Kent county. The church in Chestertown, built in 1772, was then a chapel of ease. He was Rector of both when the College was built. He was elected Principal, and continued so until he returned to Philadelphia, about 1790. Personally, of course, I was unacquainted with him, being born in 1786; but I have always heard him spoken of as eminent both as a scholar and as a minister of the Church. The life-size portrait, which I had taken from a small engraving, is hanging in the Library at Washington College, and when painted was pronounced by two aged and intelligent ladies who remembered and admired him, as a good likeness.

Of course I can know nothing personally of your renowned ancestor. I may have seen him, for he baptized me in 1786, when I was but a few days old. I was not entered at Washington College (of which I am an Alumnus) until 1794, after your ancestor had been called to Philadelphia, and I left college in 1803, the year of his death.

Please excuse this note. It would not have been written to trouble you, but I feel personally interested in the success of your researches; having been educated at the College he founded, since that a visitor of it and Professor of Chemistry in that institution, and *feeling* it is my duty to render any assistance I am able.

I remain very respectfully yours,

P. WROTH.*

---

* See Appendix, No. V.

On the 1st of July, 1789, Dr. Smith, with his wife and children, returned to Philadelphia, and went to reside upon his family-seat at the *Falls of Schuylkill.* And now—singular incident—as the village clock chimes the hour of twelve to usher in the morn of July 1st, 1879, I, his great-grandson, am preparing upon the same estate this record for the printer; *ninety* years from the time he returned to it. As I write, my mind reverts to the closing paragraph of *his* preface to the works of Nathaniel Evans, which he had collected and published as a labor of love. He there says:

The task he left to be performed was a mournful one; but it has been executed with that fidelity, which the writer of this would wish might be extended to any performance of his own, 'that may be thought worthy of the public eye, by that true friend into whose hands it may fall, when he himself shall be no more! *

In anticipation of the formal surrender of the College of Philadelphia—"*My* College" as he rightly called it—to him, he proposed that the following inscription, which is the same which was set in Queen's College, Oxford, on the Restoration, should be engraved upon the front of the edifice:

" DIVINA

OPE MISERICORDIA ET PROVIDENTIA

COLLEGIUM HOC

A CAPTIVITATE QUADAM BABYLONICA

EREPTUM

INTEGRIS ET LEGITIMIS SUIS MEMBRIS

CONSTITUITUR."

The first meeting of the Trustees of the College was held at the house of Dr. Franklin, now an aged man, upon notice given by Dr. Smith. There were fourteen Trustees surviving, *all* of whom were present:

BENJAMIN FRANKLIN, LL. D.,			DR. JOHN REDMAN,	
BENJAMIN CHEW,			JOHN LAURENCE,	
EDWARD SHIPPEN,	Esqs.		THOMAS MIFFLIN,	Esqs.
THOMAS WILLING,			SAMUEL POWEL,	

---

* See Vol. I., page 481.

RT. REV. WM. WHITE, D. D.,   GEORGE CLYMER,
ROBERT MORRIS,   } Esqs.   JAMES WILSON,   } Esqs.
FRANCIS HOPKINSON,   }   ALEX. WILCOCKS,   }

The only surviving members of the Faculty of Arts were Dr.
Smith, the Provost, and Mr. James Davidson, Professor of
Humanity and Latin and Greek Languages.

At a subsequent meeting, held April 28th, 1789, the Treasurer,
Mr. Bingham, and Col. Miles were appointed a committee to read
and report concerning the condition of the Norristown estate and
mills on the Schuylkill, of which we have already spoken. The
vacancies, ten in number, of Trustees were supplied by the choice
of the following gentlemen:

THOMAS FITZSIMONS,	WILLIAM LEWIS,
HENRY HILL,	JOHN NIXON,
REV. ROBERT BLACKWELL, D. D.,	ROBERT HARE,
SAMUEL MILES,	CASPAR WISTAR,
WILLIAM BINGHAM,	RICHARD PETERS.

The committee made the inspection, and on the 28th of May
reported. They had viewed the estate, but so unfavorable was
their statement of its condition that it was the opinion of the
Trustees that it would be to the interest of the institution to sell it
as soon as possible, and to invest the proceeds thereof in ground-
rents or some other real estate productive of a certain undimin-
ished revenue for the support of the institution. The committee
was continued, in order to advertise the estate for sale, and to
report some plan for selling it in such manner as would be agreeable to justice as well respecting the then tenant, as the engagements of the Trustees to Dr. Smith, at the time of the purchase
of the estate from him in the autumn of 1776.

Under date of the 18th of August, 1789 (Dr. Smith having
offered to take so troublesome a burden from the College), the
minutes of the Trustees continue:

At a meeting held this day it was *Resolved*, that £4,300 be the sum
demanded for the Norriton estate, exclusive of the town; £1,200 to
be paid on or before the 1st day of April and before the signing of the
deed, and that the pre-emption at that price be now offered to Dr.
Smith. An offer was made to Dr. Smith at the Board, agreeably to the
above resolve, and the Doctor accepted of the same; and the security to
be given for the remainder of the payments, to be as may be concluded

on by the Committee, viz.: the Treasurer, Col. Miles, and Mr. Bingham, formerly appointed for the advertising the estate for sale.

When the restitution of its rights to the College was made, the Professors in the medical schools came again to their places. These Professors were Dr. William Shippen, Jr., Professor of Anatomy and Surgery; Adam Kuhn, Professor of Botany and Materia Medica; and Benjamin Rush, Professor of Chemistry. Being waited upon by a committee of the Trustees, they severally expressed their satisfaction upon the renewal of their connection with the Trustees of the College, and their restoration to their Professorships under them in discharging their duties, of which, as heretofore, it was their wish and intention to continue :*

It was determined to confer no longer the degree of Bachelor of Medicine. The reason for this course was "that it would not be for the honor of the College or the advancement of sound literature to continue the degree of Bachelor of Medicine, lest young and inexperienced men under the sanction of that degree and of their collegiate education, assuming the name of Doctor, might be tempted to impose upon the public, by a too early practice. It has, therefore, been determined that the degree of Doctor in Medicine shall be the only medical degree conferred in this seminary."

On the 17th of November, 1789, the following rules, of which the original manuscript is in Dr. Smith's handwriting, respecting a medical education, having been passed by the Trustees, were published:

1. No person shall be received as a candidate for the degree of Doctor in Medicine until he has arrived to the age of twenty-one years, and has applied himself to the study of Medicine in the College for at least two years. Those students and candidates who reside in the city of Philadelphia, or within five miles thereof must have been the pupils of some respectable physician for the space of three years, and those who may come from the country and from any greater distance than five miles, must have studied with some reputable physician thereof at least two years.

2. Every candidate shall have regularly attended the lectures of the following Professors, viz.: of Anatomy and Surgery; of Chemistry and

---

* Dr. John Morgan, Professor of the Theory and Practice of Physic, was not at the time within the State. The Trustees considered him reinstated and entitled to continue in his office until his return.

the Institutes of Medicine; of Materia Medica and Pharmacy; of the
Theory and Practice of Medicine; the Botanical Lectures of the Pro-
fessor of Natural History and Botany; and a course of Lectures in
Natural and Experimental Philosophy.

3. Each candidate shall signify his intention of graduating to the
Dean of the Medical Faculty at least two months before the time of
graduation; after which he shall be examined privately by the Professors of the different branches of Medicine. If remitted to his studies,
the Professors shall hold themselves bound not to divulge the same ; but
if he is judged to be properly qualified, a medical question and case
shall then be proposed to him ; the answer and treatment of which he
shall submit to the Medical Professors. If these performances are approved, the candidate shall then be admitted to a public examination,
before the Trustees, the Provost, Vice-Provost, Professors and students
of the College. After which he shall offer to the inspection of each of
the Medical Professors a Thesis written in the Latin or English languages (at his own option) on any medical subject. This Thesis, if approved of, is to be printed at the expense of the candidate, and defended
from such objections as may be made to it by the Medical Professors, at
a commencement, to be held for the purpose of conferring degrees in
Medicine on the first Wednesday in June every year.

Bachelors in Medicine who wish to be admitted to the degree of Doctor in Medicine, shall publish and defend a Thesis agreeably to the rules
above mentioned.

The different Medical Lectures shall commence annually on the first
Monday in November, the lectures in Natural and Experimental Philosophy about the same time, and the lectures on Botany on the first Monday
in April.   BENJAMIN FRANKLIN,
                         President of the Board of Trustees.
                              WILLIAM SMITH,
        Provost of the College and Secretary of Board of Trustees.

On the 8th of June, 1790, the Commencement in the Medical
Department of the College took place. Dr. Smith, not forgetting
the recent act of restoration, sent the following polite invitation to
His Excellency the President and the Supreme Executive Council
of Pennsylvania:

                    COLLEGE OF PHILADELPHIA, June 7, 1790.
His Excellency the President and Supreme Executive Council of the
Commonwealth of Pennsylvania are requested to honor the College with
their company at the *Medical Commencement*, to be held in the College
Hall to-morrow, at 10 o'clock A. M.   WILLIAM SMITH,
                                 Provost of the College.

On the 17th of July the Public Commencement in the Department of Arts took place, and Dr. Smith sent the following:

College of Pennsylvania to the Supreme Executive Council of Pennsylvania.

Collège of Philadelphia, July 15, 1790.

The Trustees and Faculty of the College of Philadelphia request to be honored with the company of his Excellency the President and Supreme Executive Council, at a Commencement to be held in the College Hall on Saturday morning next, at 9 o'clock.

WILLIAM SMITH, Provost, etc.

The graduates in the Department of Arts were Robert Andrews, Gerardus M. Clarkson, James Coxe, of Sunbury, Henry Hutchins, William T. Meredith, William Wilson, and Benjamin Wood.

But while in one sense the triumph of Dr. Smith was complete with the restoration of the college charter, in all others, that is to say, in a practical and pecuniary sense, the victory was a barren one.* By the long cessation of its name and proper functions,

---

* I do not mean to say that Dr. Smith himself considered his triumph a " barren one." On the contrary, he looked upon the day of his victory as the proudest day of his life. He tells the following curious story, which he found in " Percy's Anecdotes," to illustrate the fate of political persecutors, and applies it to his own case.

" Lord Carnarvon in Charles Second's time is said to have never spoken in the House of Lords, but being heated by wine in the company of the Duke of Buckingham, and excited by him not to remain always a dumb Lord, he was provoked to declare before he went up to the House, that he would speak on any subject that should offer. The subject happened to be the prosecution of the Lord High Treasurer Danby. Accordingly, Lord Carnarvon stood up and delivered himself thus—' My Lords! I understand but little of Latin, but a good deal of English, and not a little of English history, from which I have learned the mischiefs of such kinds of prosecutions as this, and the ill fate of the prosecutors. I could bring many instances, and those very ancient, but I will go no farther back than the latter end of Queen Elizabeth's reign. At that time the Earl of Essex was run down by Sir Walter Raleigh, and your Lordships know very well what became of Sir Walter Raleigh. My Lord Bacon, he run down Sir Walter Raleigh, and your Lordships know what became of my Lord Bacon. The Duke of Buckingham, he run down my Lord Bacon, and your Lordships know what happened to the Duke of Buckingham. Sir Thomas Wentworth, afterwards Earl of Strafford, he run down the Duke of Buckingham, and you all know what became of him. Sir Harry Vane, he run down the Earl of Strafford, and your Lordships know what became of Sir Harry Vane. Chancellor Hyde, he run down Sir Harry Vane, and your Lordships know what became of the Chancellor. Sir Thomas Osbourn, now Earl of Danby, run down Chancellor Hyde, but what will become of the Earl of Danby your Lordships best can tell. But let me see the man that dare run down the Earl of Danby, and we shall soon see what will become of him.'

" This speech, being pronounced in an extraordinary tone and manner, the Duke of Buckingham, both surprised and disappointed, cried out: ' The man is inspired, and CLARET has done the business!'"

the college had been injured past power of any Restoring or Repealing Act to remedy. The University of the State of Pennsylvania was still in existence; a concurrent, indeed, a rival institution. Both could not survive—that much was plain. It was doubtful if even one could live. An union was agreed on. A new Board of Trustees—one-half from the Board of each institution; and so in 1791 the union was effected, Dr. Smith drawing with his own hand the charter by which they were to be consolidated.

The Trustees were these:

FROM THE COLLEGE.	FROM THE UNIVERSITY.
The Rt. Rev. Wm. White, D. D.,	Thomas McKean,
The Rev. R. Blackwell, D. D.,	Charles Pettit,
Edward Shippen,	James Spraat,
William Lewis,	Frederick Kuhl,
Robert Hare,	John Bleakly,
Samuel Powell,	John Carson,
David H. Conyngham,	Jonathan Bayard Smith,
William Bingham,	David Rittenhouse,
Thomas Fitzsimons,	Jonathan Dickinson Sergeant,
George Clymer,	David Jackson,
Edward Burd,	James Irwin,
Samuel Miles.	Jared Ingersoll.

The new institution was called the University of Pennsylvania. I do not know that Dr. Smith desired the Provostship of it. The new institution bore plainly within it the seeds of weakness and long-continuing inefficiency. With every effort to make homogeneity in the Board there was none; as any one acquainted with the history of families and men in old Philadelphia will see as he compares the columns above given. In the column from the College he sees the old aristocracy of the province and the old Church of England, in the other Presbyterianism and the Revolution—with some exceptions, the Democratic side of both. More than all, a long and bitter conflict had been endured, and

" Never could true reconcilement grow
Where wounds of deadly hate had pierced so deep."

Whether Dr. Smith would have accepted the Provostship or not, Dr. Ewing was elected to it. The connection of the former with the principal seat of learning in Pennsylvania thus ceased; it having continued for nearly thirty-seven years. The Provost Stillé remarks, in speaking of the University:

"What he made it I have endeavored to show; to what reputation and influence it might have reached had he been permitted to remain in charge of it, it is of course impossible to say. My own conviction is that the *University is suffering to this day from the ill effects of his untimely removal.* And certainly no one can doubt that had we now at its head a man with something of his broad and generous culture, of his wonderful capacity for organization, of his indomitable energy, of his large public spirit, of his perfect faith in the future of his College, and of his zealous devotion in advancing its interests—the University would soon become what its prototype was before the Revolution—*inter ignes Luna minores.*

"That he made some mistakes and many enemies in the methods he adopted for doing his share in this great work, there can be no doubt. In all his schemes he was thoroughly in earnest, and believed that he always saw clearly the end from the beginning. Hence he became, as all earnest men are apt to become, self-willed and impatient of opposition. Such men are not conciliatory, and, therefore, are often unpopular; but we must remember that the real work of the world is after all mostly done by them. Dr. Smith's prodigious energy and his large and liberal spirit secured the confidence of the best men of his time, and made him their natural leader. No better proof can be given of this than the uniform support and sympathy he received from the Trustees of the College through all the stormy scenes of his career. They felt, no doubt, that they had to do with a LIVE MAN, who, whatever might be his errors, had his whole heart in the work before him, and hence their trust in him never wavered."

Again the Provost says:

"Towards his enemies, Dr. Smith was unsparing, but as far as I can see, never vindictive. He assailed those who stood in his way, not to secure a mere personal triumph, or to gratify a desire for revenge, but because he saw in them a malignant force striving to ruin some great public interest, the success of which he had at heart. When fully roused he was a most dangerous adversary. He forgot himself in the cause with which he was identified, and he never hesitated to forsake his best friends if he found them engaged on what he considered the wrong side. He was a man of singularly frank and open temper, without any disguise as to his opinions, and too fearless to think of the personal consequences of any line of conduct which he thought it his duty to follow. It is easy to discover the failings of such men, but it is not so easy to find the grand qualities which were associated with them, and which in any fair estimate of his character should make us forget them."

It gave Dr. Smith no pleasure to observe, nor does it give me any to record, that the union of the two institutions produced under Dr. Smith's successor no good effect. The University languished. Its graduates in different years are numbered thus:

In 1794	5	In 1803	6
" 1797	3	" 1826	8
" 1801	5	" 1830	7
" 1802	5		

In 1830, therefore, the University had one single graduate more than the old College under Dr. Smith had at its first Commencement in 1757; while in 1794, 1797, 1800, 1802 and 1803 it never had as many; and in 1797, and at a date when Philadelphia was the national metropolis, but half as many. And what sort of men sent it forth at its first Commencement in 1757? Here are their names:

Jacob Duché,	Samuel Magaw,
Francis Hopkinson,	John Morgan, M. D.,
James Latta,	Hugh Williamson,

Paul Jackson.

Of these seven graduates there was not a single one who did not become eminent either in the State, in the Church, in science, or in letters.

The Provost Stillé rightly says in the paragraphs above quoted the University was suffering from the loss of Dr. Smith's services to it up to the time at which he himself was writing; that is to say up to the year 1875—yet it always had for Provosts men of ability. Dr. Ewing himself was this. Dr. John McDowell was the same. In Dr. Frederick Beasly, the institution had an acute thinker and a finished scholar and a writer much above the common. In Bishop DeLancey one of the most able, elegant, dignified, thoughtful and accomplished gentlemen that our country, and I may say that any country, ever has produced. And the praises of the respected Ludlow are yet in the mouths of many. The rest of the Faculty has been worthy of their Provosts; an assertion which is proved enough to all when I say that among this rest have been

James Davidson, Robert Patterson, Robert Walsh, Charles Willing Hare, Thomas Say, Robert Adrain, Samuel B. Wylie, the Rev. Edward Rutledge, the Rev. Christian Crusé, Henry D. Rogers, Henry Vethake, the Rev. Roswell Park, Alexander Dallas Bache, Henry Reed, and many others of hardly less if of any less abilities at all.

The Board of Trustees has ever comprised men of the first importance in this great city. Yet till the day of the Provost Stillé himself the College has ever languished. It is only in *his* day, by the curing efforts of that great physician Time, and by Dr. Stillé's own ever-active, well-directed, and most efficient labors—the devotion, the consecration I might even say—for he has made it a high and religious work—the consecration of all his best years to it—that the College is now, in 1880, beginning to be worthy of what it was when Dr. William Smith left it. William Smith was the *Fundator*, Charles J. Stillé is the *Restitutor*. Each as much as the other has been a *Conditor*. The institution with such a Provost and with a Faculty like that now there, thank God, exalts its towery head.*

Notwithstanding that Philadelphia was now the Capital of the nation and that its Congress and pulpits were filled with eloquent men from every State in the new Union, Dr. Smith was still the favorite orator of the time, especially in the eloquence of the pulpit. The 4th of July, 1790—the second "Fourth" since the operation of the Constitution—fell on Sunday. Accordingly, at a meeting of the standing committee of the Pennsylvania Society of the Cincinnati, held at the house of General Walter Stewart, June 28th, 1790, it was

Resolved, That as the Fourth of July would be on Sunday next, a sermon be delivered in celebration of American Independence in lieu of an oration; and that the Rev. Dr. William Smith, Provost of the College of Philadelphia, be requested to prepare and deliver one before the Society on said day.

---

* It is with sincere regret and with great anxiety for the future welfare of the College that just after writing these lines, I learn that there is a probability that Dr. Stillé —worn down, as it is stated, by his unintermitted and great labors, and wishing to refresh himself with European travel—desires to be relieved from his Provostship. The loss of such a man will not, at this moment, be easily supplied.

General Stewart* and Colonel Francis Johnston were appointed
to wait on Dr. Smith for this purpose.

Though the notice was a little short, Dr. Smith, who was *nunquam non paratus,* and ever ready to oblige, preached in Christ
Church, Philadelphia, before the Society agreeably to their request.
The subject of his discourse was " Temporal and Spiritual Salvation," from the text from Isaiah iii. 12.

The thanks of the Society were afterwards given to him, through
Governor McKean, General Walter Stewart and the Rev. Dr.
Rogers, who obtained from him his manuscript of the sermon, in
order to have it printed.

This sermon (published in Maxwell's edition of Dr. Smith's
Works) is a fine sample of his abilities.   Parts of it have frequently attracted attention.   I do not recall the name of any man
who seems to me to have beheld in truer vision, though the
vision then, of prophecy—the expansion over this continent of the
glories of civilization, religion and learning.   What a remarkable
passage, for example, to have been written A. D. 1790, two years
or less after the adoption of the Federal Constitution, is this ! We
have quoted it once already, in another place.   It will bear a repetition in this for a different purpose :

Transported at the thought, I am borne forward to days of distant renown !   In my expanded view these United States rise, in all their
ripened glory, before me.   I look through, and beyond, every yet peopled region of the New World, and behold period still brightening upon
period.   Where one continuous depth of gloomy wilderness now shuts

---

* General Walter Stewart died in 1796.   He was a native of Ireland, and was born
in Londonderry.   He came to America while young, and was earnest in the American
cause.   He was appointed a captain in one of the four battalions of Pennsylvania
troops for the Continental service, January 5th, 1776.   He became colonel of the Thirteenth Pennsylvania Battalion, and served during the greater part of the war.   The
Thirteenth was afterward consolidated with the Second, and Colonel Stewart remained
in command of the organization under the latter title.   After the Revolution he resided
in Philadelphia, and lived in ease on the north side of High street, between Fifth and
Sixth streets—nearly opposite the house occupied during the time that the Government
was in Philadelphia by President Washington.   He married Deborah, the daughter of
Blair McClenachan—a beautiful woman, and a leader of society.   He succeeded Major
General James Irvine as Major-General of the First Division at Philadelphia in 1794,
and had command in the city and county during the absence of Governor Mifflin with
the regular troops during the Whiskey war.   General Stewart was reputed to be one of
the handsomest men of his day.   He enjoyed the friendship of General Washington in
a marked degree.

out even the beams of day, I see new States and empires, new seats of wisdom and knowledge, new religious domes spreading around. In places now untrod by any but savage beasts, or men as savage as they, I hear the voice of happy labor, and behold towery cities growing into the skies!

The general sentiments in this address Dr. Smith tells us in a note to the address, had been published by him in a poem near fifty years before, and had been occasionally introduced into former public addresses by him, but had not before been published at large or in the present form.

After the passage above quoted, Dr. Smith concludes his sermon as follows:

Lo! in this happy picture, I behold the native Indian exulting in the works of peace and civilization! His bloody hatchet he buries deep under ground, and his murderous knife he turns into a pruning hook, to lop the tender vine and teach the luxuriant shoot to grow. No more does he form to himself a heaven after death (according to the poet) in company with his faithful dog, behind the cloud-topped hill, to enjoy solitary quiet, far from the haunts of faithless men; but, better instructed by Christianity, he views his everlasting inheritance, a house not made with hands, eternal in the heavens.

Instead of recounting to his offspring, round the blazing fire, the bloody exploits of their ancestors, and wars of savage death, showing barbarous exultation over every deed of woe; methinks I hear him pouring forth his eulogies of praise to the memory of those who were the instruments of heaven in raising his tribes from darkness to light; in giving them freedom and civilization, and converting them from violence and blood to meekness and love!

Amongst those who shall be celebrated as the instruments of this great work, I hear the names of every good citizen and Christian who is a friend to mankind, and to the gospel of Jesus Christ; and especially, methinks, I hear your names, ye illustrious patriots! who, having asserted your own and your country's rights, cheerfully join in every laudable endeavor for conveying those rights to posterity, and bringing "the utmost ends of the earth to see the salvation of our God."

Hasten, O Almighty Father, hasten this blessed period of thy Son's kingdom, which we believe shall come; and the praise and glory shall be to thy name, forever and ever! Amen.

We come now to a highly interesting event in Dr. Smith's domestic history: the engagement of marriage between his son Charles with Mary, the daughter of the Hon. Jasper Yeates, a lady of education, intelligence and amiable disposition. The letter which follows is a pleasing illustration of Dr. Smith's courtly manners, and is a tribute to his son Charles' good conduct, of which that son may have well been proud:

Dr. Smith to Jasper Yeates.

PHILADELPHIA, September 3, 1790.

MY DEAR SIR: On my return from Lancaster to Philadelphia my son Charles informed his mother and me that, having been successful in his addresses to your amiable daughter, and farther happy in obtaining yours and Mrs. Yeates's consent to their being united in wedlock at some convenient time, which he hoped might not be very remote, it was his wish that his mother and myself might assure you of our approbation, as we now readily do, and also of our desire to contribute all in our power to render the young couple permanently happy. I wish that Charles could have so far overcome his bashfulness as to have communicated himself to me on the Saturday evening after I was in company with you. I should certainly, in that case, have waited on you according to your invitation to breakfast on Sunday morning, when a few moments conversation on this business would have been better *between us* than anything by way of letter ; and it may seem disrespectful to your family that on a supposition of my being acquainted with the matter, I should leave Lancaster without waiting upon you to express the sense I have, not only of your former partiality to my son, and the advice and protection with which you favored him from his first appearance at the *Bar*, but especially this last instance of your favor to him ; a greater than which you have it not in your power to give. And I trust that such is his sensibility, and such will be his gratitude and returns of duty to you as well as of tender affection for your daughter, that you will never have cause to repent of your good offices and predilection for him. As for myself, I can only add that he is justly a favorite son, and has never in his life, by any part of his conduct, given me cause of pain, but always of much pleasure, and in no part of it more than on the present occasion of his attachment to a young lady of such amiable manners and good education, who is willing and happily qualified to accommodate herself to his situation either in a village or a city, a farm-house or a mansion, as future circumstances may require. I have done what my present situation will allow to add to his independence. If nothing adverse happens, he will have something further to expect upon the death of his mother and myself.

I have enclosed the Cincinnati sermon which you wished to see, and as a token of my affection, have inscribed it with your daughter's name.

I am with great regard and esteem,

      Your most obedient humble servant,   WILLIAM SMITH.

To JASPER YEATES, Esq., Lancaster.

21

But these domestic events were not always events of joy.   Dark clouds follow bright sunshine.   On the 19th of December in this same year Dr. Smith was called on to mourn the loss of his eldest and much loved daughter Williamina, wife of Charles Goldsborough, Esq.   The following inscription—upon a handsomely carved tombstone in the church-yard at Cambridge, Md.—is no doubt from the pen of Dr. Smith himself:

In Memory of
MRS. WILLIAMINA GOLDSBOROUGH,
Wife of Charles Goldsborough, Esq.,
Of Dorset County, Maryland,
Daughter of Dr. William Smith of
Philadelphia, and Rebecca, his wife.
She died December 19th, 1790,
Aged 28 years.

Call'd from this mortal scene in bloom of life,
Here lies a much lov'd daughter, mother, wife,
To whom each grace and excellence were given,
A saint on earth, an angel now in heaven.
Bereaved parents come to speak their woe ;
To grave it deep on monumental stone,
And with a husband's sorrows mix their own—
But ah ! no further trace this tablet bears,
Line after line is blotted with their tears.

Her mournful parents inscribe this tablet.

The poet Pope has given us many poetical epitaphs, some of which have been long admired of scholars.   I recall none more graceful and pathetic than this which an aged father puts upon his daughter's tomb.   The two letters which follow are in proper sequence to the sad events which we have been commemorating:

Dr. Smith to Charles Goldsborough.

PHILADELPHIA, January 17, 1791.

MY DEAR DISTRESSED SIR : How shall I take my pen in hand to write to you?   For many days past, although urged by every tie of affection, and solicited by your mother at every interval of her deep affliction to write to you, yet I attempted it in vain.   Inconsolable myself, unmanned, and I fear almost *unchristianed*, with the mother, sister and brothers of the angel we have lost, all in the like condition around me, what consolation could I impart to you?   Yet still there is consolation, not only in *Christianity*, but in the reason and nature of things.   She who was *loving* to all, and by all *beloved*, is now a saint in the bosom of everlasting love !   She whose delight was to make others happy, is gone where universal happiness prevails !

Let her precious memory be your consolation, and let it be preserved in those dear pledges—those sweet infant images of herself, whom she hath left behind !   While you behold *them*, you never can *forget her;* and, I trust, will even exert yourself to supply, as far as in your power, the irreparable loss which their education will sustain by the loss of her. Your endeavors will be assisted by your mother and myself during the short remainder of your lives, and therefore we wish to see and consult with you in Philadelphia as soon as your health and the situation of your family will admit.   In the meantime we are persuaded that your good Aunt Ennalls will not be wanting in her best advice to you, and kind offices to the children, and especially the dear orphan last born.   The many kindnesses of Mrs. Ennalls to our dear departed child, will never be forgotten by us.   We acknowledge them with the sincerest gratitude, and those of Mrs. Caroline Goldsborough.   In token thereof, please communicate them this letter, and particularly to your aunt, to whom I hope to write a few lines by your brother Richard.

Your mother is now able to sit up for part of the day, but I fear will never recover from the severe visitation she has sustained, but will go "mourning all the days of her life," even if longer than we can in any degree hope.   I am sincerely and affectionately yours, etc.

WILLIAM SMITH.

MR. CHARLES GOLDSBOROUGH,
  Hornes Point,
    Dorset County, Maryland.

Dr. Smith to Henry Ennalls, Esq.

PHILADELPHIA, November 14th, 1791.

DEAR SIR : The bearer, Mr. Davidson, I have engaged to go to Cambridge as a tutor to my two grandsons, children of Mr. Charles Goldsborough.   I beg your notice of him so far as to put him in the way of getting across the Bay to Cambridge as soon and with as little expense as possible.   The Cambridge packet, if in the way, will be his best conveyance.   Your kind services to him will oblige Mr. Goldsborough and
      Your most obedient servant,   WILLIAM SMITH.

On the 3d of March, 1791, Dr. Smith's son Charles, of whose engagement of marriage with Miss Mary Yeates, daughter of the Hon. Jasper Yeates, of Lancaster, Pennsylvania, we have spoken, was married.   The ceremony was performed at the house of the lady's father by the Rev. Henry Muhlenberg.   The following extract from the Yeates family Bible may not be without interest in connection with this event:

Jasper Yeates, son of *John* and *Elizabeth Yeates*, born April, 1745; died March 14th, 1817.

Sarah Burd, daughter of *James* and *Sarah Burd*, born January 1st, 1749; died October 25th, 1829.

The above were married December 30th, 1767.

Issue: *Mary Yeates*, born at Lancaster, March 13th, 1771; died August 27th, 1836.

John Yeates, born June 29th, 1772; died January 7th, 1844.

Elizabeth Yeates, born April 4th, 1778; died August 3d, 1867.

Margaret Yeates, born April 24th, 1780; died February 1st, 1855.

Catharine Yeates, born December 1st, 1783; died June 7th, 1866.

CHAPTER LIV.

DEATH OF FRANKLIN—IMPROMPTU THEREON AT A DINNER PARTY BY DR. SMITH—
CAPPED BY MR. THOMAS WILLING—FRANKLIN'S FUNERAL—DR. SMITH TO
DR. WEST—THE SAME TO THE SAME—DR. SMITH'S EULOGY ON FRANKLIN
—UNE ANECDOTE DE FAMILLE—DR. ODEL'S VERSES ON THE FRANKLIN STOVE
—FRANKLIN A NATURAL PHILOSOPHER AND NOT A STATESMAN.

ON Saturday, April 17th, 1790, died, in the 88th year of his age, the philosopher, Benjamin Franklin. On the evening of his death a company of gentlemen were seated at the dinner table of Governor Mifflin, at the Falls of Schuylkill. It consisted of Thomas McKean, Henry Hill (a private gentleman of rank in old Philadelphia), the Hon. Thomas Willing,* David Rittenhouse, and Dr. Smith. During the dinner a great thunderstorm arose, and *Primus*, a favorite negro body-servant of Dr. Smith, brought to Governor Mifflin's house the news just received from the city at Dr. Smith's of the event. Dr. Smith, under the impulse of the moment, wrote the following lines without leaving the table:

> Cease! cease, ye clouds, your elemental strife,
> Why rage ye thus, as if to threaten life?
> Seek, seek no more to shake our souls with dread,
> What busy mortal told you " Franklin's dead?"
> What, though he yields at Jove's imperious nod,
> With Rittenhouse he left his magic rod.

---

* For some notice of this eminent citizen of Philadelphia, see Appendix No. **VI.**

Mr. Willing, not to be outdone by Dr. Smith, immediately wrote the following:

> What means that flash, the thunder's awful roar—
> The blazing sky—unseen, unheard before?
> Sage Smith replies, "Our Franklin is no more."
> The clouds, long subject to his magic chain,
> Exulting now their liberty regain.

On Wednesday, the 21st of April, Dr. Franklin's remains were interred in Christ Church burying-ground, at the corner of Arch and Fifth streets. The funeral procession was large, and the streets through which it passed were crowded with a concourse of spectators, the number of whom were computed at twenty thousand. The mourners were preceded by all the clergy of the city, including the readers of the Hebrew congregation. The corpse was carried by citizens. The pall was borne by Governor Thomas Mifflin, Chief-Justice McKean, Thomas Willing, president of the Bank of North America, Samuel Powell, the mayor of the city, William Bingham and David Rittenhouse. Bells were tolled and minute guns were fired during the time that the procession was passing. In the line of the procession were the Supreme Executive Council, the General Assembly of the State, the Judges of the Supreme Court, members of the bar, the corporation of the city, the printers of the city, with their journeymen and apprentices, the Philosophical Society, the College of Physicians, the Faculty and students of the College of Philadelphia, and various other societies, besides a numerous and respectable body of citizens.*

---

* The following bills for the funeral charges of Franklin's burial, which have been preserved by his family, may interest the reader. Dolby was the sexton of " the United Churches "—Christ Church and St. Peter's.

April 21st, 1790.

The estate of Mr. Benjamin Franklin to Jos. Dolby, for his burial:

	£	s	d
To ground	0	15	0
To pall	1	0	0
To minister's attendance	0	6	0
To clerk's ditto	0	4	0
To muffling the bells	4	10	0
To invitations	3	7	6
To grave	0	10	0
	£10	12	6

The American Philosophical Society determined that one of their members should prepare and pronounce an oration commemorative of the character and virtues of their late worthy president. Dr. Smith was appointed to this office.

We now give two letters indicative of Dr. Smith's still continuing active discharge of the *details* of business, notwithstanding that years were beginning to come heavily on him.

Dr. Smith to Dr. West.

PHILADELPHIA, April 5, 1790.

DEAR SIR: By Mr. Levering, who takes this letter to you, you will receive the fifty copies of the Journal of Convention for the Western Shore, which you will distribute among the clergy and vestries at ninepence each Journal. I shall be at Chester at the Commencement of Washington College, the third Tuesday in May. I am fearful that I shall not be able to stay in Maryland till the fourth Tuesday, to meet you at Talbot Court House.

Yours, etc.,   WILLIAM SMITH.

REV. DR. WEST,
  Baltimore, Md.

Dr. Smith to Dr. West.

May 21, 1790.

DEAR SIR: I have been informed, but have not seen the advertisement, that the Visitors and Governors of St. John's College have declared their intention of filling up the office of principal of that College at the *May meeting* (viz.: next Tuesday) if any person of eminent abilities shall offer, and that it hath been notified that a preference would be given to a stranger or some gentleman of great character from Europe. Character in literature is often found to be deceitful, and a mere *literary* character, without experience in teaching and *governing*, will not be sufficient; nor will it be easy, even among those who have both great literature and experience *abroad*, to choose such as may truly suit the genius of America.

But, I doubt not, the worthy and respectable Visitors and Governors

---

Mr. Richard Bache.

Philadelphia, July 10th, 1791.

Bought of David Chambers.

A marble tombstone for the grave of his Excellency, Benjamin Franklin,
  Esq...£18   0   0
To engraving thirty letters at two pence per letter.....................   0   5   0
Porterage...   0   1   10

£18   6   10

of St. John's will duly consider every circumstance in their choice. I have the interest of that Seminary and its future success much at heart. I hope you will attend the meeting and inform me early on whom the choice shall fall, if a choice should now be made. It would have been well if the Assembly had *restored* the funds previously to an election. But, I trust, there will be no danger of their not being restored next November sessions. I am happy to hear that the number of students in the College increases, and I am persuaded that if a proper choice of a head be made, and the Legislature continue their nursing hand, the Maryland College will be an ornament to the State. The College of Philadelphia flourishes greatly, but we received back our funds in such a deranged state that I have almost repented my removing back to Philadelphia, and were I not too far advanced in years I am not certain whether I might not have offered my services once more as the head of one of the Maryland seminaries. But my family is attached to Pennsylvania, and, by a renewal of my former exertions, I hope yet to get the funds of the College of Philadelphia restored to their former footing. We have an application before the Legislature for the purpose. My sentiments respecting the choice of a Principal for St. John's, you may hint to Dr. Clagget and Mr. Sprigg, but not as expressing any doubt of the prudence and zeal of any of the worthy Visitors and Governors, nor as if I had any further wish to interfere than barely to express my hasty thoughts to you in our familiar way.

I write these lines hastily at Wilmington, where I heard from Mr. Condon, for the first time, that the election was to be on Tuesday next. Dr. Andrews has some wish, had he known in time, to offer himself for some place in one of your colleges, where his salary might be better than what we can yet give at Philadelphia.

I am yours affectionately,   WILLIAM SMITH.

To the REV. DR. WM. WEST,
  Rector of the Protestant Episcopal Church, Baltimore.

The union of the University with the College, and Dr. Smith's retirement from the Provostship, left him without stated employment, as also without any salary except the £200 allowed him by the Trustees of the old College. And being now arrived to advanced years, his pecuniary condition was in some danger of being straitened; for although he had a large amount of real property in several parts of Pennsylvania, and his wife was also in possession of some landed estate, a large portion of their joint estate was unproductive, and was held in this condition in the well-founded hope of advancement in price with the improvement of the country.

It was probably with a knowledge of the convenience which

stated employment with a money compensation would give to him, that the General Assembly of Pennsylvania having, on the 13th day of April, 1791, passed an act relating to the opening and improving of certain roads, rivers, and navigable waters in Pennsylvania, and there being requisite to the accomplishment of the work a Commission of Inquiry, that Governor Mifflin, on the 10th of the following May, appointed Dr. Smith, David Rittenhouse and William Findley joint "agents of information" relating to the work.   It seems strange that a clergyman, the late head of two colleges, the president of all the ecclesiastical councils of his church, should be put upon such a Commission, and especially that he should be made chairman of it.   But to no one could the office have been more properly entrusted.   As owner of large quantities of land in Huntingdon county—long the *Ultima Thule* of our civilization—and by his natural tastes as well, few men of the day were better acquainted with the geography, hydrography and geology of Pennsylvania.   His great physical strength, which had not yet failed him, his large acquaintance with the leading men in every part of the Commonwealth, his winning manners—when he had no cause to make them the reverse of winning—and his fine powers of business of every kind, rendered him eminently fit to be the head even of a Commission which would have been so little congenial to the disposition or capacities of most of the clergy.

In the course of his official duty Dr. Smith had many opportunities of seeing lands in different parts of the State which he was certain would rise in value.   Some of these, at a later date, he acquired, and this without the least breach of official trust, for the acquisition of bodies of land for the State or for any body in it, was no part whatever of the purposes of his appointment.

We have already mentioned that on the death of Dr. Franklin, who was President of the American Philosophical Society—an institution of which Dr. Smith was a founder at its institution in 1769, and the secretary of which he had been from that date—the Society requested Dr. Smith to pronounce a commemorative discourse upon their honored chief officer.   If any man could have had a right to refuse the office, Dr. Smith could have done so. For, united with Thomas Willing, William Allen, the Tilghmans and others of the very best men in Pennsylvania, he had been for many years in political opposition to Dr. Franklin, and Dr. Frank-

lin had suffered his political opposition to pass into personal ma-
lignancy. But such things made little impression on Dr. Smith.
If sometimes angry, as no doubt he justly was, in his anger he
sinned not. The sun never went down on his wrath. Malice,
hatred, or even the lighter kinds of uncharitableness, if we can
judge by his conduct, never rested in his heart. With the utmost
readiness he complied with the Society's request, and his eulogy
on Franklin may be taken to be one of the most skilful efforts of
his oratory. It is at this day one of the most agreeable short
biographies that we have of Franklin, and though published long
before Dr. Franklin's autobiography, in some sort anticipates it.

The eulogy was delivered on the 1st of March, 1791, in that
grand edifice of old Philadelphia, the German Lutheran Church,*
on Fourth street above Arch. Great efforts were taken by the Philosophical Society to make the scene impressive. The ceremonies
were attended by the President and Mrs. Washington, the Vice-
President and Mrs. Adams, by the Senate and House of Representatives of the United States, by the Governor and Legislature
of Pennsylvania, and by a large number of distinguished citizens.
The American Philosophical Society was there in corporate dignity, and a special place was given to the brotherhood of printers.

The orator having ascended the pulpit, opens in a grand melo-
dramatic *fugue*, worthy—had the performance been a musical
one—of Sebastian Bach himself; a fit exordium to the memory of
the man who tore lightning from heaven, and a sceptre from
tyrants :

*Citizens of Pennsylvania ! Luminaries of science ! Assembled fathers of
America !*

Heard you not that solemn interrogatory?
Who is *he* that now recedes from his labors among you?
What citizen, super-eminent in council, do you now deplore?
What luminary, what splendid sun of science, from the hallowed walks
of philosophy, now withdraws his beams?
What father of his country, what hero, what statesman, what law-
giver, is now extinguished from your political hemisphere, and invites
the mournful obsequies?
Is it *he*—your FRANKLIN? It cannot be ! Long since, full of years,

---

* This fine historic building was pulled down in 1875.

and full of honors, hath he submitted to the inexorable call, and proceeded on his fated journey.* From west to east, by land and on the wide ocean, to the utmost extent of the civilized globe, the tale hath been told—that the venerable sage of Pennsylvania, the *patriot* and patriarch of America, is no more. . . .

It seldom happens that they who are first called to give celebrity to the actions of great men, are placed in that exact situation, either in respect to time or point of view, which may enable them to delineate a whole character, in all its proportions and beauty. This is a work, of all others, the most difficult in the performance; nor is the difficulty lessened by the acknowledged lustre and eminence of the character in view. And from hence it hath happened, perhaps, that in eulogy and panegyric, but few of the moderns, and not many of the ancients have been successful. While they have been striving to weave the garlands of others, their own laurels have withered and dropped from their brow.

Yet, neither the risk of character, nor the difficulties of the subject, ought to deter us from attempting, at least, to pay the honors due to transcendent merit. . . .

The desire of fame and posthumous glory, "grasping at ages to come," as it bespeaks the native dignity of the soul of man, and anticipates his existence in another world, is also the most powerful incentive to moral excellence in this world. It is for the interest of mankind that so divine a passion should be cultivated, rewarded, and held up for imitation. The neglect of it would have an unfriendly influence on virtue and public spirit. The wisest and most renowned nations have not only voted thanks and triumphs to their illustrious citizens while living, but have celebrated them in eulogies when dead, and have erected altars of virtue and monuments of honor to perpetuate their names to succeeding ages and generations. . . .

And circumstanced as the people of these United States now are, and as our posterity, for ages to come, must be in building up and completing the glorious fabric of American empire and happiness, it might be a wise institution if we should make at least an annual pause, and consecrate a day to the review of past events, the commemoration of illustrious characters who have borne a share in the foundation and establishment of our renown, and particularly those of whom we may have been bereft during each preceding year.

In that view, how many patriots, statesmen and philosophers would now pass before us? A Livingston, a Bowdoin, a Franklin! . . .

In the earliest stages of life, he had conceived the mighty idea of American empire and glory; but like Hercules in the cradle, he was ignorant of his own strength, and had not conceived the achievements and labors which awaited him. He had not conceived that he was, one

---

* He died April 17, 1790.

day, to contend with kings and potentates for the rights of his country; to extort from them an acknowledgment of its sovereignty, and to subscribe with his name the sacred instruments* which were to give it a pre-eminent rank among the nations of the earth, and to assure its liberty and independence to the latest ages!

He was content in his humble, but honorable station of an useful private citizen, to cherish in his own bosom, and in distant view, the idea of American greatness; and he cherished those also in whom he discovered ideas congenial to his own! . . .

As the respect due to the public bodies, which compose such an illustrious part of this assembly, forbids me to trespass too long upon their precious time, I must forbear entering upon a full detail of the life and actions of this great man in those several relations, and shall, therefore, touch but briefly on such parts of his character as are either generally known in America, or have been already detailed by his numerous panegyrists, both at home and abroad. . . .

Descended from parents who first settled in America above an hundred years ago;† he was born in Boston, in January, 1706. The account of his education, which was such only as the common schools of that day afforded, the various incidents of his younger years, and the different occupations and professions for which his parents seemed to have intended him, before he was apprenticed to his brother, in the printing business, at the age of twelve years, although recorded by himself, and full of instruction, I shall leave wholly to his biographers, till his arrival at Philadelphia, about the eighteenth year of his age, to which city he came from the city of New York, partly by water, and partly by land on foot, his stock of clothes and cash at a very low ebb, to seek for employment as a journeyman printer. But by industry and the application of his great natural talents to business, he soon was enabled to procure a press, and to stand upon his own footing.

This account of his low beginnings, it is hoped, will not scandalize any of his respectable fraternity. No, gentlemen;‡ but you will exult in it when you consider to what eminence he raised himself, and raised his country, by the *right use of the press*. When you consider that the *press* was the great instrument which he employed to draw the attention of *Pennsylvania* to habits of virtue and industry; to the institution of

---

* The Declaration of American Independence, by the Congress of the United States, the treaties of amity and commerce, and of alliance with France; the definitive treaty of peace with Great Britain, acknowledging the independence of America, etc.

† His father, Josiah Franklin, settled in New England in 1682, and his mother, Abiah Folger, was the daughter of Peter Folger of Nantucket, one of the first settlers of that country.

‡ This part was more immediately addressed to the printers of Philadelphia, who attended as a body, at the delivery of this oration.

societies for the promotion of agriculture, commerce, and the mechanic arts; to the founding of schools, libraries, and hospitals, for the diffusion of useful knowledge, and the advancement of humanity—when you consider this, you will "go and do likewise;" you will, with professional joy and pride, observe, that from the torch which *Franklin* kindled by the means of his press, in the New World, "Sparks have been already stolen which are lighting up the sacred flame of liberty, virtue and wisdom over the entire face of the globe."* Be it your part still to feed that torch by means of the press, till its divine flame reaches the skies!

For the purpose of aiding his press, and increasing the materials of information, one of the first societies formed by Dr. Franklin was in the year 1728, about the twenty-second year of his age, and was called the Junto. It consisted of a select number of his younger friends, who met weekly for the "Discussion of questions in morality, politics, and natural philosophy." The number was limited to twelve members, who were bound together in all the ties of friendship, and engaged to assist each other, not only in the mutual communication of knowledge, but in all their worldly undertakings. This society, after having subsisted forty years, and having contributed to the formation of some very great men, besides Dr. Franklin himself, became at last the foundation of the *American Philosophical Society*, now assembled to pay the debt of gratitude to his memory. A book containing many of the questions discussed by the *Junto* was, on the formation of the *American Philosophical Society*, delivered into my hands, for the purpose of being digested, and in due time published among the transactions of that body. Many of the questions are curious and curiously handled; such as the following: . . .

Dr. Smith here gives several of them.

These and such similar questions of a very mixed nature, being proposed in one evening, were generally discussed the succeeding evening, and the substance of the arguments entered in their books.

But Dr. Franklin did not rest satisfied with the institution of this literary club for the improvement of himself and a few of his select friends. He proceeded, year after year, in the projecting and establishing other institutions for the benefit of the community at large.

Thus, in 1731, he set on foot the "Library Company of the City of Philadelphia," a most important institution to all ranks of people; giving them access, at a small expense, to books on every useful subject; amounting in the whole to near ten thousand volumes, and the number daily increasing. The affairs of the company have been managed from the beginning by directors of the most respectable characters. Their

---

* The Abbe Fauchet.

estate is now of very considerable value ; they have erected an elegant house, and over the front door of the building have prepared a niche for the statue of their venerable founder ; who, after the establishment of this company, still proceeded to promote other establishments and associations, such as fire-companies ; the nightly-watch for the city of Philadelphia ; a plan for cleaning, lighting and ornamenting the streets ; and an association for insuring houses against damages by fire ; to which, as collateral, he soon afterwards added his plan for improving chimnies and fire places, which was first printed at Philadelphia in 1745, entitled "An Account of the New Invented Pennsylvania Fire Places ; " which gave rise to the open stoves now in general use, to the comfort of thousands, who, assembled round them in the wintry night, bless the name of the inventor which they yet bear !

The next institution, in the foundation of which he was the principal agent, was the academy and charitable school of the city of Philadelphia ; the plan of which he drew up and published in the year 1749, as " suitable to the state of an infant country ; " but looking forward, as he did in all his plans, to a more improved state of society, he declared this academy to be "intended as a *foundation for posterity to erect into a college* or seminary of learning more extensive and suitable to future circumstances ; " and the same was accordingly erected into a college or seminary of universal learning, upon the most enlarged and liberal plan, about five years afterwards.

The Pennsylvania Hospital is the next monument of his philanthropy and public spirit ; for the establishment and endowment of which he was happily instrumental in obtaining a legislative sanction and grant, by his great influence in the general assembly, in the year 1752.

These various institutions, which do so much honor to Pennsylvania, he projected and saw established during the first twenty years of his residence in this State. Many more must have been his good offices and actions among his friends and fellow-citizens during that period, which were done in secret, and of which no record remains ; but they went before him to another world, and are written in durable characters by the pen of the recording Angel.

A life so assiduously employed in devising and executing schemes for the public good could not fail to aid him in his political career. He first became clerk of the general assembly, and then a member of the same for the city of Philadelphia, for the space of fourteen years successively.

In 1744 a Spanish privateer, having entered the bay of Delaware, ascended as high as New Castle to the great terror of the citizens of Philadelphia. On occasion of this alarm, he wrote his first political pamphlet called *Plain Truth*, to exhort his fellow-citizens to the bearing of arms, which laid the foundation of those military associations which followed, at different times, for the defence of the country.

His popularity was now great among all parties and denominations of men. But the unhappy divisions and disputes which commenced in the provincial politics of Pennsylvania in the year 1754 obliged him soon afterwards to choose his party. He managed his weapons like a veteran combatant ; nor was he opposed with unequal strength or skill. The debates of that day have been read and admired as among the most masterly compositions of the kind which our language affords; but it is happy for us, at the present day, that the subject of them is no longer interesting ; and if it were, he who now addresses you was too much an actor in the scene to be fit for the discussion of it. Dr. Franklin, by the appointment of the general assembly, quitted the immediate field of controversy, and in June, 1757, embarked for England, to contest his point at the court of Great Britain, where he continued for several years with various success in the business of his agency. In the summer of 1762 he returned to America; but the disputes which had so long agitated the province, far from being quieted by his former mission, continued to rage with greater violence than ever, and he was again appointed by the assembly to resume his agency at the court of Great Britain. Much opposition was made to his re-appointment, which seems greatly to have affected his feelings, as it came from men with whom he had long been connected both in public and private life, "the very ashes of whose former friendship," he declared, "that he revered." His pathetic farewell to Pennsylvania on the 5th of November, 1764, the day before his departure, is a strong proof of the agitation of his mind on this occasion.

"I am now," says he, "to take leave (perhaps a last leave) of the country I love, and in which I have spent the greatest part of my life. *Esto perpetua !* I wish every kind of prosperity to my *friends*, and I forgive my *enemies*."

But under whatsoever circumstances this second embassy was undertaken, it appears to have been a measure pre-ordained in the councils of heaven ; and it will be forever remembered, to the honor of Pennsylvania, that the agent selected to assert and defend the rights of a single province at the court of Great Britain became the bold asserter of the rights of America in general; "and, beholding the fetters that were forging for her, conceived the magnanimous thought of rending them asunder before they could be riveted."* And this brings us to consider him in a more enlarged view, viz. :

Secondly—As a citizen of America, one of the chief and greatest workmen in the foundation and establishment of her empire and renown.

But on this head little need be said on the present occasion. The subject has been already exhausted by his eulogists, even in distant countries. His opposition to the Stamp-Act, his noble defence of the

---

* Abbe Fauchet.

liberties of America, at the bar of parliament, and his great services, both at home and abroad, during the revolution, are too well known to need further mention in this assembly, or in the presence of so many of his compatriots and fellow-laborers in the great work. I hasten, therefore, to consider him in another illustrious point of view, viz. :

Thirdly—As a citizen of the world—successfully laboring for the benefit of the whole human race, by the diffusion of liberal science and the invention of useful arts.

Endowed with a penetrating and inquisitive genius, speculative and philosophical subjects engaged his early attention ; but he loved them only as they were useful, and pursued them no farther than as he found his researches applicable to some substantial purpose in life. His stock of knowledge and the fruits of his investigations, he never hoarded up for his own private use. Whatever he discovered—whatever he considered as beneficial to mankind—fresh as it was conceived, or brought forth in his own mind, he communicated to his fellow-citizens, by means of his newspapers and almanacs, in delicate and palatable morsels, for the advancement of industry, frugality and other republican virtues; and, at a future day, as occasion might require, he would collect and digest the parts, and set out the whole into one rich feast of useful maxims and practical wisdom.

Of this kind is his celebrated address, entitled "*The Way to Wealth,*" which is a collection or digest of the various sentences, proverbs and wise maxims, which, during a course of many years, he had occasionally published, in his *Poor Richard's Almanac,* on topics of industry, frugality, and the duty of *minding one's own business.* Had he never written any thing more than this admirable address, it would have insured him immortality as—*The Farmer's Philosopher, the Rural Sage, the Yeoman's and Peasant's Oracle.*

But greater things lay before him! Although as a philosopher, as well as a politician, he remained unconscious of the plenitude of his own strength and talents, until called into further exertions by the magnitude of future objects and occasions.

There is something worthy of observation in the progress of science and human genius. As in the natural world there is a variety and succession of seeds and crops for different soils and seasons; so (if the comparison may be allowed) in the philosophical world, there have been different æras for seed-time and harvest of the different branches of arts and sciences; and it is remarkable that, in countries far distant from each other, different men have fallen into the same tracks of science, and have made similar and correspondent discoveries, at the same period of time, without the least communication with each other. Whether it be that, at the proper season of vegetation for those different branches, there be a kind of intellectual or mental *farina* disseminated, which falling on congenial spirits in different parts of the globe, take root at the same time, and spring to a greater or less degree of perfection, according to the richness of the soil and the aptitude of the season?

From the beginning of the year 1746, till about twenty years afterwards, was the æra of electricity, as no other branch of natural philosophy was so much cultivated during that period. In America, and in the mind of Franklin, it found a rich bed: the seed took root and sprung into a great tree, before he knew that similar seeds had vegetated, or risen to any height in other parts of the world.

Before that period, philosophers amused themselves only with the smaller phenomena of electricity; such as relate to the attraction of light bodies; the distances to which such attraction would extend; the luminous appearances produced by the excited *glass tube;* and the firing spirits and inflammable air by electricity. Little more was known on the subject, than Thales had discovered 2,000 years before; that certain bodies, such as amber and glass, had this attractive quality. Our most indefatigable searchers into nature, who in other branches seemed to have explored her profoundest depths, were content with what was known in former ages of electricity, without advancing anything new of their own. Sufficient data and experiments were wanting to reduce the doctrine and phenomena of electricity into any rules or system; and to apply them to any beneficial purposes in life. This great achievement, which had eluded the industry and abilities of a Boyle and a Newton, was reserved for a Franklin. With that diligence, ingenuity, and strength of judgment, for which he was distinguished in all his undertakings, he commenced his experiments and discoveries in the latter part of the year 1746; led thereto, as he tells us, by following the directions of his friend, Peter Collinson of London, in the use of an electric tube, which that benevolent philosopher had presented to the library company of Philadelphia. The assiduity with which he prosecuted his investigations, appears from his first letter to Mr. Collinson, of March 28th, 1747:

For my own part, says he, I never was before engaged in any study that so totally engrossed my attention and my time, as this has lately done. For, what with making experiments, when I can be alone, and repeating them to my friends and acquaintance, who, from the novelty of the thing, come continually in crowds to see them, I have for some months past had leisure for little else.

He had a delight in communicating his discoveries to his friends; and such was his manner of communication, with that winning modesty, that he appeared rather seeking to acquire information himself than to give it to others; which gave him a great advantage in his way of reasoning over those who followed a more dogmatic manner.

"Possibly," he would say, "these experiments may not be new to you, as, among the numbers daily employed in such observations on your side the water, it is probable some one or other has hit on them before." From the beginning to the end of his life, he observed the same modest and cautious method of communication. The first philosophical paper inserted in his collection, in 1756, is entitled,"Physical and Meteorological Observations, Conjectures and Suppositions;" and his last at Passy, in 1784, are of a similar title, viz. : "Meteorological Imaginations and Conjectures. Loose Thoughts on an Universal Fluid," and the like.

But I return to the account of his electrical labors, and the materials on which they were grounded. Von Kliest, about the latter end of the year 1745, had accidentally discovered some of the powers and properties of what is called the Leyden-phial, and sent an account of the same to *Lieberkhun* at Berlin, which soon made this branch of science more interesting. As soon as the account of this discovery reached America (together with Mr. Collinson's tube), it excited no less curiosity here, than it had done in Europe; and Dr. Franklin writes to his friend Collinson in September, 1747, "that no less than one hundred large glass tubes had been sold in Philadelphia, in the space of four months preceding." But although Von Kliest had discovered some properties of this phial, and Muschenbroek, to his cost, had experienced others (by which the phial, or bottle received his name) it remained for Dr. Franklin to discover its true principles, and how, by means of it, to accumulate, retain, and discharge any quantity of the electric fluid, with safety. The account of this discovery and of the experiments on which it was founded, he communicated to Mr. Collinson, in his letter of September 1, 1747, with his usual caution and modesty, in the following terms :

The necessary trouble of copying long letters, which, perhaps, when they come to your hands may contain nothing new, or worth your reading (so quick is the progress made with you in electricity) half discourages me from writing more on that subject. Yet I cannot forbear adding a few observations on M. Muschenbroek's wonderful bottle.

In this letter, he discloses the whole magical powers of this bottle; by proving that it would receive an accumulation of the electric fluid on the inside, only as it discharged an equal quantity from the outside. This discovery gave him the greatest advantages over all the electricians of Europe. It put into his hands (as it were) the key which opened into all the secrets of electricity, and enabled him to make his succeeding experiments, with a sure aim, while his brethren in Europe were groping in the dark, and some of them falling martyrs to their experiments.

He was the first who fired gun-powder, gave magnetism to needles of steel, melted metals, and killed animals of considerable size, by means of electricity. He was the first who informed electricians, and the world in general, of the power of metalline-points, in conducting the electric fluid; acknowledging at the same time, with a candor worthy

22

of true philosophy, that he received the first information of this power from Mr. Thomas Hopkinson,* who had used such points, expecting by their means to procure a more powerful and concentrated discharge of the Leyden-phial; but found the effect to be directly contrary. It was, undoubtedly, the discovery of this wonderful power of metalline-points, in carrying off and silently dispersing the electric fluid when accumulated, and the similarity and resemblance which he observed between the effects of lightning and electricity, which first suggested to him the sublime and astonishing idea of draining the clouds of their *fire*, and disarming the *thunder* of its terrors; flattering himself at the same time with the pleasing hopes of gratifying a desire, long before become habitual to him, of rendering this discovery in some manner useful and beneficial to his fellow-creatures. This appears by his notes of November 7, 1749, when enumerating all the known particulars of resemblance between lightning and electricity, he concludes with saying :

The electric fluid is attracted by *points*. We do not know whether this property be in lightning; but since they agree in all the particulars in which we can already compare them, it is possible that they agree likewise in this: *Let the experiment be made.*

Difficulties, without doubt, occurred in making this experiment, both as to the manner and least expensive way of reaching the clouds with his *points;* for we do not find that he accomplished his grand experiment, till in June, 1752. In a letter to his friend Collinson, not dated, but probably written in 1749, he communicates his "Observations and suppositions towards forming a new hypothesis, for explaining the several phenomena of thunder-gusts;" which was followed in July, 1750, by another letter to the same, containing "Opinions and conjectures concerning the properties and effects of the electric matter," and giving particular directions for determining whether clouds containing lightning are electrified or not.; for ascertaining of which, his idea at this time was, "the placing a pointed iron rod on some high tower or steeple, and attempting to draw sparks from it," there being at that time no lofty spires in Philadelphia. But his ever-inventive genius, which could derive lessons of philosophy even from the play of children, soon furnished him with a more simple and less expensive method: For in June, 1752, he took the opportunity of an approaching thunder-storm, to walk into a field, where there was a shed convenient for his purpose. Dreading the ridicule which too commonly attends unsuccessful attempts in science, he communicated his intended experiment to no person but his son, who assisted him in raising a kite, which he had prepared of a large silk handkerchief, extended by two cross sticks. After

---

* "This power of points, to throw off the electrical fire, was first communicated to me by my ingenious friend, Mr. Thomas Hopkinson, since deceased; whose virtue and integrity, in every station of life, public and private, will ever make his memory dear to those who knew him, and knew how to value him."

waiting for some time, and almost beginning to despair of success, he drew the first spark with his knuckle from a key suspended to the string of the kite. Another and another succeeded; and as the string became wet, he collected fire copiously. What must have been his raptures on the success of this grand experiment; leading him to anticipate that happy and beneficent application of the principles of electricity, to the saving of life and property, which alone would have recorded his name among the benefactors of mankind; even if his discoveries of those principles could never have been extended or applied to any other useful purpose in the world. Similar must his raptures have been to those of a Newton, when by applying the laws of gravitation and projection first to the *moon,* he was enabled to extend them to the whole solar system, as is beautifully described by the poet:

> What were his raptures then! how pure! how strong!
> And what the triumphs of old Greece and Rome
> With his compar'd——When nature and her laws
> Stood all subdued by Him, and open laid
> Their every latent glory to his view.
>
> All intellectual eye; our solar round
> First gazing thro', he by the blended power
> Of *Gravitation* and *Projection* saw
> The whole in silent harmony revolve.
> First to the neighb'ring *Moon* this mighty key
> Of nature he applied—Behold! it turn'd
> The secret wards; it open'd wide the course
> And various aspects of the Queen of Night;
> Whether she wanes into a scanty orb
> Or, waxing broad, with her pale shadowy light,
> In a soft deluge overflows the sky.*

Dr. Franklin's letters, giving an account of his electrical experiments and discoveries, and, among the rest, of this grand experiment of drawing electricity from the clouds, were soon published in Europe, and translated into different languages. "Nothing was ever written on the subject of electricity," says Dr. Priestly, "which was more generally read and admired in all parts of Europe, than those letters. Electricians everywhere employed themselves in repeating his experiments, or exhibiting them for money. All the world, in a manner, and even kings themselves, flocked to see them, and all returned full of admiration for the inventor of them."

Amidst this general admiration, Dr. Franklin himself continued to communicate his knowledge and discoveries under the humble appellation of conjectures or guesses: But no man ever made bolder or happier guesses, either in philosophy or politics; He was likewise a bold experimenter in both. He had by accident received a discharge of two of

---

* Thomson's poem to the memory of Sir Isaac Newton.

his large electrical jars through his head, which struck him to the ground, but did him no lasting injury. He had likewise seen a young woman receive a still greater shock or discharge of electricity through her head, which she had inadvertently brought too near the conductor, which knocked her down; but she instantly got up, and complained of nothing further. This encouraged him to make the experiment on six men at the same time, the first placing his hand on the head of the second, and so on. He then discharged his two jars, by laying his conducting rod on the head of the first man. They all dropped together; thinking they had been struck down, as it were, by some kind of magic, or secret operation of nature; declaring when they rose that they had neither seen the flash, nor heard the report of any discharge.

For his manner of delivering his philosophical opinions, under the humble appellation of conjectures and suppositions, he makes the following apology, more humble still : " I own," (says he, in one of his letters), "that I have too strong a penchant to building hypotheses: They indulge my natural indolence." But indolence was no part of his character; and his success in this method of philosophizing will rescue it from much of the reproach which has been too liberally cast upon it. Without forming hypotheses, experimental philosophy would only be a jumble of facts, ranged under no heads, nor disposed into any system. Dr. Franklin, without troubling himself with mathematical speculations, or showing any inclination towards them, nevertheless reasoned with all the accuracy and precision of the deepest mathematician. And although he might be sometimes mistaken where the truth could be developed only by the help of pure mathematics, yet he was rarely mistaken in his mechanical and philosophical deductions.

Being on ship-board in the year 1757, an accident gave him occasion to observe the wonderful effect of oil, in stilling the waves of the sea. He immediately determined to make experiments to elucidate this new property of oil, which he did with success ; and the philosophical world is indebted to him for being now fully acquainted with a fact, which, although not unknown to Plutarch and Pliny, was for ages past known only among the Dutch fishermen, and a few seamen of other nations.

His inquiries and discoveries were confined to no limits or subjects. Through all the elements : In the *fire* and in the *water*, in the *air*, and in the *earth*, he sought for and he found new and beneficial *knowledge*.

He discovered that unaccountable agitation of the two surfaces in *contact*, when a quantity of *oil* floats on water in a vessel.

He found the *pulse-glass* in Germany, and introduced it into England, with improvements of his own.

He discovered that equal and congenial bodies acquired different degrees of heat from the sun's rays, according to their different colors.

His improvements in chimnies, stoves, etc., have been already noticed.

He made experiments to show, that boats are drawn with more diffi-culty in small canals, than in greater bodies of water.

He made and published experiments for improving the art of swim-ming, and for allaying thirst by bathing in sea-water.

He published observations on the gradual progress of northeast storms along the American coasts, contrary to the direction of the wind ; and likewise to ascertain the course, velocity, and temperature of the Gulf-stream, for the benefit of navigation.

He contrived experiments, and recommended them to the late Dr. Ingenhauz, for determining the relative powers of different metals for conducting heat, which were accordingly made.

He revived and improved the *harmonica*, or glassichord, and extended his speculations to the finer arts; showing that he could taste and criticise even the compositions of a Handel !

He left behind him some very curious thoughts and conjectures con-cerning "an universal fluid ; the original formation of the earth ; and how far, from attentive observations made during the summer, it may be possible to foretell the mildness or severity of the following winter." These were the fruits of some of his leisure hours at Passy, during his ministry at the court of France, where his time in general was devoted, with the greatest dignity, and the most splendid success, to the political objects of his mission.

That success was much promoted by the high reputation which he sustained, as a patriot and philosopher, among the patriots and philoso-phers of a generous and enlightened nation.   Of this the fullest testi-mony is to be found in the letters of condolence on his death,* from the national assembly of that country, to the *President and Congress of the United States ;* and the public mourning decreed on that occasion—an honor, perhaps the first of the kind which has ever been paid by a public body of one nation to a citizen of another.   But all nations considered themselves as being interested in him, and the homage was therefore more justly due to his *manes* and his name !

Dr. Franklin, having taken leave of the court of France, left Passy on the 12th of July, and arrived at Philadelphia, the 13th of Septem-ber, 1785, where he was welcomed with joy by his fellow-citizens of all classes; and, in testimony of their heartfelt sense of his eminent vir-tues and past services, he was unanimously elected by them to the gov-ernment of the commonwealth, for the three succeeding years; being the longest term which the constitution of Pennsylvania then allowed. During that term, he was also appointed a member of the general con-vention, for forming and establishing a constitution for the United States

* The Duke de la Rochefoucault made him acquainted with the celebrated Turgot, who wrote the memorable motto under his portrait :
" Fripuit Cœlo fulmen, mox sceptra Tyrannis."

of America; and on the 18th of September, 1787, that illustrious body having concluded their labors, Dr. Franklin, in conjunction with his colleagues of Pennsylvania, presented the result of the same, to the Speaker and House of Representatives:

SIR: I have the very great satisfaction of delivering to you and to this honorable house, the *result* of our deliberations in the late *convention*. We hope and believe that the measures recommended by that body, will produce happy effects to this commonwealth, as well as to every other of the United States.

He then presented, at the speaker's chair, the *Constitution*, agreed to in convention, for the government of the United States. The remainder of his term of office in the government, he devoted to the wise and prudent administration of its duties; so far as the growing infirmities of his years, and the painful disorder with which he had been long afflicted, would permit. During the most excruciating paroxysms of that disorder, he strove to conceal his pain, that he might not give pain to those around him; and he would often say, that he felt the greatest alleviation of his own pains, in the occasions which were offered him of doing good to others; and which he never neglected to the latest moments of his life.

One of the last public acts in which he was concerned, was to sanction with his name the memorial presented to the general government of the United States, on the subject of the slave trade, by the "Pennsylvania society for promoting the abolition of slavery, and the relief of free negroes, unlawfully held in bondage." Of this society, he was president; and the institution and design of it could not but be congenial to the soul of a man, whose life and labors had been devoted to the cause of liberty, for more than half a century; ardently striving to extend its blessings to every part of the human species, and particularly to such of his fellow-creatures, as, being entitled to freedom, are nevertheless, injuriously enslaved, or detained in bondage, by fraud or violence.

It was not his desire, however, to propagate liberty by the violation of public justice or private rights; nor to countenance the operation of principles or tenets among any class or association of citizens, inconsistent with, or repugnant to, the civil compact, which should unite and bind the whole; but he looked forward to that æra of civilized humanity, when, in consistence with the Constitution of the United States, it may be hoped, there shall not be a slave within their jurisdiction or territory! Nay, he looked more forward still, to the time when there shall not be a slave nor a savage, within the whole regions of America. He believed that this sublime æra had already dawned, and was approaching fast to its meridian glory; for he believed in Divine Revelation, and the beautiful analogy of history, sacred as well as profane! He believed that human knowledge, however improved and exalted, stood in need of illumination from on high; and that the Divine Creator has not left mankind without such illumination, and evidence of himself, both internal and external, as may be necessary to their present and future happiness.

If I could not speak this from full and experimental knowledge of his character, I should have considered all the other parts of it, however splendid and beneficial to the world, as furnishing but scanty materials for the present eulogium.

An undevout philosopher is mad.—YOUNG.

The man who can think so meanly of his own soul, as to believe that it was created to animate a piece of clay, for a few years, and then to be extinguished and exist no more, can never be a great man! But Franklin felt and believed himself immortal! His vast and capacious soul was ever stretching beyond this narrow sphere of things, and grasping an eternity! Hear himself, "although dead, yet speaking" on this awfully delightful subject! Behold here, in his own hand-writing, the indubitable testimony! In this temple of God, and before this august assembly, I read the contents, and consecrate the precious relic to his memory! It is his letter of condolence to his niece, on the death of his brother; and may be applied as a fit conclusion of our present condolences on his own death:

We have lost a most dear and valuable relation (and friend)—But, 'tis the will of God that these mortal bodies be laid aside when the soul is to enter into *real life*. Existing here is scarce to be called life; it is rather an embryo state, a preparative to living; and man is not completely born till he is dead. Why, then, should we grieve that a new child is born among the immortals, a new member added to their happy society?

We are spirits!—That bodies should be lent while they can afford us pleasure, assist us in acquiring knowledge, or doing good to our fellow-creatures, is a kind and benevolent act of God. When they become unfit for these purposes, and afford us pain instead of pleasure, instead of an aid become an incumbrance, and answer none of the intentions for which they were given, it is equally kind and benevolent that a way is provided, by which we may get rid of them—Death is that way: we ourselves prudently choose a *partial death*, in some cases. A mangled, painful limb, which cannot be restored, we willingly cut off. He who plucks out a tooth, parts with it freely, since the pain goes with it; and he that quits the *whole body*, parts at once with all the pains, and possibilities of pains and pleasures, it was liable to, or capable of making him suffer.

Our friend and we are invited abroad on a party of pleasure, that is to last forever. His chair was first ready, and he is gone before us. We could not all conveniently start together; and why should you and I be grieved at this, since we are soon to follow, and we know where to find him.

Yes, thou dear departed friend and fellow-citizen! Thou, too, art gone before us—thy chair, thy celestial car, was first ready! We must soon follow, and we know where to find thee! May we seek to follow thee by lives of virtue and benevolence like thine—then shall we surely find thee—and part with thee no more, forever! Let all thy fellow-citizens; let all thy compatriots; let every class of men with whom thou wert associated here on earth—in devising plans of government, in framing and executing good laws, in disseminating useful knowledge, in alleviating human misery, and in promoting the happiness of mankind—let them consider thee as their guardian-genius, still present and presiding amongst them; and what they conceive thou wouldst advise to be DONE, let them advise and DO likewise—and they shall not greatly deviate from the path of virtue and glory!

I hope that I make no reflection upon my ancestor, nor any, not merited, upon Dr. Franklin, when in connection with this eulogy I mention a little *anecdote de famille.* At the conclusion of the eulogy, which was delivered in Dr. Smith's best style, every one was crowding him to offer to him congratulations upon the success of his effort. When he got home, his daughter Rebecca—the one whom I have described in Volume I.* as the inspiring subject of Gilbert Stuart's divine pencil, and whose wit was equal to her beauty—was there to greet him. "Well, my daughter," said the Doctor, "I saw you seated among the *magnates* at the church. You *heard* me, I suppose?" "Oh, yes," said the girl, "I was there and heard every word." "And how did you like the eulogy, let me ask?" said the Doctor. "Oh, papa," said the daughter, looking archly into her father's face, "it *was* beautiful, very beautiful, indeed; only—papa—only—only—" "Only what?" replied the Doctor. "Only—papa—now you wont be offended—will you? I don't think you believed more than one-tenth part of what you said of old Ben Lightning-rod. Did you?" The Doctor, without either affirming or denying, laughed heartily. If he had spoken, he would probably have said: "My dear daughter, I was invited to pronounce an *eulogy*, not to analyze and describe a very complex character. In such a case you must make a picture which shall owe its effects to the skilful handling of lights; not one which shall have the truth which numerous and deep shades would give it. I have done that for which I was appointed, and that which I was expected to do. The dead can never vindicate nor defend themselves. Therefore, of *them*, is given the counsel, *nil nisi bonum.*"

It must not be supposed, by anything that I say above or by

---

* Page 472.

the insertion of this pleasant memorandum about Dr. Smith, to imply anything like want of sincerity on the part of my progenitor. In the course of their long opposition to each other in the politics of Provincial Pennsylvania, Dr. Smith had dealt some heavy blows at Franklin; no man heavier ones. I am quite ready to believe that now that the grave had closed over the remains of one who had been his earliest friend in Pennsylvania and in his latest years had not been his enemy, he desired to make even more than reparation for unintentional injustice, if injustice, which I do not believe, had ever been done.

In a note to this eulogy in Maxwell's edition of his works, Dr. Smith meant apparently to give to others, including Jefferson and Rush—*par fratrum*—the responsibility of some things which he would, perhaps, as a clerical character, have hardly been willing to assume for himself. Specifying by page the contributions of each, he says, as follows:

The assistance derived by the author in the composition of the following Eulogium, from the friendly communications of some of his learned colleagues, among the officers of the American Philosophical Society, requires his public acknowledgments to be made to them, viz.:

To DAVID RITTENHOUSE, Esq., LL. D., president of the society, for sundry papers, which have been digested into the account of Dr. Franklin's electrical and philosophical discoveries, from page 64 to 71.*

To THOMAS JEFFERSON, Esq., LL. D., one of the vice-presidents of the society, and secretary of the United States, for his letter, concerning Dr. Franklin's ministry at the court of France, pages 75 to 77.

To JONATHAN WILLIAMS, Esq., one of the secretaries of the society, for the original letter, pages 80, 81; and some papers in the appendix.

To BENJAMIN RUSH, M. D., one of the council of the society, for some sketches of Dr. Franklin's character, of which the author has availed himself, page 50.

Dr. Franklin had been elected President of the American Philosophical Society in 1769, and held the position until his death, Dr. Smith being one of the Secretaries during the whole period. In the latter years of his life many of the meetings were held at Franklin's house, in a court running south from Market street between Third and Fourth. Dr. Franklin was succeeded by David Rittenhouse, elected January 7th, 1791, who also remained

---

* The reference in this extract to pages is to the pages in Maxwell's edition of Dr. Smith's works.

in office until his death, June 26th, 1796. *He* was succeeded by Thomas Jefferson, who was elected January 6th, 1797, and continued until his resignation in 1815.

The eulogy has been printed several times; first by order of the society before which it was pronounced by Franklin's grandson, Benjamin Franklin Bache. It is also found in Maxwell's edition of Dr. Smith's works printed in 1803. In that edition Dr. Smith appends the following memorandum:

While this Eulogium was originally in the press, the following verses, beautifully poetical and descriptive of the character of Dr. Franklin, were found on the writing-desk of my study; but whether dropped there by some one of the nine muses, or by what mortal favorite of theirs, I could not then learn. They were accompanied with a request, that they might be annexed to the Eulogium; but apprehending that the publisher, Mr. Bache, who was Dr. Franklin's grandson, might think it indecent in him to give circulation to the last two stanzas, however much he might approbate the first three; they were suppressed at that time, and from a persuasion also, that, at a future day, they might more easily be endured by the warmest of Dr. Franklin's surviving friends.

The verses were found in the handwriting of my dear wife, and not recollecting, at that time, ever to have seen or read them, and asking from what original she had copied them, she laughed, as I thought, at the scantiness of my reading on a subject so recent as the death of Dr. Franklin, whose panegyrist I had been appointed, by a grave society of philosophers. I replied, with a mixture of a little raillery in my turn, that if she would not satisfy me respecting the author of the verses, or from what source she had copied them, I should consider myself as happily yoked to a very good poetess, and ascribe the composition to herself, unless clubbed between her, and her dear friend, Mrs. Ferguson. I knew either of them to be capable of the work, and from the spirit, wit and manner of it, as well as from frequent hints in their conversation, concerning Dr. Franklin, whose genius and talents they both admired, I knew also that the last two stanzas, as well as first three accorded well with their sentiments. I have discovered lately, by means of my worthy friend, Benj. R. Morgan, Esq., that the Rev. Jonathan Odell, formerly Missionary at Burlington, New Jersey, and now Secretary of the British Province of New Brunswick was the real author. I had indeed suspected him to be so, and questioned him accordingly (for he dined at my house that day), but it seems that he joined with the ladies to keep me in suspense, and in conveying a satirical hint, by means of the verses, that I was a very warm panegyrist:

Like Newton sublimely he soar'd
 To a summit before unattained;
New regions of *science* explor'd
 And the palm of philosophy gained.

With a spark that he caught from the skies,
 He display'd an unparallel'd wonder,
And we saw, with delight and surprise
 That his rod could protect us from thunder.

Oh! had he been wise to pursue
 The path which his talents design'd,
What a tribute of praise had been due,
 To the teacher and friend of mankind!

But to covet political fame
 Was in him a degrading ambition;
A spark which from Lucifer came,
 Enkindled the blaze of sedition.

Let candor then write on his urn—
 " Here lies the renowned inventor,
Whose flame to the skies ought to burn,
 But inverted, descends to the centre !"

CHAPTER LV.

Dr. Smith appointed by the Masonic Order of Pennsylvania to Prepare
an Address to President Washington, which he does—He Receives an
Answer from the President—Dr. Smith to Jonathan Williams, Esq.—
Marriage of Dr. Smith's Daughter, Rebecca, with Mr. Samuel Blodget, of Boston—Mrs. Cadwalader to Mrs. Ridgely, giving an Account
of the Wedding, etc.—Consecration of Bishop Claggett, of Maryland,
in Trinity Church, New York—Dr. Smith Preaches at the Consecration—Extracts from the Sermon—The Convention of 1792—Orders
an Address on the subject of Domestic Missions—An Address Prepared
—Signed by Dr. Smith—Authorship Uncertain.

On St. John's Day, the 27th of December, 1791, at a meeting
of the Masonic Grand Lodge of Pennsylvania, Dr. Smith and
the worshipful grand officers were appointed a Committee to prepare an address to the illustrious Brother George Washington,
President of the United States, and they were requested to report.
Dr. Smith, at the next meeting, presented the following address,
which was adopted and forwarded:

January 2d, 1792.
To George Washington, President of the United States:

Sir and Brother: The Ancient York Masons of the jurisdiction of
Pennsylvania, for the first time assembled in General Communication to

celebrate the feast of St. John the Evangelist, since your election to
the chair of government of the United States, beg leave to approach
you with congratulations from the east, and, in the pride of fraternal
affection, to hail you as the great master builder (under the Supreme
Architect) by whose labors the temple of liberty hath been reared in the
west, exhibiting to the nations of the earth a model of beauty, order
and harmony worthy of their imitation and praise. Your knowledge of
the origin and objects of our institution—its tendency to promote the
social affections and harmonize the heart—give us a sure pledge that
this tribute of our veneration, this effusion of love, will not be ungrateful to you ; nor will Heaven reject our prayer, that you may be long-
continued to adorn the bright list of master workmen, which our Fraternity produces in the terrestrial lodge ; and that you may be late
removed to that celestial lodge where love and harmony reign transcendent and divine, where the great Architect more immediately presides, and where cherubim and seraphim, wafting our congratulations
from earth to heaven, shall hail you brother.

By order and in behalf of the Grand Lodge of Pennsylvania in General Communication assembled in ample form.

Signed by the Grand Master and officers.

"Dr. Smith," so says Hayden, in "Washington and his Masonic Compeers," "delivered this address in person." On the
5th of the following March, Dr. Smith reports to the Grand
Lodge the following reply from the President :

To the Ancient York Masons of the jurisdiction of Pennsylvania :

GENTLEMEN AND BROTHERS : I received your kind congratulation with
the purest sensations of fraternal affection ; and from a heart deeply
impressed with your generous wishes for my present and future happiness, I beg you to accept my thanks.

At the same time I request you will be assured of my best wishes and
earnest prayers for your happiness while you remain in this terrestrial
mansion, and that we may hereafter meet as brethren in the celestial
temple of the Supreme Architect.*   GEORGE WASHINGTON.

On the 20th of January, 1792, there were elected into the
American Philosophical Society a number of foreigners in a body
—Count Paul Andreani, of Milan; Rudolph Vall-Travers, of Hamburg; Anthony Renatus, Charles M. de la Forest, Joseph Ceracchi,
of Rome, a sculptor, but not a philosopher, nor indeed a man of
the highest character in all things; Palisot de Beauvois, etc. I

* The original of this letter is in the Temple at Philadelphia. It is addressed to William Moore Smith, Esq., who was at that time Grand Master of Pennsylvania.—H. W. S.

am not able to say whether it was owing to some dissatisfaction about the election of one or more of these persons, or some circumstances connected with the mode of announcing the election of officers, that we find the following rather distinct sort of letter from Dr. Smith to Mr. Williams, a member of the society, related to Dr. Franklin, the president, lately deceased:

Dr. Smith to Jonathan Williams, Esq.

PHILADELPHIA, February 5, 1792.

SIR: You had yesterday my determination about signing the certificates: it was that I could not sign them till my objections were heard at a meeting of the society. The Rules require that certificates shall be signed by all the officers. I am sorry for the delay, and if the secretaries will take it upon themselves to issue the certificates without my name, rather than wait till the next meeting of the society, they may have them for that purpose. Whatever Rules may be made at the next meeting, or whatever may be found to have been the general usage, I shall submit to, or else I shall resign my appointment, that there may be no delays nor debates on my account in conducting the affairs of the society, of which I was one of the original founders and for whose honor and success I have long exerted myself. Whether the order of subscribing be according to seniority in office, or the form of return at election, according to the number of votes, in either case the present mode of signing the certificates sent to me is wrong.

I should, however, have taken no notice at present of the thing if you had not told me that you were blamed for the manner of publishing the names of the officers according to the number of votes at the last election, and that one of the vice-presidents had said that he would not subscribe unless his name stood first. I know not on what his pretensions are founded, but I am sure neither on rule or usage; and I cannot imagine that the secretaries of the society, upon any private conference among themselves, had a right to determine this point. If there be a special meeting on this business, the nature of it and the reasons for calling it must be set forth in the notices. If you think proper, I will wait upon you at Mr. Rittenhouse's to-morrow, concerning the special meeting, or send the two certificates signed by myself in the present order, provided that it be not made a precedent, and the other certificates may remain until some amicable order shall be taken at next stated meeting.

I beg you to retain this in your hands until I have the pleasure of seeing you.

I am, with great regard, your obedient servant,

WILLIAM SMITH.

To JONATHAN WILLIAMS, ESQ.

On the 10th of May, 1792, Rebecca, the daughter of Dr. Smith, of whom we spoke a little way back, was married, by Bishop White, to Samuel Blodget, Esq., of Boston.* A letter which follows will be of more interest, I fancy, to my readers of the fair sex—if any such I shall have—than all other things which, up to this time, I have given. And why shall such readers not be sometimes gratified even in the preparation of a life of a Provost and a Doctor of Divinity? I leave my said fair readers of course to translate any French word in the letter for themselves, hoping only that meanings of some of them in the year 1792 were not identical with meanings in 1880:

Mrs. Williamina Cadwalader to Mrs. Ridgely.

PHILADELPHIA, June 20, 1792.

My DEAR AUNT: What shall I say to the girls about the bride, Becky Smith's dress. She was dressed in a sprig'd muslin *chemise*, and wore a bonnet with a curtain. The young ladies, her bridesmaids, had also on *chemises*, but their hats ornamented. Did I write you that Miss Ann Hamilton, Miss Meade, and Miss Keppelé were her attendants; and that she left town the Saturday following, and saw nobody on Friday. There was great propriety both in her behavior and in all other respects. Every thing was as it ought to be, without any affectation or parade. For our sweet girls I can only tell you, that they were the most interesting creatures I ever saw, and that they were dressed in white muslin, without any thing on their heads but a white ribbon run through the hair. There was a monstrous company—forty-seven people —at supper. *That* was perfectly elegant in every respect, and not even a whisper or joke that could have raised a blush in a vestal. The young men's delicacy and propriety to their wives charmed me. They did not venture to speak or look at them the whole evening any further than that, Archibald McCall spoke to Betsy, and Tom Ringold to Maria. They had not seen them for ten days before the wedding. . . .

Yours affectionately,

W. CADWALADER.

To MRS. ANN RIDGELY, near Dover.

But we must pass from gay subjects to such grave ones as are appropriate to our pen.

In 1792 was held in Trinity Church, New York, another General Convention of the Episcopal Church. The church of Rhode Island—the last of the churches of the New England States to

---

* For an account of Samuel Blodget, Esq., see Appendix, No. VII.

Engraved by John Sartain. Phila. 1880.

MRS. REBECCA BLODGET.

From the original picture by Gilbert Stuart, painted 1806.
in the Carey Collection, the property of the Pa. Acad y of the Fine Arts.

come into the Ecclesiastical union, as the State itself had been the last to come into the Federal—now sent delegates. The clergy and laity, too, of North Carolina acceded to the union. Dr. Smith was again elected President of the House of Clerical and Lay Deputies.

At this convention an important and striking event occurred. At the last convention, that of 1789, it will be remembered that an indisposition existed on the part of Bishops White and Provoost to proceed to consecrate Dr. Bass, who had been recommended by the church in Massachusetts to the Episcopate—because those two bishops considered that when they received consecration in England, in 1787, it was understood that a third person would come from America to receive consecration at the hands of the English bishops before any bishop should be consecrated in America; a consecration which till now had not been made. All difficulty was now removed. The Rev. James Madison, D. D., of Virginia, had been consecrated at Lambeth, England, in December, 1790, so that we now had in America one bishop (Seabury) deriving Episcopal orders through the Bishops of the Church in Scotland, and three (White, Provoost and Madison) deriving them through the Church of England. Dr. Bass was not as yet quite ready to be consecrated; but the church in Maryland, understanding now that Dr. Smith did not mean to ask for consecration, elected the Rev. Thomas John Claggett, D. D., of Maryland, for their Diocesan.*

A form and manner of ordaining or consecrating a bishop having been agreed upon at the convention at Trinity Church, Monday, the 17th of September, 1792, was fixed for the consecration of Dr. Claggett; the consecration to take place in the edifice just named. Never before had the consecration of a bishop been witnessed on this continent; never before in any part of the world a consecration of a bishop deriving his orders, as with the presence of the four

---

* Dr. Claggett was born in Prince George's county, Maryland, in 1743, was graduated at Princeton in 1764, and in 1767 was ordained by Dr. Richard Terrick, Bishop of London. In 1768 he was appointed by the Governor of Maryland to the Rectorship of All Saints, in Calvert county, in which parish he continued till the beginning of the Revolution, when he retired to his residence in Prince George's, remaining without charge. He remained in this place and without charge until 1779, when he began to officiate in St. Paul's, in the county just named. In 1780 he was elected its Rector. His name appears in all kinds of early conventions of the church.

American bishops was here the case, through the blended lines of Scotland and England.

Dr. Smith was invited to preach the consecration sermon, a high compliment to him, indeed—with the presence of Seabury and White, and Provoost and Madison, all of them of a higher grade of orders—to ask of *him* to deliver the solemn charge needed by the occasion.

His text was those verses from St. Paul's Second Epistle to Timothy, chapter iv., verses 1, 5, so often preached from upon like occasions, but still ever affording a theme for new interest when handled by a man of the abilities of Dr. Smith.

I charge thee before God, and the Lord Jesus Christ, who shall judge the Quick and the Dead, at his Appearing, and his Kingdom—Preach the Word: Be instant in Season, out of Season; Reprove, Rebuke, Exhort with all Long-Suffering and Doctrine.

For the Time will come, when they will not endure sound Doctrine; but, after their own Lusts, shall they Heap to themselves Teachers having Itching Ears. And they shall turn away their Ears from the Truth, and shall be turned unto Fables.

But Watch thou in all things; Endure Afflictions; Do the work of an Evangelist; Make full Proof of thy Ministry.

He thus begins:

RIGHT REVEREND FATHERS, REVEREND BRETHREN, AND RESPECTED
    FELLOW-CITIZENS, HERE ASSEMBLED:

While, in one point of view, I consider the Nature of the Holy Solemnity and Work, upon which we are about to enter, and feel, as I do, the Weight of the Part assigned to Me on the occasion; I might well be deterred in looking forward to my task! But, in another point of glorious view, I am encouraged to proceed, when I consider that I have an Apostle, even St. Paul, the Prince of Apostles, as my leader and guide. For his second Epistle to Timothy, from which my text is taken, is nothing else but a Solemn Charge, and one of the first recorded in the Annals of Christianity—applying, at all times, and under all circumstances, to every Preacher of the Gospel, of every rank and denomination—Ministers, Pastors, Elders, Bishops—by whatsoever name they may wish to be called!

Thus guided and supported, I rise with some degree of Confidence; animated, rather than deterred, by the Venerable, but Indulgent, Presence of my clerical Brethren and Fathers; likewise by the joyful attendance, the exulting expectations, of the Lay Members of our own Church, on an occasion so long desired, so devoutly prayed for by them, as the present; together with the appearance of such a crowded Audience, of various other denominations of professing Christians;

drawn together, many no doubt for Instruction ; others, perhaps, from Curiosity, to witness a new scene in America, namely : the First Consecration of a Bishop for a Protestant Church by an authority within itself acknowledged to be valid, and sufficient to relieve it from any future necessity of sending its young candidates for the ministry across a vast ocean for receiving holy orders.

Therefore, thus guided and supported in my part of the duty, I rise not only with some degree of confidence, but even with full hopes, from the long experienced candor and indulgence of my brethren in the ministry, that where I may fall short of their expectations, it will be ascribed to the true cause, want of ability, rather than want of zeal, or earnest endeavors to do better, were it in my power.

To proceed, then, my first address should be to you, my venerable brother, elected for the office of a bishop. A long acquaintance and a happy intercourse with you, in the exchange of good offices for the support of our church, and for strengthening the hands of our brethren in the ministry, during my residence of eight or nine years in the State of Maryland, as well as other good considerations, render it unnecessary for me to say much on this part of my subject.

Of what concerns the duties of a bishop, or a chief pastor, St. Paul's Epistles to Timothy and Titus have been always considered as the true primitive uncorrupted depositary; nay, indeed, the luminous source of instruction to all preachers of the Gospel, at all times and under all circumstances, as already suggested.

The preacher then made a paraphrase of part of the Second Epistle to Timothy, from which the text is taken, and which, he says, was written under peculiar circumstances, "near the close of St. Paul's life, when he was a prisoner and in bonds at Rome— called in question for the faith of Christ, before the cruel Nero, at a time, too, when he saw persecutions springing up from without, and divisions, heresies and corruptions from within the church; and lastly, at a time when he saw and believed that his own departure, or dissolution from the body, was near at hand;" he therefore directs this last and parting charge, as a legacy of spiritual instruction, to Timothy, in the fulness of love and zeal for his future prosperity and success in the propagation of the sound doctrine of the Cross of Christ. . . . He then proceeds:

What a copious catalogue of evils does the apostle here prognosticate, which would spring up in the world among men neglecting the gospel, and not led by the power thereof. They have indeed sprung up, in these latter days especially. Our own eyes have seen them; and we could enumerate the nations and people among whom they have chiefly

23

prevailed, and do now prevail, and which the preachers of the Gospel are called by St. Paul to contend against. And he has taught us how and with what weapons to contend, in his Epistle to Titus, which immediately follows those to Timothy. It is indeed a beautiful and luminous, although a short, epistle, teaching the doctrines to be preached concerning civil and ecclesiastical affairs, order and submission in society; which, if they could prevail, would do away all the disorders and iniquities which he had enumerated above. The preacher then quotes largely from the Epistle to Titus. Such Epistles as those to Timothy and Titus, read as Dr. Smith could read them, were deeply impressive sermons. He proceeds:

Although my years—but not the station, which I have chosen to hold in the church during the short remaining span of my life—might entitle me to address you in the character of Paul to Timothy, or of a father to a son, in the Gospel of Christ; yet, as that is not necessary, after addressing you as above, in the Apostle's own words, respecting all that he thought necessary to give in charge to one of the first primitive bishops, consecrated by himself, under the authority committed to him by Jesus Christ; yet I know you will bear to be reminded, or rather forewarned, of many incidental obstructions, which, from the state of things in the present evil days, you will have to contend against in the discharge of your pastoral duty; and to this you will let me join the fruits of my own experience, and study of the Holy Scriptures, to assist you in your pious labors to struggle against infidelity and to propagate the faith as it is in Christ Jesus, and was " once delivered unto the saints."

In the discharge, therefore, of your great duty, you are to look beyond all the authorities and distinctions of men, civil or ecclesiastical; nay, and beyond the authorities of apostles, or even angels themselves, any further than as you believe, after careful examination, that they assuredly speak by divine inspiration. You will at the same time be careful to listen to the illuminations of the spirit of grace within you, and to look up steadfastly to the supreme authority of our common Lord and Master, Jesus Christ himself, in whose name St. Paul gave his charges to Timothy and Titus; referring forward to that great day when He, our said Lord Jesus, shall come to judge the world in righteousness, to make up his jewels and establish his universal and everlasting kingdom!

Here, then, I might close my notes and descend from the pulpit, being persuaded that nothing more is necessary to be addressed to you, my dear brother and bishop elect, now soon to be set apart for the great office destined you. I shall only add, that your piety and learning in the Scriptures, your exemplary life and diligence in the pastoral office, have been long known to me, long tried and approved in the church and by the public.

And thus, though I might here conclude, as I said before, yet custom forbids such a perfunctory discharge of the task committed to me on a day which we expect to be so propitious to all our church concerns. There are reciprocal duties between pastors and people which require a further detail and enforcement. There are, as enumerated before, difficulties to be encountered by the former, which can only be struggled with and overcome, or in any degree rendered tolerable, by the aid and succor of the latter.

Your greatest aid, however, you must derive from yourself; striving to be strong, nay mighty, in the Scripture. For all Scripture, according to our apostle, is given by inspiration of God; and, in your ministry, will be profitable for doctrine, for reproof, for correction, for instruction in righteousness;—that the man of God may thereby, through your care, be perfectly furnished unto all good works; and, therefore, since the time of my departure or death is so near at hand, and this may be my last address to you, my beloved son in the gospel, I charge you zealously to preach the word—preach Jesus Christ (as the word is often understood). Be instant, in season and out of season, in public and in private, as occasion may require, or necessity may call; by day and by night, in times of the peace and prosperity of the church, as well as in times of her adversity and persecution! Be not dismayed, or negligent of the gift that is in thee. Repel false preachers and false doctrines. Root out the tares from the wheat, with every weed, or new-fangled thing, which springs up at enmity to the cross of Christ, and the truth and spirit of his holy religion. But what need I add more, on a subject so fully treated of in sermons which I have delivered before many of you, on former occasions, concerning the obstructions that fall in the way to retard the success of a preached gospel.

I proceed, therefore, in addition to what I have quoted from St. Paul, to say something more concerning the peculiar and appropriated duty of a chief pastor of a Christian church. And here I need only read the charge you are speedily to hear, from the officiating bishop, before "the laying on of hands," as it hath been collected from St. Paul, by the pious and learned fathers of our church, at the time of the Reformation.

Give heed unto reading, exhortation and doctrine. Think upon the things contained in this book. Be diligent in them, that the increase coming thereby may be manifest unto all men. Take heed unto thyself, and to doctrine, and be diligent in doing them; for, by so doing, thou shalt both save thyself and them that hear thee. Be to the flock of Christ a shepherd, not a wolf. Feed them, devour them not. Hold up the weak, heal the sick, bind up the broken, bring again the outcasts, seek the lost. Be so merciful, that you be not too remiss. So minister discipline, that you forget not mercy; that, when the Chief Shepherd shall appear, you may receive the never-fading crown of glory, through Jesus Christ our Lord.—Amen.

In what a dignified point of view are pastors and bishops of the

Church of Christ spoken of in Holy Writ! By whatever names they are mentioned, their relation to Christ is always kept up.

If they are called "the salt of the earth," it is a salt that will not lose its flavor through Christ.

If they are called "ministers," they are the ministers of Christ; if laborers, they are fellow-laborers with Christ in his own vineyard.

If they are called "watchmen," they are watchmen over the souls of them whom Christ died to save.

If they are called "pastors," they are pastors of that flock whereof Christ is the chief pastor, or shepherd.

If they are called "stewards," they are stewards of the mysteries of God, and of Christ's word.

If they are called "ambassadors," they are ambassadors of Christ; and hold their commissions from an authority that is paramount to all human authority and power! They derive them from that power, which governs all things in heaven, and on earth; and are declared to be "sent of God, as though God did beseech the world through them in Christ's stead"—"Be ye reconciled unto God."

Having, therefore, such high and dignified names bestowed upon us; having our commission from such a supreme and divine authority with such a promise annexed to it*—I say, having a sure promise, from our omnipotent Master, that he will be with us, to support us in our duty, amidst all trials and sufferings; and that, as the reward of our perseverance, he will place us in the world to come, among those bright luminaries of glory, who sit at his right hand, and rejoice in the beatific vision of his refulgent presence forever and ever! Let us be strong in him.

Moreover, brethren, standing, as I think we may consider ourselves, nearly on the same primitive foundation of purity and simplicity in church government, and a free order of things among ourselves (under our happy civil constitution), as the apostles and first Christians stood, when they neither courted human authority, or human splendor, nor were courted by them; let us, I say again, be bold and diligent in the name of the Lord, carefully to hear and obey the last part of the apostle's charge, namely:

To watch and to be strong, ready to endure afflictions, and to make full proof of the gospel ministry; and to convince men that it is from God, and will be supported by him.

Thus, when it is seen that, according to the measure of grace which is given them, and of their abilities, the pastors labor, with all holy zeal and diligence, to watch over, to preserve, and duly to feed the flock, committed to their charge; it must naturally follow, as an indispensable

---

* "Go ye and teach all nations, and lo! I am with you, unto the end of the world They that turn many unto righteousness shall shine as the stars, forever and ever.'

sacred duty on the part of the flock, on the other hand, that they listen
to the voice of the pastors ; that they strengthen their hands in their
labors for the good of the flock ; that they hear the voice of the shepherds with joy, and receive it as the voice of the Great Shepherd and
Bishop of their souls !

The flock, therefore, is to be under obedience and rule in this great
case. They are to keep in mind the words of St. Paul, speaking in the
character of a great and faithful pastor :

"If we have sown unto you spiritual things, is it a great thing, or
matter, that we shall reap of your carnal or temporal things?" For if
(by the grace of the gospel) the Gentiles have been made partakers of
these spiritual things, it is their duty also to minister unto them (the
pastors) in their carnal or temporal things ; while they call them to
happiness and salvation, in the language of God, from his great mercy-
seat : "Come up thither, and I will show thee the things that must be
hereafter. Come hither, and I will show thee the Bride, the Lamb's
Wife."

My beloved brethren and hearers, pardon my zeal here, if it appears
warm ! It is by the joint efforts, both of pastors and people, that the
chief obstacles to the advancement of religion and true practical holiness, as taught by Christianity, can be overcome, and removed or surmounted.

I am persuaded that I address no person here, who will say to the
seers, "See not, and to the prophets, prophesy not unto us right things
—speak unto us smooth things—prophesy deceits ! "

No, brethren, I know you love, and will endure, sound doctrine ; and
that if any, even under the mask of an angel from heaven, were to
preach any other gospel to you than that into which you have been
baptized, and have received from Christ and his apostles through
divine revelation and the fathers of our church, according to its true
reformation, you would say, with St. Paul : "Let him be accursed ! "

I know likewise, that the plea of many for those itching ears, that
heaping up of teachers, that seeking after new doctrines and new gospels
is pretended by these seekers to be of a conscientious nature.

My charity forbids me to pry into the temple of another man's heart,
with the presumption of tracing what passes there ; I have only to say,
"Ye shall know them by their fruits." Nevertheless, it is not uncharitable to inquire what may be the causes of the great difference in the
feelings and apprehensions of men, and whence spring the effects produced among them in hearing the preached word? Why it is that some
hear unto salvation, and others forbear unto destruction?

The reason appears to be, "That the former have submitted their
spirits to the teaching of the Spirit of God ; but the latter are buoyed
up by the spirit of this world, and the pride of their own unhallowed
wisdom."

But when once the hearts of men are truly mollified, and brought to a sense of their own corruption and danger through sin; and when, by the grace of God, they are purged from the dross of pride and prejudice, they will fly to Christ, and submit to the operations of the Holy Spirit, the witness within them. They will then embrace Him as the Way and the Life; they will rejoice in hearing his Holy Word, and lay hold of his blessed Gospel as the great charter of their salvation; the richest legacy or gift which heaven could give, or man receive.

Thus touched by God and convinced of sin, the soul will pant for salvation, in his own blessed way, according to the sound doctrine of Christ and his apostles; not by cunningly-devised fables, not in man's wisdom, disputing about the means and the mystery; not conferring with flesh and blood; but by a strong faith, not wavering; an animating hope, that maketh not ashamed, and a burning love, that never can be quenched; silencing every doubt of carnal reason, and subduing the whole spiritual man to the obedience of faith under grace.

Being now brought into this holy submission, the soul no longer resists the drawings of the Father to the son; but receives that spirit of adoption promised by God, whereby we become his children, and obtain that new birth so often spoken of and so little understood; leading us to delight in hearing the word, joy in all holy exercises, conscious of the power of God in the soul, through Christ, sitting and ruling with his sceptre of righteousness in the hidden man of the heart.

But it is not so with the unregenerated, whose souls are not brought into this holy submission. Some of them are wholly listless, and loth to hear, or examine for themselves. Others of more active and restless powers, those men of itching ears already spoken of, must be doing something, although it be often worse than nothing. But in their doings they are unstable as the waves, and led, as they phrase it, to kill precious time, running about, like the Athenians of old, to tell or to hear some *new* thing; flying from altar to altar, from teacher to teacher, some of them teaching for doctrine, as St. Matthew expresses it, the commandments of men, and some of them, as St. Paul says, "giving heed to seducing spirits and the very doctrines of devils."

But, my beloved brethren, is this the way to learn or to know Christ? Alas! it is far otherwise. He is not a divided Christ, nor are his doctrines either new or uncertain. It is time, and indeed more than time, for all those who profess his blessed name, pastors as well as people, to be united in those solid and essential truths which lead to salvation; to bid adieu to whatever is new fangled and conjectural; and to deal no more in that light bread which satisfieth not the soul, but in that bread which came down from heaven, and strengtheneth a man's heart.

Could Christians be united thus, in love and in doctrine, the great obstacles to the success of the preached Gospel would more easily be removed. But although we cannot expect to arrive wholly to this point

of perfection, yet the ministers of Christ's religion are to consider it as
the great end and scope of their labors, and to persevere accordingly,
with all long-suffering, diligence and patience, unto the end.

And now to conclude, let us devoutly join in ascribing

"Glory, thanksgiving and praise to the God of heaven and earth,
who in his own good time hath been pleased to relieve our church, in
this American land, from the distress under which she hath so long
mourned and bewailed herself; by supplying us with a complete Episcopate, and the means of continuing it in a necessary succession without
having recourse to any distant or foreign land; being now enabled,
under God, on sound evangelical principles, 'to ordain elders in every
city; to send them forth to preach spiritual liberty to the miserable
captives held under the powers of darkness; and to open the prison-
doors and emancipate into the light of heaven those who are fast bound
in sin and the shadow of death.' "

In this establishment we see the whole Episcopate of the land from
whence many of us sprung, the English and Scots, happily united.

But, my venerable brother, although these circumstances are pleasing
to you and to us all, we are not to turn our sight from the difficulties
yet remaining before us: And if we behold even hosts of foes encamped
in our way, we are to look up to our aid from on high, and the promise
often already mentioned, " that Christ will be with us unto the end."
Let us never forget that to contribute, and become the chief means of
civilizing and evangelizing savage nations, was one of the great purposes, indeed among the greatest, for which God planted our fathers in
this land, then a wilderness, far distant from European scenes of felicity,
and improvements in arts and sciences.

Should we forget this, and begin to consider that this fertile land was
given us merely for our own secular uses—to eat and to drink out of its
abundance; nay, unless we seek to maintain religion among ourselves,
to impress it on our children, and to diffuse it among our unenlightened
neighbors—all our other works, our zeal and struggles for liberty, civil
or ecclesiastical, all our boasted forms of government, the complete
establishment of our independence, acknowledged by, and giving us a
rank among, the nations of the earth—all these will be in vain; for,
although they are great blessings and highly to be prized, when rightly
understood and enjoyed, we must remember that we are not independent
of God, who holds the fate of nations awfully suspended in the balance
of his justice and power, and can clearly see which scale preponderates
in virtue or vice—that, if we become remiss or negligent in the duties
assigned us on this immense continent, He can punish us for our ingratitude, by casting us out, as stubble, to be burnt; leaving us neither
root nor branch, and raising up other more worthy instruments for the
accomplishment of His own eternal purposes of love towards these yet
benighted nations.

But, my Christian brethren, I hope better things of you, although I thus speak. I hope we have all pledged ourselves, both clergy and laity, before God and the Lord Jesus Christ, who shall judge the quick and the dead at his appearing and kingdom; that we will make full proof of our zeal, and will persevere therein until the clouds of infidelity shall be dispersed by the refulgent rays " of the Sun of Righteousness arising with healing in his wings, enabling the servants of God to tread down the wicked, who shall be as ashes under the soles of their feet."

For myself, looking forward to this day-spring from on high, my bosom always expands itself into divine rapture. And I now glow again with a remnant of the warmth of more youthful days—days now half a century fled, when I first visited this American world, and, in rising prospect and poetical rhapsodies,* began to anticipate its future glories; encouraged and animated with the view, even at that time, of the rapid spread of divine knowledge; the thirst that prevailed for founding and supporting seminaries of learning, in order to aid in the propagation of true and rational religion, civil liberty, and all that can adorn or exalt human nature, in the great scale of created excellence and existence in this new world.

I would not dip farther on this occasion into the depths of prophecy. In other sermons, and according to the subjects, the line of my abilities in this way hath been extended to its utmost length, and would not now, in my feeble state, bear any further stretching.

I have only to add, then, by way of *final exhortation*, that you, who are in the active stages of life, will consider yourselves standing, as it were, in the midst of things; called upon to be conspicuous actors in the most busy and important scenes of that great drama which the Almighty is conducting towards its conclusion.

Looking forward, therefore, as well as backward, and listening to the voice of Scripture, as well as considering the analogy of things, it must appear to you that there is something more perfect and practically powerful in Christianity, tending also to its more extensive propagation, yet to be expected before the consummation of earthly things.—But as there are prophecies relating to different ages of the church which cannot be fully understood, and therefore not fully explained, until they are fully accomplished, we pretend not to say at what period of the Christian era this reformation or great change is to commence; nor how or by what means it is to be effectuated. Here let conjecture cease. Let us be silent before God; for silence will be our best praise of his incomprehensible wisdom and goodness.

AMEN! and AMEN!

---

* See verses spoken at the opening of the College of Mirania, and on the propagation of Religion, Knowledge and Liberty, chiefly written about A. D. 1740.

It is obvious, from the rhetorical structure of all parts of this discourse that it gave full scope for those elocutionary powers of which Dr. Smith, even at the age of sixty-five years, which he had now reached, remained a master. Beyond giving a venerable aspect to his fine face and figure, time had produced but little effect upon his frame or physical powers. The force, richness, and other fine qualities of his voice remained unimpaired, and his articulation was as clear, neat and distinct as it had ever been. The sermon produced great effect. It made every one feel that, even with Ashbel Green beside him, and the memory of Gilbert Tennant's best days yet fresh, Dr. Smith was still what he had been for forty years, the pulpit orator of Pennsylvania.

After the sermon, Dr. Benjamin Moore, afterwards the honored Bishop of New York, in whose house Dr. Smith always lodged during his occasional visits to that city, and with whom he was now walking home, began to speak of the sermon, and to congratulate Dr. Smith on the attention which it had drawn from the very large and mixed audience which had been in Trinity Church. "There is," said Dr. Moore, in his gayety and love of coining words, "in your manner of delivery such a *concernedness*, such an *inlookingness*, such appearance of being in earnest, that I seek nothing further to command my attention." "What," said Dr. Smith, "do *you* not look for the glittering ring, the lily-white hand and handkerchief as white, displayed and lifted up towards heaven, with the right eye pursuing it aloft; and the gilt sermon-cover in the other hand, stretching downwards towards the congregation, with the left eye squinting after it, as if to ask, ' *What think you of this?*' However," adds Dr. Smith, who records the pleasant walk and talk, "we both agreed that the truth is that neither kind of oratory, internal or external, can have any great influence on the mind of rational and judicious auditors without great care in the choice of subjects, a proper method and disposition of the matter, a correct and chaste style, and some degree of elegance, or at least neatness, in composition on the part of the preacher; things, all of them, to be felt equally by the learned and the unlearned."

The convention of 1789 was the great organizing legislature of the church, as the Congress of 1789 was the great organizing legislature of the nation. Each made those organic acts by which the system, which in that year was brought into being, first completely moved, and yet continues so to move.   In every act of one we see the hands of Hamilton, Ellsworth and Gouverneur Morris; in the other the hands of Seabury, White and Smith.   The convention of 1792 was therefore less important than the convention of 1789. Nevertheless, important legislation was made at it.   One of the most important was an act for supporting missionaries to preach the Gospel on the frontiers of the United States.   This act recommended to all the ministers of the church to preach annually a sermon and to collect money, in order to carry out the charitable design.   Treasurers were to be established in each State, and a general treasurer and secretary for all the States.   The appointment of these last was placed with the Bishop of Pennsylvania, and a standing committee to manage the charity.   This committee consisted of Bishop White, Dr. Smith, Dr. Magaw, Dr. Andrews, Dr. Blackwell, Samuel Powell and John Wood, Esqs., and these were directed to frame an address to the members of the church, recommending this charitable design to their particular attention, which address was directed to be read by every minister on the day appointed for the collection.*   Accordingly an address was made by the Bishop and Standing Committee.   The address was sent forth in April, 1793.   I am not able to affirm by what pen it was prepared.   I have seen it attributed to Dr. Smith, but it bears no strong marks of his style, though the sentiments were undoubtedly such as might have well come from his mind.   I cannot affirm it to be from the pen of Bishop White.   The style, like his in the main, strikes me as not quite like in particulars; nor is it like Dr. Magaw, whose compositions were always elegant, but usually somewhat artificial.   It may come from the pen of Dr. Blackwell or of Dr. Andrews.   I give the address, from whosever pen it came, or whether it be, as it may well be, a composition in which more than one pen participated:

When the congregations of our communion, a few years ago, by a

---

* I am not well informed of the subsequent history of this society.   In the autumn of 1816 "The Episcopal Missionary Society of Philadelphia" was made, Bishop White being its president, and his particular friends its officers.   It carried its work into Ohio, Kentucky and the western region, and was the germ of "The Domestic and Foreign Missionary Society" of the Church, established by the General Convention of 1820; this last being succeeded, if I remember, by the Board of Missions in 1835.

separation from the former centre of their ecclesiastical union, had become unconnected with one another, the first objects which engaged
the conventions, successively held, were: the reuniting of the compo-
nent parts of the body, the obtaining of the Episcopacy, and the
reviewing of the Liturgy—objects of so great magnitude and difficulty
that the measures most proper to be pursued could not be ascertained
without frequent deliberation, nor determined on without much time
and pains: although now happily carried into effect, with every appearance of stability, and, it is hoped, to general satisfaction and
edification.

Our Church being thus organized on those principles of doctrine,
discipline and worship, which we had inherited from the Church of
England, and which had been handed down to us, through her, from
the Apostles and the early fathers of the whole Christian church, it must be
seen that the principal object to be promoted by all, in their respective
stations, as the effect of so good a system, is an evangelical profession of
religion, manifesting itself in holiness of heart and life—an effect which
may be looked for wherever provision has been made for the stated
preaching of the word and the administration of the sacraments.

There are, however, many places in which no such provision can be
made by those who are to be benefited by it, owing to the difficulties
attendant on the first settlement of a country, and to the circumstances
of the settlers, which, in general, are barely competent to yield them a
subsistence. Of persons thus situated, there are very many on the extensive frontier of the United States, who, having been educated in the
faith and the worship of our Church, wish to have the benefits of its
ministry, but who are too few, in their respective neighborhoods, to
provide for it among themselves, or indeed to expect it at all, unless on
the itinerant plan now proposed; and that to be principally supported
by their richer brethren, who are also more advantageously situated for
a combined effort.

Under these circumstances, the convention have thought it a duty,
arising out of the trust committed to them by the Great Head of the
Church, to direct their attention to a people whose circumstances so
strongly claim it; and to call on the pious and liberal members of
their communion to aid them in the undertaking which these sentiments
have suggested.

It has ever been held a duty, incumbent on every branch of the
Christian Church, not to neglect, as far as opportunity shall offer, the
publishing of the glad tidings of salvation, even to heathen nations.
Accordingly, it cannot but be the desire of every member of our communion that something may be attempted by us, in due time, for assisting in every laudable endeavor for the conversion of our Indian
neighbors, notwithstanding former disappointments and discouragements. And it is the sincere wish and prayer of those who now address

you, that the day may not be far distant when Providence shall open the door, and we shall avail ourselves of the opportunity for so good a work.   But if this be a duty, how much more so is the extending of aid to those who are of one faith and one baptism with ourselves, but who, from unavoidable causes, are without those means of public worship which the Divine Author of our religion has accommodated to the wants and weaknesses of human nature ; and which he saw to be, on those accounts, necessary for upholding the profession of his name.

The promise of Christ, to be with his Church to the end of the world, will never fail; and yet particular branches of the universal church may either flourish or decline, in proportion to their continuing in a pure profession and suitable practice on the one hand, and to their falling into error, or indifference and unholy living, on the other.   However prosperous, therefore, the beginning of our Church in this new world hath been, she will have little reason to look up for a continuance of the Divine blessing if, when she contemplates so many members of her communion "scattered abroad, as sheep having no shepherd," she does not use her diligence to bring them within Christ's fold, and to secure to them a stated administration of the ordinances of his religion.

Such was the care, in times past, of the bishops and of the most eminent of the clergy and of the laity of the Church of England for the fellow-members of their communion, when struggling with the difficulties of settlement in the then infant colonies, now the independent States of our confederated republic.   The very existence of our Church in some of these States must be ascribed, under the blessing of God, to the aids, to which we here look back with gratitude.   The degree of her prosperity in every one of them must have been owing, more or less, to the same cause: and therefore the example is what we ought, in reason, to imitate ; so as to consider our brethren on the frontiers as not to be deserted because they are distant, but, from their remote situation, as the especial objects of our concern.

In accomplishing that labor of love, which has been projected by the convention, we shall be doing what may be expected of us, not only as Christians, but as good citizens of a land of liberty and law, the best security of both being moral principles and habits ; which can only be derived from the influence of religion on the minds of the people.   For however it may be contended by some, that the sense of religion is unconnected with the duties of civil life, we owe it to God and to our country to guard the members of our church against that licentious principle, and accordingly to endeavor the extension of Christian knowledge, as well with a view to temporal peace and prosperity as for the securing of the immortal happiness of a better life.

Under the impression of these sentiments, we hope for the concurrence of all the members of our church in the undertaking now proposed to them: and intending, with the Divine aid, to exert our best abilities

for a faithful administration of the trust reposed in us by the convention, we subscribe ourselves,

Your affectionate Brethren,

WILLIAM WHITE, D. D., Bishop of the Protestant
Episcopal Church in the Commonwealth of
Pennsylvania.

WILLIAM SMITH, D. D.,   ⎫
SAMUEL MAGAW, D. D.,   ⎪ The standing
JOHN ANDREWS, D. D.,   ⎬ committee ap-
ROBERT BLACKWELL, D. D.,   ⎭ pointed by the
SAMUEL POWEL,   convention.
JOHN WOOD,

PHILADELPHIA, April 22, 1793.

CHAPTER LVI.

THE YELLOW FEVER OF 1793 IN PHILADELPHIA—MR. MATHEW CAREY'S ACCOUNT
OF IT—ADVERTISEMENTS AND COMMUNICATIONS IN THE NEWSPAPERS ABOUT
IT—EXTRACTS FROM DR. SMITH'S DIARY DURING THE PESTILENCE—DEATH
OF DR. SMITH'S WIFE—ADDRESS AND EXHORTATION BY THE CLERGY OF
PHILADELPHIA—A PROCLAMATION BY THE GOVERNOR—A SERIES OF SER-
MONS IN CHRIST CHURCH BY DR. SMITH, ON THE CESSATION OF THE PESTI-
LENCE AND IN REFERENCE TO IT—PRESIDENT AND MRS. WASHINGTON ALWAYS
REGULAR ATTENDANTS ON DIVINE SERVICE AT CHRIST CHURCH, AND EARLY
PRESENT ON THE RE-OPENING OF THE CHURCH, ON THE OCCASION OF THESE
DISCOURSES.

IN the latter part of June, 1793, Philadelphia was terror-stricken
and desolated by that awful form of pestilence which has lately
visited a portion of our Southwestern States, and which is known
as the Yellow Fever.   Dreadful as were its ravages recently in that
region which seems naturally, with its great swamps and low lands,
more open to the plague, they were no more dreadful than those
which befell the city of Philadelphia, in the summer and early
autumn of 1793.   The state of affairs at the time is thus graphi-
cally told by the late noble-hearted Mathew Carey, who, during
the ravages of the pestilence, remained in the city, devoting himself to the necessities of the sick and dying:

The consternation of the people of Philadelphia at this period was
carried beyond all bounds.   Dismay and affright were visible in almost
every person's countenance.   Most of those who could by any means

make it convenient fled from the city. Of those who remained, many shut themselves up in their houses, being afraid to walk the streets. The smoke of tobacco being regarded as a preventive, many persons— even women and small boys—had cigars almost constantly in their mouths. Others, placing full confidence in garlic, chewed it almost the whole day; some kept it in their pockets and shoes. Many were afraid to allow the barbers and hairdressers to come near them, as instances had occurred of some of them having shaved the dead, and many having engaged as bleeders. Some, who carried their caution pretty far, bought lancets for themselves—not daring to allow themselves to be bled with the lancets of the bleeders. Many houses were scarcely a moment in the day free from the smell of gunpowder, burnt tobacco, nitre, sprinkled vinegar, etc. Some of the churches were almost deserted, and others were wholly closed. The coffee-house was shut up, as was the city library and most of the public offices. Three out of the four daily papers were discontinued, as were some of the others. Many devoted no small portion of their time to purifying, scouring, and whitewashing their rooms. Those who ventured abroad had handkerchiefs or sponges, impregnated with vinegar or camphor, at their noses, or smelling bottles full of thieves' vinegar. Others carried pieces of tarred rope in their hands or pockets, or camphor-bags tied round their necks. The corpses of the most respectable citizens—even of those who had not died of the epidemic—were carried to the grave on the shafts of a chair, the horse driven by a negro, unattended by a friend or relation, and without any sort of ceremony. People uniformly and hastily shifted their course at the sight of a hearse coming toward them. Many never walked on the footpath, but went into the middle of the streets, to avoid being infected in passing houses wherein people had died. Acquaintances and friends avoided each other in the streets, and only signified their regard by a cold nod. The old custom of shaking hands fell into such general disuse that many shrunk back with affright at even the offer of the hand. A person with crape or any appearance of mourning was shunned like a viper; and many valued themselves highly on the skill and address with which they got to windward of every person whom they met. Indeed, it is not probable that London, at the last stage of the plague, exhibited stronger marks of terror than were to be seen in Philadelphia from the 25th or 26th of August till late in September. When the citizens summoned resolution to walk abroad and take the air, the sick cart conveying patients to the hospital, or the hearse carrying the dead to the grave, which were traveling almost the whole day, soon damped their spirits, and plunged them again into despondency.

While affairs were in this deplorable state, and people at the lowest ebb of despair, we cannot be astonished at the frightful scenes that were acted, which seemed to indicate a total dissolution of the bonds

of society in the nearest and dearest connections. Who, without horror, can reflect on a husband, married perhaps for twenty years, desert-
ing his wife in the last agony—a wife, unfeelingly abandoning her
husband on his death-bed—parents forsaking their children—children
ungratefully flying from their parents, and resigning them to chance,
often without an inquiry after their health or safety—masters hurrying
off their faithful servants to Bush Hill, even on suspicion of the fever,
and that at a time when, almost like Tartarus, it was open to every
visitant, but rarely returned any—servants abandoning tender and
humane masters, who only wanted a little care to restore them to health
and usefulness—who, I say, can think of these things, without horror?
Yet they were often exhibited throughout our city; and such was the
force of habit that the parties who were guilty of this cruelty felt no
remorse themselves, nor met with the censure from their fellow-citizens
which such conduct would have excited at any other period. Indeed,
at this awful crisis, so much did *self* appear to engross the whole attention of many, that in some cases not more concern was felt for the loss
of a parent, a husband, a wife, or an only child, than, on other occasions, would have been caused by the death of a faithful servant.

This kind of conduct produced scenes of distress and misery of
which parallels are rarely to be met with, and which nothing could
palliate but the extraordinary public panic and the great law of self-
preservation, the dominion of which extends over the whole animated
world. Men of affluent fortunes, who have given daily employment
and sustenance to hundreds, have been abandoned to the care of a negro,
after their wives, children, friends, clerks and servants, had fled away,
and left them to their fate. In some cases, at the commencement of
the disorder, no money could procure proper attendance. With the
poor, the case was, as might be expected, infinitely worse than with the
rich. Many of these have perished without a human being to hand
them a drink of water, to administer medicines, or to perform any
charitable office for them. Various instances have occurred of dead
bodies, found lying in the streets, of persons who had no house or
habitation, and could procure no shelter.

The same state of things is more than adumbrated by the advertisements and communications which we take at random from
a package of newspaper cuttings made by Dr. Smith at the time.

Preventative against the Raging Yellow Fever.

It has been suggested, with much appositeness of reasoning, by no
means unworthy of attention, that, to avoid being infected with the
epidemic malady now prevailing in this metropolis, it is necessary to
breakfast early, and that without those appendages of the tables commonly called *Relishes*, whether of fish or flesh. To avoid lassitude and

fatigue, as much as may be; and to dine moderately, on fresh animal and vegetable food, about one o'clock in the day; drinking beer, cider, or good brandy, respectively diluted with water, as the wholesomest beverage at meals.   In the evening, tea or coffee may be drank, with simple bread and butter, as in the morning; but suppers are to be avoided. Dram-drinking (which some persons practise in the morning, and indeed at other times of the day,) is at all times an evil and destructive habit; but *at present*, is doubly pernicious in its effects.

To THE CITIZENS.—A supply of old shirts, shifts and linen, of any kind, is much wanted at the hospital for the sick.

Those who have any to spare, are requested to send them to the State House, where a person is appointed to receive them.

MATTHEW CLARKSON, Mayor.

Sept. 13, 1793.

The Printers are requested to publish this advertisement for a few days.

GENEROUS WAGES will be given to persons capable and willing to perform the services of *Nurses at the Hospital at Bushhill*, as the end desired by establishing the hospital at Bushhill much depends on good nursing and attendance.   The citizens of Philadelphia will render essential service to the sick, by aiding in procuring suitable persons for this employment.   Those who are willing to engage will please to apply to Israel Israel, Thomas Wistar, or Caleb Lownes.

EDWARD MOYSTON begs leave to inform his friends and the public, that he will shut up his Coffee-House to-morrow, the fever now prevalent being in its vicinity; as well as on account of none of the merchants having frequented the same for some days past—most of them having retired to the country.

Sept. 13, 1793.   d4t.

☞ AT this particular crisis, in which so many of the merchants and others are absent from the city, the indisposition of two of the letter-carriers renders it necessary to request all those who dwell south of and in Chesnut-street, and in Front and Water, north of Market-street, to call or send for their letters for a few days.

Sept. 13.   dtf.

A CALL FOR A MEETING.—At a meeting of a number of citizens, held at the Court House, this evening, Sept. 13th, in consequence of a verbal appointment of the Mayor and others convened at the City Hall, to take into consideration the present calamitous state of the city and its environs, having, in company with the overseers of the poor, made inquiry into the situation of the poor and afflicted, are of the opinion that, as it is not in the power of the overseers to afford the necessary

aid that the cases of the sick require, that the citizens be again convened, that some effectual means may be adopted to mitigate and, if
possible, to afford relief to the afflicted.

Upon motion, *Resolved*, That the secretary be directed to publish the
foregoing minute, and to request the citizens to attend a meeting at the
City Hall on the 14th instant, at 12 o'clock; and that, in the meantime, Israel Israel, Thomas Wistar and Caleb Lownes be requested to
confer with the physicians appointed to the care of the sick, at Bush-
Hill, obtain information of their situation, and furnish the necessary
aid and relief in their power to afford.

CALEB LOWNES.

In pursuance to this call, another meeting was held. On this
occasion it was reported that the hospital was without order or
supervision, that several superintendents and nurses were needed
there, that a sum of money ought instantly to be procured to aid
in obtaining necessaries for the sick, and that a large committee
ought to be appointed from the city, Northern Liberties and
Southwark, to aid the sick and distressed. Fifteen hundred dollars were ordered to be borrowed, if possible, from the Bank of
North America, and a committee was appointed to transact the
whole of the business relative to succoring the sick, providing
physicians, nurses, etc.

Our honored city of Philadelphia, then the metropolis of the
nation, and where the President and Congress were so lately
assembled in power, became suddenly a terror and a by-word to
the people. Its sister cities were taking every precaution to prevent the entrance within their limits of any one from Philadelphia,
and to eject such an one if in any way he came within them. The
following proclamation from the then mayor of New York will
illustrate the state of things:

BY THE MAYOR OF THE CITY OF NEW YORK.
  TO THE PRACTISING PHYSICIANS OF THE SAID CITY:

NEW YORK, Sept. 11, 1793.

GENTLEMEN: Great apprehensions are entertained by many of our
fellow-citizens that, notwithstanding every prudent and legal precaution,
the contagion of that distressing infectious disorder which now carries
off many of the citizens of Philadelphia, *may* be brought into *this* city,
by means of the open intercourse between the two cities, which cannot
lawfully be interrupted by any power in this State. You are therefore
hereby notified that the corporation of this city have taken measures to.
  24

provide a proper place as a hospital for such persons as may unhappily become subjects of that afflicting disease in this city.

And I do also hereby request each of you to report to me, in writing, to be left at my office in King street, the names of all such persons *as have arrived or shall arrive from Philadelphia*, or any other place, by *land* or *water*, and now are sick, or may be taken sick, and be under your care respectively, together with the number and street of their respective residence, and the nature of the sickness, that such as may be deemed to be subjects of *infectious disease may be removed out of the city.*

RICHARD VARICK, *Mayor.*

We have some interesting notes on the subject of this pestilence in the Diary of Dr. Smith. They are written at different times, after August 28th, 1793:

September 10, 1793.

Nathaniel Blodget, Esq.,* was buried at Christ Church. The plague, or so-called "Yellow Fever," has taken possession of the town. My friend Thomas Miller has been buried some days. The physicians have warned the people to care and cleanliness, to prevent the spread of the contagion; and to mark the houses in which it has appeared. We still stay in our town-house, as I consider it my duty as a clergyman to remain where I can be of some consolation and use. I advise my dear wife to go to our son's, at Norristown, or to let my boy drive her to our son Richard's, at Huntingdon, in the chair; but she is not willing to leave my side. We daily burn gunpowder about the house, and *Primus*† makes smoke in the cellar. The Mayor has requested the churches to cease the tolling of bells at funerals. Dr. Rush calls on us every day, and for some days gave us gentle doses of salts; but he now advises the use of barks, or of calomel and jalap. In fact, he knows not what to give.

September 13.

Francis Xavier Dupont, Consul of the French Republic, at Philadelphia, died last night at his seat at Bensalem, Bucks county. He was a firm patriot and an honest man.

September 14.

Alexander Murray, my old friend from Aberdeen, died at this date. He was buried in the evening.‡

October 13.

No service in Christ Church and St. Peter's, on account of the illness of the clerk and sexton of Christ Church and the sexton of St. Peter's.

---

* Nathaniel Blodget here mentioned was brother-in-law of Mrs. Samuel Blodget, the Doctor's daughter. He was in the navy, and had just returned from a voyage.

† The name of a favorite negro man whom the Doctor had brought with him from Maryland.

‡ For an account of this gentleman, see Appendix, No. III.

October 18.

The Rev. James Sproat died.*

19th.

The churches still closed.   I wrote to the Right Rev. Bishop White, to prevail upon him to leave the city.   He informs me that he has never slept out of the city during this whole calamity.   With others, I tell him that we consider it as a great and needless risk.

October 20.

Dr. Blackwell† was taken with the fever to-day, and was removed across the river, over to Gloucester, in the Jerseys.   I pray God to restore him to his life of usefulness.

Dr. George De Benneville‡ died at Branchtown.

---

* This was a respected clergyman of the Presbyterian Church.   An inscription upon a monument to his memory says of him:

Whatever is guiltless,
Candid and benevolent
In the human character,
Was conspicuous in him.
Amiable in domestic life,
Fervent in piety,
Mighty in the Scriptures,
Plain, practical and evangelical
In preaching,
Eminent in tenderness and charity for others,
Humble in his views of himself,
He was beloved and respected as a man,
Useful and venerable as a minister of Christ.

† Dr. Blackwell had a plantation in or among the pines of New Jersey, and to th pure and invigorating influence of the air prevalent in these woods he perhaps owed his recovery.   For a memoir of this estimable gentleman, a much respected friend of Dr. Smith, see Appendix, No. I.

‡ De Benneville's father was a Huguenot, who fled to England as a refugee from persecution, and he was employed at court by King William.   His mother was of the Granville family, and died soon after he was born, in 1703.   The orphan was taken charge of by Queen Anne, was placed on board of a ship-of-war, being destined for the navy at twelve years of age, and received his first religious impressions on the coast of Barbary by beholding the exceeding kindness of the Moors to a companion wounded by a fall.   For fifteen months he was in a state bordering on despair, by reason of inward doubting of his own salvation, and at the end of that period of suffering he was brought into the marvellous light of universal restitution.   Feeling it his duty to preach this great truth in France, he opened his testimony in the market-house of Calais about the seventeenth year of his age.   He was taken before a magistrate and sentenced to eight days' imprisonment for the offence.   Notwithstanding the warning that a repetition would endanger his life, he persisted for the space of two years in preaching in France, mostly in the woods and mountains.   In these labors Dr. Benneville had equally zealous preachers in co-operation—a Mr. Durant being of the number, a man of twenty-four years of age.   At Dieppe these two ministers were seized, tried, and condemned to death.   Durant was hanged, and while preparations were being made to behead De Benneville a reprieve arrived from Louis XV.   He was imprisoned for a

But the pestilence was walking in darkness, and in a moment was at the side of Dr. Smith himself. *He* was spared, but one dearer to him than himself was stricken down in the destruction of the noonday. The following letter to Dr. Rush gives us some interesting particulars of the sad event. It would seem that Dr. Rush, the family physician of Dr. Smith, had himself been taken ill suddenly with the fever, and was therefore unable to attend Mrs. Smith, though prior to her being taken ill he had been constantly visiting Dr. Smith's house and prescribing for his family:

Dr. Smith to Dr. Rush.

PHILADELPHIA, October 23d, 1793.

MY DEAR FRIEND: Indeed my only friend, whose own distress has permitted him to mingle his cordials of consolation in my bitter cup of affliction. How shall I thank you for your many sympathies—worthy of a physician, and (what is above all) worthy of a Christian?

The severest dispensation of Providence is now past with me, and blessed be God who has enabled me to sustain it. That dispensation which shall lay me by the side of my dear departed inestimable treasure in this life, will be but little felt, as I trust through the mercies of my God and Saviour, it will call me to share with her, her treasure in another and better life, where, as you so well express it, according to the sacred oracles, Death and the grave, and hell itself shall be "swallowed up in victory;" the genuine friendships of this life shall be revived, and love and life and light and truth reign forever and ever.

But, oh! busy recollections and memory asleep and awake, and the many tender charities and offices due to my bereaved family and children, who nearly adored the heavenly woman I have lost; the sight of the numerous remembrances of her in the lonesome house; the letters and written charges which she has left me, with the delivery of her keys to me by the faithful little black girl after her funeral, judge, my dear sir, nay feel—for your feelings are tenderly alive—how these circumstances thrill my nerves, which were never strong, and how they keep my heart and limbs and whole body in such a palpitation and trembling

---

long time in Paris, and was finally liberated by the intercession of the queen. He afterwards went to Germany, in which country he spent about eighteen years, preaching extensively, devoting himself in the meanwhile to scientific studies. In the thirty-eighth year of his age he emigrated to America, and was taken from the ship by Christopher Sauer. On recovering from his illness, De Benneville established himself in Oley, Bucks county, as a physician, and also temporarily as a teacher. He also preached and travelled much as a medical botanist among the Indian tribes in northern Pennsylvania. He intermarried with the Bartolet family, of Oley, and about 1757 removed to Milestown, where he died in 1793, aged ninety years.

that I fear the consequences. The scene of her funeral and some preceding circumstances can never depart from my mind.

On my return, with my wife, from a visit to our daughter—whom we had been striving to console on the death of Mrs. Keppele—long familiar and dear to both of us—my dear loving wife passing the gates of Christ Church Burying-ground, which stood daily open, led me through it to the graves of the two children, and calling the old grave-digger, marked out a spot for herself as close as possible to her children and the grave of Dr. Phineas Bond, whose memory she adored. By the side of the spot we found room and chose also one for me, as it was not permitted during the sickness to open a grave once closed for the burial of another. We therefore directed the grave-digger that this should be the order of our interment, and pledged ourselves to each other that this order should be observed by the survivor. But let me not be tedious to you. It gives me some ease as my children are all absent, and cannot come near me in town, to pour these circumstances into the bosom of a friend. In melancholy mood we returned to our house. Night approached. I hoped my dear wife had gone to rest, as she had chosen since her return from nursing her daughter through the fever to sleep in a chamber by herself through fear of infection to her grandchild and me. But it seems she closed not her eyes, sitting with them fixed through her chamber window,* on Mrs. Keppele's house (who had died that day), until about midnight, she saw her hearse and followed it with tearful eyes as far as it would be seen. Two days afterwards, Mrs. Rogers, her next and only surviving intimate friend, was carried past her window, and by no persuasion could we draw her from thence, nor stop her sympathetic foreboding tears, so long as her eyes could follow the funeral, which was down Arch street, two squares from Fourth street, to Second street, where, turning the corner to the Baptist Church, the hearse disappeared. She threw herself on her bed and requested me, who had stood by her side during the time of the funeral procession, to leave her to her own reflections for a few minutes, and she would soon be with me in my study, where I was writing letters to my friends and family on business to the westward. She took her pen and assisted me in copying some of them. It was Saturday; and we had persuaded our daughter to set out for Norristown next day. My wife, though she informed me on Saturday evening, that she was indisposed—and I am persuaded was sure of the nature of her case—yet she charged me not to inform her daughter, and sent me to hasten her out of town on Sunday morning, with an apology that she could not see her before she sat out, finding it necessary to take a little physic for a slight indisposition,

---

* Dr. Smith's house, to which he refers, was that fine old-fashioned one still standing at the southwest corner of Fourth and Arch, about one hundred feet below the east side of the grave-yard of Christ Church, Philadelphia.

and that if she would send the carriage back in two or three days, we hoped to follow her to Norristown. While I was getting my daughter ready and seeing her a few miles out of town, which was not until two o'clock, on Sunday, my dear wife with her own hand, had written the note which you must have in your possession, the contents of which, or her apprehensions expressed in it, I can only guess. You know the rest. My situation through the week following the Sunday evening, at six o'clock, when in much agony by a sudden and unexpected turn, after I had fondly written to all my distant family, and to my dear brother that I believed her out of danger, she breathed her last, composed and patient; her countenance appearing to brighten, as her pangs and groans ceased, into the countenance of an angel.

Decently as the time would permit, my mournful family assisted only by a worthy and pious black, Richard Allen,* she was laid in her coffin. I approached with my dear grandchild in my arms, as near as the black man would allow, to take my last view. Silent, but more awful and instructive than all the funeral pomps in the world, and short the distance we had to go, I followed her, accompanied only by the coffin-maker, and by Richard Allen, and my own weeping and faithful black boy, to the spot she had chosen, about eight o'clock in the evening to deposit all of her that was mortal.

Severe was the task that it remained for me, yesterday, to write to my daughter and other children, and to good Mrs. Cadwalader, who loved her aunt as her own parent. When these letters were finished, and an express dispatched to my son, William, to take all prudent measures possible to support his sister in her affliction. My messenger having taken his course up the street, my anxious dutiful son came to my door while I was visiting the grave to see if it had been properly covered in the night. My black boy met my son at the door of my house, and was obliged to answer his inquiry concerning his mother; that she was

---

* This was an excellent and well-known negro in his day in Philadelphia. He was born A. D. 1760, and was originally a slave of Chief Justice Chew, as afterwards of a Mr. Stokely, in Delaware. He cut wood, and was a laborer in brickyards. During the war of the Revolution he was an army teamster. By habits of economy and thrift he accumulated some money with which he purchased his freedom. He then learned the trade of shoemaking, and for many years carried on business on the south side of Spruce street below Fifth. He had several journeymen and apprentices constantly in his employ. He owned and managed at the same time a small farm in the Neck, below the city, and accumulated a considerable amount of property by various occupations. With all these he exercised the office of a preacher, preaching among the Methodist negroes. Though education had not lent her hand in his behalf, he had a capacity that few of his color exhibit, and had unbounded influence over the people of his denomination. He was eminently a humane man. In common with Absalom Jones, another colored person, he rendered invaluable services to the citizens during the prevalence of the yellow fever, in 1793. Jones was long a servant of Dr. Blackwell, and was afterwards ordained by Bishop White a minister of the Episcopal Church.

no more. I soon came from the ground and saw my dear son leaning against the wall, for he would not enter the house, nor amidst the distressing scene could we exchange a word, but such as expressed my desire, and his ready obedience that he would fly to his sister and overtake the messenger. This he did at eight miles distance from town. I have heard no more, and I dread to hear from a daughter who loved and knew the value of such a mother.

But much remains for me yet—my son Charles and his wife, my brother and his wife, my son Richard at Huntingdon, in whose bosoms she was equally precious. I can find no conveyance, and hard will be my task to write if my spirits and health can be supported so long.

For that reason only, and a few more family matters not yet arranged—especially a codicil which my dear wife's death makes necessary to my will—if it will please God, I would pray for a few days continuance of health. Then as to worldly matters I shall be prepared, and through the goodness of God I trust I am preparing, though we can never, never be fully prepared (except in his mercy) in our spiritual matters.

If God continues me longer, my worldly concerns will be in a small compass. His goodness having given me time to distribute a sufficient inheritance to my children, acquired, I trust, honestly and industriously without injury to any man, and I hope and believe from the goodness of all my children, in whom I consider myself blest, they will use it accordingly. For the rest of my days, and they cannot be many, I would willingly devote them to discharge some public engagements by assorting and leaving to the world some sermons and other writings. But if they cannot have my last hand, my executors, to be named in my proposed codicil, must suppress all, except what I have already published and avowed.

My friend, Mrs. Cadwalader, and Mrs. Bond, press me with your advise to take calomel and jalap, etc.—I know nothing of preventatives —and then to move out of town, but I wish not to remove to a distance from you for some days yet, nor until you advise. I trust you will soon be so restored that you may have a personal interview. If moving for a few days to my daughter's will change the scene a little, perhaps it may be of use.

Thus, my good friend, I have poured into your bosom, confidentially, what may be of use to my family, for to none of them have I had leisure, nor would it be yet proper to say so much. The name and memory of my dear wife I must commit to your friendly hand, who knew her virtues so well, to say to the public what may be necessary ; but of this nothing yet, as I would not have her name announced among the dead, until I find means first to notify it to my distant family. Alas ! how shall I live without her ? I never had a joy which became a joy to me until she shared it. I never had a sorrow which she did not alleviate and participate. I never did an action which I would consider as truly good, until she confirmed my opinion.

For my many failings and infirmities she had a friendly veil.

Her conversation was enlightened, and that with her correspondence by letter during my many absences, have been my joy for thirty-five years and more.   My tears now stop my hand, and will relieve you from reading more.

From your obliged and affectionate

WILLIAM SMITH.

To DR. RUSH.

Excuse inaccuracies, omissions of words, etc., for I cannot read over or correct what has flowed from my heart and pen.

On the 18th of November, Dr. Smith prepared an address and exhortation by the clergy of the city of Philadelphia to the citizens of the same, urging them to set apart a day not only as a day for Thanksgiving, but also one of confession, humiliation and prayer. Though drafted so early as November, it was not published, as its date shows, till December the 11th.   It having been the wish of Dr. Smith and Bishop White that it should be signed by some of the clergy then absent from the city, but whose presence was then daily expected.   It appeared in the *Federal Gazette,* at the date just above mentioned.

To THE CITIZENS OF PENNSYLVANIA:

The clergy of different denominations, in the city of Philadelphia, having had under deep meditation the late awful calamity, with which it hath pleased Almighty God, in his infinite wisdom, to visit and afflict this city; and devoutly considering the improvement which, as a Christian people, it becomes us to make of the dispensations of his Providence, "who doth according to his holy will in the armies of heaven and among the inhabitants of the earth," have, with one heart and voice, agreed and concluded it to be their indispensable and sacred duty to recommend and request:—

That a day be set apart, and kept holy unto the Lord, not merely as a Day of Thanksgiving for that, in all appearance, it hath pleased him, of his infinite mercy, to stay the rage of the late malignant disorder (when we had well nigh said, hath God forgot to be gracious!) but also as a day of solemn humiliation, and prayer, joined with the confession of our manifold sins, and of our neglect and abuse of his former mercies; together with sincere resolutions of future amendment and obedience to his holy will and laws; without which, our prayers, praises and thanksgivings will be vain.

In this solemn review of our past lives, and of the dealings of the Lord with us and our forefathers, let us be serious with ourselves, and search our wounds and sores to the bottom.   For, although the Almighty may manifest himself to a people, in judgment as well as mercy, by means of natural causes and with the same breath that he bids the pestilence rage, he can bid its ragings cease; yet his purposes in both are to be our chief consideration, and he hath told us, "that when his judgments are in the land, the inhabitants should learn righteousness."

On this great and humiliating occasion, the clergy consider it as needless for them to remind the inhabitants of this land of what God hath done for us, and the many instances of his divine favor and interposition, in the establishment of our civil liberties and independence, together with the enjoyment of the pure doctrines of the Gospel of Christ and the exercise of his holy religion, according to the rights of conscience, under a government of laws, and wise civil institutions of our own free and peaceable choice, there being "none to make us afraid." But the clergy must consider it as a special and most weighty part of their bounden duty to warn, to exhort, and to press the most earnest inquiry—whether we have made a due improvement of those innumerable blessings which the Almighty hath, in his goodness, even heaped upon us? Have we at all times made use of our civil liberty itself, as not seeking to abuse it? But, more especially, have we sought in good earnest, and in the fear and love of God, to improve our precious Gospel privileges, by striving to make the fruits of the same conspicuous in our lives, and "in all holy conversation and godliness?" Or whether, on the contrary, the worship of the true and living God, and the sacred ordinances of the Gospel, have not been too much slighted, or neglected, for the false pleasures of this world, its dissipations, its follies, or perhaps the too eager pursuit of its goods and enjoyments?— evils which, having their origin too generally among the gay, the rich, and those in higher stations, have, by fatal example, spread themselves downwards among all classes of our people, to the dishonor of God and the unspeakable injury of their moral and religious character, as well as the waste and ruin of their temporal substance and the distress and poverty of their families!

Together with this retrospective view of our own conduct, and of the calamity from which it hath pleased God to deliver us, who, through his mercy, survive, let us not forget to mourn with those that mourn, to sympathize with them in their distress, and to administer to their comfort and relief. This will be a fruitful subject of devout meditation; and, through divine grace, will awaken and make us feelingly alive to all holy and religious impressions: while we recall to our memory those melancholy days and nights when corps after corps of beloved husbands and wives, dutiful sons and daughters, useful citizens, venerable pastors, in quick and almost uninterrupted succession, were borne along our streets in the solitary hearse, with scarce a friend or relative to follow them to the grave! Oh! let us now consecrate their dust with our tears; and, hoping that they have departed in the Lord, thus supply the solemn rites of Christian interment which the hard necessity of the times then forbade.

Thus, prepared and humbled by deep meditation, by confession and repentance of our sins, and prayers for forgiveness and amendment— then our praises and thanksgivings to God, for our late deliverance and for stirring up the hearts of so many of our pious and benevolent brethren throughout the United States to intercede for us in their prayers, and to administer so liberally to the relief of our afflicted and suffering poor, will ascend as a sweet incense to heaven, and be a holy and acceptable sacrifice before the throne of grace, through the merits and intercession of our blessed Saviour and Redeemer Jesus Christ.

Subscribed at Philadelphia,
November 18, 1793.

Wm. White,	Friedrick Schmidt,
Wm. Smith,	John B. Smith,
John Andrews,	John Dickins,
Ashbel Green,	Joseph Turner,
Robert Annan,	Joseph Hutchins,
Henry Helmuth,	Robert Blackwell,
Samuel Magaw,	Christ. V. Keating,
Joseph Pilmore,	Thomas Ustick,
Wm. Rogers,	Nicholas Collin,

Mathew Mage.

In the meantime the Governor of the State, General Mifflin, requested Dr. Smith to furnish a draft for a proclamation of Thanks to Almighty God for having put an end to the grievous calamity that had recently afflicted the city of Philadelphia. The following is an abstract of the proclamation prepared by Dr. Smith and issued by the Governor on this great occasion:

WHEREAS, it hath pleased Almighty God to put an end to the grievous calamity that recently afflicted the city of Philadelphia; and it is the duty of all, who are truly sensible of the Divine Justice and Mercy, to employ the earliest moments of returning health in devout expressions of penitence, submission and gratitude; I have therefore deemed it proper to appoint Thursday, the Twelfth day of December, to be holden throughout this commonwealth as a day of general Humiliation, Thanksgiving and Prayer; earnestly exhorting and entreating my fellow-citizens to abstain on that day from all their worldly avocations, and to unite in confessing, with contrite hearts, our manifold sins and transgressions, and in acknowledging, with thankful adoration, the mercy and goodness of the Supreme Ruler and Preserver of the universe, more especially manifested in our late deliverance ; praying, with solemn zeal, that the same Mighty Power would be graciously pleased to instil into our minds the just principles of our duty to Him and to our fellow-creatures ; to regulate and guide all our actions by his Holy Spirit; to avert from all mankind the evils of war, pestilence and famine ; and to bless and protect us in the enjoyment of civil and religious liberty, etc.

We come now to make mention of certain discourses found in Maxwell's edition of his works, which were preached by Dr. Smith in Christ Church in the last month of 1793 and the earlier part of the following year—sermons suggested by the terrible pestilence from which the city was at last, by God's mercy, delivered. The first of these sermons was preached on the day appointed for the general humiliation, thanksgiving and prayer, by the proclamation of which some abstract has just been given. Dr. Smith, however, has himself given so interesting an account of the origin of the sermons and of some particulars connected with them, especially of President Washington's reverential attendance and deportment in connection with their delivery, that I offer to my readers an account all in his own language :

During the chief rage of the first great epidemic called the yellow fever, in Philadelphia, in the year 1793—viz. : from the latter end of September till towards the end of November—the churches had been generally shut up, except Christ Church and St. Peter's, which had been kept open by Bishop White and Dr. Blackwell, unless on the 13th and 20th of October, when the illness of the clerk and sexton of Christ Church and sexton of St. Peter's prevented their being opened. Bishop White was preserved in tolerable health, and never slept out of the city during the whole calamity, which some of his friends, myself among others, told him they considered as a great and needless risk. Dr. Blackwell was taken ill with the fever on the 27th of October, and removed across the river, into the Jerseys, near Gloucester. After about a month's severe illness he begun (almost beyond expectation) to appear on the recovery, although with but little hopes of being able soon to resume his pastoral duties in the churches. Those duties, therefore, were like to fall heavy, at least for some time, on good Bishop White, whose kind visits to myself and his other friends in the city were continued during the whole time of the affliction.

But the goodness of God now giving a prospect of a near termination of the disorder, the Bishop paid me a short visit a few days before the 1st of December, and told me that on that day the churches under his care, after the short interruption of a week or two, as mentioned above, would be on the usual footing of public service twice a day in each church; and with great delicacy and tenderness to me, in my mournful situation, he hinted a wish for some temporary assistance from me, if I was able, and that in preaching only: at the same time offering me my choice of the turn of duty. I told him that, so far as I was able, it always gave me happiness to co-operate with him in any duty, but that he must give me the choice of my subjects as well as of the turns of duty; that none but melancholy subjects—themes of distress, notes of woe—could accord with my feelings and then gloomy frame of mind. His reply was with his usual look of complacency, intimating approbation.

NINE SERMONS from 1st Thessalonians, chap. iv., verses 13–18—on Death, a Resurrection from the Dead, a Future Judgment, and an Eternal World to Come, were the fruits of that period of melancholy and deep reflection. The first was preached on Sunday, December 1st, 1793, and the last on March 9th, 1794, in Christ Church, all in the forenoon. This was understood to be according to the wish of the President and his good lady. It is certain that they were present at the delivery of all of them, and generally of every sermon preached in Christ Church, in the forenoon, during the session of Congress.

General Washington, exemplary in all his conduct, and anxious to know when it might be safe for the citizens to resume their business and stations in town, had officially consulted the physicians. Understanding by their answers to him, as well as to some of the clergy who had consulted them also, that sundry of the churches, and particularly Christ Church, where he and his lady always attended divine service, would be opened on Sunday, the first of December, that day, or the day before, he came from Germantown, and presented himself early before God in the church on Sunday. His example was followed by multitudes; and the church was more than usually crowded, before I got into it. The scene was sadly solemn: all eyes were apparently cast down in afflictive meditation. The deepest attention and silence prevailed, during the morning service; and at the delivery of the sermon, not a cheek appeared dry; for scarcely a man or woman was present, who had not to mourn the loss of a dear friend or relative. The preacher's duty was interesting. He was a fellow-sufferer and co-mourner. He does not remember that ever he lifted his eyes from his notes, which were drenched in tears. He was then, if ever, in the situation described by Luther, and impressed with the feelings of every preacher, who, like Luther, is truly interested in his subject, and, so to speak, weighed down with its truth and importance.

CHAPTER LVII.

THE visitation of pestilence, 1793, was an event in Philadelphia, at this time the metropolis of the United States, so awful; its effects, by death, upon our then society so considerable, and the terror which it continued to inspire, for some years so widespread, that I may venture to refer somewhat fully to the sermons of Dr. Smith upon the calamity.

We note primarily that, solemn and serious as most of Dr. Smith's pulpit discourses are, these are characterized by solemnity and seriousness beyond the common degree. He was now sixty-seven years old. "Uncertain," he says, "of the number of days, or months, or years remaining to me, but certain that they cannot be many, and those attended with the decay of mental as well as of bodily faculties," he naturally, after a life marked by such vicissitudes and such calamities as his had been, sought at the present moment to lead his hearers into paths of righteousness, with no thought whatever of the impression which he himself would make on any one. In sermons upon occasions of ceremonious worship, such as in the sermon before the Grand Master and Grand Officers of the Ancient and Honorable Society of Free and Accepted Masons of the State of Pennsylvania, celebrated on the anniversary of St. John the Evangelist, we see bold and lofty rhetoric. What exordium, for example, can be finer than the one in his Masonic sermon of 1778?* Bishop Atterbury's celebrated one upon the text from St. Matthew and St. Luke, *"Blessed is he that shall not be offended in me,"* where the Bishop at once breaks out, "And can any one, blessed Lord, be offended in thee?" is not more bold. It has no pretensions to rhetoric. Dr. Smith, in his discourse before the Masons, is preaching from the text of 1 Peter

---

* Works, Vol. II., p. 43.

ii. 16, "*As Free, and not using your Liberty for a cloak of licentious-ness.*" He thus opens. With his figure, his voice, his natural dramatic power, the experiment was safe, as probably it was in the case of the Bishop of Rochester, but it would be perilous indeed to the common preacher:

Liberty, evangelical and social! Jewel of inestimable price! Thou blessing, of all blessings the first! Wooed and courted by many; won and wedded by few! Ever near us, yet often at a distance fancied. Through all the modes of faith, by the saint pursued; and in every frame of government by the patriot sought. Oh, thou celestial Good, or, rather, Thou who art the Author of all good, terrestrial and celestial— Supreme Architect of the universe; who, by our great and Spiritual Master, thy Son, hast taught us the true Way of Liberty—the way of being free and accepted through Him! May I now be enlightened and enlivened by a ray from Thee!

But now, in the sermons upon the late awful epidemic, there is nothing like this. He was "no actor *here*," though his style, naturally casting itself into rhetorical forms, still preserves its habitual characteristics. His text is from a series of verses, that is to say, from the 13th to the 18th inclusive, of the 4th chapter of the First Epistle of Paul the Apostle to the Thessalonians. Every one remembers them:

But I would not have you to be ignorant, brethren, concerning them which are asleep, that ye sorrow not, even as others which have no hope.

For if we believe that Jesus died, and rose again, even so them also which sleep in Jesus will God bring with him.

For this we say unto you, by the word of the Lord, that we which are alive, and remain unto the coming of the Lord, shall not prevent them which are asleep.

For the Lord himself shall descend from heaven with a shout, with the voice of the Archangel, and with the trump of God: and the dead in Christ shall rise first.

Then we which are alive and remain, shall be caught up together with them in the clouds, to meet the Lord in the air; and so shall we ever be with the Lord.

Wherefore comfort one another with these words.

Dr. Smith thus proceeds, solemnly and grand:

Yes, brethren and sisters! ye bereaved mourners for parents, hus-bands, wives, children and dearest relatives, say a solemn Amen, and "comfort one another with these words." For if there be consolation in this world, amidst this suffering scene of man, here it is complete, and revealed to us by a divinely illuminated apostle of Christ; leading our meditations forward through all the future changes and periods of our existence and condition, as mortals and immortals, "to death, a resurrection from the dead, a future judgment, and an eternal world to come." . . .

The impressions of the dreadful calamity, from which we, who are alive, remain monuments of God's mercy in the midst of his righteous judgments, must have awakened and alarmed the most secure and thoughtless among us, and have made us feelingly alive to every sober reflection that concerns our future state and condition, viz.: death, a resurrection from the dead, a future judgment, and the opening the heavenly paradise—the everlasting kingdom of glory to the redeemed of God— "to those who sleep in the faith of Jesus." For, amidst the shafts of Providence, which have flown so thick around us and amongst us, where is the man or the woman in this assembly whose bosom is not deeply pierced, or whose tears do not this moment flow, for the loss of some of those who were lately nearest and dearest to him or to her—a husband, a wife, a father, a mother, a brother, a sister, a son, a daughter? For me—ah! my throbbing breast—deep, deep have the arrows* pierced; yet be still, in just resignation to his unerring will, who gives and takes away, by whom we live, move, and have our being—be still, while we proceed in the further review of this mournful group of departed friends and acquaintance! Who is there among us who does not recall to memory many younger and stronger than themselves, between whose summons from this life and their commitment to that long home, the grave, few were the days or hours that intervened, while we yet remain, with time and opportunity offered, to examine the past and to think of the future.

To assist your meditations in this respect, and to mingle comfort in our bitter cup of affliction, I have chosen the words of St. Paul, which have been just read as our text; a choice which I have the rather made, as the whole volumes of inspiration contain no words more evangelically comfortable or suitable to our present situation; and, as I trust, the same words and the reflections thereon arising, which, through God's grace, I have found experimentally efficacious to pour balm into my own wounds, while yet fresh and bleeding, will, through the same grace, be acceptable and effectual among you, in the like circumstances!

The text naturally divides itself into the following heads, each of which will afford subject-matter for at least one discourse:

1st. Considerations on death; the nature and cause of his awful terrors; and how, through Divine assistance, to combat and conquer them; to allay our sorrows for our departed friends, and prepare for our own departure.

2d. The certainty of a resurrection of the body from the grave; showing that death is but a temporary evil, and that our sorrow should

---

* The author lost a beloved wife, one of the most accomplished among women; whose memory remains dear to all who knew her. She died October 23, 1793.

not be without hope, as others who have no belief in the resurrection of the dead.

3d. The certainty of a future judgment, and the award of an eternity of happiness to those who sleep in the Lord, or in the faith of the Gospel—" For them that sleep in Jesus will God bring with Him, and so we shall be forever with the Lord ! "

4th. That, from all these considerations, the devout Christian may not only overcome the fear of death in himself, but derive an abundant source of consolation for the death of others, according to our apostle, who, in the sweetest accents of evangelical sympathy and love, in the last verse of our text calls us to " comfort one another with the hopes, after death and a resurrection, of being forever with the Lord ! "

I proceed now to the first head of discourse as pointed out in the text, namely: " Considerations on death, and how, through divine assistance, to subdue and overcome his mighty terrors." And oh, Thou almighty fountain of all wisdom and grace and heavenly fortitude, aid me with thy divine spirit, that the great and awful subjects which I am to handle may not suffer through my feeble endeavors; but give me, for the sake of Jesus and his Gospel, to follow, with clear and unembarrassed view, the steps and arguments of thy divinely enlightened apostle, who is everywhere superlatively instructive and sublime, but especially when he opens to us the prospects of a future world. Lo ! he stands, though with his feet on earth, his eye steadfast on heaven, considering death, not as a tyrant sent to disturb our peace, but as a messenger of God, employed to " dissolve our earthly house of this tabernacle that we may be clothed upon with our house, which is from Heaven."

" For we know," says he in another place,* " that if our earthly house of this tabernacle were dissolved, we have a building of God, an house not made with hands, eternal in the heavens. For in this (earthly) house we groan, earnestly desiring to be clothed upon with our house which is from Heaven."

Brethren, when I read this passage from our blessed apostle, in conjunction with our text, as well as many others expressive of the true spirit of primitive Christianity, I am doubtful (as saith an old commentator) whether most to admire the exalted temper of the apostles and first followers of Christ, or to deplore the low and desponding spirit of the modern professors of Christianity—so heavenly and magnanimous were the former, so earthly and abject the latter ! The former were always raising their affections to things above—to their " house not made with hands, eternal in the heavens ; " the latter too often immuring themselves deeper and still deeper within the walls of their "earthly house of this tabernacle ! "

---

* 2 Cor. v. I, 2.

And whence comes this difference between the truly primitive and modern spirit of professing Christians? Whence, brethren, but from what the apostle suggests? The former considered the present life only as a pilgrimage, and this whole world as but an inn, or short refreshing place, in their way to the regions of immortality and glory! They looked upon their passage thither as a scene of perils—a passage through a valley of sorrow and tears—and that, for the trial of their faith and exercise of their hope, they were called to a constant warfare with enemies both within and without them. The soul they considered as their truly better and immortal part, worthy of all their care; the body but as of an inferior nature—a tabernacle, a tent, a cottage, an earthen vessel, a mere temporary abode, or rather the prison-house of the soul; in itself more brittle than glass, decaying and constantly mouldering away, subject to diseases, pain and every vicissitude of the surrounding elements. And thus, daily considering the vanity and the emptiness of earthly things, their affections were more and more weaned from this world. They became impatient of the dross of body; their souls penetrated by faith through the clouds of this mortality; and they obtained some foretaste of the immense good things laid up for them in a world to come. They acquired some just and ravishing conceptions of that building of God, that house not made with hands, that celestial body, with which the soul was to be united (for the nourishment of their hope and the exercise of their charity) in the mansions of glory; and, therefore, far from being awed or terrified at the separation of the soul from the body, or apprehensions from the dissolution of their earthly tabernacle, and of its dust mixing again with its kindred dust, they groaned earnestly within themselves, waiting for the adoption, that is, the redemption of the body, that they might be clothed upon with their heavenly house, "and so be forever with the Lord."

But can we say, brethren, that this is the general temper of those who call themselves Christians in the present day? Can we say that we are always looking forward to our future end? Or rather, do we not keep ourselves blind to the future, ignorant of our destiny, or without any guesses concerning another world? We rather wish to consider the present as our only world, and death as an everlasting sleep—a total annihilation of, perhaps, soul and body! Wherefore, if we think of an approaching dissolution, we sorrow, as men having no hope beyond the narrow precincts of the grave. If any dark glimmerings of another world intrude upon our quiet, we strive to stifle the divine sparklings in the soul, and hate to converse with the God within us, or think of any future state. And thus, far from rejoicing at the notices nature gives of an approaching dissolution of our mortal part; far from groaning earnestly to be clothed upon with our immortal house, and meeting death in the full hope of glory, I may appeal to yourselves, whether the very name of death be not as a thunder-stroke to us! We startle, we

25

turn pale, we tremble before him as the king of terrors, and at his approach we cling faster and still faster to this evanescent speck of earth, loth to let go our hold. Few, too few, consider death in the right view, as a welcome messenger sent from God to summon the soul (if, peradventure, prepared) to heaven and glory. Few consider that, although his marks are sure, he shoots not an arrow but what is directed by the wisdom of our adorable Creator. In this view we consider him not; but, on the other hand, we consider him as a cruel tyrant, come to disturb our repose, to rob us of our joys and to separate us from all that we hold dear. We look upon him as the merciless ravisher of parents from children, and children from parents; wives from husbands, and husbands from wives. We view him as the despoiler of our fortune, breaking in upon all our busy projects and best prospects; tearing us from our dearest friends and relatives, levelling our fame and proudest honors with the dust, turning our beauty into deformity, our strength into rottenness and our very names into oblivion. We behold him dealing with others as with ourselves, neither sparing the young nor the old, the feeble nor the strong, the rich nor the poor, the beggar in his rags, nor the proudest ruler in his purple. We find him neither to be regardful of our pride, nor to be soothed by our flattery, tamed by our entreaties, bribed by our benefits, softened by our lamentations, nor diverted by accident or length of time. His weapons of destruction are numerous, and we are unable to draw one of them from his grip. A thousand ministers of vengeance attend his call—sword, pestilence, famine and fell disease; the air, the earth, the sea, the fire, and the beasts of the field, are the executioners of his will against man; and, more dreadful to tell, man himself—monstrous, depraved man—becomes the minister of death against his fellow-man! With scorns and with wrongs, with imprisonments, with torments, with poisons and deadly engines of destruction, man preys upon man, at thy call, O Death, and heaps up thy vast triumphs! Hence it is that thou art so terrible, and that we startle at thy name, and tremble at thy approach. Yet still, by the due use of reason, enlightened by the blessed considerations and doctrines of our text, after the example of the apostles and saints and pure professors of Christianity in every age, death might be disarmed of his sting and spoiled of his victory!

If to die were only the lot of a few, we might repine and startle at the partial decree. But since no age that is past hath been exempted from his strokes, nor shall any age that is to come, why should we, with unavailing sorrow and unprofitable stubbornness, think to oppose the universal decree, "Dust thou art, and to dust thou shalt return?" Let us think what millions have trod the path of death before us, and what millions are yet to follow! Let us think of the instability of all things, temporary and sublunary! Even kingdoms and mighty empires have submitted to their fatal periods! Great cities lie buried in the dust!   Proud towers and pyramids, the wonders of the world and the pride of ages, are overthrown and trampled under foot!   Holy temples and altars, and those also who have ministered before them, have shared the general doom!   And this great fabric of the world itself, the sun, the moon and the stars, shall submit to death, or a change similar to death; yet, like the body of man, peradventure, to be renewed again, and kindled up into fresh and everlasting lustre!

Since, then, the most solid and sumptuous works of man, and even this glorious creation, the work of God himself, are doomed to changes, to decay and to death, what are we, poor earthlings and creatures of a day, to hope for an everlasting continuance amidst this transient and perishable scene?   Or why should we be afraid when our change draws near?

The true reason is, "Our want of faith in God and union with Christ Jesus, through the grace of his divine spirit."   We do not imitate those blessed saints and first followers of Christ, who are described in our text, by striving to disentangle our souls and thoughts from this world, and to send them forward in earnest longings after heaven and immortality.   We do not seat ourselves by faith in the company of angels and archangels; nor seek to anticipate the joys of the life to come.   Our conversation is not in heaven, nor are we looking to our Redeemer from thence; nor do our souls thirst nor our flesh long after the living God.

But, on the contrary, like unweaned babes, we hang upon the breasts of this earth.   We suck poison out of it to our very souls; we cleave to it—we walk—nay, we grovel upon our bellies here, as unclean beasts, instead of lifting our eyes to heaven with the holy pride and ambition of angels!

Hence, then, comes our fear of death, because we seek to have our portion in this world, and not in the world to come, never considering what comfortable words Christ tells us, that "if any man keep his sayings he shall never see death;" for Christ hath slain death, and "brought life and immortality to light by the gospel."

The sting of death is sin, and the strength of sin is the grave; but our union with Christ gives us the victory.   If we die in the faith of Jesus, death is only a sleep in his bosom, and the grave is only the vestry-room, where we enter (as we said before) to put off the old rags of our mortality, to be clothed upon anew, and to come forth, fresh and refulgent, in the rich dress and embroidery of heaven.

It shall be my endeavor (ye mournful brethren and sisters), in my subsequent occasional discourses before you, from this luminous text, to examine and weigh, in the scales of Religion, Reason and Philosophy, those good things, commonly so-called, by which too many are drawn (as already expressed) to "hang upon the breasts of this world, and to suck poison from them to their very souls."   I shall further strive to offer such considerations as, under divine grace, may disentangle our thoughts, and wean our souls from too great an attachment to the things of this world and send them forward to another world in earnest longings after immortality; anticipating the joys above, and seating ourselves by faith in the company of angels and archangels; having our conversation in heaven, looking for the coming of our Lord, and panting to be with him forever!

The next discourse seems to have been attended, in a more particular way, by the younger class of people. It is from the same texts as the former one, and on the same general subject—" How, through divine assistance, we may subdue the fear of death." Passing over—as we must do for want of space—the earlier parts of the discourse, we come to a special address to the young. Its style recalls the full dress and form, with the gentility, unhappily, with both too much departed, of days just remembered by ourselves.

Oh, ye youth of these rising, and yet happy, American States! for whose admonition, instruction, and illumination the past and best part of my life has been devoted, through a long term of years; receive, or rather bear, the repetition of a lesson, perhaps the last, of old age!

Boast not, therefore, of your youth or strength or beauty, but in the hopes you entertain, and the resolution you have formed of preparing yourselves, to live a life of future usefulness, and to animate you in this resolution, look forward to the glorious scenes in which you will be called to act your part; and look back also "to the rock from whence you were hewed, and the hole of the pit from whence you were digged."* Think of the steps by which your virtuous and frugal ancestors rose into consideration, and say whether you can find one of their number that attained to any eminence but by virtue and industry in some settled calling or profession. Spurn from you, betimes, the syren's sloth and idleness, and seek to come forth on the theatre assigned to you, all energy and action, in the sight of mortal and immortal powers, striving to fill your post with diligence and dignity— abiding therein, but abiding with God! Spurn from you also the love of false pleasure, and seek to make a just estimate of that pleasure, which God in his goodness has ordained as the true alloy of our cares, and the reward of a virtuous course of action!

If you seek pleasure, let it be the pleasure of your whole nature and existence, considered with respect both to time and eternity! And in this view, the pleasure of a rational being, made in the image of his

---

* Isaiah li. 1.

Creator, ordained to bear his head on high, and to hold sacred intercourse with the Father of all—is not to stifle the sigh for happiness implanted in his bosom, nor bury the vital principle of action, in the in-
ordinate pursuit of animal gratifications, which serve for little else but
to enervate the soul and depress its native aspirations after the divine
life.   It is not to drink the deadly draught of poison, although served
up to us in a golden cup.   It is not to dance the giddy round of noisy
revel, thoughtless whence we came, or whither we are going!   It is not
to riot in broad day, in practices which our sober fathers would have
blushed to witness in secret.   It is not to pursue phantom after phantom, like airy bubbles, bursting in the grasp.   Nor is it to torture invention after invention, in contriving expedients to keep animal joy alive,
till the palled sense recoils, and refuses the hated load!   No, says the
wise Solomon, who spoke from experience, and had sought pleasure and
happiness through every avenue of life—no, says he—"Thou mayest rejoice, O young man, and thy heart may cheer thee in the days of thy
youth, whilst thou walkest in the ways of thy heart; but for all these
things, know that God will bring thee into judgment"*—yea, certainly
judgment in another world, and probably judgment in this—for if we
take a step among the sons and daughters of worldly pleasure, though
all seems so gay and joyous without, yet how different if we could look
within!   What distraction, weakness and dissipation of thought?   What
fretfulness, jealousies and heart-burnings of disappointed pride, dim-
ming the fair eye of fairest beauty?   What incumbrances of fortune,
what embarrassments of business, what shame, remorse and painful reflections for neglected duties and deserted families; only to be avoided
by suppressing or drowning the voice of reason, conscience and religion
by a speedy return to the round of giddy revel, till at last health and
fame and the fair paternal inheritance are shipwrecked at their feet.   I
tremble to speak the rest.   What can we behold, then, but wretchedness
complete?   "Ancestors disgraced, posterity ruined; behind, nothing
but guilt and shame, and before, nothing but inextricable misery! . . ."

The true pleasures, the sacred, substantial never-fading bliss of all who
are born into this world—high and low, old and young, is to exert the
first efforts of their reason, guided by religion and revelation, to consider for what end they were sent into it, and to discharge their part in
this life faithfully, seeking to prepare, and not afraid to take their departure for a better, always bearing in mind that the short and transient
now bears on its fleeting wing an eternity of bliss or woe.

Let no age or condition of life thrust these serious truths from the
heart.   Trust not to your youth or strength, ye whom I now more immediately address.   Look but a few months back, and consider how

* Eccl. xi. 9.

many of your age have in that short period been called to an eternal world, and what a mournful cry would have been heard, what earnest calls to repentance and sorrow for time misspent would have resounded through this city, had it pleased God then to withdraw the veil, and permit them to behold their sudden destiny.

Ye sons of pleasure, ye who glory in your health and strength, who laugh at sobriety, temperance and chastity, who count many days to come, and set death not only at a distance, but even at defiance—if any such can indeed remain among us after the late awful warnings— think of these truths and suppose it possible, nay probable, that on some day, not far distant, you may be called upon with all your unrepented sins about you, laid gasping in the burning heat of a mortal fever, and make your shameful exit, a martyr to false pleasure, under the dreadful curse which heaven has entailed upon intemperance.

With the impression of these truths, leaving the devotees of pleasure and worldly joys among the young and gay for the present, I shall proceed in my next discourse to estimate the bliss of those of higher ranks and ages, hoping the young also, if they hope for rank and age, will continue among the number of patient hearers.   AMEN!

The next sermon was preached December 12th, 1793, on the day which we have already spoken of as that for which Dr. Smith drew a Proclamation at the request of Governor Mifflin, appointing it a day of general humiliation, thanksgiving and prayer for the public deliverance from the rage of the late calamity.

The text, which the preacher remarks is changed for the day's solemnity, while the subject is not changed, is from Psalm lxxviii. verse 34, passim to verse 50:

When He slew them, then they sought Him; and they returned, and inquired early after God: and they remembered that God was their Rock, and the High God their Redeemer.   Nevertheless, they did but flatter Him with their mouth, and they lied unto him with their tongues: For their heart was not right with Him, neither were they steadfast in His covenant.   They turned back and tempted God—they remembered not His hand, nor the day when He delivered them from the enemy.   Wherefore He cast upon them the fierceness of His anger, wrath and indignation and trouble, by sending evil angels among them.   He made a way to his anger, and spared not their souls from death, but gave their life over to the pestilence.

"That there is a particular as well as a general providence," the preacher remarks in this discourse, "over the affairs of individual men, as well as whole nations; and that the Almighty holds their fate subject to his own controlling power, and weighs it in the tremendous balance of his unerring wisdom and justice, is a truth

which will not be denied by any man who professes to believe in
the existence of God."

"In vain," he continues, "are we assembled on this solemn day,
if it might be considered by any that the civil ordinance which
convokes us is only a political engine or device to awe and control the vulgar mind, and not a certain unequivocal proof 'that, as
a people, we acknowledge a God over all; supreme, almighty, and
enjoying all perfections.' It may be hoped, then," he proceeds,
"that the threshold of this holy place has not been profaned this .
day by the unhallowed step of a man or a woman who doth not
believe in the heart, as well as approach to confess with the lips,
'that there is a God who governs the affairs of his creatures in this
world, and that the Holy Scriptures of the Old and New Testament were graciously given, by his divine inspiration and authority,
to guide us in the right way through the intricate path of life and
the mazes of a mysterious Providence.'

"The dealings of the Almighty, therefore," he adds, "with a
people who acknowledge (as we do) the sovereign and uncon-
trollable power of God's special as well as general providence, in
ordering the affairs of men, will be a fit subject of our present
meditations; and the more to be chosen, as we shall have for our
guide a history authenticated on the records of Holy Scripture."

The preacher then traces the history of the Jews, upon which
his text, as he remarks, yields a prominent and irrefragable commentary, as well as a striking similitude to our own history in
many great and leading circumstances.

He notes that the Jews had for many years been without a government of their own, and sojourned in a foreign land, reduced to
a condition no better than that of the worst and most degraded
slaves; until, at last, the Almighty had compassion on their miseries, and by the hand of Moses delivered them from the rod of
Pharaoh, and conducted them through the waves of the Red Sea,
and a perilous wilderness, to the land promised to their forefather
Abraham and his seed forever.* Like the Jews, our fathers were
conducted by the hand of God through a perilous ocean, and
penetrated into a wilderness to hew out for themselves settlements
and improve them into a Canaan for the benefit of their posterity.

---

* See Gen. xiii. 14, and xxvi. 4, 5.

By the arm of the Almighty, while they were yet a small people, they were protected from surrounding dangers—the savages of the wilderness became their friends, and they grew up and multiplied into a great and prosperous people. How far we had followed the example of the Jews, in our backslidings and forgetfulness of the mercies of God, after *we* became a nation, would appear from a brief statement of their conduct, after *they* became a nation, in the promised land. This history the preacher then traces.

"The Chronicles of their kings, rulers and judges were a standing testimony," says the preacher, "of their ingratitude and forgetfulness of God, their inattention to his providence and neglect of amendment; continuing hardened in their iniquity amidst his various judgments and visitations, intended in mercy and long-suffering to lead them to reformation. The prophecies of their prophets—were they not all to the like purpose? Either filled with denunciations of judgments upon their apostasy from God, promises of forgiveness upon their repentance and amendment, or threatening of total ruin and destruction, unless they turned from the evil of their ways, to do that which is lawful and right!

"Many and various," he adds, "were the judgments inflicted on this people by the hand of Providence, for the punishment of their transgressions; but the four sorest, in extreme cases, when they became wholly hardened in their iniquity, were 'the Sword and the Famine, and the noisome Beast (to infest a desolate land), and the Pestilence, to cut off from it (by one dreadful visitation) both man and beast.' *

"The first mentioned of those four sore judgments, the sword, hath been sent," he observes, "upon us not only by the great nation from which our fathers and many of ourselves originated, but many a time likewise by the savage of the wilderness around us." And giving way to an expression of Federal politics, and to ancient dislike of France, now under Jacobin rule, more dangerous than in the days of any Louis, he adds:

Nor is it foreign to our purpose, on this solemn day, to contemplate the possibility, and even probability, of a sword against us from another great nation, once gratefully caressed, and never ungratefully offended, by us as a people.

---

* Ezek. xiv. 21.

Whether the great nation last mentioned hath in truth meditated any measures inimical to our liberty and independence, it would be wrong to pronounce absolutely in this sacred place. But we are justified in declaring our apprehensions and fears on this head; encouraged and invited, as that nation hath been, to the attempt, by the wild principles and restless conduct of their partisans here, impatient of all rule and authority, always seeking innovations, and never content long with any frame of government.

From the second and third of the sore evils by which the Jews were sometimes punished, namely: the Famine and the noisome Beast, and blast on the herbage and fruits of the earth, promotive of famine, the Almighty had been graciously pleased hitherto to spare us.

The fourth and last sore evil, the Pestilence, had indeed been permitted, or ordained, by Providence to visit our metropolis, and some others of the great towns and cities of the United States; but, in the present year, with a degree of severity and extensive calamity never experienced before. "Blessed be God," he says, "its rage is now graciously stayed, leaving us, indeed, in copious tears, to the memory of departed friends and relatives." "And, oh!" he adds, "let not those tears be too soon dried up, without deep meditation and serious improvement of the warnings given us."

After a reference in several particulars to the history of the Jews, the preacher says:

What history, ancient or modern, can exhibit a narration so concise and dignified, so marked with authentic testimony of the special inter-position of God, in his wise providence, to punish whole nations, rulers as well as people, even in this world, for the chastisement of their sins, and for their reformation and amendment?

What has been already stated gives the fullest sanction to this day's solemnity, and leads us directly to our main business and duty upon the great occasion, namely: the most serious consideration and meditation upon our own ways and works, and the improvement which, as a Chris-tian people, it becomes us to make, of our deliverance from the late awful calamity with which it pleased Almighty God, in his sovereign wisdom, to afflict this city and its vicinity.

The means of improvement pointed out and recommended by public authority,* and sanctioned by the voice and word of God, are:

---

* See an abstract of the Proclamation, p. 378.

The acknowledgment of his divine power and goodness, in the deepest humiliation and abasement of soul; the sincerest confession of our manifold sins and transgressions of our duty; contrition and sorrow for the neglect and forgetfulness of God's former mercies; earnest repentance and supplications for forgiveness, joined to sincere purposes and steadfast resolutions of future amendment and obedience to his holy will and laws.

Thus humbled, prepared and melted into love and gratitude, by a due sense of "God's mercies and long-sufferings to us ward (He not being willing that any should perish, but that all should come to repentance *)," our prayers, praises and thanksgivings this day, we trust, will ascend as a sweet incense and sacrifice, holy and acceptable before the throne of his grace. But, without this preparation of the heart, if we could pray and praise and give thanks with the tongue and voice of angels, it would all be vain and empty—nothing more than as sounding brass, or the tinkling cymbal.†

In this preparatory part of our work, therefore, let us in good earnest enter into our own hearts, examine their plagues, as in the presence of the Almighty, and not deceive ourselves, or think we can deceive him (like the people in our text) by "flattering him with our mouth, and lying unto him with our tongues, while our hearts are not right with him, and we are not steadfast in his covenant," made with our fathers, nor in our purpose of future obedience to his holy laws and commandments.

But, more especially, this becomes the duty of those who appear as the preachers of righteousness—the ministers and messengers of God (of every degree and denomination)—to stand forth, awfully impressed with the weight of their subject, and not to be afraid of the faces of men, but to speak boldly, even to authorities and dignities and powers; not to deal treacherously, or seek "to heal the hurt of the daughter of God's people slightly, with the enticing words of man's eloquence, 'saying, Peace, Peace, when there is no peace;'‡ but to probe the wounds to the bottom, by means of 'the word of God, which is quick and powerful, and sharper than any two-edged sword, piercing even to the dividing asunder of soul and spirit, and of the joints and marrow, and is a discerner of the thoughts and intents of the heart.'" ||

But although it falls to our lot, in preaching repentance, on this great occasion, more immediately to the inhabitants of the city of Philadelphia, who were among the primary and chief sufferers under the late awful visitation of the Almighty; and although great and manifold are the sins for which, in his righteous judgments, He might have inflicted this calamity upon us; yet it ought not to be considered that it was for our reproof and sins only, but those of United America, that the Lord chose us as among the first to speak to in his fierce anger. The appli-

---

* 2 Peter iii. 9.   † 1 Cor. xiii. 1.   ‡ Jer. vi. 14. || Heb. iv. 12.

cation of our Saviour's doctrine, preaching repentance, upon the punishment of the Galileans and others,* may be allowed here.

" 'Suppose ye,' says our Lord, 'that those Galileans, whose blood
Pilate mingled with their sacrifices, were sinners above all the Galileans,
because they suffered such things? I tell you, Nay; but except ye
repent, ye shall all likewise perish. Or those eighteen upon whom the
Tower in Siloam fell, and slew them, think ye that they were sinners
above all men that dwelt in Jerusalem? I tell you, Nay; but except
ye repent, ye shall all likewise perish.''

Thus warranted by the preaching and doctrine of the great Author
of our salvation, to consider particular punishments as general warnings,
the remainder of my discourse will be addressed to the whole body of
citizens, rulers as well as people, in these United States. And to this
I consider myself as more especially called, being honored with an
audience so numerous and respectable, among whom I behold the
Father of these United States, and many other characters of the first
impression, whose exempláry virtue and piety must strike deep into the
future prosperity and glory of our rising American empire—an empire
which, under the protection and favor of divine Providence, has laid the
foundation of all that can adorn and dignify man in the present world,
and guide him forward in preparations for the acquisition and enjoyment of glory, honor and immortality in a world to come!

The preacher now applies the teachings which the Scriptural
history of the Jewish nation gives as to our own country. And,
heaven knows, if my ancestor's remarks were applicable to the
United States in the apostolic days of Washington, one thousand
times more applicable are they in these licentious and degraded
times!

Keeping in view, therefore, the history of the people of Israel, and
taking up the parallel between God's providence and dealing with respect to them and ourselves, I may be allowed to recall to your mind
those times when our ancestors were but a small people in this land;
how the Almighty smoothed their passage to it through the dangers of
the stormy ocean; how he planted and supported them in a wilderness,
and made the savage beasts, and men more savage than they, who were
able in a moment to destroy them, to become their friends; commanding the solitary places to be glad around them, and the desert to rejoice
and blossom as the rose.

I might describe to you the progress of their civilization and happiness, and show, that having brought the pure Word of God in their
hand, the legacy of the Gospel of Christ as their chief riches, they were

* Luke xiii. 1–5.

not ashamed of its doctrines, nor to acknowledge the goodness of the Almighty, by promoting the ordinances of his religion; by making and executing laws for its support, and for the orderly administration of justice, constantly striving, by the purity of their lives, the simplicity of their manners, their love of truth and of one another, to give an example to their children of their obedience to the divine laws and their zeal for the prosperity of their country.

And when thus, for more than a hundred years, they had been proceeding from strength to strength, and flourishing under this simplicity of manners and regard to true religion, I might lead your attention to what the Lord did for us, their posterity, when we were called to struggle through blood and to contend for our dearest and most sacred rights. How numerous were the instances of his divine favor and interposition, in the establishment of our civil liberties and independence, assuring to us and our posterity every civil blessing, together with the free exercise of our holy religion, according to the rights of conscience, under a government of laws and a constitution of our own happy choice, there being none to make us afraid.

But what has been our sense or improvement of those numerous and invaluable blessings which the Almighty, with so liberal a hand, hath even heaped upon us? Let us not be alarmed at the question, nor shrink from the answer.

May it not be asked, then, of what avail is it that we boast of our frames of government, and that we are blessed with civil liberty, according to our highest conceptions of the name, if we know not how to respect the laws, and to distinguish liberty from licentiousness? If there remain those among us who, from pride, self-interest and the lust of power, cannot rest contented with a wise and efficacious system of joint government; but still pursuing something new, and adapted to their own phantasies, seek rather no government at all, or a government of such variant and discordant particles as to produce a Babel of confusion, rather than a Jerusalem, or city of God, happy and united within itself!

What avails it that God hath given us peace with all foreign states and powers, if with difficulty we are to be restrained from rushing voluntarily into the horrid scenes of blood and devastation in the old world from which God hath graciously set us at a distance; and where our feeble strength would scarcely weigh a grain in either balance, but might inevitably involve us in self-destruction?

What avails it that we are delivered from one late and great calamity, if we are not delivered from sin, which is the greatest calamity of all?

What avails it that God hath blessed us with a fruitful country, a happy climate and bountiful seasons, if, instead of industry, moderation of mind, thankfulness to heaven and a due improvement of His blessings, we are sapping the foundations of all our future happiness as a

people, by luxury, pride, idleness, dissipation and the eager pursuit of
false pleasure, with its never-failing attendants: infidelity and the scandalous neglect of religion, and profanation of the Lord's day!

This was one of the crying sins of the Jews, for which the severest
judgments were denounced against them: "I saw, in those days, in
Judah," says Nehemiah, "some treading wine presses on the Sabbath,
and bringing in sheaves, and lading asses; as also wine, grapes and figs,
and all manner of burdens, which they brought into Jerusalem on the
Sabbath day. And there dwelt also men of Tyre therein, who brought
fish, and all manner of ware, and sold on the Sabbath, to the children
of Judah, and in Jerusalem. Then I contended with the nobles of
Judah, and said unto them, What evil thing is this that ye do, and profane the Sabbath day? Did not your fathers thus, and did not our God
bring all this evil upon us, and upon this city? Yet you bring more
wrath upon Israel by profaning the Sabbath."*

But, notwithstanding all these judgments, this evil continued among
that people until our Saviour's days, who testified his indignation against
it by entering the temple, and, having made a scourge of small cords,
he drove them all out that sold oxen, and sheep, and doves, and poured
out the changers' money, and overthrew their tables.†

But what is all this to what we now behold?—the mere selling the
necessaries of life and the exchanging of money, which although restricted by our laws, evils of a more aggravated nature are tolerated, or
at least not restrained or corrected? The Sabbath by many is turned
into their chief day of idleness, recreation, parties of pleasure, sinful
sports and diversion, gaming, feasting, rioting and all manner of diversion! Shall I not visit for these things, saith the Lord, and shall not
my soul be avenged on such a people as this?

Oh, ye rulers and judges of the land! ye masters and heads of families, among whom, blessed be God, we have yet illustrious examples
of those who honor God's holy name and the places of his worship! I
know you will bear with the expostulations, which the faithful discharge
of my duty requires on this solemn day!

If the Jews, when under the government of God himself, and especially instructed by his inspired messengers and prophets, came to
humble themselves under his judgments, and to implore his mercy and
renew their covenant of obedience with Him; I say, if then they thought
it their duty to testify their sincerity with an oath, and to swear with a
loud voice, and with shouting, and with trumpets, and with cornets,
"That whosoever would not seek the Lord God of their fathers, whether
small or great, man or woman, should be put to death"—and if this
punishment was inflicted on those who continued in idolatry, which
was in some sort the acknowledgment of a god, or gods, although false

---

* Neh. xiii. 15–18.   † John ii. 14, 15.

ones, what punishment can be due to those who not only discountenance and refuse the worship of the true God, but openly profane, blaspheme, or deny His holy name?

I know, my brethren, the nature of persecution, and, I trust, the nature also of that civil and religious liberty which our happy constitution insures to all. But the abuse of privileges, and that licentiousness, civil or religious, which dissolves the bands of society and tends to the destruction both of soul and body, are certainly not the objects of toleration under any government. If it were possible for men of the most abundant estate, or in the higher stations of life, and who claim the unrestrained right of doing what they please with their own; I say, if it were possible for them to indulge every luxury, folly, vanity and vice, which the corrupt heart and understanding could devise (taking their chance of another world); I say again, if this were possible, without poisoning society by their fatal example in the present world, there might be some plea for their liberty of doing with their own fortune, and with their souls and bodies, according to the lusts of their own will. But would this consist with the dignity of a man, or the exercise of his rational faculties, even if he could believe that there was no world but the present; and that, after the longest life spent in the vanities here on earth, he was to lie down in the dust, like the beasts that perish, and that the trump of God would never rouse his sleeping ashes to a future judgment? No! and I am well persuaded that I do not at present address a man of this belief. On the contrary, I rather trust, that there is not a person who now hears me that does not believe he was sent into this world for nobler purposes than merely to vegetate, to rot, and to die. Wherefore, then, let us all strive to fill the sphere assigned us with dignity and diligence. If the supreme Wisdom has called us to the inferior stations of bodily labor, we are therewith to be content. It is honorable and subservient to virtue; for not the meanest calling but hath a blessing promised of God, and not the most exalted but hath its cares, its toils and temptations. Again, if, by the indulgence of heaven, we are released from the necessity of bodily labor, yet not less is the sphere of duty, nor less the joy attending the faithful discharge of it. There are liberal and ingenuous employments suited to the highest parts and estate—Go, order your affairs aright. Train up your children in the fear of God. Be an example of righteousness to your household and to society. Husband your time and your fortune for the public good. Minister out of your abundance to the necessities of others. Be hospitable; be kind; be solicitous for the advancement of justice and virtue, in all which you may be serious without gloom, cheerful without levity, and active without dissipation. For our religion enjoins no duty but what is for our own welfare, and denies no indulgence but what would cross us in our way heavenwards.

True it is, that by the precepts of this religion men blest with fortune

and abilities to serve their country in its highest offices are forbidden to
waste their prime of life and talents in scenes of dissipation and folly;
they are exhorted to spurn from their bosom and their company the
profane talker, the debauchee, the gamester, the sharper! But what is
all this, except to lead persons, born for worthy actions, to the noblest
twofold saving—a saving of time from degrading and unworthy conversation (which might be better employed in the improvement of their
own faculties, and in planning for the public weal); and a saving of
expense (which might redeem a virtuous family from distress, and make
the widow's heart sing for joy).

To stimulate us, therefore, in such fair and noble pursuits, let us
always keep in view the great objects that lie before us—the career of
glory to which we are called as a people. Let us remember that it was
not by idle hands, nor by reclining in the lap of indolence, nor by the
pursuit of false pleasure, or vanities unsuited to their condition, that our
honorable ancestors subdued a wilderness, and left this goodly heritage
to their posterity! nor is it by means like these that we can transmit
it safe and flourishing to our children and children's children.

It is always too soon when a people, even arrived at the meridian of
their glory, forget those virtues by which they were raised into importance; but for us, who have not yet half-way reached our noon; for
us, whose sun of glory has but just raised his head above the cloudy
mountains; for us, I say, to relax one jot of our industry and virtue, or
to loiter in the morning of our day—what sluggards might we be
deemed! Above all, let us do away the evil thing, and check that
growing indifference to religion which is spreading, by fatal example,
even from many of our high places to the lowest ranks of our people,
and brings us under the reproach of Solomon, when he cries out:
"Wherefore is there a price set in the hand of a fool to get wisdom,
seeing he hath no heart to it?"* "If Christ had not come and spoken
to us, we had not known sin; but now we have no cloak for sin."†
"And better had it been for us never to have known the way of righteousness, than, after we have known it, to turn from the holy commandment delivered unto us."‡ Forbid it, gracious God, that we should
ever thus turn ourselves back from the truths made known to us in
Christ Jesus! Our sins and ingratitude to thee, our great Creator,
having been in many respects like those of the Jews, let us follow their
best example, and not only resolve, but swear, as they did in the days
of good king Asa, that we will henceforth support the honor of our
Christian calling, nor suffer among us those who deny the being of their
Creator, who are enemies to the religion of their country, and trample
under foot its holy ordinances. Let us swear to amend our lives, to
walk for the future in true holiness before God; to venerate and obey

---

* Prov. xvii. 16.   † John xv. 22.   ‡ 2 Peter ii. 21.

his laws, and the laws of our country; to support its constitution, and defend our religious and civil liberties; to seek for health and wealth in honest labor and virtue; to attend to the right education of our children; to encourage and promote those arts and sciences which tend to rear up good men and good citizens; to disseminate human happiness, and to distinguish the civilized man from the barbarous savage, firmly resolving to adorn our station, in all the relations of life, whether as good magistrates, good fathers, good husbands, good brothers, faithful friends, and, in a word, as honest men and useful citizens.

Are you ready to swear to this? Yea, I trust, you have sworn already, and that we may now lift up our voice in songs of gratitude to God for our full deliverance from the late calamity, and that our prayers, praises and thanksgivings will be as a sweet incense, holy and acceptable before Him!

"Wherefore, O Lord God, who hath thus wounded us for our transgressions, by thy late heavy visitation, but now in the midst of judgment, remembering mercy, hast redeemed our souls from the jaws of death, we offer unto thy fatherly goodness ourselves, our souls and bodies, which thou hast thus delivered, to be a living sacrifice unto Thee; always praising and magnifying Thy mercies in the midst of the church, through Jesus Christ our Lord." *Amen.*

One of the finest of the series of discourses of which we are now speaking is one upon the final destruction of the world. Our author goes over the whole of the sacred Scriptures, showing from the Old Testament, as from the New, that fire, a universal conflagration, is to be the terrible agency of the great Jehovah in this awful consummation of all things. We have said elsewhere that Dr. Smith was not learned in the dogmatic or polemical writings of the Church of England. Indeed he was not so in that class of writings of any church. His tastes, whether natural or cultivated, did not incline to them; and his office of Provost did not call upon him to make an enforced acquisition of any special sort of lore, in oppugnancy to his natural and cultivated tastes. He was not a teacher of theology. But if he lacked anything of fulness here, he more than supplied it by a thorough knowledge of every part of the Holy Scriptures; the result, it must have been, of early, long and continuous reading of them. The sermon of which we now speak, and which we commend to the reading of any one who possesses Maxwell's edition of Dr. Smith's works, is an illustration as full as any other of Dr. Smith's discourses of what we say. It is a discourse from which we cannot well make extracts.

Though having fine outbreaks of eloquence and descriptive power, it is as a whole that it is most remarkable, and remarkable chiefly for the evidence which it gives of its author's wide and close reading of the Scriptures, of his capacity to arrange his Biblical lore with strength and effect, to bear upon his general proposition.

We pass, therefore, in conclusion, to a sermon upon the joys of heaven; not that it is his greatest sermon, but because it is one from which we can most easily make extracts. After some words of preface he begins:

These joys are now to be our ravishing theme. But although we may feel the consolations to be derived from the prospects and hopes of inheriting them, yet how shall we paint or describe that which "Eye * hath not seen, nor ear heard, nor hath it entered into the heart of man to conceive, the things which God hath prepared for them that love him; but God hath revealed them unto us by his Spirit; for the Spirit searcheth all things, yea, the deep things of God." Some description of them may, however, be given from the experience of what gives genuine pleasure or pain to us in this world, and especially from some passages of the inspired writers in sacred Scripture who were favored with certain visions or short glimpses of the beatific bliss and glory.

The Apostle † has said many things generally concerning the happiness of heaven, as far as human language can go, as, for example, he describes it, in comparison with all we have seen, or can see in this world, as "a far more exceeding and eternal weight of glory." "For our light afflictions, which are but for a moment, worketh for us a far more exceeding and eternal weight of glory, while we look not at the things which are seen, but at the things which are not seen; for the things which are seen are temporal; but the things which are not seen are eternal." Here, then, is the great distinction. If the things which men deem most valuable in this world were to be held forever, they would be content to enjoy them here forever; but when they know that they are perishable and temporal here, and that in heaven they will be lasting and eternal, wise men must soon be determined in their choice.

Howsoever far any description of the joys of heaven may fall short of the truth, it is hoped the souls of men may be animated by the prospect of enjoying them, and be thereby persuaded to cast off every evil habit that would render them unfit for that holy place, or stop them in their glorious progress thither; for these joys are too spiritual and sublime—too full of glory and goodness to be ever tasted by a man who carries with him a heart wedded to this world and polluted with its wickedness. It was the punishment inflicted upon Adam's first trans-

---

* 1 Cor. ii. 9, 10. Isa. iv. 4.　　　　　† 2 Cor. iv. 17, 18.

26

gression, that "the* very ground was cursed for his sake; that in sorrow he and his posterity should eat of it all the days of their lives; that it should bring forth thorns and thistles; that in sorrow and in the sweat of the face they should eat bread all the days of their lives until their return to the ground, from whence they were taken; for dust we are and unto dust we must return." "All things here," says Solomon,† "are full of labor; man cannot utter it." "Man is born unto trouble," saith Job,‡ "as the sparks fly upward." But in Christ's kingdom, where sin cannot enter and divine righteousness must forever prevail, there shall be a glorious and eternal rest from labor, both of body and soul. There shall be no more anxieties nor cares concerning the future, nor strifes, nor frauds, nor violence concerning the present; but, instead thereof, there shall be perpetual tranquillity of enjoyment; attentive to the voice of God, the harmony of the spirits of just men made perfect and of the church triumphant in heaven.

And now, first, with respect to those who labor and are heavy-laden in this world, and who may be ready to sink under their burden, heaven is described as a rest from their labor. St. John, in the Revelation, saith, "Blessed are the dead, who die in the Lord, for they rest from their labors;"§ "and there remaineth (saith St. Paul) a rest for the people of God. Let us therefore strive to enter into that rest; for it is a glorious rest, saith the prophet Isaiah."

2. The happiness of heaven is also figured to us by the metaphor of peace.

"Mark the perfect man, and behold the upright; for the end of that man is peace."‖ "The righteous are taken from the evil to come, that they may enter into peace."

This peace, to men who are born at enmity with God and all goodness, must be unspeakably desirous. To have our consciences quieted against future apprehensions of sin, disobedience and punishment; to have our souls purified from all the fell passions and inclinations of degenerate nature, from malice, anger, wrath, clamor, evil speaking; to have our hearts opened to the divine impressions and inexpressible sweets of love and friendship, which unite the spirits of the just and call them, with the accordant voice of joy and happiness, to pour forth before the throne of God their unwearied anthems of adoration and praise. This is happiness, indeed, to all who love peace and seek for relief from discord, strife and care.

3. Again, the Scriptures, addressing the devotees of worldly riches and wealth, represent the joys of heaven as a treasure—a treasure which cannot be consumed, but shall ever abound and flourish—"a treasure which neither moth nor rust can corrupt; which thieves cannot break through, nor steal; which cannot take wings and fly away in our need,

---

* Gen. iii., 17,.18, 19.   † Eccles. i. 8.   ‡ Job v. 7.   § Rev. xiv. 13.   ‖ Ps. xxxvii. 37.

and which shall remain our portion and inheritance forever." For, in
the " new Jerusalem we shall drink and be satisfied out of the rivers
that flow by the throne of God, whose waters are pure as crystal, and
shall eat the fruit of the tree of life, whose leaves heal the nations."*
Some there are, likewise, whose whole lives are devoted to the pursuit
of what they call pleasure.   Now, to draw their attention, the happiness
of heaven is called "pleasures for evermore," nay, rivers of pleasure,
which do not cloy the taste, enfeeble the body, unnerve the very soul,
and generally terminate in poverty, shame, disease and death ; but the
pleasures of heaven, when we shall have put on immortality, instead of
weakening and wearying the powers of the soul, more and more inspire
it with renewed vigor, exalting it to the strength of angels, and a taste
for happiness as boundless and sublime as are the employments in which
we shall be engaged and the objects with which we shall be forever surrounded.†

4. There are others again who, in this life, consider power and dominion and worldly grandeur as the supreme happiness.

To them, also, the bliss of heaven is represented as glory, honor,
power and dominion eternal.   "The upright shall have dominion over
the wicked in the morning of the resurrection—in that everlasting kingdom which Christ shall establish, wherein they only who are rich in faith
shall be the joyous heirs."   No outward enemy shall ever be able to rob
or despoil the righteous of this honor and dominion, to which they shall
be exalted with the angels on high, in subordination to the King of
kings, to execute his high commands and to be his ministers of love
through the infinite bounds of his creation.   We shall then have true
glory and dominion, eclipsing beyond comparison all the little pageantry
of what we call glory here.   For we shall receive from Christ himself a
crown of life and diadem of glory.   The veil of our present weakness
and ignorance shall be taken away; we shall behold with open face, and
in beatific vision, the glory of the living God ; and not only behold,
but be changed into the image of him, and advanced from glory to
glory, through endless duration.

But we must proceed a little farther in considering the circumstances
of this heavenly glory, to which we are called to aspire.   And it consists not only in the perfection to which we ourselves shall be advanced,
but in the place, the company and the employ to which we shall be
admitted—even unto Mount Zion, the city of the living God—the
heavenly Jerusalem—the company of the innumerable hosts of angels ;
the delightful employment of rising and mixing and joining in their
songs of praise, in the instruction to be derived from their conversation,
whose faculties are enlarged beyond our present comprehension ; who

---

* Rev. xxii. 1, 2.

† See a fine passage in Cudworth's " Intellectual System," which led to this thought.

are filled with the knowledge of great and wonderful things, each of them happy in himself and rejoicing in the happiness of each other.

If, therefore, love and friendship complete; if rest and peace undisturbed; if treasure and riches which cannot decay; if power and dominion secure from every foe—if these can constitute a happy society, with the everlasting God, and Jesus the Mediator of the new covenant, and the blessed Spirit of grace ruling at the head of all, and supplying and diffusing new irradiations of love and goodness, and perfection without measure, to all eternity—if this be happiness. But I am lost in the contemplation and description of its immensity—in the joy to be derived from the vision of God, the displays of his love, the fellowship of spirits so highly exalted, the raptures of converse and union, with intelligences so perfect and enlarged, so full of all that is great and good and heavenly, having the whole works of God, and all the ways and wonders of his Providence, which we now so little understand, as the everlasting objects of their investigation and praise.

"The works of the Lord are great, sought out of all them that have pleasure therein. How manifold are his works—in wisdom hath he made them all." "This is the language of good men, even in this world." But how small a portion of his ways and works do we now understand! In the blessed world above it will not be so. Here, indeed, we may examine a little corner of this little speck of earth; we may strive hardly to analyze a plant, a flower, an animated substance, and think to explain the laws of vegetable and animal motion. We may assist our dim sight to view some planets and stars, which we call distant and that traverse a small portion of universal space; but all that fills the immeasurable tracts beyond lies hid from our keenest search.

Yet, still, if that little, which is subjected to our limited view, appears so great, so beautiful, and wonderfully grand and harmonious to an inquisitive mind, with what rapture shall we be filled when, with faculties more enlarged, we shall be enabled to survey all the works of God, to have for our instructors and associates the angels that have surrounded his throne from the morning of the creation; to teach us on what the foundations of the earth were laid; from whence are the springs of the sea, and the treasures of snow and hail; what kindles the lightning's blaze, and gives the thunder its loud and solemn voice; to count all the stars and all the suns and planets that fill infinite space; to understand the laws by which they are balanced and suspended and guided in their unerring revolutions; and, when understanding this, to sing with those morning angels of joy, as they did at the first creation, as we behold world after world filled with happiness; to take the harp, in company with those that have overcome, and join in the song of Moses, the servant of God, and song of the Lamb—"Great and marvellous are thy works, Lord God Almighty! Just and true are thy ways, thou King of kings."

My Christian brethren !—candidates for eternity !—leave me not yet.
Stretch your imaginations still forward to greater objects and a more
ample field.   If such be the joy in contemplating God's works as in a
glass, by reflected vision, what must it be to contemplate and draw near
to himself, when we shall be permitted and enabled to look on his resplendent countenance, to behold him as he is, and to see even as we are
seen ?   What will it be to rise from the contemplation of created and
material worlds to the world of spirits, the history of their achievements,
and all the changes, revolutions and improvements of their condition ?
But on this subject I dare not venture a further sentiment that might
draw us from the contemplation of that final happiness, purchased for
us through the blood of our Redeemer—the consummation of which
happiness will consist in the pure vision and enjoyment of God himself,
who, if he is so good "to those whose hearts are perfect towards him on
this earth that his eyes run to and fro, to make himself strong for them;
if he withholds no good thing from those that love him in this world ;
if he openeth his hand and satisfieth the desire of every thing that
liveth," even where sin is mixed with our best services ; how great will
be the happiness to see and feel his goodness when we are exalted into
his presence ; to taste of his love flowing freely, when there is no sin to
come between our souls and his gracious countenance ; "when we are
brought fully to understand and taste the depth of the riches, both of
his wisdom and knowledge, and also of his goodness and long suffering;
who brought us out of the mire and clay of our sins ; who set our feet
upon the rock of his promises, and ordered our goings, and comforted
us on our way, until he brought us into his own holy presence ?"

Let me, then, exhort you to dwell often in the meditations of those
joys which I have endeavored to describe ; and whilst our eyes are thus
lifted towards heaven and glory, all that would fetter and bind us down
to the vain enjoyment of this world will disappear.   Let us bear our
view constantly forward to that time when, washed and made white in
the blood of the Lamb, we shall stand before the throne of God and
serve him day and night in his Temple ; when our happiness shall be
complete and without end ; "when we shall neither hunger nor thirst
any more ; neither shall the sun light on us nor any heat ; for the Lamb
which is in the midst of the throne shall feed us, and shall conduct us to
living fountains of waters, and God shall wipe all tears from our eyes."

In treating of the awful mysteries, through which our text has led us,
and especially what relates to future events, and the changes and revolutions in the destiny of man, which are yet to come, we may have erred
in part ; and we can never be secure against error, in attempting the
explanation of those mysteries which Providence has been pleased to
open to us, as yet only in part ; and which will never be fully understood, till unveiled to us by the light, to which we shall be admitted in
the world to come.

"In the meantime, let us faithfully, and with good conscience, according to our best understanding, strive to retain the form of sound words and doctrine, concerning the immortality of the soul ; the resurrection of the dead, a judgment to come, the rewards and punishments of a future life, over which Christ's throne will be established in righteousness, and his kingdom and dominion be forever."

The Christian religion has no fruits more precious than those which sweeten our cup of affliction in life, exhilarate us to combat death, and assure our hopes of a better world. Natural religion, and all the other religions which have been professed among men, could go but a short way even in teaching them how to *live ;* but in teaching them how to *die,* there remained a dismal and dreadful blank. Before the Christian revelation, death was only a leap into the dark, a wrench from the precincts of day, at which the astonished soul shuddered and recoiled. But now the gospel lifts our eye to immortal scenes. It unlocks eternity before us. It shows us a reconciled God, and Jesus the Mediator seated on his right hand. It teaches, that through his merits, the just shall live forever, passing from one degree of glory to another, and entering still more deeply into the beatific vision and enjoyment of God the Father, as their faculties are more and more enlarged and expanded. . . . .

And now, O blessed God ! Father, Son and Holy Ghost, guide and assist us in our preparations for this *celestial bliss ;* and be our rock and salvation through all the scenes we have to pass towards its attainment. Amen !

These nine sermons are among the best of Dr. Smith's discourses. They added to his fame already great. They exhibit an intimate acquaintance with all parts of the Holy Scriptures : and give evidence that his mental powers, with advancing years, had in nowise decayed, but, as usually happens, where those powers were originally good and where the moral principles and conduct had been sound, only ripened and grew more worthy of admiration and respect.

All these sermons, it is an agreeable fact for me to mention, were preached by Dr. Smith not only gratuitously, but also with the certainty that no pecuniary compensation would be received. The desolation of the city, even after the plague had been stayed, was, for a long time, great, and involved all pecuniary interests, including those of the churches. Some of the principal parishioners of the United Churches had died during the pestilence. Universal leniency towards debtors was necessary, while the de-

mands upon the church funds for the persons reduced to want by
the death of fathers, brothers and friendly protectors, was greatly
increased.   Dr. Smith, before preaching them, had been informed
that it was not in the power of the vestry to offer any expectation
of a reward : and he declared at once that he had no expectation
of any emolument; and would cheerfully perform without pecuniary compensation his part of the duties required at the two
churches as should be agreed upon between him, the rector and
Dr. Blackwell.

CHAPTER LVIII.

DR. SMITH DEVOTES HIMSELF TO INTERNAL IMPROVEMENT THROUGH THE UNION
CANAL SCHEME—HIS HALF-BROTHER, THOMAS SMITH, APPOINTED TO THE
BENCH OF THE SUPREME COURT OF PENNSYLVANIA—DEATH OF JOHN PENN—
DR. SMITH PREACHES ON THE SUBJECT OF ITINERANT MISSIONS—ALSO AT
FUNERAL OF COL. JOSEPH RUDULPH—ALSO BEFORE THE GRAND LODGE OF
PENNSYLVANIA—GENERAL CONVENTION OF 1795—CONSECRATION TO THE
EPISCOPATE OF SOUTH CAROLINA OF DR. ROBERT SMITH—DR. WILLIAM
SMITH PREACHES THE CONSECRATION SERMON, ALSO THAT OF EDWARD BASS—
OCCUPIED WITH THE PROCEEDINGS OF THE ILLINOIS AND OUACHITA LAND
COMPANIES, AND WITH INTRODUCING SUPPLIES OF DRINKING WATER INTO
PHILADELPHIA—PRESENTS A BELL TO THE COUNTY OF HUNTINGDON FOR ITS
COURT-HOUSE—BIRTH OF RICHARD PENN SMITH.

WE have nothing of a striking or of a public character to record
for some time now in the life of Dr. Smith, and are compelled,
therefore, to give to the reader such small or fragmentary matters
as we can gather from Dr. Smith's memoranda.

Just before the breaking out of the Yellow Fever, he had been
devoting his attention to matters connected with the Union Canal
Scheme, in which he had largely interested himself, visiting the
several springs and waters, tributary to the canal, at their sources
and heights.   He now sought, by working them out to their results, to give effect to his various studies and labors in this important public work.

His diary records, under date of January 31st, 1794, the appointment of his half-brother, the Hon. Thomas Smith,* to a seat
on the Bench of the Supreme Court of the State, an appointment

---

* For an account of Judge Smith, see Appendix, No. VIII.

by which Dr. Smith seems to have been much gratified; as he may well have been by the credit with which this brother filled, as he long continued to fill, this responsible and then, at least when the tenure was for life, dignified position.

On the 9th of February he notes the death of his friend, the Hon. John Penn,* at Pennsbury, Bucks county, Pennsylvania, aged sixty-seven. Mr. Penn was buried in Christ Church, Philadelphia. Among the persons present at the funeral was the Prince de Talleyrand; at that time an exile in our country from France.

On the 6th of April, in the year 1795, Dr. Smith preached in Christ Church, Philadelphia, a sermon from St. Mark, vi. 34, as an introduction to a plan for the encouragement of itinerant preachers or missionaries on the frontier settlements of the United States, as agreed upon at a convention held in New York, in September, 1792.

On the 7th of April he preached at the funeral of Colonel Joseph Rudulph, at the Swedish church at Kingsessing.

This Joseph Rudulph was the father of Mrs. Ann Smith, wife of William Moore Smith, Esq. He entered the army at the outbreak of the Revolution, took an active part in the South with Lee, spent the winter of 1778 at Valley Forge, reached the rank of colonel, and resigned his commission at the end of the war. The account of the *Rudulph* family, in the note below, is taken from an old Bible belonging to the family.†

---

* This was not the Hon. John Penn, who had taken such an interest in Dr. Smith and the college, in the years 1762-4. He was the eldest son of the Hon. Richard Penn, and was born in England in 1728. He visited America in 1753 and also in 1773, and was the last proprietary governor. He married Ann Allen, daughter of the Hon. William Allen, Chief-Justice of the Province. After the Revolution he retired to his seat at Pennsbury. His remains were subsequently transferred for interment to England.—ED.

† *John Rudulph*, born August 25th, 1719; died December 10th, 1768.
Mary Rudulph, born August 13th, 1719; died March 16th, 1795.
The above were married January 20th, 1740, and had the following issue:
Joseph Rudulph (afterwards Colonel), born December 23d, 1741; died April 4th, 1795.
Jacob Rudulph, born May 28th, 1744; died March 14th, 1795.
Ann Rudulph, born November 12th, 1746.
John Rudulph, born June 3d, 1749; died September 3d, 1789.
Hannah Rudulph, born June 6th, 1752.
Benjamin Rudulph, born May 11th, 1762; died September 23d, 1762.
Colonel Joseph Rudulph married a Swedish lady by the name *Yocum*, and had issue:
Joseph.

On St. John's day, the 24th of June, 1795, Dr. Smith preached in St. Peter's Church, Philadelphia, before the Grand Lodge of Communication. This was the last Masonic Sermon preached by him. He seems to have given satisfaction to the fraternity, since the minutes of the day record that after the discourse it was

Resolved, That the Committee of Arrangements be requested to wait on our Reverend Brother, Dr. Smith, with the thanks of this Lodge, for the discourse by him delivered on this day, and request the favor of a copy of the same for publication, and that one thousand copies thereof be printed at the expense of the Grand Lodge.

On the 8th of September, in this same year of 1795, the General Convention of the Episcopal Church met in Christ Church, Philadelphia. Dr. Smith was unanimously chosen President. Bishop Provoost preached the occasional sermon. At this convention the Rev. Dr. Robert Smith, who had been elected by the church in South Carolina as their Bishop, was consecrated on Sunday, September 13th. Dr. Smith (as he was requested to do) preached the consecration sermon. On the next day it was in convention

Resolved, unanimously, That the thanks of this House be presented to the Rev. Dr. Smith for his sermon delivered at the consecration of the Right Rev. Dr. Robert Smith, and that he be desired to furnish a copy of the same to be printed.

The convention continued its sessions until the 18th of September, when it was

Resolved, That the thanks of this house be given to the President, Dr. Smith, for his able and impartial management in his place.

Before the rising of the convention a standing committee was appointed consisting of representatives from every State. Dr. Smith was appointed to be its chairman, with power to call them together.

During the year 1796 I find but little of interest in regard to the subject of our biography. On Sunday, May 7th, he preached in Christ Church, Philadelphia, upon the occasion of the conse-

---

Ann, born 1762; married William Moore Smith, and died 1846.
Elizabeth; married Mr. Franks, of Reading, Pa.
Jacob,
Lydia, always lived with her sister, Mrs. Smith; died, unmarried, 1844.

cration of the Right Rev. Edward Bass, D.D., as Bishop of Massachusetts and New Hampshire. The reader will notice that this was the third consecration of a Bishop *in* America, and Dr. Smith preached on each occasion.

The latter part of the year found the hitherto healthy and vigorous subject of our memoir considerably broken in health. I discover in it none of his correspondence and little of his manuscript. He bemoans the loss of his friend Rittenhouse, who had died the 26th of June; records the birth of a grandson (Samuel Wemyss Smith, son of William Moore Smith), on the 1st of September; mentions the fact of his son William being elected Grand Master of the Masons; and that the roof was burnt off the old academy on Fourth street below Arch, on the night of December 30th.

I here, to some extent, lose sight of him for three years, during which time he remained chiefly at the Falls of Schuylkill; engaged, I presume, in putting into order the title papers and maps of his extensive landed estates in different parts of the Commonwealth, and in making clear and intelligible accounts of what was due him on the sales of them. During the year 1790 he gave to the public a work in 8vo., entitled,

"An account of the Proceedings of the Illinois and Ouabache Land Companies, in pursuance of their purchases made of the Independent Natives, July 5th, 1773, and October 18th, 1775, with map of New Jersey."

This volume was printed in Philadelphia. He was also much occupied with the subject of introducing water of the Schuylkill river into Philadelphia, and in January, 1799, by request of the Council of Philadelphia, he prepared and published a pamphlet on this subject, entitled,

"Remarks on a Second Publication of B. Henry Latrobe, Engineer." This was for distribution among the members of the Legislature.

In the same month of January, 1799, he presented a bell to the borough of Huntingdon, Pennsylvania, for the court-house. It was one of some size, weighing two hundred and fifty-four pounds, and had inscribed upon it:

Cast by Samuel Parker, Philadelphia, 1798. WILLIAM SMITH, D.D., to the borough of Huntingdon, Juniata.

After being used on the court-house until May, 1848, it was placed upon the public school-house, and remained in use there until December 12th, 1861, on the morning of which day, a very cold and frosty one, on ringing it for school, it was suddenly cracked.

I now find in Dr. Smith's diary the following entry:

March 13th, 1799.   The wife of my son, William Moore Smith, gave birth to a son, whom they call *Richard Penn*, after his honor, *Richard Penn*, Esq.

Of this grandson of Dr. Smith, so long a well-known citizen of Philadelphia, my readers will, I trust, excuse a son's affection, if I give, in the conclusion of this volume, some little sketch of his life and literary labors.*

On June 11th, 1799, the General Convention met again in Christ Church, Philadelphia.   Dr. Smith was again elected President.   At this convention, however, he was too feeble to take an active part.   He was placed, nevertheless, upon a Committee to draft a Course of Study, for candidates for holy orders.   I find no account of the committee having made a report.   It is probable— indeed it would seem almost certain—that the Course proposed by Bishop White at a subsequent convention, that of 1804, had from his old friend and preceptor at least a general approval.

CHAPTER LIX.

DR. SMITH ILL AT LANCASTER—LETTER TO HIS SON, WILLIAM MOORE SMITH— DEATH OF GOVERNOR MIFFLIN—DR. SMITH PREACHES A GUARDED FUNERAL SERMON UPON HIM—GILBERT STUART MAKES A PORTRAIT OF DR. SMITH— SEVERAL COPIES AND ENGRAVINGS MADE OF IT—BUST MADE BY STORKE—GEN- ERAL CONVENTION OF 1801—DR. SMITH PRESENT AT IT, BUT TOO FEEBLE TO TAKE MUCH PART IN IT—BUILDS AND INSCRIBES A MAUSOLEUM—DEATH OF HIS SISTER AND HIS MAN PRIMUS—HIS LAST WILL.

THE early part of this year (1800) found Dr. Smith ill at the house of his son, Charles, in the city of Lancaster.   He makes mention of this sickness in his will.   We have a letter to one of his sons at

---

* See Appendix No. IX.

Philadelphia, written at this time, and curiously indicative of his sense of local order and of the care which he gave his papers. I infer from the letter that the Doctor contemplated having some alterations made in his study, or to have it papered or painted, and was solicitous about keeping his "great chest" and "small red trunk" together.

Dr. Smith to William Moore Smith.*

LANCASTER, January 21st, 1800.

MY DEAR SON: I wish you to ride out now and then to Schuylkill, to see how my people there are going on; and the first time you go out get Bell (the Doctor's sister) to open my room, and in the open closet by the window you will see a small red trunk containing MSS., sermons and other papers; also some books on the shelves. I wish them all to be lifted out and laid on or by the great chest or trunk of papers, lest they should be forgot. If any occasion should be (which I hope will not be) to remove the large chest—or without your moving the little red trunk and books out of the closet—they may stand, and it may be sufficient if you put Bell in mind to move them if necessary to move anything else. If you have any windows opened in the room, you will see that they are again shut as I left them. Write to me, directing to Chambersburg, where I shall remain with the judges till the mail arrives.   Your affectionate father,

WILLIAM SMITH.

While at Lancaster, Thomas Mifflin, long the Governor of Pennsylvania, died on the 25th of January. Resolutions were passed by the Legislature expressive of his Excellency's merits and his services as a soldier and a statesman, and providing for his interment at the public expense and for the erection of a monument to his memory. Dr. Smith was requested by the new Governor, the Senate and House of Representatives, to deliver a commemorative sermon. This sermon was never published, and there was little in it not of a general nature. While Dr. Smith, of course, could not decline a public request to preach at least a "Regulation" sermon on the death of a Governor of Pennsylvania, and especially of one long his near neighbor and personal acquaintance, and while he would have been very ready to admit the considerable place that Governor Mifflin will always hold among the governors of Pennsylvania—in early days the representatives of the Demo-

---

* In the fine collection of autographs of F. J. Dreer, Esq.

cratic party, a party to which Dr. Smith did not belong—he was
too well aware of the undeniably very large part that General
Mifflin had in the "Conway cabal," of his hostility to the Commander-in-Chief, and of that commander's opinion of *him,** to go
into much eulogy either of Governor Mifflin's integrity or his
valor.   Dr. Smith asks many questions, but answers none; he
states many general truths, but leaves the hearer to apply them if
he pleases.   He is indeed amusingly cautious, saying very little
more about the subject of his discourse than this:

If we were called to power, rule and government over our fellow-
men, then shall it be known whether we bartered our favors away for
vile gain !   Whether we were open to the allurements of vice, the blandishments of flattery, and the snares or seductions of party !   Or whether
we made use of our influence and authority to support justice, to protect innocence, to encourage virtue and to reward merit.   . . .

I add no more.   To this test of the use of power and exercise of government, I may leave the character of the deceased.   The honor done
to his name by this public funeral, and the vote of a monument by the
Legislature, to perpetuate his memory, will rescue his public virtue from
public censure.   Private frailties he had, as a man; but if they were injurious, it was only to himself—never to his friends or country!

Haste we, then, to commit his mortal part, with its mortal frailties,
to its destined place—that yawning grave, where they will at last find
rest—a safe asylum from worldly distress, the shafts of malice, and the
persecutions of party.

> " His worth we seek no farther to disclose,
>   Nor draw his frailties from that dread abode—
>   Where they alike, in trembling hope, repose—
>   The bosom of his Father and his God."—GRAY.

After the funeral Dr. Smith was removed to the Falls of Schuylkill, where he remained, more or less incommoded by indisposition, during the year.   It was at this time that Gilbert Stuart
painted his celebrated picture of him.   This picture is now (1880)
in the possession of Dr. John Hill Brinton, of Philadelphia.   It
has been copied a number of times on canvas.   In 1820 two
copies were made in Lancaster, by an artist named Icholtz, for
Richard Smith, Esq., of Huntingdon.   A copy was also made by
order of Dr. Perigrine Wroth, for Washington College, Chester-

---

* See Sparks's Writings of Washington, Vol. V., pp. 483-518; 371.

town, Md. In 1857 it was copied by Thomas Sully, for St. Peter's Church, Philadelphia, and in 1872 by E. D. Marchand, by order of John Blodget Britton, Esq., for the University of Pennsylvania.* I have been informed that there is also a copy at Stoke, England, the residence of the Penn family. It has been engraved both on metal and on wood, etc. The best engraving on metal is that made by the great engraver, David Edwin, in 1803, for Maxwell's edition of Dr. Smith's works;† but a creditable one was made lately by a young artist, George Herbert White, of Philadelphia. I have also had a plaster bust modelled by a young Florentine artist of rising fame named Carl Stork, which I have presented to the University.

We have thus far seen Dr. Smith both an active and a principal person in nearly all our early church conventions. But this activity and this distinction was now soon to cease. The convention

---

* The following resolutions were adopted by the Board of Trustees of the University of Pennsylvania, March 5, 1872, at a meeting before which was laid Mr. Britton's note communicating his wish to offer the copy to the University:

Resolved, That the gift of a portrait of Dr. William Smith, the first Provost of the College of Philadelphia—since the University of Pennsylvania—which J. Blodget Britton, Esq., proposes to make to the institution, by his letter of the 10th ultimo, be and the same is hereby gratefully accepted by the trustees.

Resolved, That the eminent services rendered by Dr. Smith, in the founding of the institution, his extraordinary labors and success in procuring for it what in those early days was a magnificent endowment, and the deep, affectionate, and abiding interest which he continually manifested for its welfare and success, are deeply engraven in the history of the University and in the heart of all who have been honored with administration of its affairs.

Resolved, That the Provost of the University be requested to receive the portrait of Dr. Smith, on behalf of the trustees, whenever it shall be ready for delivery, and place the same in the chapel of the University.

Resolved, That a copy of the foregoing resolutions be transmitted to Mr. Britton by the Secretary of the Board, and that they also be published.

CADWALADER BIDDLE, Secretary.

† David Edwin, an Englishman, born at Bath, in December, 1776, was the son of John Edwin, a comedian. Young Edwin was apprenticed in his boyhood to Jossi, a Dutch engraver, who at this time was working in England, and who is said to have been a very complete artist and draughtsman. Jossi returned to Holland in 1796, and took David Edwin with him. The latter was a short time at Amsterdam, but left the country in the year 1797 in a ship bound to Philadelphia, viâ Havre, which took five months on the passage; and this conveyance Edwin obtained upon the vessel by working before the mast. Upon his arrival in Philadelphia, in December, 1797, he sought employment, and the first work which he obtained was the engraving of music—work given him by T. B. Freeman. Edwin became famous in after time as an engraver of portraits, and he obtained the best work. He engraved many of Stuart's pictures, and many portraits of public men. He died in Philadelphia, Feb. 22, 1841, aged 63.

of 1801 met in St. Michael's Church, Trenton, on Tuesday, September 8th. Dr. Smith was at first disinclined to go to it; but Dr. Blackwell, his kind friend of ancient date, offering to take him in his own carriage, he accompanied this excellent gentleman. He was, however, in a feeble condition, and declined to act as president. The Rev. Abraham Beach, D. D., of New Brunswick, in New Jersey, was accordingly elected in his stead. While observing them intelligently, Dr. Smith took but little active part in the proceedings, and his last act, in this the last convention in which he ever assisted, was to propose a canon making an addition to the first canon of 1795, on the subject of Episcopal Visitations. The addition was read and adopted, and sent to the House of Bishops, who immediately concurred in it. He was brought back to Philadelphia by Dr. Blackwell, assisted by a Maryland friend, the Rev. John Coleman,* at that time rector of St. Thomas Church, Baltimore.

During the latter part of this year Dr. Smith prepared a mausoleum on his estate, at the Falls of Schuylkill, with the following inscription, over the door:

Anno Christi 1801 GULIELMUS SMITH, S. T. P.
Tunc ætat. 75.
HOC PARVULUM MAUSOLEUM INSTITUIT
M. S.
Sui et conjugis caræ Rebeccæ.
Sobolisque Eorum.
Ouotquot hic jacent, Quotquot alibi
Cognoscere Velles
Intra disces Lector.

Among Dr. Smith's papers I find the following inscription in his handwriting directed to Mr. Latrobe, the architect, which I suppose he had intended to use:

---

* John Coleman, a native of Virginia—ordained by Bishop White in 1787. He became rector of St. John's, Baltimore and Harford counties; in 1799 of St. Thomas, Baltimore county; in 1806 of St. James, Baltimore county, and of Christ Church, Harford, also, which he erected. He was convention preacher in 1795, member of the Standing Committee seventeen times, and five times delegate to the General Convention. He published the autobiography and letters of Devereaux Jarratt. Died 1816, aged 53.

M. S.

GULIELMI SMITH, S. T. P.

Conjugis quoque ejus dilectæ Rebeccæ,

Sobolisque eorum quotquot hic inhumabuntur

Nomina intus discas.

Hanc domum Sept., 1800.

Ego G. S. tunc vivus ætat. 74 mihi et meis paravi

In qua mortui, spe Resurrectionis in Christo quiescamus

Ossibus nostris quisquis es Viator

Obsecro.

The new structure was not long without an occupant. On the 1st of February, 1801, Isabella Smith, the much-loved sister of the Doctor, died at the Falls, and on the following evening her body was deposited in the mausoleum.

The Falls soon had another visitation from "the grisly monarch." On the 10th of May, 1801, *Primus*, the faithful body-servant of Dr. Smith, died. He was buried outside the mausoleum. Dr. Smith had a great regard for *Primus*, whom he had bought as a child in Maryland, in 1783, and who had been constantly by his side for nearly twenty years. When he died, the Doctor remarked that he had been so long *Primus* in this world that he was not likely to be *Secundus*, he thought, in the world to come.

These various deaths, which in different ways were so near to him, were calculated to bring forcibly before the venerable subject of our biography a likelihood that the great change would soon overtake himself. To one so deeply reflective, however, no such warnings were necessary. His mind was always and fully awake to the necessity both of spiritual and temporal preparation for the "inevitable hour." He now made his will, a document which is so interesting, and which reveals so much of his character, that I venture to transcribe it entire:

The *last will* and testament of William Smith, D. D., of the Northern Liberties of the city of Philadelphia, and Commonwealth of Pennsylvania.

In the name of God —Amen. I, William Smith, D. D., formerly and for many years Provost of the College Academy and charitable schools of the city of Philadelphia, now resident on my farm at the Falls of Schuylkill, in the Northern Liberties of said city, and Commonwealth of Pennsylvania, being devoutly thankful to Almighty God,

my great and gracious Creator, that amidst the many visitations of
sickness and mortality which I have been called to witness in the place
of my late residence, the city of Philadelphia, and the bereavements in
my own family during those visitations, He hath been pleased to spare
me to a very advanced age, and to raise me up and restore me so far
from a late dangerous sickness, in the borough of Lancaster, during the
months of January and February, 1800, and also a late severe sickness
in February, 1802, that I am now able (in respect to strength of body
and soundness of mind, the last of which he hath at all times graciously
preserved to me both in sickness and in health during the whole period
of my life) to set my household in order and to stand prepared through
his grace for my great change. *Therefore,* I do make, publish and declare this as my last will and testament.

In the first place, I recommend and bequeath my soul to Almighty
God, who gave it, trusting in him for the forgiveness of my sins and
salvation, through the merits and intercession of his blessed Son, Jesus
Christ, grounded on a firm belief of the truths of Divine Revelation as
contained in the Scriptures of the Old and New Testament (and as I
have endeavored to teach and preach them through the grace given me)
with all zeal and fidelity, during a long period of near fifty years; striving for the propagation of heavenly knowledge and wisdom amongst all
the nations of the earth, and especially amongst those who yet sit in
darkness and the shadow of death through this American continent to
its remotest western bounds.

As to my body, whensoever God shall be pleased to call it from the
light of this world, and to close my eyes in death, I will it to a plain
Christian interment in the place and in the manner hereinafter
directed.

Concerning my worldly estate and goods with which it hath pleased
God to bless my lawful, and I trust honest, industry (being conscious
of no wrong done or intended to any man in the acquisition of the
same), I will and dispose of it as follows—that is to say:

First. My funeral expenses being first paid, I will and ordain that my
just debts (which are at present but few and small, the debt to my dear
brother Thomas excepted) be next, and as soon as possible fully and
fairly paid and discharged out of my personal estate, so far as it will
reach, and then, if need be, out of any part of my real estate, which I
empower them to sell and convey in fee for this purpose. Respecting
which, having always considered it to be the duty of a parent, after a
good and virtuous education of his children, according to his station in
life, as far as his abilities and a due measure of prudence will allow; and
having upon those principles given or conveyed to my children respectively, with an equal and impartial hand, a considerable part of my
property, as they came of age (or as their settlement and advancement
in life seemed to require), and having confirmed the same by separate

27

deeds or grants to each of them, with such limitations and reversions, etc., respecting some parts of my estate as I thought proper, this my present last will and testament needs therefore only to regard my residuary estate as it may be at the time of my death; which I will and ordain to be divided into five parts or shares as nearly of equal value (quantity and quality considered) as can be estimated.

One share or fifth part of the same to my son William. One other share or fifth among the children or legal representatives of my dear deceased daughter Williamina, share and share alike. One other share or fifth part to my son Charles in fee. One other share or fifth part to my son Richard in fee. And the remaining fifth part or share to the Hon. Thomas Smith, Esq., of the city of Philadelphia, the Right Rev. Bishop White, of the said city, and the Hon. Jasper Yeates, Esq., of the borough of Lancaster, and to the survivors and survivor and the heirs of such survivor, in trust for the use of my daughter Rebecca and her children, or legal representatives, at the time of her decease, as set forth more at large in my Deed of Trust to them.

And if such division cannot be made amicably by the devisees aforesaid, the same shall be made according to law on the application of any one or more of them.

It having now pleased God to enable me to bring this my last will towards a conclusion, although hastily, yet with a pure and sincere intention to do equal justice to all my children and family, I recommend them to the blessing of the Almighty, charging them that, from regard to my memory, the education I have bestowed on them, my anxiety to provide for and assist them in gaining comfortable settlements in life, they will always preserve a mutual affection one to another; and as I have endeavored to express my intention clearly in this will, with equal affection to all of them, I trust the said intention will be their guide and Pole star in the interpretation of the same, and that no want of legal form in the meaning or matter will ever be made a cause by any of them to contravene that intention.

Item. I do hereby direct that my funeral may be plain and decent, and that my body, wheresoever my death may happen, may be conveyed (if it can be done with any possible safety and convenience) and deposited in the middle grave prepared by me in the small mausoleum and cenotaph, which I have erected in my garden, near my present dwelling house, at the Falls of Schuylkill, and that the ashes of my dear wife and my two infant children, Phineas and Elizabeth (buried by her side in Christ Church burying-ground), be taken up and enclosed in an urn and deposited in the same grave with me during the next winter, if I should not live to execute that mournful but sacred duty myself, in pursuance of the promise which my good friend Bishop White hath given me of obtaining leave to open the ground for that purpose when I may think it convenient.

I do further direct that the figure of the angel coming down from heaven, having in one hand a little book, open, and setting his right foot on the sea and his left foot on the earth, with the other hand lifted up to heaven, in the act of swearing or proclaiming, etc. (as in Rev. x.), proposed for the top of the mausoleum, be not forgot, and that Mr. Rush, the carver, be expedited to finish and put up the same according to his promise; that the words " Time shall be no more " be cut on the small marble, above the large marble containing the inscription over the door on the outside; that the letters of the said inscription be painted black, or some other color to make them easily legible from the ground.

Item. I will and devise that a decent tombstone may be soon erected over the grave of my dear deceased son, Thomas Duncan Smith, expressive of that parental affection which he enjoyed and deserved during his life; and the singular estimation in which he was held as a physician and the first magistrate elected by the inhabitants of the county of Huntingdon after its erection, conducting himself with such benevolence, assiduities, abilities and disinterestedness in both characters that his memory continues and is likely to continue long precious to the citizens of that county, and especially among the poor, whose civil differences he generally reconciled without the rigor of legal process, and to whose bodily ails and family affliction he administered comfort and relief to the last moment of his short life, without charging, and seldom ever accepting, a fee or emolument of office. Let all this be expressed in simple and modest terms, for monuments of the dead are too often like life itself—a short and transient vanity, unless they are sanctioned by the public voice.

Item. I here ordain and direct that fourteen mourning rings, of the value of twenty dollars each, be prepared and given by my executors; that is, one ring as a token of my love to each of the following persons: my beloved relations or friends; that is to say, my dear sisters-in-law, Mrs. Williamina Bond, Mrs. Ann Ridgely and Mrs. Letitia Smith; Mrs. Ennals, of Shoal Creek, Dorset county, Maryland; my daughter-in-law, Mrs. Mary Smith, of Lancaster; my daughter Rebecca; my grand-daughter, Sarah Yerbury Goldsborough; my three sons, William Moore Smith, Charles Smith and Richard Smith, viz., one ring each; my dear brother, the Hon. Thomas Smith, Esq.; my dear friends, the Hon. Jasper Yeates, Esq., the Right Rev. William White, Bishop of the Protestant Episcopal Church in the State of Pennsylvania, and Benjamin R. Morgan, Esq., counsellor at law in the city of Philadelphia, one ring each. Lastly, I do hereby constitute and appoint my dear brother, the Hon. Thomas Smith, Esq., of the city of Philadelphia, my worthy friends, the Hon. Jasper Yeates, Esq., of the borough of Lancaster, the Right Rev. William White, Bishop of the Protestant Episcopal Church in the State of Pennsylvania, and Benjamin R. Morgan, Esq., counsellor at law, of the city of Philadelphia, and the survivors and survivor of them to be executors of this my last will and testament written in eight pages.

In witness whereof I have hereunto set my hand and seal this fourteenth day of July, in the year of our Lord one thousand eight hundred and two—hereby revoking all former wills, codicils, etc.

WILLIAM SMITH, D. D.

Signed, declared and published as and for the last will and testament of William Smith, D. D., in the presence of us who have subscribed our names as witnesses in the testator's presence and at his request.

JAMES RIDDLE,
ELIZA SMITH,
WM. RUDOLPH SMITH.

Codicil to the last will and testament of William Smith, D. D.:

WHEREAS, Since the execution of my said last will and testament, bearing date July the fourteenth, one thousand eight hundred and two, I have thought it proper, at the request of my executors therein named, to relieve them from the trouble of executorship; wherefore I do hereby revoke all that part of my said last will which constitutes and appoints my dear brother, the Hon. Thomas Smith, Esq., of the city of Philadelphia, and my worthy friends, the Hon. Jasper Yeates, Esq., of the borough of Lancaster, and the Right Rev. William White, Bishop of the Protestant Episcopal Church in the State of Pennsylvania, and the survivors or survivor of them, to be executors of my said last will and testament. And in their room and stead I do hereby constitute and appoint my dear sons, William Moore Smith, Esq., Charles Smith, Esq., and Richard Smith, Esq., together with Benjamin R. Morgan, Esq., counsellor at law, of the city of Philadelphia, and the survivors or survivor of them, to be executors of my last will and testament, before written in eight pages.

In witness whereof I have hereunto set my hand and seal this third day of February, in the year of our Lord one thousand eight hundred and three, hereby revoking all former codicils, etc.

WILLIAM SMITH, D. D.   { L. S. }

Signed, declared and published as and for the codicil to the last will and testament of William Smith, D. D., in the presence of us who have subscribed our names as witnesses in the testator's presence and at his request.

ROBERT KENNEDY,
MARTIN WHITTEM,
WM. RUDOLPH SMITH.

This will is entered in the usual form in the Register's office in Philadelphia, in Will Book No. I., page 109.

CHAPTER LX.

Dr. Smith begins to execute a purpose formed in 1789 and approved by the General Convention of that year, but by a variety of causes delayed, to publish, in a collected form, his Works—Only two volumes published out of five, which he contemplated publishing—These two printed by Maxwell, a publisher of Philadelphia during Dr. Smith's lifetime, but not published until after his death.

So far back as the year 1789, on his return from Maryland, Dr. Smith announced his intention to publish, in a collection, his sermons upon the most important branches of practical Christianity. This was made in the form of a communication to the General Convention of the church in that year, which we now give in this place.

Philadelphia, August 5, 1789.

To the Right Reverend and Reverend the Clergy, and the Worthy and Honorable Lay Members of the Protestant Episcopal Church, in the States of New York, New Jersey, Pennsylvania, Delaware, Maryland, Virginia and South Carolina, now assembled in General Convention.

My Worthy Friends and Brethren:

The sermons and discourses, whereof the texts and titles follow, are the result of the author's labors as a preacher of the blessed Gospel for near forty years past. Sundry of them, which were composed and delivered on special public occasions, have been already printed, and have passed through several editions, in Europe as well as America; but the main body of them was composed and delivered at different times, in the character of a parish minister, viz.: in the years 1764 and 176ᵣ at Christ Church and St. Peter's, in the city of Philadelphia; from thenceforward to the year 1780 in the churches of the Oxford Mission, in the county of Philadelphia; and from the latter part of the year 1780 to July 1st, 1789, in Chester parish, Kent county, Maryland.

During the foregoing long period of ministerial service the author hath frequently been solicited to print or to give manuscript copies of sundry of the sermons, and hath, as his leisure would allow, so often indulged some of his too partial friends and hearers in the latter way that copies have been multiplied in manuscript and circulated in a condition not only very incorrect, but wholly without those last improvements and touches which the best of them stand much in need of, and which the author had always designed to bestow upon a few of them, and bequeath them as a legacy to his surviving friends and hearers, if health and opportunity should permit; and if that should not be the case, he had directed those few, together with the whole remainder in the following list, to be suppressed from public view, as hasty and unfinished compositions.

But the late change in the author's situation, the resignation of his parochial as well as collegiate charge in the State of Maryland, and his return to his former station in the College of Philadelphia (added to the consideration of his advanced age) rendering it probable that he can never again engage in any stated parochial duty; the applications of some of his former friends and hearers have been renewed for the publication of sundry of those sermons which had long since been delivered before them, and of which some of them had been supplied with copies as aforesaid.

In some late conversations with judicious and worthy persons, both of the clergy and laity, respecting the present state of our churches and people in America, it hath been further suggested that the cause of religion and truth might be much promoted by the publication of a sufficient number of sermons or discourses, digested, as nearly as possible, into a system or body of divinity; comprehending the most useful and important articles of the Christian doctrine; treated of in a Scriptural and evangelical way; in an easy, affectionate and correct style; suited to the minds and apprehensions of the young and those of inferior capacity, as well as edifying to those of riper years and more improved understanding; not running out into learned niceties or debates, to disturb common readers or hearers; but avoiding all speculative and controversial subjects, or touching upon them only to improve them, as far as possible, towards the purposes of practical godliness and vital Christianity.

Although the author hath not the vanity to imagine that the following sermons are wholly sufficient to this good design, yet they may lay the foundation of a more perfect work; and he finds, upon an arrangement of them under proper heads, that in order to form a tolerably complete system, only a few sermons would be wanting, and those chiefly upon such speculative and controversial points as the author hath ever avoided in the pulpit, but which (if thought necessary in a work of this kind) might be selected from some of the ablest and most orthodox divines of our Church.

Indeed, it may be said that a complete body of sermons and divinity might be wholly selected or compiled in this way, and attempts of that kind have been made with good effect. But, as every age and country is best pleased with its own forms, compositions and phrases of speech, the author flatters himself that if it should please God to enable him to

finish those sermons in the way he proposes, they will be at least acceptable to those who have desired the publication of any of them. He
further trusts that if his design should meet with that approbation and
countenance which he affectionately solicits from the members of the
convention, they will be of use to all well-disposed Christians, and especially to those of the following descriptions, viz. :

1. To heads of families who may think it their duty to devote the
evenings of the Lord's Day to the instruction of their own households.

2. To pious and well-disposed persons (remote from places of public
worship, or unprovided with ministers or pastors) who may wish to
collect their neighbors and friends to spend some parts of a Sunday in
public worship, and in reading sermons and books of devotion.

3. To young clergymen and preachers, who, being ill-supplied with
books, or a variety of sermons on proper subjects, may be assisted in
their earlier compositions by the present work, which it is proposed to
comprise in four or five octavo volumes, in the same sized paper and
letter as this address; two volumes to be published yearly, at the rate
of one dollar per volume on the delivery of the same, in boards, to the
subscribers.   WILLIAM SMITH.

This communication was followed by a unanimous resolution
of the body, made on motion of Mr. J. Cox, a principal lay deputy
from New Jersey.

Resolved, unanimously, That the members of this Convention, being
fully persuaded that the interests of religion and practical godliness
may be greatly promoted by the publication of a body of sermons,
upon the plan proposed above, and being well satisfied of the author's
soundness in the faith, and eminent abilities for such a work, do testify
their approbation of the same, and their desire to encourage it by annexing their names thereto as subscribers.

WILLIAM WHITE, D. D., Bishop of the Protestant Episcopal Church
in the Commonwealth of Pennsylvania, and President of the
Convention.

BENJAMIN MOORE, D. D., Assistant Minister of Trinity Church, in the
city of New York; now Bishop of the Protestant Episcopal Church
in that State.

ABRAHAM BEACH, D. D., now Senior Minister of Trinity Church, in the
city of New York.

MOSES ROGERS, Lay Deputy from the State of New York.

WILLIAM FRAZER, A. M., Rector of St. Michael's Church, in Trenton,
New Jersey.

UZAL OGDEN, Rector of Trinity Church, in Newark.

HENRY WADDEL, Rector of the churches of Shrewsbury and Middle-
town, now of Trenton, New Jersey.

GEORGE H. SPIERIN, A. M., Rector of St. Peter's Church, Perth Amboy.

JOHN COX, ROBERT STRETTELL JONES, SAMUEL OGDEN, Lay Deputies from New Jersey.

SAMUEL MAGAW, D. D., Rector of St. Paul's Church, and Vice-Provost of the University of Pennsylvania; ROBERT BLACKWELL, D. D., Senior Minister in Christ Church, and St. Peter's, Philadelphia; JOSEPH PILMORE, JOSEPH G. J. BEND,* Clerical Deputies from Pennsylvania.

FRANCIS HOPKINSON, SAMUEL POWELL, TENCH COXE, GERARDUS CLARKSON, Lay Deputies from Pennsylvania.

JOSEPH COUDON, A. M., STEPHEN SYKES, A. M., Clerical Deputies from Delaware.

JAMES SYKES, Lay Deputy of Delaware.

THOMAS J. CLAGGETT, D. D., COLIN FERGUSON, D. D.,† JOHN BISSETT, A. M.,‡ Clerical Deputies from Maryland.

RICHARD B. CARMICHAEL, WM. FRISBY, Lay Deputies from Maryland.

ROBERT ANDREWS, Lay Deputy from Virginia.

ROBERT SMITH, D. D., Rector of St. Philip's Church, Principal of Charlestown College, Clerical Deputy from South Carolina.

W. W. BURROWS, WM. BRISBANE, Lay Deputies from South Carolina.

The following named clergy of the city of Philadelphia of nearly every denomination testified their approbation by annexing their names as subscribers, viz.:

FRANCIS BEESTON, Rector of the Catholic Church of St. Mary.

NICHOLAS COLLIN, D. D., Rector of the Swedish Church.

HENRY HELMUTH, D. D., Minister of Zion's and Michaelis churches.

---

* Joseph Grove John Bend, D. D., a native of New York, ordained by Bishop Provoost in 1787. He went to Pennsylvania, and was Assistant Minister of Christ Church in 1789. He afterward removed to Baltimore, and in 1791 became Rector of St. Paul's Parish, Baltimore county. He was preacher to the convention in 1808, and was always Secretary to the Maryland Convention, member of the Standing Committee, and delegate to the General Convention. He published three occasional sermons, and edited a number of works for distribution. He died in 1812, aged 53.

† Colin Ferguson, D. D., a native of Kent county, Md., brought up a Presbyterian, ordained in 1785 by Bishop Seabury, of Connecticut, and became Rector of St. Paul's, Kent, which he resigned in 1799; was President of Washington College, Chestertown, from 1789 to 1805. Died in 1806, aged 55.—*Allen.*

‡ John Bissett, A. M., a native of Scotland, brought up in the church, ordained in 1786 by Bishop Seabury, and in 1787 became Rector of South Sassafras, Kent county, Md.; in 1790 of North Sassafras, Cecil. He was Secretary to the convention, four times member of the Standing Committee, and delegate to the General Convention. Published two sermons. In 1793 removed to New York. Died in 1810, aged 48.—*Allen.*

CASPERUS WEIBERG, D. D., Minister of the German Reformed Church.

GEORGE DUFFIELD, D. D., Pastor of the Third Presbyterian Church.

SAMUEL JONES, D. D., Pastor of the Baptist Church in Lower Dublin.

WILLIAM MARSHALL, A. M., Minister of the Gospel to the Scots Presbyterian Church.

JOHN MEDER, Minister of the United Brethren's Church.

JOHN ANDREWS, D. D., Professor of Philosophy and Belles Lettres in the College and Academy of Philadelphia, and Rector of St. James's Church, Bristol.

JAMES DAVIDSON, A. M., Professor of Humanity in the College and Academy of Philadelphia.

WILLIAM ROGERS, A. M., Professor of English and Oratory, and of Practical Mathematics, in the College and Academy of Philadelphia.

The Hon. Robert Morris, Esq., acting no doubt at the suggestion of his brother-in-law, Bishop White—though he was quite competent himself to estimate rightly the literary and ecclesiastical merits of Dr. Smith—opened and received subscriptions in Congress. His subscription paper began thus:

GEORGE WASHINGTON,	WILLIAM PATTERSON,
JOHN ADAMS,	ROBERT MORRIS,
WILLIAM GRAYSON,	WILLIAM SAMUEL JOHNSON,
PH. SCHUYLER,	RALPH IZARD,

GEORGE READ.

Subscribers came in from every part of the country, indicating how widely spread was Dr. Smith's fame as a pulpit orator. The list from Maryland, in procuring which Mr. Justice Goldsborough took much interest, was especially large, and with the names of many persons in humble station, comprised the name of nearly every gentleman of rank or education in the State. We give those sent by Judge Goldsborough:

Hon. Robert Hanson Harrison, Esq., Chief Justice, etc.

Hon. Alexander Contee Hanson, Esq., Chancellor.

Hon. Robert Goldsborough, one of the Judges.

Benjamin Fred. Aug. Cæs. Dashiell, Esq., Worcester county.

Hon. Nicholas Hammond, Esq., Dorset county.
James Tilghman, Esq., Queen Anne county.
James Earle, Esq., Talbot county.
William Cooke, Esq., Annapolis county.
Gustavus Scott, Esq., Dorset county.
William Heyward, Esq., Talbot county.
William Barroll, Esq., Elkton, Cecil county.
David Kerr, Esq., Easton, Talbot county.
Mr. Jos. Haskins, Easton, Talbot county.
Edward Coursey, Esq., Queen Anne county.
Charles Blair, Esq., Dorset county.
William Hindman, Esq., Talbot county.
Edward Lloyd, Esq., Talbot county.
Pollard Edmiston, Esq., Talbot county.
Matthew Driver, Esq., Caroline county.
Robert Goldsborough, Jr., Esq., Dorset county.
Horatio Ridout, Esq., Annapolis county.
Dr. Charles Troup, Easton, Talbot county.
John Gordon, D. D., Rector of St. Michael's, Talbot county.
Dr. John Lodman Elbert, Talbot county.
Henry Dickenson, Esq., Caroline county.
Richard Spriggs, Esq., Annapolis county.
The Rev. John Bowie, D. D., Dorchester county.

The following were subscribers in Albany, etc.:

Rev. Thomas Ellison, A. M., Rector of St. Peter's.
Rev. J. Basset, A. M., Jr., Minister of the Reformed Dutch Church.
Rev. Samuel Smith, Minister of the Reformed Dutch Church in
    Saratoga.
Mr. Dudley Walsh.
Mr. Goldsborough Banyar, Jr.
Mr. P. S. Van Rensselaer.
Hon. Leonard Gansevoort, Esq.
Stephen Van Rensselaer, Esq., of Rensselaerwick.
Daniel Hale, Esq.
Barent Roorback, Esq., of Ballton.
Mr. Charles Martin, Schenectady.
John Tayler, Esq.
Mr. Daniel J. Hewson.

Dirck Ten Broeck, Esq.
John Bradstreet Schuyler, Esq., of Saratoga.
Mr. William Fryer.
Mr. William Shepherd.

I am not aware of the reasons why the publication was delayed.
The large operations in land, in which it is known that Dr. Smith
was engaged—although from my want of familiarity with their
particulars, I have not gone into any full statement of them—in
part absorbed his attention. But the Yellow Fever of 1793, and a
return of the pestilence, or something much like it, in 1795, and
again in 1797—though in these two years, especially in the former, in forms less terrible than in the first-named year—was well
calculated, attended as it was in the case of Dr. Smith with losses
so near to him and so desolating, to arrest all enterprise in the
way of publication. He himself thus refers to the case:

The distresses that followed in my family—first, the loss of a favorite
son, blessed with every literary accomplishment, especially in his medical profession, and the delight of his acquaintance;* soon afterwards the
loss of an amiable daughter, in goodness approaching that of an angel
as nearly as a mortal condition would allow;† and, more than all this,
the loss of a dear wife—a woman of whom the world was scarce worthy,
much less he whose many bereavements of this kind have brought his
gray hairs down with sorrow to the very brink of the grave—I say
these sad losses damped the preparation of the work for the public.
Little anxious to devote the melancholy moments that succeeded those
losses—especially the death of a beloved wife—to the review of old
writings and the superintending a press, my mind was carried forward
to more solemn subjects: the consummation of earthly, and the final
establishment of heavenly things; and my reading confined to such
books as I had at hand on those subjects.

However, in the year 1800 Dr. Smith began to arrange all his
writings for publication. Had he lived to see through the press
all that he thus arranged, we should have had five, if not six, 8vo.
volumes with his name. As it is, we have but two—those two
from which we have made in our biography such copious extracts. We give the table of their contents.

---

* Thomas Duncan Smith, M. D.   † Mrs. Williamina Elizabeth Goldsborough.

FIRST VOLUME.

PART I.

PART II.

Dr. Smith also left this list of ninety-eight sermons, which, as
he arranged them—and throwing out certain ones marked with an
asterisk (*), which are printed in Maxwell's two volumes or elsewhere—would have made four more volumes of sermons alone,
independent of his other works. A table of the subjects or principal heads, and of the texts of the sermons, in the proposed order
of publication, was part of the document.

PART I.

Sermons I., II. On the Being and Attributes of God.

Ex. iii. 13, 14.—And Moses said unto God, Behold, when I come unto the children of Israel, and shall say unto them, The God of your fathers hath sent me unto you; and they shall say to me, What is his name? what shall I say unto them? And God said unto Moses, I am that I am. And he said, Thus shalt thou say unto the children of Israel, I am hath sent me unto you.

Sermon III. The Holy Scriptures of the Old and New Testament are the true Word of God, and a Complete Revelation of his Divine Will to Man.

Heb. i. 1, 2.—God, who at sundry times and in divers manners, spake in time past unto the fathers by the prophets, hath in these last days spoken unto us by his Son, whom he hath appointed the Heir of all things, by whom also he made the worlds.

Sermon IV. The Folly of Infidelity.

Psalm xiv. 1.—The fool hath said in his heart, There is no God.

Sermon V. The Wisdom and Reasonableness of Faith in God.

Heb. xi. 6.—Without faith it is impossible to please him; for he that cometh to God must believe that he is, and that he is a Rewarder of them that diligently seek him.

Sermon VI. Of the Creation and Nature of Man, and the Immortality of the Soul.

Psalm viii. 5, 6; Heb. ii. 7.—Thou madest him a little lower than the angels; thou crownedst him with glory and honor, and didst set him over the works of thy hands.

Sermon VII. Of the Old and New Covenant, the Law and the Gospel.

Heb. vii. 19.—For the law made nothing perfect, but the bringing of a better hope did; by the which we draw nigh unto God.

Sermon VIII. Of the Difference between Legal and Evangelical Righteousness, or the Righteousness of Faith.

Rom. ix. 31–33.—But Israel which followed after the law of righteousness, hath not attained to the law of righteousness. Wherefore? Because they sought it not by faith, but as it were by the works of the law; for they stumbled at that stumbling-stone, as it is written, Behold, I lay in Zion a stumbling-stone and rock of offence, and whosoever believeth on him shall not be ashamed.

Sermon IX. The Honor and Dignity of the Christian Ministry and Profession.

Rom. i. 16.—I am not ashamed of the gospel of Christ; for it is the power of God unto salvation to every one that believeth.

Sermon X. The Grace and Holiness of the Christian Calling.

2 Tim. i. 9.—God hath saved us and called us with an holy calling; not according to our works, but according to his own purpose and grace, which was given us in Christ Jesus, before the world began.

Sermon XI. The Purity of the same.

Prov. xxx. 5, 6.—Every word of God is pure. He is a shield unto them that put their trust in him. Add thou not unto his words, lest he reprove thee, and thou be found a liar.

Sermon XII. On Hearing the Word of God.

John viii. 47.—He that is of God heareth God's Word.

Sermon XIII. On Doing the Word of God.

James i. 22.—Be ye doers of the word and not hearers only, deceiving your own selves.

Sermon XIV. Of Steadfastness in the Faith.

[Preached at Annapolis, June 23, 1784, before a convention of the Protestant Episcopal Church in Maryland.]

2 Tim. i. 13.—Hold fast the form of sound words which thou hast heard of me, in faith and love which is in Christ Jesus.

Sermon XV. The Victory of Faith.

I John v. 1, 4.—Whosoever believeth that Jesus is the Christ is born of God. Whatsoever is born of God overcometh the world; and this is the victory that overcometh, even our faith.

PART II.

Sermon XVI. Christ the True and Promised Messiah.   [In two Parts.]
[Preached on Christmas day.]

Luke ii. 10-14.—And the angel said unto them, Fear not; for behold I bring you good tidings of great joy, which shall be to all people; for unto you is born this day in the city of David a Saviour, which is Christ the Lord. And this shall be a sign unto you: ye shall find the Babe wrapped in swaddling clothes lying in a manger. And suddenly there was with the angel a multitude of the heavenly host, praising God and saying, Glory to God in the highest, and on earth peace, good will towards men.

Sermons XVII., XVIII. Christ the True Shepherd.

[Preached on the fourth Sunday in Advent, and on Christmas day.]

Isa. xl. 1, 2, 10, 11.—Comfort ye, comfort ye my people, saith your God. Speak ye comfortably to Jerusalem, and cry unto her that her warfare is accomplished, that her iniquity is pardoned. Behold the Lord God will come with strong hand, and his arm shall rule for him. Behold his reward is with him and his work before him.

He shall feed his flock like a shepherd: he shall gather the lambs with his arm, and carry them in his bosom, and shall gently lead those that are with young.

Sermons XIX., XX. Christ's other glorious Titles.

[Preached on Christmas day, and the Sunday following.]

Isa. ix. 6.—For unto us a Child is born, unto us a Son is given; and the government shall be upon his shoulder; and his name shall be called Wonderful, Counsellor, the Mighty God, the Everlasting Father, the Prince of Peace.

Sermon XXI. Of the Universality and Extent of Christ's Kingdom.

[Preached on the Epiphany.]

Isa. ix. 7.—Of the increase of his government and peace, there shall be no end.

28

Sermon XXII. Concerning the Conversion of the Heathen Americans, and the final Propagation of Christianity and the Sciences to the Ends of the Earth.   [In two Parts.]

[Part I. Preached before a convention of Episcopal clergy in Christ Church, Philadelphia, May 2, 1760.]

[Part II. Preached before the Trustees, Masters and Scholars, at the first Anniversary Commencement, in the college there, to which is added a Charge to the first Graduates.]

Psalm ii. 8.—Ask of me and I shall give thee the heathen for thine inheritance, and the uttermost parts of the earth for thy possession.

Sermon XXIII. On the same subject.

[Preached on the dedicaticn of Washington College, in the State of Maryland, June 23, 1789.]

Malachi i. 11.—From the rising of the sun even to the going down of the same, my name shall be great among the Gentiles; and in every place incense shall be offered unto my name and a pure offering; for my name shall be great among the heathen saith the Lord of hosts.

Sermon XXIV. On Christ's Fasting and Temptation.
[Preached in Lent.]

Matt. iv. 1–3.—Then was Jesus led up of the Spirit into the wilderness, to be tempted of the devil. And when he had fasted forty days and forty nights, he was afterwards an hungered. And when the tempter came to him, he said, If thou be the Son of God, command that these stones be made bread.

Sermon XXV. On the Institution of the Holy Sacrament.
[Preached on the Sunday before Easter.]

Luke xxii. 15, etc.—And he said unto them, With desire I have desired to eat this Passover with you before I suffer; for I say unto you, I will not any more eat thereof until it be fulfilled in the kingdom of God. And he took the cup, etc.

Sermon XXVI. On the Sufferings and Death of Christ.
From the same text.   [Preached on Good Friday.]

Sermon XXVII. On the same subject.
[Preached on Good Friday.]

Lam. i. 12.—Is it nothing unto you, all ye that pass by? Behold and see, if there be any sorrow like unto my sorrow, which is done unto me, wherewith the Lord hath afflicted me, in the day of his fierce anger.

Sermon XXVIII. On the Certainty of the Resurrection of Christ.
[Preached on Easter day.]

Job xix. 25, 26.—I know that my Redeemer liveth, and that he shall stand at the latter day upon the earth; and though after my skin worms destroy this body, yet in my flesh shall I see God.

Sermon XXIX. On the Power of the Resurrection of Christ.
[Preached on Easter day.]

Phil. iii. 8, 10.—Yea, doubtless, and I count all things but loss for the excellency of the knowledge of Christ Jesus my Lord; for whom I have suffered the loss of all things, and do count them but dung—that I may know him, and the power of his resurrection.

Sermon XXX. The Resurrection of Christ, the Pledge and Proof of Man's Immortality, and a full Evidence of the Truth of Christianity.

Col. iii. 4.—When Christ who is our life shall appear, then shall ye also appear with him in glory.

1 Cor. xv. 12–14.—If Christ be preached that he rose from the dead, how say some among you that there is no resurrection of the dead? But if there be no resurrection of the dead, then is Christ not risen; and if Christ be not risen, then is our preaching vain, and your faith is also vain.

Sermon XXXI. On the Ascension of Christ.

Psalm xxiv. 7.—Lift up your heads, O ye gates; and be ye lift up, ye everlasting doors, and the King of glory shall come in.

Sermon XXXII. On the Gift of the Holy Ghost.
[Preached on Whitsunday.]

John xiv. 16.—And I will pray the Father, and he shall give you another Comforter, that he may abide with you for ever.

Sermon XXXIII. Of the Receiving of the Holy Ghost.

Acts xix. 2, 3.—He said unto them, Have ye received the Holy Ghost since ye believed? And they said unto him, We have not so much as heard whether there be any Holy Ghost. And he said unto them, Unto what then were ye baptized?

Sermon XXXIV. On the Spirit of Adoption.
[Preached on Whitsunday.]

Rom. viii. 14, 15.—For as many as are led by the Spirit of God, they are the sons of God; for ye have not received the spirit of bondage again to fear, but ye have received the spirit of adoption, whereby we cry, Abba, Father.

FOUR SERMONS ON THE FRUITS OF THE SPIRIT.

Sermon XXXV. 1. Prayer.

Rom. viii. 15 (latter part of the foregoing text).—Whereby we cry, Abba, Father.

Sermon XXXVI. 2. Praise and Thanksgiving.

[Preached in Christ Church, Philadelphia, upon the introduction of the organ.]

Psalms xlvii. 7, and cl. 4.—Sing unto the Lord with thanksgiving. Sing praise unto our God upon the harp. Praise him with stringed instruments and organs.

Sermon XXXVII. 3. Faith, Hope and Charity.

1 Cor. xiii. 3.—And now abideth faith, hope and charity, these three; but the greatest of these is charity.

Sermon XXXVIII. 4. Love, Joy, etc. Goodness, Righteousness and Truth.

Gal. v. 22, 23.—But the fruit of the Spirit is love, joy, peace, long-suffering, gentleness, goodness, truth.

Eph v. 9.—The fruit of the Spirit is in all goodness and righteousness and truth.

Sermon XXXIX. The Danger and Sin of Resisting the Spirit, and falling away from Grace.

Heb. x. 28, 29.—He that despised Moses's law, died without mercy, under two or three witnesses; of how much sorer punishment, suppose ye, shall he be thought worthy who hath trodden under foot the Son of God, and hath counted the blood of the Covenant, wherewith he was sanctified an unholy thing, and hath done despite unto the Spirit of Grace.

Sermons XL., XLI. The Safety and Happiness of Walking after the Spirit and Loving God's Law.

Rom. viii. 1.—There is no condemnation to them which are in Christ Jesus, who walk not after the flesh, but after the Spirit.

Psalm cxix.—Great peace have they which love thy law, and nothing shall offend them.

PART III.

Sermon XLII. The Call or Invitations under the Law and the Prophets.

Isa. xlv. 22, 23.—Look unto me and be ye saved, all the ends of the earth; for I am God, and there is none else. I have sworn by myself; the word is gone out of my mouth in righteousness and shall not return, That unto me every knee shall bow, every tongue shall swear.

Sermon XLIII. The Call or Invitations under the Gospel.

Matt. xi. 28–30.—Come unto me all ye that labour and are heavy laden, and I will give you rest. Take my yoke upon you and learn of me; for I am meek and lowly in heart, and ye shall find rest unto your souls. For my yoke is easy and my burden is light.

Sermon XLIV. The Duty of Hearing the Call and drawing near to God.

Psalm lxxiii. 28.—It is good for me to draw near to God.

Sermon XLV. Of the Fear of God, under the Law.

Job xxv. 2, 4.—Dominion and fear are with him. How can man be justified with God? Or how can he be clean that is born of a woman?

Sermon XLVI. Of the Fear of God, under the Gospel.

2 Tim. i. 7.—For God hath not given us the spirit of fear, but of power, and of love, and of a sound mind.

1 John iv. 18.—There is no fear in love; but perfect love casteth out fear; because fear hath torment in it. He that feareth is not made perfect in love.

Sermons XLVII., XLVIII. Of Fear and Obedience, as the whole Duty of Man under the Law.

Eccl. xii. 13, 14.—Let us hear the conclusion of the whole matter. Fear God, and keep his commandments; for this is the whole duty of man. For God shall bring every work into judgment, with every secret thing, whether it be good, or whether it be bad.

Sermons XLIX., L. Of Love and Vital Religion, as the whole Duty of Man, under the Gospel.

1 John iii. 23, 24.—This is his commandment that we should believe on the name of his Son Jesus Christ, and love one another as he gave us commandment; and he that keepeth his commandments dwelleth in him, and he in him. And hereby we know that he abideth in us by the Spirit which he hath given us.

Sermon LI. Christ's Kingdom is not of this World.

John xviii. 36.—Jesus answered, My kingdom is not of this world.

Sermon LII. The Christian's Conversation is in Heaven.

Phil. iii. 20.—For our conversation is in heaven, from whence also we look for the Saviour, the Lord Jesus Christ.

Sermon LIII. Fellowship with God and the Works of Darkness irreconcilable.

1 John i. 5-7.—God is Light, and in him is no darkness at all. If we say that we have fellowship with him and walk in darkness, we lie, and do not the truth: but if we walk in the light as he is in the light, we have fellowship one with another, and the blood of Jesus Christ his Son cleanseth us from all sin.

PART IV.

Sermon LIV. Of Sin and the Duty of Confession.

1 John i. 8, 9.—If we say that we have no sin, we deceive ourselves and the truth is not in us; but if we confess our sins, he is faithful and just to forgive us our sins, and to cleanse us from all unrighteousness.

Sermon LV. The same subject, from the parable of the Prodigal Son, viz.:

Luke xv. 18.—I will arise and go to my father, etc.

Sermon LVI. Of Repentance and Salvation.

Ezek. xviii. 27.—When the wicked man turneth away from his wickedness that he hath committed, and doeth that which is lawful and right, he shall save his soul alive.

Sermon LVII. An Exhortation to Repentance and Good Works.

Isa. i. 16, 17.—Wash ye, make you clean; put away the evil of your doings from before mine eyes, cease to do evil; learn to do well; seek judgment, relieve the oppressed, judge the fatherless, plead for the widow.

Sermon LVIII. Want of Consideration.

Isa. i. 3.—The ox knoweth his owner, and the ass his master's crib; but Israel doth not know, my people doth not consider.

Sermon LIX. Against Presumption.

1 Cor. x. 12.—Let him that thinketh he standeth, take heed lest he fall.

Sermon LX. On Redeeming the Time.

Rom. xiii. 12.—The night is far spent, the day is at hand; let us therefore cast off the works of darkness, and let us put on the armour of light.

Sermon LXI. On Submission to the Will of God.

1 Sam. iii. 18.—And Samuel told him every whit, and hid nothing from him. And he said, It is the Lord, let him do what seemeth him good.

Sermon LXII. Of St. Peter's Want of Faith.

Matt. xiv. 30, 31.—But when he saw the wind boisterous, he was afraid; and beginning to sink, he cried, saying, Lord save me. And immediately Jesus stretched forth his hand and caught him, and said unto him, O thou of little faith, wherefore didst thou doubt?

Sermon LXIII. St. Peter's Tears and Repentance.

Luke xxii. 60–62.—While he yet spake, the cock crew; and the Lord turned and looked upon Peter. And Peter remembered the word of the Lord, how he had said unto him, Before the cock crow thou shalt deny me thrice. And Peter went out and wept bitterly.

Sermon LXIV. An Exhortation to Prayer.

Luke xxii. 46.—Why sleep ye? rise and pray, lest ye enter into temptation.

Sermon LXV. Encouragement to Prayer and Seeking God.

Jer. viii. 22.—Is there no balm in Gilead? Is there no physician there? Why then is not the health of the daughter of my people recovered?

Sermon LXVI. Of the new Creature.

Gal. vi. 15.—For in Christ Jesus neither circumcision availeth any thing, nor uncircumcision, but a new creature.

Sermon LXVII. The Knowledge of God, the Christian's true Glory.

Jer. ix. 23, 24.—Thus saith the Lord, Let not the wise man glory in his wisdom, neither let the mighty man glory in his might, let not the rich man glory in his riches; but let him that glorieth glory in this, that he understandeth and knoweth me, that I am the Lord which exercise loving kindness, judgment and righteousness in the earth; for in these things I delight, saith the Lord.

Sermon LXVIII. The Lord our Righteousness.

[An Advent Sermon.]

Jer. xxiii. 6.—In his days Judah shall be saved and Israel shall dwell safely; and this is his name whereby he shall be called, The Lord our Righteousness.

Sermon LXIX. An Advent Sermon.

Matt. xi. 5.—The poor have the gospel preached.

THREE SERMONS; OF RELATIVE DUTIES, VIZ.:

Sermon LXX. 1. Of Husbands and Wives.

Col. iii. 18, 19.—Wives, submit yourselves unto your own husbands, as it is fit unto the Lord. Husbands, love your wives and be not bitter against them.

Sermon LXXI.—Part I. 2. Of Parents and Children.

Col. iii. 20, 21.—Children, obey your parents in all things; for this is well pleasing unto the Lord. Fathers, provoke not your children to anger, lest they be discouraged.

Part II. On the Education of Children.

Prov. xxii. 6.—Train up a child in the way he should go, and when he is old he will not depart from it.

Sermon LXXII. 3. Of Masters and Servants.

Col. iii. 22, and iv. 1.—Servants, obey in all things your masters, according to the flesh; not with eye-service as men-pleasers, but in singleness of heart, fearing God. Masters, give unto your servants that which is just and equal; knowing that ye also have a Master in heaven.

Sermon LXXIII. On Destroying the Works of the Devil.

1 John iii. 8.—For this purpose the Son of God was manifested, that he might destroy the works of the devil.

Sermon LXXIV. Of Diligence in our Calling, both Temporal and Spiritual.

1 Cor. vii. 24.—Brethren, let every man wherein he is called, therein abide with God.

Sermons LXXV., LXXVI. Of Sanctification and Redemption.

1 Cor. i. 30, 31.—But of him are ye in Christ Jesus, who of God is made unto us wisdom and righteousness and sanctification and redemption; That according as it is written, He that glorieth let him glory in the Lord.

Sermon LXXVII. Of Keeping the Sabbath Day.

Ex. xx. 8.—Remember the Sabbath day to keep it holy.

Luke vi. 7–9.—And the scribes and Pharisees watched him, whether he would heal on the Sabbath day, that they might find an accusation against him. But he knew their thoughts, and said to the man which had the withered hand, Rise up and stand forth in the midst. And he rose and stood forth.

Then said Jesus unto them, I will ask you one thing, Is it lawful on the Sabbath days to do good, or to do evil? to save life, or to destroy it? And looking round about upon them all, he said unto the man, Stretch forth thy hand. And he did so, and his hand was restored whole as the other.

Sermon LXXVIII. The great Duty of Public Worship, and of Erecting and Dedicating Proper Houses for that Purpose.

[Preached in St. Peter's Church, Philadelphia, September 4, 1761, being the day appointed for the first opening and dedication of the said church; with an account of the service used on that occasion.]

1 Kings viii. 13, 27, 57, 60.—I have surely built thee an house to dwell in, a settled place for thee to abide in for ever. But will God indeed dwell on the earth? Behold the heaven and heaven of heavens cannot contain thee; how much less this house that I have builded! The Lord our God be with us, as he was with our fathers; let him not leave us nor forsake us; that all the people of the earth may know that the Lord is God, and that there is none else.

Sermon LXXIX. Of Love and Unity. Being a Farewell Sermon.

[Preached at All Saints Church, Philadelphia county, on occasion of the shutting up the churches in the Oxford Mission, on the approach of the British army towards the city of Philadelphia.]

2 Cor. xiii. 11.—Finally, brethren, farewell. Be perfect, be of good comfort, be of one mind, live in peace; and the God of love and peace shall be with you.

Sermon LXXX. Of Joy Succeeding to Sorrow.

[Preached in July, 1778, in the three churches of the Oxford Mission, on the opening of the said churches after the evacuation of the city of Philadelphia by the British army.]

Psalm cxxvi. 3, 4, 5.—The Lord hath done great things for us whereof we are glad. Turn again our captivity, O Lord, as the streams in the south. They that sow in tears shall reap in joy. He that goeth forth and weepeth, bearing precious seed, shall doubtless come again with rejoicing, bringing his sheaves with him.

THREE SERMONS AT THE CELEBRATION OF THE BLESSED SACRAMENT OF THE LORD'S SUPPER.

Sermon LXXXI. 1. On Self-examination.

1 Cor. xi. 28.—But let a man examine himself, and so let him eat of that bread, and drink of that cup.

Sermon LXXXII. 2. The Promise of Eternal Life to Worthy Partakers of the Lord's Supper.

John vi. 54.—Whoso eateth my flesh and drinketh my blood, hath eternal life; and I will raise him up at the last day.

Sermon LXXXIII. 3 and 4. An Exhortation to Frequent Communion, with an Answer to all Excuses, etc.

Luke xiv. 16, etc.—A certain man made a great supper, and bade many, and sent his servant at supper time to say to them that were bidden, Come, for all things are now ready. And they all with one consent began to make excuse. The first said, etc.

Sermon LXXXIV. Of the Progress of our Time, and the Instability of Life.

[A New Year's sermon, first preached January 1, 1781.]

James iv. 13-15.—Go to now, ye that say, To-day or to-morrow we will go into such a city, and continue there a year, and buy and sell and get gain; whereas ye know not what shall be on the morrow. For what is your life? It is even a vapour that appeareth for a little time, and then vanisheth away. For that you ought to say, If the Lord will, we shall live to do this or that.

Jer. xxviii. 16.—This year thou shalt die; because thou hast taught rebellion against the Lord.

FUNERAL SERMONS.

Sermon LXXXV. Personal Affliction and Frequent Reflection upon Human Life, of great Use to lead Man to the Remembrance of God.

[Preached in Christ Church, Philadelphia, September 1, 1754, on the death of a beloved pupil.]

Psalm xlii. 6.—O my God! my soul is cast down within me, therefore will I remember thee.

Sermon LXXXVI. The Steward's Summons.

[Preached in Christ Church, Philadelphia, January 10, 1762, at the funeral of the Rev. Robert Jenney, LL. D., Rector of that church.]

Luke xvi. 2.—Give an account of thy stewardship; for thou mayest be no longer steward.

Sermon LXXXVII. The Peaceful End of the Righteous.

[Preached in Christ Church, Philadelphia, September 6, 1772, at the funeral of Thomas Græme, Esq., M. D.]

Gen. xv. 15.—And thou shalt go to thy fathers in peace; thou shalt be buried in a good old age.

Sermon LXXXVIII. Old Age a Crown of Glory to the Righteous.

Prov. xvi. 31.—The hoary head is a crown of glory, if it be found in the way of righteousness.

Sermon LXXXIX. Longing after Immortality.

[As it was preached before the General Convention of the Protestant Episcopal Church, on Tuesday, August 4, 1789, at the funeral of the Rev. David Griffith, D. D., a member of convention for the church in Virginia, and formerly a bishop elect in that church.] *

2 Cor. v. 1, 2.—For we know that if our earthly house of this tabernacle were dissolved, we have a building of God, an house not made with hands, eternal in the heavens. For in this we groan earnestly, desiring to be clothed upon with our house which is from heaven.

Sermon XC. The Improvement of Time.

[Preached on sundry funeral occasions.]

1 Cor. vii. 29–31.—But this I say, brethren, The time is short. It remaineth that both they that have wives, be as though they had none; and they that weep, as though they weeped not; and they that rejoice, as though they rejoiced not; and they that buy, as though they possessed not; and they that use this world, as not abusing it: for the fashion of this world passeth away.

Sermon XCI. Mourning better than Mirth.

[Preached on sundry funeral occasions.]

Eccl. vii. 2.—It is better to go to the house of mourning than to go to the house of feasting, for that is the end of all men, and the living will lay it to his heart.

Sermon XCII. The Immortal Fruits of Affliction.

[Preached at the funeral of Colonel William Bordley, M. D., of Kent county, Md.

2 Cor. iv. 17.—For our light affliction, which is but for a moment, worketh for us a far more exceeding and eternal weight of glory.

Sermon XCIII. The Christian's Warfare and Crown.

[Preached in Chester Church, Maryland, February 9, 1781, at the funeral of Mrs. Rachael Coudon, wife of the Rev. Joseph Coudon, A. M.]

2 Tim. iv. 6–8.—The time of my departure is at hand. I have fought a good fight, I have finished my course, I have kept the faith; henceforth there is laid up for me a crown of righteousness, which the Lord, the righteous Judge, shall give me at that day; and not to me only, but unto all them also that love his appearing.

END OF THE FUNERAL SERMONS.

---

* This sermon, as it was at first composed, was preached January 23, 1782, at the funeral of the Rev. Hugh Neill, A. M., Rector of Chester Parish, Queen Anne's county, Maryland.

Sermon XCIV. Of the Trembling of Felix, and the Witness of Conscience.

Acts xxiv. 25.—And as he reasoned of righteousness, temperance and judgment to come, Felix trembled, and answered, Go thy way for this time, when I have more convenient season I will call for thee.

Sermon XCV. The Certainty of the last Judgment, and of a Future State of Rewards and Punishments.

2 Cor. v. 10, 11.—We must all appear before the judgment seat of Christ, that every one may receive the things done in his body, according to that he hath done, whether it be good or bad. Knowing therefore the terror of the Lord, we persuade men.

Sermon XCVI. Of the Manner of Christ's Coming to Judgment, and the Resurrection of the Dead.

1 Thess. iv. 16, 17.—For the Lord himself shall descend from heaven with a shout, with the voice of the archangel and the trump of God, and the dead in Christ shall rise first: then we which are alive and remain shall be caught up together with them in the clouds, to meet the Lord in the air; and so shall we ever be with the Lord.

Sermon XCVII. Of the Dissolution of the World by Fire at the Last Day; with an earnest Exhortation to Holiness of Life, and Preparation for Death and Judgment.

2 Pet. iii. 10, 11.—The day of the Lord will come as a thief in the night, in the which the heavens shall pass away with a great noise, and the elements shall melt with fervent heat, the earth also and the works that are therein shall be burnt up.

Seeing then that all these things shall be dissolved, what manner of persons ought ye to be in all holy conversation and godliness; looking for and hasting unto the coming of the day of the Lord.

Sermon XCVIII. Of an Eternal World, and the different State of the Righteous and the Ungodly after Judgment.

Matt. xxv. 46.—And these shall go away unto everlasting punishment, but the righteous unto life eternal.

END OF THE PAROCHIAL SERMONS.

Some of these sermons have been published. Many have not been. Where those unpublished now are I am wholly unable to discover; indeed cannot so much as conjecture. I sincerely grieve that they cannot be collected and preserved. In such institutions as the Historical Society of Pennsylvania we have now a place where any manuscripts of value are arranged, indexed, bound, and carefully preserved in fire-proof repositories. I earnestly appeal to my numerous kinsfolk, if among any of them these precious documents yet remain, to collect and deposit them in that or in some other like institution, if any there be, where they will be of some benefit to mankind. In private hands, even the best hands, they are of little or none.

But Dr. Smith contemplated, in case of his life being prolonged, the publication of other volumes than these six of which I have just written. These additional volumes were to contain his academical writings, together with many other matters, consisting of fugitive and occasional pieces; some of which had been printed in separate pamphlets, some in newspapers, magazines, and other periodical publications, and many yet in manuscript. Among these productions were to be found:

1. Addresses, Letters, etc., etc., to the people of Great Britain and Ireland, during two years and a half, while employed, under the authority of Royal Brief, in the great collection, for the better establishment and support of the colleges of New York and Philadelphia.

2. Philosophical, Astronomical and Geographical papers, to be found chiefly in the first volume of the Transactions of the American Philosophical Society; together with the Rules, Charter and Laws for its first institution, and an oration before the society.

3. An account of Thomas Godfrey, of Philadelphia, with full proofs of his being the original inventor of what has been unjustly called Hadley's Quadrant.

4. Polemical writings, viz.: Cato's Letters, containing some remarks on Paine's "Common Sense." The Anatomist, in nineteen numbers; contained in the second volume of "A Collection of Tracts, on the subject of the residence of Protestant Bishops in the American Colonies, and in answer to the writers who opposed it;" published in 1769, at New York, by John Holt. Theological Lectures, delivered to the divinity students in the College of Philadelphia; Correspondence with the Archbishop of Canterbury, in the case of the Rev. Mr. Macclenachan; Letter to the nineteen Presbyterian ministers who advocated his cause.

Political writings, viz.: Brief State and Brief View of the Politics of the Legislatures of Pennsylvania, in 1755–56, near and about the time of Braddock's defeat. Preface to a speech by J. Dickinson, Esq., in answer to Dr. Franklin's protest in the House of Assembly of Pennsylvania, with sundry other political papers, in a contest with that House, which will be noticed below.

5. Miscellaneous papers, viz.: The Rise, Progress and State of the Canal Navigation of Pennsylvania; sundry papers, addresses, etc., to be found among the proceedings of the Society for Pro-

moting Roads and Inland Navigation in the Middle States. Examination of the Connecticut claim to lands within the charter bounds of Pennsylvania, with a large Appendix, containing copies of charters, royal grants and other valuable documents; a collection of papers, drawn up at the request of Judge Sullivan, and transmitted to him by the Secretary of State, Timothy Pickering, Esq., for discovering and ascertaining the true river St. Croix.

An account of General Bouquet's expedition to Muskingum, with many papers relating to the Illinois, and the ancient boundaries between the English and French tribes.

To the above were to be added Dr. Smith's large share (which would be distinguished as far as possible from the share of his coadjutors) of tracts published in Colonel Bradford's American Magazine of 1757–58, as follows:

6. The Planter, in twenty-two numbers.
7. The Antigallican, in seven numbers.
8. The Watchman, in eight numbers.*
9. An account of the very arbitrary proceedings of the Assemblies, or Legislatures, of Pennsylvania, of which we have mentioned in our Vol. I.,† which obliged Dr. Smith to undertake a voyage to Great Britain, and which would contain many interesting papers, supported by the authority of some of the greatest characters that ever adorned the bar or the bench in the law courts of England, namely: Pratt and Yorke, then Attorney and Solicitor General, both of them afterwards Lord High Chancellors of the nation.‡

The publication was begun in an elegant way by Mr. Maxwell, a well-known publisher of Philadelphia at the beginning of this century, of whom Dr. Smith says, in a prefatory note dated Falls of Schuylkill, August 2, 1802:

I have conveyed the copyright on easy terms, induced thereto on my part by his attention to the correctness of his press, amidst the large numbers of hands which he is obliged to employ, as well as by his attention to myself, in attending me at my house in the country; to aid

---

* The "Hermit," which was first published in this American Magazine, is printed in the concluding part of the first volume of Dr. Smith's Works, published by Maxwell, in 1803.
† Pages 167–187; 203–209.
‡ By the names of Lord Camden and Lord Morden.

my failing sight, in reading and correcting the proof sheets, especially those taken from the manuscript copies.

He has taken the risk of the publication upon himself, and I hope those friends who yet remain alive, who formerly lent their names to encourage the work (many of them being, alas! now no more), were influenced by other motives than the expectation of seeing their names prefixed to a book, in a subscription list; and that whatever favor they intended towards me may be transferred to my publisher, who, being worthy of success, I pray he may be blest with it in every liberal and just undertaking.

I have given in an Appendix* a list of such things of Dr. Smith as I either know or suppose to be his, which were published in his lifetime, from the year 1750 to the year 1803.

In September of this year Mrs. Williamina Cadwalader, writing from the Falls of Schuylkill to her aunt, Mrs. Ridgely, of Dover, says:

Dr. Smith is near his end. On last Sunday he preached for St. John's Parish, in the city. I was with him, as he would have me, being afraid to go with his servant alone. I do not think he will ever preach again, at least not with my consent.

This, I have reason to think, was the last sermon which Dr. Smith ever preached. The church now called St. John's Church, Northern Liberties, was not admitted into the convention of the Protestant Episcopal Church of Pennsylvania until 1816, nor organized in form until 1815, when the Rev. George Boyd, D. D., was its rector. But the parish had a history much earlier than this; so far back as June, 1772, Dr. Smith interesting himself in originating the identical parish which forty-three years afterwards took corporate shape.†

---

* See Appendix, No. X.

† This fact is made patent by a document in Mr. Robert Coulton Davis's possession. It is a receipt, dated January 20, 1787, by "J. Booth," who promises to return it to Dr. Smith "at the town of New Castle," for a document described as in these words:

June 11th.

Whereas a certain lottery, called the Wilmington Lottery, in two classes, is set on foot for raising £2,484 Pennsylvania money, in which Richard McWilliam, Esq., and Messrs. Jonas Stedham, George Evans and Joseph Stedham, of New Castle county, are managers, who, it is declared in the scheme of the said lottery, that the money to be raised thereby is to be divided as follows, viz.: *Five-sixths of the net profits towards the building and finishing St. John's Church, in the Northern Liberties of the city of Philadelphia,* and the remaining sixth part for public uses within the county of New Castle, under the direction of the said managers, and of Rev. Dr. Richard Peters, Rev.

CHAPTER LXI.

Dr. Smith's last illness one of some length—Reads the proof-sheets of Maxwell's two volumes, at the Falls of Schuylkill, in April, 1803 —He is brought to his son's, William Moore Smith's, house, in town— Dies there May 14, 1803—Is buried in his Mausoleum at the Falls— His last official act—Mrs. Cadwalader to Mrs. Ridgely—Account of his funeral—Bills paid by his Executors—Dr. Smith's estate.

THE commencement of the year 1803 found Dr. Smith in a dying condition. The death of his sister and of his man *Primus* had left him much dependent upon those whom in some senses were strangers—strangers at least in comparison with those who had been long about him and were acquainted with all his habits and wants. His sons were affectionate; but one of them, William Moore Smith, was about to embark for England, as agent for the British claimants in America, and to take with him his own son, William Rudulph Smith, who up to that time had been constantly with his grandfather, and had been of great assistance to him in the arrangement of his papers. Charles Smith was living in the city of Lancaster, and engaged in public duties, and Richard was in Huntingdon, a town then at a great distance, as respected any ability to get to him readily, from Philadelphia. The only relatives he had near him (in the city) were his daughter-in-law (Mrs. Ann Smith), Mrs. Williamina Cadwalader, and his half-brother, Judge Thomas Smith. These, with Bishop White and Benjamin R. Morgan, Esq., were constantly by his side, and Judge Smith,

---

Dr. William Smith and Rev. Mr. Jacob Duche, of Philadelphia, and Rev. Mr. Laurence Gerelius, of Wilmington; now, that there may be no future misunderstanding relative to the disposition of the said sixth part, which, if the lottery is successful, may clear about £400, it is agreed that £70 of the same be applied by us towards the use of Trinity Church, in the borough of Wilmington, and the remainder towards the public school now erecting in the borough of Wilmington, or in that proportion if the said sixth part should prove more or less than as above estimated.

Witness our hands this 11th day of June, 1772.

Richard Peters,	Richard McWilliam,
William Smith,	Jonas Stedham,
Laurence Gerelius,	George Evans,

J. Stedham.

the Bishop and Mr. Morgan made such an arrangement that one
of them was with him every night. My grandmother (to whom I
am indebted for these facts) drove to the Falls of Schuylkill every
morning, leaving her little children to the care of her servants, at
her home, then at the southeast corner of Fifth and Chestnut
streets, in the city. Maxwell, the publisher, sent proofs of the
two volumes of his sermons daily to him, and these were corrected by himself, though the books were not so entirely completed as that they could be published in Dr. Smith's lifetime.
In the earlier part of the year we find him writing to the painter,
Gilbert Stuart, a letter too characteristic and interesting to be
omitted in our memoir:

FALLS OF SCHUYLKILL, February 28, 1803.

MY DEAR SIR: By Dr. Rush's order I am now wholly confined to
my bed-chamber; the doctor, my brother and my friends who have any
regard for me or business with me, visit me here. I grow every day
weaker; but, thank God, he keeps my mind sound and my intellect not
much impaired. I beg the pleasure and comfort of a short visit from
you in a day or two. My son, in two or three weeks, will embark for
England. I shall never see him again, as I believe. He has consented
to sit to you for his picture before he goes. I shall pay you cash down
as we may agree. An answer *per* bearer is requested by

Your affectionate   WM. SMITH.

TO MR. GILBERT STUART.

In the month of April Mrs. Ann Smith, assisted by Bishop White
and Mr. Morgan, brought the venerable sufferer from the Falls
of Schuylkill in a carriage, followed by a wagon containing his
" chest and red trunk " of papers, to her house, already mentioned,
at the southeast corner of Fifth and Chestnut streets, Philadelphia,
where he died, May 14, 1803, at midnight, in the second story
front room; the same in which my father (Richard Penn Smith)
was born, and in which Washington had sat to Gilbert Stuart for
the portrait now in the Boston Athenæum. Bishop White called
in the morning, and, in pursuance of a request which before death
had been made by his departed brother, took away the " red
trunk," containing the church papers, of which I have spoken.*
The following is the last letter I have ever found of Dr.
Smith:

---

* For account of these papers see Appendix, No. XI.

Dr. Smith to Charles Smith.

PHILADELPHIA, May 2, 1803.

DEAR CHARLES: I write you this to acknowledge the receipt of your letter and check. . . . I get weaker every day, and am wholly confined to my bedchamber, and cannot reasonably expect more than a very uncertain and short time to live, and would not wish to give you a moment's unhappiness. . . . My *two* volumes of sermons, etc., are finished, and printed, but I feel I could not rest in my grave were my wishes not carried out. But to you, my dear son, and your brother William, I trust this matter, which is of so much import to me. . . . Your wife and dear children, whom I never expect to see again, I love; I leave my blessing upon them.

Your affectionate father till death,

WILLIAM SMITH.

To CHARLES SMITH, Lancaster.

The only accounts I have of the funeral of Dr. Smith are from my grandmother and a letter from Mrs. Cadwalader. My grandmother informed me that Bishop White officiated at the mausoleum; that she and my father and uncle (Dr. Smith's two grandchildren*) were the only members of the family who followed the body to the vault. His children were all too far away to communicate to them the fact of his dissolution in time for them to be present at the funeral. Mrs. Cadwalader, widow of General John Cadwalader, was at this time residing on the estate at the Falls, near Dr. Smith's dwelling.

Mrs. Williamina Cadwalader to Mrs. Ridgely.

[Extract.]

PHILADELPHIA, May 19, 1803.

I suppose Willey will tell you that Dr. Smith died on Saturday last, and was buried on Tuesday evening in his mausoleum, at the Falls. He was carried in a hearse from his son William's house, attended by sixteen carriages, six of them filled with clergy. He had none of his children with him, but was attended affectionately by his amiable daughter-in-law, Mrs. William Moore Smith.

From your very affectionate

WILLIAMINA CADWALADER.

---

* The last official act of Dr. Smith in his position as a clergyman he makes note of thus:

"August 1, 1802.—Baptized my two grandchildren, viz.:

" 1. Samuel, who will be six years of age 1st September next.

" 2. Richard, who was three years of age 13th March last."

In the office of the Register of Wills, in Philadelphia, I find the following list of bills paid by the executors :

Dr. Benjamin Rush, medical attendance,	$334.34
James Traquair, inscription, etc., for vault,	60.94
David Edwin, for engraving portrait,	45.00
Robert Haydock, stone work for vault,	120.00
Dr. Physick, medical attendance,	32.00
Dr. Bensell, medical attendance,	12.50
Subscription to road in Huntingdon for 1803,	10.00
Funeral expenses,	199.14
For mourning rings, as per will,	280.00

The mausoleum erected by Dr. Smith was used by some members of the family as a place of sepulture until the death of my father, Richard Penn Smith, in the year 1854. This gentleman being aware that at no distant day his estate would be sold for the purpose of division, directed that a lot should be purchased in the cemetery of Laurel Hill, which is in sight of the old homestead, and that the bodies, now about fourteen in number, should be removed to that place. This was supposed to have been done with all the bodies, including that of Dr. Smith; but from the fact of their having been *buried* in the vault, those of Dr. Smith were not discovered, and so were not removed. They were subsequently disinterred by me, and it is my intention to reinter them in the grounds either of Christ Church, where he so often preached, or in those of St. Peter's, which he dedicated.

Dr. Smith left a large landed property. It was in different parts of Pennsylvania and New York, the largest part perhaps being in Huntingdon county, Pa. He had made during his lifetime a careful division among his children, who all received a fair estate, indeed I may say a large one. His property at the Falls of Schuylkill fell to the portion of my grandfather, William Moore Smith, and was in turn inherited by his son, Richard Penn Smith. From him I received a portion of the same property, which will in time be the portion of *my* son and my grandchildren.

29

CHAPTER LXII.

Causes of Dr. Smith not being consecrated Bishop of Maryland—Conclusion.

We have said, in earlier parts of this volume, that in August, 1783, Dr. Smith was elected by the Ecclesiastical Convention of Maryland—a body composed of the whole clergy of the State—to be Bishop of their diocese. The body recommended him as "a fit person and every way qualified to be invested with the sacred office of a bishop;" the convention declaring itself "perfectly satisfied that he will duly execute this office . . . to the edifying of the church and the glory of God." We have also stated that in 1786 the wardens and vestry of the parish in which he ministered for years added to this, their emphatic testimony to the correctness of his life and conversation.* With all this we know, however, that Dr. Smith was never consecrated to the Episcopal order. I am not able to say with certainty why this happened. While I think it certain that Dr. Smith would have made an imposing figure had his robe been sleeved with lawn; and indeed would have been in many ways an efficient bishop, there were certain reasons which I can conceive of as having been sufficient to cause some opposition to his consecration.

We know what transcendent qualifications are required by the apostle of him who is to be ordained to this most sacred office. With other qualifications he must be blameless, vigilant, sober, not given to wine, patient, apt to teach, not only of good behavior, but having a good *report* of them which are without. The apostle plainly intimates, I think, that a man may be of good behavior; but, from the misrepresentations, including even those that are slanderous, or from simple misapprehensions of others, may not have a good report of them that are without. Such a man, however innocent—indeed, however holy—and though the report of them that are without may be the result of wicked falsehoods and

---

*See these two documents *supra*, pp. 100, 240.

malignant persecutions, the apostle declares to us should not be
made bishop. And the reason of the apostle's view is obvious.
The work of evangelizing the world is a work to be done among
the ignorant, the prejudiced, the obstinate, the wilful, the slanderous, the wicked and profligate of every sort, and among them only
or chiefly. It is a practical work. However blameless, vigilant,
sober, patient, and of whatever good behavior, the apostle's injunction would forbid us to appoint a man to this office who would be
politically obnoxious to any in his diocese, however much more
marked by obedience to the Scripture his political conduct might
have been than theirs; or to appoint one who, however fit by all
other qualities, by weight of years could not possibly be longer
"apt to teach."

In Dr. Smith's case his years alone were such as were likely to
make him soon unfit for "the office of a bishop." In 1789, only
three years after the earliest date at which he could have been
consecrated, he resigned, "on account of his advanced age," the
presidency of a society created largely by himself, in which for
thirty years he had been the most active, intelligent and efficient
administrator, and of which the duties in 1789 had ceased to be
laborious.* Moreover, there was no salary attached to the Episcopate of Maryland. Dr. Smith was too old to find one in the
rectorship of a parochial church. His productive property was
small. The means of sustaining life were therefore wanting to
him in the good work of a bishop's office.

2. Without doubt Dr. Smith had not favored a Revolution which
involved the separation of the colonies from the mother country.
He had both written and spoken against our declaring ourselves
independent; and, in common with not a few of the most upright
and honorable citizens of Philadelphia, respected then and
venerated now, including names like those of the Willings,
the Tilghmans, the Chews, was looked upon with some dis-
favor during much of the whole war. The Church of England
had been so long and so intimately associated in popular estimation with the Crown and the British army—which, in September,
1777, had landed on or near the soil of Maryland, had, by its

---

* The Corporation for the Relief of the Widows and Children of Clergymen. See
Wallace's Century of Beneficence—1769-1879.

violence and robberies on its way to Philadelphia, left such horrid impressions even in Maryland, the adjoining State to Pennsylvania—that it would not have been wise to consecrate for the Bishop of Maryland any man who had not been notoriously in sympathy with the popular cause. Bishop Provoost had hardly any other special title to being selected for New York but that he had been a warm Whig, and had borne arms against the British invaders: and the influence even of the admirable Bishop White was without doubt much increased in a republican community by the fact that he had been a chaplain in the Congress of 1776, and from the first a friend of Washington and a supporter of the American cause.

3. A bishop, it is declared, must be "no striker." My ancestor, some persons thought, did not satisfy this requisition. He never threw the first stone. But if any one threw a first stone at him, he did not always stop with a second stone in return. He arrested the throwing of stones from the enemy's quarter by throwing them from his own side with such rapidity, force and well-directed aim, that he who began the quarrel was soon obliged to retreat precipitately from the field. Thus he dealt with the Quaker Assembly of Pennsylvania, long bearing and long forbearing; but when provoked past measure, bearding them in their den, dragging them across the ocean before the king in council, reversing all their decrees, and then compelling them to assemble in their own jurisdiction and hear, in the presence of their constituents, the royal record of their humiliation.* He acted in short, much like a man who, having been bitten by some snarling whelp, takes him with one hand by the back of the neck, and, holding his head in the air, with a whip in the other, lashes him till the animal's sides are so corrugated with welts that he never can be found again to offend anybody. This was acting, no doubt, much in accord with that good council which, while advising that a man "beware of entrance in a quarrel," yet adds:

> " But being in,
> Bear it that the opposer may beware of thee,"

though not acting with that better teaching which tells us that when smitten on one cheek we should turn the other for the

---

* See Vol. I., pp. 208, 209.

same operation upon *it*.   Dr. Smith's conduct, in short, was very
like that of a man; not quite so much like that of a clergyman.

He had been, in fact, from his first advent into Pennsylvania, in
all the political controversies which agitated the Province. His
wit was terribly keen, and left deep wounds even when upon the
surface there seemed to be smoothness. Such a man might have
attained a high degree of grace, but there was still too large a
share of nature left behind in him. This militant spirit became
more and more subject to the law of the Gospel, with his advancing
life; and in the end the spirit of Christ, we would humbly hope—
indeed, we feel well assured—quite constrained him. But in the
decline of life his physical strength rendered him incapable of any
active work.

We ought to add, in this connection, that there was never any
root of bitterness in Dr. Smith's temper. His anger was not a
sinful anger. The sun went not down upon it. This was illustrated in regard to the very Quakers of whom we have been
speaking. They had acted toward him in 1757 with a dictatorial, unjust and persecuting spirit, and had greatly injured the
interests of the Province, and especially of his college and schools.
He put an end to their power to do mischief in this way, and put
an end to it energetically and with effect. Yet in 1777, when,
amidst popular insult, the Quakers were arrested and sent off to
Virginia in exile, because they would not *promise* to abstain from
communications with General Howe, Dr. Smith entertained them
on their way and ministered to their comfort with every mark of
kindness.

4. It was a notorious fact then, as now, that Dr. Smith had been
a great speculator in real estate. He bought large quantities of
land in many parts of Pennsylvania, looking forward to peopling
and improving them, and to a rise in coming time in their value.
In this there was nothing immoral. Indeed, the great Earl of
Verulam, Francis Bacon, who tells us that "the ways to enrich are
many, and most of them foul," reckons "plantations"—within
which term Dr. Smith's purchases and purposes came—as among
"ancient, primitive and heroical works;" and says also that "the
improvement of the ground is the most natural obtaining of riches,
for it is our great mother's blessing: the earth's;" though he tells
us that is "slow."   As we have said, there was nothing immoral

in any part of this mode of acquiring wealth. Nevertheless, it did tend to entangle him with the affairs of this life, and did tend to prevent his applying himself wholly to that one great duty which lies upon the bishop as well as upon the priest, and to his "drawing all his cares and studies in that way."

It was doubtless to these tastes or pursuits of Dr. Smith that Bishop White refers when, speaking of him, he says:

His talents are in no need of my recommendation, and had they been devoted to literature, and not too much devoted to politics and speculations in land, there is no knowing the measure of celebrity which might be thought too great to be attained.

5. All the reasons which I have enumerated why Dr. Smith was not the best person for a bishop in a new, impoverished and highly republican diocese, without doubt existed, and they were all good reasons why he should not have been consecrated, though no one of them fixed upon him the stain of immorality. A graver one has been made. It is not exactly that he was "*given* to wine"— *such* a charge, in view of the strong attestations of good character from his diocese and parish, the best witnesses of his daily life, would have borne falsehood on its face—but that his habits being, in accordance with those of most gentlemen in his day, somewhat social, he was on one occasion, in the year 1785, so far overtaken as to have transcended the limits allowable to the clergy. He himself, we know, denied the charge and invited proof of it; no proof that was legal proof—by which I mean that a court of justice would have listened to—was ever, that I know of, given. That nothing like habitual impropriety in this way was ever indulged, or ever supposed to be, is shown, I think, conclusively, not only by the attestations of this diocese and parish, above referred to, but by the numberless appointments of honor and confidence with which, after this time, he was invested up to his very dying hours; the president of every house of clerical and lay deputies, from the time of the constitution of such a chamber till his physical infirmities rendered him incapable of presiding anywhere at all; the successively selected preacher year after year of all the church at the consecration of her first three bishops consecrated in America;* appointed on almost every important committee constituted by the church conventions in his time, and usually their

---

* Clagget, Bass and Smith.

chairman; the friend and companion of the most virtuous and most honored men of his age and country.

We may add, that no journal of the convention shows that Dr. Smith ever desired consecration, whatever his friends and admirers may have urged; and none of his correspondence which I have seen, either in print or in MS., shows that he ever intended so to apply. He preached, as we know, and with graceful alacrity, in 1792, at the consecration of Dr. Clagget to the Episcopate of Maryland; and, in the sermon then delivered, speaks before the assembled bishops and clergy and lay deputies, of the humble station which he himself had *chosen* to hold in the church during the remaining space in his life.

I may add that Dr. Smith, from the year 1779 till the year 1789, when it was restored, had in view, notwithstanding his residence and activity in Maryland, one great object—dearer, far, to him, I think, than a mitre—and that was the restitution to HIS college of its charter. For this, wherever he was and in whatever pursuit engaged, he was continually laboring. He never closed his residence nor took from it its furniture, at the Falls of Schuylkill, even when a citizen of Maryland, both as the head of a college and as the rector of a parish there. He left it in charge of his sister Isabella, a sister devoted to his fame, who kept it with care, subject to his wishes and interests alone. He was constantly at Philadelphia, laboring in his great object. In 1789, the year in which the charter was restored, Dr. Smith had become so much advanced in years, and ecclesiastical ambitions had so little hold on his affections, that he seems to have been indifferent to the subject.

I suppose that in times like these, when the church is agitated with much discussion upon its proper characteristics, I shall be expected to say something upon what will be called Dr. Smith's "Churchmanship"—of what sort it was: high, low, or what else.

I have already said, in different parts of this book, that Dr. Smith's cast of mind did not lead him into any of the subtleties of divinity. He was not a recluse, nor by distinction a student of divinity. He was not, except by occasion, and only then temporarily, even a parish priest, bound to set before his hearers his views upon topics important, no doubt, to be taught from the pulpit, but not in their nature relating directly to practical duties. His distinction, so far as preaching was concerned, was as a pulpit orator, wherein he was, I think, the first of his time in Philadelphia; for, though his pupil Duché was, so far as mère elocution was concerned, his equal, possibly his superior, Dr. Smith, in mental power and richness of material, was so far above him that no comparison could be made between them.

I may further say that nothing would have been so unwise in Dr. Smith as to have been largely enforcing, during his time, any one special class of views which good men in our church have, in all its history since the Reformation, entertained, in opposition to other views entertained by other men as good, and, in my view—assuming the liturgy, the rubrics, the articles and the homilies, all united, as expressing her views—as much within the church's pale as they. It must be remembered that when Dr. Smith first came to Philadelphia there was but a single church of the Church of England in all the city—old Christ Church. The Quakers, still writhing under the attacks of Keith, who had left them, were embittered towards the very name of the Church of England. *It* was the great object of their hatred, and Dr. Smith himself tells us that it was by acting on the maxim *Divide et impera*, that they hoped to destroy it.*

At a later day came on the *Illuminati*, the infidelity of France and the assaults of its revolution upon every sort of religion, and even upon the existence of a God; when all who named the name of Christ were in some degree compelled to unite, the one with the other, in order to preserve Christianity among the people at all. How inappropriate in either epoch would have been discussions, elevate though they were, upon topics not in their nature, perhaps, identical with those upon which "the others reasoned high," of providence, foreknowledge, will and fate, fixed fate, free-will, foreknowledge absolute, but ending, often much like theirs, which "found no end, in wandering mazes lost."

Indeed, during most of Dr. Smith's term of clerical life there was, if my ideas of church history are right, no great agitation

---

* See Vol. I. of this biography, page 220. We can in this day hardly form an idea of the power of the Quakers in *old* Philadelphia. Think of Bishop White devoting many months of his life to writing an answer to Barclay's Apology! He considered this answer his ablest and most finished work.

anywhere on the particular class of topics which now disturbs us; not novelties, any of them, except in the degree to which they are carried. The same class of topics, indeed, agitated the Church of England in different degrees during the reigns of Elizabeth, Edward VI., James I., and Charles I. So they did in the days of Charles II., William III., and Anne. We may even say that they were questions which embarrassed the Reformers themselves. They are, some of them, questions of essential difficulty, and about which those who think most, talk little, and dogmatize not at all. But in the days of the first and second and third Georges, the agitation had ceased. The first two were stolid Germans, and the third, though a good man and a far better king than those who believe in Byron think—not a schoolman or casuist. The theological writings of the day were of another complexion. The old questions have now in the periodicity of things of course come back. We have had the anabasis. We are now at the *acmé*. The decline will begin to-mcrrow.

But still I am asked by one, "Was not Dr. Smith a high-churchman?" and by another, "Was not Dr. Smith a low-churchman?" Αφρον! I am tempted to exclaim in response to one inquirer as to the other. Tell me, first, what *is* "a low-churchman?" What is "a high-churchman?"

In the days succeeding the English Revolution of 1688 the matter was half a political question If a man adhered to the Stuarts, he was a high-churchman. If to the House of Orange, a low-churchman.

At a later day, with us, Dr. Seabury was opposed to having the laity take any part in the government of the church, had a mitre, wrote himself "Samuel Connecticut," "Samuel, Bishop of Connecticut," and in every form, I believe, but that one which the churches in the Southern and Middle States recommended bishops to write themselves, in which the minutes of conventions in which he sat described *him*, and in which *he* described the only bishop, if I remember, that he assisted to consecrate. In popular idea this made him a *very* high-churchman. Bishop White and Bishop Provoost insisted on the admission of the laity, wrote their own names more humbly, did *not* use mitres. This made them in popular idea *low*-churchmen; not that between Bishop Seabury and both the other bishops, so far as I know the views of Bishop

Provoost, distinctions of view better making the titles did not
exist.

Bishop Hobart was called a high-churchman and denounced
through all his life as such, not because he held to any view of
the Eucharist or of the ministry, or performed any services or
offices of the church in a way largely different from many of his
brethren, but because he enforced upon his clergy strongly, and
often with fervor and with eloquence, that the church founded by
the Saviour, and which he (the bishop) considered best represented
in this day by the Protestant Episcopal Church in the United
States of America, subsisted under certain distinctive principles of
doctrine, ministry and worship, and not under all the shapes into
which fanaticism, ambition, ignorance, or interest might choose to
mould it. With no considerable difference of opinion from him
on this point, although his mode of teaching it was less fervid,
Bishop White was called a low one.

In 1826–27 we had in Pennsylvania a body of clergy whose
views and practices were unlike those of Bishop White. He then
took a strong distinction, showing in his mind great differences
between low-churchmen and low-churchmen. There were the
men known in history of *England* as low-churchmen, Tillotson, Burnet, and some others a little higher, perhaps, though
not any, lower than they, which class expressed, with more
or less precision, the Bishop's views. But those known at the
date we speak of as low-churchmen in Pennsylvania—with whose
theological opinions, though, happily, it may be reasonably
hoped, not with their tempers and practices, a part of the
clergy, I presume, remain in line—he repelled and renounced
in memorable language his affiliation with. One of them,
in a convention of the church, where the degrees of altitude
were strongly marked, alluded to the Bishop himself as being
a low-churchman—one of their party. "The gentle old man,"
says a narrator of the scene, "showed that, like flint, if struck hard
enough, he could flash fire. He rose at once, apologizing for such
an unusual thing on his part as interrupting a debate, but the personal allusion to himself must be his excuse. As the word was
used in England and a hundred years ago, perhaps it might not
be altogether incorrect to call him a low-churchman. ' But,' continued he, with an emphasis rare indeed as coming from his lips,

as the word is understood in this country, you might as well call me a Turk or a Jew.'"*

Some men are " high " on some points—" low " on others.

We have spoken in a note of Bishop Hopkins. From his first entrance into the church he was a devoted reader, lover and expositor of the fathers. Those called the apostolic ones I think he could have said by heart. There was not a line of the *Origines Sacræ* which he could not point to. Never did *he* find "ancient authors"—by whom are meant the early fathers—to contradict the Bible, whether in its parts new or old; but, on the contrary, found in them the Bible's strong supports. In all the "wrought gold" which decorates the clothing of the daughter of Zion he delighted. The ornaments of the chancel, the dress of the priesthood, the fragrance of myrrh, aloes and cassia out of the ivory palaces—all these things found interest in his beautiful tastes just as much as did those higher things, in his deeper heart, which make the church "all glorious within." These first are the matters which, in the estimation of many, make the *alto*, as in their estimation do dislikes of them the *basso*. But Bishop Hopkins's ecclesiastical views—his views of doctrine, discipline and worship alike—were in many respects very high; and they were got from the early fathers, as from the Epistles and Gospels. It is not difficult to understand his views, many of which I admire. But it is difficult to assign him to any *class* of thinkers on the Episcopal bench. Yet a party which was composed of the lowest churchmen that ever were in Pennsylvania, were desirous to make him bishop of its vast diocese, rather than to have Dr. Bird Wilson, the last of men to carry anything but holiness of life into lofty pitch, or than Henry Ustick Onderdonk, the greatest original thinker and logician of the American church, but who, if his tract on Regeneration expressed his best judgments, which I hardly think it did, was more like themselves than like any high expositor in the Church of England.

---

* Life of Bishop Hopkins, by one of his sons, second edition, page 101. I know from a person of indubitable authority yet living, and who was present in the convention where Bishop White's declaration is said to have been made, that this statement of Bishop Hopkins's son is strictly accurate; and I have heard it also from another of no less accuracy, who was present, but is now dead. I may add that from my own recollections of what I heard from many persons, witnesses of the scenes, the account of all the proceedings of 1826 and 1827, as given in the Life of Bishop Hopkins, is strictly true. *But not the idea that Bishop White voted in 1786 for his own election.*

In this day, accepting, as tests, the standards of ordinary
conversation, I am unable to say what high-churchmen and
what low-churchmen are. Indeed, if I had not certain old-
fashioned, but, as I think, very good charts, on which the "main
channel" and all important soundings are marked, I should
be unable to tell where, ecclesiastically, I am sailing—indeed,
whether to quicksands or the port. It is a good while, in the
political world, since I have found any body of men, large enough
to be called a party, in which I am willing to class myself. I
begin of late to fear that I shall be in the same condition in matters far more important.

Until, therefore, my inquiring friends define for me their terms
a little better than they do, they must excuse my not answering
very categorically their inquiries.

On certain subjects, which some persons consider as distin-
guishing the degrees of ecclesiastical altitude, and which, if they
do not distinguish them in essence, are often more or less
identified with them, we need not attempt to "locate" Dr. Smith;
for he has sufficiently "located" himself. That he abhorred all
irregularities in the performance of divine service, the use of *extempore* prayers there—declaiming against any of the church's
doctrines, as Regeneration (in the sense in which the church uses
the term)—that there was not in him the least tincture of Metho-
dism or Calvinism; all this can be inferred from the way in which
he speaks of the Rev. Mr. Macclanechan, the founder of St. Paul's
Church, Philadelphia. He is describing this reverend gentleman
to the Archbishop of Canterbury:

With a huge stature and voice more than stentorian, he started up
before his sermon; and, *instead of using any of the excellent forms provided in our Liturgy*, or a form in the nature and substance of that
enjoined by the 55th Canon, he addressed the Majesty of Heaven with a
long catalogue of epithets, such as "*sin-pardoning, all-seeing, heart-
searching, rein-trying God.*" *We thank thee that we are all here to-day,
and not in hell.* Such an unusual manner in our church sufficiently
fixed my attention, which was exercised by a strange *extempore* rhapsody
of more than twenty minutes, and afterwards a sermon of about sixty-
eight minutes more. I have heard him again and again, and still we
have the same wild, incoherent rhapsodies of which I can give no account other than that they consist of a continual ringing of the changes
upon the words "Regeneration," "Instantaneous conversion," "Im-

puted righteousness," "The new birth," etc. But I find no practical
use made of these terms, nor does he offer anything to explain them,
or to tell us what he would be at.

What sort of respect Dr. Smith had for Episcopal authority and
for the "Induction," or, as we in our American church call it, the
"Institution" of ministers, may be inferred from his further account of the reverend gentleman just named:

> Mr. Macclanechan spoke much of his popularity; the *call* he had
> from the people to be their minister, which he pretends, gives the only
> right title. The *Bishop's* authority he spoke of very disrespectfully,
> and said it could never bind the people. I replied that . . . it was
> certainly binding on *him* and *me*, who were of the clergy.*

In regard to the ministry Dr. Smith declares that the three
orders of bishops, priests and deacons are necessary to the
proper establishment of the church, and shows everywhere his
high appreciation of the threefold order.† And if, referring to
what had been enacted both by the Church and Parliament of
England, he suggested it to the Bishop of London to consider
whether anything could be done to bring into our church, without
other ordination than what they had, the German Lutheran clergy
of Pennsylvania, it must be remembered that he does not express
any opinion on the subject himself; but treats it as one which it
does not become *him* "any further to meddle with than just to
mention the facts and the great accession it might bring to our
church."‡ He considered possibly that as there was no bishop in
America who could have ordained these persons when they entered on their work, and was none now, the case fell within an
exception recognized by many learned and pious men in the
Church of England who were considered sound churchmen,
and which, *though under very different circumstances of fact*, Dr.
White recognized as temporarily dispensing with regular ordination
in our own ministers. He knew that the Church of England
recognizes the validity of the Moravian, Swedish, and perhaps the
Danish orders. We have noted the high respect paid in Philadelphia to the Lutheran body; Dr. Peters, the rector of Christ
Church, saying, in 1764, when preaching from one of its pulpits,

---

* See this work, Vol. I., p. 225.   † *Supra*, p. 97.   ‡ Vol. I., p. 404.

that he had "a very sensible pleasure in being able *publicly to declare* that between your church, the Swedish, and our own Episcopal Church there has always been, *from the very first*, a kind and loving *participation* of divine service and brotherly love." At a much later day, 1794, when the German Lutheran Church was burned down, the corporation of Christ Church put their own sacred edifice at the command, for one part of the day, Sundays and week-days, of these brethren.* My ancestor may perhaps have considered the German Lutheran body as standing in a favored position. My ecclesiastical learning will not bear me out in deciding how this may have been. Neither would it leave his integrity in any way "off color," if we were to suppose that his action in this respect—a mere suggestion to the Bishop of London for *him* to consider the matter—was done through policy, at the desire of Dr. Muhlenberg, or some other Lutheran clergyman, whom he was willing to conciliate, and without expectation that the Bishop of London would receive them.

Dr. Smith hoped to see in our large cities the churches daily open, and morning and evening prayer said daily throughout the year.†

He did NOT wish to see the services made too "naked,"‡ and we may be sure, from what he had provided on several occasions of religious solemnity,§ that he would have enjoyed the *choral* service—that form of service which, ever since the Reformation, the Church of England has in her cathedrals, her chapels-royal and collegiate churches, in her Temple church, and in the churches of her Inns of Court—everywhere, in short, throughout her beautiful land—would have enjoyed it, I say, to the very depths of his soul.

In regard to the holy communion, he assisted Bishop Seabury in making that which was a fuller consecration of the elements than the ceremony which—yielding to the demands of Puritanism—the Church of England of his day made and now makes: and was, in fact, the person who carried through the lower House of the convention of 1789 the views called high-church, of the great churchman and Bishop of Connecticut.|| He made, too, of that service an imposing celebration.¶ He enforced upon his parish-

---

* Dorr's History of Christ Church, p. 218.   † *Supra*, p. 207.   ‡ *Supra*, p. 210.
§ See Vol. I., p. 544; also Dr. Smith's Writings, Maxwell's ed., Vol. II., pp. 49, 67.
    || *Supra*, p. 290.   ¶ *Supra*, p. 199.

ioners the necessity of frequent communion; and, if we may argue from his Preface to the Proposed Book, wished to have the daily administration of it.*

Even in his Proposed Book—made in part, but in concession to prejudices—he left that ancient rubric of the Church of England which declares that a sick person, when visited by the minister of the parish, shall "be moved to make a special confession of his sins, if he feel his conscience troubled with any weighty matter;" and while he did not leave the *specific* personal absolution of the English book, he put a form which can hardly be called, and is nowhere in our Prayer Book called, but "a *declaration* of absolu¬ tion." The Church of England calls it an "absolution." Our own church abstains from saying, in terms, exactly what "*Or this*" is. *But Dr. Smith nowhere ever proposed to introduce this sort of thing as a common practice in the church, or to make the ex- treme medicine of a burthened dying soul the common daily food of him that was in no near sight of death, and every morning and every evening of his life, if the clergy did *their* duty and had the churches open, could confess his sins publicly with the rest of God's penitent people, in his holy temple, and receive full comfort in the priestly declaration or act which follows.

Neither do we anywhere perceive, in that part of his writings which are connected with the establishment of the church in America, any such dangerous view as one which has been more than adumbrated among us, that the Protestant Episcopal Church in the United States of America is, in any essential respect *of doctrine*, discipline or worship, a church different from that great bulwark of Protestantism, the Church of England, and further re- moved than it from Popish practices, whether complete, incomplete, or inchoate, whether symbolized only or substantial.† Both in the Preface, which was his entirely, to the Proposed Book—the book of 1785—and in the Preface to our Book of Common Prayer of 1789, which, if not his entirely, was based largely on what was his, such a doctrine is repelled—repelled every way; by the whole course of the argument, which shows the propriety of occasional alterations "in *forms* and *usages*," provided "the substance of the *faith* is kept entire," and repelled by specific words which say, that with all the alterations and amendments which have been

---

* See *supra*, pp. 440, 161.   † See Appendix, No. XVII.

made "this Church is *far* from intending to depart from the Church of England in *any* essential point of doctrine, discipline, or worship; or further than local circumstances may require." Dr. Smith would not, in their hour of common peril, and when beleagured by a common enemy, have turned his back upon his "mother, the Church of England"—the church of Cranmer, and Ridley, and Latimer, and of the whole glorious host of sons who have fought for and maintained that faith for which they died—in this way. He was far too wary, if he had not been too sound-headed, ever to have made such a concession to the enemy; one which surrenders the whole case to both our present enemies, though each is more opposed to each other, than either is to us.

If the Book of Common Prayer of the Church of England authorizes, though but in latency, the practices of Rome, or, even in their smouldering ashes, still preserves Rome's living doctrines; and if they who made *our* prayer book did not intend—were far from intending—to depart from that church in *any* essential point of doctrine, discipline, or worship, or further than local circumstances require, how can we defend ourselves from the "Low Papists"—sometimes called Ritualists—who are disturbing its peace and misapplying, in a disingenuous, dangerous and unwarranted way, its doctrines? And how, again, are we to answer the authors of the so-called *Reformed* Episcopal Church? They assert exactly what this view admits, adding only to it what the declarations of the Preface to our prayer solemnly affirm. And both these parties, the semi-papists and radicals, enter our citadel together! Our whole case is given up by such a position. *Non tali auxilio, nec defensoribus istis*, would Dr. Smith have dealt with the parties who are taking us, one-half of them to the gates of Rome, and the other to the shores of Geneva. *He* would have said to them, and his position would have been true: "Our church, by the changes which it has made in the English book, coupled with the solemn assurances which it has given in the new Preface, that it does not intend to depart from the Church of England in any essential point of doctrine, discipline, or worship, or further than local circumstances require; tells you that you *misinterpret* the rubrics, prayers, and other things in the book of the Church of England; that you *wrest* them from their proper sense; and that rightly interpreted—interpreted by her articles.

her homilies, her practice for generation after generation, and by
an intelligent consideration of those circumstances and difficulties
in her history under which all were made—circumstances which
presuppose both knowledge and moral and intellectual faculties
on the part of him who is to consider them, and which are not
of the class of things to be measured on a two-foot rule, or counted
on ten fingers—that thus interpreted the Church of England is
just as far from the doctrines and the practices of Rome as is her
daughter, the church in America.

And is not this argument from a change of rubric two-edged?
The English book directs that the reader of the lessons turn himself and read so as best to be heard of all.   This direction is left
out of our rubric.   Are Popish mumblings, with face averted, authorized for *us?*   Again, that book declares that though the
elements in the Lord's Supper are to be received kneeling, no
adoration is intended to them, or to any corporal presence of
Christ's natural flesh and blood.   Our book suppresses this declaration, and makes a higher "consecration."   May *we* adore the
elements and the corporal presence?

I advert with more interest to other things.   All will agree with
me, I think, that the life of Dr. Smith was a well-spent life, actively
devoted to useful and beneficent objects.   Look at the number of
young men whom he trained in the early provincial days to religion, literature, the arts and statesmanship.   We cannot begin to
tell them; but the names of William White, Jacob Duché, John
Andrews, Thomas Coombe, Thomas Hopkinson, Samuel Magaw,
James Abercrombie, among the clergy, come to our minds, as do
those of Francis Hopkinson, William Paca, Richard Peters, Alexander Wilcocks, James Tilghman, William Bingham, Benjamin
Chew, and many others among our men of State, our lawyers and
our men of worth.   Look at his early patronage of Benjamin West,
imbuing his mind with classical taste and assisting him to the
means of developing his extraordinary genius.   Look, too, at his
disinterested and kind labor in bringing the works of young
Godfrey before the world and those of Nathaniel Evans, all the
profits of which he gives to the widows and children of the clergy.
Look at that most beneficent institution, the corporation for the
relief of these widows and children of his brethren—the long,
laborious work chiefly of his hands—still subsisting in wealth and
    30

diffusing blessings the extent of which it is hard to exaggerate. Look at his labors in the pulpit for fifty years, and that great series of sermons—making a cycle of Christian duty—which we give in our preceding pages.* What a body of texts; what a field cf thought to traverse! See him ever ready to devote his splendid powers to any cause in which he could subserve the interests of humanity. *He* was the founder of the American Philosophical Society, though Franklin, who was not in the country then, nor for years afterwards, got the credit of it. An astronomer, a classical scholar, a statesman, an orator. How various his powers! how high his accomplishments!

Of his labors in the councils of the church how can we speak too highly? During much of the Provincial epoch he was its one great character. To him more than to any other person, nay, more than to all other persons in the Province, Pennsylvania owes its deserved reputation for the sound, learned and pious clergy which, unlike Virginia and some other States, it had before the Revolution. And after the peace of 1783 no man but WILLIAM WHITE—he the fruit of Dr. Smith's training from his *seventh* year till his seventeenth—stands before or, in point of splendid accomplishments, near him. In the work of internal improvements in Pennsylvania he was a pioneer. This State owes to his memory a debt, with large arrears of interest, which she has never thought of and will never discharge.

Of the University of Pennsylvania, now becoming a seat of learning which may rank with the colleges of "Oxford" and of Washington College, Maryland, to whose history "Ipswich" would afford an unjust similitude, what shall I say? How naturally the poet's words flow from my pen:

> Ever witness for him
> Those twins of learning that he raised in you!
> One of which fell with him,
> Unwilling to outlive the good that did it;
> The other, though unfinished, yet so famous,
> So excellent in art, and still so rising
> That Christendom shall ever speak his virtue.

---

* Pages 432–442.

APPENDIX.

No. I.—Page 61.

The Rev. Robert Blackwell, D. D.

THE REV. ROBERT BLACKWELL, D. D., as we learn from the "Annals of Newtown, Long Island," a historical work by James Riker, Esq.,* was descended from English ancestors of his own name. The ancient importance in England of the family of Blackwell, itself, is indicated, says Mr. Riker, by the fact that no less than six towns in that kingdom bear the name. An engraving in Mr. Riker's book, from an ancient seal, would indicate that the branch of this family from which the subject of our notice came was that one long settled in the county of Norfolk.

The great-grandfather of the Rev. Dr. Blackwell was named, like Dr. Blackwell himself, *Robert*. We find him established, A. D. 1676, more than two centuries ago, at Newtown, L. I., where he became owner of valuable estates upon the East river, and with them of the island in that water immediately opposite to New York, now and for two hundred years past known as Blackwell's island. He married, A. D. 1676, Mary Manningham, and died in or about the year 1717.

The son of this Robert was JACOB BLACKWELL, born August 4, 1692. He succeeded to his paternal estates, upon which he is supposed to have erected the fine mansion which he long occupied, yet, or lately, standing—directly opposite to Blackwell's island—and hereinafter mentioned.† He married, 10th of May, 1711, Mary, daughter of Captain William Hallet and Sarah, his wife, daughter of George Woolsey, of Jamaica, L. I. Captain Hallet, by grants dated December 1, 1652, and August, 1654, acquired large possessions at Hell-Gate and upon that portion of the island which now bears the name of Hallet's Cove.

---

* Page 354.

† Its position is indicated on Mr. Riker's map of Newtown as "The Old Blackwell House, now Rev. J. L. Thomson's."

(467)

The father of Dr. Blackwell was COLONEL JACOB BLACKWELL, born November 20, 1717, a son of the Jacob Blackwell just mentioned. Colonel Blackwell succeeded to the family estates on Long Island and on the East river, on the death of his father, December 1, 1744. He was a man of parts, and of liberal dispositions. In March, 1740, he assisted to erect and liberally endow a church edifice for the maintenance of the services of the Church of England. A petition made by him, and the other founders, to the royal authorities, for a charter, sets forth:

> That the petitioners have, at a very great expense, erected a decent church, and dedicated the same to the worship of Almighty God, according to the rites and ceremonies of the Church of England, as by law established, by the name of St. James's Church, and have obtained about a quarter of an acre of land adjoining, for the use of a cemetery, and were determined to make a suitable provision for the support of a minister or pastor, that religious duties, for the time to come, may be duly and regularly celebrated therein. But that they cannot carry on this good design to advantage except they be incorporated.*

The petition was granted, and the church incorporated by letters patent dated the 9th of September, 1761. The Rev. Samuel Seabury— afterwards the honored Bishop of Connecticut—was the first rector of the church.†

As early, too, it would seem, as 1759, along with his family connections of the name of Hallet, Colonel Blackwell was instrumental in establishing at Hallet's Cove, near their common residence, a school, where Greek and Roman literature should form a part of the ordinary course of education. It was placed under the charge of an Englishman named Rudge, from the city of Gloucester, in England, and who, Colonel Blackwell and his relatives certify, in a public advertisement of the school, had proved himself "a man of close application and sobriety, and to be capable of his office."‡

Prior to the French and Indian war of 1756–63 this member of the family of Blackwell had been appointed to a captaincy in the Newtown militia. He was afterwards promoted to the grade of colonel. He was early prominent in remonstrating against those measures of the British Crown, the attempt to enforce which caused to Great Britain the loss of her western empire. His landed interests, and his known attachment alike to the principles of government and freedom, caused him to be called, 29th of December, 1774, to preside at a convention of the Freeholders of Queen's county, which expressed in a series of resolutions, not surpassed as a declaration of true colonial policy, the con-

---

* Riker's Annals, 249–251; 354, 358.   † *Ibid.*, 16.   ‡ *Ibid.*, 167.

viction entertained in America of the impolitic and unjust character of the ministerial measures. He was subsequently elected to represent the important county just above named in the Provincial Convention of New York, a body which exercised great influence at this crisis and afterwards. While attending to his public duties in New York, his estates on Long Island were seized by the commander of the British forces, which had recently proved victorious in that region, and confiscated. "At the venerable stone house in Ravenswood," says the annalist of Newtown, Mr. Riker, writing A. D. 1852, "may still be seen the mark of the broad arrow (**T**) branded upon the front door by the British, denoting that it was the property of a rebel, and as such confiscated to the Crown. Colonel Blackwell, however, recovered his estates a short time before his death ; an event which occurred October 23, 1780, and which," says Mr. Riker, "the privations and pecuniary losses he suffered from the enemy are believed to have hastened."*

Colonel Blackwell married Frances, daughter of Joseph Sackett, Esq., of Queen's county, one of the Justices under the Crown for the Court of Common Pleas, and Hannah, his wife, daughter of Richard Alsop. By this marriage he had issue, the immediate subject of our notice.

THE REV. ROBERT BLACKWELL, D. D., was born May 6, 1748. We have no certain knowledge where he received his primary education ; probably in part at the English and classical school, which we have just mentioned that his father was instrumental in establishing. From the work of the Rev. Samuel Davies Alexander, entitled "Princeton College during the Eighteenth Century," we learn that he was graduated in the venerable college just named, with a bachelor's degree, A. D. 1768. King's College conferred on him, A. D. 1770, the same degree, and Princeton again the Master's, A. D. 1782. He seems to have been imbued with serious impressions from early years. His first studies, however, were apparently towards physic.

There was no theological school of the Church of England in the colonies. It is probable that Mr. Blackwell may have read divinity under the care of Dr. Samuel Auchmuty, Rector of Trinity Church, New York, or possibly under that of Mr. Seabury. While reading divinity he appears to have passed about two years as a tutor in the family of Colonel Frederick Philipse, a man of pre-eminent social importance in the colony of New York, partly in virtue of merits all his own, and partly from the vast wealth and political importance of his father, long a representative in the General Assembly of the colony, and proprietor by hereditary title of the Yonkers plantation, the whole

---

* Annals, 354-358; 175-181; 194.

manor of Philipsburg, in Westchester county, with the Upper Highland patent of Philipstown, in Putnam county.*

During his studies of divinity young Blackwell apparently kept up some of those studies in medicine and surgery which he began, as we have supposed, at an earlier date. It is plain, from several evidences, that Mr. Blackwell had considerable taste for the natural sciences. We know, by what we remember of him, that he was fond of horticulture, both the elegant branches of it and those merely useful, as he was also of the culture of the finer varieties of fruit-trees. His garden, attached to his city residence, was one of the largest in Philadelphia; even in its earlier days, and up to the very close of his long life, it afforded to him, in the rich collection both of plants and of fruits with which he had stocked it, an unfailing source of interest. His library, too, which came to his grandchildren undispersed, has its very good collection of theological and classical books, largely varied by books of the physical sciences, and especially by books on *materia medica*, therapeutics and surgery. It is obvious, too, that their owner read them.

The first mention which I have found of Mr. Blackwell in connection with the sacred ministry is in a letter from Dr. Auchmuty to the venerable Richard Peters, D. D., at this time Rector of the United Churches in Philadelphia. We give an extract:

New York, Sept. the 2d, 1771.

Rev. and Dear Sir:

The purpose of this letter is to introduce to your friendship and countenance the bearer of it, Mr. Blackwell, a serious, good young man. He has been reading divinity for some time, and I think I may venture to say that though he is not very showy, yet he will make a solid and good parish minister. If you Philadelphians are zealous in supplying Gloucester, I know of no one who would suit for that mission so well.† He is a single man, and at his first setting off a small income will suffice him. He intends a jaunt beyond Philadelphia, to explore the country and see if there are any vacancies. He is solicitous to be employed, and we have no employment here for him. He will

---

* A large part of the estates of which we have spoken came to the Colonel Philipse in whose family Mr. Blackwell was domesticated. But, on account of his loyalty to the Crown during the war for independence, these and all his other estates were confiscated by the Legislature of New York, and upon the withdrawal of the British troops from that State, in 1783, Colonel Philipse went to England, where he died in the city of Chester, a. d. 1785.

† The mission at Gloucester, established by the Society for the Propagation of the Gospel in Foreign Parts, a. d. 1766, had recently (a. d. 1767) become vacant by the death of the Rev. Nathaniel Evans, who had been appointed missionary there as far back as 1765. In 1769 the mission seems to have been offered to "Mr. Lyon, of Taunton." I am not aware that he performed any duty. In 1770, or early in 1771, Mr. David Griffith—the same person who was elected, in May, 1786, Bishop of Virginia, but relinquished the appointment—filled it for a short time, but was never fixed there.

be recommended by the clergy here and Colonel Philipse; and the recommendation will be no more than he deserves. I can easily procure him a letter from Governor Tryon to Governor Martin, but would choose, as North Carolina is a bad climate, that he should be more happily situated, as he is a good young man and deserves any good offices that the clergy can do for him.* I think it would be worth while once more to try to establish the mission at Gloucester (as it is so contiguous to your city), if there is the least prospect of success; and I know of no young man that in my opinion will do more to gain the love and esteem of any people than the bearer. He is a lump of good nature, and very diligent when he has anything to do.

I am, dear sir,

Your affectionate brother,

S. AUCHMUTY.

Attached to the mission at Gloucester, as would seem, was the very ancient Parish of St. Mary's, Colestown, in old Gloucester county, ten miles north of the town of Gloucester. And apparently on Dr. Auchmuty's suggestion, Dr. Peters (with whom perhaps was Dr. Smith) set measures on foot for the re-establishment of the mission.

The mission, as defined by the society and left by Mr. Evans, covered a territory of about sixty miles long by thirty wide, and a population of six thousand persons, of whom more than half were Quakers, the residue being people of the churches of England and Sweden, Lutherans and Presbyterians, all in about equal numbers. There was a church, St. Mary's, at Colestown (founded, it is said, about the year 1740—very ancient, certainly—still standing), and in 1766 the two congregations took a house with twelve acres of land for a parsonage, on a lease of five years.

The mission was now agreed to be re-established; the people at Cole's church promising *verbally* to pay to the support of the minister a portion of the expenses. Up to this date Mr. Blackwell had not been ordained even as a deacon. Before going to England for holy orders, he was desirous of seeing where he could fix himself with certainty on his return, as a parish minister. In addition to which the Society for the Propagation of the Gospel, into whose service as a missionary he proposed to enter, usually required, before establishing a mission, that the people where it was to be established should agree to contribute a certain sum towards sustaining it. The merely verbal agreement—probably undefined both as to persons and amounts—led to the letter which follows, from Mr. Blackwell to the clergy at Philadelphia who were desirous to re-establish the mission. It is singularly

---

* His Excellency, William Tryon, was at this time " Captain-General and Governor of New York and the Territories depending thereon in America, Chancellor and Vice-Admiral of the same."

characteristic of its author, as subsequently known during a long life and in transactions of much larger scope; direct, candid and kind; but decided in tone and full of integrity in matters of money. It is addressed to the Rev. Dr. Richard Peters, but was obviously intended for him and some other person; probably Dr. Smith. Thus it reads:

NEWTOWN, L. I., April 20, 1772.
REVEREND GENTLEMEN:

I have received your letter in answer to what Mr. Griffith wrote to Dr. Peters at my request concerning the mission at Cole's church, though the answer is not so plain and full as I could wish it.

You, gentlemen, are very sensible that the provision made in that parish for the support of a minister is, at best, but very small, and unless he could get the whole of what the people promise to give, I am sure, though I am a single man, I should be unable to stay among them. It never was my design to make money by the gospel. I always had, as I hope, far better views. Yet it is my opinion that any one who is worthy of that honorable and sacred character is also worthy of a comfortable maintenance from the people he serves. I shall accept the invitation you have given me, but I have one thing to request of you, which will be very easily performed by gentlemen of your influence; that is, that you will settle matters in such a manner with the people of Cole's church that when I come among them (if it be God's will that I return in safety) we may have no dispute about the payment of the salary. If they design to pay me, I cannot conceive why they are so fearful of giving bonds; for that is the usual way of settling among us, and is found very advantageous in its effects. It leaves no room for uneasiness on either side; each know what they have to depend upon, and each are contented with what they have agreed to.

Gentlemen, I know that you will do whatever lies in your power for the good of the church. I rest in the assurance of your kind endeavors. I return you my sincere thanks for your kind wishes towards me in a prosperous voyage and quick return.

I expect to sail in about a fortnight in the ship called the "Duchess of Gordon," Captain Winn, commander. I should have gone sooner, but our spring vessels have just returned. Captain Miller has sailed for London some time since; but I had only three days' notice, so that I was unable to get ready to go with him.

Reverend gentlemen, I remain your most obedient and humble servant,

ROBERT BLACKWELL.

Eighteen days previous to the date of this letter, Dr. Auchmuty had written to Dr. Peters:

Blackwell has received your letters and is now preparing for his voyage. I hope he will be despatched in a short time. We shall give him ample testimonials. He is a good lad, and will be useful.

On Thursday, the eleventh day of June, 1772—that day being the Feast of St. Barnabas—he was in England, at the little suburb of London called Fulham; and at a "special ordination," then and there held, was, by the then Bishop of London, the excellent Richard Terrick, "holding a special ordination, in the chapel of his palace at the said Fulham, admitted into the Holy Order of Deacons, according to the manner and form prescribed and used by the Church of England."

On the same day the newly ordained deacon, by a written document, declared that he would "conform to the Liturgy of the Church of England, as it is now by law established." He then received the Bishop of London's license and authority to perform the office of "a minister in Gloucester county or elsewhere within the Province of New Jersey in North America." On the 14th following he was ordained a Priest.

The reports of the Society for the Propagation of the Gospel in Foreign Parts now came to our aid. An abstract of the report for the year 1774 says:

> Mr. Robert Blackwell, missionary at Gloucester and Waterford, acquaints the society that he performs duty not only at Gloucester and Waterford (which latter goes by the name of Cole's Church) but also at Greenwich, about eighteen miles from Waterford, where there is a *new* church; not built purposely for the Church of England (the people at that time having no hopes of a missionary), but where the ministers thereof are to have the preference, and which Mr. Blackwell hopes will very shortly be an established church.*

The families belonging to each of these churches were about forty in number, many of whom, Mr. Blackwell notes, "were very ignorant, particularly in respect to the sacraments as living in the midst of Quakers, and destitute of the means of instruction. Appearances were, however, now more favorable, and Mr. Blackwell hopes, by God's blessing, to be an instrument of great good."

The grounds for the hope expressed by Mr. Blackwell that this new

---

* The "new church," to which Mr. Blackwell refers, was St. Peter's Church, Berkeley, founded and endowed A. D. 1770, by Thomas Clark. It was not incorporated until April 28, 1835, when it received the charter-title of "The Rector, Church Wardens and Vestrymen of St. Peter's Church in Berkeley." We find it in former days sometimes called "the church at Sand-town;" sometimes the church at Greenwich; and of later days "the church at Clarksborough." In the course of generations "the new church" of Dr. Blackwell's day became a very old one. It was resolved to build a new edifice; and the village of Clarksborough, which had grown up a little to the east of the church, though on ground originally of Thomas Clark, the founder of the edifice, being the residence of most of the worshippers, the new edifice was built there; a half of a mile, perhaps, west of the old situation, on the same street and same side of it with the old one, and directly opposite to the parsonage. On Monday morning, December 7, 1846, the venerable structure of Dr. Blackwell's day was reverently torn down, and on the 17th of the same month the new one was consecrated by Bishop Doane, under the charter name of "St. Peter's Church, Berkeley," in Clarksborough. It is agreeable to know that under the faithful and judicious pastoral care of the Rev. JESSE Y. BURK it is at this time one of the best ordered, flourishing and useful parishes in the State of New Jersey.

church, "not built purposely for the Church of England," would very shortly become an established church are interestingly disclosed in an ancient manuscript book, placed, through the courtesy of the rector·of the church, in my hands by Mr. William Morris Cooper, of New Jersey.

It seems that there being, prior to Dr. Blackwell's taking charge of it, no prospect of any clergyman of the church entering upon the cure, the church edifice, though built chiefly by contributions from members of the Church of England, had not been built by them exclusively; but that "Methodists"—hardly yet fully separated from the church—had assisted to build it, with an understanding that their ministers might preach in it, and that they themselves might use it for their meetings. This was not agreeable to Dr. Blackwell, who, "though he highly respected the character and motives of persons that composed other religious denominations, honored their piety and zeal, had the utmost affection for their persons, and was ever active in reciprocating the endearing charities of social life, thought it best, for the good not less of other religious bodies than of his own, that their religious operations should be kept distinct."

The church at Greenwich was not incorporated, but by its deed of foundation, dated November 29, 1770, was placed under the control of certain managers. They were now, by Dr. Blackwell's influence, assembled, and at a "regular meeting, held by appointment, June 30, 1774," this preamble and these regulations were agreed to:

1st. WHEREAS, It appears to the managers of this church, from sundry good reasons, that it would be for the advancement of religion and piety, as well as productive of the most salutary consequences, that the said church should be the property of some one particular denomination or sect of Christians : And as it appears from the subscription-paper that by far the greatest part of the monies laid out on said building was given by persons who professed themselves members of the Church of England, and still desire that this may be an Established church : We do therefore agree that it shall be so; and from the date hereof this House be an ESTABLISHED CHURCH, according to the Establishment of that part of Great Britain called England, and further that it may be included in a charter with the church at Waterford and that which is to be built at Gloucester.

2d. That if any person be dissatisfied with the above order of the managers, he, she or they, by applying personally to Thomas Clark, Esq., any time in the month of October next, and only then, and letting him know they did not subscribe for an Established church, neither are they willing that their money should remain for that use, may have their subscriptions refunded.

3d. We further agree that no person whatsoever preach in this house except the clergy of the Church of England; unless he first obtain leave under the hand of Dr. Bodo Otto, Jr., whom we appoint, during our pleasure, to inspect into the morals and abilities of such persons as shall desire to preach in said church, and to approve or disapprove of them as he thinks fit.

4th. We do appoint Mr. Gabriel D. Veber to keep the key of said church; and it is our desire that he open the church to no other preachers but such as have been agreed upon.

5th. That there be no private meetings for Divine service in said church, but that the doors be open for persons of every denomination who behave themselves with decency and good order, and desire to hear our preaching.

6th. That when there be an appointment by a minister of our clergy, there be no other on that day but such as he shall please to make.

7th. Ordered that these resolutions be published in said church immediately after Divine service; that they may be known to the people: and that they be entered in the Greenwich Church-book.

ROBERT BLACKWELL, one of the Managers, and
Clerk to the said meeting.

Present—Timothy Clark, Isaac Inskeep, Thomas Thomson, Samuel Tonkin, Jonathan Chew, Gabriel D. Veber, Bodo Otto, Jr.

GREENWICH, July 31, 1774.

This day the above resolves were published, according to the order of the Managers, by me.

ROBERT BLACKWELL.

GREENWICH, Sept. 13, 1774.

At an appointed meeting of the Managers of Greenwich Church, with Mr. Rankins, Superintendent of the Methodists in these parts, and several of the heads of them, living in Greenwich, it was agreed that the Regulations made by the Managers on June 30, 1774, shall be observed by each party.

ROBERT BLACKWELL.

In 1775 Mr. Blackwell writes to the English society in whose employment he was, that the congregation at each of his churches is somewhat increased, though he lost one of his best families by emigration. At Easter his communicants at Waterford were six, and at Greenwich twenty-five.

In 1776 he writes of the great difficulty he has in settling a mission in the general disturbance, and gives no very promising account of his congregation.

An abstract of the society's report for the next year (1777) says of the Gloucester mission, that "all is in confusion."

It is not surprising to find that a mission whose chief seat was Gloucester, in New Jersey, should be all in confusion A. D. 1777, that year memorable there and in all the country round about as the year of the assault by Count Donop on Fort Mercer, at Red Bank, and of the terrific siege of Fort Mifflin; of the marching and countermarching under the Earl of Cornwallis, and General Varnum, and Sir Henry Clinton, and General Maxwell, of hostile armies; and of constant naval engagements in the Delaware, one of the severest having been just below Gloucester, October 23, 1777, when the "Augusta" and the

"Merlin"—British ships of war—encountering our navy, exploded in the midst of the engagement.

What part in the rupture of the British Empire Mr. Blackwell took, may be surmised from the part which we have already said was taken by his father, Col. Jacob Blackwell, in New York, and from the indignities and injury suffered by him from the British invaders on Long Island. The mission at Gloucester was of course at an end. The Church of England in America had been laid prostrate by the war. Not to be useless in his sacred office, Mr. Blackwell joined the American army as a Chaplain. He had preached before it, however, anterior to his official connection with it. The venerable annalist of Philadelphia, John Fanning Watson, in a letter before me, dated June 23, 1854, says:

Dr. Robert Blackwell was once settled as a minister at an Episcopal church between Haddonfield and Mount Holly,* and while there preached a sermon to the American troops at Haddonfield, as was once told me by an elderly lady, one of his parishioners, who said it was much approved.

Mr. Blackwell followed the fortunes of our war through the gloomy winter of 1777–78, exercising the double office of both Chaplain and Surgeon to the suffering troops at the Valley Forge. An original certificate in the handwriting of Brigadier-General Anthony Wayne thus testifies to the fact, and shows that the surgical attainments of his youth came—though, probably, in a way little anticipated by him when acquiring them—to excellent and most Christian results. It thus reads:

I do certify that Dr. Robert Blackwell was Chaplain to the First Pennsylvania Brigade, and *Surgeon to one of the regiments* in the year 1778, and that he took and subscribed the oath as directed by Congress before me at the Valley Forge, in common with other officers of the Line.

Given at Philadelphia, this 10th October, 1783.

ANTHONY WAYNE, B. G.

[Endorsed in Dr. Blackwell's handwriting.]

General Wayne's Certificate that R. B. hath taken the oath of allegiance.

We have no record testimony how long Dr. Blackwell's connection with the army continued. As he was with it both as Chaplain and Surgeon—"an officer of the Line"—in the year 1778, and at the Valley Forge, we may assume, almost with certainty, that he followed it on its sudden departure from Pennsylvania to overtake the flying British, and was with it at Monmouth, and afterwards. Indeed, in the absence of anything whatever to show that he left it before, the presumption

---

* Cole's Church answers this description.

would be that he stayed with it until the beginning of 1780, on the 17th of January, in which year he was married.   On the 23d of October, 1780, his father, Colonel Jacob Blackwell, died, and on the 26th of March, 1781, he was residing "near Philadelphia," and then for the first time, so far as we see, since the breaking up of his mission and his joining the army, ready to enter into ordinary parochial work.

By the demise of his father, at the date above mentioned—October 23, 1780—Dr. Blackwell succeeded to the possession of considerable real estate in the East river and on Long Island, just opposite to New York.   An immense increase in its value, in connection with property which passed to him in marriage, assisted to make him what for forty years and more before his death he was; not only the richest of the Episcopal clergy in the United States, but one of the richest men of his day in Philadelphia.

Dr. Blackwell remained without a parochial cure, so far as we know —though no doubt preaching frequently where an opportunity for being useful offered itself—until the year 1781.   In the spring of that year began that connection with the United Churches which associates his name inseparably with their history ; a connection long and honorable to him, and beneficent to them.*   It remained of an official sort till 1811, and constant and ecclesiastical, though not official, till 1831—a term of half a century; Bishop White during the whole time being Rector of the two churches.

The situation of the United Churches as respected political matters, when Dr. Blackwell was called to them, in 1781, was delicate.   It required great discretion on the part of their clergy, and conduct that should be at once conciliatory and controlling, to keep the congregations in anything like ancient steadiness and place.   The Church of England had never been strong in Pennsylvania.   Outside of Philadelphia its settled clergy had not been more than six.   During the war of the Revolution some had returned to England,† and some had died. In 1781 they numbered only three: Mr. White, Mr. Magaw, Rector of St. Paul's, and Mr. Blackwell.   The body of worshippers in the United Churches—that is to say, the worshippers most influential in point of education, wealth, social standing and moral worth, had not been inclined to the Revolution, and had reluctantly acquiesced in it.

---

* His engagement, which, at the first, was "to assist Mr. White on Sundays," began on Easter Day, April 14, 1781.   At a meeting of the Vestry, held September 19, 1781, for the purpose of choosing " an Assistant Minister of Christ Church and St. Peter's," he was unanimously elected to be such.

† Dr. Duché, Mr. Coombe, Dr. Alexander Murray, Mr. Thomas Barton, and I suppose others, returned to England.

Some of these were disposed to give but slender support to churches which acknowledged a new allegiance, and both whose officiating ministers had been officially in the service of either the Congress or the army. But the class called "the hot Whigs" were more difficult yet to manage. *They* were intolerant and bitter; and they were glad to see excluded and departing from the churches every one who had not been violent in the cause of the Revolution, and who was not as vindictive as themselves. No men but men like Dr. White and Dr. Blackwell, both of them gentlemen by birth—both of unquestioned devotion to the cause of independence, and whose conduct was marked by decision, candor, toleration, discretion and suavity of manner—could have kept such elements of discord from breaking forth into political animosities which, in the then state of the United Churches, would have been fatal to the prosperity, and indeed perhaps to the existence of the parishes. But the men were suited to the time as completely as they harmonized with each other. The parishes remained united in fact as in name— united to each other and united in themselves. The churches, largely depopulated for some time after the occupation of the city by the British army, thus reacquired by degrees their ancient numbers.

Dr. Blackwell was ever faithful in the discharge of the various and, as before long they became, onerous duties which they imposed upon him.

For thirty years he performed steadily or assisted to perform divine service and to preach, not only twice a day on Sundays, but to perform service also on Wednesdays and Fridays, and upon the festivals and fasts recognized more particularly in the church; upon all of which days both Christ Church and St. Peter's, in accordance with what is contemplated in the Book of Common Prayer, were opened, as they also daily were in the holy season of Lent, for divine service. Regarding the "Catechism" as an admirable compend of the Church's doctrine and teachings, and looking at the Church's teachings as ever better than his own, he was never neglectful of the rubric which makes it the duty of the minister of every parish diligently upon Sundays and Holy Days, or on some other convenient occasion, openly, in the church, to instruct or examine so many children of his parish sent unto him as he should think convenient, in some part of that excellent compend. And there yet survive those who recall with animated feelings his venerable figure and his air of sweet and paternal dignity as he would move before the lines of little people arranged on both sides of the middle aisle of Christ Church or St. Peter's; his Prayer Book, with his gold spectacles, in one hand, while the other, left free, he would put, with affectionate commendation, upon the head of some little innocent who seemed to need encouragement or to deserve commendation. His private Registry of Baptisms, Marriages and Burials, in the archives of the Historical Society of our State, and carefully treasured by it as among its more precious possessions, exhibits a large amount of duties faithfully performed for every class, including the poorest and most ignorant. And they were all as faithfully recorded.

In parishes having a circuit so wide as had those of the United Churches in Dr. Blackwell's day, and with parishioners so numerous, the discharge of such external duties as make part of every clergyman's office, imposed upon both their ministers constant labor and many duties requiring the best qualities of a pastor's character. All these, in Dr. Blackwell's case, were called into special requisition during those visitations of contagious pestilence which desolated Philadelphia on more than one occasion during his ministry, and one of which came near, by his fidelity to his parochial duties, to involve his own life. Dreadful as have been the visitations of the Yellow Fever of late times in the southern parts of the United States, they do not appear to have been more dreadful than those visitations of it under which Philadelphia came in 1793 and 1797. The visitation of 1793 was perhaps the most alarming. A letter before us from an eminent physician of Philadelphia to a friend thus speaks of it:

Though every one is not confined, yet from the general diffusion of the contagion through every street in the city, nobody is perfectly well. One complains of giddiness; one of headache; another of chills; others of pains in the back, or stomach; and all have more or less quickness of pulse and redness or yellowness in the eyes. No words can describe the distress which pervades all ranks of people, from the combined operations of fear, grief, poverty, despair and death. . . . Never can 1 forget the awful sight of mothers wringing their hands, fathers dumb for awhile with fear and apprehension, and children weeping aloud before me; all calling upon me to hasten to the relief of their sick relations. This is but a faint picture of the distress of our city. It is computed that one hundred persons, on an average, have been buried every day for the last eight or ten days. The sick suffer, not only from the want of physicians, bleeders, nurses and friends, but from want of the common necessaries of life. Five physicians, four students of medicine, and three bleeders have died of the disorder. But the mortality falls chiefly on the poor, who, by working in the sun, excite the contagion into activity. Whole families of these have been swept away by it. . . . The former sources of charity in money are dried up or carried into the country. There is little credit now given for anything. Every service to the sick is purchased at a most exorbitant rate. The price of bleeding is seven shillings and sixpence, and nurses' wages are three dollars and three dollars and a half per day. Families who lived by the daily labor of journeymen or day laborers suffer greatly from the death of persons by whom alone their daily wants were supplied. My heart has been rent a thousand times, in witnessing distress from that cause as well as from sickness. I have, in vain, endeavored to relieve it. The resources of a prince would not have relieved one-half of it. . . . Some of the wealthy are at last affected. Mr. Van Berkle, Mr. Powel, Mrs. Blodget and Mrs. Clymer are at present confined by it. Mr. Van Berkle is in danger. Continue, my dear friend, to pray for our distressed and desolated city.

It was in the midst of scenes like these that Dr. Blackwell, with his fearless rector and associate, Bishop White, was most active. Advising their parishioners everywhere to flee to places of safety, neither was willing himself to leave Philadelphia for a day. Dr. Blackwell was not unfamiliar with spectacles of terror. For a long and dreadful winter he had made his daily and nightly rounds through the hospitals of the Valley Forge, ministering to the souls and bodies alike of the six thousand sick and wounded soldiers who were there, without blankets or clothes, freezing and dying in the wards. He saw, in the new scenes of plague and pestilence, only new work which his Divine Master put now before him. Clergy, not the Church's, might leave the city. The Church, by solemn rubric, forbade any minister of Hers to do so; and though, "for fear of the infection," the whole residue of the parish should flee, and no neighbor be near, HE was to remain, and, "upon special request of the diseased, ALONE to communicate with him." In his combined character of physician, priest and man, rich in this world's goods, the entry of his house was filled night and day with applicants for aid; and, so long as he remained unattacked himself, few went away without some benefit from their application. On the 20th of October, 1793, having endured the rage of the pestilence unharmed, at a moment when it seemed to exhibit some signs of approaching decline, he was, in the midst of his active efforts to relieve others, himself suddenly stricken down. Fortunately, he was taken at once to a country residence, near Gloucester, and his restoration, for some time despaired of, ultimately took place; though his constitution never recovered perfectly from the shock of this attack.

Dr. Blackwell's sermons were characterized by solid sense, abundant scholarship, pious feeling, and a pervading tone of purity and sweetness. On occasions and in passages they rose to high solemnity. He uttered nothing crude, questionable or jejune. In conversation with the writer of this sketch, the late Horace Binney, who had known him from childhood, and was for many years one of his parishioners, spoke of them "as to *him* never uninteresting;" a higher tribute than which, to the solidity of their merits, no sermons could receive. Their structure had little of the arts of rhetoric. His voice was agreeable and well modulated, but neither in it nor in his gestures was there much elocutionary display. He addressed himself to the understandings, the consciences and the hearts of his hearers; and the effects which he produced were effects which endured, and to this day bring forth good fruit.

Dr. Rufus Wilmot Griswold, in his "Republican Court," refers to him more than once as a conspicuous person of society in the days of

Washington. After speaking of him as "a man of large fortune, fine appearance and singularly pleasant temper and manner," he says:

He was "a scholarly and sensible preacher of the English University cast. His sermons, of the homiletical kind, were, like those of the higher classes of the English clergy in the last century, calculated for educated hearers more than to arouse an indifferent or slumbering congregation."

Dr. Griswold adds:

Being withal a man of unquestioned piety and great propriety of life, he maintained a dignified position, and was extensively deferred to by an opulent and worldly class, who would probably have deferred to no one else less blessed with adventitious influence.

At the distance of near a century since Dr. Blackwell was called to minister in them, and of more than fifty years since he has been lying in the grave beside St. Peter's, it is interesting to look at the condition of the United Churches. It is a condition which testifies in part of his work, and of what sort it was.

While almost all the Protestant churches which existed in his time in the eastern part of Philadelphia have been demolished, or delivered over to secular and sometimes to impious uses, the old United Churches remain in strength and usefulness, and are likely to remain. Their ancient worshippers have disappeared; but worshippers in lines of straight succession still crowd their sacred aisles. The congregations of these old churches at this day are as active as were those of earlier days in works of charity and usefulness; and as active in such works as any anywhere, or of the newest.

Nor did this venerable gentleman confine his labors to offices sacerdotal or clerical only. In every department of religion—indeed in every sphere of humanity or science where he moved—he verified, unconsciously, the prediction which, A. D. 1770, in his early life Dr. Auchmuty made of him, that he would be "useful."

He was among the first persons who set themselves at work to reestablish the Episcopal Church after it had been prostrated by the war of the Revolution; one of those ten clergymen who, with six laymen, met May 11, 1784, at New Brunswick, N. J.—HE having been the person to propose that time and to approve that place,* by whom were set a-going measures for the purpose of forming a "Continental Represen-

---

* In a letter I received from Mr. Blackwell some time ago, he proposed Tuesday, 11th May, as a proper time for the meeting, and acquiesced with my proposal of Brunswick for the place.—(*Letter of the Rev. Abraham Beach to the Rev. Dr. White of March 22d, 1784, in Bishop W. S. Perry's "Half Century of Legislation of the American Church," Vol. III., p. 9.*)

tation" of the church, and for "the better management" of its concerns. With his fellow-workers—Mr. White, Mr. Beach, Mr. Magaw, Dr. Smith and others—he did faithful labor in this behalf: so faithful and with such success that in one year afterwards, 1785, a convention of seven out of ten of the States where the church was, was held,* the first in the series of those great conventions which still continue to represent triennially the church in her corporate dignity, and which, all may pray, may continue to represent her in the future with as much good result to the end of time.

Of the first convention Dr. Blackwell was a member, as he was of the convention of 1786, one which like that composed representatives from seven States; of that of 1789, the first of our General Conventions, in the sense which included any States of New England; and of those, its successors, of 1795, of 1799, of 1801, of 1804 and 1808, after which date, retiring from parochial charge, he was no longer eligible to any.

In all these conventions he was called upon for active service, and placed in positions showing reliance on his learning, his intelligence and practical wisdom. In the General Convention of 1789 he is appointed on various important committees; on one to take into consideration the proposed Constitution of the Protestant Episcopal Church, and to recommend such alterations, additions and amendments as the committee should think necessary and proper; on another to prepare a Morning and Evening Service for the use of the church; on a third to report what further measures were then necessary to perpetuate the succession of Bishops in America; on a fourth to superintend the printing of the Book of Common Prayer as then adopted and still existing; and finally, on the adjournment of the body, on a Standing Committee to act during the recess of the convention.†

In the General Convention of 1792 he is again appointed a member of the Standing Committee;† appointed also on the Committee for Carrying into Effect an act or plan which the convention had previously passed for Supporting Missions.‡

In the convention of 1795 we find him presiding in Committee of the Whole, to take into consideration the General State of the Church; appointed also at the same convention on a joint committee of the two Houses, "to arrange the Canons and principal papers belonging to the Church; causing them to be fairly transcribed in a properly bound book,

---

* This convention had representatives from New York, New Jersey, Pennsylvania, Delaware, Maryland, Virginia and South Carolina.

† See Minutes of July 30, October 3, October 15, October 16, 1789.

‡ See Minutes of 19th September, 1792

in order that they may be faithfully preserved for the perpetual use of the House of the General Convention of this Church, to recur to as occasion may require;" appointed again on the Standing Committee.*

In the convention of 1804 he is a member of a committee "to prepare an office of Induction in the Rectorship of Parishes;" Chairman of a committee to settle "a very unhappy difference," subsisting between the Rev. Uzal Ogden, D. D., and the then congregation of Trinity Church, Newark, which appeared to threaten the existence of that church, and which its vestry brought before the convention, asking *it* "to devise some means for their relief;" Chairman "to manage, on the part of the House of Clerical and Lay Deputies, a Conference with the House of Bishops on certain points where differences of opinion prevailed," but where perfect harmony was arrived at by patience and learning of the committees of the respective bodies.†

He was Treasurer both of General conventions and of State conventions; his plentiful fortune and his liberal disposition making him a very acceptable officer in situations like these then were, and still are, where funds were limited and demands upon them large.

For fifty-nine years he was an active and valuable member of that beneficent corporation, now so opulent, but long very feeble, and for some years after its organization scarce existent, "for the Relief of the Widows and Clergymen in the Communion of the Protestant Episcopal Church;" becoming a member of it A. D. 1773, and ending his services to it only with his life. From the year 1803 until 1814 he was its Treasurer, for Pennsylvania. As late as 1828 Bishop White, in an address to the convention of the clergy and laity of his State, speaks of the assistance which that "reverend brother, then present," had rendered to him "after the shock received by the fund from the currency at the Revolutionary war," not only in reorganizing the society, but also in rescuing the remnant of the fund from the further danger into which it had fallen. He was a Trustee from its origin, A. D. 1812, of that useful institution of the church in Pennsylvania, the Society for the Advancement of Christianity, and a constant contributor to its funds.

He was a Manager of "The Philadelphia Dispensary," a beneficent institution established A. D. 1786, and still beneficently existing for the relief of the indigent sick, and early and long a contributor to its funds; a "Visitor"—personally interesting himself—of the incorporated

---

* See Minutes of September 12, September 17, September 18, 1795.

† See Minutes of September 13, September 15 and September 18, 1804.

"Young Ladies' Academy of Philadelphia,"* one of the best schools for young ladies which ever existed in Philadelphia; a Trustee of the Episcopal Academy of Philadelphia; a Trustee of the University of Pennsylvania; a member of the American Philosophical Society, and one of the Counsellors;† a member of the Society for Political Inquiries, a society established A. D. 1787, and composed of the first men of the nation, and of such alone, or chiefly.‡ He was an earnest promoter of that important institution of the church, The General Theological of New York, and by his testamentary dispositions gave to it $2,500 to establish in it a scholarship.§

In 1810, the city growing, even then, rapidly toward the west, St. James's Church, in Seventh street above Market, was built and a !ded to the ancient parishes as one of the United Churches. Dr. Blackwell now availed himself of the claims of advancing years, and of health not longer robust, to retire from official connection with the corporation, whose enlarged form and wide circuit seemed likely to place upon him duties that were more suited to youthful strength. We have in the records of the United Churches‖ a tribute to his services and worth both from the vestry of the two churches and from the venerable rector of them, the first Bishop of this diocese, than whom no one living had so good opportunities of knowing Dr. Blackwell's usefulness and virtue.

The Minutes of the Corporation record that on the 18th of September, 1810, "the Right Rev. Dr. White read a letter which he had written to the Rev. Dr. Blackwell, and Dr. Blackwell's answer thereto." The Resolution mentioned in Bishop White's letter had been passed by the Vestry on the 6th of August, 1810. The letter and answer are thus:

August 7, 1810.

REVEREND AND DEAR SIR:

Last evening, agreeable to your desire, I informed the Vestry of your intended resignation, which produced the request expressed in the Minutes following:

* See "The Rise and Progress of the Young Ladies' Academy, at Philadelphia." Philadelphia, 1794. 12mo., pp. 1, 15, 117.

† January 19, 1788.

‡ This society was established February 9, 1787, and was limited to fifty members. Dr. Franklin, Major William Jackson, Francis Hopkinson, Samuel Powel, James Wilson, William Bradford, Jr., John Nixon, George Clymer, Jared Ingersoll, Thomas Fitzsimons, Robert Morris, Edward Shippen, Edward Tilghman, Gouverneur Morris, William Bingham, and a few other persons were members. It met, except in the summer months, and in deference to his age and eminence, at the house generally of Dr. Franklin, who was its President.

§ The Blackwell Scholarship; in the gift of the Bishop of the Diocese of Pennsylvania.

‖ See the Rev. Dr. Dorr's History of Christ Church, pp. 221-223.

August 6. The Right Rev. Dr. White informed the Vestry that the Rev. Dr. Blackwell had expressed his determination to decline his place as Assistant Minister in the United Churches, whenever a suitable person can be obtained in his room. It was further expressed that the cause of his resignation was occasional indisposition; but that he was willing to continue to officiate to allow sufficient time to choose another minister. Whereupon,

Resolved, That the Right Rev. Dr. White be requested to express to Dr. Blackwell the regret with which the Vestry have received the foregoing intimation; and more particularly for the cause which has induced it; and that he at the same time communicate to Dr. Blackwell the sense of the Vestry of the services rendered by him in the discharge of the duties of his office, and acquaint him of the resolution of the Vestry to take early measures for releasing him from his station by the election of a successor.

In performing the duty thus laid on me by the Vestry, I participate in the respectful and affectionate sentiments which they have expressed; and I further take the opportunity of mentioning that during whatever may remain to me of life, I shall reflect with satisfaction on the harmony which has subsisted between us, and the friendly intercourse in which we have trod, through so long a space of time, and that of our united parochial ministry.

With my best wishes and my prayers for your happiness,

I remain, Reverend and dear sir,

Your humble servant,

WM. WHITE.

To the REV. ROBERT BLACKWELL, D. D.

[DR. BLACKWELL'S ANSWER.]

RIGHT REVEREND AND DEAR SIR:

When I look back on the long and happy connection that has for so many years subsisted between us as ministers of the United Churches, the many kind attentions you have shown me, and the affectionate behavior I have always experienced from you, you may be assured that I am very sensibly affected at the dissolution of a connection so happily begun, and continued so long with such uninterrupted harmony and good will. I am fully persuaded that nothing will interrupt the friendly understanding that now subsists between us; but that, as we pass down the vale of years, our brotherly affection will know no change, but in its increase; and that, as we draw nearer the close of life, our hopes of happiness will become brighter and brighter.

My dear sir, you will please to express to the Vestry the satisfaction I feel at the kind and friendly notice they have taken of my past services; and assure them that they were always performed with a willing heart, a sincere mind, and an ardent desire that they might be useful and acceptable to the congregation.

It is my earnest prayer that their labors in promoting the interest and welfare of the United Churches may be crowned with full success. My best wishes shall ever attend them.

Right reverend and dear sir, with the highest esteem and veneration for your many amiable and Christian virtues, and with the sincerest wishes for your long life, health and happiness,

I am your affectionate friend and brother,

8th August, 1810.   ROBERT BLACKWELL.

The RIGHT REV. WILLIAM WHITE, D. D., Bishop of the Protestant Episcopal Church in the State of Pennsylvania.

On the 14th of May, 1811, the Rev. Jackson Kemper (afterwards the first Missionary Bishop of the West) was elected an Assistant in the place of Dr. Blackwell; and we fix the termination of Dr. Blackwell's official relation to the United Churches from that day. On the same day the Vestry makes this request:

> The Vestry request that the Church Warden present their thanks to the Rev. Dr. Blackwell for his past service, and at the same time express their hope that, notwithstanding his resignation, he will occasionally favor them with his sermons when the Rector or either of the Assistant Ministers may request.

In the year 1788 Dr. Blackwell received from the University of Pennsylvania the degree of Doctor of Divinity.

Dr. Blackwell was twice married:

First, January 17, 1780, by the Rev. William White, to Rebecca Harrison, daughter of Joseph and Ann Harrison, of Gloucester county, New Jersey. This lady died February 25, 1782, aged 25 years. Family affection has preserved an old manuscript which contains an account of her death and some graceful elegiac lines to her memory. I am unable to state with certainty the author of them. They have been attributed, not without some probability, to the accomplished first Provost of the College of Philadelphia. If *he* was not the author of them, it is difficult to say to whom in Philadelphia at that time we can assign them. *Second*, November 2, 1783, to Hannah Benezet, relict of John Benezet, Esq., and daughter of William and Mary Bingham. This lady died December 16, 1815.

No issue by the latter marriage survived. By the former, Dr. Blackwell left one child, a daughter, Rebecca Harrison, who became, November 26, 1800, the wife of George Willing, of Philadelphia.

Dr. Blackwell's dwelling-house in Philadelphia was on the south side of Pine street below Third, and within a hundred yards of the church in which he most frequently ministered. At the distance of more than a century from the time of its erection it still stands, shorn, indeed, of its spacious and well-kept grounds, but, as respects the house itself, absolutely unimpaired, we may say, in solidity or even in appearance ; a conclusive evidence of the superiority of its materials and modes of structure. The house, its occupant, the surrounding houses, and the occupants of these, made in their day so considerable a feature of the city that the local historian of Philadelphia, Mr. Thompson Westcott, in a chapter devoted to "Notable Mansions in the City built between 1750 and 1776," gives us quite an extended mention of them. He says:*

---

* History of Philadelphia, chapter ccxix.

In the year 1761 the Proprietaries, Thomas and Richard Penn, granted the whole front on Pine street, from Second to Third, being four hundred and sixty feet in width by one hundred and two feet in depth, to John Stamper, in consideration of £1100 sterling and a yearly quit-rent of five shillings. Stamper was an Englishman who had been a successful merchant. He was a member of the Common Council and an alderman, and in 1759 was mayor of the city. After the purchase from the Penns he bought forty feet of ground south of the original grant, which made his lot one hundred and forty-two feet deep, to an alley, which was called, after him, Stamper's alley. At this time Mr. Stamper lived in Second street, at the southwest corner of Stamper's alley. Upon this large lot on Pine street Mr. Stamper built, some time before the Revolution, a fine three-story brick house, which was formerly No. 50, and which is now known as No. 224. It will be readily distinguished by its red and blue glazed brick, its ancient columnar doorway, and its low steps. The cornice and dormer windows are fine specimens of old-fashioned woodwork. The interior of the house was finished, according to the taste of the ante-Revolutionary times, with elaborate paneling, wainscoting, surbases, heavy doors, etc., which still remain. The stable and coach-house in Stamper's alley are also still standing. Stamper had two daughters. One of these—Mary Stamper—married William Bingham the elder, and was the mother of the Hon. William Bingham, afterwards Senator of the United States, whose property finally went, through the marriage of one of his daughters, to the English family of the Barings. Hannah, the other daughter, married, in second marriage, the Rev. Robert Blackwell, D. D., and, upon the division of her grandfather's (Stamper's) estate, this fine house, running to within about thirty feet of Third street, passed into the possession of Dr. Blackwell, who was one of the ministers of Christ Church and St. Peter's. Dr. Blackwell lived in this until his death, which occurred in the year 1831—nearly half a century. It is yet one of the best specimens of stately city architecture which now remains in Philadelphia.

On the west end of this lot Dr. Blackwell, before the marriage of his only daughter, Rebecca Harrison Blackwell, with George Willing, built on the Pine street front of the lot the fine house formerly No. 64, now No. 238, in which Mr. Willing long lived, and which is still standing. It is now inhabited by the Hon. J. R. Burden. It was one of the best houses of the modern style, with chimneys against the sides, and with folding-doors in the middle of the parlors. The garden attached to Dr. Blackwell's house was filled with flowers, shrubbery and fruit trees, and was common to the Blackwell and the Willing families.

At the southeast corner of Pine and Third streets Mr. Stamper built, before the Revolution, a fine house for his son, Joseph Stamper, on the occasion of his marriage with Miss Sarah Maddox, the granddaughter of Joshua Maddox, Esq., one of the Justices of the Province. Mrs. Stamper, who survived her husband for many years, remained in this old house until her death, which occurred about the year 1826. The property was then bought by Dr. Philip Syng Physic, who pulled down the old house and erected on the lot a row of houses facing upon Third street, which are still standing. They extended from Pine street to Stamper's alley.

At the southwest corner of Pine and Second streets another house, which is still standing, was built about the year 1773, and was long owned by Dr. Blackwell. In this house, at the time of the Revolution, there dwelt a Mr. Franklin, and here boarded, during this period, Elias Boudinot, LL. D., at one time President of the Continental Congress, Commissary General of prisoners during the Revolutionary war, subsequently member of the Congress of the United States, and finally Director of the

Mint under President Washington. His memory is specially maintained in our local annals by the bequest of lands bordering on the Susquehanna river, which he made to the city of Philadelphia in trust for the purpose of supplying poor housekeepers with fuel.

No. II.—Page 64.

William Moore, of Moore Hall, and his Origin.

As to the origin of the Moore family, of America, the first of whom I have any information is Sir John Moore, who had for his family seat Fawley, in Berkshire, England. This gentleman was passed to the order of Knighthood by Charles I., King of England, on the 21st day of May, 1627; probably as a reward for some important services rendered to the country and to the crown. The motto on his coat of arms was: "Nihil utile quod non honestum."

He was, beyond a doubt, a monarchist in politics and a churchman in religion, as he lost both his fortune and his life in those revolutionary excitements—produced more by a blind and ignorant religious bigotry than a love of rational liberty—which deprived the unfortunate monarch of his crown, and brought him to an ignominious end upon the scaffold. It was a sacrifice professedly made to establish the rights of his subjects, and the freedom of conscience in religion. But the light which succeeding events have thrown upon the character of the agents, and of the sufferers in that tragedy, has led many to contemplate it as a case of martyrdom in the cause of God and his church.

Sir John Moore was succeeded by his son, Sir Francis Moore, who was the father of John and James Moore, who came to America and settled in South Carolina about 1680, where James remained and became Governor from the year 1700 until 1703, when he was deposed.

"Drake" informs us that in 1719 he undertook an expedition against Florida, which was a failure. This expedition caused the first issue of paper money in America, under the name of Bills of Credit.

John Moore, it appears, came with his wife and family to Philadelphia some time prior to 1700, and became the king's collector at that port; this we know from his commission, which is before me, dated 1703, signed by Evelyn, etc. He had several children when he came to Philadelphia, and as we are informed by his will, bearing date November 16, 1731, had seven at his death.

Upon his coming to Philadelphia it appears he bought a large tract of land on "ye 2nd street," north of High or Market street, and built his family residence at the corner of a small street running from Second to the river, then known as Gardener's alley, now Coombe's. He was a prominent member of Christ Church, being one of the vestrymen up to the time of his death. I shall now give such an account of his children as I have been able to obtain. His wife's name was Rebecca.

His eldest son, John Moore, was born in Carolina, in 1686; and at an early age was sent to England to receive his education, and upon his return to America settled in the city of New York, and became an eminent merchant of that city in colonial times. He was an alderman, for many years a member of the Legislature, and at the time of his death, colonel of one of the New York regiments, and a member of the King's council for the province. He died in 1749, at 63 years of age. He was the first person buried in Trinity churchyard, and the title of the family vault is still in the name of the family.

Mr. John Moore married Frances Lambert, and was blest through her with eighteen children, among whom were three pairs of twins. The descendants of Mr. Moore married into the Bayard, Livingston, Hoffman, Onderdonk, Bailey, Tredwell and Rogers families, which are among the most respectable families of the North.

Stephen, the seventeenth child, owned West Point, which he sold to the United States, and removed to North Carolina. Upon the invasion of the Southern States by the British, in 1779, he commanded a regiment of North Carolina militia. He was afterwards taken prisoner at the first battle of Camden. Being exchanged, he returned to his beautiful seat, Mount Tirza, in North Carolina, where he died, leaving in that State a highly respectable family.

The seventh of the thirteen sons of John Moore was Lambert, who married Elizabeth Channing. He was born in 1722—was sent to England for education, and was bred a scholar in Westminster school. At twenty-one years of age he returned to his native country, and settled in that part of the State of New York which was called the neutral ground. Here he lost all his property amidst the devastation and plunder which desolated that part of the country. His house at West Point, where he resided during the early part of the Revolutionary war, was plundered by the Hessians, when the British took the posts of the Highlands, and his family was turned out of doors in a destitute condition. He removed thence to the city of New York, where he obtained an appointment in the Customs. and lived in comfort until the conclusion of the war. After this event he removed to his brother John's, in Norwich, Connecticut, where he died of a pulmonary disease, on the

19th of June, 1784, in the communion of the church. In the spring of 1785 his remains were removed to New York, and deposited in the family vault in Trinity churchyard, by his son, Richard Channing Moore, the late Bishop of Virginia, who then resided in that city.

The mother of Bishop Moore was descended of a highly respectable family. Being left an orphan at two years of age, she was brought up in the family of her uncle, John Pintard, Esq., one of the aldermen of New York. She was an accomplished lady, having received the best education which New York afforded, and was highly esteemed in the best society of her native city. She was polished in her manners, of the most amiable disposition and exemplary piety, and was remarkable for sound judgment and strong good sense. To the early religious instructions, the prayers, and lovely and pious example of this exemplary Christian mother, Bishop Moore often delighted to revert, with tears of gratitude in his eyes, and a bosom swelling with filial affection and reverence. To her early nurture and admonition in the Lord, he ascribed, under God, all his happiness and usefulness in this world, and his hopes of a blessed immortality in the next. She entered upon her eternal rest at his house, on Staten Island, on the 7th of December, 1805, in the 78th year of her age.

Of the eleven brothers and sisters of Bishop Moore, our limits will allow us only to say that they were all honorably connected in marriage, were respectable, virtuous and useful.

Richard Channing Moore, the late Bishop of Virginia, was born in the city of New York, on the 21st of August, 1762. He received a liberal education, and was bred a physician; but after practising medicine for several years, in 1787 he resolved to devote himself to the ministry of the Gospel of Christ, and was ordained by Bishop Provoost in New York. The first two years of his ministry were spent at Rye, in the county of West Chester, most acceptably to the congregation among whom he labored, and usefully for the church at whose altar he ministered. Thence he was called to a wider field of labor by the congregation of St. Andrew's Church, at Richmond, on Staten Island.

Here Dr. Moore labored for twenty-one years with eminent success. His faithfulness in all the departments of ministerial duty, his zeal in the advancement of true religion, his love of his Divine Master and of his work, his unaffected love of all men, his amenity of manners and entire freedom from spiritual pride and all moroseness in his theological views, gave him not only an unbounded popularity among his people, but won for him their warm admiration and sincere attachment.

In 1809 Dr. Moore was called by God's providence to a still more important sphere of usefulness in St. Stephen's Church, in the city of New York. Here he continued five years. His labors were very great; but neither the strength of his fine constitution nor the ardor of his zeal failed, and he was again, as on Staten Island, richly rewarded for all his toils by the abundant bestowment of God's blessing on the work of his ministry. He found a small congregation, and only about thirty communicants. After a short ministry of five years he left a crowded church and between four and five hundred communicants. There is, I believe, to this day, in St. Stephen's Church, an honorable monument to the zeal and efficiency of his ministry while there. When the whole church had become crowded, every pew, not only in the body of the church, but also in the galleries being occupied, a gentleman called on the rector and applied for a pew. "There is none," was the reply. "Will you permit me to build one?" was the answer. "Where?" said the doctor. "There, over the gallery, against the wall," said the persevering applicant. "But how will you obtain access to it?" said the doctor. "By cutting a small door in the wall, and building a private stairway outside of the church," said the zealous man; and there, I understand, high up against the wall, is that pew to this day, a lasting memorial of pastoral zeal, fidelity and eloquence, such as few ministers of Christ are cheered by.

The next important change which occurred in the life of Dr. Moore was his call to the Rectorship of the Monumental Church, at Richmond, and to the Episcopate of Virginia. These events occurred in the spring of 1814. The peculiar history of the church of which he now became Rector is too well known to require more than the remark, that it was built upon the site of the old theatre—the burning of which had caused the death of more than a hundred persons, and involved Richmond in the deepest distress.

Dr. Moore enjoyed all the real blessings of life to the last; with unusual physical strength, and mental faculties but little impaired, except his memory, he continued his duties even to the end. Two days only before the last visitation on which he died, he officiated and preached at a funeral. His address was *ex tempore,* and such was his energy, animation and fervor, and such the influence of his exhortation, that an old Christian of another Christian society said, "Surely this must be his last, last message to Richmond." It was so; two days after he obeyed the call of duty, and commenced, in his 80th year, a journey of one hundred and fifty miles, to Lynchburg, to perform Episcopal functions. He arrived in Lynchburg on Thursday, the 5th of November. On Friday he attended Divine service in the forenoon; in the afternoon he met at the Rector's house the candidates for confirmation, and made them a very admirable address on the qualifications for that holy rite; in the evening he attended service again, and after a sermon by one of his presbyters he made an address, which is represented to have been characterized by pathos, animation and energy in the highest degree. Eyes that seldom wept were suffused with tears; and some of the most hardened in impenitency were softened when the old and venerable servant of God, in tenderest accents, and with outstretched and trembling hands, and fervent love, heralded for the last time the good tidings of the Gospel, and entreated them for Christ's sake to be reconciled to God. That night, after a day spent so usefully in his sacred office, and only about three hours after his voice had proclaimed, in the temple of God, the gracious invitations of his beloved Saviour, the fatal shaft which no skill could extract pierced him. Feeling unwell a little after midnight, he arose to call for help; but his strength failing him, he fell on the floor, and lay there helpless for some time before his returning strength enabled him to make himself heard. When raised and placed on his bed, he was found to be laboring under a violent attack of pneumonia. He lived for five days, suffering but very little pain, and during most of the time none. Generally he was in a profound stupor, but occasionally he roused up, and his eyes and countenance would for a little while resume their usual intelligent and benevolent expression. When thus himself, he was resigned, calm, full of peace and hope, and free from all fear. When asked whether there was anything to be done in reference to his temporal affairs, he said no, that everything had been attended to—that nothing remained but to bid the Rev. Mr. Atkinson to bear his love to his dear children. When told (by Mr. Atkinson, at whose house he died, and who, with his wife, were son and daughter to him in the absence of his own children) that death was at hand, he said, "It is well; I trust I am prepared either for this world or the next." On Thursday, November 10, 1842, at about half past one A. M., after hours of entire freedom from pain, and in the gentlest and most peaceful manner, without a struggle or a groan, this good man died.

The second child of John and Rebecca Moore was Thomas, born in Carolina, 1689; he was likewise sent to England for his education. He graduated at Oxford, and took orders and became the Chaplain to Dr. Atterbury, Bishop of Rochester, one of the most eminent scholars and celebrated preachers of his age. The well-known sermons of this admired prelate were edited and published under the direction of Dr. Moore. He died in Little Britain, in London, leaving a highly respectable family, among whom was Thomas Moore, D. D., rector of North Bray, in Kent.

Daniel, sixth child of John Moore, of Philadelphia, was also sent to

England, and received his education at Oxford, and became an eminent lawyer; made a large estate, and was a member of Parliament for many years. His daughter, *Frances Moore*, married the celebrated Lord Chancellor of England, Erskine. "Burke" gives the following account of this union:

LINEAGE.

THE HON. THOMAS ERSKINE, born January 21, 1750, third son of Henry David, fifth Earl of Buchan (see that dignity), having served both in the army and navy, devoted at length his talents to the bar, to which he was called in 1778. Gifted with the most powerful eloquence, Mr. Erskine attained at once the summit of his profession as an advocate, in which capacity he continued until the year 1806, when he was appointed Lord High Chancellor of Great Britain, and elevated to the peerage, April 8th, in the same year, as Baron Erskine, of *Restormel Castle*. His lordship married, first, May 29, 1770, Frances, daughter of Daniel Moore, Esq., M. P., by whom (who died December 22, 1805) he had issue:

I. David Montagu, present peer.

II. Henry David, in holy orders, Rector of Kirby Underdale, York county; married May 4, 1813, Mary Harriet, third daughter of John, first Earl of Portarlington, by whom (who died December 16, 1827) he has issue: 1. Henry; 2. George; 3. Harriet; 4. Louisa-Lucy, married, May 21, 1845, to the Rev. Thomas Frederick Rudston Read; 5. Caroline; 6. Fanny-Louisa, married, September 16, 1847, to Henry Linwood Strong, Esq., barrister-at-law; 7. Agnes; and 8. Julia-Henrietta, married, February 17, 1846, to Captain Broadley Harrison, Tenth Hussars.

III. Thomas (the Right Hon.), late one of the Judges of the Court of Common Pleas, born March 12, 1788; married, December 10, 1814, Henrietta-Eliza, only daughter of the late Henry Trail, Esq., and has surviving issue:

1. Henry Trail, born December 25, 1815; 2. Thomas, born November 12, 1828; 3. Anne; 4. Julia.

IV. Esme-Stewart, Lieutenant-Colonel in the army, born in 1789, married, in 1809, Eliza Bland, daughter of the late Lieutenant-Colonel Smith, and by her (who married, secondly, James Norton, Esq., and died in 1833) had issue:

1. Thomas, born March 29, 1810; 2. Esme-Stewart, born September 8, 1811, died in 1833; 3. Harry, born August 11, 1814.

Colonel Erskine was Deputy Adjutant-General in the battle of Waterloo, where he lost an arm. He died August 26, 1817.

V. Frances, married, in 1802, to the Rev. Dr. Holland, prebendary and precentor of Chichester.

VI. Elizabeth, married, in 1798, to Sir David Erskine, Knt., and died August 2, 1800.

VII. Margaret.

VIII. Mary, married, in 1805, to David Morris, Esq., who died in 1815.

Lord Erskine married, secondly, Miss Sarah Buck, by whom he also left issue. The success of this eminent lawyer is, probably, the most remarkable upon record as to promptitude; for almost immediately after he was called to the bar he was fortunate enough to find an opportunity for the display of his extraordinary powers. Captain Baillie, who had been removed from the superintendence of Greenwich Hospital, by the Earl of Sandwich, was proceeded against by that nobleman for the publication of a libel, and the attorney-general having to move the Court of King's Bench for his lordship upon the subject, Mr. Erskine was retained by Captain Baillie to oppose the motion; upon which he displayed so much eloquence and spirit that he received, when leaving the court, no less than thirty retainers from attorneys who happened to be present. But of all Erskine's cases, those which raised the advocate's reputation the highest were his splendid defences of Lord George Gordon and of Admiral Keppel. He was likewise distinguished in an eminent degree for the prisoners in the memorable state prosecutions against John Horne Tooke, Hardy, etc.

His lordship died of inflammation of the chest, November 17, 1823, at Amondell, near Edinburgh, the seat of his nephew, the Hon. Henry Erskine. The following is the inscription upon the tomb of his wife:

> Near this place lies buried
> THE HONORABLE FRANCES ERSKINE,
> The most faithful and most
> Affectionate of women.
> Her husband,
> Lord Thomas Erskine,
> An inhabitant of this parish,
> Raised this monument
> To her lamented memory.
> A. D. 1807.

John Moore, the collector, left, as we see by his will, two daughters—Rebecca and Mary. Of Rebecca I have been able to find no account, and am led to believe she died unmarried. Mary became the wife of Peter Evans, Esq., who was high sheriff of the city of Philadelphia. He was born in the city of London, and was an attorney by profession. He styles himself, in his will (May 13, 1745), "of the Inner Temple, London." He died in Philadelphia, May 25, 1745, leaving four children, viz.: John, Mary, Margaret and Ann. I find no record of John. Mary married a Peter Robinson. Ann died a child, and Margaret married Mr. David Franks, December, 1743, and had issue—

1. ABIGAIL, born January 6, 1744–5.
2. JACOB, born January 7, 1746–7.
3. MARY, born January 25, 1747–8; died August 26, 1774.
4. REBECCA.

David Franks was British agent in Philadelphia as late as 1779. His eldest daughter,

I. **Abigail** married Andrew Hamilton, Esq., of the "Woodlands," near Philadelphia, January 6, 1768, and had issue as follows:

5. MARGARET, born October 4, 1768.
6. ANN, born December 18, 1769; died 1798.
7. MARY, born August 21, 1771.

8. JAMES, born July 31, 1774; died July 20, 1817.

9. ANDREW, born November 6, 1776; died May 16, 1825.

10. FRANKS, born May 22, 1779; died August 4, 1798.

11. REBECCA, born November 7, 1783; died February 2, 1842.

IV. **Rebecca Franks** married Sir Henry Johnson, Bart., for an account of whom see "Burke's Peerage."

VI. **Ann Hamilton** married James Lyle, October 17, 1792, and had issue:

12. MARY, born January 22, 1796; died November 1, 1829.

13. ELLEN, born October 21, 1797; died February 8, 1852.

James Lyle was a broker of the firm of Lyle & Newman. He died at Long Branch, August 10, 1826.

IX. **Andrew Hamilton** married Eliza, only daughter of the Rev. D. H. Urquhart, of Brondmayne, Dorset, England, June 11, 1817, and had issue:

14. MARY ANN, born January 8, 1822; died January 24, 1851.

Andrew Hamilton died in 1825, and his widow married Mr. John Gardiner; she died March 12, 1834.

XI. **Rebecca Hamilton** married Francis Lewis O'Beirne, November 28, 1809, and had issue:

15. THOMAS ORMSBY, born 1810; died October 25, 1839.

16. JAMES HAMILTON.

17. REBECCA JANE, died 1839.

Francis Lewis O'Beirne was the son of the Lord Bishop of Meath, who styles himself "of Arabraccan House, in the county of Meath, in that part of the United Kingdom called Ireland, but now, 1809, residing in London." After marriage they resided at Fern Cottage, Heston, near Southwell, in the county of Middlesex, England. In 1818 Mrs. O'Beirne returned to America (Philadelphia), where she died February 2, 1842. *Francis Lewis O'Beirne* died July 7, 1840. Their son, *Thomas Ormsby O'Beirne*, entered the English army, and became a captain in the Twenty-fifth Regiment Bengal Native Infantry, "near Shause," where he died, single, October 25, 1839, leaving a will which is of record in the Register of Wills' office, Philadelphia.

XII. **Mary Lyle** married Henry Beckett, November 12, 1818; had issue:

18. MARY ANN; died 1844.

19. HAMILTON.

Henry Beckett was the son of Sir Henry Beckett. See "Burke" (Hamilton).

XIII. **Ellen Lyle** married Hartman Kuhn, December 15, 1818; had issue:

20. MARY.
21. ELLEN.
22. ELIZABETH, born February 17, 1826; died April 2, 1830.
23. JAMES HAMILTON (killed in the Rebellion).
24. CHARLES.
25. ROSALIE, born April 23, 1829; died December 20, 1841.
26. HARTMAN, born February 22, 1831.
27. ELIZABETH (2d), born October 24, 1833.
28. SOPHIA, born June 5, 1835.

Hartman Kuhn was the son of Adam Kuhn, M. D., of Philadelphia; he was born February 4, 1784; died November 6, 1860.

XIV. **Mary Ann Hamilton** married Septimus Henry Palairet, May 1, 1843. By this marriage there was no issue.
Septimus Henry Palairet died June, 1854.

XVI. **James Hamilton O'Beirne** married Henrietta Francis; had issue:

29. HAMILTON KUHN, born January 8, 1866.
30. FRANCES STUART.
31. LEWIS ORMSBY.
32. ARMINE JAMES.
33. EMILY.
34. CHARLES BURGOYNE.
35. WILLIAM HENRY DE LANCEY.
36. EVELINE FANNY AMELIA.

XVII. **Rebecca Jane O'Beirne** married Major Armine Simcoe Henry Mountain, June 10, 1837; had issue:

37. JENNY (died an infant).

Major (afterwards Colonel) Armine Simcoe Henry Mountain was in her Britannic Majesty's service, in the Twenty-sixth (Cameronian) Regiment. Upon the death of his wife, in 1839, he again married Miss Charlotte Anna Dundas, and died February 8, 1854.

XVIII. **Mary Ann Beckett** married Sir Thomas Whichcote, Bart.; died May, 1844.

XIX. **Hamilton Beckett** married Sophia, daughter of Lord Lyndhurst.—(See "Burke.")

XX. **Mary Kuhn** married (her cousin) Hartman Kuhn (son of Charles), February 3, 1842.

    38. FREDERICK, born December 16, 1843; died December 23, 1844.
    39. WILLIAM.
    40. MARY.
    41. ELLEN.
    42. CORNELIUS HARTMAN.
    43. CHARLES.

XXI. **Ellen Kuhn** married Manlius Evans.

    44. CADWALADER.
    45. ELLEN LYLE.
    46. ROSALIE.
    47. HARTMAN KUHN.

XXIV. **Charles Kuhn** married Louisa, daughter of the Hon. Charles Francis Adams, of Massachusetts.

XXVI. **Hartman Kuhn** married Grace McCarey.

Another son of John Moore was William Moore (known as of Moore Hall), from his seat on the banks of the Schuylkill, above Valley Forge. He was born in Philadelphia, May 6, 1699, and at the age of fourteen was sent to England to finish his education. He graduated at the University of Oxford in 1719, and returned to America, where he married Williamina, daughter of David, fourth Earl of Wemyss.* She had, to-

---

* A recent writer in "Frazer's Magazine" gives the following account of the Wemyss of Fifeshire:

The Wemyss family has claims to great antiquity, being descendants of Gillimachus, fourth Earl of Fife. Their great ancestor, the first Earl, is the Macduff of Shakspeare, whose important service to King Malcolm was rewarded by that monarch with the Earldom of Fife. Three special privileges were also bestowed upon him at the same period: First, that he and his successors should conduct the king to the chair of state at coronations; second, that they should lead the van of the army in battle; and, third, that unpremeditated murder on the part of any of Macduff's kin to the ninth degree was expiable by certain fines or offerings at the cross of Macduff. "Our judicious Skeen," as Sibbald calls him, thus refers to this curious privilege: "The croce of clan Mackduff had privelege and liberty of girth, in sik sort, that when onie manslayer, being within the ninth degree of kin and bluid to Mackduff, sometime Earl of Fyffe, come to that croce, and gave nyne kie (cows) and an colpindach or young kow, he was free of the slaughter committed be him." A dangerous privilege, it will be thought, in those lawless times. Very little now remains of this famous cross. There:

32

gether with her brother James (afterwards fifth Earl of Wemyss), been driven from Scotland in the year 1716, on account of their father having espoused the cause of the Pretender.

"Burke," in his Peerage of Scotland, gives the following

LINEAGE.

This ancient family traces its origin to John, baronial Lord of Weems, whence the surname was probably derived, who was younger son of the celebrated Macduff, Thane of Fife, the vanquisher of the tyrant Macbeth.

Sir Michael de Wemyss was sent, according to Fordun, in 1290, with Sir Michael Scot, to Norway, by the lords of the regency in Scotland, to conduct the young Queen Margaret to her dominions; but her majesty unfortunately died upon the journey, at the Orkneys. Sir Michael swore fealty to Edward I., in 1296, and he witnessed the act of settlement of the crown of Scotland by King Robert I., at Ayr, in 1315. From Sir Michael lineally descended:

Sir John Wemyss, of Wemyss, who married, first, in 1574, Margaret, eldest daughter of William, Earl of Morton, but by that lady had no issue; and, secondly, in 1581, Anne, sister of James, Earl of Moray, by whom he had, with other issue,

Sir John Wemyss, of Wemyss, who was created a Baronet May 29, 1625; and elevated to the peerage of Scotland, as *Baron Wemyss, of Elcho,* April 1, 1628. His lordship was advanced to the dignities of Earl of Wemyss, in the county Fife, and *Lord Elcho and Methel,* June 25, 1633. This nobleman, although indebted for his honors to King Charles I., took part against his royal master, and sided with the Parliamentarians. He married, in 1610, Jane, daughter of Patrick, seventh Lord Gray, by whom he had six children, and was succeeded in 1649 by his only son,

David, second earl. This nobleman married, first, in 1628, Jean, daughter of Robert Balfour, Lord Burleigh, by whom he had an only surviving daughter,

Jane, who became, first, the wife of Archibald, Earl of Angus; and, after his lordship's decease, of George, Earl of Sutherland.

The Earl of Wemyss married, secondly, Lady Eleanor Fleming, daughter of John, second Earl of Wigton, but by that lady had no issue. He married, thirdly, Margaret, daughter of John, sixth Earl of Rothes (widow successively of James, Lord Balgony, and Francis, Earl of Buccleuch), by whom he had an only surviving daughter, Margaret, in whose favor his lordship, having resigned his peerage to the crown, obtained, August 3, 1672, a new patent, conferring the honors of the family, with the original precedency, upon her ladyship. He died in 1680, when the baronetcy became dormant, but the other dignities descended accordingly to his daughter,

---

can be no doubt that these early Earls of Fife exercised absolute and almost royal state and jurisdiction within their territories, forming a kind of *imperium in imperio.* A manuscript referred to by Sibbald says: "He had all his earldom (Fife) erected into a principality, that is to say, to exime his tenants and subjects from all other courts and judgement, and give justice to all his, in his own countries." Very likely it is owing to this, rather than to its general wealth and importance, that the county, which at that time included Kinross, Clackmannan, and portions of Perthshire and Stirlingshire, came to be designated "the Kingdom of Fife." The Wemyss branch of the Macduffs broke off from the main stem at the fourth earl, in the twelfth century, and the present Fife branch of the family is descended from James, third son of the fifth Earl of Wemyss. The chief of the blood is the Earl of Wemyss.

Lady Margaret Wemyss, as Countess of Wemyss. Her ladyship married Sir James Wemyss, of Caskyerry, who was created, April 15, 1672, for life, *Lord Burntisland*, having had previously a charter of the castle of Burntisland. The issue of this marriage were:

David, successor to the countess's honors.

Anne, who married David, Earl of Leven and Melville, and had issue.

Margaret, married to David, Earl of Northesk.

The Countess of Wemyss married, secondly, George, first Earl of Cromarty, but had no issue by his lordship; she died in 1705, and was succeeded by her only son,

David, fourth earl. This nobleman, who was appointed by Queen Anne, Lord High Admiral of Scotland, sworn of the Privy Council, and constituted one of the Commissioners for concluding the treaty of union, married, first, in 1697, Lady Anne Douglas, daughter of William, first Duke of Queensberry, and sister of James, Duke of Queensberry and Dover, and of William, first Earl of March, by whom he had one surviving son,

James, his successor.

Williamina (afterwards Mrs. Moore).

There is a tradition in the family that the wife of David Wemyss died in childbed, and, believing her expected child to be a boy, requested that it be christened *William*, after William of Orange; being a girl, it was christened *Williamina*.

David Wemyss married twice afterwards, but had no male issue. He died March 15, 1720.

Upon his marriage, William Moore settled upon an estate presented to him by his father, John Moore, which was situated upon the river Schuylkill, some twenty-five miles from Philadelphia. This property consisted of about twelve hundred acres of land, which he farmed with the help of a large number of slaves and redemptioners. He built upon it a large house (still, in 1880, standing). It was known as "Moore Hall."

William Moore died at Moore Hall, May 30, 1782. His will, which is written "with his own hand," is a singular document, being mainly a tribute to his wife, to whom he gives his whole estate, and of whom he says: "Never frightened by the rude rabble, or dismayed by the insolent threats of the ruling powers—happy woman, a pattern of her sex, and worthy the relationship she bears to the Right Honorable and noble family from whence she sprang." He was a staunch Royalist, but during the stay of the army at Valley Forge he invited Colonel Clement Biddle and his staff to make Moore Hall his headquarters. Mrs. Moore survived him until December 6, 1784, when the family removed to Philadelphia.

The following notice of the death of William Moore, Esq., appeared in the *Pennsylvania Gazette* of June 18, 1782:

On Friday, May 30th, died at his seat in Chester county, William Moore, Esq., of Moore Hall, in the 84th year of his age, and was interred on the Sunday following, in his family burying-ground, at Radnor churchyard. His funeral was attended by a large concourse of his most respectable neighbors, and an excellent sermon was preached by the Rev. William Currie. At an early period of his life Mr. Moore was a member of the Assembly, a Colonel of militia, one of the Justices of the Peace, and President of the County Courts of Chester, which last office he filled with great and acknowledged abilities for about forty years. He has left a numerous family of children, grandchildren and great-grandchildren to bewail his memory; and more especially a mournful and beloved wife, with whom he lived upwards of sixty-one years in the most perfect and uninterrupted conjugal felicity.

The following inscription is on a slab at Radnor Church, Delaware county, Pennsylvania:

"To the memory of
WILLIAM MOORE, Esq., of Moore Hall, in the
County of Chester,
and of WILLIAMINA his wife.
He departed this life on the 30th day of
May, 1783, aged 84 years.
She died on the 6th day of December, 1784,
in the 80th year of her age.

"This venerable pair lived together in perfect love and unremitted harmony and confidence for the long period of sixty-three years; dispensing the best duties of life in ardent and uninterrupted zeal; beloved by their children and by their friends, respected by the community in which they passed their lengthened days. Benevolence and urbanity beamed on all who sought their hospitable mansion; they administered comfort to the worthy poor, protecting humble honesty though cursed with poverty.

"He presided in the Common Pleas, Quarter Sessions, and Orphans' Courts in Chester county for a great length of time. As a judge and a magistrate he was indefatigable in executing the solemn charge of these important stations, acquitting himself with intelligence, impartiality and dignity. He was a kind father, a warm friend and an indulgent master. She was one of the brightest patterns of excelling nature. Possessing a bright and cultivated heart and understanding, she was mild, considerate, kind and good; she was consequently distinguished by her amiable disposition and unassuming manners. With calmness, but with resignation, she bore the heaviest afflictions, the severest trials of an uncertain world, and placed her firm reliance upon a state of happiness beyond the grave—

"'That place Celestial, where no storm assails,
No ills approach—where bliss alone prevails.'"

The foregoing inscription was written by Phineas Bond, a grandson of the Moores. For a full account of the issue and descendants of William and Williamina Moore, of Moore Hall, see Appendix XI.

No. III.—PAGE 237.

Alexander Murray, D. D.

[By John A. Childs, D. D.]

THE REV. ALEXANDER MURRAY, D. D., was a native of Scotland, born in 1727. He was educated in King's College, Aberdeen. After his ordination to the ministry he was induced, it appears, most probably by the Rev. William Smith, D. D., who was a graduate of the same college, on his visit to England, his native land, to come to Pennsylvania, under an appointment by the Society for the Propagation of the Gospel. He arrived in Pennsylvania in 1763, and immediately began his ministry at Reading and Morlatten. His ecclesiastical views were of a very decided character, and his work as a missionary very extensive. He laid the foundations of a church at Reading, called St. Mary's, and the people of that town were very solicitous for the continuance of his appointment by the society, and addressed the officers to that effect. During the agitation which existed previous to the war of independence, he sympathized largely with the colonies, and in 1775 signed a paper, with a number of clergy, hoping and praying for some method of conciliation, and satisfaction of a reasonably discontented people.

When, however, a separation became not only imminent, but a *fait accompli* to all intents, he refused to discontinue the prayers for the royal family. He was threatened with some violence, and thereafter sailed to London. He continued to reside there during the Revolutionary war, and being always a strong advocate for an Episcopate in the church in the colonies, he used his influence with the Bishop of London, as well as with the Archbishop of Canterbury, in seeking for the consecration of bishops in the United States. In accomplishing this he kept up a correspondence with the Rev. William White, D. D., communicating the conditions under which consecration would be imparted. His advice and influence contributed to that end, and deserved, as has been said, honorable mention and grateful remembrance.

In 1790 Dr. Murray returned to America, and continued to reside in Philadelphia until his death, September 14, 1793. His body lies interred with those of the Sims, Morgan, Evans and Clark families, with which he was connected by marriage—families particularly prominent in the early history of the church in Philadelphia. Upon his decease he left by his will directions to found bursaries in connection with the university at which he graduated.

No. IV.—Pages 185, 258.

The Case of the Episcopal Church Considered.

[By Mr. Thomas H. Montgomery.]

Bishop White begins the concluding paragraph of his "Episcopal Charge on the subject of Revivals, delivered before the Forty-eighth Convention of the Diocese of Pennsylvania, and addressed to the Clerical Members of the Convention, printed by order of the Convention, Philadelphia, 1832," with the following words:

Brethren, it is bordering on the half of a century since the date of the incipient measures of your bishop, for the organizing of our church out of the wreck of the Revolution.

On a copy of this charge in my possession the Bishop has added, on the last blank pages, the following note:

"Those measures began with the author's pamphlet, entitled 'The case of the Episcopal Churches in the United States considered.'

"The circumstances attached to that publication are the following:

"The congregations of our communion throughout the United States were approaching to annihilation. Although within this city three Episcopal clergymen, including the author, were resident and officiating; the church over the rest of the State had become deprived of their clergy during the war, either by death or by departure for England. In the Eastern States, with two or three exceptions, there was a cessation of the exercises of the pulpit; owing to the necessary disuse of the prayers for the former civil rulers. In Maryland and in Virginia, where the church had enjoyed civil establishments, on the ceasing of these, the incumbents of the parishes, almost without exception, ceased to officiate. Further south the condition of the church was not better, to say the least. At the time in question there had occurred some circumstances which prompted the hope of a discontinuance of the war: but that it would be with the acknowledgment of American independence there was little reason to expect.

"On the 6th of August, 1782, the Congress, as noticed on their printed journal of that day, received a communication from Sir Guy Carleton and Admiral Digby, dated the 2d of that month, which gave the first opening of the prospect of peace. The pamphlet had been advertised for sale in the *Pennsylvania Packet* of the 6th, and some copies had been previously handed by the author to a few of his friends. This suspended the intended proceedings in the business; which, in the opinion of the author, would have been justified by necessity, and by no other consideration.

"It was an opinion commonly entertained, that if there should be a discontinuance of military operations, it would be without the acknowledgment of independence, as happened after the severance of the Netherlands from the crown of Spain. Of the like issue there seemed probable causes, in the feelings attendant on disappointed efforts for conquest; and in the belief cherished, that the successes of the former colonists would be followed by dissensions, inducing return to the domination of the mother country. Had the war ended in that way, our obtaining of the succession from England would have been hopeless. The remnant of the Episcopal Church in Scotland, laboring under penal laws not executed, would hardly have regarded the bringing down on themselves of the arm of government. Fear of the like offence would have operated in any other quarter to which we might have had recourse. In such a case, the obtaining of the succession in time to save from ruin, would seem to have been impossible."

No. V.—Page 309.

Peregrine Wroth, M. D., of Baltimore, Md.

THE great interest taken in this work by the *late* venerable Dr. Peregrine Wroth, of Baltimore, in furnishing information in regard to Dr. Smith's life in Maryland, prompted me to write to him to get some of the particulars of his life, out of which to prepare a notice of him in event of his death, which I felt sure would occur ere its publication. I therefore give such extracts from his letters, which will be found *entire* in the Historical Society of Pennsylvania, as may tend to that purpose. He says, under date April, 1877:

It is a rather difficult task, especially to one whose life is not such as to serve as an example for the imitation of others. But this I can say, that my family (in America), beginning with James Wroth, Esq., who emigrated from England in or about 1660, can trace back the name to one who bore the name of *De Wrotham*, in the reign of King John.

The family in England held a very respectable rank in society, as a genealogy sent to me by John Newton Lane, Esq., of King's Bromley Manor, near Lichfield, in 1854, informs me. Mr. Lane descended from Mary Wroth, the eldest daughter of Sir Henry Wroth. I was of the fifth generation after James, and was born April 7, 1786, being now 91 years old on the 7th of this month. Before I left college I was adopted by a cousin of my father, and intended as a student of law under Hon. James A. Bayard, of Delaware, the grandfather of Hon. T. F. Bayard, now a Senator of the United States, the office held by his father and grandfather. But he who had adopted me dying before my father, I was persuaded to study medicine, and began to practise in 1807, and after the age of 70 retired from public life, and, 1868, removed to Baltimore. Having been baptized by your distinguished ancestor, the first Principal of my (Washington) college, I have always felt an interest in that college, and finished my course there in 1803 under Rev. Dr. C. Ferguson, the second Principal, the successor of your ancestor, then Provost (I think) of the University of Pennsylvania.

I practised fifty years, lacking two months. Of myself I can only say that I think I held a respectable rank among my contemporary physicians, and about 1840 or 1841 published a small volume under the title of "Clinical Aphorisms," *for beginners.* I afterwards wrote Brief Memoirs of the twelve physicians of my county (Kent) who were in practice before the act of "Incorporating the Medical and Chirurgical Faculty of Maryland" was passed—at the request of the eminent Dr. George C. M. Roberts, late of this city, who contemplated a work on *that* portion of the faculty; but which of course was not published.

Under date February 8, 1872, he says:

Your ancestor, Rev. William Smith, D. D., was Rector of I. U. Parish, Kent county, the church in Chestertown being at that time a chapel of ease, where he regularly preached, and lived in Chestertown. I have many, many times been in the house where he lived, and almost feel as if I had been acquainted with him—having been baptized by him and afterwards an alumnus of the college of which he was the first Principal. I will here send you one or two anecdotes which, I am confident, are authentic.

On some occasion a man from the country was in his house, and being in the library with the doctor, and amazed at the great number of books, exclaimed, "My— my! Doctor, did you ever read all these books?" The doctor replied: "Hoot, mon, no; but I know what's in 'em." This was during the doctor's residence in Chester— from about 1780 to —. Before that time he lived in Philadelphia. About the commencement of the Revolution of 1776 the gentlemen of Philadelphia were in the habit of meeting every day in the old City Hall, in Market street below Third. One day the meeting had taken place, and after a while Dr. Smith entered the hall. Dr. Benjamin Rush was there, and, walking up to the doctor, said: "Dr. Smith, we have come to the conclusion that you are the author of ———" (*Publius*, I think, an article which had appeared in one of the newspapers). The doctor regarded Rush with a glance of dignified contempt, and said: " Ben. Rush, I knew you when you were *so* high," holding his hand about three feet from the floor. " You are no higher yet, mon." No more was said on that subject.

These anecdotes I heard, I am almost sure, from Dr. Morgan Browne, an eminent physician of Chestertown, and my preceptor, and had been a pupil of Dr. Smith, and may be considered authentic. Of his daughter (I will not be sure of her name. If he had another daughter living with him in Chestertown, it may not have been William- ina), I heard from the same authority, I suppose, that she was walking in the street, and the mud took one of her shoes off. She did not stop to take it up (at that time the sidewalks for foot-passengers were not paved), but walked on, stepping on with the foot which had a shoe on ; then, drawing up the shoeless foot to it, again advanced the foot that had a shoe on, etc. After walking on in this way, she was met by a friend, who asked: " What are you doing?" Miss Smith replied: " I'm putting my best foot foremost."

These little things seem at first sight of little value, but they serve to *indicate char- acter*. Such as they are, I offer them—to be used as you think proper.

I do not remember to have given you the history of the *endowment* of Washington and St. John's Colleges—the former at Chestertown, the latter at Annapolis, Maryland. If I have not, and such account shall be desired and in time for your work, I will send it when you let me know.*   I have the account, and will copy it off—to send as soon as I hear that it may suit your plan—if I live.

Very truly yours,   P. WROTH.

H. W. SMITH, ESQ.

Again he writes :

We have a life-size painting (bust) of Dr. Smith in the Library at Washington Col- lege. It was painted by W. W. McLane, from a print in a volume of Dr. Smith's sermons, which belonged to *me*, and very closely resembles, I think, the likeness you sent me. The painting was *retouched* by Unger, a distinguished portrait painter of Pennsylvania—a native of Prussia.

Dr. Wroth had been married four times.   He died at Baltimore, June 13, 1879, in his 94th year.

No. VI.—Page 324.

The Hon. Thomas Willing, Esq.

It was my hope to be able to present a somewhat full biographical sketch of this distinguished citizen of Philadelphia. I find myself, however, unable to do so. The following genealogical notice, which is

---

* For this account see Vol. II., page 308.

understood to come from the papers of one of the most eminent genealogists of our city, now for some years deceased, and who contemplated preparing, and did in part prepare, bestowing much labor on it, "A Dictionary of our Philadelphia Genealogies," may in part supply the loss; and I have the greater satisfaction in presenting it in these volumes since a portion of it, the poetical tribute to an early member of the family, is from the pen of my ancestor, Dr. Smith; whose ready talents, often called on in this way, rarely found a worthier subject for their exercise. The Willings belonged to the Proprietary party,* and until Dr. Smith was displaced from the college by the confisČatory act of 1779, were munificent friends of that institution. On these accounts, as for others, they were highly valued by Dr. Smith.

The Willings came into England from the neighboring district of Wales. The name, which in its present form is not a common one either in England or America, has been regarded, on traditional report, as a change upon that of Wellyn, or Llewellyn.

JOSEPH WILLING, of Gloucestershire, England, married, July 1, 1672, Elizabeth Plaver, by which lady (who died October 4, 1675) he had issue:

(1) George, born September 12, 1673.

(2) Joseph, born September 22, 1675.

He married, secondly, May 24, 1676, Ava Lowle, of Gloucester, an heiress of ancient family and of good estates, descended to her through several generations from her Saxon ancestors. By this lady, whose arms, in place of the proper arms of his own family, he took with her estates, and who died December 31, 1717, he had issue, six children, among whom were Mary, born June 3, 1678; married, October 11, 1705, to Stephen Burcomb, of Monmouth, by whom she had issue:

(1) Ann.

(2) THOMAS, of whom presently.

(3) Richard, born May 26, 1681; died September 6, 1736, and is buried in the Mayor's Chapel at Bristol; married, February 21, 1790, Mary Syms, by which lady he had issue, three children, among whom were

(1) CHARLES, born November 23, 1712; married December 22, 1735, Chadery Tudsbury.

(2) Mary Syms, born May 2, 1725; died at Temple Cloud, in the

---

* Mr. Thomas Willing was one of the persons who, along with Lynford Lardner, Richard Hockley, William Peters and some others, "applauded" when Dr. Smith, A. D. 1758, had his great quarrel with the Quaker Assembly, and were arrested by order of the Assembly for a breach of privilege. See Vol. I., p. 177.

city of Somerset, being the last survivor of her family of the name of Willing in that district of country.

THOMAS WILLING, the oldest son of Joseph and Anne Willing, born January 16, 1679–80, visited America with his younger brother Richard, first in 1720. Returning to Bristol, England, he died in that the city of his residence, 1760. He married, July 16, 1704, Anne, granddaughter, on her paternal side, of Major-General Thomas Harrison, a lawyer of the Inns of Court, a member of the Long Parliament, Major-General in Cromwell's time, one of the judges who sat on the trial of King Charles I.; also granddaughter on her mother's side, as has been traditionally said, though this is not so certain, we believe, to Simon Mayne (more properly written Meyn), a gentleman of Lincolnshire, a principal actor in Cromwell's time, and another of the persons who sat on the trial of this unfortunate monarch. By this lady, who was born in 1684 and died in 1747, and whose character, distinguished by sweetness of temper, by great accomplishment, and by deep piety, seems to have been "dulcified" in its flow of two generations from "the hard, acidulous, metallic tincture" of its Puritan and military spring, he had issue, among other children,

(1) Charles, of whom presently.

(2) Thomas, who resided in the Temple, London, and is hereafter spoken of.

(3) Dorothy, married —— Hand, in England, where she remained.

CHARLES WILLING, whom we may regard as the founder of the American family (he having been the first who permanently resided here), born May 18, 1710, was taken to Philadelphia, in the then Province of Pennsylvania, at the age of 18, on a second visit to that country by his father, who, during his previous residence of five years there, had foreseen its rising greatness, and was determined to establish his oldest son there, at Philadelphia, its metropolis. In this city the subject of our notice pursued with great success and with noble fidelity to its best principles, the profession of a merchant, in which career he obtained, both at home and abroad, high and permanent consideration by the scope, vigor and forecast of his understanding, by his great executive power, by his unspotted integrity, and by the amenity of his disposition and manners. His enlarged and successful operations, and his well-founded credit, assisted in early establishing with foreign countries a high reputation for American commerce; and contributed to give to the city of his adoption, then the chief city of the confederacy, and afterwards the seat of its Congress, that reputation for public honor and for private wealth which it enjoyed at the opening of the Revolution, and which was of such eminent importance to the nation in its negotiations with France and Holland in the struggles of that contest. He was active in establishing the "Philadelphia Associators," in 1744, and one of the founders and first trustees of the University of Pennsylvania, a warden and active member of Christ Church. Towards the close of his life he discharged with dignity, justice and efficiency the important functions of Chief Magistrate of Philadelphia, in the Mayoralty of which city, now filling it for a second time, he died, not yet having attained the age of 45 years, respected and lamented by a whole community, November 30, 1754.

His death, in the bloom of life, was justly regarded as a civic calamity to Philadelphia. The *Pennsylvania Gazette* of December 5, 1754, contains a tribute to his memory, with some elegiac stanzas, by the Rev. William Smith, D. D., first Provost of the College of Philadelphia. They are in these words:

Last Saturday, after a short illness, departed this life, in the 45th year of his age, Charles Willing, Esq., mayor of this city. As it may be truly said that this community had not a more useful member, his death is justly lamented as a public loss to his country, as well as an almost irretrievable loss to his family and friends.

In the character of a magistrate, he was patient, indefatigable, and actuated by a steady zeal for justice. As a merchant, it was thought that no person amongst us understood commerce in general, and the trading interests of the Province in particular, better than he; and his success in business was proportionably great. As a friend, he was faithful, candid and sincere. As a husband and parent, few ever exceeded him in tenderness and affection. Being himself a sincere Christian, he was strictly attentive to the education of his children in every virtuous qualification; and in a particular manner he was remarkable in the discharge of that essential part of a parent's duty, so little considered—a regular attendance, together with his numerous family, on the public worship of God. And for this, accordingly, they will now have reason to bless his memory; since the impressions thereby received will go farther to teach them how to bear their present heavy affliction, and recommend them to the favor of the world (degenerate as it is), than all the external advantages—all the fortune, graces and good nature he has left them possessed of.

ODE TO THE MEMORY OF CHARLES WILLING, Esq.

1. Once more I seek the cypress shade,
To weave a garland for the dead,
    Alone, dejected, wan!
Shall WILLING quit this mortal strife,
And not a verse show him, in life
    And death—AN HONEST MAN?

2. Forbid it every grateful muse—
The world itself will patriot-views,
    With transient tears, commend;
But nobler far your task, ye Nine!
'Tis yours th' immortal wreath to twine,
    And consecrate each friend.

3. Be present then—this boon bestow!
   A friend is lost! Now bind his brow
     And bid each age proclaim
   How first among th' illustrious band
   That fix'd your mansions in this land,
     Stands Willing's honor'd name.*

4. Bid helpless innocence reliev'd,
   The widow's hopeless state retriev'd,
     And orphan's right restor'd—
   Tell how he graced the judgment seat,†
   Still incorrupt and firmly great,
     Alike to slave or lord.

5. How nicely he the various plan
   Of bounteous commerce‡ knew to scan,
     And raise his country's weal—
   Her trade by him enlarg'd, her good
   Thro' every secret maze pursu'd,
     To distant times will tell.

6. What more he did to bless the State,
   And all the deeds of life complete,
     Should any seek to know!
   Bid them behold his num'rous race,
   And read in each illumined face
     What language cannot show!

7. Bid them look up to Celia's eyes,
   Where all the soul of softness lies,
     And reason beams through truth.
   Or, should this risk be deem'd too bold,
   Bid them each manly grace behold,
     Rip'ning in Damon's youth.

8. Damon, attend! proceed to shine!
   To fill a father's place be thine,
     And soothe a mother's care!
   This done—still mindful of his hearse,
   Whose doom was sudden, write this verse,
     And drop a filial tear.

EPITAPH.

If to be all the wise and good commend,
The tender husband, father and the friend;
At home belov'd and blest, esteem'd abroad;
Studious to serve mankind, and please his God;
If this from death one useful life could save,
  Thou hadst not read that Willing fills this grave!

---

* As a trustee of the Academy.   † As a magistrate.   ‡ As a merchant.

MORAL.

But ah! what boots it that, with ceaseless toil,
We court renown, or bask in fortune's smile?
In midst of all our fond enchanting dreams,
E'en while our souls are bent on patriot schemes,
Death lurks behind to cut life's thin-spun thread;
Then swift as noontide shadows all is fled!
One only thought remains to cheer the mind—
If human aims are just—" That Heaven is kind!"

This Charles Willing built, A. D. 1749, the large and imposing dwelling house, till lately standing, at the southwest corner of Willing's alley and Third street, whose character and history is eloquently dwelt on by Dr. Griswold in the "Republican Court." An engraving on wood, giving a good representation of it and its spacious grounds, is in " Watson's Annals," Vol. II., page 619, Hazard's Edition.

He married, in Philadelphia, January 21, 1730, Anne, daughter of Joseph and Abigail Shippen, and granddaughter of Edward Shippen, a man of pre-eminent consideration in the early history of Pennsylvania; Speaker, in 1695, of the Assembly of the Province; appointed by its charter, in 1701, first mayor of the city of Philadelphia; President from 1702 to 1704 of the Governor's Council, and appointed by William Penn, proprietary of the Province, to be one of the executors of his will. By this lady, who was born in Philadelphia, August 5, 1710, died in the same place, June 23, 1791, he had issue, eleven children, among whom were:

(1) THOMAS, of whom presently.

(2) Ann, born July 10, 1733, died January 2, 1812; married, February 8, 1762, to Tench Francis, of Philadelphia.

(3) Dorothy, born July 16, 1735; died in Scotland, 1782.

(4) Mary, born September 24, 1740, died March 28, 1814; married William Byrd, Esq., of Westhover, in Virginia.

(5) Elizabeth, born February 10, 1742, died 1830; married, August 7, 1769, Samuel Powel.

(6) Richard, born January 2, 1744, died January 30, 1798.

(7) Margaret, born January 15, 1753, died September 21, 1816; married Robert Hare.

THOMAS, the oldest son, was taken by his father, at a tender age, to England, and educated in liberal studies at Bath, under the eye of his grandmother, Anne Willing, already spoken of. He afterwards went to London, where he was placed under the care of his uncle, Thomas Willing, Esq., a gentleman of fortune, abilities and reputation, residing on the Temple. Under his uncle's supervision, the subject of our present notice was entered a student of law in that venerable seat of legal learning, and pursued for several months with great assiduity the studies of a barrister. Returning to his native city, the opulence, powerful connections and established reputation of his father's commercial house, pointed to commerce as a profession. And on the death of his father, in 1754, he assumed the exclusive control of that gentleman's large concerns. He associated with himself the late Hon. Robert Morris, Esq., afterwards well known as "the Financier of the Revolution," but separated himself from that gentleman upon Mr. Morris's great enterprises of landed purchase, which, ending disastrously, clouded the latter years of his distinguished and useful life. Mr. Willing was in many places of public trust in the Province, occupying among them a seat on the Bench of the Supreme Court. He was among the persons who early opposed the unconstitutional measures of Great Britain. His name stands at the head of that great list of merchants and traders who signed the non-importation resolutions of 1764. He was President of the Provincial Meeting of Deputies, chosen by the several counties of Pennsylvania, which met in Philadelphia, July 15, 1774, one of whose resolves was in these memorable words:

That, although a suspension of the commerce of this large trading Province with Great Britain would greatly distress multitudes of our industrious inhabitants, yet that sacrifice and a much greater we are ready to offer for the preservation of our liberties. But in tenderness to the people of Great Britain as well as of this country, and in hopes that our just remonstrances will at length reach the ears of our gracious sovereign, and be no longer treated with contempt by any of our fellow-subjects in England, it is our earnest desire that the Congress should first try the gentler mode of stating our grievances and making a firm and decent claim of redress.

Mr. Willing was in the Congress of 1775, and in that one more celebrated, though composed of less able men, of 1776. He voted steadily and fearlessly against the Declaration of Independence, considering that he had not received power from the assembly, by whom he was appointed a delegate, to vote for a revolution; and that, whether or not, the time had not arrived in which Pennsylvania should come into the measure. He remained also in the city during the occupation of it by the British army. But when Sir William Howe sent a person to administer the oath of allegiance to George III., he refused to take it. For all this no one ever questioned his political integrity; though many did that of men about him who were vigorous in declaring their devotion to the cause of independence. During the session of the Congress of 1774 he was in constant and confidential intercourse of the great men who strove to make Great Britain yield to the solicitations of the colonies, and repeal her obnoxious acts of legislation. John Adams, after speaking, in his Diary, of numerous persons of great fame whom he met in Philadelphia during the session of the Congress, says:

Sunday, 11 October, 1774.

There is such a quick and constant succession of new scenes, characters, persons and events turning up before me, that I can't keep any regular account. . . . Dined at Mr. Willing's, who is a Judge of the Supreme Court here, and the gentlemen from Virginia, Maryland and New York a most splendid feast again; turtle and everything else. Mr. Willing is the most sociable, agreeable man of all.*

When, in the year 1781, with a view of enabling the United States of America to carry on the war for independence, the Bank of North America was chartered by Congress—a time when our finances were almost desperate, when public credit was at an end, when no means were afforded adequate to the public expense, when the money and credit of the United States were at so low an ebb that some members of the Board of War declared that they had not the means of sending an express to the army— it was made a part of the enactment by that body, such was the confidence had by it in his integrity, skill and solid wealth, that THOMAS WILLING be the present President of the Institution. At a later day, March 26, 1782, when the State of Pennsylvania came to act on the charter, certain members of the Assembly opposed this feature of the enactment, arguing that Mr. Willing had voted against the Declaration of Independence, had remained in the city during the occupation, etc., etc. "We think," said they, "that loading with honors a man who so lately contributed what he could to enslave his country, is a discouragement to the Whigs, is a wound to the cause of patriotism, and is trampling on the blood of those heroes and martyrs who have fallen in the defence of our liberty." But, upon the question being taken, the objectors— country members, and mostly of the Democratic side—were overwhelmed, and, by a vote of thirty-eight to sixteen, the Congressional enactment left undisturbed. Mr. Willing entered at once upon the Presidency of the Bank of North America, and until taken from it, eight or nine years afterwards, to be placed in the higher office of President of the Bank of the United States, then lately chartered by the Federal government, administered it with the most satisfactory results; its dividends being for years of a magnitude previously unheard of in the history of banks. The bank to this day maintains the highest reputation. His administration of the Bank of the United States was

---

* Among "the gentlemen from Virginia, Maryland and New York," were George Washington, Patrick Henry, Peyton Randolph, William Paca, Samuel Chase, John Jay and Philip Livingston.—Works, Vol. II., page 378.

not less beneficent; and when, in 1816, having been hunted down by a political party, its charter ceased and its affairs were wound up, it paid in gold, during the prevalence of a paper currency which placed gold at a high premium, $116 for each $100 of its capital

We have not a sufficient acquaintance with the history of Mr. Thomas Willing to give any particular account of his enterprises in trade. They were of the largest and most successful kind in that day, and we believe chiefly with the Indies.

Mr. Morris has justly been called the Financier of the Revolution; and it is not easy to overestimate his services to the country in the dark days of 1780-81. But it was largely owing to the solid wealth, inherited and acquired, of his partner, Mr. Willing, put into the partnership of Willing & Morris, by Mr. Willing; to the executive capacity of that gentleman; to his great discretion and to the various qualities, not always easily defined, but always easily perceived as surely felt, which go to make up that combination which gives weight and influence to men in the community where they live, that Mr. Morris was able to do the great things that he did. The National Bank of North America was the agent by which Mr. Morris produced his wonderful effects upon the Revolution; and of that bank Mr. Willing was the head, both titular and real.

The following inscription is from the pen of the Hon. Horace Binney, upon a monument in the grounds of Christ Church, Philadelphia, in which, along with both his parents, his wife and many of his descendants, the subject of this part of our notice is interred:

" In memory of
THOMAS WILLING, ESQ.,
Born 19th of December, 1731, O. S.: died 19th of January, 1821,
Aged 89 years and 30 days.

" This excellent man, in all the relations of private life and in various stations of high public trust, deserved and acquired the devoted affection of his family and friends, and the universal respect of his fellow-citizens.

" From 1754 to 1807 he successively held the offices of Secretary to the Congress of Delegates at Albany, Mayor of the city of Philadelphia, her Representative in the General Assembly, President of the Provincial Congress, Delegate to the Congress of the Confederation, President of the first chartered bank in America, and President of the first Bank of the United States.

" With these public duties he united the business of an active, enterprising and successful merchant, in which pursuit, for sixty years, his life was rich in examples of the influence of probity, fidelity and perseverance, upon the stability of commercial establishments, and upon that

33

which was his distinguished reward upon earth, public consideration and esteem. His profound adoration of the Great Supreme, and his deep sense of dependence on his mercy, in life and in death, gave him, at the close of his protracted years, the hope of a superior one in Heaven.''

The following obituary notice in the *Pennsylvania Packet* of February 10, 1781, is upon the wife of Thomas Willing, of the family name, we believe, of McCall:

On Monday last died, greatly and deservedly regretted, Mrs. Ann Willing, wife of Thomas Willing, Esq., and her remains were, on Wednesday, interred in Christ Church burying-ground, with the tribute of many a tear to her memory.

With every virtue that can adorn the female character, she possessed the most amiable and endearing manners. It is not the frail memorial, inscribed on the fugitive page, that can do her justice. A more durable monument of her virtue and her worth is erected in the hearts of her surviving friends, stamped in such strong characters that nothing but the passing hand of death can ever efface them.

I have seen some handsome lines to the memory of Anne Willing, of the family name of Shippen, wife of Charles Willing and mother of Thomas Willing, said to be from the pen of the well-known and accomplished Mrs. Ferguson, of Græme Park. I regret not to be able to recover them.

No. VII.—Page 350.

Samuel Blodget, Jr.

[By Lorin Blodget, Esq.]

Samuel Blodget, Jr., who married Rebecca, the favorite daughter of Rev. William Smith, in 1792, was the son of Samuel Blodget,* of Concord, N. H., who was born at Woburn, Mass., but subsequently resided at Concord, and was distinguished as a member of the expe-

---

* Samuel Blodget, Sr., of Woburn and Concord, was grandson of Thomas Blodget, of London, merchant, who came over in the ship "Increase," in 1635, and who was sworn in "Freeman" of Boston, March 3, 1635. He was accompanied by his wife, Susanna, and his infant sons, Daniel and Samuel, from whom are descended all bearing this name in the United States. See Encyclopædia Britannica, Johnson's Universal Cyclopædia, etc., for biographical notices of Samuel Blodget, of Woburn and Concord; also for notices of Benjamin Thompson, afterward Count Rumford, who was himself a native of Woburn; his mother, whose maiden name was Susanna Blodget, was a

dition against Louisburg, in 1745, and as Judge in Hillsboro' county, N. H.; also as an extensive manufacturer at Blodget's Mills, near Concord, during the Revolutionary war, and supplied the patriot service with the product of his mills.

Samuel Blodget, Jr., was born at Woburn, in 1755, and at the time of the encampment of the patriot forces at Cambridge, in July, 1775, entered into the military service, and became acquainted with the new Commander-in-Chief, General Washington, with whom his father was also personally intimate, and afterwards a correspondent. He was especially interested in the two favorite projects then entertained by General Washington, the founding of a "federal city," or national capital, and the establishment of a national university; and after three years of arduous service in the army, a part of the time on the staff of the Commander-in-Chief, left the service in broken health in 1778, and engaged in the East India trade, in Boston, visiting Europe in 1784, and again in 1790. These visits and much of his time and efforts for many years were devoted to the carrying out of the great enterprises which enlisted his patriotism early in the war, and subsequently brought him to Philadelphia and to Washington, and induced him to invest his entire fortune in the founding of the city of Washington and the establishment of a national university. The account of his earlier efforts in this direction is briefly given in a work published at Washington in 1806,* and he was almost alone among prominent citizens in the

---

daughter of Samuel Blodget, Sr. (Savage's Genealogical Dictionary; Bond's Genealogy of Watertown, etc.)

Samuel Blodget published A Prospective Plan of the Battle near Lake George, on the Eighth Day of September, 1755, with an Explanation thereof; containing a full, though short, History of that important affair. By Samuel Blodget, occasionally at the camp when the battle was fought. Boston, N. E.: Richard Draper. MDCCLV., 4to. Title, pp. 5. Plan. London: T. Jefferys. MDCCLVI. 4to, pp. (2), 5.

* "The writer needed not the recommendation of his former commander to persuade him to purchase, as he did in 1791, property to the amount of above $100,000 in and adjoining the city, one day to become the noblest of the universe. Of the first purchase he made he gave above 1,500 lots to the United States, or one-half of his property, in common with other proprietors of the lands, on the site selected for the permanent seat of the government."—(Economica, page 24.)

"From the time of the first mention of a federal city and a national university, every opportunity to expand the mind of the writer has been embraced. The opportunities for inquiry were but few, until when, in an impaired state of health, originating in the army by the severe campaigns of 1775 to 1778, occasioned in 1784 a visit to Europe, where no time was lost to search for such information as was deemed worth transporting to America. After a second visit to Europe, the writer returned in 1791 and informed President Washington of the plans he had attempted from the best points only of the ancient and modern cities of the old world, and adapted to his ideas for a

Northern States to join his fortunes to the enterprises on which Washington had set his heart. At the time of the original action by Congress, authorizing the establishment of the national capital on the Potomac, no money was appropriated and no expenditure directed or authorized by the general government itself. It was a permissive act merely, providing that if the friends of the site on the Potomac should found a city and erect public buildings there fit for the occupation of Congress before the year 1800, then the seat of government should be removed to and established at that city. Beyond this the work was that of Washington, Jefferson, the States of Virginia and Maryland, and their personal friends in the Northern States. The commissioners authorized to conduct the negotiations began their work March 11, 1791, and formed an agreement with the proprietors of the lands chosen as the site of the city, March 31 of the same year, by which it was stipulated that one-half of the lots and squares into which these lands should be laid out, should remain the property of the original owners, and one-half should become the property of the new city, and be sold to raise money to erect the public buildings. Mr. Blodget at that time purchased 500 acres, being one of the largest of the private properties on the site, and it was duly laid out in squares and lots under the terms of the agreement. He also purchased several hundred single lots at a public sale of lots held for the benefit of the city, in October, 1791, being much the largest individual purchaser at the sale, and bringing to the new city several of his personal friends, from Boston, as purchasers. The State of Virginia had appropriated $70,000, and Maryland $120,000, toward the cost of the Capitol and President's House, but no money being obtainable from these State appropria-

---

federal heart or capital for his country. But his views for the university were what he most prized, designed in part at the Hague, and completed at Oxford, where he had all the universities of ancient and modern times to guide his pencil."

The suggestion as to a national university was first made at the camp at Cambridge, in October, 1775, "when Major William Blodget went to the quarters of General Washington to complain of the ruinous state of the colleges from the conduct of the militia quartered therein. The writer of this being in company with his friend and relation, and hearing General Greene join in lamenting the then ruinous state of the eldest seminary of Massachusetts, observed, merely to console the company of friends, that to make amends for these injuries, after our war he hoped we should erect a noble university, at which all the youth of the world might be proud to receive instruction. What was thus pleasantly said, Washington immediately replied to: '*Young man, you are a prophet, inspired to speak what I am confident will one day be realized.*'" The original of the design for this university is in the Library of Congress at Washington. —(*Ibid.*, pp. 21-23.)

tions,* a plan for a general loan of $500,000 was proposed by Mr. Blodget, and carried out in part by the commissioners: 500 bonds of $1,000 each being prepared, and Mr. Blodget advancing $10,000 of his own money,† which sum was actually paid to them July 17, 1792.

At this time the plans for the President's House and Capitol were so far matured that the foundations of each were begun, and, as it happened, these advances by Mr. Blodget were directly applied to that purpose.‡

During this and the following year Mr. Blodget gave his entire time to the interests of the new city, buying very largely himself, and inducing many of his Boston friends to buy of the government lots sold on October 8, 1792, for which the commissioners tendered him their thanks, officially, in letters to the President. Soon after this sale Mr. Jefferson suggested to the commissioners the appointment of a Supervisor, or General Superintendent of the work of erecting the public buildings, naming Mr. Blodget as a suitable person, and on June 5, 1793, the commissioners duly appointed him Supervisor as follows: "———— You are retained for one year, commencing the 1st instant, as Supervisor of the buildings and in general of the affairs committed to our care, for which you are to receive £600, payable in money or in lots at their just value," etc.

In pursuance of this appointment, he entered at once on the most active duties, the greatest difficulty existing in obtaining the money appropriated by the States of Virginia and Maryland, only a small portion as yet being received. In this emergency, and as the project of a general loan on pledge of the real estate of the city had failed, owing

* Mr. Jefferson, then Secretary of State, writes to the Commissioners, May 11, 1792: "I had informed you that the catastrophe among the paper dealers would retard the completion of the loan. I now enclose you a letter from Mr. Blodget, by which you will perceive its effect to be greater than he had at first supposed. He thinks that the payment of June, which if the loan had been filled up, would have been of $50,000, must now be thrown back and consolidated with that of November, except as to $10,000 which he undertakes to pay on the 15th of June for eighty shares he takes himself, and twenty shares he has disposed of. After consultation with the President we concluded nothing better was to be done than to leave the matter in Mr. Blodget's hands. I therefore yesterday delivered his 500 warrants for which I enclose his receipt."

† See letter of Thomas Jefferson to the commissioners, dated at Philadelphia, July 11, 1792, in which he says: "I enclose you a letter received from him (Samuel Blodget) this day, informing you that the deposit of $10,000 is made in the Boston Bank, and will be paid to your orders."

‡ See also letter of acknowledgment of the commissioners to Samuel Blodget, July 18, 1792, in which they accept the money, and advise him that the foundations of the buildings will at once be entered upon.

to the general financial depression, the commissioners resorted to a lottery, which was drawn in the latter part of the year, and yielded a moderate sum for the use of the new city. A second lottery was less fortunate, and it resulted in claims which embarrassed the commissioners and their agent for years afterwards. Mr. Blodget ascribes the losses and misfortunes of the new city then and subsequently to the refusal of Congress to guarantee any loans or make any appropriations for erecting the public buildings or laying out the city. Even after the seat of government was duly established there, in 1800, the same neglect continued, and Mr. Blodget found himself, as did other proprietors, actually unable to continue the payment of taxes on the large number of lots and squares, placed at a high valuation, but wholly unsalable. He paid taxes on much the largest amount of property in the city from 1791 to 1807; most of the speculative purchases by Robert Morris, James Greenleaf, Nicholson and others, were not kept up by the purchasers, and ultimately reverted to the city, and other proprietors were, as Mr. Blodget was, nearly ruined by the burden of carrying large properties which could not be sold.*

At this time, or more particularly in 1804 to 1806, Mr. Blodget published several editions of a statistical and financial volume, which had a wide reputation and was frequently quoted in standard European works. This work was published in the completest form in 1806, under the title "ECONOMICA; *A Statistical Manual for the United States of America*," pp. 202, with Appendix, containing the first general tables of population, commerce, industry and social statistics, prepared for general circulation. This work has been frequently quoted as an excellent authority for events of its time.†

From 1793 to 1814 Mr. Blodget resided chiefly at Washington, although he was much at Philadelphia, and had large business interests there. He was active in promoting the business interests of both cities, was a large stockholder in the first insurance company, marine and fire, founded in Philadelphia, and which sustained heavy losses from the French spoliations. He had an estate in Mantua, West Philadelphia, which continued in possession of his family. In Washington the fine mansion on his original purchase was located just north of the junction of Rhode Island and Massachusetts avenues. Thirty-eight entire squares,

---

* The assessed value of his estate in Washington in 1803 was $75,199, embracing 5606.903 square feet of city lots.

† At page 96 of this volume will be found a letter of President Washington to Samuel Blodget, Jr., written about the time of his appointment as Supervisor at Washington, complimenting him on his services to the city, and sending his good wishes to his venerable father at Concord, N. H.

twelve half squares, and 186 single lots were standing to his name on the assessment books for many years, most of them so remaining in 1807.

In 1812 to 1814 his health was much broken, and further misfortunes to his property interests, resulting from the war, induced his final return to Philadelphia, in 1814, where he died in April of that year. In pursuit of his purpose of founding a national university, he made at one time a large donation of his property in the city of Washington—1,500 lots—and stocks in various companies were left to the same purpose in President Washington's will, at his death, in 1799. The estimated value of these stocks was $25,000, but in both cases the intended donation was not realized. Several thousand dollars were, however, deposited by Mr. Blodget in a bank at Georgetown, and a form of organization of trustees was maintained for many years afterwards, Judge Bushrod Washington being the principal and last surviving trustee.

The enterprises and efforts which engaged his attention almost from 1775 to the day of his death were peculiarly difficult, and their success doubtful or remote. But the city of Washington, which was looked on as being impracticable at the time it was founded, and for which Congress then absolutely refused all aid, was actually prepared for occupation as the seat of government, in 1800, in a great degree by his own efforts and sacrifices. The records of the commissioners—Daniel Carroll, Thomas Johnson and David Stuart—are full of testimony to the vital character of the aid rendered them at every step by Mr. Blodget, and the money given by him personally was the first considerable amount applied to the erection of the two most necessary structures, the Capitol and the President's House.

With him it was a labor of love and a work of supreme patriotism to aid in founding the city Washington had chosen, and Congress had reluctantly permitted Washington and Jefferson to build, if they could, in the comparatively remote locality on the Potomac. Other cities looked on the effort as unwise, and opposed it as being injurious to their interests; but the commissioners, without money, finally triumphed—a few devoted friends of Washington, who became attached to him when in New England, in 1775, came to their relief, and adhered to them to the end. Mr. Blodget left four children (see genealogy). His portrait, painted by Trumbull, is in existence. His remains are buried in Christ Church ground, Philadelphia.

No. VIII.—Page 407.

The Hon. Thomas Smith.

My chief knowledge of this collateral ancestor of my own—a half-brother of my great-grandfather, Dr. William Smith, the Provost—is derived from an obituary notice of him in the *United States Gazette* of April, 1809. I am not able to say who the author of it was, possibly Mr. Enos Bronson,* long the editor of that paper: a gentleman of talents at once versatile, strong and graceful, with an education various and finished. This gentleman was an acquaintance and friend of Judge Smith, as were almost all that high class of gentlemen, members of the bar and leading Federalists of Philadelphia, who gave tone to society in our city at that time: Edward Tilghman, William Rawle, William Lewis, Joseph Hopkinson, Charles Willing Hare, Horace Binney, Charles Chauncey, John B. Wallace, William Meredith and others. Mr. Bronson may very well have written it, though a literary friend familiar with his style, as also with that of the late Chief Justice Tilgh-

---

* Enos Bronson, as we learn from Mr. Eugene H. Munday's valuable Historical Sketch of the *North American and United States Gazette*, was a native of Waterbury, Conn., and born March 31, 1774. He was graduated at Yale College, and afterwards began the study of the law. He did not, however, long continue this pursuit. Removing to Philadelphia, he became a teacher in the Academy of the Protestant Episcopal Church. His tastes were towards literature and political acquisitions, etc. He soon afterwards (A. D. 1801) purchased the *Gazette of the United States*, succeeding John Ward Fenno in the editorship, and conducting the paper in the interest of Federal politics. About the time of our declaration of war against Great Britain (A D. 1812), party spirit ran very high. In Baltimore a riot occurred, and the printing office of a Federal newspaper was destroyed by a mob. The office of Mr. Bronson was threatened with a similar fate if he did not cease from his unfavorable criticisms upon the administration and its Democratic leaders. Mr. Bronson was not to be intimidated, nor to cease the expression of his just political views at the dictation of ruffians. At last, however, the threats of violence against his office took actual shape. He received intelligence from a good source that on a night fixed the office would be sacked. On that same night the late Nathaniel Chapman, M. D., Charles Chauncey, the Hon. Bird Wilson, John B. Wallace, Horace Binney, Thomas Biddle, with a few other gentlemen (all intimate friends of Mr. Bronson), Federalists all, of vigorous strength, came to the office of the *Gazette* with muskets well loaded with ball, bayonets set, and gave evidence of what any band of ruffians might expect. The ringleaders of the mob came and looked;

man, suggests to me that a certain plainness of manner gives it rather to the eminent Chief Justice of Pennsylvania just named, who was warmly attached to his Associate, and was one of the executors, I think, of his last will. Come from what source it may, it is worthy of preservation in the biographies of the eminent Judges of Pennsylvania.

OBITUARY.

HON. THOMAS SMITH was a native of North Britain, from whence he emigrated in early life to this continent. On the 9th of February, 1769, he was appointed deputy surveyor of an extensive frontier district, and established his residence at the town of Bedford. In the execution of his official duties he displayed integrity and abilities which could not have been exceeded. His fidelity in this important and interesting trust was so strongly marked that no individual has been able to complain of injury; and exemption from law suits, and certainty of titles to property, have been almost the invariable result. So high was his sense of honor, so inflexible his principles of justice, that he would never suffer even suspicion to cast a shade over his official character. His private interests yielded to the firmness of his mind; and although landed property was then so easily to be acquired, he scrupulously avoided all speculation, determined that the desire of gain should neither warp his rectitude nor give birth to jealousy in others.

When the county of Bedford was erected, he received commissions from the then proprietors to execute the offices of Prothonotary, Clerk of the Sessions, Orphans' Courts, and Recorder of Deeds for that county; and such was the uniform tenor of his conduct as to insure the respect, esteem and attachment of all who had any transactions with him.

At the commencement of the late Revolution he zealously espoused the cause of his adopted country, and at the head of his regiment of militia performed his tour of duty

---

looked again and went away. An hour or two after midnight they came again and found the guard still on duty. They then disappeared, and never renewed their visits or their menaces. While proprietor of the *United States Gazette*, Mr. Bronson published several works, including "Roscoe's Life of Lorenzo de Medecis," and "Leo X.," by the same author. They are beautiful specimens of typography. "Under much coldness of manner, amounting almost to apathy, Mr. Bronson," said the *Baltimore Chronicle*, when noticing his death, which occurred in April, 1823, "possessed a warm and benevolent heart, alive to all tender impulses, blended with uncommon boldness and decision. His facility in writing and his powers of abstraction were remarkable. With his office filled with men like Joseph Dennie, Nathaniel Chapman, Thomas Biddle and others, the wits and conversation men of Philadelphia at that day—talking, telling stories and laughing, he would hand sheet after sheet of his ready composition to the printer's boy, and read proofs in which not an error would be left."

Mr. Bronson married Mary, daughter of the venerable Bishop White. Two of his seven children survive: one the widow of the late accomplished Prof. Henry Reed, who was lost at sea on the ill-fated "Arctic;" the other the Rev. William White Bronson, a minister of the Protestant Episcopal Church, distinguished for his theological learning and valued by all who know him for his devotion to the sick and poor and suffering of every class who need his service. I owe to him my many thanks for services rendered to me in the presentation of this work.

in her service; and his attachment to the liberties and independence of these United States was inviolable.   By the citizens of his county he was chosen to represent them in the convention which formed the first constitution of this commonwealth, but it is just to add, that instrument did not meet his entire approbation.   As a member of the Legislature, frequently elected, his talents were useful, his exertions and industry unremitted; and when, towards the close of the Revolutionary war, he was appointed to represent this State in Congress, he carried with him into that body the same invaluable qualities, the same firm and inflexible integrity.

The law was his profession, and he practised with industry and success, seeking to do justice, but abhorring iniquity and oppression; never greedy of gain, he was moderate in receiving the honorable reward of his professional services.   He was a father to those who confided in him, however poor or afflicted.   He delighted to encourage merit and virtue wherever he found them; but he exposed, with severity, violence, fraud and iniquity, whether clothed in rags or shrouded behind the mantle of wealth or influence.   To those who sought it, he gave honest and sound advice in questions of law, according to the best of his skill and judgment.   He discouraged law suits, and scorned to foment litigation for the sake of gain.   He may have frequently erred—more frequently may have been deceived by statements imposed upon him by clients; but he never, knowingly, recommended the prosecution of an unjust cause.

When the judiciary department, under the present constitution of Pennsylvania, was organized, he was appointed President of the district composed of the counties of Cumberland, Mifflin, Huntingdon, Bedford and Franklin, in which office he continued until, upon the resignation of Mr. Bradford, he was appointed a Judge of the Supreme Court of Pennsylvania.   The arduous duties of both those stations he performed with skill and integrity.   He spared not himself in sickness or in health—he shrunk from no labor or fatigue.   Although his constitution was wearing away, his high sense of duty foreclosed from his view his approaching danger; or, though he beheld it, it appeared to him trivial in comparison with what he considered the obligations of conscience.   He never tasted the bread of idleness; nor would he have touched the emoluments of office if unable to perform its duties.   But he sunk under this too zealous attention to rigid duty, at an age not greatly advanced; and when, by a little indulgence and self-denial (most surely justifiable), he might yet have been spared to his afflicted family.

The expressions of his features were apparently austere: his outward manners were not marked with grace or softness.   In conversation, his sentiments were delivered with blunt sincerity, and were sometimes supposed, by those who knew him, not to designate the character of harshness—but his heart was replete with the finest qualities which could adorn it—humane, benevolent and just.—In his friendships ardent and sincere, and his acts of friendship executed with peculiar delicacy and grace.   In all his dealings he was scrupulously exact, and there exists no man who can truly say he has received from him an injury.   Those who knew him well will not hesitate to acknowledge the correctness of this brief eulogium on departed worth.

To his family his loss is irreparable; as a husband and a father, he was affectionate, mild, indulgent.   The happiness of his family was the great object of his life.   Domestic harmony reigned in his household.   His mansion was the abode of hospitality; long, very long will his loss be mourned; the memory of his virtues will remain as their sweetest consolation; but the deep felt sorrows of his afflicted widow and children cannot recall the husband, father, friend.

The following are the inscriptions from the tombs in Christ church-yard, Philadelphia, over the graves of Judge Smith and his family:

THOMAS SMITH,
One of the Judges of the Supreme Court of Pennsylvania,
Rests beneath this marble.
He sustained various public offices with ability and fidelity;
His integrity was inviolable.
An affectionate husband and father. In his friendships
Benevolent and sincere.
He conscientiously discharged his public duties
Until the last day of his life with
Unremitted industry and zeal,
And died March 31, 1809,
Aged 64 years.

Also
LETITIA SMITH,
Wife of the above, died March 8, 1811,
Aged 52 years,
Reposes here. Her last request prohibits more.
Let angels speak her praises.

FRANCES SOPHIA SMITH,
Daughter of Thomas and Letitia Smith,
Died in Savannah,
Feb. 8, 1829,
Aged 50,
Reposes here.

REBECCA SMITH,
Died March 16th,
1855.

LETITIA SMITH,
Died October 15, 1832.

GEORGE WASHINGTON SMITH,
Died April 22, 1876. Aged 76.

George Washington Smith, whose name is the last upon the list of Judge Smith's children, was the only son of Judge Smith. The following notice of him appeared in one of the papers of the day:

DEATH OF GEORGE WASHINGTON SMITH, Esq.

It is with sincere regret that we announce the death of Mr. George Washington Smith, who expired on Saturday last, April 22, 1876, after an illness of some length, at his residence, No. 911 Clinton street. Mr. Smith never having been in public office, nor in the practice of a profession of any kind; having been a good deal reserved in general intercourse, and having, moreover, been a frequent traveller and resident abroad, was not much known to the present generation of Philadelphians. But he was well deserving of the honor and respect of them all. His father was the Hon. Thomas Smith, one of the Judges of the Supreme Court of Pennsylvania, a native of Scotland (born near Aberdeen), and half-brother of the able and accomplished Dr. William Smith, Provost, and in fact the founder, of the old College of Philadelphia, now the University of Pennsylvania, both being sons of Thomas Smith, a man of property in Scotland.

Thomas Smith, coming to this country, went to Carlisle, Pa., where he practised law successfully, and built the large house there afterwards occupied by Mr. Hamilton. In 1790 he came to this city, and resided on the south side of Market street, between Tenth and Eleventh. He was appointed in 1794 a Judge of our Supreme Court, and died in 1809, leaving the reputation of an able and most upright judge. He was devotedly attached to the Federal party—the party of Washington and Hamilton, of Jay and Marshall; and he named his son after Washington, with whom he was on terms of personal friendship. His wife, who, if a picture of her by the elder Peale, still preserved, does not exaggerate her personal attractions, must have been distinguished by beauty, was of the family name of Van Dearen.

Mr. George Washington Smith was born, as appears by a record in his own handwriting in our Historical Society, on the 4th of August, 1800. His mother died while he was a mere infant, and his father in 1809, before he had completed his ninth year. He was then committed to the care of the late Chief Justice Tilghman and Edward Shippen Burd, as his guardians, the actual guardianship being discharged by the former, for whom Mr. Smith, in common with all who knew him intimately, ever entertained the warmest affection and respect. He received his primary instructions in classical literature from the well-known James Ross, the author of the Grammar, and in 1818 graduated at Princeton, where the late gifted Joseph McIlvaine, Esq., afterwards Recorder of this city and a Representative in the Legislature, was his classmate. He studied law in the office of the late Hon. Horace Binney, and was in due time admitted to the bar. But his circumstances were such as raised him above the necessity of practising his profession, and he never did so. He, however, engaged actively in matters of public interest, especially those relating to railroads, which then occupied the attention both of practical and scientific men, Mr. Moncure Robinson, yet surviving in honor among us, being in those days at the head of them. He was also greatly interested in the subject of prison discipline.

Two papers signed with his initials, "G. W. S.," in the *Views of Philadelphia*, published by the late Mr. Cephas Childs, give evidence of his ability in the discussion of what is now known as Penology. He had already been abroad, and paid much attention to the subject of railways in England and on the continent, and was often before committees at Harrisburg, where it was remarked by the late John B. Wallace— a leading member of the House of Representatives, and much interested in the subject of internal improvements, then representing, for about three years (from 1830 to 1833), one of our western counties in the Legislature—"that his information could always be depended upon for its accuracy." During some years Mr. Smith afterwards resided in Edinburgh and London, where he was engaged in vindicating before the Superior Courts of England, and finally before the House of Lords, the rights of a sister, who had married a Scotch gentleman of rank and fortune, to a large amount of property which, in his idea, she had, in disregard of her rights, surrendered to her husband's family, in the settlement of a family difficulty. The case came finally before the

British House of Peers, and is reported. The House adjudged, as we recall the matter, that his views were correct; though a majority of the Peers, acting on an old rule, made in the interests of family peace and harmony, that a family settlement will not be disturbed, even though a party have surrendered rights, unless the case be very grievous, refused to break up what had been once signed and sealed.

Of late years Mr. Smith had travelled much, not only in Europe, but also in Africa and Asia, spending much time in the regions which make the subject of Sallust's Jugurthine war, exploring its antiquities, and also in Palestine, where he sought to widen and to deepen the foundations of a religious faith that from early life he ever professed.

Mr. Smith, at the time of his death, was the senior Vice-President of the Historical Society of Pennsylvania, of which, with Benjamin Horner Coates, he was in 1822 a founder, and in which he ever took a deep interest. This he testified quite lately by a munificent donation of money. He was also a warden and a vestryman of Christ Church, in whose general welfare, and especially in the welfare of whose Sunday schools—where he personally labored as a teacher—he took a deep interest. During such time as his health allowed he was to be seen regularly in the ancient pew of the family, near to that of the same as occupied by Washington while President of the United States. He was for several years, and up to the very close of his life, a munificent benefactor of the Episcopal Hospital, devoting his large income to this and to other objects of charity, religion, or literature, in the most unostentatious manner, and without one charge upon it in his own favor for luxury, or avarice, or personal aggrandizement of any kind. In his politics, Mr. Smith belonged to the school of which his father was a well-known advocate, and from the principles of that school he never swerved. He was distinguished by a very high sense of political and personal honor; and though, as we have said, not widely known in this city at this day, his death will be lamented by a most respected class of persons among us.

Resolutions of respect to his memory were adopted by the Vestry of Christ Church this morning. Mr. Smith was one of the vestrymen of that venerable church for more than thirty years, and was one of its most liberal benefactors. For several years past he had annually deposited in the basin at the offertory at Christ Church, on Thanksgiving Day, for the benefit of the Episcopal Hospital, the sum of $5,000. He also gave largely to the new parish building fund, and constantly gave to the current charities and expenses of the parish, which will greatly feel his loss. The funeral of Mr. Smith will take place from Christ Church on Wednesday morning.

No. IX.—Page 411.

Richard Penn Smith.

RICHARD PENN SMITH was born at his parental residence, the venerable edifice still standing at the southeast corner of Chestnut and Fifth streets, Philadelphia. He received his early education at Joseph Neif's grammar school, at the Falls of Schuylkill, with whom he remained until he was ten years of age. He and his brother, Samuel Wemyss Smith, were for some years under the care of a private tutor by the name of Sanderson,* whom their father, William Moore Smith, Esq., had found reading the classics in the original upon one of his annual tours up the Juniata. He took a fancy to him, and brought him to Philadelphia as the tutor and companion of his two sons above mentioned.

When Mr. Neif quit his school these boys were sent to one at Mount Airy, kept by Mr. John T. Carré. After some years spent at Mount Airy, Mr. Smith went to Huntingdon, Pa., and was placed under the care of the Rev. John Johnson, a Presbyterian clergyman, who had there established a school, and was for many years well known as a successful teacher of the Greek and Latin languages. In 1818 he returned to Philadelphia and entered the office of William Rawle, Esq., to study the law. His fellow-students in the office were David Paul

---

* John Sanderson, who was born in Carlisle in 1783, studied the classics with a clergyman living some six or seven miles from his home, and in 1806 came to Philadelphia as private tutor to the children of William Moore Smith. In 1808 he became a teacher in Clermont Seminary, which was established near Frankford, the Principal of which was John T. Carré. Afterward Sanderson married a daughter of Mr. Carré's, and became a partner in the management of the school. He was a contributor to the *Portfolio.* While residing in the family of Mr. Smith he designed "The Lives of the Signers of the Declaration of Independence," which was the first attempt to combine their biographies. The first and second volumes of this book were written by John Sanderson, assisted by his pupils. The life of Hopkinson was written by Richard Penn Smith, and that of Chancellor Wythe by William Rudulph Smith; but the work was not published until 1820. The remaining seven volumes are attributed to Robert Waln, Jr., Henry Dilworth Gilpin, and others. Mr. Sanderson published, in 1826, "Remarks on the Plan of a College to Exclude the Latin and Greek Languages." His views were adverse to the establishment of such an institution. After the death of Stephen Girard he advocated, in accordance with those opinions, the introduction of the languages in the course of studies at Girard College. These arguments were enforced through the medium of the press, in a series of letters signed "Roberjot." He went to Paris in 1835, and remained there one year. His impressions were given to the world in "Sketches of Paris, in Familiar Letters to his Friends, by an American Gentleman. Two volumes. 1838;" "The American in Paris. Two volumes. 1838." These are light, agreeable, and abounding in wit and humor. Theodore Hook suggested the publication of this book in England. Jules Janin translated it into French, and it was published in 1843. He commenced a work to be entitled "The American in Paris," portions of which were published in the *Knickerbocker Magazine.* Upon his return to Philadelphia he opened a private school, and when the High School was established he was Professor of Greek and Latin. The writer was long his pupil. He died in 1844.

Brown, Thomas White* (afterwards of Indiana, Pa.), and Thomas S. Smith. He was admitted to practice as a member of the bar in 1820. He inherited from his family a taste for letters, and was early distinguished for the extent and variety of his acquirements. His first appearance as an author was in the columns of the *Union*, where he published a series of letters, moral and literary, under the title of the "Plagiary." About the close of the year 1822 he purchased the newspaper establishment, the *Aurora* (which long before this date had lost its violent political caste), from Mr. Duane, and assumed the arduous

---

* Upon the death of Judge Thomas White, which occurred in 1880, the following notice appeared in a Philadelphia paper:

A citizen of Philadelphia, through your journal, desires to offer a memorial tribute to the late Judge Thomas White, of Indiana county, Pennsylvania, who departed this life at his residence on the 23d inst. The deceased was a worthy descendant of a highly aristocratic family in Dublin, and born about 1799, in Sussex, England, where his father was barrack-master in the British army. At a very early age he was brought to our city, where he was raised and educated. Under the friendly auspices of the late John Vaughan, Esq., he was entered as a student of law in the office of the venerable William Rawle, where he graduated with his fellow-student, Richard Penn Smith, in 1820, with flattering encomiums, and was admitted to practice. He soon after settled in Indiana county, this State, in which circuit he rapidly rose to professional honors and wealth. Thus distinguished, he sought not political station, because it was uncongenial to his nature. Imbued with literary taste, he was at home in his well-selected library, and while he cultivated literature he also devoted his energies to agriculture and to the breeding of blooded stock animals—thus blending the elegant pursuit of letters and judicial learning with the useful science of modern farming. Nothing more honorable can be said of Thomas White.

To delineate a character so amiable and pure as that of the deceased, wherein eminent integrity was combined with all the domestic virtues of the husband, father, brother and friend, may prove a task more difficult than the writer of this may with propriety undertake, or truth unadorned can draw. The simplicity of his manners was proverbial. He was guided by the fixed principles of religion and good morals. On the election of Governor Ritner, in 1834, he received the appointment of President Judge for his district.

Governor Curtin—in view of his conservative but loyal predilections, and to avert, if possible, an ultimate appeal to arms to sustain the Union cause—appointed Judge White one of the commissioners to the Peace Convention that assembled at Washington before the rebellious die was cast. Alas! his eloquent appeals were fruitless.

Domestic affliction during the latter part of Judge White's life did its work to enfeeble his constitution. The sudden loss of an only daughter in the first bloom of womanhood—the death of his eldest son, Colonel Richard White—the long captivity of his son, Brigadier-General Harry White—with the additional loss of a very promising favorite grandson—so sapped his health and mind that he yielded at length his harassed spirit to that Supernal Power that gave it sixty-seven years ago. His body is buried in peace with his offspring—but his memory will live in the hearts of his widow and his family.

and responsible duties of an editor. At this work he continued about five years, when, finding it both wearisome and unprofitable, he abandoned it and resumed his profession. A good classical scholar, and a tolerable linguist, with a decided bent for the pursuits of literature, his mind was well stored with the classics, both ancient and modern; and amid the vexations and drudgery of a daily newspaper, he wooed the muses with considerable success. Perhaps to the discipline which editorship necessarily imposes, and the promptness which it requires, may in part be attributed the great facility he possessed in composition. While engaged in the duties of a profession, generally considered uncongenial to the successful prosecution of literary adventure, he produced a number and variety of pieces, both in prose and verse, which showed considerable versatility of talent. His favorite study was the drama, and with this department of literature he was thoroughly familiar. With the dramatists of all nations he had an extensive acquaintance, and in the dramatic history of England and France he was profoundly versed. Perhaps there are few who studied the old English masters in this art with more devoted attention, and with a keener enjoyment of their beauties. But it is not alone in the keen enjoyment and appreciation of others that he deserves attention. He has given ample evidence that he possessed no ordinary power for original effort in this most difficult department of literature.

We do not know how many plays he has produced, but the following, all from his pen, have been performed at different periods, and in most instances with complete success: "Quite Correct;" "Eighth of January;" "The Disowned; or, the Prodigals;" "The Deformed; or, Woman's Trial;" "A Wife at a Venture;" "The Sentinels;" "William Penn;" "The Triumph of Plattsburg;" "Caius Marius;" "The Water Witch;" "Is She a Brigand?" "My Uncle's Wedding;" "The Daughter;" "The Actress of Padua;" "The Bravo."

As an evidence of his facility in composition, it may be mentioned that several of his pieces have been written and performed at a week's notice. The entire last act of "William Penn" was written on the afternoon of the day previous to its performance, yet this hasty production ran ten successive nights, drawing full houses, and has since been several times revived. His "Deformed" and "Disowned," two dramas which may be compared favorably with any similar production of this country, were both performed with success in London.

In 1831 Mr. Smith published a work in two volumes, called the "Forsaken," the scene of which is laid in Philadelphia and the adjoining country during our Revolutionary struggle. Many years ago American novels—with the exception of Cooper's—were not received with the same favor as now; but a large edition of the "Forsaken" was even then disposed of, and it obtained from all quarters strong commendation.

In 1836 Mr. Smith wrote for Carey & Hart, of Philadelphia, a "Life of David Crockett," and one of "Martin Van Buren," and also published two volumes, entitled "The Actress of Padua, and other Tales," which have been eminently successful. As a writer of short tales, he was natural and unaffected in manner, correct in description, concise in expression, and happy in the selection of incidents. He possessed, moreover, a quiet humor, and an occasional sarcasm, which make his productions both pleasant and pungent.

Mr. Smith wrote much for the periodical literature of the day, both political and literary, and his poetical pieces, if collected, would make a large volume; but these appear to have been scattered abroad, without any purpose of reclamation. His name is attached to a limited number, which are distinguished by a healthy tone of thought, neatness of expression, and harmony of versification; but as, generally, they were produced for some particular occasion, they have—most of them, at least—passed into oblivion with the occasion that called them into existence.

Mr. R. P. Smith married Mrs. Elinor Matilda Lincoln, on the 5th of May, 1823, the ceremony being performed in Christ Church, Philadelphia, by the Rev. Dr. Abercrombie. Five children were the offspring of this union, of whom I am the only survivor. My mother died September 16, 1833, and we were alone—he made me his companion. Well do I remember how proud I was of him; he took me with him wherever he went, and his associates and companions (child as I was) became mine. James N. Barker, Robert M. Bird, Joseph C. Neal, Edwin Forrest, James Goodman, Edgar A. Poe, Louis A. Godey, William E. Burton, Robert T. Conrad, Joseph R. Chandler and Morton McMichael were the literary magnates of Philadelphia, and of all that intellectual coterie *my* father's star was the brightest, his wit the gayest, and his sarcasm the most cutting; as a writer he was admired; as a dramatist, at that day the most successful in the country, and with some fame as a poet, he was beloved as a companion and a gentleman.

In 1836 my father again married, retired from active life and went to reside upon the family-seat at the Falls of Schuylkill, near Philadelphia. Here he died, August 12, 1854.

His social qualities made him a great favorite among his acquaintances, and the remembrance of his brilliant conversation will long preserve his name from oblivion. His papers I carefully collected, which, with a full set of his printed works, have been deposited in the archives

34

of the Historical Society of Pennsylvania, with the fond hope that he may some day have a great-grandson to edit them and give them to the public.

James Reese, Esq. ("Colley Cibber"), in his "Life of Edwin Forrest," the tragedian, speaking of my father, says:

There are numerous anecdotes related of Richard Penn Smith, all of which display the most ready wit and sarcastic humor. Indeed, he was so celebrated for repartee and off-hand sayings that he was actually dreaded in company, and very few had the courage to measure lances with him when wit was the prize. A few we give here:

Richard Penn Smith avowedly wrote for money, and he required something more substantial than the blandishments of the Muses to tempt him to put his pen to paper. If Green Room anecdotes are to be depended upon, he was blessed with a thicker skin than usually falls to the lot of the *genus irritabile vatum*. It is told of him that upon one occasion he happened to enter the theatre during the run of one of his pieces, just as the curtain was falling, and met with an old school-fellow, who had that day arrived in Philadelphia, after an absence of several years. The first salutation was scarcely over when the curtain fell, and the author's friend innocently remarked: "Well, this is really the most insufferable trash that I have witnessed for some time." "True," replied Smith, "but as they give me a benefit to-morrow night as the author, I hope to have the pleasure of seeing you here again."

At another time a friend met him in the lobby, as the green curtain fell on one of his progeny, and, unconscious of its paternity, asked the author, with a sneer, what the piece was all about. "Really," was the grave answer, "it is now some years since I wrote that piece, and though I paid the utmost attention to the performance, I confess I am as much in the dark as you are."

When Mr. Smith was a young man, he was introduced by his father to a well-known Philadelphian by the name of Wharton, who, from the fact of having a very large nose with a wart on it, was called "Big-nosed Wharton," to distinguish him from another gentleman of the same name. When out of hearing, the father said to the son: "They call that gentleman Big-nosed Wharton." The son quickly replied: "They have made a mistake; they should call him *Wart-on Big nose.*"

Upon going one day into a hotel in which some of his friends were holding an argument about the city of Dumfries, Scotland, they made an appeal to him to decide the question. "I know nothing of *the* Dumfries of Scotland, but I know *a Dumb-freas* of Germantown." Mr. Freas, of the Germantown *Telegraph*, an excellent gentleman, who was deaf and talked but little, was sitting within hearing at the time.

He was at a dinner given to the Judges of the Supreme Court by the Bar of Philadelphia, on the change of the constitution, in 1837. Mr. Smith had his health drank, and when he arose to reply, a lawyer by the name of Lee, of a character almost infamous, and every way low, pulled him by the coat and urged him to toast *him*. As Mr. Smith closed his remarks he said: "Gentlemen, *you* have toasted the Binneys, the Chaunceys, the Rawles and Sergeants of the bar; allow me to offer the *Lees* of the Philadelphia Bar." Mr. Lee did not see the joke, and replied, to the amusement of all present.

Mr. Smith always raised his own pigs. On one occasion he had them killed on the *eighth* of January (the anniversary of the battle of New Orleans, where Sir Edward Packenham was killed). The next day he met a friend, who remarked: "Smith, yesterday was a fine day for killing pigs." "Yes," replied Smith, "but a bad day for Packing-ham."

The reader will excuse me for the insertion of some extracts from my father's letters to me, but they tend to show his character as a parent.

To HORACE W. SMITH, Nazareth Hall, Pennsylvania:

PHILADELPHIA, October 16, 1837.

MY DEAR SON:

You must not imagine that you are forgotten from my not having written to you; there is never a day passes but we talk about you. Your mother* is getting the clothes made, that you require, and in a few days they shall be put in a box and forwarded to you. We are at a loss to find a lid to any of the boxes about the house, as you cut them all up to make ships and toys, so that you have occasioned unnecessary trouble for want of thought. Before you throw away or destroy anything, you should always reflect whether it will not be of use to you at some future day. A little reflection of this kind will save you a great deal of trouble throughout life.

We are all well, and little brother Richard† has grown to be a fine big boy. He crows and laughs, and to-day we bought him a basket chair to teach him to sit alone. Grandmother is well, and takes great interest in your letters. She keeps them, and reads them over and over again. You must write to her without delay, and in your letter say something to aunt Lydia, who loves you very much, as we all do, and feel a deep interest in hearing a favorable report of your conduct and attention to your studies.

Mr. Godey was a good deal amused at receiving a letter from you, and told me that he would write to you. You should have borne in mind to have paid the postage on that letter, as you wrote to him on *your own business, alone;* but as it was to Mr. Godey, it did not matter. However, make it a rule always to pay the postage when you write to gentlemen on business in which you are solely interested. Your letter was very well put together, and afforded us all much amusement.

Mr. Forrest has returned from England; I went to see him, and he enquired after you. . . . Mother laughs a good deal at your sending for a *white satin* vest, for she was not aware that you owned one. You shall have a *new black velvet* one, out of my old one.

I have but to repeat to you, to attend to your studies, and by correct and amiable deportment endeavor to secure the esteem of your preceptors and schoolmates. If you are unfortunately at any time placed under restraint, for neglect of your lessons or any other cause, bear in mind that it is a temporary punishment for your own good, and instead of being annoyed at those who punish you, blame yourself, and endeavor to avoid a repetition of the cause. Do not view your teachers as taskmasters, but be grateful to them for the information they endeavor to impart, and set about all that is required of you with a cheerful spirit.

Do not neglect to write to grandmother, and address your letter to me. Write soon. Bless you, my dear boy; I wish to see you very much.

Your affectionate father,

RICHARD PENN SMITH.

Give my respects to Mr. and Mrs. Van Vleck.

---

* My stepmother—my father's second wife.

† This was my half brother, Richard Penn Smith, Jr. He took a prominent part in the suppression of the late rebellion as Colonel of the California regiment.

Again :

PHILADELPHIA, January 24, 1838.

DEAR SON:

You have neglected to write to me since your return, and I find that I must write to you, or remain ignorant of your health and condition. We expected to hear all about your journey up, your safe arrival, and happy reunion with your teachers and school-fellows; but it appears that you have not a single word to say, though you spoke, when here, in such high terms of the kindness you had received, and your perfect satisfaction. You must repair this neglect, and write without delay, for we are all anxious to hear from you, and grandmother is becoming quite impatient.

I have nothing new to communicate. Your uncle William is still at Washington, and has not been here since he first went. There has been a remarkable exhibition at the Walnut Street Theatre—a man seven feet eight inches high, from Kentucky, and but twenty-one years old. Think what a creature! he is half a yard taller than Mr. Traquair, and you have never yet seen a man who could not walk under his arm-pits. There was also a nice little man with him, scarcely a yard high, who is nearly twice his age—a mere Liliputian. I went behind the scenes and had a conversation with them both, to satisfy myself that there was no deception. The big man was feeble, possessed but little muscular power, and his health was delicate. He had outgrown his strength. He told me that he grew thirteen inches in one year, during a great portion of which time he was confined to his bed through rheumatism and weakness. The little fellow was as brisk as a bee, and though twice as old, bids fair to outlive his friend, "the man mountain." My dear son, nature, in her works, goes immeasurably beyond the extent of human comprehension; objects are daily presented to our eyes, of whose magnificence our feeble intellects could form no conception, and we pass them by without even noticing their beauty; but when, as in the present instance, she deviates from some well-established rule, our dull senses are shocked at the enormity, we recoil from her works, and cry "Unnatural!" Still it is her work; for what purpose thus formed—inscrutable; but though disfigured, not the less entitled to respect.

That which is coarse and grotesque seizes hold of the imagination of all; it is the lot of a chosen few to have a keen perception, and relish for the beautiful. I would have you rather look for beauties than defects. Cultivate a taste of this kind, and it will be an inexhaustible source of enjoyment to you. The world is full of beauty. The sky, glittering with myriads of unknown worlds, the green fields, the flowing rivers—I would have you love them all. They are mighty volumes, which God has spread before all his creatures; we see them daily, and it is wicked to blindly turn away, and refuse to read his works as illustrated there. Study and love these, my son, and your mind will be as young and joyous as at present, even when your head is gray.

We are all well, and send you a great deal of love. Your mother has been urging me to write to you for several days, but I have been much engaged in my office, and constantly writing. Say something to please grandmother, and write to her soon. Your uncle Britton died on Sunday, and was buried yesterday in the city. I went to the funeral. He had been sick for some time. Little brother Dick grows like a man, and I hope will soon write you a letter. I am going to Trenton, New Jersey, to-morrow.

Give my respects to Mr. Van Vleck, and tell him that whenever he thinks proper to draw upon me for the amount of your bill for tuition, etc., he can do so, and it shall be paid. Attend to your studies with diligence, and, above all, endeavor to do nothing—not even the slightest thing—that will tend to humble you in your own esteem. Respect yourself, and others will respect you. I scratch this hastily, with a very incorrigible pen, and fear you will not be able to read it. God bless you, my dear boy.   Your affectionate father,

RICHARD PENN SMITH.

Under date

PHILADELPHIA, April 25, 1838.

MY DEAR SON:

Shortly after the receipt of your letter I procured a copy of the "Actress of Padua" for you, and left it at the stage office; about two weeks after I called to ascertain whether you had received it, and found that it had not been forwarded, but the clerk promised to send it the next day, so I presume you have received it before this time. You shall have your music book, but I fear it will be attended with similar difficulties to transmit it.

The picture came safe, and your mother has had it handsomely framed and hung in the parlor. The frame cost three dollars, so your present has been somewhat expensive to me; but it was an evidence of your good feeling, and it afforded us all much satisfaction. It looks quite flashy, I assure you.

Thomas wrote to you from Harrisburg, and doubtless mentioned Anne's marriage to Mr. Hobart, and the melancholy death of poor David.* Within a few hours of his dissolution he was talking cheerfully of his speedy recovery. We are truly in the midst of death. My dear boy, you are but twelve years old; and yet in the brief scope of your memory how many of your friends and acquaintance, both younger and older than yourself, have departed!—within little more than one year, five or six of your own immediate relatives. Think at times seriously upon this, but not with a gloomy spirit. It is as much a condition upon which we receive life, as the necessity of breathing, and remember that death is divested of all terrors to the enlightened and pure in mind. It is the act of a wise man to live in such a way that the close of life will become more cheerful, and hold out far brighter promises than even the sunny days of his boyhood. In this manner I trust you will live. . . . .

Your uncle William went to Sunbury a few days ago. His book on "Wisconsin" has been published. Aunt Lydia is living with grandmother at the Falls. Why don't you say a kind word to them in your letters? They are always thinking and talking about you, and as soon as they learnt that you required new clothing, they both came to me privately, and wished to pay for a suit. Our sources of gratification in this world, my dear boy, are manifold, and not a few somewhat mysterious. It is beyond your philosophy to understand what pleasure they could derive in spending their money for you, when I cheerfully furnish you with everything necessary; but still it is so, and when you have made some progress in metaphysics, you may amuse yourself in tracing the motive to its pure fountain. You want your clothes by the time of the examination, but you have not stated when it takes place, and really I do not know. They shall be sent soon.

Little Dick grows finely. He has been very sick with a cold for three weeks, but is recovering. He endeavors to talk, can shake *day-day*, and pushes a chair from one end of the office to the other. He looks very much like what you were, and has a rousing big head. Mother scolded at your saying nothing to her in your last letter;

* David Conden, a bound boy, raised in the family of my grandmother.

she wished me to send you a dollar when she received the picture, but I thought I could spend it better, so declined. She sends you a great deal of love.

Attend to your studies with diligence, for in four or five years your school-education must terminate. I intend you for a man of business, for such are the most independent and happy. To become such will require the attention of several years, so you will perceive the importance of your time. I hope to see you industrious and provident. These are virtues enjoined upon us in the Sacred Writings, and their effects are forcibly illustrated in the following passages: " The ants are a people not strong, yet they prepare their meat in the summer; " " The spider taketh hold with his hands, and is in kings' palaces."

I enclose you a dollar, which your mother insists must go this time. Our best respects to Mr. and Mrs. Van Vleck. We all send you our best wishes and love, and hope you'll write soon. Affectionately your father,

RICHARD PENN SMITH.

No. X.—Page 445.

Printed Works of William Smith, D. D.

From the year 1750 to the year 1803, so far as known, or supposed to exist, by me.— H. W. SMITH.

A Memorial for the Established or Parochial Schoolmasters in Scotland, addressed to the great men in Parliament, etc. By William Smith, as Commissioner of said Schoolmasters. *London, Jan.* 31, 1750.

An Essay on the Liberty of the Press. *London, July,* 1750.

A Scheme for Augmenting the Salaries of Established or Parochial Schoolmasters in Scotland, dated at Abernethy, November 5, 1749. *Scott's Magazine, October,* 1750.

Essay on Education. *Published in a New York paper, Nov.* 7, 1752.

New Year's Ode. *January* 1, 1753.

A General Idea of the College of Mirania. With some Account of its Rise, etc. 8vo. *J. Parker & W. Weyman, New York,* 1753.

A Compendium of Logic, including Metaphysics, and one of Ethics, by Samuel Johnson, D. D. ; with a Philosophical Meditation and Religious Address to the Supreme Being, for the use of young students in Philosophy, by William Smith, A. M. *Published in Phila., in* 1753, *by B. Franklin, and in London,* 1754.

Letter to Archbishop Herring, giving an Account of the Death of Sir Danvers Osborne, Governor of New York.

London, Dec. 15, 1753.

Historical Account of the Charity for the Instruction of the Poor Germans in America. *Franklin, Phila.*, 1753.

Several Essays on Education were published during 1754 in the *Antigua Gazette.*

Sermon preached in Christ Church, Philadelphia, on the Death of a Beloved Pupil, September 1, 1754.

Published by Benjamin Franklin, 1754.

A Sermon Preached in Christ Church, Philadelphia, before the Ancient and Honorable Society of Free and Accepted Masons. 8vo.

B. Franklin & D. Hall, Philadelphia, 1755.

A Brief State of the Province of Pennsylvania. 8vo.

R. Griffiths, London, 1755.

A Brief View of the Conduct of Pennsylvania for 1755 : being a sequel to the last. 8vo. *R. Griffiths, London,* 1756.

The American Magazine, for 1757 and 1758. From October, 1757, to October, 1758, with a supplement ; 13 numbers in all. 8vo.

Wm. Bradford, Philadelphia.

A Charge, delivered May 17, 1757, at the First Anniversary Commencement in the College and Academy of Philadelphia, to the Young Gentlemen who took their Degrees on that occasion, by W. Smith; to which is added an Oration in Latin, by Paul Jackson. 12mo.

Printed by B. Franklin & D. Hall, Philadelphia, 1757.

A True and Impartial State of the Province of Pennsylvania, being an Answer to the pamphlets entitled "A Brief State," and "A Brief View." 8vo. *W. Dunlap, Philadelphia,* 1759.

Recommendation of William Smith, D. D., to the University of Oxford. 4to, large paper. (50 copies. *Privately printed at Philadelphia,* 1865.) *London,* 1759.

Discourses on Public Occasions during the War in America. 8vo.

London, 1759.

A Discourse Concerning the Conversion of the Heathen Americans. 8vo. *W. Dunlap, Philadelphia,* 1760.

An Exercise, consisting of a Dialogue and Ode, sacred to the Memory of his late Gracious Majesty George II. Performed at the Public Commencement in the College of Philadelphia, May 23, 1761. The ode set to music and sung with the organ.
Philadelphia : Printed and sold by Andrew Steuart, in 2d street, and by Andrew Gaine, in New York.

Discourses on Public Occasions during the War in America. Second edition. 8vo. *London,* 1762.

The Last Summons, a Sermon Preached in Christ Church, Philadelphia, on January 10, 1762, at the Funeral of Robert Jenny, Rector of the said Church. 12mo. *A. Steuart, Philadelphia,* 1762.

Exercise on the Accession of George III., at the College, 18th of May, 1762. 4to. *Philadelphia,* 1762.

Speech by John Dickenson, Esq., in Assembly of Pennsylvania, May 24, 1764; with Preface by William Smith. *Phila.,* 1764.

Answer to Mr. Franklin's Remarks on a late Protest. 8vo.
Printed by William Bradford, Philadelphia, 1764.

Juvenile Poems on Various Subjects, with the Parthia, a Tragedy, with some account of the Author and his Writings. 4to. By Thomas Godfrey, Jr. (This was edited by William Smith, D. D., and an account of the author inserted.) *Henry Miller, Phila.,* 1765.

Dialogue, etc., for the Commencement in the College, 30th of May, 1765. 8vo. *Philadelphia,* 1765.

An Historical Account of the Expedition Against the Ohio Indians, in the year 1764, under the Command of Henry Bouquet. Illustrated with a map and copper plates.
William Bradford, Philadelphia, 1765 ; *at the London Coffee-House.* (This work was reprinted in *London* in 1766, in *Paris* in 1769, and in *Cincinnati* in 1868.)

Four Dissertations on the Reciprocal Advantages of a Perpetual Union between Great Britain and her American Colonies; written for Mr. Sargent's Prize Medal, to which is prefixed an Eulogium spoken on the Delivery of the Medal. 8vo.
William & Thomas Bradford, Philadelphia, 1766.

An Exercise containing a Dialogue and Two Odes, performed at the Public Commencement in the College of Philadelphia, May 20, 1766.
Philadelphia : Printed by W. Dunlap, in Market street, 1766.

An Exercise containing a Dialogue and Two Odes, performed at the Public Commencement in the College of Philadelphia, November 17, 1767.
Philadelphia : William Goddard, in Market street, 1767.

Some Account of the Charitable Association lately erected ; also a Sermon Preached in Christ Church, October 10, 1769. 4to.
D. Hall & W. Sellers, Philadelphia, 1769.

Cato's Letters, containing some Remarks on Paine's Common Sense, etc.
Published by John Holt, New York, 1769.

Some Account of the Charitable Corporation, and also a Sermon Preached in Christ Church. 8vo.
D. Hall & W. Sellers, Philadelphia, 1770.

An Exercise containing a Dialogue and Two Odes, performed at the Commencement of the College of Philadelphia, June 5, 1770.
Printed by J. Cruikshank & J. Collins.

Works of Nathaniel Evans. *John Dunlap, Philadelphia, 1772.*

An Oration, delivered January 22, 1773, before the American Philosophical Society. 4to. *J. Dunlap, Philadelphia, 1773.*

An Examination of the Connecticut Claim to Lands in Pennsylvania. With an Appendix, containing Extracts and Copies from Original Papers. 8vo. *Joseph Cruikshank, Philadelphia, 1774.*

A Sermon on the Present Situation of American Affairs, preached in Christ Church, 1775. 8vo. *J. Humphreys, Jr., Philadelphia, 1775.*

A Fast Sermon and Prayer, at All Saints Church, Philadelphia, July 20, 1775, on Occasion of the first Fast appointed by the American Congress. *Philadelphia, 1775.*

An Oration in Memory of General Montgomery, and of the Officers and Soldiers who fell with him, December 31, 1775, before Quebec. 8vo. *J. Dunlap, Philadelphia, 1776.*

A Sermon Preached in Christ Church (for the benefit of the poor), by appointment of and before the General Communication of Masons, on December 28, 1778. Dedicated to George Washington. 8vo.
J. Dunlap, Philadelphia, 1779.

Ahiman Rezon, abridged and digested as a help to all that are or would be Free and Accepted Masons, to which is added a Sermon (see last pamphlet). 8vo. *Hall & Sellers, Philadelphia, 1783.*

An Account of Washington College, in the State of Maryland, published by order of the Visitors and Governors of the said College, for the Information of its Friends and Benefactors.   51 pp., 8vo.
Philadelphia, 1784.

An Address to the General Assembly of Pennsylvania, in the Case of the Violated Charter of the College, etc., of Philadelphia. 12mo.
R. Aitken & Son, Philadelphia, 1788.

Two Sermons delivered in Christ Church. 8vo.
Dobson & Lang, Philadelphia, 1789.

Eulogium on Benjamin Franklin.
Benjamin Franklin Bache, Philadelphia, 1792.

An Historical Account of the Rise, Progress and Present State of the Canal Navigation in Pennsylvania.   Map.   4to.
Zachariah Poulson, Jr., Philadelphia, 1795.

An Account of the Proceedings of the Illinois and Ouabache Land Companies, in Pursuance of their Purchases made of the Independent Natives, July 5, 1773, and October 18, 1775. 8vo.
William Young, Philadelphia, 1796.

Remarks on the second Publication of B. Harvey Latrobe, Esq.
Z. Poulson, Philadelphia, 1790.

The Works of William Smith, D. D., late Provost of the College and Academy of Philadelphia.   2 vols., 8vo.   Portrait.
Hugh Maxwell, Philadelphia, 1802–3.

No. XI.—Page 447.

Account of Dr. Smith's Papers.

My respected friend, Mr. Thomas H. Montgomery, great-grandson of Bishop White, is good enough to give me, at my request, the subsequent history of the papers of Dr. Smith taken by Dr. White upon the death of the former.

" 2320 Spruce Street, Philadelphia,
" 14 November, 1879.

" My Dear Sir :

" The MSS. of Bishop White, composed of his correspondence and other writings, which accumulated in his hands during the organization of the American church, were lent by him to the late Rev. Dr. F. L. Hawks, as an aid to that eminent historian in compiling his records of our ecclesiastical history. With him they remained for many years, as his work was a vast one and demanded time; and Bishop White, it appears, never sought to recover them, nor did his executors, after his death, give the matter prompt attention. Both of the executors predeceased Dr. Hawks by some years, and upon the death of the latter the Bishop's descendants took steps to obtain the MSS. from Dr. Hawks's estate. When it was ascertained that since Dr. Hawks's death they had practically been in the custody of the House of Bishops, Bishop White's descendants, with entire unanimity, decided that it was eminently proper they should remain in such custody; and under date of 15 October, 1868, presented the following Memorial to the Bishops:

"To the Right Reverend the Bishops of the Protestant Episcopal Church of the United States of America in Convention assembled:

"The Memorial of the undersigned, descendants of the late Right Rev. William White, Bishop of the Protestant Episcopal Church in the Diocese of Pennsylvania, respectfully show:

"That the said Bishop White, some few years prior to his death, loaned to the Rev. Francis L. Hawks, D. D., LL. D., for the purpose of historical examination, the major portion of his collection of MSS., consisting of correspondence between himself and many bishops, clergymen and laymen, in this and other countries; as also other papers, bearing principally on the establishment of the church in America, and being of very great value. That these papers were in Dr. Hawks's custody at the death of Bishop White, but were not claimed by the latter's executors, because of their understanding that Dr. Hawks had not concluded his investigations, and so remained with Dr. Hawks until his decease, September 26, 1866, no claim having as yet been laid to them for the reason above stated. That on the 27th of October, 1866, subsequently to Dr. Hawks's death, a descendant of Bishop White, and agent of your memorialists, called upon one of the executors of his estate, and there did make claim, to which answer by letter was returned under date of November 16, 1866, by the said executor, to the effect that he would be heard from in due time upon the subject; that, notwithstanding this reply, nothing further has been heard, nor was anything known as regards these papers by your memorialists, until a few months since, when information was received that they had all been placed by Dr. Hawks's executors in the custody of your venerable body.

"Your memorialists further show that they represent all the descendants of the said Bishop White, with the exception of two, who are now residents of distant parts of the United States, and with whom your memorialists have put themselves in communication; that they have every reason to believe, and do believe, that the assent and ratification of the same will in due course be had to this action of your memorialists, although it has been impossible up to this date to obtain it for presentation herewith.

"Your memorialists therefore pray that your Reverend Body take into consideration their claim to the said papers, and acknowledge the same, if in your wisdom it seems just; and that they be permitted hereby to put upon record their wish to make a gift

of the same to the House of Bishops and their successors, when such gift can be perfected by all the parties interested therein.*

"This Memorial was, on motion of the Bishop of Pennsylvania, who
had presented it, referred to the Committee on Memorials and Petitions, namely, the Bishops of Delaware, Virginia and Western New
York, who submitted the following report :

"The Standing Committee on Memorials and Petitions, to whom was referred the
Memorial of the descendants of the late Right Rev. William White, D. D., Bishop of
the Diocese of Pennsylvania, and Presiding Bishop, setting forth that certain papers
of much historical interest had been loaned by their venerable ancestor to the late Rev.
Francis L. Hawks, D. D., LL. D., and upon the decease of Dr. Hawks had been
placed in the custody of the House of Bishops, asking of this House a recognition of
their right of property, and permission to put upon record their wish to make a gift
of the same to the House of Bishops, when such gift can be perfected by all the parties
interested therein, report the following resolutions :

"*Resolved*, That the House of Bishops hereby acknowledge that the right of property
in the papers loaned by the late Bishop White, of Pennsylvania, to the Rev. Francis L.
Hawks, D. D., LL. D., remains in the heirs and descendants of Bishop White.

"*Resolved*, That this House highly appreciate the generous proposal of the memorialists to present to the Bishops the above-mentioned papers, and return their cordial
thanks for the promise of a donation of so much historic value.

"Which resolutions were on motion adopted.†

"At the meeting of the House of Bishops, in the General Convention
of 1871, 'the Bishop of Pennsylvania presented a communication from
the descendants of the late Bishop White, together with a deed conveying certain historical documents to the sole custody of the House,'
when, on his motion, it was

"*Resolved*, That the House of Bishops gratefully acknowledge the reception of the
deed of gift by the descendants of Bishop White, conveying to this House the papers
mentioned therein, and return to Thomas H. Montgomery, Esq., and through him to
all represented by that gift, the thanks of this House for the important trust now confided to their sole custody.‡

"In the interesting report of the Special Committee to the House,
in 1868, in the papers left by Dr. Hawks reference is first made to the
transcripts made in England, at the expense of the General Convention,
from original documents, 'in all eighteen folio volumes of historical
matter, the value of which cannot be too highly estimated.' The report
proceeds to say that, 'besides these important folios, this collection
comprises the correspondence of Bishop White, Bishop Hobart and
Bishop Ravenscroft, and the Rev. Drs. William Smith and Samuel
Peters.‖

---

* Journal of the General Convention of 1868, pp. 216, 431.
† *Ibid.*, 1868, p. 227.   ‡ *Ibid.*, 1871, p. 274.   ‖ *Ibid.*, 1868, p. 228.

"Trusting that the above narration may afford you the desired state-ment as to the destination which the valuable MSS. of your distin-guished ancestor finally took,

"I remain, truly yours,

"THOS. H. MONTGOMERY.

"HORACE WEMYSS SMITH, ESQ., Falls of Schuylkill."

No. XII.

Genealogical Account of the Descendants of William Moore, Esq., of Moore Hall, Penna., whose Daughter Dr. Smith Married.

William Moore (known as of "Moore Hall") married WILLIAM-INA, daughter of DAVID, fourth Earl of Wemyss,* 1722.

1. REBECCA, born at Moore Hall, February 21, 1724–5; died January 9, 1728.

2. WILLIAM, born at Moore Hall, October 5, 1726.

3. WILLIAMINA, born at Moore Hall, February 21, 1727–8.

4. JOHN, born at Philadelphia, October 1, 1729; died February 2, 1730.

5. JOHN (second), born at Moore Hall, January 21, 1730.

6. REBECCA, born at Philadelphia, February 21, 1732–3; died October 20, 1793.

7. THOMAS WILLIAM, born at Moore Hall, June 12, 1735.

8. MARGARET, born at Moore Hall, March 26, 1738; died July 17, 1745.

9. MARY, born at Moore Hall, July 8, 1741.

10. ANNE, born at Moore Hall, October 4, 1742; died December 20, 1810.

11. FRANCES, born at Moore Hall, March 10, 1744–5.

12. JAMES WEMYSS, born at Moore Hall, July 22, 1747.

III. **Williamina Moore** married PHINEAS BOND, M. D., August 4, 1748.

13. PHINEAS, JR., born July 15, 1749; died 1816.

14. WILLIAMINA, born February 26, 1753.

15. ANN, born August 5, 1756; died December 13, 1796.

---

* See pages 498–9.

16. Rebecca.

17. Elizabeth, died January 26, 1820.

Dr. Phineas Bond was born in Virginia, in the year 1717; died in Philadelphia, June 11, 1773.

IV. **John Moore** married Miss Ann O'Niel, December 3, 1758.

18. Williamina, born November 17, 1759.

VI. **Rebecca Moore** married William Smith, D. D., July 3, 1758.

19. William Moore, born June 1, 1759; died March 12, 1821.

20. Thomas Duncan,* born November 18, 1760; died July 9, 1789.

21. Williamina Elizabeth, born July 4, 1762; died December 19, 1790.

22. Charles,† born March 4, 1765; died April 18, 1836.

23. Phineas, born January 31, 1767; died August 16, 1770.

24. Richard,‡ born January 25, 1769; died October 1, 1823.

25. Rebecca, born April 11, 1772; died March 9, 1837.

26. Eliza, born May 16, 1776; died September 25, 1778.

VII. **Thomas William Moore** married Mrs. Anne, widow of *Dr. Richard Ascough*, a surgeon in the British army, July 6, 1761.

27. Janet Forman.

28. Thomas William.

Thomas William Moore, Sr., was a merchant in New York city, of the firm of Moore & Lynsen. He was admitted to membership in the Chamber of Commerce, October 4, 1765, and in 1769 was made free-man of the city under the appellation of gentleman. He died in England.

X. **Ann Moore** married Dr. Charles Ridgely, June 2, 1774.

29. Williamina Moore, born February 20, 1775; died April 21, 1808.

30. Mary, born August 9, 1777; died March 9, 1855.

31. Henry Moore, born August 6, 1779; died August 6, 1847.

32. George Wemyss, born April 4, 1781; died at sea, 1800.

33. Ann, born February 12, 1784; died August 29, 1805.

Dr. Charles Greenbury Ridgely was born January 26, 1738; was educated at the College of Philadelphia. He generally wrote his name Charles Ridgely, dropping the Greenbury. He died November 25, 1785; he was buried at Dover; Dr. Smith officiated. For an account of him see this volume, page 252.

---

* See Appendix No. XIII.   † *Ibid.*, No. XIV.   ‡ *Ibid.*, No. XV.

XIV. **Williamina Bond** married GENERAL JOHN CADWALADER, January 30, 1779.

34. THOMAS, born October 29, 1779; died October 31, 1841.
35. FRANCES, born June 25, 1781; died March 25, 1843.
36. JOHN, born May 1, 1784; died July 10, 1785.

General John Cadwalader was a son of Dr. Thomas Cadwalader, born in Philadelphia, January 10, 1742; died at Shrewsbury, Md., February 10, 1786, aged 44 years.

XVII. **Elizabeth Bond** married JOHN TRAVIS, of Philadelphia, 1792.

37. ANN BOND, born August 8, 1793.
38. JOHN PHILLIPS, born April 18, 1795; died 1817.
39. FRANCES BOND, born September 4, 1797.
40. ELIZABETH, born 1799.
41. WILLIAMINA WEMYSS, born 1802; died 1876.

XIX. **William Moore Smith** married ANN RUDULPH, June 3, 1786.

42. WILLIAM RUDULPH,* born August 31, 1787; died August 22, 1868.
43. SAMUEL WEMYSS, born September 1, 1796; died January 6, 1819.
44. RICHARD PENN,† born March 13, 1799; died August 12, 1854.

XXI. **Williamina Elizabeth Smith** married CHARLES GOLDS-BOROUGH, ESQ., of Horn's Point, Dorchester county, Md., May 15, 1783.

45. ROBERT, born February 18, 1784; died June 22, 1817.
46. WILLIAM SMITH, born September 26, 1786; died 1813.
47. SARAH YEABERY, born August 8, 1787; died 1862.
48. WILLIAMINA, born December 1, 1790; died 1792.

Mr. Charles Goldsborough was the son of Robert Goldsborough, barrister-at-law. He was born November 21, 1761, and died June 12, 1801.

XXII. **Charles Smith**‡ married MARY YEATES, of Lancaster, Pa., March 3, 1791.

49. JASPER, born March 15, 1792; died November 19, 1823.
50. WILLIAM WEMYSS, born March 20, 1795; died March 27, 1825.
51. WILLIAMINA ELIZABETH, born October 3, 1797; died January 9, 1848.
52. SARAH YEATES, born March 24, 1802; died March 4, 1847.
53. CHARLES EDWARD, born March 6, 1804; died January 2, 1829.

---

*See Appendix No. XVI. †See Appendix No. IX., page 525. ‡See Appendix No. XIV.

54. MARY MARGARET, born October 16, 1806; died January 11, 1870.

55. THEODORE HORATIO, born January 20, 1809; died March 27, 1837.

56. CATHERINE YEATES, born December 31, 1810; died July 3, 1817.

Mrs. Mary Smith was the daughter of the Hon. Jasper Yeates, Associate Justice of the Supreme Court of Pennsylvania. She was born March 13, 1770, and died August 27, 1836.

XXIV. **Richard Smith*** married LETITIA NIXON COAKLEY, of Lancaster. No issue.

Mrs. Letitia Smith was the daughter of John Coakley and Letitia Nixon, his wife.

XXV. **Rebecca Smith** married SAMUEL BLODGET, JR., ESQ., May 10, 1792.

57. THOMAS SMITH, born August 25, 1793; died 1836.

58. JULIA ANN ALLEN, born November 13, 1795; died July 26, 1877.

59. ELINOR MATILDA, born 1797; died September 16, 1833.

60. JOHN ADAMS, born December 28, 1799; died March 5, 1870.

For an account of *Samuel Blodget, Jr.*, see Appendix No. VII

XXVII. **Janet Forman Moore** married LIEUTENANT JACOB JONES,† of the navy.

61. WILLIAMINA.

62. RICHARD AYSCOUGH.

XXVIII. **Thomas William Moore, Jr.,** married (first) MARY,

---

* See Appendix No. XV.

† Commodore Jacob Jones was born about the year 1770, near the village of Smyrna, Kent county, Delaware. His father was an independent and respectable farmer. The subject of our memoir was at first intended for the practice of medicine; accordingly he graduated, but did not continue long in practice. The clerkship of the Supreme Court of the State of Delaware was conferred upon him; in this office he continued for some time, but as it did not agree with his health, he resolved to enter as midshipman in the service of his country. On the breaking out of the war with Tripoli he was stationed on the ill-fated "Philadelphia;" he was there taken prisoner, and kept in confinement about a year and a half. He was now promoted to a lieutenancy; he was shortly after appointed to command the "Argus," and gave such entire satisfaction that he was appointed a captain. In 1811 he was transferred to the command of the "Wasp," and distinguished himself in several engagements with the enemy's vessels; he was afterwards captured and placed on his parole. In 1821 he took command of a squadron, in which he continued for three years. On his return he was ordered to the command of the Baltimore station, in which capacity he served until transferred as Post-Captain of the Harbor of New York. Commodore Jones died August 3, 1850,

daughter of George Gibbs, who died in 1813; married (second) Miss BIBBY, of New York.

63. THOMAS BIBBY.

XXX. **Mary Ridgely** married WILLIAM WINIDER MORRIS, M. D., November 5, 1807.

64. WILLIAM RIDGELY, born January 23, 1811.
65. EMILY RIDGELY, born 1814.
66. ANNIE M., born 1819.

XXXI. **Henry Moore Ridgely** married SARAH, daughter of John Banning, Esq., of Dover, Del., November 21, 1803.

67. ANN, born February 21, 1815.
68. HENRY, born April 15, 1817.
69. NICHOLAS, born December 18, 1820; died December 1, 1849.
70. EUGENE, born May 4, 1822.
71. WILLIAMINA ELIZABETH.
72. EDWARD, born January 30, 1831.

XXXIV. **Thomas Cadwalader** married MARY BIDDLE, 1804.

73. JOHN, born April 1, 1805; died January 26, 1879.
74. GEORGE, born May 16, 1806, died February 30, 1879.
75. THOMAS, born August 27, 1808; died January 19, 1844.
76. HENRY, born January 21, 1817; died July 2, 1844.
77. WILLIAM, born October 2, 1820; died October 15, 1875.

Mrs. Mary Cadwalader was the daughter of Clement Biddle, Esq., of Philadelphia. She was born January 6, 1781.

XXXV. **Frances Cadwalader** married DAVID MONTAGU ERSKINE, of Restormel Castle, county Cornwall, England, 1800.

78. THOMAS AMERICUS.
79. JOHN CADWALADER.
80. EDWARD MORRIS.
81. JAMES STUART.
82. FRANCES.
83. MARY.
84. SEVILLA, died March 12, 1835.
85. STEWARTA.
86. ELIZABETH.
87. HARRIET.
88. JANE PLUMER.

Lady Frances Erskine died March 25, 1843. His lordship married

35

(second) Ann Bond, daughter of John Travis, Esq., of Philadelphia, she being first cousin to his first wife.   No issue.

XXXV. **Frances Travis** married J. G. Williamson.   No issue.

XL. **Eliz ibeth Travis** married WILLIAM GREENE COCHRAN, 1825.
89. FANNY TRAVIS, born March 8, 1825.
90. ELIZABETH.
91. TRAVIS, born March 7, 1830.
92. WILLIAM, born February 3, 1832.
93. ANNIE BOND, born October 10, 1834.
94. HENRY, born January 9, 1836.
95. GEORGE, born April 14, 1838.

XLII. **William Rudulph Smith** married ELIZA ANTHONY, March 16, 1809.
96. WILLIAM ANTHONY, born November 13, 1809.
97. THOMAS DUNCAN, born February 7, 1812.
98. HENRIETTA WILLIAMINA, born May 2, 1814; died November 27, 1873.
99. ANNE AMELIA, born March 13, 1816.
100. ALGERNON SIDNEY, born February 3, 1818; died October 10, 1818.
101. ELIZA, born October 27, 1820; died June 5, 1825.
Mrs. Eliza Smith was the daughter of Joseph Anthony, of Philadelphia, born August 12, 1789; died January 10, 1821.

XLII. **William Rudulph Smith** married MARY H. VANDYKE (second wife), October 25, 1823.
102. RUDULPH VANDYKE, born September 5, 1825; died June 17, 1857.
103. RICHARD MOORE, born October 1, 1828.
104. PENELOPE CAMPBELL, born August 2, 1830; died December 17, 1852.
105. JOHN MONTGOMERY, born October 26, 1834.
106. LETITIA NIXON, born January 5, 1833; died February 24, 1833.
107. MARIA LETITIA, born September 10, 1836; died December 26, 1852.
108. SAMUEL WEMYSS, born April 10, 1840.
109. MARY ELIZA, born January 24, 1845.
110. HENRY HOBART, born May 21, 1848; died April 18, 1850.
Mary Hamilton Vandyke, fourth daughter of Dr. Thomas James Van-

dyke, United States army, and his wife, Penelope Smith Campbell, born at Maysville, Tenn., April 17, 1805.

XLIV. **Richard Penn Smith** married Mrs. ELINOR MATILDA LINCOLN, May 5, 1823.

111. ELINOR MATILDA, born September 13, 1824; died November 19, 1825.

112. HORACE WEMYSS, born August 13, 1825.

113. DUNCAN MOORE, born September 15, 1827; died March 6, 1829.

114. HELEN WEST, born May 9, 1831; died July 20, 1832.

115. EMMA MATILDA, born October 26, 1832; died 1834.

Mrs. Elinor M. Smith, see No. 59.

XLIV. **Richard Penn Smith** married (second) ISABELLA STRATTON KNISELL, 1836.

116. RICHARD PENN (second), born May 9, 1837.

117. ISABELLA PENN, born January 22, 1839.

118. WILLIAM MOORE, ⎫
119. ELIZA ARNOLD, ⎬ twins, born January 4, 1841.

120. MARIA LEWIS, born January 23, 1844; died April 1, 1869.

Mrs. Isabella Stratton Smith was the daughter of Christopher and Elizabeth Knisell, born November 27, 1812; died May 17, 1880.

XLV. **Robert Goldsborough** married MARY NIXON, 1810.

121. NICHOLAS LOCHERMAN, born 1810; died December 5, 1850.

122. LOUISA NIXON, born May 21, 1813.

123. SARAH YEABURY, born November 5, 1815.

124. WILLIAMINA ELIZABETH ENNALS, born 1818.

Mrs. Mary Goldsborough was the daughter of the Hon. Charles Nixon, of Dover, Del., and the niece of Nicholas Vandyke. After the death of Robert Goldsborough (June 22, 1817) she married Mr. Gardner Baily, November 1, 1825.

XLVII. **Sarah Yeabury Goldsborough** married CHARLES GOLDSBOROUGH, ESQ., of Shoal Creek, Md., 1803.

125. CHARLES YEABURY, born 1805; died 1807.

126. JOHN McDOWELL, born 1806; died 1807.

127. WILLIAM TILGHMAN, born 1808; died 1876.

128. GEORGE WASHINGTON, born 1810; died 1812.

129. CHARLES McDOWELL, born 1811; died 1815.

130. ROBERT F., born 1814; died 1819.

131. WILLIAMINA E. E., born 1813; died 1865.

132. MARY TILGHMAN, born 1816; died 1849.
133. CAROLINE F., born 1820; died 1854.
134. WILLIAM HENRY, born 1818.
135. ROBERT F., born 1822; died 1824.
136. SARAH LLOYD, born 1824; died 1825.
137. RICHARD TILGHMAN, born 1826.
138. HENRIETTA MARIA, born 1828; died 1845.
139. CHARLES F., born 1830.
Charles Goldsborough, Esq., born 1765. He was a State Senator of Maryland, member of Congress from 1804 to 1817, and Governor of Maryland in 1819; died 1834.

LI. **Williamina Elizabeth Smith** married THOMAS B. MCELWEE, ESQ., February 6, 1822.
140. MARY REBECCA, born May 14, 1823.
141. CHARLES JOHN, born April 4, 1825; died January 7, 1850.
142. SARAH YEATES, born April 23, 1827.
143. ANNA, born June 12, 1829; died May 15, 1842.
144. CATHERINE YEATES, born October 16, 1831.
Thomas B. McElwee was a member of the bar, born October 31, 1792; died August 23, 1843.

LII. **Sarah Yeates Smith** married LEONARD KIMBALL, ESQ., January 29, 1823.
145. CHARLES EDMUND, born December 22, 1823.
146. THEODORE HORATIO, born June 17, 1825; died February 22, 1874.
147. WILLIAM DOUGLAS, born February 14, 1827; died 1838.
Leonard Kimball, Esq., son of Edmund and Rebecca Kimball, born December 11, 1785, at Bradford, Essex county, Mass.; was an attorney; died at Philadelphia, January 28, 1847.

LIII. **Charles Edward Smith** married MISS OWEN, of Baltimore.
148. MARY YEATES, born 1829; died in Baltimore, October 28, 1854.

LIV. **Mary Margaret Smith** married GEORGE BRINTON, ESQ., of Philadelphia, July 27, 1831.
149. JOHN HILL, born May 21, 1832.
150. MARY YEATES, born November 22, 1834.
151. SARAH FREDERICA, born January 23, 1839.
152. MARGARET YEATES, born August 3, 1843.

George Brinton was the son of John Hill and Sarah Brinton, born at Philadelphia, March 7, 1804; died June 30, 1858.

LVII. **Thomas Smith Blodget** married Miss Anna Marshall.
153. An infant.

LVIII. **Julia Ann Allen Blodget** married John Britton, Jr., of Philadelphia.
154. Ellen Matilda.
155. John Blodget.
156. Maria Louisa, died 1831.
157. Harriet Emily.
158. George Edward, born September 10, 1825; died July 3, 1861.
159. Isabella Smith, died 1854.
160. Mary Yeates, died 1853.
161. William Henry, died July 10, 1851.
John Britton, Jr., died January 20, 1838.

LIX. **Elinor Matilda Blodget** married Abel Lincoln, Esq., of Massachusetts, 1810.
162. William Smith, born November 10, 1811.
163. Thomas Blodget, born 1813.
164. Julia Maria, born February 7, 1816.
165. John George, born 1818; died 1842.
Abel Lincoln, Esq., died of yellow fever in New Orleans, June 5, 1822. Mrs. Lincoln married Richard Penn Smith, as will be seen under No. 44.

LX. **John Adams Blodget** married Nancy Fletcher, of Bedford, Pa., 1825.
166. Rebecca Smith, born March 27, 1826.
167. Eliza Duncan, born 1828.
Mr. John Blodget was an attorney at law, and practised his profession in Bedford, Pa.; he died in Philadelphia, July 5, 1872.

LXII. **Richard Ayscough Jones.**
168. John M.

LXIV. **William Ridgely Morris** married Catharine Harris, May 15, 1845.
169. Mary M., born June 20, 1847.
170. Walter, born February 18, 1849.
171. Julia, born May 13, 1857; died 1858.

LXVI. **Annie M. Morris** married Judge CALEB S. LAYTON.

LXVII. **Ann Ridgely** married CHARLES IRENEE DU PONT, ESQ., May 11, 1841.

172. AMELIA E., born February 26, 1842.

173. HENRY RIDGELY, born November 19, 1848.

Charles Irenee du Pont was born in Charleston, S. C., March 29, 1797. He was the son of Victor du Pont and Gabrielle Josephine Lafitte de Pelleport. His grandfather was Pierre Samuel du Pont de Nemours; he was educated at Mount Airy, Germantown. In manhood he engaged in various manufacturing employments on the Brandywine. He died January 31, 1869, aged 72 years.

LXVIII. **Henry Ridgely** married VIRGINIA JENKINS.

174. RUTH ANN, born June 28, 1848.

LXIX. **Nicholas Ridgely** married MARY TILDEN, December 18, 1845.

175. MARY TILDEN, born August 11, 1849.

LXX. **Eugene Ridgely** married M. A. MIFFLIN.

176. DANIEL MIFFLIN.

LXXI. **Williamina M. Ridgely** married ALEXANDER JOHNSON.

177. HENRY RIDGELY, born March, 1847.

178. NICHOLAS RIDGELY.

179. ANN DU PONT, born December, 1856.

LXXII. **Edward Ridgely** married ELIZABETH COMEGYS.

180. HARRIET MOORE.

181. EDWARD DU PONT.

182. SARAH BANING.

183. HENRY.

LXXIII. **John Cadwalader, Sr.,** married (first) MARY, daughter of Hon. Horace Binney, of Philadelphia, October, 1828.

184. MARY BINNEY, born September 22, 1829; died May 26, 1861.

185. ELIZABETH BINNEY, born September 22, 1831.

Mrs. Mary Cadwalader, born February 27, 1805; died 1830.

LXXIII. **John Cadwalader** married (second) MRS. HENRIETTA MARIA McILVAINE, daughter of Charles N. Bancker, 1833.

186. SARAH BANCKER, born 1834.

187. FRANCES, born 1835.

188. THOMAS, born 1837; died August, 1841.

189. CHARLES E., born November 5, 1839.

190. ANNE, born 1841.

191. JOHN, JR., born June 27, 1843.

192. GEORGE, born 1845.

Hon. John Cadwalader was born at No. 172 (old number) Chestnut street, Philadelphia. He was educated at the University of Pennsylvania, and graduated in the Department of Arts in 1821. He entered the office of the Hon. Horace Binney, and was admitted to the Philadelphia bar September 30, 1825. He at once took a high position as a lawyer, and was distinguished for the thoroughness, accuracy and variety of his learning and his success as a counsellor. In 1855 he was elected a member of Congress for the Fifth Congressional District, composed of a portion of Philadelphia and Montgomery counties, and served for a single term, when he was succeeded by the late Owen Jones. Upon the death of the Hon. John K. Kane, Mr. Cadwalader was appointed to fill the vacancy in the United States District Court, by President Buchanan. Judge Cadwalader died January 26, 1879.

LXXIV. **George Cadwalader** married FRANCES MEASE.

193. FRANCES, died an infant.

General George Cadwalader was born in Philadelphia (see No. 74). He was educated at the University of Pennsylvania, and graduated at that institution in 1823. He did not engage in any profession, but became the assistant of his father, General Thomas Cadwalader, who was the agent of the Penn estates—to which position he succeeded his father.

He in early manhood manifested a taste for military affairs, and at the age of 18 joined the First Troop of Philadelphia City Cavalry. During the Mexican war General Cadwalader served in that country under General Scott. He was breveted Major-General for gallant service at Chapultepec. In 1861, at the breaking out of the rebellion, he was assigned to a command under General Robert Patterson in the Shenandoah valley. He continued in the service during the entire war, and held a number of responsible positions. General Cadwalader married Miss Fanny Mease, a daughter of Dr. Mease, of Philadelphia.

General Cadwalader died February 3, 1879. His wife died January 9, 1880.

LXXVIII. **Thomas Americus Erskine** married LOUISA,

daughter of G. Newnham, Esq., of New Timber Place, Sussex, and relict of Thomas Adlington, Cheshire, May 12, 1830.

LXXIX. **John Cadwalader Erskine,** in the East India C. C. S., Bengal, married MARGARET, daughter of John Martyn, Esq., of county Tyrone.

    194. WILLIAM MACNAGHTEN, born January 7, 1841.
    195. FANNY MACNAGHTEN.

LXXX. **Edward Morris Erskine** married MRS. CAROLINE LOUGHNAN.

LXXXII. **Frances Erskine** married GABRIEL SHAWE, ESQ., 1824.

LXXXIII. **Mary Erskine** married HERMAN COUNT DE BAUMGARTEN, of Bavaria, June 16, 1832.

LXXXIV. **Sevilla Erskine** married HENRY FRANCIS HOWARD, ESQ.

LXXXV. **Stewarta Erskine** married YATES BROWN, ESQ., October 26, 1828.

LXXXVI. **Elizabeth Erskine** married ST. VINCENT KEENE HAWKINS WHITSHED, ESQ., only son of Admiral Sir James Hawkins Whitshed, Bart., K. C. B., April 1, 1832.

LXXXVII. **Harriet Erskine** married CHARLES WOODMASS, ESQ., of Alveston, county Warwick, August 29, 1833.

XCI. **Travis Cochran** married MARY, daughter of Isaac Norris, Esq., of Philadelphia, April 30, 1857.

    196. MARY NORRIS.
    197. JOHN TRAVIS.
    198. ISAAC NORRIS.
    199. FANNY TRAVIS.

XCII. **William Cochran** married ELIZA, daughter of John R. Penrose, Esq., of Philadelphia, March 20, 1857.

    200. WILLIAM GREENE, born December 27, 1857.
    201. HARRIET PENROSE, born November 5, 1860.

XCIII. **Annie Bond Cochran** married SAMUEL L. SHOBER, November 16, 1858.

    202. JOHN BEDFORD.
    203. ELIZABETH TRAVIS.
    204. SAMUEL L.

205. FANNY COCHRAN.
206. ANNE BOND.
207. REGINALD.

XCV. **George Cochran** married AUGUSTA, daughter of Andrew K. Hay, Esq., of Winslow, N. J.
208. GEORGE BOND.
209. ELIZABETH L.

XCVI. **William Anthony Smith** married MISS REBECCA C. BELLAS, of Sunbury, Pa., May 23, 1842.
210. WILLIAM BELLAS, born April 13, 1843; died December 5, 1865.
211. THOMAS RUDOLPH, born August 12, 1844.
212. HENRY HOBART, born June 30, 1846.
213. HUGH BELLAS, born March 23, 1850.
Mrs. Rebecca C. Smith died August 8, 1861.

XCVII. **Thomas Duncan Smith** married MISS SARAH W. BARNS, February 3, 1847.
214. MARY BARNS, born November 27, 1847.
215. THOMAS DUNCAN, born November 21, 1849; died December 31, 1860.
216. WILLIAM RUDOLPH, born October 13, 1851.
217. CATHERINE, born 1853; died 1855.
218. SARAH WURTS, born May 5, 1855.
219. ANNE HOBART, born December 20, 1860.
220. HENRY A., born February 3, 1864.

XCVIII. **Henrietta Williamina Smith** married ROBERT ENOCH HOBART, of Pottstown, Pa., July 30, 1835.
221. WILLIAM SMITH, born April 4, 1836.
222. SARAH MAY, born March 2, 1838.
223. ELIZA ANTHONY, born August 4, 1840.
224. ROBERT ENOCH, born February 20, 1843; died November 14, 1843.
225. JOHN HENRY, born September 25, 1844.
226. HENRIETTA, born May, 1847.

XCIX. **Anne Amelia Smith** married JOHN POTTS HOBART, ESQ., April 5, 1838.
227. ELIZA SMITH, born March 14, 1839.
228. JULIA BIDDLE, born March 29, 1841; died June 13, 1879.
229. JOANNA HOLLAND, born February 12, 1843.

230. MARY, born February 3, 1845.

231. NATHANIEL POTTS.

232. CECIL, died 1877.

233. DAVID McKNIGHT.

Mr. John Potts Hobart is an attorney at law, son of Nathaniel P. and Joanna Hobart.

CIII. **Richard Moore Smith** married MISS FRANCES BOYDEN, January 3, 1856.

234. PENELOPE EUNICE, born October 13, 1858; died January 23, 1859.

235. MARY FRANCES, born February 18, 1860; died March 22, 1861.

CIV. **Penelope Campbell Smith** married WILLIAM HENRY, ESQ., August 2, 1848.

CV. **John Montgomery Smith** married MISS ANTONIA HILDEBRAND, October 14, 1862.

236. WILLIAM HILDEBRAND, born July 10, 1863; died January 1, 1869.

237. RICHARD MONTGOMERY, born April 21, 1866.

238. HENRIETTA WILLIAMINA, born July 14, 1867; died January 16, 1869.

Mrs. Antonia Smith died August 17, 1868.

CV. **John Montgomery Smith** married (second) MRS. JANE M. CRAWFORD, November 23, 1870.

239. HAMILTON VANDYKE, born August 13, 1871; died March 24, 1872.

240. FRANCES AMELIA, born July 24, 1872; died December 1, 1872.

241. ETTA MILTON, born September 1, 1873.

CVIII. **Mary Eliza Smith** married GEORGE W. DEDRICK.

CXI. **Horace Wemyss Smith** married REBECCA, daughter of Isaac Dorland, Esq., of Huntingdon, Pa., April 26, 1849.

242. ELEANOR MATILDA, born February 2, 1850; died April 20, 1865.

243. RICHARD PENN (third), born November 6, 1851.

CXVI. **Richard Penn Smith*** (second) married LUCY PIPER, daughter of John George and Mary A. Woods, of Pittsburgh, Pa., November 16, 1863.

---

* Commonly known as " *Colonel*" Richard Penn Smith.

244. RICHARD PENN (fourth), born May 31, 1865.
245. MARY FLEMING, born August 17, 1867.
246. MORTON WISTAR, born June 23, 1872
247. EDWARD GOULD, born December 15, 1875
Mrs. Lucy Piper Smith, born May 5, 1843

CXVII. **Isabella Penn Smith** married JAMES E. FLEMING, April 28, 1859.
248. LIZZIE SCHRODER, born January 20, 1860; died June 23, 1860.
249. WILLIAMINA, born September 17, 1863; died January 27, 1864.
250. MARIA SMITH, born June 22, 1865, died July 11, 1865.
251. ELIZA GOULD, born July 31, 1866; died August 1, 1866.
252. MARIA LEWIS, born August 8, 1871.
253. ISAAC WISTAR, born November 17, 1875; died December 5, 1875.

CXVIII **William Moore Smith** married ELIZABETH BEEBE MELVILLE, August 4, 1865
254. WILLIAM MOORE, born January 19, 1867; died January 7, 1877.
255. ISABELLA KNISELL, born February 10, 1868.
256. EDNA GOULD, born May 7, 1874.
Mrs. Elizabeth Beebe Smith was born May 1, 1841.

CXIX. **Eliza Arnold Smith** married EDWARD WANTON GOULD, December 24, 1861.
257. DAVID JAMES, born March 24, 1863.
258. EDWARD WANTON, JR., born November 5, 1866.

CXXII. **Louisa Nixon Goldsborough** married WILLIAM E. HARRISON, Esq., May 15, 1844.
259. WILLIAM E., born May 3, 1845; died October, 1846.

CXXIII **Sarah Yeabury Goldsborough** married MR. JAMES B. STEELE, of Eldon, Md., 1839.
260. LOUISA NIXON.
261. WILLIAMINA E. E., born 1844.
262. ELLEN GOLDSBOROUGH, born December 12, 1846.
263. SOPHIA ISABELLE.
264. CLARENCE.

CXXIV. **Williamina Elizabeth Ennals Goldsborough** married MR. FRANCIS JENKINS HENRY, 1836.
265. MARY NEVITT, born 1837.
266. JOHN CAMPBELL, born 1840.

267 NANNIE OGLE BUCHANAN, born 1842.
268. ELIZABETH NIXON, born 1844.
269. WILLIAMINA G., born 1846.
270. FRANCIS JENKINS, born 1847.
271. ROBERT G., born 1849.
272. NICHOLAS G., born 1852.
273. HAMPTON, born 1853.

CXXVII. **William Tilghman Goldsborough** married Miss ELLEN LLOYD, of Wye House, Talbot county, Md., 1838.

274. CHARLES, born 1839.
275. WILLIAM TILGHMAN, born 1840.
276. EDWARD LLOYD, born 1843.
277. ELLEN LLOYD, born 1848.
278. FITZHUGH, born 1849.
279. NANNIE LLOYD, born 1852.
280. SALLY MURRAY, born 1854.
281. RICHARD TILGHMAN, born 1855.
282. ALICE LLOYD, born 1858.
283. MARY LEE, born 1863.

CXXXI. **Williamina Elizabeth Ennals Goldsborough** married WILLIAM W. LAIRD, ESQ., son of Rev. James Laird.

284. JAMES WINDER, born 1838; died 1864.
285. CHARLES G., born 1840; died 1840.
286. WILLIAM HENRY, born 1842.
287. MARTHA PIERCE, born 1845.
288. PHILIP DUNDRIGE, born 1846.

CXXXII. **Mary Tilghman Goldsborough** married WILLIAM GOLDSBOROUGH, of Myrtle Grove.

289. ROBERT H., born 1841; died 1865.
290. SUSAN ELIZABETH, born 1842.
291. WILLIAM, born 1843.
292. CHARLES.
293. MARY T., died 1849.

CXXXIII. **Caroline F. Goldsborough** married MR. P. P. DAVIDSON, of Virginia.

294. MARY F., born 1840; died 1845.
295. NANNIE S., born 1842.
296. PHILIP P., born 1843.
297. SARAH G., born 1845.

298. CHARLES G., born 1846.

299. WILLIAM F., born 1848.

CXXXIV. **William Henry Goldsborough** married MISS ROSA J. PACKARD, daughter of Professor Packard, of the Theological Seminary of Virginia.

CXXXVII. **Richard T. Goldsborough** married MISS MARY HENRY.

CXXXVIII. **Henrietta Maria Goldsborough** married MR. D. M. HENRY.

CXXXIX. **Charles F. Goldsborough** married MISS CHARLOTTE A. P. HENRY.

CXL. **Mary Rebecca McElwee** married J. M. SLEEK, June 30, 1841.

300. MARY REBECCA.

301. GEORGE.

CXL. **Mary Rebecca McElwee** married (second) WILLIAM J. ROCK, April 23, 1857.

302. FREDERICK JACKSON, born 1857.

303. WALLACE SHIPPEN, born 1859.

304. FLORENCE KATHERINE, born 1862.

305. FRANK MARBURG, born 1866.

CXLII. **Sarah Yeates McElwee** married TOWNSEND WHELEN, October 21, 1847.

306. HENRY, born August 20, 1848.

307. CHARLES SMITH, born July 28, 1850.

308. KINGSTON GODDARD, born October 5, 1851.

309. ALFRED WHELEN, born June 9, 1854.

310. SARAH YEATES, born August 7, 1856.

Townsend Whelen, son of Israel and Mary Whelen, born in Philadelphia, April 3, 1822; died October 26, 1875.

CXLIV. **Catharine Yeates McElwee** married EVANS W. SHIPPEN, November 25, 1852.

311. FRANCES HUIDEKOPER, born November 18, 1853.

312. CATHARINE YEATES, born November 5, 1857.

313. FRANKLIN, born September 9, 1865.

314. HERMAN HUIDEKOPER, born September 4, 1869.

315. HARBERT, born November 1, 1870; died November 15, 1870.
316. HARRY HOUSTON, born February 12, 1872.
317. MARY ELIZABETH, born November 23, 1873; died October 25, 1876.

CXLV. **Charles Edmund Kimball** married MISS SIGISMUNDA STRIBLING, daughter of Commodore Stribling.
318. THEODORE HORATIO, born November 8, 1854.
319. WILLIAM WARE, born August 3, 1857.

CXLVI. **Theodore Horatio Kimball** married MISS ELIZABETH FULLER, daughter of Richard Fuller, Esq., of Baltimore, April 13, 1858.
320. RICHARD FULLER, born November 3, 1859.
Mrs. Elizabeth Kimball died November 27, 1861.

CXLIX. **John Hill Brinton, M. D.,** married SARAH WARD, daughter of Rev. F. DeWitt Ward, D. D., of Geneseo, N. Y.
321. GEORGE, born April 11, 1868.
322. JOHN HILL, born December 13, 1870.
323. WARD, } twins, { born May 27, 1873.
324. JASPER YEATES, } { born May 27, 1873; died September 22, 1876.
325. JASPER YEATES (second), born October 5, 1878.

CLI. **Sarah Frederica Brinton** married J. M. DACOSTA, M. D., April 26, 1860.
326. CHARLES FREDERICK, born December, 1874.

CLII. **Margaret Yeates Brinton** married NATHANIEL CHAPMAN MITCHELL, November 5, 1868.
327. MARY BRINTON, born October 20, 1869.
328. JOHN KEARSLEY, born October 15, 1871.
329. ELIZABETH KEARSLEY, born October 31, 1877.

CLIV. **Ellen Matilda Britton** married CORNELIUS MOORE, M. D., of North Carolina.

CLIV. **John Blodget Britton** married MISS FANNY B. HORNER, daughter of Joseph Horner, Esq., of Warrington, Va., October 1, 1874.

CLVII. **Harriet Emily Britton** married MR. S. R. BOWEN, of the Eastern Shore of Maryland, August 15, 1844.
330. JOHN JOSEPH, born December 13, 1848.
331. WILLIAM CORNELIUS, born November 11, 1851.

CLXII. **William Smith Lincoln** married MARY, daughter of Robert Given, Esq., of Centreville. Pa., December 1, 1842.

332. JOHN GEORGE, born October 1, 1844.
333. MARGARET TAYLOR, born January 26, 1846.
334. ROBERT GIVEN, born September 12, 1847.
335. JULIA MATILDA, born September 23, 1849.
336. WILLIAM SMITH, born September 25, 1851.
337. ELINOR MATILDA.
338. HATTIE BELL, born March 4, 1856.
339. HARRY, born 1858.

CLXIII. **Thomas Blodget Lincoln** married SOPHIA, daughter of Michael W. Ash, Esq., of Philadelphia, March 1, 1835.

340. ELINOR MATILDA.
341. HARRIET.
342. SOPHIA.
343. JAMES RUSH.

Mrs. Thomas B. Lincoln died at Belmont, Philadelphia, January, 1844.

CLXIV. **Julia Maria Lincoln** married ROBERT WILLIAMS, ESQ., of Hollidaysburg, Pa., 1840.

344. ELINOR MATILDA, born April 19, 1841.
345. ROBERT BERKLEY, born July 1, 1845.
346. SARAH BARNS, born August 24, 1848.
347. WILLIAM LINCOLN.
348. RICHARD CURRIE, born June 10, 1855; died March 29, 1879.

CLXVI. **Rebecca Smith Blodget** married SAMUEL CALVIN, ESQ., attorney at law, December 26, 1843.

349. ELIZA BLODGET, born November 27, 1844.
350. MATTHEW CALVIN, born January 1, 1847.
351. JOHN BLODGET, born April 24, 1853; died July 14, 1853.

CLXVII. **Eliza Duncan Blodget** married MR. ALFRED ADAMS CRAINE, June 24, 1853.

352. JOHN BLODGET, born March 5, 1854, died February 25, 1860.
353. REBECCA CALVIN, born July 31, 1859.

CLXIX. **Mary M. Morris** married CALEB S. PENNEWILL, June 17, 1869.

CLXXII. **Amelia E. du Pont** married EUGENE DU PONT, July 5, 1866.

354. ANNE RIDGELY, born April 22, 1867.
355. ALEXIS IRENEE, born August 2, 1869.
356. EUGENE.
357. AMELIA.
358. JULIA SOPHIA, born 1877.

CLXXIV. **Ruth Ann Ridgely** married RICHARD HARRINGTON.
359. HENRY RIDGELY.
360. SAMUEL M.

CLXXVI. **Daniel Mifflin Ridgely** married MISS ELLA MADDEN.

CLXXXIV. **Mary Binney Cadwalader** married WILLIAM HENRY RAWLE, September 13, 1849.
361. MARY CADWALADER, born December 12, 1850.
362. WILLIAM, born September 3, 1855; died April 25, 1860.
363. EDITH, born April 29, 1861.
Mrs. Mary Binney Rawle died May 26, 1861.

CLXXXV. **Elizabeth Binney Cadwalader** married GEORGE HARRISON HARE, of the United States navy.
No issue.

CXC. **Anne Cadwalader** married REV. HENRY J. ROWLAND, 1878.
364. JOHN CADWALADER, born February 10, 1879.

CXCI. **John Cadwalader, Jr.,** married MARY HELEN, third daughter and child of Joshua Francis Fisher, of Philadelphia, April 17, 1866.
365. SOPHIA, born February 6, 1867.
366. MARY HELEN, born March 19, 1871.
367. JOHN, born February 24, 1874.
Mrs. Mary Helen Cadwalader was born July 1, 1844.

CCXVI. **William Rudulph Smith** married ELIZABETH R., daughter of Dr. George Bailey, October 7, 1875.
368. LAURA.

CCXVIII. **Sarah Wurts Smith** married ALFRED WHELEN, ESQ., April 21, 1876.
369. TOWNSEND, born March 6, 1877 (see 309).

CCXXI. **William Smith Hobart** married FRANCES LAURA, daughter of Isaac Sanborn, Esq., of Peru, N. Y., January 5, 1865.

370. MARY HENRIETTA, born October 3, 1868.
371. ROBERT ENOCH HOBART, born June 15, 1874.

CCXXII. **Sarah May Hobart** married WILLIAM J. RUTTER.
ESQ., of Pottstown, Pa.
372. ROBERT HOBART.
373. JESSIE IVES.
374. CHARLES.
375. WILLIAM IVES.

CCXXIII. **Eliza Anthony Hobart** married JOHN W. ROYER,
ESQ., October 25, 1865.
376. HENRIETTA HOBART.
377. SARAH WHELEN.
378. JOHN W.
379. ELIZA HOBART.

CCXXVII. **Eliza Smith Hobart** married JOHN W. HUNT, M. D.
380. MYRA.

CCXXIX. **Joanna Holland Hobart** married MR. E. F. CHAM-
BERS DAVIS, of Pottsville, September, 1873.
381. JOHN HOBART, born July 27, 1874.
382. GEORGE LINN LACHLAN.

CCXXXI. **Nathaniel Potts Hobart** married MISS ANNE ROSE-
BERRY, October, 1875.
383. BLANCHE ROSEBERRY.

CCXLIII. **Richard Penn Smith** (third) married KATE CECELIA,
daughter of Joseph Russell, of Philadelphia, April 28, 1874.
384. RICHARD PENN (fifth), born October 13, 1875.
385. RUSSELL MOORE, born January 26, 1877.
386. EDGAR WEMYSS, born September 2, 1879.

CCLX. **Louisa Nixon Steele** married MR. JOSEPH HENRY
HOOPER.
387. MARY MERITT.
388. WILLIAM HENRY.
389. HARRY ENNALS.
390. AGNES PITT.
391. MUNCY.

CCLXII. **Ellen Goldsborough Steele** married MR. J. D.
RICHARDS, of Pennsylvania.
36

CCLXIII. **Sophia Isabella Steele** married WALTER MEAD BUCK, ESQ., of England.

CCLXV. **Mary Nevitt Henry** married MR. SELBY SPENCE, of Worcester county, Maryland.

CCLXVI. **John Campbell Henry** married MISS NANNIE LAKE.
392. BESSY TRYON.

CCLXVII. **Nannie Ogle Buchanan Henry** married MR. J. N. STEELE.
393. JAMES.

CCLXVIII. **Elizabeth Nixon Henry** married WILLIAM T. GOLDSBOROUGH.

CCLXIX. **Williamina Goldsborough Henry** married MR. D. S. MEESE.
394. ROBERT G.
395. MARY NIXON, born September 10, 1877.

CCCVI. **Henry Whelen** married LAURA, daughter of William S. Baker, Esq., of Philadelphia, October 21, 1875.
396. WILLIAM BAKER, born July 6, 1877.
397. LAURA, born September 6, 1878.

CCCVII. **Charles Smith Whelen** married MIGNONETTE, daughter of William A. Violett, Esq., of New Orleans, January 14, 1880.

CCCVIII. **Kingston Goddard Whelen** married MISS MARY ROBERTS HARBERT, October 15, 1874.
398. SARAH YEATES, born December 21, 1875.
399. REBECCA HARBERT, born May 25, 1877.
400. VIRGINIA HARBERT, born October 19, 1879.

CCCIX. **Alfred Whelen, M.D.,** married SARAH WURTS SMITH (see No. 218).

CCCXI. **Frances Huidekoper Shippen** married WILLIAM ROBERT GILL, ESQ., May 3, 1875.

CCCXXXIII. **Margaret Taylor Lincoln** married MR. W. B. WATSON, February 6, 1878.

CCCXXXIV. **Robert Given Lincoln** married MISS MARTHA CAMPBELL, of McConnellstown.

    401. WILLIAM CAMPBELL.

CCCXLIII. **James Rush Lincoln** married ELIZA ALDRIDGE, daughter of Benjamin R. Blake, Esq., of Virginia, March 28, 1865.

    402. RUSH ALDRIDGE HUNT, born April 8, 1866.

Mrs. Lincoln died May 12, 1866.

CCCXLIX. **Eliza Blodget Calvin** married GEORGE W. SMITH, M. D., of Hollidaysburg, Pa., April 16, 1874.

    403. REBECCA CALVIN, born January 7, 1875.

    404. MARY MCDONALD, born March 16, 1876.

CCCLXI. **Mary Cadwalader Rawle** married FREDERIC RHINELANDER JONES, March 22, 1870.

    405. BEATRICE CADWALADER.

I have completed, so far as I have been able, the record through six generations of the descendants of William and Williamina Moore, of Moore Hall.

Of necessity, as in every case of a genealogy so long, and where the progeny has been so numerous, there are many omissions, and I suppose there must be some mistakes; but I have done the best that I could do under the circumstances.

As to the character of these descendants, the reader will have noticed they intermarried with prominent and influential families of England and America. Many have gained high and honorable places in the learned professions, and others deserve a fair place in the ranks of literature. I have known many, too, who, without any worldly eminence, and with no distinctions which literary *fame* gave to them, have held a place which, in any true view, ranks more highly than the highest of this poor earth; men and women, in private stations—some in private stations that were but humble—who discharged through long lives, and under many and trying vicissitudes, their duty to God and to man, "having their eyes only on the Master's service, and looking forward to 'the recompense of reward.'" They have not been borne to honors on the corrupted currents of this world. Their reward will come where there is " no shuffling," and " where the action lies in his true nature."

No. XIII.—Page 542.

Thomas Duncan Smith.

THOMAS DUNCAN SMITH, second son of Rev. William Smith, D. D., and Rebecca Smith, was born at Philadelphia, on the 18th of November, 1760, and was baptized by the Rev. J. Duchè, the Rev. Dr. Peters and Mr. Thomas William Moore being sponsors.

Of his youth we know but little. He was educated at the College and Academy of Philadelphia, where, under the training and watchful care of his father, he became an excellent classical scholar, and graduated with honor at the commencement held in June, 1776. Upon leaving college he studied medicine, and, having completed his studies, settled himself at Huntingdon, then a small town on the Juniata river, which had been laid out by Dr. Smith in 1767. It subsequently became and still remains the county town of Huntingdon county, which was erected in pursuance of an act of the Legislature on the 20th day of September, 1787. The new county had formerly been embraced within the limits of Bedford county, from which it was stricken off in compliance with the necessities and demands of the people; but the measure met at that day the most strenuous opposition, and it was only after a determined struggle that it was accomplished. Immediately after the erection of the county, offices were established for the transaction of the public business, and appointments made to fill them. Among others, Thomas Duncan Smith, of the town of Huntingdon, was duly commissioned one of the Justices of the county on the 23d day of November, 1787. Here in his dual capacity as physician and magistrate he continued to reside until his death, which took place, after a severe attack of fever, on the 9th day of July, 1789. As a young physician he is said to have been very successful in his practice, and by his talents and deportment to have enjoyed the confidence of all. As a magistrate he was firm and decisive, requiring from all obedience to the laws, and often adjusting difficulties among neighbors without legal process. A beautiful tribute to his memory, by his father, may be seen in his will, on page 419 of this volume, and his tomb may be found in the large cemetery on the hill overlooking the town of Huntingdon, and from which; looking up and down the Juniata river, can be had one of the finest views along its whole course. During his short life he had passed through "stirring times," and not the least of them in that portion of our State where he had located, and which was then becoming settled by a wild and adventurous population. He was a good and useful citizen, and died in the prime of life and in the midst of his usefulness, deeply regretted by the community in which he lived.

Cotemporaneous with the erection of Huntingdon county was the framing of the Constitution of the United States, which was signed at Philadelphia on the 17th day of September, 1787. Its adoption, as is well known, met with much opposition in several of the States, and in Huntingdon county became violent and riotous. The leader of the opponents was General William McAlevy, who had acquired a military title during the Revolutionary war, being mentioned as Colonel Mc-Alevy in the records of that struggle, and in connection with the alarms caused by the Tories and Indians. His residence was at McAlevy's Fort, in Standing Stone valley, a place that still bears his name, and he possessed much political influence among the people. The excitement of the times led to attempts by large bodies of armed men to obstruct the performance of public duty by the officials of the county, and to the offering of the grossest indignities to them personally, of which Thomas Duncan Smith came in for his share. Minute details of the events of those days may be found in the "Colonial Records;" but to give some idea of the feelings governing the people, I shall quote somewhat from M. S. Lytle's "History of Huntingdon County:"

"Colonel John Cannan, member of the Supreme Executive Council from Huntingdon county, was the first against whom there was any manifestation of enmity. On the first day of the court, in March, 1788, a number of men, bearing bludgeons and carrying an effigy of Colonel Cannan, entered the town. Justices Phillips and Henderson left the bench, the courts being then in session, and met the mob at the upper end of Allegheny street, and endeavored to dissuade them from a disturbance of the peace, which they seemed to have in contemplation. This effort, however, was unsuccessful. They marched down the street to the house in which the courts were sitting. There they made so much noise that it was impossible to proceed with business, and, after they had been several times warned to desist from this outrage, the sheriff was directed to arrest the one who seemed the most turbulent, and commit him to prison. When he had been taken into custody a riot ensued, and he was rescued by those who were acting with him in this violation of the law. An indictment was immediately drawn against the principals, presented to the Grand Jury, returned a true bill, and entered upon the records of the Court of Quarter Sessions;

but as preparations could not then be made for trial, the case was continued until the next sessions.

"In the following May a battalion of militia, which had been organized by Benjamin Elliott, Lieutenant of the county, was ordered to assemble in Hartslog valley. Some of the riotous element was present, and after falling into ranks made an objection to mustering under Colonel Cannan and Major Spencer, two field officers who had been commissioned when the battalion belonged to Bedford county, and who, it was alleged, had not been fairly elected—Colonel Woods, then lieutenant of that county, having obtained the return of such men as pleased himself. An assault was made upon Colonel Elliott, and he received many severe blows from several persons. A friend of his who undertook to protect him and restore order, was treated in the same violent manner. Elliott, in an account of this affair, says that 'they met, some for the purpose of doing their duty, and others for the purpose of making a riot, which they effected, about the Federal government, in which riot I was very ill used by a senseless banditti, who were inflamed by a number of false publications privately circulated by people who were enemies of the Federal government.'

"A commander was then selected for the battalion, who, according to previous arrangement, ordered that all who were unwilling to serve under the field officers heretofore named should withdraw from the ranks. More than one-third of those in line marched out and formed a new line in front of the rest. Colonel Elliott and the field officers, finding that the roll could not be called, and that to remain longer would be unavailing, retired from the field, accompanied by that part of the battalion which had shown a disposition to render obedience to those who had a right to command them.

"A few days afterwards warrants were issued by Thomas Duncan Smith, one of the justices, for the arrest of three of the leaders in this demonstration. The prisoners were taken by the constable before Thomas McCune, another justice, who merely required them to enter into their own recognizances for their appearance in five days before Justice Smith. In the meantime they gathered a large force of men, and when they came before the justice on the day appointed, his office was instantly filled by the crowd. They refused to give bail, and insisted that they should be committed. As he was aware of their designs, and as he was unwilling to give them a pretext for the commission of further outrages, he declined to comply with their request. There was, besides, no safe prison in the county, none having been yet erected. He reminded them of this, that the jail was but a 'block house,' and told them that, as two of them were owners of real estate, and that as it was but eight days until the June Sessions of the court, he would release them without security. Finding that he was unalterable in his determination, one of them, who was subsequently discovered to have a cutlass concealed under his coat, grossly insulted him and threatened him with violence.

"The accused and the crowd left the office and the town, and in the afternoon, about one o'clock, returned, more than ninety in number, sixty of them armed with rifles and muskets, and the remainder with clubs, scalping knives and tomahawks. They marched down Allegheny street to Second, up Second to Penn, up Penn to the Diamond, where they formed into a circle. Justice Smith was then called into the centre, and it was demanded that he would tear up the warrants upon which the arrests had been made. He refused to do so; but, having them in his pocket, he delivered them to one of the leaders. They were then passed into the hands of a man who must have been the greatest desperado of the party, as he had previously presented a rifle three times to Justice Smith's breast, and was only prevented by the interference of others from taking the Justice's life. He stepped from the ranks, and tearing the warrants threw some of the pieces at the Justice, saying, 'See now what it is to be a magistrate.'

"The Clerk of the Court of Quarter Sessions was next required to deliver to them the indictment that had been found at the March Sessions. It was also destroyed.

"Justices Smith and Henderson, having gone to the house on Allegheny street in which the courts were held, were followed by a number of armed men, who demanded possession of the Quarter Sessions docket. On obtaining it they obliterated the record of the proceedings against the rioters, the part which was obnoxious to them.

"The compliance of the officers with these demands was compelled by intimidation and threats. The order-loving portion of the community was completely overawed.

"Information was then brought to Smith and Henderson that personal injury was intended them. Both sought safety, the former by secreting himself and the latter by flight. Their own houses and several others were searched for them. The sheriff and David McMurtrie, the latter of whom had incurred their enmity at the review, had gone from town the day before, and avoided unpleasant consequences to themselves. Two constables were obliged to leave their homes to save their lives. The sheriff could not with safety go into the country to serve writs, and all kinds of business was affected by this unhappy state of affairs.

"Another visit was feared, and on the 5th of June, 1788, a full statement of these occurrences was sent to the Council, with the assurance that, without the interposition of the government, order could not be preserved.

"The Council took action in regard to the matter on the 25th of June. The chief justice and one of the judges attended, and a conference was held relative to these disturbances. The following were the proceedings, as found in the minutes:

"A letter from two of the magistrates in Huntingdon county, stating that the daring and violent outrages were committed by a lawless set of men, that the officers of the government have been insulted and their lives endangered, and that part of the records of the court have been destroyed and erased, was read, praying the support of the government, etc. Thereupon,

"*Resolved*, That the most proper and effectual measures be immediately taken to quell the disturbances in Huntingdon county, and to restore order and good government, and that the Honorable the Judges of the Supreme Court be informed that the Supreme Executive will give them aid and assistance, which the laws of the State will warrant, and shall be found necessary to accomplish this end.

"The language of this resolution was more vigorous than the action which followed it. Nothing further was then done to suppress these high-handed acts, approaching so nearly to a revolt that they can scarcely be called by any other name.

"After the Council had been informed of them, and before the passage of the resolution, other violence had been committed. Samuel Clinton, who had made himself notorious as a rioter, Abraham Smith and William McCune, came into town at the head of about twenty men, and beat Alexander Irwin, a citizen. The same party, joined perhaps by others, assaulted the houses of the county officers at night with showers of stones. The persons against whom there seemed to be the greatest hatred were Robert Galbraith, President Judge of the County Court of Common Pleas, etc., Thomas Duncan Smith, Justice, Andrew Henderson, Recorder of Deeds, etc., and Benjamin Elliott, Sheriff and Lieutenant of the County.

"Threats were sent from all parts of the county that death, cropping, tarring and feathering, should be inflicted upon these or any other officers who should attempt to enforce the laws. And these threats were not made without an intention of carrying them into execution. About the middle of August, one hundred and sixty men, collected from all parts of the county, some of them from Huntingdon, led by General McAlevy, Abraham Smith, John Smith and John Little, paraded the streets, not armed as before, but with muskets secreted, as was supposed by those who had reason to fear them. The officers and a few others, who gave their support to the government under the constitution, took refuge in the house or Benjamin Elliott, and there, with arms, were determined to defend themselves and to repel force with force. Thus protected, no attack was made upon them. The enemy was content with marching through the streets, under flying colors and to the music of the fife. They met at William Kerr's house and elected delegates to a convention to be held at Lewisburg. At this election all were permitted to vote who had marched in the ranks that day, and all others were excluded.

"This political animosity continued for more than a year. The subject was again before the Council in June, 1789. On the 12th day of that month a committee, to whom the matter had been referred, made a report, which, if it had been published or preserved, would have thrown greater light upon these transactions than can now be obtained from any source. By order of Council, the next day was assigned for further action upon the report. On the 13th the following resolution was adopted:

"*Resolved*, That the consideration of the report of the committee to whom was referred the representation from the Justices and others of Huntingdon county, relative to some late disturbances in that county, be postponed.

"As the Council had delayed so long, and as the excitement had subsided, perhaps no wiser course could have been pursued at that time. This daring opposition to the execution of the laws, formidable as it seemed, was not sufficiently powerful to accomplish its purposes, and its interference with the functions of government in Huntingdon county could not retard their progress elsewhere. Unassisted by similar combinations in other parts of the State or nation, its ultimate failure and discontinuance were necessary consequences; and while it was the duty of the Executive to protect the incumbents of places of trust in their official capacities, and the lives and liberty of the people, yet it was good policy to refrain from the employment of military power until it became absolutely unavoidable. That the fury of this political tempest would soon exhaust itself must have been apparent. It ended without loss of life or limb, and with but slight personal injury to any. We cannot excuse those who instigated and encouraged this unlawful conduct, but the civil authorities were competent to bring them to punishment. We have not ascertained whether this was done. One of them was under bonds in February, 1790, for his appearance at the next Supreme Court in this county, but whether he was brought to trial, and if so, whether it resulted in conviction, we are not informed.

"It has generally been stated and believed by those who have had nothing but traditionary accounts of these occurrences, that the records of the court were burned by McAlevy and his men, but there is no official evidence that such was the case. There are in existence authentic and reliable documents which seem to prove conclusively that some of the records were torn and others obliterated by erasures. It has been said that a copy of the Constitution of the United States was burned, and this may be correct, and may have given rise to the statement that other papers were destroyed in the same way."

No. XIV.—Page 543.

Hon. Charles Smith.

CHARLES SMITH, the *third* son of Rev. William Smith, D. D., and Rebecca Smith, was born at Philadelphia, on the 4th of March, 1765, and was baptized by the Rev. Mr. Sturgeon; John Moore, Esq., and Mr. Charles Smith, both of London, being sponsors.

His early education was under the care of his father, in Philadelphia, and subsequently at Washington College, Maryland, where he graduated at the commencement held on the 14th day of May, 1783, delivering the valedictory oration on that occasion.*

Having completed his collegiate education, he commenced the study of the law with his eldest brother, William Moore Smith, at Easton, Northampton county, Pa., and was admitted to the bar in Philadelphia in June, 1786.

After his admission to the bar he opened his office in the town of Sunbury, Northumberland county, Pa., where his industry and rising talents soon procured for him the business and confidence of the people. He was elected a delegate, with his colleague, Simon Snyder, to the convention which framed the constitution for the State of Pennsylvania, adopted in 1790, and was looked on as a very distinguished member of that talented body of men. Although differing in the politics of that day from his colleague, yet Mr. Snyder for more than thirty years afterwards remained the firm friend of Mr. Smith, and when the former became the Governor of the State for three successive terms, it is well known that Mr. Smith was his confidential adviser in many great State matters.

Mr. Smith was married on the 3d day of March, 1791, to Mary, daughter of Jasper Yeates, one of the Supreme Court judges of the

* See *Maryland Journal,* and *Baltimore Advertiser,* July 8, 1783.

State, and soon after removed from Sunbury to Lancaster, where Judge Yeates resided.

Under the old Circuit Court system it was customary for most of the distinguished country lawyers to travel over the northern and western parts of the State with the judges, and hence Mr. Smith, in pursuing this practice, soon became associated with such eminent men as Thomas Duncan, David Watts, Charles Hall, John Woods, James Hamilton, and a host of luminaries of the middle bar. Among them Mr. Smith always held a conspicuous station, and his practice was consequently lucrative and extended. The settlement of land titles at that period became of vast importance to the people of the State, and the foundation of the law had to be laid with regard to settlement rights, the rights of warrantees, the doctrine of surveys, and the proper construction of lines and corners. In the trials of ejectment cases the learning of the bar was best displayed, and Mr. Smith soon was looked on as an eminent land lawyer. In after years, when called on to revise the old publications of the laws of the State, and under the authority of the Legislature to frame a new compilation of the same (generally known as "Smith's Laws of Pennsylvania"), he gave to the public the result of his knowledge and experience on the subject of land law in the very copious note on that subject which may well be termed a Treatise on the Land Laws of Pennsylvania. In the same work his notes on the Criminal Law of the State are elaborate and instructive to the student and the practitioner.

Mr. Smith was appointed. on the 27th day of March, 1819, President Judge of the Judicial District composed of the counties of Cumberland, Franklin and Adams, where his official learning and judgment, and his habitual industry rendered him a useful and highly popular Judge.

On the erection of the District Court of Lancaster City and County, he became the first President Judge, and was duly commissioned April 28, 1820, which office he held for some years. He afterwards removed with his family to Baltimore, where he lived a few years, and finally removed to Philadelphia, where he spent the last years of his life, and died in that city on March 18, 1836, aged 71 years. He was buried from his residence, No. 12 Clinton square, in his family vault, in the yard of the Church of the Epiphany.

No. XV.—Page 542.

Richard Smith.

RICHARD SMITH, the *fifth* son of Rev. William Smith, D. D., and Rebecca Smith, was born at Philadelphia, on the 25th of January, 1769, and was baptized in Christ Church, on the 19th of March following, by the Rev. Dr. Peters, his sponsors being Dr. Smith and Richard Hockley, Esq., Receiver-General of the Province of Pennsylvania.

His youth passed during the troublesome times of the Revolution, and the early impressions then made upon his mind appear never to have been forgotten. Carefully educated by his father, he soon became a good classical scholar, and imbibed a love for literature which he retained and enjoyed until the day of his death.

Soon after leaving college he commenced the study of law, and was admitted to the bar in Philadelphia on the 27th day of February, 1792. He subsequently located himself at Huntingdon, the seat of justice for Huntingdon county, which had been erected in 1787; but the precise time of his going there is not known. In the act erecting the county and fixing the seat of justice, it recited "that the proprietor of said town had agreed to lay off and set apart a proper and sufficient quantity of grounds, for the site of a court house, county gaol and prison, and hath engaged to give, assure and convey the same to the Commonwealth, in trust and for the use and benefit of the said county;" therefore certain trustees were named and appointed to carry the same into effect. On the 25th of August, 1791, in pursuance of the agreement under which Huntingdon had been made the county seat, Dr. Smith conveyed lot No. 41, on the east side of St. Clair (now Second) street, to Benjamin Elliott, Ludwig Sell, George Ashman, William McAlevy, RICHARD SMITH and Andrew Henderson, Trustees, as a site for a county prison.

The first appearance of Mr. Smith in the courts of the county seems to have been in 1795, as he was there admitted as a member of the bar in that year. He was regarded as a ripe scholar, an ornament to the bar, and soon occupied a prominent position at it. He was personally popular, and spoken of as being "the pride of the village." From 1797 to 1801 he represented the district composed of the counties of Huntingdon, Bedford and Somerset in the State Senate in a manner highly satisfactory to his constituents, and then resumed his professional duties.

He was married at Lancaster, Pa., on the 7th day of May, 1804, to Miss Letitia Nixon Coakley, the marriage ceremony being performed by the Rev. Joseph Clarkson, at the house of William Montgomery, Esq. Then returning home, he settled down at the place he had selected for his future residence, on the bank of the Juniata, about half a mile above the town of Huntingdon, and well known as "Cypress Cottage." Here he continued to reside until his death, which occurred suddenly, on the 1st day of October, 1823.

The "cottage" stood upon elevated ground, a short distance from the river, surrounded by shade and fruit trees, as well as shrubbery, with its several out-houses and fences, all neatly whitewashed, presenting an air of comfort, and making it a most inviting spot. To the right of the cottage a handsome lawn extended down to the bank of the river, well shaded by large buttonwood and other trees, and which became the resort of the young people of the town for their pic-nic parties, and where, on each annual return of our national birthday, it was duly celebrated in a most patriotic manner. Here the military and citizens of the town marched in procession to hear the reading of the Declaration of Independence and the usual oration, and then all participated in a good dinner spread on a long table erected under the shade of the grand old trees. The farm attached to the cottage as well as the one on the island were both well cultivated, and about thirty feet to the right of the dwelling stood a two-story building called "The Study." In this was a large and well-selected library, and here, amidst his books, Mr. Smith spent many happy hours, either quietly attending to his business or perusing his favorite authors.

The walk along the river bank was a very pleasant one, and much used by the young people. Calls were almost daily made (especially in summer) at the cottage, where all were hospitably welcomed, as the "latch-string was always out." And in return, it is but just to say that "Uncle Richard" and "Aunt Lettie," as they were familiarly called by all, were respected and loved by both old and young in the town.

Thus time passed on. Mr. Smith had inherited and also acquired much landed property, but eventually, from various causes, found himself financially embarrassed, and had to see much of his property sacrificed to satisfy his creditors. The hard times following the war in 1815, the worthless paper currency then in circulation, and the depreciation in real estate, can only be appreciated by those who witnessed the scenes occurring at that day.

In February, 1821, Mr. Smith was appointed, by Governor Heister,

Recorder of Deeds and Register of Wills for Huntingdon County, which offices he accepted, and continued to discharge their duties until the day of his death.

To add to his difficulties, he now found himself involved in a law suit about the title to a piece of property in the borough of Huntingdon, the amount involved not being large, according to the valuation of property in the town at that day, yet he had come to consider it as the great event of his life. He prepared for the trial with much anxiety of mind, as if his future prosperity depended upon its result, or he feared something serious would happen. At length the day of trial came, and its progress was watched by him with the most intense interest until its close, when the jury returned a verdict in his favor. A motion was made by his opponent for a new trial, and this was argued upon the second day after the rendition of the verdict. Upon the argument he was grossly insulted, and statements made by his opponent which Mr. Smith promptly arose to deny. He was sternly ordered by the court to sit down, when he slowly sank down in his seat, his head fell forward and rested upon the counsel table, having been seized with apoplexy. His nephew, General William R. Smith, one of the members of the bar, caught him in his arms and had him carried to the open air at the door of the court room, where Dr. Henderson immediately attempted to bleed him, but all in vain, and in less than ten minutes he was dead!

The consternation and confusion this event occasioned in court caused it to immediately adjourn, and nothing further was done in the cause. His funeral took place in a few days, his body being followed to the grave by the members of the bar and a large concourse of citizens of the town and county, among whom he had so long resided. The following inscription covers his grave and that of his elder brother, by the side of whom he was buried:

Sacred

To the memory of

THOMAS DUNCAN SMITH, M. D.,

Born Nov. 18, 1760,

Died July 9, 1789;

And of

RICHARD SMITH, ESQ.,

Born Jan. 25, 1769,

Died Oct. 1, 1823,

Sons of

WILLIAM SMITH, D. D.

In life

United in brotherly love;

In death

They are not divided.

In personal appearance Mr. Smith is described by those who knew him "as a large, portly, fine-looking gentleman of the old school, possessing the most attractive social qualities, and all the elements of popularity were combined in him."

His widow, Letitia Nixon Smith, was a refined and intelligent lady, and continued to reside in Huntingdon for some years after the death of her husband, devoting her time to the interests of education, Sunday schools and the church. She finally removed to Athens, Tenn., and spent the remainder of her days with her nephew, Thomas Nixon Vandyke, Esq. There she died and was buried, some thirty years or more after the death of her husband.

Among the fugitive pieces written by my father, Richard Penn Smith, I find the story of "My Uncle Nicholas," and no doubt he had his uncle in view when it was written. As an evidence of his style of writing, I here add it :

"MY UNCLE NICHOLAS.

" BY RICHARD PENN SMITH.

"'Call no man happy 'till you know the nature of his death; he is at best but fortunate.'—*Solon to Crœsus.*

"Time eats the children he begets, and the memories of few men outlive their monuments; nay, myriads pass into oblivion even before the elements have sullied their epitaph. My uncle Nicholas, notwithstanding his deserts, has not escaped this order of things. I knew him in the April of my years—the flower-time of my life; and as my mind reverts to those sunny days, the first object it rests upon is the beloved image of my uncle Nicholas.

"He was a placid being, overflowing with the best of humanities. His heart and his doors were open to all his fellow-beings, and there was not a creature endued with animal life towards which he did not studiously avoid giving pain. His dogs loved him, and he could not walk abroad into his fields but his cattle followed him, and fed out of his hand.

"'He was a scholar, a ripe and a good one,' at least I viewed him as such in my boyhood. His mind was stored with good learning, but his favorite companions were those hearty old poets who have retained their freshness for centuries, and who possess a reproductive faculty that will make them blossom through succeeding ages. With what delight would he pore over the harmonious numbers of Spencer, and Drayton, and Drummond, and the vigorous dramatists of those times! and there was scarcely a gem of the minor poets that he had not culled to grace his memory. These he would recite with all the feeling and enthusiasm of early life, and at times I imagined they were golden links that inseparably bound him to his boyhood. They appeared to possess the faculty of making him young again.

"He was a quiet humorist, but with no more gall than might be found in a dove. His face was ever mantling with some pleasant thought, and his mind flowed on as gently as a secret brook, that ever and anon dimples and smiles at its own babbling.

"He was married, and my aunt was one of the gentlest of creatures. You might have searched the world without finding a pair whose hearts and minds so perfectly harmonized. She was a delicately attuned instrument, ever breathing the softest music; never depressed to sadness, and seldom exhilarated beyond a placid smile. If perchance she laughed, it was at some jest of my uncle Nicholas; not that it excited her risible faculties, but that she perceived by the mantling of his countenance there was more intended than came within the scope of her apprehension; and she would laugh outright that he might more fully enjoy the freak of his imagination. How they loved each other!

"My uncle dwelt on a farm on the outskirts of a village. He had selected it as a residence in early life, and had lived long enough to see the primitive settlement assume something like a name on the map of his country. He was identified with the spot; all the villagers in a measure looked upon him as a patriarch, and even the children would break off their amusements to salute him as he passed; and he ever had a kind word and a jest to bestow upon the humblest of the little troglodytes. They all called him uncle Nicholas, and he was so kind to them that many grew up in the belief that he was actually the uncle of the whole village.

"His residence was a delightful spot. His farm was well cultivated, and his buildings, while they afforded every comfort, were not so ostentatious as to awaken the envy of his less prosperous neighbors. A river flowed beside it, and in the rear were shady walks of sugar maple, to which the villagers would resort of a summer afternoon for recreation, and few would fail in returning to stop at my uncle's cottage and partake of the hospitality of his board. Indeed he and his were looked upon as common property.

"At these social gatherings all the belles of the village would rival each other to secure my uncle's attention. He was ever the gayest among the gay, while his gentle manners and playful fancy ministered to the delight of all; and it was amusing to behold the quiet complacency of my aunt as she gazed on his little gallantries, and to watch her countenance gradually light up, as her mind would pass from the scene before her to the halcyon days when he wooed and won her, and then she would turn to her next neighbor and whisper, in a tone mingled with pride and fondness, 'You see his winning ways have not yet left him.' And then she would smile and look on in silence, as if life could afford no delight like gazing on my uncle Nicholas when he was happy.

"Happy!—the heavens themselves are never so bright and clear but that a cloud overshadows some portion, and there lives not that man whose mind is so free but that at some period a phantom pursues it, from which he fears escape is impossible. My uncle's phantom was the dread of poverty. He had lived generously, and from his habits and tone of mind was ill calculated to increase his possessions. As he advanced in life he perceived that his property had imperceptibly wasted away; and to increase his terrors, there was a lawsuit against him that had been pending many years. He dreaded its termination would result in ruin, though convinced that justice was on his side; but the boasted trial by jury is by no means as infallible as its encomiasts pretend, for it is a difficult matter for one man who does not understand his case to explain to twelve who frequently are incapable of comprehending the matter under any circumstances. And by this frail tenure do we cling to our possession of liberty and life. The sword of Damocles is a type of the trial by jury.

"It was a melancholy sight to behold the old gentleman, term after term, attending court to learn the issue of his cause. It absorbed all his faculties and sapped the very foundation of his mind. He was wont to have a word and a cheerful smile for all he met, but now he would pass his next neighbor without token of recognition. His little friends, the children, no longer followed him. His favorite volumes remained undusted on the shelves—their charm had passed away, and those vernal fancies, that were wont to make his heart like a singing bird in spring, had died and it sung no more.

"He would at times struggle to disengage his mind from the phantom that embraced it with iron clutches, and affect more cheerfulness in the presence of my aunt, for he perceived that his melancholy was contagious. How tenderly she watched over him, and soothed him and encouraged him! God bless her! At one of those tender interviews, which were frequent, he appeared suddenly animated with hope —the world was open to him—he was a man, and could labor like other men—his countenance brightened, and he exclaimed, exultingly:

"'The spider taketh hold with her hands and is in kings' palaces.' He fondly looked into the recess of his wife's heart through her glistening eyes, and continued: 'The ants are a people not strong.' He

37

paused, and finished the proverb in a tone scarcely audible—'yet they prepare their meat in the summer. Alas! the snows of many winters are on my head.' A tear dropped from his eye on the pale forehead of the partner of his bosom. She consoled him no more that day.

"He had contracted various small debts with the tradesmen of the village, among whom were some newcomers who had not known him in his palmy days. And even if they had, the chances are that it would not have altered their conduct towards him. Few men make an ægis of the past to shield them from present evils. True, he has been as liberal as the sun that shines on all alike without distinction, but how soon do we forget the splendor of yesterday if the sun rise in clouds to-morrow.

"His creditors became impatient, and though there was some hesitation in taking out the first execution, yet that being done, others followed as regularly as links of the same chain. There was a time when he felt as confident and secure among the villagers as in the bosom of his own family; but now there was no longer safety for the sole of his foot on his hearthstone. He was humbled, and he moved among his neighbors, a broken down man, with fear and trembling, dreading all whom he chanced to meet.

"At length his library was seized upon and sold. His books were of no great value to any other than himself, but he prized them beyond every thing. He had bought them in his boyhood; to lose them was to sever the chain that bound him to happier days, and as he beheld them scattered one by one, he wept as if they had been things of life that had abandoned him in his misfortunes.

"It was a melancholy sight to behold him after this event, seated in his study, gazing on the empty shelves, and repeating various choice passages from his favorite volumes. I witnessed him once, looking intently on the vacant spot where a fine old copy of 'Herrick's Poems' had stood for near half a century. I knew the place well, for at that time it was my delight to delve for the pure ore of that 'very best of English lyric poets.' A melancholy smile came over his bland countenance, and he repeated, in a low tremulous voice:

"Call me no more,
　As heretofore,
　　The music of the feast
　Since now, alas!
　The mirth that was
　　In me, is dead or ceased.

" Before I went
 To banishment
  Into the loathed west;
 I could rehearse
 A lyric verse
  And speak it with the best.

" But time, ah me!
 Has laid, I see,
  My organ fast asleep;
 And turn'd my voice
 Into the noise
  Of those that sit and weep.

" His eyes slowly moved along the empty shelves until they rested upon a place that had been occupied by a collection of the old dramatists. He smiled, though he shed tears:

" 'Beshrew me, but thy song hath moved me.' I turned from the window through which I was gazing, unperceived, and left him breathing fragment upon fragment.

" My uncle was accustomed to rise with the sun, and continued his habit to the last. But he no longer enjoyed the songs of the birds, the babbling of the waterfall, nor the fresh breeze of the morning laden with fragrance—their influence had departed from them; still, he adhered to his custom, and would wander from his green meadows to the maple grove, and from the grove to the river, as if in pursuit of something—he knew not what. On his return his usual remark was, 'Is it not strange that the flowers should have lost their fragrance, and the little birds their skill in singing!' In happier days how he would praise the flowers and the birds!

"As term-time approached, his malady ever increased. His morning meal would scarcely be over when he would adjust his dress, and call for his hat and cane, and on being asked whither he was going, he would invariably reply: 'To the village to see my friends. Of late they have ceased to come here, and it is right that I should see them.' He would for hours walk from one end of the village to the other, and bow to all who accosted him, yet pause to converse with none; and on his return, when my good aunt would inquire whether he had seen his friends, the constant reply was, 'No, I have fallen in with none of them.' Alas! my poor uncle, how thy brain must have been shattered to imagine that a man in adversity can ever find his friends!

"At length the dreaded day arrived—his cause was marked for trial, and in a few hours the result would be known. The matter in dispute was not of such a great moment, but he had brooded over it until his fears had magnified it to vital importance. His opponent was a coarse and brutal man, and in their protracted contest the abruptness of his demeanor had awakened whatever latent asperity had found a hiding-place in my uncle's bosom. He looked upon that cause, trifling as it was, as the most important matter of his life. His daily thoughts and irritated feeling had magnified it. Even the little ant, by constant application, can create a mound altogether disproportionate to its size, and there is not a column so beautiful that may not be defaced by the trail of a slimy snail. My poor uncle feared the ant-hill, and recoiled at the filth of the worm.

"The morning his cause was to be tried he dressed himself with unusual care, and my aunt, knowing the bent of his mind, exercised all her little appliances to encourage him. He went to the court-house and took his seat, a dejected man. He looked around as if in search of some one to sit beside him to aid and sustain him, but none such were present, and he sat alone.

"The caus was called, the jury empanelled, and the investigation proceeded. Every question that arose, in its progress wrought up my uncle's mind to painful intensities. In the ardor of his feelings he at times interrupted the proceedings, and was rudely ordered by the court to sit down and be silent. He obeyed, while every fibre of his frame shook with passion and offended pride. His opponent smiled in triumph as he beheld his confusion. He sat alone; no one approached to sympathize with him, and he felt as if deserted by all. In consequence of the distracted state of his mind, his defence, though a just one, had been imperfectly made out. Facts had escaped his memory; papers were missing that should have been produced, and the result was, the jury returned a verdict against him without leaving the box. It fell like a thunderbolt upon him; he fancied the last business of his life was over, and in the triumph of the moment his adversary taunted him, and openly charged him with dishonesty. The old man rose to repel the insult, while every limb shook with passion as if palsy-struck. All was confusion. The judges interfered to preserve order. My uncle heard them not. He was commanded to sit down, but still persisted to vindicate his character. A second, a third time was he called upon to sit down and be silent, which awakened him to a sense of his position. He beheld his antagonist still smiling; he slowly sunk into his seat, and, as if abashed, his head hung over his bosom, and gradually descended until it rested on the desk before him. Order was again restored, and the court proceeded in its business. A few moments after some one approached my uncle, and on raising him he was found to be dead !

"Thus died that good old man. There was a time when I looked upon him being secure from the shafts of fate; but who may boast of to-morrow! He was wealthy, had health and friends, and his gentle spirit made his home a paradise. His sources of enjoyment were bound-less, for all nature, from her sublimest mysteries even down to the petals of a simple flower, was one mighty minister, and he drew wisdom and delight from all. And yet a single cloud was magnified until it over-shadowed his heaven of happiness, and he died friendless and heart-broken; all had vanished that made earth beautiful. But is this strange?—The flowers of life pass away as the flowers of the seasons, without our being conscious of the cause of their decay, and there breathes not that man, however prosperous, but, like my poor uncle, hath his phantom, and in time discovers that 'even in laughter the heart is sorrowful and the end of that mirth is heaviness.'"

No. XVI.—Page 551.

William Rudolph* Smith.

[By Richard Moore Smith.]

WILLIAM RUDOLPH SMITH, the eldest son of William Moore Smith, was born at La Trappe, in Montgomery county, Pa., on the 31st day of August, A. D. 1787. The family removing to Philadelphia in 1792, he was placed at school under the tuition of Mr. James Little and his ushers, this being at that time the largest and best preparatory school in the city. In 1799 he was placed in the Latin school of the Rev. James McRea; but soon afterwards the whole care of his education was as-sumed by his grandfather, the Rev. William Smith, D. D., who received him into the old family residence at the Falls of Schuylkill, where he remained, under a rigid course of instruction, until April, 1803, when, as private secretary, he accompanied his father to England, the latter being one of the commissioners, under the 6th article of the Jay treaty, to adjust and settle the demands of the British claimants.

During their protracted residence in England the father and son travelled much together at various times, journeying along the south coast from Dover to Falmouth, visiting all points of interest in the in-terior of the south and west, and making frequent and extended jour-

---

* The Rudulph family spelt their name with a *u*. My uncle always spelt his Rudolph.

neys into other parts of the kingdom. In London their time was happily spent at the houses of many friends, and particularly at the house of Charles Dilly, Queen's Square, so often mentioned by Boswell in his life of Johnson. Mr. Dilly took great satisfaction in showing to his guests the arm-chair in which Dr. Johnson always sat at his table, and where he enjoyed himself, perhaps, more than at any other house in London. It was at this hospitable table that Dr. Johnson met with and learned to tolerate the great radical leader, John Wilkes.

In Mr. Dilly's house the young secretary had the gratification to meet with the venerable Pascal Paoli, with Richard Cumberland, with a brother of James Boswell, and with many of the literary celebrities and other notorieties of the day. And Benjamin West, the President of the Royal Society, in his attentions to the father and son, did not forget the obligations which, in early life, he owed to his friend and patron, Dr. William Smith.

In the home of Mr. West, in Great Newman street, and in the picture-gallery, young William Rudolph Smith met and formed friendships with many of the great painters and artists of England and of the continent, for in those stirring times London was the city of refuge for the emigrès and for all classes of refugees seeking safety from the whirlwind of strife then sweeping over every country in Europe. George Cadoudal, the great Vendean chief, and General Pichegrou, both afterwards concerned in the attempt to assassinate Napoleon, were among the acquaintances thus formed. These London days, teeming with the recollections of Sarah Siddons, of John and Stephen Kemble, of the old crazy King George III., to whom he had been presented at court, of the Prince of Wales and Beau Brummel, of the soldiers and statesmen who were then shaping the destiny of the civilized world, were the solace of many an hour in after years, and, related in his inimitable way, the delight of three succeeding generations of listening friends.

Intended by his father for the bar, young Smith, during his residence in England, commenced a preparatory course of study under the direction of Thomas Kearsley, Esq., of the Middle Temple, and from this period until the autumn of 1808 he was a diligent student—for the first two years after their return to America under the direction of his father, at his country residence, five miles from the city, on the Old York road, and afterwards in the office of James Milnor, in Philadelphia; in after years Mr. Milnor removed to the city of New York, and, having taken orders, became a distinguished minister of the Episcopal Church. In 1808 Mr. Smith was admitted to the bar in Philadelphia; his examiners were Richard Rush, Thomas Ross and Peter A. Browne; the Judge was Jacob Rush. The following year he removed to Huntingdon, Pa., where he entered into the practice of his profession. On the 17th of March, 1809, he was married to Eliza Anthony, of Philadelphia, who was descended on the father's side from the Rhode Island family of that name, and on the mother's side from Michael Hillegas, the Treasurer of the United States during the Revolution.

For the ensuing eleven years Mr. Smith led a busy life; assuming at once a leadership in his profession, he soon became extensively known as one of the most profound lawyers in the State. He was appointed, in 1811, Deputy Attorney-General for Cambria County, under Walter Franklin; he was reappointed to the same office by Richard Rush, Attorney-General, and in 1812 was again reappointed by Jared Ingersoll, Attorney-General.

A boy's love for a military career had impelled Mr. Smith, in early life, to connect himself with the Third Troop of Philadelphia Light-Horse, and, whilst a member of this body, he had the satisfaction of riding the same horse which had carried his father, when a member of this same troop, in the expedition to suppress the celebrated Whiskey Insurrection. His taste for military affairs strengthened with advancing years, and caused Mr. Smith to study carefully the question of the national defences and the organization of the State militia forces. He devoted a large portion of his time to the study of field tactics, and was active and energetic in the thorough organization and drilling of the Pennsylvania militia, in which he served in various grades up to the rank of major-general. In the war of 1812–15 with England, he was Colonel of the 62d Regiment of Pennsylvania Reserves, and commanded that regiment when ordered up to Erie to support General Scott in the movement on Canada, which resulted in the victory at Lundy's Lane. General Smith was in Baltimore during the siege of that city; he witnessed the disaster at Bladensburg, the subsequent occupation of Washington, and the burning of the Capitol by the British.

In civil life General Smith filled with distinguished ability the various offices to which he was, at intervals, elected or appointed. He served in both branches of the Pennsylvania Legislature, held many offices of civil trust and honor, and in January, 1836, was admitted Counsellor of the Supreme Court of the United States, at Washington

In January, 1821, General Smith lost his wife, her death occurring very suddenly, after a brief illness of a few hours only. Three years afterwards he married again, his second wife being Mary Hamilton Van Dyke, whose family, originally from Delaware, had removed to and settled in the State of Tennessee.

In 1827 General Smith removed from Huntingdon to Bedford county, where he continued to reside until the year 1837, when he was appointed Commissioner of the United States, in conjunction with Governor Henry Dodge, to treat with the Chippewa Indians for the purchase of their pineries on the Mississippi river and its tributaries. The journey into the Northwest, in the fulfilment of this trust, forms an important epoch in the life of General Smith. The wonderful resources of the country in all that makes a nation happy, rich and great, impressed him profoundly as a statesman; with prophetic vision he saw the sceptre of Empire passing from the East to settle firmly in the grasp of the Mighty West; instantly he resolved to be one of those earnest pioneers who turned heroically from the attractions of Eastern life to devote their lives to the work of formulating the legislation and shaping the destiny of these States of glorious promise. His letters to his brother, Richard Penn Smith, afterwards published in Philadelphia, under the title of "Observations on Wisconsin Territory," are filled with glowing descriptions of this paradise for farmers. That the magic beauty of the scenery deeply touched his poetic nature may be witnessed by the following lines dashed off in a moment of tender recollection:

All hail, Wisconsin! Prairie land,
   In summer decked with flowers,
As scattered by some fairy hand
   'Midst sylvan shades and bowers.

Thy soil abundant harvests yields,
   Thy rocks give mineral wealth;
And every breeze that sweeps thy fields
   Comes redolent of health.

Perennial springs and inland seas
   Give other beauties zest;
Long may thy dwellers live in ease,
   Gem of the fertile West!

Returning to Pennsylvania, General Smith, in 1838, removed his family to Wisconsin and settled in Iowa county, at Mineral Point. In 1839 he was appointed Adjutant General of the Territory of Wisconsin, by Governor Dodge, which office he continued to fill, under successive administrations, for more than twelve years. He also received from Governor Dodge the civil appointment of District Attorney of Iowa county, retaining this office also for many years. In 1840 he was called to preside over the first Democratic convention that assembled at the seat of government of Wisconsin Territory, and he drafted the address sent forth by that body to the people. He was elected Secretary of the Legislative Council of Wisconsin, and in 1846 was elected delegate to the Convention to form a Constitution for the State of Wisconsin; the journals of that convention show that General Smith originated many of the great legislative reforms that have since become law, not only in Wisconsin, but have been widely adopted in other and older States of the Union, notably the "Homestead Exemption Law," and the Rights of Married Women to hold their own earnings and to own property, independently of and beyond the control of their husbands. In 1849 General Smith was elected Chief Clerk of the Senate, and again in 1850 was re-elected to the same office, receiving a *unanimous vote.* In 1849 he, together with a few other citizens of kindred spirit and with similar tastes, all deeply interested in collecting and preserving matters of historical interest, founded the "State Historical Society of Wisconsin." The immediate success of the society in this work induced the Legislature to place the institution under State patronage. A room in the Capitol was assigned for their use, and annual appropriations of money made to carry out and enlarge the designs of the society.

By a special act of the Legislature, in 1852, General Smith was authorized to compile a "Documentary History of Wisconsin from its Earliest Settlement to the Present Time." To this work he devoted several years of his life, and the first two volumes of the history were published by the State in 1854.

In 1856 General Smith was elected Attorney-General of the State of Wisconsin, and filled the office with marked ability for two years; then having reached the ripe age of 71 years, he deemed it best to rest from his labors and retire from active professional and political life, intending for the remainder of his days to quietly enjoy his home, his library, and the society of his family and intimate friends. Here for eleven years more he was the delight of all who approached him, his ripe scholarship and varied information, his sparkling wit and kindly disposition, gave a charm to his conversation that will never be obliterated from the memories of those who knew him. His reminiscences of Washington and the statesmen of his day, and the leading incidents of those early days of the republic, were related with dramatic effect; the hands of Washington had rested upon his head, he had listened to the first reading of the Farewell Address, and was present in the German Lutheran church in Philadelphia when Major-General Lee, by the appointment of Congress, pronounced the funeral oration of Washington. He was present in the theatre on the night when the now national anthem of "Hail Columbia" was first sung, and was witness to the enthusiasm with which the song was greeted. It had been his strange fortune to see every President of the United States from Washington to Lincoln; these and similar recollections served to entrance a generation of listeners who could look upon them as events belonging to, to them, almost a remote antiquity.

In 1868 General Smith, still active and in good health, made the tour of Wisconsin, visiting many of his old friends in the northern and eastern part of the State; then proceeding to Quincy, in the State of Illinois, he finished his tour in a visit to his youngest daughter, residing in that city with her husband, Mr. Robert H. Deaderick. And here, in the fulness of years, this long and brilliant life came to a quiet and peaceful close.

General Smith during all his life was an active and prominent Mason, passing through all the degrees of that order, from the Blue Lodge to the Royal Arch Chapter. He was several times made Grand Secretary, and was twice Grand Master of the Grand Lodge of Wisconsin. He had a singular love and veneration for the order while he lived, and he was buried with Masonic honors on the 26th day of August, A. D. 1868, at Mineral Point, Wis. A Masonic monument marks his place of rest.

No. XVII.—Page 463.

In asserting what I here do, I do not forget that in "The Form of Prayer for the Visitation of Prisoners" it is said, in that part of the form provided for "persons under sentence of death," that after a particular confession, by the person under sentence, of the sin for which he stands condemned—which confession the visiting clergyman is to exhort him to make—such clergyman shall "*declare* to him *the pardoning mercy of God, in the form which is used in the communion service;*" that form being admitted by all to be one more capable of being interpreted to be a form of "absolution" than any other in our Prayer Book. The inference drawn therefore by some is that the church here puts an interpretation on that form generally, interpreting it wherever it occurs in the Prayer Book as but "a declaration of God's pardoning mercy."

Conversing not long since with a layman of our church, whom I have often consulted in the preparation of this biography, he made some remarks of which what follows, so far as I remember, is the substance. I adopt them as expressing my own views:

I do not consider that the church in this rubric says in terms exactly what these words, brought from the communion service, are or do, except, perhaps, as when they are said to a malefactor convicted of crime for which he has been judicially sentenced to death, and who now, confessing the crime, admits his awful guilt. And I think that the same words which are uttered at the communion-table over bishops, priests, deacons and baptized laity professing to be religious—all presumably known to the minister, and all presumably guiltless of heinous crimes—may properly be left to have whatever meaning the said words have in themselves, or as read by the light of postures prescribed, or by the light of other things existing in connection with them; while those same words may well be restricted in meaning by a rubric, when said to a malefactor judicially sentenced to death for what may be the most dreadful crime known to laws, both human and divine, which crime he now confesses that, with perhaps numberless others like it, he has perpetrated. The minister, we must remember, in visiting the person under sentence of death, may have never seen or heard of him until the morning of the execution, and just before the minister is about to utter over the wretched man the commendatory "prayer for a person at the point of departure." In the sincerity of repentance of such a person—a person whose whole life may have been marked by atrocious crimes, and who may be a most hardened sinner, having, besides, in the hope of a pardon from the government, a motive to appear repentant when not so in reality—the minister may utterly and rightly disbelieve. *The convict, as yet, has not communicated, and he may wish never to communicate.*

The service for the Visitation of Prisoners is not in the English Prayer Book. It comes to us from a form (somewhat altered, I doubt not) set forth by the Convocation and Parliament of Ireland, and first appeared in the Proposed Book. That book obliterated the word *priest* from its rubrics, substituting for it the word *minister.* This word includes deacons. But as by the practice of the Church of England, deacons do not pronounce "absolution," the Proposed Book characterizes as "a Declaration concerning the forgiveness of sins" those same words which the English book calls "The Absolution or Remission of sins." In the Visitation of Prisoners it therefore made its rubric read thus:

"After his confession the *minister* shall *declare* to him the pardoning mercy of God"—

Adding—

"in the form which is used in the Communion Service."

The Convention of 1789, ignoring very much the Proposed Book, used as the basis of *its* work, the English Prayer Book, and generally restored the word *priest* in the rubrics, or, where it did not, as in the Visitation and Communion of the Sick, guarded the use of the word "minister" by references—"out." But, as I have said, this service of the Visitation of Prisoners was not in the English book, and a service of the sort being thought a most fit one to be in a Prayer Book, the Convention took it from the Proposed Book; the rubric above quoted, with its word "minister," coming in as part.

Most other services in our Book of 1789 were referred to committees, were reported on, amended and discussed; but about this one there was no such advisement. It was adopted on the last day of the Convention's session, "originating," as the minutes tell us, in the House of Bishops, and being "passed" by the Deputies.

Haste and its usual concomitant, mistake, seems to be shown by what followed as a result in the Prayer Book of 1789, then made. Those same words which in the daily and evening service that book allows the priest, alone, to say, and to say only in a certain posture (that is, standing), and which the people are allowed to hear only in a certain other posture (that is, kneeling), and which in the communion service a Bishop (if a Bishop is present) alone may say, we here allowed a deacon to say, in any posture, to a malefactor under sentence of death in any posture, the same or other; the posture before the "declaration" of both parties having been, according to probabilities, that of sitting. Indeed Bishop White himself tells us that the use of the word "minister," in the book of 1789, instead of the word "priest," must have been from "oversight" (Brownell's Family Prayer Book, *Ed.* of 1875, p. 493).

This inconsistency was too great to be left, and in the standard Prayer Book of 1838 the rubric was changed by putting the word *priest* in the place of the word *minister.* This change of the word *minister* to the word priest may perhaps of itself "tone up" the word "declare" from a low meaning (as *ex. gr.:* "state" or "make known"), to a higher one (as *ex. gr.:* "declare officially;" that is, "pronounce.") If it does not do this, why was the change made?

The Proposed Book prescribed "the form which s used in the communion service," instead of the form in the morning and evening service of the same book (the form of the English book, and the first of the two forms in our book of 1789), from the impropriety, I suppose, of making a convict who is on the point of being executed praying that "the *rest*" of his life *"hereafter"* may be pure and holy, "so that *at the last*" he may come to God's eternal joy.

The change made by the standard of 1838 leaves the rubric defective and awkwardly mended. Is the "priest" alone, under *it*, to "visit" persons under sentence of death? Is "absolution," of any kind, to be given to one who has been confessedly a heinous malefactor, and who has not communicated? If no "absolution" is intended, why, as I have already asked, do we not allow the thing to be said by a "minister," as of old? I recognize, of course, the old distinction of absolutions declarative, precatory and judicial. But, under it, the form in the communion is not the declarative one.

The fact is that the committee who issued the standard of 1838 had a difficulty too great for any committee not having larger power than it had to manage. They were trying to raise by the change of *one* word the tone of a rubric improvidently imported from a book of a low plane of churchmanship throughout (the Proposed Book), and with whose other rubrics this one was in unison, to a pitch which should accord with the better considered rubrics of a book of a much higher plane of churchmanship (our Book of Common Prayer of 1789), and with whose rubrics this rubric was not in unison. If I remember, the committee had but power to change errors in typography. I am not sure about this. But I am sure that in their present state, matters are not fully enough stated to be clear. The thing, however, was a dangerous one to handle.

On the whole case, neither the old rubric nor the new one can be looked on as interpreting "the form which is used in the communion service" anywhere but in the service of the Visitation of Prisoners itself, if, indeed, it interprets that form even there.

I may add, that even in the Proposed Book, except as this rubric there may so characterize it, *this* form—the form, I mean, used in the communion service—is not characterized as a "Declaration" of any sort, although another form, in language truly declarative—though with an entreaty appended—and which other form the Church of England calls "the Absolution, or Remission of Sins"—is.

For Dr. Smith's private declarations that the Proposed Book—which went further in the way of reform of the English Prayer Book than does our Prayer Book of 1789—did not proceed on the idea that the Church of England was in anything erroneous, see *supra,* p. 178.

INDEX.

38

Religion in America
Series II

An Arno Press Collection

Adler, Felix. **Creed and Deed:** A Series of Discourses. New York, 1877.

Alexander, Archibald. **Evidences of the Authenticity, Inspiration, and Canonical Authority of the Holy Scriptures.** Philadelphia, 1836.

Allen, Joseph Henry. **Our Liberal Movement in Theology:** Chiefly as Shown in Recollections of the History of Unitarianism in New England. 3rd edition. Boston, 1892.

American Temperance Society. **Permanent Temperance Documents of the American Temperance Society.** Boston, 1835.

American Tract Society. **The American Tract Society Documents,** 1824-1925. New York, 1972.

Bacon, Leonard. **The Genesis of the New England Churches.** New York, 1874.

Bartlett, S[amuel] C. **Historical Sketches of the Missions of the American Board.** New York, 1972.

Beecher, Lyman. **Lyman Beecher and the Reform of Society:** Four Sermons, 1804-1828. New York, 1972.

[Bishop, Isabella Lucy Bird.] **The Aspects of Religion in the United States of America.** London, 1859.

Bowden, James. **The History of the Society of Friends in America.** London, 1850, 1854. Two volumes in one.

Briggs, Charles Augustus. **Inaugural Address and Defense,** 1891-1893. New York, 1972.

Colwell, Stephen. **The Position of Christianity in the United States,** in Its Relations with Our Political Institutions, and Specially with Reference to Religious Instruction in the Public Schools. Philadelphia, 1854.

Dalcho, Frederick. **An Historical Account of the Protestant Episcopal Church, in South-Carolina,** from the First Settlement of the Province, to the War of the Revolution. Charleston, 1820.

Elliott, Walter. **The Life of Father Hecker.** New York, 1891.

Gibbons, James Cardinal. **A Retrospect of Fifty Years.** Baltimore, 1916. Two volumes in one.

Hammond, L[ily] H[ardy]. **Race and the South:** Two Studies, 1914-1922. New York, 1972.

Hayden, A[mos] S. **Early History of the Disciples in the Western Reserve, Ohio;** With Biographical Sketches of the Principal Agents in their Religious Movement. Cincinnati, 1875.

Hinke, William J., editor. **Life and Letters of the Rev. John Philip Boehm:** Founder of the Reformed Church in Pennsylvania, 1683-1749. Philadelphia, 1916.

Hopkins, Samuel. **A Treatise on the Millennium.** Boston, 1793.

Kallen, Horace M. **Judaism at Bay:** Essays Toward the Adjustment of Judaism to Modernity. New York, 1932.

Kreider, Harry Julius. **Lutheranism in Colonial New York.** New York, 1942.

Loughborough, J. N. **The Great Second Advent Movement:** Its Rise and Progress. Washington, 1905.

M'Clure, David and Elijah Parish. **Memoirs of the Rev. Eleazar Wheelock, D.D.** Newburyport, 1811.

McKinney, Richard I. **Religion in Higher Education Among Negroes.** New Haven, 1945.

Mayhew, Jonathan. **Observations on the Charter and Conduct of the Society for the Propagation of the Gospel in Foreign Parts;** Designed to Shew Their Non-conformity to Each Other. Boston, 1763.

Mott, John R. **The Evangelization of the World in this Generation.** New York, 1900.

Payne, Bishop Daniel A. **Sermons and Addresses,** 1853-1891. New York, 1972.

Phillips, C[harles] H. **The History of the Colored Methodist Episcopal Church in America:** Comprising Its Organization, Subsequent Development, and Present Status. Jackson, Tenn., 1898.

Reverend Elhanan Winchester: Biography and Letters. New York, 1972.

Riggs, Stephen R. **Tah-Koo Wah-Kan; Or, the Gospel Among the Dakotas.** Boston, 1869.

Rogers, Elder John. **The Biography of Eld. Barton Warren Stone, Written by Himself:** With Additions and Reflections. Cincinnati, 1847.

Booth-Tucker, Frederick. **The Salvation Army in America:** Selected Reports, 1899-1903. New York, 1972.

Satolli, Francis Archbishop. **Loyalty to Church and State.** Baltimore, 1895.

Schaff, Philip. **Church and State in the United States** or the American Idea of Religious Liberty and its Practical Effects with Official Documents. New York and London, 1888. (Reprinted from *Papers of the American Historical Association,* Vol. II, No. 4.)

Smith, Horace Wemyss. **Life and Correspondence of the Rev. William Smith, D.D.** Philadelphia, 1879, 1880. Two volumes in one.

Spalding, M[artin] J. **Sketches of the Early Catholic Missions of Kentucky;** From Their Commencement in 1787 to the Jubilee of 1826-7. Louisville, 1844.

Steiner, Bernard C., editor. **Rev. Thomas Bray:** His Life and Selected Works Relating to Maryland. Baltimore, 1901. (Reprinted from *Maryland Historical Society Fund Publication,* No. 37.)

To Win the West: Missionary Viewpoints, 1814-1815. New York, 1972.

Wayland, Francis and H. L. Wayland. **A Memoir of the Life and Labors of Francis Wayland, D.D., LL.D.** New York, 1867. Two volumes in one.

Willard, Frances E. **Woman and Temperance:** Or, the Work and Workers of the Woman's Christian Temperance Union. Hartford, 1883.

Belmont University Library